Subscription Notice

This Wiley product is updated on a periodic basis with supplements to reflect important changes in the subject matter. If you purchased this product directly from John Wiley & Sons, Inc., we have already recorded your subscription for this update service.

If, however, you purchased this product from a bookstore and wish to receive (1) the current update at no additional charge, and (2) future updates and revised or related volumes billed separately with a 30-day examination review, please send your name, company name (if applicable), address and the title of the product to:

Supplement Department
John Wiley & Sons, Inc.
One Wiley Drive
Somerset, NJ 08875
1-(800)-225-5945

Financial Products

Taxation, Regulation, and Design

Financial Products
Taxation, Regulation, and Design

ANDREA S. KRAMER

Formerly *Taxation of Securities, Commodities, and Options*

Wiley Law Publications
JOHN WILEY & SONS, INC.
New York • Chichester • Brisbane • Toronto • Singapore

In recognition of the importance of preserving what has
been written, it is a policy of John Wiley & Sons, Inc., to
have books of enduring value published in the United States
printed on acid-free paper, and we exert our best efforts
to that end.

Copyright © 1991 by John Wiley & Sons, Inc.

All rights reserved. Published simultaneously in Canada.

Reproduction or translation of any part of this work
beyond that permitted by Section 107 or 108 of the
1976 United States Copyright Act without the permission
of the copyright owner is unlawful. Requests for
permission or further information should be addressed to
the Permissions Department, John Wiley & Sons, Inc.

This publication is designed to provide accurate and
authoritative information in regard to the subject
matter covered. It is sold with the understanding that
the publisher is not engaged in rendering legal, accounting,
or other professional service. If legal advice or other
expert assistance is required, the services of a competent
professional person should be sought. *From a Declaration
of Principles jointly adopted by a Committee of the
American Bar Association and a Committee of Publishers.*

Library of Congress Cataloging in Publication Data:

Kramer, Andrea S.
  Financial products: taxation, regulation, and design / Andrea S. Kramer.
    (Nonprofit law, finance, and management series)
  Rev. ed. of: Taxation of securities, commodities, and options. c1986.
  Includes index.
  ISBN 0-471-51272-9 (set).—ISBN 0-471-54372-1 (vol. 1).—ISBN 0-471-54373-X
(vol. 2).
    1. Taxation of bonds, securities, etc.—Unites States.
2. Commodity exchanges—Taxation—Law and legislation—United States. 3. Options
(Finance)—Taxation—Law and legislation—United States. 4. Investments—
Taxation—Law and legislation—United States.   I. Kramer, Andrea S. Taxation of
securities, commodities, and options.   II. Title.   III. Series.
KF6415.K73   1991
343.7305'246—dc20   91-15525
[347.3035246]   CIP

Printed in the United States of America

10 9 8 7 6 5 4 3 2 1

Summary Contents

Volume 1

Abbreviations

PART ONE   OVERVIEW OF THE MARKETS

1 Overview of the Corporate Equity and Debt Securities Markets
2 Overview of the Government Securities Markets
3 Overview of the Municipal Securities Markets
4 Overview of the Commodity Markets
5 Overview of the Options Markets
6 Overview of Notional Principal Contracts
7 Overview of Asset-Backed Securities

PART TWO   TAXATION OF MARKET PARTICIPANTS

8 Overview of Market Participants
9 Investors
10 Traders
11 Dealers

12 Hedgers
13 Brokers

PART THREE TAXATION OF CAPITAL TRANSACTIONS

14 General Principles
15 Computation of Gains or Losses
16 Basis
17 Holding Period
18 Short Sales of Capital Assets
19 Wash Sales of Stock or Securities
20 Identification of Capital Assets

PART FOUR TAXATION OF ORDINARY INCOME TRANSACTIONS

21 General Principles
22 Identification of Ordinary Income Property
23 Hedging Transactions

PART FIVE TAXATION OF DIVIDEND INCOME, INTEREST INCOME, AND SECURITY LOANS

24 Dividend Income
25 Interest Income
26 Security Loans

PART SIX TAXATION OF STOCK AND OTHER EQUITY SECURITIES, OPTIONS ON SECURITIES, PUBLICLY TRADED PARTNERSHIP INTERESTS, AND PUBLICLY TRADED TRUST INTERESTS

27 Stock and Equity Securities
28 Partnership Interests
29 Publicly Traded Trust Interests
30 Options on Stock

Summary Contents
Volume 2

Abbreviations

PART SEVEN   TAXATION OF DEBT SECURITIES AND OPTIONS ON DEBT SECURITIES

31   General Principles for Taxation of Debt Securities

32   Government Securities

33   Municipal Securities

34   Convertible Debt Securities

35   Options on Debt Securities

PART EIGHT   TAXATION OF ASSET-BACKED SECURITIES

36   Tax Considerations for Entities Used to Pool Asset-Backed Securities

37   Taxation of Pass-Through Certificate Owners

38   Taxation of Pay-Through Bond Owners

39   Taxation of Owners of Equity Interests in Entities Issuing Pay-Through Bonds

Summary Contents

40 Taxation of Owners of Pass-Through Debt Certificates

41 Taxation of REMIC Interest Owners

PART NINE TAXATION OF PHYSICAL COMMODITIES AND OPTIONS ON COMMODITIES

42 Physical Commodities

43 Options on Commodities

PART TEN TAXATION OF SECTION 1256 CONTRACTS

44 Statutory Definitions

45 General Tax Rules for Section 1256 Contracts

46 Exceptions to Section 1256 Treatment

PART ELEVEN TAX CONSEQUENCES OF HOLDING OFFSETTING POSITIONS (STRADDLES)

47 Background on Pre-ERTA Rules

48 Straddle Definitions

49 Limitation on Recognition of Straddle Losses While Holding an Offsetting Position

50 Losses Carried Forward

51 Attribution Rules

52 Disclosure of Unrecognized Gain

53 Penalties

54 Modified Wash Sales and Short Sales Rules

55 Capitalization of Straddle Interest and Carrying Charges

56 Exceptions to Application of the Straddle Rules

57 Mixed Straddles

PART TWELVE TREATMENT OF GAIN OR LOSS ON TERMINATIONS OF CERTAIN CONTRACT RIGHTS AND OBLIGATIONS

58 Terminations of Contract Rights and Obligations

PART THIRTEEN   FOREIGN CURRENCY

59   Foreign Currency Transactions

PART FOURTEEN   NOTIONAL PRINCIPAL CONTRACTS

60   Notional Principal Contracts

Table of Cases

Table of Internal Revenue Code Sections

Table of Statutory Sections

Table of Treasury Pronouncements

Treasury Regulations

Temporary Treasury Regulations

Proposed Treasury Regulations

Revenue Rulings

Revenue Procedures

General Counsel's Memoranda

Income Tax Unit Rulings

Internal Revenue News Releases

Internal Revenue Announcements

Internal Revenue Notices

Treasury Decisions

Private Letter Rulings

Technical Advice Memoranda

Table of Legislative History

Commodity Futures Improvements Act of 1989

Deficit Reduction Act of 1984

Economic Recovery Tax Act of 1981

Internal Revenue Bill of 1921

Summary Contents

Internal Revenue Code of 1939

Internal Revenue Code of 1954

Omnibus Budget Reconciliation Act of 1987

Revenue Act of 1950

Revenue Act of 1978

Revenue Reconciliation Act of 1989

Secondary Mortgage Market Enhancement Act of 1984

Tax Equity and Fiscal Responsibility Act of 1982

Tax Reform Act of 1969

Tax Reform Act of 1976

Tax Reform Act of 1985

Tax Reform Act of 1986

Technical and Miscellaneous Revenue Act of 1988

Technical Corrections Act of 1982

Technical Corrections Bill of 1988

Regulation of Government Securities

Special Reports, Studies, and Legislation

Index

About the Author

Detailed Contents
Volume 2

Abbreviations xl

PART SEVEN TAXATION OF DEBT SECURITIES AND OPTIONS ON DEBT SECURITIES

31 General Principles for Taxation of Debt Securities   825

§ 31.1 In General 825
§ 31.2 Original Issue Discount 826
    (a) Corporate and Government Debt Securities Issued After July 1, 1982 827
    (b) Corporate Debt Securities Issued After May 27, 1969, and Before July 2, 1982 829
    (c) Corporate Debt Securities Issued Before May 28, 1969, and Government Debt Securities Issued Before July 2, 1982 830
    (d) Short-Term Corporate and Government Obligations 831
        (1) Law in Effect Before July 19, 1984 831
        (2) Law in Effect After July 18, 1984 832
            (i) In General 832

Detailed Contents

      (ii) Election 833
    (3) Interest Deferral 834
    (4) Characterization of Amounts Received on Retirement or Sale 835
  (e) Tax-Exempt Securities 836
  (f) Foreign Investors 837
  (g) Applicable High Yield Discount Obligations 838
    (1) In General 838
    (2) Applicable High Yield Discount Obligations 839
      (i) Payment-in-Kind Bonds 839
      (ii) Significant Original Issue Discount 840
        (a) Accrual Period 841
        (b) Calculation of Significant Original Issue Discount 841
    (3) Taxation of Issuers 842
      (i) Original Issue Discount 842
      (ii) Earnings and Profits 842
      (iii) S Corporations Exempt 842
    (4) Taxation of Holders 843
    (5) Effective Date and Exceptions 843
  (h) Corporate Reorganizations 844
  (i) Contingent Payment Obligations 845
  (j) Investment Units 845
  (k) Pass-Through Certificates 846
  (l) Pay-Through Bonds 846
  (m) Real Estate Mortgage Investment Conduit Regular Interests 846
  (n) Information Reporting 848
    (1) Information to be Set Out on the Debt Security 848
    (2) Information to be Reported to the IRS 849
    (3) Reporting OID Payments to the IRS 850
    (4) Reporting for Real Estate Mortgage Investment Conduit Regular Interestsand Certain Similar Debt Securities 852
§ 31.3 Market Discount Bonds 852

(a) Overview 852
(b) Market Discount and Market Discount Bonds Defined 854
(c) Market Discount Bonds Acquired at Original Issue 855
(d) Transfers to Controlled Corporations 856
(e) Corporate Reorganizations 856
(f) Accrued Market Discount 856
   (1) In General 856
   (2) Elections to Accrue Market Discount 857
      (i) Ratable Accrual 857
      (ii) Accrual on a Constant Interest Rate Method 857
(g) Election to Include Market Discount Currently 858
(h) Gain on Sale 858
(i) Installment Instruments 859
(j) Pass-Through Certificates 860
(k) Pay-Through Bonds 860
(l) Real Estate Mortgage Investment Conduit Regular Interests and Certain Similar Debt Instruments 860
(m) Interest Deferral 861
   (1) In General 861
   (2) Disallowed Deductions Allowed in Later Years 862
      (i) Election 862
      (ii) Year of Disposition 862
      (iii) Nonrecognition Transactions 862

§ 31.4 Purchase Premiums 863
(a) In General 863
   (1) Taxable Securities 863
      (i) Election to Amortize Purchase Premiums 864
      (ii) Special Rules for Decedents 865
   (2) Tax-Exempt Securities 866
      (i) In General 866
      (ii) Dealers in Tax-Exempt Securities 866
(b) Determination of Amortizable Bond Premiums 868

		(c) Callable Securities 870
		(1) Taxable Securities 870
		(2) Tax-Exempt Securities 871
		(d) Convertible Debt Securities 872
		(e) Amortization of Capitalized Expenses 873
		(f) Pass-Through Certificates 873
		(g) Pay-Through Bonds 874
		(h) Real Estate Mortgage Investment Conduit Regular Interests 874
	§ 31.5	Zero Coupon Securities 874
		(a) Taxable Securities 875
		(b) Tax-Exempt Securities 876
	§ 31.6	Stripped Bonds 877
		(a) In General 877
		(b) Stripped Bonds Disposed of Before July 2, 1982 878
		(1) Treatment of the Seller 878
		(2) Treatment of the Purchaser 880
		(c) Stripped Bonds Disposed of After July 1, 1982, and Acquired Before October 23, 1986 880
		(1) Treatment of the Seller 881
		(2) Treatment of the Purchaser 882
		(3) Treatment of the Issuer 883
		(4) Tax-Exempt Securities 883
		(d) Stripped Bonds Acquired After October 22, 1986 884
		(1) Taxable Securities 884
		(2) Tax-Exempt Securities 884
		(i) Acquired Before June 11, 1987 884
		(ii) Acquired After June 10, 1987 886
		(e) Stripped Pass-Through Certificates 886
		(1) Law in Effect Before July 18, 1984 886
		(2) Current Law Considerations 887
		(i) In General 887
		(ii) Taxation of Taxpayer Stripping the Bond 888
		(iii) Taxpayer Owning Stripped Bonds 889
		(f) Stripped Pay-Through Bonds 890

	(g) Reconstituted Stripped Bonds 891
§ 31.7	Foreign Currency Transactions 891
	(a) Original Issue Discount 891
	(b) Market Discount 892
	(c) Bond Premium 893
§ 31.8	Securities in Default 893
§ 31.9	Exchanges of Debt Securities 896
	(a) In General 896
	(b) Corporate Reorganizations 897
	(c) Bankruptcy Proceedings 898
§ 31.10	Retirement, Redemption, and Disposition of Debt Securities 900
	(a) Originally Issued at a Discount 900
	(b) Market Discount Bonds 900
	(c) Reissuances 901
§ 31.11	Repurchase Agreements and Reverse Repurchase Agreements 901
	(a) In General 901
	(1) Types of Repurchase Agreements 902
	(2) Considerations for Real Estate Investment Trusts 903
	(3) Tax Considerations 903
	(b) Sales or Financing Transactions 903
	(1) Loans 904
	(2) Sales 906
	(3) Sham Transactions 907
	(4) Economic Substance 909
	(c) Alternative Minimum Tax 910
	(d) Reporting Requirement 911
	(e) Straddle Rules 911
§ 31.12	Registration Requirements 911
	(a) In General 911
	(b) Registration-Required Securities 915
	(1) In General 915
	(2) Treasury Authority to Require Registration 915
	(3) Registered Form 916
	(4) Foreign-Issued Obligations 916
	(i) In General 916
	(ii) Restrictions on Offers and Sales 916
	(iii) Restrictions on Delivery 918

Detailed Contents

                    (iv) Certification
                         Requirements   918
                         (a) In General   918
                         (b) Electronic
                             Certification   919
                         (c) Exceptions for Certain
                             Obligations   920
                    (v) Effective Date and Special
                        Rules   921
               (c) Noncompliance with Registration
                   Requirements   921
               (d) Exceptions to Loss Denial and Ordinary
                   Income Treatment   922
                    (1) In General   922
                    (2) Financial Institution Investment
                        Accounts   924
               (e) Securities Sold Outside of the United
                   States Subsequently Acquired by a United
                   States Person   926
               (f) Real Estate Mortgage Investment Conduit
                   Regular Interests   926
    § 31.13 Wash Sales   927
    § 31.14 Short Sales   928
    § 31.15 Straddle Rules   928

32 Government Securities   929

    § 32.1   Treasury Securities   929
             (a) Treasury Bills   930
                 (1) In General   930
                 (2) Payment of Federal Taxes with
                     Certain Treasury Bills   931
                 (3) Capital Assets   931
             (b) Savings Bonds   932
                 (1) Series EE Savings Bonds   932
                     (i) In General   932
                     (ii) Election to Defer Taxes   932
                     (iii) Transfers to Spouses and
                           Former Spouses   934
                     (iv) Co-owners   935
                     (v) College Savings Bonds   936
                         (a) In General   936
                         (b) Qualified Savings
                             Bonds   937

(c) Qualified Higher Education Expenses 937
(d) Amount of Excludable Interest 938
(e) Recordkeeping 938
(2) Series HH Savings Bonds 939
(3) Dispositions 939
(c) Payment of Estate Taxes with Certain Treasury Bonds 940
(d) Tax-Free Exchanges 943
(1) General Rule 943
(2) Application of Original Issue Discount Rules 945
(i) Nonmarketable Securities 946
(ii) Marketable Securities 946
§ 32.2 Federal Agency Debt Securities 946
(a) Test for Exemption from State and Local Tax 947
(b) Federal National Mortgage Association Bonds 948
(c) Government National Mortgage Association Certificates 948
§ 32.3 Repurchase Agreements and Reverse Repurchase Agreements 949
§ 32.4 When-Issued Securities 949
§ 32.5 Zero Coupon Securities 949

33 Municipal Securities 951

§ 33.1 In General 951
§ 33.2 Types of Municipal Securities 952
(a) General Obligation Bonds 952
(b) Municipal Revenue Bonds 953
(c) Private Activity Bonds 953
(1) In General 954
(i) Private Activity Bonds Issued After August 16, 1986 955
(ii) Limits on Aggregate Amount of Private Activity Bonds 956
(2) Private Activity Bond Financing 957
(i) Exempt Facility Private Activity Bonds 957

     (ii) Qualified Mortgage Bonds and Qualified Veterans' Mortgage Bonds 959
       (a) Qualified Mortgage Bonds 959
       (b) Qualified Veterans' Mortgage Bonds 961
     (iii) Small Issue Exemption 962
     (iv) Qualified Student Loan Bonds 963
     (v) Qualified Redevelopment Bonds 963
     (vi) Qualified 501(c)(3) Bonds 964
       (a) In General 964
       (b) Qualified Hospital Bonds 966
       (c) Mixed-Use Facilities 968
       (d) Volume Limitation 968
       (e) Rental Housing Projects 968
       (f) Land Acquisitions 969
§ 33.3 General Tax Principles 969
  (a) Interest Income 969
    (1) Federal Income Tax 969
     (i) In General 969
       (a) Municipal Securities with Interest in Default 970
       (b) Original Issue Discount 970
       (c) Premiums 970
       (d) Sales 970
     (ii) Federal Guarantees 971
     (iii) Registration Requirements 972
     (iv) Acquisition of a Put Option 973
     (v) Insurance 974
     (vi) Arbitrage Bonds and Taxable Municipal Securities 975
     (vii) Limitations on Advance Refundings 978
     (viii) Information Reporting 980
     (ix) Hedge Bonds 980
    (2) Estate and Gift Taxes 982
    (3) Social Security Benefits 982

　　　　　　　　　(4) Original Issue Discount and Market Discount 983
　　　　　　(b) State Taxation 983
　　　　　　(c) Sales of Tax-Exempt Securities 984
　　　　　　(d) Interest to Purchase or Carry Tax-Exempt Securities 985
§ 33.4　Defaulted Tax-Exempt Securities 985
§ 33.5　Flow-Through Entities 986
　　　　　(a) Partnerships 986
　　　　　(b) S Corporations 987
　　　　　(c) Regulated Investment Companies 987
§ 33.6　Investments by Financial Institutions in Tax-Exempt Securities 988
§ 33.7　Alternative Minimum Tax 989
§ 33.8　Losses Incurred by Property and Casualty Insurance Companies 990
§ 33.9　Depreciation Deductions for Bond Financed Property 990
§ 33.10　Use of Bond Financed Property 990
§ 33.11　Branch Profits Tax 991
§ 33.12　Superfund Environmental Tax 991

34　Convertible Debt Securities　　　　　　　　　　993

§ 34.1　In General 993
§ 34.2　Tax Treatment of an Issuing Corporation 994
　　　　　(a) Issuance of Convertible Debt Securities 994
　　　　　(b) Original Issue Discount 998
　　　　　(c) Premiums 1000
　　　　　　　(1) In General 1000
　　　　　　　(2) Conversion Features 1000
　　　　　　　(3) Unamortized Premiums on Conversion 1001
　　　　　(d) Exercise of Conversion Rights 1001
　　　　　(e) Accrued Interest on Conversions 1002
　　　　　(f) Repurchase by the Issuer 1003
§ 34.3　Tax Treatment of a Convertible Debt Security Owner 1006
　　　　　(a) Acquisition of Convertible Debt Securities 1006
　　　　　(b) Original Issue Discount 1007
　　　　　(c) Premiums 1008
　　　　　(d) Change in Conversion Ratios or Conversion Prices 1009

Detailed Contents

	(e) Conversion into Common Stock 1011	
§ 34.4	Adjustable Rate Convertible Notes 1012	
§ 34.5	Mandatory Convertible Notes 1013	
§ 34.6	Exchangeable Debt Securities and Portfolio Exchangeables 1014	
	(a) Exchangeable Debt Securities 1014	
	(b) Portfolio Exchangeables 1014	
§ 34.7	Discount Convertible Debt Securities 1015	

35 Options on Debt Securities   1017

- § 35.1   Pre-DRA Transactions   1017
- § 35.2   Post-DRA Transactions   1018

PART EIGHT   TAXATION OF ASSET-BACKED SECURITIES

36 Tax Considerations for Entities Used to Pool Asset-Backed Securities   1021

- § 36.1   Participation Certificates   1021
- § 36.2   Pass-Through Certificates   1022
  - (a) In General   1023
  - (b) Prohibition Against Varying Investments   1024
  - (c) Prohibition Against Multiple Interests   1025
  - (d) Stripped Pass-Through Certificates   1028
  - (e) Senior and Subordinated Pass-Through Certificates   1029
- § 36.3   Pay-Through Bonds   1031
- § 36.4   Equity Interests in Entities Issuing Pay-Through Bonds   1033
  - (a) Special Purpose Corporations   1034
  - (b) Owner Trusts   1034
  - (c) Phantom Income Considerations   1035
- § 36.5   Pass-Through Debt Certificates   1036
  - (a) In General   1036
  - (b) Form over Substance Considerations   1037
  - (c) Sale or Secured Loan for Tax Purposes   1037
  - (d) Partnership Tax Status   1039
- § 36.6   Regulated Investment Companies   1039
- § 36.7   Real Estate Investment Trusts   1040

§ 36.8 Real Estate Mortgage Investment Conduits 1041
    (a) In General 1041
    (b) Prior Legislative Proposals 1044
    (c) Investor Interests 1045
        (1) Regular Interests 1046
            (i) In General 1046
            (ii) Requirements 1047
            (iii) Fixed Rate Regular Interests 1048
            (iv) Variable Rate Regular Interests 1048
            (v) Senior and Subordinated Regular Interests 1051
            (vi) Stripped Regular Interests 1052
        (2) Residual Interests 1053
    (d) Asset Test 1053
        (1) Qualified Mortgages 1055
            (i) In General 1055
            (ii) Regular Interests Transferred on Startup Day 1057
            (iii) Qualified Replacement Mortgages 1057
            (iv) Credit Enhancements 1058
        (2) Permitted Investments 1058
            (i) Cash Flow Investments 1058
            (ii) Qualified Reserve Assets 1059
                (a) Qualified Reserve Fund Defined 1060
                (b) Potential Problems 1060
                (c) Prompt and Appropriate Reductions 1061
                (d) Prohibition Against Active Trading of Reserve Fund Assets 1062
            (iii) Foreclosure Properties 1062
    (e) Reasonable Arrangement Rules 1063
    (f) Inadvertent Terminations 1063
    (g) Prohibited Transactions 1064
    (h) Tax on Contributions to a REMIC after the Startup Day 1066
    (i) Tax on Net Income from Foreclosure Property 1067

Detailed Contents xxii

- (j) Compliance and Reporting 1067
  - (1) Books and Records 1067
  - (2) OID Reporting 1068
  - (3) Reporting Market Discount or Premiums 1068
  - (4) Reports to Regular Interests 1068
  - (5) Information to Be Supplied to the IRS 1069
- (k) REMIC Election 1070
- (l) Treatment of Allocable Investment Expenses 1071
- (m) Qualified Liquidations 1071
- (n) Credit Enhancements 1072
- (o) Taxable Mortgage Pools 1073
- (p) Policy Considerations for Applying REMIC Treatment to Pools of Nonmortgage Assets 1076

37 Taxation of Pass-Through Certificate Owners 1077

- § 37.1 General Tax Principles 1077
- § 37.2 Purchases at the Principal Amount 1079
- § 37.3 Purchases at a Premium 1079
- § 37.4 Purchases at a Discount 1080
  - (a) Original Issue Discount 1081
  - (b) Market Discount 1082
- § 37.5 Stripped Pass-Through Certificates 1083
  - (a) Taxation of Taxpayer Stripping the Bond 1083
  - (b) Taxpayer Owning Stripped Bonds 1085
- § 37.6 Senior and Subordinated Pass-Through Certificates 1086
- § 37.7 Special Considerations for Graduated Payment Mortgages 1086

38 Taxation of Pay-Through Bond Owners 1089

- § 38.1 General Tax Principles 1089
- § 38.2 Purchase at the Principal Amount 1090
- § 38.3 Purchase at a Premium 1091
- § 38.4 Purchase at a Discount 1091
- § 38.5 Stripped Pay-Through Bonds 1092
- § 38.6 Senior and Subordinated Pay-Through Bonds 1092

39 Taxation of Owners of Equity Interests in Entities Issuing Pay-Through Bonds — 1093

§ 39.1 Equity Interests in Corporations 1093
§ 39.2 Equity Interests in Owner Trusts 1094
    (a) Owner Trusts Classified as Investment Trusts 1094
    (b) Owner Trusts Classified as Partnerships 1094
    (c) Phantom Income 1094

40 Taxation of Owners of Pass-Through Debt Certificates — 1095

41 Taxation of REMIC Interest Owners — 1097

§ 41.1 Regular Interests 1098
    (a) Debt Treatment 1098
        (1) Purchase at the Principal Amount 1098
        (2) Purchase at a Premium 1099
        (3) Purchase at a Discount 1099
    (b) Issue Price 1100
    (c) Gain on Disposition 1101
§ 41.2 Residual Interests 1102
    (a) In General 1102
    (b) Distributions 1102
    (c) Disallowed Losses 1102
    (d) Subsequent Holders 1103
    (e) Calculation of Income or Loss 1103
    (f) Tax Basis 1104
    (g) Excess Inclusions 1104
        (1) Policy Reasons for Excess Inclusion Rules 1104
        (2) General Rule 1105
        (3) Daily Accrual 1106
        (4) Residual Interests Without Significant Value 1106
    (h) Issue Price 1107
    (i) Residual Interests Received in Exchange for Property 1107
    (j) Wash Sales Rule 1108
    (k) Phantom Income 1109
§ 41.3 Real Estate Investment Trusts 1109
    (a) Investment in REMIC Interests 1109

Detailed Contents xxiv

             (b) Excess Inclusion Allocation to REIT Shareholders 1110
§ 41.4 Financial Institutions 1110

PART NINE TAXATION OF PHYSICAL COMMODITIES AND OPTIONS ON COMMODITIES

42 Physical Commodities   1115

§ 42.1 Outright Purchases of Commodities 1116
      (a) Acquisition Pursuant to a Long Futures Contract Position 1117
      (b) Acquisition Pursuant to a Long Forward Contract Position 1118
      (c) Acquisition Pursuant to a Long Call Options Position 1119
      (d) Acquisition Pursuant to a Short Put Options Position 1120
      (e) Sale of a Commodity 1120
§ 42.2 Financed Purchases of Commodities 1121
§ 42.3 Purchases of Commodities with Offsetting Positions 1122
§ 42.4 Cash and Carry Transactions 1123
§ 42.5 Leverage Transactions 1124
§ 42.6 Exchange of Futures for Physicals 1124

43 Options on Commodities   1127

§ 43.1 In General 1127
§ 43.2 Options on Physical Commodities 1128
      (a) Unlisted Cash Options 1128
      (b) Listed Cash Options 1128
§ 43.3 Options on Futures Contracts 1128
      (a) Futures Option Positions Before November 1, 1983 1128
      (b) Futures Option Positions After October 31, 1983 1129

PART TEN TAXATION OF SECTION 1256 CONTRACTS

44 Statutory Definitions   1133

§ 44.1 Regulated Futures Contracts 1133
      (a) Cash Settlement Contracts 1135

§ 44.2   (b) Qualified Boards or Exchanges   1136
§ 44.2   Foreign Currency Contracts   1137
       (a) Pre-TRA '86 Treatment   1137
       (b) Treatment as a Result of TRA '86 and TMRA '88   1140
§ 44.3   Nonequity Options   1140
       (a) Treasury Designation   1142
       (b) Futures Option Positions After October 31, 1983   1142
       (c) Futures Option Positions Before November 1, 1983   1143
           (1) Position That Futures Options Are Eligible for 60/40 Treatment   1143
               (i) Short Futures Options as Regulated Futures Contracts   1144
               (ii) Long Futures Options as Subject to the 60/40 Rule   1144
           (2) Position That Futures Options Are Ineligible for 60/40 Tax Treatment   1146
§ 44.4   Dealer Equity Options   1148
§ 44.5   DRA Transitional Year Elections for Section 1256 Options   1150
§ 44.6   Expanded Definition of Section 1256 Contracts for "Qualified Funds"   1152

45 General Tax Rules for Section 1256 Contracts   1155

§ 45.1   Mark-to-Market Rule   1155
       (a) Constructive Receipt Doctrine   1157
       (b) Subsequent Gain or Loss   1157
§ 45.2   60/40 Rule   1159
       (a) Dealers in the Underlying Property   1160
       (b) Commodity Dealers and Option Dealers   1161
       (c) Dealer Equity Options Unavailable to Limited Partners and Limited Entrepreneurs   1163
           (1) Unintended Tax Result   1164
           (2) General Partners as Limited Entrepreneurs   1164
§ 45.3   Straddles Made Up Exclusively of Section 1256 Contracts   1165

Detailed Contents xxvi

§ 45.4 Loss Carry-Back Rules for Section 1256 Contract Losses   1166
  (a) In General   1166
  (b) Mixed Straddle Accounts   1170
  (c) Restricted Interest   1171
§ 45.5 Termination of Section 1256 Contracts Before Delivery or Exercise Date   1173
§ 45.6 Making or Taking Delivery and Exercising or Being Exercised on Section 1256 Positions   1175
  (a) Delivery Under Futures Contracts   1175
  (b) Exercise of Option Positions   1176
  (c) Delivery or Exercise of Part of a Straddle   1177

46 Exceptions to Section 1256 Treatment   1179

§ 46.1 Mixed Straddles   1179
§ 46.2 Hedging Transactions   1179
  (a) Qualified Hedging Transactions   1179
  (b) Section 988 Hedging Transactions   1180

PART ELEVEN   TAX CONSEQUENCES OF HOLDING OFFSETTING POSITIONS (STRADDLES)

47 Background on Pre-ERTA Rules   1185

§ 47.1 Explanation of Straddle Transactions   1185
§ 47.2 Tax Rules in Effect for Pre-ERTA Transactions   1189
  (a) Revenue Ruling 77-185   1192
  (b) *Smith v. Comm'r*   1192
  (c) Legislative, Judicial, and Administrative Solutions for Certain Pre-ERTA Straddles   1194
  (d) *Miller v. Comm'r*   1201
    (1) Tax Court Decision   1201
    (2) The Tenth Circuit Decision   1204
  (e) Subsequent Judicial Decisions   1205

48 Straddle Definitions   1211

§ 48.1 Straddle   1211
§ 48.2 Personal Property   1212
  (a) Actively Traded   1212

(b) United States Currency 1213
(c) Certain Stock Positions 1214
   (1) In General 1214
   (2) Stock Offsetting Options or Substantially Similar or Related Property 1216
   (3) Treasury Regulations 1218
   (4) Offsetting Position Stock 1219
(d) Examples 1220

§ 48.3 Positions 1221
(a) Definition 1221
(b) Repurchase Agreements and Reverse Repurchase Agreements 1222
   (1) Definition 1222
   (2) Tax Analysis 1223
      (i) Repos as Financing Transactions 1223
      (ii) Repos as Sales Transactions 1224
      (iii) Short-Term Obligations and Market Discount Obligations 1225
   (3) Summary If Straddle Rules Apply 1226
(c) Foreign Currency 1226

§ 48.4 Offsetting Positions 1227
(a) In General 1227
(b) Option Positions 1229
(c) Debt Securities 1233

§ 48.5 Unrecognized Gain 1235

49 Limitation on Recognition of Straddle Losses While Holding an Offsetting Position — 1237

§ 49.1 Loss Deferral Rule 1237
§ 49.2 Coordination of Loss Deferral and Modified Wash Sales Rules 1239

50 Losses Carried Forward — 1241

51 Attribution Rules — 1245

§ 51.1 General Rules 1245
§ 51.2 Statutory Elections 1246
§ 51.3 Section 1256 Contracts 1247

Detailed Contents

§ 51.4 Mixed Straddles 1247

52 Disclosure of Unrecognized Gain 1249

§ 52.1 Generally Required 1249
§ 52.2 Exceptions 1250
§ 52.3 Examples 1251

53 Penalties 1253

§ 53.1 Penalties for Failure to Disclose Unrecognized Gain 1253
   (a) Penalties Under Pre-TRA '86 Law 1253
   (b) Penalties Under Current Law 1254
§ 53.2 Increased Interest Rate 1255

54 Modified Wash Sales and Short Sales Rules 1257

§ 54.1 Coordination with the Wash Sales and Short Sales Rules 1258
§ 54.2 Coordination with the Loss Deferral Rule 1259
§ 54.3 Modified Wash Sales Rule 1263
§ 54.4 Modified Short Sales Rule 1264
   (a) Application 1265
   (b) Mixed Straddles 1270
   (c) Regulated Investment Companies 1271
   (d) Married Put Transactions 1272

55 Capitalization of Straddle Interest and Carrying Charges 1275

§ 55.1 Pre-ERTA Transactions 1276
§ 55.2 Capitalization Requirements 1284
   (a) In General 1285
   (b) Straddle Income 1287
   (c) Short Sales 1288
   (d) Mixed Straddle Accounts 1289
   (e) Application After Certain Provisions 1290
   (f) Hedging Transactions 1291

56 Exceptions to Application of the Straddle Rules 1293

§ 56.1 Identified Straddles 1293
   (a) Requirements 1293
   (b) Subsequent Transactions 1295
§ 56.2 Hedging Transactions 1296

§ 56.3	Qualified Covered Calls 1297	
	(a) Scope of Exemption 1297	
	(b) Definition 1298	
	(c) Exceptions to the General Rule to Determine the Lowest Qualified Bench Mark 1299	
	(d) Limitations on the Exemption 1299	
	(1) Subsequent Stock Sale 1300	
	(2) In-the-Money Call Options Established After June 30, 1984 1300	
	(3) Treasury Regulations 1301	
§ 56.4	Married Put Transactions 1301	
§ 56.5	Certain Stock Positions 1302	
§ 56.6	Short-Term Stock Option Positions Established Before July 18, 1984 1303	
§ 56.7	Straddles Made Up Exclusively of Section 1256 Contracts 1304	

57 Mixed Straddles   1307

§ 57.1 Summary of Choices Available When Holding a Mixed Straddle   1313

§ 57.2 Identified Section 1256(d) Mixed Straddles   1315
   (a) One-Time Mixed Straddle Election   1315
   (b) Limited Scope of Election   1316
   (c) Mixed Straddles Created by Taking Delivery Under or Exercising a Long Section 1256 Contract   1317

§ 57.3 Straddle-by-Straddle Netting with Section 1092(b)(2) Identified Mixed Straddles   1318
   (a) Clear Identification   1318
      (1) Separate Accounts   1320
      (2) Confirmations   1321
      (3) Other Methods   1321
   (b) Summary of Rules to Net Gains and Losses   1322
   (c) Accrued Gain and Loss on Establishing Straddles   1323
   (d) Same Day Disposition of All Positions   1326
   (e) Non-Section 1256 Positions Disposed of First   1327

Detailed Contents

           (f) Section 1256 Positions Disposed of First   1328
           (g) Partial Disposition of Straddle Positions   1329
           (h) Loss Deferral and Holding Period Rules   1331
§ 57.4 Mixed Straddle Accounts   1332
           (a) Account Contents   1334
           (b) Daily Mark-to-Market   1336
           (c) Annual Account Net Gain or Loss   1337
           (d) Capitalization of Interest and Carrying Charges   1340
           (e) Total Annual Account Net Gain or Loss   1342
           (f) Account Cap   1342
           (g) Yearly Mixed Straddle Elections   1342
           (h) Manner for Making Election   1344
           (i) Transitional Elections Provided in 1984   1345
§ 57.5 Methods of Identifying and Netting Mixed Straddles May Not Be Mutually Exclusive   1347
§ 57.6 Limitations on Who Can Make Section 1092(b)(2) Identified Mixed Straddle and Mixed Straddle Account Elections   1348
           (a) Section 1092(b)(2) Identified Mixed Straddles   1348
           (b) Mixed Straddle Accounts   1349
           (c) Conclusion   1349
§ 57.7 Treatment of Mixed Straddles Where at Least One Position Is Capital and at Least One Position Is Ordinary   1350
§ 57.8 Summary of Effective Dates   1351

PART TWELVE   TREATMENT OF GAIN OR LOSS ON TERMINATIONS OF CERTAIN CONTRACT RIGHTS AND OBLIGATIONS

58 Terminations of Contract Rights and Obligations   1355

    § 58.1 Pre-ERTA Cancellation Transactions   1355
    § 58.2 Capital Gain or Loss on Terminations   1364

PART THIRTEEN FOREIGN CURRENCY

59 Foreign Currency Transactions   1369

§ 59.1   Introduction   1369
§ 59.2   General Rules for Foreign Currency Transactions   1370
- (a) In General   1370
  - (1) Section 988 Transactions Defined   1370
  - (2) Qualified Funds   1374
  - (3) Personal Transactions   1375
  - (4) Realization of Exchange Gains and Losses   1376
- (b) Character of Gains and Losses   1377
  - (1) In General   1377
  - (2) Regulated Investment Companies   1378
  - (3) Election to Treat Certain Gains or Losses as Capital   1379
  - (4) Election to Treat Regulated Futures Contracts and Nonequity Options as Section 988 Transactions   1379
- (c) Timing   1380
  - (1) General   1380
  - (2) Deliveries   1381
  - (3) Exception Where Economic Benefit Is Derived   1382
- (d) Source   1382
  - (1) Exchange Gains and Losses   1382
  - (2) Residence   1383
    - (i) Individuals   1383
    - (ii) Corporations   1383
    - (iii) Partnerships   1383
    - (iv) Estates and Trusts   1384
- (e) Separately Computed Gain or Loss   1384
- (f) Foreign Currency Gain or Loss   1384
  - (1) Booking Date   1385
  - (2) Payment Date   1385
  - (3) Computing Gain or Loss   1385
- (g) Functional Currency Rules   1387
  - (1) Functional Currency   1387
    - (i) In General   1387

- (ii) Application of Treasury Regulations 1388
- (iii) U.S. Dollar Functional Currency 1388
- (iv) Economic Environment 1389
- (v) Single Functional Currency of a Foreign Corporation 1390
- (2) Nonfunctional Currency 1391
- (3) Qualified Business Units 1393
  - (i) In General 1393
  - (ii) Corporations 1393
  - (iii) Individuals 1393
  - (iv) Partnerships, Trusts, and Estates 1394
  - (v) Trade or Business 1394
  - (vi) Separate Books and Records 1396
  - (vii) Transitional Rules for Certain QBUs Using a Profit and Loss Method of Accounting Before January 1, 1987 1397
  - (viii) Functional Currency of a QBU 1397
- (h) Mixed Straddles 1398
- (i) Foreign Currency Transactions of Certain Commodity Funds 1399
  - (1) In General 1399
  - (2) Expanded Definition of Section 1256 Contracts 1400
  - (3) Requirements for a Qualified Fund 1400
  - (4) Election 1402
    - (i) Procedure 1402
    - (ii) Time for Making the Election 1403
    - (iii) Transitional Rule for the 1988 Calendar Year 1404
- (j) Election into Section 988 Treatment for Regulated Futures Contracts and Nonequity Options 1404
  - (1) Procedure 1405
  - (2) Time for Making the Election 1407
  - (3) Late Elections 1407

		(4) Transitional Rule for the 1988 Calendar Year 1408
§ 59.3		Foreign Currency Hedging Transactions 1408
§ 59.4		Steps to Analyze Foreign Currency Transactions 1408

§ 59.3 Foreign Currency Hedging Transactions 1408
§ 59.4 Steps to Analyze Foreign Currency Transactions 1408
    (a) Regulated Futures Contracts and Nonequity Options 1409
        (1) Positions Entered into Before 1986 1409
        (2) Positions Entered into After Enactment of I.R.C. § 988 and Before October 22, 1988 1409
        (3) Positions Entered into After October 21, 1988 1410
    (b) Futures and Options That Are Not Section 1256 Contracts 1410
        (1) Positions Entered into Before 1986 1410
        (2) Positions Entered into After Enactment of I.R.C. § 988 and Before October 22, 1988 1410
        (3) Positions Entered into After October 21, 1988 1411
        (4) Election Available for Tax Years Beginning After September 20, 1989 1411
    (c) Foreign Currency Contracts That Are Section 1256 Contracts 1411
        (1) Positions Entered into Before 1986 1411
        (2) Positions Entered into After Enactment of I.R.C. § 988 and Before October 22, 1988 1412
        (3) Positions Entered into After October 21, 1988 1412
        (4) Election Available for Tax Years Beginning After September 20, 1989 1412
    (d) Forward Contracts That Are Not Section 1256 Contracts 1413
        (1) Positions Entered into Before 1986 1413

Detailed Contents xxxiv

            (2) Positions Entered into After Enactment of I.R.C. § 988 and Before October 22, 1988   1413
            (3) Positions Entered into After October 21, 1988   1413
            (4) Election Available for Tax Years Beginning After September 20, 1989   1413
       (e) Spot Contracts   1414
§ 59.5   Translation Rules   1414
       (a) Foreign Subsidiaries   1415
       (b) Foreign Branches   1416
§ 59.6   Mark-to-Market Accounting   1417
§ 59.7   Straddle Rules   1418

PART FOURTEEN   NOTIONAL PRINCIPAL CONTRACTS

60 Notional Principal Contracts   1421

§ 60.1   Introduction   1421
§ 60.2   Swap Transactions   1424
       (a) Introduction   1424
       (b) Interest Rate Swaps   1425
           (1) Interest Rate Swap Hedge Transactions   1425
                (i) Periodic Swap Payments Prior to Swap Maturity   1425
                (ii) Up-Front and Assignment Fees   1430
                (iii) Termination Payments   1431
           (2) Interest Rate Swaps That Are Not Hedge Transactions   1433
                (i) Periodic Swap Payments for Swaps That Are Not Hedges   1433
                    (a) Character of Periodic Swap Payments   1433
                        (1) Swap Payments Are Not Interest   1434
                        (2) Swap Payments Are Not Made for the Purchase of Property   1436

     (3) Swap Payments Might Be Made for the Rendering of Services 1436
     (4) Income Equivalent to Interest 1436
    (b) Timing and Amount of Periodic Swap Payments 1436
    (c) Up-Front and Assignment Fees 1437
    (d) Source of Income for Periodic Swap Payments 1437
   (ii) Treatment of Termination of Swaps That Are Not Hedges 1437
  (c) Foreign Currency Swaps 1440
   (1) Introduction 1440
   (2) Definition of Foreign Currency Swaps 1441
   (3) Foreign Currency Swaps Are Not Section 1256 Contracts 1441
   (4) Section 988 Treatment 1442
   (5) Timing of Income and Expenses 1443
    (i) Lump-Sum Payments 1443
    (ii) Periodic Interim Payments 1444
    (iii) Principal Payments 1445
    (iv) Anti-Abuse Rule 1445
    (v) Disposition or Termination 1446
   (6) Source 1446
   (7) Character 1446
  (d) Commodity Swaps 1446
   (1) Commodity Swap Hedge Transactions 1447
    (i) Periodic Swap Payments Prior to Swap Maturity 1447
    (ii) Up-Front and Assignment Fees 1448
    (iii) Termination Payments 1448

(2) Commodity Swaps Not Used as Hedges 1448
   (i) Periodic Swap Payments 1448
   (ii) Timing and Amount 1449
(e) Swap Options 1449
   (1) In General 1449
   (2) Character 1449
   (3) Timing 1449
   (4) Source 1451
(f) Zero Coupon Swaps 1451
(g) Withholding Tax Obligations 1452
   (1) On Fixed or Determinable, Annual or Periodical Income 1452
   (2) Withholding Under Temporary Treasury Regulation § 1.861-7T 1453

§ 60.3 Interest Rate Caps, Floors, and Collars 1453
(a) Caps, Floors, and Collars Entered into to Hedge 1455
   (1) Up-Front Fees 1455
      (i) Timing 1455
      (ii) Character 1456
   (2) Periodic Payments 1457
      (i) Timing 1457
      (ii) Character 1457
   (3) Termination and Assignment Fees 1458
      (i) Timing 1458
      (ii) Character 1458
   (4) Analogy to Options 1458
(b) Caps, Floors, and Collars Not Entered into to Hedge 1459

§ 60.4 Forward Rate Agreements 1460
(a) In General 1461
   (1) Forward Rate Agreements as Futures Contracts 1461
   (2) Forward Rate Agreements as Forward Contracts 1462
   (3) Forward Rate Agreements as Interest Rate Swaps 1462
(b) Character 1463
(c) Timing 1463
(d) Source 1463

	(e)	Offsetting Positions Where One Position Is a Forward Rate Agreement 1464
	(f)	Speculative Positions 1464
§ 60.5	Sourcing Rules 1465	
	(a)	Sourcing Rules for Notional Principal Contracts 1465
	(b)	Sourcing Rules for Liability Hedges 1468
		(1) Interest Equivalent Treatment for Gains and Losses for Swaps and Other Financial Products 1468
		(2) Treatment Where Liability Hedges Are Not Properly Identified 1469
	(c)	Sourcing Rules for Asset Hedges 1469
§ 60.6	Mark-to-Market Treatment for Dealers 1469	
§ 60.7	Straddle Rules 1470	
	(a)	Notional Principal Contracts on United States Currency 1470
	(b)	Notional Principal Contracts on Foreign Currency 1471

Table of Cases — T-1

Table of Internal Revenue Code Sections — T-31

Table of Statutory Sections — T-55

Table of Treasury Pronouncements — T-65

   Treasury Regulations   T-65
   Temporary Treasury Regulations   T-70
   Proposed Treasury Regulations   T-76
   Revenue Rulings   T-76
   Revenue Procedures   T-81
   General Counsel's Memoranda   T-82
   Income Tax Unit Rulings   T-82
   Internal Revenue News Releases   T-82
   Internal Revenue Announcements   T-83
   Internal Revenue Notices   T-83
   Treasury Decisions   T-84
   Private Letter Rulings   T-84
   Technical Advice Memoranda   T-86

Detailed Contents   xxxviii

Table of Legislative History   T-89

   Commodity Futures Improvements Act of 1989   T-89
   Deficit Reduction Act of 1984   T-89
   Economic Recovery Tax Act of 1981   T-90
   Internal Revenue Bill of 1921   T-91
   Internal Revenue Code of 1939   T-91
   Internal Revenue Code of 1954   T-91
   Omnibus Budget Reconciliation Act of 1987   T-92
   Revenue Act of 1950   T-92
   Revenue Act of 1978   T-93
   Revenue Reconciliation Act of 1989   T-93
   Secondary Mortgage Market Enhancement Act of 1984   T-93
   Tax Equity and Fiscal Responsibility Act of 1982   T-93
   Tax Reform Act of 1969   T-94
   Tax Reform Act of 1976   T-94
   Tax Reform Act of 1985   T-94
   Tax Reform Act of 1986   T-95
   Technical and Miscellaneous Revenue Act of 1988   T-97
   Technical Corrections Act of 1982   T-97
   Technical Corrections Bill of 1988   T-97
   Regulation of Government Securities   T-98
   Special Reports, Studies, and Legislation   T-98

Index   I-1

About the Author

Abbreviations

Many abbreviations are used in this book. The most common abbreviations include the following:

ACC	AMEX Commodities Corporation
ACRNs	adjustable rate convertible notes
ADRs	American Depository Receipts
AMEX	American Stock Exchange
ARM	adjustable rate mortgage
ARPS	adjustable rate preferred stocks
BBA	British Banker's Association
BTCC	Board of Trade Clearing Corporation
CAPS	convertible adjustable preferred stocks
CATS	Certificate of Accrual on Treasury Securities
CBOE	Chicago Board Options Exchange, Inc.
CBT	Chicago Board of Trade
CCC	Commodity Credit Corporation
CDC	Certified Development Company
CEA	Commodity Exchange Act
CSAC	Central Securities Administrators Council
CFTC	Commodity Futures Trading Commission
Circuses	combined interest rate and currency swaps
CME	Chicago Mercantile Exchange
CMECH	Clearing House of the Chicago Mercantile Exchange
CMO	collateralized mortgage obligation

Abbreviations

CMS	collateralized mortgage security
COD	cash on delivery
Code	Internal Revenue Code
COMEX	Commodity Exchange, Inc.
CRB	Commodity Research Bureau
CRC	Chicago Rice and Cotton Exchange
CSC	Coffee, Sugar & Cocoa Exchange, Inc.
DRA	Deficit Reduction Act of 1984
DVP	delivery versus payment
ECU	European Currency Unit
EFP	exchange of futures for physicals
ERISA	Employee Retirement Income Security Act of 1974
ERTA	Economic Recovery Tax Act of 1981
ESOPs	Employee Stock Ownership Plans
Farmer Mac	Federal Agricultural Mortgage Corporation
FASB	Financial Accounting Standards Board
FCC	Federal Communications Commission
FCM	futures commission merchant
FDAPI	fixed or determinable, annual or periodical income
FDIC	Federal Deposit Insurance Corporation
FFIEC	Federal Financial Institutions Examination Council
FHA	Federal Housing Administration
FHLB	Federal Home Loan Bank
FHLBB	Federal Home Loan Bank Board
FHLMC	Federal Home Loan Mortgage Corporation
FICO	Financing Corporation
FIFO	first-in, first-out
FIRREA	Financial Institutions Reform, Recovery, and Enforcement Act of 1989
FNMA	Federal National Mortgage Association
FRAs	forward rate agreements
FRB	Federal Reserve Board
FRCNs	floating rate convertible notes
FSLIC	Federal Savings and Loan Insurance Corporation
FTAPI	fixed or taxable, annual, or periodic income
G.C.M.	General Counsel's Memoranda
GEM	growing equity mortgage
GMAC	General Motors Acceptance Corporation
GMCs	guaranteed mortgage certificates
GNMA	Government National Mortgage Association
GO	general obligation

GPM	graduated payment mortgage
GSCC	Government Securities Clearing Corporation
HIC	hold-in-custody
HUD	Housing and Urban Development
IB	introducing broker
ICA	Investment Company Act of 1940
IDB	industrial development bond
INTEX	International Futures Exchange (Bermuda) Limited
IO	interest only
IPs	index participations
IPMA	International Primary Market Association
I.R.C.	Internal Revenue Code
I.R.	Internal Revenue News Releases
IRS	Internal Revenue Service
ISDA	International Swap Dealers Association
ISDA Code	Code of Standard Wording Assumptions and Provisions for Swaps
I.T.	Income Tax Unit Ruling
JCAH	Joint Commission on Accreditation of Hospitals
KCBT	Kansas City Board of Trade
LBO	leveraged buyout
LIBOR	London interbank offered rate
LIFO	last-in, first-out
LME	London Metals Exchange
LTM	leverage transaction merchants
LTR	Private Letter Ruling
LYONS	liquid yield option notes
MBS	mortgage-backed security
MBSCC	MBS Clearing Corporation
MCF	mortgage cash flow
MGE	Minnesota Grain Exchange
MidAm	MidAmerica Commodity Exchange
MLP	master limited partnership
MSE	Midwest Stock Exchange
MSRB	Municipal Securities Rulemaking Board
Munis	municipal securities
NASAA	North American Securities Administrators Association
NASD	National Association of Securities Dealers
NASDAQ	National Association of Securities Dealers Automated Quotation System
NFA	National Futures Association

Abbreviations

NSCC	National Securities Clearing Corporation
NYCE	New York Cotton Exchange
NYFE	New York Futures Exchange
NYME	New York Mercantile Exchange
NYSE	New York Stock Exchange
OBRA ("1987 Act")	Omnibus Budget Reconciliation Act
OCC	The Options Clearing Corporation
OID	original issue discount
OTC	over-the-counter
OTS	Office of Thrift Supervision
PABs	private activity bonds
PACs	planned amortization class bonds
PBOT	Philadelphia Board of Trade
PC	mortgage participation certificate
PERLS	principal exchange-rate linked securities
PHLX	Philadelphia Stock Exchange
PIK bonds	payment-in-kind bonds
PO	principal only
Prop. Treas. Reg.	Proposed Treasury Regulations
PSA	Public Securities Association
PSE	Pacific Stock Exchange
PTC	Participants Trust Company
PTPs	publicly traded partnerships
QBU	qualified business unit
QPIP	qualified periodic interest payment
Refcorp	Resolution Funding Corporation
REIT	real estate investment trust
REMIC	real estate mortgage investment conduit
Rev. Proc.	Revenue Procedures
Rev. Rul.	Revenue Ruling
RFC	regulated futures contract
RICs	regulated investment companies
RRA '89	Revenue Reconciliation Act of 1989
RRA '90	Revenue Reconciliation Act of 1990
RTC	Resolution Trust Corporation
RULPA	Revised Uniform Limited Partnership Act (1976)
SBA	Small Business Administration
SBIA	Small Business Investment Act of 1958
SBIC	small business investment company
SBO	settlement balance order
SEA	Securities Exchange Act of 1934

SEC	Securities and Exchange Commission
Section 108	Section 108 of the DRA
Securities Act	Securities Act of 1933
SIMEX	Singapore International Monetary Exchange Limited
SLMA	Student Loan Marketing Association
SMBS	stripped mortgage-backed security
SMMEA	Secondary Mortgage Market Enforcement Act of 1984
STRIPS	Separate Trading of Registered Interest and Principal of Securities
TACs	targeted amortization class bonds
TAM	Technical Advice Memorandum
TAP	transaction adjustment payment
TCA '82	Technical Corrections Act of 1982
T.D.	Treasury Decisions
TEFRA	Tax Equity and Fiscal Responsibility Act of 1982
Temp. Treas. Reg.	Temporary Treasury Regulations
TIA	Trust Indenture Act of 1939
TIGRs	Treasury Investment Growth Receipts
TIM	Trust for Investment in Mortgages
TIN	taxpayer identification number
TMP	taxable mortgage pool
TMRA '88	Technical and Miscellaneous Revenue Act of 1988
TRA '69	Tax Reform Act of 1969
TRA '76	Tax Reform Act of 1976
TRA '85	Tax Reform Act of 1985
TRA '86	Tax Reform Act of 1986
Treas. Reg.	Treasury Regulation
UBTI	unrelated business taxable income
U.K.	United Kingdom
ULPA	Uniform Limited Partnership Act
VA	Veterans Administration
WAL	weighted average life
Zeros	zero coupon bonds

Part Seven

Taxation of Debt Securities and Options on Debt Securities

Thirty-one

General Principles for Taxation of Debt Securities

§ 31.1 IN GENERAL

In general, interest expense on debt securities is deductible for tax purposes (subject to the limitations on investment interest[1] and personal interest),[2] and includable in the income of the holders of the debt securities. Dividends paid on corporate stock are not deductible by the issuer, although certain corporate shareholders are eligible for the intercorporate dividends received deduction.[3] As a result, many corporations have favored the issuance of debt over stock issuances to raise additional funds.[4]

This chapter addresses general tax principles for the taxation of debt securities. It discusses the special tax rules that apply to tax-exempt securities and to short-term obligations. The OID rules are discussed in section 31.2. Market discount bonds are discussed in section 31.3, and purchase premiums on taxable and tax-exempt securities are discussed in section 31.4. Taxable and tax-exempt zero coupon securities are

---

[1] *See* section 9.2(e).
[2] *See* section 9.2(h).
[3] *See* section 24.9.
[4] *See* Roach, *Living with Corporate Debt*, 2 J. APPLIED CORP. FIN. 19 (Spring 1989); Taylor & Aidinoff, *Approaches to Debt: Is Integration the Answer?*, 67 TAXES 931 (1989).

discussed in section 31.5. Stripped bonds are discussed in section 31.6. Foreign currency transactions are discussed in section 31.7. Securities in default are discussed in section 31.8. Exchanges of debt securities are discussed in section 31.9. The tax rules that apply to retirements, redemptions, and dispositions of debt securities are addressed in section 31.10. The tax rules and considerations that apply to repurchase agreements and reverse repurchase agreements are set out in section 31.11. The registration requirements imposed on certain debt securities are addressed in section 31.12.

The wash sales rule,[5] the short sales rule,[6] and the Straddle Rules[7] apply to taxpayers owning debt securities unless specific exemptions are available. In addition, investors and traders are subject to the general rules for capital transactions,[8] while dealers, hedgers, and certain financial institutions are subject to the general rules for ordinary income transactions.[9]

§ 31.2 ORIGINAL ISSUE DISCOUNT

In general, OID is the difference between the issue price of a debt security and its stated redemption price at maturity.[10] If a debt security is originally issued at a price that is less than its redemption value at maturity, this discount amount is viewed as a form of interest that must be included in the owner's income and it can be deducted by the issuer. This discount is allocated over the life of the security through a series of adjustments to the security's issue price.

The OID method used to adjust the issue price depends on the date the security is issued and whether it is a corporate, government, short-term, or tax-exempt security. OID on a security is carried over from one purchaser to the next. The OID rules have changed in many ways since they were initially introduced into the Code. First applied to corporate securities in 1969, the OID rules were expanded to include government securities in 1982, and they were amended in 1984 to treat all taxable securities in the same way. In addition, special rules apply to short-term securities and tax-exempt securities.

---

[5] *See generally* Chapter 19.
[6] *See generally* Chapter 18.
[7] *See generally* Part Eleven.
[8] *See generally* Part Three.
[9] *See generally* Part Four.
[10] I.R.C. § 1273(a)(1).

An in-depth analysis of the OID rules is beyond the scope of this book.[11] Nevertheless, a brief explanation is critical to any understanding of the tax treatment of debt securities. The remainder of this section discusses the OID rules.

(a) CORPORATE AND GOVERNMENT DEBT SECURITIES ISSUED AFTER JULY 1, 1982

Owners of either corporate or government debt securities issued after July 1, 1982, with a term to maturity exceeding one year, must include in income the sum of the daily portion of OID determined for each day during the taxable year the security is held by the taxpayer.[12] The issuer's interest deduction is also subject to these rules.[13] For taxable securities, OID is ignored under a de minimis exception if the difference is less than .25 percent per year of the stated redemption price at maturity when multiplied by the number of complete years to maturity.[14]

For debt securities issued before January 1, 1985, OID is allocated over the life of the security through a series of adjustments to the issue price (i.e., adjustments made under I.R.C. § 1272)[15] for each "bond period" (i.e., the first one-year period beginning on the security's issue date and each subsequent anniversary, or the shorter period to maturity for the last period). The increase in the adjusted issue price for any bond period is allocated ratably to each day in the bond period.[16] In the case of securities issued after December 31, 1984, adjustments are made on the basis of six-month "accrual periods" that end on the day in the calendar year that corresponds to the maturity date, or the date six months before the

---

[11] For an excellent analysis of the Treasury regulations issued to address OID, see A PRACTICAL GUIDE TO THE ORIGINAL ISSUE DISCOUNT REGULATIONS (D. Garlock principal author & ed. 1988). *See also* New York State Bar Association, Tax Section, *Report of Ad Hoc Committee on Proposed Original Issue Discount Regulations, reprinted in Special Report*, 34 TAX NOTES 363 (1987).

[12] I.R.C. § 1272(a)(1). On April 2, 1986, the Treasury issued proposed rules on the tax treatment of debt securities issued after July 1, 1982, that contain OID. The proposed regulations explain and expand upon the OID provisions contained in the Code. *See generally* Prop. Treas. Reg. §§ 1.163-7, 1.1271-1 to 1.1273-2, 1.1275-1 to 1.1275-5. For a discussion of the proposed regulations, see American Bar Association, Section of Taxation, *Report on the Proposed Original Issue Discount Regulations*, 40 TAX LAW. 481 (1987); McCawley, *OID and Imputed Interest: Comments and Observations*, 28 Tax Mgmt. (BNA) Memorandum 227, 227—34 (1987); Lokken, *The Time Value of Money Rules*, 42 TAX L. REV. 1 (1986).

[13] I.R.C. § 163(e).

[14] I.R.C. § 1273(a)(3).

[15] I.R.C. § 1272(a)(4).

[16] I.R.C. § 1272(a)(3).

maturity date.[17] Each adjustment is allocated ratably to each day in the period that is included in the taxpayer's income for each day he holds the securities during the taxable year.[18]

The adjustment to a debt security's issue price, which is made each "bond period" or "accrual period" (whichever is applicable), increases the issue price as adjusted from the previous period. The adjustment made each period equals the adjusted issue price of the debt security at the beginning of the period, multiplied by the security's yield to maturity, minus the interest payable during the period.[19]

A subsequent owner of an OID security purchased for more than its adjusted issue price (i.e., the issue price plus the daily portions of OID for all days prior to the purchase) can offset the amount of OID included in income. For debt securities purchased before July 19, 1984, this "acquisition premium" is allocated on a straight-line basis over the number of days remaining to maturity. For debt securities purchased after July 18, 1984, the excess purchase price is amortized by reducing the daily portion of OID by the amount that would be the daily portion multiplied by a fraction reflecting the ratio of the acquisition premium to the total unaccrued OID at purchase.[20]

The taxpayer's basis in a security is increased by the amount of OID included in his income.[21] If there was an intention (at the time of issuance) to call the debt security before maturity, gain on the sale or redemption of debt securities is treated as interest to the extent of the OID, minus that portion of the OID previously included in income.[22] Redemptions pursuant to a mandatory sinking fund may evidence an intent to call debt securities before maturity. A mandatory sinking fund can also accelerate the inclusion of OID under the rules that apply to debt securities with serial maturity provisions as well. Gain realized on the exchange of OID debt securities issued with an intention to call the securities before maturity is not taxed as ordinary income if the gain is not otherwise recognized because of a nonrecognition Code provision such as I.R.C. § 354(a).[23]

A corporate issuer of debt securities issued in registered form at a discount must furnish the registered owner and the IRS with an informa-

---

[17] I.R.C. § 1272(a)(5).
[18] I.R.C. § 1272(a)(1).
[19] I.R.C. § 1272(a)(3).
[20] I.R.C. § 1272(a)(7).
[21] I.R.C. § 1272(d)(2).
[22] I.R.C. § 1271(a)(2)(A).
[23] Rev. Rul. 75-39, 1975-1 C.B. 272.

tion statement on IRS Form 1099-OID for the calendar year, if there is at least $10 of OID for the calendar year.[24]

Because the amount of OID includable in the owner's gross income is treated as interest, it is subject to backup withholding. The amount to be withheld is limited to cash payments made to payees (e.g., payments of stated interest and payments on redemption or maturity).[25]

(b) CORPORATE DEBT SECURITIES ISSUED AFTER MAY 27, 1969, AND BEFORE JULY 2, 1982

The owners of corporate debt securities with maturities in excess of one year issued after May 27, 1969, and before July 2, 1982, must include in income the "ratable monthly portion" of OID (i.e., OID divided by the number of complete months from the date of issuance through the day before the stated maturity) multiplied by the number of complete months and fractions thereof that they held such securities during the taxable year.[26] The basis of the debt security is increased by the amount of OID that was included in his income.[27]

On the sale or exchange of corporate debt securities issued after May 27, 1969, the purchaser of a security is treated as stepping into the shoes of the seller. Thus, the untaxed balance of the OID that is not includable in the income of prior owners is included in the subsequent owner's income ratably over the remaining life of the security. The amount is prorated on a daily basis for corporate and government securities issued after July 1, 1982.[28] The amount is prorated on a monthly basis for corporate securities issued after May 27, 1969, and before July 2, 1982.[29] If a subsequent owner purchases a debt security for an amount in excess of its adjusted basis in the hands of the prior security owner, however, the ratable amount of the excess is allowed as a reduction or offset. The subsequent owner determines his ratable monthly portion by dividing the amount by which the debt security's stated redemption price at maturity exceeds the security's cost to him by the number of complete months, plus any fractional months from the date he purchased the security and ending on

---

[24] Treas. Reg. § 1.6049-6(a) (1983). For a discussion of information reporting, see section 31.2(n).

[25] Temp. Treas. Reg. § 35a.9999-2 (A-15) (1983). The time and the manner of OID backup withholding depends on the type of security on which the OID is earned. *See generally* I.R.C. § 3406 and the temporary Treasury regulations issued thereunder.

[26] I.R.C. § 1272(b)(1); Treas. Reg. § 1.1232-3A(a)(2) (1975).

[27] I.R.C. § 1272(d)(2).

[28] I.R.C. § 1272(a)(1).

[29] I.R.C. § 1272(b)(1).

the day before maturity.[30] Future purchasers are treated in a similar manner.[31]

Any corporate issuer of debt securities in registered form issued at a discount after May 27, 1969, must furnish the registered owner and the IRS with an information statement[32] for the calendar year if two conditions are met. First, there must be at least $10 of OID for the calendar year. Second, the term of the security must be for more than one year.[33]

(c) CORPORATE DEBT SECURITIES ISSUED BEFORE MAY 28, 1969, AND GOVERNMENT DEBT SECURITIES ISSUED BEFORE JULY 2, 1982

For corporate debt securities issued after December 31, 1954, and before May 28, 1969, and for government securities issued after December 31, 1954, and before July 2, 1982, the owner does not pay tax on the OID until the security is sold, exchanged, or redeemed.[34] This allows a cash basis taxpayer that holds such debt securities the opportunity to defer discount income until he is actually paid. Upon sale or redemption of such securities, any gain is treated as ordinary income to the extent of an amount equal to the OID multiplied by a fraction, the numerator of which is the number of full months the owner holds the security, and the denominator of which is the number of months from the date of issuance to maturity.[35] For investors[36] and traders,[37] any excess gain is capital gain (long-term or short-term depending on the taxpayer's holding period).[38] Dealers,[39] hedgers,[40] and certain financial institutions[41] report ordinary income on the entire gain.

---

[30] I.R.C. § 1272(b)(4); Treas. Reg. §§ 1.1232-3A(a)(2), (3) (1975).

[31] I.R.C. § 1272(b)(4); Treas. Reg. §§ 1.1232-3A(a)(2), (3) (1975).

[32] This statement is provided on IRS Form 1099-OID. For a discussion of OID information reporting, see section 31.2(n).

[33] Treas. Reg. § 1.6049-6(a) (1983).

[34] I.R.C. § 1271(c)(2).

[35] *Id.*; Treas. Reg. § 1.1232-3(c) (1980).

[36] *See* section 8.1.

[37] *See* section 8.2.

[38] I.R.C. § 1271(c)(2)(A).

[39] *See* section 8.3.

[40] *See* section 8.4.

[41] *See* section 8.8.

(d) SHORT-TERM CORPORATE AND GOVERNMENT OBLIGATIONS

A short-term corporate or government obligation is a bond, debenture, note, certificate, or other evidence of indebtedness[42] that has a fixed maturity date that is not more than one year from the date of issue.[43] Short-term obligations are generally subject to the rules set out in I.R.C. §§ 1281–1283, as well as the rules in I.R.C. §§ 163(e)(2)(C), 1271(a)(3), and 1271(a)(4).

This section addresses the rules that apply to short-term corporate and government obligations.

(1) LAW IN EFFECT BEFORE JULY 19, 1984

Under the law in effect prior to July 19, 1984, OID on a short-term debt security was not generally included in income by a cash basis taxpayer prior to sale or redemption unless the taxpayer elected to include OID in income as it accrues.[44] Under the law in effect prior to the DRA changes in 1984,[45] the Code exempted short-term government securities payable without interest and due in one year or less (i.e., Treasury bills)[46] from the periodic inclusion of OID for all taxpayers.[47] A similar exemption from the OID rules was available for the obligations of natural persons[48] and tax-exempt securities.[49] In addition, interest on indebtedness incurred to purchase or carry securities eligible for these exemptions was currently deductible against unrelated income.[50]

---

[42] *See* I.R.C. § 1275(a)(1)(A) for the definition of a debt instrument.
[43] *See* I.R.C. §§ 1271(a)(3)(B), 1272(a)(2)(C), 1283(a)(1)(A).
[44] I.R.C. §§ 1281, 1282(b)(2), 1283(c).
[45] Pub. L. No. 98-369, 98 Stat. 494 (1984) [hereinafter DRA].
[46] *See* section 2.1(a)(1).
[47] I.R.C. § 1232A(a)(2)(C) (1983), *repealed by* DRA, *supra* note 45, § 42(a)(1).
[48] I.R.C. § 1232A(a)(2)(A) (1983), *repealed by* DRA, *supra* note 45, § 42(a)(1).
[49] I.R.C. § 1232A(a)(2)(B)(ii) (1983), *repealed by* DRA, *supra* note 45, § 42(a)(1). For a discussion of tax-exempt securities, see generally Chapter 33.
[50] I.R.C. § 163(a).

(2) LAW IN EFFECT AFTER JULY 18, 1984

(i) In General

For short-term debt securities acquired by certain taxpayers after July 18, 1984, acquisition discount (i.e., the difference between the stated redemption price at maturity and the taxpayer's basis in the security)[51] on short-term securities is accrued if the securities are held by any of the following taxpayers:

1. A taxpayer using the accrual method of accounting[52]
2. A bank[53]
3. A taxpayer that holds the securities primarily for sale to customers in the ordinary course of the taxpayer's trade or business[54]
4. A taxpayer that identifies the securities under I.R.C. § 1256(e)(2) as being part of a hedging transaction[55]
5. A RIC[56]
6. A common trust fund[57]
7. A taxpayer holds a stripped bond or stripped coupon if the taxpayer stripped the bond or coupon (or it was stripped by any other person) and the bond's or coupon's basis is determined by reference to the basis in the hands of such person[58]
8. A partnership, S corporation, trust, or other flow-through entity if more than 20 percent of the value of the entity is owned for 90 days by taxpayers that are subject to the rule for mandatory accrual,[59] and
9. Any flow-through entity that is formed or availed of to avoid mandatory accrual[60]

---

[51] I.R.C. § 1283(a)(2).
[52] I.R.C. § 1281(b)(1)(A).
[53] I.R.C. § 1281(b)(1)(C).
[54] Id.
[55] I.R.C. § 1281(b)(1)(E).
[56] I.R.C. § 1281(b)(1)(D).
[57] Id.
[58] I.R.C. § 1281(b)(1)(F).
[59] I.R.C. §§ 1281(b)(2)(C), (D).
[60] I.R.C. § 1281(b)(2)(A).

A "short-term obligation" is defined as any bond, debenture, note, or certificate or other evidence of indebtedness with a fixed maturity date not more than one year from the date of issue.[61] It does not include any tax-exempt obligation as defined in I.R.C. § 1275(a)(3).[62]

Acquisition discount accrued on a daily basis is computed so that each daily portion is equal to the amount of the discount divided by the number of days from the day after the acquisition to the maturity date.[63]

(ii) Election

For taxable years ending after July 18, 1984, a transitional year election to accrue acquisition discount is available to taxpayers subject to mandatory accrual for all short-term securities held during the taxable year that includes July 18, 1984.[64] If the election is made, the accrual of discount is treated as a change in the taxpayer's accounting method. The net adjustments to income required by the new rules are made over a five-year period, beginning with the year in which the election is made.[65]

For short-term government securities issued after July 18, 1984, a cash basis taxpayer can elect to include acquisition discount in income. Such an election applies to all short-term taxable securities acquired on or after the first day of the first year for which the election is made, and continues in effect unless the IRS consents to a revocation.[66] Acquisition discount accrues ratably on a daily basis; the discount is divided by the number of days after the date the taxpayer acquires the security, up to and including the date of maturity.[67]

A taxpayer can elect, however, to use a constant interest rate (based on yield to maturity) for certain short-term securities and ratable accrual on other short-term securities.[68] This election applies on a security-by-security basis. As a practical matter, cash basis taxpayers may decide to elect to accrue acquisition discount so they can currently deduct interest expense.

---

[61] I.R.C. § 1283(a)(1)(A).
[62] I.R.C. § 1283(a)(1)(B).
[63] I.R.C. § 1283(b)(1).
[64] I.R.C. § 1282(b)(2).
[65] DRA, *supra* note 45, § 44(e)(2).
[66] I.R.C. § 1282(b).
[67] I.R.C. § 1283(b)(1).
[68] I.R.C. § 1283(b)(2).

Gain or loss on the sale or redemption of a short-term security is generally treated as capital gain or loss for investors[69] and traders,[70] and ordinary income or loss to dealers,[71] hedgers,[72] and certain financial institutions.[73] For all taxpayers (including investors and traders), any OID recovered on a sale or redemption of a short-term security is treated as interest.[74]

(3) INTEREST DEFERRAL

I.R.C. § 1282 was added to the Code in 1984, as a rule to prevent cash method taxpayers not subject to I.R.C. § 1281[75] from deferring taxable income while obtaining deductions to carry (finance) short-term obligations.[76] Basically, I.R.C. § 1282 postpones a deduction for net direct interest expense on short-term obligations to the extent that accrued acquisition discount or OID is not taken into income by the holder. The interest deductions are available when the security matures.

A taxpayer's ability to currently deduct interest is limited for indebtedness incurred to purchase or carry short-term securities not subject to mandatory accrual under I.R.C. § 1281. If a taxpayer is not subject to mandatory accrual, his "net direct interest expense" (defined as the excess of interest paid or accrued to carry a security over the interest or OID included in income from the security)[77] with respect to a short-term security is deductible only to the extent that the interest expense exceeds the sum of (1) the daily portions of acquisition discount for each day during the taxable year on which the taxpayer held the security,[78] and (2) the amount of any interest payable on the security (other than interest taken into account in determining the amount of acquisition discount), which accrues during the taxable year while the taxpayer held the

---

[69] *See* section 8.1.
[70] *See* section 8.2.
[71] *See* section 8.3.
[72] *See* section 8.4.
[73] *See* section 8.8.
[74] United States v. Midland-Ross Corp., 381 U.S. 54 (1965), *rev'g* 335 F.2d 561 (6th Cir. 1964), *aff'g* 214 F. Supp. 631 (N.D. Ohio 1963); Treas. Reg. § 1.1232-3A(b)(2) (1975); STAFF OF THE JOINT COMM. ON TAXATION, 98TH CONG. 2D SESS., GENERAL EXPLANATION OF THE REVENUE PROVISIONS OF THE DEFICIT REDUCTION ACT OF 1984, at 103 (Joint Comm. Print 1984).
[75] For a discussion of I.R.C. § 1281, see section 31.2(d)(2).
[76] DRA, *supra* note 45, § 41(a).
[77] I.R.C. § 1277(c).
[78] I.R.C. § 1282(a)(1).

security (and is not included in the taxpayer's gross income for the year under the taxpayer's accounting method).[79]

When the interest expense on the loan incurred to finance the purchase or the short-term security does not exceed the yield on the security (and there are no payments made on the security during the taxable year), the entire interest expense is deferred until the security matures. On the other hand, a deduction may be available under I.R.C. § 1282 to the extent that the interest expense on the loan exceeds the yield on the short-term debt security, and for any interest income taxable in the year the security is issued.

(4) CHARACTERIZATION OF AMOUNTS RECEIVED ON RETIREMENT OR SALE

TRA '86[80] changed the rules for determining the ordinary income portion of any gain on the disposition of short-term obligations, both governmental and nongovernmental, and for the economic accrual of discount. Prior to amendment in 1986, I.R.C. § 1271 did not apply to nongovernmental short-term obligations. Nongovernmental obligations were covered by the addition of I.R.C. § 1271(a)(4). For tax years ending after July 18, 1984, any gain realized (by any taxpayer) on the retirement, sale, or exchange of a short-term nongovernmental obligation is treated as ordinary income (interest) to the extent of the ratable share of accrued OID.[81] The ratable share of accrued OID is computed by multiplying the total OID of the obligation by a fraction, the numerator of which is the number of days the obligation was held, and the denominator of which is the total days from issuance to maturity.[82] However, TRA '86 permits taxpayers to irrevocably elect to accrue OID on short-term nongovernmental obligations using a constant interest rate formula.[83] Under this method, the ratable share of OID is the portion of the OID that accrues while the taxpayer holds the obligation, determined by using the yield to maturity and compounding daily.[84]

An irrevocable election to accrue acquisition discount using a constant interest rate method is also available to owners of taxable short-term,

---

[79] I.R.C. § 1282(a)(2).
[80] Pub. L. No. 99-514, 100 Stat. 2085 (1986) [hereinafter TRA '86].
[81] I.R.C. § 1271(a)(4), *added by* TRA '86, *supra* note 80, § 1803(a).
[82] I.R.C. § 1271(a)(4)(C).
[83] I.R.C. § 1271(a)(4)(D).
[84] *Id.*

governmental obligations.[85] Such obligations are defined as any obligation (other than a tax-exempt obligation) of the United States or a United States possession, a state or its political subdivisions, or the District of Columbia that matures within one year of its date of issuance.[86] Upon the sale or exchange of these instruments, any gain that does not exceed an amount equal to the ratable share of the acquisition discount is treated as ordinary income.[87] Acquisition discount is defined as the excess of the stated redemption price at maturity over the taxpayer's basis. Taxpayers can elect to accrue acquisition discount compounding daily using the taxpayer's yield to maturity on the obligation. This rule is generally effective for tax years ending after July 18, 1984.[88]

Because I.R.C. § 1271 limits ordinary income recapture to the amount of gain that is realized, accrued acquisition discount or OID can avoid ordinary income treatment. In addition, because I.R.C. § 1271(a)(3) (certain short-term government obligations) and I.R.C. § 1271(a)(4) (certain nongovernment short-term obligations) do not apply to the disposition of a security for which acquisition discount or OID was accrued currently under I.R.C. § 1281, the holder's basis in the security is increased by the amount of accrued discount.[89]

(e) TAX-EXEMPT SECURITIES

Under IRS rulings issued prior to the DRA changes to the Code in 1984, OID on tax-exempt securities was apportioned among the original owner and subsequent owners of a security on a straight-line basis over the term of the security.[90] In many cases, the straight-line method resulted in artificially large portions of the OID attributed to its earlier bond periods. Further, because the owner of a tax-exempt security reduced the amount he realized on disposition of the security by the accrued (but tax-exempt) OID, the straight-line method also resulted in the recognition of an artificial loss on the disposition of the security for its market price.[91]

---

[85] I.R.C. § 1271(a)(3)(E).

[86] I.R.C. § 1271(a)(3)(B).

[87] I.R.C. § 1271(a)(3)(A).

[88] TRA '86, *supra* note 80, § 1803(a)(3).

[89] I.R.C. § 1283(d).

[90] HOUSE CONFERENCE REPORT, DEFICIT REDUCTION ACT OF 1984, H.R. CONF. REP. NO. 861, 98th Cong., 2d Sess. 810, *reprinted in* 1984 U.S. CODE CONG. & ADMIN. NEWS 1445, 1498 [hereinafter H.R. CONF. REP. NO. 861]; Rev. Rul. 73-112, 1973-1 C.B. 47.

[91] HOUSE WAYS AND MEANS COMM. REPORT, DEFICIT REDUCTION ACT OF 1984, H.R. REP. NO. 432, 98th Cong., 2d Sess. 1178, *reprinted in* 1984 U.S. CODE CONG. & ADMIN. NEWS 697, 851 [hereinafter H.R. REP. NO. 432].

Such artificial losses are not available to taxpayers for tax-exempt securities issued after September 3, 1982, and acquired after March 1, 1984. OID on tax-exempt obligations is now accrued in the same manner as that required since 1982 for OID on taxable debt securities,[92] except that there is no de minimis exception. Thus, all discounts (including those that are less than .25 percent) are accounted for and accrued.[93] OID on tax-exempt securities is accrued under the "economic" or "constant" (compound) interest method, which reflects the actual market appreciation of these securities.[94]

For purposes of tax-exempt obligations under I.R.C. § 1288, OID has the meaning it has under I.R.C. § 1273(a) (without regard to 1273(a)(3))—which provides the de minimis rule for determining the amount of OID.[95] In addition, the term "tax-exempt obligation" has the meaning given to the term by I.R.C. § 1275(a)(3),[96] which includes obligations for which the interest is not includable in gross income under I.R.C. § 103,[97] or the interest is exempt from tax (without regard to the identity of the holder) under any other provision of law.[98]

(f) FOREIGN INVESTORS

The DRA in 1984 initially provided that a foreign investor that receives a taxable interest payment on an obligation with OID, is taxed on an amount equal to the OID accrued on the obligation since the last payment of interest. TRA '86 amended this provision to provide that, when a foreign investor receives a payment (whether interest or principal) on an OID obligation, the taxable amount is equal to the amount of OID accrued on the obligation and that has not before been subject to tax, whether or not such OID accrued since the last payment of interest.[99] This amendment applies retroactively to payments made on or after September 16, 1984, with respect to obligations issued after March 31, 1972.[100]

A foreign investor, on the sale, exchange, or retirement of an OID obligation, is taxed on the amount of any gain not in excess of the OID

---

[92] I.R.C. § 1288(a); *see* section 31.2(e).
[93] I.R.C. § 1288(b)(1).
[94] *See* H.R. REP. No. 432, *supra* note 91, at 1178–79.
[95] I.R.C. § 1288(b)(1).
[96] I.R.C. § 1288(b)(2).
[97] I.R.C. § 1275(a)(3)(A).
[98] I.R.C. § 1275(a)(3)(B).
[99] I.R.C. § 871(a)(1)(C), *as amended by* TRA '86, *supra* note 80, § 1810(e).
[100] TRA '86, *supra* note 80, § 1810(e).

accruing while the foreign investor held the obligation (to the extent not previously taxed). TRA '86 provides that the foreign investor is taxed on the amount of OID accrued while the investor held the obligation (to the extent not previously taxed), whether or not the amount exceeds the foreign investor's gain on the sale, exchange, or retirement.[101] The TRA '86 amendment applies retroactively to payments made on or after September 16, 1984, with respect to obligations issued after March 31, 1972.[102]

Under the DRA, OID on an obligation held by a related foreign lender was not deductible by the issuer until paid. TRA '86 provides that this rule does not apply to the extent that the OID income is effectively connected with the lender's conduct of a United States trade or business unless the OID income is exempt from United States tax, or is subject to a reduced rate pursuant to a tax treaty.[103] The TRA '86 amendment applies to obligations issued after June 9, 1984.[104]

(g) APPLICABLE HIGH YIELD DISCOUNT OBLIGATIONS

(1) IN GENERAL

The RRA '89[105] added I.R.C. §§ 163(e)(5) and 163(i) to address Congressional concerns over the tax treatment of debt securities that (1) are issued with substantial OID and do not pay interest currently ("high yield OID securities"), and (2) call for interest to accrue at a fixed rate, but that give the issuer the option to make interest payments in the form of cash or additional bonds of the issuer ("payment-in-kind" or "PIK" bonds). The RRA '89 provisions—as modified retroactively by the RRA '90—limit the issuer's deduction of interest that is accrued as discount or paid in kind. They do not limit deductions for cash payments.[106] RRA '89 calls for bifurcation of the OID on high yield OID securities and PIK bonds:

1. A portion of the issuer's deduction is deferred until the issuer actually pays interest (not in additional bonds). The holder

---

[101] I.R.C. § 881(a)(3), *as amended by* TRA '86, *supra* note 80, § 1810(e)(2)(B).

[102] TRA '86, *supra* note 80, § 1810(e).

[103] *Id.*; I.R.C. § 163(e)(3)(A).

[104] TRA '86, *supra* note 80, § 1810(e).

[105] Pub. L. No. 101-239, 103 Stat. 2301 (1989) [hereinafter RRA '89]. The RRA '90 (Pub. L. No. 101-508, 104 Stat. 1388 (1990)) amended these sections retroactively as if the amendment were included in RRA '89.

[106] *See* Sheppard, *Ring Around the Interest Disallowance Rules*, 15 DAILY TAX HIGHLIGHTS & DOCUMENTS 2471 (1989).

reports OID on this portion as income as it accrues under applicable OID rules.

2. A "disqualified portion" is basically treated as a nondeductible return on equity that is never deductible by the issuer (if the yield exceeds a specified amount). The holder reports the income on this portion as it accrues under the applicable OID rules. A corporate holder can qualify for the intercorporate dividends received deduction.[107]

The remainder of this section addresses application of I.R.C. §§ 163(e)(5) and (i) to high yield OID securities and PIK bonds.

(2) APPLICABLE HIGH YIELD DISCOUNT OBLIGATIONS

"Applicable high yield discount obligations" are subject to I.R.C. §§ 163(e)(5) and 163(i). In general, bifurcation applies to any "applicable high yield discount obligation" that has a term of more than five years, "significant OID," and a yield that is at least five percentage points above the applicable federal rate in effect for the calendar month in which the obligation is issued.[108] In addition, the security must be issued by a corporation.[109]

(i) Payment-in-Kind Bonds

PIK bonds permit (or require) the issuer to make payments-in-kind rather than in cash for interest payments.[110] Even though the PIK bonds call for interest to accrue at a fixed rate, the issuer has the option—or is required to—make some or all of the interest payments (typically except for the last payment) in cash or additional baby bonds. If the issuer pays interest by giving the holder an additional bond, the interest is basically accrued and is added to the principal amount of the PIK bond.[111]

---

[107] For a discussion of the intercorporate dividends received deduction, see section 24.9.
[108] I.R.C. § 163(i)(1).
[109] I.R.C. § 163(e)(5) provides that the issuer must be a corporation for I.R.C. § 163(e)(5) to apply.
[110] Bonds that are issued in lieu of cash interest payments are often referred to as "baby bonds," while the PIK bonds are often referred to as "parent bonds."
[111] PIK bonds have been quite popular in LBO financings. In general, the payments in kind are made for the first three to six years after the bonds are issued. *See generally* Clark, *Pay-in-kind Pfd. Gains Following in Leveraged Deals*, CORP. FINANCING WK., Apr. 13, 1987, at 1.

PIK bond interest is treated in the same manner as OID under I.R.C. § 163(i)(3)(B), which provides that "any payment to be made in the form of another obligation of the issuer (or a related person within the meaning of [I.R.C.] section 453(f)(1) shall be assumed to be made when such obligation is required to be paid in cash or in property other than such obligation)." Any reference to an "obligation" in I.R.C. § 163(i)(3)(B) is treated as including a reference to stock except for purposes of I.R.C. § 163(i)(1)(B). This means that if interest on PIK bonds is paid in the form of another obligation of the issuer (or a related person), the interest is treated as paid at the maturity date of the obligation received as payment, or when the stock (preferred or common) is redeemed.

Any payment under the PIK bond is assumed to be made on the last day permitted under the instrument.[112] This means that if the issuer has the option to pay interest on its PIK bonds in cash or with a payment-in-kind, the PIK bond is viewed as being issued with OID. It is assumed under I.R.C. § 163(i)(3)(A) that the issuer will not pay interest in cash until the maturity date.

(ii) Significant Original Issue Discount

An applicable high yield discount obligation must have "significant original issue discount,"[113] which is defined in I.R.C. § 163(i)(2), based on a formula set out in the Code. A debt instrument is treated as having significant OID if (1) the aggregate amount that would be includable in gross income with respect to the instrument for periods before the close of any "accrual period" (as defined in I.R.C. § 1272(a)(5)) ending after the date five years after the date of issue,[114] *exceeds* (2) the *sum* of (a) the aggregate amount of interest to be paid under the instrument before the close of the accrual period, and (b) the product of the issue price of the instrument (as defined in I.R.C. §§ 1273(b) and 1274(a)) and its yield to maturity.[115]

---

[112] I.R.C. § 163(i)(3)(A).
[113] I.R.C. § 163(i)(1)(C).
[114] I.R.C. § 163(i)(2)(A).
[115] I.R.C. § 163(i)(2)(B). Its yield to maturity is generally an amount equal to the first 12 months' yield on the instrument. I.R.C. §§ 163(i)(2), (3).

(a) ACCRUAL PERIOD

"Accrual period," for purposes of calculating whether there is significant OID, is defined in I.R.C. § 1272(a)(5).[116] "Except as otherwise provided in [Treasury] Regulations," accrual period "means a 6-month period (or shorter period from the date of original issue of the debt instrument) which ends on a day in the calendar year corresponding to the maturity date of the debt instrument or the date 6 months before such maturity date."[117] Prop. Treas. Reg. § 1.1272-1(d),[118] however, defines "accrual period" as (1) regular intervals of one year or less, during which a debt instrument either pays or compounds interest, (2) any short period from the date of issue to the first regular accrual period, and (3) any short period from the end of the last regular accrual period to maturity of the instrument.[119]

(b) CALCULATION OF SIGNIFICANT ORIGINAL ISSUE DISCOUNT

A debt instrument is treated as having significant OID if, at the time the instrument is issued, the issuer is not required to pay all interest and OID that accrued on the debenture by the end of the period beginning on the fifth year after issuance and ending before the sixth year after issuance—except for an amount equal to the first 12 months' yield that accrued after the instrument was issued.

In addition, a debt instrument is viewed as issued with significant OID if, at the time it is issued, the issuer is not required to have paid by the end of each accrual period all interest and OID accrued on the debt instrument—except for an amount equal to the first 12 months' yield that accrued after the instrument was issued. Because it is assumed, for determining whether a debt instrument is an applicable high yield discount obligation, that any payment under the instrument is made on the last day permitted under the instrument,[120] the calculation of significant OID is based on the instrument's terms when it is issued.

---

[116] I.R.C. § 163(i)(2)(A).

[117] I.R.C. § 1272(a)(5).

[118] (1989).

[119] Because I.R.C. § 1272(a)(5) provides for regulatory exceptions to the definition of accrual period, the reference in I.R.C. § 163(i)(2)(A) to the accrual period as defined in I.R.C. § 1272(a)(5) appears to incorporate any modifications by future Treasury regulations to the six-month statutory definition.

[120] I.R.C. § 163(i)(3)(A).

(3) TAXATION OF ISSUERS

(i) Original Issue Discount

OID on an applicable high yield discount obligation is bifurcated under I.R.C. § 163(e)(5). First, a portion of the issuer's interest deduction is deferred until the issuer actually pays interest (not in additional bonds). Second, a portion is disqualified and treated as a nondeductible return on equity that is never deductible by the issuer if the yield exceeds the adjusted federal rate, plus six percentage points (which is one point higher than the yield to maturity under I.R.C. § 163(i)(1)(B)).[121] As a result, the issuer can deduct interest payments when paid on the deferred portion although the issuer can never deduct interest paid on the nondeductible portion.

(ii) Earnings and Profits

In general, I.R.C. § 163(e)(5)(E) provides that the provisions of I.R.C. § 163(e)(5) do not apply "for purposes of determining earnings and profits." There is an exception provided in I.R.C. § 163(e)(5)(E) "for purposes of determining the dividend equivalent portion of any amount includible in gross income under [I.R.C.] section 1272(a) in respect of an applicable high yield discount obligation, no reduction shall be made for any amount attributable to the disqualified portion of any original issue discount on such obligation."[122] As a result, a corporate holder will not be denied the intercorporate dividends received deduction because the issuer's earnings and profits were reduced by the disqualified portion of OID.

(iii) S Corporations Exempt

The provisions of I.R.C. § 163(e)(5) do not apply to any obligation issued by any corporation for any period during which the corporation is an S corporation.[123] The Conference Report that accompanied RRA '89 states that the "conferees intend that if a C corporation issues an applicable

---

[121] I.R.C. § 163(e)(5)(C).
[122] I.R.C. § 163(e)(5)(E).
[123] I.R.C. § 163(e)(5)(D).

instrument and subsequently converts to S corporation status, previously accrued but deferred interest will be deductible when paid."[124]

(4) TAXATION OF HOLDERS

Although OID on an applicable high yield discount obligation is bifurcated for purposes of the issuer, I.R.C. § 163(e)(5) does not address the OID rules that apply to holders. As a result, the holder reports OID income as it accrues under the applicable OID rules for both the issuer's deferred and nondeductible portions of OID.

A corporate holder of an applicable high yield discount obligation can qualify for the intercorporate dividends received deduction.[125] In general, I.R.C. § 163(e)(5)(B)(i) provides that solely for purposes of I.R.C. §§ 243, 245, 246, and 246A, "the dividend equivalent portion of any amount includible in gross income of a corporation under I.R.C. § 1272(a) in respect of an applicable high yield discount obligation shall be treated as a dividend received by such corporation from the corporation issuing such obligation." The "dividend equivalent portion" is "the portion of the amount so includible (I) which is attributable to the disqualified portion of the original issue discount on such obligation, and (II) which would have been treated as a dividend if it had been a distribution made by the issuing corporation with respect to stock in such corporation."[126] This means that a corporate holder reports as interest income all OID calculated under I.R.C. § 1272 and it might also be entitled to the intercorporate dividends received deduction under I.R.C. § 163(e)(5)(B).[127]

(5) EFFECTIVE DATE AND EXCEPTIONS

The rules for applicable high yield discount obligations generally apply to debt securities issued after July 10, 1989. There are four exceptions to the general effective date.

---

[124] HOUSE CONFERENCE REPORT, REVENUE RECONCILIATION ACT OF 1989, H.R. CONF. REP. NO. 386, 101st Cong., 1st Sess. 521, 554, *reprinted in* 1989 U.S. CODE CONG. & ADMIN. NEWS 3124, 3157.

[125] I.R.C. § 163(e)(5)(B). For a discussion of the intercorporate dividends received deduction, see section 24.9.

[126] I.R.C. § 163(e)(5)(B)(ii).

[127] In determining the amount of stock the holder owns in the issuer, it appears as if the applicable high yield discount obligation is not treated as "stock." In addition, it appears as if the basis reduction required by I.R.C. § 1059 does not apply to the dividend equivalent portion of interest received under I.R.C. § 163(e)(5)(B) because I.R.C. § 163(e)(5)(B)(i) does not provide that this amount is a dividend for purposes of I.R.C. § 1059 and the applicable high yield discount obligation is not "stock."

First, the provisions of I.R.C. §§ 163(e)(5) and (i) do not apply to certain debt instruments issued in connection with an acquisition (1) made on or before July 10, 1989, (2) for which there is a written binding contract in effect on July 10, 1989, and at all times thereafter before such acquisition, or (3) a tender offer was filed with the SEC on or before July 10, 1989.[128] To meet this exception, the terms of the instrument must meet the provisions set out in RRA '89 § 7202(c)(2)(A)(ii), and the use of the instrument in connection with the acquisition was determined and evidenced by written documents before July 10, 1989.[129]

Second, the provisions of I.R.C. §§ 163(e)(5) and (i) do not apply to "any instrument issued pursuant to the terms of a debt instrument issued on or before July 10, 1989," or excepted under RRA '89 § 7202(c)(2).[130]

Third, the provisions of I.R.C. §§ 163(e)(5) and (i) do not apply to any instrument issued to refinance an OID instrument to which I.R.C. §§ 163(e)(5) and (i) do not apply, if the refinancing does not (1) postpone the maturity date on the old instrument, (2) the issue price of the new instrument does not exceed the adjusted issue price of the old instrument, (3) the stated redemption price of the new instrument is not greater than the stated redemption price at maturity of the old instrument, and (4) the interest payments under the new instrument before maturity are not less than (and are paid no later than) the interest payments required under the old instrument.[131]

Fourth, the provisions of I.R.C. §§ 163(e)(5) and (i) do not apply "to instruments issued after July 10, 1989, pursuant to a reorganization plan in a title 11 or similar case (as defined in [I.R.C.] section 368(a)(3))" if the amount of the proceeds and the maturity of such instruments do not exceed the amount or maturities specified in the last reorganization plan filed in the case on or before July 10, 1989.[132]

(h) CORPORATE REORGANIZATIONS

The proposed Treasury regulations on OID do not address debt securities issued in corporate reorganizations, although Treas. Reg. § 1.1232-3(b)(1)(iv) of the prior regulations provided that the owner would carry over to the new debt security the amount of unaccrued OID from the old debt security, reduced by the amount of any ordinary income on the

---

[128] RRA '89, *supra* note 105, § 7202(c)(2)(A)(i).
[129] RRA '89, *supra* note 105, § 7202(c)(2)(A)(iii).
[130] RRA '89, *supra* note 105, § 7202(c)(2)(B).
[131] RRA '89, *supra* note 105, § 7202(c)(2)(C).
[132] RRA '89, *supra* note 105, § 7202(c)(2)(D).

exchange. I.R.C. § 1275(a)(4) provides that the issue price of a new debt security is at least equal to the adjusted issue price of a debt security received in exchange for it.[133]

(i) CONTINGENT PAYMENT OBLIGATIONS

The basic premise in the OID rules that interest should be reported as income as it accrues does not apply in the case of contingent payment obligations. This is because all of the interest that accrues might not actually be paid and the yield on the obligation cannot be calculated on the issue date because the timing and the amount of future payments is contingent. For a discussion of the proposed Treasury regulation that addresses the application of the OID rules to debt instruments that provide for one or more contingent payments, see Prop. Treas. Reg. § 1.1275-4.[134]

(j) INVESTMENT UNITS

I.R.C. § 1273(c)(2) addresses the case of "any debt instrument and an option, security, or other property issued together as an investment unit."[135] First, the issue price for the unit is determined in accordance with the rules of I.R.C. §§ 1273(c)(2) and 1273(b) as if the unit were a debt instrument.[136]

Second, the issue price determined for the investment unit is allocated to each element of the unit on the basis of the relationship of the fair market value of such element to the fair market value of all elements in the unit.[137] An allocation of basis on the fair market value of the elements in an investment unit can be made easily if the elements trade independently in a public market. If not, the determination of fair market value obviously becomes more difficult.

---

[133] I.R.C. § 1275(a)(4), *added by* TCA '82, Pub. L. No. 97-448, § 306(a)(9)(c)(ii), 96 Stat. 2365 (1983) [hereinafter TCA '82]. It applies to debt securities issued after December 12, 1982.

[134] (1989). Under Prop. Treas. Reg. § 1.1275-4(c), contingent interest is treated as a separate obligation. Contingent interest is accounted for separate from the noncontingent obligation. Contingent interest is not deductible until the amount becomes fixed. The most controversial portions of the proposed regulations under I.R.C. § 1275 are the rules for contingent payment obligations. *See, e.g.,* Sheppard, *IRS Officials Preview Upcoming Changes to OID Rules,* 46 TAX NOTES 1243 (1990).

[135] Prop. Treas. Reg. § 1.1273-2(d)(1) defines an investment unit as a debt instrument and a property right, such as a security or option.

[136] I.R.C. § 1273(c)(2)(A).

[137] I.R.C. § 1273(c)(2)(B).

And third, the issue price of any debt instrument included in the investment unit is the portion of the issue price allocated to the debt instrument under I.R.C. § 1273(c)(2)(B).[138] The proposed Treasury regulations address investment units at Prop. Treas. Reg. § 1.1273-2(d).[139]

In LTR 8851047,[140] the IRS ruled that reset notes and preferred stock received in exchange for preferred stock is an investment unit under I.R.C. § 1273(c).

(k) PASS-THROUGH CERTIFICATES

Pass-through certificates are a popular form of asset-backed securities.[141] Pass-through certificates can be purchased with OID. For a discussion of the tax treatment of pass-through certificates purchased with OID, see section 37.4.

(l) PAY-THROUGH BONDS

Pay-through bonds are a popular form of asset-backed securities.[142] Pay-through bonds can be purchased with OID. For a discussion of the tax treatment of pay-through bonds purchased with OID, see section 38.4.

(m) REAL ESTATE MORTGAGE INVESTMENT CONDUIT REGULAR INTERESTS

REMIC regular interests are debt securities subject to the OID rules. For a discussion of regular interests, see generally sections 7.2(g) and 36.8(c)(1). REMIC regular interests purchased at a discount are generally taxed in the same manner as pay-through bonds. For a discussion of pay-through bonds purchased with OID or market discount, see section 38.4.

Regular interests may be subject to the OID rules if the stated redemption price at maturity exceeds the issue price. I.R.C. § 1272(a)(6), which provides rules to determine the daily portion of OID, applies to "any regular interest in a REMIC or qualified mortgage held by a REMIC."[143] I.R.C. § 1272(a)(6) also applies to "any other debt instrument if payments under such debt instrument may be accelerated by reason of

---

[138] I.R.C. § 1273(c)(2)(C).
[139] (1989).
[140] (Sept. 27, 1988).
[141] For a discussion of pass-through certificates, see generally Chapters 7 and 36.
[142] For a discussion of pay-through bonds, see generally Chapters 7 and 36.
[143] I.R.C. § 1272(a)(6)(C).

prepayments of other obligations securing such debt instrument (or, to the extent provided in regulations, by reason of other events)."[144] This means that I.R.C. § 1272(a)(6) applies to qualified mortgages held by a REMIC (and other debt instruments issued after December 31, 1986), if the payments can be accelerated because of prepayments.

In calculating OID (or market discount) on the mortgages a REMIC holds and on the REMIC's regular interests, the REMIC must include any "prepayment assumption" used in calculating the yield to maturity.[145] In addition, the REMIC must take into account actual prepayments when it calculates the OID (or market discount) that has accrued for each day in any accrual period.[146] The "prepayment assumption to be used . . . will be that used by the parties in pricing the particular transaction," while prepayment assumptions for the regular interests must be "determined by the assumed rate of prepayments on qualified mortgages." The TRA '86 Conference Report that accompanied the REMIC legislation provides that "prepayment assumptions used must not be unreasonable based on comparable transactions, if comparable transactions exist."[147] In addition, "unless otherwise provided by [Treasury] regulations, the use of . . . prepayment assumptions based on a Public Securities Association standard . . . an industry recognized standard" would be permitted.[148] Further, "in the case of publicly offered instruments, a prepayment assumption will be treated as unreasonable only in the presence of clear and convincing evidence."[149]

There can never be negative OID. This means that if the OID for an accrual period is negative, "the amount of OID attributable to such accrual period would be treated as zero, and the computation of OID for the following accrual period would be made as if such . . . period and the preceding . . . period were a single accrual period."[150]

---

[144] *Id.*
[145] I.R.C. § 1272(a)(6)(B)(iii).
[146] I.R.C. § 1272(a)(6)(A).
[147] STAFF OF THE JOINT COMM. ON TAXATION, 99TH CONG., 2D SESS., TAX REFORM BILL OF 1986, FINAL CONFERENCE COMM. DECISIONS II-238 to II-239 (Joint Comm. Print 1986) [hereinafter TRA '86 Conf. Rep.].
[148] *Id.* at II-239.
[149] *Id.* n.23.
[150] *Id.* at II-239.

(n) INFORMATION REPORTING

Issuers of debt securities with OID are subject to various information reporting requirements if the securities have more than a de minimis amount of OID and they are not exempt under I.R.C. § 1272(a)(2).

(1) INFORMATION TO BE SET OUT ON THE DEBT SECURITY

I.R.C. § 1275(c)(1)(A) provides that Treasury regulations can require any debt security with OID to set out on the instrument (1) the amount of OID, and (2) the issue date. If the debt security is not publicly offered, Treasury regulations need not require the information to be set out on the face of the instrument "before any disposition of such instrument by the first buyer."[151]

For OID securities issued after May 8, 1986, the issuer must provide the following information:

1. The amount of the OID (as defined in I.R.C. § 1273(a)(1) and Prop. Treas. Reg. § 1.1273-1(a))[152]
2. The issue date (as defined in I.R.C. § 1275(a)(2) and Prop. Treas. Reg. § 1.1275-1(c))[153]
3. The yield to maturity (as defined in Prop. Treas. Reg. § 1.1272-1(f))[154]
4. The method used to determine yield where there is a short accrual period, and
5. The amount of OID allocable to the short accrual period[155]

In addition, Temp. Treas. Reg. § 1.6049-7T(g)[156] sets out the information requirements for those OID securities under I.R.C. § 1272(a)(6)— REMIC regular interests, qualified mortgages held by a REMIC, or any debt security that may be accelerated by reason of prepayments of other obligations securing such debt instrument—that are issued after April 8, 1988. Information requirements are the same as the general require-

---

[151] I.R.C. § 1275(c)(1)(B). This provision applies to instruments first disposed after May 8, 1986, by the first holder.
[152] (1986).
[153] (1986).
[154] (1986).
[155] Prop. Treas. Reg. § 1.1275-3(a) (1989).
[156] (1989).

ments set out above, except that two additional statements must be added:

1. The rate at which interest is payable (if any) as of the issue date,[157] and
2. The assumption made under I.R.C. § 1272(a)(6)(B)(iii) for the rate of prepayments of the obligations underlying the interest[158]

There is a $50 penalty imposed for each debt instrument on which the issuer fails to provide the required information, unless the failure "is due to reasonable cause and not to willful neglect."[159]

(2) INFORMATION TO BE REPORTED TO THE IRS

Issuers of publicly offered debt instruments with OID issued after August 16, 1984, file IRS Form 8281, which contains the following information:

1. The name, address, telephone number, and taxpayer identification number of the issuer
2. The issue date (as defined in I.R.C. § 1275(a)(2)), maturity date, and CUSIP number of the issue
3. The amount of original issue discount for the entire issue (as defined in I.R.C. § 1273(a))
4. A schedule of the amount of original issue discount per unit of original principal amount for each accrual period and specifying the unit of original principal amount if other than $1000
5. The issue price (as defined in I.R.C. § 1273(b)) expressed as a percentage of the principal amount
6. The stated redemption price at maturity of the entire issue, or of each debt instrument within the issue if in denominations of other than $1000
7. The stated interest rate and the interest payment dates
8. The yield to maturity
9. A description of the debt instrument, or, in place of the description, a copy of the offering circular or prospectus, which

---

[157] Temp. Treas. Reg. § 1.6049-7T(g)(3) (1989). The issue date refers to the REMIC startup date as defined in I.R.C. § 860G(a)(9).
[158] Temp. Treas. Reg. § 1.6049-7T(g)(4) (1989).
[159] I.R.C. § 6706(a).

description shall include a statement of any terms and conditions of the instrument that govern—

    a. Whether payments of principal may be made prior to maturity of the debt instrument

    b. Whether the debt instrument is part of an investment unit

    c. Whether the debt instrument is issued in an exchange described in I.R.C. § 368(a)

    d. Whether the debt instrument is a variable rate debt instrument described in Prop. Treas. Reg. § 1.1275-5(a)

    e. Whether the debt instrument is part of a serial issue, and

    f. Whether the debt instrument is a stripped bond or stripped coupon

10. The method selected for computing the amount of original issue discount allocable to a short accrual period, and

11. Such other information as is required by the form[160]

The Form 8281 must be filed within 30 days after the issue date for debt securities issued after May 31, 1985.[161] Failing to file or late filing of a Form 8281 is subject to a penalty equal to one percent of the aggregate issue price of the issue up to a maximum penalty of $50,000 for the issue, unless it is shown that the failure is due to reasonable cause and not willful neglect.[162]

(3) REPORTING OID PAYMENTS TO THE IRS

Every person that pays interest or OID to any other person during a calendar year, in the aggregate of $10 or more, must report the aggregate amount of the payment and the name and address of the recipient.[163]

Interest and OID, for I.R.C. § 6049 reporting purposes, do not include OID in the following circumstances:

1. OID on any obligation issued by a natural person[164]

---

[160] Prop. Treas. Reg. § 1.1275-3(b)(2) (1989).
[161] Prop. Treas. Reg. § 1.1275-3(b)(3) (1989).
[162] I.R.C. § 6706(b); Prop. Treas. Reg. § 1.1275-3(b)(4) (1989).
[163] I.R.C. § 6049; Prop. Treas. Reg. § 1.6049-5(c) (1989). The term "person" is defined to include "any governmental unit and any agency or instrumentality thereof and any international organization and any agency or instrumentality thereof. I.R.C. § 6049(d)(1).
[164] See I.R.C. § 6049(b)(2)(A).

2. OID on tax-exempt debt securities exempt under I.R.C. § 103(a) or any other Code provision[165]

3. Except as provided in regulations, any amount paid to a person described in I.R.C. § 6049(b)(4),[166] or any amount described in I.R.C. § 6049(b)(5)[167]

OID should be reported as if paid at the time it is includable in gross income under I.R.C. § 1272 (which sets out the instruments for which OID must be included in current income) except that the amount reportable with respect to any subsequent holder is determined as if he were the original holder.[168] If I.R.C. § 1272 does not apply to the obligation, OID should be reported at the earlier of the maturity or redemption of the security.[169] These provisions do not apply to any obligation not in registered form issued before January 1, 1983.[170] The OID amount is reported on IRS Form 1099-INT.[171]

Every person required to file a Form 1099-OID with the IRS must also furnish a written statement to each person whose name appears on the form, showing the name and address of the person required to make the return, and the aggregate amount of payments to, or includable in the gross income of, the person whose name is required to be shown on the return.[172] The Form 1099-OID for tax years beginning with calendar year 1991, will need to be prepared for each person that is a holder of record at any time during the calendar year, reporting the OID that accrued for the

---

[165] *See* I.R.C. § 6049(b)(2)(B).

[166] "Person" is defined in I.R.C. § 6049(b)(4) to include a corporation; an organization exempt from taxation under I.R.C. § 501(a) or an individual retirement plan; the United States or any of its wholly owned agencies or instrumentalities; a State, the District of Columbia, a possession of the United States, any subdivision, or any wholly owned agency or instrumentality of any of the foregoing; a foreign government, political subdivision, or any wholly owned agency or instrumentality; an international organization or any wholly owned agency or instrumentality; a foreign central bank of issue; a dealer in securities or commodities required to register as such under certain laws; a REIT as defined in I.R.C. § 856; an entity registered under the ICA; a common trust fund as defined in I.R.C. § 584(a); or any trust that is exempt from tax under I.R.C. § 664(c) (charitable remainder trusts and charitable remainder unitrusts), or is described in I.R.C. § 4947(a)(1) (certain other charitable trusts). I.R.C. § 6049(b)(4).

[167] Amounts described in I.R.C. § 6049(b)(5) include amounts subject to withholding for nonresident aliens and foreign corporations by the person paying the amount, or the amounts would be subject to withholding but for certain facts set out in I.R.C. § 6049(b)(5).

[168] I.R.C. § 6049(d)(6)(i).

[169] I.R.C. § 6049(d)(6)(ii).

[170] I.R.C. § 6049(d)(6).

[171] Treas. Reg. § 1.6049-4(b)(2) (1983).

[172] I.R.C. § 6049(c).

§ 31.3   Financial Products: Taxation, Regulation, and Design

actual holding period during the year. Under the rules in effect prior to January 1, 1991, a person required to send a Form 1099-OID was allowed to send the form only to those persons that were holders of record on the semiannual record date, or on June 30 and December 31. Under prior rules, the person required to send the form could treat holders as holding the debt obligations for the entire year. The Form 1099-OID must include a legend stating that the reported amount is also being reported to the IRS.[173]

(4) REPORTING FOR REAL ESTATE MORTGAGE INVESTMENT CONDUIT REGULAR INTERESTS AND CERTAIN SIMILAR DEBT SECURITIES

For REMIC regular interests and other debt instruments where the payments under the instruments may be accelerated by reason of prepayments of other obligations securing the debt instruments,[174] the method for calculating OID is set out in I.R.C. § 1272(a)(6). In general, a REMIC regular interest or similar debt instrument will have the daily portion of OID determined by allocating to each day in the accrual period its ratable share of the excess (if any) of (1) the *sum* of (a) the present value of the remaining payments under the debt instrument as of the close of the period, and (b) the payments during the accrual period of amounts included in the stated redemption price of the debt instrument, *over* (2) the adjusted issue price of the debt instrument at the beginning of the period.[175] Because this information is usually only available to the issuers of the REMIC regular interest and the similar debt instruments, I.R.C. § 6049(d)(7) provides more detailed reporting requirements on the issuers of REMIC regular interests and similar debt instruments. The issuer of an I.R.C. § 1272(a)(6) instrument must file with the IRS on IRS Form 8811 for each issue identifying the instrument.[176]

§ 31.3   MARKET DISCOUNT BONDS

(a) OVERVIEW

There are two types of discount on debt securities—OID and market discount. If a security is issued at a discount, the difference between the

---

[173] Treas. Reg. § 1.6049-6(b)(1)(iv) (1983).
[174] I.R.C. § 1272(a)(6)(C).
[175] I.R.C. § 1272(a)(6).
[176] Temp. Treas. Reg. § 1.6049-7T(b)(1) (1989).

issue price and the redemption price is OID,[177] which is deemed to be additional interest income to the holder[178] and additional interest expense to the issuer. OID is allocated over the term of the security.[179] For a discussion of OID, see section 31.2.

Market discount is the difference between the purchase price of a debt security after it has been issued and its redemption price. The prices of debt securities fluctuate as interest rates change and as the issuer's financial condition and credit ratings change. As a result, debt securities issued without OID can be acquired at a discount (or a premium) from the original issue price.[180] A debt security purchased at a price that is less than its issue price has market discount. There is this type of market discount whenever the value of a debt security declines after issuance (typically because of an increase in prevailing interest rates).[181]

Under the law in effect before the DRA changes to the Code in 1984, a taxpayer that was an investor or trader and that purchased a security at a price below its issue price (i.e., a market discount bond) could treat the difference on sale or at maturity as a capital gain rather than as additional interest income.[182] Congress recognized that from the standpoint of an owner of a debt security, market discount is indistinguishable from OID.[183] By financing a purchase of a debt security with market discount, some taxpayers, under the law in effect before the DRA changes in 1984, effectively converted ordinary income (that would be offset by current interest deductions for interest incurred to carry the obligation) into capital gain (taxed on a deferred basis on the disposition of the security).[184] Taxpayers accomplished this by purchasing market discount bonds with borrowed funds, while deducting interest on the indebtedness currently and reporting the difference between the purchase price and the total principal payments as capital gain.

Two Code provisions, initially added by the DRA in 1984, now eliminate this opportunity for conversion for certain securities acquired with

---

[177] I.R.C. §§ 1278(a)(5), 1273(a)(1).

[178] I.R.C. § 1272(a)(1).

[179] I.R.C. § 163(e).

[180] For a discussion of market premiums, see section 31.4.

[181] H.R. REP. No. 432, *supra* note 91, at 1170.

[182] *See, e.g.*, Darby Inv. Corp. v. Comm'r, 37 T.C. 839 (1962), *aff'd per curiam*, 315 F.2d 551 (6th Cir. 1963); Vancoh Realty Co. v. Comm'r, 33 B.T.A. 918 (1936), *nonacq*. XV-2 C.B. 49. H.R. REP. No. 432, *supra* note 91, at 1170.

[183] H.R. REP. No. 432, *supra* note 91, at 1170.

[184] *Id.*

market discount.[185] First, market discount is recharacterized as additional interest.[186] Second, interest incurred to purchase or carry a market discount bond is not currently deductible and must be deferred.[187] I.R.C. § 1278 provides definitions and special rules. The rule that market discount is recharacterized as additional interest is addressed in section 31.3(f). The rule that interest incurred to purchase or carry market discount bonds is deferred is addressed in section 31.3(m).

(b) MARKET DISCOUNT AND MARKET DISCOUNT BONDS DEFINED

Market discount is defined as the amount by which the stated redemption price of a security (i.e., a revised issue price in the case of a security issued with OID) exceeds the security's basis immediately after acquisition—if it was issued at par.[188] Market discount also includes the amount by which a security is purchased in the market for less than it was issued for, after its price is increased by the amount of OID accruing from issue until the date of purchase.[189]

A market discount bond is defined in I.R.C. § 1278(a)(1) as any bond having market discount. I.R.C. § 1278(a)(3) defines a bond as any bond, debenture, note, certificate, or other evidence of indebtedness.[190] Market discount bonds do not include the following obligations:

1. Short-term securities with fixed maturities not exceeding one year from the date of issue[191]

2. Tax-exempt securities, as defined in I.R.C. § 1275(a)(3)[192]

3. United States savings bonds[193]

---

[185] Despite the fact that Congress stated that market discount is indistinguishable from OID, it adopted separate Code provisions for market discount and OID.

[186] I.R.C. § 1276(a)(3) for securities acquired before October 22, 1986, and I.R.C. § 1276(a)(4), for securities acquired after October 22, 1986. TRA '86, *supra* note 80, § 1803(a)(13)(A)(i).

[187] I.R.C. § 1277.

[188] I.R.C. § 1278(a)(2)(A).

[189] I.R.C. § 1278(a)(2).

[190] This definition of a bond is the same as the definition of a debt instrument in I.R.C. § 1275(a)(1)(A) (for purposes of the OID rules).

[191] I.R.C. § 1278(a)(1)(B)(i).

[192] I.R.C. § 1278(a)(1)(B)(ii).

[193] I.R.C. § 1278(a)(1)(B)(iii); *see* sections 2.1(a)(4) and 32.1(b).

4. Securities where the total market discount is de minimis—that is less than .25 percent of the stated redemption price at maturity, multiplied by the number of years until maturity,[194] and

5. Certain installment bonds to which I.R.C. § 453B applies[195]

(c) MARKET DISCOUNT BONDS ACQUIRED AT ORIGINAL ISSUE

TRA '86 amends the definition of a market discount bond for tax years ending after July 18, 1984, to provide that, except in two specified situations or as provided by Treasury regulations, market discount is not created on the original issuance of a debt security.[196] Further, as may be the case in a nontaxable exchange, if the adjusted basis of any debt security is determined by its adjusted basis in the hands of the person that acquired the bond when it was originally issued, the bond does not create market discount for the owner.[197]

The first statutory exception—which applies to tax years ending after July 18, 1984—provides that market discount is created on the original issuance of a bond offered to the public if the owner has a cost basis that is less than the issue price.[198] This may result, for example, if a large investor obtains a deeper discount than is available to retail customers. Because issue price is defined for OID purposes as the initial offering price to the public at which a substantial amount of the debt instrument is sold, the discount available to the large investor would not otherwise be covered by the OID rules. The market discount rules apply and the amount of market discount is the difference between the issue price and the holder's basis.[199]

Under the second exception—which also applies to tax years ending after July 18, 1984—[200] market discount is deemed to be created when, pursuant to a plan of reorganization, a bond is issued in exchange for a market discount bond.[201] This exception prevents the owner of a market discount bond from eliminating the taint of accrued market discount by swapping the bond for a new bond. For purposes of the market discount

---

[194] I.R.C. § 1278(a)(2)(C).
[195] I.R.C. § 1278(a)(1)(B)(iv).
[196] TRA '86, *supra* note 80, § 1803(a)(6); I.R.C. § 1278(a)(1).
[197] TRA '86, *supra* note 80, § 1803(a)(6); I.R.C. § 1278(a)(1).
[198] I.R.C. § 1278(a)(1)(C)(ii).
[199] De minimis amounts are not treated as market discount under I.R.C. § 1278(a)(2)(C).
[200] TRA '86, *supra* note 80, § 1803(a)(6).
[201] I.R.C. § 1278(a)(1)(C)(iii).

rules of I.R.C. § 1276, however, this exception does not apply to a newly issued bond that is exchanged for a market discount bond issued on or before July 18, 1984, if the terms and interest rates of the two bonds are identical.[202] This exception applies to tax years ending after July 18, 1984.

(d) TRANSFERS TO CONTROLLED CORPORATIONS

Accrued market discount is taxed to the transferor of a market discount bond in an I.R.C. § 351 exchange.[203] I.R.C. § 351 provides for nonrecognition of gain where appreciated property is transferred to a controlled corporation in exchange for the stock or securities of the corporation. Therefore, taxpayers cannot avoid the market discount rules by exchanging a bond with accrued market discount for stock in a transaction that qualifies as an I.R.C. § 351 exchange. These rules apply to obligations issued after July 18, 1984, in tax years ending after that date.[204]

(e) CORPORATE REORGANIZATIONS

If a debt security is originally issued pursuant to a plan of reorganization as part of a reorganization (within the meaning of I.R.C. § 368(a)(1)) in exchange for another bond that has market discount, I.R.C. § 1278(a)(1)(C)(i) does not apply to the bond that is issued pursuant to the reorganization.[205] As a result, the new bond is treated as retaining the character of the original market discount bond.

(f) ACCRUED MARKET DISCOUNT

(1) IN GENERAL

Gain on the disposition of market discount securities issued and acquired after July 18, 1984, must generally be recognized as interest income to the extent of the amount of market discount accrued by the taxpayer during the period he owns the security.[206] Accrued market discount for any security is an amount that bears the same ratio to the market discount on

---

[202] *Id.*
[203] I.R.C. § 1276(d)(1)(C).
[204] TRA '86, *supra* note 80, § 1803(a)(5).
[205] I.R.C. § 1278(a)(1)(C)(iii).
[206] I.R.C. §§ 1276(a)(1), 1276(a)(3) for securities acquired before October 22, 1986, and I.R.C. § 1276(a)(4) for securities acquired after October 22, 1986. TRA '86, *supra* note 80, § 1803(a)(13)(A)(i).

the security as the number of days during which the taxpayer held the security bears to the number of days from the date the taxpayer acquired the security until its maturity date.[207] At the election of the taxpayer, market discount can be computed using the constant (compound) interest method used to determine daily portions of OID accruing on debt securities issued after July 18, 1982.[208]

(2) ELECTIONS TO ACCRUE MARKET DISCOUNT

Taxpayers can elect to accrue market discount under one of two elections—ratably under I.R.C. § 1276(b)(1), or on the basis of a constant interest rate method under I.R.C. § 1276(b)(2). The remainder of this section addresses the two methods under which taxpayers can elect to accrue market discount.

(i) Ratable Accrual

Accrued market discount is generally treated as interest, which can be accrued ratably under I.R.C. § 1276(b)(1). Under this election, the accrued market discount on any bond is an amount that bears the same ratio to the market discount on the bond as (1) the number of days the taxpayer held the bond bears to (2) the number of days after the date the taxpayer acquired the bond and up to (and including) the date of its maturity.[209] The ratable accrual method is a straight-line method that reflects simple interest with no compounding of market discount from prior periods.

(ii) Accrual on a Constant Interest Rate Method

A taxpayer can irrevocably elect under I.R.C. § 1276(b)(2) to use a constant interest rate (i.e., the method used for OID on debt securities issued after July 1, 1982) for market discount on any particular securities. I.R.C. § 1276(b)(2) provides that a taxpayer can elect on a bond-by-bond basis to accrue market discount on any bond on the basis of a constant interest rate in lieu of ratable accrual under I.R.C. § 1276(b)(1). The accrued market discount is the aggregate amount that would have been includable in the gross income of the taxpayer under I.R.C. § 1272(a)(2) with respect to the bond, for all periods during which the bond was held by the taxpayer, if the bond had been (1) originally issued on the date on

---

[207] I.R.C. § 1276(b)(1).
[208] I.R.C. § 1276(b)(2).
[209] I.R.C. § 1276(b)(1).

which the bond was acquired by the taxpayer, (2) for an issue price equal to the basis of the taxpayer in the bond immediately after acquisition.[210]

If a market discount bond has OID, the computation of accrued market discount for the constant interest rate can be very confusing. To apply I.R.C. § 1276(b)(2)(A) to a market discount bond with OID, (1) the stated redemption price at maturity is treated as equal to its revised issue price, and (2) the determination of the portion of the OID that would have been includable in the taxpayer's gross income under I.R.C. § 1272(a) is to be made under Treasury regulations.[211]

Once an election is made to accrue market discount on a bond on the constant interest basis, the election is irrevocable.[212]

(g) ELECTION TO INCLUDE MARKET DISCOUNT CURRENTLY

A taxpayer (cash or accrual) need not include market discount in income until the security is sold or redeemed. For taxable years ending after July 18, 1984, however, a taxpayer can elect—for certain securities—to include market discount in gross income as it accrues for the taxable years to which it is attributable, as determined under I.R.C. § 1276(b).[213] Once an election is made, it applies to all market discount bonds (as defined to *exclude* short-term debt securities, tax-exempt securities, United States savings bonds, and certain installment securities) acquired by the taxpayer in the tax year of the election and in subsequent years.[214] The election is irrevocable unless the taxpayer receives IRS approval to revoke the election.[215]

The basis of any bond in the hands of the taxpayer is increased by the amount of market discount that is included in gross income under I.R.C. § 1278(b).[216]

(h) GAIN ON SALE

Gain on the sale of a market discount bond is generally treated as interest income to the extent of accrued but untaxed market discount up to the

---

[210] I.R.C. § 1276(b)(2)(A).
[211] I.R.C. § 1276(b)(2)(B).
[212] I.R.C. § 1276(b)(2)(C).
[213] I.R.C. § 1278(b)(1).
[214] I.R.C. § 1278(b)(2).
[215] I.R.C. § 1278(b)(3).
[216] I.R.C. § 1278(b)(4).

date of disposition.[217] If the taxpayer elects to currently include market discount in income, none of the gain upon disposition is treated as market discount.[218] If the taxpayer does not recognize any gain on the disposition, none of the market discount is taken into account. If the market discount bond provides for more than one principal payment, each principal payment is treated as ordinary income to the extent of accrued market discount that has not been taken into account.[219]

(i) INSTALLMENT INSTRUMENTS

Market discount on debt instruments where the principal is paid in more than one installment is taken into income upon receipt of amounts includable in the debt instrument's stated redemption price at maturity, to the extent of the amounts so received.[220] This rule applies to bonds acquired after October 22, 1986 (the date of enactment of TRA '86). To avoid double counting, the amount of any partial principal payment included in income under this provision reduces the amount of accrued market discount with respect to subsequent partial principal payments.[221] Accrued market discount is also reduced for purposes of the rule that gain on the disposition of a market discount bond is ordinary income to the extent of accrued market discount already included in income.[222]

The manner in which accrued market discount on installment obligations is to be computed has been left to Treasury regulations.[223] Pending such regulations, the Conference Report accompanying TRA '86 states the intention of the Conferees to allow owners to accrue market discount using either (1) a constant interest rate method, or (2) one of two formulas, depending on whether the obligation has OID.[224]

For debt instruments with OID, accrued market discount for a period is equal to the total remaining discount multiplied by a fraction, the numerator of which is the OID for the period, and the denominator of which is the total remaining OID at the beginning of the period.[225]

---

[217] I.R.C. §§ 1276(a), (e).
[218] I.R.C. § 1278(b).
[219] I.R.C. § 1276(a)(3).
[220] TRA '86, *supra* note 80, § 1803(a)(13)(A); I.R.C. §§ 1276(a), (b)(3).
[221] TRA '86, *supra* note 80, § 1803(a)(13)(A); I.R.C. §§ 1276(a), (b)(3).
[222] I.R.C. § 1276(a)(3)(B).
[223] I.R.C. § 1276(b)(3).
[224] TRA '86 Conf. Rep., *supra* note 147, at II-842. For a discussion of the constant interest rate method, see section 31.3(f)(2)(ii).
[225] TRA '86 Conf. Rep., *supra* note 147, at II-842.

For debt instruments without OID, accrued market discount for a period is equal to the total remaining discount multiplied by a fraction, the numerator of which is the stated interest paid in the accrual period, and the denominator of which is the total stated interest remaining to be paid at the beginning of the period.[226]

(j) PASS-THROUGH CERTIFICATES

Pass-through certificates are a popular form of asset-backed securities.[227] Pass-through certificates can be purchased with market discount. For a discussion of the tax treatment of pass-through certificates purchased with market discount, see section 37.4(b).

(k) PAY-THROUGH BONDS

Pay-through bonds are a popular form of asset-backed securities.[228] Pay-through bonds can be purchased with market discount. For a discussion of the tax treatment of pay-through bonds, see section 38.1.

(l) REAL ESTATE MORTGAGE INVESTMENT CONDUIT REGULAR INTERESTS AND CERTAIN SIMILAR DEBT INSTRUMENTS

REMIC regular interests and certain other debt instruments—where payments under the debt instruments may be accelerated by reason of prepayments of other obligations securing such debt instruments (or, to the extent provided in Treasury regulations, by reason of other events)—are addressed in I.R.C. § 1272(a)(6)(C).[229] At the date of this writing, Treasury regulations have not been issued. Until regulations are issued under I.R.C. § 1276(b)(3), owners of such debt instruments can elect to accrue market discount under either the ratable method or the constant interest rate method.[230]

---

[226] *Id.*

[227] For a discussion of pass-through certificates, see generally Chapters 7 and 36.

[228] For a discussion of pay-through bonds, see generally Chapters 7 and 36.

[229] For a discussion of the application of the OID rules to REMIC regular interests and certain similar debt instruments, see section 31.2(n)(4).

[230] For a discussion of the ratable method of accruing market discount, see section 31.3(f)(2)(i). For a discussion of the constant interest rate method, see section 31.3(f)(2)(ii). For a discussion of the taxation of REMIC regular interests purchased at a discount, see section 41.1(a)(3).

(m) INTEREST DEFERRAL

(1) IN GENERAL

For debt securities acquired after July 18, 1984, I.R.C. § 1277 provides that a taxpayer cannot deduct interest for indebtedness incurred to purchase or carry securities with market discount. For such securities, net interest expense is only deductible to the extent that the expense exceeds the amount of market discount allocable to the days during the taxable year in which the taxpayer owned the securities (as determined under the rules of I.R.C. § 1276(b)).[231] I.R.C. § 1277 acts to defer the excess of interest expense over the interest income on a market discount bond to the extent of the market discount that accrues during the taxable year.

For market discount bonds issued before July 18, 1984, any gain on the disposition of the securities is treated as interest income to the extent of any deferred interest expense.[232]

Net direct interest expense is the excess (if any) of (1) the amount of interest paid or accrued during the taxable year on indebtedness that is incurred to purchase or carry the bond, over (2) the aggregate amount of interest (including OID) includable in gross income for the taxable year with respect to the market discount bond.[233]

To prevent avoidance of this rule by financing debt securities through short sales,[234] the deduction of short sales expenses is also deferred if short sales of property are used to generate funds for the purchase of market discount bonds.[235] Short sale expenses (as defined in I.R.C. § 265(a)(5)) are treated as interest expenses.[236] Interest expenses and other deferred costs are allowed as a deduction for the taxable year in which the taxpayer disposes of the market discount securities,[237] or earlier at the taxpayer's election if—and to the extent that—the taxpayer has net interest income in the earlier year.

---

[231] I.R.C. § 1277(a).
[232] I.R.C. § 1277(d).
[233] I.R.C. § 1277(c).
[234] *See generally* Chapter 18.
[235] H.R. CONF. REP. NO. 861, *supra* note 90, at 806.
[236] I.R.C. § 1277(c).
[237] I.R.C. § 1277(b)(2)(A).

(2) DISALLOWED DEDUCTIONS ALLOWED IN LATER YEARS

The owner of a market discount bond with interest expense deferred under I.R.C. § 1277 can deduct those expenses in later years.

(i) Election

The owner of a market discount bond can elect to treat any disallowed interest expense "as interest paid or accrued by the taxpayer during such taxable year to the extent such disallowed interest expense does not exceed the net interest income with respect to such bond."[238] This election operates independent of the election to accrue market discount on a constant interest rate method. The amount of disallowed interest expense is determined as of the close of the preceding taxable year and does not include any amount already taken into account under I.R.C. § 1277(b)(1)(A).[239] Net interest income is defined as the excess of the amount of interest income over interest expense from the bond (determined under I.R.C. § 1277(c)(2) over the amount under I.R.C. § 1277(c)(1)).[240]

(ii) Year of Disposition

Any disallowed expense is treated as interest paid or accrued by the taxpayer in the taxable year when the market discount bond is disposed of.[241]

(iii) Nonrecognition Transactions

If a market discount bond is disposed of in a nonrecognition transaction (1) the disallowed interest expense is treated as interest paid or accrued in the year of disposition, and (2) the disallowed interest expense is treated as either (A) disallowed interest expense of the transferee with respect to transferred basis property described in I.R.C. § 1276(c)(2), or (B) disallowed interest expense with respect to the exchanged basis property described in I.R.C. § 1276(c)(2).[242]

---

[238] I.R.C. § 1277(b)(1)(A).
[239] I.R.C. § 1277(b)(1)(B).
[240] I.R.C. § 1277(b)(1)(C).
[241] I.R.C. § 1277(b)(2)(A).
[242] I.R.C. § 1277(b)(2)(B).

§ 31.4 PURCHASE PREMIUMS

A purchase premium is the amount that a purchaser pays to acquire a debt security in excess of its face value. A purchaser may be willing to buy a debt security at a premium if the security's interest rate or yield to maturity exceeds current market interest. I.R.C. § 171 provides the rules on the amortization of purchase premiums on debt securities. It does not apply to debt securities held during years before January 1, 1942, although it applies to the amount of the bond premium attributable to taxable years beginning after 1941. Premium attributable to periods prior to January 1, 1942, is treated as a capital loss at the time of the disposition of the securities.

I.R.C. § 171 provides for the amortization of premiums on any interest-bearing bond, debenture, note, certificate, or other evidence of indebtedness. For bonds issued before September 27, 1985, the bonds must have been issued by a corporation, government, or political subdivision.[243] A debt security need not be issued by a corporation, government, or political subdivision for obligations issued after September 27, 1985. I.R.C. § 171 does not apply to any securities (1) that are stock in trade of the taxpayer,[244] (2) that are properly included in the taxpayer's inventory if on hand at the end of the taxable year,[245] (3) held by the taxpayer primarily for sale to customers in the ordinary course of business,[246] or (4) held by dealers for purposes other than investment.[247] Amortization applies regardless of whether the security is in registered form or has interest coupons held or acquired in tax years beginning after December 31, 1953, and ending after August 16, 1954.[248]

(a) IN GENERAL

(1) TAXABLE SECURITIES

Bond premiums paid on taxable debt securities are deductible.[249] A taxpayer can elect, on taxable bonds only, to deduct the amount of the amortizable premium for the taxable year in computing taxable in-

---

[243] I.R.C. § 171(d), *prior to amendment by* TRA '86, *supra* note 80, § 1803(a)(11)(B).

[244] I.R.C. § 171(d); Treas. Reg. § 1.171-4(a) (1957).

[245] I.R.C. § 171(d); Treas. Reg. § 1.171-4(a) (1957).

[246] I.R.C. § 171(d); Treas. Reg. § 1.171-4(a) (1957).

[247] Treas. Reg. § 1.171-4(c) (1957).

[248] Treas. Reg. § 1.171-4(a) (1957).

[249] I.R.C. § 171(a)(1); Treas. Reg. §§ 1.171-1(b)(2), (3)(ii) (1957).

come.[250] If a taxpayer does not elect to amortize premiums, he reports a loss on redemption. Such a loss is either capital or ordinary, depending on whether the debt security is a capital or ordinary asset in his hands. For a discussion of the tax treatment of bond premiums paid on tax-exempt securities, see section 31.4(a)(2).

(i) Election to Amortize Purchase Premiums

If a taxpayer amortizes premiums, he must reduce the basis of the securities to account for the amount of the premium deducted each year.[251] Basis is adjusted to the extent of the amortizable bond premium attributable to the taxable year.[252]

A taxpayer that elects to amortize premiums and sells the debt securities before maturity at a price above the amortized cost basis reports a capital gain if he is an investor[253] or a trader,[254] but not if he is a dealer[255] or a financial institution.[256] If a taxpayer amortizes a security's premium from the date of acquisition, redemption at par should have no tax effect. If a taxpayer has not amortized all of the security's premium, however, its sale or redemption at face value results in a capital loss (for taxpayers that are neither dealers nor financial institutions).

Generally, for bonds acquired before October 23, 1986, amortizable premium of taxable bonds is an itemized deduction not subject to the two percent of adjusted gross income limitation. As a result, a taxpayer cannot deduct amortizable premiums if he computes his taxes based on the optional tax tables,[257] or if he elected the standard deduction.[258] A taxpayer that does not itemize but has elected to amortize bond premiums, must reduce his basis in the debt security to the extent that deductions for premium would have been allowed.[259]

Corporations, unlike other taxpayers, can only amortize bond premiums for taxable securities.[260] Only the owners of common trust funds or

---

[250] I.R.C. § 171(c); Treas. Reg. § 1.171-1(b)(2) (1957).
[251] I.R.C. § 1016(a)(5); Treas. Reg. § 1.1016-5(b) (1980).
[252] I.R.C. §§ 171(a), 1016(a)(5); Treas. Reg. §§ 1.171-1(b)(2), (3) (1957).
[253] *See* section 8.1.
[254] *See* section 8.2.
[255] *See* section 8.3.
[256] *See* section 8.8.
[257] I.R.C. § 3.
[258] I.R.C. § 144 (repealed in 1976).
[259] Treas. Reg. § 1.171-1(b)(5) (1957).
[260] Treas. Reg. § 1.171-3(a) (1957).

foreign personal holding companies can authorize the election to amortize premiums of any bonds held by the common trust funds or the foreign personal holding companies.[261] Only the fiduciary of a trust or estate can elect to amortize premiums.[262]

An election to amortize the premium on any debt security applies to all debt securities held by the taxpayer at the beginning of the taxable year in which the election first applies, and it applies to all debt securities acquired in subsequent taxable years.[263] Once such an election is made, the IRS must consent to any revocation of the election.[264] The appropriate premium amounts must be deducted in the first taxable year for which the election applies. In addition, a taxpayer must attach a statement to his tax return showing the computation of the premium.[265] A taxpayer cannot subsequently decide to amortize premiums for prior years by filing an amended return or a refund claim.[266] Further, a taxpayer that did not amortize bond premiums in the year a security was acquired cannot report increased deductions in the remaining years to maturity. If a taxpayer did not originally elect to amortize premiums, he computes the applicable deduction by reducing the amount of the premium by the amount of premium that could have been taken in prior years, and dividing that amount by the number of years remaining to maturity.[267]

(ii) Special Rules for Decedents

Specific provisions prescribe the tax treatment of amortizable premium on a debt security held by a decedent. For decedents who used the cash basis accounting, interest earned on a debt security until the decedent's date of death is included in either the estate's or legatee's gross income.[268] The amount of amortizable bond premium attributable to the period prior to a decedent's death is not allowed as a deduction for the estate or legatee.[269] For decedents that used the accrual method of accounting, the interest earned on the securities during the period prior to the decedent's

---

[261] I.R.C. § 171(c)(2).
[262] I.R.C. § 171(c).
[263] I.R.C. § 171(c)(2); Treas. Reg. § 1.171-3(a) (1957).
[264] I.R.C. § 171(c)(2); Treas. Reg. § 1.171-3(a) (1957).
[265] Treas. Reg. § 1.171-3(a) (1957).
[266] Barnhill v. Comm'r, 241 F.2d 496 (5th Cir. 1957), aff'g Woodward v. Comm'r, 24 T.C. 883 (1955), acq. 1956-1 C.B. 6.
[267] I.R.C. § 171(b)(1)(C); Treas. Reg. § 1.171-2(a)(4) (1968).
[268] Treas. Reg. § 1.171-1(c)(1) (1957).
[269] Id.

death is included in the decedent's income.[270] The deduction attributable to the amortizable bond premium is also taken into account in computing the decedent's gross income.[271]

(2) TAX-EXEMPT SECURITIES

(i) In General

A taxpayer that owns tax-exempt securities must treat the amortizable bond premium he paid for the securities as an adjustment to the basis or adjusted basis of the bond. The amortizable amount is not deductible.[272] For example, if a premium on a tax-exempt bond is $1, the basis or adjusted basis of the bond is reduced by $1.[273] A deduction for a premium paid to acquire tax-exempt securities—if allowed—would allow the taxpayer to reduce his income by an expense attributable to earning tax-exempt interest.[274] Thus, the premium paid, in effect, reduces the annual interest on tax-exempt securities because a portion of the interest received represents a partial return of premium.

The premium that must be amortized (but not deducted) on a tax-exempt security is the amount by which the security's basis for determining loss (as adjusted to reflect a prior amortization) exceeds the face amount of the security at its maturity (or call date for callable securities).[275]

(ii) Dealers in Tax-Exempt Securities

I.R.C. § 171(f) provides special rules in the case of dealers in tax-exempt securities that are set out in I.R.C. § 75. Special provisions in I.R.C. § 75 require the reduction of a taxpayer's "cost of goods sold" deduction by the amount of amortizable bond premiums to a dealer in "municipal bonds," defined to include all securities issued by governments or political subdivisions if the interest is excludable from gross income.[276] For these

---

[270] Treas. Reg. § 1.171-1(c)(3) (1957).
[271] *Id.*
[272] I.R.C. §§ 171, 1016(a); Treas. Reg. § 1.171-1(b)(1) (1957).
[273] Treas. Reg. § 1.171-1(b)(1) (1957).
[274] *See generally* sections 9.3 and 33.3(a).
[275] *See* section 31.4(c). For a discussion of the calculation of the mandatory amortization of premiums on tax-exempt bonds, see Gelband, *Tax Free? Not Really—But What's Owed to IRS?*, BARRON'S, Dec. 25, 1989, at 15, col. 1.
[276] I.R.C. § 75(b); Treas. Reg. § 1.75-1(a)(2) (1963).

purposes, a municipal bond does not include any security if (1) the dealer sells or otherwise disposes of it within 30 days after its acquisition, or the earliest maturity or call date is more than five years from the date the dealer acquired it, and (2) the amount realized from its sale (or the fair market value at the time of its disposition) exceeds its adjusted basis computed without regard to I.R.C. §§ 75(b) and 1016(a)(6).[277]

In computing the gross income of a taxpayer subject to I.R.C. § 75 that uses inventories valued on any basis other than cost, the "cost of securities sold" is reduced by an amount equal to the amortizable bond premium that would be allowed as a deduction under I.R.C. § 171(a)(2).[278] In the case of taxpayers subject to I.R.C. § 75 that compute their gross incomes without the use of inventories or with inventories valued at cost, the adjusted basis of a municipal security is reduced by the amount of the adjustment required under I.R.C. § 1016(a)(5) for amortizable bond premiums.[279] The term "cost of securities sold" is the amount obtained by subtracting the value of the closing inventory of a taxable year from the sum of (1) the value of the opening inventory for such year, and (2) the cost of securities and other property purchased during the year that is included in the taxpayer's inventory if on hand at the close of the year.[280] The cost of securities sold is not reduced where the earliest call or maturity date is more than five years from the date the security is acquired and the security is owned by the taxpayer at the close of the taxable year.[281]

In the year a municipal bond is sold or otherwise disposed of, the cost of securities sold for the year is reduced by the amounts provided by I.R.C. § 1016(a)(5),[282] without regard to the dealer's method of inventory valuation. If the dealer values his inventories at cost or does not use inventories, the adjusted basis of his municipal securities is not reduced until the taxable year in which the securities are sold or disposed of.[283]

Dealers are generally not required to amortize bond premiums.[284] Because a dealer in tax-exempt securities may receive tax-free interest income, however, he may be more willing to pay a premium to acquire the securities. The adjustments required by I.R.C. § 75 were designed to

---

[277] I.R.C. § 75(b)(1); Treas. Reg. § 1.75-1(a)(2) (1963).
[278] I.R.C. § 75(a)(1).
[279] I.R.C. § 75(a)(2).
[280] I.R.C. § 75(b)(2); Treas. Reg. § 1.75-1(a)(3) (1963).
[281] Treas. Reg. § 1.75-1(b)(2) (1963).
[282] *Id.*
[283] I.R.C. § 75(a)(2); Treas. Reg. § 1.75-1(c) (1963).
[284] I.R.C. § 171(d).

eliminate the artificial loss and accompanying tax advantage that a dealer would otherwise receive by purchasing tax-exempt securities.

Example 31-1

Assume that a dealer must pay $1250 to acquire a bond that matures in five years and pays interest of $70 per year and $1000 at maturity. The premium is $250. If he holds the bond until maturity, he receives $350 in tax-exempt interest. Without the adjustments required by I.R.C. § 75, the dealer would have a loss of $250 on the disposition of the bond at maturity. This is an artificial loss because the bond actually provided $100 of revenue ($350 minus $250). To prevent an artificial loss, I.R.C. § 75 reduces the bond's tax basis, or adjusted basis.

(b) DETERMINATION OF AMORTIZABLE BOND PREMIUMS

In general, a security's bond premium is the excess of the taxpayer's basis (for determining the loss on a sale or exchange) for the security over the amount payable at maturity.[285] A security is acquired on the date it was ordered under a firm commitment to buy (i.e., the trade date), and not the date it is delivered to the taxpayer (i.e., the settlement date).[286] Debt securities are considered to be acquired on the trade date even if the purchaser pays accrued interest through the settlement date.[287] The amount of premium amortizable during a taxable year is the amount of the premium attributable to that year.[288] The amortizable bond premium for the taxable year is the amount of the bond premium attributable to the year.[289]

For securities acquired after October 22, 1986, and before December 31, 1987, TRA '86 treats the deduction for amortizable bond premiums as an interest deduction, unless otherwise provided by Treasury regulations.[290] I.R.C. § 171(e) was amended to provide that except as provided in Treasury regulations, in the case of any taxable bond (1) the amount of any bond premium shall be allocated among the interest payments on the

---

[285] *See* I.R.C. § 171(b)(1); Treas. Reg. § 1.171-2(a) (1968).
[286] Treas. Reg. § 1.171-2(a)(2)(i) (1968).
[287] Rev. Rul. 66-97, 1966-1 C.B. 190.
[288] I.R.C. § 171(b)(2); Treas. Reg. § 1.171-2(a)(6) (1968).
[289] I.R.C. § 171(b)(2).
[290] I.R.C. § 171(e), *prior to amendment by* TMRA '88, Pub. L. No. 100-647, § 1006(j)(1)(A), 102 Stat. 3342 (1988).

bond under rules similar to the rules of I.R.C. § 171(b)(3), and (2) in lieu of any deduction under I.R.C. § 171(a), the amount of any premium so allocated to any interest payment is applied against (and operates to reduce) the amount of the interest payment. Thus, for example, bond premium is treated as interest for purposes of applying the investment interest limitations of I.R.C. § 163(d).[291]

For bonds issued after September 27, 1985, the amount of bond premium that can be amortized for a taxable year (and deducted currently in the case of a taxable bond) is calculated under a constant yield method (except as provided otherwise by Treasury regulations).[292] Also, this treatment of a bond premium is extended to obligations issued by individuals in addition to corporate and government bonds.[293]

Under the constant yield method, amortizable bond premium is computed on the basis of the taxpayer's yield to maturity, using the taxpayer's basis for the bond, and compounding at the close of each accrual period. The accrual periods are generally the six-month periods ending on the date corresponding to the maturity date of the bond or the date that is six months before the maturity date. According to the Conference Report accompanying TRA '86, regulations to be issued for the accrual of market discount on installment obligations will also apply to amortizing bond premium.[294]

Bond premium is generally the amount paid for a bond in excess of the amount payable at maturity, or at an earlier call date if the bond is callable and this amount would result in a smaller deduction.[295] For purposes of the constant yield method, if the amount payable on an earlier call date is used to determine the amount of the bond premium attributable to the period before the call date, the bond is treated as if it matured on the call date for the redemption amount and that it had been reissued on that date for the same amount.[296]

Taxpayers that have an election to amortize and deduct bond premium in effect can choose (subject to regulations) whether that election will apply to obligations issued after September 27, 1985.[297]

For bonds received in exchange for other property—in which the basis of the bond is determined at least in part by the basis of the property—the

---

[291] For a discussion of investment interest, see section 9.2(e).

[292] I.R.C. § 171(b)(3).

[293] I.R.C. § 171(d).

[294] TRA '86 Conf. Rep., *supra* note 147, at II-842.

[295] I.R.C. § 171(b)(3)(B).

[296] *Id.*

[297] TRA '86, *supra* note 80, § 1803(a)(11).

basis of the bond cannot exceed its fair market value for purposes of determining the amount of amortizable premium.[298] This rule, effective for exchanges after May 6, 1986, does not apply to exchanges of one bond for another pursuant to a reorganization.[299]

(c) CALLABLE SECURITIES

Callable securities are securities that an issuer can retire at a certain date or dates prior to the stated maturity date. To retire callable securities prior to the stated maturity date, the issuer must usually pay the owners an amount that exceeds face value.

This section addresses both taxable and tax-exempt callable securities.

(1) TAXABLE SECURITIES

Amortizable premium on callable securities is often calculated differently from the premium on noncallable securities. Under some circumstances, the earlier call date is considered to be the maturity date for purposes of determining the amortization period.[300] The term "earlier call date" can have several meanings. It can be (1) the earliest call date specified in the security as a day certain, (2) the earliest interest payment date if the security is callable at such date, (3) the earliest date at which the security is callable at par, or (4) such other call date, prior to maturity, specified in the security as selected by the taxpayer.[301]

In the case of taxable securities that were issued after January 22, 1951, and acquired after January 22, 1954, but before January 1, 1958, the earlier call date can be used to compute the amortizable bond premium only if the earlier call date is more than three years from the date the securities were originally issued. If the call date on such securities falls within three years of issue, the amortizable premium is determined by computing the difference between the security's basis and the amount payable at maturity.[302] In the case of callable securities acquired after December 31, 1957, the earlier call date is used to calculate the bond premium only if the excess of the security's basis over the amount payable on an earlier call date results in a smaller amortizable premium attribut-

---

[298] I.R.C. § 171(b)(4).
[299] TRA '86, *supra* note 80, § 1803(a)(12).
[300] Treas. Reg. § 1.171-2(b) (1968).
[301] *Id.*
[302] Treas. Reg. § 1.171-2(a)(2)(i) (1968).

able to the period between the acquisition date and earlier call date than results by calculating the bond premium for that period using the excess of the security's basis over the amount payable at maturity.[303]

If a security has multiple call dates, the amount of the amortizable premium is initially calculated with reference to the earliest call date. If not called on that date, any remaining unamortized premium is amortized to a subsequent call date or maturity.[304]

If a callable security is redeemed prior to its maturity date, a compensating amortizing adjustment may be necessary in the year the bond is redeemed. The amount of the amortizable premium attributable to the tax year in which the security is called includes an amount equal to the excess of the security's adjusted basis, as of the beginning of that taxable year, over the amount received on redemption of the security at an earlier call date.[305]

If a taxpayer holding a callable security also has a "buy back agreement" or put option with the seller, the amount of the amortizable premium is nevertheless determined with reference to the call price.[306]

(2) TAX-EXEMPT SECURITIES

Special rules apply to tax-exempt callable securities. Where there is more than one call date, the premium must be amortized to the earliest call date.[307] If the security is not called at the earliest call date, the premium is then amortized to the next call date or, if no other call date exists, to maturity.[308] The basis of the security is reduced accordingly.

Example 31-2

Assume that a taxpayer purchased two $1000 tax-exempt bonds on January 1, 1973, that mature in 20 years (1993) for $2200. The bonds

---

[303] I.R.C. § 171(b)(1); Treas. Reg. § 1.171-2(a)(2)(i) (1968).

[304] Treas. Reg. § 1.171-2(b)(2) (1968).

[305] I.R.C. § 171(b)(2); Treas. Reg. § 1.171-2(a)(2)(iii) (1968).

[306] Industrial Research Prods., Inc. v. Comm'r, 40 T.C. 578, 588 (1963), *acq.* 1966-1 C.B. 2.

[307] Pacific Affiliate, Inc. v. Comm'r, 18 T.C. 1175, 1208 (1952), *aff'd*, 224 F.2d 578 (9th Cir. 1955), *cert. denied*, 350 U.S. 967 (1956).

[308] Rev. Rul. 60-17, 1960-1 C.B. 124. A premium paid on the call of a tax-exempt security before maturity is taxable as a capital gain (or ordinary income for dealers and certain financial institutions) not as tax-exempt interest. Rev. Rul. 72-587, 1972-2 C.B. 74, *modified by* Rev. Rul. 80-143, 1980-1 C.B. 19; *see also* Rev. Rul. 74-172, 1974-1 C.B. 178; Bryant v. Comm'r, 2 T.C. 789 (1943), *rev'g* 38 B.T.A. 618 (1938); District Bond Co. v. Comm'r, 1 T.C. 837 (1943).

are callable on January 1, 1977, for $2120. For the four-year period between January 1, 1973, and January 1, 1977, the taxpayer must reduce the basis of these bonds by $80 ($2200 minus $2120), which is the amount of the nondeductible, amortizable bond premium. If the bonds were not called on January 1, 1977, however, the remaining $120 premium is amortized over the remaining 16 years to maturity. If there is no call date between the first call date and maturity, the remaining unamortized premium is amortized on a straight-line basis to maturity.[309]

(d) CONVERTIBLE DEBT SECURITIES

Amortization of premium applies to convertible debt securities.[310] Under no circumstances, however, can any amount of the premium attributable to the owner's conversion privilege be amortized.[311] The value of a debt security's conversion feature is determined as of the date of the security's acquisition by subtracting from the security's cost at acquisition the price that would have been paid for the security on the open market if it had not been convertible.

The determination of the assumed price for a nonconvertible security is a two-step procedure. First, the yield on nonconvertible securities of a similar character is determined. Second, the price currently paid is ascertained by using standard bond tables to determine the current price of securities at the same yield that have the same classification and grade.[312]

If a security is converted before the full amount of the premium not attributable to the conversion feature is amortized, the taxpayer cannot deduct the unamortized premium in the year of conversion. Rather, the portion of the premium remaining unamortized is treated as part of the tax basis of the new security received on conversion of the old security. Thus, the basis of the new security is the same as that of the security relinquished.[313]

An issuing corporation cannot deduct a premium paid or incurred upon the repurchase of a convertible debt security into stock of (1) the

---

[309] Because there is only one call date in this example, the remaining premium of $120 is amortized at an annual rate of $7.50 over the next 16 years.

[310] For a discussion of convertible securities, see sections 1.1(d) and 34.1.

[311] I.R.C. § 171(b); Treas. Reg. § 1.171-2(c)(1)(1968); National Can Corp. v. United States, 687 F.2d 1107 (7th Cir. 1982), aff'g 520 F. Supp. 567 (N.D. Ill. 1981).

[312] Treas. Reg. § 1.171-2(c)(2) (1968).

[313] See Ades v. Comm'r, 38 T.C. 501, 512 (1962), aff'd per curiam, 316 F.2d 734 (2d Cir. 1963).

issuing corporation, or (2) a company in control of or controlled by the issuing corporation to the extent that the repurchase prce of the debt security exceeds the adjusted issue price plus a normal call premium on nonconvertible securities.[314] The issuing corporation can claim a deduction, however, to the extent it can prove that the excess premium is attributable to the cost of borrowing and not to the conversion feature.[315] In addition, the issuer cannot deduct a premium on the redemption of its stock under I.R.C. § 162(k).

(e) AMORTIZATION OF CAPITALIZED EXPENSES

A taxpayer can elect to amortize capitalized expenses, such as buying commissions, as a premium if he (1) regularly amortizes capitalized expenses and uses a reasonable method, (2) amortizes capitalized expenses and uses the method of amortization prescribed by Treasury regulations, or (3) uses a reasonable amortization method but does not amortize capitalized expenses.[316]

If there is a premium exclusive of capitalized expenses, two different methods are available to capitalize expenses. First, a taxpayer that regularly amortizes capitalized expenses and uses a reasonable method of amortization must treat the capitalized expenses as part of the premium.[317] Second, if a taxpayer does not generally use an amortization method that treats capitalized expenses as part of the premium for purposes of amortization, the taxpayer can (but is not required to) treat the capitalized expenses as part of the premium.[318]

(f) PASS-THROUGH CERTIFICATES

Pass-through certificates can be purchased at a premium, although it is unlikely that a purchaser will pay a premium if the certificate offers either limited or no call protection. For a discussion of the tax considerations for pass-through certificates purchased at a premium, see section 37.3.

---

[314] I.R.C. § 249(a); Treas. Reg. § 1.249-1(a) (1973).
[315] I.R.C. § 249(a); Treas. Reg. § 1.249-1(b) (1973); see section 34.2.
[316] Treas. Reg. § 1.171-2(d)(1) (1968).
[317] Treas. Reg. § 1.171-2(d)(2)(i) (1968).
[318] Treas. Reg. § 1.171-2(d)(2)(iii) (1968).

(g) PAY-THROUGH BONDS

Pay-through bonds can be purchased at a premium. For a discussion of the tax considerations for pay-through bonds purchased at a premium, see section 38.3.

(h) REAL ESTATE MORTGAGE INVESTMENT CONDUIT REGULAR INTERESTS

REMIC regular interests that are purchased at a premium are subject to the general tax rules that apply to premiums on taxable securities. For a discussion of these tax rules, see generally section 31.4.

§ 31.5 ZERO COUPON SECURITIES

Zero coupon securities are debt securities payable without interest at a fixed maturity date.[319] They trade at very deep discount. The difference between the original discounted price and the par amounts represents a compounded annual yield at the original interest rate. There is no reinvestment risk because the original rate is locked in. In other words, the owner's yield is assured as long as the issuer meets its payment obligations when the zero coupon security matures.[320]

For tax purposes, zeros issued after July 1, 1982, are considered to be OID securities so that OID is accrued in accordance with the OID rules.[321] As a result, the rules in I.R.C. §§ 163(e)(5) and 163(i) for so-called applicable high yield debt obligations can apply to zero coupon securities. For a discussion of applicable high yield debt obligations, see section 31.2(g). Because of the stripped bond rules, zeros are not attractive products for all taxpayers. They may be attractive, however, for tax-exempt entities (e.g., pension funds), certain foreign investors, and low bracket taxpayers. Zeros can also be attractive to fund a known future liability at a specified date with a guaranteed rate. Of course, locking in an interest rate for a long time is only beneficial if the general level of interest rates remains constant or decreases. If interest rates increase, the market value of the securities declines to compensate for its low yield in relation to the market rate of interest.

---

[319] *See generally* section 2.2(e).

[320] For a discussion of investment strategies using zeros, see section 2.2(e). *See also* Donnelly, *Rate Gamblers Put Their Chips on 'Zeros,'* Wall St. J., June 16, 1989, at C1.

[321] *See generally* section 31.2.

This section looks first at taxable zeros and then at tax-exempt zeros.

(a) TAXABLE SECURITIES

Owners of taxable zeros report income on interest earned on a yearly basis. The United States Treasury issues STRIPS,[322] and some brokerage firms[323] and federal government agencies also issue taxable zeros.[324] In addition, there are certificate of deposit zeros that are insured by the FDIC and corporate zeros. Finally, there is a market for zero coupon convertible bonds.[325]

Example 31-3

A taxpayer buys a $1000 STRIPS security for $880. The taxpayer receives $1000 when the STRIPS security matures. The taxpayer is taxed each year on the interest as it accrues.

TEFRA[326] significantly altered the timing of interest deductions for issuers and the reporting of interest income for owners of zeros. For corporate debt securities issued after May 27, 1969, and before July 1, 1982, an owner was required to include in income the ratable monthly portion of OID multiplied by the sum of the complete months he held the security during the taxable year.[327]

As to zero coupon convertibles, the zero coupon bond is convertible into the common stock of the issuer at a price set at issuance. These securities typically have more price volatility than normal coupon bonds. Allocation of the tax basis to the conversion feature is not appropriate. Conversion is not a taxable event.

---

[322] For a discussion of Treasury zeros, see section 2.2(e).
[323] Salomon Brothers issues CATS and Merrill Lynch issues TIGRs. (The brokerage firms detach the interest coupons from the principal, deposit them with a trustee, and issue their own instruments.)
[324] For example, SLMA has offered zero coupon bonds aimed at foreign investors. *See* Monroe, *Sallie Mae Offers Zero-Coupon Bonds Aimed at European, Japanese Investors*, Wall St. J., Aug. 2, 1984, § 2, at 33, col. 2.
[325] *See* Mitchell, *Zero Coupon Convertibles Find a Market*, Wall St. J., Dec. 11, 1989, at C1.
[326] Pub. L. No. 97-248, § 232, 96 Stat. 324, 499-501 (1982) [hereinafter TEFRA].
[327] *See* section 31.2.

(b) TAX-EXEMPT SECURITIES

Zero coupon municipal securities do not pay interest currently. Because one of the major attractions of tax-exempt securities is the receipt of tax-free interest,[328] zero coupon municipal securities are generally an attractive investment only if they sell at a very deep discount where the compounded return is very high.

Example 31-4

A taxpayer pays $5000 for a zero coupon municipal security that matures in seven years at $7000 to provide for future college expenses for his child. At maturity, the taxpayer receives $7000 tax-free (a 10 percent yield).

Prior to the DRA changes in 1984, several tax strategies were used with zero coupon tax-exempt securities. One was to purchase a zero and hold it for less than the current long-term capital gain holding period (which was one year at that time). The taxpayer could obtain a nontaxable short-term gain and a deductible short-term capital loss. The DRA changed this tax result for those zero coupon securities issued after September 3, 1982, that are purchased after March 1, 1984,[329] thereby ending the practice of selling zero coupon municipal securities to generate tax losses.[330] The OID rules now apply to adjust the basis of zero coupon municipal securities.

Example 31-5

Assume that under pre-DRA law, a taxpayer paid $5353 for zero coupon municipal securities with a compounded annual return of 10 percent redeemable for $100,000 in 30 years. Under the law in effect before the DRA changes in 1984, if the taxpayer sold the securities before maturity, the taxpayer reported gain or loss on a straight-line basis over the 30-year period (i.e., $3155 per year). If the taxpayer held the securities for less than the long-term capital gain holding period, the taxpayer's basis was $8508 ($5353 plus $3155).

Assume further that interest rates had not changed in this period. Because interest is determined on a compound basis, the market value of the securities was $5902. The taxpayer had a $549 tax-free

---

[328] *See generally* section 33.3(a).
[329] DRA, *supra* note 45, § 44(f).
[330] *See* section 31.2(e).

gain ($5902 minus $5353) and a short-term capital loss of $2606 ($8508 basis minus $4902 sales price).[331]

§ 31.6 STRIPPED BONDS

(a) IN GENERAL

Stripped bonds and coupons are quite popular. For example, the United States Treasury issues STRIPS, which are the zero coupon portion of Treasury securities.[332] In addition, stripped asset-backed securities are another type of stripped bonds and coupons. For a discussion of stripped asset-backed securities, see sections 7.2(c)(2) and 7.2(d)(7).

In general, there are four ways that debt securities can be stripped. First, a debt security with the right to interest can be purchased. The coupons can be stripped and retained, while the principal portion is sold. Second, a debt security with the right to interest can be purchased, stripped, and the principal portion retained while the coupon is sold. Third, a taxpayer can purchase already separated coupons. Fourth, a taxpayer can purchase the principal portion only (which is economically equivalent to zero coupon security). Although coupon stripping was often used under old tax laws to modify the timing and character of income, it has been used more recently to create additional value by allowing the separation of the interest and principal portion.

Stripped bonds are debt securities issued with interest coupons[333] where the unmatured coupons are separated from ownership of the debt security.[334] In other words, the security is divided into two pieces: a right to receive principal and a right to receive interest. The principal portion of a stripped bond is economically equivalent to a zero coupon security because it no longer carries the right to receive periodic interest payments.[335] The principal and coupon receipts must represent interrelated

---

[331] Under the law in effect after the DRA changes in 1984, the OID rules apply to adjust the basis of the securities. *See* section 31.2(e).

[332] For a discussion of coupon stripping transactions, see McGrath, *Coupon Stripping Under Section 1286: Trees, Fruits, and Felines*, 38 TAX LAW. 267 (1985).

[333] "Coupon" is defined broadly in I.R.C. § 1286(e)(5) to include any right to receive interest on a security (whether or not evidenced by a coupon).

[334] I.R.C. § 1286(e)(2); *see also* SENATE FINANCE COMM. REPORT, TAX EQUITY AND FISCAL RESPONSIBILITY ACT OF 1982, S. REP. NO. 494, 97th Cong., 2d Sess. 215 (1982), *reprinted in* 1982 U.S. CODE CONG. & ADMIN. NEWS 781 [hereinafter S. REP. NO. 494].

[335] *See* section 31.5.

ownership interests, so the stripped bond rules do not apply to separate, independent evidences of indebtedness.[336]

(b) STRIPPED BONDS DISPOSED OF BEFORE JULY 2, 1982

In 1982, the Treasury issued a release proposing certain legislative changes in the tax treatment of stripped bonds.[337] The Treasury proposed that sellers of stripped bonds be prohibited from claiming "artificial losses" and that purchasers treat the separated interest and principal portions as OID securities, including amounts in income that reflect the increase in value of the debt security for that year. This section discusses stripped bonds prior to the Code changes made by TEFRA.

(1) TREATMENT OF THE SELLER

Under pre-TEFRA law (i.e., prior to July 2, 1982), a seller of a stripped bond that retained the right to receive the interest and sold the principal portion would take the position that all of his basis in the debt security was properly allocated to the principal portion.[338] The seller thus claimed so-called artificial losses to the extent of the difference between the amount for which he bought the debt security (with the right to receive interest) and the amount he received on the sale of the principal portion (without the right to receive interest).[339] Dealers[340] and certain financial institutions[341] would report an ordinary loss on the sale of a stripped bond, while investors[342] and traders[343] would report a capital loss.[344]

In addition, taxpayers with net operating losses could strip the bonds and sell the stripped coupons to accelerate the inclusion of ordinary income.[345]

---

[336] See LTR 8939014 (June 30, 1989).

[337] Treasury Release No. R-822, TREASURY NEWS (June 9, 1982) [hereinafter Treasury Release No. R-822].

[338] S. REP. NO. 494, *supra* note 334, at 215.

[339] *Id.* at 216.

[340] See section 8.3.

[341] See section 8.8.

[342] See section 8.1.

[343] See section 8.2.

[344] S. REP. NO. 494, *supra* note 334, at 215.

[345] See Rev. Rul. 58-536, 1958-2 C.B. 21.

Further, under pre-TEFRA law, the seller could accelerate income by selling only the right to receive the interest and retaining the principal portion.[346]

In TAM 8827002,[347] the IRS ruled that, for purposes of computing loss on the sale of stripped bonds under pre-TEFRA law, a taxpayer must allocate his basis in the bonds between the interest coupons that were detached and held and the principal note amount that the taxpayer transferred, based on the relative fair market values of the coupon and principal amount items.

In TAM 8827002, the taxpayer owned stock in banks that routinely purchased United States Treasury and FNMA notes with interest coupons attached. The bank detached the interest coupons before selling the notes, and deducted ordinary losses calculated by taking the difference between its tax basis and amount realized on the sale of the notes without the interest coupons.

The IRS, in TAM 8827002, analyzed I.R.C. § 1286, which was added by TEFRA to cover the tax treatment of stripped bonds disposed of after July 1, 1982. Those rules prevent taxpayers from gaining an "unwarranted tax advantage" by selling the principal amount of stripped bonds to generate a large tax loss.

Because the transaction at issue in TAM 8827002 involved a disposition before July 1, 1982, the IRS applied the law in effect before enactment of I.R.C. § 1286. The IRS found that the courts generally require a basis allocation where taxpayers sell a partial interest and retain a partial interest in property. The IRS also found that Treas. Reg. § 1.61-6(a) supported the requirement that the allocation must be made according to the relative fair market values of the two separate items making up the bond.

The IRS compared the sale of detached coupon bonds to the transfer of a remainder interest and a life estate in real property. The IRS found that the bond itself is like a remainder interest, to which the owner is entitled at the expiration of the preceding interest (in this case, the coupon, which entitles the holder to the right to receive interest until the bond's

---

[346] *See generally* Shafer v. United States, 204 F. Supp. 473 (S.D. Ohio 1962), *aff'd per curiam*, 312 F.2d 747 (6th Cir.), *cert. denied*, 373 U.S. 933 (1963) (where owners of Japanese government bonds on which interest payments had been suspended during World War II, but for which the Japanese government agreed to service after the war, were allowed—under NYSE rules—to strip the bonds and sell the coupons at a price that accelerated income. The court held that the taxpayers received ordinary income, not capital gain, on the sale of the new and old coupons.).

[347] (Mar. 30, 1988).

maturity). Based on this analysis, the IRS found that the basis allocation rules should be applied to the transaction.

(2) TREATMENT OF THE PURCHASER

Under pre-TEFRA law, the purchaser of stripped coupons allocated his tax basis among the coupons he purchased.[348] When a coupon was redeemed, the taxpayer typically reported ordinary income equal to the difference between the amount received for the coupon and his basis.[349] In the case of coupons disposed of prior to maturity, a taxpayer that was not a dealer or a financial institution reported capital gain on all of the gain not attributable to accrued interest,[350] even if the increase in value was due to the passage of time.

A purchaser of a stripped bond could defer the inclusion of discount as income until the disposition of the stripped bond. As a result, purchasers of stripped coupons could convert ordinary income into capital gain by selling stripped coupons before their maturity.

(c) STRIPPED BONDS DISPOSED OF AFTER JULY 1, 1982, AND ACQUIRED BEFORE OCTOBER 23, 1986

TEFRA made substantive changes to the taxation of stripped bonds in 1982 by enacting I.R.C. § 1232B,[351] which the DRA[352] redesignated as I.R.C. § 1286 without any substantive changes.[353] Congress enacted I.R.C. § 1232B as part of TEFRA in 1982 to eliminate artificial tax losses.[354] The stripped bond rules provide basis allocation rules and treat stripped bonds as subject to OID at the time the security is stripped.

---

[348] S. REP. NO. 494, *supra* note 334, at 215.

[349] *Id.*

[350] Treasury Release No. R-822, *supra* note 337.

[351] TEFRA, *supra* note 326, § 232.

[352] DRA, *supra* note 45, § 41(a).

[353] The only minor DRA change made to I.R.C. § 1286(a) in 1984 was a provision that a stripped bond or coupon was treated as originally issued on the purchase date. Because a "purchase" is defined in I.R.C. § 1286 as any "acquisition"—and the term "acquisition" presumably has a broader meaning than "purchase"—a person that received a stripped bond as a gift after July 1, 1982—even though that debt security may have been purchased prior to July 1, 1982—most likely must comply with the requirements set forth in I.R.C. § 1286.

[354] *See, e.g.*, S. REP. NO. 494, *supra* note 334, at 215–18; HOUSE CONF. REPORT, TAX EQUITY AND FISCAL RESPONSIBILITY ACT OF 1982, H.R. CONF. REP. NO. 760, 97th Cong., 2d Sess. (1982), *reprinted in* 1982 U.S. CODE CONG. & ADMIN. NEWS 1190.

A stripped bond is defined as a "bond" issued at any time with interest coupons where there is a separation in ownership between the bond and any coupon that has not yet become payable.[355] A stripped coupon is defined as any coupon relating to a stripped bond (irrespective of whether it was stripped from the bond).[356]

The remainder of ths section addresses stripped bonds disposed of after July 1, 1982, and acquired before October 23, 1986.

(1) TREATMENT OF THE SELLER

When a debt security is stripped, any interest accrued on that security prior to the time it is disposed of, not including any interest that had been previously included in the seller's gross income, must be included in taxable income.[357] This accrued interest increases the basis of the stripped bond.[358] Immediately before the disposition of either the stripped corpus or the coupons, the seller must allocate his basis between what he disposed of and what he retained in proportion to their respective fair market values on the date of disposition.[359] After a disposition, the seller must treat the retained portion of the security as an OID security with a purchase price equal to the cost basis allocated to it.[360] The seller was, therefore, subject to the OID periodic inclusion rules.[361]

Example 31-6

Assume a taxpayer sells the principal portion of a debt security on January 1 for $578,435 when there are four years until the security matures for $1 million. Assume that the taxpayer retains the eight semiannual interest coupons, each with a face amount of $100,000. The taxpayer must allocate $578,435 of his basis to the principal and the remaining $421,565 to the interest coupons. The taxpayer does not realize any gain or loss on this sale. In addition, each coupon the taxpayer retains is allocated a portion of the remaining basis of

---

[355] I.R.C. § 1286(e)(2).
[356] I.R.C. § 1286(e)(3).
[357] I.R.C. § 1286(b)(1), *prior to amendment by* TRA '86, *supra* note 80, § 1803(a)(13)(B)(i); I.R.C. § 1232B(b)(1) (1982), *repealed by* DRA, *supra* note 45, § 42(a)(1) (1984).
[358] I.R.C. § 1286(b)(2), *prior to amendment by* TRA '86, *supra* note 80, § 1803(a)(13)(B)(ii); I.R.C. § 1232B(b)(2) (1982), *repealed by* DRA, *supra* note 45, § 42(a)(1).
[359] I.R.C. § 1286(b)(3); I.R.C. § 1232B(b)(3) (1982), *repealed by* DRA, *supra* note 45, § 42(a)(1).
[360] I.R.C. § 1286(b)(4); I.R.C. § 1232B(b)(4) (1982), *repealed by* DRA, *supra* note 45, § 42(a)(1).
[361] S. REP. No. 494, *supra* note 334, at 216; *see* section 31.2(a).

$421,565. Further, income accrues on each coupon as if each coupon were a separate security issued with OID.

(2) TREATMENT OF THE PURCHASER

The purchaser of the principal portion of a debt security (without the right to receive interest) must treat it as an OID security subject to the OID rules.[362] OID is equal to the stated redemption price at maturity over the security's ratable share of the purchase price allocable to the principal portion and coupon,[363] which is equal to the fair market value of the principal portion and coupon of the security on the date of purchase.[364] For purchases after July 1, 1982, the term "purchase" is defined broadly to include: "any acquisition of a debt instrument, where the basis of a debt instrument is not determined in whole or in part by reference to the adjusted basis of such debt instrument in the hands of the person from whom acquired."[365]

The purchaser of the interest portion of a stripped bond must report as income under the OID rules the amount of the excess of the coupon's face amount at maturity over its ratable share of the purchase price,[366] which equals its fair market value on the date of purchase.[367] This OID is included in income periodically between the date of purchase and the maturity date of the coupon.

Example 31-7

Assume a taxpayer purchases stripped coupons that give him the right to receive interest when each coupon matures. Each coupon is allocated a portion of the basis that is allocated among the coupons and the principal portion. (This basis is equal to the difference between the face amount of the debt security and the amount of basis allocated to the principal portion.) Income accrues from each coupon as if it were a separate security issued with OID. If the face amount of the security equals $750,000 and the basis allocated to the principal equals $550,000, the remaining basis is $200,000. This

---

[362] I.R.C. § 1286(a); I.R.C. § 1232B(a) (1982), *repealed by* DRA, *supra* note 45, § 42(a)(1).
[363] I.R.C. § 1286(a); I.R.C. § 1232B(a) (1982), *repealed by* DRA, *supra* note 45, § 42(a)(1).
[364] S. REP. No. 494, *supra* note 334, at 216.
[365] I.R.C. §§ 1272(d)(1), 1286(e)(6).
[366] I.R.C. § 1286(a); I.R.C. § 1232B(a) (1982), *repealed by* DRA, *supra* note 45, § 42(a)(1).
[367] S. REP. No. 494, *supra* note 334, at 216.

$200,000 of remaining basis is allocated to the interest amounts each year according to the OID rules.

(3) TREATMENT OF THE ISSUER

The issuer of a stripped bond can deduct interest equal to the aggregate daily portion of the OID for the days in the taxable year.[368] The aggregate daily portion is calculated under I.R.C. § 1272(a). Because I.R.C. § 1286 treats stripped bonds as OID securities for purposes of I.R.C. § 1272(a) but not for purposes of I.R.C. § 163(e), issuers can presumably still obtain interest deductions, notwithstanding the fact that the security may have been stripped.[369]

(4) TAX-EXEMPT SECURITIES

I.R.C. § 1286(d) provides special rules for tax-exempt securities. Different rules apply, depending on when sales of stripped tax-exempt obligations or stripped coupons occur. The following rules apply for purchases and sales of stripped tax-exempt obligations or stripped coupons on or before June 10, 1987, and to any sales of stripped tax-exempt obligations or stripped coupons held by a person on June 10, 1987, for sale in the ordinary course of such person's trade or business, or to any such obligations or coupons during the time they are held by another person that purchased them from such a holder.[370] A seller that strips a tax-exempt security and disposes of either the principal portion or the coupon is deemed to purchase the portion he retains.[371] Because the seller is treated as having purchased an OID security, he must allocate his basis between the items disposed of and the items retained.[372] In addition, subsequent sales of the retained items are treated as if I.R.C. § 1232(c) of pre-TEFRA law (in 1982) were still in effect.[373] The accrued interest rules of I.R.C. § 1286(b)(1) do not apply to tax-exempt securities.[374]

---

[368] I.R.C. § 163(e), *prior to amendment by* TRA '86, *supra* note 80, §§ 1803(a)(4), 1810(e)(1)(A), 1810(e)(1)(B).

[369] I.R.C. §§ 163(e), 1286. I.R.C. § 163(e) was amended by TRA '86, *supra* note 80, §§ 1803(a)(4), 1810(e)(1)(A), 1810(e)(1)(B).

[370] TRA '86, *supra* note 80, §§ 1018(g)(4)(B)(i)-(ii). *See* section 31.6(d)(2) for the other rules applicable to stripped tax-exempt obligations and coupons.

[371] I.R.C. § 1286(d)(2), *prior to amendment by* TRA '86, *supra* note 80, § 1879(s)(1).

[372] S. REP. No. 494, *supra* note 334, at 217.

[373] I.R.C. § 1286(d)(3), *prior to amendment by* TRA '86, *supra* note 80, § 1879(s)(1).

[374] I.R.C. § 1286(d)(1), *prior to amendment by* TRA '86, *supra* note 80, § 1879(s)(1).

Purchasers of stripped tax-exempt securities are not subject to the OID inclusion rules.[375] Also, if the purchaser disposes of the stripped tax-exempt security, I.R.C. § 1286(d)(3) applies I.R.C. § 1286(c) without regard to the date of purchase.[376]

Because any OID on tax-exempt securities is also tax-free, application of the rule for stripped bonds would allow purchasers and sellers of tax-exempt securities to increase their tax bases in the principal and interest portions.

Sellers are required, however, to allocate the cost of the securities between principal and interest portions to assure that artificial losses are not available on the sale of the stripped bond. Finally, a purchaser of the stripped principal portion of a tax-exempt security and the seller of the interest portion have taxable gain on a subsequent sale or redemption of a stripped bond—to the extent of the portion of the cost allocated to the detached interest portion.

(d) STRIPPED BONDS ACQUIRED AFTER OCTOBER 22, 1986

(1) TAXABLE SECURITIES

For debt securities acquired after October 22, 1986, TRA '86 provides that a person that strips a coupon from a bond and disposes of either the bond or the coupon must include in his gross income the accrued market discount on the bond up to the date of disposition.[377] This amount is in addition to any interest accrued on the bond. Although this rule does not apply to stripped tax-exempt securities, other rules treat a purchaser of such a bond or coupon as having acquired an OID bond.[378]

(2) TAX-EXEMPT SECURITIES

(i) Acquired Before June 11, 1987

When a stripped tax-exempt bond or coupon is purchased after October 22, 1986, and before June 11, 1987, the amount of OID is equal to the amount that produces a yield to maturity equal to the lower of (1) the coupon rate on the original tax-exempt bond, or (2) the actual yield to

---

[375] *Id.*

[376] I.R.C. § 1286(d)(3), *prior to amendment by* TRA '86, *supra* note 80, § 1879(s)(1).

[377] TRA '86, *supra* note 80, § 1803(a)(13); I.R.C. § 1286(b).

[378] I.R.C. § 1286(d).

maturity of the stripped bond or coupon (based on its purchase price).[379] According to the Conference Report accompanying TRA '86, a taxpayer that can establish the actual yield of a bond (with all coupons attached) at the time of the original issue can elect to use that yield instead of the coupon rate.[380] The following example is adapted from the Conference Report that accompanied TRA '86.

Example 31-8

A tax-exempt security with a face amount of $1000, two years remaining to maturity, and a coupon rate of 10 percent (payable annually) is stripped and the right to the $1000 principal payment is sold for $797.20 (a 12 percent yield, compounded annually). The amount of OID is limited to $167.40 (the total OID on the stripped bond, assuming a 10 percent yield and a $797.20 purchase price). The amount of OID is tax-exempt, and the holder will adjust his basis accordingly.

The person that strips the tax-exempt bond must increase his basis in the bond or coupon by the interest accrued but not paid prior to the sale. The rules for stripped tax-exempt bonds apply to the purchase or sale of stripped bonds or coupons after October 22, 1986, and before June 11, 1987.[381]

For purposes of I.R.C. § 1286(d), a tax-exempt obligation has the same meaning as it does under I.R.C. § 1275(a)(3). For purchases and sales of stripped tax-exempt bonds and coupons after June 10, 1987, I.R.C. § 1286(d) provides that the purchaser of the stripped tax-exempt obligation or coupon treats a portion of the OID as if it is from a tax-exempt obligation, while any excess OID is treated as if it is from a taxable security.[382] For purposes of stripped bonds or coupons from October 22, 1986, to June 11, 1987, the total amount of OID equals the OID that produces a lower yield to maturity as of the purchase date, which is equal to the lower of (1) the coupon rate of interest on the bond before the coupon is separated, or (2) the yield to maturity based on the purchase price of the stripped bond or stripped coupon.[383] The tax-exempt portion of OID determined under I.R.C. § 1286(a) is the excess of the amount of the

---

[379] *Id.*
[380] TRA '86 Conf. Rep., *supra* note 147, at II-842 to II-843.
[381] I.R.C. §§ 1286(b), (d); TRA '86, *supra* note 80, §§ 1803(a)(13)(B), 1018(g)(4)(B)(i)–(ii).
[382] I.R.C. § 1286(d)(1).
[383] TRA '86 Conf. Rep., *supra* note 147, at 842.

bond's stated redemption price at maturity (or the amount that is payable on the coupon's due date) over the issue price that would produce a yield to maturity as of the purchase date equal to the lower of (1) the coupon rate of interest on the obligation from which the coupons were separated, or (2) the yield to maturity (on the basis of the purchase price) of the stripped obligation or coupon.[384] This preserves as tax-exempt OID the original amount of tax-exempt interest and OID on the obligation, while it converts market discount on the unstripped obligation into taxable OID.

(ii) Acquired After June 10, 1987

I.R.C. § 1286(d) was amended for tax-exempt securities acquired after June 10, 1987, to determine the amount of OID attributable to stripped tax-exempt bonds or coupons. Because the purchaser's tax basis in the bond or coupon is adjusted for the accrual of OID, the calculation is obviously quite important. If one or more coupons is stripped from a tax-exempt security, a portion of the OID is treated as OID on a tax-exempt obligation, while the excess is treated as OID on an obligation that is not a tax-exempt obligation. According to the Conference Committee Report, a purchaser that can establish the actual yield of a bond (with all coupons attached) at the time of original issue, may elect to use the original yield to maturity instead of the coupon rate for purposes of this calculation.[385]

(e) STRIPPED PASS-THROUGH CERTIFICATES

(1) LAW IN EFFECT BEFORE JULY 18, 1984

Under the law in effect prior to July 18, 1984, the OID rules did not apply to obligations of an issuer that was not a corporation.[386] As a result, there was no requirement for the owner of a noncorporate debt security to accrue OID.[387] Under the law in effect prior to July 18, 1984, however, there was a different result if a debt security became a stripped bond or stripped coupon. For purposes of the stripped bond provisions, it does not matter who the issuer is. The definition of a bond in I.R.C. § 1286(e)(1) is broad enough to include a bond, debenture, note, or certificate or other evidence of indebtedness.

---

[384] I.R.C. § 1286(d)(2).
[385] TRA '86 Conf. Rep., *supra* note 147, at II-843.
[386] I.R.C. § 1271(b).
[387] *See generally* section 31.2.

The question raised with respect to mortgage pools under the law in effect before July 18, 1984, was whether the packaging in a pool of residential mortgages (predominately consisting of debt obligations of individuals) and the sale of pass-through certificates involves coupon stripping. A committee of the New York State Bar Association addressed this issue in a report in response to the Treasury's request for recommendations for Treasury regulations under the pre-DRA OID and stripped bond provisions.[388] The committee asserted that the pooling of mortgages for resale did not involve any form of coupon stripping "if the seller of the mortgages receives a servicing fee for services rendered but retains no other interest in the pool, or if the seller retains a pro rata interest in mortgage principal or interest."[389] If, on the other hand, "the seller retains disproportionate interests in mortgage principal and interest in order to adjust for the difference between the rate of interest on the mortgages and current market rates," the committee stated that the pooling involves coupon stripping.[390]

(2) CURRENT LAW CONSIDERATIONS

(i) In General

Stripped pass-through certificates reflect the "stripping" of the interest component of cash flows on asset-backed securities.[391] Interest can be separated from principal in the pass-through certificate structure without running afoul of the prohibition against multiple interests because of the specific example in the Treasury regulations that allows the stripping of bonds from coupons. In Example (4) of Treas. Reg. § 301.7701-4(c),[392] a trust with multiple classes of ownership was taxed as a trust because "the multiple classes simply provide each certificate holder with a direct interest in what is treated under [I.R.C.] section 1286 as a separate bond."[393] This means that the multiple classes "merely facilitate direct investment in the assets held by the trust."[394] Because of the specific

---

[388] New York State Bar Association, Ad Hoc Committee on Original Issue Discount and Coupon Stripping, *Report to Treasury, reprinted in* 22 TAX NOTES 993 (1984).

[389] *Id.* at 1023.

[390] *Id.*

[391] For a detailed discusson of stripped pass-through certificates, see section 7.2(c)(2). *See also The Stripped Mortgage-Backed Security, Innovations,* INTERMARKET, Mar. 1987, at 70.

[392] (1986). *See* sections 7.2(c)(2)(i) and 36.2(c).

[393] Treas. Reg. § 301.7701-4(c), Example (4) (1986).

[394] *Id.*

reference in Example (4) to I.R.C. § 1286, it is possible that expansive interpretations of the stripped bond rules may result in an expansion of the scope of Example (4).[395] In fact, some securitized assets offerings have combined stripped and subordinated certificates.

(ii) Taxation of Taxpayer Stripping the Bond

In a typical stripped pass-through certificate transaction, the originator or promoter (collectively referred to as the "promoter") sells principal balances and rights to receive interest on the underlying pooled debt obligations at a particular interest rate, while retaining the excess of the yield on the underlying pooled assets over the interest rate on the pass-through certificates.[396] This transaction is subject to the stripped bond rules in I.R.C. § 1286.

The underlying pooled debt obligations are "evidences of indebtedness" that are treated as bonds as defined in I.R.C. § 1286(e)(1).[397] The right to receive interest is treated as a "coupon" under I.R.C. § 1286(e)(5).[398] Separating a portion of the interest from the bond is treated as a "stripped bond" under I.R.C. § 1286(e)(2),[399] equal to the excess of each payment due on an underlying pooled asset over the sum of the portions of each underlying asset allocable to amortization of principal, interest on a monthly principal balance at the interest rate on the pass-through certificate, and the monthly servicing fees.[400]

The promoter (i.e., the "person stripping the bond") allocates its tax basis among the items it retains and the items it disposes of. If an amount is received in excess of the promoter's tax basis, there is a taxable gain on the sale.[401] When the promoter disposes of any of the retained coupons and bond, it must include in income any accrued interest or market discount on the stripped bonds.[402] The tax basis of the bond and coupons is

---

[395] *See, e.g.,* LTR 8618065 (Feb. 7, 1986).

[396] For a detailed discussion of the transaction, see section 7.2(c)(2).

[397] A bond is defined in I.R.C. § 1286(e)(1) as a "bond, debenture, note, or certificate or other evidence of indebtedness."

[398] A coupon is defined in I.R.C. § 1286(e)(5) to include "any right to receive interest on a bond (whether or not evidenced by a coupon)."

[399] A stripped bond is defined in I.R.C. § 1286(e)(2) as "a bond issued at any time with interest coupons where there is a separation in ownership between the bond and any coupon which has not yet become payable."

[400] *See generally* LTR 8640012 (June 30, 1986); LTR 8625048 (Mar. 24, 1986); LTR 8620016 (Feb. 7, 1986).

[401] I.R.C. § 1286(b).

[402] I.R.C. § 1286(b)(1).

increased by the amount of this income.[403] Basis is allocated between the retained coupons and the bonds that the promoter sells to the certificate owners on the basis of fair market value of the coupons and bonds.[404] If the promoter sells the retained bonds and coupons, it recognizes gain in an amount equal to the extent of the retained yield (i.e., the retained interest rate). In addition, the amount that the promoter retains—that is, the retained coupons—is viewed as having been originally issued as of the purchase date with OID equal to the excess of the amount payable on the due date of the coupon, which is the originator's share of the scheduled interest payments over the tax basis allocated to the coupons.[405]

(iii) Taxpayer Owning Stripped Bonds

An owner of a stripped pass-through certificate has an undivided ownership interest in the underlying pool of stripped debt obligations. Under I.R.C. § 1286, the underlying obligations are viewed as having been originally issued on the date the certificate owner purchased the certificate with OID equal to the excess of their stated redemption price at maturity over their ratable share of the purchase price. The owners of the pass-through certificates—under the provisions of I.R.C. § 1272—must accrue the OID on the coupons and bonds, although it is unclear exactly how these rules are to be applied.[406] Pass-through certificates that are subject to the stripped bond rules of I.R.C. § 1286 are also subject to the OID rules. Those pass-through certificates that are not subject to the stripped bond rules, on the other hand, are not subject to the OID rules unless interest on the underlying pooled debt obligations is scheduled to increase over time.[407]

The pass-through certificate owner has a tax basis in his certificate equal to its purchase price.[408] The price paid for the certificate is allocated

---

[403] I.R.C. § 1286(b)(2).

[404] I.R.C. § 1286(b)(3). If the promoter "originated" the underlying pooled assets, it will most likely have a tax basis in each debt obligation equal to its face value.

[405] For a discussion of OID, see section 31.2.

[406] If stripped bonds and coupons are characterized as debt obligations on which payments may be accelerated by reason of the prepayment of other obligations securing the debt instruments, OID accrual might be calculated under I.R.C. § 1272(a)(6). For a discussion of OID, see section 31.2.

[407] For a detailed discussion of pass-through certificates subject to the stripped bond rules, see J. PEASLEE & D. NIRENBERG, FEDERAL INCOME TAXATION OF MORTGAGE BACKED SECURITIES 137 (1989). For a discussion of pass-through certificates not subject to the stripped bond rules, see *id.* at 144. For a discussion of graduated payment mortgages, see section 37.7.

[408] For a discussion of tax basis, see Chapter 16.

among each of the pooled debt obligations in accordance with their respective fair market values.[409]

An investment trust holding a pool of stripped debt obligations might be viewed as holding separate stripped bonds and coupons for each principal and interest payment on each debt obligation. This is because interest on stripped bonds might be viewed as stripped coupons under I.R.C. §§ 1286(e)(2) and (3). The stripped bonds and coupons might represent multiple stripped bonds. Because stripped pass-through certificate owners must allocate their purchase price among all of the stripped bonds and coupons in the pool, this allocation can be difficult, if not impossible.

To minimize the problems in allocating basis and payments among all of the underlying pooled debt obligations, certificate owners might be able to aggregate payments of principal and interest from all of the stripped bonds and coupons in the underlying pool into one debt instrument. Aggregation is allowed under the rules contained in the proposed Treasury regulations on OID. Aggregation is allowed if the debt obligations are "issued in connection with the same transaction or a series of related transactions or a part of the same issue shall be treated together as a single debt instrument with a single issue price, maturity date, yield, and stated redemption price at maturity.[410] The proposed Treasury regulations further provide that "[w]hether debt instruments are issued in connection with the same transaction or a series of related transactions shall be determined in accordance with all the facts and circumstances surrounding the issuance of the debt instrument."[411]

(f) STRIPPED PAY-THROUGH BONDS

Pay-through bonds can be issued as stripped bonds where the interest coupons (defined broadly to include any right to receive interest on a security whether or not evidenced by a coupon)[412] are separated from ownership of the debt security.[413] In other words, the security is divided into two pieces: a right to receive principal and a right to receive interest. Stripped bonds and coupons purchased after July 1, 1982, are subject to I.R.C. § 1286. For a discussion of stripped pay-through bonds, see section

---

[409] I.R.C. § 1286(a).
[410] Prop. Treas. Reg. § 1.1275-2(d) (1986).
[411] Id.
[412] I.R.C. § 1286(e)(5).
[413] I.R.C. § 1286(e)(2).

7.2(d)(7). For a discussion of the stripped bond rules, see generally the discussion in section 31.6(a).

(g) RECONSTITUTED STRIPPED BONDS

A subsequent purchaser of stripped bonds and stripped coupons can acquire interests in bonds and coupons that basically reconstitute the bond and coupon back into the bond that was originally stripped. It appears that once a taxpayer owns all of the stripped bonds and stripped coupons with respect to a single bond, the stripped bond rules cease to apply. This is because I.R.C. § 1286(e)(2) defines a stripped bond as "a bond issued at any time with interest coupons where there is a separation in ownership between the bond and any coupon which has not yet become payable." Once the taxpayer holds all of the stripped bonds and stripped coupons, there is no longer a separation in ownership between the bond and any coupon which has not yet become payable.

§ 31.7 FOREIGN CURRENCY TRANSACTIONS

TRA '86 introduced I.R.C. § 988, which applies to all debt securities issued by a United States taxpayer and that are denominated in foreign currencies.[414] OID on debt securities denominated in foreign currencies for any accrual period is determined in terms of units of foreign currency.

(a) ORIGINAL ISSUE DISCOUNT

The Treasury has regulatory authority to prescribe rules for the accrual of OID on nonfunctional currency-denominated securities. The Senate Report that accompanied TRA '86 provides that until such regulations are issued, OID is to be determined in terms of units of the nonfunctional currency using the average exchange rate for the accrual period.[415] To determine the adjusted issue price, the functional currency amount of OID included in income for an accrual period is then added to the basis of a security.

At the date of this writing, Treasury regulations have not been issued to address OID on debt securities denominated in foreign currencies or determined by reference to the value of one or more foreign currencies. In

---

[414] For a discussion of foreign currency transactions, see generally Part Thirteen.

[415] SENATE FINANCE COMM. REPORT, S. REP. NO. 313, 99th Cong., 2d Sess. 461 (1986) [hereinafter S. REP. NO. 313].

Announcement 86-92,[416] the IRS announced that the rules contained in Prop. Treas. Reg. § 1.1275-4 (dealing with contingent payment rules for OID) originally proposed on April 8, 1986, are not intended to apply to lending transactions "merely because some or all of the payments are denominated in or determined by reference to the value of one or more foreign currencies." The IRS also stated that it "is actively considering the application of the original issue discount rules to foreign currency borrowings and solicits the comments of interested practitioners and taxpayers."[417] It appears as if Announcement 86-92 covers all payments for which their dollar values are determined by the value of one or more foreign currencies. The temporary Treasury regulations under I.R.C. § 988 also provide that a debt instrument "is not considered a contingent payment debt instrument merely because some or all of the payments are denominated in, or determined by reference to, a nonfunctional currency."[418]

(b) MARKET DISCOUNT

Market discount, as defined in I.R.C. § 1278(a)(2), is determined in units of nonfunctional currency in which the market discount bond is denominated (or in which the payments are determined).[419] Accrued market discount (other than market discount currently included in income pursuant to I.R.C. § 1278(b)) is translated into functional currency at the spot rate on the date the market discount bond is disposed of.[420] None of the accrued market discount is treated as exchange gain or loss.[421] Market discount includable in income under I.R.C. § 1278(b) is translated into functional currency at the average exchange rate for the accrual period.[422] Exchange gain or loss with respect to accrued market discount includable currently in income under I.R.C. § 1278(b) is determined in accordance with Temp. Treas. Reg. § 1.988-2T(b)(3) (addressing accrued interest income).

---

[416] 1986-32 I.R.B. 46 (Aug. 11, 1986).
[417] Announcement 86-92, 1986-32 I.R.B. 46 (Aug. 11, 1986).
[418] Temp. Treas. Reg. § 1.988-2T(b)(2)(i) (1989).
[419] Temp. Treas. Reg. § 1.988-2T(b)(11) (1989).
[420] *Id.*
[421] *Id.*
[422] *Id.*

(c) BOND PREMIUM

The rules for computing bond premium on debt securities denominated in foreign currency will also be provided by Treasury regulations. Until regulations were released, bond premiums could be translated into U.S. dollars at the average exchange rate in effect during the accrual period.[423]

Temp. Treas. Reg. § 1.988-2T(b)(10)[424] addresses the treatment of amortizable bond premium on a debt instrument, defined in Temp. Treas. Reg. § 1.988-2T(a)(2)(i) as a debt instrument where all payments are denominated in, or determined with reference to, a single nonfunctional currency.[425] Amortizable bond premium on such a security is computed in the units of nonfunctional currency in which the bond is denominated (or in which the payments are determined).[426] Amortizable bond premium properly taken into account under I.R.C. § 171 or Treas. Reg. § 1.61-12 (or the successor provision thereof) reduces interest income or expense in units of nonfunctional currency.[427]

Exchange gain or loss is realized with respect to the bond premium by treating the amortized portion of the premium with respect to any period as a return of principal.[428]

If the taxpayer does not elect to amortize bond premium under I.R.C. § 171, the amount of bond premium constitutes a market loss when the bond matures.[429]

§ 31.8 SECURITIES IN DEFAULT

Securities with interest payments in default are generally traded "flat," which means that they are traded at their full principal amount without any allocation between unpaid accrued interest and principal. These securities are often referred to as "flat bonds." The owner of such securi-

---

[423] S. REP. NO. 313, *supra* note 415, at 461. For a discussion of bond premium issues for debt securities denominated in foreign currencies, see generally O'Neill & Lee, *Federal Income Tax Treatment of Foreign Currency Transactions After the Tax Reform Act of 1986, Special Report*, 33 TAX NOTES 185, 191–93 (1986).

[424] (1989).

[425] For a discussion of nonfunctional currency, see section 59.2(g)(2).

[426] Temp. Treas. Reg. § 1.988-2T(b)(10) (1989).

[427] *Id.* For a discussion of bond premiums, see section 31.4.

[428] *Id.*

[429] Temp. Treas. Reg. § 1.988-2T(b)(10) (1989) (referring to Temp. Treas. Reg. § 1.988-2T(b)(8) (1989)) (which limits the exchange gain or loss on the payment or disposition of a debt instrument).

ties has the right to principal and any unpaid accrued interest without any additional or separate charges. The tax rules that apply to securities in default take into account the fact that accrued interest is likely to never be paid. Both cash and accrued basis taxpayers do not include interest as it "accrues" on securities in default. Rather, taxpayers only include such interest when it is paid, or the securities are sold at a price in excess of their tax basis and a portion of the gain is attributable to interest.

Payments of interest that accrued prior to the date on which the taxpayer purchases the securities are treated as a recovery of cost (i.e., a return of capital)[430] that reduces the basis of the securities. The taxpayer is first allowed to recover his cost before reporting taxable income because it is not certain that the taxpayer will ever recover his investment.[431] Additional payments that relate to interest that accrued prior to purchase that exceed the taxpayer's cost are treated as capital gain.[432] These payments are not treated as interest.[433] As a result, the payment of interest accrued prior to acquisition of tax-exempt securities in default is first treated as a return of capital, with any excess treated as a capital gain, not as tax-exempt interest.[434]

Payments of interest that accrue after the taxpayer purchases defaulted securities are treated as interest income when received by the taxpayer.[435] Such interest is taxable, irrespective of whether the amounts are paid by the issuer or a subsequent purchaser.[436]

If securities in default are subsequently resold by the taxpayer at a flat price that exceeds the taxpayer's basis in the securities, any gain that represents interest that accrued while the taxpayer owned the securities is treated as ordinary income.[437] The portion of gain attributable to interest is determined on the basis of the ratio that the sales proceeds

---

[430] Treas. Reg. § 1.61-7(c) (1966). For a discussion of the considerations on when holders of defaulted loans and debt securities can cease accruing interest income, see Calvin & Farias, *When Can Holders of Defaulted Debt Cease Accruing Interest Income?*, 73 J. TAX'N 378 (1990).

[431] Hewitt v. Comm'r, 30 B.T.A. 962, 965 (1934), *acq.* VIII-2 C.B. 9.

[432] Rickaby v. Comm'r, 27 T.C. 886, 891 (1957), *acq.* 1960-2 C.B. 6; Rev. Rul. 60-284, 1960-2 C.B. 464.

[433] First Kentucky Co. v. Gray, 190 F. Supp. 824, 825 (W.D. Ky. 1960), *aff'd*, 309 F.2d 845 (6th Cir. 1962).

[434] R.O. Holton & Co. v. Comm'r, 44 B.T.A. 202, 206 (1941); Noll v. Comm'r, 43 B.T.A. 496, 502 (1941).

[435] Rev. Rul. 60-284, 1960-2 C.B. 464.

[436] Fisher v. Comm'r, 209 F.2d 513, 515 (6th Cir. 1954), *aff'g* 19 T.C. 384 (1952), *cert. denied*, 347 U.S. 1014 (1954); Jaglom v. Comm'r, 303 F.2d 847, 849 (2d Cir. 1962), *aff'g* 36 T.C. 126 (1961); Tobey v. Comm'r, 26 T.C. 610, 618 (1956), *acq.* 1956-2 C.B. 8.

[437] *Jaglom*, 303 F.2d at 849; United States v. Langston, 308 F.2d 729, 731 (5th Cir. 1962), *rev'g* 62-1 U.S. Tax Cas. (CCH) ¶ 9243 (S.D. Fla. 1961).

bears to the sum of the face amount of principal and all accrued but unpaid interest at the time of sale.[438]

If flat securities in default are sold short, it appears as if the payments made by the borrower to the short seller in lieu of interest are deductible as nonbusiness expenses if the requirements to deduct, rather than capitalize, these amounts are complied with.[439] If the owner recovers his securities before the payment of interest that accrued prior to purchase, the payment should generate short-term capital gain to the owner.

The redemption of securities in default raises the question of whether the payments are retirement proceeds, which are generally viewed as an exchange of the securities.[440] The case law is clear that the proceeds received on retirement of securities in default include any payments of accrued but unpaid interest that accrued prior to the taxpayer's purchases.[441]

There are two conflicting private letter rulings on the proration of principal and interest on defaulted securities. In the first private ruling, LTR 8821018,[442] the IRS ruled that amounts paid on defaulted tax-exempt securities were allocated solely to principal. As a result, bondholders could not recognize tax-free interest and could not report a capital loss on the transaction. In LTR 8821018, a municipality issued bonds to provide tax-exempt financing to a corporation for the construction of a medically supervised retirement home. Under the terms of the financing, the corporation was required to make principal and interest payments to a trustee. When the corporation did not make these payments, the property secured by the bonds was sold. The sales proceeds, minus certain administration costs, were distributed to the bondholders as a "final payment." The bond indenture provided that payments were to be prorated between principal and interest. The bondholders requested an "interest first" allocation (rather than an allocation between principal and interest as provided in the indenture). Such a result would have given the bondholders tax-exempt interest, although I.R.C. § 57(a)(5) provides that interest on certain private activity bonds is a tax

---

[438] *Jaglom*, 303 F.2d at 850, where the court suggested—although it did not decide the issue—that if a sale occurs in anticipation of an imminent payment by the issuer, the fair market value of principal and interest would be more appropriate than face value. *Id.*

[439] *See generally* section 18.6.

[440] *See generally* section 31.9.

[441] *Tobey*, 26 T.C. at 618; *Hewitt*, 30 B.T.A. at 965 (1934); *Chase v. Comm'r*, 44 B.T.A. 39, 51, nonacq. 1941-1 C.B. 13, *aff'd per curiam sub nom. Helvering v. Chase*, 128 F.2d 740 (2d Cir. 1942); *Adrian & James, Inc. v. Comm'r*, 4 T.C. 708, 715 (1945), *acq.* 1945 C.B. 1.

[442] (Feb. 23, 1988).

preference item.[443] Treating this payment as interest would have also yielded a larger capital loss. The IRS reasoned that the normal considerations allowing a principal and interest proration were not present. Thus, the IRS ruled in LTR 8821018 that the agreement between the issuer and the bondholders to reallocate the payments between principal and interest had no effect and the entire amount would be treated as a return of principal.

In the second private ruling, LTR 8819068,[444] the IRS reached a different result from the result it reached in LTR 8821018. In LTR 8819068, involving taxable bonds, the IRS ruled that amounts paid on defaulted taxable bonds could be prorated between principal and interest. In this private ruling, an insolvent company, pursuant to a sale of all its assets and a subsequent liquidation, offered to purchase all of its outstanding debentures. There was no arrangement for the allocation of the payment. The IRS concluded that proration was appropriate because the facts were similar to *Warner Co. v. Comm'r*,[445] where a principal and interest proration was allowed after a financially distressed taxpayer repurchased some of its bonds without an allocation arrangement.

§ 31.9 EXCHANGES OF DEBT SECURITIES

(a) IN GENERAL

Without a specific statutory provision for tax-free status, exchanges of debt securities are taxable.[446] Exchanges of debt securities of the same issuer are taxable if there are any material changes in the terms of the debt securities.[447] Exchanges of substantially identical securities of the same issuer are viewed as debt refundings and are not taxable.[448]

---

[443] *See generally* section 33.2(c).

[444] (Feb. 17, 1988).

[445] 11 T.C. 419 (1948), *aff'd*, 181 F.2d 599 (3d Cir. 1950).

[446] *See* I.R.C. § 1031(a)(2), which states that tax-free exchanges of property do not apply to bonds, notes, securities, or other evidences of indebtedness. For a discussion of debt-for-debt exchanges, see Kohl, *The Fundamentals of Debt Swaps*, 48 TAX NOTES 1037 (1990).

[447] Mutual Loan & Sav. Co. v. Comm'r, 184 F.2d 161, 165 (5th Cir. 1950), *rev'g* 8 T.C.M. (CCH) 203 (1949); Rev. Rul. 81-169, 1981-1 C.B. 429 (an exchange was taxable where there were differences in interest rates, maturity dates, and sinking fund provisions); LTR 7902002 (June 29, 1978) (an exchange of New York City Notes for Municipal Assistance Corporation Bonds, referred to as "Big MAC" bonds, was taxable because the securities were not viewed as substantially identical; Rev. Rul. 73-328, 1973-2 C.B. 296 (where an exchange of a note for corporate bonds was a taxable exchange).

[448] Rev. Rul. 56-435, 1956-2 C.B. 506, *as modified by* Rev. Rul. 81-169, 1981-1 C.B. 429.

Where no physical exchange of securities takes place, there can be a constructive exchange if there is a significant change in terms so that a new or materially different security is deemed to be issued.[449] It may also be possible that an "in-substance defeasance" can be a constructive exchange.[450] In an in-substance defeasance, a corporation typically transfers assets to a trust that it has established for the sole purpose of making payments of principal and interest on its outstanding debt securities.

In Rev. Rul. 87-19,[451] the IRS ruled that a financial institution is deemed to have exchanged original tax-exempt securities for new tax-exempt securities, under I.R.C. § 1001, if it waives its right under an interest adjustment clause to receive a higher interest rate. The IRS, citing Rev. Rul. 81-169,[452] found that the waiver results in a "material change in the terms of the bonds."[453]

(b) CORPORATE REORGANIZATIONS

Special Code provisions allow for tax-free exchanges of debt securities in connection with reorganizations pursuant to I.R.C. §§ 354, 368, and 371. Because it is beyond the scope of this book to discuss tax-free corporate reorganizations in detail, it is sufficient to point out that the exchange of debt securities for other corporate bonds, securities, and stock may be tax-free if the exchange qualifies under one of the specific Code provisions.[454]

Special rules apply to Treasury securities and municipal securities. Treasury securities can be exchanged tax-free in accordance with the provisions of I.R.C. § 1037.[455] Municipal securities do not qualify for the

---

[449] See Rev. Rul. 79-155, 1979-1 C.B. 153 (where gain was not realized under I.R.C. § 354); Rev. Rul. 73-160, 1973-1 C.B. 365 (where a change in the terms of the debt securities did not create a deemed exchange).

[450] See Rev. Rul. 85-42, 1985-1 C.B. 36.

[451] 1987-1 C.B. 249.

[452] 1981-1 C.B. 429.

[453] 1987-1 C.B. at 250.

[454] See generally Sheppard, *Debt-For-Debt Exchanges—Issue Price in Reorganizations*, 48 TAX NOTES 954 (1990); McCall & Walker, *Debt Securities Revisited*, 108 BANKING L.J. 73 (1991). For an excellent discussion of reorganizations, see B. BITTKER & J. EUSTICE, FEDERAL INCOME TAXATION OF CORPORATIONS AND SHAREHOLDERS ch. 14 (5th ed. 1987); R. WILLENS, TAXATION OF CORPORATE CAPITAL TRANSACTIONS: A GUIDE FOR CORPORATE, INVESTMENT BANKING, AND TAX ADVISERS ch. 8 (1984).

[455] See section 32.1(d).

corporate reorganization provisions of I.R.C. § 368(a)(1), which only apply to private corporations.[456]

For a discussion of the OID rules that apply to debt securities received in corporate reorganizations, see section 31.2(h). For a discussion of the market discount rules that apply to debt securities received in corporate reorganizations, see section 31.3(e).

(c) BANKRUPTCY PROCEEDINGS

The treatment of bankruptcy proceedings is beyond the scope of this book, so it is sufficient to point out that the treatment of bond-for-bond exchanges in bankruptcy proceedings raise questions about cancellation of indebtedness and when income should be realized.[457]

§ 31.10 RETIREMENT, REDEMPTION, AND DISPOSITION OF DEBT SECURITIES

The retirement[458] of a taxable debt security is generally considered to be a taxable sale or exchange,[459] resulting in capital gain or loss except for OID,[460] market discount,[461] or for certain securities that are required to be issued in registered form.[462] If at the time of original issue there was an intention to call a debt security before maturity, any gain realized on a sale or exchange is treated as ordinary income up to the amount of the

---

[456] *See* section 33.4; *see also* Emery v. Comm'r, 166 F.2d 27, 30–31 (2d Cir. 1948), *aff'g* 8 T.C. 979 (1947); Girard Trust Co. v. United States, 166 F.2d 773, 775 (3d Cir. 1948), *aff'g* 69 F. Supp. 874 (E.D. Pa. 1946).

[457] *See* Treasury, *IRS Officials Discuss Possible Changes to Financial Instrument Rules*, Daily Tax Rep. (BNA) No. 90, at G-7 (May 9, 1990); Sheppard, *Debt-for-Debt Exchanges—Issue Price in Reorganizations*, 48 TAX NOTES 954 (1990).

[458] The term "retirement" is read broadly to include redemptions, repurchases, and cancellations by the issuer. McClain v. Comm'r, 311 U.S. 527, 530 (1941), *aff'g* 110 F.2d 878 (5th Cir. 1940); Estate of Monroe v. Comm'r, 45 B.T.A. 1060 (1941), *acq.* 1942-1 C.B. 12, *aff'd per curiam sub nom.* Pinnell v. Comm'r, 132 F.2d 126 (3d Cir. 1942), *amended sub nom.* Pinnell v. Comm'r, 43-1 U.S. Tax Cas. (CCH) ¶ 9255 (3d Cir. 1943); MacDougald v. Comm'r, 44 B.T.A. 1046 (1941).

[459] I.R.C. § 1271(a)(1).

[460] *See* section 31.2.

[461] *See* section 31.3.

[462] *See* section 31.12. In addition, debt securities issued prior to 1955 must either have interest coupons or be in registered form for a taxpayer to obtain capital gain treatment. I.R.C. § 1271(c)(1).

OID, reduced by the amount of OID previously included in the owner's income.[463]

There are several exceptions to the requirement for ordinary income treatment. First, the provisions for ordinary income do not apply to tax-exempt securities.[464]

Second, it does not apply to any owner that purchases a debt security at a premium.[465] Third, I.R.C. § 1271 does not apply to any obligations issued by natural persons or to any obligations issued before July 2, 1982, by noncorporate or nongovernmental issuers.[466]

In G.C.M. 39,543,[467] the IRS Chief Counsel's Office, in response to a request from the Joint Committee on Taxation, concluded that a call premium received by a holder on the early redemption of a debt security subject to the provisions of I.R.C. § 1271 is treated as capital gain. The Chief Counsel noted that former I.R.C. § 1232(a) had provided that gain in excess of earned OID received by a holder on the redemption of evidences of indebtedness was considered to be gain from the sale or exchange of a capital asset.[468] In the G.C.M., the Chief Counsel's Office noted that "Congress did not specifically intend the elimination of [I.R.C. § 1232] to change the holder's treatment of call premiums" when it enacted I.R.C. § 1271.[469] "The lack of an affirmative provision in section 1271 that call premiums be treated as interest income, given their treatment under section 1232 as capital gain," was viewed as evidence that "Congress did not intend to change their treatment by a holder."[470]

In LTR 8551025,[471] the IRS reviewed a proposed convertible debenture issuance that included a put option provision that would be triggered by an adverse IRS audit. In the private ruling, the shareholders of a national bank would receive convertible debentures in exchange for their stock. Under the terms of the indenture, if the IRS asserted on audit that the debentures constituted an equity interest (rather than a bona fide indebtedness), up to 35 percent of the principal amount of the debentures received by each shareholder could be redeemed at the shareholder's

---

[463] I.R.C. § 1271(a)(2).

[464] I.R.C. § 1271(a)(2)(B).

[465] *Id.*

[466] I.R.C. § 1271(b).

[467] Fed. Taxes (P-H), [1986 Transfer Binder] Internal Memoranda of the IRS, ¶ 128(86)-34 (July 29, 1986, numbered on Aug. 4, 1986).

[468] *Id.* at 636.

[469] *Id.* at 635.

[470] *Id.* at 638.

[471] (Sept. 23, 1985).

election. Under the proposed debenture issuance, a final determination by a court or an IRS closing agreement was not necessary to trigger the put. Because of the convertibility feature and certain other hybrid debt and equity characteristics, the issuer recognized that, on audit, the debentures were subject to attack as equity. In the private ruling, the IRS stated that a determination of whether the debentures constitute debt or equity would be made "upon examination."

(a) ORIGINALLY ISSUED AT A DISCOUNT

Gain on the retirement or disposition of debt securities issued after 1954 at a discount of more than .25 percent held by an investor[472] is covered by separate provisions.[473] That portion of the gain representing OID in excess of this de minimis amount that has not been previously taxed is treated as ordinary income.[474] Excess gain, if any, is treated as capital gain.

To determine OID for convertible debt securities,[475] the issue price is not reduced by the value of the conversion feature.[476]

For debt securities with detachable warrants,[477] a portion of the issue price is allocated to the warrants, based on the respective fair market values of the two components.[478] The fact that the warrants are not exercised does not affect the amount of OID, if any, determined at the time the debt securities were issued.[479]

(b) MARKET DISCOUNT BONDS

For debt securities issued before July 19, 1984, capital gain or loss results on the retirement or disposition of a debt security with market discount.[480] Gain is ordinary, up to the amount of interest expense allowed under I.R.C. § 1277(b)(1), if the debt security was purchased after July 18, 1984, and was directly financed.[481] Certain debt securities are exempt

---

[472] *See* section 8.1.
[473] I.R.C. §§ 1271(c)(2)(A), 1273(a)(3).
[474] Rev. Rul. 75-117, 1975-1 C.B. 273.
[475] *See* section 1.1(d).
[476] Treas. Reg. § 1.1232-3(b)(2) (1980); *see also* section 34.3(b).
[477] *See* section 1.1(c).
[478] *See* Treas. Reg. § 1.1232-3(b)(2) (1980).
[479] Rev. Rul. 72-46, 1972-1 C.B. 50.
[480] I.R.C. § 1277(d). For a discussion of market discount bonds, see generally section 31.3.
[481] I.R.C. § 1277(d). For a discussion of the interest deferral provisions applicable to market discount bonds, see section 31.3(m).

from the market discount rules if they are one of the following types of debt securities:

1. Short-term obligations[482]
2. Tax-exempt securities[483]
3. United States savings bonds[484]
4. Certain installment obligations,[485] or
5. Securities where the discount is less than .25 percent of the stated redemption price of a debt security at maturity, multiplied by the number of complete years remaining to maturity of the security[486]

(c) REISSUANCES

When the terms of debt securities are modified, there may be a reissuance, retirement, or a sale or exchange.[487] I.R.C. § 1001 must be considered. At the date of this writing, the Treasury is considering when gain or loss is triggered under I.R.C. § 1001 when the issuer materially modifies the terms of the debt instrument.[488]

§ 31.11 REPURCHASE AGREEMENTS AND REVERSE REPURCHASE AGREEMENTS

(a) IN GENERAL

Repos and reverse repos (collectively "repo transactions") are generally financing transactions where securities (typically government securities, municipals, and mortgage-backed securities) are financed pursuant to an agreement between the parties to return substantially identical securi-

---

[482] I.R.C. 1278(a)(1)(B).
[483] *Id.*
[484] *Id.* For a discussion of United States savings bonds, see section 32.1(b).
[485] I.R.C. § 1278(a)(1)(B).
[486] I.R.C. § 1278(a)(2)(C).
[487] For a discussion of the tax considerations raised by a reissuance, see Henry, *Reissuance Revisited, Special Report,* 42 TAX NOTES 91 (1989).
[488] *See* Sheppard, *Tax Officials Consider Debt Securities Questions,* 47 TAX NOTES 1044 (1990).

ties at the end of the loan term.[489] Repo transactions "are frequently used by dealers in Government securities, financial institutions, and others for temporary cash management, interest rate arbitrage, or the borrowing of securities used in the course of a dealer's business."[490] In a repo transaction, a taxpayer (referred to as the "seller-debtor") borrows money using securities he owns as collateral by "selling" the securities to the other party (referred to as the "buyer-creditor") while agreeing to repurchase equivalent securities from the buyer-creditor at a future date. In a reverse repo transaction (so named because the transaction is the reverse side of a repo), the buyer-creditor purchases securities from the seller-debtor and agrees to sell equivalent securities back to the seller-debtor at a future date.

(1) TYPES OF REPURCHASE AGREEMENTS

Repo transactions can be overnight, for a longer specified period (referred to as "term repos"), for the maturity of the underlying security, or with an open settlement date (referred to as "open repos"). Open repos can generally be terminated by either side on one business day's notice. The buyer-creditor may or may not take physical possession of the securities and, depending on the terms of the agreement and the type of securities involved, may or may not reregister the securities in his name.

Repo transactions are generally terminated in one of two ways. First, the securities can be returned to the seller-debtor at the same price as they were transferred to the buyer-creditor, plus charges representing an agreed-upon interest rate added to the principal at the maturity of the contract. Or, second, the securities can be returned to the seller-debtor at a predetermined price that is higher than the price at which they were transferred to the buyer-creditor.

On the date when a repo transaction is terminated, the money and securities equivalent to those securities first "sold" are returned to their original owner. The seller-debtor receives the same or equivalent securities back from the buyer-creditor, while the buyer-creditor receives his funds plus an additional amount back from the seller-debtor.

---

[489] *See* Bowsher, *Repurchase Agreements*, FRB ST. LOUIS REV., Sept. 1979, at 17; Lucas, Jones & Thurston, *Federal Funds and Repurchase Agreements*, FRBNY Q. REV., Summer 1977, at 33. For a discussion of repos, see section 2.2(c).

[490] Price v. Comm'r, 88 T.C. 860, 864 (1987).

(2) CONSIDERATIONS FOR REAL ESTATE INVESTMENT TRUSTS

For REITs, repos do not qualify as real estate assets, cash or cash items (including receivables), or government securities under I.R.C. § 856(c)(5).[491] In addition, a REIT entering into repos is not considered to be holding property primarily for sale to customers in the ordinary course of business within the meaning of I.R.C. § 856(a)(4).[492] This characterization of repos can be a disadvantage to REITs because they are subject to varying tax consequences, depending on whether 75 percent of their assets qualify as the types of assets mentioned above.[493]

(3) TAX CONSIDERATIONS

The major tax questions with repo transactions are whether they qualify as a sale or a loan and whether the Straddle Rules apply. The issue of whether the seller-debtor is the owner of the repoed security for tax purposes may arise, independent of whether the interest rate on the repo is fixed or floating, or whether the repo is a term repo or an open repo. This section discusses the tax considerations for repo transactions involving both taxable and tax-exempt securities. It also addresses sham transactions and the recent application of economic substance arguments to deduct expenses. For a discussion of possible application of the Straddle Rules to repos, see section 48.3(b).

(b) SALES OR FINANCING TRANSACTIONS

A repo transaction can be characterized as either a sale or a loan. In Rev. Rul. 79-195,[494] the IRS addressed whether a repo was a sale or a loan. The IRS found that the characterization is based on the facts and depends on whether there has been "a relinquishment of substantial incidents of ownership and a shifting of the economic risk of loss."[495] In general, repos

---

[491] Rev. Rul. 77-59, 1977-1 C.B. 196.
[492] *Id.*
[493] *See generally* I.R.C. §§ 851–855; *see also* section 8.10.
[494] 1979-1 C.B. 177.
[495] Rev. Rul. 79-195, 1979-1 C.B. 177.

are treated as secured loans.[496] In certain circumstances, however, repo transactions are viewed as sales.[497]

(1) LOANS

When a repo is treated as a loan, neither gain nor loss is recognized by the seller-debtor on the initial transfer. The securities are "sold" as collateral to secure the loan. As with other financing transactions, repos may be subject to the OID rules for short-term obligations[498] and to the market discount rules.[499] The accrual of OID on the repoed security does not qualify for capital treatment.

Congress enacted I.R.C. § 1058 in 1976 to remove some of the uncertainty that surrounded the correct income tax treatment of certain securities lending transactions. Congress wanted to clear up this uncertainty to encourage persons to lend their securities to brokers because those loans can have a favorable impact on the liquidity of the securities markets.[500] Although I.R.C. § 1058 was intended to clarify existing law, it appears as if the security loan provisions of I.R.C. § 1058 may impose additional requirements on a repo to assure that the transaction qualifies as a loan.[501] For a securities lending transaction to fit within I.R.C. § 1058(b)(3), the transfer of securities must "not reduce the risk of loss or opportunity for gain of the transferor of the securities on the securities transferred." Proposed Treasury regulations provide that in order not to reduce a security lender's (i.e., the seller-debtor) risk of loss or increase his opportunity for gain, the agreement under which securities are borrowed

---

[496] Rev. Rul. 74-27, 1974-1 C.B. 24 (a repo was a loan where the security subject to the repo was returnable on demand of the seller-creditor "on or before" a fixed date); Rev. Rul. 77-59, 1977-1 C.B. 196 (a repo was a loan where the securities subject to the repo agreement were transferred "generally overnight or not more than several days"); American Nat'l Bank of Austin v. United States, 421 F.2d 442 (5th Cir.), cert. denied, 400 U.S. 819 (1970); First Nat'l Bank in Wichita v. Comm'r, 57 F.2d 7 (10th Cir. 1932), aff'g 19 B.T.A. 744 (1930), cert. denied, 287 U.S. 636 (1932).

[497] Citizens Nat'l Bank of Waco v. United States, 551 F.2d 832, 843 (Ct. Cl. 1977); American Nat'l Bank of Austin v. United States, 573 F.2d 1201, 1205 (Ct. Cl. 1978), aff'g 77-1 U.S. Tax Cas. (CCH) ¶ 9316 (Ct. Cl. 1977).

[498] See section 31.2(d).

[499] See section 31.3.

[500] SENATE FINANCE COMM. REPORT, INTERNAL REVENUE CODE OF 1954—NONMEMBER TELEPHONE COMPANIES—INCOME, S. REP. NO. 762, 95th Cong., 2d Sess., reprinted in 1978 U.S. CODE CONG. & ADMIN. NEWS 1286, 1289 [hereinafter S. REP. NO. 762].

[501] See generally Chapter 26.

must provide that the lender can terminate the loan upon notice of not more than five business days.[502]

If a seller-debtor has a term repo under which he cannot demand the return of the repoed securities until the term expires, the IRS may assert that I.R.C. § 1058 does not apply. If I.R.C. § 1058 does not apply, gain or loss may be recognized on the initial transfer of the repoed securities and again on reacquisition of the securities at the termination of the repo.[503] However, it appears the transaction still could qualify as a loan if it would have qualified as a loan under the law in effect before enactment of I.R.C. § 1058 in 1976.[504] It is the author's view that a fixed rate term repo for less than the maturity of the security should be viewed as a loan. It does not protect a seller-debtor from risk of loss, or preclude an opportunity for gain.

In a series of cases, banks that acquired tax-exempt securities in reverse repo transactions (i.e., as buyer-creditors) claimed they were the owners of the securities and, therefore, entitled to tax-exempt interest during the period they held the securities. If repos are secured loans rather than sales, the interest on the tax-exempt securities is taxable to the buyer-creditor;[505] it remains tax-exempt, however, to the seller-debtor.[506]

It is unclear whether the seller-debtor in a repo transaction remains the owner of a repoed security for tax purposes when the repoed security is transferred by the buyer-creditor to a third party.[507] The transfer by the buyer-creditor of the collateral to a third party in a repo that is structured

---

[502] Prop. Treas. Reg. § 1.1058-1(b)(3) (1983).

[503] *See* section 26.3.

[504] "The committee does not intend to change the tax treatment of 'repurchase Agreements' in which loans of money collateralized by securities are structured as sales and repurchases of securities." S. REP. NO. 762, *supra* note 500, at 1294 n.5. *See* Prop. Treas. Reg. § 1.1058-1(e)(1) (1983). This proposed regulation provides that if a transaction is intended to comply with I.R.C. § 1058, but fails to do so because it does not meet the requirements of I.R.C. § 1058(b) and Prop. Treas. Reg. § 1.1058-1(b), gain or loss is recognized on the initial transfer of the security. The American Bar Association Section of Taxation's Securities Loan Task Force drafted a report that advocates that if a transaction fails to qualify under I.R.C. § 1058, gain or loss should be recognized only if gain or loss would be recognized without regard to I.R.C. § 1058. The IRS is reexamining this proposed regulation. For a discussion of the Task Force Report, see Sheppard, *On the Border: IRS Contemplates Narrow Mission of Section 1058*, 48 TAX NOTES 1083 (1990).

[505] *American Nat'l Bank of Austin*, 421 F.2d at 453; Union Planters Nat'l Bank of Memphis v. United States, 426 F.2d 115, 118 (6th Cir. 1970), *rev'g* 295 F. Supp. 1151 (W.D. Tenn. 1968), *cert. denied*, 400 U.S. 827 (1970).

[506] Interest may be taxable to the seller-debtor, however, if the buyer-creditor subsequently transfers the securities to a third party.

[507] *See generally* Chapter 26.

as a loan may be viewed the same as borrowing the securities (as with margin accounts and short sales). In that case, the seller-debtor (i.e., the lender of the securities) receives ordinary income (not dividends or interest) in amounts equivalent to interest, dividends, and other distributions that the owner of the securities is entitled to receive during the period the securities are transferred.[508] In addition, if the buyer-creditor transfers the collateral to a third party, the seller-debtor may not be able to accrue OID.[509] The seller-debtor no longer owns the securities; instead he owns an obligation representing a claim against the buyer-creditor. Further, interest received by the seller-debtor on repos of tax-exempt securities is not tax-exempt interest to him.

(2) SALES

When a repo is treated as a sale, the buyer-creditor becomes the owner of and entitled to the income from the tax-exempt securities acquired subject to repo agreements.[510] As a result, the seller-debtor cannot treat the interest he receives as tax-exempt, and any gain or loss is recognized on the transfer of the securities.

Several factors are relevant in determining whether the initial transfer of securities under a repo is a sale. A fixed rate term repo with a term to maturity of the security subject to the repo may be viewed as a sale for tax purposes at the time the repo is entered into. The seller-debtor may not be viewed as having any remaining risk of loss or opportunity for gain on the securities.[511] With a sale, the seller-debtor does not have an economic interest in the securities, is not liable on any debt on which interest can be deducted, and is not entitled to accrue any interest or OID on the repoed securities.

In addition, there may be a sale if the seller-debtor cannot repurchase the securities unless he is requested to do so by the buyer-creditor.[512] Similarly, there may be a sale if the buyer-creditor has no right to resell the securities to the seller-debtor unless he is so requested by the seller-debtor.[513]

---

[508] Rev. Rul. 80-135, 1980-1 C.B. 18; Rev. Rul. 60-177, 1960-1 C.B. 9; Prop. Treas. Reg. § 1.1058-1(d) (1983); *see generally* S. REP. NO. 762, *supra* note 500, at 1288–95.
[509] For a discussion of OID, see section 31.2.
[510] *Citizens Nat'l Bank of Waco*, 551 F.2d at 843.
[511] *But see* I.R.C. § 1058; Prop. Treas. Reg. § 1.1058-1 (1983).
[512] *Citizens Nat'l Bank of Waco*, 551 F.2d at 842.
[513] *American Nat'l Bank of Austin*, 421 F.2d at 453.

A taxpayer may finance the purchase of a security with a repo. In that case, the taxpayer would purchase the security from a seller. As part of the transaction, the purchaser would immediately resell the security to the original seller and agree to repurchase the security at a future date. In effect, the seller is financing the purchase of the security until the purchaser completes the future repurchase of the security.

If the interest rate is fixed, then the price the taxpayer (now a seller-debtor) must pay to repurchase the security in the future would be fixed. Because the price is fixed, the IRS may argue that the taxpayer actually purchased a forward contract from the seller. The IRS might seek to collapse the transaction and argue that all the taxpayer has is the obligation to purchase a security at a specified price on a future date.

The only case known to the author which specifically discusses this argument is Judge Wells' opinion, which dissented in part and concurred in part to the majority opinion in *Sheldon v. Comm'r*.[514] In *Sheldon*, the majority opinion of the Tax Court did not discuss the forward contract issue because it found the repurchase agreements lacked economic substance.[515] However, Judge Wells found that the transactions had economic substance and addressed the issue of whether repurchase agreements are forward contracts, as argued by the IRS, or financing transactions.

Judge Wells, in his concurring and dissenting opinion, observed that "the principle is well established that the tax consequences should be determined by the economic substance of the transaction, not the labels put on it for property law (or tax avoidance) purposes."[516] He describes the true substance of a repurchase agreement as a financing transaction. Although the buyer-creditor nominally is the owner of the security for the duration of the repurchase agreement, the buyer-creditor bears no market risk of a decline in the security's value and no market benefit from any increase in the security's value. The buyer-creditor simply has made a loan in exchange for an interest payment.

(3) SHAM TRANSACTIONS

The IRS may attempt to prevent a taxpayer from treating a repo as a financing transaction by arguing that the repo transaction is a sham transaction. In *Price v. Comm'r*,[517] the Tax Court disallowed deductions

---

[514] Tax Ct. Rep. (CCH) 46,602, at 2939 (May 29, 1990).
[515] *See* discussion at section 31.11(b)(4).
[516] *Sheldon*, Tax Ct. Rep. (CCH) 46,602, at 2960.
[517] 88 T.C. 860 (1987).

for interest expenses and other losses claimed by participants in repos because the Tax Court found the transactions to be shams.[518] "[T]o obtain the desired tax advantages, the transactions have to be real rather than illusory."[519]

Although the repo agreements in *Price* purported to sell, purchase, and borrow billions of dollars of securities, the Tax Court found that, in most of the repo transactions it reviewed, no securities existed. The court noted that because no securities existed, the repo participants "were playing a football game without the football."[520]

In determining that the transactions were not bona fide, the Tax Court looked behind the form of the transaction to determine its true economic substance. The transactions addressed in *Price* were found to be contrived and fictitious, not on the basis of one factor, but on a combination of the following factors:

- The transactions purportedly were for billions of dollars in government securities, yet it did not appear that the dealers involved in the transactions had the ability to acquire, own, or possess the amount of the securities allegedly sold.[521]
- The court found that the transactions were prearranged to provide a specified loss to some parties and a specified profit to others.[522]
- A relatively small amount of margin deposits were required in comparison to the magnitude of the alleged trades.[523]

Because the repo transactions were not bona fide, the Tax Court denied all of the claimed deductions for the interest expense and the losses sustained as a result thereof.[524]

---

[518] *See* Zigas, *So You Thought You'd Seen the Last of Tax Straddles*, Bus. Wk., June 15, 1987, at 90.
[519] *Price*, 88 T.C. at 883.
[520] *Id.* at 884.
[521] *Id.*
[522] *Id.*
[523] *Id.*
[524] *Id.* (citing Glass v. Comm'r, 87 T.C. 1087 (1986), *aff'd sub nom.* Herrington v. Comm'r, 854 F.2d 755 (5th Cir. 1988), *and aff'd sub nom.* Yosha v. Comm'r, 861 F.2d 494 (7th Cir. 1988), *cert. denied,* 1989 U.S. LEXIS 2370). For a case in which the repurchase agreements were held to be bona fide and not fictitious, see *Sheldon v. Comm'r*, Tax Ct. Rep. (CCH) 46,602, at 2939 (May 29, 1990).

(4) ECONOMIC SUBSTANCE

If the court finds that the repurchase agreements are not sham transactions, the IRS may argue that the transaction lacks economic substance.[525] In *Sheldon v. Comm'r*,[526] although the Tax Court, in a divided opinion, held that Treasury bill repurchase agreements were not fictitious, the court disallowed the interest deductions by holding that the repurchase agreements lacked economic substance.

The tax benefit sought by the taxpayers (partners in a limited partnership) in *Sheldon* was based on the fact that the discount income on the Treasury bills was not taxable—under the tax law in effect in 1981—until maturity of the Treasury bills. The taxpayer financed the Treasury bill purchase with repos and deducted the interest expense on the repos. Current tax laws now require an accrual of Treasury bill discount for most taxpayers.[527]

The majority court in *Sheldon* stated that interest is not deductible if it "is incurred in a transaction that cannot with reason be said to have purpose, substance, or utility apart from their anticipated tax consequences."[528] In one year, the taxpayer locked in an actual loss of about $60,000, and locked in an actual profit of $18,000 in the following year. In the first year, the taxpayer deducted more than $5 million of interest expense. Although the Tax Court found a potential for profit in the transactions, in the court's view, the potential profit was "infinitesimally nominal and vastly insignificant" when compared to the claimed tax deductions. As a result, the transactions were found to lack economic purpose or substance apart from the tax consequences.

The Tax Court noted that in four consecutive years, the taxpayers structured repurchase agreements toward the end of the year to straddle the end of the year to incur interest expense immediately, but postpone income until the following year. The court found the timing of the transactions to be critical and of overriding importance. The court observed that the taxpayers

> were content because the $60,000 [of locked in loss] was a small "price" to pay for the more than $5 million in interest deductions that permitted offset

---

[525] Economic substance arguments have been considered in determining whether transactions similar to repos have constituted sales. *See, e.g.*, Rev. Rul. 79-195, 1979-1 C.B. 177; Rev. Rul. 77-59, 1977-1 C.B. 196; Rev. Rul. 74-27, 1974-1 C.B. 24.

[526] Tax Ct. Rep. (CCH) 46,602, at 2939 (May 29, 1990).

[527] For a discussion of the requirement to accrue discount under I.R.C. § 1282(b)(2), see section 31.2(d)(2).

[528] *Sheldon*, Tax Ct. Rep. (CCH) 46,602, at 2956.

against their ordinary income and deferral of that income to the next taxable year, when a new plan of deferral could be employed at year end.[529]

Judge Wells filed a vigorous dissent to the majority court's holding in *Sheldon* that the repo transactions lacked economic substance. Judge Wells stated that the economic substance inquiry has been whether a transaction was imbued with tax-independent considerations. According to Judge Wells, the majority improperly evaluated the transactions in this case for economic substance by applying a test that until now has been used only to determine whether a taxpayer had an actual and honest profit objective for purposes of I.R.C. § 183 (denying deductions for activities not engaged in for profit). Judge Wells stated that it is inappropriate for the court to substitute its business judgment for that of the taxpayer and inquire into whether a transaction offers *enough* profit in light of the expected tax benefits.[530]

(c) ALTERNATIVE MINIMUM TAX

Interest deductions on repo transactions can result in the imposition of alternative minimum tax for noncorporate taxpayers.[531] Repo interest deductions can be viewed as excess itemized adjusted deductions for the taxable year. In *Wallach v. United States*,[532] the United States Court of Claims granted an IRS motion for summary judgment on the grounds that there was no genuine issue in the case, and that repo interest deductions that exceed 60 percent of the taxpayers' adjusted gross income are tax preference items. In 1978 and 1979, the taxpayers engaged in repo transactions whereby they purchased Treasury securities, federal agency securities, and a bank certificate of deposit with a total purchase price of $12,760,000 from a securities dealer. The taxpayers paid $229,000, borrowed the rest of the purchase price, and sold the securities back to the dealer, subject to their obligation to repurchase the securities at the same price. Although the taxpayers' borrowing costs fluctuated depending on the cost of money, the "yield to maturity" on the securities was fixed and did not fluctuate. During both 1978 and 1979, the taxpayers' interest expense on the repo transaction exceeded their interest income (by $95,000 in 1978, and $322,000 in 1979). Their total repo interest expense for 1978 and 1979, when added to other deductions,

---

[529] *Id.* at 2955.
[530] *Id.* at 2956.
[531] For a discussion of the alternative minimum tax, see section 15.4(a)(2)(ii).
[532] 8 Ct. Cl. 631 (1985), *aff'd*, 800 F.2d 1121 (Fed. Cir. 1986).

caused their adjusted itemized deductions for each year to exceed 60 percent of their adjusted gross income for each year. The Court of Claims found, as a matter of law, that the excess deductions were tax preference items.[533]

(d) REPORTING REQUIREMENT

Because a repo transaction structured as a loan is a financing arrangement for tax purposes—involving the payment of interest—the interest must be reported on Form 1099-INT, Statement for Recipients of Interest Income, if interest in an amount of $10 or more is paid.[534] For each unintentional failure to file such an information return, the penalty is $50 for each failure, up to a maximum amount of $50,000 for any one year.[535]

For intentional disregard of the filing requirement, the penalty is increased to not less than 10 percent of the aggregate unreported amounts and the $50,000 maximum penalty ceiling does not apply.[536] Although the interest income and expense in some repo transactions can net out to very little in the aggregate, the penalties for failure to file can be based on the gross amounts of the securities, which can obviously prove very costly.

(e) STRADDLE RULES

For a discussion of possible application of the Straddle Rules to repos and reverse repos, see section 48.3(b). For a discussion of the Straddle Rules, see generally Part Eleven.

§ 31.12 REGISTRATION REQUIREMENTS

(a) IN GENERAL

The government's concern with securities issued in bearer form is that taxable interest income and gains on the sales of both taxable and tax-exempt securities may not be reported and tax may not be paid by the holder. In 1982, TEFRA established a registration requirement for cer-

---

[533] *Id.*

[534] IR-83-92, 10 Stand. Fed. Tax Rep. (CCH) ¶ 6630 (June 30, 1983).

[535] I.R.C. § 6652(a)(1) (applies to payments made before January 1, 1984); I.R.C. § 6652(a)(2) (applies to payments made after December 31, 1983).

[536] I.R.C. § 6652(a)(2) (applies to payments made before January 1, 1984); I.R.C. § 6652(a)(3) (applies to payments made after December 31, 1983).

tain debt securities[537] and imposes penalties on issuers that issue unregistered securities and taxpayers that own unregistered securities.[538] With registration, the IRS can identify security owners (both past and present) and assure that transfers (by sale, gift, or inheritance) are properly reflected on the tax returns of transferors and transferees.[539]

TEFRA originally provided a December 31, 1982 effective date for the Code amendments concerning registration requirements, and a September 3, 1982 effective date for amendments to the Second Liberty Bond Act.[540] TCA '82 delayed the effective date until July 1, 1983, for tax-exempt securities (i.e., debt securities that were not required to be in registered form prior to TEFRA).[541] Under current law, a registration-required security issued after December 31, 1982, must be in registered form.[542]

The registration requirements do not apply to any debt security issued pursuant to the exercise of a warrant or convertible security issued before August 10, 1982, if the security was offered or sold outside of the United States without registration under the Securities Act.[543]

On December 12, 1986, the IRS issued proposed, temporary, and final regulations dealing with registration-required securities.[544] The regulations address the term "registration-required" securities.[545] They also address the repeal by the DRA in 1984 of the 30 percent withholding tax on certain types of interest and the imposition of sanctions on (1) those issuers that issue registration-required obligations in bearer form, and (2) persons holding registration-required obligations in bearer form.[546]

---

[537] TEFRA, *supra* note 326, § 310.
[538] *See* section 31.12(c).
[539] *See* Herman, *Bearer Bonds: There's Value but Also Risk*, Wall St. J., Mar. 30, 1990, at C1.
[540] TEFRA, *supra* note 326, § 310(d)(1); Second Liberty Bond Act, ch. 56, 40 Stat. 288 (1917), amended by TEFRA, *supra* note 326, § 310(d)(2).
[541] TCA '82, *supra* note 133, § 306(b)(2).
[542] T.D. 8111, 1987-1 C.B. 69.
[543] TEFRA, *supra* note 326, § 310(d)(3). For a discussion of registered convertible debt securities, see generally letter from Goldman, Sachs & Co. to Fred T. Goldberg, Jr., Commissioner of Internal Revenue (Oct. 9, 1989) (discussing issuance of convertible, registered-form obligations), *reprinted in* 15 DAILY TAX HIGHLIGHTS & DOCUMENTS 750 (1989); letter from Morgan Stanley & Co. Incorporated to Fred T. Goldberg, Jr., Commissioner of Internal Revenue (Oct. 6, 1989) (discussing convertibility of foreign-registered obligations into bearer obligations), *reprinted in* 15 DAILY TAX HIGHLIGHTS & DOCUMENTS 749 (1989).
[544] T.D. 8110, 1987-1 C.B. 81; INTL-53-86, 1987 C.B.-1 796; T.D. 8111, 1987-1 C.B. 69, *as amended* May 19, 1988, in T.D. 8203, 1988-1 C.B. 77, *as further amended* May 10, 1990 in T.D. 8300, 1990-1 C.B. 31.
[545] T.D. 8110, 1987-1 C.B. 81.
[546] *Id.*

The proposed[547] and temporary[548] regulations address the definition of "registration-required" as it applies to securities and the repeal of the 30 percent withholding tax. The proposed and temporary regulations clarify the definition of "registered form" as it applies to certain types of obligations, addressing questions and answers under Treas. Reg. § 35a.9999-5, which provides guidance in defining a registration-required security.

The final Treasury regulations[549] address the definition of the term "registration-required obligation" as it relates to securities issued to certain foreign persons. Specifically, the regulations contain rules for determining "whether an issuer may claim an interest deduction for interest paid on an obligation in bearer form, which is otherwise a registration-required obligation, because the issuer satisfies the conditions set forth in I.R.C. § 163(f)(2)(B)."[550]

I.R.C. § 163(f)(2)(B) provides that an obligation is not "registration-required" if three conditions are met. First, in the case of obligations not in "registered form," interest on the obligation is payable only outside of the United States and its possessions.[551] Second, in the case of obligations not in "registered form," there is a statement on the face of the obligation that any person that holds the obligation will be subject to limitations under the tax laws.[552] And third, arrangements are in place that are reasonably designed to ensure its sale or resale in connection with its original issue only to a person that is not a United States person.[553]

In Treas. Reg. § 46.4701-1,[554] the IRS issued final regulations clarifying that issuers of obligations that would otherwise be exempt under I.R.C. § 103(a) are not subject to tax imposed on issuers of registration-required obligations if the obligations are not in registered form. The regulation provides that Form 720 (Quarterly Federal Excise Tax Return) must be filed by persons liable for tax.[555] And, the definition of "issue price" is cross-referenced to the definition provided in I.R.C. § 1273(b).[556]

---

[547] INTL-53-86, 1987-1 C.B. 796.
[548] T.D. 8111, 1987-1 C.B. 69.
[549] T.D. 8110, 1987-1 C.B. 81.
[550] *Id.*
[551] I.R.C. § 163(f)(2)(B)(ii).
[552] *Id.*
[553] I.R.C. § 163(f)(2)(B)(i).
[554] T.D. 8102, 1986-2 C.B. 182.
[555] *Id.*
[556] *Id.*

In Treas. Reg. § 46.4701-1, the IRS addressed the excise tax imposed on the issuer of registration-required obligations that are not issued in registered form. The Treasury regulation provides that an excise tax is imposed on any person that issues a registration-required obligation not in registered form. The amount of the tax is one percent of the principal amount multiplied by the number of years from the date of issuance to the date of maturity.[557] The tax is not levied on obligations that are exempt from tax under I.R.C. § 103(a), or any other provision of federal law. The rules generally apply to obligations issued after December 31, 1982.[558]

The final Treasury regulations delete a conversion rule that was strongly criticized in written comments on the proposed regulations filed with the IRS. They also clarify that, in specified circumstances, a bearer obligation may be offered and sold outside the United States to a financial institution purchasing the obligation for the account of a customer that is a United States person.

The Supreme Court has upheld the constitutionality of TEFRA § 310(b)(1), which requires registration of state and local bonds as a condition of tax exemption for interest earned on those securities. This provision of TEFRA effectively requires states to issue bonds in registered form by denying a tax exemption for interest earned on bearer bonds. In *South Carolina v. Baker*,[559] the Supreme Court found that the TEFRA provision does not violate the Tenth Amendment, constitutional principles of federalism, or the doctrine of intergovernmental tax immunity.[560]

The Supreme Court concluded that mere allegations by the State of South Carolina—to the effect that Congress was uninformed and chose an ineffective remedy to prevent tax evasion—did not amount to an allegation that the political process had operated in a defective manner.[561] In addition, the Supreme Court found that although the provision regulates state activities, it does not seek to control or influence the manner in which states regulate private parties.[562] Finally, the Supreme Court found that TEFRA § 310 does not violate the doctrine of intergovernmental tax immunity by taxing the interest earned on unregistered state bonds.[563]

---

[557] Treas. Reg. § 46.4701-1(c) (1986).
[558] Treas. Reg. § 46.4701-1(e) (1986).
[559] 485 U.S. 505, *reh'g denied*, 486 U.S. 1062 (1988).
[560] *Id.* at 526–27.
[561] *Id.* at 511–12.
[562] *Id.* at 512–13.
[563] *Id.* at 526.

Owners of unregistered state bonds are not constitutionally entitled to a tax exemption with respect to interest earned from the bonds.[564]

(b) REGISTRATION-REQUIRED SECURITIES

(1) IN GENERAL

Registration is required for "registration-required obligations" and "registration-required bonds," defined in both I.R.C. §§ 149(a)(2) and 163(f)(2).[565] A registration-required obligation is defined in I.R.C. § 163(f)(2) to mean any security other than a security that:

1. Is issued by a natural person
2. Is not of a type offered to the public
3. Has a maturity (at issue) of not more than one year, or
4. Is described in I.R.C. § 163(f)(2)(B), which describes certain securities not subject to registration where there are arrangements reasonably designed to ensure that the securities will be sold (or resold in connection with the original issue) only to persons that are not United States persons

(2) TREASURY AUTHORITY TO REQUIRE REGISTRATION

Although registration is not required for short-term debt securities (i.e., maturity at issue of not more than one year) and securities not offered to the public, the Treasury has authority to require registration of short-term and privately placed securities if the Treasury determines, by regulation, that the securities are "used frequently in evading federal taxes."[566] Any regulations expanding the registration requirements can have prospective effect only and can apply only to debt securities issued after the regulations are promulgated.[567]

---

[564] *Id.* at 526–27.
[565] The same definition applies to the various Code provisions amended by TEFRA in 1982. In some places the Code language repeats the rules, while in other places it merely provides a cross-reference.
[566] I.R.C. § 163(f)(2)(C).
[567] *Id.*

(3) REGISTERED FORM

A registration-required obligation must be "in registered form." This phrase can be viewed as requiring registration of both principal and interest elements. For purposes of registration-required obligations, however, registration can be in book-entry form if the securities can be transferred in a manner consistent with Treasury regulations.[568] In addition, it is contemplated that the regulations will address the registration of securities held by nominees to assure proper identification of owners.[569]

(4) FOREIGN-ISSUED OBLIGATIONS

(i) In General

On May 7, 1990, the Treasury issued final regulations that set out the registration requirements for obligations issued to certain foreign persons and the imposition of an excise tax on the issuers of registration-required obligations issued in bearer form.[570] The regulations are generally effective May 10, 1990, although the text of the regulations states the dates of applicability of the rules to various transactions and taxpayers. The regulations apply to obligations originally issued after September 7, 1990, although the issuer may choose to apply rules set out in Treas. Reg. §§ 1.163-5(c)(2)(i)(A), (B), or (D).

The final regulations reflect a number of changes based on difficulties commentators raised with the proposed regulations (issued on August 24, 1989).[571] They also reflect, and incorporate by reference, certain SEC requirements under Regulation S (which governs sales of United States securities offshore).[572] The Treasury notes, however, that its "final regulations are separate and independent from the rules and interpretations that the SEC chooses to adopt in its administration of the securities laws. The SEC's interpretations will be considered by the Service where appropriate; however, the Service must ultimately base its interpretations on the tax policies underlying [I.R.C.] section 163(f)(2)(B)."[573]

---

[568] See I.R.C. §§ 149(a)(3)(A), 163(f)(3).

[569] I.R.C. § 149(a)(3)(B).

[570] T.D. 8300, 1990-1 C.B. 31. See generally Connors & Hiltz, Final Regs. Ease Rules for Portfolio Bearer Debt Offerings, 73 J. Tax'n 166 (1990).

[571] Id.

[572] Id. Regulations can be found at 54 Fed. Reg. 30,063 (1989).

[573] T.D. 8300, 1990-1 C.B. 31.

The regulations contain three requirements: (1) restrictions on offers and sales, (2) restrictions on delivery, and (3) certification requirements. As to offers and sales, "the issuer and distributor must not offer or sell the obligation during the restricted period to a person within the United States or its possessions or to a United States person. (The obligation may, however, be sold to a United States person in certain circumstances if the person is a financial institution or acquires and holds through a financial institution.)"[574] As to delivery of obligations sold during the restricted period, "neither the issuer nor any distributor may deliver the obligation in definitive form within the United States or its possessions."[575] With respect to certification, "[c]ertification is required on the earlier of the date of the first payment of interest on the obligation or the date of delivery by the issuer of the obligation in definitive form."[576]

(ii) Restrictions on Offers and Sales

During the restricted period (defined in Treas. Reg. § 1.163-5(c)(2)(i)(D)(7) as beginning on the earlier of the closing date or the first date on which the obligation is offered to persons other than a distributor and ending on the expiration of 40 days beginning on the closing date or the date on which the issuer receives the proceeds), an obligation issued after September 7, 1990 must meet the following requirements. First, the issuer does not offer or sell the obligation during the restricted period to a person who is within the United States or its possessions, or to a United States person.[577]

Second, the distributor does not offer or sell the obligation during the restricted period to any person who is within the United States or its possessions, or to a United States person.[578] A distributor is deemed to satisfy these requirements if it (1) covenants that it will not offer or sell the obligation during the restricted period to a person who is within the United States or its possessions, or to a United States person, and (2) has in effect "procedures reasonably designed to ensure that its employees or agents who are directly engaged in selling the obligation are aware that the obligation cannot be offered or sold during the restricted period to a person who is within the United States or its possessions, or is a United States person."[579]

[574] *Id.*
[575] *Id.*
[576] *Id.*
[577] Treas. Reg. § 1.163-5(c)(2)(i)(D)(1)(i) (1990).
[578] Treas. Reg. § 1.163-5(c)(2)(i)(D)(1)(ii)(A) (1990).
[579] Treas. Reg. § 1.163-5(c)(2)(i)(D)(1)(ii)(B) (1990).

An offer or sale is considered to be made to a person who is within the United States or its possessions "if the offeror or seller of the obligation has an address within the United States or its possessions for the offeree or buyer of the obligation."[580] The offer or sale is not so viewed if it is made to (1) an exempt distributor (as defined in Treas. Reg. § 1.163-5(c)(2)(i)(D)(5)), (2) an international organization (as defined in I.R.C. § 7701(a)(18)) or a foreign central bank (as defined in I.R.C. § 895), or (3) the foreign branch of a United States financial institution (as described in Treas. Reg. § 1.163-5(c)(2)(i)(D)(6)(i).[581]

(iii) Restrictions on Delivery

In connection with a sale of an obligation issued after September 7, 1990, it must meet the following delivery requirement during the restricted period (defined in Treas. Reg. § 1.163-5(c)(2)(i)(D)(7) as the earlier of the closing date or the first date on which the obligation is offered to persons other than a distributor, and ending on the expiration of 40 days beginning on the closing date or the date on which the issuer receives the proceeds). Neither the issuer nor any distributor can deliver the obligation in definitive form within the United States or its possessions during the restricted period.

(iv) Certification Requirements

For obligations issued after September 7, 1990, they must meet the following certification requirements.

(a) IN GENERAL

In general, a certificate must be provided to the issuer of the obligation stating that—on the *earlier* of the date of the first actual payment of interest by the issuer on the obligation, or the date of delivery of the obligation in definitive form—(1) the obligation is owned by a person that is not a United States person; (2) the obligation is owned by a United States person that is described in Treas. Reg. § 1.163-5(c)(2)(i)(D)(6) (as a foreign branch of a United States financial institution purchasing for its own account or for resale, or a United States person that acquires the obligation through the foreign branch of a United States financial institution and holds the obligation through the financial institution on that

---

[580] Treas. Reg. § 1.163-5(c)(2)(i)(D)(1)(iii)(A) (1990).
[581] Treas. Reg. § 1.163-5(c)(2)(i)(D)(1)(ii)(B) (1990).

date); or (3) the obligation is owned by a financial institution for purposes of resale during the restricted period, and the financial institution also certifies that it has not acquired the obligation for purposes of resale directly or indirectly to a United States person (or to a person within the United States or its possessions).[582]

If the issuer does not make the obligation available for delivery in definitive form within a reasonable period of time after the end of the restricted period, the obligation is viewed as not satisfying the certification requirements.[583]

The certificate must be signed (or sent by electronic certification as set out in Treas. Reg. § 1.163-5(c)(2)(i)(D)(3)(ii)) by either the owner of the obligation or by a financial institution or clearing organization through which the owner holds the obligation, directly or indirectly.[584] A certificate provided by a clearing organization must be based on statements provided to it by its member organizations.[585]

The certification requirements are not satisfied if the issuer "knows or has reason to know that the certificate" is false.[586]

The issuer must retain the certificate (and the clearing organization must retain the statements provided to it by its member organizations) for four calendar years after the year in which the certification is received.[587]

(b) Electronic Certification

The certificate required to be provided to the issuer of obligations issued after September 7, 1990, to non-United States persons can be provided electronically if the following requirements are met. First, the person receiving the electronic certificate must maintain adequate records for the retention period establishing that the certificate was received.[588] Second, there must be a written agreement that was entered into prior to the time of certification, to which the sender and the recipient are subject, that the electronic certificate has the same effect as a signed certificate.[589]

---

[582] Treas. Reg. §§ 1.163-5(c)(2)(i)(D)(3)(i)(A), (B), (C) (1990).

[583] Treas. Reg. § 1.163-5(c)(2)(i)(D)(3)(i) (1990).

[584] Id.

[585] Id.

[586] Id.

[587] Id.

[588] Treas. Reg. § 1.163-5(c)(2)(i)(D)(3)(ii) (1990).

[589] Id. The written agreement includes, for these purposes, the written membership rules of a clearing organization.

(c) EXCEPTIONS FOR CERTAIN OBLIGATIONS

The certification requirements do not apply, and no certificate is required, for obligations sold during the restricted period if *all* of the following requirements are met.

1. The interest and principal with respect to the obligation are denominated only in the currency of a single foreign country.[590]

2. The interest and principal with respect to the obligation are payable only within that foreign country.[591]

3. The obligation is offered and sold in accordance with practices and documentation customary in that foreign country.[592]

4. The distributor covenants to use reasonable efforts to sell the obligation within that foreign country.[593]

5. The obligation is not listed, or the subject of an application for listing, on an exchange located outside that foreign country.[594]

6. The IRS has designated the foreign country as a foreign country in which certification is not permissible.[595]

7. Issuance of the obligation is subject to guidelines or restrictions imposed by governmental, banking, or securities authorities in the foreign country.[596]

8. More than 80 percent of the value of the obligations in the offering are sold to nondistributors maintaining an office located in the foreign country.[597]

For purposes of the exception for those obligations that meet all of the requirements set out above, foreign currency-denominated obligations that are convertible into U.S. dollar-denominated obligations, or that are linked to the U.S. dollar in a way that effectively converts the obligations

---

[590] Treas. Reg. § 1.163-5(c)(2)(i)(D)(3)(iii)(A) (1990).
[591] Treas. Reg. § 1.163-5(c)(2)(i)(D)(3)(iii)(B) (1990).
[592] Treas. Reg. § 1.163-5(c)(2)(i)(D)(3)(iii)(C) (1990).
[593] Treas. Reg. § 1.163-5(c)(2)(i)(D)(3)(iii)(D) (1990).
[594] Treas. Reg. § 1.163-5(c)(2)(i)(D)(3)(iii)(E) (1990).
[595] Treas. Reg. § 1.163-5(c)(2)(i)(D)(3)(iii)(F) (1990).
[596] Treas. Reg. § 1.163-5(c)(2)(i)(D)(3)(iii)(G) (1990).
[597] Treas. Reg. § 1.163-5(c)(2)(i)(D)(3)(iii)(H) (1990).

to U.S. dollar-denominated obligations, do not satisfy these requirements and are not eligible for the exception.[598]

A foreign currency-denominated obligation is not treated as linked to the U.S. dollar "solely because the obligation is the subject of a swap transaction."[599]

(v) Effective Date and Special Rules

The regulations for registration-required obligations for foreign-issued obligations generally apply to obligations issued after September 7, 1990.

If an obligation is originally issued after September 7, 1990, pursuant to the exercise of a warrant or the conversion of a convertible obligation and the warrant or obligation with the conversion privilege was issued on or before May 10, 1990, then the issuer can choose to apply the rules of Treas. Reg. § 1.163-5(c)(2)(i)(A), Treas. Reg. § 1.163-5(c)(2)(i)(B), or Treas. Reg. § 1.163-5(c)(2)(i)(D).[600]

For obligations issued after May 10, 1990, and on or before September 7, 1990, the issuer can choose to apply the rules of Treas. Reg. §§ 1.163-5(c)(2)(i)(A) or (B), or Treas. Reg. § 1.163-5(c)(2)(i)(D).[601]

If the issuer chooses to apply the rules of Treas. Reg. § 1.163-5(c)(2)(i)(A), the issuer must apply the definition of United States person used for such purposes on December 31, 1989, and must obtain any certificates that would have been required under the law in effect on December 31, 1989.[602]

(c) NONCOMPLIANCE WITH REGISTRATION REQUIREMENTS

The registration requirements for registration-required securities are contained in six separate Code sections and the Second Liberty Bond Act. Some of these provisions apply to issuers, while others apply to security owners. Both types of sanctions do not appear to apply to the same securities:

---

[598] Treas. Reg. § 1.163-5(c)(2)(i)(D)(3)(iii) (1990).
[599] Id.
[600] Treas. Reg. § 1.163-5(c)(3)(ii) (1990).
[601] Id.
[602] Id.

- I.R.C. § 103(j) provides that registration-required tax-exempt securities must be issued in registered form for interest to be exempt from federal tax.[603]
- I.R.C. § 163(f) prohibits an issuer from deducting interest paid on unregistered registration-required securities.
- I.R.C. § 165(j) denies any loss on the sale, exchange, theft, loss, or other disposition of unregistered registration-required securities.
- I.R.C. § 312(m) prohibits any reductions to a corporate issuer's earnings and profits for interest paid on unregistered registration-required securities.
- I.R.C. § 1287 denies capital gain treatment on the disposition of unregistered registration-required securities.
- I.R.C. § 4701 imposes an excise tax on issuers of unregistered registration-required securities equal to one percent of the principal amount multiplied by the number of calendar years (or portions thereof) from the date the securities are issued until their maturity.[604]
- The Second Liberty Bond Act requires registration of most long-term United States securities offered to the public.[605] Certain government securities held by non-United States persons are exempt from the registration requirements.

(d) EXCEPTIONS TO LOSS DENIAL AND ORDINARY INCOME TREATMENT

(1) IN GENERAL

In certain circumstances, an owner of an unregistered security can deduct losses under I.R.C. § 165(j), or obtain capital gain on the sale of the securities under I.R.C. § 1287. The remainder of this section first sets out the Code provisions and then lists regulatory provisions that elaborate on the exemptions.

It is important to note that these exceptions only apply to a loss denial under I.R.C. § 165(j) and a capital gain denial under I.R.C. § 1287.[606] These exceptions do not affect I.R.C. § 163(f) (which denies interest deductions

---

[603] *See* section 33.3(a)(1)(iii).
[604] I.R.C. § 4701(a); T.D. 8102, 1986-2 C.B. 182; Treas. Reg. § 46.4701-1 (1986) (excise tax on the issuer of obligations not in registered form).
[605] TEFRA, *supra* note 326, § 310(a).
[606] I.R.C. § 165(j)(3).

for interest paid) or I.R.C. § 149(a) (which denies tax-exempt status on interest earned on unregistered registration-required securities).[607]

The Code exemptions from the registration requirements to obtain a loss or a capital gain are as follows:

1. The securities are held in connection with a trade or business outside of the United States.[608]

2. The owner of the securities is a broker-dealer (registered under federal or state law) that holds the securities for sale to customers in the ordinary course of business.[609]

3. The owner complies with reporting requirements as the Treasury may require with respect to the ownership, transfer, and payment.[610]

4. The owner promptly surrenders the securities to the issuer for the issuance of new securities in registered form.[611]

Treasury regulations elaborate on the Code exemptions listed above and provide exemptions for the following persons from the loss denial and ordinary income rules:

1. Underwriters, brokers, dealers, or other persons that hold unregistered securities for a non-United States trade or business[612]

2. Broker-dealers that hold such unregistered securities for sale to customers if the securities are not delivered to any person in bearer form, except upon receipt of a certificate signed by the customer stating that the securities are not being acquired by a United States person, unless the person is otherwise exempt[613]

---

[607] For a discussion of the controversy over the registration requirements for municipal securities, see section 33.3(a)(1)(iii).
[608] I.R.C. § 165(j)(3)(A).
[609] I.R.C. § 165(j)(3)(B).
[610] I.R.C. § 165(j)(3)(C).
[611] I.R.C. § 165(j)(3)(D).
[612] Treas. Reg. § 1.165-12(c)(1) (1986).
[613] *Id.*

3. Financial institutions (including broker-dealers)[614] that hold unregistered securities through an entity engaged in the business of holding such securities for members if it credits or debits members' accounts without physical delivery[615]

4. Any person that owns a registration-required security through a financial institution[616]

5. Any person that surrenders to the issuer or transfer agent an unregistered registration-required security within 30 days after acquisition to convert the security into registered form[617]

If any of the above exemptions are available, registration is not required and the loss denial and capital gain denial provisions do not apply.

(2) FINANCIAL INSTITUTION INVESTMENT ACCOUNTS

One of the exceptions to loss denial and ordinary income treatment is available to a financial institution (defined in Treas. Reg. § 1.165-12(c)(l)(v) (1986) to include a broker-dealer) that holds the obligation in bearer form for its own account and that reports any interest payments or any gain or loss from the disposition of the obligation on its tax return for the year.

In the case of a resale of the obligation inside the United States, the financial institution resells the obligation only to another financial institution for its own account or for the account of an exempt organization and the transaction consists of a purchase of a block of obligations, the total denominations of which are *at least* $1 million;[618] and the financial institution holding the obligation *delivers* the obligation in accordance with the following restrictions. First, the financial institution can only *deliver* such obligations outside of the United States.[619] "Delivery" includes the transfer of an obligation evidenced by a book-entry,

---

[614] Financial institutions are defined as any person or a 50 percent or more owner of the total voting power of stock entitled to vote for any person that (1) conducts a banking, financing, or similar business; (2) engages in the business as a broker or dealer in securities; (3) is an insurance company; (4) is a pension or profit sharing plan; (5) is an investment advisor; (6) is a RIC; or (7) is a finance corporation where a substantial portion of its business is making loans, servicing debt obligations, acquiring accounts receivable notes, or acquiring installment obligations. Treas. Reg. § 1.165-12(c)(1)(v) (1986).

[615] Treas. Reg. § 1.165-12(c)(2) (1986).

[616] Treas. Reg. § 1.165-12(c)(3) (1986).

[617] Treas. Reg. § 1.165-12(c)(4) (1986).

[618] Treas. Reg. § 1.165-12(c)(1)(ii) (1986).

[619] Treas. Reg. § 1.165-12(c)(1)(iv) (1986).

including a book-entry notation by a clearing organization evidencing transfer of the obligation from one member of the organization to another member.

Second, if the financial institution *delivers* an obligation that is offered or sold inside the United States, it must be delivered to a financial institution that states (under penalties of perjury) that it is a financial institution that is purchasing (1) for its own account, or (2) for the account of another financial institution or exempt organization that will in turn comply with one of the exceptions from I.R.C. § 165(j).[620] In addition, the financial institution delivering the obligation must have no actual knowledge that the purchaser's statement is false.[621]

Third, if the selling financial institution delivers an obligation that is offered and sold outside the United States to another financial institution, it must deliver a confirmation stating that any United States taxpayer that holds the obligation and is not otherwise exempt is denied any loss or capital gain treatment with respect to the obligation.

Fourth, if the selling financial institution delivers an obligation that is offered and sold outside the United States to a nonfinancial institution, it must have sufficient documentary evidence that the person is not a United States person.[622]

In conclusion, a financial institution (including a broker-dealer) can hold a registration-required obligation for its own investment account without being subject to any gain or loss restrictions if one of two conditions is met. First, the financial institution must offer to sell and sell only outside of the United States. Or, second, it offers to sell or sells inside the United States to another financial institution for its own account or for the account of another financial institution or exempt organization. Moreover, the sale inside the United States must involve at least $1 million in obligations. In addition, delivery of the obligations must always be outside the United States. Finally, the delivery of obligations must include either a signed statement by the purchaser (in the case of obligations sold outside the United States) or a confirmation statement of the seller (in the case of obligations sold outside the United States).

---

[620] *Id.*
[621] *Id.*
[622] *Id.*

(e) SECURITIES SOLD OUTSIDE OF THE UNITED STATES SUBSEQUENTLY ACQUIRED BY A UNITED STATES PERSON

Certain unregistered securities can be sold to non-United States persons if interest is payable outside the United States and the securities are properly legended.[623] If such unregistered securities are subsequently acquired by United States persons, this acquisition does not trigger the so-called issuer penalties. In addition, the issuer can still deduct interest payments and reduce its earnings and profits for interest paid. The United States person acquiring the securities, however, is subject to two penalties denying a loss or a capital gain on the sale of the securities. First, the United States person cannot deduct a loss on the sale, exchange, theft, loss, or other disposition of the unregistered securities.[624] Second, any gain from the sale or other disposition of the securities is taxed at ordinary income, not capital gain, rates.[625]

(f) REAL ESTATE MORTGAGE INVESTMENT CONDUIT REGULAR INTERESTS

On May 7, 1990, the Treasury issued temporary regulations that set out the registration requirements of REMIC regular interests.[626] A regular interest in a REMIC (as defined in I.R.C. §§ 860D and 860G) is a "registration-required obligation" under I.R.C. § 163(f)(2)(A) and Treas. Reg. § 1.163-5(c) if the regular interest is described in those sections.[627] For a discussion of REMIC regular interests, see sections 7.2(g) and 36.8(c).

An obligation held by a REMIC is considered to be described in I.R.C. §§ 163(f)(2)(A) or (B) if the obligation is described in either of those sections, without regard to whether the REMIC regular interests are so considered.[628]

For purposes of I.R.C. § 4701, a regular interest in a REMIC is considered to be issued solely by the recipient of the proceeds from the issuance of the regular interest (referred to as the "sponsor").[629] The sponsor is liable for any excise tax imposed under I.R.C. § 4701 that may be imposed

---

[623] I.R.C. § 163(f)(2)(B); Second Liberty Bond Act § 28(b)(2), 31 U.S.C. 3121(g)(2) (1982).
[624] I.R.C. § 165(j).
[625] I.R.C. § 1287.
[626] T.D. 8300, 1990-1 C.B. 31.
[627] Temp. Treas. Reg. § 1.165-5T(e)(1) (1990).
[628] Temp. Treas. Reg. § 165-5T(e)(2) (1990).
[629] Temp. Treas. Reg. § 1.163-5T(e)(3) (1990).

with reference to the principal amount of the regular interest.[630] For a discussion of the excise tax imposed under I.R.C. § 4701, see sections 31.12(a) and 31.12(c).

The IRS is granted broad authority under the temporary regulations to "characterize a regular interest in a REMIC and any obligation held by such a REMIC in accordance with the substance of the arrangement they represent and may impose the penalties provided under [I.R.C.] sections 163(f)(1) and 4701 in the appropriate amounts and on the appropriate persons."[631] This provision can be illustrated by the following example taken from Temp. Treas. Reg. § 1.163-5T(e)(4).

Example 31-9

Assume a corporation issues an obligation that is purportedly in registered form and that will qualify as a "qualified mortgage" within the meaning of I.R.C. § 860G(a)(3) in the hands of a REMIC, contributes the obligation to a REMIC as its only asset, and arranges for the sale to investors of regular interests in the REMIC in bearer form that do not meet the requirements of I.R.C. § 163(f)(2)(B).

If the provision that allows the IRS to look to the substance of the arrangement is applied, the obligation held by the REMIC is not considered to be issued in registered form or to meet the requirements of I.R.C. § 163(f)(2)(B). The corporation will not be allowed a deduction for the payment of interest on the obligation held by the REMIC, and the excise tax under I.R.C. § 4701, calculated with reference to the principal amount of the obligation held by the REMIC, will be imposed on the corporation and may be collected from the corporation and its agents.[632]

§ 31.13 WASH SALES

The wash sales rule applies to taxpayers that are not dealers in debt securities. For a discussion of the wash sales rule, see generally Chapter 19.

---

[630] *Id.*
[631] Temp. Treas. Reg. § 1.163-5T(e)(4) (1990).
[632] *Id.*

§ 31.14 SHORT SALES

The short sales rule may apply to debt securities that are capital assets in the hands of the taxpayer. For a discussion of the short sales rule, see generally Chapter 18.

§ 31.15 STRADDLE RULES

The Straddle Rules apply to offsetting positions in debt securities. For a discussion of the Straddle Rules, see generally Part Eleven.

Thirty-two
Government Securities

This chapter addresses the tax treatment of Treasury and federal agency securities. The wash sales rule,[1] short sales rule,[2] and the Straddle Rules[3] apply to taxpayers holding debt securities unless specific exceptions are available.[4] For a discussion of the tax provisions that apply generally to debt securities, see Chapter 31.

§ 32.1 TREASURY SECURITIES

Treasury securities include both marketable securities (i.e., Treasury bills, notes, and bonds) and nonmarketable securities (e.g., savings bonds).[5] With some exceptions discussed in this section, Treasury securities are generally treated for federal income tax purposes in the same way as other debt securities. Treasury securities, however, are exempt from all taxes imposed by state and local governments, except for estate or inheritance taxes, franchise taxes, and other nonproperty taxes imposed on corporations.[6] Interest income earned on Treasury securities issued

---

[1] *See generally* Chapter 19.
[2] *See generally* Chapter 18.
[3] *See generally* Part Eleven.
[4] For example, the wash sales and short sales rules typically do not apply to dealers in the particular debt security.
[5] *See* section 2.1(a).
[6] 31 U.S.C.A. § 3124(a) (1983). This statute essentially codifies the Supreme Court's ruling in McCulloch v. Maryland, 17 U.S. (4 Wheat.) 316 (1819), which provides that all properties, functions, and instrumentalities of the federal government are exempt from state and local taxation.

after 1941 is included in a taxpayer's gross income.[7] Treasury securities issued prior to 1941 are exempt from all federal taxes.

Like other types of debt securities, Treasury securities are capital assets in the hands of investors[8] and traders.[9] They are ordinary income property in the hands of dealers,[10] hedgers,[11] commercial banks, mutual savings banks, savings and loans, and small business investment companies.[12]

Redemption of Treasury securities at maturity is generally taxable unless the securities are exchanged in a tax-free exchange that qualifies under I.R.C. § 1037 or I.R.C. § 454(c).[13] Tax provisions generally applicable to debt securities, including the rules on OID, market discount, premiums, and stripped bonds, are discussed in Chapter 31.

(a) TREASURY BILLS

(1) IN GENERAL

Treasury bills are short-term obligations issued at a discount and payable without interest at a fixed maturity date not exceeding one year from the date of issue.[14] Income derived from Treasury bills is taxable for federal purposes.[15] The amount of discount at which Treasury bills are originally sold by the United States is considered to be interest and is subject to tax for federal tax purposes.[16] However, a cash basis taxpayer need not recognize interest or OID from a Treasury bill until it is sold or matures, whichever is earlier.[17]

---

[7] Public Debt Act of 1941 § 4(a), 55 Stat. 7, 9 (1941).
[8] *See* section 8.1.
[9] *See* section 8.2.
[10] *See* section 8.3.
[11] *See* section 8.4.
[12] *See* section 8.8.
[13] *See* section 32.1(d).
[14] 31 U.S.C.A. § 3104 (1983); 31 C.F.R. § 309.1 (1988). *See* section 2.1(a)(1).
[15] *See* section 2.1(a).
[16] *See* section 31.2(d).
[17] I.R.C. §§ 454, 1272(a)(2).

(2) PAYMENT OF FEDERAL TAXES WITH CERTAIN TREASURY BILLS

The Treasury has the authority to issue regulations to allow Treasury bills of any series to be accepted at maturity value, whether at or before maturity, to pay income taxes.[18] Although authorization and the procedure to tender Treasury bills at par is in place, the Treasury has not issued any such regulations. At this writing, Treasury bills are not available to pay taxes at par value prior to maturity.

(3) CAPITAL ASSETS

Prior to enactment of ERTA in 1981,[19] Treasury bills were excluded from the definition of capital assets in I.R.C. § 1221.[20] Under pre-ERTA law, taxpayers that were not dealers,[21] hedgers,[22] or certain financial institutions[23] could seek to convert ordinary income into long-term capital gain through the use of Treasury bill futures contract spreads. Taxpayers established Treasury bill futures contract spreads to attempt to generate capital gains and ordinary losses. Treasury bills were ordinary income assets, and the IRS had ruled in Rev. Rul. 78-414[24] that Treasury bill futures contracts were capital assets. Under the law in effect before the ERTA tax changes in 1981, long Treasury bill futures contract positions that declined in value could be closed out by taking delivery of a Treasury bill and selling it to generate an ordinary loss. To generate capital gains, appreciated positions were closed out by offset.

Under current law, Treasury bills are capital assets unless they are held for sale by dealers, acquired as part of a hedging transaction, or held by certain financial institutions. Therefore, if an investor or trader closes out a long Treasury bill futures contract position by taking delivery and he immediately resells the Treasury bills, the sale generates a capital gain or loss just as if he had closed out the position by offset.

---

[18] I.R.C. § 6312(a); 31 C.F.R. § 309.5(b) (1989).

[19] Pub. L. No. 97-34, 95 Stat. 172 (1981) [hereinafter ERTA].

[20] I.R.C. § 1221 (1976), *amended by* ERTA, *supra* note 19, § 505(a).

[21] *See* section 8.3.

[22] *See* section 8.4.

[23] *See* section 8.8.

[24] 1978-2 C.B. 213. For a discussion of Treasury bill repurchase transactions and Sheldon v. Comm'r, Tax Ct. Rep. (CCH) 46,602, at 2939 (May 29, 1990), see sections 31.11(b)(2), 31.11(b)(3), and 31.11(b)(4).

(b) SAVINGS BONDS

Savings bonds are nonnegotiable, nontransferable Treasury securities, which can be issued at a discount or pay interest semiannually.[25] They are the most common nonmarketable securities issued by the Treasury. The income tax treatment of interest earned on United States savings bonds is spelled out in the Treasury's offering for new bonds.[26] The federal tax treatment of interest income on savings bonds can be determined by looking at the Treasury Department Circular that offers the particular bond issue to the public. This section discusses tax considerations for savings bonds currently available to purchasers.

(1) SERIES EE SAVINGS BONDS

(i) In General

Series EE bonds (which replaced Series E bonds) are zero coupon securities[27] issued at a discount.[28] Accrued interest is added to the issue price at stated intervals, although interest is payable only at redemption of the bonds as part of the redemption value.[29] The difference between the price paid for a Series EE bond and its redemption value is interest, and is generally subject to all taxes imposed under the Code.[30]

(ii) Election to Defer Taxes

An owner of Series EE bonds can elect to defer federal tax on the interest income (the cash method), or pay it currently (the accrual method).[31] If a taxpayer elects to use the cash method, he can change the method to accrual without IRS consent.[32] Once a taxpayer elects the accrual method, however, he cannot change his method of reporting interest

---

[25] *See* section 2.1(a)(4).

[26] The terms of the current Treasury offerings for Series EE and Series HH bonds are contained in Treasury Department Circular No. 3-80. 31 C.F.R. § 353.0 (1989).

[27] *See* sections 2.2(e) and 31.5.

[28] *See* section 2.1(a)(4).

[29] 31 C.F.R. § 353.30 (1989).

[30] 31 C.F.R. § 351.8(a) (1989).

[31] 31 C.F.R. § 351.8(b) (1989).

[32] I.R.C. § 454(a); 31 C.F.R. § 351.8(b)(3) (1989).

income to the cash method without first obtaining IRS approval.[33] The election applies to all savings bonds owned by the taxpayer at the beginning of the taxable year and to all savings bonds acquired thereafter.[34] The election does not bind anyone to whom the savings bonds are subsequently transferred.[35]

In Rev. Proc. 89-46,[36] the IRS announced guidelines for changing a method of accounting for interest on Series E or EE bonds. The purpose of the revenue procedure "is to provide a procedure for certain cash basis taxpayers to obtain expeditious consent to change their method of reporting the increase in the redemption value (interest) of Series E or EE U.S. savings bonds."[37] Taxpayers that comply with the procedures set out in Rev. Proc. 89-46 will be deemed to have obtained consent to change their method of reporting this income.

In Rev. Proc. 89-46, the IRS stated that I.R.C. § 454 provides that the taxpayer can elect to treat the increase in redemption value (interest) as income for the year in which it occurs. I.R.C. § 446 provides that the application must be filed within 180 days after the beginning of the tax year in which the proposed change is to be made. Rev. Proc. 89-46—in accordance with Treas. Reg. § 1.446-1(e)(3)(ii)—waives the 180-day rule "for tax years beginning on or after January 4, 1989."[38] In addition, the IRS consents to a taxpayer's election to change from the accrual method to the cash method. This consent, provided by Rev. Proc. 89-46, "is granted for the tax year for which a taxpayer requests a change (year of change) by filing a current form 3115 in the manner described in . . . this revenue procedure [89-46]."[39]

In *West v. United States*,[40] the district court granted the government's motion for summary judgment, finding that an estate cannot retroactively revoke an election under I.R.C. § 454(a) to treat interest on Series E bonds on the accrual method. In *West*, the decedent owned Series E bonds

---

[33] I.R.C. § 454(a); 31 C.F.R. § 351.8(b)(3) (1989). The election cannot be made on an amended tax return. Rev. Rul. 55-655, 1955-2 C.B. 253. This election to avoid tax until the bonds are cashed in has been referred to as a "travesty—giving windfalls to the rich and fleecing the financially unsophisticated." Thuronyi, *Tax Reform for 1989 and Beyond, Special Report*, 42 TAX NOTES 981, 992 (1989).

[34] I.R.C. § 454(a). The taxpayer must include the actual increase in redemption value that occurs on the stated intervals in each year. Treas. Reg. § 1.454-1(a)(2) (1971).

[35] Treas. Reg. § 1.454-1(a) (1971).

[36] 1989-2 C.B. 597.

[37] Rev. Proc. 89-46, 1989-2 C.B. 597.

[38] *Id.*

[39] *Id.*

[40] 701 F. Supp. 695 (W.D. Ark. 1988).

that she had kept in a safe deposit box and she entered into an agreement to lease the safe deposit box with another couple, as joint tenants with rights of survivorship. The decedent's estate believed the couple owned the bonds and elected the accrual method of accounting under I.R.C. § 454(a). Once the Arkansas Supreme Court held that the couple did not own the bonds, the estate sought to revoke the election. The IRS claimed that the election was irrevocable and binding, and the Court agreed. The Court rejected the estate's argument that it had acted on a material mistake of fact and found that "although [the election was] most unwise from the standpoint of the estate, [the election] was clearly authorized by law and hence not illegal."[41]

(iii) Transfers to Spouses and Former Spouses

In Rev. Rul. 87-112,[42] the IRS ruled that deferred, accrued interest on Series E and Series EE bonds transferred to a spouse (or to a former spouse pursuant to a divorce) is includable in the transferor spouse's income in the year of the transfer. The transferor spouse in this case had not elected yearly reporting of the increments of interest income on the savings bonds pursuant to the elective provisions of I.R.C. § 454. As a result, the transferee spouse is taxable on interest accrued from the date of the transfer to the date the savings bonds are redeemed. The IRS also ruled that the transferee spouse's basis in the savings bonds is a carryover basis increased by the amount of accrued interest income taxed to the transferor spouse.

I.R.C. § 1041(a) provides that gain or loss is not recognized on a transfer to a spouse or, if incident to a divorce, to a former spouse. Pursuant to I.R.C. § 1041(b)(1), the property is treated as acquired by the transferee as a gift. Thus, the basis of the property to the transferee spouse is the same as the transferor spouse's adjusted basis.[43] In Rev. Rul. 87-112, the IRS found that although I.R.C. § 1041(a) prohibits gain on disposition of property, it does not protect income that ordinarily is recognized as an assignment of income. The accrued interest on the savings bonds was viewed as income, not gain. Under this analysis, the IRS concluded that I.R.C. § 454(c) required the donor to include the accrued interest upon making the gift.[44] The IRS found that the transferee spouse's basis was the sum of the transferor's basis immediately prior to the transfer, plus the

---

[41] *Id.* (citing Mamula v. Comm'r, 346 F.2d 1016 (9th Cir. 1965), *rev'g* 41 T.C. 572 (1964)).
[42] 1987-2 C.B. 207.
[43] Rev. Rul. 87-112, 1987-2 C.B. 207.
[44] *Id.*

income recognized from the transfer.[45] In other words, the basis was increased to reflect the income recognized on the transfer.

(iv) Co-Owners

In *Apkin v. Comm'r*,[46] the Tax Court held that interest on Series E bonds accrued up to the time of a decedent's death is taxable to the decedent's co-owner in the year of redemption. In *Apkin*, the decedent's son was a co-owner of Series E bonds that he inherited from his mother. The court found, under I.R.C. § 691(a)(1)(B), that the co-owner must include in his income in the year of redemption, as income in respect of a decedent, all of the accrued interest to the date of the decedent's death.[47]

The Tax Court in *Apkin* found that the decedent never made an express election under I.R.C. § 454(a) to include the interest in income in the year when it accrued. The court concluded that "by remaining silent [the decedent] in effect made an election to have the interest included in her reportable income in the year or years of maturity (as extended) or of redemption prior thereto."[48]

In *Fletcher v. Comm'r*,[49] the Tax Court held the full value of jointly owned Series E bonds are included in the estate of the second spouse to die in a simultaneous death. "Federal regulation preempts state property law or court decisions"[50] that, in this case, treated the second spouse to die and each of two adult children as entitled to one-third of the property of the first spouse to die.

In reaching its conclusion in *Fletcher*, the Tax Court stated that the value of all property owned by the decedent at the time of death is includable in the gross estate.[51] When a co-owner of joint property dies, I.R.C. § 2040 "provides rules to determine how much, if any, of the jointly held property is includable in the gross estate of the deceased co-owner."[52] The court found that I.R.C. § 2040 does not apply because it is the second estate of a co-owner of jointly held property that is before the court. The court had to determine the interest the decedent held after the death of her husband. The Tax Court looked "to state law to determine

---

[45] *Id.*
[46] 86 T.C. 692 (1986).
[47] *Id.* at 693–94.
[48] *Id.* at 694.
[49] Tax Ct. Rep. (CCH) 46,358, at 2625 (Jan. 31, 1990).
[50] *Id.* at 2627.
[51] *Id.* at 2626 (citing I.R.C. §§ 2031, 2033).
[52] *Id.*

whether the decedent possessed an interest in property at the date of death."[53] Notwithstanding state law, a controlling federal statute or regulation "overrides or preempts any inconsistent state property law, including the decision of the highest state court."[54] The Tax Court found that federal regulation preempts state law with respect to Series E bonds, which are "issued by the Secretary of the Treasury under authority granted in title 31 U.S.C. section 3105 (1982)."[55] And, within that authority, the Treasury has issued regulations concerning co-ownership of savings bonds. The regulations provide that "[i]f one of the coowners named on a bond has died, the surviving coowner will be recognized as its sole and absolute owner, and payment or reissue will be made as though the bond were registered in the name of the survivor alone."[56] As a result, the second spouse to die became the sole owner of the bonds on the death of the first spouse.

(v) College Savings Bonds

(a) IN GENERAL

Congress, in 1988, enacted I.R.C. § 135 as a way to help with the skyrocketing cost of tuition for college educations.

Beginning in 1990, interest on Series EE bonds issued after December 31, 1989, may be exempt from federal taxes if the bond proceeds are used to pay the college tuition of the bond owner's designated beneficiary.[57] Certain cash basis taxpayers may exclude interest income on a qualified Series EE bond that is used to pay qualified educational expenses of the taxpayer, his spouse, or his dependent.[58] The exclusion is limited to bonds purchased after December 31, 1989, and to taxpayers, or their spouses, that have purchased such bonds after having attained 24 years of age.

---

[53] *Id.* at 2627 (citing Helvering v. Stuart, 317 U.S. 154, 161 (1942), *rev'g* 124 F.2d 772 (7th Cir. 1941), *modifying* 42 B.T.A. 1421 (1940); Tracy v. Comm'r, 70 T.C. 397, 402 (1978), *acq.* 1978-2 C.B. 3).

[54] *Id.* (citing Free v. Bland, 369 U.S. 663, 669 (1962), *rev'g* 162 Tex. 72, 344 S.W.2d 435 (1961), *rev'g* 337 S.W.2d 805 (Tex. Civ. App. 1960); United States v. Chandler, 410 U.S. 257, 262 (1973), *rev'g* 460 F.2d 1281 (9th Cir. 1972), *aff'g* 312 F. Supp. 1263 (N.d. Cal. 1970)).

[55] *Id.*

[56] *Id.* (citing 31 C.F.R. § 315.61 (1989)).

[57] Notice 90-7, 1990-3 I.R.B. 5 (Jan. 16, 1990), *implementing* the Technical and Miscellaneous Revenue Act of 1988, Pub. L. No. 100-647, § 6009, 102 Stat. 3342, 3688-90 (1988) [hereinafter TMRA '88].

[58] TMRA '88, *supra* note 57, § 6009.

The exclusion is limited by a ratio consisting of the qualified educational expenses and the aggregate bond principal and interest redeemed. Moreover, the exclusion is phased out for joint filers and individuals with adjusted gross incomes of $90,000 and $55,000, respectively.[59] This exemption is not available to taxpayers filing joint returns with an adjusted gross income in excess of $90,000, or to single taxpayers whose adjusted gross income exceeds $55,000.[60] For couples with an adjusted gross income between $60,000 and $90,000, and for single taxpayers with an adjusted gross income of between $40,000 and $55,000, a declining portion of interest from Series EE bonds is exempt from federal taxation.[61]

(b) QUALIFIED SAVINGS BONDS

To be eligible for the exclusion, the bonds must be issued in the name of the taxpayer (as sole owner), or in the names of the taxpayer and the taxpayer's spouse (as co-owners).[62] The taxpayer must be at least 24 years old before the date the bonds are issued.[63] A taxpayer that purchases a qualified bond can designate any individual (including a child) as a beneficiary of the bond (payable on death).[64]

(c) QUALIFIED HIGHER EDUCATION EXPENSES

Expenses that can be paid with the proceeds of qualified savings bonds are limited to tuition and required fees at eligible educational institutions.[65] Qualified higher education expenses must be reduced by "amounts received as scholarships, fellowships, veteran's benefits, or other tax-exempt educational benefits."[66] In addition, expenses for courses or other education "involving sports, games, or hobbies, other than as part of a degree or certificate granting program are not qualified educational expenses."[67]

---

[59] Notice 90-7, 1990-3 I.R.B. 5 (Jan. 16, 1990).
[60] *Id.*
[61] *Id.*
[62] *Id.*
[63] *Id.* Bonds are issued as of the first day of the month in which they are purchased.
[64] Notice 90-7, 1990-3 I.R.B. 5 (Jan. 16, 1990).
[65] *Id.*
[66] *Id.*
[67] *Id.*

(d) AMOUNT OF EXCLUDABLE INTEREST

The amount of interest on qualified savings bonds that is excludable under I.R.C. § 135 is limited by "the amount of redemption proceeds (interest and principal) used to pay qualified higher education costs during the same tax year as the redemption."[68]

Example 32-1

Assume that 50 percent of the total qualified savings bond redemption proceeds a taxpayer receives are used to pay qualified higher education expenses in the same year as the redemption. Only 50 percent of the interest portion of the qualified savings bond redemption proceeds is excludable interest under I.R.C. § 135.[69]

The interest exclusion is phased out for joint filers with "modified adjusted gross incomes" between $60,000 and $90,000.[70] Married individuals must file joint returns to claim an interest exclusion.[71] The phase-out range for single filers and heads of households is between $40,000 and $55,000.[72] The phase-out limits will be indexed for inflation after 1990 "and then rounded to the nearest multiple of $50,000."[73]

(e) RECORDKEEPING

Taxpayers can use IRS Form 8818, Optional Form to Record Redemption of College Savings Bonds, to maintain records on redeemed bonds to substantiate the interest exclusion available under I.R.C. § 135.

---

[68] *Id.*

[69] Example taken from Notice 90-7, 1990-3 I.R.B. 5 (Jan. 16, 1990).

[70] Modified adjusted gross income is adjusted gross income modified by adding back certain exclusions for income from foreign sources, certain United States possessions, and Puerto Rico, and after taking into account taxable social security benefits, the Individual Retirement Account deduction, and the passive activity loss limitation. Notice 90-7, 1990-3 I.R.B. 5 (Jan. 16, 1990).

[71] *Id.*

[72] *Id.*

[73] *Id.*

(2) SERIES HH SAVINGS BONDS

Series HH bonds, referred to as "current income bonds," have a maturity of 10 years and pay interest on a current basis, semiannually.[74] At the present time, Series HH bonds are only issued in exchange for Series E and EE bonds.[75] However, the face amount of Series H bonds purchased for cash that have reached final maturity may be reinvested in Series HH bonds.[76]

Series HH bonds are issued in registered form[77] and cannot be transferred or pledged as collateral.[78] In addition, the Treasury announced that effective October 1, 1989, interest payments for all new issues of Series HH bonds will be made only by electronic funds transfer.[79] Interest will be paid directly to the account specified by the bond owner.[80]

Unlike Series EE bonds, no election is available for holders of Series HH bonds to defer recognition of interest income at the federal level. Interest on Series HH bonds is paid semiannually, beginning six months from the issue date.[81] Interest on Series HH bonds ceases at maturity, or if the bond is redeemed before maturity, interest ceases as of the end of the preceding interest payment period.[82] The interest on the bonds is subject to all taxes imposed by the Code when the interest is paid (for cash method taxpayers) or accrues (for accrual method taxpayers).[83] Interest income is not taxable at the state or local level.[84]

(3) DISPOSITIONS

Savings bonds can only be transferred under very limited circumstances.[85] The IRS has not viewed the transfer of Series E bonds to a grantor trust (where the transferor is treated as the trust's owner for tax

---

[74] 31 C.F.R. § 352.2 (1989).
[75] 31 C.F.R. § 352.0 (1989).
[76] 31 C.F.R. § 352.8 (1989).
[77] 31 C.F.R. §§ 352.2, 353.5 (1989).
[78] 31 C.F.R. §§ 353.15, .16 (1989).
[79] *Capital Developments*, 53 Banking Rep. (BNA) No. 14, at 510 (Oct. 9, 1989).
[80] *Id.*
[81] 31 C.F.R. § 353.31(a) (1989).
[82] *Id.*
[83] 31 C.F.R. § 352.10 (1989).
[84] 31 C.F.R. § 352.10 (1989).
[85] *See* section 2.1(a)(4).

purposes) as a disposition triggering tax on the accrued interest.[86] Some savings bonds (e.g., Series E and Series EE bonds) are issued at a discount, and the owner can elect to accrue interest income currently or to defer taxation until retirement, redemption, or disposition.[87] Other savings bonds (e.g., Series HH bonds) are current income bonds issued at par and paying interest semiannually. Taxpayers holding savings bonds issued at a discount can defer taxation on the interest income by using the cash method, which can be continued if zero coupon savings bonds are exchanged for other Treasury securities in a tax-free exchange under I.R.C. § 1037.[88]

Series EE savings bonds can be redeemed at any time after six months from issue at the current redemption value shown in Treasury Circular No. 1-80.[89] Those Series HH savings bonds issued in a tax-free exchange are redeemed at face amount, while those issued for cash are redeemed at the current redemption value shown in Treasury Circular No. 2-80, Second Revision.[90] If a Series HH bond is redeemed at less than face value, the difference represents an interest adjustment.[91]

(c) PAYMENT OF ESTATE TAXES WITH CERTAIN TREASURY BONDS

Certain Treasury bonds can be redeemed at their face amounts, plus accrued interest, regardless of their redemption dates to pay estate taxes due on the death of the bond owner.[92] These bonds are referred to as "flower bonds" (perhaps because they "bloom" into full value when their owner dies). They have low interest rates and frequently sell at a substantial discount.[93] Flower bonds can be a potentially important estate planning device for an individual with a short life expectancy. Because of the low yield, an individual would not purchase flower bonds unless he thought his death was imminent and he wanted his estate to use the

---

[86] Rev. Rul. 58-2, 1958-1 C.B. 236; LTR 7729003 (Apr. 19, 1977).

[87] I.R.C. § 454(a).

[88] *See* section 32.1(d).

[89] 31 C.F.R. § 353.35(b) (1989).

[90] 31 C.F.R. § 353.35(c) (1989).

[91] *Id.*

[92] 31 C.F.R. § 306.28(a) (1989); Treas. Reg. § 20.6151-1(c) (1958); Rev. Rul. 69-489, 1969-2 C.B. 172; Rev. Proc. 69-18, 1969-2 C.B. 300.

[93] Certain Treasury bonds issued between 1953 and 1963 with interest rates between three percent and 4.25 percent, and maturity dates in 1985, 1990, 1992 through 1995, and 1998, are redeemable at par to pay estate taxes. A current list of eligible flower bond issues can be obtained from any Federal Reserve bank or branch, or from the Bureau of the Public Debt.

flower bonds to pay his estate taxes.[94] The Treasury has not been authorized to issue new flower bonds since 1971.[95] As a result, outstanding flower bond issues continue to decrease over time.

Flower bonds are redeemable at par only to the extent they are included in the decedent's gross estate for federal estate tax purposes. They are redeemable at par by the representative of the estate or, if there is none, by certain persons holding or receiving assets included in the decedent's gross estate. Flower bonds can be redeemed only to the extent of the net amount of the federal estate tax, after taking into account all allowable credits (including the credit for federal gift taxes paid).[96]

In determining a decedent's gross estate, flower bonds are valued at par rather than at their fair market value to the extent that they may be applied to pay federal estate taxes. Bonds that exceed the amount applied to pay the estate tax are valued at the mean between their highest and lowest quoted selling prices on the estate's valuation date.[97] Accrued interest to the date of death is taxed as part of the estate regardless of whether the bonds could have been used to pay estate taxes.[98] This reduces the overall tax benefit of flower bonds to the part that remains after paying the additional estate tax attributable to the discount from par.[99] This means that greater benefits are available to taxpayers with lower marginal estate tax rates.

If an estate has excess flower bonds remaining after the payment of estimated federal estate tax, there can be a problem if any additional federal estate taxes become due after the representative of the estate sells the excess bonds at their fair market value. If the IRS subsequently assesses an estate tax deficiency, flower bonds sold at the market price are

---

[94] The yield on a flower bond is less than that offered by a comparable Treasury issue with the same maturity date.

[95] I.R.C. § 6312 (1970), *repealed by* Public Debt Limit—Interest Rate—Social Security Wage Base Act, Pub. L. No. 92-5, § 4(a)(2), 85 Stat. 5 (1971) for Treasury securities issued after March 3, 1971. 31 U.S.C. § 3121(b)(2) (1983).

[96] Rev. Rul. 76-367, 1976-2 C.B. 259.

[97] Even if bonds are not actually used to pay estate taxes, they must be valued at par to the extent they could have been used to pay estate taxes. Bankers Trust Co. v. United States, 284 F.2d 537, 538 (2d Cir. 1960), *rev'g* 178 F. Supp. 267 (S.D.N.Y. 1959), *cert. denied*, 366 U.S. 903 (1961).

[98] Rev. Rul. 69-489, 1969-2 C.B. 172.

[99] For example, a bond purchased for $900 that is redeemable to pay estate taxes at $1000 can generate a tax savings of $60 to an estate in the 40 percent bracket ($100 less the $40 increase in estate taxes caused by converting the $900 of cash into the $900 flower bond).

valued at their higher par value to the extent of any additional taxes. This can increase an estate's total federal estate tax.[100]

If a redemption of flower bonds at par is contemplated, careful planning is necessary prior to an individual's death.[101] Four conditions must be met to redeem flower bonds at par.

- First, the bonds must have been owned by the decedent at the time of his death.[102]
- Second, bonds held in trust are redeemable at par (1) if the trust actually terminates in favor of the decedent's estate, (2) if the trustee is required to pay the decedent's estate tax, or (3) to the extent that the debts of the decedent's estate (including costs of administration, state inheritance taxes, and federal estate taxes) exceed the estate's assets, without taking the trust estate into account.[103]
- Third, bonds held in joint ownership are redeemable at par if (1) the bonds actually became the property of the decedent's estate, or (2) to the extent that the surviving joint owner is required to contribute toward payment of the federal estate tax.[104]
- Fourth, bonds held as community property are redeemable at par only to the extent of the decedent's one-half interest in the bonds.[105]

In *Estate of Piper v. United States*,[106] the Court of Claims found that when the IRS erroneously refunded cash for estate taxes paid with flower bonds, the estate was required to repay the refund, plus statutory interest from the date of the refund. In addition, the IRS was required to reinstate the flower bonds with interest from the date of the refund.[107] The interest

---

[100] Estate of Simmie v. Comm'r, 69 T.C. 890, 896 (1978), *aff'd*, 632 F.2d 93 (9th Cir. 1980), where the estate's representative sold what he believed to be excess flower bonds at the market price (which was less than par) after the estate tax return was filed and before an estate tax deficiency was assessed. The flower bonds sold at the market price were included in the estate at par value. *But see* Colorado Nat'l Bank v. United States, 27 A.F.T.R.2d (P-H) ¶ 147,575, at 1829 (D. Colo. 1971).

[101] For a general discussion of estate planning considerations in using flower bonds, see J. Price, Contemporary Estate Planning, Text and Problems 768–71 (1983).

[102] 31 C.F.R. § 306.28(b)(1) (1989).

[103] 31 C.F.R. § 306.28(b)(1)(iii) (1989).

[104] 31 C.F.R. § 306.28(b)(1)(i) (1989).

[105] 31 C.F.R. § 306.28(b)(1)(i)(A) n.6 (1989).

[106] 57 A.F.T.R.2d (P-H) ¶ 148,833 (Ct. Cl. 1986).

[107] *Id.* at 86-1523.

that the IRS owed the estate on the flower bonds could not be used to offset the estate's liability to the IRS for the erroneous cash refund.[108]

(d) TAX-FREE EXCHANGES

The exchange of Treasury securities is generally taxable, unless the provisions for tax-free exchanges of property under different Code provisions apply independently. The Treasury is authorized, however, to issue regulations to provide for the tax-free surrender of certain Treasury securities issued under chapter 31 of title 31 of the United States Code in exchange for certain other Treasury securities issued under the same chapter.[109] An exchange not covered under I.R.C. § 1037 is taxable. In addition, any noncorporate cash basis taxpayers that retain Series E and EE savings bonds past maturity can elect to retain their investments in certain United States discount obligations without current tax.[110] The remainder of this section discusses tax-free exchanges under I.R.C. § 1037.

(1) GENERAL RULE

Exchanges are tax-free under I.R.C. § 1037 only if Treasury regulations specifically provide tax-free status. The appropriate Treasury Department Circular can be used to ascertain whether an exchange of Treasury securities is tax-free.[111] Also, each offering circular announcing a new Treasury security states the specific terms for an exchange and whether the exchange is completely or partially tax-free. For example, the exchange of Series E and Series EE savings bonds for Series HH bonds on a tax-free basis was first offered to the public in 1982.[112] As a result, a taxpayer can exchange Series E or EE bonds for Series HH bonds with a continued deferral of untaxed interest until the new bonds are ultimately redeemed.[113]

---

[108] *Id.*
[109] I.R.C. § 1037(a).
[110] I.R.C. § 454(c).
[111] Treas. Reg. § 1.1037-1(a) (1971).
[112] 31 C.F.R. pts. 351, 352 (1989); *see* section 32.1(b).
[113] 31 C.F.R. §§ 351.8(c), 352.0 (1989); *see* sections 2.1(a)(4) and 32.1(b).

Example 32-2

Assume a taxpayer purchased a Series E bond for $800 and elects not to accrue the interest for tax purposes. The bond is redeemable at maturity for $1000 ($800 plus accrued interest). Rather than pay tax on the interest when the bond is redeemed, the taxpayer elects to exchange the Series E bond for a $1000 Series HH bond. Pursuant to the provisions of I.R.C. § 1037(a), the accrued interest is not recognized in the year of the exchange.[114]

An owner of Treasury securities that has not reported interest on the accrual basis can exchange those securities for new securities authorized for exchange by the Treasury until the taxable year in which the new securities reach final maturity, or are otherwise disposed of.[115] Each new security issued in a tax-free exchange bears a legend showing how much of its issue price represents untaxed interest on the old securities that were exchanged.[116] Untaxed interest is taxable when the new securities mature, are redeemed, or are otherwise disposed of.

Example 32-3

Assume a taxpayer owns a $1000 Series E savings bond purchased for $750 with an issue date of May 1, 1948. The taxpayer surrenders the bond to the United States in exchange for a Series HH bond on March 15, 1985, when the Series E bond has a redemption value of $1304.80. If the taxpayer pays an additional $195.20 to the United States government and obtains three $500 face amount Series HH bonds, none of the $554.80 gain ($1304.80 redemption value minus the $750 tax basis) is recognized at the time of the exchange.[117]

If a taxpayer receives any cash in an otherwise nontaxable exchange, gain is recognized up to the amount of the cash received in the exchange.[118] Loss, however, is not recognized.[119]

---

[114] 31 C.F.R. §§ 352.0, 352.7(g)(1) (1989).
[115] *See, e.g.*, 31 C.F.R. § 352.7(g)(1) (1989).
[116] *See, e.g.*, 31 C.F.R. § 352.7(g)(2) (1989).
[117] *See* Treas. Reg. § 1.1037-1(a), Example (1) (1971).
[118] I.R.C. § 1031(b).
[119] I.R.C. § 1031(c).

Example 32-4

In 1983, a taxpayer purchases for $970 a Treasury bond that was originally issued at its par value of $1000. In 1984, he surrenders the bond to the United States in an exchange authorized by the Treasury solely for a new Treasury bond with a fair market value of $950. The taxpayer's $20 loss on the exchange ($970 tax basis minus $950 redemption value) is not recognized at the time of the exchange.[120]

The basis of securities acquired in a completely nontaxable exchange is determined under I.R.C. § 1031.[121] The basis of the new securities is the cost of the old securities, increased by any gain recognized, and reduced by any cash received. Any premium paid by the owner on the exchange (i.e., cash paid other than for accrued interest on the new bonds) is added to the basis of the new securities.[122] For capital assets, the holding period of the new securities received in the exchange includes the holding period of the old securities.[123]

Example 32-5

Assume the facts are the same as in Example 32-4. The taxpayer's basis in the new bond, which has a market value of $950, is $970.[124] Assume further that it is necessary for the taxpayer to pay an additional $10 to acquire the new bond. His basis in the new bond is now $980—to reflect his additional $10 cash payment.[125]

(2) APPLICATION OF ORIGINAL ISSUE DISCOUNT RULES

The OID[126] rules are generally applied to tax-free exchanges under I.R.C. § 1037 in accordance with the following provisions. If an exchange is tax-free under I.R.C. § 1037(a) and the new securities received in the exchange are disposed of or redeemed at a gain, ordinary income is realized in an amount equal to the OID on the old securities that, but for I.R.C. § 1037,

---

[120] *See* Treas. Reg. § 1.1037-1(a)(3), Example (2) (1971).
[121] Treas. Reg. § 1.1037-1(d) (1971).
[122] For a discussion of premiums, see section 31.4.
[123] Treas. Reg. § 1.1037-1(c) (1971); *see* section 31.9.
[124] *See* I.R.C. § 1031(d).
[125] Treas. Reg. § 1.1037-1(a)(3), Example (2) (1971).
[126] *See* section 31.2.

would have been taxable as ordinary income at the time of the exchange.[127] In other words, if a security that was originally issued at a discount is exchanged tax-free, a portion or all of the gain on the sale or exchange of the new security may be considered gain from the sale or exchange of property that is not a capital asset.[128]

In addition, different provisions apply to nonmarketable and marketable securities.[129] The remainder of this section looks at the provisions that apply to nonmarketable and marketable securities.

(i) Nonmarketable Securities

If a nonmarketable security originally issued at a discount is exchanged,[130] the amount that would have been ordinary income on the exchange of the old security cannot exceed the difference between the issue price and the stated redemption price of the old security at the time of the exchange.[131] The issue price of the new security received in the exchange is treated as the stated redemption price of the old security plus any consideration paid to the United States as part of the exchange.[132]

(ii) Marketable Securities

If a marketable security issued at not less than par (e.g., a Treasury bond) is exchanged, the issue price of the new security received is treated as the issue price of the old security, plus any consideration paid to the United States as part of the exchange.[133]

§ 32.2 FEDERAL AGENCY DEBT SECURITIES

Various federal agencies issue debt securities to help finance their operations.[134] Federal agency debt securities are generally taxed in the same

---

[127] Treas. Reg. § 1.1037-1(b) (1971).

[128] For a discussion of the rules used in computing OID on the disposition of debt securities, see section 31.2.

[129] *See* section 2.1(a).

[130] *E.g.*, I.R.C. § 454(c) (on Series E or Series EE bonds).

[131] I.R.C. § 1037(b)(1).

[132] I.R.C. § 1037(b)(1)(B); Treas. Reg. § 1.1037-1(b)(2)(ii) (1971).

[133] I.R.C. § 1037(b)(2); Treas. Reg. § 1.1037-1(b)(5) (1971).

[134] *See* section 2.1(b).

way as Treasury securities.¹³⁵ Interest paid on debt securities issued by federal agencies is exempt from income taxation by state and local governments under 31 U.S.C. § 3124, but is not exempt from federal income taxes. This statute essentially codifies the Supreme Court's ruling in *McCulloch v. Maryland*,¹³⁶ which provides that all properties, functions, and instrumentalities of the federal government are exempt from state and local taxation.

(a) TEST FOR EXEMPTION FROM STATE AND LOCAL TAX

In *Smith v. Davis*,¹³⁷ the Supreme Court established a four-part test to determine whether a security is exempt from state and local taxation. Specifically, the Supreme Court noted that securities exempt from state and local tax "have been characterized by (1) written documents, (2) the bearing of interest, (3) a binding promise by the United States to pay specified sums at specified dates, and (4) specific congressional authorization, which also pledged the faith and credit of the United States in support of the promise to pay."¹³⁸ The four-part test set out in *Smith v. Davis* has been cited with approval in *Montgomery Ward Life Insurance Co. v. State Department of Local Government Affairs*.¹³⁹ In *Montgomery Ward Life*, the court held that GNMA pass-through certificates were not exempt from state and local taxation.¹⁴⁰ The court specifically noted that GNMA pass-through certificates did not meet the four-pronged test in *Smith v. Davis*. The obligation of the United States was not primary but rather "a contingent and speculative obligation requiring default by the issuer before it arises."¹⁴¹ The court indicated that "obligation[s] issued to secure money for a governmental purpose" come under the exemption from state and local taxation.¹⁴²

The Supreme Court has indicated, albeit in dicta, that debt securities issued by federal agencies and instrumentalities—even though not issued directly by the United States—qualify for the exemption from state and local taxation. In *Memphis Bank & Trust Co. v. Garner*,¹⁴³ the Supreme

---

¹³⁵ For a discussion of the taxation of debt securities, see generally Chapter 31.
¹³⁶ 17 U.S. (4 Wheat.) 316 (1819).
¹³⁷ 323 U.S. 111 (1944), *aff'g* 197 Ga. 95, 28 S.E.2d 148 (1943).
¹³⁸ 323 U.S. at 115.
¹³⁹ 89 Ill. App. 3d 292, 297, 301, 411 N.E.2d 973, 976, 980 (1980).
¹⁴⁰ For a discussion of GNMA pass-through certificates, see sections 2.1(b)(2) and 36.2.
¹⁴¹ *Montgomery Ward Life*, 89 Ill. App. 3d at 297, 411 N.E.2d at 977.
¹⁴² *Id.* at 298, 411 N.E.2d at 978.
¹⁴³ 459 U.S. 392, 394 (1983), *rev'g* 459 U.S. 816 (1982).

Court noted that the exemption established in the predecessor section to 31 U.S.C. § 3124 applies not only to Treasury securities but also to debt securities of instrumentalities of the United States.

(b) FEDERAL NATIONAL MORTGAGE ASSOCIATION BONDS

In *First Federal Savings and Loan v. Oklahoma Tax Commission*,[144] the Oklahoma Supreme Court found that income earned (1) from overnight demand deposits placed in the Federal Home Loan Bank, (2) from bonds issued by the FNMA, and (3) from the secondary reserve maintained by the FSLIC, is subject to Oklahoma state tax. The interest on the demand deposit was not exempt from tax because the term "obligations," as used in the exemption clause of 12 U.S.C. 1433, was not all-embracing.[145] The court reasoned that corporate income earned on the FNMA bonds is taxable under 12 U.S.C. 1719(b), which provides that FNMA bonds must contain disclaimers that the obligations are not notes or obligations of the United States and, therefore, are subject to taxation.[146] Finally, the court noted that federally insured savings banks have a property interest in their share of the secondary reserve maintained for them by the FSLIC, and the interest earned on that share was also found to be taxable.[147]

(c) GOVERNMENT NATIONAL MORTGAGE ASSOCIATION CERTIFICATES

In *Rockford Life Insurance Co. v. Illinois Department of Revenue*,[148] the United States Supreme Court held that GNMA certificates are not tax-exempt. The Court reasoned that GNMA certificates were not "obligations" of the United States subject to exemption under the Constitution or the intergovernmental immunity statute. More specifically, the Supreme Court noted that because the United States was only secondarily liable on the certificates (as guarantor), the GNMA certificates did not fall within the statutory definition of "other obligations of the United States."[149] In addition, in applying the four-part test set forth in *Smith v.*

---

[144] 743 P.2d 640 (1987), *cert. denied*, 480 U.S. 901 (1988).
[145] 743 P.2d at 645.
[146] *Id.* at 646.
[147] *Id.* at 647.
[148] 482 U.S. 182 (1987), *aff'g* 479 U.S. 947 (1986), *noting jur.* 112 Ill. 2d 174, 492 N.E.2d 1278 (1986), *aff'g* 128 Ill. App. 3d 302, 470 N.E.2d 596 (1984).
[149] 482 U.S. at 188.

Davis,[150] the Court held that the constitutional doctrine of intergovernmental tax immunity did not apply because the element requiring "a binding promise by the United States to pay specified sums at specified dates" was not present.[151]

§ 32.3 REPURCHASE AGREEMENTS AND REVERSE REPURCHASE AGREEMENTS

Repos and reverse repos commonly involve Treasury and federal agency securities. For a discussion of the tax treatment of repos and reverse repos, see section 31.11.

§ 32.4 WHEN-ISSUED SECURITIES

There is an active when-issued, or wi, market for Treasury and federal agency securities. For a discussion of the tax considerations for when-issued securities, see section 27.3(d).

§ 32.5 ZERO COUPON SECURITIES

Zero coupon securities, or zeros, are bonds that have had their coupons removed, creating two different types of securities. The most popular zeros are based on Treasury securities. For a discussion of the tax considerations for zeros, see section 31.5.

---

[150] 323 U.S. 111 (1944), *aff'g* 197 Ga. 95, 28 S.E.2d 148 (1943); *see* section 32.2(a).
[151] 482 U.S. at 189.

Thirty-three

Municipal Securities

§ 33.1 IN GENERAL

Interest received on the debt securities of a state, territory, or possession of the United States, or any political subdivision of the foregoing, or the District of Columbia, is excluded from gross income for federal tax purposes.[1] The securities of states and their political subdivisions, referred to as "municipal securities," constitute the most significant category of tax-exempt securities.[2] This section specifically addresses municipal securities used to finance or refinance government operations and public projects or activities. Nevertheless, it is important to note that the following discussion on the general tax principles of tax-exempt interest also applies to other types of tax-exempt securities.[3]

Despite the broad tax exemption contained in I.R.C. § 103(a), interest on certain municipal securities (e.g., private activity bonds that are not qualified, and arbitrage bonds) may not be exempt from tax. Also, interest on private activity bonds other than "qualified 501(c)(3) bonds"[4] is, in the hands of certain owners, subject to alternative minimum tax.[5] The interest on all municipal bonds, in the hands of certain holders, is subject to

---

[1] I.R.C. § 103(a)(1). *See generally* HOUSE WAYS AND MEANS COMM., 101ST CONG., 2D SESS., OVERVIEW OF THE FEDERAL TAX SYSTEM (Comm. Print 1990), *reprinted in Special Supplement*, 17 DAILY TAX HIGHLIGHTS & DOCUMENTS S1 (1990).

[2] *See generally* Chapter 3.

[3] For a discussion of collateral tax consequences, see generally Mentz, *The Collateral Tax Consequences of Investments in Municipal Obligations*, 35 TAX LAW. 603 (1982).

[4] *See* section 33.2(c)(2)(vi).

[5] I.R.C. §§ 55, 56(b)(1)(C)(iii), 56(c)(1). *See* section 33.7.

the Superfund environmental tax[6] and the branch profits tax.[7] In addition, proposals are frequently introduced in Congress to repeal or limit applicability of the tax exemption for certain types of municipal securities.[8] The remainder of this section discusses tax considerations for various types of municipal securities and mentions general tax principles applicable to tax-exempt securities.

§ 33.2 TYPES OF MUNICIPAL SECURITIES

Municipal securities are defined in the Treasury regulations as "obligations issued by or on behalf of any state or local governmental unit by constituted authorities empowered to issue such obligations."[9] In addition, municipal securities include "[c]ertificates issued by a political subdivision for public improvements . . . which are evidence of special assessments against specific property . . . even though the obligations are satisfied out of special funds and not out of general funds or taxes."[10] Interest on special bills and special assessment bonds for municipal purposes may also be tax-exempt.[11] In short, the obligations must be incurred in the exercise of the borrowing power of a state or a political subdivision (e.g., counties, special districts, cities, and towns).[12]

(a) GENERAL OBLIGATION BONDS

General obligation, or "GO," bonds are secured by the issuing municipality's general taxing powers.[13] Some GO bonds are also secured by certain identified fees or charges, which provide an additional source of revenue to secure the bonds. Interest on GO bonds is tax-exempt and is not a

---

[6] I.R.C. § 59A. *See* section 33.12.

[7] I.R.C. § 884. *See* section 33.11.

[8] *See, e.g., 1985 Tax Reform, President's Tax Proposals to Congress for Fairness, Growth, and Simplicity*, Stand. Fed. Tax Rep. (CCH) Rep. No. 25, Extra Ed., ch. 11 (May 29, 1985); Hoerner, *Major Overhaul of Taxation of Tax-Exempts in the Offing*, 15 DAILY TAX HIGHLIGHTS & DOCUMENTS 2121 (1989).

[9] Treas. Reg. § 1.103-1(b) (1972).

[10] *Id.*

[11] Bryant v. Comm'r, 111 F.2d 9, 12 (9th Cir. 1940), *acq.* 1944 C.B. 4; Avery v. Comm'r, 111 F.2d 19, 23 (9th Cir. 1940).

[12] *See* Rev. Rul. 69-171, 1969-1 C.B. 46 (interest paid to a bank by a political subdivision on behalf of a student borrower was taxable); *see also* LTR 8142048 (July 21, 1981).

[13] *See* section 3.2(a).

preference item for calculation of alternative minimum taxable income.[14] In the hands of certain holders, however, the interest on general obligation bonds is subject to the Superfund environmental tax[15] and the branch profits tax.[16]

TRA '86[17] imposes new arbitrage restrictions, information reporting requirements, and restrictions on advance refundings.[18] Also, if more than $15 million of the proceeds of any governmental use bond issue is used in a private, nongovernmental use—even if the bonds are not characterized "private activity bonds"[19] the issuer must allocate a portion of its volume cap[20] to the nonqualified amount in excess of $15 million for the interest on such bonds to remain tax-exempt.[21]

(b) MUNICIPAL REVENUE BONDS

Revenue bonds are usually issued by a municipality to finance or refinance a particular governmental project. The municipality pledges the revenues generated by the project to meet interest and principal payment obligations. It does not pledge its full taxing power in support of its payment obligations. Depending on the use of the proceeds of any issue of revenue bonds, those bonds are treated as either governmental bonds, subject to the same requirements as GO bonds, or private activity bonds, subject to the requirements set forth below.[22] If the use of the bond proceeds does not cause the bonds to become private activity bonds, the interest on the revenue bonds is tax-exempt and is not a preference item for calculation of alternative minimum taxable income.[23]

(c) PRIVATE ACTIVITY BONDS

Private activity bonds are a type of revenue bond issued by a municipality, where a major part of the project or facility financed by the bond is

---

[14] For a discussion of the justification for the tax exemption, see section 33.3(a).

[15] I.R.C. § 59A. *See* section 33.12.

[16] I.R.C. § 884. *See* section 33.11.

[17] Pub. L. No. 99-514, 100 Stat. 2085 (1986) [hereinafter TRA '86].

[18] For a discussion of arbitrage restrictions, see section 33.3(a)(1)(vi); for information reporting requirements, see section 33.3(a)(1)(viii); and for restrictions on advance refundings, see section 33.3(a)(1)(vii).

[19] For a discussion of private activity bonds, see section 33.2(c).

[20] For a discussion of the volume cap, see section 33.2(c).

[21] I.R.C. § 141(b)(5).

[22] I.R.C. § 141.

[23] For a discussion of the justification for the tax exemption, see section 33.3(a).

leased, owned, or generally used by a private business or any person other than a governmental unit. In addition, the payment of principal or interest is secured—at least in major part—by the project, facility, or revenues of a trade or business of a person other than a government unit.[24] The attraction of private activity bond financing is that the cost of borrowing the funds is lower than in the case of taxable bonds or loans from financial institutions.

Because of abuses in the types of facilities that were financed with private activity bonds, the tax exemption has been eliminated in many cases and restricted in others. In addition, proposals are frequently introduced in Congress to repeal or further limit the tax exemption available for certain private activity bonds,[25] although it is not likely that those private activity bonds already outstanding will be affected by any future legislation. The remainder of this section briefly discusses the current tax treatment of private activity bonds.[26]

(1) IN GENERAL

A private activity bond is a security that is nominally issued by a municipality and the payment of the principal or interest on the bond is secured, in whole or major part, by any interest in (1) property used in a trade or business of any person other than a governmental unit, (2) payments with respect to such property, or (3) is derived from payments from the property or borrowed money used (or to be used) in a trade or business of any person other than a government unit. In addition, a major portion of the proceeds from the bond issue are used in the trade or business of any person other than a government unit; and either interest and principal payments may be secured by a lien or mortgage on the property used in a trade or business, including by an I.R.C. § 501(c)(3) organization for its exempt purposes, or the proceeds of the issue are used in such a manner to make the bonds private loan bonds.[27]

---

[24] *See* section 25.4(b).

[25] H.R. 157, 101st Cong., 1st Sess. (1989); H.R. 5215, 100th Cong., 2d Sess. (1988); H.R. 1767, 2551, 3092, 3838, 99th Cong., 1st Sess. (1985); S. 981, 99th Cong., 1st Sess. (1981).

[26] It is possible that the tax provisions applicable to private activity bonds will be modified by future legislation. *See, e.g.*, Marty-Nelson & Blatter, *Tax-Exempt Financing in the Aftermath of the Technical and Miscellaneous Revenue Act of 1988, Special Report*, 41 TAX NOTES 557 (1988); Spector, *State Revolving Funds and Tax-Exempt Bonds, Special Report*, 42 TAX NOTES 601 (1989).

[27] I.R.C. § 141(a).

Generally, the phrase "major portion of the proceeds" is defined as more than 10 percent of the proceeds of an issue.[28] An issue of bonds can fail the "major portion" test, however, if more than five percent of the proceeds of the issue are used for a private business use that is not related to or disproportionate to the governmental use financed by the issue.[29] A lower limitation is imposed on an issue of bonds if five percent or more of the issue is used by an output facility (other than a facility for the furnishing of water) where the nonqualified portion exceeds the excess of $15 million over the aggregate unqualified amount of such issues.[30]

Private loan bonds are bonds, the lesser of five percent or $5 million of the proceeds of which is used directly or indirectly to make or finance loans (other than certain tax assessment related loans) to persons other than governmental units.[31]

(i) Private Activity Bonds Issued After August 16, 1986

To be tax-exempt, private activity bonds issued after August 16, 1986 must meet additional requirements. Some of these requirements apply to all private activity bonds, but some apply only to private activity bonds that are not qualified 501(c)(3) bonds, mortgage revenue bonds, or qualified student loan bonds.[32] Four requirements apply to all private activity bonds. First, the average maturity of any issue of private activity bonds cannot exceed 120 percent of the average, reasonably expected, economic life of the financed facilities.[33] This provision does not apply to mortgage revenue bonds or qualified student loan bonds.[34]

Second, a public hearing must be held after reasonable notice, prior to issuance of the bonds, and issuance must be approved after the hearing.[35]

Third, no more than two percent of the aggregate face amount of any issue can generally be spent on issuance costs (other than fees for credit enhancement, such as letters of credit or bond insurance premiums).[36]

---

[28] I.R.C. § 141(b).
[29] I.R.C. § 141(b)(3).
[30] I.R.C. § 141(b)(4).
[31] I.R.C. § 141(c).
[32] I.R.C. § 147.
[33] I.R.C. § 147(b).
[34] *See* I.R.C. § 147(h)(1).
[35] I.R.C. § 147(f).
[36] I.R.C. § 147(g); STAFF OF THE JOINT COMM. ON TAXATION, 99TH CONG., 2D SESS., TAX REFORM BILL OF 1986, FINAL CONFERENCE COMM. DECISIONS II-730 (Joint Comm. Print 1986) [hereinafter TRA '86 Conf. Rep.].

And fourth, no portion of such issue can generally be used to provide any airplane, skybox or other private luxury box, health club facilities, facilities primarily used for gambling, or liquor stores.[37]

Three requirements only apply to private activity bonds that are not qualified 501(c)(3) bonds, mortgage revenue bonds, or qualified student loan bonds. First, such bonds cannot be held by any person that is a substantial user of the bond-financed facilities, or by a person related to such substantial user.[38]

Second, less than 25 percent of the net proceeds from the bond issue can be used to acquire land, and no part of the proceeds can be used to directly or indirectly acquire farm land.[39] An exception is available for first-time farmers and for land acquired for certain environmental purposes.[40]

Third, bond proceeds cannot be used to acquire property unless the first use of the property is pursuant to the bond-financed acquisition, or the property is substantially rehabilitated.[41]

(ii) Limits on Aggregate Amount of Private Activity Bonds

The Code now limits the aggregate amount of certain types of private activity bonds that a state can issue during any calendar year.[42] The Code now limits the aggregate amount of private activity bonds other than qualified 501(c)(3) bonds,[43] certain refunding bonds,[44] qualified veterans' mortgage bonds,[45] qualified exempt facility bonds for airports, docks and wharves,[46] and certain government-owned solid waste disposal facilities.[47]

The state limit for 1987 was $75 multiplied by the state's population, or $250 million.[48] After 1987, each state's calendar year volume limitation is

---

[37] I.R.C. § 147(e). Proceeds of qualified 501(c)(3) bonds can be used to finance certain health club facilities.
[38] I.R.C. § 147(a).
[39] I.R.C. § 147(c)(1).
[40] I.R.C. §§ 147(c)(2), 147(c)(3).
[41] I.R.C. § 147(d).
[42] I.R.C. § 146.
[43] I.R.C. § 146(g)(2).
[44] I.R.C. § 146(i).
[45] I.R.C. § 146(g)(1).
[46] I.R.C. § 146(g)(3).
[47] I.R.C. § 146(h).
[48] I.R.C. § 146(d)(1).

the greater of $50 multiplied by the state's population, or $150 million.[49] Each state's volume cap is allocated among state agencies and other issuing authorities, including, in Illinois, constitutional home rule cities.[50] Also, under certain circumstances, an issuer can elect to carry forward its unused volume cap for specified purposes.[51]

(2) PRIVATE ACTIVITY BOND FINANCING

The remainder of this section addresses in broad brush the tax requirements of private activity bonds. It is intended to merely acquaint the reader with private activity bond financing; it is not intended to be a comprehensive analysis.

Numerous statutory exceptions, special rules, and transitional provisions apply to private activity bonds.[52] Even if a security meets the definition of a private activity bond under the general rule of I.R.C. § 103(b) and it complies with the applicable requirements of I.R.C. §§ 146 and 147, the security is taxable unless it falls within one of the specific exemptions contained in I.R.C. § 141(e). These exemptions include exempt facility bonds,[53] qualified mortgage bonds,[54] qualified veterans' bonds,[55] qualified small issue bonds,[56] qualified student loan bonds,[57] qualified redevelopment bonds,[58] and qualified 501(c)(3) bonds.[59] The remainder of this section discusses each of these exemptions.

(i) Exempt Facility Private Activity Bonds

If a private activity bond is issued for one of the purposes of financing an exempt facility described in I.R.C. § 142 and the bond meets all of the Code requirements, it qualifies for tax exemption under I.R.C. § 103(a). There is no limitation on the dollar amount available to finance exempt

---

[49] I.R.C. § 146(d)(2).
[50] I.R.C. §§ 146(b), 146(c), 146(d)(3), 146(d)(4), 146(e).
[51] I.R.C. § 146(f).
[52] *See, e.g.*, TRA '86, *supra* note 17, §§ 1312-1317.
[53] I.R.C. §§ 141(e)(1)(A), 142.
[54] I.R.C. §§ 141(e)(1)(B), 143(a).
[55] I.R.C. §§ 141(e)(1)(C), 143(b).
[56] I.R.C. §§ 141(e)(1)(D), 144(a).
[57] I.R.C. §§ 141(e)(1)(E), 144(b).
[58] I.R.C. §§ 141(e)(1)(F), 144(c).
[59] I.R.C. §§ 141(e)(1)(G), 145.

facilities for airports, docks, and wharves.[60] All other exempt facility bonds, however, are subject to a volume cap.[61]

A private activity bond issue is exempt under the exempt facility exemption if substantially all of its proceeds are used to provide one of the following facilities:

1. Governmentally owned airports or storage or training facilities directly related to such airports[62]
2. Governmentally owned docks and wharves or storage or training facilities directly related to the foregoing[63]
3. Mass commuting facilities or storage or training facilities directly related to the foregoing[64]
4. Facilities for furnishing water[65]
5. Sewage facilities[66]
6. Solid waste disposal facilities[67]
7. Qualified residential rental projects[68]
8. Facilities for the local furnishing of electric energy or gas[69]
9. Local district heating or cooling facilities[70]
10. Qualified hazardous waste facilities[71]
11. High-speed, intercity rail facilities[72]

I.R.C. § 142 thus sets out a wide range of facilities that are eligible for tax-exempt financing.

TRA '86 removed the tax exemption for exempt facility financing of parking facilities (unless functionally related and subordinate to an exempt facility), mass commuting vehicles, hydroelectric generating

[60] I.R.C. § 146(g)(3).
[61] I.R.C. § 146.
[62] I.R.C. §§ 142(a)(1), 142(b), 142(c).
[63] I.R.C. §§ 142(a)(2), 142(b), 142(c).
[64] I.R.C. §§ 142(a)(3), 142(b), 142(c).
[65] I.R.C. §§ 142(a)(4), 142(e).
[66] I.R.C. § 142(a)(5).
[67] I.R.C. § 142(a)(6).
[68] I.R.C. §§ 142(a)(7), 142(d).
[69] I.R.C. §§ 142(a)(8), 142(f).
[70] I.R.C. §§ 142(a)(9), 142(g).
[71] I.R.C. §§ 142(a)(10), 142(h).
[72] I.R.C. §§ 142(a)(11), 142(i).

facilities, industrial parks, pollution control facilities, sports facilities, and convention or trade show facilities. Qualified hazardous waste facilities,[73] on the other hand, were granted eligibility for tax-exempt financing by TRA '86.

Offices cannot be financed unless the office is located on the premises of an exempt facility.[74] In addition, if the functions performed at such offices are not related to the day-to-day operations at the exempt facility, the unrelated functions performed in such offices must be de minimis to preserve tax-exempt treatment.[75]

(ii) Qualified Mortgage Bonds and Qualified Veterans' Mortgage Bonds

Mortgage bonds, issued by municipalities, provide that all of the proceeds are used directly or indirectly to provide mortgages or other financing for owner-occupied residences.[76] Interest on mortgage bonds issued after April 24, 1979, is generally taxable unless the bonds meet a comprehensive list of requirements as to the types of residences, their locations, the aggregate amount of bonds, and arbitrage limits.[77] The remainder of this section discusses the two types of tax-exempt mortgage bonds—qualified mortgage bonds and qualified veterans' mortgage bonds.

(a) QUALIFIED MORTGAGE BONDS

Qualified mortgage bonds issued before December 31, 1991, as part of a qualified mortgage issue[78] are tax-exempt if eleven conditions are met. First, all proceeds of the issue (except for issuance costs and a debt service reserve fund) must be used to finance owner-occupied residences.[79]

Second, each residence must be a single-family residence that can reasonably be expected to become the principal residence of the mortgagor.[80] Each residence must be located within the jurisdiction of the issuer.

---

[73] I.R.C. § 142(a)(10).
[74] I.R.C. § 142(b)(2)(A).
[75] I.R.C. § 142(b)(2)(B).
[76] I.R.C. §§ 143(a), 143(b).
[77] *See generally* I.R.C. § 143.
[78] I.R.C. § 143(a)(1)(B), *as amended by* Pub. L. No. 101-508, § 11408, 104 Stat. 1388 (1990) [hereinafter RRA '90].
[79] I.R.C. § 143(a)(2)(A)(i).
[80] I.R.C. § 143(c).

Third, at least 95 percent of the net proceeds must be used to finance residences of mortgagors that, within three years prior to the mortgage, had no present ownership interest in their principal residences.[81]

Fourth, the purchase price for each residence must not exceed 90 percent (110 percent in targeted areas) of the applicable average area purchase price for residences.[82]

Fifth, the aggregate amount of all private activity bonds—including qualified mortgage bonds—issued by the municipality during any calendar year must not exceed the volume limitation applicable to such municipality.[83]

Sixth, no financing can be provided for any mortgagor whose family income exceeds 115 percent of the applicable median family income. If the housing is located in a "high housing cost area," however, the limitation is increased for bonds issued after December 31, 1988.[84]

Seventh, the mortgages must be new mortgages.[85]

Eighth, at least 20 percent of the issue proceeds must, with reasonable diligence, be made available to targeted areas.[86] Targeted areas residences are defined in I.R.C. § 143(j).

Ninth, the bonds must not be arbitrage bonds and must meet certain additional arbitrage requirements applicable only to qualified mortgage bonds.[87]

Tenth, for loans originated from bonds issued after December 31, 1988, a 3.5-year loan origination period is imposed.[88]

Eleventh, for loans originated after December 31, 1990, the qualified mortgage bond/mortgage credit certificate subsidy is recaptured from certain high income recipients, whose incomes increase after the financing is received and who sell the homes purchased subject to such subsidy within 10 years of purchase.[89]

TRA '86 permitted issuers of qualified mortgage bonds to elect to issue mortgage bonds, or mortgage credit certificates, to first-time home buy-

---

[81] I.R.C. § 143(d).
[82] I.R.C. § 143(e).
[83] I.R.C. § 146.
[84] I.R.C. § 143(f).
[85] I.R.C. § 143(i).
[86] I.R.C. § 143(h).
[87] I.R.C. §§ 143(a), 148; *see* section 33.3(a)(1)(vi).
[88] I.R.C. § 143(a)(2)(D).
[89] I.R.C. § 143(m).

ers for up to 25 percent of the amount of their qualified mortgagor bond capacity.[90] This authority expires on December 31, 1991.[91]

(b) QUALIFIED VETERANS' MORTGAGE BONDS

Qualified veterans' mortgage bonds are tax-exempt if 95 percent or more of the net proceeds are used to finance single-family owner-occupied residences for veterans.[92] Qualified veterans' mortgage bonds issued after July 18, 1984, must meet seven additional requirements. First, each mortgagor must be a "qualified veteran" that applies for financing before the later of January 1, 1985, or 30 years after he left active military service. A qualified veteran is defined as any veteran that served on active duty at some time before January 1, 1977.[93]

Second, the municipality's mortgage program for veterans must have been in effect before June 22, 1984.[94]

Third, the aggregate amount of all private activity bonds issued by the municipality, including qualified veterans' mortgage bonds, during the calendar year must not exceed the volume limitation applicable to such municipality.[95]

Fourth, each residence must be a single-family residence that can reasonably be expected to become the principal residence of the mortgagor.[96] Each residence must be located within the jurisdiction of the issuer.

Fifth, the bonds must not be arbitrage bonds and must meet certain additional arbitrage requirements applicable only to qualified veterans' mortgage bonds.[97]

Sixth, the mortgages must be new mortgages.[98]

Seventh, both interest and principal repayment obligations for qualified veterans' mortgage bonds must be secured by the general obligation of the municipality.[99] Qualified mortgage bonds are subject to the volume limitation imposed by I.R.C. § 146.

---

[90] I.R.C. §§ 25(d)(2)(A), 25(f)(2).
[91] I.R.C. §§ 25(h), 143(a)(1)(B), *as amended by* RRA '90, *supra* note 78, § 11408.
[92] I.R.C. § 143(b)(1).
[93] I.R.C. §§ 143(b)(1), 143(l)(4).
[94] I.R.C. § 143(l)(2).
[95] I.R.C. § 146.
[96] I.R.C. § 143(c).
[97] I.R.C. § 143(g).
[98] I.R.C. § 143(i)(1).
[99] I.R.C. § 143(b)(2).

(iii) Small Issue Exemption

Certain private activity bonds that qualify for the small issue exemption generate tax-exempt interest.[100] The $1 million small issue exemption is available to private activity bond issues with an aggregate authorized face amount of $1 million or less. At least 95 percent of the net proceeds of private activity bonds must be used for one of two purposes. Either 95 percent of the proceeds must be used for the acquisition, construction, reconstruction, or improvement of land (subject to the 25 percent limit), or property of a character subject to an allowance for depreciation, or 95 percent must be used to redeem all or part of a prior issue that was used for such purposes.[101] The proceeds of a small issue exemption financing are not available to finance inventory or to provide working capital for a business.[102]

The IRS has ruled that the simultaneous issuance of several series of qualified small issue bonds of $1 million can qualify for the small issue exemption if (1) the qualified small issue bonds are not sold at substantially the same time, (2) the qualified small issue bonds are not sold pursuant to a common plan of marketing, (3) the qualified small issue bonds are not sold at substantially the same rate of interest, and (4) a common or pooled security is not used or available to pay debt service on the qualified small issue bonds.[103]

For bonds issued after December 31, 1978, a $10 million small issue limitation can be elected in certain cases.[104] Expenses of issuing bonds are capital expenditures that must be included in determining whether the $10 million limitation is met.[105] To compute the $10 million limitation—for three years before and three years after the date of issuance of the bonds—all capital expenditures relating to facilities in the same municipality and used by the same or related user must be aggregated.[106] The proceeds of a $10 million issue must be used for the same purposes authorized for the $1 million exemption.

---

[100] I.R.C. §§ 103(a), 144(a).

[101] I.R.C. § 144(a).

[102] Treas. Reg. § 1.103-10(b)(1)(ii) (1986).

[103] Rev. Rul. 81-216, 1981-2 C.B. 21 (revoked by IR-81-102, 10 Stand. Fed. Tax Rep. (CCH) ¶ 6750 (Sept. 3, 1981)), *revoking* Rev. Rul. 74-380, 1974-2 C.B. 32; Rev. Rul. 77-55, 1977-1, C.B. 18; Rev. Rul. 78-159, 1978-1 C.B. 27.

[104] I.R.C. § 144(a)(4).

[105] Rev. Rul. 77-234, 1977-2 C.B. 39.

[106] I.R.C. § 144(a)(4)(A)(ii); LTR 840639 (Nov. 7, 1983); LTR 8347050 (Aug. 22, 1983); LTR 8347043 (Aug. 22, 1983); LTR 8347040 (Aug. 22, 1983); LTR 8345007 (Aug. 5, 1983); LTR 8234122 (May 27, 1982); G.C.M. 38,597 (Dec. 30, 1980).

Not more than $40 million of tax-exempt qualified small issue bonds can be outstanding with respect to any person or related persons who owns, occupies, or leases a substantial portion of the bond-financed facilities.[107] Authority for the issuance of qualified small issue bonds for commercial facilities (except for current refunding bonds meeting certain statutory requirements) expired on December 31, 1986.[108] Authority for the issuance of qualified small issue bonds for manufacturing facilities and certain first time farmers is scheduled to expire on December 31, 1991.[109]

Qualified small issue bonds are subject to the volume limitation imposed by I.R.C. § 146.

(iv) Qualified Student Loan Bonds

Qualified student loan bonds generate interest that is excluded from gross income for federal income tax purposes.[110] Loans financed by qualified student loan bonds must be made with at least 90 percent of the net proceeds of such bonds in conjunction with a qualified program established under the federal Higher Education Act of 1965,[111] or with at least 95 percent of the net proceeds of such bonds as part of an eligible state supplemental student loan program.[112]

Qualified student loan bonds are subject to slightly different arbitrage rebate requirements than are other private activity bonds.[113] Qualified student loan bonds are subject to the volume limitation imposed by I.R.C. § 146.

(v) Qualified Redevelopment Bonds

TRA '86 added the tax exemption for the interest on qualified redevelopment bonds.[114] Qualified redevelopment bonds are tax increment bonds where 95 percent or more of the net proceeds are used for redevelopment purposes in any blighted area.[115] The payment of principal, premium (if

---

[107] I.R.C. § 144(a)(10).
[108] I.R.C. § 144(a)(12)(A).
[109] I.R.C. §§ 144(a)(12)(B), 144(a)(12)(C), *as amended by* RRA '90, *supra* note 78, § 11408.
[110] I.R.C. §§ 103(a), 144(b).
[111] Pub. L. No. 89-329, 79 Stat. 1219 (1965); I.R.C. §§ 144(b)(1)(A), 144(b)(2)(A).
[112] I.R.C. §§ 144(b)(1)(B), 144(b)(2)(B).
[113] I.R.C. § 148; *see, e.g.*, I.R.C. §§ 148(f)(4)(D), 148(g).
[114] I.R.C. § 144(c).
[115] I.R.C. § 144(c)(1).

any), and interest on such bonds can only be primarily secured by (1) taxes of general applicability imposed by a general purpose governmental unit, or (2) any increase in real property tax revenues attributable to such increase in assessed value by reason of the redevelopment. (Any increase in real property tax revenues must be reserved exclusively for debt service on the bonds (and similar bonds) to the extent the increase does not exceed debt service.)[116]

Proper redevelopment purposes are defined to include the acquisition of real property, the clearing and preparation for redevelopment of such land, the rehabilitation of such real property, and the relocation of occupants of the real property. It does not include new construction or the enlargement of an existing building.[117]

A designated blighted area is an area so designated by a general purpose local governmental unit in the jurisdiction of the designated area.[118] The designated blighted area must (1) meet certain standards of blight,[119] (2) not exceed 20 percent of the total assessed valuation in the designating governmental unit's jurisdiction,[120] and (3) meet certain minimum acreage requirements.[121] In addition, special user fees or charges cannot be imposed within the redevelopment area.[122] Further, there are also limitations on the use of bond proceeds for certain types of facilities and the land on which they are located, such as food service and certain recreational facilities.[123] The private activity bond limitation on the use of bond proceeds for the acquisition of land imposed by I.R.C. § 147(c) does not apply to qualified redevelopment bonds, except with respect to land for farming purposes and for first time farmers.[124] Qualified redevelopment bonds are subject to the volume limitation imposed by I.R.C. § 146.

(vi) Qualified 501(c)(3) Bonds

(a) IN GENERAL

The interest on bonds issued on behalf of I.R.C. § 501(c)(3) organizations, such as private universities and nonprofit hospitals, is excluded from

---

[116] I.R.C. § 144(c)(2)(B).
[117] I.R.C. § 144(c)(3)(B).
[118] I.R.C. § 144(c)(4)(A).
[119] I.R.C. § 144(c)(4)(B).
[120] I.R.C. § 144(c)(4)(C).
[121] I.R.C. § 144(c)(4)(D).
[122] I.R.C. § 144(c)(5).
[123] I.R.C. § 144(c)(6).
[124] I.R.C. § 144(c)(8).

gross income for federal income tax purposes only if two requirements are met. First, all of the property acquired by the net proceeds of the issue must be owned by one or more I.R.C. § 501(c)(3) organizations or governmental units. Second, 95 percent of the net proceeds of the bonds must be used for an exempt use.[125] The use of such bond proceeds by an I.R.C. § 501(c)(3) organization in an unrelated trade or business—as determined under I.R.C. § 513(a)—does not qualify as a use for an exempt purpose.[126]

Qualified 501(c)(3) bonds, at least 95 percent of the net proceeds of which are used "with respect to a hospital," are "qualified hospital bonds" and, accordingly, are not subject to the $150 million nonhospital bond limitation. Generally, no I.R.C. § 501(c)(3) organization or group of organizations under common management and control can have outstanding at any one time more than $150 million of qualified 501(c)(3) bonds that are not "qualified hospital bonds."[127] TRA '86 does not define "with respect to a hospital." Some guidance can be derived from the House Committee Report,[128] however, which elaborates on a provision of the House Bill[129] that is similar to the $150 million nonhospital bond limitation found in TRA '86.

The House Bill and House Committee Report appeared to narrow financeable expenditures to those expenditures for "facilities,"[130] arguably precluding working capital financing. TRA '86 does not require that financeable expenditures be made only with respect to "facilities," but can be made "with respect to a hospital." This means that working capital financings should be permissible.

The House Committee Report defines the term "hospital" as a "facility" that meets the following requirements. First, it must be accredited by the Joint Commission on Accreditation of Health Care Organizations ("JCAH"), or it must be accredited or approved by a program of the qualified governmental unit in which the facility is located if the Secretary of Health and Human Services has found that the accreditation or comparable approval standards of such qualified governmental unit are essentially equivalent to those of the JCAH. Second, the facility is primarily used to provide diagnostic services and therapeutic services for medical diagnosis, treatment, and care of injured, disabled, or sick

---

[125] I.R.C. § 145(a).

[126] I.R.C. § 145(a)(2)(A).

[127] I.R.C. § 145(b).

[128] HOUSE WAYS AND MEANS COMM. REPORT, H.R. REP. NO. 426, 99th Cong., 1st Sess. 540–41 (1985) [hereinafter H.R. REP. NO. 426].

[129] H.R. 3838, *as passed by* the House of Representatives on December 18, 1985, § 144(b).

[130] *Id.*; H.R. REP. NO. 426, *supra* note 128, at 540–41.

persons as hospital in-patients, under the supervision of physicians (the Joint Committee Report includes persons who are mentally ill in the term "sick persons"). Third, the facility must have a requirement that every patient be under the care and supervision of a physician. Fourth, the facility must provide 24-hour nursing services rendered or supervised by a registered professional nurse, and a licensed practical nurse or registered nurse must be on duty at all times. The term "hospital" does not include rest or nursing homes, day care centers, medical school facilities, research laboratories, or ambulatory care facilities (e.g., surgicenters).[131]

For interest on any qualified 501(c)(3) bond that is not a "qualified hospital bond" to be excluded from gross income for income tax purposes, two conditions must be met. First, the bond must *not* be a part of an issue of nonhospital bonds, the principal amount of which exceeds $150 million. Second, when the principal amount of the bond is added to the principal amount of tax-exempt nonhospital bonds of any 501(c)(3) organization that is a "test period beneficiary"[132] (or certain organizations related to such 501(c)(3) organization), the total nonhospital bonds outstanding for all such organizations cannot exceed $150 million.[133]

Only qualified 501(c)(3) bonds are subject to the $150 million nonhospital bond limitation. I.R.C. § 501(c)(3) organizations can avoid the $150 million nonhospital bond limitation by electing to have nonhospital bonds issued after August 15, 1986, treated as "exempt-facility bonds" or "qualified redevelopment bonds."[134]

For bonds issued after October 21, 1988, state and local governmental units are effectively prevented from issuing qualified 501(c)(3) bonds to purchase rental housing units in other jurisdictions due to a technical amendment to the arbitrage rules characterizing "investment property."[135]

(b) QUALIFIED HOSPITAL BONDS

If the proceeds of qualified 501(c)(3) bonds are used "with respect to a hospital," the bonds are "qualified hospital bonds" and, accordingly, are not subject to the $150 million nonhospital bond limitation. Generally, no I.R.C. § 501(c)(3) organization or group of organizations under common management and control can have outstanding at any one time more

[131] H.R. REP. NO. 426, *supra* note 128, at 540–41.
[132] I.R.C. § 145(b)(4).
[133] I.R.C. § 145(b).
[134] I.R.C. § 145(e).
[135] I.R.C. § 148(b)(2)(E).

than $150 million of qualified 501(c)(3) bonds that are not "qualified hospital bonds."[136]

TRA '86 does not define "with respect to a hospital," although some guidance can be derived from the House Committee Report that accompanied TRA '86,[137] which elaborates on a provision of the House Bill[138] that is similar to the $150 million nonhospital bond limitation found in TRA '86. The House Bill and the House Committee Report appear to narrow financeable expenditures to those expenditures for "facilities,"[139] thereby arguably precluding working capital financing.

Because TRA '86 does not require financeable expenditures to be made only with respect to "facilities"—but "with respect to a hospital"—working capital financings should also be permissible.

The House Committee Report defines the term "hospital" as a "facility" that meets the following requirements. First, it must be accredited by the JCAH, or it must be accredited or approved by a program of the qualified governmental unit in which the facility is located if the Secretary of Health and Human Services has found that the accreditation or comparable approval standards of such qualified governmental unit are essentially equivalent to those of the JCAH.[140] Second, the facility is primarily used to provide diagnostic services and therapeutic services for medical diagnosis, treatment, and care of injured, disabled, or sick persons as hospital in-patients, under the supervision of physicians (the Joint Committee Report includes persons who are mentally ill in the term "sick persons").[141] Third, the facility must have a requirement that every patient be under the care and supervision of a physician.[142] Fourth, the facility must provide 24-hour nursing services rendered or supervised by a registered professional nurse, and a licensed practical nurse or registered nurse must be on duty at all times.[143] The term "hospital" does not include rest or nursing homes, day care centers, medical school facilities, research laboratories, or ambulatory care facilities (e.g., surgicenters).[144]

---

[136] I.R.C. § 145(b).
[137] H.R. REP. NO. 426, *supra* note 128, at 540–41.
[138] H.R. 3838, *supra* note 129, § 144(b).
[139] *Id.*; H.R. REP. NO. 426, *supra* note 128, at 540–41.
[140] H.R. REP. NO. 426, *supra* note 128, at 540–41.
[141] *Id.* at 541; TRA '86 Conf. Rep., *supra* note 36, at II-727.
[142] H.R. REP. NO. 426, *supra* note 128, at 541.
[143] *Id.*
[144] *Id.*

(c) MIXED-USE FACILITIES

Certain bond-financed facilities are treated as mixed-use facilities if a portion of the facilities is used as a hospital and a portion is used as a part of a nonhospital related facility (e.g., a laboratory that serves both a hospital and private physicians' offices). The Conference Report accompanying TRA '86 anticipates that the Treasury will promulgate allocation formulas for such situations. The Conferees suggest, until Treasury guidance is provided, treating bonds as qualified hospital bonds to the extent of the proportionate share of the use of the bond-financed facilities for in-patient hospital services.[145] If 90 percent or more of the net proceeds of an issue are used with respect to a hospital, however, the 10 percent or less used for nonhospital purposes is not counted toward the $150 million limitation.[146]

(d) VOLUME LIMITATION

Unlike most other private activity bonds, qualified 501(c)(3) bonds are not subject to the volume limitation.[147]

(e) RENTAL HOUSING PROJECTS

Provisions of TMRA '88[148] subject qualified 501(c)(3) bonds issued after October 21, 1988, for the acquisition of existing rental housing projects where there will be no substantial rehabilitation, to the income limits already in effect for private purpose multifamily housing bonds.[149] Also, for bonds issued after October 21, 1988, state and local governmental units are effectively prevented from issuing qualified 501(c)(3) bonds to purchase rental housing units in other jurisdictions due to a technical amendment to the arbitrage rules characterizing "investment property."[150]

---

[145] TRA '86 Conf. Rep., *supra* note 36, at II-727.
[146] I.R.C. § 145(b)(3).
[147] I.R.C. § 146(g)(2).
[148] Pub. L. No. 100-647, 102 Stat. 3342 (1988) [hereinafter TMRA '88].
[149] I.R.C. § 145(d).
[150] I.R.C. § 148(b)(2)(E).

(f) LAND ACQUISITIONS

The limitation on use of bond proceeds for land acquisition does not apply to qualified 501(c)(3) bonds.[151] If 25 percent or more of the proceeds of an issue of qualified 501(c)(3) bonds is used to acquire land, the land is assigned a 30-year useful life for calculation of the average maturity limitation, instead of being assigned a zero useful life.[152]

§ 33.3 GENERAL TAX PRINCIPLES

This section addresses the general tax principles that apply to tax-exempt securities. Section 33.3(a) addresses interest income. Section 33.3(b) addresses state taxation. Section 33.3(c) addresses sales of tax-exempt securities. Section 33.3(d) addresses interest to purchase or carry tax-exempt securities.

(a) INTEREST INCOME

This section discusses current issues with respect to the interest exemption from federal income tax.

(1) FEDERAL INCOME TAX

(i) In General

Interest income earned on municipal securities is not includable in gross income for federal income tax purposes,[153] which makes municipal securities attractive investments for taxpayers in high marginal tax brackets. The Supreme Court recently held in *South Carolina v. Baker*,[154] that owners of municipal bonds are not constitutionally entitled to an exemption from taxes on the income they earn from municipal bonds, and upheld the constitutionality of section 310(b)(1) of TEFRA,[155] which requires long-term municipal bonds to be issued in registered form in

---

[151] I.R.C. §§ 147(c), (h)(2).
[152] I.R.C. § 147(b)(3)(B).
[153] I.R.C. § 103(a).
[154] 485 U.S. 505, *reh'g denied*, 486 U.S. 1062 (1988).
[155] Pub. L. No. 97-248, 96 Stat. 324 (1982) [hereinafter TEFRA].

order for the interest on such bonds to be excluded from gross income for federal income tax purposes.[156]

(a) Municipal Securities with Interest in Default

If municipal securities are purchased when interest payments are in default, any amounts subsequently paid on the outstanding unpaid interest amount are treated as a return of capital, not as the payment of tax-exempt interest.[157] The taxpayer's remaining cost basis is thereby reduced. For a discussion of flat bonds generally, see section 31.8.

(b) Original Issue Discount

Any OID on municipal securities is treated as interest, which means that the discount is exempt from federal income taxes.[158] If municipal securities are sold before maturity, each holder of the security is entitled to apportion the amount of OID.[159]

(c) Premiums

A premium received on a redemption of tax-exempt securities is not interest. Rather, it is taxable as an amount received in exchange for the securities.[160]

(d) Sales

Gain on the sale of municipal securities, except to the extent attributable to accrued interest or OID, is also taxable income.[161]

---

[156] The Code has provided a tax exemption for municipal securities since 1913. For a discussion of *South Carolina v. Baker*, see Note, *Municipal Bond Financing After South Carolina v. Baker and the Tax Reform Act of 1986: Can State Sovereignty Reemerge?*, 42 TAX LAW. 147 (1988) (authored by Patricia Trujillo).

[157] Clyde E. Pierce Corp. v. Comm'r, 120 F.2d 206, 208 (5th Cir. 1941); R.O. Holton & Co. v. Comm'r, 44 B.T.A. 202, 206 (1941); Treas. Reg. § 1.61-7(c) (1966); G.C.M. 39,586 (June 24, 1986).

[158] Rev. Rul. 73-112, 1973-1 C.B. 47.

[159] For a discussion of how OID is allocated for tax-exempt securities, see generally section 31.2(e).

[160] For a discussion of premiums, see section 31.4.

[161] Willcuts v. Bunn, 282 U.S. 216, 224 (1931), *rev'g* 35 F.2d 29 (8th Cir. 1929), *aff'g* 29 F.2d 132 (D.C. Minn. 1928).

(ii) Federal Guarantees

If municipal securities that are otherwise tax-exempt are directly or indirectly guaranteed by the United States government (or its instrumentalities or agencies), interest income on the securities is not exempt from tax.[162] This prohibition against federal guarantees generally applies to all municipal securities issued after December 31, 1983.[163]

There are three different ways in which a security is viewed as federally guaranteed. First, an obligation is federally guaranteed if the payment of principal or interest is guaranteed in whole or in part by the United States government, any federal agency, or federal instrumentality.[164] Second, a security is federally guaranteed if five percent or more of the proceeds is used to make loans (where the payment of principal or interest is guaranteed by the United States, any federal agency, or federal instrumentality) or the proceeds are invested directly or indirectly in federally insured deposits or accounts.[165] Third, a security is federally guaranteed if the payment of principal or interest is indirectly guaranteed by the United States government, any federal agency, or federal instrumentality.[166] Letters of credit are not considered to be federal guarantees for this purpose.[167]

There are several exceptions to the prohibition against federal guarantees. First, a security is not deemed to be federally guaranteed by reason of certain insurance programs, such as the insurance programs of FNMA, FHLMC, GNMA, SLMA, the Federal Housing Administration, or the Veteran's Administration (or the Bonneville Power Authority for certain bonds).[168] I.R.C. § 149(b)(3)(B) provides that investments in addition to those listed in the Code can be exempt from the prohibitions if permitted under regulations. On October 10, 1990, the Treasury issued temporary regulations providing for an exception from the prohibition of federal guarantees for investments in obligations issued by Resolution Funding

---

[162] I.R.C. § 149(b).

[163] Pub. L. No. 98-369, § 631(c)(1), 98 Stat. 494 (1984) [hereinafter DRA].

[164] I.R.C. § 149(b)(2)(A). Interest on debt securities issued to develop geothermal energy is taxable if the repayment of principal or interest is guaranteed under Title V of the Department of Energy Act of 1978—Civilian Applications (Pub. L. No. 95-238, 92 Stat. 47 (1978)). Rev. Rul. 80-161, 1980-1 C.B. 21.

[165] I.R.C. § 149(b)(2)(B).

[166] I.R.C. § 149(b)(2)(C).

[167] Federal Deposit Ins. Corp. v. Philadelphia Gear Corp., 476 U.S. 426 (1986), *on remand*, 795 F.2d 903 (10th Cir. 1986), *rev'g* 474 U.S. 918 (1985), *aff'g in part, rev'g in part* 587 F. Supp. 294 (W.D. Okla. 1984).

[168] I.R.C. § 149(b)(3)(A).

Corporation pursuant to FIRREA.[169] As a result, obligations issued by Resolution Funding Corporation are exempt from the prohibition against federal guarantees for investments made on or after October 2, 1990.[170]

Second, some securities generate tax-exempt interest even though they are federally insured (e.g., securities to finance residential rental property occupied by low or moderate income individuals,[171] qualified mortgage bonds,[172] and qualified veterans' mortgage bonds),[173] provided the proceeds are not invested in federally insured deposits or accounts.[174] Other exceptions allow certain temporary investments, investments in Treasury obligations, investments in a reasonably required reserve and replacement fund, and investments of a bona fide debt service fund.[175]

In the past, certain municipal securities have been issued that were secured by certificates of deposit that are federally insured by either the FSLIC or the FDIC in amounts up to $100,000 for each security holder. Municipal securities issued after April 14, 1983 (or issued pursuant to a binding contract in effect on or after March 4, 1983) are not tax-exempt if the proceeds of the issue are invested in federally insured deposits or accounts.[176]

(iii) Registration Requirements

Municipal securities issued after December 31, 1982, must be issued in registered form in order for interest on them to be tax-exempt.[177] This provision, originally enacted as part of TEFRA in 1982,[178] provides certain exemptions for securities not issued to the public,[179] securities with a maturity of not more than one year after issuance,[180] and certain obligations intended to be sold to non-United States persons.[181] TEFRA originally provided a December 31, 1982, effective date for registration

---

[169] T.D. 8313 (1990-44 I.R.B. 7).
[170] *Id., amending* Temp. Treas. Reg. § 1.149(b)(3)-1T (1990).
[171] I.R.C. § 149(b)(3)(C)(i)(I).
[172] I.R.C. § 149(b)(3)(C)(i)(II); *see* section 33.2(c)(2)(ii).
[173] I.R.C. § 149(b)(3)(C)(i)(III); *see* section 33.2(c)(2)(ii).
[174] I.R.C. § 149(b)(3)(C)(ii).
[175] I.R.C. § 149(b)(3)(B).
[176] I.R.C. § 149(c)(2).
[177] I.R.C. § 149(a).
[178] TEFRA, *supra* note 155, § 310(b)(1).
[179] I.R.C. § 149(a)(2).
[180] *Id.*
[181] *Id.*; Temp. Treas. Reg. § 1.163-5T(c) (1984).

requirements.[182] TCA '82 delayed, until July 1, 1983, the effective date for those tax-exempt securities that were not required to be in registered form on the day before TEFRA's enactment (i.e., September 2, 1982).[183]

An additional penalty is imposed on owners of nonregistered tax-exempt securities that are required to be in registered form. Loss on the sale, exchange, theft, loss, or other disposition of nonregistered securities is not deductible if the security should be—but is not—in registered form.[184] In addition, gain on the disposition of securities required to be registered that would otherwise be tax-exempt (except that they are not issued in registered form) is taxed as ordinary income, not capital gain.[185]

These registration requirements were found to be constitutional by the Supreme Court in *South Carolina v. Baker*.[186]

(iv) Acquisition of a Put Option

Certain municipal securities have a put option feature that grants the owner the right to sell the securities back to the issuer at par prior to maturity.[187] If interest rates increase, a municipal securities owner would most likely exercise the put option. The tax question is whether the put option affects the tax-exempt status of the interest.

The IRS has ruled that a RIC that purchases municipal securities with put option features is the owner of the tax-exempt securities, despite the fact that the risk of loss on the security is shifted by simultaneously purchasing separate put options.[188] The IRS considered the following factors in reaching this decision. First, the taxpayer paid an arm's length price for the put options, which represented the parties' estimate of the value of the risk.[189] Second, the primary purpose for the taxpayer's acquisition of the put options was to increase liquidity, not to shift the risk of loss.[190] Third, the taxpayer would still benefit from any appreciation in the value of the tax-exempt securities. Fourth, the period during which the risk could be shifted was substantially less than the term of the

---

[182] TEFRA, *supra* note 155, § 310(d)(1).

[183] TCA '82, Pub. L. No. 97-448, § 306(b)(2), 96 Stat. 2365, 2405–06 (1983).

[184] I.R.C. § 165(j)(1).

[185] I.R.C. § 1287. For a discussion of these penalty provisions, see section 31.12.

[186] 485 U.S. 505 (1988), *reh'g denied*, 486 U.S. 1062 (1988).

[187] *See* section 3.3.

[188] Rev. Rul. 82-144, 1982-2 C.B. 34; LTR 8317017 (Jan. 21, 1983); LTR 8247025 (Aug. 18, 1982).

[189] Rev. Rul. 82-144, 1982-2 C.B. 34.

[190] *Id.*

municipal security.[191] Because of this last factor used in the IRS's analysis, it is not clear what effect, if any, a put option feature built into a municipal security that is conterminous with the term of the security would have on the tax-exempt status of the security.

In 1983, without revoking this ruling, the IRS announced that it would not issue rulings "as to the true owner" of securities subject to put options.[192] The Treasury has announced that it has a regulations project pending that will deal with when and whether a put option on a tax-exempt security results in a reissuance of such securities.[193]

(v) Insurance

Municipal securities are frequently backed by a form of insurance, an indemnity, or a guarantee (insuring the issuer's payment obligations), without subjecting the interest income to tax.[194] In the event of a default, the insurance company typically pays the owner of the securities any principal and interest that has not been paid by the issuer.

The IRS has ruled that insuring municipal securities against a default in principal and interest does not affect the tax-exempt status of the interest paid on the securities.[195] In addition, if defaulted interest is eventually paid by the third party, the payment is not included in the gross income of the security owners.[196] Insurance proceeds representing defaulted interest on tax-exempt securities is exempt from gross income, irrespective of whether the insurance is paid for by the issuer, the underwriters, or the security owners.[197] If the securities are guaranteed by

---

[191] *Id.*

[192] Rev. Proc. 83-55, 1983-2 C.B. 572, *superseded by* Rev. Proc. 84-22, 1984-1 C.B. 449.

[193] 55 Fed. Reg. 16,636 (1990). According to the Abstract, "Proposed Regulations would provide guidance regarding whether changes in the terms of an outstanding obligation result in that obligation being treated as retired and reissued as a new obligation."

[194] *See* section 3.3.

[195] Rev. Rul. 76-78, 1976-1 C.B. 25; Rev. Rul. 72-134, 1972-1 C.B. 29, *amplified by* Rev. Rul. 72-575, 1972-2 C.B. 74, *amplified by* Rev. Rul. 76-78, 1976-1 C.B. 25; LTR 8347058 (Aug. 25, 1983); LTR 7801017 (Oct. 7, 1977), *modified by* LTR 7816004 (Jan. 17, 1978).

[196] Rev. Rul. 76-78, 1976-1 C.B. 25; Rev. Rul. 72-134, 1972-2 C.B. 29, *amplified by* Rev. Rul. 72-575, 1972-2 C.B. 74, *amplified by* Rev. Rul. 76-78, 1976-1 C.B. 25; LTR 8347058 (Aug. 25, 1983); LTR 7801017 (Oct. 7, 1977), *modified by* LTR 7816004 (Jan. 17, 1978).

[197] Unlike the line of rulings concerning tax-exempt interest, payments made by an insurance company or surety company to cover defaulted dividend payments may preclude application of the intercorporate dividends received deduction. *See* UNITED STATES STEEL CORPORATION, PROSPECTUS (Supp. Jan. 24, 1985).

the federal government, the interest income on the securities is generally not tax-exempt.[198]

(vi) Arbitrage Bonds and Taxable Municipal Securities

An arbitrage bond is a municipal security where any portion of the proceeds of the issue is reasonably expected to be used directly or indirectly to (1) acquire securities expected to produce a higher yield, or (2) replace funds that were used directly or indirectly to acquire higher yielding investments.[199] Prior to 1969, some municipalities would issue their own tax-exempt securities with the intention of investing a major portion of the proceeds in taxable debt securities with higher interest rates. As a result, the municipality's interest expense was less than the interest income it could earn on its investment in taxable debt securities. It would benefit from this interest rate spread between its arbitrage bonds and the taxable securities.

Interest on arbitrage bonds issued after October 9, 1969 is taxable.[200] The IRS has ruled that the arbitrage limits were violated by a municipality that entered into repurchase agreements as a way of investing its funds.[201] The municipality (i.e., the seller-debtor) transferred its notes pursuant to a repo agreement to a securities dealer in exchange for cash, which the municipality invested in a local government investing pool at a "materially higher" yield.[202]

Some municipalities have issued securities that intentionally do not comply with the arbitrage limitations and that generate taxable interest income. As a result, the municipal issuers can invest the proceeds of the issue at the highest rates available without regard to the arbitrage restrictions. Taxable debt securities pay higher interest rates and thus have a higher interest cost to the municipalities. Nevertheless, because the municipalities are free to invest the funds at a higher rate than they otherwise could if they had to comply with the arbitrage restrictions, this may benefit the issuers. For example, municipal issuers issued $283 million of taxable debt in the first quarter of 1988, $725 million in the first

---

[198] *See* section 33.3(a)(1)(ii).

[199] I.R.C. § 148.

[200] I.R.C. § 103(b)(2). For a discussion of acceptable arbitrage transactions, see Buschman & Winterer, *Legal Arbitrage*, in 1 THE MUNICIPAL BOND HANDBOOK 204 (F. Fabozzi, S. Feldstein, I. Pollack & F. Zarb eds. 1983).

[201] Rev. Rul. 79-108, 1979-1 C.B. 75.

[202] *Id.*

§ 33.3(a)   Financial Products: Taxation, Regulation, and Design   976

quarter of 1987, and $164 million in the first quarter of 1986.[203] In the same month, the Indiana Housing Authority also issued taxable securities.

The remainder of this section provides a brief overview of arbitrage bonds. A detailed discussion is beyond the scope of this book. The arbitrage regulations issued by the Treasury are complex and difficult to apply.[204] TRA '86 extends to all tax-exempt securities (including refunding issues) additional arbitrage restrictions that previously applied to IDBs and single-family housing bonds.[205] These restrictions include the rebate of certain arbitrage profits to the federal government,[206] additional limitations on the investment of bond proceeds,[207] a prohibition against recouping issuance costs (other than credit enhancement fees) from arbitrage earnings,[208] and reducing the amount of bond proceeds that can be used to fund a reasonably required reserve and replacement fund from 15 percent to 10 percent.[209]

Somewhat different requirements apply to different kinds of municipal securities. For example, certain governmental units that issue $5 million or less of tax-exempt securities (other than private activity bonds) in any year can issue certain small issues ($5 million or less in any year) that are not subject to the rebate requirements.[210] Also, governmental bonds and qualified 501(c)(3) bonds are not subject to the limitations on investment in nonpurpose investments.[211] Nonpurpose investments are defined as investments that are not acquired to carry out the governmental purpose of the issuer.[212]

---

[203] See Carlson, *Los Angeles County Discovers Benefits in Taxable Securities*, Wall St. J., Dec. 10, 1985, at 33, col. 1; Yacik, *Municipal Issuers Sell $1.93 Billion of Taxable Debt So Far This Year*, THE BOND BUYER, Sept. 2, 1986, at 1, col. 2; Datta, *First Quarter Taxable Sales Fall to $283 Million, Lowest Since 1986*, THE BOND BUYER, Apr. 21, 1988, at 4, col. 1.

[204] In fact, the regulations were amended six times in a six-year period prior to adoption of final regulations.

[205] See generally Report of the Anthony Commission on Public Finance—Preserving the Federal—State—Local Partnership: The Role of Tax-Exempt Financing, reprinted in Special Report, 15 DAILY TAX HIGHLIGHTS & DOCUMENTS 1291 (1989).

[206] I.R.C. § 148(f).

[207] I.R.C. §§ 148(c), 148(d), 148(e).

[208] I.R.C. § 148(h).

[209] I.R.C. § 148(d).

[210] I.R.C. § 148(f)(4)(C).

[211] I.R.C. § 148(d)(3).

[212] I.R.C. § 148(f)(6).

The Treasury Department recently released lengthy rebate regulations[213] which apply to private activity bonds issued after December 31, 1985, and governmental bonds issued after August 31, 1986. These regulations have been the source of considerable controversy. On May 25, 1990, the Committee on Ways and Means recommended simplification of both the statutory and regulatory framework of rebate.[214] The rebate regulations are characterized as "impos[ing] administrative burdens significantly in excess of those necessary to ensure compliance with Congressional objectives in enacting the rebate requirement."[215]

Whether a security is an arbitrage bond depends on the issuer's reasonable expectations—on the date of issue—as to the amount and use of the proceeds.[216] The Treasury regulations contemplate that issuers can issue "no arbitrage certificates" to express their reasonable expectations that the bonds are tax-exempt.[217] Although the applicable Treasury regulations state that subsequent events do not affect a certification made in accordance with the issuer's reasonable expectations on the date of issue,[218] TRA '86 provides that a bond is treated as an arbitrage bond if the issuer intentionally and improperly invests bond or replacement proceeds.[219] Certificates issued in bad faith, however, where a municipality reasonably expected to use all or a major portion of the proceeds to acquire higher yield securities, cannot be relied on and such bonds are arbitrage bonds.[220]

The IRS, in published rulings, has taken the position that certain outstanding municipal securities are taxable.[221] The IRS found that, after the securities had been issued, the issuers acted in a manner that violated the arbitrage rules. The investors had relied on "no arbitrage certifications" based on the reasonable expectations of the issuers at the time the securities were issued. In another published ruling, improper arbitrage actions of the issuer were found to have occurred at the time the securities

---

[213] Temp. Treas. Reg. §§ 1.148-0T, 1.148-1T, 1.148-2T, 1.148-3T, 1.148-4T, 1.148-5T, 1.148-6T, 1.148-7T, 1.148-8T, 1.148-9T, 1.150-0T (1989).

[214] HOUSE WAYS AND MEANS COMM., 101ST CONG., 2D SESS., WRITTEN PROPOSALS ON TAX SIMPLIFICATION (Comm. Print 1990), *reprinted in* 17 DAILY TAX HIGHLIGHTS & DOCUMENTS 2871 (1990).

[215] *Id.* at 31.

[216] Treas. Reg. § 1.103-13(a)(2)(i) (1979).

[217] Treas. Reg. § 1.103-13(a)(2)(ii)(B) (1979).

[218] Treas. Reg. § 1.103-13(a)(2)(ii)(F) (1979).

[219] I.R.C. § 148(a).

[220] Rev. Rul. 85-182, 1985-2 C.B. 39.

[221] *See* Rev. Rul. 80-91, 1980-1 C.B. 29; Rev. Rul. 80-92, 1980-1 C.B. 31; Rev. Rul. 85-182, 1985-2 C.B. 39.

were issued.[222] The IRS found the securities to be taxable. In addition, a municipality cannot rely on its no arbitrage certification if the certification is made in bad faith.[223] The major impact of these published rulings is that investors that acquire securities which they believe to be tax-exempt may subsequently find themselves taxed on interest earned on those securities if the issuer acts in violation of the arbitrage regulations. The IRS has announced, under certain limited circumstances, it will consider entering into closing agreements with issuers that agree to give up their arbitrage profit to preserve the tax-exempt status of interest paid on their securities issued before April 30, 1982, or with respect to which a private ruling was sought before that date.[224]

(vii) Limitations on Advance Refundings

TRA '86 imposes stricter limitations on the ability of issuers to advance refund tax-exempt bonds with a second issue of tax-exempt bonds issued after August 15, 1986.[225] Because many tax-exempt bonds are not callable for redemption until 10 years or more after issuance, advance refunding is often used by issuers to reduce their interest costs. In an advance refunding, the proceeds of a second issue of tax-exempt bonds are invested—typically in direct or fully guaranteed obligations of the federal government—in an irrevocable account held by a trustee. The proceeds are in an amount sufficient (when added to their earnings) to pay the principal of, premium (if any), and interest on the first issue of bonds to the date fixed for redemption of the first issue.

Virtually all tax-exempt bonds may be refunded on a current basis (i.e., where the refunded bonds are called for redemption within 90 days after the issuance of tax-exempt refunding bonds).[226] Advance refunding bonds (bonds issued more than 90 days prior to the redemption of the refunded bonds), however, must meet a variety of requirements. First, only governmental bonds and most qualified 501(c)(3) bonds can be advance refunded on a tax-exempt basis.[227]

---

[222] Rev. Rul. 80-328, 1980-2 C.B. 53.

[223] Rev. Rul. 85-182, 1985-2 C.B. 39.

[224] Announcement of Rev. Rul. 82-101, 1982-1 C.B. 21, in the Internal Revenue Bulletin, IRS News Release I.R. 82-51, 10 Stand. Fed. Tax Rep. (CCH) ¶ 6488 (Apr. 30, 1982).

[225] I.R.C. § 149(d).

[226] I.R.C. § 149(d)(3)(B)(ii).

[227] I.R.C. § 149(d)(2). Certain qualified 501(c)(3) bonds issued to acquire rental housing projects can only be currently refunded and also must meet certain maturity and amount requirements. See TMRA '88, supra note 148, § 5053(c)(3).

Second, refunding bonds must meet one of two requirements. If the original bonds are issued after 1985, the refunding bonds must be the first advance refunding of the original bonds, or if the original bond was issued before 1986, the refunding bonds must be the first or second advance refunding of the original bonds. Bonds issued prior to 1986 may be refunded one more time, however, even if they have been refunded more than twice before.[228]

Third, if the issuer can realize present value debt service savings (without regard to provision for administrative expenses), the refunded bonds must be redeemed in one of two ways. If the refunded bond was issued after 1985, it must be redeemed on the first call date,[229] or if the refunded bond was issued before 1986, it must be redeemed on the first call date at which such redemption may be made at a redemption price of 103 percent or less.[230]

Fourth, the initial temporary periods during which bond proceeds can be invested at an unrestricted yield are reduced to (1) 30 days from the date of issuance for the refunding bond proceeds, and (2) the temporary periods applicable to new issues under TRA '86 for the refunded bond proceeds.[231]

Fifth, upon issuance of the advance refunding bonds, the minor portion of the refunded bond issue that can be invested at an unrestricted yield is reduced to the lower level applicable to new bonds issued pursuant to TRA '86 (an amount equal to the lesser of five percent of the proceeds of the refunded bonds or $100,000 instead of the 15 percent permissible under prior law).[232] Compliance with this provision may be difficult or impossible in transactions where the refunded bonds were refunding bonds when they were issued and where escrow investments established for the bonds that were refunded by the refunded bonds took advantage of the former, higher, minor portion limitation. Many of these escrows were established as irrevocable escrows with no right of substitution of investments. Even when investments can be substituted in such an escrow, if the initial investment was made in U.S. Treasury Securities, State and Local Government Series, a substantial penalty can be assessed if these investments are redeemed prior to their maturity.[233]

---

[228] I.R.C. §§ 149(d)(3)(A), 149(d)(6).
[229] I.R.C. § 149(d)(3)(A)(ii).
[230] I.R.C. § 149(d)(3)(A)(iii).
[231] I.R.C. § 149(d)(3)(A)(iv).
[232] I.R.C. § 149(d)(3)(A)(v).
[233] 31 C.F.R. § 344.5 (1989).

Sixth, TRA '86 prohibits certain abusive transactions designed to obtain a material financial advantage (based on arbitrage) apart from savings attributable to lower interest rates.[234]

Seventh, RRA '89[235] requires an analysis of refunding bonds to see if they are taxable hedge bonds. For a description of the hedge bond provisions, including their application to refunding bonds, see section 33.3(a)(1)(ix).

(viii) Information Reporting

TRA '86 extends to all tax-exempt securities the requirement that issuers file an information report with the IRS with respect to certain tax-exempt bonds.[236] The report contains certain information regarding the issuer, the bond issue, the property financed, the principal users (for private activity bonds), a certification with respect to compliance with the volume cap (if applicable) and any other information that is required by the IRS.[237]

(ix) Hedge Bonds

RRA '89 imposed a new category of taxable municipal bonds, called "hedge bonds,"[238] to address a perceived abuse in which an issuer would issue tax-exempt bonds to "lock in" current interest rates, investing the proceeds until the issuer was ready to proceed with the intended use of the bond proceeds. If interest rates were higher when time arrived to spend the bond proceeds, the hedge bond proceeds would be used for governmental purposes; if interest rates had fallen, the hedge bonds would be retired with the invested proceeds and new bonds, with the then existing lower interest rates, would be issued to fund the issuer's purposes.

Under the new hedge bond rules, a bond issue is a "hedge bond" issue if either: (1) more than 50 percent of its proceeds are invested in nonpurpose investments having a substantially guaranteed yield for four years or more;[239] or (2) the issuer does not reasonably expect that 85 percent or more of the spendable proceeds will be used to carry out the governmen-

---

[234] I.R.C. § 149(d)(4).
[235] Pub. L. No. 101-239, 103 Stat. 2301 (1989) [hereinafter RRA '89].
[236] I.R.C. § 149(e)(1).
[237] I.R.C. § 149(e)(2).
[238] I.R.C. § 149(g).
[239] I.R.C. § 149(g)(3)(A)(ii).

tal purpose of the issue within three years of the bonds' issuance.[240] Hedge bonds are taxable unless two conditions are met. First, at least 95 percent of the reasonably expected costs of issuance are paid within 180 days of the date of issue and the payment of such costs is not contingent.[241] And second, at issuance, the issuer reasonably expects to spend for the governmental purposes of the issue:

1. 10 percent of the spendable proceeds of the issue within 12 months after the date of the issue.[242] A transition rule of RRA '89 increases this to 15 percent for bonds issued before January 1, 1991, which received appropriate governmental approval prior to November 18, 1989.[243]
2. 30 percent within 24 months after the date of the issue.[244]
3. 60 percent within 36 months after the date of the issue.[245] A transition rule of RRA '89 reduces this to 50 percent for bonds issued before January 1, 1991, which received appropriate governmental approval prior to November 18, 1989.[246]
4. 85 percent within 60 months after the date of the issue.[247]

Generally, refunding bonds are not treated as hedge bonds if the bonds they refund are not hedge bonds.[248] Special rules apply to refundings of bonds issued before the effective date of the hedge bond rules[249] and bonds, the proceeds of which are used for construction projects having a construction period in excess of five years.[250]

A narrow exception allows issuers to avoid characterization of a bond issue as hedge bonds if 95 percent of the net proceeds of the issue (excluding amounts invested in a bona fide debt service fund, and investment earnings held for not more than 30 days pending reinvestment) is invested in tax-exempt bonds not subject to alternative minimum tax.[251]

---

[240] I.R.C. § 149(g)(3)(A)(i).
[241] I.R.C. §§ 149(f)(3), 149(g)(1)(B).
[242] I.R.C. § 149(g)(2)(A).
[243] RRA '89, *supra* note 235, § 7651(b)(4).
[244] I.R.C. § 149(g)(2)(B).
[245] I.R.C. § 149(g)(2)(C).
[246] RRA '89, *supra* note 235, § 7651(b)(4).
[247] I.R.C. § 149(g)(2)(D).
[248] I.R.C. § 149(g)(3)(C)(i).
[249] I.R.C. §§ 149(g)(3)(C)(ii), (iii).
[250] I.R.C. § 149(g)(4)(A).
[251] I.R.C. § 149(a)(3)(B).

These provisions generally apply to bonds issued after September 15, 1989.[252] Certain exceptions to the hedge bond effective date provisions exist for bonds sold or offered for sale prior to September 15, 1989.[253] Also, the hedge bond provisions do not apply to bonds issued to fund a self-insurance fund prior to July 1, 1990, if the issue received appropriate governmental approval prior to September 15, 1989.[254]

(2) ESTATE AND GIFT TAXES

Municipal securities are subject to estate and gift taxes.[255] The tax exemption provided in I.R.C. § 103(a) is limited to federal income tax on interest income. Estate tax[256] and gift tax[257] are both viewed as excise taxes on the transfer of property, not as a tax on the property transferred. For estate tax purposes, a decedent's gross estate includes all property, real or personal, tangible or intangible, wherever situated.[258] In addition, a decedent's estate includes the value of all property to the extent of the decedent's interest in the property at the time of his death.[259] The same rationale applies to gifts.

(3) SOCIAL SECURITY BENEFITS

Gross income includes up to one-half of a taxpayer's social security and railroad retirement benefits received in any taxable year after 1983.[260] The amount included in gross income is the lesser of one-half of the benefit, plus modified adjusted gross income, minus the base amount.[261] Modified adjusted gross income includes tax-exempt interest received or accrued by the taxpayer during the taxable year.[262] This means that some

---

[252] RRA '89, *supra* note 235, § 7651(b)(1).

[253] The hedge bond provisions do not apply if the bonds were sold before September 15, 1989, and issued before October 15, 1989 (*Id.* § 7651(b)(2)), or if preliminary offering materials were mailed to the underwriting syndicate prior to September 15, 1989 (*Id.* § 7651(b)(3)).

[254] *Id.* § 7651(b)(5).

[255] United States v. Wells Fargo Bank, 485 U.S. 351 (1988), *rev'g* Rosenberg v. United States, 481 U.S. 107 (1987); Greiner v. Lewellyn, 258 U.S. 384 (1922); Knowlton v. Moore, 178 U.S. 41 (1900); *contra* DRA, *supra* note 163, § 641.

[256] Treas. Reg. § 20.2033-1(a) (1963).

[257] Willcuts v. Bunn, 282 U.S. at 230; I.R.C. § 2511(a); Treas. Reg. § 25.2511-1(a) (1983).

[258] I.R.C. § 2031(1).

[259] I.R.C. § 2033.

[260] I.R.C. §§ 86(a), (d)(1).

[261] I.R.C. § 86(b)(1).

[262] I.R.C. § 86(b)(2); Goldin v. Baker, 809 F.2d 187 (2d Cir.), *cert. denied*, 484 U.S. 816 (1987).

recipients of social security and railroad retirement benefits that also receive tax-exempt interest income have a greater portion of their benefits subject to tax.

(4) ORIGINAL ISSUE DISCOUNT AND MARKET DISCOUNT

The IRS has ruled that to the extent discount on municipal securities is OID, it is treated as tax-exempt interest.[263] Market discount, on the other hand, is not treated as tax-exempt interest.[264] Prior to the DRA in 1984,[265] OID on tax-exempt securities was apportioned among the original holder and subsequent holders of a tax-exempt security on a straight-line basis over the term of the security.[266] In many cases, the straight-line method resulted in artificially large portions of a security's OID being attributed to its earlier periods, thereby increasing its owner's tax basis in the security. Furthermore, because the security owner reduces the amount realized on disposition by accrued (albeit tax-exempt) OID, the use of the straight-line method also frequently results in the recognition of a loss on a sale of the security at the market price.[267]

The DRA amended the Code in 1984 to eliminate so-called artificial losses. OID on tax-exempt securities is now accrued in the same manner as is required for OID on debt securities issued by corporations and other entities.[268] This means that for tax-exempt securities issued after September 3, 1982, and acquired after March 1, 1984, OID is accrued under the economic or constant interest method (a compound interest method) to reflect the actual market appreciation of these securities.[269] For a discussion of OID, see section 31.2. For a discussion of market discount, see section 31.3.

(b) STATE TAXATION

State, city, and other local taxes (collectively "state taxes") are beyond the scope of this book. Nevertheless, because state taxation frequently

---

[263] Rev. Rul. 73-112, 1973-1 C.B. 47.

[264] *Id.*

[265] DRA, *supra* note 163, § 41(a).

[266] Rev. Rul. 73-112, 1973-1 C.B. 47; *see also* HOUSE CONFERENCE REPORT, DEFICIT REDUCTION ACT OF 1984, H.R. CONF. REP. NO. 861, 98th Cong., 2d Sess. 810 (1984).

[267] HOUSE WAYS AND MEANS COMM. REPORT, DEFICIT REDUCTION ACT OF 1984, H.R. REP. NO. 432, 98th Cong., 2d Sess. 1178, *reprinted in* 1984 U.S. CODE CONG. & ADMIN. NEWS 697, 851 [hereinafter H.R. REP. NO. 432].

[268] I.R.C. § 1288(a).

[269] See H.R. REP. NO. 432, *supra* note 267, at 1178; section 31.2.

plays an important part in a taxpayer's decision to acquire municipal securities, this section briefly mentions some state tax considerations. Typically, a decision to acquire a municipal security is based on the security's after-tax yield, which requires consideration of state, as well as federal taxes. With state taxes currently deductible from gross income for federal tax purposes, the benefit of this deduction must also be factored in to determine the after-tax yield of a particular security.[270]

Interest income on municipal securities is not always subject to state taxes. This is because there are basically three approaches to state taxation. First, some states do not tax municipal securities at all. Second, some states tax only nonlocal municipal securities. Third, other states tax all municipal securities. Furthermore, if a state imposes tax on municipal securities, the tax is typically in one of the three following forms: Some states impose a tax on interest, others impose a tax on personal property, while others tax gains on the sale of municipal securities. For a state-by-state discussion of state taxes, see *State Tax Reports (CCH)*.

(c) SALES OF TAX-EXEMPT SECURITIES

Although interest income on municipal securities is exempt from federal income taxes, gains on the sale of such securities are taxable. The definition of gross income includes "gains derived from dealings in property,"[271] without any exemption for gains on the sales of tax-exempt securities. Capital gain or loss results on the sale of municipal securities held as capital assets by investors[272] and traders.[273] Ordinary income results from the sale of municipal securities held by dealers,[274] hedgers,[275] and certain financial institutions.[276]

As with all types of property, gain or loss is computed by subtracting the adjusted basis of the property from the amount realized.[277] With tax-exempt securities, however, there can be difficulties in determining the basis of the securities and the proceeds from their sale. For a discussion of

---

[270] Of course, future legislative proposals to repeal the deduction for state income taxes would affect the municipal security market. *See, e.g.*, Proctor & Rappaport, *Federal Tax Reform and the Regional Character of the Municipal Bond Market*, FRBNY Q. REV., Autumn 1985, at 6.

[271] I.R.C. § 61(a)(3).

[272] *See* section 8.1.

[273] *See* section 8.2.

[274] *See* section 8.3.

[275] *See* section 8.4.

[276] *See* section 8.8.

[277] I.R.C. § 1001(a); *see generally* Chapter 16.

premiums on tax-exempt securities, see section 31.4(a)(2). For a discussion of discounts and their effect on basis, see sections 31.2(e) and 31.3.

If a tax-exempt security is sold between interest payment dates for a specified price plus accrued interest, the accrued interest is treated as tax-exempt income and is neither part of the sales proceeds nor the cost basis of the security.[278] Parties to a sale of a tax-exempt security cannot arbitrarily adjust the amount of tax-exempt interest on the sale. If the parties agree to allocate interest in a manner different from the interest accrual during their respective holding periods, the allocation adjusts the purchase price and does not affect the allocation of tax-exempt interest income.[279]

(d) INTEREST TO PURCHASE OR CARRY TAX-EXEMPT SECURITIES

An interest deduction is not available for interest on any indebtedness incurred or continued to purchase or carry tax-exempt securities.[280] For a discussion of the limitation on interest deductions, see sections 9.3(b), 10.3(b), 11.3(b), and 33.6.

§ 33.4 DEFAULTED TAX-EXEMPT SECURITIES

In general, I.R.C. § 1001(a) provides the rules on calculating the gain or loss on the disposition of property, including exchanges of securities that do not qualify as tax-free reorganizations under I.R.C. § 368(a)(1). Similarly, if changes in the terms of a security are so material as to virtually amount to the issuance of a new security, the transaction is taxable.[281] A municipality cannot exchange its securities in a transaction that qualifies as a Type E recapitalization under I.R.C. § 368(a)(1)[282] because the recapitalization provisions are only available to private corporations.[283]

---

[278] Rev. Rul. 72-224, 1972-1 C.B. 30.
[279] Rev. Rul. 74-482, 1974-2 C.B. 267.
[280] I.R.C. § 265(a)(2).
[281] Rev. Rul. 73-160, 1973-1 C.B. 365.
[282] Emery v. Comm'r, 166 F.2d 27, 30 (2d Cir. 1948), aff'g 8 T.C. 979 (1947); Girard Trust Co. v. United States, 166 F.2d 773, 775 (3d Cir. 1948), aff'g 69 F. Supp. 874 (E.D. Pa. 1946).
[283] *Emery*, 166 F.2d at 30; *Girard Trust Co.*, 166 F.2d at 775.

An exchange of defaulted municipal securities is generally a taxable transaction.[284]

If a municipal refunding is merely viewed as an extension of an outstanding loan agreement and not as an exchange, the IRS has ruled that there is no tax on the transaction.[285] A refunding that merely extends an outstanding loan agreement is not an exchange that gives rise to gain or loss. The transaction is taxable under I.R.C. § 1001 if the new securities have terms materially different from the old securities.[286]

§ 33.5 FLOW-THROUGH ENTITIES

(a) PARTNERSHIPS

A partner's adjusted basis in his partnership interest is increased by various items, including his distributive share of partnership income exempt from tax.[287] A basis adjustment is ordinarily made as of the end of the partnership's taxable year.[288] This increase in a partner's adjusted basis reflects his pro rata share of the tax-exempt interest earned by the partnership for the partnership's tax year. A basis adjustment assures that tax-exempt interest is not indirectly taxed if a partner disposes of his partnership interest or it is liquidated. Without such a basis adjustment, a tax would be imposed on the partner's share of the tax-exempt interest on a subsequent disposition or liquidation of his partnership interest, or upon a distribution of cash in excess of basis.

---

[284] *See Emery*, 166 F.2d at 30; *Girard Trust Co.*, 166 F.2d at 775; Rev. Rul. 81-169, 1981-1 C.B. 429.

[285] Rev. Rul. 81-169, 1981-1 C.B. 429 (modifying Rev. Rul. 56-435, 1956-2 C.B. 506) (which removed the "implication that nontaxability is conditioned on the equality of fair market value rather than the fact that there are no material differences in the terms of the bonds").

[286] *See* Mutual Loan & Sav. Co. v. Comm'r, 184 F.2d 161, 164 (5th Cir. 1950), *rev'g* 8 T.C.M. (CCH) 203 (1949) (where securities issued in exchange for defaulted municipal securities with a different date of issue and interest rate were held to be an extension or renewal of the original loan agreement); City Bank Farmers Trust Co. v. Hoey, 52 F. Supp. 665, 666 (S.D.N.Y. 1942), *aff'd per curiam*, 138 F.2d 1023 (2d Cir. 1943); West Mo. Power Co. v. Comm'r, 18 T.C. 105, 110 (1952); *see also* TAM 8451012 (Aug. 23, 1984); TAM 8052023 (Sept. 25, 1980) (revoking LTR 7948011 (Aug. 24, 1979)); LTR 7929061 (Apr. 19, 1979); TAM 7845001 (June 29, 1978).

[287] I.R.C. § 705(a).

[288] Treas. Reg. § 1.705-1(a)(1) (1956).

(b) S CORPORATIONS

A shareholder's basis in his S corporation stock is increased by his pro rata share of the corporation's "items of income," which include tax-exempt income.[289] This basis adjustment—reflecting a shareholder's pro rata share of tax-exempt income—allows an S corporation to distribute tax-exempt interest to its shareholders without triggering tax because of a low stock basis.

(c) REGULATED INVESTMENT COMPANIES

By way of background, the tax-exempt character of interest on municipal securities does not flow through to shareholders of C corporations. In addition, the earnings and profits of a C corporation are increased by tax-exempt interest income that the corporation receives.[290] Because dividends paid out of earnings and profits are taxable to the shareholders, irrespective of the tax-exempt nature of the original source, a shareholder in a C corporation may incur an indirect tax on tax-exempt income. This indirect tax is avoided, however, on certain dividends paid by RICs.[291]

Prior to 1976, tax-exempt interest did not flow through to shareholders from RICs that owned tax-exempt securities. Hence, there was no incentive—under the law in effect prior to 1976—for a RIC to acquire tax-exempt securities. Although the interest on tax-exempt securities was not taxable to the company, tax-exempt interest increased the RIC's earnings and profits, resulting in taxation as ordinary dividends when distributed to its shareholders.[292] For taxable years beginning after 1975, RICs can pay "exempt-interest dividends" if at least 50 percent of the value of their total assets at the end of each quarter consists of tax-exempt securities.[293]

To qualify as exempt-interest dividends, dividends from a RIC must meet certain conditions. First, they must be dividends (other than capital gain dividends) paid by a RIC and designated as exempt-interest dividends in a written notice mailed to the company's shareholders not less than 45 days after the close of the taxable year.[294] Second, the aggregate amount designated as an exempt-interest dividend must be greater than

---

[289] I.R.C. § 1367(a)(1).
[290] Treas. Reg. § 1.312-6(b) (1955).
[291] *See* section 8.9.
[292] I.R.C. § 852(b) (1970), *amended by* TRA '76, Pub. L. No. 94-455, § 2137(c), 90 Stat. 1520, 1931 (1976).
[293] I.R.C. § 852(b)(5).
[294] I.R.C. § 852(b)(5)(A).

the excess of the amount of tax-exempt interest over the amounts disallowed as deductions under I.R.C. §§ 265 and 171(a)(2).[295] Basically, I.R.C. § 265 prevents a RIC from deducting the expenses allocable to tax-exempt portfolios.[296] It also prevents the shareholders from obtaining an interest deduction on indebtedness incurred by them to purchase or carry RIC shares on which exempt-interest dividends are received during the taxable year.[297] Finally, a shareholder's loss on a sale or exchange of his shares in a RIC is not allowed to the extent of exempt-interest dividends he has received, unless the shares have been held by him for at least 31 days.[298]

§ 33.6 INVESTMENTS BY FINANCIAL INSTITUTIONS IN TAX-EXEMPT SECURITIES

Banks and certain other financial institutions own municipal securities for various reasons, such as to lower their own taxes, in the course of underwriting or making a market in these securities, and to collateralize public deposits if required by state law. In fact, banks have historically been major participants in the municipal securities market.[299] But since 1981, banks have sharply reduced their purchases of municipal securities, which may be explained in large part by changes in the tax laws since ERTA in 1981. TEFRA amended the Code in 1982 to deny a deduction for 15 percent of the interest expense incurred to purchase or carry tax-exempt securities acquired after December 31, 1982.[300] The 15 percent nondeductible amount was increased to 20 percent by the DRA in 1984, and it was increased to 100 percent for certain bonds by TRA '86.[301] Banks cannot deduct 20 percent of their interest expense incurred to purchase or carry tax-exempt securities acquired after December 31, 1982, but before August 8, 1986.[302]

---

[295] *Id.* For a discussion of I.R.C. § 265, see sections 9.3, 10.3, and 11.3.
[296] I.R.C. § 265(3).
[297] I.R.C. § 265(4).
[298] I.R.C. § 852(b)(4)(B).
[299] *See* Proctor & Donahoo, *Commercial Bank Investment in Municipal Securities*, FRBNY Q. REV., Winter 1983–84, at 26.
[300] I.R.C. § 291(a)(3) (1982), *amended by* DRA, *supra* note 163, § 68(a); *see* section 11.3(b)(3); *see also* Proctor & Donahoo, *supra* note 299, at 31–32.
[301] I.R.C. § 265(b).
[302] I.R.C. § 265(b).

For tax years ending after December 31, 1986, banks and savings and loans cannot deduct any of their interest expense incurred to purchase or carry governmental purpose or private activity tax-exempt securities, except for "qualified tax-exempt obligations," which are still subject to the 20 percent interest disallowance.[303] Qualified tax-exempt obligations are either governmental purpose or qualified 501(c)(3) bonds.[304] Also, they must be issued by an issuer that reasonably expects that it and its subordinate entities will issue no more than $10 million of such bonds during that calendar year. In addition, the issuer must designate which of the bonds it intends to be eligible for the more favorable 20 percent disallowance treatment. No more than $10 million of such bonds can be so designated in any calendar year.[305] For a further discussion of the rules for financial institutions, see section 11.3(b)(3). Other factors that may explain decreased bank investments in recent years include bank profitability, the level and volatility of interest rates, and credit risks.

Certain financial institutions (defined to include commercial banks, mutual savings banks, savings and loan associations, cooperative banks, business development corporations, and small business investment corporations) realize ordinary income and loss on the sale or exchange of tax-exempt securities.[306]

§ 33.7 ALTERNATIVE MINIMUM TAX

Under Code amendments made by TRA '86, "tax-exempt income" may be subject to the alternative minimum tax. Generally, for purposes of calculating corporate and individual minimum tax, tax-exempt interest on all private activity bonds issued after August 7, 1986, except for qualified 501(c)(3) bonds, is a preference item.[307] Tax-exempt interest on certain refunding bonds issued after August 7, 1986, however, is not a preference item.[308]

Also, all tax-exempt interest received by a corporation (excluding any S corporation, RIC, REIT, or REMIC) may be an adjustment to alterna-

---

[303] I.R.C. § 265(b)(3). See Lodge, *Bank Appetites for Tax-Exempt Investments Slacken Under Interest Disallowance Rule*, 1 BANKING L. REV. 43 (Winter 1989).

[304] See section 33.2(c)(2)(vi).

[305] I.R.C. § 265(b)(3). This section imposes no limit, however, on the private activity bonds (other than qualified 501(c)(3) bonds) that an issuer can issue.

[306] I.R.C. § 582(c)(1); see section 8.8.

[307] I.R.C. §§ 56(b)(1)(C)(iii), 56(c)(1), 57(a)(5)(C)(ii).

[308] I.R.C. § 57(a)(5)(C)(iii).

tive minimum taxable income if it is included in the calculation of either "adjusted net book income" or "adjusted current earnings."[309] For a discussion of the alternative minimum tax, see generally sections 15.4(a)(2)(ii), 15.5(c), and 15.5(d).

§ 33.8 LOSSES INCURRED BY PROPERTY AND CASUALTY INSURANCE COMPANIES

For tax years after 1986, the amount of losses a property and casualty insurance company can otherwise deduct in computing its federal income tax liability was reduced by 15 percent of the tax-exempt interest received or accrued during such tax year with respect to bonds issued after August 7, 1986.[310]

§ 33.9 DEPRECIATION DEDUCTIONS FOR BOND FINANCED PROPERTY

TRA '86 provides an alternative depreciation system for certain categories of property, including property placed in service after December 31, 1986, financed with the proceeds of tax-exempt securities issued after March 1, 1986.[311] This alternative depreciation system provides that the cost of property subject to it must be recovered on a straight-line basis over the property's class life, thereby resulting in longer and slower depreciation of such assets.[312]

§ 33.10 USE OF BOND FINANCED PROPERTY

For property financed with the proceeds of private activity tax-exempt bonds issued after August 15, 1986, interest deductions are not allowed if the bond financed property is not used on a continuous basis by qualifying persons for qualifying purposes or the property is transferred to nonqualifying persons.[313] For a discussion of private activity bonds, see section 33.2(c).

[309] I.R.C. § 56(c)(1).
[310] I.R.C. § 832(b)(5)(B)(i).
[311] I.R.C. §§ 168(g)(1)(C), 168(g)(5).
[312] *See generally* I.R.C. § 168.
[313] I.R.C. §§ 150(b), 150(c).

§ 33.11 BRANCH PROFITS TAX

A 30 percent tax is imposed by TRA '86 on adjusted "effectively connected earnings and profits" of domestic branches of foreign corporations.[314] Effectively connected earnings and profits include tax-exempt interest from any tax-exempt securities received by the domestic branches.[315]

§ 33.12 SUPERFUND ENVIRONMENTAL TAX

The Superfund Revenue Act of 1986 imposes a tax on a corporation's "modified alternative minimum taxable income," which is defined to include interest on all tax-exempt securities.[316]

---

[314] I.R.C. § 884.
[315] TRA '86 Conf. Rep., *supra* note 36, at II-647.
[316] I.R.C. § 59A.

Thirty-four

Convertible Debt Securities

This chapter addresses convertible debt securities. The wash sales rule,[1] short sales rule,[2] and the Straddle Rules[3] apply to taxpayers holding debt securities unless specific exceptions are available.[4] For a discussion of the tax provisions that apply generally to debt securities, see Chapter 31.

§ 34.1 IN GENERAL

Convertible debt securities are typically "convertible" into the common stock of the issuing corporation.[5] The taxation of convertible debt securities is not governed by any particular Code provision. Rather, one must look to various Code provisions, Treasury regulations, often conflicting judicial decisions, and IRS pronouncements to ascertain the appropriate

---

[1] *See generally* Chapter 19.
[2] *See generally* Chapter 18.
[3] *See generally* Part Eleven.
[4] For example, the wash sales and short sales rules typically do not apply to dealers in the particular debt security.
[5] For a discussion of convertible securities, see section 1.1(d).

tax treatment of convertible debt securities.[6] In addition, the rules for high yield discount obligations enacted as part of RRA '89[7] can have application. For a discussion of high yield discount obligations, see section 31.2(g).

Section 34.2 discusses general tax principles applicable to convertible debt securities from the perspective of corporate issuers, while section 34.3 addresses owners of convertible debt securities. Section 34.4 addresses adjustable rate convertible notes. Section 34.5 addresses mandatory convertible notes issued by bank holding companies. Section 34.6 addresses exchangeable debt securities and portfolio exchangeables. Section 34.7 addresses discount convertible debt securities.

§ 34.2 TAX TREATMENT OF AN ISSUING CORPORATION

This section addresses the tax treatment of a corporation issuing convertible debt securities.

(a) ISSUANCE OF CONVERTIBLE DEBT SECURITIES

The major tax consideration when a corporation issues convertible debt securities is whether the securities are treated as debt obligations of, or equity interests in, the issuer. There have been many conflicting judicial decisions as to whether a security is a debt or an equity interest.[8] The classification of securities as debt or equity interests is important for the

---

[6] *See generally* Fleischer & Cary, *The Taxation of Convertible Bonds and Stock*, 74 HARV. L. REV. 473 (1961); Panel Discussion, *Convertible Debentures and Strange Securities*, 28 N.Y.U. INST. ON FED. TAX'N 331 (1970); Thrower, *Conglomerates and Convertibles*, 1 TAX ADVISER 4 (1970); Strasen, *The Taxation of Convertible and Other Equity-Flavored Debt Instruments*, 65 TAXES 937 (1987); Madison, *The Deductibility of "Interest" on Hybrid Securities*, 39 TAX LAW. 465 (1986); Donnelly, *Convertible Bonds Regain Some Luster After Being Battered in October Crash*, Wall St. J., Dec. 3, 1987, at 3; *Treasurers Advised to Repurchase Corporate Debt*, CORP. FINANCING WK., Nov. 30, 1987, at 2; Zigas, *In Bumpy Markets, Cushion the Ride with a Convertible*, BUS. WK., Jan. 18, 1988, at 94; Heston, *How to Get Stocks and Bonds in One Package*, FUTURES, Sept. 1986, at 50; Rose, *A Little-Known Type of Convertible Bond Can Be a Profitable Investment for Some*, Wall St. J., June 9, 1986, at 21; Rundle, *Convertible Securities Holders Can Lose Out If Issue Is Called and Underlying Stock Is Low*, Wall St. J., May 1, 1986, at 53; Donnelly, *Convertible-Bond Game Becomes Riskier*, Wall St. J., Mar. 7, 1989, at Cl; Schultz, *Convertible Bond Funds: Safety Plus the Sizzle of Stocks*, FORTUNE, July 17, 1989, at 29; Liscio, *Best of All Worlds—Convertibles Never Had It So Good*, BARRON'S, Aug. 7, 1989, at 16.

[7] Pub. L. No. 101-239, 103 Stat. 2301 (1989) [hereinafter RRA '89].

[8] *See generally* B. BITTKER & J. EUSTICE, FEDERAL INCOME TAXATION OF CORPORATIONS AND SHAREHOLDERS ¶¶ 4.01–4.04, at 4-2 to 4-27 (5th ed. 1987).

tax treatment of new security products with conversion features. Recharacterization of debt interests as equity interests can have significant—usually detrimental—tax consequences.[9]

I.R.C. § 385 was enacted in 1969 to provide some guidance on debt and equity interests. It granted the Treasury authority to issue regulations "as may be necessary or appropriate to determine whether an interest in a corporation is to be treated . . . as stock or indebtedness."[10] It was amended in 1989 to expand Treasury authority to determine whether an interest is "in part stock and in part indebtedness."[11] Any regulations issued pursuant to the expanded authority granted to the Treasury effective December 19, 1989, "shall only apply with respect to instruments issued after the date on which the Secretary of the Treasury or his delegate provides public guidance as to the characterization of such instruments whether by regulation, ruling, or otherwise."[12] In other words, regulatory coverage of instruments that are determined to be part stock and part indebtedness cannot be applied retroactively. I.R.C. § 385 lists some factors to consider as to whether there is a debtor–creditor relationship or a corporation–shareholder relationship. First, is there a written, unconditional promise to pay a fixed sum on demand or on a specified date, and a fixed rate of interest, in return for an adequate consideration in money or money's worth?[13]

Second, is the debt subordinated, or does it have a preference over any indebtedness of the corporation?[14]

Third, what is the corporation's ratio of debt to equity?[15] For example, in LTR 8523009,[16] the IRS ruled that convertible debt securities issued in a leveraged buyout qualified as debt even though the issuer had an enormous amount of debt compared to equity.

---

[9] *See* sections 34.4 and 34.5.
[10] I.R.C. § 385(a).
[11] I.R.C. § 385(a), *as amended by* RRA '89, *supra* note 7, § 7208(a)(1).
[12] RRA '89, *supra* note 7, § 7208(a)(2).
[13] I.R.C. § 385(b)(1).
[14] I.R.C. § 385(b)(2).
[15] I.R.C. § 385(b)(3). For a discussion of the denial of an interest deduction on so-called earnings stripping transactions, see section 34.2(e).
[16] (Feb. 25, 1985).

§ 34.2(a)   Financial Products: Taxation, Regulation, and Design

Fourth, is the security convertible into stock of the corporation?[17]

Fifth, what is the relationship between the shareholders and the owners of the interest in question?[18]

All of these factors are to be considered in light of all facts and circumstances. For a discussion of debt and equity considerations, see section 27.2.

If convertible debt securities are classified as equity interests rather than debt securities, six consequences result: (1) interest is not deductible, (2) there is no issue premium or discount, (3) retirement premiums and discounts are tested for capital gain or ordinary income under the stock redemption rules, (4) installment reporting is not available under I.R.C. § 453, (5) the securities cannot be issued in Type B or Type C reorganizations under I.R.C. § 368(a)(1) (because the securities do not qualify as voting stock), and (6) conversion into other stock might be tax-free.[19]

For convertible debt securities that are treated as debt interests, the issuing corporation treats the securities in the same way as other debt obligations, and the corporation services the debt according to its terms.[20]

In addition, I.R.C. § 385(a) specifically authorizes the Treasury to issue debt-equity regulations. At this writing, after several attempts to issue such regulations, all proposed and final regulations have been withdrawn.[21] In fact, Congress amended I.R.C. § 385(a), effective December 19, 1989, to extend Treasury authority to address instruments that are "in part stock and in part indebtedness."[22] At this writing, the only available guidelines as to whether a security is a debt instrument or an equity interest are those listed in I.R.C. § 385(b), IRS rulings, and often conflicting judicial decisions.

---

[17] I.R.C. § 385(b)(4). If warrants are issued with preferred stock or debentures, the securities can be treated as either separate property or as a single exchangeable security. The Treasury regulations withdrawn under I.R.C. § 385 treated the warrant and other security as separate securities. The position taken in the withdrawn Treasury regulations was contrary to case law. See, e.g., Universal Castings Corp. v. Comm'r, 37 T.C. 107 (1961), aff'd, 303 F.2d 620 (7th Cir. 1962).

[18] I.R.C. § 385(b)(5).

[19] B. BITTKER & J. EUSTICE, supra note 8, ¶ 4.02, at 4–6.

[20] For a discussion of debt securities, see generally Chapter 31.

[21] The effective date of the final Treasury regulations, issued on December 31, 1980, was continually delayed until the regulations were formally withdrawn by the Treasury on August 5, 1983.

[22] RRA '89, supra note 7, § 7208(a)(1).

Two IRS rulings are worth mentioning because they provide guidance on debt-equity considerations. In LTR 8523009,[23] the IRS addressed convertible securities issued to a seller in a leveraged buyout transaction. If the securities were classified as debt instruments, the transaction would not be tax-free under I.R.C. § 351 (transfers to controlled corporations). The IRS set out 13 factors that the courts have used to address debt and equity issues:

1. The name given to the instrument
2. Fixed maturity date, if any
3. The source of principal payment
4. The right to enforce payment of principal or interest
5. Management participation
6. Status relative to corporate creditors
7. Intent of the parties
8. Is the corporation thinly capitalized?
9. Identity of interest between creditors and shareholders
10. The source of interest payments
11. Corporate ability to obtain loans from outside lending institutions
12. Are the funds used to acquire capital assets?
13. Is there a failure to repay on the due date?

In LTR 8523009, after reviewing the facts and circumstances, the IRS found that the notes had more debt than equity characteristics. The IRS would consider convertible securities as equity if it was likely they would be converted.[24]

In Rev. Rul. 85-119,[25] the IRS addressed the debt or equity considerations for subordinated capital notes issued by a bank holding company to meet its capital requirements. The IRS ruled that the notes were debt securities.[26]

If debt securities (including bonds, debentures, notes, certificates, or other evidences of indebtedness issued by a corporation and bearing

---

[23] (Feb. 25, 1985).
[24] This analysis was applied in Rev. Rul. 83-98, 1983-2 C.B. 40. For a discussion of Rev. Rul. 83-98, see section 34.4.
[25] 1985-2 C.B. 60.
[26] For a discussion of Rev. Rul. 85-119, see section 34.5.

interest) are issued at their face value, the corporation realizes no gain or loss.[27] Expenses incurred by the corporation to issue the debt securities are treated as capital expenditures, recoverable over the term of the debt securities in the same manner as discount is recoverable.[28]

It is well established that, upon conversion of the debt security, no gain or loss will be recognized by the corporate issuer. The conversion is tax-free to a corporate issuer under I.R.C. § 1032, which provides that gain or loss is not recognized by a corporation on receipt of property in exchange for its stock.

(b) ORIGINAL ISSUE DISCOUNT

A detailed description of OID is beyond the scope of this book. Nevertheless, a brief discussion is necessary to understand its effect on convertible debt securities. OID is the excess that a corporation must pay on the retirement of its debt securities over the amount of consideration it receives from purchasers on the issuance of the securities.[29] OID is basically a cost of borrowing money, which is deductible by the corporation ratably over the life of the debt.[30] For corporate debt securities issued at a discount, the net amount of the discount is treated as an additional cost of borrowing and is deductible by the corporation ratably over the life of the debt securities.[31]

No part of the issue price of convertible debt securities is deemed to be attributable to the conversion feature. The issue price of a convertible debt security includes any amount paid for the conversion factor.[32] Therefore, a convertible debt security sold at par is not issued at a discount, regardless of the value of the conversion feature, because the issue price

---

[27] Treas. Reg. § 1.61-12(c)(1) (1980).
[28] Helvering v. Union Pac. R.R. Co., 293 U.S. 282, 287 (1934), *aff'g* 69 F.2d 966 (2d Cir. 1934), *denying reh'g to* 69 F.2d 67 (2d Cir. 1934), *rev'g* 26 B.T.A. 1126 (1932), *acq. and nonacq.* XII-1 C.B. 13, 23; Denver & Rio Grande W.R.R. v. Comm'r, 32 T.C. 43, 51-52 (1959), *aff'd on other grounds*, 279 F.2d 368 (10th Cir. 1960); Leach Corp. v. Comm'r, 30 T.C. 563, 579 (1958), *acq.* 1959-1 C.B. 4; Rev. Rul. 59-387, 1959-2 C.B. 56.
[29] For a discussion of OID, see generally section 31.2.
[30] Treas. Reg. § 1.1232 (1980); Treas. Reg. §§ 1.163-3(a)(1), 4(a)(1) (1973).
[31] Treas. Reg. § 1.163-3(a)(1) (1973) (for corporate debt securities issued on or before May 27, 1969); Treas. Reg. § 1.163-4(a)(1) (1973) (for corporate debt securities issued after May 27, 1969); *see also* Treas. Reg. § 1.1232 (1980); *see* section 31.2.
[32] Treas. Reg. § 1.1232-3(b)(2)(i) (1980).

and the maturity amount of the debt security are equal. A conversion feature does not affect OID calculations.[33]

If the debt security's stated redemption price at maturity exceeds its issue price and such excess is more than a de minimis amount (.25 of 1 percent of the stated redemption price at maturity, multiplied by the number of full years to maturity), then such excess is OID that is deductible by the issuer and includable in income by the holder on a constant yield basis under the provisions of I.R.C. §§ 1271–1275 and the proposed OID Treasury regulations.[34] The proposed Treasury regulations provide that no portion of the issue price of the debt security should be allocated to the conversion feature in computing OID.

In *Honeywell Inc. v. Comm'r*,[35] the Tax Court addressed *Chock Full O'Nuts Corp. v. United States*,[36] finding that its rationale applies "a fortiori where, as here, the *issuer* pays no more upon redemption of a debenture than was received on the issuance of the debenture."[37]

The *Honeywell* decision struck a substantial blow to corporate issuers that hoped to claim OID on exchangeable and convertible debt securities. In *Honeywell*, the Tax Court examined debentures issued by Honeywell Overseas Finance Corp. that were exchangeable for stock in the finance subsidiary's parent, Honeywell. Honeywell claimed OID on the convertible debentures issuer's stock, and it hired an outside securities consultant to appraise the value of the exchangeability feature.[38]

Honeywell claimed, unsuccessfully, that the exchangeability created a separate security, and because the debentures were issued at par, the difference between the value of the exchangeability feature and the debentures' price could be considered OID.[39] The Tax Court did not agree.

It appears as if an exchangeable debt security—exchangeable into the shares of another corporation that is owned by the issuer—does not generate OID. Rather, the exchangeable debt instrument would most likely be treated as a single security that does not require bifurcation of

---

[33] Chock Full O'Nuts Corp. v. United States, 453 F.2d 300, 305 (2d Cir. 1971), *aff'g* 322 F. Supp. 772 (S.D.N.Y. 1971); *accord* Hunt Foods & Indus., Inc. v. Comm'r, 57 T.C. 633, 638 (1972), *aff'd per curiam*, 496 F.2d 532 (9th Cir. 1974); AMF, Inc. v. United States, 476 F.2d 1351, 1353 (Ct. Cl. 1973), *cert. denied*, 417 U.S. 930 (1974); *see* Note, *Original Issue Discount Does Not Occur When a Corporation Issues Convertible Bonds at Par—Chock Full O'Nuts Corp. v. United States, 453 F.2d 300 (2d Cir. 1971)*, 39 BROOKLYN L. REV. 1305 (1973).

[34] For a discussion of OID, see generally section 31.2.

[35] 87 T.C. 624 (1986), *acq.* 1988-1 C.B. 1.

[36] 453 F.2d 300 (2d Cir. 1971), *aff'g* 322 F. Supp. 772 (S.D.N.Y. 1971).

[37] 87 T.C. at 639 (emphasis in original).

[38] *Id.* at 636–37.

[39] *Id.* at 638–39.

the issue price between the bond element and the exchangeability feature.[40]

(c) PREMIUMS

(1) IN GENERAL

If debt securities are issued at a premium, the net amount of the premium (excluding any portion attributable to a conversion premium)[41] is treated as corporate income to be prorated or amortized over the life of the debt securities.[42] This also applies to convertible debt securities issued at a premium.[43] The amount of the premium is not reduced by any amount attributable to the conversion feature.[44]

(2) CONVERSION FEATURES

The portion of the purchase price of convertible debt securities that is attributable to a conversion feature is not treated as a premium.[45] The value of a conversion feature on a debt security is determined as of the date the security is acquired—the market price for the security, if it had not been convertible, is subtracted from the purchase price of the convertible security.[46]

Determining the assumed price for a nonconvertible security is a two-step procedure. First, a taxpayer must determine the yield on nonconvertible debt securities with a similar character. Second, the price currently paid on such a security (at the specified yield, classification, and grade) is determined using standard bond tables.[47] Once the value of the conversion feature is determined, it is subtracted from the issue price to determine the amount of premium, if any, relating to the debt element of the security.

---

[40] *But see* Prop. Treas. Reg. § 1.1273-2(e) (1989), which provides that "[t]he issue price of a debt instrument which is convertible into stock or another debt instrument of the issuer shall include any amount paid with respect to the conversion privilege."

[41] *See* section 34.2(c)(2).

[42] Treas. Reg. § 1.61-12(c)(2) (1980). For a general discussion of premiums, see section 31.4.

[43] Treas. Reg. § 1.61-12(c)(6) (1980).

[44] *See* section 34.2(c)(2).

[45] National Can Corp. v. United States, 687 F.2d 1107, 1112 (7th Cir. 1982), *aff'g* 520 F. Supp. 567 (N.D. Ill. 1981); I.R.C. § 171(b); *see* Treas. Reg. § 1.171-2(c)(1) (1968).

[46] *See* Crawford, *Amortization of Conversion Feature Discount: What Is the Proper Treatment?*, 32 J. TAX'N 102 (1970).

[47] Treas. Reg. § 1.171-2(c)(2) (1968).

(3) UNAMORTIZED PREMIUMS ON CONVERSION

If a debt security is converted before the full amount of the premium that is not attributable to the conversion feature is included in the income of the corporate issuer, the unamortized premium is not taxable to the issuer at conversion. Rather, the unamortized premium is treated as additional proceeds from the sale of stock.[48]

(d) EXERCISE OF CONVERSION RIGHTS

Prior to DRA[49] amendments to the Code in 1984, gain or loss was not recognized by the corporate issuer on the exchange of its convertible debt securities for its stock. The stock was considered to be a form of payment for the debt securities. It was not viewed as a discharge of indebtedness, irrespective of whether the par value or market value of the stock was different from the face amount of the debt securities.[50]

The DRA revoked this so-called debt-equity exception contained in I.R.C. § 108(e)(10) in all cases except where the issuer is in bankruptcy or is insolvent.[51] For transfers after July 18, 1984, in tax years ending after such date, cancellation income results to the extent that the adjusted issue price of the debt securities exceeds the value of the stock issued on the retirement.[52] In 1986, I.R.C. § 108(e)(10) was again amended to repeal the exception for transfers in certain workout plans, under which stock was transferred to creditors in satisfaction of indebtedness if the corporation was having trouble meeting its liabilities and certain statutory requirements contained in I.R.C. § 108(e)(10)(c) were met.[53]

---

[48] I.R.C. § 171(b)(1).

[49] Pub. L. No. 98-369, 98 Stat. 494 (1984) [hereinafter DRA].

[50] Commissioner v. Motor Mart Trust, 156 F.2d 122, 127 (1st Cir. 1946), *aff'g* 4 T.C. 931 (1945), *acq.* 1947-1 C.B. 3.

[51] DRA, *supra* note 49, § 59.

[52] I.R.C. § 108(e)(10).

[53] TRA '86, Pub. L. No. 99-514, § 621(e)(1), 100 Stat. 2085 (1986). *See* Seas Shipping Co. v. Comm'r, 371 F.2d 528 (2d Cir. 1967), *aff'g* 24 T.C.M. (CCH) 1222 (1965), *cert. denied*, 387 U.S. 943 (1967); Southern Natural Gas Co. v. United States, 412 F.2d 1222 (Ct. Cl. 1969); Rev. Rul. 90-16, 1990-1 C.B. 12.

(e) ACCRUED INTEREST ON CONVERSIONS

A corporate issuer on the accrual basis can deduct interest that accrues on convertible securities as the interest accrues.[54] In addition, accrued interest is generally deductible, even if payment is deferred under the terms of the securities until after the final payment of principal and interest on other securities issued by the corporation.[55]

If the provision in the debt security as to the proper treatment for accrued interest is ambiguous—so it is not clear whether interest is forfeited or paid through the issuance of stock—the corporation may be denied an interest deduction. In *Columbia Gas System, Inc. v. United States*,[56] for example, a corporate taxpayer issued convertible debt securities. The securities provided for interest payable semiannually and a provision that relieved the issuer of any interest that was accrued but unpaid at the date of conversion. The clause provided that "there shall be no adjustment in respect of interest or dividends on the conversion of any Debenture or Debentures."[57] The court found the clause unclear as to whether the debenture intended a discharge of accrued interest or a payment. It, therefore, construed the ambiguity against its drafter (i.e., the corporate issuer) and denied the corporation an interest deduction.[58]

If under the terms of a debt security an owner forfeits his right to accrued interest on conversion, the corporate issuer cannot deduct the accrued interest from the period after the last interest date to the date of the conversion.[59] Similarly, the corporate issuer, at the end of its taxable year, cannot deduct interest that has accrued between payment dates

---

[54] I.R.C. § 163(a); Hummel-Ross Fibre Corp. v. Comm'r, 40 B.T.A. 821 (1939), *acq.* 1940-1 C.B. 3; Shamrock Oil & Gas Co. v. Comm'r, 42 B.T.A. 1016 (1940), *acq.* 1940-2 C.B. 6; Central Elec. & Tel. Co. v. Comm'r, 47 B.T.A. 434 (1942), *acq.* 1942-2 C.B. 4.

[55] Natco Corp. v. United States, 240 F.2d 398 (3d Cir. 1956), *aff'g* 56-2 U.S. Tax Cas. (CCH) ¶ 9642 (W.D. Pa. 1956).

[56] 473 F.2d 1246, 1247 (2d Cir. 1973), *aff'g* 334 F. Supp. 1279 (S.D.N.Y. 1971).

[57] 473 F.2d at 1246.

[58] *Id.* at 1249; *see* Comment, *Tax Treatment of Accrued Interest on Convertible Bonds—A Dilemma for Corporate Taxpayers*, 15 Wm. & Mary L. Rev. 192 (1973); *see also* Bethlehem Steel Corp. v. United States, 434 F.2d 1357 (Ct. Cl. 1970); Tandy Corp. v. United States, 79-1 U.S. Tax Cas. (CCH) ¶ 9160 (N.D. Tex. 1979), *aff'd*, 626 F.2d 1186 (5th Cir. 1980).

[59] Rev. Rul. 74-127, 1974-1 C.B. 47; Rev. Rul. 68-170, 1968-1 C.B. 71, *clarified by* Rev. Rul. 74-127, 1974-1 C.B. 47.

because the payment obligation does not become fixed until the interest payment is actually due.[60]

In addition, a corporate issuer cannot deduct interest payments made to its parent corporation upon the conversion of the issuer's convertible debt securities into the common stock of its parent. In *Husky Oil Co. v. Comm'r*,[61] the Tax Court held that the owners of the convertible debt securities have alternative rights to demand either payment from the corporate issuer or shares of common stock from the issuer's parent. When one right is exercised by the security owner, the alternate obligation is discharged.[62] A debt security owner's election to convert the debt security to common stock extinguishes the corporate issuer's obligations to accrue interest.[63]

(f) REPURCHASE BY THE ISSUER

A corporate issuer's deduction for a retirement premium is limited to a normal call premium on nonconvertible debt securities. A corporate issuer cannot deduct any premium[64] paid or incurred after April 22, 1969, to repurchase a security convertible into stock of the issuer or a company in control of or controlled by the issuing corporation,[65] to the extent that the repurchase price of such a security exceeds the adjusted issue price plus a "normal call premium" on securities that are not convertible.[66]

I.R.C. § 249(a) provides that

> [n]o deduction shall be allowed to the issuing corporation for any premium paid or incurred upon the repurchase of a bond, debenture, note, or certificate or other evidence of indebtedness which is convertible into the stock of the issuing corporation, or a corporation in control of, or controlled

---

[60] Scott Paper Co. v. Comm'r, 74 T.C. 137, 165–66 (1980); Rev. Rul. 74-127, 1974-1 C.B. 47. *See generally* Capento Sec. Corp. v. Comm'r, 47 B.T.A. 691 (1942), *nonacq.* 1943 C.B. 28, *aff'd*, 140 F.2d 382 (1st Cir. 1944); *Hummel-Ross Fibre Corp.*, 40 B.T.A. 821 (1939), *acq.* 1940-1 C.B. 3, *Shamrock Oil & Gas Co.*, 42 B.T.A. 1016 (1940), *acq.* 1940-2 C.B. 6; *Central Elec. & Tel. Co.*, 47 B.T.A. 434 (1942), *acq.* 1942-2 C.B. 4; *Columbia Gas Sys.*, 473 F.2d 1244 (2d Cir. 1973), *aff'g* 334 F. Supp. 1279 (S.D.N.Y. 1971); *Bethlehem Steel Corp.*, 434 F.2d 1357 (Ct. Cl. 1970); *Tandy Corp.*, 79-1 U.S. Tax Cas. (CCH) ¶ 9160 (N.D. Tex. 1979), *aff'd*, 626 F.2d 1186 (5th Cir. 1980).

[61] 83 T.C. 717, 735 (1984), *aff'd sub nom.* Marathon Oil v. Comm'r, 838 F.2d 1114 (10th Cir. 1987).

[62] 83 T.C. at 735.

[63] *Id.*

[64] *See* section 31.4.

[65] Control means the ownership of stock possessing at least 80 percent of the total combined voting power of all classes of stock entitled to vote, and at least 80 percent of the total number of the shares of all classes of stock. I.R.C. §§ 249(b)(2), 368(c)(1).

[66] I.R.C. § 249(a); Treas. Reg. §§ 1.249-1(a), (c) (1973).

by, the issuing corporation, to the extent the repurchase price exceeds an amount equal to the adjusted issue price plus a normal call premium on bonds or other evidences of indebtedness which are not convertible.

This means that I.R.C. § 249(a) denies a deduction for the repurchase of that portion of the convertible debt security attributable to the conversion feature. The issuer can establish that the premium is not due to the conversion feature. (An issuer is not allowed a deduction for the repurchase of its own stock.)[67]

A normal call premium is defined as an amount equal to a normal call premium on a nonconvertible debt security that is comparable to the convertible debt security.[68] It is a call premium specified in dollars under the debt security's terms.[69] As a result, if a specified call premium is constant over the entire term of the debt security, the normal call premium is the amount specified.[70] If, on the other hand, the specified call premium varies during the period in which a comparable nonconvertible debt security is callable (or if it is not callable over its entire term), the normal call premium is the amount specified for the period during the term of such comparable nonconvertible debt security, which corresponds to the period during which the convertible debt security was repurchased.[71] In addition, a call premium of a convertible debt security specified in dollars is treated as a normal call premium on a nonconvertible debt security if the call premium at the time of repurchase does not exceed an amount equal to one year's interest payable on the security, increased by the amount of deductible discount.[72]

A corporate issuer can deduct a redemption premium in excess of a normal call premium on convertible debt securities to the extent it can establish that the excess premium is attributable to the cost of borrowing funds, not to the conversion feature.[73] The portion of a repurchase premium attributable to the conversion feature is the amount by which the selling price of the convertible debt security increased between the date it was issued and the date it was repurchased, due to a general decline in yields on comparable nonconvertible securities.[74]

---

[67] Treas. Reg. § 1.249-1(e) (1973).
[68] Treas. Reg. § 1.249-1(d)(1) (1973).
[69] Id.
[70] Id.
[71] Id.
[72] Treas. Reg. § 1.249-1(d)(2) (1973).
[73] I.R.C. § 249(a); Treas. Reg. § 1.249-1(e)(1) (1973).
[74] Treas. Reg. § 1.249-1(e)(2) (1973).

In *Clark Equipment Co. v. United States*,[75] the district court for the Western District of Michigan held that the corporation could not deduct the difference between the value of stock and cash it exchanged for convertible debentures, and the face value of the convertible debentures, because I.R.C. § 249 provides that a deduction is not allowed for any bond premium paid upon the repurchase of a debt security that is convertible into stock of the issuing corporation, to the extent that the premium exceeds the normal call premium on nonconvertible securities. In *Clark Equipment*, a wholly owned subsidiary issued debentures, guaranteed by its parent corporation, convertible at the holder's option into stock of the parent. The obligation to convert was later transferred to the subsidiary and when the holders exercised their options to convert, they received stock in the parent and cash in lieu of fractional shares.

The district court found that "the case law is sparse on this issue" and looked at *National Can Corp. v. United States*[76] where the court denied the deductions claimed by the corporate taxpayer "for the excess of the fair market value of the taxpayer's stock exchanged by the taxpayer to effect the conversion of convertible debentures."[77] The court acknowledged that the parent corporation in *National Can* "effected the conversions, exchanging its own stock for the convertible debentures issued by its subsidiary."[78] In the facts before the *Clark Equipment* court, "the subsidiary exchanged its parent's stock for the convertible debentures issued by the subsidiary."[79] The Seventh Circuit in *National Can* reasoned that the purpose behind I.R.C. § 249 "was to disallow corporate taxpayers deductions for premiums attributable to essentially capital transactions."[80] The court found that the "relevant exchange" before the court in *Clark Equipment* is "essentially a capital transaction" and that I.R.C. § 249 applies to deny the loss upon conversion.[81]

On a procedural note, the taxpayer asserted that I.R.C. § 249 did not apply to its transaction because I.R.C. § 249 was enacted as part of the Tax Reform Act of 1969 to apply to any repurchase of a convertible obligation occurring after April 22, 1969, "other than a convertible obligation repurchased pursuant to a binding obligation incurred on or before April 22, 1969, to repurchase such convertible obligation at a specified call

---

[75] 89-2 U.S. Tax Cas. (CCH) ¶ 9471 (W.D. Mich. 1989), *aff'd*, 912 F.2d 113 (6th Cir. 1990).
[76] 687 F.2d 1107 (7th Cir. 1982), *aff'g* 520 F. Supp. 567 (N.D. Ill. 1981).
[77] *Clark Equip. Co.*, 89-2 U.S. Tax Cas. (CCH) ¶ 9471, at 89,323.
[78] *Id.*
[79] *Id.*
[80] *Id.* (citing *National Can*, 687 F.2d at 1115–16).
[81] *Id.* at 89,323.

premium."[82] The district court found that the debentures were issued before April 22, 1969, but the binding obligation was not the obligation of the party attempting to claim the exception. The wholly owned subsidiary had no obligation until 1971, when the obligation was transferred from the parent to the wholly owned subsidiary. Before 1971, the obligation was the parent's; after 1971, it was the subsidiary's obligation.[83]

The Sixth Circuit Court of Appeals affirmed the district court's decision in *Clark Equipment*,[84] finding that all of the five elements must be present as a condition of applicability of I.R.C. § 249.[85]

§ 34.3 TAX TREATMENT OF A CONVERTIBLE DEBT SECURITY OWNER

This section addresses the tax treatment of an owner of a convertible debt security.

(a) ACQUISITION OF CONVERTIBLE DEBT SECURITIES

A taxpayer can acquire a convertible debt security in either a taxable or nontaxable transaction. In a taxable transaction, the taxpayer's basis in the security is his cost basis,[86] which is subject to various adjustments.[87] In a nontaxable transaction, the taxpayer's basis is either a carry-over basis (for transactions other than certain acquisitions from decedents), or a stepped-up basis (for certain acquisitions from decedents).[88] A taxpayer obtains a new holding period for securities acquired in a taxable transaction and a tacked holding period for securities acquired in a nontaxable

---

[82] *Id.* (citing Treas. Reg. § 1.249-1 (1973)).

[83] *Id.* at 89,324.

[84] 912 F.2d 113 (6th Cir. 1990).

[85] The five elements set out by the Sixth Circuit are as follows:

    1) The *issuing corporation* is attempting to claim the deduction;

    2) that corporation *paid or incurred a premium* in the conversion transactions;

    3) that corporation *repurchased* debentures;

    4) the debentures were *convertible into the stock of a corporation in control of the issuing corporation*, and

    5) the amount disallowed as a deduction is *attributable to the conversion feature*.

912 F.2d at 916.

[86] *See* section 16.2.

[87] *See, e.g.,* section 31.2(b).

[88] *See* section 16.3.

transaction.[89] As with other types of debt securities, convertible debt securities are capital assets in the hands of investors[90] and traders,[91] and are ordinary assets in the hands of dealers,[92] hedgers,[93] and certain financial institutions.[94]

(b) ORIGINAL ISSUE DISCOUNT

A detailed discussion of OID is beyond the scope of this book. Nevertheless, a brief discussion is necessary to understand its effect on convertible debt securities. OID is the excess that a corporation must pay on the retirement of its debt securities over the amount of consideration it receives from purchases on the issuance of the securities.[95] The tax treatment of OID has changed greatly in recent years. As a result, the owner of a convertible debt security includes OID in income in accordance with the rules in place for debt securities issued at the time when the securities were issued without adjustment for the portion of the issue price allocable to the conversion feature.

- The sum of the daily portion of OID determined for each day during the tax year in which a convertible debt security issued after July 1, 1982 is owned, is included in the owner's income for debt securities issued after July 1, 1982.[96]
- For convertible debt securities issued after May 27, 1969, and before July 2, 1982, the owner must include in income his ratable monthly portion of OID, multiplied by the number of complete months and fractions thereof during which he has held the convertible debt security.[97]
- For convertible debt securities issued before May 28, 1969, a taxpayer is not required to report OID until the year the convertible debt security is sold, exchanged, or redeemed.[98]

---

[89] *See generally* Chapter 17.
[90] *See* section 8.1.
[91] *See* section 8.2.
[92] *See* section 8.3.
[93] *See* section 8.4.
[94] *See* section 8.8.
[95] For a discussion of OID generally, see section 31.2.
[96] I.R.C. § 1272(a)(1); *see* section 31.2.
[97] I.R.C. § 1272(b)(1); *see* section 31.2(b).
[98] I.R.C. § 1271(c)(2)(A); *see* section 31.2(c).

If a taxpayer pays cash for a convertible debt security, the OID rules can be relatively simple. The tax issues concerning OID become much more complicated if a security is acquired as part of a package offering,[99] or is acquired in a tax-free exchange of property worth less than the convertible debt security.[100] Finally, the conversion feature of convertible debt securities does not create OID even if both parties acknowledge that the securities would have been sold for less than face value if the securities had not been issued with conversion privileges.[101]

In a Tenax Co. convertible debt securities offering in 1985, the corporate issuer took the position that its debt securities convertible into the stock of its parent, the Timken Co., generate OID in an amount equal to the portion of the issue price allocable to the conversion feature.[102] The issuer took this position notwithstanding the decision in *National Can Corp. v. United States*,[103] based on Rev. Rul. 69-265,[104] in which the IRS ruled—in the context of a reorganization—that a conversion feature is an item of property separate and distinct from the debt security to which it relates.[105] The rationale for the creation of OID in the Tenax-Timken offering was that unlike *National Can Corp.*, where the subsidiary was obligated to honor the conversion, Timken, the parent corporation, is not obligated to honor the conversion.

(c) PREMIUMS

The fact that a debt security is convertible into stock does not, in itself, deny the security owner a deduction under I.R.C. § 171 for a premium paid.[106] The security is within the scope of I.R.C. § 171 if the owner of the security has control over whether to convert the security.[107] The amount

---

[99] For a discussion of package offerings of convertible debt securities, see Burns & Levitt, *Package Offerings of Convertible Debentures*, 19 TUL. TAX INST. 307–35 (1970).

[100] For a discussion of OID generally, see Paine & Westheimer, *Original Issue Discount Regulations Revised but Remain Controversial*, 35 J. TAX'N 282–85 (1971); Sheffield, *Debt Issued for Traded and Nontraded Property*, 62 TAXES 1022 (1984); Lee, *The Tax Reform Act and Convertible Debt Securities*, 44 ST. JOHN'S L. REV. 1081 (special ed. 1970).

[101] National Can Corp. v. United States, 687 F.2d 1107, 1111–12 (7th Cir. 1982), *aff'g* 520 F. Supp. 567 (N.D. Ill. 1981).

[102] *Tenax Offering May Open Door to Big Savings on Convertibles*, CORP. FINANCING WK., Sept. 16, 1985, at 1.

[103] 687 F.2d at 1107.

[104] 1969-1 C.B. 109.

[105] The purchasers of the convertible debt securities of the Tenax Co. were mostly tax-exempt entities that do not pay tax on OID income as it accrues.

[106] Treas. Reg. § 1.171-2(c)(1) (1968).

[107] *Id.*

of the premium, however, must be reduced by the portion of the issue price attributable to the conversion feature.[108] The value of the conversion feature is ascertained as of the time of acquisition by reference to an assumed price for the same security without a conversion feature.[109]

If a convertible debt security is converted at a time when a portion of the premium remains unamortized, the security owner cannot deduct the unamortized amount of premium remaining at conversion. Rather, the unamortized premium is treated as part of the cost basis of the new security acquired. The basis of the new security is the same as that of the debt security that preceded it.[110]

In summary, if the debt security is issued for an amount in excess of the amount payable at maturity, the holder of the security may elect to deduct such excess over the life of the debenture, as amortizable bond premium under I.R.C. § 171. The issuer must report income in a like amount, under the applicable regulations. TRA '86 brought the treatment of bond premium into conformity with the treatment of OID, requiring amortizable bond premium to be computed on the basis of the holder's yield to maturity, determined by using the holder's basis for each debt security and compounding at the close of each accrual period. The Code provides that the amount of bond premium on a convertible debt security does not include any amount attributable to the conversion features of the debt security.

(d) CHANGE IN CONVERSION RATIOS OR CONVERSION PRICES

A change in the conversion ratio or the conversion price of convertible debt securities can be treated as a deemed distribution, that is, taxable to those security owners deemed to have received the distribution under I.R.C. § 305(b)(2).[111] In general, a stock dividend (or a series of distributions) is taxable if some shareholders receive cash or other property, while other shareholders receive an increase in their proportionate interests in the assets or earnings and profits of the corporation.[112] Any

---

[108] I.R.C. § 171(b); Treas. Reg. § 1.171-2(c)(1) (1968).
[109] Treas. Reg. § 1.171-2(c)(2) (1968); *see* section 34.2(c)(2).
[110] *See* Ades v. Comm'r, 38 T.C. 501, 512 (1962), *aff'd per curiam*, 316 F.2d 734 (2d Cir. 1963).
[111] For a discussion of dividends generally, see Chapter 24.
[112] I.R.C. § 305(b)(2); *see* section 24.2(b)(2).

disproportion in the deemed distribution—no matter how minor—can trigger taxability under I.R.C. § 305(b)(2).[113]

A change in a conversion ratio or redemption price is treated as a distribution for any shareholder whose proportionate interest is increased in either the earnings and profits or assets of the corporation.[114] To determine whether any shareholder's proportionate interest has been increased, the outstanding stock of the distributing corporation is deemed to include securities that are convertible into such stock, regardless of whether the securities are convertible during the taxable year.[115] This creates a serious obstacle to paying stock dividends when convertible securities are outstanding—unless the convertible securities provide for a "full adjustment" in the conversion ratio or conversion price to reflect all stock dividends.[116] The "presence of convertible debentures functions as a 'spoiler' for other equity shareholders . . . the payment of interest on the debentures apparently will trigger taxability for stock dividends paid to common shareholders."[117]

The IRS has ruled in Rev. Rul. 75-513[118] that an increase in the conversion ratio of convertible debt securities is a deemed distribution to the debt security owners if the conversion ratio is adjusted each year to reflect the differential between the interest rate of the securities and the yield that could have been obtained by investing in the corporation's stock on the date the debt securities were issued. In Rev. Rul. 75-513, a corporation paid a cash dividend to its shareholders and adjusted the conversion ratio of the debt securities to entitle the debt security owners to acquire additional shares. The IRS ruled that the distribution was a deemed taxable distribution to the debt holders and that I.R.C. § 301 applies by reason of I.R.C. §§ 305(b)(2) and 305(c).[119] The adjustment of the conversion ratio resulted in a cash dividend to the shareholders and an increase in the interest of the debt security owners. The distribution was found to be disproportionate.

---

[113] The Senate Finance Committee had proposed a de minimis exception in the Tax Reform Act of 1969, but it was rejected by the Conference Committee. SENATE FINANCE COMM. REPORT, TAX REFORM ACT OF 1969, S. REP. NO. 552, 91st Cong., 1st Sess. 154, *reprinted in* 1969 U.S. CODE CONG. & ADMIN. NEWS 2027, 2186; HOUSE CONFERENCE REPORT, TAX REFORM ACT OF 1969, H.R. CONF. REP. NO. 782, 91st Cong., 1st Sess. 309–10, *reprinted in* 1969 U.S. CODE CONG. & ADMIN. NEWS 2392, 2424.

[114] I.R.C. § 305(c).

[115] Treas. Reg. § 1.305-3(b)(5) (1974).

[116] Treas. Reg. § 1.305-3(d)(1)(i) (1974).

[117] B. BITTKER & J. EUSTICE, *supra* note 8, ¶ 7.43.10, at 7-81 to 7-82.

[118] 1975-2 C.B. 114.

[119] *Id.*

(e) CONVERSION INTO COMMON STOCK

A taxpayer does not generally recognize gain or loss when he exchanges a convertible debt security for stock in the corporation that issued the debt security.[120] A taxpayer's basis in the stock received in the conversion is the same as his basis in the convertible debt security.[121] Gain or loss is recognized only when the stock is subsequently disposed of.[122] The exchange is viewed as a transformation of the security, rather than a disposition.[123] Additionally, the conversion right must be contained in the terms of the debt security.[124]

The Code does specifically require the recognition of gain on an exchange of debt securities for stock in certain circumstances. One such situation is on the disposition of installment obligations under I.R.C. § 453.[125]

Conversion of convertible debt securities of one corporation into common stock of another corporation can also be taxable.[126] The IRS has ruled that gain or loss is not recognized on conversion into a parent's stock where—pursuant to a Type A reorganization—the acquiring corporation and its parent were liable for convertible securities acquired in the merger, the securities were convertible into the parent's stock, and the securities' interest rate and maturity date would change.[127] The IRS has also ruled that the nonrecognition provisions of the Code do not apply to a conversion where convertible debt securities are issued by one corporation and the stock is issued by a separate and distinct corporation.[128] As a result, gain or loss is recognized to the extent of the difference between the

---

[120] Rev. Rul. 72-265, 1972-1 C.B. 222 (which superseded and restated G.C.M. 18,436, 1937-1 C.B. 101, under the 1954 Code and regulations).

[121] *Id.*

[122] For a discussion of the holding period of stock acquired by conversion of a convertible security, see section 17.3(a)(3).

[123] *See* Fleischer & Cary, *The Taxation of Convertible Bonds and Stock*, 74 HARV. L. REV. 473, 478 (1961).

[124] Rose v. Trust Co. of Ga., 77 F.2d 355, 356 (5th Cir. 1935); G.C.M. 18,436, 1937-1 C.B. 101, *superseded by* Rev. Rul. 72-265, 1972-1 C.B. 222.

[125] Rev. Rul. 72-264, 1972-1 C.B. 131 (where the IRS ruled that deferred installment proceeds evidenced by convertible debt securities were taxable when the taxpayer subsequently disposed of the securities).

[126] International Tel. & Tel. Corp. v. Comm'r, 77 T.C. 60, 78, *supp. op.* 77 T.C. 1367 (1981), *aff'd per curiam*, 704 F.2d 252 (2d Cir. 1983); Rev. Rul. 69-135, 1969-1 C.B. 198, *distinguished by* Rev. Rul. 79-155, 1979-1 C.B. 153; *see also* Eisenberg, *IRS Position on Right to Convert into Another Corporation's Stock Is Confusing*, 33 J. TAX'N 25 (1970).

[127] Rev. Rul. 79-155, 1979-1 C.B. 153.

[128] Rev. Rul. 69-135, 1969-1 C.B. 198, *distinguished by* Rev. Rul. 79-155, 1979-1 C.B. 153.

fair market value of the common stock received on conversion and the cost (or other) basis of the debt securities converted into the stock.[129]

§ 34.4 ADJUSTABLE RATE CONVERTIBLE NOTES

The IRS ruled in Rev. Rul. 83-98[130] that ACRNs are equity interests, rather than debt obligations, of the corporate issuer. In most cases, ACRNs will be converted into common stock.[131] Moreover, it is to the advantage of the issuing corporation to force conversion so as not to pay additional cash to ACRN owners. ACRNs usually do not represent a promise to pay a certain sum because of the high probability of conversion.[132] As a result, "interest" payments are not deductible as interest by the issuer and are taxed as dividends to the ACRN owners. Corporate ACRN owners can qualify for the intercorporate dividends received deduction.[133]

ACRNs, first offered in 1982, were structured to comply with the requirements for hybrid debt instruments under the final Treasury regulations issued pursuant to I.R.C. § 385(a). These regulations were subsequently withdrawn by the Treasury.[134] ACRNs are typically convertible into stock, callable after a few years for a principal amount that is low in relation to the value of the common stock into which they are convertible. In addition, "interest" payments on ACRNs are unreasonably low when compared to other debt instruments issued at the same time. Further, the future annual yield on ACRNs is based on the level of dividends paid on the corporation's common stock.

In LTR 8523009,[135] the IRS ruled that convertible debt issued in a leveraged buyout qualified as debt even though the amount of debt was substantially in excess of the equity. The private ruling addressed Rev. Rul. 83-98[136] and appears to have narrowed the "high probability of conversion" test stated in the ruling. The IRS found that to the extent the newly acquired assets of the issuers are purchased at fair market value,

---

[129] *Id.*

[130] 1983-2 C.B. 40.

[131] Rev. Rul. 83-98, 1983-2 C.B. 40. ACRNs are also referred to as "floating rate convertible notes," or "FRCNs."

[132] Rev. Rul. 83-98, 1983-2 C.B. 40.

[133] *See* section 24.9.

[134] For a discussion of the debt-equity regulations, see section 34.2(a).

[135] (Feb. 25, 1985).

[136] 1983-2 C.B. 40.

there is not a sufficient economic incentive to convert the debt securities into the stock of the issuer.[137] On the other hand, to the extent the assets are acquired for less than fair market value, there is an economic incentive to convert the debt securities into the issuer's stock, which reflects the higher value of the newly acquired assets.[138]

§ 34.5 MANDATORY CONVERTIBLE NOTES

Mandatory convertible notes are securities issued by some domestic bank holding companies to meet capital requirements imposed by the FRB and the Comptroller of the Currency. In 1982, the FRB and the Comptroller of the Currency issued capital adequacy guidelines for assessing the capital of banks and bank holding companies. Under those guidelines, mandatory convertible notes are deemed to be primary capital.[139] Even though mandatory convertible notes qualify for bank regulatory capital, the IRS ruled in Rev. Rul. 85-119[140] that mandatory convertible notes are debt securities for tax purposes. As a result, under I.R.C. § 163(a), the periodic payments made to noteholders are deductible as interest by the bank holding company that issues the notes. The mandatory convertible notes considered by the IRS provided that the rights of the noteholders are subordinated to the bank's general creditors. In addition, at maturity (or call), the notes can be exchanged for equity interests in the bank holding company, although they are generally expected to be redeemed for cash.

The IRS limited Rev. Rul. 85-119 to the mandatory convertible notes it considered in the ruling. Although explicitly limited to its facts, Rev. Rul. 85-119 is very significant; it provides usable guidelines for bank holding companies that want to expand their regulatory capital without issuing equity interests. On the facts, the IRS found the notes—designated as debt by the parties—created a debtor-creditor relationship.[141] Some of the factors considered by the IRS in the ruling include the following.

---

[137] LTR 8523009 (Feb. 25, 1985).

[138] *Id.*

[139] *See generally* Saunders, *Lord, Make Me Chaste, but Not Just Yet*, FORBES, Sept. 9, 1985, at 56; *Fed Seeks Comments on Perpetual Debt*, BANKING EXPANSION REP., Nov. 18, 1985, at 15; *Too Much Preferred Stock Is a No-No*, BANKING EXPANSION REP., Dec. 16, 1985, at 2. *See also* 50 Fed. Reg. 46,739 (Nov. 13, 1985); *Subordinated Capital Notes Seeing Renewed Activity*, CORP. FINANCING WK., Apr. 7, 1986, at 4.

[140] 1985-2 C.B. 60.

[141] Rev. Rul. 85-119, 1985-2 C.B. 60 (citing Rev. Rul. 68-54, 1968-1 C.B. 69 and Rev. Rul. 73-122, 1973-1 C.B. 66, both of which were distinguished by Rev. Rul. 83-98, 1983-2 C.B. 40).

- First, the mandatory convertible notes were issued for cash at 100 percent of their face amount in a public offering and were not held in proportion to the bank holding company's stock.
- Second, the notes could not be called for 12 years and were freely transferable.
- Third, the noteholders could neither vote nor participate in the management of the bank holding company.
- Fourth, the notes bore a market rate of interest payable irrespective of earnings.
- Fifth, the noteholders could sue to compel payment of any amounts in default.
- Sixth, the bank holding company was not thinly capitalized and its debt-to-equity ratio was within industry standards.

It appears that the IRS took a liberal view of the definition of debt in Rev. Rul. 85-119 to include convertible securities that are likely to be converted.[142]

§ 34.6 EXCHANGEABLE DEBT SECURITIES AND PORTFOLIO EXCHANGEABLES

(a) EXCHANGEABLE DEBT SECURITIES

Exchangeable debt securities are exchangeable for shares of common stock of a corporation, other than the issuer. The exchange of exchangeable debt securities for the shares of common stock in another corporation is taxable to the issuer, although the amount of the gain is unclear.

(b) PORTFOLIO EXCHANGEABLES

Variations on the theme of exchangeable debt securities now include debentures that are convertible into other forms of underlying property, such as commodities or real estate. These debt securities are often referred to as "portfolio exchangeables." The Treasury regulations on OID—which prevent allocation of value to a conversion privilege in an investment unit—are expressly applicable only to rights to convert into stock or debt of the issuer. However, it is very likely that the portfolio exchangeables would be viewed as single instruments for tax purposes.

[142] For a discussion of a more narrow interpretation, see the discussion of Rev. Rul. 83-98 in section 34.4 and the discussion of LTR 8523009 in section 34.2(a).

The exchange of the portfolio exchangeable for the underlying property should be a taxable transaction to both parties to the transaction. Gain or loss should be recognized by the holder, measured by the difference between the fair market value of the stock received and the cost or other basis of the debt security. At the same time, the issuer should recognize gain or loss, measured by the difference between the adjusted issue price of the debt security and the issuer's basis in the underlying property.

§ 34.7 DISCOUNT CONVERTIBLE DEBT SECURITIES

A discount convertible debt security is a debt security that is convertible into the issuer's common stock at a specified number of shares per debt security. The debt securities are redeemable prior to an anniversary date, only if the price of the issuer's stock exceeds a certain level. Thereafter, the debt securities may be redeemed at prices reflecting accrued OID and a declining redemption premium. The holder has a right to put the debt security to the issuer at any time after a given anniversary date at specified prices. This debt instrument is similar to a conventional convertible debt security, with the important difference that it bears no stated interest and is, therefore, issued at a discount. Discount convertibles have been marketed by Merrill Lynch Capital Markets as "liquid yield option notes," or "LYONS."

The central tax question raised by discount convertibles is the proper treatment of the OID. Most issuers believe that OID that accrues prior to the conversion of the debt security can be deducted by the issuer and must be included in income by the holder. There is a danger that the courts will hold that if the debt securities do not, in fact, receive any payment for accrued interest if the debt securities are converted, the issuer will be denied a deduction on the basis that no interest ever really accrued.

The issuers of discount convertibles have been careful to provide in their indentures that the share of stock issued upon conversion of an instrument is deemed to be paid first in satisfaction of accrued OID up to the date of conversion. The accrued OID is deemed to be paid rather than cancelled, extinguished, or forfeited.

Conversion of LYONS is not a taxable event to the holder. The holder's obligation to include in gross income daily portions of OID terminates upon conversion. The holder's basis in the debt security is carried over and becomes the basis in the stock. Conversion has no effect on OID previously deducted by the issuer, although the unamortized OID amount cannot be deducted after conversion.

Thirty-five

Options on Debt Securities

Options on physical debt securities commenced trading on option exchanges in 1982.[1] (The various types of options on debt securities are discussed in section 5.2(a)(2).) In addition, options on futures contracts on debt securities (e.g., Treasury bonds) trade on commodity exchanges.[2] Options on futures contracts are discussed generally in Chapter 43.

§ 35.1 PRE-DRA TRANSACTIONS

Prior to the DRA amendments to I.R.C. § 1256 in 1984,[3] options on debt securities (whether listed or unlisted options) were not eligible for section 1256 treatment. As a result, the same tax rules that apply to equity options were applied to options on debt securities established prior to the DRA amendments. For a discussion of the tax treatment of equity call options, see section 30.3(b). For a discussion of equity put options, see section 30.3(c).

Offsetting positions on debt options—established after the enactment of ERTA in 1981 and prior to DRA's 1984 extension of section 1256 treatment to additional products (including exchange-traded options on

---

[1] *See* section 5.1.
[2] *See* section 5.2(b).
[3] DRA, Pub. L. No. 98-369, 98 Stat. 494 (1984).

§ 35.2　　Financial Products: Taxation, Regulation, and Design

debt securities)—were subject to the Straddle Rules.[4] This is because options on debt securities qualify as both personal property[5] and positions in personal property,[6] which are subject to the Straddle Rules.

§ 35.2　POST-DRA TRANSACTIONS

The tax treatment of debt option positions established after enactment of the DRA in 1984 depends on whether the options are listed for trading on an exchange. Listed option positions on debt securities (i.e., options on debt securities traded on commodity exchanges, national security exchanges, and other markets designated by the Treasury)[7] established generally after July 18, 1984,[8] are nonequity options[9] subject to section 1256 treatment.[10] For a discussion of the DRA transitional rules, see section 44.5. For a discussion of nonequity options, see section 44.3. For a discussion of section 1256 treatment, see generally Part Ten.

Unlisted debt security options are taxed in the same manner as unlisted equity options (i.e., options on stock and narrow-based stock indexes), that is, in accordance with the provisions of I.R.C. § 1234.[11] For a discussion of equity call options, see section 30.3(b). For a discussion of equity put options, see section 30.3(c).

---

[4] *See generally* Part Eleven.
[5] *See* section 48.2.
[6] *See* sections 48.3, 48.4(b), and 48.4(c).
[7] I.R.C. §§ 1256(g)(5), (7).
[8] The date of enactment of the DRA.
[9] I.R.C. § 1256(g)(3).
[10] I.R.C. § 1256(b)(3).
[11] *See* section 30.3.

Part Eight
Taxation of Asset-Backed Securities

Tax treatment is a major factor in structuring asset-backed securities offerings. With the exception of REMICs, RICs, and REITs, which are statutorily created, the tax treatment of asset-backed securities is a hodgepodge of provisions based on Treasury pronouncements, judicial decisions, and an assortment of Code provisions. Asset pools are quite popular because pooling assures that owners of asset-backed securities do not have any direct responsibility for collecting payments generated from the underlying assets in the pool. The traditional tax concern for asset-backed securities has been to avoid corporate tax at the level where the assets are "pooled." This has been a critical factor in structuring asset-backed securities offerings. A common form of asset pooling has been an investment trust, in which the investors are issued pass-through certificates. In an investment trust, income is taxed only to the certificate owners, not to the trust.[1]

The concern with using an investment trust is that multiple classes of certificate owners with different rights would reclassify the trust as an association taxable as a corporation.[2] A relatively recent development in structuring asset-backed securities has been the formation of corporations that issue debt securities, referred to as "pay-through bonds," collateralized by mortgages.[3] The pay-through bond structure was first

---

[1] I.R.C. §§ 671–679. For a discussion of pass-through certificates, see sections 7.2(c) and 36.2.
[2] *See* sections 7.2(c)(1) and 39.2(a).
[3] For a discussion of pay-through bonds, see sections 7.2(d) and 36.3.

introduced in 1983 by FHLMC to provide one vehicle that could offer debt securities with different payment priorities for investors.[4] With pay-through bonds, tax at the corporate level is minimized because deductions are available for the interest paid to the owners of the debt securities.[5] A popular type of pay-through bond is a CMO, which is a series of bonds issued by a corporation in various classes with different payment priorities and payment schedules.[6]

For real estate assets, the Tax Reform Act of 1986[7] created a new form of flow-through entity—a REMIC—for multiple-class investments in mortgage-backed securities.[8]

This Part Eight discusses tax considerations for the structure of asset-backed securities and the major tax considerations for owners of asset-backed securities.

---

[4] *See* section 2.1(b)(3).

[5] For a discussion of the tax treatment of pay-through bonds, see Chapter 38.

[6] For a discussion of CMOs issued by FHLMC, see sections 1.1(e) and 2.1(b)(3). For a discussion of CMOs generally, see sections 7.2(d)(2) and 36.3. *See also* Golden, *Collateralized Mortgage Obligations: Probing the Limits of National Bank Powers under the Glass-Steagall Act*, 36 CATH. U.L. REV. 1025 (1987).

[7] TRA '86, Pub. L. No. 99-514, 100 Stat. 2085 (1986).

[8] *See* sections 7.2(g), 36.8, and Chapter 41.

Thirty-six

Tax Considerations for Entities Used to Pool Asset-Backed Securities

Entities that hold pooled assets can be classified for tax purposes as corporations, partnerships, trusts, REMICs, RICs, or REITs. REMICs, RICs, and REITs are subject to specific Code provisions to determine their classification as such entities. For all other entities, the tax classification is determined under Treasury regulations, tax pronouncements, and judicial decisions. This chapter addresses the tax considerations involved in the selection of a structure to pool assets and issue securities.

§ 36.1 PARTICIPATION CERTIFICATES

Loan participations are a traditional form of securitization, whereby the loan originator resells portions of the loan to other investors, typically under a participation agreement.[1] Participations are structured as trusts or partnerships for tax purposes. Under applicable state law, a participation agreement might not establish a trust, so such a participation agreement would most likely be viewed as a partnership for tax purposes.[2] A partnership is defined in I.R.C. § 761(a) as "a syndicate, group,

---

[1] For a discussion of participation certificates, see section 7.2(b).
[2] For a discussion of the factors in determining the tax status of a partnership, see section 28.1.

pool, joint venture or other unincorporated organization through or by means of which any business, financial operation, or venture is carried on, and which is not . . . a corporation or a trust or estate." A loan participation agreement that creates a partnership might—under certain limited circumstances—be able to elect out of the partnership tax rules. Under Treasury regulations, a partnership can elect out of the partnership tax provisions for tax purposes if it "is availed of—(1) for investment purposes only and not for the active conduct of a business, (2) for the joint production, extraction, or use of property . . . or (3) by dealers in securities for a short period for the purpose of underwriting, selling, or distributing a particular issue of securities, if the income of the members of the organization may be adequately determined without the computation of partnership taxable income."[3] Given the conditions set out in the regulations, it may be difficult for most participation arrangements to elect out of the partnership tax rules.

§ 36.2 PASS-THROUGH CERTIFICATES

Pass-through certificates are issued by a trust that holds and services a fixed pool of assets.[4] Each certificate represents a pro rata interest in each of the underlying assets making up the pool. Payments received by the trust are distributed (i.e., passed through) to the certificate owners minus all fees and expenses incurred to service the assets and administer the pool (including expenses, if any, for credit enhancements).[5] Because the fees attributable to servicing pooled assets are usually fixed in advance, certificate owners are generally assured a fixed rate of interest on the principal balance of their certificates.

The investment trust was once the most common and desirable vehicle for securitizing assets. Given the burdensome tax requirements, however, entities that issue pay-through bonds are often more attractive. In an investment trust, the trust issues "pass-through certificates" representing fractional ownership interests in a pool of identified property.[6] Cash flow from the pooled assets is distributed or "passed-through" pro rata to certificate holders—without taxation at the trust level. Shortfalls or deficiencies in the scheduled cash flow from the pooled assets are

---

[3] I.R.C. § 761(a). *See also* Treas. Reg. § 1.761-2 (1972).

[4] For a discussion of pass-through certificates, see section 7.2(c).

[5] *See generally* Treas. Reg. § 1.671-3(a) (1969).

[6] The fact that a pass-through certificate holder is treated as owning the assets that make up the pool can be of significance to certain entities, such as savings and loan associations.

reflected in reduced payments on the certificates, unless these payments are in some manner guaranteed with a form of credit enhancement.[7] On the other hand, faster than expected payments on the trust's pooled assets lead to retirement of its interests earlier than its investors had planned.

(a) IN GENERAL

To avoid taxation at the pool level, the investment trust structure is used for pass-through certificates.[8] The trust is generally ignored for tax purposes, so the certificate owners, rather than the trust, are subject to tax.[9] For tax purposes, the term "corporation" includes unincorporated "associations" that have corporate characteristics.[10] Such pools are structured to avoid classification as an association taxable as a corporation. Although an entity may be a trust or a partnership for state law purposes, it can, under certain circumstances, be deemed an association and treated as a corporation for tax purposes.[11]

A mortgage pool structured as a trust is treated as an investment trust if the "grantor" holds "the beneficial enjoyment of the corpus or the income therefrom" and has a power to dispose of the corpus "without the approval or consent of any adverse party."[12] Equitable ownership in each separate mortgage is transferred, on a pro rata basis, to the certificate owners that own undivided interests in the pool. The certificate owners include in income all items of income, deductions, and credits attributable to their pro rata interests.[13] Certificate owners (whether on the cash or accrual method of accounting) report income at the time the payments

---

[7] For a discussion of credit enhancements, see section 7.1(b).

[8] *See generally* I.R.C. §§ 671–679. For a discussion of REMIC treatment for multiple-tranche mortgage-backed securities, see sections 7.2(g) and 36.8(a).

[9] The trustee of the investment trust files IRS Form 1041, U.S. Fiduciary Income Tax Return, with a statement that identifies the certificate holders and shows items of income, loss, deductions, and credits allocable to the certificate holders. Treas. Reg. § 1.671-4(a) (1981).

[10] I.R.C. § 7701(a)(3). *See* section 28.1.

[11] If a trust is classified as an association taxable as a corporation, the following tax consequences result. First, the entity is subject to corporate tax. Second, those owners of the pass-through certificates that are not tax-exempt entities are taxed on any distributions made to them. Third, certificate owners that are corporations should be entitled to the intercorporate dividends received deduction. *See* section 24.9(a). If a trust is classified as an association taxable as a partnership, the following tax consequences result. First, assuming the PTP rules do not apply, there should not be a tax at the entity level. *See* Chapter 28. Second, any tax imposed on "partnership income" might be allocated between the originator or promoter and the certificate owners in an unexpected way.

[12] I.R.C. § 674(a).

[13] Treas. Reg. § 1.671-3(a) (1969).

§ 36.2(b)   Financial Products: Taxation, Regulation, and Design

on the pooled assets are received by the trust, even if distributions are not made to them at that time. The trustee is simply viewed as an agent acting on behalf of the certificate holders. This tax result has been confirmed in numerous revenue rulings addressing pass-through certificates guaranteed by GNMA, FNMA, FHLMC, and private mortgage pools with private insurance.[14]

Under Treasury regulations, an investment trust is treated as a nontaxable conduit if—and only if—two conditions are met. First, the trustee must not have the power to vary the trust's investments.[15] Therefore, asset pools organized as investment trusts permit the trustee to exercise only ministerial powers and to vary the pool assets only by disposing of any assets in default. Second, there must be only a single class of ownership interests.[16] An investment trust cannot have multiple classes, or "tranches," of ownership interests. The prohibition against varying investments is discussed in section 36.2(b). The prohibition against multiple ownership interests is discussed in section 36.2(c).

(b)   PROHIBITION AGAINST VARYING INVESTMENTS

To avoid reclassification as an association taxable as a corporation, the enabling documents for an investment trust must provide that the trustee has no power to vary the investments in the asset pool.[17] An entity will only be classified as a trust for tax purposes if its activities are limited to conserve and protect property for the benefit of the beneficiaries of the trust. This means that an investment trust must not grant the trustee (or any other person) power to change the trust's investments.

Notwithstanding this broad prohibition, investment trust status has been upheld where trust provisions allow a minimal level of activity on the part of the trustee. Minor activities have been approved by the IRS in

[14] *See generally* Rev. Rul. 84-10, 1984-1 C.B. 155; Rev. Rul. 81-204, 1981-2 C.B. 157, *amplified by* Rev. Rul. 85-125, 1985-2 C.B. 180; Rev. Rul. 81-203, 1981-2 C.B. 137; Rev. Rul. 80-96, 1980-1 C.B. 317; Rev. Rul. 77-349, 1977-2 C.B. 20; Rev. Rul. 74-300, 1974-1 C.B. 169; Rev. Rul. 74-221, 1974-1 C.B. 365; Rev. Rul. 74-169, 1974-1 C.B. 147; Rev. Rul. 72-376, 1972-2 C.B. 647; Rev. Rul. 71-399, 1971-2 C.B. 433; Rev. Rul. 70-545, 1970-2 C.B. 7; Rev. Rul. 70-544, 1970-2 C.B. 6; Rev. Rul. 61-175, 1961-2 C.B. 128.

[15] Commissioner v. North Am. Bond Trust, 122 F.2d 545, 546 (2d Cir.), *cert. denied*, 314 U.S. 701 (1941); Treas. Reg. § 301.7701-4(c) (1986); Rev. Rul. 78-149, 1978-1 C.B. 448; Rev. Rul. 75-192, 1975-1 C.B. 384.

[16] Treas. Reg. § 301.7701-4(c)(1) (1986).

[17] *See generally* Pennsylvania Co. for Ins. on Lives and Granting Annuities v. United States, 146 F.2d 392 (3d Cir. 1944), *aff'g* 48 F. Supp. 972 (E.D. Pa.), *and aff'g* 48 F. Supp. 969 (1942); Commissioner v. North Am. Bond Trust, 122 F.2d 545, 546 (2d Cir.), *cert. denied*, 314 U.S. 701 (1941).

published rulings. For example, the IRS has ruled that a trust that holds mortgages and makes quarterly distributions to its certificate owners can, under certain circumstances, reinvest the monthly payments it receives on the pooled mortgages in high quality obligations. To so qualify, the obligations must mature prior to the next trust distribution date and must be held to maturity.[18]

The IRS has also allowed—without subjecting a trust to tax as a corporation—a trustee two years to accept new mortgages in exchange for mortgages that were initially included in the trust and that did not conform to representations and warranties.[19] (It is unclear whether an exchange period that extends beyond two years might change the tax result.)[20] The power to sell a trust's assets is allowed if the sales proceeds cannot be reinvested in new assets.[21] Where there has been a failure to deliver the obligations on a "when, as, and if issued basis" under a contract, minimal powers to acquire substantially similar obligations have not tainted an investment trust's tax status as a trust.[22] And, a trustee can exchange old obligations for new obligations if the debtor is in default, or might be in default in the near future.[23] "[I]t is evident that the power to take advantage of variations in the market is critical to the determination of whether the trustee has power to vary the investment. If the trustee has this power, the trust will be treated as an association taxable as a corporation.[24]

(c) PROHIBITION AGAINST MULTIPLE INTERESTS

An investment trust cannot have multiple classes of ownership interests and still be viewed as a trust for tax purposes. The tax theory behind the prohibition against multiple interests—advanced by the Treasury Department in the Treasury decision that accompanied the regulations that prohibit multiple interests—is that the tax-free trust vehicle is not

---

[18] Rev. Rul. 75-192, 1975-1 C.B. 384. *See* G.C.M. 36,132 (Jan. 8, 1975).

[19] *See generally* Rev. Rul. 84-10, 1984-1 C.B. 155; Rev. Rul. 81-203, 1981-2 C.B. 137; Rev. Rul. 80-96, 1980-1 C.B. 317; Rev. Rul. 74-300, 1974-1 C.B. 169; Rev. Rul. 74-221, 1974-1 C.B. 365; Rev. Rul. 72-376, 1972-2 C.B. 647; Rev. Rul. 71-399, 1971-2 C.B. 433; Rev. Rul. 70-545, 1970-2 C.B. 7. *See also* LTR 8918026 (May 9, 1989).

[20] For a discussion of mortgage pools taxable as trusts, see J. PEASLEE & D. NIRENBERG, FEDERAL INCOME TAXATION OF MORTGAGE BACKED SECURITIES 33, 33–58 (1989).

[21] Rev. Rul. 78-149, 1978-1 C.B. 448; Rev. Rul. 73-460, 1973-2 C.B. 424.

[22] Rev. Rul. 86-92, 1986-2 C.B. 214.

[23] Rev. Rul. 73-460, 1973-2 C.B. 424, *distinguished by* Rev. Rul. 78-149, 1978-1 C.B. 448.

[24] K. LORE, MORTGAGE-BACKED SECURITIES: DEVELOPMENTS AND TRENDS IN THE SECONDARY MORTGAGE MARKET ch. 6, at 6–8 (Clark Boardman, Securities Law Series 1988–89).

available to provide investors with a means of acquiring economic interests that could not have been acquired by a direct investment in the trust's assets.[25] On March 21, 1986, the Treasury issued final regulations, effective as of April 28, 1984, on the tax classification of trusts with multiple ownership classes.[26]

The regulations, first proposed in 1984, provide that investment trusts with multiple ownership classes are "associations" taxable as "corporations."[27] The regulations provide that "trust classification may be appropriate for a multiple class trust if the trust is formed to serve the traditional custodial purposes of a fixed investment trust and the existence of multiple classes of beneficial interests is incidental to such purposes."[28] In Rev. Proc. 86-29,[29] the IRS modified Rev. Proc. 86-3[30] when it announced that it would issue private letter rulings addressing the classification of an arrangement as a fixed investment trust when the arrangement has multiple classes of equitable ownership. In Rev. Proc. 83-52,[31] the IRS amended Rev. Proc. 83-22[32] to provide that the IRS would not issue advance rulings concerning the classification of trusts with multiple ownership classes.[33]

The Treasury regulations provide that "[a]n investment trust with multiple classes of ownership interests will ordinarily be classified as an association or partnership."[34] Nevertheless, an investment trust is taxed as a trust if "there is no power under the trust agreement to vary the investment" and "the trust is formed to facilitate direct investment in the assets of the trust and the existence of multiple classes of ownership interests is incidental to that purpose."[35] The regulations set out examples of multiple ownership interests that are acceptable and those that

---

[25] T.D. 8080, 1986-1 C.B. 371.

[26] The regulations were issued in response to an offering by Dean Witter Reynolds, Inc. on behalf of Sears Mortgage Securities Corporation to issue $500 million of multiple trust interests (i.e., fast pay and slow pay interests). For this reason, the regulations are often referred to as the "Sears regulations" or, less frequently, the "Dean Witter regulations."

[27] Treas. Reg. § 301.7701-4 (1986). The proposed regulations had a prospective effective date so they did not affect the first Sears fast pay and slow pay offering. When the regulations were issued in final form, they were effective as of April 28, 1984, which was the date the regulations were first proposed.

[28] T.D. 8080, 1986-1 C.B. 371.

[29] 1986-1 C.B. 659.

[30] 1986-1 C.B. 416.

[31] 1983-2 C.B. 569.

[32] 1983-1 C.B. 680.

[33] The IRS superseded Rev. Proc. 83-52 in Rev. Proc. 89-3, 1989-1 C.B. 761.

[34] Treas. Reg. § 301.7701-4(c)(1) (1986).

[35] *Id.*

are not. Three examples in the regulations apply the "incidental to facilitate direct investment" standard. These examples are discussed in the remainder of this section.

In Example (1) of Treas. Reg. § 301.7701-4(c)(2),[36] a corporation purchases a portfolio of residential mortgages and transfers the mortgages to a bank under a trust agreement. The corporation receives from the trustee two classes of certificates evidencing the rights to payments from the pooled mortgages. Class A holders are entitled to all payments of mortgage principal—both scheduled and prepaid—until their certificates are retired.[37] Holders of Class B certificates receive payments of principal only after all Class A certificates have been retired.[38] The corporation sells the Class A and Class B certificates to the public. In Example (1), the Treasury finds that the trust is not taxable as a trust. Instead, it is taxable as an association or a partnership. Holders of the Class B certificates have "call protection" because the risks of prepayment are shifted to the Class A certificates. This call protection means that "[t]he trust thus serves to create investment interests with respect to the mortgages held by the trust that differ significantly from direct investment in the mortgages."[39] In other words, "the existence of multiple classes of trust ownership is not incidental to any purpose of the trust to facilitate direct investment."[40]

In Example (2) of Treas. Reg. § 301.7701-4(c)(2),[41] an originator transfers mortgages to a bank under a trust agreement under which the trustee has no power to reinvest the proceeds or to vary the investments. The originator receives back two classes of certificates evidencing rights to payments from the pooled mortgages. Class C certificate holders are entitled to receive 90 percent of the payments of principal and interest on the mortgages. Class D certificate holders are entitled to receive the remaining 10 percent.[42] The only difference between the two classes is that, in the event of a default, the payment rights of Class D certificates are subordinated to the rights of Class C certificate holders. The originator sells the Class C certificates to investors and retains the Class D certificates.[43] In Example (2), the Treasury finds that the trust is taxed as a trust although it has multiple ownership interests ("given the greater security

---

[36] (1986).
[37] Treas. Reg. § 301.7701-4(c)(2), Example (1) (1986).
[38] *Id.*
[39] *Id.*
[40] *Id.*
[41] (1986).
[42] Treas. Reg. § 301.7701-4(c)(2), Example (2) (1986).
[43] *Id.*

provided to the holders of Class C certificates"); the interests "are substantially equivalent to undivided interests in the pool of mortgages, coupled with a limited recourse guarantee running from [the originator] to the holders of Class C certificates."[44] As a result, the Treasury finds that "the existence of multiple classes of ownership interests is incidental to the trust's purpose of facilitating direct investment in the assets of the trust."[45]

In Example (4) of Treas. Reg. § 301.7701-4(c)(2),[46] a trust is formed to hold a portfolio of bonds and the trust certificates are sold to public investors. Each certificate represents a right to receive "a particular payment with respect to a specific bond."[47] For tax purposes, under the rules of I.R.C. § 1286,[48] "stripped coupons and stripped bonds are treated as separate bonds."[49] In Example (4), the Treasury finds that "[a]lthough the interest of each certificate holder is different . . . and the trust thus has multiple classes of ownership, the multiple classes simply provide each certificate holder with a direct interest in what is treated under [I.R.C.] section 1286 as a separate bond."[50] The trust is taxed as a trust because "the multiple classes of trust interests merely facilitate direct investment in the assets held by the trust."[51]

(d) STRIPPED PASS-THROUGH CERTIFICATES

Stripped pass-through certificates reflect the "stripping" of the interest component of cash flows on asset-backed securities.[52] Interest can be separated from principal in the pass-through certificate structure without running afoul of the prohibition against multiple interests because of the specific example in the Treasury regulations that allows the stripping of bonds from coupons. In Example (4) of Treas. Reg. § 301.7701-4(c)(2),[53] a trust with multiple classes of ownership was taxed as a trust because "the multiple classes simply provide each certificate holder with a direct

---

[44] *Id.*

[45] *Id.*

[46] (1986).

[47] Treas. Reg. § 301.7701-4(c)(2), Example (4) (1986).

[48] For a discussion of the stripped bond rules, see generally section 31.6. *See also* discussion at section 36.2(d).

[49] Treas. Reg. § 301.7701-4(c)(2), Example (4) (1986).

[50] *Id.*

[51] *Id.*

[52] For a detailed discussion of stripped pass-through certificates, see section 7.2(c)(2). *See also The Stripped Mortgage-Backed Security*, INTERMARKET, Mar. 1987, at 70.

[53] (1986). *See* sections 7.2(c)(2)(i) and 36.2(c).

interest in what is treated under [I.R.C.] section 1286 as a separate bond."[54] This means that the multiple classes "merely facilitate direct investment in the assets held by the trust."[55] Because of the specific reference in Example (4) to I.R.C. § 1286, it is possible that expansive interpretations of the stripped bond rules may result in an expansion of the scope of Example (4).[56] In fact, some securitized assets offerings have combined stripped and subordinated certificates.

(e) SENIOR AND SUBORDINATED PASS-THROUGH CERTIFICATES

Senior and subordinated classes of pass-through certificates provide a form of credit enhancement.[57] The senior class, frequently rated by a nationally recognized rating organization, has a priority claim to cash flow from the underlying pooled assets. Distributions to the subordinated class are reduced by the amount of any payment defaults and late payments, thereby protecting the senior class up to the distributions otherwise allocated to the subordinated class. The subordinated class, which most likely is not rated by a rating agency, provides excess collateralization, or the cash that is needed for a reserve fund to protect the senior class.[58] To minimize the risks of possibly tainting trust tax status, reserve funds are typically maintained outside of the trust. The subordinated pass-through certificate holders are generally treated as the owners of the reserve fund, which is itself a trust for tax purposes if structured to meet applicable tax rules.[59]

For a trust to be taxed as a trust for tax purposes, it must not provide investors with a means of acquiring economic interests that could not have been acquired by a direct investment in the trust's assets.[60] Example (2) of Treas. Reg. § 301.7701-4(c)(2)[61] allows senior and subordinated

---

[54] Treas. Reg. § 301.7701-4(c)(2), Example (4) (1986).

[55] *Id.*

[56] *See, e.g.,* LTR 8618065 (Feb. 7, 1986).

[57] For a detailed discussion of senior and subordinated pass-through certificates, see section 7.2(c)(3).

[58] If a reserve fund is used, it should not affect the classification of the trust as a trust for tax purposes. *See* G.C.M. 38,311 (Mar. 19, 1980), *revoked by* G.C.M. 39,040 (Sept. 27, 1983); Rev. Rul. 75-192, 1975-C.B. 384.

[59] In LTR 8918045 (Feb. 6, 1989), the IRS addressed the definition of a qualified reserve as it relates to credit enhancements in a trust that elected REMIC status. For a discussion of LTR 8918045, see section 36.8(n).

[60] T.D. 8080, 1986-1 C.B. 371.

[61] (1986).

pass-through certificates under the facts set out in the example. For a discussion of Example (2), see section 36.2(c). T.D. 8080, which accompanied the regulations, appears to require the pool originator or promoter to retain the subordinated certificate. It states that "the subordinated interest is retained as a security device by the originator of the mortgages, and is in lieu of a direct guarantee to investors."[62] Given this statement, there was concern that a transfer of subordinated pass-through certificates to unrelated third parties would taint trust status. The IRS confirmed this "no transfer" position in a private letter ruling released in mid-1989.

The IRS reviewed a securitization structure for auto loan receivables in the trust structure in LTR 8929030.[63] A company purchased a pool of self-amortizing, fixed-rate, level-payment auto loans from a bank and immediately assigned the contracts to a trustee in exchange for two classes of certificates (Class A and Class B). Each certificate class represented an equal, undivided interest in the pool, entitling the certificate holder to a percentage of the principal and interest. The company acted as the master servicer of the loans, in exchange for a fee based on a percentage of the outstanding loans plus a percentage of interest received. The company subcontracted the servicing obligations to the bank.

In the situation examined in the private letter ruling, Class A certificate holders have essentially the same rights as holders of Class B certificates, with two differences:

1. While the payments to Class B holders are reduced by losses recognized on the contracts during the prior month, Class A holders' payments are not so reduced.

2. Also, while Class A certificates may be freely exchanged, Class B certificates may not be transferred unless the transferor furnishes to the trustee an opinion of counsel concluding that the transfer will not affect the tax classification of the trust.

When the company wanted to sell the Class B certificates to unrelated buyers at fair market value, it requested a ruling from the IRS that the sale of the Class B certificates would not affect the trust's status as a trust for tax purposes. The IRS disagreed with the company's ruling position and ruled instead that a sale of the Class B certificates would preclude continued status as a trust for tax purposes; the trust, therefore, would be

[62] T.D. 8080, 1986-1 C.B. 371.
[63] (dated Apr. 21, 1989 and issued July 21, 1989).

classified as an association or partnership under Treas. Reg. § 301.7701-2.[64] The IRS distinguished the arrangement from Example (2) of Treas. Reg. § 301.7701-4(c)(2)[65] because the subordinated interest would be transferred to unrelated buyers. (In Example (2), the subordinated interest is retained by the originator.)

The IRS found in the private letter ruling that the two classes of ownership interests, if held by investors, would satisfy diverse investment goals, not facilitate investment in the pool by a single class of investors. On this basis, the IRS found that a transfer of the subordinated interests would taint the trust's tax status.

In light of LTR 8929030, it is clear that the IRS is limiting the scope of the Treasury regulations to the four corners of the examples set out in the regulations.[66]

Given the chill LTR 8929030 placed on transfers of subordinated ownership interests, a few possible ways to transfer subordinated pass-through certificates without running afoul of the limitations imposed on transfer follow. First, it might be possible to transfer subordinated certificates to an affiliate of the originator or sponsor without a tax problem—especially if the sponsor and the affiliate file consolidated tax returns. Second, if a partnership holds the pooled assets, partnership interests in the entity can be transferred to third parties as long as the partnership does not terminate under the provisions of I.R.C. § 708(b)(1)(B).[67]

§ 36.3 PAY-THROUGH BONDS

Because of the limitations on multiple ownership classes, also referred to as "tranches," in investment trusts, it is nearly impossible to issue multiple classes of ownership interests in trusts holding pooled assets while maintaining classification as a trust for tax purposes.[68] This means—given the body of Treasury pronouncements and regulations—that a pass-through vehicle with multiple tranches is not available except

---

[64] (1983).

[65] (1986). For a discussion of Example (2), see section 36.2(c).

[66] Some securitized asset offerings have combined stripped and subordinated certificates by relying on two examples at the same time.

[67] I.R.C. § 708(b)(1)(B) provides that "a partnership shall be . . . terminated only if within a 12-month period there is a sale or exchange of 50 percent or more of the total interest in partnership capital and profits."

[68] *See* discussion at section 36.2(a).

§ 36.3   Financial Products: Taxation, Regulation, and Design

for those limited exceptions discussed in section 36.2(d). The way around this obstacle, while minimizing entity level tax, is to use debt (rather than equity) in a pay-through (rather than pass-through) structure.[69] This typically utilizes a corporation or owner trust, which, in either case, includes multiple-debt tranches and a residual ownership class (or classes) that constitutes equity rather than debt.[70]

Pay-through bonds, including CMOs, are structured as debt securities issued by a corporation subject to corporate tax, or if the issuer is an owner trust, the trust is usually subject to the partnership tax provisions.[71] Interest payments made to the bond owners are deductible by the corporation or owner trust in determining its taxable income. This means that the corporation's taxable income is based on the difference between the yields on the mortgage (income) and the payment obligations of the pay-through bonds (deductible by the corporation as interest expense).[72] Typically, to collateralize pay-through bonds, the corporation or owner trust uses the proceeds from the sale of its bonds to acquire the assets to be pooled (and sometimes it acquires pass-through certificates that represent ownership interests in other asset pools).

The introduction of CMOs by FHLMC in 1983 revolutionized the pay-through bond market.[73] CMO pay-through bonds provide investors with a way to hold different ownership interests in the entity issuing the interests. CMOs—and all pay-through bonds—are an attractive concept, especially in light of Treasury regulations that generally define investment trusts to preclude trust tax status for trusts with more than one ownership class, except in limited circumstances.[74] Pay-through bonds offer substantial flexibility in tailoring maturities and average lives of debt securities to meet investor demands.[75] They also provide, through the prioritization of cash flows, a measure of call protection. Pay-through bonds attempt to reduce the uncertainty of the timing of cash flow created

---

[69] For a discussion of pay-through bonds, see section 7.2(d).

[70] For entities that hold real estate mortgages, the REMIC rules and the TMP provisions must be considered. *See generally* sections 7.2(g), 36.8, and 36.8(o).

[71] For a discussion of the issues raised over whether an interest qualifies as debt or equity in the issuer, see generally section 27.2. To support debt treatment for tax purposes, the owners of the equity interests might need to hold an ownership interest in the underlying pooled assets that is more than a nominal residual interest.

[72] If a debt interest is treated as equity, the entity issuing the "ownership interest" cannot deduct the "interest payments" made to the owners of the interest. For a discussion of equity interests in entities issuing pay-through bonds, see section 7.2(e).

[73] For a discussion of FHLMC/CMOs, see section 2.1(b)(4).

[74] Treas. Reg. § 301.7701-4(c)(1) (1986) (effective for interests issued after April 28, 1984); *see* section 36.2(a).

[75] For a detailed discussion of CMOs, see section 7.2(d)(2).

by mortgage prepayments by creating—from the underlying pooled collateral—bonds that mature serially.[76] All scheduled and unscheduled principal paydowns are typically allocated sequentially to the first class of bonds until it has been fully paid, and then all principal payments are applied to the next class until it has been fully paid, until all classes are fully paid. The classes are divided into tranches, ranging from fast pay to slow pay. As a result, each class receives—at a scheduled time—all of the principal payments from the collateralized asset pool.

For multiple-class pay-through bonds that hold real estate mortgages, REMICs replace all vehicles used under pre-TRA '86 law to issue the interests. In fact, after 1991, REMICs will be the exclusive way to issue, without two levels of tax, multiple-class securities backed by real estate. For a discussion of REMICs, see sections 7.2(g) and 36.8. For a discussion of the taxable mortgage pool provisions, see section 36.8(o).

§ 36.4 EQUITY INTERESTS IN ENTITIES ISSUING PAY-THROUGH BONDS

Pay-through bonds are typically issued by special purpose corporations or owner trusts. Regardless of whether pay-through bonds are issued by a corporation or an owner trust, the entity that holds the pooled assets cannot simply issue bonds. Someone has to be at risk with an equity investment and come last in line behind the bondholders. Without a sufficient equity investment, the pay-through bonds would be treated as equity—not debt—precluding an interest deduction by the corporation or trust.[77] If this equity layer is sold to third parties, such investors will typically demand a high return, adding an economic cost to the debt structure that would not be present in the absence of tax requirements.[78]

In addition, to assure debt treatment for tax purposes, the owners of the equity interests must hold more than a nominal interest in the underlying pooled assets. It has been suggested by some commentators that the equity interest in an entity that issues pay-through bonds should equal one and one-half to two percent of the face amount of the bonds.

---

[76] Standard pass-through certificates pass through interest and principal received on the underlying pooled collateral on a pro rata basis to the certificate holders. Prepayments of the underlying assets make the cash flow received by such certificate holders irregular and widely dispersed over time. Moreover, the certificates remain outstanding as long as any of the mortgages in the pool remain outstanding.

[77] For a discussion of the issues raised over whether an interest is debt or equity, see generally section 27.2.

[78] For a general discussion of equity interests in pay-through bonds, see section 7.2(e).

This equity can be structured as the residual interest in the underlying pooled assets.

(a) SPECIAL PURPOSE CORPORATIONS

A special purpose corporation issuing pay-through bonds has minimal tax at the corporate level because it deducts all of the interest it pays to its bondholders. The corporation's taxable income (or loss) is based on the difference between the yields on its assets and the payment obligations on its pay-through bonds. These are typically designed to match as closely as possible.[79] The pay-through bonds must be viewed as the corporation's debt obligations for the corporation to deduct the interest it pays on the bonds. For a discussion of debt and equity considerations, see section 27.2.

(b) OWNER TRUSTS

An owner trust is not taxed at the entity level if the trust qualifies as an investment trust or as a partnership for tax purposes.[80] Taxation as a partnership results if a trust is not taxable as a trust but it has more "partnership" than "corporate" characteristics.[81] It is highly unlikely that an owner trust will be taxed as an investment trust. This means that—to avoid tax classification as a corporation—it must qualify as a partnership. To so qualify, the trust must have at least two owners at all times (referred to as "associates"),[82] an objective to carry on business and divide the gains from that business, significant restrictions on the transfer of the ownership interests, and personal liability of the trust's owners for the trust's operating expenses and liabilities, except for payments on the bonds that are collateralized by the underlying pooled assets. Typically, owner trusts have continuity of life, but they often lack centralized management. In addition, their equity owners typically have personal liability. And their ownership certificates are not freely transferable.

If an owner trust qualifies as a partnership for tax purposes, each item of its income, loss, deduction (including interest payments to holders of

---

[79] For a detailed discussion of pay-through bonds, see section 7.2(d).

[80] Owner trusts became popular to address financial accounting concerns (such as the fact that the issuer must generally carry pay-through bonds on its balance sheet for accounting and regulatory purposes). For a discussion of these issues, see K. LORE, *supra* note 24, ch. 3, at 3-29 to 3-31, ch. 7, at 7-1 to 7-21.

[81] For a discussion of partnerships, see generally Chapter 28.

[82] Associates are owners that have a beneficial interest in the entity and that act together for the business objective.

its pay-through bonds and any other deductible expenses), and credit is allocated to the trust's owners. In short, the owners receive the residual income or loss from the trust's activities—just as does a special purpose corporation when it issues pay-through bonds. Because the residuals have not been previously taxed at the entity level, an owner trust generally avoids double taxation (first at the special purpose entity level and then when the owner receives the residuals). As the issuer of pay-through bonds, an owner trust has the important advantage over a corporation because it avoids an additional layer of federal income tax at the entity level.

(c) PHANTOM INCOME CONSIDERATIONS

"Phantom income" is generally allocated to the equity interests in a special purpose corporation or owner trust in a multiple-tranche pay-through bond offering. Phantom income results when there is taxable income in excess of the cash flow on the underlying pooled assets. Phantom income results because of the timing difference between the payments received on the underlying pooled assets and the payment obligations on the pay-through bonds. Income and deductions do not match up; because a portion of the interest income received on the pooled assets is almost always used by the corporation or trust to make nondeductible principal payments to its pay-through bondholders. Phantom income is inevitable.[83] Indeed, precisely because the objective of the pay-through bond structure is to provide investors with an amortization schedule that is different from the amortization of the underlying pooled assets, it is difficult—if not impossible—to avoid phantom income.[84]

Although phantom income is generally offset in future years by an equal amount of phantom loss, the timing difference is a real economic expense. Equity owners have income in the earlier years and losses in the later years. Income is equal to the interest received on the underlying pooled assets while there are deductions for interest that is paid or accrued on the pay-through bonds for that year. Because some nondeductible principal is typically paid off during the year, the interest deduction is less than the income on the underlying assets. "[A] sale [of an ownership interest] before maturity may have the effect of moving the tax

---

[83] There is also a phantom income problem for holders of REMIC residual interests. *See* section 41.2(k).

[84] For a discussion of phantom income and illustrations of sources of phantom income, see Lupo, *Phantom Income*, in FEDERAL INCOME TAXATION OF MORTGAGE BACKED SECURITIES, *supra* note 20, at 265 app. A, 267–302.

benefits inherent in the reduced future taxable income (or loss) up to the point of sale. Thus, such a sale can mitigate the phantom income problem."[85]

A corporation issuing multiple-tranche pay-through bonds must maintain a reserve to pay taxes and cannot pay out all of its funds to its bondholders.[86] Likewise, trust owners must be prepared to come up with money out of their own pockets to pay taxes on phantom income if there is no reserve fund or it is inadequate to meet tax obligations.

§ 36.5 PASS-THROUGH DEBT CERTIFICATES

Pass-through debt certificates are interests in trusts that are treated as the debt obligations of the originator or sponsor of the offering. In the pass-through debt certificate structure, the sale of the certificates is characterized as a sale, rather than a pledge, of trust assets for financial and (possibly) regulatory accounting purposes. The originator typically retains the residual—or equity—ownership interest in the trust, and investors purchase trust certificates that are treated as debt securities for tax purposes.[87] This structure is not used for pooling real estate mortgages eligible for REMIC status. For a discussion of REMICs, see sections 7.2(g) and 36.8.

(a) IN GENERAL

Pass-through debt certificates are structured as debt for tax purposes.[88] The entity does not try to qualify as an investment trust; instead it treats the transaction as a secured borrowing for tax purposes.[89] A major tax issue that has to be addressed is whether the transaction is treated as a

---

[85] *Id.* at 268.

[86] Nationally recognized rating organizations typically rate only those bonds that have sufficient reserves to pay taxes.

[87] For a discussion of pass-through debt certificates, see section 7.2(f).

[88] *See id.*

[89] For regulatory and financial accounting purposes, the transfer of the assets to the trust is typically treated as a sale.

secured borrowing or a sale.[90] It is important that the transaction be viewed as a secured borrowing to get the desired tax result.

(b) FORM OVER SUBSTANCE CONSIDERATIONS

The IRS can challenge—subject to judicial review—the tax position of treating pass-through debt certificates as debt securities, even if the originator and the pass-through certificate owners all treat the certificates as debt securities.[91] In pass-through debt certificate offerings, the originator and the certificate holders (as a condition to acquisition of the certificates) agree to treat the certificates as the originator's liability for federal and state tax purposes.[92] Based on the economic substance of the transaction, the originator and certificate holders report the tax on the transaction as if the certificates are debt securities.

(c) SALE OR SECURED LOAN FOR TAX PURPOSES

If the transaction is treated as a sale, the trust is not an investment trust if the proceeds from the pooled assets are reinvested in new assets.[93] A sale is viewed as a transfer of property for money, or an obligation to pay

---

[90] For convenience, the following discussion treats pass-through debt certificates as a single security for tax purposes:

> Technically, the holder of a pass-through [debt] certificate should calculate income or loss for each mortgage separately by allocating among the mortgages, in proportion to their respective fair market values, the price paid for the certificate and the price received on resale. Such an allocation is rarely necessary in practice, however, because in most instances the tax results obtained by viewing the mortgages alternatively in isolation and as a single aggregated debt instrument would be the same.

J. PEASLEE & D. NIRENBERG, *supra* note 20, at 114.

[91] *See* Helvering v. F. & R. Lazarus & Co., 308 U.S. 252, 255 (1939), *aff'g* 101 F.2d 728 (6th Cir. 1939), *aff'g* 32 B.T.A. 633 (1935), *acq.* XIV-2 C.B. 35; Gregory v. Helvering, 293 U.S. 465, 470 (1935); Rothstein v. Comm'r, 90 T.C. 488 (1988). *See also* Commissioner v. P.G. Lake, Inc., 356 U.S. 260, 265–67 (1958), *rev'g* 241 F.2d 71 (5th Cir. 1957), *aff'g* 24 T.C. 1016 (1955), *nonacq.* 1956-2 C.B. 10, *reh'g denied*, 356 U.S. 964 (1958); Commissioner v. Court Holding Co., 324 U.S. 331, 334 (1945), *rev'g* 143 F.2d 823 (5th Cir. 1944), *rev'g* 2 T.C. 531 (1943), *acq.* 1943 C.B. 5 (withdrawn in part), *nonacq.* 1968-2 C.B. 3, 1969-2 C.B. XXVI; Commissioner v. Danielson, 378 F.2d 771 (3d Cir. 1967), *vacating* 44 T.C. 549 (1965), *cert. denied*, 389 U.S. 858 (1967), *on remand*, 50 T.C. 782 (1968). *Cf.* Comdisco, Inc. v. Comm'r, 756 F.2d 569, 577–78 (7th Cir. 1985), *rev'g* 83-2 U.S. Tax Cas. (CCH) ¶ 9245 (N.D. Ill. 1983).

[92] *See, e.g.*, CALIFORNIA CREDIT CARD TRUST 1987-A, PROSPECTUS (Feb. 25, 1987) at 31–32 [hereinafter California Credit Card Trust 1987-A]. For a discussion of the pass-through debt certificates issued pursuant to the prospectus, see section 7.2(f).

[93] Treas. Reg. § 301.7701-4(c) (1986).

money.[94] If, on the other hand, the transaction is treated as a secured borrowing, the trust qualifies as a security arrangement.[95] A loan is viewed as a transaction where title to property is transferred as "security," not as a sale.[96]

The tax characterization as a sale or loan turns on whether the originator or sponsor gives up the significant incidents of ownership in the pooled assets.[97] Whether a transfer constitutes a sale or a loan is a question of fact, which means that all of the facts and circumstances that evidence economic ownership must be considered.[98] Although many factors reflect the incidents of ownership, the most important factors turn on whether the originator or certificate holders have the burdens and benefits of ownership. Some significant factors include the following:

- Does legal title pass to the certificate owners?[99]
- Does the risk of loss or default on the pooled assets belong to the originator or the certificate owners?[100]
- Does the originator or the certificate owner have control over and possession of the pooled assets?[101]
- Does the originator retain the potential for gain on the pooled assets, or do the certificate owners have the potential for gain?[102]
- Are the substantive terms of the pass-through debt certificates similar to the terms of the underlying pooled assets, or is there a mismatch of timing payments, interest rates, and economics?[103]

---

[94] Commissioner v. Brown, 380 U.S. 563 (1965), *aff'g* 325 F.2d 313 (9th Cir. 1963), *aff'g* 37 T.C. 461 (1961).

[95] Treas. Reg. § 1.61-13(b) (1957); Rev. Rul. 76-265, 1976-2 C.B. 448.

[96] *See* Stein v. Director of Internal Revenue, 135 F. Supp. 356, 357 (E.D.N.Y. 1955); Gatlin v. Comm'r, 34 B.T.A. 50, 56 (1936); United Nat'l Corp. v. Comm'r, 33 B.T.A. 790 (1935), *nonacq.* XV-1 C.B. 47. *See generally* section 31.11.

[97] *See* United Surgical Steel Co. v. Comm'r, 54 T.C. 1215, 1228–31 (1970), *acq.* 1971-2 C.B. 3; Grodt & McKay Realty, Inc. v. Comm'r, 77 T.C. 1221 (1981); Town & Country Food Co. v. Comm'r, 51 T.C. 1049, 1056–57 (1969), *acq.* 1969-2 C.B. XXV.

[98] *See* Haggard v. Comm'r, 24 T.C. 1124 (1955), *aff'd*, 241 F.2d 288 (9th Cir. 1956).

[99] *See* Commissioner v. Segall, 114 F.2d 706 (6th Cir. 1940), *rev'g* 38 B.T.A. 43 (1938), *nonacq.* 1938-2 C.B. 58, *cert. denied*, 313 U.S. 562 (1941).

[100] *See United Surgical Steel*, 54 T.C. at 1230; Rev. Rul. 54-43, 1954-1 C.B. 119, 121; G.C.M. 39,584 (Oct. 10, 1986); G.C.M. 37,848 (Feb. 5, 1979); G.C.M. 34,602 (Sept. 9, 1971).

[101] *See United Surgical Steel*, 54 T.C. at 1229–30; Mathers v. Comm'r, 57 T.C. 666, 674–76 (1972), *acq.* 1973-2 C.B. 2; G.C.M. 39,584 (Oct. 10, 1986).

[102] *See United Surgical Steel*, 54 T.C. at 1229.

[103] *See id.* at 1230–31; *Town & Country Food*, 51 T.C. at 1057; Bogatin v. United States, 78-2 U.S.T.C. ¶ 9733, at 85,470–71 (W.D. Tenn. 1978); Schaeffer v. Comm'r, 41 T.C.M. (CCH) 752, 756 (1981).

- Is the originator responsible for taxes, fees, and all expenses for servicing the pooled assets?
- Are the pass-through debt certificates subject to the types of financial covenants typically contained in secured loan agreements?[104]

(d) PARTNERSHIP TAX STATUS

If pass-through debt certificates are not found to be debt securities, originators try to avoid classification of the trust as an "association" taxable as a "corporation." Originators do this by structuring the trust so that it qualifies as a partnership. This "fall back" position assures that the trust is not subject to tax at the trust level.[105] Instead—if the trust has more partnership than corporate characteristics—the originator and certificate holders are treated as partners, and the trust is treated as a partnership.[106] To support partnership tax status, the trust documents typically restrict the transferability of the trust certificates, provide personal liability for the certificate owners, and give the equity owners (typically by majority vote) the power to control management over certain management issues.

If the transaction is classified as a partnership for tax purposes, the partnership's assets are treated as the pooled assets. The interests of the originator and the certificate holders are measured by the cash flow on the pooled assets. A "partner's" distributive share of income, gain, loss, deduction, and credit is determined under I.R.C. § 704 and the Treasury regulations promulgated thereunder.[107]

§ 36.6 REGULATED INVESTMENT COMPANIES

RICs can be used to issue and hold asset-backed securities. To meet and maintain RIC tax status, the issuer must comply with all of the requirements of the ICA, including the registration requirements. For a general

---

[104] G.C.M. 39,584 (Oct. 10, 1986).

[105] The fall back position attempts to assure flow-through tax treatment under the partnership tax provisions.

[106] *See generally* Chapter 28. For a discussion of publicly traded partnerships, see section 28.4. For a discussion of the consequences of partnership status to pass-through debt certificate holders that are not United States persons for tax purposes, see J. PEASLEE & D. NIRENBERG, *supra* note 20, at 26–27.

[107] For a discussion of the possible classification of issuing pass-through debt certificates as a partnership transaction, see California Credit Card Trust 1987-A, *supra* note 92, at 33–34.

discussion of RICs, see section 8.9. For a discussion of the ICA requirements that apply to asset-backed securities offerings, see generally section 7.6(d).

§ 36.7 REAL ESTATE INVESTMENT TRUSTS

REITs can be used to pool mortgages directly, or to hold pass-through certificates or pay-through bonds issued by other entities.[108] In general, a REIT must have more than 100 shareholders and must satisfy various income tests based on the types of income it earns.[109] Although REITs can be formed as either trusts or corporations, they are taxable as corporations. Unlike regular corporations, however, REITs are allowed deductions in computing taxable income for qualified dividends paid to their shareholders.[110]

REITs have not been widely used for pooling mortgages because of structural limitations on their use. In fact, at the time of this writing, there has only been one public offering of mortgage-backed securities in the REIT structure.[111] With the enactment of TRA '86, interest increased in the formation of REITs to issue and hold single-class investments in mortgage-backed securities. At this writing, however, REITs are not viable entities to qualify as REMICs.[112]

To deduct dividends paid to its shareholders, REITs must hold most of their assets in the form of real property and real property loans.[113] Mortgage-backed pass-through certificates qualify as "real estate assets."[114] In addition, interest income on pass-through certificates qualifies as "interest on obligations secured by mortgages on real property or

---

[108] For a discussion of REIT requirements generally, see section 8.10.

[109] *See generally* I.R.C. §§ 851–859. *See also* Kies, *Improved REITs as Sole Vehicle for Passive Real Estate Investment—An Alternative to Other Proposed Limitations*, 31 TAX NOTES 923 (1986); Noteware, *The Securitization of Real Estate*, 1 J. REAL EST. DEV. 57 (1986); Blumberg, *Why Real Estate Investment Trusts Are Good Investments*, 15 REAL EST. REV. 90 (1986); Mai & Greenfield, *The New Uses of Real Estate Investment Trusts*, 32 PRAC. LAW. 27 (1986).

[110] *See* section 24.6.

[111] *See* Emerald Mortgage Investments Corporation, Registration No. 33-27092 (July 21, 1988) (NYSE Listing July 21, 1988).

[112] *See* section 36.8(a); *see also Tax Bill Casts Uncertainty over Availability of REITs to Issue REMICs*, CORP. FINANCING WK., Oct. 6, 1986, at 2.

[113] I.R.C. § 856(c)(5). *See* Rev. Rul. 84-10, 1984-1 C.B. 155; Rev. Rul. 77-349, 1977-2 C.B 20; Rev. Rul. 74-300, 1974-1 C.B. 169; Rev. Rul. 74-169, 1974-1 C.B. 147; Rev. Rul. 70-545, 1970-2 C.B. 7; Rev. Rul. 70-544, 1970-2 C.B. 6.

[114] I.R.C. § 856(c)(5)(A).

on interests in real property."[115] On the other hand, pay-through bonds and other debt obligations do not qualify as real estate assets. As a result, REITs are more likely to acquire pass-through certificates than to acquire pay-through bonds. Investments in pay-through bonds could adversely affect a REIT's tax treatment.

A second problem encountered in using REITs to pool mortgages is that REITs must distribute at least 95 percent of their taxable income to their shareholders as dividends.[116] This distribution requirement further limits the usefulness of REITs to pool mortgages because payment obligations may not allow at least 95 percent of the entity's taxable income to be distributed as dividends.

§ 36.8 REAL ESTATE MORTGAGE INVESTMENT CONDUITS

Since their introduction in 1983, pay-through bonds, including CMOs, have been a fast growing mortgage-backed security product.[117] Flexibility was drastically curtailed, however, by Treasury regulations—first proposed in 1984 and finalized in 1986—that would tax as corporations those entities issuing securities representing multiple classes of interests.[118]

(a) IN GENERAL

TRA '86 made major changes to the developing multiple-ownership interest market. For taxable years beginning after December 31, 1986, a new investment entity, referred to as a "REMIC," can be used to hold fixed mortgage pools where multiple classes of interests are held by investors. The new REMIC rules supersede the tax treatment that applied under pre-TRA '86 law to entities that hold pooled mortgage assets and sell multiple classes of interests.

In 1986, Congress went a long way toward eliminating the tax difficulties encountered in issuing securities with multiple ownership tranches. One major difficulty is that an investment trust cannot issue multiple-tranche pass-through certificates. Another is that pay-through bonds will not be viewed as debt securities if the tranches too closely

---

[115] I.R.C. § 856(c)(3)(B); Rev. Rul. 74-300, 1974-1 C.B. 169; Rev. Rul. 70-545, 1970-2 C.B. 7; Rev. Rul. 70-544, 1970-2 C.B. 6.
[116] I.R.C. § 857(a)(1).
[117] For a discussion of pay-through bonds, see sections 7.2(d) and 36.3(c).
[118] For a discussion of the Treasury regulations, see section 36.2(c).

reflect the payments received on the pooled assets. The answer to these, as well as other difficulties, is REMICs—entities created by Congress to replace all other structures for issuing multiple tranches of mortgage-backed securities.

Through the end of 1991, REMIC treatment is elective, but after that date REMICs are the only way to issue multiple-tranche mortgage-backed securities in a tax-advantageous manner. REMICs replace all vehicles used under pre-TRA '86 law to issue multiple-class mortgage-backed securities.

REMICs allow issuers a way to structure mortgage-backed securities that provide the desired economic, accounting, and regulatory treatment—without the tax treatment turning on the type of entity selected to pool these assets. This means that REMICs can be structured as corporations, trusts, partnerships, or simply as segregated pools of assets. The legal form is disregarded for tax purposes, to assure that the tax treatment of REMICs allows originators or promoters to operate under tax rules "flexible enough to accommodate most legitimate business concerns while preserving the desired certainty of income tax treatment."[119] Because REMICs hold a pool of real estate mortgages that liquidates over time, mortgage prepayments, when received, are distributed to the holders of the REMIC's interest in accordance with the terms of the REMIC's documentation.

Although REMICs were off to a slow start after they were first introduced on January 1, 1987, they now dominate the multitranche mortgage-backed securities market. Early REMIC offerings were structured to look like existing MBS structures, although more recent REMIC offerings take advantage of the unique REMIC provisions. REMICs have an obvious advantage over investment trusts because multiple-payment tranches can be offered to investors. They also have major advantages over traditional pay-through structures. There is no need for an equity investment, thereby allowing the pooled mortgages to be stripped of all cash flow and reinvestment proceeds. Unlike a corporate issuer of pay-through bonds, a REMIC has no tax at the entity level. Unlike an owner trust, there need not be any personal liability on the owners of any of the REMIC's obligations. And further, owners of REMIC residual interests can freely transfer their interests without any tax at the entity level. In summary, REMICs allow the flexibility of the pay-through bond structures without many of the major tax and other disadvantages attendant

---

[119] STAFF OF THE JOINT COMM. ON TAXATION, 99TH CONG., 2D SESS., GENERAL EXPLANATION OF THE TAX REFORM ACT OF 1986, at 411 (Joint Comm. Print 1986) [hereinafter General Explanation of TRA '86].

to those structures. It is likely that REMIC offerings will continue to evolve in ways that take advantage of the unique REMIC provisions.

TRA '86 provides that REMICs are not subject to tax at the entity level[120]—they are not treated as corporations, partnerships, or trusts.[121] Instead, income is allocated to the owners of REMIC interests under special rules provided in newly enacted I.R.C. §§ 860A through 860G. Regular interests are treated as debt securities.[122] Regular interest owners generally take into income that portion of the income of the REMIC that would be recognized by accrual method taxpayers holding debt securities with the same terms as the regular interests.[123] Residual interest owners take into account all income or loss not taken into account by regular interest owners.[124]

Any entity—including a segregated pool of assets—can elect to be treated as a REMIC if it meets the following statutory requirements.[125] First, an election to be treated as a REMIC must be made or must be in effect for the taxable year and all of the entity's prior taxable years.[126] Second, all of its interests must be either regular or residual interests.[127] Third, it must have only one class of residual interests that provides that all distributions are pro rata.[128] Fourth, as of the close of the fourth month after the so-called startup day and each quarter ending thereafter, substantially all of its assets must consist of "qualified mortgages" and "permitted investments."[129] The startup day is defined as any day selected by the REMIC that is on or before the first day on which REMIC

---

[120] REMICs are subject to certain penalty taxes, including the tax on prohibited transactions, the tax on contributions to the REMIC after the startup day, and certain withholding taxes. For a discussion of the penalty taxes that can be assessed against a REMIC, see sections 36.8(h) and 36.8(i).

[121] I.R.C. § 860A(a). *See generally* Rosenthal, *Mortgage-Backed Securities Industry Identifies Wrinkles in Technical Corrections Act REMIC Rules*, 39 TAX NOTES 427 (1988); Pozdena, *Mortgage Securitization & REMICs*, FRBSF Weekly Letter, May 8, 1987, at 1; Johnson, *Real Estate Mortgage Investment Conduits—A Flexible New Tax Structure for Issuers and Investors*, 34 TAX NOTES 911 (1987); *Participating Forwards, REMICs*, INTERMARKET, Jan. 1987, at 14.

[122] For a discussion of regular interest owners, see section 36.8(c)(1).

[123] I.R.C. § 860B.

[124] For a discussion of residual interest owners, see section 36.8(c)(2).

[125] I.R.C. § 860D. The term "entity" is not defined in the Code, but it includes a segregated pool of assets, a partnership, trust, or corporation. STAFF OF THE JOINT COMM. ON TAXATION, 99TH CONG., 2D SESS., TAX REFORM BILL OF 1986, FINAL CONFERENCE COMM. DECISIONS II-226 (Joint Comm. Print 1986) [hereinafter TRA '86 Conf. Rep.]. Popular REMIC structures include the owner trust, the multiple-ownership class trust, and the two-tier REMIC.

[126] I.R.C. § 860D(a)(1); *see* section 36.8(k).

[127] I.R.C. § 860D(a)(2); *see* section 36.8(c).

[128] I.R.C. § 860D(a)(3); *see* section 36.8(c)(2).

[129] I.R.C. § 860D(a)(4); *see* section 36.8(d).

interests are issued.[130] (An entity might not be able to make a REMIC election if it receives an equity investment before the startup day if the residual interest is viewed as having been issued before the startup day.)[131] Fifth, it must have a calendar year for its taxable year.[132]

(b) PRIOR LEGISLATIVE PROPOSALS

Prior to enactment of the REMIC provisions, various legislative proposals were made to change the tax treatment of mortgage related and other asset-backed securities.[133] In 1983, a legislative proposal was introduced in Congress to create a new type of pass-through entity, referred to as a "Trust for Investment Mortgages," or a "TIM." A TIM would have been available to pool mortgages, while providing flow-through benefits similar to those available to REITs and RICs.[134] In the original TIM proposal, TIMs would have been able to hold pass-through securities guaranteed by GNMA, FNMA, and FHLMC.[135] Because the Treasury viewed the proposal to allow TIMs to hold government-guaranteed mortgage-backed securities as abusive, the Treasury distributed an alternative TIM proposal in 1984 that would have prohibited GNMA, FNMA, and FHLMC from issuing TIMs or similar instruments.[136]

In late 1985, two legislative proposals on mortgage-backed securities were introduced in Congress. One of the proposals provided rules under which an entity that held real estate mortgages could issue interests tied to specified cash flows from the mortgages without characterizing the entity as an association taxable as a corporation.[137] These interests would have been known as "collateralized mortgage securities" or "CMSs," which could have been issued (1) by a corporation, trust, or partnership;

---

[130] I.R.C. § 860G(a)(9); *see* section 36.8(c)(2).

[131] J. PEASLEE & D. NIRENBERG, *supra* note 20, at 61 n.6.

[132] I.R.C. § 860D(a)(5).

[133] *See generally* JOINT COMM. ON TAXATION, DESCRIPTION OF BILLS RELATING TO THE TAX TREATMENT OF MORTGAGE RELATED SECURITIES (S. 1959 AND S. 1978) AND ENVIRONMENTAL ZONES (S. 1839) (JCS-3-86) Jan. 30, 1986, *reprinted in* Daily Tax Rep. (BNA) No. 21, at J-1 (Jan. 31, 1986) [hereinafter Joint Comm. Description of Bills on Mortgage Related Securities].

[134] JOINT COMM. ON TAXATION, 98TH CONG., 1ST SESS., DESCRIPTION OF S. 1822 (RELATING TO TRUSTS FOR INVESTMENTS IN MORTGAGES) 10 (Joint Comm. Print 1983).

[135] *Id.*

[136] 21 TAX NOTES 629 (1983). For a discussion of the 1983 TIM proposal, see Liles, *Mortgage-Backed Securities—Current Status and Recent Proposals*, 25 Tax Mgmt. (BNA) Memorandum 123, 126–28 (1984). For a discussion of the Treasury's alternative TIM proposal, see K. LORE, MORTGAGE-BACKED SECURITIES: DEVELOPMENT AND TRENDS IN THE SECONDARY MORTGAGE MARKET ch. 6, at 6-70 & app. 6-A, 6-88 to 6-105 (Clark Boardman, Securities Law Series 1986-87).

[137] S. 1959, 99th Cong., 1st Sess., 131 CONG. REC. 36,864-70 (1985).

(2) in the form of an ownership interest or debt obligation; and (3) with different classes of maturities.[138]

The second proposal suggested in 1985, would have amended the investment trust rules to permit a trust with multiple classes of interests to be treated as an investment trust in certain circumstances.[139] It would have allowed multiple classes of interests in trusts that hold financial instruments (including most debt obligations, accounts receivable, and lease receivables) if the trust met two requirements. First, the financial instruments would need to have been identified when the trust interests were issued. Second, the financial instruments could not have been substituted for other financial instruments except in very limited circumstances.[140]

(c) INVESTOR INTERESTS

REMICs can issue two types of investor interests—regular and residual interests—which means that all of the interests must meet the requirements of these investor interests. A REMIC can have one or more classes of regular interests. Although the term "interest" is not defined in the Code or the legislative history accompanying enactment of the REMIC provisions, the Conference Report to TRA '86 identifies one transaction that is not an "interest." Any rights to receive payment for goods or services rendered in the ordinary operation of a REMIC are not treated as interests in the REMIC.[141]

REMICs can have only one class of residual interests (all distributions to residual interests must be pro rata). Both regular and residual interests must generally be issued on the same day, referred to as the "startup day."[142] If an equity contribution is received before the startup day, it might be viewed as a prohibited issuance of a residual interest before the startup day.[143]

This section briefly identifies the types of investor interests in a REMIC. The tax treatment of owners of regular and residual interests is discussed in sections 41.2 and 44.1.

---

[138] *See generally* Joint Comm. Description of Bills on Mortgage Related Securities, *supra* note 133.

[139] S. 1978, 99th Cong., 1st Sess., 131 CONG. REC. 17,984–86 (1985).

[140] For a description of the amendments proposed by S. 1978, see generally Joint Comm. Description of Bills on Mortgage Related Securities, *supra* note 133.

[141] TRA '86 Conf. Rep., *supra* note 125, at II-229.

[142] For a discussion of the startup day, see section 36.8(a).

[143] J. PEASLEE & D. NIRENBERG, *supra* note 20, at 61 n.6.

(1) REGULAR INTERESTS

(i) In General

A REMIC can have one or more classes of regular interests issued on the startup day. They can be issued in the form of debt, stock, partnership interests, interests in a trust, or any other form permitted by state law. They can be structured to look like multiple tranches of CMOs and those entities issuing pay-through bonds. Regular interests need not have a specified principal amount as long as there is a specified amount that can be identified as a principal amount if the interest had been issued in the form of debt.[144]

I.R.C. § 860D(a)(3) provides that there must be "1 (and only 1)" class of residual interests. There is no similar statutory language regarding the number of regular interests. The Conference Report to TRA '86 provides, however, that REMICs must have one or more classes of regular interests and a single class of residual interests.[145] It has been suggested that there is "no limit on the number of classes of regular interests and, apparently, no requirement that there be even one."[146] A rationale advanced for such a position is as follows:

> While the REMIC rules could not function unless a REMIC has at all times a class of residual interests to which the taxable income of the REMIC can be allocated, there is no similar reason that compels the presence of any classes of regular interests. Thus, an entity should not lose its status as a REMIC merely because all of its regular interests are retired or because no regular interests were ever issued.[147]

Regular interests that relate to only a portion of the qualified mortgages owned by a REMIC can be issued in compliance with the REMIC provisions. Each interest must have a fixed principal amount and bear interest at a fixed or variable rate (as allowed by Treasury regulations).[148]

A REMIC cannot issue regular interests with the amount of interest (or similar payments) disproportionate to the specified principal amount. In

---

[144] TRA '86 Conf. Rep., *supra* note 125, at II-228.
[145] *Id.*; General Explanation of TRA '86, *supra* note 119, at 411.
[146] J. PEASLEE & D. NIRENBERG, *supra* note 20, at 60.
[147] *Id.* at 60 n.4.
[148] For a discussion of fixed rate regular interests, see section 36.8(c)(1)(iii). For a discussion of variable rate regular interests, see section 36.8(c)(1)(iv).

addition, the interest rate on the debt must not substantially exceed prevailing market rates.[149]

(ii) Requirements

Even if regular interests are not viewed as debt securities under state law, they are treated as debt securities for tax purposes.[150] The requirements for regular interests are discussed in this section. First, a regular interest has all of its terms fixed on the startup day.[151] TMRA '88[152] added the requirement that a regular interest must be designated on the startup day.[153]

Second, the owner must get the unconditional right to receive a specified principal (or other similar) amount.[154] The requirement to "unconditionally entitle" a regular interest owner to principal "does not imply that the owner must be protected against losses resulting from defaults or delinquencies on the underlying mortgages. Indeed, the legislative history goes further and states that a regular interest will not fail to be a regular interest because it is subordinated to other regular interests in the event of defaults or delinquencies on the underlying mortgages."[155]

Third, a regular interest must provide that interest, or any similar payment (if any), at or before maturity must be based on a fixed rate (or a variable rate if one is provided in Treasury regulations).[156] An interest can qualify as a regular interest if the timing—but not the amount—of the principal payments (or other similar payments) is contingent on the extent of prepayments on qualified mortgages and the amount of income from permitted investments.[157]

The amount of interest (or similar payments) on a regular interest cannot be contingent. Nevertheless, it can be subordinated to payments on other regular interests. In addition, it can depend on the absence of defaults on qualified mortgages. The amount of interest (or similar

---

[149] TRA '86 Conf. Rep., *supra* note 125, at II-229.
[150] I.R.C. § 860B(a).
[151] I.R.C. § 860G(a)(1).
[152] Pub. L. No. 100-647, 102 Stat. 3342 (1988) [hereinafter TMRA '88].
[153] *Id.* § 1006(t)(5)(A).
[154] I.R.C. § 860G(a)(1)(A).
[155] J. PEASLEE & D. NIRENBERG, *supra* note 20, at 71–72 (citing TRA '86 Conf. Rep., *supra* note 125, at II-228).
[156] I.R.C. § 860G(a)(1)(B); *see* section 41.1.
[157] I.R.C. § 860G(a)(1).

payments) on a regular interest cannot be disproportionate to the specified principal amount.[158]

(iii) Fixed Rate Regular Interests

Regular interests that are payable "based on a fixed rate" are authorized in I.R.C. § 860G(a)(1)(B). The term "based on a fixed rate" is not defined in the Code or legislative history, which means that there are many open questions in interpreting whether a regular interest is payable based on a fixed rate. What if a mortgage is prepaid and interest on the mortgage therefore ceases? If the interest shortfall is passed through to regular interests issued in the form of pass-through trust certificates, the regular interests should be considered to be "based on a fixed rate" even if the interest rate varies because of a mortgage prepayment. Or, what if a regular interest has a so-called stepped interest rate that increases or decreases in accordance with a fixed formula? In light of proposed Treasury regulations addressing the OID rules, interests with stepped interest rates may not be "based on a fixed rate."[159]

(iv) Variable Rate Regular Interests

Regular interests can provide that interest payments (or other similar amounts) with respect to such interest are payable based on a variable rate to the extent provided in Treasury regulations.[160] This means that the Treasury has enormous power to authorize regular interests with variable interest rates. This power is important because "[v]ariable rate [debt securities] are currently an attractive investment for many investors. By providing for market-based yields, the price impact of prepayment is minimized."[161]

Two IRS Notices—Notice 87-41[162] and Notice 87-67[163]—announce that Treasury regulations, when issued, will authorize certain variable rate regular interests of the types described in the notices. Until Treasury regulations are issued, the notices, effective for regular interests issued on or after June 15, 1987, can be relied on for issuing variable rate regular

---

[158] Taxation of regular interest owners is discussed in section 41.1.
[159] *See* Prop. Treas. Reg. § 1.1273-1(b)(1) (1986). For a discussion of fixed rate regular interests, see generally *REMICs*, H1 Tax Transactions Library (CCH) ¶ 305.011 (July 1989).
[160] I.R.C. § 860G(a)(1)(B).
[161] K. LORE, *supra* note 136, at 6-42.
[162] 1987-1 C.B. 500 (June 15, 1987) [hereinafter Notice 87-41].
[163] 1987-2 C.B. 377 (Oct. 5, 1987) [hereinafter Notice 87-67].

interests. These notices have paved the way for certain variable rate debt investments. If "future guidance is inconsistent with the guidance provided by [these notices], such future guidance will be given prospective effect only."[164] The remainder of this section discusses variable rate regular interests authorized by Notice 87-41 and Notice 87-67.

In Notice 87-41, the IRS found that interests qualify as regular interests if they bear interest at a variable rate based on current values of an objective interest index—as the term "objective interest index" is defined in Treasury regulations proposed under the OID rules.[165]

The IRS has announced that variable rate regular interests are permitted if such interests qualify as "variable rate debt instruments" within the meaning of Prop. Treas. Reg. §§ 1.1275-5(a), (b), and (c).[166] Treasury regulations, when issued, "will permit interest expressed as a fixed multiple of an objective interest index plus or minus a constant number of basis or percentage points to qualify as interest based on an objective interest index,"[167] as that phrase is used in Prop. Treas. Reg. § 1.1275-5(a) (1986). Regulations, when issued, will be effective for interests issued on or after June 15, 1987.

Among other things, the proposed regulations under § 1.1275-5 provide that variable rate instruments must have interest rates that are based on the current value of an objective interest index. An objective interest index is defined in the proposed OID regulations as either "(1) [a] rate which, as of the issue date of the debt instrument, is made known publicly and offered currently to unrelated borrowers in private lending transactions by a financial institution, or (2) [a] rate reflecting an average (based on a statistically significant sample) of current yields on a class of publicly traded debt instruments."[168] Examples of "objective interest indices" include "the prime rate of a designated financial institution, LIBOR . . . , the applicable Federal rate, and the average yield on Treasury securities as published in Federal Reserve bulletins."[169] "[I]nterest expressed as a fixed multiple of an objective interest index or as a constant number of percentage or basis points more or less than an objective interest index shall constitute interest based on an objective interest index."[170] The proposed regulations also state that "interest expressed as

---

[164] Notice 87-41, *supra* note 162.
[165] Prop. Treas. Reg. § 1.1275-5(a) (1986).
[166] (1986). Notice 87-41, *supra* note 162.
[167] *Id.*
[168] Prop. Treas. Reg. § 1.1275-5(b) (1986).
[169] *Id.*
[170] *Id.*

§ 36.8(c)   Financial Products: Taxation, Regulation, and Design   1050

a fixed multiple of an objective interest index plus or minus a constant number of percentage or basis points shall not constitute interest based on an objective interest index."[171]

Notice 87-67 acknowledges that a mortgage can have a fixed interest rate for one or more accrual periods and a variable rate for other accrual periods.[172] The index used to calculate the qualified variable interest rate need not be the same in all periods. This means that REMICs can hold mortgages with a fixed interest rate for one or more accrual periods and a variable interest rate for the other accrual periods.[173] Notice 87-67 also authorizes the payment of interest on a regular interest at a variable rate based on the weighted average of the interest rates on the qualified mortgages held by the REMIC.

The regulations for variable rate debt instruments also provide that an interest in a REMIC will not fail to qualify as a regular interest merely because the rate of interest may not exceed a maximum or may be less than a minimum rate.[174] This means that interest rate caps and floors are permissible on objective interest index rates. It appears as if caps and floors need not be the same in each period. Variable rate debt instruments can include caps and floors that vary from period to period.[175]

Notice 87-41 treats variable rate pay-through bonds as regular interests in REMICs. Notice 87-41 "does not allow pass-through certificates to qualify as regular interests in any case where the pass-through rate varies because of differences between the rates of interest on underlying mortgages."[176] This problem was addressed by Notice 87-67, which permits "a regular interest to have a variable rate that is based on a weighted average of the interest rates on the qualified mortgages held by the REMIC" if—and only if—"interest on each qualified mortgage is payable in each accrual period during its life either at a fixed rate or at a qualified variable rate."[177]

In Notice 87-67, the IRS also supplemented Notice 87-41 to allow REMICs to pay interest on their regular interests at variable rates based on a weighted average of the interest rates on qualified mortgages held by that REMIC. To satisfy this rule, interest on each qualified mortgage must be payable, during each accrual period, at either a fixed rate or a variable

---

[171] *Id.*
[172] Notice 87-67, *supra* note 163.
[173] Prop. Treas. Reg. §§ 1.1275-5(d)(4), (d)(5), Example (5) (1986).
[174] Notice 87-67, *supra* note 163.
[175] *See* Prop. Treas. Reg. § 1.1274-3(d)(1)(v), Example (2) (1986).
[176] J. PEASLEE & D. NIRENBERG, *supra* note 20, at 68–69.
[177] *Id.* at 69.

rate based on current values of an objective interest index (within the meaning of Prop. Treas. Reg. §§ 1.1275-5(a), (b), and (c) (1986)).[178]

As to the determination of whether interest on a qualified mortgage is payable at a variable rate, Notice 87-67 provides that the phrase "objective interest index" (as discussed in Notice 87-41) appearing in Prop. Treas. Reg. § 1.1275-5(b) (1986) is applied to include a rate reflecting the average cost of funds of one or more financial institutions.[179] This provision addresses the problem raised after Notice 87-41 was released, as to whether certain commonly used interest indices were "objective interest indices" if they did not meet the literal definition because they were not offered to borrowers and did not reflect an average of current yields.

(v) Senior and Subordinated Regular Interests

Regular interests can be structured with different rights and priorities provided for classes of senior and subordinated interests. For a discussion of the senior and subordinated structure, see section 7.1(b). The Conference Report that accompanied TRA '86 provides that "[t]he conferees intend that an interest in a REMIC would not fail to be treated as a regular interest if the payment of principal (or similar) amounts with respect to such interest are subordinated to payments on other regular interests in the REMIC, and are dependent upon the absence of defaults on qualified mortgages."[180] Regular interests can "resemble the types of interests described in Treas. Reg. sec. 301.7701-4(c)(2) (Example 2)."[181] The Joint Committee Report acknowledges that the payment of interest can also be subordinated to payments on other regular interests.[182]

The senior and subordinated REMIC structure can have several attractions over a similar structure in an investment trust that issues pass-through certificates. For example, the originator of the REMIC need not retain the subordinated interests. Instead, subordinated regular interests in a REMIC can be sold to third parties. The Conferees support this view in the Conference Report that accompanied enactment of the REMIC legislation, which provides that "[t]he status of an interest as a regular

---

[178] Notice 87-67, *supra* note 163.

[179] *Id.*

[180] TRA '86 Conf. Rep., *supra* note 125, at II-228.

[181] *Id.* Example (2) in the regulations allows investment trusts to issue senior and subordinated interests while still being treated as trusts for tax purposes. For a discussion of Example (2), see section 36.2(c).

[182] General Explanation of TRA '86, *supra* note 119, at 415.

interest in this case does not depend on whether the subordinated regular interest is sold or retained."[183]

The IRS, in LTR 8918045,[184] found that a REMIC structured with senior and subordinated certificates and credit enhancements qualified as a REMIC. In the private letter ruling, the IRS looked at credit enhancements issued in connection with the REMIC offering and did not even address the fact that the REMIC had issued both senior and subordinated interests. For a discussion of LTR 8918045, see section 36.8(n).

(vi) Stripped Regular Interests

A regular interest can be a stripped bond and still qualify as a regular interest under certain circumstances. The issuance of stripped regular interests is discussed in the remainder of this section. A regular interest can have interest payments that "consist of a specified portion of interest payments on qualified mortgages and such portion does not vary during the period such interest is outstanding."[185] This provision, added to the Code by TMRA '88, means that an issuer can structure a regular interest as an IO strip if the requirements for a regular interest are met.[186] For example, an interest must be "issued on the startup day with fixed terms and which is designated as a regular interest."[187] In addition, the interest must "unconditionally" entitle the owner "to receive a specified principal amount (or other similar amount)."[188]

Prior to the TMRA '88 amendments, it was believed that stripped regular interests could not be issued by a REMIC. Under the law in effect prior to July 1, 1987 (for REMICs with a startup day before that date), the interest must have provided that "interest payments (or other similar amounts), if any, with respect to such interest at or before maturity are payable based on a fixed rate (or to the extent provided in regulations, at a variable rate)."[189] In addition, the TRA '86 Conference Report that accompanied the REMIC legislation provided that "an interest in a REMIC may not qualify as a regular interest if the amount of interest (or similar

---

[183] TRA '86 Conf. Rep., *supra* note 125, at II-228 n.7.
[184] (Feb. 6, 1989).
[185] I.R.C. § 860G(a)(1)(B)(ii).
[186] For a discussion of stripped pass-through certificates, see generally sections 7.2(c)(2) and 36.2(d). For a discussion of IO strips, see section 7.2(c)(2)(ii). For a discussion of stripped pay-through bonds, see sections 7.2(d)(7) and 38.5.
[187] I.R.C. § 860G(a)(1); *see* section 36.8(c)(1)(ii).
[188] I.R.C. § 860G(a)(1)(A); *see* section 36.8(c)(1)(ii).
[189] I.R.C. § 860G(a)(1)(B), *prior to amendment by* TMRA '88, *supra* note 152, § 1006(t)(5)(A).

payments) is disproportionate to the specified principal amount."[190] This prohibition in the Conference Report against a disproportionately high interest rate relative to the principal amount was viewed as prohibiting stripped regular interests in a REMIC.

In 1988, Congress amended I.R.C. § 860G(a)(1)(B) to provide that interest payments can "consist of a specified portion of the interest payments on qualified mortgages" as long as "such portion does not vary during the period [the regular] interest is outstanding."[191] The legislative history accompanying the TMRA '88 change provided that "the definition of regular interest is broadened to encompass interests which entitle the holder to interest payments consisting of a specified portion of the interest payments on qualified mortgages if such portion does not vary during the period the regular interest is outstanding. The broadening of the definition is intended to permit such interests in a REMIC to qualify as a regular interests [sic] even if the amount of interest is disproportionate to the specified principal amount."[192]

An interest will now be treated as a regular interest if it meets the requirements of I.R.C. § 860G(a)(1)(B)—first, it must consist of a specified portion of the interest payments on qualified mortgages. Second, the interest portion must not vary during the period the regular interest is outstanding. Because I.R.C. § 860G(a)(1)(A) provides that a regular interest must "unconditionally" entitle "the holder to receive a specified principal amount (or other similar amount)," a regular interest must provide for at least a small amount of principal in addition to interest. Given the requirement that an owner of a regular interest must be entitled to receive a "specified principal amount," it appears as if interest only (i.e., IO) strips cannot be issued by REMICs. Rather, stripped regular interests are authorized as long as the owner is entitled to receive some principal.[193]

(2) RESIDUAL INTERESTS

A residual interest is a REMIC interest that meets three requirements. First, it is issued on the startup day.[194] (The startup day is generally

---

[190] TRA '86 Conf. Rep., *supra* note 125, at II-229.

[191] I.R.C. § 860G(a)(1)(B)(ii).

[192] HOUSE WAYS AND MEANS COMM. REPORT H.R. REP. NO. 795, 100th Cong., 2d Sess. 81 (1988); SENATE FINANCE COMM. REPORT, S. REP. NO. 445, 100th Cong., 2d Sess. 87, *reprinted in* 1988 U.S. CODE CONG. & ADMIN. NEWS 4515, 4606.

[193] For a discussion of the TMRA '88 changes made to I.R.C. § 860G(a)(1), see Peaslee, Nirenberg & Gunther, *Interest-Only REMIC Regular Interests, Special Report*, 41 TAX NOTES 855 (1988).

[194] I.R.C. § 860G(a)(2).

defined in I.R.C. § 860G(a)(9) as "the day on which the REMIC issues all of its regular and residual interests.")

Second, it is not a regular interest in a REMIC.[195] The Code and the legislative history are silent as to whether a residual interest must have provisions that make it economically different from the regular interest.

And third, it is designated as a residual interest.[196] A REMIC can only have one class of residual interests.[197] If there is more than one class of residual interests, the REMIC election is terminated. The single-class requirement simplifies reporting of residual income so that all residual income is allocated to the residual interests. Distributions—if any—among residual interest owners must be pro rata.[198]

Residual interests need not provide for distributions or have a minimum value. "[A]n interest in a REMIC could qualify as a residual interest regardless of value. Thus, for example, an interest need not entitle the holder to any distributions in order to qualify as a residual interest."[199] In fact, REMIC originators and sponsors frequently want the residual interest to be only a nominal amount, to assure that the maximum amount of the cash flows from the pooled mortgages are used for the operations of the REMIC and to meet its principal and interest obligations. Given the position set out in the General Explanation of TRA '86 that a residual interest can qualify as a residual interest "regardless of value," it appears as if a residual interest need not have any minimum value ascribed to it.

The Conference Report that accompanied TRA '86 provides that REMIC interests that are "economically" contingent are residual interests, even if they have interest and principal payments that are only nominally fixed:

> [A]n interest in a REMIC may not qualify as a regular interest if the amount of interest (or similar payments) is disproportionate to the specified principal amount. For example, if an interest is issued as a debt security with a coupon rate of interest that is substantially in excess of prevailing market interest rates (as adjusted for risk), the conferees intend that the interest would not qualify as a regular interest. Instead, the conferees intend that such an interest may be treated either as a residual interest, or as a combination of a regular interest and a residual interest.[200]

[195] *Id.* For a discussion of regular interests, see section 36.8(c)(1).
[196] I.R.C. § 860G(a)(2).
[197] I.R.C. § 860D(a)(3).
[198] *Id.*
[199] General Explanation of TRA '86, *supra* note 119, at 416. Taxation of residual interests is generally discussed in section 41.2.
[200] TRA '86 Conf. Rep., *supra* note 125, at II-229.

(d) ASSET TEST

To qualify as a REMIC, substantially all of the entity's assets must be held in "qualified mortgages" and "permitted investments."[201] The TRA '86 Conference Report provides that a de minimis amount can be held in other assets.[202] Treasury regulations can set a "safe harbor" amount of nonqualified assets that will not taint a REMIC election. There is an exception to the assets requirements for the initial and liquidation periods of the REMIC. The initial period runs from the startup day to the close of the third month beginning after the startup day.[203] The liquidation period begins when a plan of liquidation is adopted and ends when the REMIC is liquidated.[204]

The remainder of this section discusses the types of assets that qualify under the REMIC rules as "qualified mortgages" and "permitted investments."

(1) QUALIFIED MORTGAGES

A qualified mortgage is defined to include three types of items. First, it includes any obligation principally secured by an interest in real estate. Second, it includes regular REMIC interests transferred on the startup day. Third, it includes qualified replacement mortgages. A debt obligation not principally secured by an interest in real property cannot be a qualified mortgage. The remainder of this section addresses each of these qualified mortgages.

(i) In General

A qualified mortgage includes "any obligation (including any participation or certificate of beneficial ownership therein) which is principally secured, [sic] by an interest in real property."[205] Neither the Code nor the legislative history defines the phrase "interest in real property." What qualifies as real property is determined under state law. This means that receivables from assets that are not real estate assets cannot be qualified mortgages. Qualified mortgages also include substituted mortgages and regular interests in other REMICs.[206]

---

[201] I.R.C. § 860D(a).
[202] TRA '86 Conf. Rep., *supra* note 125, at II-226.
[203] I.R.C. § 860D(a)(4).
[204] I.R.C. § 860D(a).
[205] I.R.C. § 860G(a)(3)(A).
[206] I.R.C. § 860G(a)(3).

Stripped instruments can be qualified mortgages if they arise from instruments that would have been qualified mortgages if they had not been stripped.[207] Participations or certificates of beneficial ownership—that is, pass-through certificates—can be qualified mortgages. Investment trust interests are also qualified mortgages to the extent that the trust's assets qualify as qualified mortgages.[208] GNMA, FNMA, and FHLMC pass-through certificates are also "qualified mortgages." Senior and subordinated classes of interests are also treated as qualified mortgages.

In addition, to be a qualified mortgage, the obligation must meet one of two conditions. First, it must be "transferred to the REMIC on the startup day," that is, "the day on which the REMIC issues all of its regular and residual interests. To the extent provided in regulations, all interests issued (and all transfers to the REMIC) during any period (not exceeding 10 days) permitted in such regulations shall be treated as occurring on the day during such period selected by the REMIC for purposes of this paragraph."[209] As provided in TMRA '88 § 1006(t)(5)(F), the amendment does not apply to any REMIC where the startup day was in effect before July 1, 1987. Or, second, the obligation must be "purchased by the REMIC within the 3-month period beginning on the startup day if, except as provided in the regulations, such purchase is pursuant to a fixed contract in effect on the startup day."[210]

Qualified mortgages include "any obligation secured by stock held by a person as a tenant-stockholder as defined in [I.R.C.] section 216 in a cooperative housing corporation (as so defined)."[211] Such loans are "treated as secured by an interest in real estate."[212] The IRS has ruled that installment land sales contracts are qualified mortgages for a REMIC.[213]

In addition, Notice 87-41 provides that Treasury regulations, when issued, will allow the term "qualified mortgages" to include, among other things, manufactured housing or mobile homes that are single-family

---

[207] TRA '86 Conf. Rep., *supra* note 125, at II-227 n.5.
[208] *Id.*
[209] I.R.C. § 860G(a)(9), *amended by* TMRA '88, *supra* note 152, § 1006(t)(5)(E).
[210] TRA '86 Conf. Rep., *supra* note 125, at II-227 n.5.
[211] I.R.C. § 860G(a).
[212] *Id.*
[213] LTR 8946013 (Aug. 15, 1989); LTR 8921018 (Feb. 16, 1989); LTR 8849033 (Sept. 12, 1988); LTR 8832017 (May 13, 1988).

residences.²¹⁴ Treasury regulations will clarify that recreational vehicles, campers, and similar vehicles do not qualify as real property under the REMIC rules.²¹⁵

(ii) Regular Interests Transferred on Startup Day

A qualified mortgage is defined to include "any regular interest in another REMIC transferred to the REMIC on the startup day in exchange for regular or residual interests in the REMIC."²¹⁶

(iii) Qualified Replacement Mortgages

When a mortgage pool is formed, some of the loans in the pool may not meet the terms and conditions set out by the parties. To allow a limited opportunity to replace nonconforming mortgages, the term qualified mortgage is defined to include "any qualified replacement mortgage."²¹⁷ Certain mortgages can replace such nonconforming mortgages if the qualified replacement mortgage is any obligation that meets one of two conditions. First, the replacement mortgage is any obligation received in exchange for any qualified mortgage within three months after the startup day.²¹⁸ Or second, the replacement mortgage would have been a qualified mortgage if it had been transferred to the REMIC on or before the startup day and was received in exchange for a qualified mortgage with a default or threatened default by the obligor (referred to as a "defective qualified mortgage") within two years after the startup day.²¹⁹ Treasury regulations, when issued, will hopefully provide guidance as to when an obligation is a "defective qualified mortgage."

If a mortgage does not meet the definition of a qualified mortgage, two adverse consequences result. First, all income from the mortgage is taxed

---

²¹⁴ Notice 87-41, *supra* note 162. I.R.C. § 25(e)(10) defines "single family residence" to include "any manufactured home which has a minimum of 400 square feet of living space and a minimum width in excess of 102 inches and which is of a kind customarily used at a fixed location."

²¹⁵ Notice 87-41, *supra* note 162.

²¹⁶ I.R.C. § 860G(a)(3)(C).

²¹⁷ I.R.C. § 860G(a)(3)(B).

²¹⁸ I.R.C. § 860G(a)(4)(B).

²¹⁹ *Id.* The TRA '86 Conference Report defines a defective mortgage as "a qualified mortgage with respect to which there is a default or threatened default by the obligor." TRA '86 Conf. Rep., *supra* note 125, at II-227 n.6. The Joint Committee Report expands the group of defective qualified mortgages to include defective mortgages as that term applies in the case of investment trusts. General Explanation of TRA '86, *supra* note 119, at 413 n.68.

as a prohibited transaction.[220] Second, the REMIC election would terminate if the mortgage and other nonpermitted assets make up more than a de minimis amount of the REMIC's assets. "A REMIC can meet the assets test even if it holds only a single qualified mortgage. Thus, the REMIC rules can be used to create partial ownership interests in a single loan as an alternative to relying on the stripped bond rules of [I.R.C.] section 1286."[221] (If an entity with subsidiaries makes a REMIC election, elections would also need to be made for the subsidiaries to assure that the debt obligations of the subsidiaries meet the "qualified mortgage" requirements.)[222]

(iv) Credit Enhancements

Credit enhancements should not affect an entity's status as a REMIC and should not taint a mortgage's status as a qualified mortgage. Nevertheless, the use of credit enhancements by REMICs is not specifically addressed in the Code or the legislative history. In LTR 8918045,[223] the IRS ruled that certain credit enhancements proposed by the REMIC seeking the ruling did not taint REMIC status. For a discussion of LTR 8918045, see section 36.8(n).

(2) PERMITTED INVESTMENTS

In addition to qualified mortgages, REMICs can hold "permitted investments." A permitted investment is defined as any one of three investments: "cash flow investments," "qualified reserve assets," or "foreclosure property."[224] The remainder of this section discusses those assets that qualify as permitted investments under the REMIC rules.

(i) Cash Flow Investments

A cash flow investment is a form of a permitted investment. It is defined as "any investment of amounts received under qualified mortgages for a temporary period before distribution" to the REMIC interest holders.[225]

---

[220] *See generally* section 36.8(g).

[221] J. PEASLEE & D. NIRENBERG, *supra* note 20, at 79.

[222] For a discussion of REMIC subsidiaries and integration considerations, see generally J. PEASLEE & D. NIRENBERG, *supra* note 20, at 98–107.

[223] (Feb. 6, 1989).

[224] I.R.C. § 860G(a)(5).

[225] I.R.C. § 860G(a)(6).

The Conference Report that accompanied the REMIC legislation provides that although cash flow investments need not be mortgage related, they must be paid out by the next succeeding regular payment date, and they must be limited to those types of investments that produce passive interest income.[226] Based on this broad interpretation, cash flow investments should include most types of temporary investments.

Guaranteed investment contracts qualify as cash flow investments if the payments are made to owners of regular or residual interests at regular payment dates.[227] In a guaranteed investment contract, a REMIC remits payments from qualified mortgages to third parties that agree to return the amounts, plus interest, at times coinciding with the times that the payments are to be made to holders of the regular or residual REMIC interests.

There are limitations on the types of cash flow investments that are permitted investments for a REMIC. As a starting point, the cash flow from qualified mortgages must be "invested temporarily in passive-type assets, and paid out to the investors at the next succeeding regular payment date."[228] In addition, the cash flow investment must not be a prohibited transaction subject to a 100 percent tax.[229] The 100 percent tax on prohibited transactions obviously deters a REMIC from intentionally acquiring long-term or speculative assets.

(ii) Qualified Reserve Assets

A qualified reserve asset is a form of permitted investment that serves as a form of credit enhancement to meet the payment obligations of a REMIC if there is a default on a qualified mortgage. A qualified reserve asset is defined as any "intangible property which is held for investment and as part of a qualified reserve fund."[230]

---

[226] TRA '86 Conf. Rep., *supra* note 125, at II-227.

[227] *Id.*

[228] *Id.*

[229] For a discussion of prohibited transactions, see section 36.8(g).

[230] I.R.C. § 860G(a)(7). "[T]he phrase 'held for investment' was meant only to prevent the holding of active business assets." J. PEASLEE & D. NIRENBERG, *supra* note 20, at 81. The reserve is established to set aside the funds needed for the reserve and to hold passive, rather than active, assets.

(a) QUALIFIED RESERVE FUND DEFINED

A qualified reserve fund is defined as any "reasonably required reserve" maintained by a REMIC (1) to "provide for full payment" of certain expenses, and (2) to provide additional security for payments due on its regular interests that otherwise might be delayed or defaulted upon because of defaults and late payments on qualified mortgages.[231] A reasonable amount is viewed as an amount that is appropriate to take into account the creditworthiness of the qualified mortgages and the extent and nature of any guarantees relating to the qualified mortgages.[232]

A nationally recognized rating organization typically requires a reserve fund to be of a particular minimum size for the rating organization to provide a credit rating for the transaction. If a minimum reserve fund is specified by such a rating organization, this should demonstrate that the minimum amount of the reserve fund is a reasonably necessary reserve.[233] This position was supported in LTR 8918045,[234] where the IRS found that a subordination reserve fund set up to provide credit support for owners of a senior class of REMIC certificates is a qualified reserve within the meaning of I.R.C. § 860G(a)(7)(B).[235] The reserve reviewed by the IRS was found to comply with the "prompt and appropriate reduction" requirement "of I.R.C. § 860G(a)(7)(B) as long as the reserve is reduced in accordance with the [Trust] Agreement, because the size of the reserve is to be determined by [the] Surety's standards, which are in turn largely determined by reference to independent rating agencies' continuing appraisal of Surety's claims paying ability."[236]

(b) POTENTIAL PROBLEMS

Although "any intangible property which is held for investment" can be held in a qualified reserve fund,[237] holding qualified reserve assets inside a REMIC may result in serious problems if more than five percent of a REMIC's assets are qualified reserve assets. There are three major con-

---

[231] I.R.C. § 860G(a)(7)(B); TRA '86 Conf. Rep., *supra* note 125, at II-227. The reference to defaults includes late payments. TRA '86 Conf. Rep., *supra* note 125, at II-227.

[232] TRA '86 Conf. Rep., *supra* note 125, at II-227.

[233] For a discussion of nationally recognized rating agencies and credit enhancements, see section 7.1(b).

[234] (Feb. 6, 1989).

[235] LTR 8918045 (Feb. 6, 1989).

[236] *Id.*

[237] I.R.C. § 860G(a)(7)(A).

cerns. First, such REMIC interests may pose investment problems for REITs.[238] This is because a REMIC interest is treated as a "real estate asset" only if more than 95 percent of the REMIC's assets are real estate assets.[239]

Second, a REMIC interest is treated as a "qualifying real property loan" for determining the bad debt reserves of a thrift only to the extent a REMIC's assets consist of qualifying real property loans.[240]

Third, a REMIC interest is viewed as a qualifying asset for a domestic building and loan association only to the extent the REMIC's assets consist of assets of the sort allowed for domestic building and loan associations.[241] A domestic building and loan association is described as a domestic building and loan association, a domestic savings and loan association, and a federal savings and loan association which meets the requirements of I.R.C. § 7701(a)(19).

To avoid application of any of these tax rules that can limit the investment in REMIC interests by REITs, thrifts, and domestic building and loan associations, the REMIC should consider using a form of credit enhancement different from a qualified reserve fund (e.g., a letter of credit, a reserve fund held outside the REMIC, or senior and subordinated classes of regular interests) that is secured with assets held outside of the REMIC. Notwithstanding application of these tax rules, however, nationally recognized rating agencies—as well as prospective purchasers of the REMIC interests—may demand that credit enhancement assets be held in a qualified reserve fund. The IRS has ruled in a private letter ruling that a reserve held outside of a REMIC is not an asset of the REMIC.[242] The outside reserve considered by the IRS could include "either separate assets of the pledging party or amounts otherwise distributable directly to such party from [the REMIC] (e.g., servicing fees)."[243]

(c) PROMPT AND APPROPRIATE REDUCTIONS

As the REMIC's regular interests are retired and payments on qualified mortgages are received, amounts in a reserve fund must be reduced

---

[238] I.R.C. § 856(c)(6)(E).
[239] *Id. See* sections 36.7 and 41.3(a).
[240] I.R.C. § 593(d)(4).
[241] I.R.C. § 7701(a)(19)(C)(xi).
[242] LTR 8918045 (Feb. 6, 1989).
[243] *Id.*

"promptly and appropriately."[244] Treasury regulations, when issued, will need to clarify the requirement to "promptly and appropriately" reduce a reserve fund. "The requirement that a reserve be *promptly and appropriately reduced* as payments are received should not prevent the buildup of reserves over time . . . as long as the reserve does not at all times exceed the size required to provide adequate default protection or to pay expenses."[245]

(d) PROHIBITION AGAINST ACTIVE TRADING OF RESERVE FUND ASSETS

Given the passive nature of a REMIC, active trading of reserve fund assets is prohibited by the rule set out in I.R.C. § 860G(a)(7)(C). A reserve will not be a qualified reserve fund if more than 30 percent of the gross income from the assets in a qualified reserve fund is generated from the sale or other disposition of property held for less than three months.[246] For this computation, gain on the disposition of a qualified reserve asset is not taken into account if the asset is disposed of to prevent a default on a regular interest where the "threatened default" results from a default on one or more qualified mortgages.[247]

(iii) Foreclosure Properties

Foreclosure property is a form of a permitted REMIC investment. It is defined as property that (A) "would be foreclosure property under [I.R.C.] section 856(e) (without regard to [the permitted investment definition]) if acquired by a [REIT], and (B) which is acquired in connection with the default or imminent default of a qualified mortgage held by the REMIC."[248] The foreclosure property concept, taken from the REIT rules, is important with respect to those qualified mortgages that are not covered by a guarantee of the federal government. But, until Treasury regulations are issued, it is not clear as to what extent the REIT foreclosure rules are to apply to REMICs.

---

[244] I.R.C. § 860G(a)(7)(B). I.R.C. § 860G(e)(1) grants the Treasury authority to adopt regulations "to prevent unreasonable accumulations of assets in a REMIC."
[245] J. PEASLEE & D. NIRENBERG, *supra* note 20, at 81–82 (emphasis in the original).
[246] I.R.C. § 860G(a)(7)(C). The 30 percent limitation is similar to the 30 percent limitation on short-term trading for RICs set out in I.R.C. § 851(b)(3). *See generally* section 8.9.
[247] I.R.C. § 860G(a)(7)(C).
[248] I.R.C. § 860G(a)(8).

(e) REASONABLE ARRANGEMENT RULES

A REMIC must have in place "reasonable arrangements" designed to ensure that two conditions are met. First, "residual interests in such entity are not held by disqualified organizations (as defined in [I.R.C.] section 860E(e)(5))."[249] Second, the REMIC must make available "information necessary for the application of [I.R.C.] section 860E(e)."[250] The reasonable arrangement rules assure that the "excess inclusion rules" are not avoided when owned by a tax-exempt entity.[251] The "reasonable arrangement" concept acknowledges the fact that it may be difficult for many REMICs to determine with certainty all of the beneficial owners of their residual interests because many REMIC interests are held in street name or on behalf of undisclosed principals.

A disqualified organization is defined in I.R.C. § 860E(e)(5) to include three broad groups of organizations. First, a disqualified organization includes "the United States, any State or political subdivision thereof, any foreign government, any international organization, or any agency or instrumentality of any of the foregoing."[252] Second, a disqualified organization includes "any organization (other than a cooperative described in [I.R.C.] section 521) which is exempt from tax imposed by this chapter unless such organization is subject to the tax imposed by [I.R.C.] section 511."[253] Third, a disqualified organization includes "any organization described in section 1381(a)(2)(C)."[254] RICs, REITs, and pass-through entities are not disqualified organizations, which means that they can acquire residual interests in REMICs without violating the reasonable arrangement rules.

(f) INADVERTENT TERMINATIONS

If an entity that once satisfied the REMIC rules fails to meet the REMIC requirements at a later date, the entity will lose its status as a REMIC unless the termination is deemed to be "inadvertent."[255] Whether a termination is inadvertent is an important consideration because the

---

[249] I.R.C. § 860D(a)(6), which was added to the Code by TMRA '88, *supra* note 152, § 1006(t)(19), is effective as if it were included in TRA '86.

[250] I.R.C. § 860D(a)(6).

[251] For a discussion of the excess inclusion rules, see section 41.2(g).

[252] TMRA '88, *supra* note 152, § 1006(t)(16)(B).

[253] I.R.C. § 860E(e)(5)(B).

[254] I.R.C. § 860E(e)(5)(C).

[255] I.R.C. § 860D(b)(2)(B).

termination of a REMIC can create adverse tax consequencs for both the entity and the owners of its interests. As a result, Congress gave the Treasury the authority to issue regulations to provide some relief for inadvertent failures to comply with the REMIC requirements,[256] as long as the inadvertent failures occur in good faith.[257] First, the Treasury must determine that the cessation of REMIC status was inadvertent.[258] Second, the REMIC must take steps "no later than a reasonable time after discovery of the event resulting in such cessation"[259] to once again qualify as a REMIC. Third, the "entity, and each person holding an interest in such entity at any time during the period specified . . . agrees to make such adjustments . . . as may be required by the Secretary [of the Treasury] with respect to such period."[260] If these requirements are met, "then, notwithstanding such terminating event, such entity shall be treated as continuing to be a REMIC (or such cessation shall be disregarded for purposes of [I.R.C. § 860D(b)(2)(A)]), whichever the Secretary determines to be appropriate."[261]

(g) PROHIBITED TRANSACTIONS

In general, a REMIC is not a taxable entity if it meets the REMIC requirements and makes a REMIC election. Instead of taxing the REMIC, its income is taken into account by the owners of its regular and residual interests.[262] Because the types of activities a REMIC can engage in are limited, a tax is imposed at the entity level for all transactions outside of those that a REMIC may engage in.

A "prohibited transaction," as defined in I.R.C. § 860F(a)(2), is subject to a tax equal to 100 percent of the REMIC's net income from such a transaction.[263]

Prohibited transactions include four types of transactions:

---

[256] *Id.*
[257] TRA '86 Conf. Rep., *supra* note 125, at II-229.
[258] I.R.C. § 860D(b)(2)(B)(ii).
[259] I.R.C. § 860D(b)(2)(B).
[260] I.R.C. § 860D(b)(2)(B)(iv).
[261] I.R.C. § 860D(b)(2).
[262] *See* section 36.8(a).
[263] I.R.C. § 860F(a)(1). Assets that do not meet the asset test can be held in a de minimis amount at any time, or in a larger amount until the end of the third month beginning after the startup day. *See* section 36.8(d).

1. The disposition of a qualified mortgage (except as provided below)[264]

2. The receipt of any income attributable to any assets other than assets permitted to be held by a REMIC (i.e., qualified mortgages or permitted investments)[265]

3. The receipt of any amount representing a fee or other compensation for services,[266] and

4. The gain from the disposition of any cash flow investment, other than pursuant to a qualified liquidation[267]

For purposes of imposing the tax on prohibited transactions, net income is computed without taking into account any losses or deductions from prohibited transactions.[268] This means that any item attributable to a prohibited transaction that generates a loss (and expenses attributable to the transaction) cannot be taken into account in computing net income.

If a qualified mortgage is disposed of in one of the following four ways, it is not a prohibited transaction. First, a disposition is not a prohibited transaction if it is pursuant to "the substitution of a qualified replacement mortgage for a qualified mortgage (or the repurchase in lieu of substitution of a defective obligation)."[269] Second, a mortgage disposition is not a prohibited transaction if it results from "the foreclosure, default, or imminent default of the [qualified] mortgage."[270] Third, a disposition is not a prohibited transaction if a mortgage is disposed of because of "the bankruptcy or insolvency of the REMIC."[271] Fourth, a disposition is not a prohibited transaction if it is pursuant to a "qualified liquidation."[272]

In addition, a disposition is not a prohibited transaction if it is "required to prevent default on a regular interest where the threatened

---

[264] I.R.C. § 860F(a)(2)(A).
[265] I.R.C. § 860F(a)(2)(B).
[266] I.R.C. § 860F(a)(2)(C).
[267] I.R.C. § 860F(a)(2)(D). For a discussion of a qualified liquidation, see section 36.8(m).
[268] I.R.C. § 860F(a)(3). *See also* TRA '86 Conf. Rep., *supra* note 125, at II-230.
[269] I.R.C. § 860F(a)(2)(A)(i).
[270] I.R.C. § 860F(a)(2)(A)(ii).
[271] I.R.C. § 860F(a)(2)(A)(iii).
[272] I.R.C. § 860F(a)(2)(A)(iv). A qualified liquidation results if a REMIC adopts a plan of complete liquidation, sells all of its assets (other than cash) within 90 days, and distributes all of the cash and liquidation proceeds to its interest holders within the 90-day period. I.R.C. § 860F(a)(4). For a discussion of qualified liquidations, see section 36.8(m).

default results from a default on 1 or more qualified mortgages."[273] Further, a disposition is not a prohibited transaction if it is entered into "to facilitate a clean-up call (as defined in [Treasury] regulations)."[274]

(h) TAX ON CONTRIBUTIONS TO A REMIC AFTER THE STARTUP DAY

For REMICs with startup days after July 1, 1987, a tax is imposed on any contributions made to the REMICs after the startup day. In general, any amount contributed after the startup day is subject to a 100 percent tax on the amount of the contribution.[275] Exceptions from this tax are provided for contributions made in cash that meet the following requirements. First, a cash contribution is not subject to the penalty tax if the contribution is "to facilitate a cleanup call (as defined in regulations) or a qualified liquidation."[276]

Second, a cash contribution "in the nature of a guarantee" is not subject to the penalty tax.[277]

Third, "any contribution during the 3-month period beginning on the startup day" is not subject to the penalty tax.[278]

Fourth, any cash contribution "to a qualified reserve fund by any holder of a residual interest in the REMIC" is not subject to the penalty tax.[279]

And fifth, any cash contribution "permitted in regulations" is not subject to the penalty tax.[280]

Although the purpose of this tax on contributions to a REMIC after the startup day is not discussed in the Code or the legislative history accompanying enactment of I.R.C. § 860G(d), it appears as if the tax might be intended to prevent unreasonable accumulations of assets and partial redemptions of REMIC regular interests.

---

[273] I.R.C. § 860F(a)(5).
[274] I.R.C. § 860F(a)(5)(B).
[275] I.R.C. § 860G(d)(1).
[276] I.R.C. § 860G(d)(2)(A).
[277] I.R.C. § 860G(d)(2)(B).
[278] I.R.C. § 860G(d)(2)(C).
[279] I.R.C. § 860G(d)(2)(D).
[280] I.R.C. § 860G(d)(2)(E).

(i) TAX ON NET INCOME FROM FORECLOSURE PROPERTY

A tax is imposed on the net income from foreclosure property of each REMIC.[281] The tax on foreclosure property is computed for each taxable year by multiplying the net income from foreclosure property by the highest corporate tax rate specified in I.R.C. § 11(b).[282] "Net income from foreclosure property" is defined as "the amount which would be the REMIC's net income from foreosure property under [I.R.C.] section 857(b)(4)(B) if the REMIC were a real estate investment trust."[283]

The IRS has ruled in a private letter ruling that payments made to a REMIC by a surety company or a provider of credit enhancement are treated as a guarantee and are not subject to the tax on contributions to a REMIC after the startup day.[284] The IRS further ruled that any advances of funds by the mortgage loan servicer under an agreement to advance funds for various costs and expenses and to replace delinquent payments on mortgage loans are not subject to the tax on contributions to a REMIC after the startup day.[285]

(j) COMPLIANCE AND REPORTING

There are detailed compliance and reporting requirements for a REMIC and its residual and regular interest owners. A few of these requirements are addressed in this section.

(1) BOOKS AND RECORDS

A REMIC must maintain its books and records on the calendar year.[286] In addition, the REMIC must file information returns as if it were a partnership for tax purposes.[287]

---

[281] TMRA '88, *supra* note 152, § 1006(t)(8)(B), effective as if included in the TRA '86 provisions that established REMICs.

[282] I.R.C. § 860G(c)(1).

[283] I.R.C. § 860G(c)(2).

[284] LTR 8918045 (Feb. 6, 1989).

[285] *Id.*

[286] I.R.C. § 860D(a)(5).

[287] I.R.C. § 860F(e). Residual interest owners are treated as partners. *Id.*

(2) OID REPORTING

The OID rules require detailed calculations that are based on information more readily available to the issuer of an OID security than to the owner or any other person.[288] As a result, TRA '86 requires broad reporting of interest payments and OID accruals by REMICs (as well as any other issuer of debt securities subject to the OID rules imposed by TRA '86).[289] Amounts includable in the gross income of the owners of regular interests are treated as interest for reporting purposes.[290] In addition, a REMIC (or similar issuer) must report interest and OID to a broader group of debt security owners than was initially required under pre-TRA '86 law.[291] Reporting is required to owners that include corporations, certain dealers in commodities and securities, common trust funds, REITs, and certain other trusts.[292]

(3) REPORTING MARKET DISCOUNT OR PREMIUMS

A "REMIC or similar issuer is required to report sufficient information to allow owners to compute the accrual of any market discount or amortization of any premiums."[293] The Treasury has authority to issue regulations that can require more frequent or more detailed reporting.[294] The TRA '86 amendments are effective for tax years beginning after December 31, 1986.[295]

(4) REPORTS TO REGULAR INTERESTS

In March 1988, the IRS issued temporary regulations that set out the manner in which a REMIC must provide reports to its regular interest owners.[296]

---

[288] For a discussion of OID, see section 31.2.
[289] General Explanation of TRA '86, *supra* note 119, at 424.
[290] I.R.C. § 6049(d)(7)(A).
[291] I.R.C. § 6049(d)(7)(B).
[292] *Id.*; TRA '86 Conf. Rep., *supra* note 125, at II-237.
[293] I.R.C. § 6049(d)(7)(B); TRA '86 Conf. Rep., *supra* note 125, at II-237.
[294] I.R.C. § 6049(d)(7)(D).
[295] Pub. L. No. 99-514, § 675(a), 100 Stat. 2085, 2320 (1986) [hereinafter TRA '86].
[296] T.D. 8186, 1988-1 C.B. 37; Temp. Treas. Reg. §§ 1.67-3T, 1.860-1T, 1.860F-4T, 1.6049-7T (1988).

Various information is reported on IRS Form 1099, while other information is reported on Schedule Q of IRS Form 1066.[297]

IRS Notice 89-72[298] provides simplified reporting procedures for REMICs and other issuers of collateralized debt obligations (as described in I.R.C. § 1272(a)(6)(C)(ii)). These rules replace those set out in the temporary Treasury regulations to "ensure that both the [IRS] and investors will receive timely and accurate tax information."[299] The notice states that new temporary regulations will differ from existing temporary regulations in two important ways. "First, the new regulations will contain information reporting rules not only for REMIC regular interests but also for other collateralized debt obligations. Second, the new regulations will generally eliminate the chain of reporting by requiring only the nominee who holds an interest for the actual owner (the last middleman in the chain) to report tax information to the investor and to the [IRS]."[300]

(5) INFORMATION TO BE SUPPLIED TO THE IRS

IRS Form 1066 is used by REMICs to report their income, deductions, gains, and losses, and to report and pay tax on net income for prohibited transactions.[301] Form 1066 must be filed by the 15th day of the fourth month after the end of the tax year. Schedule Q (Form 1066), Quarterly Notice to Residual Interest Holder of REMIC Taxable Income or Net Loss Allocation, must also be used.[302]

Treasury regulations, when issued, will require a REMIC or other issuer of collateralized debt obligations to file with the IRS new IRS Form 8811, Information Return for Real Estate Mortgage Investment Conduits (REMICs) and Issuers of Collateralized Debt Obligations.[303] On IRS Form 8811, the REMIC or other issuer must list its name, employer, identification number, and the CUSIP number assigned to each class of REMIC regular interests or collateralized debt obligations.[304] In addition, the issuer "must provide the name, address, and telephone number of a person who can be contacted by a broker or other middleman to obtain

---

[297] For a discussion of reporting requirements, see K. LORE, *supra* note 24, at 6-72 to 6-83.
[298] 1989-1 C.B. 738 (June 26, 1989) [hereinafter Notice 89-72].
[299] *Id.*
[300] *Id.*
[301] Announcement 88-18, 1988-5 I.R.B. 29 (Feb. 1, 1988).
[302] Announcement 88-83, 1988-21 I.R.B. 32 (May 23, 1988) provides a change affecting item C of Schedule Q of Form 1066.
[303] Notice 89-72, *supra* note 298.
[304] *Id.*

(k) REMIC ELECTION

To qualify as a REMIC, an entity must elect to be taxed as a REMIC.[306] In March 1988, the Treasury issued temporary regulations that prescribe the manner in which an entity can elect REMIC status.[307] A REMIC must annually file an income tax return with the IRS on IRS Form 1066, U.S. Real Estate Mortgage Investment Conduit Income Tax Return.[308] The REMIC election is irrevocably made on Form 1066 for the first taxable year of the entity's existence.[309] The election must be made on the return filed for the year that includes the startup day.[310] The return, due on April 15 of the following year,[311] remains in effect unless and until there is an event that causes the entity to no longer qualify as a REMIC.

Temp. Treas. Reg. § 1.860D-1T(a) (1988) provides that an entity—or a segregated pool of assets within an entity—can elect to be treated as a REMIC by furnishing certain information and by computing its REMIC taxable income (or loss) in accordance with I.R.C. § 860C(b) and the regulations issued thereunder.[312]

If a REMIC election terminates, the termination is effective as of the beginning of the year in which the event occurs.[313] For a discussion of inadvertent terminations, see section 36.8(f). If the REMIC is liquidated and it qualifies as a REMIC for all periods in which it is in existence, termination should not relate back to the beginning of the tax year of the liquidation. "Otherwise, a REMIC could not liquidate and remain a REMIC throughout its life, except in a case where the liquidation happens to take place on January 1."[314]

---

[305] *Id.*
[306] I.R.C. § 860D(a)(1).
[307] T.D. 8186, 1988-1 C.B. 37.
[308] Temp. Treas. Reg. § 1.860F-4T(b) (1988).
[309] Temp. Treas. Reg. § 1.860D-1T(a) (1988).
[310] I.R.C. § 860D(b)(1).
[311] I.R.C. § 6072(a).
[312] But note that regular and residual interests must be designated and must be issued on the startup day. *See* discussion at section 36.8(a).
[313] I.R.C. § 860D(b)(2)(A).
[314] J. PEASLEE & D. NIRENBERG, *supra* note 20, at 92.

(l) TREATMENT OF ALLOCABLE INVESTMENT EXPENSES

A REMIC must allocate to each of its "pass-through interest holders" a proportionate share of the aggregate amount of the REMIC's allocable investment expenses for the calendar quarter.[315] A pass-through interest holder is defined as any holder of a residual interest that is either an individual (other than certain nonresident aliens), a person that computes his income in the same manner as an individual, or a pass-through entity.[316] A single-class REMIC must report to both its pass-through interest holders and the IRS the proportionate share of each holder's allocable investment expenses.[317]

(m) QUALIFIED LIQUIDATIONS

A REMIC can adopt a plan of complete liquidation and dispose of its assets without being subject to the tax on prohibited transactions.[318]

If a REMIC sells its assets pursuant to a qualified liquidation, it is not a prohibited transaction.[319] If a REMIC sells all of its assets, other than cash, within the "liquidation period," it does not recognize any gain or loss on the sale of its assets.[320] A REMIC can choose to liquidate for any reason, and the liquidation can still qualify as a qualified liquidation.

To meet the requirements for a qualified liquidation, the REMIC must first adopt a plan of complete liquidation.[321] Second, the REMIC must sell "all of its assets (other than cash) within the liquidation period."[322] And third, on or before the last day of the liquidation period, the REMIC must credit or distribute all of the liquidation proceeds, plus its cash (except for amounts to meet the claims of creditors), to the holders of its regular or residual interests.[323] The term "liquidation period" is defined as the period beginning on the date of the adoption of the plan of liquidation, and ending at the close of the 90th day after that date.[324]

---

[315] Temp. Treas. Reg. § 1.67-3T(a)(1) (1988).

[316] Temp. Treas. Reg. § 1.67-3T(a)(2)(i)(A) (1988).

[317] Temp. Treas. Reg. § 1.860F-4T(e)(4) (1988).

[318] For a discussion of prohibited transactions, see section 36.8(g).

[319] I.R.C. § 860F(a)(2)(A).

[320] I.R.C. § 860F(a)(4).

[321] I.R.C. § 860F(a)(4)(A)(i).

[322] I.R.C. § 860F(a)(4)(A)(ii).

[323] I.R.C. § 860F(a)(4)(A)(iii); TRA '86 Conf. Rep., *supra* note 125, at II-236.

[324] I.R.C. § 860F(a)(4)(B).

Allowing a REMIC to liquidate without recognizing any gain or loss on the sale of its assets is consistent with the conduit (i.e., pass-through) nature of a REMIC. "A holder of a [REMIC's] regular or residual interest, [on the other hand] recognizes gain or loss on the liquidation of the REMIC."[325]

(n) CREDIT ENHANCEMENTS

The use of credit enhancements by REMICs is not specifically addressed in the Code or the legislative history that accompanied enactment of the REMIC provisions.[326] The IRS has addressed the use of credit enhancements in a private letter ruling issued in 1989. In LTR 8918045,[327] the IRS addressed the tax consequences of several types of credit enhancements used by a REMIC formed as a trust that issued pass-through certificates. This private ruling provides some guidance as to where the IRS stands on the use of credit enhancements by REMICs. The remainder of this section addresses this private ruling.

In LTR 8918045, a pool of mortgages was transferred to a trust in exchange for senior and subordinated pass-through certificates. The trust agreement provided for the establishment of several forms of credit enhancements. First, the pass-through certificates were issued in both senior and subordinated form. Second, the trustee was required to establish a "subordination reserve fund to provide further credit support for the holders of the senior certificates."[328] Third, the trustee would purchase a "Certificate Guaranty Insurance Policy" from a surety company, whereby the surety would guarantee to the senior pass-through certificate holders "timely payment on each distribution date of principal and interest then due on their certificates."[329] If the surety made any payments to the senior pass-through certificate holders, the surety could look to the trustee for reimbursement (as a direct reimbursement right against the trust, as a right of subrogation, or a combination of these rights). In addition, the surety could require a right of reimbursement against the mortgage loan servicer or the prior owner of the mortgages and this right could be secured by a pledge of a reserve of assets held outside of the trust, which could include separate assets of the pledging parties or amounts otherwise distributable directly to the pledging parties from the trust

---

[325] General Explanation of TRA '86, *supra* note 119, at 424.
[326] For a discussion of credit enhancements, see generally section 7.1(b).
[327] (Feb. 6, 1989).
[328] LTR 8918045 (Feb. 6, 1989).
[329] *Id.*

(e.g., servicing fees).[330] Further, the surety could also require additional types of credit enhancements, such as a letter of credit or mortgage pool insurance.[331]

In LTR 8918045, the IRS ruled that the Certificate Guaranty Insurance Policy issued by the surety and the additional credit enhancements that the surety may require, are incidents of the mortgage loans and not separate assets of the trust.[332] This means that the requirement of I.R.C. § 860D(a)(4)—that substantially all of a REMIC's assets must be qualified mortgages and permitted investments—is not violated by these credit enhancements.[333] Any deferred payment obligations and the proceeds of payment will continue to be treated as incidents of the mortgage loans notwithstanding a default, foreclosure, or extinguishment of rights with respect to a mortgage loan or loans.[334]

The IRS also ruled in LTR 8918045 that the credit enhancements are viewed as incidents of the mortgage loans for determining the tax treatment of REMIC interests owned by REITs.[335]

In LTR 8918045, the IRS ruled that the reimbursement rights of the surety or another provider of additional credit enhancement did not create an ownership interest in the trust.[336] The reimbursement rights are not considered in determining whether all of the interests are regular or residual interests.[337] This is an important finding because an entity—to qualify as a REMIC—can only have regular and residual interests designated as such on the startup day.[338] Credit enhancements do not create a class of interests that taint an entity's REMIC status.

(o) TAXABLE MORTGAGE POOLS

After 1991, REMICs are the exclusive way to issue—without two levels of tax—multiple-class securities backed by real estate. All other entities, pools, or other arrangements that hold mortgages with multiple classes of ownership interests (and with payments tied to the timing of mortgage

[330] *Id.*
[331] *Id.*
[332] *Id.*
[333] For a discussion of the asset requirements for a REMIC, see section 36.8(d).
[334] *Id.*
[335] LTR 8918045 (Feb. 6, 1989), *referring to* I.R.C. §§ 593(d)(4), 856(c)(6)(E), 7701(a)(19)(C). *See* section 41.3(a).
[336] LTR 8918045 (Feb. 6, 1989).
[337] *Id.*
[338] I.R.C. § 860D(a). For a discussion of requirements of regular and residual interests, see sections 36.8(c)(1) and 36.8(c)(2).

payments) will be treated as taxable mortgage pools, or TMPs, if a REMIC election is not made.[339] If the entity, pool, or other arrangement is classified as a TMP, it is taxed as a separate corporation subject to corporate tax and cannot file a consolidated tax return with any corporation.[340] The TMP rules will force most entities that can make REMIC elections to do so to avoid the TMP rules.[341]

A TMP is defined in I.R.C. § 7701(i) as an entity—other than a REMIC—that meets the following four conditions. First, "substantially all of the assets . . . consists of debt obligations (or interests therein)."[342] Second, "more than 50 percent of such debt obligations (or interests) consists of real estate mortgages (or interests therein)."[343] Third, the "entity is the obligor under debt obligations with 2 or more maturities."[344] (This third requirement gives the Treasury the right to treat preferred stock that is collateralized with assets as a TMP.) Fourth, under the terms of the debt obligations . . . (or underlying arrangements), payments on such debt obligations bear a relationship to payments on the debt obligations (or interests)."[345] Although a REMIC must have a calendar year as its taxable year, there is no calendar year requirement for a TMP.

Any portion of an entity that meets the definition of a TMP is treated as a TMP. The General Explanation of TRA '86 provides that the TMP provisions apply if "an entity segregates mortgages . . . and issues debt obligations in two or more maturities, which maturities depend upon the timing of payments on the [underlying] mortgages."[346] In addition, "[d]ebt instruments that may have the same stated maturity but different rights relating to acceleration of that maturity, are to be treated as having different maturities."[347]

To determine whether an entity is a TMP, "equity interest of varying classes which correspond to [differing] maturity classes of debt [to the extent provided in Treasury regulations] shall be treated as debt."[348]

---

[339] I.R.C. § 7701(e).
[340] I.R.C. § 7701(i)(1).
[341] Corporate issuers will generally make the REMIC election if available because a TMP cannot file consolidated returns with affiliated corporations.
[342] I.R.C. § 7701(i)(2)(A)(i).
[343] Id.
[344] I.R.C. § 7701(i)(2)(A)(ii).
[345] I.R.C. § 7701(i)(2)(A)(iii).
[346] General Explanation of TRA '86, supra note 119, at 427.
[347] Id.
[348] I.R.C. § 7701(i)(2)(D).

There are two major exceptions to the TMP rules. First, a domestic building and loan association that would otherwise be treated as a TMP is specifically exempt from the TMP provisions.[349] A "domestic building and loan association" is defined as a domestic building and loan association, a domestic savings and loan association, and a federal savings and loan association that meets the requirements of I.R.C. § 7701(a)(19).

Second, REITs are exempt from the TMP rules. If "an entity that otherwise would be treated as a TMP" also meets the requirements to be treated as a REIT, it "can elect to be treated as a REIT" and thereby avoid the TMP provisions.[350] "If a portion of a REIT is treated as a TMP, such portion may qualify as a REIT subsidiary."[351] In addition, adjustments relating to the inclusion of "excess inclusion income" will—under Treasury regulations when issued—apply to the REIT's shareholders.[352] The excess inclusion calculation "is to be made as if the equity interests in the REIT were the residual interest in a REMIC."[353] Under I.R.C. § 860E(d), REIT shareholders—not the REIT that is holding the residual interest in a REMIC—are subject to the tax on excess inclusion income. REIT shareholders are subject to the tax on income earned under the TMP provisions.[354]

Although the TMP provisions are generally effective after 1991, a grandfather rule is provided for certain entities that would otherwise fall under the TMP rules. The TMP provisions do not apply to any entity or arrangement in existence on December 31, 1991, unless there is a "substantial transfer" of costs or property to the entity after that date.[355] Although the legislative history that accompanied the enactment of the REMIC legislation as part of TRA '86 does not identify the types of transfers that are viewed as substantial, the General Explanation of TRA '86 provides that transfers in payment of obligations held by the entity will not affect availability of the grandfather provision.[356]

---

[349] I.R.C. § 7701(i)(2)(C).

[350] General Explanation of TRA '86, *supra* note 119, at 427.

[351] *Id.* at 428.

[352] Excess inclusion income is defined at I.R.C. § 860E(c). For a discussion of excess inclusion income, see section 51.2(g).

[353] General Explanation of TRA '86, *supra* note 119, at 428.

[354] REIT status may be preferable to REMIC status under certain situations, so an ability to elect REIT status is attractive to such entities.

[355] TRA '86, *supra* note 295, § 675(c)(2).

[356] General Explanation of TRA '86, *supra* note 119, at 428.

(p) POLICY CONSIDERATIONS FOR APPLYING REMIC TREATMENT TO POOLS OF NONMORTGAGE ASSETS

The author believes there is no policy justification for limiting the availability of REMIC-type tax treatment to pools of real estate mortgage assets. This position has been advanced by the American Bar Association.[357] In enacting the REMIC provisions, Congress recognized the increasing use of multiple-class arrangements in packaging mortgages and acknowledged the considerable tax uncertainties in such structures. The REMIC provisions were enacted to provide rules "prescribing (1) the Federal income tax treatment of the REMIC, (2) the treatment of taxpayers who exchange mortgages for interests in the REMIC, (3) the treatment of taxpayers holding interests in the REMIC, and (4) the treatment of disposition of interests in the REMIC."[358] But the same uncertainties that apply to the packaging of real estate mortgages also apply to the securitization of other assets. The author believes that it makes no sense to have tax treatment turn on the type of assets placed into a pool, or the selection of the entity utilized to pool those assets. Rather, all securitized assets should be taxed in a consistent manner, which means that REMIC-type treatment should be available for all securitized assets.

It is important to note, of course, that REMICs do not provide answers for all of the concerns to reform the tax treatment of asset-backed securities. For example, a REMIC is an entity that can only conduct limited activities to hold a fixed pool of assets. In addition, REMICs cannot engage in broad management activities. And, under current rules, REMICs cannot enter into swaps and other notional principal contracts because such contracts do not meet the asset test. Notwithstanding these limitations, it appears appropriate to allow pools of asset-backed securities to elect REMIC-type tax treatment.

---

[357] See ABA Members Support Creation of "Asset Securitization Investment Conduits" to Supplant REMICs, 19 DAILY TAX HIGHLIGHTS & DOCUMENTS 1981 (1990).

[358] TRA '86 Conf. Rep., *supra* note 125, at II-225.

Thirty-seven
Taxation of Pass-Through Certificate Owners

This chapter discusses the tax treatment of pass-through certificate owners. Section 37.1 sets out the general tax principles that apply to holders of pass-through certificates. Section 37.2 looks at pass-through certificates purchased at their principal amount. Section 37.3 looks at pass-through certificates purchased at a premium. Section 37.4 looks at pass-through certificates purchased at a discount. Section 37.5 looks at the taxation of stripped pass-through certificates. Section 37.6 looks at the taxation of senior and subordinated classes of pass-through certificates. Section 37.7 looks at the special considerations for graduated payment mortgages.

§ 37.1 GENERAL TAX PRINCIPLES

Pass-through certificates—typically ownership interests in trusts—represent undivided ownership interests in each asset making up the pool.[1] This characterization can be significant for mutual savings banks, cooperative banks, domestic building and loan associations, and other savings institutions as defined in I.R.C. § 591(a). This is because such

---

[1] *See* Rev. Rul. 84-10, 1984-1 C.B. 155; Rev. Rul. 77-349, 1977-2 C.B. 20; *see also* sections 1.1(e) and 36.2.

institutions must own real estate mortgages to qualify for the special bad debt reserve deduction provided in I.R.C. § 593(b)(1). This characterization can also be significant for REITs because they must own real estate interests to deduct dividends paid to their shareholders.[2] Certificate owners compute their tax liability by including all items of income, deductions, and credits attributable to their pro rata pool interests in income (irrespective of whether on the cash or accrual method of accounting) at the time the mortgage payments, or payments on other assets in the pool, are received by the trust, even if the distributions are not made to the certificate owners at that time.[3] The trustee is simply viewed as the agent of the certificate owners.

A pass-through certificate owner, as the beneficial owner of each underlying asset, should technically calculate income or loss on each asset separately. As a practical matter, however, allocation to each asset is usually not necessary because the tax results are usually the same if the assets are viewed separately or in the aggregate.

Each payment a certificate owner receives includes interest, principal, and payments for various charges and fees. Repayment of principal is a tax-free return of capital.[4] Interest and fees received by the trust are taxable as ordinary income. Fees paid to service the assets, custodian fees, and other "business expenses" are generally deductible under I.R.C. § 162. Trust expenses deductible under I.R.C. § 212 will be taken into account by certificate owners to the extent allowable by I.R.C. § 67 (which limits the deductions for miscellaneous itemized deductions to the extent such deductions exceed, in the aggregate, two percent of the taxpayer's adjusted gross income).[5]

A certificate owner's gain or lss on the sale of a pass-through certificate is based on the difference between the certificate's tax basis and the net proceeds on the sale.[6] Investors[7] and traders[8] obtain capital gain or loss, reduced by any gain attributable to interest or discount income,

---

[2] I.R.C. § 856(c)(3).
[3] Treas. Reg. § 1.671-3(a) (1969); Rev. Rul. 81-203, 1981-2 C.B. 137; Rev. Rul. 80-96, 1980-1 C.B. 317; Rev. Rul. 77-349, 1977-2 C.B. 20; Rev. Rul. 74-300, 1974-1 C.B. 169; Rev. Rul. 74-221, 1974-1 C.B. 365; Rev. Rul. 72-376, 1972-2 C.B. 647; Rev. Rul. 71-399, 1971-2 C.B. 433.
[4] Rev. Rul. 84-10, 1984-1 C.B. 155; Rev. Rul. 70-545, 1970-2 C.B. 7.
[5] *See* section 9.1(d).
[6] *See generally* Chapter 16.
[7] *See* section 8.1.
[8] *See* section 8.2.

which is taxable at ordinary income rates. Dealers,[9] hedgers,[10] and certain financial institutions[11] obtain ordinary income.

The price paid for a pass-through certificate is allocated to the owner's undivided interest in the pooled assets based on the fair market value of the pooled assets. This means that there may be market discounts, OID, or premiums on the acquisition of pass-through certificates. Taxation of pass-through certificates purchased at discounts[12] or premiums[13] can be very confusing. As a result, it is necessary to separately consider the tax treatment of pass-through certificates purchased at their principal amount, a premium, and a discount to determine the appropriate tax treatment for an owner of a pass-through certificate. The remainder of this chapter discusses some of these major issues.

§ 37.2 PURCHASES AT THE PRINCIPAL AMOUNT

The taxation of pass-through certificates purchased at their principal amounts is relatively straightforward. The only interest element is the stated interest amount. Principal payments are a tax-free return of capital. If a certificate is sold for an amount different from the amount of the principal balance outstanding at the time of sale, there is gain or loss on the sale. Capital gain or loss (long-term or short-term depending on the owner's holding period) is available to investors[14] and traders.[15] Ordinary income is available to dealers,[16] hedgers,[17] and certain financial institutions.[18]

§ 37.3 PURCHASES AT A PREMIUM

If a pass-through certificate owner purchases the certificate at a price that is greater than the redemption price at maturity of the owner's undivided

---

[9] *See* section 8.3.
[10] *See* section 8.4.
[11] *See* section 8.8.
[12] *See* section 37.4.
[13] *See* section 37.3.
[14] *See* section 8.1.
[15] *See* section 8.2.
[16] *See* section 8.3.
[17] *See* section 8.4.
[18] *See* section 8.8.

ownership interest in the underlying pooled assets, the owner has purchased the certificate at a premium. Although it is possible to purchase pass-through certificates at a premium, it is unlikely that an investor will make such a purchase because investors are typically unwilling to pay a premium for certificates that—at most—offer either limited or no call protection. For pass-through certificates with a premium, Rev. Rul. 84-10[19] provides that certificate owners can amortize their proportionate shares of premium to the extent allowed by I.R.C. § 171.

Under pre-TRA '86 law, premiums on residential mortgages originated on or before September 27, 1985, generally could not be amortized because I.R.C. § 171 did not apply to obligations of individuals.[20] This meant that only premiums on those mortgages that were issued by corporations could be amortized. All premiums paid on the purchase of a residential mortgage or pass-through certificate evidencing such a mortgage had to be allocated among the principal payments in proportion to the principal amounts.[21] The premium paid was then deductible as an ordinary loss as the principal payments to which the premium amounts were allocated (for cash method taxpayers) or accrued (for accrual method taxpayers).

TRA '86 amended I.R.C. § 171(d) by eliminating the requirement that a bond with amortizable premium must have been issued by a government or corporation. I.R.C. § 171(d) now provides that a bond with amortizable premium can be issued by individuals, not just governments or corporations. This change is effective for obligations issued after September 27, 1985.[22] The Conference Report that accompanied TRA '86 can be read to allow the amortizable premium on an obligation to be amortized by taking into account prepayments in a way consistent with I.R.C. § 1272(a)(6).[23]

§ 37.4 PURCHASES AT A DISCOUNT

The treatment of pass-through certificates purchased at a discount depends on whether the discount is OID[24] or market discount.[25] OID is

---

[19] 1984-1 C.B. 155.

[20] I.R.C. § 171(d). For a general discussion of premiums, see section 31.4.

[21] *See* Peaslee & Nirenberg, *Federal Income Tax Treatment of Mortgage-Backed Securities*, in THE HANDBOOK OF MORTGAGE-BACKED SECURITIES 1297, 1368–70 (F. Fabozzi rev. ed. 1988).

[22] TRA '86, Pub. L. No. 99-514, § 1803(a)(11)(B), 100 Stat. 2085, 2795 (1986).

[23] STAFF OF THE JOINT COMM. ON TAXATION, 99TH CONG., 2D SESS., TAX REFORM BILL OF 1986, FINAL CONFERENCE COMM. DECISIONS II-842 (Joint Comm. Print 1986) [hereinafter TRA '86 Conf. Rep.].

[24] *See generally* section 31.2.

[25] *See generally* section 31.3.

included in the certificate owner's income as the discount accrues,[26] while market discount is included in income only when the principal payments are received for cash method taxpayers, accrued for accrual method taxpayers, or when the certificate is sold.[27] TRA '86 provides that a holder of a debt instrument payable in installments takes accrued market discount into income upon receipt of principal payments.[28]

(a) ORIGINAL ISSUE DISCOUNT

It is not likely that a pass-through certificate will have OID, unless the stripped bond rules apply,[29] interest payments on the underlying mortgages increase over time,[30] the originator charges "excessive" points or similar charges, or interest on the mortgage loan does not meet the definition of qualified periodic interest payment, or QPIP. Excessive points reduce the issue price of the mortgage loan, thereby creating OID. Interest may not meet the QPIP definition if the loans have variable rates not based on an established index.

Many pass-through certificates in real estate mortgage pools represent interests in residential mortgage obligations of individuals. Because the rules that require the inclusion in income of OID on obligations of individuals (i.e., natural persons) only apply to mortgages closed after March 1, 1984,[31] one must determine the date when a mortgage obligation is incurred. As a rule of thumb, gain from a sale of a pass-through certificate issued after July 18, 1984, is treated as ordinary income to the extent of the market discount that accrued during the period the seller owned the security.[32] To further confuse the issue, the way in which discount is allocated among principal payments depends on whether the certificate is subject to the provisions in effect before or after the DRA changes in 1984.

Gain realized on the sale of a pass-through certificate that represents OID that was not previously included in income is treated as ordinary

---

[26] I.R.C. § 1272.
[27] See I.R.C. §§ 1276–1278.
[28] See section 31.3(f).
[29] The stripped bonds and coupons would be viewed as zero coupon bonds under I.R.C. § 1286(a) and the OID rules would apply. See section 31.6.
[30] See generally New York State Bar Association, Tax Section, Report of Ad Hoc Committee on Proposed Original Issue Discount Regulations, reprinted in Special Report, 34 TAX NOTES 363, 413–14 (1987). For an excellent discussion of the application of the OID, market discount, and stripped bond rules as they apply to pass-through certificates, see J. PEASLEE & D. NIRENBERG, FEDERAL INCOME TAXATION OF MORTGAGE BACKED SECURITIES 120, 120–55 (1989).
[31] DRA, Pub. L. No. 98-369, § 41(a), 98 Stat. 494, 531 (1984) (codified at I.R.C. § 1272(a)(2)(D)).
[32] I.R.C. § 1276(a)(1).

income if the mortgage is an obligation of an individual. This is because I.R.C. § 1271(a)(1) does not apply to natural persons.[33] Therefore, any gain on amortized or prepaid principal is treated as ordinary income, irrespective of the certificate owner's holding period. Treating amortized or prepaid principal as ordinary income can be a substantial tax disadvantage to an owner of a pass-through certificate.[34] Once the certificate is sold, gain or loss on the remaining principal balance, if any, is treated as a capital gain or loss (long-term or short-term, depending on the owner's holding period).

In general, the amount of OID allocable to any accrual period is calculated based on the adjusted issue price of a debt obligation at the beginning of that accrual period and the yield to maturity, reduced by payments of QPIP allocable to that accrual period.[35] This general rule does not consider the acceleration of payments due to unscheduled prepayments. Acceleration of payments. was addressed in I.R.C. § 1272(a)(6), enacted as part of TRA '86, to determine the accrual of OID on debt obligations on which payments are accelerated because of prepayments. The provisions of I.R.C. § 1272(a)(6) should not apply to mortgage loans held by an investment trust because the prepayments do not depend on the prepayment of any other obligations securing the loans. I.R.C. § 1272(a)(6)(C)(i) provides that this rule does apply to a REMIC's regular interests. If I.R.C. § 1272(a)(6) does not apply to mortgage loans, prepayments result in capital gain or ordinary income, but not accelerated OID.[36]

(b) MARKET DISCOUNT

An owner of a pass-through certificate may be subject to the market discount rules found at I.R.C. §§ 1276–1278 if his undivided interest in an underlying loan is purchased at a discount. For a discussion of market discount, see generally section 31.3. Market discount generally equals the excess of the certificate owner's allocable portion of the principal balance of the underlying loan over the purchase price for the certificate.[37] Unless

---

[33] I.R.C. § 1271(b)(1).

[34] This may explain, in part, why tax-exempt entities invest in pass-through certificates, while many taxable entities and individuals invest much less frequently in pass-through certificates.

[35] Prop. Treas. Reg. § 1.1272-1(c)(2)(i) (1986).

[36] *See generally* I.R.C. §§ 1271(a), 1271(b)(1), 1272(a)(6).

[37] I.R.C. §§ 1278(a)(1), (a)(2)(A), (a)(2)(B).

a certificate owner elects, under I.R.C. § 1278(b), to currently include market discount in income, gain on the disposition of a loan with market discount is treated as ordinary income to the extent the gain does not exceed the accrued market discount not previously included in income.[38] In addition, payments of amounts included in the stated redemption price at maturity are also treated as ordinary income to the extent these payments do not exceed accrued market discount not already included in gross income.[39] If a pooled asset consists of a loan with OID, a pass-through certificate owner might be able to accrue market discount in a manner similar to the OID provisions if the owner is viewed as having purchased an undivided interest in the loan at a market discount.[40]

§ 37.5 STRIPPED PASS-THROUGH CERTIFICATES

Stripped pass-through certificates can be issued by an investment trust with the trust retaining its status as a trust for tax purposes. For a discussion of stripped pass-through certificates, see sections 7.2(c)(2) and 36.2(d). Stripped bonds and coupons purchased after July 1, 1982, are subject to the stripped bond provisions of I.R.C. § 1286. For a discussion of the stripped bond rules, see section 31.6.

Stripped pass-through certificates can be issued as stripped bonds where the interest coupons (defined broadly to include any right to receive interest on a security whether or not evidenced by a coupon)[41] are separated from ownership of the debt security.[42] In other words, the security is divided into two pieces: a right to receive principal and a right to receive interest.

(a) TAXATION OF TAXPAYER STRIPPING THE BOND

In a typical stripped pass-through certificate transaction, the originator or promoter (collectively referred to as the "promoter") sells principal balances and rights to receive interest on the underlying pooled debt obligations at a particular interest rate while retaining the excess of the yield on the underlying pooled assets over the interest rate on the pass-

---

[38] I.R.C. § 1276(a)(1).
[39] *See* I.R.C. § 1276(a)(3)(A); TRA '86 Conf. Rep., *supra* note 23, at II-842.
[40] *See* I.R.C. § 1277(a).
[41] I.R.C. § 1286(e)(5).
[42] I.R.C. § 1286(e)(2).

through certificates.[43] This transaction is subject to the stripped bond rules in I.R.C. § 1286.

The underlying pooled debt obligations are "evidences of indebtedness" that are treated as bonds as defined in I.R.C. § 1286(e)(1).[44] The right to receive interest is treated as a "coupon" under I.R.C. § 1286(e)(5).[45] Separating a portion of the interest from the bond is treated as a "stripped bond" under I.R.C. § 1286(e)(2),[46] equal to the excess of each payment due on an underlying pooled asset over the sum of the portions of each underlying asset allocable to amortization of principal, interest on a monthly principal balance at the interest rate on the pass-through certificate, and the monthly servicing fees.[47]

The promoter (i.e., the "person stripping the bond") allocates its tax basis among the items it retains and the items it disposes of. If an amount is received in excess of the promoter's tax basis, there is a taxable gain on the sale.[48] When the promoter disposes of any of the retained coupons and bond, it must include in income any accrued interest or market discount on the stripped bonds.[49] The tax basis of the bond and coupons is increased by the amount of this income.[50] Basis is allocated between the retained coupons and the bonds that the promoter sells to the certificate owners on the basis of fair market value of the coupons and bonds.[51] If the promoter sells the retained bonds and coupons, it recognizes gain in an amount equal to the extent of the retained yield (i.e., the retained interest rate). In addition, the amount that the promoter retains—that is, the retained coupons—is viewed as having been originally issued as of the purchase date with OID equal to the excess of the amount payable on the due date of the coupon, which is the originator's share of the scheduled interest payments over the tax basis allocated to the coupons.[52]

---

[43] For a detailed discussion of the transaction, see section 7.2(c)(2).

[44] A bond is defined in I.R.C. § 1286(e)(1) as a "bond, debenture, note, or certificate or other evidence of indebtedness."

[45] A coupon is defined in I.R.C. § 1286(e)(5) to include "any right to receive interest on a bond (whether or not evidenced by a coupon)."

[46] A stripped bond is defined in I.R.C. § 1286(e)(2) as "a bond issued at any time with interest coupons where there is a separation in ownership between the bond and any coupon which has not yet become payable."

[47] *See generally* LTR 8640012 (June 30, 1986); LTR 8625048 (Mar. 24, 1986); LTR 8620016 (Feb. 7, 1986).

[48] I.R.C. § 1286(b).

[49] I.R.C. § 1286(b)(1).

[50] I.R.C. § 1286(b)(2).

[51] I.R.C. § 1286(b)(3). If the promoter "originated" the underlying pooled assets, it will most likely have a tax basis in each debt obligation equal to its face value.

[52] For a discussion of OID, see section 31.2.

(b) TAXPAYER OWNING STRIPPED BONDS

An owner of a stripped pass-through certificate has an undivided ownership interest in the underlying pool of stripped debt obligations. Under I.R.C. § 1286, the underlying obligations are viewed as having been originally issued on the date the certificate owner purchased the certificate with OID equal to the excess of their stated redemption price at maturity over their ratable share of the purchase price. The owners of the pass-through certificates—under the provisions of I.R.C. § 1272—must accrue the OID on the coupons and bonds, although it is unclear exactly how these rules are to be applied.[53] Pass-through certificates that are subject to the stripped bond rules of I.R.C. § 1286 are also subject to the OID rules. Those pass-through certificates that are not subject to the stripped bond rules, on the other hand, are not subject to the OID rules unless interest on the underlying pooled debt obligations is scheduled to increase over time.[54]

The pass-through certificate owner has a tax basis in his certificate equal to its purchase price.[55] The price paid for the certificate is allocated among each of the pooled debt obligations in accordance with their respective fair market values.[56]

An investment trust holding a pool of stripped debt obligations might be viewed as holding separate stripped bonds and coupons for each principal and interest payment on each debt obligation. This is because interest on stripped bonds might be viewed as stripped coupons under I.R.C. §§ 1286(e)(2) and (3). The stripped bonds and coupons might represent multiple stripped bonds. Because stripped pass-through certificate owners must allocate their purchase price among all of the stripped bonds and coupons in the pool, this allocation can be difficult, if not impossible.

To minimize the problems in allocating basis and payments among all of the underlying pooled debt obligations, certificate owners might be able to aggregate payments of principal and interest from all of the

---

[53] If stripped bonds and coupons are characterized as debt obligations on which payments may be accelerated by reason of the prepayment of other obligations securing the debt instruments, OID accrual might be calculated under I.R.C. § 1272(a)(6). For a discussion of OID, see section 31.2.

[54] For a detailed discussion of pass-through certificates subject to the stripped bond rules, see J. PEASLEE & D. NIRENBERG, *supra* note 30, at 137–43. For a discussion of pass-through certificates not subject to the stripped bond rules, see *id.* at 144–47. For a discussion of graduated payment mortgages, see section 37.7.

[55] For a discussion of tax basis, see Chapter 16.

[56] I.R.C. § 1286(a).

stripped bonds and coupons in the underlying pool into one debt instrument. Aggregation is allowed under the rules contained in the proposed Treasury regulations on OID. Aggregation is allowed if the debt obligations are "issued in connection with the same transaction or a series of related transactions or as part of the same issue shall be treated together as a single debt instrument with a single issue price, maturity date, yield, and stated redemption price at maturity."[57] The proposed Treasury regulations further provide that "[w]hether debt instruments are issued in connection with the same transaction or a series of related transactions shall be determined in accordance with all the facts and circumstances surrounding the issuance of the debt instrument."[58]

§ 37.6 SENIOR AND SUBORDINATED PASS-THROUGH CERTIFICATES

Senior and subordinated classes of pass-through certificates are established as a form of credit enhancement. For a detailed discussion of senior and subordinated pass-through certificates, see generally section 7.2(c). Senior and subordinated classes do not affect the tax status of an investment trust issuing the certificates if the subordinated class is retained by the originator or promoter. For a detailed discussion of the limitations imposed on transfer, see section 36.2(e). This means that both the senior and subordinated classes that do not taint the trust's tax status as an investment trust are pass-through certificates subject to the tax rules that generally apply to pass-through certificates.

§ 37.7 SPECIAL CONSIDERATIONS FOR GRADUATED PAYMENT MORTGAGES

GPMs are different from traditional mortgages because the monthly mortgage payments on a GPM are not all equal.[59] GPM payments are generally smaller in the early years and increase during the life of the mortgage. Owners of GPM certificates on the accrual method must pay

[57] Prop. Treas. Reg. § 1.1275-2(d) (1986).
[58] *Id.*
[59] *See* section 2.1(b)(2). *See also*, Senft, *Mortgages*, 19–24; Waldman & Gordon, *Determining the Yield of a Mortgage Security*, 295–96; Askin & Lowell, *The Rating of Mortgage-Backed Securities*, 313, all in THE HANDBOOK OF MORTGAGE-BACKED SECURITIES (F. Fabozzi rev. ed. 1988).

taxes on the entire amount of interest that would be paid if the GPM were a traditional mortgage, even though less interest is received on the GPM mortgage. The interest shortfall is treated as a deferred item, and any mortgage prepayments are used to reduce any deferred interest outstanding.[60]

---

[60] *See* Senft, *Pass-Through Securities*, in THE HANDBOOK OF FIXED INCOME SECURITIES 469, 503 (F. Fabozzi & I. Pollack eds. 1983).

Thirty-eight
Taxation of Pay-Through Bond Owners

This chapter discusses the tax treatment of pay-through bond owners. Section 38.1 sets out the general tax principles that apply to holders of pay-through bonds. Section 38.2 addresses the purchase of pay-through bonds at their principal amount. Section 38.3 addresses the purchase of pay-through bonds at a premium. Section 38.4 addresses the purchase of pay-through bonds at a discount. Section 38.5 looks at stripped pay-through bonds. Section 38.6 addresses senior and subordinated pay-through bonds.

§ 38.1 GENERAL TAX PRINCIPLES

Pay-through bonds are the debt obligations of corporate and owner trust issuers,[1] which means that an owner of a pay-through bond simply owns a debt security subject to all of the tax rules that generally apply to debt securities.[2] In brief summary, a pay-through bond owner does not own an interest in the underlying assets used to collateralize the loan.[3] Pay-through bond owners are taxed on the payments they receive from the

---

[1] *See* sections 7.2(d) and 36.3.
[2] *See generally* Chapter 31.
[3] This can be a disadvantage to thrift institutions and REITs because they are subject to various tax rules, depending on whether their assets are characterized as mortgages and real estate investments. *See* sections 41.3 and 41.4.

entity that issues the pay-through bonds (for cash method taxpayers) or as they accrue (for accrual method taxpayers), not on the payments the entity is entitled to receive on the pooled assets it owns. Interest received on the bonds is taxable as ordinary income. Gain or loss on the sale of the pass-through bonds is equal to the difference between the owner's tax basis in the bonds and the net proceeds from their sale. Investors and traders obtain capital gain or loss[4] to the extent there is any gain not attributable to interest or discount income. Dealers,[5] hedgers,[6] and certain financial institutions[7] obtain ordinary income or loss.

REMICs, which, after 1991, replace all vehicles used under pre-TRA '86 law to issue multiple-class mortgage-backed securities without two levels of tax, are discussed in sections 7.2(g) and 38.8.

The tax rules that apply to owners of debt securities turn on whether the securities are purchased at their principal amount, purchased at a premium, or purchased at a discount. As a result, it is necessary to separately consider the tax treatment of pay-through bonds purchased in these ways to determine the appropriate tax treatment for an owner of a pay-through bond. The remainder of this section highlights these issues.

§ 38.2 PURCHASE AT THE PRINCIPAL AMOUNT

Taxation of pay-through bonds purchased at their principal amount is relatively straightforward. The only interest element is the stated interest amount. Principal repayments are viewed as a return of capital that is not taxable to the owner of the pay-through bond. A bondholder recognizes gain or loss on the sale of the bond if it is sold for an amount different from the principal amount, that is, if the net sales proceeds exceed the bondholder's tax basis in the bond.[8]

Investors[9] and traders[10] obtain capital gain or loss (long-term or short-term depending on the owner's holding period). Dealers,[11] hedgers,[12] and certain financial institutions[13] obtain ordinary income.

---

[4] *See* sections 8.1 and 8.2.
[5] *See* section 8.3.
[6] *See* section 8.4.
[7] *See* section 8.8.
[8] For a discussion of tax basis, see Chapter 16.
[9] *See* section 8.1.
[10] *See* section 8.2.
[11] *See* section 8.3.
[12] *See* section 8.4.
[13] *See* section 8.8.

Accrued but unpaid interest on a pay-through bond (i.e., the interest that accrues between interest payment dates) is viewed as interest and is taxable as such to the bondholder.[14] The purchaser can offset accrued interest paid to purchase a pay-through bond on the next interest payment date.[15]

§ 38.3 PURCHASE AT A PREMIUM

If a pay-through bond is purchased at a premium, the owner can elect to amortize the premium as an offset to interest income under a constant yield method over the life of the bond.[16] The owner of such a corporate obligation can use any method of amortizing bond premium which is regularly employed by him as long as the method is reasonable.[17] TRA '86 amended I.R.C. § 171(d) by eliminating the requirement that a bond with amortizable premium must have been issued by a government or corporation. This change, effective for obligations issued after September 27, 1985, means that premiums on bonds issued by persons and entities other than government and corporations can be amortized under I.R.C. § 171.[18] In all other cases, bond premium is amortized under the straight-line method unless the owner elects the constant yield method.[19]

§ 38.4 PURCHASE AT A DISCOUNT

Pay-through bonds are frequently purchased at a discount because the mortgages used as collateral for pay-through bonds are frequently purchased at a discount.[20] Taxation of pay-through bonds purchased at a discount depends on whether the bonds have OID[21] or market discount.[22] In general, OID is included in the bond owner's income as the discount

---

[14] Treas. Reg. § 1.61-7(d) (1966).
[15] L.A. Thompson Scenic Ry. Co. v. Comm'r, 9 B.T.A. 1203 (1928), *acq.* VIII-1 C.B. 31.
[16] I.R.C. § 171. For a discussion of premiums generally, see section 31.4.
[17] I.R.C. § 171(b)(3); Treas. Reg. § 1.172-2(f)(1) (1968).
[18] TRA '86, Pub. L. No. 99-514, § 1803(a)(11)(B), 100 Stat. 2085, 2795 (1986).
[19] *See* Treas. Reg. § 1.171-2(f) (1968).
[20] J. PEASLEE & D. NIRENBERG, FEDERAL INCOME TAXATION OF MORTGAGE BACKED SECURITIES 113, 122–36 (1989).
[21] *See* section 31.2.
[22] *See* section 31.3.

accrues,[23] while market discount is included in income only when the principal payments are received (for cash basis taxpayers) or accrued (for accrual method taxpayers), or when the bonds are sold.[24] TRA '86 provides that a holder of a debt instrument payable in installments takes accrued market discount into income upon receipt of principal payments.[25] A bond owner that purchases a pay-through bond with OID must include in income that portion of the OID that accrues in each year during which he owns the bond.[26]

§ 38.5   STRIPPED PAY-THROUGH BONDS

Pay-through bonds can be issued as stripped bonds where the interest coupons (defined broadly to include any right to receive interest on a security whether or not evidenced by a coupon)[27] are separated from ownership of the debt security.[28] In other words, the security is divided into two pieces: a right to receive principal and a right to receive interest. Stripped bonds and coupons purchased after July 1, 1982, are subject to I.R.C. § 1286. For a discussion of stripped pay-through bonds, see section 7.2(d)(7). For a discussion of the stripped bond rules, see generally section 31.6.

§ 38.6   SENIOR AND SUBORDINATED PAY-THROUGH BONDS

Senior and subordinated classes of pay-through bonds are a form of credit enhancement that does not affect the tax status of the bonds as debt securities. This means that both the senior and subordinated classes are subject to the tax rules that generally apply to pay-through bonds. For a discussion of senior and subordinated pay-through bonds, see generally section 7.2(d)(9).

---

[23] I.R.C. § 1272(a)(1). The rules requiring the current inclusion in income of OID have applied to corporate debt securities since 1969. For a discussion of the OID rules, see Kayle, *Where Has All the Income Gone? The Mysterious Relocation of Interest and Principal in Coupon Stripping and Related Transactions*, 7 VA. TAX REV. 303 (1987). *See also* New York State Bar Association, Tax Section, *Report of Ad Hoc Committee on Proposed Original Issue Discount Regulations*, reprinted in Special Report, 34 TAX NOTES 363, 363–425.

[24] *See* I.R.C. §§ 1276–1278.

[25] *See* section 31.3(f).

[26] I.R.C. § 1272(a)(1). For a discussion of how the OID and market discount rules apply to pay-through bonds, see J. PEASLEE & D. NIRENBERG, *supra* note 20, at 116–37.

[27] I.R.C. § 1286(e)(5).

[28] I.R.C. § 1286(e)(2).

Thirty-nine

Taxation of Owners of Equity Interests in Entities Issuing Pay-Through Bonds

For pay-through bonds to be treated as debt securities for tax purposes, the entity issuing the bonds must be treated as the owner of the pooled assets for tax purposes, and the owners of the entity's equity interests must have an equity investment in the entity. The entities that issue pay-through bonds are corporations and owner trusts. This chapter addresses the tax treatment of owners of equity interests in corporations and owner trusts. For a discussion of equity interests in entities issuing pay-through bonds, see generally sections 7.2(e) and 36.3.

§ 39.1   EQUITY INTERESTS IN CORPORATIONS

Owners of equity interests in corporations that issue pay-through bonds own stock interests subject to all of the tax rules that apply to corporate stock. For a discussion of stock, see Chapter 27.

§ 39.2 EQUITY INTERESTS IN OWNER TRUSTS

Owner trusts are not taxed at the entity level if the trust qualifies as an investment trust or as a partnership for tax purposes.[1] Instead, owners of equity interests include in income their pro rata shares of the taxable income or loss of the owner trust. The remainder of this section addresses those owner trusts classified as investment trusts and those classified as partnerships.

(a) OWNER TRUSTS CLASSIFIED AS INVESTMENT TRUSTS

If an owner trust is classified as an investment trust, the trust is ignored for tax purposes. Each equity interest owner is treated as if he purchased an undivided pro rata interest in the underlying pooled assets.[2] If the owner of a trust interest is a cash basis taxpayer, his pro rata share of trust income is reported when it is received by the trust. If the owner is on the accrual basis, his pro rata share of income is reported when it accrues to the trust. When an owner of a trust interest sells his equity interest, it is viewed as a sale of the underlying pooled assets.

(b) OWNER TRUSTS CLASSIFIED AS PARTNERSHIPS

If an owner trust is classified as a partnership, the trust is treated as a partnership for tax purposes. Each item of income, gain, deduction, and credit is calculated at the entity level, frequently under the accrual method.[3] Each owner of a trust interest is a partner of the owner trust partnership and is taxed on his pro rata share of partnership taxable income earned in the partnership's taxable year. He is not viewed as owning an undivided interest in the pooled assets.

(c) PHANTOM INCOME

For a discussion of phantom income considerations, see section 36.4(c).

---

[1] For a discussion of the tax treatment of owner trusts, see section 36.4(b).
[2] *See* discussion at sections 36.2(a), (b), and (c).
[3] *See* I.R.C. § 448.

Forty

Taxation of Owners of Pass-Through Debt Certificates

Pass-through debt certificates are structured as debt securities for tax purposes. For a discussion of pass-through debt certificates, see generally section 7.2(f). Pass-through debt certificates are subject to the general tax rules that apply to debt securities. For a discussion of the tax rules that apply to debt securities, see Chapter 31. For a discussion of the tax rules as they apply to pay-through bonds, see generally Chapter 38.

Forty-one
Taxation of REMIC Interest Owners

All interests in entities that qualify as REMICs for tax purposes are either regular or residual interests, as defined in the Code. Regular interests are treated as debt securities for tax purposes, while residual interests are allocated all REMIC income that is not otherwise allocated to the regular interests.[1] The term "interest" is not defined in the Code, and the legislative history to TRA '86, which enacted the REMIC rules, provides no guidance. The Conference Report to TRA '86 simply identifies one transaction that is not an "interest." It provides that any rights to receive payment for goods or services rendered in the ordinary operation of a REMIC are not treated as interests in the REMIC.[2]

This chapter addresses the taxation of REMIC interest owners. Section 41.1 addresses regular interests and section 41.2 addresses residual interests. The wash sales rule, which generally applies to the disposition of residual interests, is addressed in section 41.2(j). The treatment of REITs that hold REMIC interests is discussed in section 41.3(a). The treatment of financial institutions is discussed in section 41.4. And, finally, phantom income considerations are discussed in section 41.2(k).

---

[1] *See* section 7.2(g).

[2] STAFF OF THE JOINT COMM. ON TAXATION, 99TH CONG., 2D SESS., TAX REFORM BILL OF 1986, FINAL CONFERENCE COMM. DECISIONS II-229 (Joint Comm. Print 1986) [hereinafter TRA '86 Conf. Rep.].

§ 41.1 REGULAR INTERESTS

(a) DEBT TREATMENT

Regular interests in a REMIC are taxed for all purposes as if they are debt securities.[3] For example, a regular interest is treated as a market discount bond if its revised issue price exceeds its owner's basis in the regular interest.[4] Any market premiums can be amortized currently.[5] In addition, regular interests are also subject to the reporting requirements under I.R.C. § 1275.[6] Further, regular interest owners must account for interest and all amounts includable in gross income on the accrual method, regardless of their methods of accounting for tax purposes.[7] This means that cash basis taxpayers, as well as accrual basis taxpayers, must always report income from regular interests when it accrues, not when it is paid.

For a regular interest that is not treated as a debt security under state law, the amount of its fixed unconditional payment is treated as the stated principal amount. Periodic payments, if any, are treated as stated interest payments.[8] In other words, owners of regular interests generally take into account that portion of the REMIC's income that would be taken into account by an accrual basis owner of a debt security with the same terms.[9] If this amount exceeds the REMIC's income, the amount is not reduced.[10] The remainder of this section addresses the tax treatment of REMIC regular interests purchased at the principal amount, purchased at a premium, and purchased at a discount.

(1) PURCHASE AT THE PRINCIPAL AMOUNT

The tax treatment of REMIC regular interests purchased at their principal amount is relatively straightforward and similar to the tax treatment that applies to pay-through bondholders. For a discussion of pay-through bonds purchased at the principal amount, see section 38.2.

Two exceptions from general tax rules apply to REMIC regular interests. First, owners of REMIC regular interests must report income on the

---

[3] I.R.C. § 860B(a).
[4] TRA '86 Conf. Rep., *supra* note 2, at II-231.
[5] *Id.*
[6] *Id.* For a discussion of REMIC reporting requirements, see section 36.8(j).
[7] I.R.C. § 860B(b).
[8] TRA '86 Conf. Rep., *supra* note 2, at II-231.
[9] *Id.*
[10] *Id.* n.13.

accrual method.[11] Second, gain on the disposition of a regular interest is treated as ordinary income to the extent that the amount of ordinary income is the excess, if any, of "the amount which would have been includible in the gross income of the taxpayer with respect to such interest if the yield on such interest were 110 percent of the applicable Federal rate" over "the amount includible in gross income with respect to such interest by the taxpayer."[12]

(2) PURCHASE AT A PREMIUM

REMIC regular interests purchased at a premium are subject to the general tax rules that apply to premiums.[13]

(3) PURCHASE AT A DISCOUNT

REMIC regular interests purchased at a discount are generally taxed in the same manner as pay-through bonds. For a discussion of pay-through bonds purchased with OID or market discount, see section 38.4.

Regular interests may be subject to the OID rules if the stated redemption price at maturity exceeds the issue price.[14] I.R.C. § 1272(a)(6), which provides rules to determine the daily portion of OID, applies to "any regular interest in a REMIC or qualified mortgage held by a REMIC."[15] I.R.C. § 1272(a)(6) also applies to "any other debt instrument if prepayments under such debt instrument may be accelerated by reason of prepayments of other obligations securing such debt instrument (or, to the extent provided in regulations, by reason of other events)."[16] This means that I.R.C. § 1272(a)(6) applies to qualified mortgages held by a REMIC (and other debt instruments issued after December 31, 1986), if the payments can be accelerated because of prepayments.

In calculating OID or market discount on the mortgages a REMIC holds and on the REMIC's regular interests, the REMIC must include any "prepayment assumption" used in calculating the yield to maturity.[17] In addition, the REMIC must take into account actual prepayments when it

---

[11] I.R.C. § 860B(b).

[12] I.R.C. § 860B(c). For a discussion of the calculation of the gain on disposition, see generally section 41.1(c).

[13] *See generally* sections 31.4 and 36.8(j)(iii).

[14] For a discussion of OID, see generally section 31.2.

[15] I.R.C. § 1272(a)(6)(C).

[16] *Id.*

[17] I.R.C. § 1272(a)(6)(B)(iii).

calculates the OID or market discount that has accrued for each day in any accrual period.[18] The "prepayment assumption to be used . . . will be that used by the parties in pricing the particular transaction," while prepayment assumptions for the regular interests must be "determined by the assumed rate of prepayments on qualified mortgages." The TRA '86 Conference Report that accompanied the REMIC legislation provides that "prepayment assumptions used must not be unreasonable based on comparable transactions, if comparable transactions exist."[19] In addition, "unless otherwise provided by [Treasury] regulations, the use of . . . prepayment assumptions based on a Public Securities Association standard . . . an industry recognized standard" would be permitted.[20] Further, "in the case of publicly offered instruments, a prepayment assumption will be treated as unreasonable only in the presence of clear and convincing evidence."[21]

There can never be negative OID. This means that if the OID for an accrual period is negative, "the amount of OID attributable to such accrual period would be treated as zero, and the computation of OID for the following accrual period would be made as if such . . . period and the preceding . . . period were a single accrual period."[22]

(b) ISSUE PRICE

The issue price of a regular interest is determined under I.R.C. § 1273(b), which sets out the method to determine the issue price of a debt security for purposes of determining OID.[23] This means that the issue price is the initial offering price to the public. There is a special rule for regular interests issued in exchange for property. The issue price of a regular interest issued in exchange for property is equal to the fair market value of the property without regard to whether the requirements of I.R.C. § 1273(b) are met.[24] Fair market value is determined by reference to the fair market value of the regular interests received in the exchange.[25]

A regular interest owner's basis is generally equal to his cost, except that the basis of any regular interest received in exchange for property is

---

[18] I.R.C. § 1272(a)(6)(A).
[19] TRA '86 Conf. Rep., *supra* note 2, at II-238 to II-239.
[20] *Id.* at II-239.
[21] *Id.* n.23.
[22] *Id.* at II-239.
[23] *Id.* at II-231.
[24] *Id.* at II-232.
[25] *Id.*

equal to the basis of the property exchanged for it.[26] If property is transferred in exchange for more than one class of regular or residual interests, the basis of the property transferred is allocated in proportion to the fair market value of the interests so received.

If property is exchanged for a regular interest, any excess of the issue price of the regular interest over the basis of the interest in the hands of the transferor immediately after the transfer is currently includable in the owner's gross income under rules similar to I.R.C. § 1276(b).[27] In other words, the owner of a regular interest is treated like a holder of a market discount bond for which an election under I.R.C. § 1278(b) is in effect.[28] Any excess of the basis of the regular interest in the transferor's hands immediately after the transfer over the issue price of the interest is treated like market premium allowable as a deduction under rules similar to the rules of I.R.C. § 171.[29]

(c) GAIN ON DISPOSITION

Gain on the disposition of a regular interest is treated as ordinary income to the extent of the fraction set out in the following sentence.[30] The amount of ordinary income is the excess, if any, of the amount that would have been includable in the taxpayer's gross income with respect to the regular interest if the yield on the interest were 110 percent of the applicable federal rate[31] when the interest was acquired, divided by the total amount of ordinary income includable by the taxpayer with respect to the interest prior to disposition.[32] The applicable federal rate is, in general, equal to an average yield of U.S. Treasury securities with different maturities published by the IRS on a monthly basis. The requirement to treat a portion of the gain on the sale of a regular interest as ordinary income is intended to assure that gain—up to the 110 percent level set out in the fraction—is taxed as ordinary income.

---

[26] *Id.*
[27] *Id.*
[28] For a discussion of market discount, see section 31.3.
[29] For a discussion of market premium, see section 31.4.
[30] I.R.C. § 860B(c).
[31] I.R.C. § 1274(d).
[32] I.R.C. § 860B(c).

§ 41.2 RESIDUAL INTERESTS

(a) IN GENERAL

Residual interest owners are subject to tax on the income of the REMIC not otherwise allocated to the regular interests. This tax includes "excess inclusions" (which also includes phantom income).[33] At the end of each calendar quarter, an owner of a residual interest takes into account as ordinary income or loss his daily portion of the taxable income or net loss of the REMIC for each day during the taxable year that he held the residual interest.[34] The daily portion is determined "by allocating to each day in any calendar quarter its ratable portion of taxable income (or net loss) for such quarter, and by allocating the amount so allocated to any day among the holders (on such day) of residual interests in proportion to their respective holdings on such day."[35]

(b) DISTRIBUTIONS

Distributions from a REMIC to residual interest owners are tax-free to the extent they do not exceed the owner's adjusted basis in the residual interest.[36] Any distribution in excess of adjusted basis is treated as gain from the sale or exchange of the residual interest.[37] This means that an owner of a residual interest is taxed without regard to actual cash distributions.

(c) DISALLOWED LOSSES

The net loss of a REMIC that is taken into account by an owner of a residual interest is limited to the adjusted basis of the interest as of the first to occur of either the close of the quarter or the time of disposition. The adjusted basis is determined without taking into account the net loss for the quarter.[38] Any disallowed loss can be carried forward indefinitely by the owner and can be used to offset any income generated by the same REMIC.

---

[33] *See generally* I.R.C. § 860E. For a discussion of phantom income, see section 41.2(k).
[34] I.R.C. § 860C(a)(1).
[35] I.R.C. § 860C(a)(2). It may be difficult to apply these allocation rules.
[36] I.R.C. § 860C(c)(1).
[37] I.R.C. § 860C(c)(2).
[38] TRA '86 Conf. Rep., *supra* note 2, at II-233.

(d) SUBSEQUENT HOLDERS

The Conference Report accompanying TRA '86 acknowledges that it may be necessary to modify the rules governing the taxation of residual interest owners if the owners that purchase residual interests from prior holders after a significant change in the interest's value could substantially accelerate or defer income because of any premium or discount in the price paid by such a purchaser.[39] Treasury regulations or future legislation is needed to clarify the types of adjustments that may be necessary.

(e) CALCULATION OF INCOME OR LOSS

The amount of taxable income or loss of a REMIC that is taken into account by residual interest owners is determined in the same manner as for an individual using the accrual method of accounting with a calendar year as his tax year.[40] This general rule is subject to five modifications.

First, a deduction is allowed for those amounts that would be deductible as interest if the REMIC's regular interests were treated as indebtedness of the REMIC.[41]

Second, in computing a REMIC's gross income, market discount on any market discount bonds held by the REMIC is includable for the year in which the discount accrues under the provisions of I.R.C. § 1276(b)(2).[42] The provisions of I.R.C. §§ 1276(a) and 1277 do not apply.[43]

Third, no items of income, gain, loss, or deduction allocable to a prohibited transaction are taken into account for purposes of determining the REMIC's taxable income or net loss.[44]

Fourth, those deductions not allowed to partnerships under I.R.C. § 703(a)(2) are not allowed except for investment expenses that are deductible under I.R.C. § 212.[45] Deductions allowable under I.R.C. § 212 will be addressed in Treasury regulations when issued. The Conference Report accompanying TRA '86 states that for those REMICs that are similar to single-class grantor trusts under pre-TRA '86 law, deductions

---

[39] *Id.* n.15.
[40] I.R.C. § 860C(b)(1).
[41] I.R.C. § 860C(b)(1)(A).
[42] I.R.C. § 860C(b)(1)(B).
[43] *Id.*
[44] I.R.C. § 860C(b)(1)(C).
[45] I.R.C. § 860C(b)(1)(D). *See* section 9.1.

allowable under I.R.C. § 212 are allocated to all REMIC interest owners.[46] For all other REMICs, such deductions are allocated to the holders of the residual interests.[47]

Fifth, the amount of net income from foreclosure property (if any) is reduced by the amount of the tax on foreclosure property imposed by I.R.C. § 860G(c).[48]

(f) TAX BASIS

A residual interest owner's tax basis is determined in a way that is similar to a partner's basis in a partnership. The owner's basis in the residual interest is increased by the amount of taxable income he takes into account.[49] The basis of the residual interest is reduced (but not below zero) by the amount of any distributions received from the REMIC and by any net loss that the owner takes into account.[50] When a residual interest is disposed of, the basis adjustment made on account of the owner's daily portions of the REMIC's taxable income or net loss is deemed to occur immediately before the disposition.[51]

(g) EXCESS INCLUSIONS

(1) POLICY REASONS FOR EXCESS INCLUSION RULES

The rules on excess inclusions and the REMIC wash sales rule are designed to assure that a REMIC's phantom income is taxed to the residual interest holders.[52] The excess inclusion rules assure that an amount that is roughly equivalent to phantom income is taxed, regardless of a taxpayer's net operating losses or status as a tax-exempt entity. This means that net operating losses cannot be used to offset phantom income, and tax-exempt entities that hold residual interests with phantom income cannot avoid taxation. In addition, because residual inter-

---

[46] TRA '86 Conf. Rep., *supra* note 2, at II-234 n.16.
[47] *Id.*
[48] I.R.C. § 860C(b)(1)(E). For a discussion of the tax on foreclosure property, see section 36.8(i).
[49] I.R.C. § 860C(d)(1).
[50] I.R.C. § 860C(d)(2).
[51] *Id.*
[52] For a discussion of the REMIC wash sales rules, see section 41.2(j). For a discussion of phantom income, see section 41.2(k).

ests in REMICs are not required to have minimal value,[53] residual interests could otherwise generate phantom income without any tax liability. Without the excess inclusion provisions, "the after-tax yield on a residual interest for a low marginal rate taxpayer would exceed the after-tax yield for a high marginal rate taxpayer by an amount that reflected more than the differences in marginal rates."[54] The excess inclusion rules "tend to reduce the excessive differences in after-tax yields for high and low marginal rate taxpayers."[55] This means that the excess inclusion rules "promote neutrality among potential holders of such interests by attempting to assure that differences in after-tax yields for different taxpayers bear a closer relationship to the differences in those taxpayers' marginal tax rates than otherwise would be the case."[56] The excess inclusion rules thereby reduce "the otherwise powerful incentive for low marginal rate taxpayers to hold residual interests" and protect tax "revenues that would be lost if residual interests were to be held primarily by these taxpayers."[57]

(2) GENERAL RULE

Excess inclusions are taxed to the residual interest holders under I.R.C. § 860E(a)(1), which provides that "the taxable income of any holder of a residual interest in a REMIC for any taxable year shall in no event be less than the excess inclusion for such taxable year."[58] The portion of income that is subject to these rules is the excess, if any, of the amount of net income of the REMIC that an owner takes into account for any calendar quarter, divided by the sum of the daily accruals with respect to the interest while it is held by the owner.[59] Excess inclusions are, therefore, almost always taxed—even if the residual interest is owned by a tax-exempt entity or a taxpayer with an otherwise available net operating loss.[60]

---

[53] *See* section 36.8(c)(2).
[54] Kayle, *Where Has All the Income Gone? The Mysterious Relocation of Interest and Principal in Coupon Stripping and Related Transactions*, 7 VA. TAX REV. 303, 351 (1987).
[55] *Id.*
[56] *Id.*
[57] *Id.*
[58] For nonresident aliens and foreign corporations, excess inclusions are subject to a 30 percent withholding tax. I.R.C. § 860G(b)(2).
[59] I.R.C. § 860E(c).
[60] For a discussion of excess inclusions as they relate to REITs, see section 41.3(b).

Special rules apply to a portion of a REMIC's net income. First—except for residual interests held by certain thrift institutions—a portion of the REMIC's net income taken into account by the residual interest owners cannot be offset by the owner's net operating losses.[61] The special exception for thrift institutions was provided because "of the difficulties currently being experienced" by such industry when the REMIC rules were enacted in 1986.[62] This exception can be revoked by Treasury regulations if "necessary or appropriate to prevent avoidance of tax."[63]

Second, the same portion of net income that cannot offset net operating losses is treated as unrelated business taxable income for tax-exempt organizations (including qualified pension and profit sharing plans) subject to the unrelated business income tax under I.R.C. § 511.[64] Because the statute specifically limits application of the excess inclusion rules to those organizations "subject to the tax imposed by [I.R.C.] section 511," it, therefore, does not appear to cover other tax-exempt organizations—such as governments or their subdivisions—that are not subject to tax on unrelated business taxable income.

(3) DAILY ACCRUAL

Daily accrual is determined by allocating to each day in the calendar quarter a ratable portion of the product of the adjusted issue price of the residual interest at the beginning of the accrual period and 120 percent of the federal long-term rate.[65] The "Federal long-term rate" is defined as the "rate which would have applied to the residual interest under [I.R.C.] section 1274(d) (determined without regard to [the determination of daily accruals in I.R.C. § 860E(c)(2)]) if it were a debt instrument."[66]

(4) RESIDUAL INTERESTS WITHOUT SIGNIFICANT VALUE

The Conference Report accompanying TRA '86 provides that Treasury regulations, when issued, can treat all of the income from a residual interest as an excess inclusion if the interest does not have significant value. Any such regulations can be retroactively applied and will take into account the value of residual interests in relation to the regular

---

[61] I.R.C. § 860E(a).
[62] TRA '86 Conf. Rep., *supra* note 2, at II-234.
[63] I.R.C. § 860E(a)(2).
[64] I.R.C. § 860E(b).
[65] I.R.C. § 860E(c)(2).
[66] I.R.C. § 860E(c)(2)(C).

interests, although they cannot apply in cases where the value of the residual interest is at least two percent of the combined value of the regular and residual interests.[67]

For residual interests without significant value, the entire amount of income that is taken into account by the owners is treated as an excess inclusion.[68] As a result, a tax-exempt entity subject to tax under I.R.C. § 511 that holds such a residual interest is subject to tax on the excess inclusion as unrelated business taxable income.[69]

To determine whether a residual interest has significant value, the Conference Report that accompanied TRA '86 provides that "the [Treasury] regulations . . . [when issued will] take into account the value of the residual interest in relation to the regular interests."[70] In addition, the Conference Report goes on to state that the value of the residual interest would be treated as significant under Treasury regulations if the value of the residual interest "is at least two percent of the combined value of the regular and residual interests."[71]

(h) ISSUE PRICE

A residual interest is treated as having an issue price equal to the amount of money paid for the interest when it is issued, or, if the interest was issued in exchange for property, the fair market value of the interest when issued.[72]

(i) RESIDUAL INTERESTS RECEIVED IN EXCHANGE FOR PROPERTY

If a residual interest is received in exchange for property, any excess of the issue price of the residual interest over the basis of the interest in the hands of the transferor immediately after the transfer is amortized and included in the residual owner's income on a straight-line basis over the expected life of the REMIC.[73] Any excess of basis over the issue price is deductible by the owner on a straight-line basis over the expected life of

---

[67] TRA '86 Conf. Rep., *supra* note 2, at II-235.
[68] I.R.C. § 860E(c)(1).
[69] I.R.C. § 860E(b). TRA '86 Conf. Rep., *supra* note 2, at II-235.
[70] TRA '86 Conf. Rep., *supra* note 2, at II-235.
[71] *Id.*
[72] *Id.*
[73] *Id.* at II-236.

the REMIC.[74] The assumptions used in calculating OID and any binding agreement to liquidate a REMIC are taken into account in determining the REMIC's expected life.[75]

(j) WASH SALES RULE

The wash sales rule of I.R.C. § 1091 applies in a modified fashion to dispositions of residual interests in REMICs.[76] The REMIC wash sales rule and the excess inclusion rule[77] are designed to assure that the owners of residual interests pay tax on phantom income.[78]

REMIC residual interests are treated as a security.[79] The REMIC wash sales rule applies if a seller of a REMIC residual interest—during the period beginning six months before and ending six months after the interest's disposition—acquires (or enters into any other transaction that results in application of the wash sales rule) a residual interest in a REMIC, or any interest in a TMP that is comparable to a residual interest.[80]

Because of phantom income imposed on residual interests, the basis of REMIC residual interests in early years will often exceed the fair market value of the interests. As a result, it is likely that a sale at fair market value will accelerate the recognition of the phantom income that would be realized in subsequent tax years. The REMIC wash sales rule means that a seller of a residual interest cannot recognize a loss if the seller acquires another residual interest "or has entered into a contract or option to acquire" a residual interest substantially identical to the residual interest. Treasury regulations can provide circumstances under which the wash sales rule will not apply.[81] For purposes of applying the wash sales rule, the TMP definition is effective for any entity in existence after December 31, 1986.[82]

---

[74] *Id.*
[75] *Id.*
[76] I.R.C. § 860F(d). For a discussion of wash sales, see generally Chapter 19.
[77] *See* section 41.2(g)(1).
[78] For a discussion of phantom income, see sections 36.4(c) and 41.2(k).
[79] I.R.C. § 860F(d)(1).
[80] I.R.C. § 860F(d).
[81] I.R.C. § 860F(d)(2)(A).
[82] TRA '86, Pub. L. No. 99-514, § 675(c)(3), 100 Stat. 2085, 2320 (1986).

(k) PHANTOM INCOME

A residual interest owner can have "phantom income" when there is a timing difference between income recognized for tax purposes before the receipt of cash flow on the underlying pooled assets. For a discussion of phantom income, see generally section 36.4(c). Nondeductible principal repayments can result in phantom income because the deduction for interest expense is smaller than the REMIC's income.[83]

§ 41.3 REAL ESTATE INVESTMENT TRUSTS

(a) INVESTMENT IN REMIC INTERESTS

REMICs are legal investments for REITs.[84] Regular and residual interests of REMICs are treated as qualifying real property loans and real estate assets for REITs.[85] REMIC interests held by a REIT are "real estate assets" as that phrase is defined in I.R.C. § 856(c)(5)(A). Interest on a REMIC interest is viewed as "interest on obligations secured by mortgages on real property or on interests in real property"[86] if at least 95 percent of the REMIC's assets are "interests in real property."[87] The REMIC interests are treated as such in the same proportion that the assets of the REMIC would be treated as qualifying real property loans or real estate assets.[88] If 95 percent of a REMIC's assets are treated as qualifying real property loans or real estate assets at all times during a calendar year, then the entire regular or residual interest is treated as qualifying real property loans or real estate assets for the year.[89]

For residual interests, the amount treated as qualifying real property loans cannot exceed the owner's adjusted basis in the residual interest.[90] For a residual interest, its fair market value—rather than the fair market

---

[83] For a discussion of phantom income as it relates to REMIC residual interests, see J. PEASLEE & D. NIRENBERG, FEDERAL INCOME TAXATION OF MORTGAGE BACKED SECURITIES 175, 175-190 (1989); K. LORE, MORTGAGE-BACKED SECURITIES: DEVELOPMENTS AND TRENDS IN THE SECONDARY MORTGAGE MARKET ch. 6, at 6-62 to 6-63 (Clark Boardman, Securities Law Series 1988–89).

[84] For a review of REIT ownership of REMICs, see section 36.7.

[85] *See* section 8.10.

[86] I.R.C. § 856(c)(3)(B).

[87] I.R.C. § 856(c)(6).

[88] TRA '86 Conf. Rep., *supra* note 2, at II-237.

[89] *Id.* nn.20 & 21.

[90] *Id.*

value of all of the REMIC's assets—is used in applying the asset test of I.R.C. § 856(c)(5).[91]

In addition, if a REIT owns interests in a REMIC, the income derived from the interests is treated as interest income.[92]

A REIT that issues its own debt obligations may want to issue pay-through bonds instead of REMIC interests because a REIT cannot obtain more than 30 percent of its gross income from the sale of real estate held for less than four years.[93] In addition, a REIT must be careful not to be deemed to be a dealer in mortgages or else it could be subject to a tax on 100 percent of the gain.[94]

(b) EXCESS INCLUSION ALLOCATION TO REIT SHAREHOLDERS

Although a REIT can avoid tax on excess inclusion income from a REMIC's residual interest through the dividends paid deduction, the excess inclusion income is passed through to the REIT's shareholders. If a REMIC's residual interest is held by a REIT, the Treasury can issue regulations so that the "aggregate excess inclusions" over the REIT's taxable income within the meaning of I.R.C. § 857(b)(2) (excluding any net capital gains) "shall be allocated among the shareholders of such [REIT] in proportion to the dividends received by such shareholders from trust."[95] "[A]ny amount allocated to a [REIT] shareholder under [I.R.C. § 860E(d)(1)] shall be treated as an excess inclusion with respect to a residual interest held by such shareholder."[96]

§ 41.4 FINANCIAL INSTITUTIONS

Regular and residual interests are treated as evidences of indebtedness for purposes of I.R.C. § 582(c).[97] This means that certain financial institutions (defined to include commercial banks, mutual savings banks,

---

[91] *Id.*
[92] *Id.*
[93] I.R.C. § 856(c)(4).
[94] I.R.C. § 857(b)(6).
[95] I.R.C. § 860E(d)(1).
[96] I.R.C. § 860E(d)(2). Rules similar to the rules for REITs set out in I.R.C. § 860E(d) will also apply to RICs, common trust funds, and organizations to which "part I of subchapter T applies." I.R.C. § 860E(d).
[97] I.R.C. § 582(c)(1).

savings and loan associations, cooperative banks, business development corporations, and small business investment corporations) obtain ordinary income and loss on regular and residual interests.[98]

If two conditions are met, REMIC interests qualify as "qualifying real property loans"[99] if held by those financial institutions taxed as "mutual savings banks, cooperative banks, domestic building and loan associations, and other savings institutions chartered and supervised as savings and loan or similar associations under Federal or State law."[100] First, 95 percent of the REMIC's assets must be "qualifying real property loans."[101] Second, if the REMIC is part of a tiered structure (e.g., one REMIC owns another REMIC), the REMICs comprising the tiered structure "shall be treated as 1 REMIC for purposes of [the 95 percent rule]."[102]

---

[98] *See* section 8.8.
[99] I.R.C. § 593(d).
[100] I.R.C. § 591(a).
[101] I.R.C. § 593(d)(4).
[102] *Id.*

Part Nine
Taxation of Physical Commodities and Options on Commodities

Forty-two
Physical Commodities

The acquisition, maintenance, and sale of physical commodities in cash transactions embodies many of the tax rules that apply to all commodity transactions.[1] Therefore, the discussion of cash transactions in this chapter introduces many of the tax rules that apply to all types of commodity positions. A taxpayer can acquire, maintain, and sell physical commodities in cash transactions with or without financing and with or without establishing an offsetting position.

First, a taxpayer can simply purchase a physical commodity for immediate or deferred delivery, paying the entire purchase price with his own funds (outright purchase). The taxpayer can accept immediate delivery or agree to take delivery at a later date. Upon subsequent sale of the commodity at the prevailing market price, the taxpayer can (theoretically) obtain an unlimited economic profit or a total loss of his investment.

Second, a taxpayer can finance all or a portion of the purchase price (financed purchase). Tax questions include whether the interest expense is deductible, and whether the financing is included in the basis for the property.[2] The taxpayer is not protected from the risk that the commodity will decline in value, and has the potential for unlimited economic profit or a total loss of his investment. Moreover, the taxpayer can lose more than the down payment on the purchase.

Third, a taxpayer can purchase a commodity outright and establish an offsetting position, subject to the Straddle Rules.[3] This reduces the risk of

---

[1] For a discussion of the cash market for commodities, see section 4.2(a).

[2] For a discussion of tax basis, see generally Chapter 16.

[3] For a discussion of the Straddle Rules, see generally Part Eleven.

loss in owning a commodity. The offsetting position might sell the commodity for a fixed price at a future date (futures or forward contract) or establish an options position or other offsetting position. By entering into an offsetting position, the taxpayer can lock in the sales price, thereby reducing both the risk of market price fluctuations and the profit potential.

Finally, a taxpayer can both finance a purchase and establish an offsetting position subject to the Straddle Rules.

§ 42.1 OUTRIGHT PURCHASES OF COMMODITIES

A taxpayer can acquire a physical commodity in the cash or spot market by purchasing it outright, for immediate or deferred delivery, paying cash or other consideration on delivery for the entire purchase price.[4] The taxpayer can purchase the commodity for deferred delivery by:

1. Entering into a long futures contract position
2. Privately negotiating a forward contract
3. Establishing a short put options position (which may or may not result in delivery), or
4. Establishing a long call options position

The taxpayer closes out the position by taking delivery of the underlying commodity. He does not own the commodity until he actually acquires it. Commissions and fees to purchase the commodity are part of its cost and are added to its basis.[5]

The remainder of this section sets out the acquisition of a commodity in the four ways enumerated above.[6] It also addresses the sale of a commodity.

---

[4] *See* section 4.2(a).
[5] Commissioner v. Covington, 120 F.2d 768, 770 (5th Cir. 1941), *aff'g in part, rev'g in part* 42 B.T.A. 601 (1940), *cert. denied*, 315 U.S. 822 (1942); *see* sections 9.1(c)(1), 10.1(d), and 11.1(b).
[6] Although there are other ways to acquire a commodity, these ways are the most common.

(a) ACQUISITION PURSUANT TO A LONG FUTURES CONTRACT POSITION

A taxpayer can acquire a commodity by taking delivery pursuant to a long futures contract position. To establish the initial futures contract position (i.e., an opening transaction), the taxpayer purchases a standardized futures contract traded on a commodity exchange; the only open term is the price at which the underlying commodity is to be purchased.[7] The taxpayer holds the long futures contract position until the delivery month, taking delivery when the contract matures at the agreed purchase price.[8] If a taxpayer wants to close out his long position without accepting delivery, he can enter into a short futures contract position to sell the same amount of the same underlying commodity for delivery in the same month as the long position (i.e., a closing transaction).

For those commodities for which options on futures contracts are traded, a taxpayer can enter into a long call options position, exercise the option, and receive the underlying futures contract.[9] A taxpayer can also enter into a short put options position[10] that may result in the purchase of a long futures position. With a short put position, however, the taxpayer will never receive the underlying property unless the holder of the long position decides to exercise. In both instances, as described above, the taxpayer can hold the long futures contract until it matures, thereby taking delivery of the commodity pursuant to the futures contract position.

The underlying property acquired by delivery under a futures contract is a capital asset in the hands of investors[11] and traders;[12] it is ordinary income property in the hands of hedgers[13] and dealers.[14] At delivery, the futures contract is valued (i.e., marked-to-market) and gain or loss is recognized for tax purposes (just as if it had been closed out by offset).[15] If a taxpayer takes delivery under a futures contract position that is part of a straddle consisting of two or more futures contract positions, any futures

---

[7] *See* section 4.2(b).
[8] *See* section 45.6(a).
[9] For a discussion of call options, see section 5.4(a).
[10] For a discussion of put options, see section 5.4(b).
[11] *See* section 8.1.
[12] *See* section 8.2.
[13] *See* section 8.4.
[14] *See* section 8.3.
[15] *See* section 45.6.

contracts open on the delivery date are treated as if sold for their fair market value on the delivery date.[16] This allows the taxpayer to treat the remaining futures contract positions as if terminated and acquired on that date. Moreover, the taxpayer can make a section 1256(d) identified mixed straddle election on the date of delivery.[17] For a discussion of mixed straddle elections generally, see Chapter 57. For a discussion of section 1256 contracts, see generally Part Ten.

The holding period of property acquired by taking delivery pursuant to a long futures contract position subject to section 1256 treatment begins to run on the date of delivery.[18] (Prior to amendment by TCA '82, the holding period of a long futures contract was added to that of the property received under the long futures contract.)[19] Thus, the holding period of property acquired pursuant to a futures contract subject to section 1256 treatment does not include the period during which the futures contract was held.[20] On the other hand, the holding period for a commodity acquired pursuant to a non-section 1256 futures contract position includes the period during which the long position was held.[21] This "tacked on" holding period applies, for example, to futures contracts traded on foreign exchanges. It also applies to futures contracts that are part of an identified section 1256(d) mixed straddle where there is a mixed straddle election in effect.[22]

(b) ACQUISITION PURSUANT TO A LONG FORWARD CONTRACT POSITION

A taxpayer can acquire a commodity by taking delivery pursuant to a long forward contract position.[23] The owner of a long forward contract position does not own the underlying property for tax purposes. Forward contracts cannot generally be terminated prior to delivery unless both

---

[16] I.R.C. § 1256(c)(2); *see* section 45.6.

[17] *See* HOUSE WAYS AND MEANS COMM. REPORT, TECHNICAL CORRECTIONS BILL OF 1982, H.R. REP. NO. 794, 97th Cong., 2d Sess. 24 (1982); SENATE FINANCE COMM. REPORT, TECHNICAL CORRECTIONS ACT OF 1982, S. REP. NO. 592, 97th Cong., 2d Sess. 26, *reprinted in* 1982 U.S. CODE CONG. & ADMIN. NEWS 4149, 4173; *see also* section 57.2. The mixed straddle elections under I.R.C. § 1092(b), which were enacted in 1984, should also apply.

[18] I.R.C. § 1223(8).

[19] I.R.C. § 1223(8) (1976), *amended by* TCA '82, Pub. L. No. 97-448, § 105(c)(4), 96 Stat. 2365, 2385 (1983).

[20] *See* section 17.3(b).

[21] I.R.C. § 1223(8); *see* section 17.3(b).

[22] *See* section 57.2. For a discussion of mixed straddle elections generally, see Chapter 57.

[23] For a discussion of forward contracts, see sections 4.2(a) and 4.3(b).

parties agree. Although unusual, a forward contract is assignable or can be offset. The holder of the long position can dispose of his forward contract position prior to its maturity, taking his profit or loss at that time.

In addition, a holder of a long forward contract position that wants to profit from a rise in the market price of the underlying commodity (or to stop his losses in a declining market) prior to maturity of the forward contract, can sell short an equivalent amount of the underlying commodity. The short sale could be closed using the commodity acquired pursuant to the long forward contract. For application of the Straddle Rules, see generally Part Eleven.

The character of gain or loss on forward contracts is determined by the status of the taxpayer—that is, as an investor,[24] trader,[25] dealer,[26] or hedger.[27] Gain or loss is recognized only at the time of sale or complete disposition of the asset.

Because no special rules apply to govern the tax consequences of gain or loss inherent in or realized by a party that enters into a forward contract, the tax consequences are governed by the general rules applicable to gain or loss realized on the sale or disposition of an asset. As a privately negotiated contract not traded on or subject to the rules of a qualified board of exchange, a forward contract is not subject to the Mark-to-Market Rule or the 60/40 Rule of I.R.C. § 1256.[28] Theoretically, a forward contract itself is not subject to the Straddle Rules of I.R.C. § 1092 because it is not actively traded. However, a forward contract can be an interest in actively traded property if there is a ready market for the underlying commodity. For this reason, most forward contracts that hedge actively traded property are subject to the Straddle Rules.[29]

(c) ACQUISITION PURSUANT TO A LONG CALL OPTIONS POSITION

A taxpayer can establish a long call options position, whereby he pays the holder of the short position (i.e., the writer or grantor) a premium for granting him the option to purchase the underlying commodity at the

---

[24] *See* Chapter 9. Investors receive capital gain or loss.
[25] *See* Chapter 10. Traders receive capital gain or loss.
[26] *See* Chapter 11. Dealers receive ordinary income or loss.
[27] See Chapter 12. Hedgers receive ordinary income or loss.
[28] *See* Part Ten.
[29] *See* Chapter 58.

option's strike price.[30] Options are traded on certain futures contracts (futures options), which means there is an exchange market for trading in certain options for which the underlying property is a futures contract.[31]

If a taxpayer decides not to exercise the option, it expires worthless and he has lost the amount of the premium he paid for the option; he does not obtain the underlying property.[32] For a discussion of the taxation of securities options, see Chapter 30. For a discussion of the taxation of commodity options, see Chapter 42 and section 44.3.

(d) ACQUISITION PURSUANT TO A SHORT PUT OPTIONS POSITION

A taxpayer can write a put option (short position), whereby he receives a premium for granting the holder of the option (long position) the option to sell the underlying property to the taxpayer at the option's strike price.[33] Certain futures options are currently traded where the property underlying the option is a futures contract on a physical commodity.[34]

By establishing a short put position, the taxpayer has no control over, and may never obtain, the underlying property. If the holder of the long position does not exercise the option, the option expires worthless, although the taxpayer can keep the premium income he received from the long position. For a discussion of the taxation of commodity options, see Chapter 42 and section 44.3. For a discussion of securities options, see Chapter 30.

(e) SALE OF A COMMODITY

In an outright cash purchase, irrespective of whether the commodity is acquired immediately or its delivery is deferred, a taxpayer can realize an unlimited economic profit on the sale of the commodity if the price of the commodity rises, or a total economic loss if the price of the commodity declines in value. If the taxpayer reduces his risk of loss by entering into an offsetting position (to sell the commodity he now owns at a specified date in the future), his profit potential is also minimized.[35]

---

[30] *See* section 5.1.

[31] For a discussion of futures options, see section 43.3.

[32] *See* section 5.4(a).

[33] *See* section 5.4(b).

[34] Options on futures contracts (futures options) are discussed in section 43.3.

[35] The tax consequences of holding offsetting positions in personal property are discussed in Part Eleven.

For investors and traders, the sale of a physical commodity generates capital gain or loss,[36] long-term or short-term, depending on the taxpayer's holding period.[37] For a commodity acquired pursuant to a long section 1256 futures contract position, the holding period does not begin to run until the taxpayer actually acquires the commodity.[38] In addition, closing out a futures contract position by taking delivery of the underlying commodity is a taxable event subject to special rules.[39] On the other hand, if delivery is made under a long non-section 1256 futures contract (e.g., futures contracts traded on foreign exchanges), the holding period includes the time period during which the long futures contract was held.[40] Losses are deferred on offsetting positions.[41]

Dealers and hedgers receive ordinary income or loss on their sales of physical commodities in the ordinary course of business.[42] Of course, dealers and hedgers can purchase commodities for investment purposes, where sales generate capital gain or loss treatment.[43] If a dealer or hedger holds an offsetting position, losses are deferred unless the transaction qualifies for the statutory hedging exemption,[44] or as a section 988 hedging transaction.[45]

§ 42.2 FINANCED PURCHASES OF COMMODITIES

A taxpayer can finance the purchase of a physical commodity, subject to the obligation to repay the borrowed funds. The taxpayer can purchase the commodity for immediate or deferred delivery.[46] Theoretically, the taxpayer can obtain unlimited profits or a total loss of his investment; he is not protected against any risk of loss on a decline in the market value of the commodity.

---

[36] *See generally* Part Three.
[37] I.R.C. § 1222.
[38] I.R.C. § 1223(8).
[39] I.R.C. § 1256(c); *see* section 45.6.
[40] I.R.C. § 1223(8); *see* section 17.3(b).
[41] *See generally* Part Eleven.
[42] *See generally* Part Four.
[43] *See generally* Part Three.
[44] *See generally* Chapter 23.
[45] *See* section 59.3.
[46] The techniques for purchasing a commodity for deferred delivery are discussed in section 42.1.

With a financed purchase, a taxpayer incurs interest expenses that might not be deductible. First, a current deduction for interest expense is not available under the provisions of I.R.C. § 263(g) if the taxpayer holds an offsetting position in the commodity (e.g., a futures contract, forward contract, or options position). Interest on a financed position with offsetting positions must be capitalized.[47]

Second, if the commodity is an investment asset, the amount of interest currently deductible is subject to the statutory limitation on investment interest under I.R.C. § 163(d).[48] The investment interest limitation applies to investors and may apply to traders as well. However, a taxpayer may be able to assert that the financed purchases are part of a "trade or business" and that the investment interest limitation does not apply. In a trade or business, the taxpayer may be required to inventory the purchased commodities and the commodities may be considered ordinary income property, not capital assets.[49]

Third, interest expense from a passive activity is subject to the passive loss rules.[50]

Fourth, interest expense incurred in a so-called portfolio investment is subject to the portfolio investment rules.[51]

§ 42.3 PURCHASES OF COMMODITIES WITH OFFSETTING POSITIONS

To reduce the risk of economic loss from owning a physical commodity, a taxpayer can generally sell a futures contract position, enter into a privately negotiated forward contract, or establish a long put option or a short call option. The taxpayer holds offsetting positions. The short position (or long put option) reduces the risk of holding the long physical commodity position. The remainder of this section merely highlights some of the tax issues for offsetting positions. Offsetting positions are discussed in detail in Part Eleven.

By entering into an offsetting position, a taxpayer can lock in the price at which he can sell the commodity. Both his risk from holding the commodity and the potential for gain are limited. Because it is possible

---

[47] *See generally* Chapter 55.
[48] For a discussion of the investment interest limitations, see sections 9.2(e), 10.2(e), and 11.2.
[49] *See generally* Part Two.
[50] *See* section 9.8.
[51] *See* section 9.9.

for prices in the spot market to behave differently from prices for the futures, options, and forward markets, there is some risk of loss and some possibility for profit even with offsetting positions. Interest expense while holding offsetting positions is not deductible and must be added to the commodity's basis.[52]

Offsetting positions are generally subject to the Straddle Rules,[53] which defer losses on closing out one position while there is an unrecognized gain inherent in the remaining open straddle position.[54] Interest and carrying charges must be capitalized.[55] If a taxpayer holds a short futures contract position (or short call option or long put option) in a section 1256 contract[56] while also holding a physical commodity, the futures contract and nonequity options positions are subject to section 1256 treatment, unless the taxpayer elects to treat the position as an identified section 1256(d) mixed straddle,[57] or the taxpayer otherwise qualifies for a mixed straddle election.[58] The modified wash sales rule[59] and the modified short sales rule[60] may also apply. Qualified hedging transactions[61] and section 988 hedging transactions[62] are exempt from the Straddle Rules, section 1256 treatment, and the requirement to capitalize interest and carrying charges.

§ 42.4 CASH AND CARRY TRANSACTIONS

Cash and carry transactions involve a financed purchase of a commodity in the cash market and the sale of a futures contract or forward contract for the same commodity.[63] The tax treatment of cash and carry transactions changed dramatically with ERTA in 1981,[64] which requires capital-

---

[52] I.R.C. § 263(g)(1). For a discussion of cash and carry transactions, see sections 4.3(d) and 55.1.
[53] *See generally* Part Eleven.
[54] *See generally* Chapter 49.
[55] I.R.C. § 263(g)(1); *see* section 55.2.
[56] I.R.C. § 1256(b); *see generally* Part Ten.
[57] I.R.C. § 1256(d)(4); *see* section 57.2.
[58] *See* Chapter 57.
[59] *See* section 54.3.
[60] *See* section 54.4.
[61] *See generally* Chapter 23.
[62] *See* section 59.3.
[63] *See* sections 4.3(d) and 55.1.
[64] ERTA, Pub. L. No. 97-34, § 502, 95 Stat. 172, 327 (1981).

ization of interest and carrying charges on offsetting positions.[65] Prior to ERTA, taxpayers that held a physical commodity (long position) and a futures contract or forward contract to sell the commodity in the future (short position) were able to deduct their expenses while limiting their risk of loss.[66]

§ 42.5 LEVERAGE TRANSACTIONS

Leverage transactions are contracts for the purchase of commodities, usually precious metals, on a deferred delivery basis.[67] Leverage contracts are taxed in the same manner as non-section 1256 forward contracts.[68] In addition, if a taxpayer holds offsetting positions, the Straddle Rules apply.[69]

§ 42.6 EXCHANGE OF FUTURES FOR PHYSICALS

EFP transactions involve transfers of futures contracts not executed on a commodity exchange floor by open and competitive outcry.[70] The taxation of EFP transactions varies, depending on the particular transactions. EFPs typically are entered into by commercial firms to effect delivery of physicals that are not deliverable on a futures contract (for instance, physicals not in the mandated location or of deliverable quality). Such EFP transactions may qualify as part of a hedging transaction.[71] Basically, there are two types of EFP transactions. In the first, both parties initially own opposite futures positions. One trader is long a cash position and short a futures position, and a second trader is long a futures contract. After the EFP, the first trader has offset his long futures position by the short futures contract from the second trader. The second trader has the cash position from the first trader. In the second, only one party initially

---

[65] I.R.C. § 263(g)(1); *see* section 55.2.

[66] *But see* Julien v. Comm'r, 82 T.C. 492 (1984); Mortensen v. Comm'r, 49 T.C.M. (CCH) 94 (1984); Hirai v. Comm'r, 48 T.C.M. (CCH) 1134 (1984); Ostrower v. Comm'r, 48 T.C.M. (CCH) 1144 (1984); King v. Comm'r, 87 T.C. 1213 (1986), *later proceeding* King v. Comm'r, 89 T.C. 445 (1987), acq. 1988-2 C.B. 1, *action on decision*, 1988-009 (Apr. 11, 1988); Ganz v. Comm'r, Tax Ct. Mem. Dec. (CCH) ¶ 46,586 (May 21, 1990).

[67] *See* section 4.3(e).

[68] For a discussion of forward contracts, see sections 4.3(c) and 42.1(b).

[69] *See generally* Part Eleven.

[70] *See* section 4.3(f).

[71] *See generally* Chapter 23.

owns a futures contract position. The first trader is long the cash position, while the second trader is long the futures contract. After the EFP, the first trader is long the futures contract, while the second trader is long the cash position. In other words, the two parties have substituted their positions.

If both parties initially hold opposite futures contract positions, the EFP transaction results in the transfer of a physical commodity and the offset of the opposite futures contract obligations of both parties. One side sells the futures contract and purchases the physical commodity, while the other side closes a futures contract and sells the physical commodity. When the futures contract position is offset, this is a taxable transaction.[72] Gain or loss is computed at 60/40 rates for futures contracts that qualify for section 1256 treatment,[73] and at ordinary income rates for hedging and ordinary income transactions.[74]

If only one of the parties to the EFP transaction initially owns a futures contract position, that position is transferred to the other party, which assumes all obligations associated with the transferred futures contract position. The party transferring the futures contract is taxed on the transfer, at 60/40 rates for capital transactions,[75] and ordinary income rates for hedging transactions[76] and other ordinary income transactions.[77]

EFP transactions are not executed at competitive prices in the futures market. As a result, there is a possibility for the manipulation of the prices of the components of the EFP.[78] If there is a pattern of trading EFPs on commodities deliverable under futures contracts outside the price range established in the futures market or a comparable commodity market, the IRS may seek to adjust the price of an EFP to the comparable futures contract price for that day.

---

[72] *See* sections 45.5 and 45.6.
[73] *See generally* Part Ten.
[74] *See* section 23.2(b)(3).
[75] *See generally* Part Ten.
[76] *See generally* Chapter 23.
[77] *See* section 23.2(b)(3).
[78] Even though pricing does not reflect the commodity's price in the futures market for that day, the EFP price, nevertheless, may reflect the prevailing price for the commodity in a different, yet legitimate, market.

Forty-three

Options on Commodities

§ 43.1 IN GENERAL

The types of options on physical commodities (referred to as "cash options") and options on futures contracts (referred to as "futures options") are discussed generally in Chapter Five. (Cash options and futures options are collectively referred to as "commodity options.") Certain options on commodities are listed options,[1] which means that they are traded on commodity exchanges designated as contract markets by the CFTC or other markets designated by the Treasury.[2] Futures options must be traded on commodity exchanges. Therefore, futures options qualify as listed options. Those cash options traded on exchanges or markets designated by the Treasury are listed options, while those cash options that are not so traded are unlisted options.[3] For a discussion of stock options, see generally Chapter 30. For a discussion of options on debt securities, see generally Chapter 35.

The tax treatment of cash options and futures options depends on whether the options are listed for trading on an exchange. All listed option positions on commodities established after October 31, 1983, are nonequity options subject to section 1256 treatment.[4] Unlisted cash

---
[1] *See* section 30.1(a).
[2] I.R.C. §§ 1256(g)(5), (7).
[3] *See* section 44.3(a).
[4] I.R.C. § 1256(a)(1), *as amended by* Pub. L. No. 98-369, 98 Stat. 494 (1984) [hereinafter DRA]; *see* section 43.3(b).

options are taxed in the same way as unlisted equity options, that is, in accordance with the provisions of I.R.C. § 1234.[5]

§ 43.2 OPTIONS ON PHYSICAL COMMODITIES

(a) UNLISTED CASH OPTIONS

The tax treatment of unlisted cash options follows the tax treatment of equity options (i.e., options on stock and narrow based stock indexes). For a discussion of the taxation of equity call options, see section 30.3(b). For a discussion of equity put options, see section 30.3(c).

(b) LISTED CASH OPTIONS

Cash options listed for trading on an exchange[6] are nonequity options subject to section 1256 treatment. For a discussion of nonequity options, see section 44.3. For a discussion of section 1256 treatment, see generally Part Ten.

§ 43.3 OPTIONS ON FUTURES CONTRACTS

(a) FUTURES OPTION POSITIONS BEFORE NOVEMBER 1, 1983

When ERTA[7] established section 1256 treatment for RFCs in 1981, futures options had been banned from trading on commodity exchanges.[8] This may explain, in part, why ERTA made no mention of the tax treatment of futures options. The result is that when futures options commenced trading in 1981,[9] the tax consequences were not clearly established in the Code. This uncertainty was resolved for futures options established after October 31, 1983. In 1984, the DRA provided that such options are nonequity options subject to section 1256 treatment.[10]

---

[5] *See generally* section 30.3.
[6] 47 Fed. Reg. No. 56,996 (Dec. 22, 1982).
[7] ERTA, Pub. L. No. 97-34, 95 Stat. 172 (1981).
[8] *See* section 5.2(b).
[9] 6 Fed. Reg. No. 54,500 (Nov. 3, 1981).
[10] DRA, *supra* note 4, § 102(a)(2).

Because the DRA amendments to I.R.C. § 1256 only apply to option positions established after October 31, 1983, however, taxpayers have taken conflicting reporting positions with respect to futures option positions established prior to November 1, 1983. Some taxpayers have taken the position that such futures options were section 1256 contracts,[11] while other taxpayers have taken the position that such futures options were not eligible for section 1256 treatment.[12] For a discussion of the conflicting reporting positions for futures options prior to the DRA change, see section 44.3(c).

(b) FUTURES OPTION POSITIONS AFTER OCTOBER 31, 1983

All futures option positions established after October 31, 1983, are nonequity options subject to section 1256 treatment. For a discussion of nonequity options, see section 44.3. For a discussion of section 1256 treatment, see generally Part Ten.

---

[11] *See* section 44.3(c)(1).
[12] *See* section 44.3(c)(2).

Part Ten

Taxation of Section 1256 Contracts

Part Ten discusses the special tax regime that is applied to section 1256 contracts. Section 1256 treatment was first provided for regulated futures contracts, later to foreign currency contracts,[1] and then to cover nonequity options and dealer equity options.[2]

In general, gains and losses from section 1256 contracts are subject to both the Mark-to-Market Rule and the 60/40 Rule, collectively referred to as "section 1256 treatment." Section 1256 treatment does not apply to qualified hedging transactions,[3] identified section 1256(d) mixed straddles (where a mixed straddle election has been made), or mixed straddle accounts.[4] In addition, 60/40 treatment does not apply to section 1256 transactions entered into by dealers in the underlying property.[5]

The Mark-to-Market Rule provides that open section 1256 contracts are treated as if closed, and unrecognized gains and losses are taken into account for tax purposes at the end of the tax year. In other words, each section 1256 contract held at the close of a tax year is treated as if it were sold for its fair market value on the last business day of that taxable year, and all gains and losses are tallied up at year-end for computing taxable

---

[1] TCA '82, Pub. L. No. 97-448, § 105(c)(5)(B), 96 Stat. 2365, 2386 (1983).
[2] DRA, Pub. L. No. 98-369, § 102(a)(2), 98 Stat. 494, 620 (1984).
[3] *See generally* Chapter 23.
[4] *See generally* Chapter 57.
[5] *See* section 45.2(a).

income. Such year-end reporting prevents the deferral of income using straddle transactions.[6]

Under the 60/40 Rule, section 1256 contracts are taxed as 60 percent long-term and 40 percent short-term capital gain or loss, irrespective of the length of time the taxpayer held such positions.

Example 10-1

To illustrate how the Mark-to-Market and 60/40 Rules work, assume that on the last business day of 1985, a noncorporate taxpayer has $100 of gain from section 1256 contracts on open, as well as closed, positions. The 60/40 Rule automatically characterizes the gain as $60 of long-term and $40 of short-term capital gain. Because 60 percent of the long-term capital gain is excluded from tax under pre-TRA '86 law,[7] only $24 (60 percent of the $60 long-term capital gain portion) was taxable under pre-TRA '86 law. The entire $40 of short-term capital gain portion was taxable under pre-TRA '86 law. Hence, a total of $64 ($24 plus $40) of the $100 gain from section 1256 contracts is reported as income. Assuming the taxpayer was in the 50 percent tax bracket (the maximum rate in 1985), the tax due on $64 was $32. Therefore, the maximum tax on $100 of section 1256 contract gain was $32, yielding a maximum tax rate of 32 percent.

After the TRA '86 changes, the long-term capital gains exclusion was removed. This means that all of the short-term and long-term capital gains are included in income at the taxpayer's tax rate unless a long-term capital gain preference is reenacted in the Code.[8]

Part Ten discusses section 1256 contracts and summarizes the rules generally affecting them.

---

[6] *See* sections 47.1 and 47.2.

[7] I.R.C. § 1202(a), *prior to repeal by* TRA '86, Pub. L. No. 99-514, § 1202(a), 100 Stat. 2085 (1986); *see* section 15.4(a)(2)(i).

[8] The RRA '90 (Pub. L. No. 101-508, 104 Stat. 1388 (1990)) provides a maximum tax rate of 28 percent for individuals.

Forty-four
Statutory Definitions

Section 1256 contracts consist of regulated futures contracts, foreign currency contracts, nonequity options, and dealer equity options.[1] A discussion of each type of section 1256 contracts follows. In addition, there is an expanded definition of section 1256 contracts for certain so-called qualified funds that trade foreign currency contracts. This expanded definition is discussed at section 44.6.

§ 44.1 REGULATED FUTURES CONTRACTS

RFCs, first subject to section 1256 treatment in 1981, formed the original basis for the entire tax system embodied in section 1256. In fact, the justification for imposing section 1256 treatment on futures contracts—with a year-end mark-to-market calculation—was based on the special way futures contracts are traded and how they are subject to a daily mark-to-market system. The value of futures contracts is recalculated each day, based on the closing or settlement price for that particular contract on that day.[2] Despite this initial justification, the scope of section 1256 treatment has been expanded since 1981 to include types of property within its scope that are not subject to a mark-to-market system like futures contracts. Because mark-to-market amounts are added to or subtracted from the value of a futures contract, taxing unrealized gains

---

[1] I.R.C. § 1256(b).
[2] *See* section 4.4(b)(1).

and losses makes some sense for futures contracts under an expanded view of the doctrine of constructive receipt.[3]

An RFC must meet two requirements. First, the contract must require that amounts to be deposited or allowed to be withdrawn follow a system of marking-to-market.[4] Second, the contract must be traded on or made subject to the rules of a qualified board or exchange,[5] defined as a national securities exchange registered with the SEC, a domestic board of trade designated as a contract market by the CFTC, or any other market determined by the Treasury to have rules adequate to carry out the purposes of I.R.C. § 1256.[6]

The RFC definition originally contained two additional requirements. One requirement has been eliminated completely and the other one has been liberalized. First, the RFC definition originally provided that the contract itself had to require delivery of personal property.[7] This requirement was eliminated in 1982[8] and retroactively applied back to ERTA's date of enactment in 1981.[9] Second, the contract had to be traded on a domestic commodity exchange registered with the CFTC (or another market authorized by the Treasury).[10] For positions entered into after July 18, 1984, this requirement was eliminated at the same time that the concept of a qualified board or exchange was introduced into the Code.[11] As a result, RFCs can be traded on national securities exchanges, as well as commodity exchanges, without the need for prior Treasury approval.

The IRS has ruled in technical advice that taxpayers were not entitled to apply section 1256 treatment to the futures contracts that they held during the 1981 tax year because there was nothing on their joint return to indicate a valid election allowed by ERTA § 509(a)(1).[12] The problem was that the taxpayers addressed in TAM 8620004 did not comply with the 1981 transitional election requirements set out in Temp. Treas. Reg. § 5c.1256-2 (1982). The taxpayers did not include any reference to the

---

[3] *See* section 45.1(a).

[4] I.R.C. § 1256(g)(1)(A). For a discussion of how futures contracts are marked-to-market, see section 4.4(b).

[5] I.R.C. § 1256(g)(1)(B).

[6] I.R.C. § 1256(g)(7); *see* section 44.1(b).

[7] I.R.C. § 1256(b)(1), *prior to amendment by* Pub. L. No. 97-448, § 105(c)(5)(A), 96 Stat. 2365, 2385 (1983) [hereinafter TCA '82].

[8] TCA '82, *supra* note 7, § 105(c)(5)(A).

[9] ERTA, Pub. L. No. 97-34, 95 Stat. 172 (1981); TCA '82, *supra* note 7, § 105(c)(5)(D)(ii)(I).

[10] I.R.C. § 1256(b)(3) (1981), *amended by* TCA '82, *supra* note 7, § 105(c)(5)(A).

[11] Pub. L. No. 98-369, § 102(a)(3), 98 Stat. 494, 620 (1984) [hereinafter DRA]; *see* section 44.1(b).

[12] TAM 8620004 (Feb. 3, 1986).

number or the nature of the futures contracts or the dates the contracts were acquired or disposed of. Moreover, the taxpayers faled to state how they had computed the reported gain, whether the contracts were RFCs within the meaning of section 1256, or whether any elections were being made with respect to the contracts. Consequently, the IRS found that no election had been made. The IRS concluded that an amended return could not be filed to conform the election to the essential filing requirements. The special relief provision only applies to taxpayers that had timely filed an election in the first place. Because the time for filing the election in question is fixed by the Code provisions, no filing extension was available.

In TAM 8742005,[13] the IRS ruled that information provided on an addendum to Schedule D of the taxpayers' joint return did not constitute a valid election under ERTA § 509(a)(1). The couple had listed, on a separate statement attached to their Schedule D, their gains and losses resulting from RFCs entered into before June 23, 1981. They reported the RFCs in a manner consistent with the rules for reporting RFCs at that time. Further, the couple referred to the section 1256 ratio and ERTA "sections 501 through 507." The IRS found, however, that these steps did not constitute a valid election, citing *Knight-Ridder Newspapers, Inc. v. United States*,[14] which held that a clear statement of election is an "essential element" to obtain deferred tax treatment.

TMRA '88[15] made substantial changes to the tax treatment of foreign currency-related contracts in general, and foreign currency-related RFCs in particular. Among the changes, certain foreign currency commodity pools can now obtain section 1256 treatment on foreign currency-related RFCs, even if the contract is traded on a board or exchange that is *not* a qualified board or exchange under I.R.C. § 1256(g)(7).[16]

(a) CASH SETTLEMENT CONTRACTS

When I.R.C. § 1256 was enacted in 1981, the RFC definition was broad enough to cover all futures contracts traded on domestic commodity exchanges. This was because all futures contracts traded in 1981 called for the delivery of personal property. Subsequently, however, trading commenced in futures contracts that settled in cash (referred to as "cash

---

[13] (June 30, 1987).
[14] 743 F.2d 781 (11th Cir. 1984).
[15] TMRA '88, Pub. L. No. 100-647, 100 Stat. 3342 (1988).
[16] For a detailed discussion of the changes resulting from TMRA '88, see section 44.6 and Chapter 59.

settlement contracts") rather than by the delivery of a physical commodity. Under the RFC definition, it was unclear whether cash settlement contracts (e.g., futures contracts on stock indexes and Eurodollar futures contracts) qualified for section 1256 treatment. In fact, the only reference to cash in ERTA's legislative history indicated that United States currency was not personal property.[17] To eliminate this uncertainty, TCA '82 retroactively eliminated the requirement for delivery of personal property.[18] Cash settlement contracts—which call for payment of trading profits or losses by a cash payment (rather than by delivery of personal property) and which are traded on domestic commodity exchanges (now expanded to qualified boards or exchanges)—were retroactively made eligible for section 1256 treatment.[19]

(b) QUALIFIED BOARDS OR EXCHANGES

Under the rules as originally enacted in 1981, RFCs had to be traded on domestic commodity exchanges or in other markets determined by the Treasury to have rules adequate to carry out the purposes of I.R.C. § 1256.[20] The Treasury has designated markets, other than CFTC registered markets, as markets adequate to carry out the purposes of section 1256. In 1984, the IRS ruled that an exchange seeking a ruling had rules adequate to carry out the purposes of I.R.C. § 1256 and that its contracts qualified for section 1256 treatment.[21] The exchange maintains a system of marking its contracts to the settlement price. Each clearing member calculates the mark-to-market payments and collects the deficits or reimburses the excess amounts for each account it carries on a daily basis. In turn, the clearing organization affiliated with the exchange, on a daily basis, pays out any profit, or demands payment of any loss incurred, by settling its members' accounts.[22] In 1986, the IRS found in Rev. Rul. 86-7 that a foreign exchange was found to be a qualified board or exchange.[23] The IRS ruled that the Mercantile Division of the Montreal Exchange is a

---

[17] STAFF OF THE JOINT COMM. ON TAXATION, 97TH CONG., 1ST SESS., GENERAL EXPLANATION OF THE ECONOMIC RECOVERY TAX ACT OF 1981, at 289 (Joint Comm. Print 1981) [hereinafter General Explanation of ERTA].

[18] TCA '82, *supra* note 7, §§ 105(c)(5)(A), 105(c)(5)(D)(ii)(I).

[19] *Id.* § 105(c)(5)(D)(ii)(I).

[20] I.R.C. § 1256(g)(7)(B) (1981), *amended by* TCA '82, *supra* note 7, § 105(c)(5)(A).

[21] LTR 8437122 (June 18, 1984).

[22] *Id.*

[23] Rev. Rul. 86-7, 1986-1 C.B. 295.

qualified board or exchange. In Announcement 86-58,[24] the IRS provided that the effective date for Rev. Rul. 86-7 is April 18, 1985, which is also the determination date of the ruling that concluded that the Mercantile Division of the Montreal Exchange is a qualified board or exchange within the meaning of I.R.C. § 1256(g)(7)(C).

Under current law, RFCs can be traded on a qualified board or exchange (defined to include securities exchanges as well as commodity exchanges). As a result, RFCs entered into after June 18, 1984, technically can be traded on national securities exchanges registered with the SEC without prior designation of the market by the Treasury.

§ 44.2 FOREIGN CURRENCY CONTRACTS

(a) PRE-TRA '86 TREATMENT

Gains and losses on forward contracts[25] are generally not eligible for section 1256 treatment. Rather, forward contracts are personal property of the type subject to the Straddle Rules.[26] There is an exception, however, for foreign currency contracts, defined to cover forward contracts on certain foreign currencies traded through the interbank markets.[27] Foreign currency contracts, made subject to section 1256 treatment in 1982[28] (when such treatment was only available to RFCs), are afforded section 1256 treatment even though these contracts are not subject to a mark-to-market system.[29] This expansion was the first departure from the original rationale of section 1256 treatment.

To qualify for section 1256 treatment, a foreign currency contract must meet three requirements. First, the contract must require delivery of a foreign currency of a type in which RFCs are traded, or the contract's settlement value depends on such a currency.[30] At this writing, domestic exchanges, the Mercantile Division of the Montreal Exchange, and the International Futures Exchange (Bermuda) Ltd. are qualified boards or

---

[24] 1986-17 I.R.B. 35 (Apr. 28, 1986).
[25] *See* sections 4.2(a) and 4.3(b).
[26] *See generally* Part Eleven.
[27] I.R.C. § 1256(g)(2)(A).
[28] TCA '82, *supra* note 7, at § 105(c)(5) (codified at I.R.C. § 1256(b)).
[29] SENATE FINANCE COMM. REPORT, TECHNICAL CORRECTIONS ACT OF 1982, S. REP. NO. 592, 97th Cong., 2d Sess. 26, *reprinted in* 1982 U.S. CODE CONG. & ADMIN. NEWS 4149, 4172.
[30] I.R.C. § 1256(g)(2)(A)(i).

exchanges.[31] This means that section 1256 treatment only applies to forward contracts traded in those foreign currencies traded on any of those exchanges. Section 1256 treatment does not apply to other currencies that do not have individual futures contracts traded on those exchanges. In other words, the contract must either require the delivery of a foreign currency that is also deliverable under a futures contract traded on a qualified board or exchange, or the contract must have its settlement depend on the value of such a currency. The DRA expands this provision to include cash settlement forward contracts.[32]

Second, the forward contract must be traded in the interbank market,[33] which is an informal market among certain commercial banks for trading foreign currencies. Contracts traded in the interbank market generally include contracts between a commercial bank and another person and contracts entered into with an FCM or other similar market participants.[34] The typical interbank forward contract obligates a party to buy or sell a fixed amount of currency for a fixed price on a future date. Any contract with different terms would not be traded in the interbank market. Questions are raised about the scope of the requirement that foreign currency contracts must be traded in the interbank market to be eligible for section 1256. For example, a multinational company's forward contracts might not be assignable and might not be traded on the interbank market. This requirement is satisfied if the bank with which the contract is entered into trades in the interbank market. The House Report accompanying TCA '82 states that "a contract between two persons, neither of whom is a futures commission merchant or other similar participant in the interbank market, is not a foreign currency contract."[35] Does this mean that if one of the parties is a participant in the interbank market, the "traded on the interbank market" requirement is satisfied? Is it enough that the contracts *could be* traded in the interbank market? What are the relevant characteristics of such a contract? The Conference Report accompanying TCA '82 states that bank forward contracts with maturities longer than the maturities available for RFCs are within the

---

[31] Rev. Rul. 86-7, 1986-1 C.B. 295; Rev. Rul. 86-72, 1986-1 C.B. 286.

[32] DRA, *supra* note 11, at § 102(a)(3) (codified at I.R.C. § 1256(g)(2)(A)(i)).

[33] I.R.C. § 1256(g)(2)(A)(ii).

[34] HOUSE CONFERENCE REPORT, TECHNICAL CORRECTIONS ACT OF 1982, H.R. CONF. REP. NO. 986, 97th Cong., 2d Sess. 25, *reprinted in* 1982 U.S. CODE CONG. & ADMIN. NEWS 4203, 4213 [hereinafter H.R. CONF. REP. NO. 986].

[35] REPORT OF THE COMM. ON WAYS AND MEANS, TECHNICAL CORRECTIONS ACT OF 1982, H.R. REP. NO. 794, 97th Cong., 2d Sess. 25 (1982).

definition of a foreign currency contract, if the requirements of I.R.C. § 1256(g) are otherwise satisfied.[36]

Third, the contract must be "entered into at arm's length at a price determined by reference to the price in the interbank market."[37] It is not clear exactly what the "arm's length price" requirement covers. For example, is a contract viewed as a foreign currency contract if its arm's length price is determined by a standard that is different from "the price in the interbank market"? A price is determined by reference to the interbank market if it is a price that would be obtainable from a bank that is a substantial participant in the interbank market.[38] Certain adjustments are allowed for differences attributable to contract variations customary in the interbank market, including provisions relating to commissions, the amount of currency under the contract, and the creditworthiness of the parties.[39] The Treasury has broad authority to issue regulations to carry out the purpose of granting section 1256 treatment to foreign currency contracts.[40] The TCA '82 legislative history assumes that the IRS will publish periodic rulings or statements to provide guidance as to whether a price is determined by reference to the interbank market and specify a type of contract (or identify specific contracts) excluded from the definition of foreign currency contracts.[41] At the date of this writing, no such rulings or statements have been issued by the IRS.

If the parties to a foreign currency contract are changed, the original contract is deemed to terminate and a new contract is deemed to be created. Thus, a foreign currency contract that originally qualifies for section 1256 treatment can lose section 1256 status if the new party does not meet all of the statutory requirements, and—in addition—the new contract must also independently qualify as a foreign currency contract.[42]

---

[36] H.R. Conf. Rep. No. 986, *supra* note 34, at 25.
[37] I.R.C. § 1256(g)(2)(A)(iii).
[38] H.R. Conf. Rep. No. 986, *supra* note 34, at 25.
[39] *Id.*
[40] I.R.C. § 1256(g)(2)(B).
[41] H.R. Conf. Rep. No. 986, *supra* note 34, at 25.
[42] *Id.*

(b) TREATMENT AS A RESULT OF TRA '86 AND TMRA '88

TRA '86 added comprehensive rules for the treatment of foreign currency transactions.[43] TRA '86 treatment of section 988 transactions (which generally provides for ordinary treatment of gains and losses from these transactions), however, included a special "carve-out" for these section 988 transactions that were subject to section 1256. Thus, pre-TRA '86 treatment remained applicable to those section 1256 foreign currency contracts (as therein defined), except that such contracts would be exempt from the section 1256 treatment if the contract were a foreign currency hedging transaction as set forth in I.R.C. § 988(d).

TMRA '88 substantially altered the section 1256 "carve-out" from section 988 treatment. A taxpayer can now choose capital or ordinary treatment on all foreign currency transactions that were once subject solely to section 1256 treatment.[44] TMRA '88 also made significant changes to the tax treatment of foreign currency-related transactions of certain foreign currency commodity pools.[45]

§ 44.3 NONEQUITY OPTIONS

Nonequity option positions established after July 18, 1984, receive section 1256 treatment.[46] In addition, DRA also provided special transitional year elections with different effective dates.[47] The definition of a nonequity option is somewhat circular, defined by reference to other terms also created by the DRA: listed options, equity options, and qualified boards or exchanges.

A nonequity option is defined as any listed option that is not an equity option.[48] Hence, listed options and equity options must also be defined in order to define a nonequity option.

A listed option is any option (other than a right to acquire stock from an issuer) that is traded on or subject to the rules of a qualified board or exchange.[49]

---

[43] TRA '86, Pub. L. No. 99-514, 100 Stat. 2085 (1986). *See* Chapter 59 for a detailed discussion of these changes.

[44] For a discussion of the changes, see section 59.2.

[45] For a discussion of these changes, see section 44.6 and Chapter 59.

[46] DRA, *supra* note 11, § 102(a)(2) (codified at I.R.C. § 1256(b)(3)).

[47] *See* section 44.5.

[48] I.R.C. § 1256(g)(3); *see* sections 30.3 and 44.4.

[49] I.R.C. § 1256(g)(5).

An equity option is defined as any option to buy or sell stock, or any option, the value of which is determined directly or indirectly by reference to stock, a group of stocks, or a stock index.[50] An equity option, however, does not include any option on any group of stocks or stock indexes if either (1) the CFTC has designated the exchange where it is traded as a contract market for the option, or (2) the Treasury has determined that the option meets the requirements for such a designation.[51] In Rev. Rul. 86-8,[52] the IRS determined that an option on the High Technology Index of the Pacific Stock Exchange is a nonequity option within the meaning of I.R.C. § 1256(g)(3). In Announcement 86-58,[53] the IRS announced that the effective date for Rev. Rul. 86-8 is April 1, 1985, which is the determination date of the ruling.

In Rev. Rul. 87-67,[54] the IRS ruled that an option on the Institutional Index of the AMEX is a nonequity option within I.R.C. § 1256(g)(3) for positions established on or after July 27, 1987.

In Rev. Rul. 87-43,[55] the IRS ruled that futures or option contracts established through a Mutual Offset System between the CME and the SIMEX are treated as traded on or subject to the rules of the exchange that assumes the contract for purposes of section 1256. Thus, contracts assumed by the CME will be treated as traded on or subject to the rules of a qualified board or exchange, while contracts assumed by the SIMEX will not be treated as traded on or subject to the rules of a qualified board or exchange. The IRS also ruled that use of the Mutual Offset System will not affect the sourcing rules of gains or losses from futures and option contract transactions.

In summary, after reviewing the relevant definitions, it appears that a nonequity option is any option—whether traded on securities exchanges or commodity exchanges—on commodities, futures contracts, debt instruments, foreign currencies, and broad-based stock indexes. Even if an option's value is determined by reference to stocks or stock indexes, it is a nonequity option if futures contracts are—or could be—traded on such contracts. Nonequity options do not include options on individual stocks, small groups of stocks, or narrow-based stock indexes.

---

[50] I.R.C. § 1256(g)(6)(A).
[51] I.R.C. § 1256(g)(6)(B).
[52] 1986-1 C.B. 295.
[53] 1986-17 I.R.B. 35.
[54] 1987-2 C.B. 212.
[55] 1987-1 C.B. 252.

(a) TREASURY DESIGNATION

Several stock index options that are traded on securities exchanges have not been, but could be, designated for trading by the CFTC.[56] These options only qualify for section 1256 treatment after the Treasury determines such contracts could be designated, if a designation was requested, for trading on an exchange regulated by the CFTC.[57] In LTR 8526035,[58] the Treasury adopted the joint guidelines promulgated by the CFTC and the SEC for determining whether an index is a nonequity option as defined by I.R.C. § 1256(g)(3).[59] It is important to note that Treasury designations might have prospective effect only, raising questions about the tax treatment of contracts traded prior to designation.[60]

(b) FUTURES OPTION POSITIONS AFTER OCTOBER 31, 1983

Section 1256 treatment applies to options on futures contract positions established after October 31, 1983, ending the uncertainty over the tax treatment of such options. Futures options were banned from trading in 1978, which may explain why ERTA (which enacted section 1256 in 1981) made no special reference to the tax problems raised by commodity options. In late 1981, however, the CFTC approved a pilot program for exchange-traded futures options, and trading commenced on various domestic commodity exchanges. Because futures options appeared to be subject to both the option rules under I.R.C. § 1234 *and* the rules for RFCs under I.R.C. § 1256, the tax treatment of futures options was not clear under the law in effect at that time. Although a request for a revenue ruling on the tax treatment of options on futures was submitted to the Treasury in early 1982, a revenue ruling was never issued. Legislative action was necessary to resolve the issue of whether futures options were subject to 60/40 treatment. Because the DRA provisions only apply to futures option positions established after October 31, 1983, the tax treatment for futures options entered into prior to that date remains unsettled.

---

[56] House Conference Report, Deficit Reduction Act of 1984, H.R. Conf. Rep. No. 861, 98th Cong., 2d Sess. 909, *reprinted in* 1984 U.S. Code Cong. & Admin. News 1597 [hereinafter H.R. Conf. Rep. No. 861].

[57] I.R.C. §§ 1256(b)(3), (g)(6)(B).

[58] (Apr. 1, 1985).

[59] SEA Release No. 20,578 (Jan. 18, 1984), 49 Fed. Reg. 2884 (1984). *See, e.g.,* Rev. Rul. 86-8, 1986-1 C.B. 295.

[60] H.R. Conf. Rep. No. 861, *supra* note 56, at 909.

For a discussion of the tax treatment of futures options before November 1, 1983, see section 44.3(c).

(c) FUTURES OPTION POSITIONS BEFORE NOVEMBER 1, 1983

Because futures option positions established after October 31, 1983, are section 1256 contracts, the question of how futures options entered into before November 1, 1983, are taxed remains an open question. Some taxpayers may take the position that futures options entered into before November 1, 1983, are eligible for section 1256 treatment, while other taxpayers may take the position that such futures options are governed by the option rules contained in I.R.C. § 1234. Under these circumstances, contradictory reporting positions are inevitable. The commodity exchanges have advanced the position that futures options prior to the DRA amendments are eligible for 60/40 treatment. The securities exchanges have advanced the position that futures options are not eligible for 60/40 treatment but, rather, are taxed as capital assets (for traders and investors) and as ordinary income property (for dealers and hedgers). The remainder of this section summarizes the conflicting tax positions for futures options entered into before November 1, 1983.

(1) POSITION THAT FUTURES OPTIONS ARE ELIGIBLE FOR 60/40 TREATMENT

On May 13, 1982, the CSC filed a ruling request with the Treasury concerning the tax treatment of futures options on sugar futures contracts to be traded on that exchange.[61] In addition, the CBT has endorsed the views of the commodity exchanges in a brochure published jointly by the CBT, CSE, and COMEX.[62] The principal rulings that the CSC requested were that (1) a short futures option is an RFC, and (2) gain or loss on the lapse or closing of a long futures option is taxable under the 60/40 Rule but not the Mark-to-Market Rule.[63]

---

[61] Letter from Donald Schapiro of Barrett Smith Schapiro Simon & Armstrong to Assistant Commissioner (Technical), IRS (May 13, 1982).
[62] CBT, CSC & COMEX, TAX CONSEQUENCES OF FUTURES OPTIONS TRADING (1982).
[63] *See* sections 45.1 and 45.2.

(i) Short Futures Options as Regulated Futures Contracts

The commodity exchanges claimed that a short futures option met the definition of an RFC for two reasons. First, the amount required to be deposited by the grantor of a futures option and the amount that may be withdrawn by such grantor depend on a system of marking-to-market. Second, the futures options are traded on markets that are designated as contract markets by the CFTC.

In the view of the commodity exchanges, there was no inconsistency under pre-DRA law between the statutory provisions of I.R.C. § 1256 (which govern RFCs) and the provisions of I.R.C. § 1234 (which govern the tax treatment of options). I.R.C. § 1234(b) (which clearly applies to futures options) provides that a grantor's gain or loss from any closing transaction with respect to, and gain from the lapse of, an option is treated as gain or loss from the sale or exchange of a capital asset held for not more than one year. The commodity exchanges argued that because I.R.C. § 1256 applied to RFCs held by a taxpayer as capital assets (and provided that gains and losses are subject to the 60/40 Rule, irrespective of the actual holding period of the RFC), it followed that even though an option was deemed to have been held for less than the long-term holding period under I.R.C. § 1234(b), gain or loss from its disposition was 60/40 gain or loss by application of I.R.C. § 1256. Moreover, the commodity exchanges argued that even if a conflict did exist between the provisions of I.R.C. §§ 1256 and 1234(b), the conflict should be resolved in favor of I.R.C. § 1256 because that section was enacted after I.R.C. § 1234(b).

Although both I.R.C. §§ 1234(b) and 1256 appeared to apply to short futures options, their provisions were incompatible under pre-DRA law. First, I.R.C. § 1256 provides that gain or loss from the disposition of an RFC is treated as 60 percent long-term and 40 percent short-term capital gain or loss without regard to the actual holding period. Second, I.R.C. § 1234(b) provides that gain or loss from the disposition of an option is treated as 100 percent short-term capital gain or loss without regard to the actual holding period. If a short futures option was both an RFC and a short option, the Code would have provided for two completely inconsistent methods of taxation for the same product. The determination of what treatment was dominant did, in fact, require legislative action.

(ii) Long Futures Options as Subject to the 60/40 Rule

The commodity exchanges conceded that long futures options did not meet the statutory definition of an RFC because the holder of a futures option was not subject to a mark-to-market system governing deposits and withdrawals. Nevertheless, the commodity exchanges pointed out that under I.R.C. § 1234(a), the "character" of gain or loss attributable to the lapse, sale, or exchange of an option to buy or sell property was the same as the "character" that the underlying property would have in the hands of the taxpayer. It was their view that I.R.C. § 1256(a)(3) directed that any gain or loss with respect to an RFC "be treated" as part long-term and part short-term. Therefore, under this interpretation, because the underlying property of a futures option is an RFC, gain or loss from the sale or exchange of the futures option should be subject to the 60/40 Rule.

As used in I.R.C. § 1234(a), the term "character" refers only to the capital or ordinary aspect of the underlying property and not to the holding period. Indeed, it would be impossible to determine the holding period that such property "would have in the hands of the taxpayer if acquired by him" as I.R.C. § 1234(a) requires. The determination of whether capital gain or loss with respect to an option is long-term or short-term is made by reference to the period of time for which the taxpayer held the option.[64] If the holding period of the option were determined by reference to the holding period of the underlying property (presumably the current owner's holding period in the case of a long call or the taxpayer's holding period in the case of a short put), then the disposition of a one-day old option on property held by its current owner for over one year would generate long-term capital gain or loss for the holder.

The commodity exchanges advanced the argument that, in enacting I.R.C. § 1256, Congress intended to create a new category of assets. These assets—section 1256 assets—are neither capital nor ordinary, but simply are taxed as if they were capital assets, 60 percent of which were held for over a year and 40 percent for less than a year. This interpretation would have allowed long futures options to be taxed as RFCs because I.R.C. § 1234(a) provides that long options have the same character (in this case, section 1256 asset status) as the underlying property. However, the legislative history of ERTA makes clear that RFCs are capital assets and that the rules in I.R.C. § 1256 are simply intended to provide a holding period assumption:

> Any capital gain or capital loss on a regulated futures contract which is marked-to-market is treated as if 40 percent of the gain or loss is short-term capital gain or loss, and as if 60 percent of the gain is long-term capital gain or loss. . . . Regulated futures contracts continue to constitute capital assets in all cases in which they would have constituted capital assets under

[64] Treas. Reg. § 1.1234-1(a)(1) (1979).

prior law. Treatment of gains and losses as partially short-term and partially long-term is not intended to affect the character of such contracts as capital assets.[65]

In summary, the tax rules that had been urged by the commodity exchanges for futures option transactions of traders or investors prior to November 1, 1983, are as follows. First, all gain or loss taken into account by holders or grantors of futures options would be subject to the 60/40 Rule. Second, grantors (writers) of futures options that were required to provide and were entitled to receive daily mark-to-market payments would recognize gain or loss on termination of their obligations under the option and on positions open at the end of the tax year under the Mark-to-Market Rule. Third, holders of futures options not subject to a mark-to-market system were not subject to the Mark-to-Market Rule—long futures options were not RFCs. No gain or loss would be recognized by holders of futures options on their exercise and acquisition of the underlying RFCs. The premium paid for the option would be treated as an adjustment when gain or loss on the RFC was recognized (thereby increasing loss or decreasing gain). Gain or loss would be taken into account by holders of futures options on lapse of the options, or on their termination by offset. Of course, commodity dealers that use futures options for hedging transactions would receive ordinary income or loss treatment.

(2) POSITION THAT FUTURES OPTIONS ARE INELIGIBLE FOR 60/40 TAX TREATMENT

On August 19, 1982, the AMEX, CBOE, and PHLX submitted a memorandum to the Treasury urging rejection of the positions advanced by the commodity exchanges.[66] The securities exchanges argued that, as a matter of policy, futures options should not be entitled to more favorable tax treatment than options on debt securities and physical commodities traded on domestic securities exchanges. Moreover, the securities exchanges argued that the tax treatment of futures options proposed by the commodity exchanges was not authorized under existing law.

According to the securities exchanges' view of pre-DRA law, a long futures option was not an RFC because it was not a contract with respect to which the amount required to be deposited and the amount that could

---

[65] General Explanation of ERTA, *supra* note 17, at 297.
[66] Letter from Robert A. Rudnick of Cadwalader, Wickersham & Taft to John E. Chapoton, Assistant Secretary of the Treasury (Aug. 19, 1982).

be withdrawn did not depend on a system of marking-to-market. Because futures options were not entitled to RFC treatment, their taxation was governed by the rules in I.R.C. § 1234. The securities exchanges took issue with the commodity exchanges' position that the "character" of gain or loss for an option holder was determined by reference to the "character" of the gain or loss on the underlying property, that is, 60/40 treatment. Rather, the securities exchanges asserted that the "character" of the underlying property—as the term is used in I.R.C. § 1234(a)—refers to its status as a capital or ordinary asset and that the character of property does not encompass the special tax rate provided in I.R.C. § 1256.

Furthermore, the securities exchanges argued that under I.R.C. § 1234, the exercise of an option was not a taxable event in itself. Rather, the gain or loss that inures to a holder or writer during the option period was recognized when the underlying property was sold. This argument, if accepted, would have opened a substantial opportunity for tax avoidance. If a futures option holder could choose how his gain or loss was to be taxed, he could structure his transactions to convert short-term capital gain into 60 percent long-term and 40 percent short-term capital gain. This opportunity could have been maximized by using straddles in futures options that, when closed out by offset and exercise, would generate short-term capital loss and gain subject to the 60/40 Rule. The Straddle Rules would not affect such straddles in futures options because the option holder would not be recognizing losses while deferring unrealized gain in offsetting positions. Rather, the holder would simply choose to recognize the gains as 60/40 under section 1256 and the losses as short-term capital loss.

To avoid the conversion possibility inherent in this position, the securities exchanges argued that Congress intended to limit section 1256 treatment to gain or loss with "respect to" RFCs. Thus, they asserted that if a futures option was exercised, the gain or loss from the option element had to be "segregated" from any gain or loss attributable to the RFC. The segregated amount had to either be recognized upon the exercise of the option or suspended until the RFC gain or loss was recognized.[67]

In summary, the tax rules proposed by the securities exchanges apply the following tax treatment to futures options entered into by investors or traders prior to November 1, 1983.[68] First, holders of futures options

---

[67] There was no legal precedent for this "segregation" concept and, therefore, this part of the securities exchanges' argument was, in effect, a proposal for new legislation to deal with the conversion problem.

[68] The proposals do not affect the tax treatment of hedgers and dealers that would receive ordinary gain or loss treatment on their futures option transactions.

recognized capital gain or loss, either long-term or short-term, depending on their holding period in the option, on the lapse or offset of the futures options. The 60/40 Rule did not apply to option holders and the option was treated as a separate asset. On exercise of a futures option, gain or loss was calculated and recognized at such time or segregated and suspended for future recognition. If recognized when exercised, gain or loss was either short-term or long-term, depending on the holding period of the option. If segregated and suspended, the gain or loss was long-term or short-term, depending on the period for which the RFC and any property delivered pursuant to the RFC were held. Second, grantors of futures options recognized short-term capital gain or short-term capital loss on lapse or closing of futures options. On an assignment of the option, gain or loss was calculated and either recognized at that time or segregated and suspended for later recognition.

§ 44.4 DEALER EQUITY OPTIONS

Dealer equity options established after July 18, 1984, are subject to section 1256 treatment.[69] To qualify as dealer equity options, the options must meet four requirements. First, all dealer equity options must be held by an options dealer, defined as any person registered with an appropriate national securities exchange as a market maker or specialist in listed options.[70] This definition of an options dealer can be expanded with Treasury approval to include any person that performs similar functions to the extent appropriate to carry out the purposes of I.R.C. § 1256.[71] Indeed, under this authority, the definition of an options dealer can include those dealers that trade options in the over-the-counter market and in certain foreign markets.

Second, the option must be a listed option that is also (1) an equity option,[72] (2) traded on or subject to the rules of a qualified board or exchange,[73] and (3) either an option on stock or an option that has its value determined (directly or indirectly) by reference to stock, a group of stocks, or a stock index.[74]

---

[69] DRA, *supra* note 11, at § 102(a)(2) (codified at I.R.C. § 1256(b)(4)).
[70] I.R.C. § 1256(g)(8)(A); *see* sections 8.2(b) and 8.3(d).
[71] I.R.C. § 1256(g)(8)(B).
[72] I.R.C. § 1256(g)(4).
[73] I.R.C. § 1256(g)(5).
[74] I.R.C. § 1256(g)(6)(A).

Third, a dealer equity option must be purchased or granted by an options dealer in the normal course of his trade or business.[75] It is not clear from the Code or legislative history whether any sort of identification might be required of an options dealer to demonstrate that his trading is in the normal course of business, or what the tax treatment might be if he cannot meet this requirement.

Fourth, a dealer equity option must be listed on the qualified board or exchange on which the options dealer is "registered."[76] It is not clear from the Code or legislative history what type of registration is contemplated by this requirement.

Granting option dealers capital gain and loss treatment under the 60/40 Rule is a radical departure from prior law as viewed by such taxpayers. Under the law in effect before the DRA changes in 1984, option dealers viewed themselves as dealers for tax purposes and reported their transactions in options and the stock underlying such options as ordinary income and loss.[77] If option dealers are not dealers in the underlying property, they receive section 1256 treatment on their dealer equity options, notwithstanding the fact that they continue to view themselves as dealers for all other purposes. The House Conference Report of the DRA states that the treatment of option dealers as obtaining capital gain or loss, changes the claimed tax treatment of option dealers, except to the extent that an option is acquired to hedge property that would generate ordinary loss.[78] The Conference Committee amendments require losses on hedge property to be treated as ordinary.[79] Option dealers need not treat their dealer equity options as investment assets and need not comply with the identification requirements otherwise imposed on securities dealers for investment assets under I.R.C. § 1236.[80]

Finally, limited partners and limited entrepreneurs, including S corporation shareholders that do not actively participate in the management of the business, cannot report gains and losses from dealer equity options allocated to them as 60 percent long-term and 40 percent short-term capital gain or loss. Rather, any gain or loss with respect to dealer

---

[75] I.R.C. § 1256(g)(4)(B).

[76] I.R.C. § 1256(g)(4)(C).

[77] *But see* Laureys v. Comm'r, 92 T.C. 101 (1989), *acq. and nonacq.* 1990-1 C.B. 1, where the Tax Court ruled that a CBOE market maker's option losses were capital in nature because the transactions were not undertaken in connection with his being "called to the post" (i.e., when he was required by the CBOE to make a market in a particular option).

[78] *See* H.R. CONF. REP. No. 861, *supra* note 56, at 909.

[79] *See id.*

[80] *Id.*

equity options allocable to limited partners or limited entrepreneurs is marked-to-market and taxed as short-term capital gain or loss.[81]

§ 44.5 DRA TRANSITIONAL YEAR ELECTIONS FOR SECTION 1256 OPTIONS

The Straddle Rules apply to nonequity options and dealer equity options established after December 31, 1983.[82] The extension of section 1256 treatment applies to option positions established after July 18, 1984.

The DRA provides a transitional rule for nonequity options and dealer equity options held during a taxpayer's taxable year in which the DRA was enacted. Under the DRA provisions, a taxpayer could elect section 1256 treatment either for (1) all of the positions held by him on July 18, 1984 (referred to as "date of enactment election"), or (2) all of the positions held by him during the full taxable year in which July 18, 1984, was included (referred to as "full year election").[83] Under the date of enactment election, a taxpayer applied section 1256 treatment to all positions held on that date. The Straddle Rules—but not section 1256 treatment—applied to all positions acquired after December 31, 1983, and disposed of before July 18, 1984. If a taxpayer made a full year election to have section 1256 treatment apply to all positions at any time during the transitional year, all nonequity options (and equity options held by an options dealer at any time during the transitional year) were marked-to-market on the last business day of such year.[84] Thus, a calendar year taxpayer could elect section 1256 treatment for his entire 1984 tax year.

If a flow-through entity (including a partnership, trust, or S corporation) held a position made subject to section 1256 during the period or date covered by the election, only the flow-through entity could make an election with respect to such contracts.[85] For example, if a partnership held nonequity options or dealer equity options on July 18, 1984, only the partnership—not the partners—could elect to treat those options as section 1256 contracts.[86] A taxpayer that was a partner in a partnership, however, could make an election with respect to contracts held by him

[81] I.R.C. § 1256(f)(4); *see* section 45.2(c).
[82] DRA, *supra* note 11, § 101(e)(1).
[83] *Id.* § 102(g).
[84] *Id.* § 102(h)(1)(B)(ii)(II).
[85] Temp. Treas. Reg. § 1.1256(h)-2T(d) (1985).
[86] *Id.*

outside the partnership, without regard to whether the partnership also makes such an election.[87]

If a taxpayer made the full year election or held an interest in a flow-through entity that had made the full year election, he could elect to pay part or all of the deferrable tax in two or more (but not more than five) equal installments.[88] This election was made at the same time and with the same tax return as the full year election.[89] If a taxpayer elected to defer the payment of tax, the first installment had to be paid on or before the due date for filing the return for the taxable year that included July 18, 1984, with the succeeding installment paid on or before the date that is one year after the last date prescribed for payment of the preceding installment.[90]

The "deferrable tax amount" is defined as the excess of (1) the tax applying the amendments made by the DRA to all section 1256 contracts held by the taxpayer during the transitional year, over (2) the tax computed by applying the DRA amendments to all section 1256 contracts held during the transitional year.[91] Stock options that were section 1256 contracts and stock positions held as part of option straddles that were held as ordinary assets on the last day of the preceding taxable year are treated as having been acquired for their market value in the preceding tax year.[92] The deferrable tax amount definition restricts the benefit of the five-year pay-in provision to those option dealers that treated their stock and option positions as inventory prior to the DRA. The definition allows option dealers to pay, in installments, the tax relating to unrecognized gains in both stock and options "pushed" into the transitional year from prior years. Option dealers electing the full year election were also entitled to elect to pay the portion of the tax liability attributable to the unrealized appreciation of their stock and stock option positions for years prior to the transitional year in two to five equal annual installments, with interest.[93] The five-year pay-in provision was limited to unrealized appreciation in stock and stock option positions that would have generated ordinary income if the positions had been disposed of on the last day of the preceding year. Elections had to be made on IRS Form 6781 by the

---

[87] *Id.*
[88] Temp. Treas. Reg. § 1.1256(h)-3T(a) (1985).
[89] *See* Temp. Treas. Reg. § 1.1256(h)-3T(c) (1985).
[90] Temp. Treas. Reg. § 1.1256(h)-3T(d) (1985).
[91] Temp. Treas. Reg. § 1.1256(h)-3T(b)(1) (1985).
[92] Temp. Treas. Reg. § 1.1256(h)-3T(b)(2)(ii) (1985).
[93] DRA, *supra* note 11, § 102(h)(1)(A); Temp. Treas. Reg. § 1.1256(h)-3T(a) (1985).

due date of the income tax return (taking valid extensions into account) for the transitional year.[94]

To obtain the benefits of the multiyear pay-in, option dealers with interests in flow-through entities (such as partners in partnerships) that made the full year election must have also made an individual election to pay the deferrable tax in installments.[95] This requirement created an unexpected problem for taxpayers with a different taxable year than that of their flow-through entities. For example, a partner with a September 30 fiscal year-end that was a partner in a calendar year partnership receives a distribution of the income from the full year election in a taxable year that does not include July 18, 1984. Because the full year election only allows a taxpayer to defer the payment of taxes relating to years *including* July 18, 1984, it appears as if such a taxpayer cannot qualify for the five-installment pay-in election.

§ 44.6 EXPANDED DEFINITION OF SECTION 1256 CONTRACTS FOR "QUALIFIED FUNDS"

TMRA '88 narrowed, but did not eliminate, the section 1256 carve-out.[96] In response to pressure from large commodity pools, Congress went precisely the opposite way. These commodity pools wanted to have all their commodity holdings taxed in the same way—as capital assets. But the 1986 tax scheme upset this pattern by specifying ordinary gain or loss treatment for foreign currency products while leaving other commodity products with capital treatment. In 1988, these commodity pools sought to retain the section 1256 carve-out and to obtain capital gain treatment of products that are not section 1256 contracts, despite being subject to I.R.C. § 988 under the 1986 tax scheme.

Congress' response in 1988 was to specify that, irrespective of I.R.C. § 988, foreign currency products held by certain commodity trading partnerships can be treated as capital. Commodity trading partnerships that elect to be treated as "qualified funds" are entitled to capital treatment on foreign currency products that meet an expanded definition of section 1256 contracts. This expanded definition, available only to qualified funds, brings within I.R.C. § 1256 all present section 1256 contracts, plus forwards and futures on foreign currencies that had not previously met section 1256 requirements. And the Treasury, by regula-

---

[94] Temp. Treas. Reg. § 1.1256(h)-3T(c) (1985).
[95] Temp. Treas. Reg. § 1.1256(h)-3T(a) (1985).
[96] *See* discussion of the carve-out at section 59.2.

tion, can designate "similar financial instruments" (such as over-the-counter options) as special section 1256 contracts. The conferees expressly stated that they did not expect the Treasury to include foreign currency swaps in the expanded definition of section 1256 contracts.

All products falling within this expanded definition of section 1256 contracts are marked-to-market at year-end, but the 60/40 Rule only applies to products within the standard definition of section 1256 contracts. Thus, products within the expanded definition generate 100 percent short-term capital gains or losses. In other words, the price the commodity pools paid for consistent capital treatment of their assets is a mark-to-market at year-end with no opportunity for long-term capital gains.

As for which taxpayers can elect to be qualified funds, they must be partnerships that meet an ownership test (at least 20 unrelated partners), a principal activity test (the principal activity must be buying and selling commodity futures, options, and forwards), and an income test (90 percent of income must come from interest, dividends, and commodity product trading).[97] Once the election is made, a partnership is treated as a qualified fund for that year and all subsequent years, unless the partnership fails to meet one or more of the qualification tests.

If a qualified fund fails to meet these tests during a taxable year, it must use yet another set of special tax rules: net gains on products within the expanded definition of section 1256 contracts are treated as ordinary; net losses on products within the expanded definition are treated as 100 percent short-term; and traditional section 1256 contracts are subject to the 60/40 Rule.

---

[97] For a detailed discussion of these requirements, see section 59.2(i).

Forty-five

General Tax Rules for Section 1256 Contracts

Section 1256 contracts[1] are subject to two unique tax rules: the Mark-to-Market Rule and the 60/40 Rule, collectively referred to as "section 1256 treatment." The Mark-to-Market Rule applies to all section 1256 contracts, while the 60/40 Rule only applies to section 1256 contracts that are capital assets in the hands of the taxpayer. The Mark-to-Market Rule eliminates the tax advantage previously available for certain straddle transactions used under law in effect before the ERTA tax changes in 1981,[2] to defer the payment of tax by currently reporting losses while deferring unrecognized gains on offsetting positions.[3] General tax rules for section 1256 contracts are discussed in this chapter.

§ 45.1 MARK-TO-MARKET RULE

Under the Mark-to-Market Rule, a section 1256 contract open at the end of a taxable year is marked-to-market; that is, it is treated as if it were sold for its fair market value on the last business day of the taxable year.[4] Additionally, when a taxpayer terminates a section 1256 contract position during the year (by offset or otherwise), the contract is marked-to-

---

[1] For a discussion of section 1256 contracts, see generally Chapter 44.
[2] Pub. L. No. 97-34, 95 Stat. 172 (1981) [hereinafter ERTA].
[3] *See* section 47.1.
[4] I.R.C. § 1256(a)(1).

market. In other words, mark-to-market treatment is required if a taxpayer (1) offsets a section 1256 position, (2) makes or takes delivery under a section 1256 contract, (3) exercises or is exercised on a section 1256 option position, (4) makes or is the recipient of an assignment under a section 1256 option, or (5) closes a position by lapse or otherwise.[5]

The fair market value of a section 1256 contract is its settlement price, determined by the qualified board or exchange on which the contract is traded on the last business day of the taxable year, or on the day during the tax year when the contract is terminated.[6] The Mark-to-Market Rule applies to all section 1256 contracts unless the contracts are (1) part of a qualified hedging transaction,[7] (2) part of an identified section 1256(d) mixed straddle for which a mixed straddle election has been made,[8] (3) has been included in a mixed straddle account,[9] or (4) part of a section 988 hedging transaction.[10] The Mark-to-Market Rule also applies even if nonrecognition of gain or loss might result from the application of other Code sections.[11]

TMRA '88[12] provides special rules for transactions in foreign currency-related forward contracts, futures, options, and similar instruments held by "qualified funds." Commodity trading partnerships that elect to be treated as "qualified funds" are entitled to capital treatment on foreign currency products that meet an expanded definition of section 1256 contracts.[13] All products that fall within the expanded definition of section 1256 contracts are marked-to-market at year-end, but the 60/40 Rule only applies to products within the standard definition of section 1256 contracts. This means that products within the expanded definition generate 100 percent short-term capital gains or losses.

---

[5] I.R.C. § 1256(c)(1).

[6] I.R.C. § 1256(c)(3). *See* STAFF OF THE JOINT COMM. ON TAXATION, 97TH CONG., 1ST SESS., GENERAL EXPLANATION OF THE ECONOMIC RECOVERY TAX ACT OF 1981, at 296–97 (Joint Comm. Print 1981) [hereinafter General Explanation of ERTA]. For a discussion of those entities that are treated as qualified boards or exchanges, see section 44.1(b).

[7] I.R.C. § 1256(e); *see generally* Chapter 23.

[8] I.R.C. § 1256(d)(1); *see* section 57.2.

[9] I.R.C. § 1092(b)(2)(B); *see* section 57.4.

[10] I.R.C. § 988(d)(1); *see* section 59.3.

[11] General Explanation of ERTA, *supra* note 6, at 297.

[12] TMRA '88, Pub. L. No. 100-647, 102 Stat. 3342 (1988).

[13] For a discussion of the expanded definition of section 1256 contracts for qualified funds, see section 44.6.

(a) CONSTRUCTIVE RECEIPT DOCTRINE

The Mark-to-Market Rule applies an expanded constructive receipt concept to unrecognized section 1256 contract gains at year-end, and it expands the doctrine to cover the recognition of losses.[14] It was first applied to futures contracts on the grounds that such contracts were subject to a unique mark-to-market system for daily cash settlement purposes that could justify such treatment.[15] The Mark-to-Market Rule, however, applies the concept of constructive receipt of cash under the daily cash settlement system (used to adjust futures contract prices to the market price)[16] to all section 1256 contracts (including contracts not subject to a daily mark-to-market settlement process). The Mark-to-Market Rule treats funds subtracted from or added to a taxpayer's section 1256 contract account as taxable gains and losses on the last day of the tax year. As a result, the Mark-to-Market Rule effectively eliminates the use of section 1256 contract straddle transactions to defer the payment of tax. With the application of section 1256 treatment to contracts not subject to daily cash settlement—first to foreign currency contracts in 1982, later to nonequity options and dealer equity options in 1984, and to certain foreign currency contracts traded by qualified funds in 1988—the doctrine of constructive receipt was extended well beyond its original justification for expansion to futures contracts. In fact, section 1256 treatment now applies to contracts for which the constructive receipt doctrine simply cannot be used to justify section 1256 treatment.

(b) SUBSEQUENT GAIN OR LOSS

Because the Mark-to-Market Rule requires taxes to be paid on unrecognized, as well as recognized, section 1256 contract gains, taxpayers can be required to pay tax on gain that, in fact, may never be realized.[17] If a taxpayer continues to hold a section 1256 contract that was marked-to-

---

[14] General Explanation of ERTA, *supra* note 6, at 296.

[15] *See id.* at 296 (where the Joint Committee refers to the mark-to-market system as margin adjustments); *see also* section 4.4(b).

[16] *See* section 4.4(b). The BTCC Bylaws provide, for example, that open futures contract positions are marked to the settlement price of the day. On each day the positions remain open, payments are made to bring the positions to the settlement price of that day, and "after such payments have been made, the buyer shall be deemed to have bought and the seller shall be deemed to have sold such commodity to the Clearing Corporation at the settlement price of such day." BTCC Bylaw 503.

[17] On the other hand, a taxpayer can be required to report a loss on a section 1256 contract that is never realized.

market at the end of a taxable year, any gain or loss realized on the section 1256 contract in a subsequent tax year is adjusted to reflect any gain or loss taken into account in the preceding year.[18] This means that the Mark-to-Market Rule can distort a taxpayer's income, sometimes causing substantial economic hardship if gains are reported in the first year that do not materialize in a subsequent tax year.

Example 45-1

Assume that on the last business day of the taxable year, a taxpayer holds a section 1256 contract position with an unrealized gain of $100. Under the Mark-to-Market Rule, the gain is included in the taxpayer's income for the year. In addition, the taxpayer's basis in the contract is increased by $100 in the second year to reflect the tax reported in the first year. Further, suppose that at the beginning of the second year the market moves against the taxpayer's position so the section 1256 contract declines in value by $150. The taxpayer then closes out the section 1256 contract in the second year with an actual loss of $50 on the position. Irrespective of this actual loss, the taxpayer reports a $100 gain in the first year and a $150 loss in the second year. This is because the contract's tax basis was adjusted in the second year to reflect the tax paid in the first year. This basis adjustment may be small comfort, given that the taxpayer is out-of-pocket the amount of his tax liability for at least 12 months on the $100 gain reported as income in the first year.

To ameliorate some of the harsh effects of the Mark-to-Market Rule, special provisions exempt qualified hedging transactions from the Mark-to-Market Rule;[19] section 988 hedging transactions (introduced by TRA '86),[20] a new type of hedging transaction for foreign currency risks (amended by TMRA '88);[21] and identified section 1256(d) mixed straddles (composed of section 1256 contracts and non-section 1256 positions in personal property).[22]

---

[18] I.R.C. § 1256(a)(2).
[19] I.R.C. § 1256(e); *see generally* Chapter 23.
[20] TRA '86, Pub. L. No. 99-514, 100 Stat. 2085 (1986).
[21] I.R.C. § 988(d). For a discussion of section 988 hedging transactions, see section 23.3. For a discussion of the TMRA '88 changes to section 988 transactions, see Chapter 59.
[22] I.R.C. § 1256(d)(1); *see generally* Chapter 57.

§ 45.2 60/40 RULE

Under the 60/40 Rule, section 1256 contracts that are capital assets in the hands of a taxpayer are taxed as 60 percent long-term and 40 percent short-term capital gains and losses.[23] The 60/40 Rule applies to all positions—whether short or long—without regard to the length of time a taxpayer holds the contracts.[24] This means that the capital gain holding period requirement is eliminated for those section 1256 contracts subject to section 1256 treatment.[25] With the highest individual income tax rate under pre-TRA '86 law at 50 percent, the maximum tax rate on section 1256 contracts taxed under the 60/40 Rule was 32 percent.[26] Under TRA '86 tax rates for 1987, individuals were subject to a maximum tax rate of 28 percent for long-term capital gain and 32 percent for short-term capital gain. Under the TRA '86 tax rates for 1988 and thereafter, the maximum 60/40 rate is the same 28 percent rate (or "rate adjusted" 33 percent) applicable to all other forms of income. Under RRA '90,[27] capital gains of individuals are taxed at the same rate applicable to all other forms of income up to a maximum rate of 28 percent.

TMRA '88 provides special rules for transactions in foreign currency-related forward contracts, futures, options, and similar instruments held by "qualified funds." These "qualified funds" are basically currency commodities funds or similar partnerships that elect to be treated as "qualified funds" to obtain capital treatment for instruments falling within a broader definition of the term "section 1256 contract." All of such section 1256 contracts of "qualified funds" will be subject to the Mark-to-Market Rule. The 60/40 Rule (60 percent long-term and 40 percent short-term capital gain), however, only applies to those instru-

---

[23] I.R.C. § 1256(a)(3). The Senate, in considering enactment of TRA '86, had proposed to tax 60/40 gains as 100 percent short-term capital gain for a maximum tax rate equal to the top individual rate. Ultimately, this Senate proposal was not enacted as part of TRA '86. If it had been enacted, it would only have affected the 60/40 Rule; it would not have affected the Mark-to-Market Rule. What the Senate proposal of 1986 demonstrates is that the 60/40 allocation could be amended by future congressional actions.

[24] *See* I.R.C. § 1256(a)(3).

[25] For exceptions to section 1256 treatment, see sections 46.1 and 46.2. For the special rules that apply to mixed straddle accounts, see section 57.4.

[26] Under the pre-TRA '86 exclusion of 60 percent of long-term capital gain for noncorporate taxpayers under I.R.C. § 1202, 60 percent of the long-term portion was excluded from taxable income and only 40 percent of the long-term capital gain amount was taxable. Because the entire short-term capital gain portion remained taxable, this meant that on $100 of section 1256 gain, a total of $64 ($24 plus $40), rather than $100, is taxable. For a taxpayer in the 50 percent tax bracket, the tax due was $32, or a tax rate of 32 percent.

[27] Pub. L. No. 101-508, 104 Stat. 1388 (1990).

ments falling within the general definition of a "section 1256 contract." Those instruments falling within the expanded definition of "section 1256 contracts" for "qualified funds" are accorded 100 percent short-term gains or losses (as opposed to 60/40 treatment).[28]

(a) DEALERS IN THE UNDERLYING PROPERTY

To the extent section 1256 contracts are held for purposes of hedging underlying property, dealers in the underlying property obtain ordinary income treatment on both the underlying property for which they are dealers and on their section 1256 contract transactions.[29] Section 1256 contracts not held as a hedge under the statutory hedging exemption are subject to the Mark-to-Market and the 60/40 Rules (unless the asset is an ordinary income asset). If dealers holding section 1256 contracts to hedge their dealer positions in the underlying property do not meet the statutory hedging exemption, they are subject to the Straddle Rules—the loss deferral rule of I.R.C. § 1092, and the requirement to capitalize interest and carrying charges under I.R.C. § 263(g).[30]

The 60/40 Rule does not apply to those section 1256 contracts that are ordinary assets in the hands of a taxpayer.[31] Section 1256 contracts that are ordinary income property continue to generate ordinary income or loss.[32] Such ordinary income contracts open at year-end are marked-to-market at ordinary income rates.[33] Section 1256 contracts are not marked-to-market at year-end[34] if they are (1) identified as section 1256(d) mixed straddles,[35] (2) part of qualified hedging transactions,[36] or (3) part of section 988 hedging transactions.[37]

The *Corn Products* doctrine[38] (prior to modification by *Arkansas Best Corp. v. Comm'r*)[39] was codified in I.R.C. § 1256(f)(3)(B) to provide that

---

[28] For a general discussion of TMRA '88, see Chapter 59.

[29] *See* sections 8.3 and 8.4.

[30] *See generally* Chapter 23. For a discussion of the Straddle Rules, see Part Eleven.

[31] I.R.C. § 1256(f)(2).

[32] General Explanation of ERTA, *supra* note 6, at 297.

[33] *Id.*

[34] I.R.C. §§ 1256(d)(1), (e)(1).

[35] *See* section 57.2.

[36] *See generally* Chapter 23.

[37] *See* section 59.3.

[38] Corn Prods. Ref. Co. v. Comm'r, 350 U.S. 46 (1955), *aff'g* 215 F.2d 513 (2d Cir. 1954), *aff'g* 20 T.C. 503 (1953), *aff'g* 11 T.C.M. (CCH) 721 (1952), *aff'g* 16 T.C. 395 (1951), *reh'g denied*, 350 U.S. 943 (1956).

[39] 485 U.S. 212 (1988), *aff'g* 800 F.2d 215 (8th Cir. 1986), *aff'g in part, rev'g in part* 83 T.C. 640 (1984).

capital asset treatment is not available to any section 1256 contract to the extent that the contract is held to hedge other property and any loss with respect to the property is an ordinary loss.[40] The fact that a taxpayer actively deals or trades in section 1256 contracts is not taken into account to determine whether gain or loss on the underlying property is ordinary.[41] Legislative history that accompanied the DRA[42] in 1984 explains that the reference to the hedging exemption in I.R.C. § 1256(f)(3)(B) is not intended to limit the scope of the hedging exemption under the current law.[43] In other words, a section 1256 contract may hedge property to be acquired, or obligations to be incurred, to the extent those results are obtained under the hedging exemption of I.R.C. § 1256(e).[44] The taxation of financial products for businesses using these products in the ordinary course of their business was thought to be settled by the *Corn Products* doctrine. After *Arkansas Best*, however, tax policy in this area is in chaos. Taxpayers now have the opportunity to choose the most advantageous tax treatment for their transactions (ordinary treatment for losses, capital treatment for gains). This may be possible by characterizing losses as representing ordinary income transactions (under the Supreme Court's footnote in *Arkansas Best*), and gains in accordance with the strict language of *Arkansas Best*. The Treasury and the IRS, on the other hand, must be truly befuddled. Unlike taxpayers, who can follow their individual self-interests in any given case, the government must ultimately reach a consistent approach. The *Arkansas Best* decision raises real questions as to what the government will do to reach a consistent approach.

(b) COMMODITY DEALERS AND OPTION DEALERS

Taxpayers that are commodity dealers under I.R.C. § 1402(i)(2)(B), or option dealers under I.R.C. § 1256(g)(8), are granted special tax treatment in a number of areas. (The criteria to determine whether a taxpayer is eligible for either designation are discussed in sections 8.2(b), 8.2(c), 8.3(d), and 8.3(e).) I.R.C. § 1256(f)(3) makes it clear that professional commodity and option dealers (i.e., traders) obtain capital gains and losses on their section 1256 contract transactions. Because gain and loss from section 1256 contracts is treated as from the sale or exchange of a

---

[40] I.R.C. § 1256(f)(3)(B).
[41] I.R.C. § 1256(f)(3)(C).
[42] Pub. L. No. 98-369, 98 Stat. 494 (1984) [hereinafter DRA].
[43] HOUSE CONFERENCE REPORT, DEFICIT REDUCTION ACT OF 1984, H.R. CONF. REP. NO. 861, 98th Cong. 2d Sess. 909 (1984) [hereinafter H.R. CONF. REP. NO. 861].
[44] *Id.*

capital asset,[45] both option dealers (which claimed ordinary income treatment prior to the DRA in 1984, and viewed themselves as securities dealers that traded options and underlying securities)[46] and professional commodity traders report capital gain and loss on section 1256 contracts, except to the extent that the position is a hedge against ordinary income property.[47]

Under the law in effect before the DRA changes in 1984, a dealer in options was viewed as a dealer in the underlying property simply because he was a dealer in the options overlaying the property.[48] This position was reversed in 1984 by the DRA, in that the Code now provides that in determining whether gain or loss is ordinary income or loss, "the fact that the taxpayer is actively engaged in dealing in or trading section 1256 contracts related to such property shall not be taken into account."[49] As a result, an options dealer does not report ordinary income or loss with respect to his transactions in property underlying the options he trades *unless* he is a dealer in the underlying property under general tax rules.[50]

DRA changes the treatment of option market makers by providing that market makers, defined as "option dealers," are treated as buying and selling capital assets unless the option positions are acquired as a hedge against ordinary income property.[51] Accordingly, a market maker does not report ordinary income or loss on transactions in options, stock, or securities unless he is also a dealer—independent of his options business—in the underlying stock or securities.[52] Under current law, option dealers generally receive 60/40 treatment under section 1256 for their option transactions and capital gain or loss on their transactions in the underlying property (unless they qualify as dealers—under general tax rules—in the underlying property).

---

[45] I.R.C. § 1256(f)(3)(A).

[46] In Laureys v. Comm'r, 92 T.C. 101 (1989), *acq. and nonacq.* 1990-1 C.B. 1, the Tax Court ruled that a CBOE market maker's option losses were capital in nature because the transactions were not undertaken in connection with his being "called to the post" (i.e., when he was required by the CBOE to make a market in a particular option).

[47] HOUSE WAYS AND MEANS COMM. REPORT, DEFICIT REDUCTION ACT OF 1984, H.R. REP. NO. 432, Pt. II, 98th Cong., 2d Sess. 1270, *reprinted in* 1984 U.S. CODE CONG. & ADMIN. NEWS 697, 932 [hereinafter H.R. REP. NO. 432].

[48] I.R.C. § 1234(a)(1); *see also* H.R. CONF. REP. NO. 861, *supra* note 43, at 915.

[49] I.R.C. § 1256(f)(3)(C).

[50] H.R. REP. NO. 432, *supra* note 47, at 1270.

[51] *Id.*

[52] *Id.*

Section 1256 treatment is not available to any property underlying section 1256 positions.[53] This means that gain or loss on the underlying property is only recognized upon a sale or exchange of that property, not on a mark-to-market basis. Furthermore, market makers that are not dealers in the underlying securities are no longer treated as trading ordinary income assets.[54] Any gain or loss from the sale or exchange of stock or securities underlying the options in which the option market makers trade is capital gain or loss, irrespective of whether the option positions are held for investment, or in the course of making a market in options.[55] Under the modified short sales and wash sales rules in I.R.C. § 1092(b), the Treasury has issued regulations, discussed generally in Chapter 54, that may preclude long-term capital gain treatment for stock or securities positions used to hedge or offset option positions established in the course of making a market in options.

(c) DEALER EQUITY OPTIONS UNAVAILABLE TO LIMITED PARTNERS AND LIMITED ENTREPRENEURS

Limited partners and limited entrepreneurs of partnerships, S corporations, and other entities that qualify as option dealers cannot report their allocable gain or loss from dealer equity options as 60/40 gains or losses.[56] Rather, all such gains and losses are treated as short-term capital gains and losses for such taxpayers.[57] This limitation on 60/40 treatment precludes the flow-through of 60/40 gains and losses from dealer equity options to passive investors and those members of option dealer firms that do not actively participate in the entity's management.[58] This section discusses the impact of this limitation on the tax treatment of such taxpayers and the possible impact of option dealer partnerships on general partners.

---

[53] Section 1256 treatment applies only to section 1256 contracts as defined in I.R.C. § 1256(b).
[54] *Compare* I.R.C. § 1234(a)(1) *with* I.R.C. § 1256(f)(3)(C) (which was first introduced by the DRA, *supra* note 42, § 102(b)).
[55] I.R.C. § 1256(f)(3)(C); *see* sections 8.2(b) and 8.3(d).
[56] I.R.C. § 1256(f)(4).
[57] *Id.*
[58] For a discussion of limited entrepreneurs, see section 23.2(c)(3).

(1) UNINTENDED TAX RESULT

Because of the way the exclusion for 60/40 gains or losses for limited partners and limited entrepreneurs is structured, it is possible that an option dealer firm could generate gains on section 1256 contracts at 60/40 rates, while also generating losses on dealer equity options, which flow through to its limited partners and limited entrepreneurs as short-term capital loss. The short-term capital loss could then be used to offset the short-term capital gain portion of other section 1256 contracts. As a result, it is possible that limited partners and limited entrepreneurs could receive an unintended tax benefit by being able to shelter their short-term capital gains.

(2) GENERAL PARTNERS AS LIMITED ENTREPRENEURS

Certain general partners of option dealer partnerships might be viewed as limited entrepreneurs, recharacterizing their allocable share of gains and losses on dealer equity options as short-term capital gain or loss. Because the term "limited entrepreneur"[59] is a vague concept—it was introduced into the Code in 1976 to deny farm losses for certain entities with passive investors—it is unclear whether the limited entrepreneur designation applies to certain general partners.

Treasury regulations proposed under I.R.C. § 464 provide that a limited entrepreneur is someone with an interest other than as a limited partner that does not actively participate in the management of the enterprise.[60] The standard for when a taxpayer is a limited entrepreneur is not clear. To avoid limited entrepreneur status, I.R.C. § 464(e) might be read to require active participation in the "enterprise," while I.R.C. § 1256(e) might be read to require active participation in the "entity." Literal application of the proposed Treasury regulation to general partners may require a general partner to actively participate in both the enterprise, as required in I.R.C. § 464(e), and the entity, as required in I.R.C. § 1256(e) (which incorporates I.R.C. § 464(e) by reference). It is unclear which, if either, requirement must be complied with to assure a general partner is not viewed as a limited entrepreneur. It is the author's view that neither requirement is appropriate and that the exclusion from 60/40 treatment should only apply to those general partners that do not participate in the business and that have limited their risks.

---

[59] I.R.C. § 464(e)(2).
[60] Prop. Treas. Reg. § 1.464-2(a)(3) (1983).

In addition, it is not clear what activities a general partner must engage in to assure he is not viewed as a limited entrepreneur. Although all partners might actively participate in a partnership's business, some partners—if they trade at all—may trade only equity options while others may trade other products. Are all of the partners sufficiently involved in the business to avoid limited entrepreneur classification and to obtain 60/40 treatment on the firm's dealer equity options? What if some partners are active in the general management and operation of the partnership, while others are involved in trading activities? Are those partners involved in general firm management viewed as limited entrepreneurs? Or, what if the partnership agreement delegates certain management rights to a management committee or to a managing partner? Are all of the partners that are not active in management viewed as limited entrepreneurs?

The answers to these questions are not clear, although it seems appropriate to assert that the exclusion from 60/40 treatment should apply only to general partners that, much like limited partners, have entered into agreements to limit their risk of loss from the business and that do not participate in the management of the partnership. If the "at risk" rule under I.R.C. § 465(b)(4) is examined to provide guidance as to when a general partner has limited his risk, the partner would be protected against loss through nonrecourse financing, guarantees, stop loss agreements, or similar arrangements.

§ 45.3 STRADDLES MADE UP EXCLUSIVELY OF SECTION 1256 CONTRACTS

If all positions in a straddle consist of section 1256 contracts, the Straddle Rules do not apply and the positions are subject to section 1256 treatment.[61] In addition, interest and carrying charges need not be capitalized.[62] According to the legislative history of ERTA in 1981, Treasury regulations (yet to be promulgated) will define the manner in which such straddle positions in section 1256 contracts are to be matched.[63] This exemption is consistent with the policy behind the Straddle Rules because there is no opportunity to defer income. All offsetting positions

---

[61] I.R.C. §§ 1092(d)(5)(A), 1256(a)(4); *see* section 56.7.
[62] I.R.C. §§ 263(g)(1), 1256(a)(4).
[63] SENATE FINANCE COMM. REPORT, ECONOMIC RECOVERY TAX ACT OF 1981, S. REP. NO. 144, 97th Cong., 1st Sess. 147–48, *reprinted in* 1981 U.S. CODE CONG. & ADMIN. NEWS 105, 247 [hereinafter S. REP. NO. 144].

composing a straddle made up exclusively of section 1256 contracts are subject to section 1256 treatment, which means that recognized and unrecognized gains and losses are reported for tax purposes at year-end.[64]

In addition, straddles made up exclusively of section 1256 contracts can be designated as identified straddles.[65] This means that the positions of the identified straddle cannot be paired up with any other position not part of the identified straddle that otherwise offsets an identified straddle position.

Under the law in effect before clarification by the DRA in 1984, it was unclear whether straddles made up exclusively of RFCs could qualify as identified straddles. The statutory language of I.R.C. § 1256(a)(4), when enacted by ERTA, provided that if all positions making up a straddle were RFCs, the provisions of I.R.C. § 1092 did not apply.[66] Because the identified straddle provisions are found in I.R.C. § 1092(a)(2), however, it appeared under pre-DRA law as if the identified straddle provisions were unavailable to RFC straddles.[67] It also appeared inequitable to permit positions of an RFC straddle (where the positions were identified in accordance with the identified straddle provisions) to be matched up with other positions outside of the straddle.[68] DRA resolved this issue in 1984 by providing that I.R.C. § 1256(a)(4) does not preclude an identified straddle election for a straddle that consists exclusively of section 1256 contracts.[69] There is no risk of having a section 1256 contract position paired up with another position that is not part of an identified section 1256 straddle.

§ 45.4 LOSS CARRY-BACK RULES FOR SECTION 1256 CONTRACT LOSSES

(a) IN GENERAL

Special loss carry-back rules are available for section 1256 contract losses. Taxpayers can use section 1256 losses incurred in one year to

---

[64] I.R.C. § 1256(a).

[65] *See* section 56.1.

[66] ERTA, *supra* note 2, § 503(a).

[67] *See* STAFF OF THE JOINT COMM. ON TAXATION, 98TH CONG., 2D SESS., GENERAL EXPLANATION OF THE REVENUE PROVISIONS OF THE DEFICIT REDUCTION ACT OF 1984, at 311 (Joint Comm. Print 1981).

[68] *Id.*

[69] I.R.C. § 1092(d)(5)(B).

reduce income generated on such contracts in a prior tax year, thereby providing a form of income averaging generally not available to other taxpayers.[70] ERTA introduced a three-year carry-back rule for losses from section 1256 contracts subject to the Mark-to-Market Rule ("loss carry-back election").[71] This carry-back rule is quite complicated, applying only after netting section 1256 contracts with unrelated capital gains and losses, which results in a net capital loss that could otherwise be carried forward under I.R.C. § 1212(b). If a taxpayer other than a corporation, estate, or trust makes a loss carry-back election, "net section 1256 contract losses" recognized under the Mark-to-Market Rule can be carried back to each of the three preceding years and applied against net section 1256 contract gain recognized under the Mark-to-Market Rule during such periods.[72]

Net section 1256 contract loss is defined as the lesser of (1) the net capital loss for the taxable year from section 1256 contracts, or (2) the sum of net short-term and net long-term capital loss for the taxable year.[73] Net section 1256 contract gain is defined as the lesser of (1) the capital gain net income for the taxable year from section 1256 contracts, or (2) the net capital gain income for the taxable year.[74]

The loss carry-back election is available after netting capital losses from section 1256 contracts under the Mark-to-Market Rule with capital gains from other sources if two requirements are met. First, a net capital loss must exist for the year.[75] Second, the net capital loss must be a capital loss that could be carried forward under the provisions of I.R.C. § 1212(b).[76] Losses on stock underlying options are capital losses for all taxpayers except for hedgers and dealers in the stock.[77] For option dealers

---

[70] Prior to ERTA's enactment in 1981, taxpayers, other than corporations, were not allowed to carry back capital losses. Although individual taxpayers with significant increases in income can qualify for income averaging (a gain carry-back provision), taxpayers with significant decreases in income are not eligible for income averaging. See I.R.C. §§ 1301–1305. The inability under pre-ERTA law to carry back capital losses was a significant tax disadvantage to commodity traders in light of the volatility of the commodity markets. General Explanation of ERTA, *supra* note 6, at 305. Commodity traders could not use trading losses from one year to offset trading gains in prior years; losses could only be carried forward under general tax rules.

[71] I.R.C. § 1212(c).
[72] *Id.*
[73] I.R.C. § 1212(c)(4).
[74] I.R.C. § 1212(c)(5).
[75] I.R.C. § 1212(c)(4)(A).
[76] I.R.C. § 1212(c)(4)(B).
[77] I.R.C. § 1221.

eligible for 60/40 treatment on their dealer equity option positions,[78] stock positions established after July 18, 1984 (giving effect to their transitional year elections) generate capital gain or loss,[79] and the loss carry-back election can be used (for post-DRA years) to reduce stock gains.

Losses that are carried back are treated as if 60 percent of the losses were long-term and 40 percent were short-term capital loss.[80] Carry-back losses cannot be used to increase or produce a net operating loss for the taxable year.[81] In addition, such losses are carried back to the earliest of the three preceding taxable years in which there is a net section 1256 contract gain.[82] Any portion of the loss not absorbed in the earliest of the three preceding years can then be carried forward to the next taxable year and, if any loss remains, to the next (most recent) taxable year.[83] Any net section 1256 contract loss carried forward from the first carry-back year is again recharacterized as 60 percent long-term and 40 percent short-term capital loss.[84]

Example 45-2

Assume that in 1986, a taxpayer has net section 1256 contract losses of $100,000 and has $50,000 in long-term capital gain from other sources. The section 1256 contract loss is characterized as $60,000 long-term and $40,000 short-term capital loss.[85] The net section 1256 contract losses are applied against the $50,000 long-term capital gain, thereby leaving a net section 1256 contract loss of $50,000 for 1986.

Assume that the taxpayer does not make the loss carry-back election. In this case, the remaining loss of $50,000 from section 1256 contracts can be carried forward to 1987.[86] Because the $100,000 of section 1256 contract loss is treated under the 60/40 Rule as 60 percent long-term ($60,000) and 40 percent short-term ($40,000) capital loss, $10,000 is treated as long-term capital loss ($60,000

---

[78] I.R.C. §§ 1256(a)(3), (b)(4).
[79] DRA, *supra* note 42, § 102(f)(1).
[80] I.R.C. § 1212(c)(1).
[81] I.R.C. § 1212(c)(3).
[82] I.R.C. § 1212(c)(2).
[83] *Id.*
[84] I.R.C. § 1212(c)(6)(A).
[85] I.R.C. § 1256(a)(3).
[86] I.R.C. § 1212(b).

minus $50,000 from the long-term capital gain from other sources) and $40,000 as short-term capital loss.

On the other hand, assume that the taxpayer decides to make the loss carry-back election. Net losses from section 1256 contracts are carried back three years. Net losses are carried back first (in this example) to 1983, but only to the extent of $50,000, which is the net section 1256 contract loss which could have been carried forward to 1987. However, the amount carried back to 1983 is recharacterized under the 60/40 rule and is treated as 60 percent long-term and 40 percent short-term capital loss, rather than $10,000 long-term and $50,000 short-term capital loss as in the previous example where the taxpayer did not make the loss carry-back election. Hence, in 1983, the $50,000 carry-back loss yields $30,000 of long-term and $20,000 of short-term capital loss.

Assume further that in 1983 the taxpayer had net section 1256 contract gains of $20,000.[87] This $20,000 of section 1256 gains is composed of $12,000 long-term and $8000 short-term capital gain. When the section 1256 contract loss to be carried back under the loss carry-back election is carried back to 1983, there remains $30,000 in unused 1986 section 1256 contract losses ($50,000 minus $20,000), which can then be carried forward to 1984. This $30,000 once again is recharacterized as 60/40 loss and, therefore, is recharacterized as $18,000 long-term (60 percent of $30,000) and $12,000 short-term capital loss (40 percent of $30,000), which can be used to offset any section 1256 contract gain in 1984. Remaining loss, if any, can be carried forward to 1985. If, after application to the relevant carry-back periods, any section 1256 contract losses remain, these losses can be carried forward to years after 1986 to offset capital gains incurred in those years.

Under the TRA '86 changes to the Code, 60/40 treatment for section 1256 contract losses is generally not as disadvantageous after 1987 as it was under pre-TRA '86 law, although it retained some of the old law disadvantages for losses reported in 1987. For losses reported in 1987, short-term capital losses were still generally preferred over long-term capital losses because there was a transitional rate preference in 1987 for net long-term capital gain (technically "net capital gain").

Under the TRA '86 changes to the Code, all capital losses reported after 1987 are treated identically, irrespective of whether the losses are long-

---

[87] The only section 1256 contracts traded in 1983 were RFCs and certain foreign currency contracts.

term or short-term. RRA '90 provided a preferential maximum tax rate of 28 percent for the long-term capital gains of individuals. First, long-term gains, against which long-term losses are first offset, are not preferred over short-term gains. Second, the deduction of an individual's capital losses against ordinary income (up to the ceiling of $3000 for joint returns or $1500 for individual tax returns) is equally available for long-term and short-term losses.

Capital losses carried back to pre-1987 years are generally treated more favorably if the losses are short-term rather than long-term. Capital losses in the case of a corporation can be carried back (for three years). In the case of an individual, capital losses can be carried back (for three years) if—and only if—the individual's losses arose from section 1256 contracts and are offset against gains from section 1256 contracts in the carry-back year or years.

(b) MIXED STRADDLE ACCOUNTS

There is some question as to whether a section 1092(b) mixed straddle election,[88] which can alter the treatment of section 1256 contracts that are part of a mixed straddle, will preclude the carry-back election on the grounds that treatment under section 1092(b)—although referring to the 60/40 treatment of section 1256—is not treatment under section 1256 as is required by I.R.C. § 1212(c). This argument was advanced by the government in *Roberts v. United States*,[89] a case involving a section 1092(b) mixed straddle account election. The magistrate assigned to *Roberts* recommended to the district court on September 19, 1988, that the plaintiffs' motion for summary judgment on the I.R.C. § 1212(c) issue be granted, noting that the carry-back provisions applied to net section 1256 losses arising in a mixed straddle account because "nothing in the statutory language [of I.R.C. § 1212] indicate[d] that such losses [could] *not* be carried back."[90] Moreover, the magistrate noted that the IRS Forms allow for such carry-backs and (while not binding) do "parallel the requirements of the tax code."[91]

---

[88] *See* Chapter 57 for a discussion of mixed straddles.
[89] Nos. 86 C 9934, 86 C 9935, 86 C 9936 (N.D. Ill. Sept. 19, 1988) (Report and Recommendation of the Magistrate).
[90] *Id.* at 15 (emphasis in original).
[91] *Id.*

On April 6, 1990, the District Court for the Northern District of Illinois decided *Roberts*,[92] adopting the magistrate's report and recommendation. In *Roberts*, the court acknowledged that it raised "an issue of first impression, namely whether the taxpayers are allowed under Internal Revenue Code section 1212(c) to carry back their section 1256 contract losses incurred in 1986 in commodity futures and mixed straddles . . . to offset section 1256 contract gains in 1984 regardless of whether or not such losses were part of their mixed straddle account elections made pursuant to Temp. Treas. Reg. section [1.1092(b)-4T]."[93] The court, "[a]fter a *de novo* review of the record, and the memoranda of counsel," found that the magistrate's report "is in accordance with law."[94] As a result, the court adopted the report and recommendations of the magistrate and granted the taxpayers' motions for summary judgment.[95]

(c) RESTRICTED INTEREST

The government must pay interest on the overpayment of tax that results from a carry-back, unless the carry-back fits a specific exception to the general rule provided in I.R.C. § 6611(a). The issue has been raised on audit as to whether a "net section 1256 contracts loss" under I.R.C. § 1212(c) is treated as a "net capital loss" for purposes of the restriction on interest under I.R.C. § 6611(f). It is the author's view that "net section 1256 contracts loss" carry-backs are exempt from the restricted interest limitations in I.R.C. § 6611(f). The so-called restricted interest rules in I.R.C. § 6611(f) only apply to net operating loss, net capital loss, and credit carry-backs. Restricted interest does not apply to carry-backs of "net section 1256 contracts losses" as defined in I.R.C. § 1212(c)(4). As a result, interest on a tax refund generated by a carry-back of a "net section 1256 contracts loss" should be subject to the mandatory payment rules of I.R.C. § 6611(a), and interest should accrue from the date the tax return was filed for the year in which such taxes were paid or accrued, regardless of when the carry-back claim is filed.[96] The remainder of this section addresses that analysis.

In general, I.R.C. § 6611(a) provides that interest is "allowed and paid upon any overpayment in respect of any internal revenue tax at the

[92] 734 F. Supp. 314 (N.D. Ill. 1990), *adopting* 1988 U.S. Dist. LEXIS 17336, *rereporting* 1988 U.S. Dist. LEXIS 17334.
[93] 734 F. Supp. at 316.
[94] *Id.* at 317.
[95] *Id.*
[96] *See* Rev. Rul. 85-65, 1985-1 C.B. 366.

§ 45.4(c)

overpayment rate established under [I.R.C.] section 6611." In Rev. Rul. 85-65,[97] the IRS stated that "[p]ayment of interest is mandatory on underpayments and overpayments of any internal revenue tax unless specifically prohibited by law or by mutual agreement." Under I.R.C. § 6611(b)(1), interest is allowed and paid for credits from the date of the overpayment to the due date of the amount against which the credit is taken. In addition, I.R.C. § 6611(e) provides that if any overpayment of tax is refunded within 45 days after the last date prescribed for filing the return of such tax (determined without regard to any extension of time for filing the return) or, in case the return is filed after such last date, is refunded within 45 days after the date the return is filed, no interest is allowed under I.R.C. § 6611(a) on such overpayment.

I.R.C. § 6611(f) sets out restrictions on the government's obligations to pay interest on refunds of income tax caused by certain carry-backs and adjustments. Overpayments with respect to net operating losses and net capital loss carry-backs are "deemed not to have been made prior to the filing date for the taxable year in which such net operating loss or net capital loss arises."[98] The terms "net operating loss" and "net capital loss" are not defined in I.R.C. § 6611(f). Rather, I.R.C. § 6611(f)(3)(C) addresses a taxpayer's right to file "a claim for refund for any overpayment" described in I.R.C. §§ 6411(a)(1) or (2). For these purposes, "a net operating loss" is defined as it is in I.R.C. § 172(b) and a "capital loss carry-back" is defined as it is in I.R.C. § 1212(a)(1).[99]

I.R.C. § 172(b) defines net operating losses by a cross-reference to I.R.C. §§ 172(c) and (d), which specifically exclude from the computation any net capital losses incurred by individuals.[100] In addition, I.R.C. § 1212(a) deals only with capital loss carry-backs of a corporation. Furthermore, a "net capital loss" is defined in I.R.C. § 1222(1) as "the excess of the losses from sales or exchanges of capital assets over the sum allowed under I.R.C. § 1211." In the case of a corporation, for the purpose of determining losses under I.R.C. § 1211, amounts that are short-term capital losses under I.R.C. § 1212 are excluded.

I.R.C. § 1211(b) limits the allowance of capital losses for individuals to the lesser of $3000, or the excess of such losses over such gains. In the case of a taxpayer that is not a corporation, a net capital loss is carried forward as specified in I.R.C. §§ 1212(b)(1)(A) or (B).[101] A "net capital loss" of an

---

[97] 1985-1 C.B. 366.
[98] I.R.C. § 6611(f)(1).
[99] I.R.C. § 6411(a).
[100] I.R.C. § 172(d)(2).
[101] I.R.C. § 1212(b).

individual, therefore, is the amount of the loss not allowed or allowable on the current year's tax return and is an amount that can be carried forward as a "short-term capital loss"[102] or as a "long term capital loss"[103] to the succeeding taxable year. Individuals cannot carry net capital losses back to prior years and cannot have net capital losses subject to a carry-back.

"Net section 1256 contracts losses," defined in I.R.C. § 1212(c)(4), are the lesser of (1) the net capital loss for the taxable year, determined by taking into account only gains and losses from section 1256 contracts, or (2) the sum of the amounts that, but for I.R.C. § 1212(6)(A), would be treated as capital losses in the succeeding taxable year under I.R.C. §§ 1212(b)(1)(A) and (B). "Net section 1256 contracts loss" carry-backs are only available to individuals. These losses are not, for carry-back purposes, the same as net operating losses or net capital losses. Furthermore, "net section 1256 contracts loss" carry-backs cannot be used to offset other types of capital gains from prior years.

§ 45.5 TERMINATION OF SECTION 1256 CONTRACTS BEFORE DELIVERY OR EXERCISE DATE

To terminate rights and obligations under a section 1256 contract prior to its delivery or exercise, the taxpayer must enter into a closing transaction, that is, the acquisition of a long position to liquidate a short position or a short position to liquidate a long position. A closing transaction for a futures contract covers the same number of units of the same underlying commodity for delivery in the same month. With respect to an option, a closing transaction covers the same quantity and strike price as the option position previously established.[104] Gain or loss on a closing transaction is the difference between the price of the opening transaction and the price of the closing transaction. When the opening transaction is a long position, the trade is profitable if the closing transaction's contract price is greater than the opening transaction's contract price. When the opening transaction is a short position, the trade is profitable if the contract price of the opening transaction is greater than the contract price for the closing transaction.

---

[102] I.R.C. § 1212(b)(1)(A).
[103] I.R.C. § 1212(b)(1)(B).
[104] For a discussion of closing transactions, see section 4.3(c).

§ 45.5   Financial Products: Taxation, Regulation, and Design   1174

If a taxpayer transfers his rights in a section 1256 contract, the transfer is treated as a termination.[105] Gains and losses are taken into account at the transfer as if the section 1256 contract was terminated by offset or delivery.[106] Thus, transfers made to and from partnerships and other flow-through entities are viewed as terminations.[107] Presumably, transfers of all other sorts—even those not permitted under the rules of a domestic commodity exchange—are also treated as terminations.

A termination or transfer segregates any 60/40 gain or loss inherent in an open section 1256 contract from any gain or loss subsequently realized by the taxpayer. In general, the rules of section 1256 apply if the taxpayer terminates (or transfers) his obligations or rights with respect to a section 1256 contract by offset, making or taking delivery, exercise or being exercised, assignment or being assigned, lapse, or otherwise.[108] Gain or loss is determined on the basis of the contract's fair market value at the time of termination (or transfer), which is usually the actual price received or paid.[109] Under the 60/40 Rule, any gain or loss at termination (or transfer) is treated as 60 percent long-term and 40 percent short-term capital gain or loss.[110]

Example 45-3

Assume a taxpayer entered into a futures contract position to purchase wheat for delivery in June at $3.50 per bushel (long position). Two months later, when June wheat is trading for $4 per bushel, the taxpayer decides to liquidate his long position. Under the rules of all domestic commodity exchanges, the taxpayer cannot privately negotiate with a third party to sell his rights to purchase the wheat, nor can he negotiate with the clearing organization to release him from his rights and obligations under his long futures contract position. Instead, the taxpayer must enter into a closing transaction by entering into a short position to sell June wheat at $4 per bushel. As a result, the taxpayer's long and short positions are

---

[105] I.R.C. § 1256(c)(1).

[106] This rule does not apply to the transfer of contracts of third party taxpayers between FCMs. HOUSE WAYS AND MEANS COMM. REPORT, TECHNICAL CORRECTIONS ACT OF 1982, H.R. REP. NO. 794, 97th Cong., 2d Sess. 24, n.4 (1982) [hereinafter H.R. REP. NO. 794]; SENATE FINANCE COMM. REPORT, TECHNICAL CORRECTIONS ACT OF 1982, S. REP. NO. 592, 97th Cong., 2d Sess. 27, n.4, *reprinted in* 1982 U.S. CODE CONG. & ADMIN. NEWS 4149, 4173 [hereinafter S. REP. NO. 592].

[107] H.R. REP. NO. 794, *supra* note 106, at 24; S. REP. NO. 592, *supra* note 106, at 27.

[108] I.R.C. § 1256(c)(1).

[109] S. REP. NO. 144, *supra* note 63, at 158.

[110] I.R.C. § 1256(c)(1).

netted and closed out by the clearing organization affiliated with the domestic commodity exchange on which the futures contract is traded. The taxpayer receives a gain of $.50 per bushel (minus commissions). The contracts are extinguished, that is, they are no longer open, and the taxpayer has no remaining rights or obligations with respect to either the long or short position.

Example 45-4

Assume that when XYZ foreign currency is trading for $.45 per unit, a taxpayer purchases, for a $1000 premium, one July 50 call option granting him the option, at any time before the July expiration date, to purchase 100,000 units of XYZ currency at $.50 per unit. If the taxpayer wants to close out the option position when the currency is trading for $.55 per unit, he enters into an offsetting short position by selling one July 50 call option on XYZ currency. At the sale, the taxpayer has a profit equal to the price at which he sold his option minus the $1000 he paid for the option and any transaction costs.

Example 45-5

Assume two option dealers, as defined in I.R.C. § 1256(g)(8)(A), enter into a partnership to trade section 1256 option contracts. Notwithstanding the rules of all domestic securities and commodity exchanges, which prohibit the private transfer of positions off the exchange floors, the two option dealers agree to contribute their open section 1256 contracts to the capital of their newly formed partnership. This transfer is treated as a termination. All gain or loss on section 1256 contracts is marked-to-market at their fair market value at the time of contribution to the partnership's capital. Gain or loss is 60 percent long-term and 40 percent short-term.

§ 45.6 MAKING OR TAKING DELIVERY AND EXERCISING OR BEING EXERCISED ON SECTION 1256 POSITIONS

(a) DELIVERY UNDER FUTURES CONTRACTS

Delivery is made pursuant to a futures contract when the taxpayer holding a long (or short) futures contract position has the obligation during the delivery month to take (or make) delivery of the underlying property or cash. The short position is obligated to deliver the property or

§ 45.6(b)   Financial Products: Taxation, Regulation, and Design

cash to the long position. The property acquired upon delivery is a capital asset for investors and traders, and it is ordinary income property for hedgers and dealers.[111]

If the holder of a long futures contract position takes delivery under the futures contract, the futures contract is valued, that is, marked-to-market, on the delivery date.[112] Gain or loss is recognized on the long futures contract position just as if it had been closed out by offset.[113] Under the 60/40 Rule, the character of the gain or loss for capital assets is 60 percent long-term and 40 percent short-term. The tax basis of the property acquired pursuant to a long futures contract position, that is, the contract price, is increased or decreased to reflect any gain or loss recognized upon termination of the futures contract.[114] Delivery segregates any gain or loss inherent in the section 1256 contract from the gain or loss on the underlying property.

Example 45-6

Assume that the taxpayer holds a long futures contract position to acquire wheat for $3.50 per bushel and holds the position until its delivery date, when wheat is selling at $4.50 per bushel. The taxpayer has a $1 per bushel gain inherent in his position. The taxpayer takes delivery of the wheat pursuant to his futures contract position, which has a value equal to the settlement price of the contract on the date of delivery. Therefore, if the value of June wheat is $4.50 per bushel at the time of delivery, the taxpayer recognizes a $1 per bushel gain at 60/40 rates on the date of delivery ($4.50 minus $3.50). The taxpayer's tax basis for the wheat acquired is $4.50 per bushel ($3.50 per bushel paid under the futures contract position plus $1 of gain recognized at delivery under the futures contract position).

(b) EXERCISE OF OPTION POSITIONS

The holder of an unprofitable option (put or call) does not generally exercise the position, simply letting it expire worthless. The holder of a profitable long option position (put or call) that wants to close out the

---

[111] *See generally* Part Two.
[112] *See* General Explanation of ERTA, *supra* note 6, at 297–98.
[113] I.R.C. § 1256(c)(1).
[114] The provision to tack on the holding period under I.R.C. § 1223(8) does not apply to a commodity acquired pursuant to a futures contract that is taxed under I.R.C. § 1256. *See* section 17.3(b).

position has two choices. Either he can exercise the option or enter into a closing transaction (by selling the option itself at a profit).[115] With a call option, the taxpayer can exercise the option, take delivery of the underlying property, and sell it for a profit.[116] In the case of a put option, the holder of the long position can buy the underlying property (if he does not already own it), and after exercising the option he can deliver it to the short position.[117] If the holder of a long position exercises a call option, he thereby agrees to buy the property underlying the option from the short position at the option price. For a put option, the holder of a long position that exercises the option thereby agrees to sell the underlying property to the short position at the option price.

(c) DELIVERY OR EXERCISE OF PART OF A STRADDLE

A special rule applies when a taxpayer takes delivery or exercises any section 1256 contracts that are part of a straddle consisting of two or more section 1256 contracts. At the delivery or exercise of any section 1256 contract that is part of a straddle, each of the remaining section 1256 contracts is treated as if terminated and sold for its fair market value on the day the taxpayer takes delivery of the underlying property.[118] The taxpayer treats the remaining section 1256 positions as if terminated on the date of delivery and as if new positions are acquired on that date. Therefore, the taxpayer can make a section 1256(d) identified mixed straddle election on the date of delivery, even though the short position was previously acquired.[119]

Example 45-7

Assume a taxpayer holds a silver straddle consisting of long and short futures contract positions. Assume further that the taxpayer takes delivery of the physical silver under the long futures contract. On the delivery date, both positions are treated as sold for their fair

---

[115] *See* section 5.1.

[116] By exercising the option and selling the underlying property, the call holder loses whatever time value remains in the option. In addition, transaction costs are generally higher when buying and selling the property underlying an option rather than simply entering into a closing transaction.

[117] Purchasing the underlying property to deliver upon exercise of the option is generally more costly than simply entering into a closing transaction.

[118] I.R.C. § 1256(c)(2).

[119] S. REP. NO. 592, *supra* note 106, at 27; *see* section 57.2.

market value on that date.[120] For section 1256 positions that are capital assets, gain or loss is treated as 60/40 gain or loss. The holding period of the long futures contract position is not tacked on to the period of time the taxpayer holds the physical silver to determine the holding period for the physical silver.[121]

Example 45-8

Assume a taxpayer holds a straddle position consisting of a July 40 long call position on ABC stock and an ABC September 40 short call position. The taxpayer holds a straddle as defined in I.R.C. § 1092(c)(1). Assume that the long position increases in value and the short position incurs a loss. The taxpayer decides to exercise his rights under the long position prior to its expiration, to take delivery of the ABC stock at the strike price (exercise price) of $40 per share. His securities broker provides a notice of exercise to OCC, thereby obligating the taxpayer to pay the aggregate exercise price for the underlying security on the exercise settlement date, regardless of the market price of ABC stock on that date.[122]

---

[120] I.R.C. § 1256(c)(3).
[121] *See* section 17.3(b).
[122] The taxpayer, as an exercising holder of a put option (long position), is contractually obligated to deliver the specified number of units of the underlying property on the exercise settlement date. *See* section 5.4(b).

Forty-six

Exceptions to Section 1256 Treatment

The Code provides exceptions to application of the Mark-to-Market Rule and the 60/40 Rule for certain mixed straddles and hedging transactions. These exceptions are mentioned briefly in this chapter with cross-references provided for detailed discussions of these exceptions.

§ 46.1 MIXED STRADDLES

Mixed straddles, that is, straddles comprised partially of section 1256 contracts and partially of other positions,[1] are exempt from section 1256 treatment if the taxpayer makes one of several elections. For a discussion of the scope and application of the various mixed straddle elections, see generally Chapter 57.

§ 46.2 HEDGING TRANSACTIONS

(a) QUALIFIED HEDGING TRANSACTIONS

Hedging transactions that qualify under I.R.C. § 1256(e) are exempt from section 1256 treatment. As a result, such transactions are not marked-to-market and are not eligible for 60/40 treatment. The positions making up

---

[1] I.R.C. § 1256(d)(4).

qualified hedging transactions are taxed at ordinary income rates when the positions are closed and are not subject to the Mark-to-Market Rule. For a discussion of the scope and application of the hedging exemption, see generally Chapter 23. For a discussion of hedgers generally, see section 8.4.

(b) SECTION 988 HEDGING TRANSACTIONS

For taxable years beginning after December 31, 1986, TRA '86 introduced a new type of hedging transaction for foreign currency risks. So-called section 988 hedging transactions are exempt from section 1256 treatment.[2] This means that a taxpayer has some flexibility in identifying transactions as section 988 hedging transactions, which avoids application of 60/40 treatment or the mark-to-market requirement under I.R.C. § 1256. A section 988 hedging transaction is any transaction that meets two requirements. First, the transaction must be identified by the IRS or the taxpayer as being a section 988 hedging transaction. Second, the transaction is entered into by a taxpayer primarily to reduce the risk of currency fluctuations on (1) property held or to be held by the taxpayer, or (2) borrowings made or to be made, or obligations incurred or to be incurred, by the taxpayer.[3] Section 988 treatment applies to hedging transactions regardless of whether a position would otherwise be subject to section 1256 treatment.[4] For a discussion of the scope and application of the section 988 hedging exemption, see generally section 59.3. The hedging exemption for foreign currency-related transactions may not be as critical for taxpayers seeking ordinary treatment on hedging transactions given the recent flexibility provided for section 988 transactions by TMRA '88. For a discussion of these changes, see generally Chapter 59.

---

[2] I.R.C. § 988(d)(1).
[3] I.R.C. § 988(d).
[4] *Id.*

Part Eleven

Tax Consequences of Holding Offsetting Positions (Straddles)

Positions making up a straddle are referred to as "offsetting positions." Several tax rules, which vary depending on the type of property making up the straddle, apply to straddle transactions. This Part Eleven addresses the rules that apply to positions in personal property, defined to include any personal property, including certain positions in stock, of a type that is actively traded.[1] Part Eleven does not deal with a straddle where all of its positions consist of section 1256 contracts, as that term is defined in I.R.C. § 1256(b). Such a straddle is not subject to the rules discussed in Part Eleven.[2] Rather, section 1256 straddles are subject to section 1256 treatment.[3]

In 1981, ERTA introduced the tax regime now in place for offsetting positions.[4] This regime was first applied to commodities and securities other than corporate stock.[5] It was expanded by the DRA in 1984 to include exchange-traded stock options ("listed options") and certain

---

[1] I.R.C. § 1092(d)(1).
[2] I.R.C. §§ 1092(d)(5)(A), 1256(a)(4).
[3] *See generally* Part Ten.
[4] ERTA, Pub. L. No. 97-34, §§ 501–509, 95 Stat. 172, 323–35 (1981).
[5] I.R.C. § 1092(d)(2) (1982), *amended by* Pub. L. No. 98-369, § 101(a)(1), 98 Stat. 494, 616 (1984) [hereinafter DRA].

stock positions.⁶ I.R.C. § 1092, entitled "straddles," embodies the loss deferral rule, which requires deferral of a loss on one position up to the unrecognized gain inherent in an offsetting position.⁷ It also includes the modified wash sales rule that prevents a deduction for the disposition of a position at a loss if the taxpayer has an unrecognized gain in a successor position.⁸ The holding period for a position is suspended under the modified short sales rule during the period a taxpayer holds offsetting positions and positions that are successor positions to the initial offsetting position.⁹ In addition, a taxpayer must capitalize interest and carrying charges allocable to personal property that are part of a straddle.¹⁰ All of these rules—the loss deferral rule, the modified wash sales rule, the modified short sales rule, and the requirement to capitalize interest and carrying charges—are referred to collectively as the Straddle Rules. A taxpayer that does not hold offsetting positions can deduct losses and expenses incurred with respect to personal property, subject to limitations imposed under other tax principles without regard to the Straddle Rules.¹¹

The separate rules that compose the Straddle Rules are summarized below as a brief introduction to the chapters contained in Part Eleven. The key concept underlying the loss deferral rule is that losses incurred with respect to a position in personal property are not deductible if the taxpayer holds an offsetting position in personal property with an inherent unrecognized gain.¹² If the loss deferral rule applies, a taxpayer must defer the losses realized on any position in personal property while he holds the offsetting position.¹³

The Treasury has broad authority to issue regulations to cover offsetting positions that are similar to the wash sales rule in effect for stocks and securities¹⁴ and the short sales rule in effect for the short sales of capital assets.¹⁵ This regulatory authority, expanded by the DRA in 1984, required the Treasury to issue regulations on mixed straddles not later

---

⁶ DRA, *supra* note 5, § 101(a)(1).

⁷ I.R.C. § 1092(a)(1)(B).

⁸ Temporary Treasury regulations provide guidance on coordination of the loss deferral rule and modified wash sales rule.

⁹ Temp. Treas. Reg. § 1.1092(b)-2T(a)(1) (1986).

¹⁰ I.R.C. § 263(g).

¹¹ *See, e.g.*, section 42.1.

¹² I.R.C. § 1092(a)(1)(A).

¹³ I.R.C. § 1092(a)(1)(B).

¹⁴ I.R.C. § 1091.

¹⁵ I.R.C. § 1092(b).

than January 18, 1985.[16] Although regulations were issued to meet this Congressional requirement, and have since been amended, many additional issues remain unresolved and need to be addressed.

The modified wash sales rule prevents a taxpayer from disposing of the loss position of a straddle to obtain a loss deduction while replacing the loss position with a substantially identical position 30 days before or after the disposition.[17] When a taxpayer holds a position that offsets a loss position, any loss incurred on disposing of the loss position cannot be recognized if he replaces it within 30 days with a substantially identical position.[18] Without such a rule, a taxpayer could report a tax loss for positions not covered by the loss deferral rule and protect the unrecognized gain in the open position by remaining in a balanced position.[19] Temporary Treasury regulations expand the loss deferral rule and the modified wash sales rule to "successor positions."[20]

The modified short sales rule suspends the holding period for property that is part of a straddle until the taxpayer disposes of the offsetting positions (and successor positions).[21] It supplements the loss deferral rule by preventing the use of offsetting positions to extend, without risk of loss, the holding period of positions in personal property.[22]

The capitalization requirement, contained in I.R.C. § 263(g), provides that a taxpayer must capitalize "interest and carrying charges" allocable to personal property that is part of a straddle. Interest and carrying charges that must be capitalized while holding offsetting positions include (1) interest expense incurred to purchase or carry property; (2) expenses incurred to store, insure, or transport personal property; and (3) amounts paid or incurred in connection with personal property used in a short sale.[23]

The consequences of holding offsetting positions in personal property, as well as the scope and application of the Straddle Rules, are discussed in this Part Eleven.

---

[16] DRA, *supra* note 5, § 103(b).
[17] I.R.C. § 1091(a).
[18] *Id.*
[19] *See* section 54.3.
[20] Temp. Treas. Reg. § 1.1092(b)-1T(a) (1986).
[21] Temp. Treas. Reg. § 1.1092(b)-2T(a)(1) (1986).
[22] *See* section 54.4.
[23] *See* section 55.2.

Forty-seven

Background on Pre-ERTA Rules

§ 47.1 EXPLANATION OF STRADDLE TRANSACTIONS

The taxation of spreads, referred to as "straddles" for tax purposes, was totally changed in 1981 by the enactment of ERTA and the imposition of the Straddle Rules.[1] These tax changes did not wipe out spread trading because such positions are still established to obtain profits as part of legitimate trading strategies.[2]

From an economic perspective, a taxpayer's gain or loss on a pre-ERTA straddle transaction may have been small in relation to the tax deferral available—or at least asserted by the taxpayer.[3] Transaction costs and margin requirements on futures contracts are low when one looks at the value of the underlying commodity. The amount of margin required to enter into a straddle transaction is based on the price spread between the long and short positions.[4] This is much smaller in absolute value than the margin requirements to establish separate futures contract positions. Furthermore, because the unrealized gain in a profitable position of a straddle approximately equals the unrealized loss in the losing position of the straddle, the taxpayer generally does not need to deposit additional margin or mark-to-market payments to maintain the losing position.

---

[1] For a discussion of the Straddle Rules, see generally Part Eleven.
[2] *See* section 4.3(c). In fact, many spread trading strategies increase—rather than decrease a taxpayer's risk of loss in holding either position by itself.
[3] *See* section 47.2.
[4] For a discussion of futures margin and mark-to-market payments, see section 4.4(b).

Accordingly, significant leverage is available and a taxpayer can lose (or make) a substantial amount of money by opening a futures contract position with a small deposit.

In its simplest form, a taxpayer establishes a straddle by entering into a futures contract obligating him to purchase a fixed amount of a commodity for delivery in a future month (long position) and a futures contract obligating him to sell the same quantity of the identical commodity for delivery, usually in a different month (short position).[5]

To establish a straddle, a taxpayer may, for example, enter into a long futures contract position to purchase wheat for delivery in September and a short futures contract position to sell wheat for delivery in December. Because the long and short positions call for delivery in different calendar months, the positions do not cancel out each other and they are not offset (as in the case of a closing transaction) by the clearing organization affiliated with the commodity exchange on which the wheat futures contracts are traded.[6] As the market price moves up or down, there is a gain in one position and a loss in the other.

Under the pre-ERTA rules in effect before 1981, a taxpayer might have waited until there had been sufficient market movement before closing out the losing position ("lift" the losing "leg" of the straddle) in the current taxable year, hoping to generate a deductible tax loss. After recognizing the loss for tax purposes, the taxpayer might immediately reestablish a straddle in the current taxable year (to protect the "naked" leg of the straddle and "lock in" his gain) by purchasing or selling a new futures contract position for a different delivery month on the same side of the market (either long or short) as the position that had been closed out at a loss (referred to by the IRS as a "switch transaction"). In the next taxable year, the taxpayer liquidated all of the positions in the new straddle (lift both "legs" of the straddle) and recognized a taxable gain approximately equal to the loss reported in the first taxable year.

A common type of tax-motivated straddle is a butterfly straddle, referred to as such because the positions that make up the two spreads of the straddle resemble a butterfly's wings when diagrammed. Basically, a butterfly straddle consists of at least two spreads established as mirror images of each other with the same intermediate delivery date, and involving the purchase and sale of nonoffsetting futures contract positions. For example, a butterfly straddle consists of a long position in a

---

[5] Straddles in options and cash commodities can also be established if a taxpayer acquires long and short positions.

[6] Futures positions for delivery in different calendar months are not viewed as substantially identical property for short sales purposes. *See* section 18.4(e).

near delivery date (e.g., January), a similar long position in a distant delivery date (e.g., November), and two short positions with a delivery date in between the long and short positions (e.g., June).[7] Of course, the positions could be entered into in the reverse order so that the butterfly straddle consists of one near and one distant short position and two long positions with delivery dates in between the delivery dates for the short positions.[8]

Because the two spreads making up the butterfly mirror each other, a butterfly straddle provides some protection against a change in the price of the underlying commodity, irrespective of whether the market price moves up or down. In addition, the positions of the two spreads making up the butterfly provide protection against a change in the price of the positions making up the other spread. Butterfly straddles that mirror each other further reduce the risk of price changes in the underlying commodity.

Example 47-1

Assume that a taxpayer purchases one December Treasury bond contract at 89 (long position), sells two March Treasury bond contracts at 88 16/32 (short position), and buys one June Treasury bond contract at 88 4/32 (long position). Assume further that the taxpayer closes out these positions with the following results. The one short December contract is closed out at 85, the two long March contracts are closed out at 84 28/32, and the one short June contract is closed out at 84 28/32. The taxpayer loses $4000 on the December contract, makes $7250 on the March position, and loses $3250 on the June position. The net profit or loss to the taxpayer was zero.

This butterfly straddle is made up of two separate spread trades. In this example, the taxpayer is long one December and March Treasury bond spread (i.e., long one December Treasury bond futures contract, short one March Treasury bond futures contract) and short one March and June Treasury bond spread (short one March Treasury bond futures contract, long one June Treasury bond futures contract).

In outright long or short positions, gains and losses result from changes in absolute price levels. In spread positions, gains and losses result only from changes in the relative prices of the spread positions, not from absolute price changes. In butterfly positions,

---

[7] This transaction is referred to as "selling a butterfly."
[8] This transaction is referred to as "buying a butterfly."

gains or losses result from changes in the relative prices of the two spreads. In this example, even though the price of the December contract fell four points and the December and March spread went from 16/32 to 4/32, the net value of the position did not change at all.

Example 47-2

A taxpayer enters into a futures contract to buy gold at $340 for delivery in February (i.e., a long position with a near delivery date), buys a gold futures contract at $410 for delivery in October (i.e., a long position with a distant delivery date), and sells two gold futures contracts at $387 for delivery in June (i.e., two short positions with identical intermediate delivery dates).[9] The taxpayer now holds a butterfly straddle consisting of two separate spreads—one spread consists of a long February position and a short June position, while the other spread consists of a long October position and a short June position. Assume that the price of gold increases so that the short positions decline in value and the long positions increase in value. Assume further that the price of gold on December 20 is at $390, $417, and $440 for February, June, and October delivery, respectively. Prior to the enactment of ERTA in 1981, a taxpayer that wished to generate tax losses would close out the short positions for delivery in June on December 20 by buying two June gold contracts at $417, thereby generating a $6000 loss. To lock in the appreciation inherent in the February and October long contracts, the taxpayer would either replace the June position by selling two June contracts at $417 (i.e., a switch) or would "sell around" the June delivery date by selling one April gold contract trading at $405 and an August contract trading at $429.

At the end of the day on December 20, the taxpayer would have two balanced straddles (i.e., short April against long February and short August against long October), which effectively lock in a $6000 gain. He would also have a $6000 short-term capital loss to use against capital gains from other transactions. In the next tax year, the taxpayer liquidates all of the remaining positions in the new

---

[9] Gold futures contracts traded on the COMEX are traded for delivery in February, April, June, August, October, and December.

straddle (lifts the "legs" of the spread) and recognizes a taxable gain approximately equal to the loss incurred in the first tax year.[10]

Spread transactions using futures contract positions thus were used before 1981 under pre-ERTA law to "push" a taxpayer's income forward into the subsequent tax year. Furthermore, if the loss in the first year was on the short position, the loss would be short-term capital loss because gain or loss on closing a short position is short-term.[11] When the gain recognized in the second year was on the long side and the long position had been held for more than six months (half as long as the then current holding period to receive long-term capital gain for other capital assets), the taxpayer would have converted short-term capital gain into long-term capital gain.[12] If the loss was on the long position, it was short-term or long-term capital loss, depending on whether the long position had been held for more than six months.[13]

Certain other tax straddle transactions (such as spreads using actual Treasury bills and Treasury bill futures contracts) were also used to convert ordinary income into short-term capital gain, and taxpayers would enter into futures contract spreads to convert the short-term capital gain generated on the initial spread transactions into long-term capital gain.[14]

§ 47.2 TAX RULES IN EFFECT FOR PRE-ERTA TRANSACTIONS

Prior to the enactment of ERTA in 1981, public attention focused on the taxation of commodity transactions because a number of gaps in the Code allowed taxpayers to receive—or at least to attempt to claim—certain tax advantages using commodity and government security transactions. Congress was concerned with the growing perception that "it was possible—indeed, perhaps legitimate—to pay no tax at ordinary income

---

[10] For an example of the economic and tax consequences of holding a butterfly straddle, see *Commodity Tax Straddles: Hearing on S. 626 Before the Subcomm. on Taxation and Debt Management and the Subcomm. on Energy and Agricultural Taxation of the Senate Comm. on Finance*, 97th Cong., 1st Sess. 33–35 (1981).

[11] *See* I.R.C. § 1233(b).

[12] I.R.C. § 1222(3). Futures contracts under pre-ERTA law had a more than six-month holding period to obtain long-term capital gain.

[13] I.R.C. §§ 1222(2), (4).

[14] *See* section 47.2.

rates."[15] Revelations about the substantial tax revenues lost by the use of futures contract straddles (and other commodity-related transactions) ultimately resulted in enactment of ERTA's commodity provisions.[16] In addition, Congress believed that the revenue loss to the government might grow substantially and that widespread tax sheltering activities were threatening to disrupt the commodity markets.[17] Congress was prepared to change the law even though it acknowledged that the "commodity futures markets play an important role in the economy" and that the "efficiency of these markets be preserved and the liquidity of these markets maintained."[18]

To understand the tax framework for commodity transactions, it is useful to consider the tax rules in effect prior to enactment of ERTA in 1981—many of which continue to apply in certain circumstances. Before ERTA, gains and losses from commodity transactions were generally treated in the same manner as all other gains and losses from the sale of capital assets. This was the case for traders and investors alike.[19] The exceptions to capital asset treatment were for dealers in physical commodities that derived ordinary income with respect to their inventory transactions,[20] and hedgers that received ordinary income treatment with respect to their hedging transactions.[21] As capital assets, physical commodities were subject to the customary holding period of more than one year to qualify for long-term capital gain or loss treatment. Commodity futures contracts had a shortened holding period of more than six months to receive long-term capital treatment.[22] Physical commodities

---

[15] STAFF OF THE JOINT COMM. ON TAXATION, 97TH CONG., 1ST SESS., GENERAL EXPLANATION OF ECONOMIC RECOVERY TAX ACT OF 1981, at 282 (Joint Comm. Print 1981) [hereinafter General Explanation of ERTA]; FINANCE COMM. REPORT, ECONOMIC RECOVERY TAX ACT OF 1981, S. REP. NO. 144, 97th Cong., 1st Sess. 146, *reprinted in* 1981 U.S. CODE CONG. & ADMIN. NEWS 105, 246 [hereinafter S. REP. NO. 144].

[16] The General Explanation of ERTA stated that enactment of the tax straddle provisions would increase fiscal year budget receipts by an estimated $37 million in 1981, $623 million in 1982, $327 million in 1983, and $273 million in 1984. General Explanation of ERTA, *supra* note 15, at 315.

[17] *See id.* at 282–83; S. REP. NO. 144, *supra* note 15, at 146–47.

[18] General Explanation of ERTA, *supra* note 15, at 283; S. REP. NO. 144, *supra* note 15, at 146.

[19] *See* sections 8.1 and 8.2.

[20] *See* section 8.3.

[21] *See* section 8.4.

[22] I.R.C. § 1222 (1977), *amended by* Pub. L. No. 98-369, § 1001(a), 98 Stat. 494, 1011 (1984) [hereinafter DRA]. In 1984, the DRA reduced to six months the long-term holding period for assets acquired after June 22, 1984, and before January 1, 1988.

and futures contracts held for less than their respective long-term holding periods generated short-term capital gain or loss.[23]

Neither the wash sales rule of I.R.C. § 1091 (disallowing losses on the disposition of stocks and securities if a taxpayer acquires substantially identical property within 30 days before or after the disposition),[24] nor the short sales rule of I.R.C. § 1233 (preventing conversion of short-term capital gain to long-term capital gain or long-term capital loss to short-term capital loss)[25] applies to futures contracts with different delivery months. In addition, the IRS ruled in 1971 that the wash sales rule of I.R.C. § 1091 did not apply to futures contracts.[26] This was confirmed in *Smith v. Comm'r*,[27] when the Tax Court held that neither the statutory wash sales rule of I.R.C. § 1091 nor a nonstatutory wash sales rule applies to straddles of futures contracts. Furthermore, prior judicial decisions had supported the view that the sale of one futures contract position in a straddle is a closed and completed transaction, even though the taxpayer simultaneously purchases a similar futures contract position with a different delivery date.[28]

The IRS attack on pre-ERTA commodity straddle transactions was widespread. The first published attempt by the IRS to disallow losses claimed by taxpayers arising from straddle losses was in 1977 with Rev. Rul. 77-185.[29] The first court case to address the deductibility of straddle losses under pre-ERTA law was *Smith v. Comm'r*.[30] Since the *Smith* decision, a legislative solution was enacted in 1984 as section 108 of the DRA ("Section 108"), which was subsequently amended and which basically limited the arguments that the IRS could advance to deny straddle losses to the issue of whether the taxpayer had a profit motive sufficient to allow a loss deduction. Several judicial decisions interpret the scope of Section 108.

The remainder of this chapter discusses Rev. Rul. 77-185, Section 108, and judicial decisions concerning pre-ERTA straddles. Because stock options and certain stock positions are subject to the Straddle Rules—

---

[23] These general tax rules continue to be applicable, subject to the modifications discussed in the remainder of this Part Eleven.

[24] *See generally* Chapter 19.

[25] *See generally* Chapter 18.

[26] Rev. Rul. 71-568, 1971-2 C.B. 312.

[27] 78 T.C. 350, 385–86, 388 (1982), *aff'd without op.* 820 F.2d 1220 (4th Cir. 1987).

[28] *See* Valley Waste Mills v. Page, 115 F.2d 466, 468 (5th Cir. 1940), *aff'g* 40-1 U.S. Tax Cas. (CCH) ¶ 9382 (M.D. Ga. 1940), *cert. denied*, 312 U.S. 68 (1941); Harriss v. Comm'r, 143 F.2d 279, 282 (2d Cir. 1944), *aff'g* 44 B.T.A. 999 (1941), *acq.* 1941-2 C.B. 6.

[29] 1977-1 C.B. 48, *amplified by* Rev. Rul. 78-414, 1978-2 C.B. 213; *see* section 47.2(a).

[30] 78 T.C. at 350.

but are not afforded the protection of Section 108—many of the arguments that were advanced by the IRS for commodity transactions that are now covered by Section 108 remain important for taxpayers that entered into pre-DRA option and stock spread positions.[31]

(a) REVENUE RULING 77-185

In Rev. Rul. 77-185,[32] the IRS denied a deduction for certain straddle losses in silver futures contracts and out-of-pocket expenses on the grounds that the taxpayer had no reasonable expectation of deriving an economic profit from the transactions.[33] Although not relying on any specific Code provisions, the IRS ruled that straddle transactions were shams without economic substance and were not completed and closed out until the year in which the last straddle position was closed out. The IRS's rationale for not allowing a short-term capital loss on closing out the losing position of the straddle in the first year was that a taxpayer that reestablished a similar position with a different delivery date had not really changed his position in a true economic sense. The IRS further ruled that a lack of profit motive precluded a deduction for out-of-pocket expenses incurred to close out the straddle in the second year.[34] Rev. Rul. 77-185, which has been the subject of both controversy and litigation, ignored court cases that supported the view that the sale of one futures contract position in a straddle was a closed and completed transaction even though a similar futures contract position with a different delivery date was simultaneously purchased.[35] Rev. Rul. 77-185 has also been cited by the IRS to deny deductions for pre-DRA option straddles.

(b) *SMITH V. COMM'R*

The first case to address the issue of the deductibility of pre-ERTA commodity straddle losses was *Smith v. Comm'r*.[36] In *Smith*, the Tax Court accepted the legitimacy of commodity straddle transactions. Under the particular facts before it, however, the Tax Court denied the

---

[31] For a discussion of option and stock spread transactions before enactment of the DRA in 1984, see section 30.2.
[32] 1977-1 C.B. 48, *amplified by* Rev. Rul. 78-414, 1978-2 C.B. 213.
[33] The IRS ruled in Rev. Rul. 78-414, 1978-2 C.B. 213, that the positions it advanced in Rev. Rul. 77-185, 1977-1 C.B. 48, apply to straddle transactions in Treasury bills.
[34] *See* I.R.C. § 165(c).
[35] *E.g., Valley Waste Mills*, 115 F.2d at 468; *Harriss*, 143 F.2d at 282.
[36] 78 T.C. 350 (1982), *aff'd without op.* 820 F.2d 1220 (4th Cir. 1987).

straddle losses because the straddles were not entered into for profit within the meaning of I.R.C. § 165(c)(2). The *Smith* victory was somewhat hollow for the government because of the need to establish a lack of profit motive on a case-by-case basis (motive being a matter of subjective expectation). The Tax Court found that the four elements necessary to recognize capital losses under I.R.C. § 165 were present in a commodity straddle. First, property was acquired by the taxpayer. Second, a closed and completed transaction, fixed by identifiable events, occurred in the taxable year in which the taxpayer claimed the capital loss. Third, the taxpayer had a tax basis in the property. And fourth, the amount realized by the closing transaction was ascertainable. Therefore, the elements necessary to claim a capital loss were present in closing one leg of a commodity straddle position.[37]

In analyzing commodity straddles generally, the Tax Court held that the transactions were neither shams nor devoid of economic substance.[38] The Tax Court based its determination, in part, on the fact that futures contracts are binding on the parties to the contracts under the rules of the applicable commodity exchange, and impose substantial rights and obligations with respect to the underlying commodities on the parties to the contracts.[39] In addition, the Tax Court held that a futures contract straddle could not be treated as a single indivisible unit for tax purposes.[40] In so holding, the court concluded that the separate long and short positions must be treated as independent positions and, as such, disposition of either position of the straddle constitutes a closed and completed transaction. As a matter of law, the wash sales rule of I.R.C. § 1091 does not apply to futures contracts.[41] Moreover, neither a nonstatutory wash sales rule nor the step transaction doctrine could be applied to disallow losses arising from futures contract straddle transactions.[42]

With respect to profit motive, the Tax Court held that as long as a taxpayer had a nontax profit motive for his commodity futures transactions, he was entitled to recognize losses even if there was a strong tax avoidance purpose for the transactions.[43] A taxpayer with a profit motive

---

[37] 78 T.C. at 371–83.

[38] The Tax Court did not accept the market values assigned to the straddle positions because the values were assigned to the positions after the trade was executed. Hence, the Tax Court readjusted the amount of losses to reflect the settlement prices for the positions on the days the positions were closed out. *Id.* at 384 n.26.

[39] *Id.* at 385.

[40] *Id.* at 376.

[41] *See generally* Chapter 19.

[42] 78 T.C. at 388.

[43] *Id.* at 391. *But see* Fox v. Comm'r, 82 T.C. 1001 (1984).

could recognize a loss under I.R.C. § 165. He must only have had a bona fide expectation of a profit and his expectation need not be reasonable.[44]

The Tax Court only addressed the taxation of the commodity futures transactions occurring in the first taxable year of the straddle and did not consider whether the gain recognized in the second taxable year on closing the straddle was taxable in that year. Therefore, in an attempt to force the Tax Court to modify its decision, the IRS filed a motion for reconsideration of *Smith*, advising the Tax Court that unless the court changed its decision, the IRS "intend[ed] . . . to follow the logical consequences of the . . . opinion and seek the disallowance of the tax straddle losses, coupled with the recognition of tax straddle gains."[45] Such a result—if supported by the courts—would have placed a taxpayer in the worst possible position: straddle losses would be denied in the first taxable year and straddle gains would be recognized in the second taxable year. The IRS further stated that it would continue to litigate straddle cases based on the analysis of Rev. Rul. 77-185, where "[l]osses and gains are netted at the termination of the tax straddle [with] the losses essentially cancel[ing] out the gains."[46] On April 8, 1982, the Tax Court denied the IRS motion, thus rejecting by implication the IRS interpretation of *Smith*, but leaving open the possible disallowances of straddle losses in one year without requiring offset of those losses with gains generated in subsequent years. This argument has been precluded by Section 108 for positions subject to its coverage.[47]

(c) LEGISLATIVE, JUDICIAL, AND ADMINISTRATIVE SOLUTIONS FOR CERTAIN PRE-ERTA STRADDLES

After *Smith*,[48] the IRS continued to challenge deductions for pre-ERTA straddle losses. A major reason the IRS continued its attack appears to be that Congress, in enacting the commodity provisions of ERTA, did not take a position on whether Rev. Rul. 77-185 was a correct interpretation of pre-ERTA law.[49] The Tax Court in *Smith* specifically stated its belief that the ERTA changes in 1981 did not affect the pre-ERTA case before it

---

[44] 78 T.C. at 391.
[45] IRS Motion for Reconsideration, ¶ 6(c), Smith v. Comm'r, 78 T.C. 350 (1982).
[46] *Id.*
[47] *See* section 47.2(c).
[48] 78 T.C. at 350.
[49] *See* General Explanation of ERTA, *supra* note 15, at 279, 281–83; SENATE CONFERENCE REPORT, ECONOMIC RECOVERY TAX ACT OF 1981, S. CONF. REP. NO. 176, 97th Cong., 1st Sess. 258 (1981); S. REP. NO. 144, *supra* note 15, at 145–47.

and that Congress did not intend to influence the resolution of the issues in that case.[50] In 1982, however, Senators Dole, Moynihan, Percy, and Dixon acknowledged that "there were straddles that appeared to have been legitimate for tax purposes" and urged adoption of Treasury regulations that did not penalize taxpayers who "rolled" income.[51]

The commodities industry actively lobbied for a legislative solution to the audit issues raised by the IRS on pre-ERTA straddles. As a result, Section 108, as enacted as part of the DRA, in effect codified the Tax Court's decision in *Smith*, thereby limiting the ability of the IRS to challenge straddle losses predating the effective date of ERTA for certain straddles other than straddles in stock or stock options.[52] Section 108 was enacted to provide "certainty" as to the tax treatment of commodity straddles entered into by taxpayers prior to the effective date of ERTA.[53]

Taxation of pre-ERTA commodity straddles has shifted in favor of and against taxpayers several times since commodity straddles were outlawed in 1981. In 1984, during early discussions about the tax changes leading up to the DRA changes, Congress expressed concern over the mounting backlog of pre-ERTA commodity straddle cases. Congress responded by enacting Section 108, which, as originally enacted in 1984, provided a new, more lenient definition of the profit motive standard necessary for a taxpayer to prove his intent for entering into commodity straddle transactions. The new profit motive standard was that there had to be "a reasonable prospect of any profit from the transaction." Under Section 108, as enacted as part of the DRA, commodity dealers and persons regularly engaged in investing in futures contracts were pro-

---

[50] Throughout the consideration of [ERTA], constant reference was made to the fact that the Internal Revenue Service disputed the tax benefits claimed by pre-1981 tax straddles. . . . Tax benefits from pre-1981 tax straddles were referred to only as "allegedly available" in the Senate Finance Committee Report. . . . In committee prints prepared by the Joint Committee on Taxation to explain the proposed Senate and House versions of the new tax straddle legislation, specific references were made to the instant cases, both by name and Tax Court docket number. . . . Rarely can a court be as certain as we are here that the provisions of a new law were not to affect the case before it.

78 T.C. at 394–95 (citations omitted).

[51] *See* Letter from Senator Bob Dole to Roscoe Egger, Jr., Director of the IRS (June 23, 1982); Letter from Senator Daniel Patrick Moynihan to Roscoe Egger, Jr., Director of the IRS (Apr. 29, 1982); Letter from Senators Charles H. Percy and Alan J. Dixon to Roscoe Egger, Jr., Director of the IRS (Mar. 15, 1982). It is interesting to note that both Senators Moynihan and Dole were actively involved in the enactment of the commodity provisions of ERTA.

[52] DRA, *supra* note 22, § 108.

[53] ERTA's effective date is generally June 23, 1981. January 1, 1981 is the effective date of ERTA for those taxpayers that elected retroactive treatment back to the beginning of 1981. ERTA, Pub. L. No. 97-34, § 509(a)(1), 95 Stat. 172, 333–34 (1981).

vided with a rebuttable presumption of the requisite profit motive. "Commodity dealers" were defined as individuals who, before 1982, were actively engaged in trading section 1256 contracts and were registered with a domestic board of trade. "Persons regularly engaged in investing in regulated futures contracts" were not specifically defined.

Under Section 108, the IRS could not advance the arguments it had advanced in Rev. Rul. 77-185,[54] Rev. Rul. 78-414,[55] or *Smith*[56] to deny straddle losses. Rather, the IRS could attempt to deny pre-ERTA commodity straddle losses if—and only if—the taxpayer did not have a profit motive for entering into the transaction. Under Section 108, losses incurred through the disposition of pre-ERTA commodity straddle positions can generally be deducted in the year the loss positions were disposed of if the straddle was entered into for a profit.[57] The Conference Committee Report of DRA stated that the profit motive requirement is satisfied "if there is a reasonable prospect of any profit from the transaction."[58] Because of TRA '86[59] changes that follow the House Bill, the profit motive standard was made more stringent than the original standard of a "reasonable prospect of any profit from the transaction."[60]

In *Fox v. Comm'r*,[61] the Tax Court disallowed the taxpayer's straddle losses from Treasury bill option straddles because a profit motive was not the taxpayer's *primary* motive for entering into the transaction. If applied to pre-ERTA commodity straddle transactions, a primary motive standard could be difficult to satisfy. Section 108, as originally enacted, and the accompanying legislative history appeared to make the *Fox* standard inapplicable to pre-ERTA commodity straddles.[62] The *Fox* standard, however, applies pre-ERTA commodity straddles after the TRA '86 amendment of Section 108, as well as to straddles in stock options and stock positions specifically not covered by Section 108. *See* section 30.2.

Section 108, as originally enacted as part of DRA, also provided that if a straddle was not entered into for profit, the loss could not be deducted in the year the loss position was disposed of, although the loss could be used

---

[54] 1977-1 C.B. 48.
[55] 1978-2 C.B. 213.
[56] 78 T.C. at 350.
[57] For a discussion of the profit motive standard, see sections 47.2(d) and 47.2(e).
[58] HOUSE CONFERENCE REPORT, DEFICIT REDUCTION ACT OF 1984, H.R. CONF. REP. NO. 861, 98th Cong., 2d Sess. 917 (1984) [hereinafter H.R. CONF. REP. NO. 861].
[59] Pub. L. No. 99-514, 100 Stat. 2085 (1986) [hereinafter TRA '86].
[60] *See infra* text beginning at note 69.
[61] 82 T.C. at 1023.
[62] *See* section 47.2(d).

to offset the gain realized on closing the straddle.[63] Thus, the taxpayer could ultimately net the losses against the gains from a straddle not entered into for profit, with the loss deferred until the year when the gain was recognized.[64]

Section 108, as originally enacted by the DRA, established a rebuttable presumption of profit motive for pre-ERTA straddles if the taxpayer was (1) a commodities dealer, defined as a person actively engaged in trading futures contracts and who is registered with a commodity exchange, or (2) any other person regularly engaged in investing in futures contracts.[65] Taxpayers eligible for the presumption are collectively referred to as "professional traders." To qualify for the presumption of profit motive available to professional traders, a pre-ERTA commodity straddle must meet two requirements. First, there must be a reasonable possibility of profit.[66] A significant factor in determining profit motive is the amount of transaction costs.[67] Second, a professional trader that entered into the pre-ERTA straddle cannot be a syndicate, defined as any partnership or S corporation where more than 35 percent of the losses were allocated to limited partners or shareholders that did not actively participate in the management of the business.[68] If either of these requirements is not met, the profit motive presumption is not available to a professional trader. For professional traders eligible for the presumption, Section 108 shifts the burden of proof to the IRS to establish that there was no profit motive. Other taxpayers for whom the profit motive presumption does not apply must prove they entered into pre-ERTA commodity straddle transactions for profit.

After enactment of Section 108, the IRS continued to challenge the deductibility of losses from pre-ERTA straddles for the open audits and docketed court cases, including cases against professional traders eligible for the profit motive presumption. Also, because exchange-traded stock options were not covered by Section 108, the IRS continued to challenge straddle losses involving pre-DRA stock options.

In addition, the Treasury responded to Section 108 by issuing temporary regulations to require a profit motive standard more stringent than

---

[63] DRA, *supra* note 22, § 108(c).

[64] Section 108 precludes the IRS assertion, made in its motion for reconsideration in *Smith*, that straddle losses can be denied while straddle gains in a subsequent tax year are recognized. *See* section 47.2(b). *See supra* text accompanying note 45.

[65] DRA, *supra* note 22, § 108(b).

[66] H.R. CONF. REP. NO. 861, *supra* note 58, at 917.

[67] *Id.*

[68] DRA, *supra* note 22, § 108(h).

"a reasonable prospect of any profit from the transaction." Under the temporary regulations, a taxpayer was required to prove that his *primary motive* for entering into commodity straddles was an economic profit. The temporary regulations also attempted to restrict the availability of the presumption for commodity dealers to transactions in those futures contracts that were the subject of the dealer's regular trading activity.[69]

In 1985, the Tax Court decided *Miller v. Comm'r*, where it held that the test to be applied under Section 108 is "whether there is reasonable prospect of a profit from the transaction."[70] In 1986, the Tax Court reaffirmed its position in *Miller* in the context of a commodity floor trader's straddle transactions.[71]

In 1988, the Tenth Circuit Court of Appeals reversed the *Miller* case, holding that taxpayers could not deduct short-term capital losses from pre-ERTA commodity straddles because tax avoidance was the dominant purpose for the transactions.[72] The Court found that before a taxpayer could deduct straddle losses under Section 108—as originally enacted—the taxpayer "must prove that his primary motive for entering into a straddle transaction was one of economic profit."[73] For a detailed discussion of *Miller*, see section 47.2(d).

While the IRS waged war on commodity straddles in the courts after enactment of Section 108 in 1984, the commodity industry sought new legislative solutions for pre-ERTA straddles. In 1986, TRA '86 amended Section 108 to make it less favorable to investors and more favorable to commodity dealers. Congress also instructed the IRS to bring all pending pre-ERTA straddle cases to a "speedy resolution."[74] The amendment to Section 108 effected by TRA '86 originated in the House of Representatives and was adopted verbatim by the Conference Committee. The House Report states "it was not the intention of Congress in enacting Section 108 to change the profit motive standard of section 165(c)(2) or to enact a new profit motive standard."[75] The House Report also states that "a taxpayer who does not satisfy the indicia of trade or business status, such

---

[69] Temp. Treas. Reg. § 1.165-13T (1984).

[70] 84 T.C. 827 (1985), *rev'd*, 836 F.2d 1274 (10th Cir. 1988); *see* section 47.2(d).

[71] Perlin v. Comm'r, 86 T.C. 388 (1986).

[72] 836 F.2d 1274 (10th Cir. 1988), *rev'g* 84 T.C. 827 (1985).

[73] 836 F.2d at 1287.

[74] STAFF OF THE JOINT COMM. ON TAXATION, 99TH CONG., 2D SESS., TAX REFORM BILL OF 1986, FINAL CONFERENCE. COMM. DECISIONS II-845 (Joint Comm. Print 1986) [hereinafter TRA '86 Conf. Rep.].

[75] HOUSE WAYS AND MEANS COMM. REPORT, H.R. REP. NO. 426, 99th Cong., 1st Sess. 911 (1985) [hereinafter H.R. REP. NO. 426].

as the taxpayer in *Miller v. Comm'r*, [citation omitted][76] would not be considered in the trade or business of trading commodities."[77] The Conference Committee Report accompanying TRA '86 states that "the Conference agreement follows the House bill," but it makes no reference to any profit motive standard. The statement of managers discusses various aspects of the classification of commodities dealers, but it does not deal with investors.[78]

In a colloquy on the Senate floor between Senators Dole and Packwood following the Conference Committee's action, Senator Packwood concurred in a statement made by Senator Dole that "I understand that the Conference Report does not amend the provisions of the 1984 Act as they affect investors and that the Conferees rejected any additional benefit for those investors."[79] Senator Dole also stated that "a further understanding of the statement of managers explaining the Conference Report did not include the language of the House Report that discussed investors and the Conference Report is the entire agreement of the Conferees." Senator Packwood's concurrence with this statement is also included in this colloquy. In a floor statement on October 2, 1986, House Ways and Means Committee Chairman Dan Rostenkowski stated that "as I indicated in my opening remarks to the House on September 25, 1986, I feel that a floor colloquy interpreting a provision of a Conference Report can only be considered valid by taxpayers and appropriate government officials at the Treasury Department and IRS if it appears in substantially the same form in both the House and Senate." Chairman Rostenkowski went on to say that Senator Dole's colloquy with Senator Packwood regarding the treatment of investors in pre-ERTA commodity straddles did not reflect the House's interpretation of the Conference agreement.[80] Therefore, it is entirely unclear from the legislative actions whether the TRA '86 amendment to Section 108 overrules *Miller* as to the profit motive standard to which investors are subject. Under TRA '86, commodity dealers must simply prove that they are engaged in a trade or business and that the loss was incurred in this trade or business.[81] The rebuttable presumption of profit motive for commodity dealers has been eliminated. Losses of a "commodity dealer" are *automatically* treated as having been incurred in

---

[76] 84 T.C. 827 (1985), *rev'd*, 836 F.2d 1274 (10th Cir. 1988).
[77] H.R. REP. NO. 426, *supra* note 75, at 911.
[78] TRA '86 Conf. Rep., *supra* note 74, at II-845.
[79] 132 CONG. REC. S13,956 (daily ed. Sept. 27, 1986) (statement of Sen. Dole).
[80] 132 CONG. REC. E3389 (daily ed. Oct. 2, 1986) (statement of Chairman Rostenkowski).
[81] TRA '86, *supra* note 59, § 1808(d).

a trade or business.[82] A commodity dealer is defined to include *any* person owning a seat on a contract market.[83] The definition of a commodities dealer was also expanded to cover certain members of a dealer's family to the extent they engaged in commodities trading through an organization consisting only of dealers and their families.

What does the TRA '86 provision mean for pending pre-ERTA commodity straddle cases? With respect to investors, they do not have much (except the Senate floor colloquy) to hang their hats on. *In Glass v. Comm'r*,[84] the Tax Court tested the transactions generating the losses alone (not the overall investment) to determine whether a taxpayer had the requisite profit motive.

On April 16, 1987, the IRS announced a special procedure to provide taxpayers an opportunity to settle pre-ERTA commodities straddles cases as well as other long-standing tax shelter cases.[85]

In two news releases, the IRS stated that its settlement offer, which affected 75,000 taxpayers with pending commodities cases and audits, would apply to those taxpayers that choose to settle. Those taxpayers that do not choose to settle could take their cases to the IRS Appeals Division, or to court. In the releases, the IRS emphasized that the offers would not get better unless there were significant new factual or legal developments.

The IRS announced it would concede losses claimed by dealers on trades entered into on regulated commodity exchanges because of Section 108, while dealers in off-the-market transactions would be offered settlements.

The IRS also announced it would settle trades made by investors that engaged in transactions on a regulated exchange by allowing approximately 30 percent of the claimed loss. It would settle trades made by investors in off-the-market cases that were not designated as "tax shelter projects" by allowing approximately 20 percent of the loss.

Settlements for litigation projects (made up of tax shelters identified by common issues of fact and law and organized by a single promoter or group of promoters and including one or more tax shelters) would be based on the merits of the individual litigation projects.

---

[82] I.R.C. § 108(b), *as amended by* TRA '86, *supra* note 59, § 1808(d).

[83] I.R.C. § 108(f), *as amended by* TRA '86, *supra* note 59, § 1808(d); TRA '86 Conf. Rep., *supra* note 74, at II-845.

[84] 87 T.C. 1087 (1986), *aff'd sub nom.* Herrington v. Comm'r, 854 F.2d 755 (5th Cir. 1988), *and aff'd sub nom.* Yosha v. Comm'r, 861 F.2d 494 (7th Cir. 1988), *cert. denied*, 1989 U.S. LEXIS 2370.

[85] IR-87-56, 10 Stand. Fed. Tax Rep. (CCH) ¶ 6454 (Apr. 16, 1987); IR-87-57, 10 Stand. Fed. Tax Rep. (CCH) ¶ 6455 (Apr. 16, 1987).

In IR-87-57, the IRS announced that in most instances it would not assert penalties as part of the settlements but it would generally assert additional interest because a straddle, by definition, is a "tax-motivated transaction." Where gains from straddles entered into before June 23, 1981, are reported in years after 1981, the IRS announced it would make necessary adjustments for the commodities issue in all years.

(d) MILLER V. COMM'R

The Tax Court decision in *Miller v. Comm'r*,[86] and its subsequent reversal on appeal, illustrate the confusion and controversy that surrounded enactment of Section 108 in 1984. The remainder of this section addresses both the Tax Court decision and the Tenth Circuit decision in great detail.

(1) TAX COURT DECISION

On May 13, 1985, the Tax Court issued the first decision interpreting Section 108.[87] In *Miller v. Comm'r*,[88] the Tax Court held that the taxpayer's commodity straddle losses were deductible pursuant to the provisions of Section 108. The court made clear that in the absence of Section 108, however, it would have denied the deductions because the taxpayer lacked the otherwise necessary profit motive.[89]

The taxpayer opened a commodity trading account in 1974 and traded commodities through 1983. During the period 1975 through 1983, the taxpayer entered into 158 commodity futures trades for his own account. Of these transactions, 114 were outright positions and 44 were straddles. Of the 44 straddles, only four gold futures contract transactions involved "switches," defined by the court as closing out the loss leg to realize a tax loss and reestablishing a similar position in a different delivery month. Three of these switches were challenged by the IRS and were at issue in the case.

The taxpayer's switches, unlike his other trades, were done in consultation with his broker's "Tax Straddle Department." The court noted that

---

[86] 84 T.C. 827 (1985), *rev'd*, 836 F.2d 1274 (10th Cir. 1988).

[87] *See* section 47.2(c). *See also supra* text beginning at note 69.

[88] 84 T.C. 827, 846 (1985), *rev'd*, 836 F.2d 1274 (10th Cir. 1988).

[89] The *Miller* case was decided by the full Tax Court, 10 judges voting with the majority and eight judges dissenting. TRA '86 basically reversed *Miller* and made clear that by enacting Section 108, Congress did not intend to change the standard for a profit motive sufficient to justify a tax deduction; that is (at least for customers), the standard in *Fox*, not that in *Miller*, is the law. The difference between the "primarily for profit" and the "reasonable expectation of any profit" standards could be significant.

these trades were contrary to the taxpayer's customary trading practices. Hence, but for Section 108, the losses would have been denied under the prior straddles cases—*Smith v. Comm'r,*[90] and *Fox v. Comm'r,*[91]—because the transactions were not entered into primarily to make a profit. According to the Conference Committee Report that accompanied DRA, however, Section 108 allows the deduction of losses "if there is a reasonable prospect of any profit from the transaction."[92] Therefore, the court was asked to decide whether, in transactions governed by Section 108, the taxpayer must establish that his straddle was entered into primarily for profit (applying the *Smith* and *Fox* standards) or whether he can prevail if he can show merely a reasonable prospect of any profit from the transaction.

The IRS attempted to disallow the taxpayer's deductions on two principal grounds. First, under the temporary Treasury regulations issued shortly after enactment of Section 108—which reflected the *Smith* and *Fox* "primarily for profit" standards—the taxpayer lacked the requisite profit motive. Second, the taxpayer's straddles did not have economic substance.[93] Under the temporary Treasury regulations, a pre-ERTA commodity straddle transaction was considered to have been entered into for profit only if it satisfied the requirements of I.R.C. § 165(c)(2).[94] In *Fox*, the Tax Court held that I.R.C. § 165(c)(2) is not satisfied unless the *primary* motive behind the transaction is to realize an economic profit.[95] The Tax Court in *Miller* held that Section 108 does not require satisfaction of the I.R.C. § 165(c)(2) standard and that the temporary Treasury regulations were invalid insofar as they required the taxpayer to establish anything beyond "a reasonable prospect of any profit" from the transaction.[96] The court simply concluded that Section 108 precluded the IRS's "economic substance" argument.[97]

Given the Tax Court's interpretation of Section 108, the only issue remaining in *Miller* was whether the taxpayer actually had a reasonable prospect of any profit from the "switches." The Tax Court found that, although relatively remote, there was indeed a possibility that the taxpayer's gold straddles—even as modified by the switches—could have

---

[90] 78 T.C. at 350.
[91] 82 T.C. at 1001.
[92] H.R. Conf. Rep. No. 861, *supra* note 58, at 917.
[93] *See* Temp. Treas. Reg. § 1.165-13T (1984).
[94] Temp. Treas. Reg. § 1.165-13T (A-2) (1984).
[95] 82 T.C. at 1021.
[96] 84 T.C. at 842.
[97] *Id.* at 845.

resulted in an economic profit. As a result, the court found it was bound by the intent of Congress, as reflected in Section 108 and the Conference Committee Report, to decide the case in favor of the taxpayer.[98]

The court in *Miller* did not make clear whether it viewed the taxpayer as a professional trader entitled to the presumption of profit motivation. There are two possible explanations for this. First, it may be that the court found that both the taxpayer and the government had offered sufficient evidence to establish their positions and, thus, each had met any burden of proof that the presumption (or its absence) would have assigned to either position. Second, some of the dissenting judges found that the majority opinion rendered the presumption useless. Practically all taxpayers that entered into pre-ERTA straddles—whether professional traders or not—can establish the minimal profit motive standard required by the majority's opinion.[99] Whatever the reason for the lack of attention paid by the court to the taxpayer's possible status as a professional trader, it is clear that the presumption of profit motive in Section 108 may turn out to be less important in the resolution of straddle cases than many commentators had previously assumed.

Obviously, for pre-ERTA commodity straddle cases, the Tax Court decision in *Miller* appeared enormously important. Indeed, taxpayers under audit or with pending litigation involving straddle deductions taken before 1982 took great comfort from the Tax Court's decision in *Miller*. After the Tax Court's decision, several issues became clear. First, Section 108 does not apply to straddles involving stock options. Therefore, *Miller* did not affect the IRS's ability to disallow stock option losses that do not satisfy the requirements in *Smith* and *Fox*. Indeed, the *Fox* case has been reaffirmed for non-Section 108 cases by the *Miller* decision, and the "primarily for profit" test appears to be the standard that must be met in non-Section 108 situations.

Second, it remained unclear just how far Section 108 extended beyond futures contracts. For example, does Section 108 apply to forward contracts, options on government securities, or actual government securities? The *Miller* decision did not provide any guidance with respect to these issues.

Third, the IRS could succeed in challenging loss deductions for pre-ERTA commodity straddles if the taxpayer did not have any profit motive. There must be some prospect for an economic gain over the cash investment and transaction costs if the deductions are to stand up.

---

[98] *Id.* at 846.

[99] *Id.* at 855 (Simpson, J., dissenting).

Fourth, the significance of the professional trader's presumption remained unclear after *Miller*. Regardless of whether the IRS or the taxpayer has the burden of proof, the taxpayer, as a practical matter, has to show that there was at least some possibility of profit from the transaction.

Fifth, to survive an IRS challenge, pre-ERTA straddles subject to Section 108 must have been properly established by the taxpayer and cannot be shams, fakes, or fictitious trades. All transactions must also have been properly priced. Section 108 is not applied if the transactions did not take place as reported.

(2) THE TENTH CIRCUIT DECISION

The Tenth Circuit reversed the Tax Court decision in *Miller* on January 11, 1988.[100] On appeal, the Court found that before a taxpayer could deduct straddle losses under Section 108 as originally enacted, he "must prove that his primary motive for entering into a straddle transaction was one of economic profit."[101] The Tenth Circuit found the legislative history on Section 108 in error as a matter of law,[102] refusing to view the reference in Section 108 to "transactions entered into for profit" as ambiguous enough to require reference to the DRA legislative history.

The Tenth Circuit looked at prior case law interpreting the profit motive requirement. In the past, the Tax Court disallowed tax straddle losses not connected with a trade or business because such losses were not incurred in transactions entered into for profit.[103] Case law for 50 years sustained the profit motive requirement.[104]

The Tenth Circuit found that the Tax Court in *Miller* would have disallowed the losses had it not found an interpretative problem in Section 108.[105] The Tax Court found Section 108 to be ambiguous and had used the legislative history to interpret the words "if such a position is part of a transaction entered into for profit."[106] The Tenth Circuit noted

---

[100] 836 F.2d 1274 (10th Cir. 1988), *rev'g* 84 T.C. 827 (1985).

[101] 836 F.2d at 1287.

[102] *Id.* at 1281–83.

[103] *Id.* at 1278 (citing Smith v. Comm'r, 78 T.C. 350 (1982), *aff'd without op.* 820 F.2d 1220 (4th Cir. 1987); Fox v. Comm'r, 82 T.C. 1001 (1984)).

[104] *Id.* at 1278–79 (citing, inter alia, Helvering v. National Grocery Co., 304 U.S. 282 (1938), *rev'g* 92 F.2d 931 (3d Cir. 1937), *rev'g* 35 B.T.A. 163 (1936); Weir v. Comm'r, 109 F.2d 996 (3d Cir. 1940), *aff'g* 39 B.T.A. 400 (1939), *cert. denied*, 310 U.S. 637 (1940); King v. United States, 545 F.2d 700 (10th Cir. 1976)).

[105] *Id.* at 1279.

[106] *Id.* at 1279–80.

that the Tax Court had correctly observed that this language did not require either a subjective or objective standard, but it concluded that, given the long-standing judicial interpretation, the language was not sufficiently ambiguous to require a review of the legislative history.[107]

The Tenth Circuit held that the statute itself must be the primary source of any interpretation, and that the statute is conclusive when its language is unambiguous.[108] The Tenth Circuit held that the discrepancy between Section 108 as enacted and the legislative history indicated that while the Conference Committee addressing the DRA may have intended one test, Congress had actually enacted another.[109] The court found it was bound to apply the law, not rewrite it.[110] On this basis, the Tenth Circuit reversed *Miller*.[111]

(e) SUBSEQUENT JUDICIAL DECISIONS

As Section 108 was considered and revised, the judicial decisions reflected the confusion. After the amendment to Section 108 by TRA '86, cases interpreting pre-ERTA straddles were decided. This section provides a brief overview of some of the cases addressing Section 108.

The Tax Court ruled in two memoranda decisions, *Landreth v. Comm'r*,[112] and *Kurtz v. Comm'r*,[113] that pre-ERTA straddle losses are allowable under Section 108. In *Landreth*, the taxpayer entered into a commodity straddle program to defer taxes on his capital gains from the sale of a sawmill business. The taxpayer's straddle trades in Treasury bill and gold futures were executed between December 1978 and March 1979 and resulted in economic losses. Judge Scott found that the taxpayer's motive in entering into the straddle transactions was to generate tax losses and the preference for an economic profit was "merely incidental."[114] Nevertheless, Judge Scott, finding that the holding in *Miller*[115]

---

[107] *Id.* at 1283.

[108] *Id.*

[109] *Id.* at 1284.

[110] *Id.* at 1284–85.

[111] The Tax Court in *Miller* invalidated Question and Answer No. 2 in Temp. Treas. Reg. § 1.165-13T (1984). The Tenth Circuit, however, was not prepared to invalidate this portion of the regulations, although the court did note that the regulation does have the potential for invalid application. 836 F.2d at 1286.

[112] 50 T.C.M. (CCH) 728 (1985), *rev'd*, 859 F.2d 643 (9th Cir. 1988).

[113] 50 T.C.M. (CCH) 695 (1985), *rev'd sub nom.* Miller v. Comm'r, 836 F.2d 1274 (10th Cir. 1988).

[114] *Landreth*, 50 T.C.M. (CCH) at 733.

[115] 84 T.C. at 827.

controlled the case, ruled that the taxpayer could deduct his losses because each of his straddles had a reasonable (though small) prospect for some profit at the time it was acquired.[116] On April 26, 1988, the Ninth Circuit Court of Appeals affirmed the Tax Court's decision in *Landreth*.[117] In its decision, the Ninth Circuit affirmed the Tax Court's ruling, citing the legislative history to Section 108 and a previous case handled by the panel, *Wehrly v. United States*.[118]

The IRS argued in *Landreth* that the Ninth Circuit should make note of TRA '86 amendments to Section 108, which adopted a "primarily for profit" test. This test was used by the Tenth Circuit in *Miller*,[119] where the Tenth Circuit reversed the Tax Court's decision, concluding that losses incurred by taxpayers from pre-ERTA commodity straddles are not deductible.

The Ninth Circuit used a "reasonable prospect of any profit" standard, as it did in the *Wehrly* case. In *Landreth*, the Ninth Circuit noted that it agreed with the Tenth Circuit that the meaning of the term "entered into for profit" in Section 108 is "unambiguous" because it is identical to language in I.R.C. § 165(c)(2), which has interpreted "entered into for profit" to mean "primarily for profit."

The IRS asked the Ninth Circuit to reconsider its decision to allow the deductibility of losses from commodity futures straddles when taxpayers can reasonably expect a profit.[120] On October 4, 1988, the Ninth Circuit vacated its April 26, 1988 opinion.[121] The Ninth Circuit determined that it was not required to follow *Wehrly*, and it then remanded the case for proceedings consistent with its October opinion.

In *Kurtz v. Comm'r*,[122] pre-ERTA commodity straddle losses from gold and silver futures contracts were held to be deductible even though the Tax Court found that the transactions were primarily tax motivated. Judge Whitaker acknowledged that the taxpayers "had a genuine interest, hope, and perhaps expectation, of substantial profits from their straddle investments."[123] Nevertheless, Judge Whitaker found that the taxpayers would not "have undertaken this course of investment activity,

---

[116] *Landreth*, 50 T.C.M. (CCH) at 733.
[117] 859 F.2d 643, 644 (9th Cir.), *withdrawing* 845 F.2d 828 (1988).
[118] 808 F.2d 1311 (1986).
[119] 836 F.2d 1274 (10th Cir. 1988), *rev'g* 84 T.C. 827 (1985).
[120] IR-88-80, 10 Stand. Fed. Tax Rep. (CCH) ¶ 6533 (May 2, 1988).
[121] *Landreth*, 859 F.2d 643 (9th Cir. 1988).
[122] 50 T.C.M. (CCH) 695 (1985), *rev'd sub nom.* Miller v. Comm'r, 836 F.2d 1274 (10th Cir. 1988).
[123] 50 T.C.M. (CCH) 695, 699 (1985).

over a preordained 6-month period and totally in reliance upon the advice of others, if they had not been convinced that it would result in substantial tax savings at little if any cost."[124] Although the "tax objective was predominate [sic],"[125] application of Section 108 and the *Miller* decision[126] controlled to allow deductions for pre-ERTA straddle losses.

In *Perlin v. Comm'r*,[127] the Tax Court held that a commodity trader's futures transactions were not shams for tax purposes and that they satisfied the "entered into for profit" requirement of Section 108. The IRS alleged that portions of the taxpayer's straddles were prearranged trades established in a noncompetitive manner and disallowed the resulting tax losses. The Tax Court dismissed the IRS's allegations and found that all of the taxpayer's trades had been established by open outcry in accordance with the rules of the CBT (notwithstanding the testimony of some members of the exchange who claimed that the taxpayer had not traded in the pit on the dates in question).

In *Perlin*, the IRS also contended that the taxpayer's straddles were invalid pursuant to provisions in the temporary Treasury regulations promulgated under Section 108.[128] (The temporary regulations provided that, for Section 108 to apply, a professional trader's futures transactions must be in property that is the subject of his regular trading activity.) For example, the temporary Treasury regulations specify that a commodity dealer that regularly trades only in agricultural futures does not qualify for the profit motive presumption for a silver futures straddle transaction. The Tax Court found that the taxpayer's trading activity was broad enough to include the straddles challenged by the IRS. Although the Tax Court found that the temporary Treasury regulations did not reflect the wording of the statute approved by Congress, the Tax Court found it unnecessary to invalidate that portion of the temporary regulations.

The IRS also charged that the taxpayer's straddles had no possibility of a profit as a result of the transaction costs that the taxpayer incurred. The Tax Court, upon examination of the actual transaction costs involved, disagreed with this contention and found that there was a possibility of a profit despite these transaction costs.

The IRS also contended that the taxpayer's straddles had tax results that were disproportionate to their economic consequences. The temporary Treasury regulations provide that the extent to which straddle

---

[124] *Id.*
[125] *Id.* at 700.
[126] 84 T.C. at 827.
[127] 86 T.C. 388 (1986).
[128] Temp. Treas. Reg. § 1.165-13T (1984).

transactions have tax results that are disproportionate to their economic consequences is a factor in determining whether they were entered into with a profit motive. The Tax Court ruled that this provision of the temporary Treasury regulations is invalid and refused to apply the disproportionate results test in determining whether the taxpayer's straddles were profit motivated.[129]

As their final assault, the IRS alleged that the taxpayer's straddles were shams because he utilized special instructions to prevent the BTCC's computer from offsetting positions acquired during the same day. As a result of the special instructions, the computer used FIFO when calculating the effects of each trade. The Tax Court noted that, under the CFTC's regulations, a trader can specifically identify the position that he wishes to close out and it is only if no such identification is made that the clearing organization will offset the positions on a FIFO basis. The court held that the taxpayer's use of the special instructions was consistent with the requirements of these regulations and was perfectly valid for tax purposes.

In *Glass v. Comm'r*,[130] the Tax Court examined option straddle transactions entered into in London in light of the TRA '86 amendments to Section 108. Despite finding that (1) the trades were executed at market prices, (2) the trades were "layed off" in a manner consistent with proper brokerage practices, and (3) that the trading strategies used by the taxpayers could have been profitable, the Tax Court still found the trades to be "shams in substance" (i.e., economic shams), simply because the taxpayers always closed out loss positions before year-end. Therefore, the court found that even though the trades were correctly executed, they were "shams" because the taxpayers' probable motivations for selling unprofitable positions at the end of the year were to recognize tax losses.

In *King v. Comm'r*,[131] the Tax Court granted the taxpayer's motion for a partial summary judgment. In *King*, the Tax Court held that the taxpayer, who was a commodities dealer under Section 108(b), was entitled to deduct his commodity losses without regard to either a profit motive or whether the losses were incurred as part of his regular trading activities.

In *Wehrly v. United States*,[132] the taxpayers sued for refunds after they paid tax assessments imposed on their forward contract cancellation

---

[129] Invalidating Question and Answer No. 5 of Temp. Treas. Reg. § 1.165-13T (1984).

[130] 87 T.C. 1087 (1986), *aff'd sub nom.* Herrington v. Comm'r, 854 F.2d 755 (5th Cir. 1988), *and aff'd sub nom.* Yosha v. Comm'r, 861 F.2d 494 (7th Cir. 1988), *cert. denied*, 1989 U.S. LEXIS 2370.

[131] 87 T.C. 1213 (1986), *later proceeding* King v. Comm'r, 89 T.C. 445 (1987), *acq.* 1988-2 C.B. 1, *action on decision*, 1988-009 (Apr. 11, 1988).

[132] 808 F.2d 1311 (9th Cir. 1986).

transactions. In *Wehrly*, a three-judge panel of the Ninth Circuit Court of Appeals held that pre-ERTA straddle losses covered by Section 108 were deductible if the straddle trades were real transactions (i.e., were not shams) and were entered into with "a reasonable prospect of profit." The court rejected the IRS's argument that the straddle transactions had to be entered into "primarily for profit" to be deductible. The IRS asked the full Ninth Circuit to review and reconsider the three-judge panel decision in light of the TRA '86 amendments to Section 108. On December 23, 1986, the Ninth Circuit denied the IRS's motion for a reconsideration and rehearing. The conclusion in *Wehrly* was later rejected by the Ninth Circuit in *Landreth v. Comm'r*,[133] which held that the correct standard is the primarily for profit standard.

In *Cook v. Comm'r*,[134] the Tax Court, in a reviewed decision, held that in order for commodities dealers to take advantage of the per se profit motive presumption provided in Section 108, the losses incurred by the dealer must not be prearranged or fictitious. The Tax Court found that the taxpayer's straddle losses were prearranged and lacked economic substance. Under this analysis, the Tax Court affirmed the deficiency determinations relating to the taxpayer that were sustained in *Glass*.

The Tax Court in *Cook* found that although the language of Section 108(b) is "straightforward enough," the provision's legislative history could be consulted.[135] The House Report states that "the presumption would not be available in any cases where the trades were fictitious, prearranged, or otherwise in violation of the rules of the exchange in which the dealer is a member."[136] In conclusion, the Tax Court held that "it is appropriate before applying the per se rule of Section 108(b) to enquire whether straddle transactions were fictitious, prearranged, or otherwise in violation of the rules of the exchange, and if so, whether there were losses actually incurred."[137]

In *Boswell v. Comm'r*,[138] the Tax Court, in a reviewed decision, held that the taxpayer's straddle losses were not deductible because his primary motive for entering into the transactions was not to realize an economic profit. The Tax Court announced that because of the 1986 amendment to Section 108(a), it would no longer follow its decision in *Miller*.[139]

---

[133] 859 F.2d 643 (9th Cir. 1988), *vacating* 845 F.2d 828 (9th Cir. 1988).
[134] 90 T.C. 975, 980 (1988).
[135] *Id.* at 984.
[136] *Id.* (citing H.R. REP. NO. 426, *supra* note 75, at 911).
[137] *Id.* at 986 (citations omitted).
[138] 91 T.C. 151 (1988).
[139] 84 T.C. at 827.

Although cases continue to be decided, the line of pre-ERTA cases seems to have been resolved with *Boswell*.[140] Investors must have entered into their commodity straddle transactions primarily to realize an economic profit. Meanwhile, dealers are only eligible for the profit motive presumption if their transactions were not prearranged or fictitious.

In *Kovner v. Comm'r*,[141] the Tax Court held that an investor that is registered with the CFTC as an "associated person" is not a commodities dealer for purposes of Section 108. The taxpayer in *Kovner* was not a member of a commodity exchange, and he was neither a floor broker nor a floor trader. As an associated person, he placed orders through a floor broker for customer orders, as well as for his own trades. The Tax Court found that although he was "engaged full-time in commodities transactions . . . this does not necessarily make him eligible to deduct losses under Section 108(b)."[142] Because the Conference Report for the DRA states that "[a] commodity dealer is any person registered with a domestic board of trade designated as a contract market by the CFTC who buys or sells options or RFCs subject to the rules of such board,"[143] the Tax Court found that associated persons were excluded from the definition of commodities dealers. In a dissenting opinion, Judge Whalen objected to the construction of the term "'commodities dealer' to exclude everyone other than floor traders, floor brokers, and members of an exchange."[144] Judge Whalen found that "[b]y limiting the term 'commodities dealers' [under I.R.C. § 1402(i)] to floor traders, floor brokers, and members of an exchange, the majority limits the application of self-employment taxes [under I.R.C. §§ 1401–1403] to the same group. Other commodities traders escape self-employment taxes on the gains and losses realized from their trading of section 1256 contracts."[145] Rather, Judge Whalen contended, the Tax Court should have applied the "trading section 1256 contracts" standard on the basis of the facts and circumstances of the case.

---

[140] In *Etshokin v. Comm'r*, 59 T.C.M. (CCH) 753 (1990), the Tax Court found that the taxpayer's commodity straddle transactions were entered into primarily for a profit and were deductible under Section 108. Although the taxpayer was "also concerned with tax consequences" of his transactions, the court found that his tax "concern was secondary" to his profit motive. *Id.* at 762.
[141] Tax Ct. Rep. (CCH) 46,664, at 3010 (June 20, 1990).
[142] *Id.* at 3015.
[143] *Id.* at 3016 (citing H. Rept. 98-861, at 910 (1984), 1984-3 C.B. [vol. 2] 164).
[144] *Id.* at 3019 (dissent of Judge Whalen).
[145] *Id.*

Forty-eight
Straddle Definitions

The starting point for any inquiry on the applicability of the Straddle Rules is with the statutory definitions of certain key terms. Basically, the Straddle Rules apply to positions in personal property if the taxpayer holds a position in personal property that offsets the position from which the loss (or expense) arose. Hence, the statutory definitions are crucial to ascertain whether the Straddle Rules apply to a taxpayer's position.

§ 48.1 STRADDLE

A straddle consists of "offsetting positions with respect to personal property."[1] Simply stated, a taxpayer holds a straddle when he holds two or more positions in personal property if holding one position reduces his risk of loss from holding the other position. In fact, if one position protects the other, this is enough to establish a straddle even if the other position is not protected in the same manner.

Example 48-1

Assume that a taxpayer owns gold bullion and enters into a futures contract position to sell the same amount of gold bullion at a future date. The taxpayer has substantially reduced his risk of loss in holding gold bullion (long position) because he simultaneously holds a position to sell gold bullion in the future (short position). The

[1] I.R.C. § 1092(c)(1).

taxpayer holds offsetting positions with respect to gold bullion and has thus entered into a straddle.

Example 48-2

Assume a taxpayer enters into a long futures contract position to buy gold bullion and enters into a forward contract to sell gold coins (short position). The taxpayer has reduced his risk of loss in holding the gold bullion and in agreeing to sell the gold coins in the future because he holds the other position. The taxpayer has reduced his risk even though the property is not of the same kind (i.e., gold bullion and gold coins) and the interests in gold are not the same types of positions (i.e., a futures contract and a forward contract). The positions are deemed to be offsetting and the taxpayer holds a straddle.

§ 48.2 PERSONAL PROPERTY

Personal property is defined as any personal property of a type that is actively traded.[2] Because real estate is not actively traded, it is excluded, by definition, from the term "personal property." The remainder of this section addresses the terms "actively traded," "United States currency," and "certain stock positions." It also sets out some examples of personal property.

(a) ACTIVELY TRADED

To be subject to the Straddle Rules, personal property must be actively traded. The Code provides no guidance as to when property is actively traded. In addition, the legislative history of ERTA (which enacted the Straddle Rules in 1981) provides only minimal guidance, stating that "[i]n order to be treated as actively traded, property need not be traded on an exchange or in a recognized market."[3] Hence, the definition of personal property is broader than the types of property traded on an exchange or in a recognized market, and the definition of personal property may include

---

[2] I.R.C. § 1092(d)(1).
[3] STAFF OF THE JOINT COMM. ON TAXATION, 97TH CONG., 1ST SESS., GENERAL EXPLANATION OF THE ECONOMIC RECOVERY TAX ACT OF 1981, at 289 (Joint Comm. Print 1981) [hereinafter General Explanation of ERTA].

items not generally thought of as actively traded property. Treasury regulations are needed to clarify which property is actively traded. The temporary regulations that have already been issued provide no such clarification.

Interests in personal property—such as futures contracts, forward contracts, and options—are positions in personal property, as well as personal property—if the interests are actively traded.[4] For taxable years beginning after December 31, 1986, foreign currency for which there is an active interbank market is presumed to be actively traded.[5]

Example 48-3

A debt security that entitles its holder to cash at a future date (e.g., a Treasury bill, note, or bond traded in a recognized market) constitutes personal property if the debt security, itself, is actively traded.

Example 48-4

Index options and futures contracts that settle in cash are personal property because these products are traded on a securities or commodity exchange.

Example 48-5

An agreement to sell the assets of a business for future delivery is neither personal property nor a position in personal property; the agreement is not actively traded and the assets sold under the agreement are not actively traded.

(b) UNITED STATES CURRENCY

Although the statutory definition of personal property does not address this point, United States currency is not viewed as personal property. The only reference to currency in ERTA's legislative history in 1981 indicates that United States currency does not fall into this category. Personal property, as defined, only includes "property or interests in property that

---

[4] *Id.*
[5] I.R.C. § 1092(d)(7)(B).

may result in gain or loss on their disposition."[6] There is no gain or loss on the disposition of United States currency.

(c) CERTAIN STOCK POSITIONS

Certain stock positions are now subject to the Straddle Rules. This section addresses the general application of the Straddle Rules to stock positions. It also addresses stock positions that offset options or substantially similar or related property. Further, it addresses the Treasury regulations. And finally, it looks at so-called offsetting position stock.

(1) IN GENERAL

Prior to January 1, 1984, personal property subject to the Straddle Rules did not include stock within its scope.[7] This was changed by the DRA in 1984, which repealed the blanket exemption for corporate stock from the definition of personal property for stock positions established after December 31, 1983.[8] As a result of the DRA change, certain stock positions are now personal property.[9] TRA '86[10] clarifies that the exemption from the Straddle Rules for certain stock positions does not extend to positions in stock (including exchange-traded stock options that do not qualify for the qualified covered call exemption).[11]

First, stock is defined as personal property if the stock is part of a straddle where at least one of the offsetting positions in the straddle is (1) an option with respect to such stock (or substantially identical stock or securities), or (2) Treasury regulations view it as a position with respect to substantially similar or related property (other than stock).[12] Hence, corporate stock is personal property if it is held in a straddle with an option on the same stock, or substantially identical stock or securities (such as convertible debt securities).

In addition, stock is personal property if the stock is part of a straddle where the offsetting position is stock in a corporation formed or availed of

---

[6] *Id.*
[7] I.R.C. § 1092(d)(1).
[8] Pub. L. No. 98-369, § 101(b)(1), 98 Stat. 494, 618 (1984) [hereinafter DRA].
[9] I.R.C. § 1092(d)(3).
[10] Pub. L. No. 99-514, 100 Stat. 2085 (1986) [hereinafter TRA '86].
[11] I.R.C. § 1092(d)(3)(A), *as amended by* TRA '86, *supra* note 10, § 1808(c).
[12] I.R.C. § 1092(d)(3)(B)(i).

to take positions that offset positions taken by any shareholder of the corporation ("offsetting position stock").[13]

The term personal property does not include stock if all of the positions in the straddle consist of stock positions or the short sale of stock. TRA '86 makes it clear that the exception for stock in I.R.C. § 1092(d)(3)(A) is limited to stock and does not apply to interests in stock.[14]

In *Rivera v. Comm'r*,[15] the Tax Court examined the scope of the definition of personal property prior to the January 1, 1984, change to determine whether to include stock within its scope. The Tax Court found that forward contracts in stock were not subject to the Straddle Rules because they did not constitute positions in personal property.[16] The court also found that the IRS failed to establish that the taxpayer's purchase of forward contracts in stock resulted in a substantial underpayment of tax due to a tax-motivated transaction.[17]

In *Rivera*, the taxpayer purchased forward contracts in stock. She entered into many "spread" transactions, in which she purchased both long and short forward contracts on the same underlying securities with different delivery dates and different contract prices.[18] On her 1981 tax return, she claimed losses from her investments in forward contracts.

In its deficiency notice, the IRS determined that the taxpayer was not entitled to the losses claimed, because among other things, the transactions were subject to I.R.C. § 1092. The Tax Court granted summary judgment in favor of the taxpayer, finding as a matter of law that stock forward contracts did not constitute positions in personal property within the meaning of I.R.C. § 1092 prior to the DRA amendments in 1984. Because I.R.C. § 1092 did not, on its face, clearly exclude stock from the definition of personal property, the court looked to its legislative history. The Senate Finance Committee Report and the Conference Committee Report that accompanied ERTA in 1981 both indicated that the Straddle Rules were intended to apply only to commodity-related property and to certain stock options.[19]

---

[13] I.R.C. § 1092(d)(3)(B)(ii). DRA, *supra* note 8, § 101(e)(2) makes this provision applicable to positions taken by a shareholder on or after May 23, 1983, in taxable years ending after such date.

[14] TRA '86, *supra* note 10, § 1808(c). Other rules can apply to limit losses on stock. *See generally* Chapter 18 and section 19.3(f).

[15] 89 T.C. 343, 347 (1987).

[16] *Id.* at 349.

[17] *Id.* at 351.

[18] *Id.* at 345.

[19] *Id.* at 349.

The Tax Court rejected the IRS's argument that the legislative history of the DRA, which repealed the exception for stock, indicated that the exclusion of "stock" from the definition of personal property under prior law applied only to "direct positions in stock."[20]

(2) STOCK OFFSETTING OPTIONS OR SUBSTANTIALLY SIMILAR OR RELATED PROPERTY

Turning first to the situation where a stock position offsets options or substantially similar or related property, the Straddle Rules apply to certain options, futures contracts, and stock indexes. In addition, the position is a mixed straddle subject to the mixed straddle rules.[21] Options and futures contracts are traded on securities and commodity exchanges on stock indexes (e.g., the Standard & Poor's 100 and 500 Indexes, the Major Market Index, the New York Stock Exchange Composite Stock Index, Value Line Stock Index, Computer Technology Index, Oil Index, Standard & Poor's OTC Industrial Stock Price Index, and Gold/Silver Stock Index). A taxpayer might create a straddle if he holds a "basket" of stocks (short or long) and enters into an opposite stock index option or stock index futures contract position (collectively referred to as "index contract positions") where some of the stock making up the index contract also make up his stock position. The risk of loss of holding the stock position may be substantially diminished by holding the opposite index contract position.

The DRA Conference Report provides examples of straddles consisting of stock and substantially similar or related property. First, a straddle consists of offsetting positions of stock and a convertible debt security of the same corporation, where the price movements of the two positions are related.[22]

Second, a straddle includes a short position in a stock index RFC (or option on the RFC or stock index, itself) and stock in a RIC where its principal holdings mimic the performance of the stocks included in the stock index.[23]

Third, holding an index and a portfolio of stocks where their performance mimics the performance of an index is a straddle.[24]

---

[20] *Id.* at 350.

[21] *See generally* Chapter 57.

[22] HOUSE CONFERENCE REPORT, DEFICIT REDUCTION ACT OF 1984, H.R. CONF. REP. NO. 861, 98th Cong., 2d Sess. 908 (1984) [hereinafter H.R. CONF. REP. NO. 861].

[23] *Id.* For a discussion of RFCs, see section 44.1.

[24] H.R. CONF. REP. NO. 861, *supra* note 22.

The DRA Conference Committee makes the point, however, that stock offset by another position (other than an option) in substantially related stock might reduce a corporate taxpayer's holding period for the intercorporate dividends received deduction,[25] but is not a straddle.[26]

Extension of the Straddle Rules to stock offset by positions in substantially similar or related property raises potential problems in applying the Straddle Rules. A taxpayer might own a portfolio of various stocks and enter into an S&P 500 futures contract or an S&P 100 option contract. If the taxpayer's stock portfolio consists of less than all of the 500 or 100 stocks underlying the index contract positions, at what point is the risk of loss in holding a particular stock position viewed as substantially diminished by holding the index contract position? Or, what if a taxpayer constructs a portfolio of stocks, the value of which correlates (to some degree) to the value of an index contract? Or, what if an index contract is based on a specific industry where one company makes up a major portion of the market share for the industry, and the taxpayer holds stock in the company with the stock value that makes up a major portion of the price in the index? In this last situation, it is likely that the taxpayer holds a straddle. These questions and many other gray areas need to be addressed in Treasury regulations.

Portfolios of stocks (long or short) are traded against opposite stock index positions (short or long). Program trading may result in application of the Straddle Rules. In program trading, a trader arbitrages stocks against stock indexes if the value of those stocks reflected in the price of a stock index future is "out of line."[27] The following discussion, based on two articles from The New York Times on August 30, 1985,[28] demonstrates how program trading uses stock positions to offset what may be viewed for tax purposes as offsetting positions of substantially identical property. Positions so established are subject to the Straddle Rules and are mixed straddles subject to the mixed straddle rules.[29] Program trading typically is conducted by institutional investors and other professionals that buy or sell shares in 100 or more large companies that they view as a surrogate for the broader S&P 500 index. (Although there are several types of stock index futures, the S&P 500 futures index has been commonly used and is used in this discussion.) By buying a stock index

---

[25] *Id.; see* sections 17.7 and 24.9.
[26] H.R. CONF. REP. NO. 861, *supra* note 22, at 908.
[27] *See* section 8.7.
[28] *See* Sterngold, *Those Strange Market Turns*, N.Y. Times, Aug. 30, 1985, at D1, col. 3; *What Catches the Arbitrageur's Eye?*, N.Y. Times, Aug. 30, 1985, at D4, col. 4.
[29] *See generally* Chapter 57.

future, an investor or trader expects that the market will rise above its current level prior to the date when the contract expires. When the difference in price between the actual level of the current S&P 500 index and the level of a futures contract is out of line, investors or traders lock in a profit by buying futures contracts in one market and selling stocks in another, or vice versa.[30]

Example 48-6

A taxpayer buys an S&P futures contract and sells stocks included in the index with an equal value to the settlement value of the futures contract. At current futures margin rates, the taxpayer margins his S&P futures contract position for $3000. The taxpayer holds property substantially identical to the stock position. The short and long positions are offsetting positions subject to the Straddle Rules. In addition, the taxpayer holds a mixed straddle.[31]

Portfolio insurance typically involves the use of futures contracts to offset stock portfolios by selling stock index futures after stock prices decline by a predetermined amount. It is often viewed as "a synthetic option that represents the purchase of a protective put on stock."[32] The "insurance" is the "cost of selling underpriced futures and buying them back at higher prices."[33] As with program trading, if part of the portfolio mimics the futures contract index used as the portfolio insurance, the Straddle Rules may apply.[34]

(3) TREASURY REGULATIONS

For positions entered into after January 1, 1984, the DRA directs the Treasury to promulgate regulations to identify which stock positions are

---

[30] For more information on program trading, see CME, *Informational Materials on Program Trading* (Dec. 1989). *See also* Powers, *The Basket Program Business,* INTERMARKET, Jan. 1986, at 43; Seligman, *Don't Fret About Program Trading,* FORTUNE, Oct. 13, 1986, at 87.

[31] For a discussion of the mixed straddle rules, see Chapter 57.

[32] Commins, *Fad or Revolution? While Portfolio Insurance Has Its Critics, the Technique Is Still Proliferating and at the Same Time Adapting Itself to New Applications,* INTERMARKET, June 1987, at 18.

[33] *Id.* at 19.

[34] For a discussion of various forms of portfolio insurance, see Nutt, Farra & Grannan, *Hedging with Portfolio Insurance: Understanding Derivatives Can Reduce the Cost,* INTERMARKET, Sept. 1987, at 8.

to be viewed as offset by index contract positions.[35] At this writing, the only Treasury regulations that mention positions that offset stock are temporary regulations in the area of mixed straddle accounts.[36] At this writing, there are no regulations that specifically identify those index contract positions that are viewed as offsetting corporate stock. In fact, objective and workable standards will be difficult to develop, which may explain why regulations have not been issued.

The temporary Treasury regulations provide an example of a taxpayer holding stock in three corporations and options on a broad-based stock index futures contract. The values of the corporate stocks are included in the index.[37] The example assumes that a reasonable person, on the basis of all of the facts and circumstances, would expect the stocks in these corporations to be offsetting positions with respect to the options on the broad-based stock index future.[38] It is unlikely, however, that stock in three corporations could offset a broad-based stock index. The example seems more appropriate as an illustration of a narrow-based index than a broad-based index.

(4) OFFSETTING POSITION STOCK

The Straddle Rules apply to "offsetting position stock," defined as any stock in a corporation "formed or availed of" to take positions opposite to positions taken by the shareholders of the corporation.[39] This provision defers losses from trading in personal property by a shareholder to the extent of any unrecognized gain in the stock of the corporation. The phrase "availed of" might not require any kind of intentional or purposeful matching of offsetting positions.[40] As a result, stock might be treated as offsetting position stock without any intentional matching of positions.

What about the situation where a corporation may have been "formed or availed of" to take positions that offset the positions of its shareholders? Do the Straddle Rules make the stock of the corporation the relevant position, or are the corporation's positions in personal property the relevant positions? When should stock be treated as a position? If the

---

[35] DRA, *supra* note 8, § 103(c).
[36] Temp. Treas. Reg. § 1.1092(b)-4T(b) (1985).
[37] Temp. Treas. Reg. § 1.1092(b)-4T(b)(3), Example (1985).
[38] *Id.*
[39] I.R.C. § 1092(d)(3)(B)(ii).
[40] *See* Garrett v. United States, 479 F.2d 598, 602 (5th Cir. 1973), *aff'g* 73-2 U.S. Tax Cas. (CCH) ¶ 16,094 (N.D. Tex. 1972).

test looks only to the intention of forming or utilizing the corporation, the Straddle Rules might be circumvented. Or, should the definition of offsetting position stock look to objective criteria, such as the assets of the corporation and the extent to which the corporation has other characteristics that avoid the Straddle Rules?

(d) EXAMPLES

To be subject to the Straddle Rules, the products in question must fall within the definition of personal property. Some assets that qualify as personal property and others that do not include the following:

- Actively traded physical commodities (e.g., corn, wheat, or silver) are personal property.
- Foreign currency that is freely convertible into other currencies and that is actively traded is personal property. It is not necessary for futures contracts to be traded on the foreign currency for the currency to be viewed as personal property.
- Corporate stock positions offset by other stock positions are not personal property.
- Corporate stock offset by an option on the same stock or substantially identical stock or securities (such as convertible debt securities) is personal property.
- A portfolio of corporate stock offset by a stock index (futures contract or option) is personal property if the value of the stocks correlate to a significant degree to the value of the index.
- Real estate is not personal property.
- Actively traded options to purchase or sell commodities, stock, or other securities are personal property.
- Government securities are personal property.
- Actively traded debt securities are personal property.
- An option, futures contract, or forward contract is personal property if it is actively traded.
- A futures contract or option that does not require delivery of personal property or shares of stock but calls for cash settlement is personal property if the contract is actively traded.

§ 48.3 POSITIONS

The Straddle Rules apply to offsetting positions, so it becomes necessary to determine what a position is. A position is defined as "an interest (including a futures contract or forward contract or option) in personal property."[41] There is no requirement that there be active trading in the position; the only requirement is that it be an interest in personal property. Positions in personal property can offset other positions even if they are not in the same underlying property, or are not the same types of interests in property.[42]

(a) DEFINITION

A position consists of an interest in property, including a futures contract, forward contract, or option contract. This definition, however, does not provide sufficient guidance for many of the complex issues that arise when a taxpayer holds interests in property. Some examples of positions, which may or may not meet the definition of personal property, include the following:

- An owner of a physical commodity that is actively traded, such as gold or silver bullion, holds a position.
- A party to either a long or short futures contract or exchange-traded options contract holds a position.
- An owner of foreign currency of a type that is convertible into other currencies holds a position.
- An owner of United States currency does not hold a position because he does not hold personal property or an interest in personal property.
- A party to a contract to buy or sell a physical commodity of a type that is actively traded (e.g., gold or silver bullion) holds a position, irrespective of whether the contract is actively traded. The contract, itself, is an interest in personal property, and if the contract is actively traded it is also personal property. On the other hand, if the contract is not actively traded, it is not personal property.
- A party to a forward contract to buy or sell a physical commodity that is actively traded (e.g., corn, wheat, or soybeans) holds a position, irrespective of whether the contract itself is actively

---

[41] I.R.C. § 1092(d)(2).
[42] I.R.C. § 1092(c)(2)(A).

traded. If the contract is actively traded, the contract is both a position and personal property.

(b) REPURCHASE AGREEMENTS AND REVERSE REPURCHASE AGREEMENTS

It is not settled whether a transaction structured as a repo or a reverse repo is a position subject to the Straddle Rules.[43] The remainder of this section discusses tax issues concerning application of the Straddle Rules to repo transactions.

(1) DEFINITION

Repos and reverse repos are generally financing transactions where securities are financed pursuant to the terms of an agreement. One party is viewed as the borrower and the other party is viewed as the lender. In a repo transaction, a taxpayer that owns securities borrows funds and uses his securities as collateral. He obtains cash by "selling" the securities to the other party and agrees to repurchase equivalent securities from the other party at a future date. In a reverse repo transaction (so named because the transaction is the reverse side of a repo), the taxpayer purchases securities from the other party and agrees to sell equivalent securities to the other party at a future date. In both repo and reverse repo transactions, the initial seller is referred to as the "seller-debtor," while the initial buyer is referred to as the "buyer-creditor."

On the date when the repo or reverse repo transaction is terminated, the money (plus an interest factor to reflect the use of the money) and securities equivalent to those securities first "sold" are returned to their original owners. The seller-debtor receives the same or equivalent securities back from the buyer-creditor, while the buyer-creditor receives his funds (plus an interest factor) back from the seller-debtor.

Example 48-7

A taxpayer purchases Treasury bills in one year that mature in the following taxable year. The taxpayer (in this case the seller-debtor) enters into an agreement to sell the Treasury bills to a buyer-creditor and to buy them back at a later date. When looked at from the side of the seller-debtor, this is a repo transaction. It is a reverse

---

[43] For a discussion of repos, see sections 2.2(c) and 31.11.

repo when looked at from the side of the buyer-creditor. The repurchase price is the original cash received plus an additional amount reflecting interest on the financing.

(2) TAX ANALYSIS

If a repo or a reverse repo transaction is treated as a position, it might be subject to the Straddle Rules. In addition, any interest expense incurred on the transaction (except for hedging transactions eligible for the statutory hedging exemption) would need to be capitalized under the provisions of I.R.C. § 263(g).[44]

(i) Repos as Financing Transactions

For tax purposes, a repo transaction is generally treated as a secured loan. The seller-debtor gives the securities to the buyer-creditor as collateral to secure the seller-debtor's obligations under the loan.[45] It is the author's view that the seller-debtor's side of the repo transaction is not a position. Borrowing United States currency does not meet the definition of a position under I.R.C. § 1092(d)(2) because United States currency is not personal property.[46] Hence the seller-debtor does not have an interest in personal property as defined in I.R.C. § 1092(d)(1).[47]

In addition, the buyer-creditor simply lends money to the seller-debtor, taking the securities as collateral for the loan. The buyer-creditor holds the seller-debtor's obligation to repay the borrowed funds. The obligation to repay borrowed funds could be viewed as personal property in the hands of the creditor. The buyer-creditor's side of the transaction should not be a position if, as typically is the case, either the seller-debtor's obligation to repay the borrowed funds is not actively traded or the property is not personal property (i.e., it is not of a type that is actively traded). A borrowing creates a property interest in the buyer-creditor with the right to receive payment under the debt. It does not create a property interest in the seller-debtor that is obligated to repay borrowed funds:

---

[44] *See generally* Chapter 55.
[45] American Nat'l Bank of Austin v. United States, 421 F.2d 442, 452 (5th Cir.), *cert. denied*, 400 U.S. 819 (1970); *see* Rev. Rul. 79-108, 1979-1 C.B. 75; Rev. Rul. 77-59, 1977-1 C.B. 196; Rev. Rul. 74-27, 1974-1 C.B. 24; *cf.* Rev. Rul. 82-144, 1982-2 C.B. 34 (the taxpayer was not holding the position as security on a loan or for the benefit of the seller).
[46] General Explanation of ERTA, *supra* note 3, at 289; *see also* section 48.2(b).
[47] General Explanation of ERTA, *supra* note 3, at 289.

> [D]ebts ... are not property of the debtors in any sense; they are obligations of the debtors, and only possess value in the hands of the creditors. With [creditors] they are property. ... To call debts property of the debtors is simply to misuse terms. All the property there can be in the nature of things in debts of corporations, belongs to the creditors, to whom they are payable.[48]

Thus, an obligation on the side of the buyer-creditor, which has a right to receive repayment of the debt in the transaction, should not be a "position" if the seller-debtor's obligation to repay the borrowed funds is not actively traded.[49]

(ii) Repos as Sales Transactions

If a repo transaction goes beyond borrowings of the types typically found in financing transactions, it is possible that a repo transaction is a "position" that may be subject to the Straddle Rules. With a seller-debtor, he can hold no more than one position (i.e., the obligation to buy the security). With a buyer-creditor, he can arguably hold two positions (i.e., the security and the obligation to sell the security).

Officials at the Treasury have indicated that it is the Treasury's view that repos can be positions subject to the Straddle Rules.[50] Deferral and conversion opportunities, present in certain types of repo transactions, have raised concern at the Treasury. Treasury regulations addressing repos have not been promulgated to date, but the Treasury has announced that the applicability of the Straddle Rules to repo transactions is an issue that Treasury regulations, if and when issued, will address.[51]

The IRS has taken the position on audit that repo transactions may, under certain circumstances, be the economic equivalent of a forward contract.[52] In certain circumstances, repo transactions have been held to

---

[48] Case of State Tax on Foreign-Held Bonds, 82 U.S. 300, 320 (1872).

[49] The IRS, on audit, has taken the position that a repo is a "position" subject to the Straddle Rules. However, the IRS has not set out any analysis as to why a repo would so qualify, and it is unknown whether this position has been taken consistently by the IRS.

[50] *See* Address by John E. Chapoton, Assistant Secretary of the Treasury for Tax Policy, National Conference on Domestic and International Uses of Options and Futures, in New York City (Sept. 26, 1983), *reprinted in* 21 TAX NOTES 347 (1983).

[51] *Id.*

[52] *See* Sheldon v. Comm'r, Tax Ct. Rep. (CCH) 46,602, at 2939 (May 29, 1990). In *Sheldon*, the Tax Court majority did not address the issue. However, Judge Wells, concurring in part, stated that the repo transactions were not forward contracts. For a discussion of *Sheldon*, see section 31.11(b)(2). *See also* Sheppard, *Economic Substance and the Case of the T-Bill Rolls*, 48 TAX NOTES 396 (1990).

be sales.⁵³ This has been supported by the IRS's view of repos as purchases and sales and is the position of some other commentators. One commentator has stated that "a repo of fixed term with a fixed interest rate can be the economic equivalent of a long forward contract to purchase the shirttail security on termination of the repo, and might be treated as such under the tax law."⁵⁴ The view that repos might be forward contracts may be limited to those transactions where the securities are bought and "sold" at the same time and "there has been a reduction of the repo borrower's 'risk of loss or opportunity for gain.' "⁵⁵ In addition, the repo borrower might lose the ownership of the securities under I.R.C. § 1058 (security loan agreements) and the Treasury regulations proposed thereunder.⁵⁶

(iii) Short-Term Obligations and Market Discount Obligations

For obligations acquired after July 18, 1984, the DRA may make the question of whether a repo transaction is a position less important with respect to certain taxpayers for short-term obligations, including Treasury bills, and market discount obligations.⁵⁷ The DRA changed the rules for short-term obligations and contains two provisions designed to eliminate the opportunity for conversion of market discount obligations—the first recharacterizes market discount as additional interest and the second defers deductions for interest incurred to carry a market discount bond.

Under pre-DRA law, if a Treasury bill was used in a repo transaction, it was believed that the seller-borrower could defer interest accrual until the Treasury bill matured or was sold.⁵⁸ Short-term government obligations payable without interest and due in one year or less were exempted from the general rule requiring the periodic inclusion of OID.⁵⁹ A similar exemption from the OID rules was available for nongovernmental short-term obligations held by cash basis taxpayers.⁶⁰ Interest on

---

[53] Citizens Nat'l Bank of Waco v. United States, 551 F.2d 832 (Ct. Cl. 1977).
[54] Schapiro, *Sheltering the Revenue from Shelters: A Legislative Proposal Involving the Minimum Tax and Accounting Provisions*, 22 TAX NOTES 811, 820 n.40 (1984).
[55] *Id.*
[56] *See generally* Chapter 26 and section 31.11.
[57] *See* sections 31.2(d)(2) and 31.3(m).
[58] See I.R.C. § 454(b); H.R. CONF. REP. NO. 861, *supra* note 22, at 806.
[59] H.R. CONF. REP. NO. 861, *supra* note 22, at 807; *see* section 31.2.
[60] H.R. CONF. REP. NO. 861, *supra* note 22, at 807.

indebtedness incurred to purchase or carry obligations eligible for these exemptions had been deductible from unrelated income.

Also under pre-DRA law, if a market discount security was used in a repo transaction, the seller-borrower claimed the accrual of market discount as capital gain. A taxpayer purchasing an obligation at a price below its issue price treated the difference upon the sale or at maturity as capital gain rather than additional interest income.[61] Under pre-DRA law, a taxpayer could convert ordinary income into capital gain by entering into a repo if the value of the obligation declined after its issuance (typically because of an increase in prevailing interest rates).

(3) SUMMARY IF STRADDLE RULES APPLY

In conclusion, if repos and reverse repos are positions in personal property (i.e., interests in personal property that are actively traded), they are subject to the Straddle Rules unless the transactions qualified for the hedging exemption.[62] Under the Straddle Rules, losses (if any) with respect to the repo transactions are deferred to the extent of unrecognized gains until all of the positions are closed out.[63] Moreover, interest and carrying charges are capitalized and cannot be currently deducted.[64] Inability to deduct interest expense would be the major problem.

(c) FOREIGN CURRENCY

Because hedged currency positions are offsetting positions (i.e., straddles) for purposes of the Straddle Rules, the Straddle Rules apply to defer losses and capitalize interest and carrying charges unless an exemption is available. Prior to enactment of TRA '86, however, it was unclear as to whether a debt security denominated in a foreign currency was a "position" for purposes of the Straddle Rules. For tax years beginning after December 31, 1986, TRA '86 adds I.R.C. § 1092(d)(7), which makes it clear that an obligor's interest in a foreign currency denominated debt obligation is a position for purposes of the Straddle Rules.[65]

---

[61] *See id.* at 805; *see also* section 31.3.
[62] *See generally* Chapter 23.
[63] I.R.C. § 1092(a)(1).
[64] I.R.C. § 263(g)(1).
[65] I.R.C. § 1092(d)(7)(A).

The rationale for this treatment is that a foreign currency borrowing is economically equivalent to a short position in the foreign currency.[66] Second, for taxable years beginning after December 31, 1986, a foreign currency is presumed to be actively traded for application of the Straddle Rules if there is an active interbank market for the currency.[67]

§ 48.4 OFFSETTING POSITIONS

Losses realized on a position in personal property cannot be recognized for tax purposes to the extent that the taxpayer has unrecognized gains in offsetting positions.[68] In other words, once a taxpayer holds positions in personal property, losses on closing out any of those positions cannot be deducted to the extent there is unrecognized gain in any positions that reduce the risk of holding the position closed out at a loss. Determining which positions offset other positions is critical to ascertain whether losses are currently deductible.

The remainder of this section addresses offsetting positions in general. It then discusses options as offsetting positions. And finally, it addresses debt securities as offsetting positions.

(a) IN GENERAL

When a taxpayer has a substantial diminution of risk of loss from holding any position in personal property by reason of holding one or more other positions in personal property (whether or not of the same kind), he holds offsetting positions.[69] Where one or more positions offset only a portion of one or more other positions, the positions are treated as offsetting only to the extent of the portion that is balanced.[70] Positions can be offsetting even if they are not in the same underlying property or they are not the same types of interests in property.[71] The Code provides rebuttable presumptions for determining offsetting positions and explicitly authorizes

---

[66] SENATE FINANCE COMM. REPORT, S. REP. NO. 313, 99th Cong., 2d Sess. 469 (1986) [hereinafter S. REP. NO. 313].
[67] I.R.C. § 1092(d)(7)(B).
[68] I.R.C. § 1092(a)(1)(A).
[69] I.R.C. § 1092(c)(2)(A).
[70] General Explanation of ERTA, *supra* note 3, at 288.
[71] *Id.*

the Treasury to establish additional presumptions by regulations,[72] which have not yet been issued. Positions are presumed to be offsetting if:

1. The positions are in the same personal property or the property and a contract for such property (e.g., gold and a short gold futures contract), if the value of one position increases when the value of the other position decreases.

2. The positions are in the same personal property or any altered form of the property (e.g., soybeans and a short soybean oil futures contract), if the value of one position increases when the value of the other position decreases.

3. The positions are in debt securities with similar maturities if the value of the positions ordinarily move inversely to each other (e.g., holding a long Treasury bill position and a short Treasury note position with scheduled maturities in sufficiently close proximity to each other, such that a change in the value of one will correspond substantially to a change in the value of the other).

4. The positions are sold or marketed as offsetting, irrespective of whether the positions ordinarily change in value inversely.

5. The aggregate margin requirements for maintaining the positions are lower than the sum of the margin requirements for each position if held separately, irrespective of whether the positions ordinarily change in value inversely.

6. Other factors (including subjective or objective tests) as may be defined in Treasury regulations—if and when issued—will indicate that the positions are offsetting.[73]

Any of these presumptions can be rebutted (by either the taxpayer or the government) by demonstrating that there is no substantial diminution of risk of loss from holding the positions presumed to be offsetting.[74] Neither the Code nor the legislative history to ERTA provides guidance regarding the extent to which the risk of loss in holding positions must be diminished to be deemed substantially reduced. The only references in the legislative history indicate that mere diversification of assets usually does not substantially diminish the risk of loss, and a taxpayer is not

[72] I.R.C. § 1092(c)(3)(A).
[73] *Id.*
[74] I.R.C. § 1092(c)(3)(B).

generally considered to be holding offsetting positions if he holds no short positions.[75] Thus, a taxpayer holding a portfolio of government securities does not hold offsetting positions if he holds no short positions in the same or similar securities.[76] In addition, if a taxpayer holds short positions, the positions should only be treated as offsetting other positions to the extent that the positions are balanced.[77] As of this writing, Treasury regulations have not been issued on the question of what constitutes a substantial diminution of risk of loss. It is not likely that clarifying regulations will, in fact, be issued.

Loss is deferred to the extent of unrecognized gain in an offsetting position. The deferred loss is the amount of gain the taxpayer would recognize if the gain position was sold or otherwise transferred at its fair market value on the last business day of the taxable year. For a section 1256 contract subject to the loss deferral rule,[78] fair market value is determined by the final settlement price established by the securities or commodity exchange on which the contract is traded on the final trading day of the year.[79] The applicable settlement price for other personal property is normally considered as its fair market value.[80]

Even if a taxpayer enters into an offsetting position in the ordinary course of his business, the Straddle Rules apply unless the transaction qualifies as a hedging transaction or a section 988 hedging transaction.[81] If a taxpayer enters into offsetting positions using investment assets, the hedging exemption does not apply and the transactions are subject to the Straddle Rules.

(b) OPTION POSITIONS

Options are subject to the Straddle Rules if a taxpayer substantially reduces his risk of loss in holding one or more positions in personal property by reason of holding an option in personal property. The hard question in most situations is: Does holding an options position substan-

---

[75] General Explanation of ERTA, *supra* note 3, at 288; SENATE FINANCE COMM. REPORT, ECONOMIC RECOVERY TAX ACT OF 1981, S. REP. NO. 144, 97th Cong., 1st Sess. 150, *reprinted in* 1981 U.S. CODE CONG. & ADMIN. NEWS 105, 249 [hereinafter S. REP. NO. 144].

[76] General Explanation of ERTA, *supra* note 3, at 288.

[77] *Id.*

[78] I.R.C. § 1092(d)(5)(A); *see generally* Chapter 57.

[79] General Explanation of ERTA, *supra* note 3, at 285.

[80] *Id.* at 285–86.

[81] I.R.C. § 1092(e); *see generally* Chapter 23. *See also* section 59.3.

tially reduce the risk of holding another position? Or, is the options position capable of being protected by another position?

This section addresses those options that compose offsetting positions subject to the Straddle Rules.[82] This section does not, however, address straddles consisting entirely of options that are section 1256 contracts because such options are subject to section 1256 treatment and are exempt from the Straddle Rules.[83]

Actively traded options are personal property.[84] Furthermore, if the options are on property that is actively traded, they are positions in personal property.[85] In either of these situations, offsetting positions involving options are subject to the Straddle Rules.[86] Options subject to the Straddle Rules include options (whether traded on securities exchanges, commodity exchanges, or in the over-the-counter market) on physical commodities, futures contracts, foreign currencies, stock, other securities, stock groups, and stock indexes. Any of these option positions can substantially reduce the risk of holding another position in personal property.

The Straddle Rules now apply to most option spreads. Nevertheless, there are some gray areas. For instance, the Straddle Rules should not apply to the purchase of a put option (long position) and a purchase of a call option (long position) on the same underlying property. Holding both positions of such a "long option straddle" does not reduce the risk of holding either position. In other words, a taxpayer's risk of loss in holding one position is not reduced by holding the other position. As the long call option goes up in value, the long put option declines in value and vice versa, but the two positions increase or decrease in value independently of each other.

On the other hand, the Straddle Rules are likely to apply to a sale of a put (short position) and a sale of a call (short position). Unlike the situation where the taxpayer purchased both option positions (long positions), the premium income from one position serves to offset the loss from holding the other position. The Straddle Rules certainly apply to conversion and reverse conversion transactions. Determining when an

---

[82] For a discussion of the tax treatment of options that are not subject to the Straddle Rules, see sections 44.3 and 44.4.
[83] I.R.C. §§ 1092(d)(5)(A), 1256(a)(4); *see generally* Part Ten.
[84] *See* I.R.C. § 1092(d)(1); *see also* General Explanation of ERTA, *supra* note 3, at 289.
[85] I.R.C. § 1092(d)(2); *see also* General Explanation of ERTA, *supra* note 3, at 289. For a discussion of personal property, see section 48.2.
[86] *See* I.R.C. § 1092(a)(1)(A); *see also* General Explanation of ERTA, *supra* note 3, at 287–88.

option substantially reduces the risk of holding another position or when the option position is protected by another position can be quite difficult.

Example 48-8

A taxpayer holds offsetting option positions when he holds long and short call option contracts for the same underlying stock. Ownership of the long contract protects the taxpayer from the risk of loss on owning the short contract. Risk of loss on the short contract is reduced by the taxpayer's holding the long contract. The long option is capable of protecting the short position, and it is also capable of being protected by the short position. The short option has the same characteristic—it is capable of protecting the long position and it is also capable of being protected by the long position.

With respect to an option writer (short position), the risk of loss on the potentially offsetting position is reduced only to the extent of the premium received on writing the option. The short position may not protect the long position, but the long does protect the short, or vice versa. This is enough to have offsetting positions. Whether an option writer holds offsetting positions may depend upon the relationship between the market value and volatility of the underlying property and the premium the option writer received to write the option. An option writer (short position) transfers to the option holder (long position) a profit opportunity in return for a measure of protection against loss. The greater the profit opportunity transferred to the holder, presumably the higher the premium and hence the greater the protection provided to the writer.

Example 48-9

A taxpayer holding a share of stock with a market value of $50 sells an option to buy the stock at $60 for a $2 premium.

The taxpayer has reduced the risk of loss on his long position by $2, or four percent. If the same taxpayer had sold an option to buy the stock at $50 for, say, $8, he would have reduced his risk of loss by $8, or 16 percent.

At a minimum, an option holder should be viewed as holding offsetting positions based on the relationship between the market value and volatility of the underlying property and the sum of the strike price plus the premium paid for the option. Just because a taxpayer holds an option to buy property does not mean he has substantially reduced the risk of carrying a short position in that property. Nevertheless, the positions may be viewed as offsetting.

Example 48-10

A taxpayer agrees to sell silver at $50 (short position) and purchases a call option to buy silver at $60 (long position), paying a $2 premium. If the market price of the silver drops below $48, the taxpayer makes money. If the market price goes up, the taxpayer can lose up to $12 before his option gives him any protection from loss. All the taxpayer did by buying the call option position was provide insurance against the price of silver going above $62. There has been a substantial risk reduction and this may be an offsetting position.

In addition, an option that is out-of-the-money is capable of protecting another position, but may not be capable of being protected itself.[87] If a taxpayer holds both a long and a short put option or a long and a short call option at the same exercise price, regardless of whether the exercise price is in-the-money, the long and short options are offsetting positions, that is, they protect each other. Further, the writer of a put or call that is out-of-the-money has a position that is capable of being protected but is not generally capable of protecting another position. These positions can still be a straddle subject to the Straddle Rules.

On the other hand, in-the-money options are like bilateral contracts and thus are capable of being protected, as well as providing protection for another position. In Rev. Rul. 80-238,[88] the IRS ruled for purposes of the intercorporate dividends received deduction that a taxpayer does not reduce his holding period under I.R.C. § 246(c)(1)(A) by writing a call option, but noted that in-the-money call options were explicitly excluded from this holding.[89] For purposes of the dividends received deduction, the issue is whether the long stock position is protected; the issue of protection of a put or call position is irrelevant.

---

[87] For a discussion of in-the-money, out-of-the-money, and at-the-money options, see section 5.1.
[88] 1980-2 C.B. 96.
[89] *See* sections 17.7 and 24.9.

(c) DEBT SECURITIES

Debt security positions are presumed to be offsetting if they have similar maturities and the value of the positions ordinarily move inversely to each other.[90] To determine whether debt security positions are offsetting, one first must examine whether the positions are in personal property as defined in the Code. This is because the Straddle Rules only apply to offsetting positions in personal property.[91] Next, one should determine whether the debt securities are of similar maturities and have values that move inversely to each other. An open issue is whether the debt securities, to be viewed as offsetting positions, must be from the same issuer.

Debt securities are subject to the Straddle Rules if the securities themselves—or the positions in the securities (options, futures, forward contracts, or other interests)—are actively traded. To qualify as personal property, the positions or the property underlying the positions must be actively traded.[92]

Example 48-11

Assume a taxpayer owns United States Treasury bills in the principal amount of $100,000 that mature in March (long position), and he agrees to sell Treasury notes in the same principal amount that also mature in March (short position). The taxpayer holds offsetting positions. The debt securities are from the same issuer, that is, the Treasury Department. Furthermore, the debt securities are actively traded and fall within the definition of personal property. And, because the maturities of the two Treasury securities are in the same calendar month, there is no question but that the scheduled maturities are sufficiently close to each other to assume that a change in the value of one position corresponds inversely to a change in the value of the other position. It is expected that as the value of the long Treasury bill position increases, the value of the short Treasury note position decreases and vice versa.

Offsetting positions might not be as obvious as in the previous example. Currently, there are no guidelines to determine whether two positions are offsetting. It is not clear when debt securities are deemed to be of a similar maturity and treated as presumptively offsetting. To date,

---

[90] I.R.C. § 1092(c)(3)(A).
[91] For a discussion of personal property, see section 48.2.
[92] I.R.C. § 1092(d)(1).

neither case law nor Treasury regulations provide any guidance.[93] It appears that the length of time until a debt security matures should indicate how close the maturity dates of "offsetting" securities positions (long and short) need to be to substantially diminish the risk of loss in holding opposite positions.

Example 48-12

If a debt security matures in 24 months, it might be viewed as offsetting another debt security that matures in 18 months. On the other hand, if a debt security matures in six years, it should not offset another debt security that matures in 12 years, because holding one debt security would not substantially reduce the risk of loss in holding the other position.

Certain debt securities might not need to be of the same issuer to be offsetting. With securities of different issuers possibly offsetting each other, complicated problems in comparing debt instruments must be addressed. It is one thing to view a Treasury security (i.e., a Treasury bill, note, or bond) as possibly offsetting a federal agency security guaranteed by the federal government (e.g., a GNMA security). It is another thing to view the debt instrument of one corporation as offsetting the debt instrument of another unrelated corporation. When should debt securities be treated as offsetting? Must the issuers have the same creditworthiness? Or must the debt securities have the same rating from a nationally recognized rating agency? What other factors should be considered for debt security positions of different issuers to be viewed as offsetting? Treasury regulations, if and when issued, should provide some guidance.

A taxpayer with a portfolio of debt securities that does not hold any short positions in the same or similar securities does not hold offsetting positions. (The legislative history of ERTA makes it clear that a taxpayer does not generally hold offsetting positions if he holds no short positions.)[94] Mere diversification of assets does not substantially diminish the risk of loss in holding positions.[95] Finally, if a taxpayer holds both short and long positions, the positions are viewed as offsetting only to the

---

[93] For a discussion of substantially identical bonds for wash sales purposes, see section 19.9(g).
[94] General Explanation of ERTA, *supra* note 3, at 288.
[95] *Id.*; S. Rep. No. 144, *supra* note 75, at 150.

extent that the positions are balanced.[96] Therefore, where positions are not balanced, only part of the loss from a single position might be subject to the Straddle Rules.

Example 48-13

A taxpayer holds a short position in one debt security in the principal amount of $1000 and a long position in the same security (i.e., same issuer, same maturity date, and same interest rate) in the principal amount of $100,000. The positions offset each other to the extent of $1000. Loss, if any, incurred on the remaining $99,000 worth of the principal amount of the long position should not be subject to the Straddle Rules.

The Treasury is authorized to issue regulations prescribing the method for determining the portion of a position that is taken into account as offsetting.[97] At the date of this writing, regulations have not been issued.

§ 48.5 UNRECOGNIZED GAIN

Losses incurred on closing a position in personal property are currently deductible only to the extent that the losses exceed unrecognized gain on an offsetting position acquired before the loss was realized.[98] The concept of unrecognized gain, therefore, is important to ascertain whether losses incurred in one taxable year are deductible in that year, or whether such losses must be deferred until the offsetting position is closed out.

Unrecognized gain is the amount of gain that would be taken into account if a position were sold at its fair market value on the last business day of the taxable year.[99] Under the cash method of accounting, gains from the sale of property are not generally recognized until the sale proceeds are actually or constructively received, while losses are recognized as of the contract date.[100] Furthermore, unrecognized gain includes

---

[96] *Id.*

[97] I.R.C. § 1092(c)(2)(B); General Explanation of ERTA, *supra* note 3, at 288.

[98] I.R.C. § 1092(a)(1)(A).

[99] I.R.C. § 1092(a)(3)(A)(i).

[100] After TRA '86 amendments, securities traded in an established market (e.g., an exchange or over-the-counter market), both cash and accrual taxpayers recognize gain or loss on the day the trade is executed (i.e., the trade date) even if the settlement date occurs several business days later. S. REP. NO. 313, *supra* note 66, at 131.

the amount of gain that has been realized on the sale or exchange of a position even if that gain has not been recognized.[101] The distinction between realized gain and recognized gain, under tax accounting rules, is that realization refers to actual gain, while recognition addresses the year when gain is taken into account for tax purposes.[102] The difference between recognized and unrecognized gain is that unrecognized gain is generally not reported for tax purposes until some further event occurs.

Inclusion of "unrealized gain" in the definition of "unrecognized gain" prevents the deferral of gains into the subsequent year and the deduction of losses in the current year. In 1981, the Straddle Rules originally provided for losses to be deferred on closing out the losing position of a straddle only to the extent that there were unrealized gains. Deferring losses only to the extent of unrealized gains, however, was perceived as a loophole available to a cash basis taxpayer that sold property in one tax year and received the sales proceeds in the next tax year. Such a cash basis taxpayer was not subject to the loss deferral rule as originally enacted, because he had no unrealized gains in the first year. A cash basis transaction locked in the gain to be received at a future time not subject to the occurrence of any further legal event. Such a taxpayer, however, did have unrecognized gain insofar as he had a right to receive proceeds in the subsequent year. Hence, to close this loophole, the word "unrecognized" was substituted for "unrealized" by TCA '82.[103] The continued deferral for a cash basis taxpayer that realized—but did not recognize—gain was thereby eliminated by the TCA '82 change.

---

[101] I.R.C. § 1092(a)(3)(A)(ii).
[102] *See* sections 14.3 and 14.4.
[103] TCA '82, Pub. L. No. 97-448, § 105(a)(1), 96 Stat. 2365, 2384 (1983); SENATE FINANCE COMM. REPORT, TECHNICAL CORRECTIONS ACT OF 1982, S. REP. NO. 592, 97th Cong., 2d Sess. 25, *reprinted in* 1982 U.S. CODE CONG. & ADMIN. NEWS 4149, 4171.

Forty-nine

Limitation on Recognition of Straddle Losses While Holding an Offsetting Position

The concept of the loss deferral rule—that a taxpayer cannot deduct losses while holding an offsetting position—is taken one step further with the modified wash sales rule.[1] These rules apply to straddles consisting of non-section 1256 positions and to certain mixed straddles; they do not apply to straddles consisting solely of section 1256 positions.[2] This chapter first discusses the limitations on recognition of straddle losses provided by the loss deferral rule. Then it discusses the attempt made by temporary Treasury regulations to coordinate the loss deferral rule with the modified wash sales rule.

§ 49.1 LOSS DEFERRAL RULE

The Code provides that losses on closing out a position in personal property are postponed and cannot be recognized for tax purposes to the

---

[1] *See* section 54.3.
[2] I.R.C. § 1256(a)(4); *see* section 56.7.

extent that there is an unrecognized gain inherent in offsetting positions in personal property.[3] In other words, losses are currently deductible only to the extent that they exceed unrecognized gains in an offsetting position acquired before the loss position was closed out.

The Code provides rebuttable presumptions to determine when a taxpayer holds offsetting positions and explicitly authorizes the Treasury to establish additional presumptions by regulation.[4] It is assumed that one dollar of unrecognized gain in a position that remains open at the end of any taxable year will at most defer only one dollar of recognized loss in an offsetting position closed out during the same year.[5]

The amount of loss that is deferred is the amount of gain a taxpayer would recognize if the gain position were sold (or otherwise disposed of) at its fair market value on the last business day of the taxable year.[6] Fair market value for a section 1256 contract that is subject to the loss deferral rule[7] and remains open at the end of the year is determined by the final settlement price for that contract on its last trading day of the year.[8] The settlement price for personal property not traded on an exchange is normally considered to be its fair market value.[9]

Example 49-1

On December 1, a taxpayer enters into offsetting long and short positions in physical gold that are not subject to section 1256 treatment. On December 10, the taxpayer disposes of the short position at an $11 loss, at which time there is $5 of unrealized gain in the offsetting long position. At year-end there is still $5 of unrecognized gain in the offsetting long position. Under these circumstances, $5 of the $11 loss is not deductible in the taxable year because there is $5 of unrecognized gain in the offsetting long position; the remaining $6 of loss, however, is taken into account in the first taxable year.[10]

---

[3] I.R.C. § 1092(a)(1)(A).

[4] I.R.C. § 1092(c)(3)(A); see section 48.4.

[5] *See* STAFF OF THE JOINT COMM. ON TAXATION, 97TH CONG., 1ST SESS., GENERAL EXPLANATION OF ECONOMIC RECOVERY TAX ACT OF 1981, at 284 (Joint Comm. Print. 1981) [hereinafter General Explanation of ERTA].

[6] *Id.* at 285.

[7] I.R.C. § 1092(d)(5)(A). *See generally* Chapter 57.

[8] General Explanation of ERTA, *supra* note 5, at 285.

[9] *See id.* at 285–86.

[10] Temp. Treas. Reg. § 1.1092(b)-1T(g), Example (1) (1986).

§ 49.2 COORDINATION OF LOSS DEFERRAL AND MODIFIED WASH SALES RULES

This section provides a brief summary of the coordination between the loss deferral and the modified wash sales rules. Coordination between these rules is discussed in detail in section 54.2, which also provides illustrative examples.

If a taxpayer disposes of less than all of the positions of a straddle, any loss is disallowed to the extent there is unrecognized gain in (1) a successor position, (2) positions that are offsetting with respect to the loss position, and (3) positions that are offsetting with respect to the successor position.[11] The terms "straddle" and "offsetting position" are defined in I.R.C. § 1092. Basically, a taxpayer holds a straddle if he holds offsetting positions.[12] This means that a taxpayer holds a straddle if there is a substantial diminution of risk of loss in holding any position with respect to personal property by reason of holding one or more other positions with respect to such property (whether or not of the same kind).[13]

A successor position is defined in the temporary Treasury regulations as any position that offsets (at any time) a second position in either of two situations: (1) the second position offsets a loss position that was disposed of by the taxpayer, or (2) the successor position is entered into during a period commencing 30 days prior to and ending 30 days after the disposition of the loss position.[14] A successor position is one that is on the same side of the market as the loss position.

When the temporary regulations were initially released in January 1985, the definition of a successor position was substantially broader than the current definition. A successor position was defined in the first set of temporary regulations to include any position offsetting a successor position that was entered into within 30 days after the loss position was no longer part of the straddle. Under such a broad definition, loss could be deferred because of unrecognized gains in positions that were never part of the original straddle.[15]

The successor position rule is a hybrid of the wash sales rule and the loss deferral rule. Basically, Temp. Treas. Reg. § 1.1092(b)-1T incorpo-

---

[11] Temp. Treas. Reg. § 1.1092(b)-1T(a) (1986).
[12] I.R.C. § 1092(c)(1).
[13] I.R.C. § 1092(c)(2)(A).
[14] Temp. Treas. Reg. § 1.1092(b)-5T(n) (1986).
[15] The author believes that the first definition of a successor position was well beyond the intent of Congress in enacting I.R.C. § 1092(b) and that the current definition of a successor position is more appropriate.

rates the loss deferral rule in its scope by providing that a loss can be taken into account only to the extent it exceeds year-end unrecognized gain in offsetting positions or successor positions. The concept of loss deferral is applied not only to offsetting positions but also to successor positions. The modified wash sales rule is embodied in the definition of a successor position.

Any loss that is disallowed by operation of the loss deferral rule of I.R.C. § 1092 is treated as sustained in the succeeding taxable year (subject to operation of the loss deferral rule once again in the succeeding taxable year).[16] For stock or securities that are part of a straddle, any disallowed loss is subject to further application of Temp. Treas. Reg. § 1.1092(b)-1T(a)(1) and to the limitations of Temp. Treas. Reg. § 1.1092(b)-1T(a)(2).[17] A loss for a stock or securities position disallowed in one year under the rule set out in Temp. Treas. Reg. § 1.1092(b)-1T(a)(1) is not allowed in the succeeding taxable year, however, unless two conditions are met. First, substantially identical stock or securities (the acquisition of which caused the loss to be disallowed in the first year) must be disposed of during the second year. And second, neither Temp. Treas. Reg. § 1.1092(b)-1T(a)(1) nor Temp. Treas. Reg. § 1.1092(b)-1T(a)(2) can apply in the second year to disallow the loss.[18] If the disposition of a loss position would (except for application of the loss deferral rule) result in a capital loss, the loss allowed in the carry-over year is also treated as a capital loss.[19] Conversely, a disallowed ordinary loss is carried over to the succeeding taxable year as an ordinary loss.[20] If the disposition of a section 1256 contract position at a loss would (but for application of these deferral rules) result in 60 percent long-term and 40 percent short-term capital loss, the carried-over loss is treated as 60/40 loss, irrespective of whether any gain or loss on any successor position would be treated as 100 percent long-term or short-term capital gain or loss.[21]

---

[16] Temp. Treas. Reg. § 1.1092(b)-1T(b) (1986).
[17] *Id.*
[18] *Id.*
[19] Temp. Treas. Reg. § 1.1092(b)-1T(c)(1) (1986).
[20] *Id.*
[21] Temp. Treas. Reg. § 1.1092(b)-1T(c)(2) (1986).

Fifty

Losses Carried Forward

Losses that are not deductible in one taxable year ("deferred losses") can be carried forward to the succeeding taxable year.[1] Once carried forward, deferred losses are treated as incurred in the succeeding taxable year and are again subject to the loss deferral rule.[2] This procedure may require a continued deferral of the loss until the position offsetting it is closed out.[3] In addition, the character of the deferred loss (i.e., capital or ordinary) is determined at the time when the loss is realized, rather than at the time the loss is allowed as a deduction to the taxpayer.[4] If the disposition of a loss position would result in 60 percent long-term and 40 percent short-term capital loss, the loss allowed on disposition is treated as a 60/40 loss, irrespective of whether any gain or loss with respect to a successor position would be treated as 100 percent long-term or short-term capital gain or loss.[5] Carrying deferred losses forward creates complex problems in determining when such losses are deductible.

Example 50-1

In 1986, assume that a taxpayer enters into a forward contract position to sell gold (short position) and purchases gold bullion

---

[1] I.R.C. § 1092(a)(1)(B).

[2] Temp. Treas. Reg. § 1.1092(b)-1T(b) (1986). If a stock or securities position is part of a straddle, loss on one position is disallowed under Temp. Treas. Reg. § 1.1092(b)-1T(a)(1) until the substantially identical stock or securities position is also disposed of. *Id.*

[3] *See* I.R.C. § 1092(a)(1)(B).

[4] Temp. Treas. Reg. § 1.1092(b)-1T(c)(1) (1986).

[5] Temp. Treas. Reg. § 1.1092(b)-1T(c)(2) (1986).

(long position). The taxpayer holds offsetting positions in personal property. If before the end of 1986, the taxpayer closes out the short forward contract position at a $10 loss, that loss is deductible only to the extent it exceeds any appreciation in the gold bullion he still holds at the end of the year. If at the end of 1986, the gold bullion position had an unrecognized gain of $6, only $4 of the $10 loss was deductible in 1986. The $6 deferred loss is carried forward into 1987 as a capital loss (long-term or short-term depending upon the taxpayer's holding period).[6] In addition, the holding period regulations may apply.[7]

Deferred loss is carried forward until there is no offsetting gain inherent in a position acquired before the loss position was closed out.[8] It should be noted that the legislative history to ERTA refers to "unrealized," not "unrecognized," gains. The concept was changed by TCA '82[9] to close the "loophole" that is discussed in section 48.5. In fact, gain may arise before an offset is recognized, or after an offsetting position is disposed of. This is a technical glitch in the Code that provides curious results.

Example 50-2

Assume that throughout 1987 the taxpayer in Example 50-1 maintained the long gold bullion position that he acquired prior to closing out the short forward contract position at a loss. The $6 deferred loss carried forward from 1986 cannot be recognized in 1987 because the offsetting gain inherent in the gold bullion has not been recognized. Even if the amount of the unrecognized gain in the gold bullion drops below $6, the entire loss must be deferred because there continues to be offsetting gain in a position (i.e., the gold bullion) that was acquired before the loss position (i.e., the short

---

[6] ERTA, enacted in 1981, provides that a taxpayer's straddle losses are deferred to the extent the taxpayer has unrealized gains in offsetting positions. If a taxpayer realizes a loss on closing out one or more positions, the amount of loss he can deduct is the excess of the loss over the unrealized gain (if any) in the positions that offset the loss position and which are acquired before disposing of the loss position. STAFF OF THE JOINT COMM. ON TAXATION, 97TH CONG., 1ST SESS., GENERAL EXPLANATION OF THE ECONOMIC RECOVERY TAX ACT OF 1981, at 283–84 (Joint Comm. Print 1981) [hereinafter General Explanation of ERTA]; FINANCE COMM. REPORT, ECONOMIC RECOVERY TAX ACT OF 1981, S. REP. NO. 144, 97th Cong., 1st Sess. 147, *reprinted in* 1981 U.S. CODE CONG. & ADMIN. NEWS 105, 247 [hereinafter S. REP. NO. 144].
[7] Temp. Treas. Reg. §§ 1.1092(b)-2T(a), (b) (1986).
[8] General Explanation of ERTA, *supra* note 6, at 284; S. REP. NO. 144, *supra* note 6, at 147.
[9] TCA '82, Pub. L. No. 97-448, § 105(a)(1)(A), 96 Stat. 2365, 2384 (1983).

forward contract) was closed out. If the taxpayer disposed of the gold bullion in 1988, he could recognize the $6 deferred loss in that year, notwithstanding any other long gold positions held at the end of 1988 if these other positions were established *after* the original short position was closed out in 1986.[10]

---

[10] General Explanation of ERTA, *supra* note 6, at 284; S. REP. NO. 144, *supra* note 6, at 147.

Fifty-one

Attribution Rules

§ 51.1 GENERAL RULES

In determining whether a taxpayer holds offsetting positions that are subject to the Straddle Rules, positions held by certain related parties are deemed to be held by the taxpayer.[1] Attribution is applied before determining whether two or more positions are offsetting.[2]

There are two general attribution rules. First, positions are treated as if held by a taxpayer[3] if held by the taxpayer's spouse or a corporation that files a consolidated return with a corporate taxpayer.[4] This limits attribution to those parties (such as the taxpayer's spouse)[5] with income that can be reported on the same tax return.[6] Hence, positions established by a taxpayer's wholly owned corporation are generally not attributed to the taxpayer unless a consolidated return is filed with the taxpayer. There is attribution if the stock is viewed as "offsetting position stock."[7]

Another attribution rule provides that positions held by a flow-through entity in which the taxpayer has an interest, such as a trust, partnership, or S corporation, are treated as if the positions were held by the taxpayer

---

[1] I.R.C. § 1092(d)(4).
[2] I.R.C. § 1092(d)(4)(A).
[3] I.R.C. § 1092(d)(4).
[4] I.R.C. § 1501.
[5] I.R.C. § 1092(d)(4)(B).
[6] *See* STAFF OF THE JOINT COMM. ON TAXATION, 97TH CONG., 1ST SESS., GENERAL EXPLANATION OF THE ECONOMIC RECOVERY TAX ACT OF 1981, at 290 (Joint Comm. Print 1981); FINANCE COMM. REPORT, ECONOMIC RECOVERY TAX ACT OF 1981, S. REP. NO. 144, 97th Cong., 1st Sess. 151, *reprinted in* 1981 U.S. CODE CONG. & ADMIN. NEWS 105, 250.
[7] For a discussion of offsetting position stock, see section 48.2(c)(4).

as beneficiary, grantor, partner, or shareholder if part (or all) of the gain or loss from the positions held by the flow-through entity would be taken into account in determining the taxpayer's own offsetting positions.[8] Treasury regulations, not yet promulgated, may identify circumstances where positions held by flow-through entities will not be attributed to a taxpayer.[9]

§ 51.2 STATUTORY ELECTIONS

A number of questions must be addressed to determine how statutory elections can be made when the attribution rules are applied to a particular taxpayer. At what levels can elections be made? Assuming the proper election requirements or the specific identification requirements are met, can positions held, for example, by a taxpayer and his spouse, become part of an identified section 1256(d) straddle, a section 1092(b)(2) identified mixed straddle, or a mixed straddle? Can one corporation in a consolidated group make a hedging exemption election for another corporate member of the consolidated group? It is unclear under the statutory provisions and the legislative history of both ERTA and the DRA whether a taxpayer can make a valid election for another party that holds positions that are attributed to the taxpayer. Regulatory guidance is necessary.

The only information concerning elections provided at the date of this writing is contained in an IRS announcement on elections under ERTA's transitional rules for positions held by partnerships[10] and temporary regulations under the DRA.[11] The IRS announced that elections made under ERTA's transitional rules[12] were to be made at the partnership level.[13] In addition, partners in partnerships that made one election could make an additional separate election with respect to individually held positions either to pay their tax in installments or make no election at

---

[8] I.R.C. § 1092(d)(4)(C).
[9] *Id.*
[10] IRS News Release No. IR-82-13, 10 Stand. Fed. Tax Rep. (CCH) ¶ 6330 (Jan. 22, 1982) [hereinafter IRS News Release No. IR-82-13].
[11] Temp. Treas. Reg. § 1.1092(b)-4T(f) (1985).
[12] *See* ERTA, Pub. L. No. 97-34, §§ 508(c), 509, 95 Stat. 172 (1981) (concerning the effective date for application of the Straddle Rules and section 1256 treatment).
[13] IRS News Release No. IR-82-13, *supra* note 10, at 71,420.

all.[14] The same provisions should apply to DRA elections because there have been no changes to the attribution rules by the DRA.[15]

§ 51.3 SECTION 1256 CONTRACTS

What is the scope of the attribution rules for section 1256 contract positions subject to the Mark-to-Market Rule?[16] One of the attribution rules provides that positions held by a partnership are treated as if such positions are held by its partners.[17] This attribution rule leaves important issues open. Suppose a partner dies or sells his partnership interest so that he ceases to be a partner in the partnership. Is there a deemed disposition of the partner's proportionate share of the section 1256 contracts held by the partnership? Such a deemed disposition would treat the former partner as having realized gain or loss on his proportionate share of the partnership's section 1256 contracts at the date he died or disposed of his partnership interest. It is not clear on what date section 1256 contracts held by a partnership are to be marked-to-market and reported on the partner's tax return.

§ 51.4 MIXED STRADDLES

Various elections are provided for establishing mixed straddle accounts and specifically identifying section 1092(b)(2) identified mixed straddles. For a discussion of these elections, see generally Chapter 57. The temporary Treasury regulations provide that the terms "related person" or "flow-through entity," as used in the regulations, are defined in I.R.C. §§ 1092(d)(4)(B), (C).[18] Although the attribution rules apply to identify those positions that are part of a straddle, it is not clear whether the attribution rules are available for making elections with respect to positions that are attributed to the taxpayer.

---

[14] *Id.*
[15] *See* DRA, Pub. L. No. 98-369, § 101(b)(2), 98 Stat. 494, 618–19 (1984).
[16] For a discussion of the Mark-to-Market Rule, see section 45.1.
[17] *See* I.R.C. § 1092(d)(4)(C).
[18] Temp. Treas. Reg. § 1.1092(b)-5T(j) (1986); *see* section 51.1.

Fifty-two

Disclosure of Unrecognized Gain

§ 52.1   GENERALLY REQUIRED

To verify that a loss is deductible, a taxpayer must, with some exceptions, disclose on his tax return all unrecognized gains in positions in personal property, regardless of whether the positions are part of a straddle.[1] Obviously, this reporting requirement enables the IRS to determine which tax returns to select for audit and to identify possible offsetting positions by comparing positions closed out at a loss with gain positions open at year-end.

The Treasury is authorized to issue regulations prescribing the time, manner, and form for a taxpayer to disclose unrecognized gain and the amount of unrecognized gain in open positions.[2] At the date of this writing, the only required reporting rules for use by taxpayers to disclose unrecognized gains are set out in IRS Form 6781.[3] Part III of Form 6781 generally requires reporting of each position for which there is unrecognized gain (whether or not part of a straddle) if the position is held by the taxpayer at the end of the tax year.

---

[1] I.R.C. § 1092(a)(3)(B).
[2] I.R.C. § 1092(a)(3)(B)(i).
[3] IRS Form 6781, Gains and Losses from Section 1256 Contracts and Straddles, Pt. III.

§ 52.2 EXCEPTIONS

There are five statutory exceptions to the disclosure requirements.[4]

- First, reporting is not required for unrecognized gains that are part of an identified straddle.[5]
- Second, reporting is not required for inventory items.[6]
- Third, disclosure is not required for positions that are part of hedging transactions.[7]
- Fourth, reporting is not required for depreciable property or real property used in a taxpayer's trade or business.[8]
- And fifth, reporting is not required where a taxpayer incurred no loss during the taxable year on any position (including section 1256 contracts), or where the only loss the taxpayer incurred for the year is in a position described in the three previous exceptions.[9]

If a taxpayer carries a deferred loss forward from a prior year to the current taxable year, the taxpayer must report his unrecognized gain positions.[10]

Another exception to disclosure, which is discussed in the Joint Committee Report on ERTA, states that taxpayers that have incurred losses from the disposition of long positions and that have neither disposed of nor held any short positions during the taxable year, "generally would not hold offsetting positions and would not be expected to report unrealized gain."[11] Although there is no statutory basis for this rule, it is sensible to exclude from reporting obligations those taxpayers with portfolios of appreciated property if they have not engaged in any short transactions during the year.

---

[4] I.R.C. §§ 1092(a)(3)(B)(ii)(I)–(III).
[5] I.R.C. § 1092(a)(3)(B)(ii)(I); *see* section 56.1.
[6] I.R.C. § 1092(a)(3)(B)(ii)(II).
[7] *Id.*; *see generally* Chapter 23.
[8] I.R.C. § 1092(a)(3)(B)(ii)(II).
[9] I.R.C. § 1092(a)(3)(B)(ii)(III).
[10] STAFF OF THE JOINT COMM. ON TAXATION, 97TH CONG., 1ST SESS., GENERAL EXPLANATION OF THE ECONOMIC RECOVERY TAX ACT OF 1981, at 286 (Joint Comm. Print 1981).
[11] *Id.*

§ 52.3 EXAMPLES

Example 52-1

Assume a gold dealer holds gold bullion in his inventory (long position) and enters into a forward contract to sell gold in the future (short position). The dealer holds offsetting positions. Assume further that the dealer fails to comply with the requirements to qualify the straddle as a qualified hedging transaction[12] so that his gold positions are subject to the Straddle Rules.[13] Also, assume that before the end of the year the dealer disposes of the short forward contract position at a loss, and at the end of the year he has gain in the long gold position. Finally, assume that the dealer maintains the appreciated gold position.

Under these assumptions, the dealer need not report his unrecognized gain because the gain is on inventory property that is exempt from the disclosure requirements.[14] But because the dealer did not comply with the requirements of a qualified hedging exemption,[15] the loss deferral rule still applies to preclude him from recognizing—to the extent of the unrecognized gain inherent in the gold inventory—his loss on closing out the short forward contract position.

Example 52-2

Assume the facts in Example 52-1, but that the price of gold fell drastically prior to the end of the year. Based on the assumptions in Example 52-1, the dealer's short forward contract has unrecognized gain while his gold inventory has an inherent unrecognized loss. If the dealer sells his gold inventory at a loss and the only losses sustained by the dealer are on inventory positions in that taxable year, the dealer does not need to report the unrecognized gain on the short forward contract.[16] Provided the dealer does not have other types of losses that need to be reported for the year, unrealized gains need not be reported.

---

[12] *See generally* Chapter 23.
[13] *See generally* Part Eleven.
[14] I.R.C. § 1092(a)(3)(B)(ii)(II).
[15] *See* I.R.C. §§ 1092(e), 1256(e).
[16] I.R.C. § 1092(a)(3)(B)(ii)(II).

In conclusion, because the transaction does not qualify for the hedging exemption, the loss deferral rule precludes recognition of loss on the sale of the gold to the extent of the unrecognized gain inherent in the short forward contract position.[17]

---

[17] I.R.C. § 1092(a)(1)(A).

Fifty-three
Penalties

§ 53.1 PENALTIES FOR FAILURE TO DISCLOSE UNRECOGNIZED GAIN

The Code imposes penalties on a taxpayer for failure to disclose unrecognized gain. These penalties are discussed in the remainder of this section. Penalties under the law in effect before the changes in 1986 are discussed in section 53.1(a). The penalties under current law are discussed in section 53.1(b).

(a) PENALTIES UNDER PRE-TRA '86 LAW

Under the law in effect before TRA '86,[1] a taxpayer that failed to report, without reasonable cause, all unrecognized gains required to be reported under I.R.C. § 1092(a)(3)(B), was subject to a penalty if he (1) held an offsetting gain position during the taxable year, and (2) had a tax deficiency attributable (in whole or in part) to the denial of the loss deduction.[2] Failure to report unrecognized gains was treated as negligent or intentional disregard of the rules and regulations, without an intent to defraud.[3]

Under pre-TRA '86 law, the penalty for failure to disclose unrecognized gain was equal to five percent of the amount of the underpayment.[4] In

---
[1] Pub. L. No. 99-514, 100 Stat. 2085 (1986) [hereinafter TRA '86].
[2] I.R.C. § 6653(f), *prior to amendment by* TRA '86, *supra* note 1, § 1503(c)(3). I.R.C. § 6653(f) was amended by redefining an underpayment as due to negligence.
[3] I.R.C. § 6653(f), *prior to amendment by* TRA '86, *supra* note 1, § 1503(c)(3).
[4] I.R.C. § 6653(a)(1), *prior to amendment by* TRA '86, *supra* note 1, § 1503(a).

addition, a penalty equal to 50 percent of the interest payable on the deficiency was also imposed.[5] This penalty was computed for the period commencing on the date the tax return was due (determined without regard to any extensions) and ending on the date the tax is assessed or paid, whichever occurred first.[6] The penalty was imposed for a failure to report unrecognized gains, irrespective of whether the taxpayer held offsetting positions. Hence, a taxpayer was subject to a penalty if he did not report the gain, even if he obtained an opinion of counsel that the gain position did not offset a loss position. Although a taxpayer can rely on an opinion of counsel that he holds no offsetting gain position to claim a loss deduction, he must still disclose all unrealized gain positions and indicate that none of the disclosed gain positions offset the loss position.[7]

Example 53-1

Assume a taxpayer with unrecognized gain positions open at year-end obtains a legal opinion that these positions did not offset any positions for which he reported loss during the tax year for positions in personal property. Assume further that the taxpayer does not report any of his unrecognized year-end gain positions on his tax return. The taxpayer is subject to the penalty because he did not disclose his unrecognized gain positions.[8] The taxpayer must disclose all of his unrecognized gain positions[9] and, further, must indicate that none of the gain positions he disclosed are considered offsetting positions.[10]

(b) PENALTIES UNDER CURRENT LAW

TRA '86 made major changes to the negligence and fraud penalties under I.R.C. § 6653. The TRA '86 amendments to I.R.C. § 6653(f) for failures to

---

[5] I.R.C. § 6653(a)(2), *prior to amendment by* TRA '86, *supra* note 1, § 1503(a).

[6] I.R.C. § 6653(a)(2)(B), *prior to amendment by* TRA '86, *supra* note 1, § 1503(a).

[7] STAFF OF THE JOINT COMM. ON TAXATION, 97TH CONG., 1ST SESS., GENERAL EXPLANATION OF THE ECONOMIC RECOVERY TAX ACT OF 1981, at 291 (Joint Comm. Print 1981) [hereinafter General Explanation of ERTA]; SENATE FINANCE COMM. REPORT, ECONOMIC RECOVERY TAX ACT OF 1981, S. REP. NO. 144, 97th Cong., 1st Sess. 152, *reprinted in* 1981 U.S. CODE CONG. & ADMIN. NEWS 105, 251.

[8] I.R.C. § 6653(f), *prior to amendment by* TRA '86, *supra* note 1, § 1503(c)(3).

[9] I.R.C. § 1092(a)(3)(B)(i).

[10] General Explanation of ERTA, *supra* note 7, at 291.

disclose unrecognized gains conform I.R.C. § 6653(f) to the new, expanded definition of negligence now contained in I.R.C. § 6653(a).

TRA '86 "expands the scope of the negligence penalty by making it applicable to all taxes under the Code. . . . and generally redrafts the negligence penalty to make it clearer and more comprehensible."[11] First, the definition of negligence is expanded to cover "any failure to make a reasonable attempt to comply with the [Code] provisions . . . as well as any careless, reckless, or intentional disregard of rules or regulations."[12] Because new I.R.C. § 6653(a) does not limit the definition of negligence to any particular items, "all behavior that is considered negligent under present law . . . and any behavior that is considered negligent by the courts . . . is also subject to the negligence penalty."[13]

Because Treasury regulations have not yet been issued providing exemptions from the reporting requirements, it is possible that the penalty provisions would not apply to a failure to fully report all positions with unrecognized gain.

§ 53.2 INCREASED INTEREST RATE

In 1984, the DRA increased the interest rate applied to underpayments of tax if the underpayment was attributable to tax-motivated transactions and if the underpayment exceeds $1000.[14] Generally, interest is imposed on any amount not paid on or before the last date prescribed for payment without regard to any extension of time for payment.[15] The annual rate of interest (on amounts not paid by the last date prescribed for payment) is established on a semiannual basis by the Treasury and is equal to the adjusted prime rate charged by banks for the six-month period ending on September 30 and March 31 of any calendar year.[16] For taxable years beginning after December 31, 1986, the annual rate of interest is the underpayment rate. Any adjusted rate of interest established for the six-month period ending September 30 becomes effective January 1 of the

---

[11] STAFF OF THE JOINT COMM. ON TAXATION, 99TH CONG., 2D SESS., TAX REFORM BILL OF 1986, FINAL CONFERENCE COMM. DECISIONS II-780 (Joint Comm. Print 1986) [hereinafter TRA '86 Conf. Rep.].

[12] I.R.C. § 6653(a)(3).

[13] TRA '86 Conf. Rep., *supra* note 11, at II-781.

[14] I.R.C. § 6621(d) (originally enacted as Pub. L. No. 98-369, § 144(a), 98 Stat. 494, 682-83 (1984)) [hereinafter DRA].

[15] I.R.C. § 6601(a), *prior to amendment by* TRA '86, *supra* note 1, § 1511(c)(11).

[16] I.R.C. § 6621(d)(1), *prior to amendment and redesignation as* I.R.C. § 6621(c) by TRA '86, *supra* note 1, §§ 1511(c)(1)(A), (B), (C).

succeeding year, whereas an adjusted rate of interest established for the six-month period ending March 31 becomes effective on July 1 of the same year.[17]

In the event an underpayment of tax is substantial and attributable to a tax-motivated transaction, the annual rate of interest is 120 percent of the rate established for each six-month period ending September 30 and March 31.[18] An underpayment of tax is considered substantial if the underpayment for any taxable year exceeds $1000.[19] A substantial underpayment of tax is attributable to a tax-motivated transaction if, among other things, the underpayment arises from a straddle.[20] For purposes of this section, a straddle is defined as offsetting positions with respect to personal property,[21] without regard to either the special rules contained in I.R.C. § 1092(d)[22] or the hedging exemption contained in I.R.C. § 1092(e).[23]

Any underpayment of tax in excess of $1000 that is attributable to a straddle bears interest at a rate equal to 120 percent of the rate established by the Treasury. The 120 percent rate applies to interest accruing after December 31, 1984.[24]

For purposes of determining whether a substantial underpayment is attributable to a straddle or other tax-motivated transaction—including any sham or fraudulent transaction for purposes of determining interest for periods after December 31, 1986—the tax liability is calculated as if all items of income, gain, loss, deduction, or credit had been reported properly on the income tax return of the taxpayer.[25] The difference between the tax liability based on this computation and the tax liability computed without taking into account any adjustments to items attributable to tax-motivated transactions equals the amount of the tax-motivated underpayment.[26]

---

[17] I.R.C. § 6621(b), *prior to amendment by* TRA '86, *supra* note 1, § 1511(a).

[18] I.R.C. § 6621(d)(1), *prior to amendment and redesignation as* I.R.C. § 6621(c) by TRA '86, *supra* note 1, §§ 1511(c)(1)(A), (B), (C).

[19] I.R.C. § 6621(d)(2), *prior to amendment and redesignation as* I.R.C. § 6621(c) by TRA '86, *supra* note 1, §§ 1511(c)(1)(A), (B), (C).

[20] I.R.C. § 6621(d)(3)(A), *prior to amendment and redesignation as* I.R.C. § 6621(c) by TRA '86, *supra* note 1, §§ 1511(c)(1)(A), (B), (C).

[21] I.R.C. §§ 1092(c), 6621(d)(3)(A), *prior to redesignation as* I.R.C. § 6621(c) by TRA '86, *supra* note 1, §§ 1511(a)(1)(A), (B), (C); *see generally* Chapter 48.

[22] I.R.C. § 1092(d) provides various definitions and special rules for application of the Straddle Rules.

[23] *See generally* Chapter 23.

[24] DRA, *supra* note 14, § 144(c).

[25] *Id.*

[26] Temp. Treas. Reg. § 301.6621-2T (Q-5) (1984).

Fifty-four
Modified Wash Sales and Short Sales Rules

The Treasury has broad authority to issue regulations to establish modified wash sales and modified short sales rules to apply to straddles.[1] This regulatory authority, originally granted by ERTA in 1981,[2] was expanded by the DRA in 1984.[3] Temporary regulations were issued on January 18, 1985,[4] and amended on January 13, 1986.[5] ERTA called for regulations imposing rules for straddle transactions that were to be "similar" to the wash sales rule applicable for stock and securities[6] and the short sales rule already established for substantially identical property.[7] The DRA expanded the Treasury's authority to issue regulations "with respect to gain or loss on positions which are part of a straddle as may be appropriate" to carry out the purposes of the Straddle Rules and "to apply the principles" of the wash sales and short sales rules to straddle transactions.[8] The DRA's grant of regulatory authority is sub-

---

[1] I.R.C. § 1092(b)(1).
[2] ERTA, Pub. L. No. 97-34, 95 Stat. 172, 324 (1981).
[3] Pub. L. No. 98-369, 98 Stat. 494 (1984) [hereinafter DRA].
[4] Temp. Treas. Reg. §§ 1.1092(b)-1T to 1.1092(b)-5T (1986).
[5] T.D. 8070, 1986-1 C.B. 291.
[6] I.R.C. §§ 1091(a), (d).
[7] I.R.C. §§ 1092(b)(1), 1233(b), 1233(d); ERTA, *supra* note 2, § 501(a).
[8] I.R.C. § 1092(b)(1).

stantially broader than the original authority to issue rules "similar" to the wash sales and short sales rules.

The modified wash sales and short sales rules were enacted because of Congressional concern that the loss deferral rules in I.R.C. § 1092(a) would not defer losses on straddle positions in all of the circumstances Congress viewed as appropriate. As a result, these rules were enacted to preclude the deduction of losses on a position that was part of a straddle while the taxpayer remained in a balanced—that is, offsetting—position.

There are exceptions to application of these rules. Hedging transactions that qualify for the hedging exemption are exempt from all of the Straddle Rules, including the modified wash sales and modified short sales rules.[9] In addition, these rules do not apply to loss positions included in a mixed straddle account, or to losses on positions in a straddle that only consists of section 1256 contracts.[10]

This chapter addresses the modified wash sales and short sales rules that apply to straddles.

§ 54.1 COORDINATION WITH THE WASH SALES AND SHORT SALES RULES

The modified wash sales and short sales rules apply, unless a specific exemption is available, to positions that are part of a straddle. In many cases the wash sales rule of I.R.C. § 1091 or the short sales rule of I.R.C. § 1233 may also apply. The short sales rule of I.R.C. § 1233[11] explicitly provides that "property" subject to the short sales rule does not include any position to which the modified short sales rule applies.[12] As a result, the scope of the short sales rule of I.R.C. § 1233 can now be read narrowly and may, in fact, be limited to short sales of stock.[13]

On the other hand, in 1984, when the Straddle Rules were extended to stock options and certain stock positions,[14] it was unclear whether the wash sales rule of I.R.C. § 1091, the modified wash sales rule, or both rules applied to stock or securities positions that were part of a straddle. Because some transactions clearly fall within the statutory language of both rules, the coordination of these rules had to be addressed in Treasury

---

[9] *See generally* Chapter 23. *See also* Temp. Treas. Reg. § 1.1092(b)-1T(d)(1)(i) (1986).
[10] Temp. Treas. Reg. § 1.1092(b)-1T(d) (1986).
[11] *See generally* Chapter 18.
[12] I.R.C. § 1233(e)(2).
[13] *See* section 18.1.
[14] *See* section 48.2(c).

regulations or clarifying legislation. On January 14, 1986, the Treasury amended the temporary regulations issued in 1985 under I.R.C. § 1092(b), to "coordinate" the application of the wash sales rule, modified wash sales rule, and the loss deferral rule for stock and securities positions that are part of a straddle. The amended temporary regulations, which apply retroactively to dispositions of loss positions on or after January 24, 1985,[15] provide that I.R.C. § 1092(b) applies in lieu of I.R.C. § 1091 to defer losses incurred from the disposition of stock and securities positions in a straddle.[16] After January 24, 1985, the wash sales rule contained in I.R.C. § 1091 applies only to stock or securities positions that are not part of a straddle (e.g., outright stock positions and the short sale of stock).[17] The temporary Treasury regulations do not provide any clarification regarding preemption of I.R.C. § 1233 by I.R.C. § 1092(b).

§ 54.2 COORDINATION WITH THE LOSS DEFERRAL RULE

The temporary Treasury regulations, as amended, generally provide that if a taxpayer disposes of less than all of the positions of a straddle, any loss on the disposition of the loss position is not deductible to the extent there is unrecognized gain as of the close of the taxable year in one or more of the following positions: (1) successor positions, (2) offsetting positions to loss positions, and (3) offsetting positions to any successor positions.[18] The provisions of Temp. Treas. Reg. § 1.1092(b)-1T do not apply to losses sustained on (1) positions that are part of a hedging transaction, (2) positions included in a mixed straddle account (as defined in Temp. Treas. Reg. § 1.1092(b)-4T), or (3) positions that are part of a straddle consisting only of section 1256 contracts.[19] Any loss that is not deductible because of this general rule is carried over and is treated as sustained in the succeeding taxable year.[20]

A special rule is applied first to losses from the disposition of stock or securities positions that are part of a straddle before the general rule mentioned above is applied. Any loss on the disposition of stock or securities is not taken into account if, within a period beginning 30 days

---

[15] T.D. 8070, 1986-1 C.B. 291.

[16] Temp. Treas. Reg. § 1.1092(b)-1T(e) (1986).

[17] For a discussion of application of the Straddle Rules to certain stock positions, see section 48.2.

[18] Temp. Treas. Reg. § 1.1092(b)-1T(a)(2) (1986).

[19] Temp. Treas. Reg. § 1.1092(b)-1T(d) (1986).

[20] Temp. Treas. Reg. § 1.1092(b)-1T(b) (1986).

before the date of disposition and ending 30 days after such date, the taxpayer has acquired (by purchase or in a taxable exchange) substantially identical stock or securities, or entered into a contract or option to acquire such securities.[21] This rule does not apply to losses sustained by a dealer in securities if the losses are sustained in transactions made in the ordinary course of business.[22] The term "substantially identical" has the same meaning as it has when it is used in I.R.C. § 1091(a).[23] The term "securities" has the same meaning as it has in I.R.C. § 1236(c).[24] If any loss on the disposition of stock or securities remains deductible after application of this special rule,[25] the general rule[26] applies and may further defer a deduction for the remaining losses. The temporary Treasury regulations incorporate a restrictive wash sales rule for stock or securities.[27]

The term "successor position" is defined in the temporary Treasury regulations as any position that is or was at any time offsetting to a second position if (1) the second position was offsetting to a loss position disposed of, and (2) the position is entered into during a period commencing 30 days before and ending 30 days after the disposition of the loss position.[28] The temporary regulations acknowledge that a position entered into after all of the straddle positions are disposed of will not be considered a successor position.[29] If all positions of the original straddle are disposed of in the same tax year, then all of the economic gain or loss is reported in that year and the Straddle Rules do not apply. In short, a successor position is one that is on the same side of the market as the loss position.

The successor position rule is a hybrid of the wash sales rule and the loss deferral rule. Basically, Temp. Treas. Reg. § 1.1092(b)-1T incorporates the loss deferral rule by providing that a loss can be taken into account only to the extent it exceeds year-end unrecognized gain in offsetting positions or successor positions. The concept of loss deferral is applied to not only offsetting positions but to successor positions as well.

---

[21] Temp. Treas. Reg. § 1.1092(b)-1T(a)(1) (1986). Any loss on the stock or securities positions that results while the positions are not part of a straddle is subject to the wash sales rule of I.R.C. § 1091. For a discussion of the wash sales rule, see generally Chapter 19.

[22] Temp. Treas. Reg. § 1.1092(b)-1T(d)(2) (1986). For a discussion of dealers in securities, see generally section 8.3.

[23] Temp. Treas. Reg. § 1.1092(b)-5T(p) (1986). See section 19.9.

[24] Temp. Treas. Reg. § 1.1092(b)-5T(q) (1986). See section 19.6(a).

[25] Temp. Treas. Reg. § 1.1092(b)-1T(a)(1) (1986).

[26] Temp. Treas. Reg. § 1.1092(b)-1T(a)(2) (1986).

[27] This rule assures that a taxpayer cannot avoid both the wash sales rule in I.R.C. § 1091 and the loss deferral rule in I.R.C. § 1092.

[28] Temp. Treas. Reg. § 1.1092(b)-5T(n) (1986).

[29] See Temp. Treas. Reg. §§ 1.1092(b)-5T(n), (p), (q) (1986).

The modified wash sales rule is embodied in the definition of a successor position.

Any loss disallowed by the modified wash sales rule is carried forward and treated as if sustained in the succeeding taxable year (when it will again be subject to these deferral rules). For stock or securities that are part of a straddle, any disallowed loss is subject to further application of Temp. Treas. Reg. § 1.1092(b)-1T(a)(1) and to the limitations of Temp. Treas. Reg. § 1.1092(b)-1T(a)(2).[30] A loss on a stock or securities position that is disallowed in one year under the rule set out in Temp. Treas. Reg. § 1092(b)-1T(a)(1) is not allowed in the succeeding taxable year, however, *unless* (1) substantially identical stock or securities (the acquisition of which caused the loss to be disallowed in the first year) are disposed of during the second year, and (2) neither Temp. Treas. Reg. § 1092(b)-1T(a)(1) nor Temp. Treas. Reg. § 1092(b)-1T(a)(2) applies in the second year to disallow the loss.[31]

If capital loss is deferred in this manner, the loss allowed in the subsequent taxable year is also treated as a capital loss.[32] In all other cases, the loss is an ordinary loss.[33] If the disposition at a loss of a section 1256 contract position would (but for application of these deferral rules) result in 60 percent long-term and 40 percent short-term capital loss, the carried-over loss is treated as a 60/40 loss, irrespective of whether any gain or loss on any successor positions would be treated as 100 percent long-term or short-term capital gain or loss.[34] All other deferred losses are treated as ordinary.

Example 54-1

On December 1, a taxpayer enters into offsetting long and short positions. On December 10 he disposes of the short position at an $11 loss, when the long position has a $5 unrealized gain. At the end of the year, the long position still has a $5 unrecognized gain inherent in it. As a result, $5 of the $11 loss is not deductible in the first tax year because there is $5 of unrecognized gain in the offsetting long position.[35]

---

[30] Temp. Treas. Reg. § 1.1092(b)-1T(b) (1986).
[31] *Id.*
[32] Temp. Treas. Reg. § 1.1092(b)-1T(c)(1) (1986).
[33] *Id.*
[34] Temp. Treas. Reg. § 1.1092(b)-1T(c)(2) (1986).
[35] Temp. Treas. Reg. § 1.1092(b)-1T(g), Example (1) (1986).

Example 54-2

Assume the facts are the same as in Example 54-1, except that at year-end there is $11 of unrecognized gain in the offsetting long position. In this example, the entire $11 loss is not deductible in the taxable year in which it is incurred because of the $11 unrecognized gain in the long position.[36]

Example 54-3

On November 1, a taxpayer enters into offsetting long and short positions. On November 10, he disposes of the long position at a $10 loss. On November 11, he enters into a new long position that is a successor position to the long position disposed of, and that is not substantially identical to the long position disposed of. Assume further that both the original short position and the successor long position are open at year-end, and there is $10 of unrecognized gain in the successor long position and no unrecognized gain in the offsetting short position. The entire $10 loss is not deductible for the taxable year because there is $10 of unrecognized gain inherent in the successor long position.[37]

Example 54-4

Assume the facts are the same as in Example 54-3, except that at year-end there is $4 of unrecognized gain in the successor long position and $6 of unrecognized gain in the short position. The entire $10 loss on the original long position is not deductible for this year because there is a total of $10 of unrecognized gain in both the successor long position and the short position.[38]

Example 54-5

Assume the facts are the same as in Example 54-3, except that year-end there is $8 of unrecognized gain in the successor long

---

[36] Temp. Treas. Reg. § 1.1092(b)-1T(g), Example (2) (1986).
[37] Temp. Treas. Reg. § 1.1092(b)-1T(g), Example (4) (1986).
[38] Temp. Treas. Reg. § 1.1092(b)-1T(g), Example (5) (1986).

position and $8 of unrecognized loss in the short position. Only $8 of the total $10 realized loss on the original long position is disallowed for the taxable year because of the $8 of unrecognized gain in the successor long position.[39] The remaining $2 loss is deductible.

Example 54-6

On November 1, a taxpayer enters into offsetting long and short positions. By November 10, the market has moved so that there is $20 of unrecognized gain in the long position, and the taxpayer disposes of the short position at a $20 loss. By November 15, the value of the long position has declined, thereby eliminating all unrealized gain in the position. On November 15, the taxpayer establishes a second short position that is a successor position that offsets the long position. The successor position is not substantially identical to the short position disposed of on November 10. Assume further that at year-end there is no unrecognized gain in the offsetting long position or the successor short position. The entire $20 loss incurred on the disposition of the original short position is allowed for the year because there is no unrecognized gain in the successor short position or the offsetting long position.[40]

§ 54.3 MODIFIED WASH SALES RULE

In general, the modified wash sales rule prevents a taxpayer from disposing of a loss position in a straddle to obtain the benefit of a loss deduction when he immediately replaces the loss position with a substantially identical position or a successor position. Although the Code does not establish a priority between the modified wash sales rule and the loss deferral rule, the legislative history of ERTA provides that when the modified wash sales rule applies, it disallows losses prior to application of

---

[39] *Id.*
[40] Temp. Treas. Reg. § 1.1092(b)-1T(g), Example (10) (1986).

the loss deferral rule.[41] Under this analysis, the modified wash sales rule should prevent a taxpayer with offsetting positions from disposing of the loss position and recognizing a loss while he remains in a balanced position by virtue of his unrecognized gain position. Far-reaching attribution rules are used to apply the modified wash sales rule.[42]

The statutory mandate to the Treasury to issue regulations left many open questions on the scope and application of the modified wash sales rule. Some, but not all, of these questions have been resolved by the temporary Treasury regulations. Because positions can be opened and closed in rapid succession throughout the year, a mechanism to trace positions subject to the modified wash sales rule is necessary.

§ 54.4 MODIFIED SHORT SALES RULE

Congress enacted the modified short sales rules for straddles to assure that the principles of I.R.C. § 1233 (which prevent taxpayers from converting short-term to long-term capital gain, and long-term to short-

---

[41] The legislative history of ERTA assumes that the replacement position of a straddle subject to the modified wash sales rule has a tax basis equal to its cost, plus the amount of loss not deductible after the application of the modified wash sales rule. STAFF OF THE JOINT COMM. ON TAXATION, 97TH CONG., 1ST SESS., GENERAL EXPLANATION OF ECONOMIC RECOVERY TAX ACT OF 1981, at 286-87 (Joint Comm. Print 1981) [hereinafter General Explanation of ERTA]; SENATE FINANCE COMM. REPORT, ECONOMIC RECOVERY TAX ACT OF 1981, S. REP. No. 144, 97th Cong., 1st Sess. 149, *reprinted in* 1981 U.S. CODE CONG. & ADMIN. NEWS 105, 244 [hereinafter S. REP. No. 144]. For example, if a position in a straddle was acquired at a cost of $100, was sold for $50, and was replaced with a new position that cost $60, the $50 loss (not allowed under the modified wash sales rule) is added to the basis of the replacement position. In this example, the replacement position has a tax basis of $110 ($60 purchase price plus $50 of denied loss).

By analogy to the wash sales rule of I.R.C. § 1091, which disallows losses if a taxpayer acquires a substantially identical security 30 days before or 30 days after the sale (i.e., a 61-day prohibited period), it was assumed after enactment of ERTA that the modified wash sales rule would substitute the concept of "offsetting positions" for the apparently broader concept of "substantially identical property." General Explanation of ERTA at 287; S. REP. No. 144, at 149. It was also assumed after enactment of ERTA that Treasury regulations would provide that a deduction be denied for a loss incurred on closing out a position in a straddle that subsequently is replaced with another position (whether or not substantially identical) that offsets the remaining position (or positions) in the same straddle. *See* General Explanation of ERTA at 286; S. REP. No. 144, at 149. In other words, it was assumed that a loss position and the position that replaces it would be subject to the modified wash sales rule if any other position offsets both positions. It was also assumed that a loss allowed under the modified wash sales rule could be deferred by subsequent application of the loss deferral rule. General Explanation of ERTA at 286; S. REP. No. 144, at 149. This is because the loss deferral rule applies irrespective of whether the taxpayer replaces a loss position, thereby applying to more transactions than those covered by the modified wash sales rule.

[42] I.R.C. § 1092(d)(4). *See generally* Chapter 51.

term capital loss)[43] apply to straddle transactions where such a conversion is also possible. The remainder of this section addresses the modified short sales rules that apply to straddle positions.

(a) APPLICATION

The modified short sales rule substitutes the concept of offsetting positions for substantially identical property contained in the original short sales rule of I.R.C. § 1233.[44] Presumably, this prevents a taxpayer from either converting short-term capital gain into long-term capital gain, or long-term capital loss into short-term capital loss. It was thought that the modified short sales rule prevented the use of offsetting positions to extend, without risk of loss, the holding period of positions in personal property. Therefore, the modified short sales rule applies to offsetting positions so that the holding period for property that is part of a straddle is suspended and does not begin to run again until the offsetting position is disposed of by the taxpayer.

While offsetting positions remain open, no position in the straddle should increase its holding period. Presumably, for investors[45] and traders,[46] any gain from the disposition of the short position is short-term capital gain and the holding period of the long position begins on the earlier of the date on which the short position is disposed of, or the date on which the long position is disposed of.[47] In addition, any loss on one position of a straddle is long-term capital loss if, at the time the straddle was established, the other position was held for the long-term holding

---

[43] *See generally* Chapter 18.

[44] The General Explanation of ERTA provides some suggestions on the scope of the modified short sales rule. For example, it indicates that a short futures contract is equivalent to the short sale of a long futures contract for the same commodity, or of the short sale of the commodity itself. General Explanation of ERTA, *supra* note 41, at 287; S. REP. No. 144, *supra* note 41, at 149. Additionally, the General Explanation of ERTA assumes that regulations will provide rules to suspend the commencement of the holding period for any positions that are part of a straddle subject to the Straddle Rules. General Explanation of ERTA, *supra* note 41, at 287; S. REP. No. 144, *supra* note 41, at 149. This means that the modified short sales rule terminates the holding period of a long position in a straddle unless the long-term holding period requirement was already satisfied with respect to that position. General Explanation of ERTA, *supra* note 41, at 287; S. REP. No. 144, *supra* note 41, at 149.

[45] *See* section 8.1.

[46] *See* section 8.2.

[47] I.R.C. § 1233(b).

period.[48] Attribution rules are used in applying the modified short sales rule.[49]

The temporary Treasury regulations provide that the holding period of any position that is part of a straddle does not begin until the date the straddle is terminated—that is, the date the taxpayer no longer holds (either directly or indirectly through a related person or flow-through entity) an offsetting position with respect to that position.[50] The holding period rules do not apply to section 1256 contracts.[51] This rule does not apply to a position held by a taxpayer for the long-term capital gain holding period (or longer) before a straddle that includes such position is established.[52] Similarly, loss incurred on the disposition of one or more positions of a straddle is treated as a long-term capital loss if (1) on the date the taxpayer entered into the loss position the taxpayer held, directly or indirectly, one or more offsetting positions with respect to the loss position, and (2) one or more positions in the straddle constitute capital assets that have been held for the long-term holding period on the day the loss position was acquired.[53] This rule applies to section 1256 contracts. If a taxpayer acquires a section 1256 contract at a time when he has held an offsetting position for more than the long-term capital asset holding period, the loss on the section 1256 contract is treated as a long-term capital loss, not a 60/40 loss.[54]

There is an exception (often referred to as the "killer rule") to the holding period rule for positions that do not qualify for section 1256 treatment, but are part of a mixed straddle.[55] Losses from the disposition of one or more loss positions that are part of a mixed straddle and that are non-section 1256 positions are treated as 60 percent long-term and 40 percent short-term capital losses if (1) gain or loss from the disposition of one or more of the section 1256 contracts in the mixed straddle would be considered gain or loss from the sale or exchange of a capital asset, (2) the disposition of no position in the straddle (other than a section 1256 contract) would result in long-term capital gain or loss, and (3) a valid

---

[48] I.R.C. § 1233(d).

[49] I.R.C. § 1092(d)(4); *see also* Chapter 51.

[50] Temp. Treas. Reg. § 1.1092(b)-2T(a)(1) (1986).

[51] Temp. Treas. Reg. § 1.1092(b)-2T(f), Example (6) (1986); *see* Example 54-10.

[52] Temp. Treas. Reg. § 1.1092(b)-2T(a)(2) (1986).

[53] Temp. Treas. Reg. § 1.1092(b)-2T(b)(1) (1986).

[54] Temp. Treas. Reg. § 1.1092(b)-2T(f), Example (7) (1986).

[55] For a discussion of mixed straddles, see Chapter 57. For a discussion of the scope of the modified short sales rule to mixed straddles, see section 54.4(b). For a discussion of the killer rule, see text commencing at note 19 in Chapter 57.

election relating to either straddle-by-straddle identification or mixed straddle accounts has *not* been made by the taxpayer.[56]

Example 54-7

On October 1, 1984, a taxpayer acquires gold. On January 1, 1985, the taxpayer enters into an offsetting forward contract position to sell gold (short position). On April 1, 1985, the taxpayer disposes of the short gold forward contract at no gain or loss. On April 10, 1985, he sells the gold for a profit. Because the gold has not been held for more than six months before the offsetting short position was entered into (the then current long-term capital gain holding period), the holding period for the gold begins no earlier than the time the straddle is terminated. Thus, the holding period of the original gold purchased on October 1, 1984, and sold on October 10, 1985, begins on April 1, 1985, the date the straddle was terminated. Consequently, gain recognized with respect to the gold is short-term capital gain.[57]

Example 54-8

On January 1, 1985, the taxpayer enters into a forward contract to buy gold (long position) and on August 4, 1985, enters into an offsetting short forward contract to sell gold (short position). On September 1, 1985, the taxpayer disposes of the short position at a loss. Because an offsetting long position had been held by the taxpayer for more than six months prior to the acquisition of the offsetting short position (the then current long-term capital gain holding period), the loss with respect to the closing of the short position is treated as a long-term capital loss.[58]

Example 54-9

On March 1, 1985, the taxpayer enters into a long forward contract and on July 17, 1985, the taxpayer enters into an offsetting short gold futures contract. He does not make any election with respect to mixed straddles. On August 10, 1985, the taxpayer disposes of the

---

[56] Temp. Treas. Reg. § 1.1092(b)-2T(b)(2) (1986).
[57] Temp. Treas. Reg. § 1.1092(b)-2T(f), Example (1) (1986).
[58] Temp. Treas. Reg. § 1.1092(b)-2T(f), Example (4) (1986).

long gold forward contract at a loss. Because the forward contract was part of a mixed straddle—and the disposition of none of the positions in the straddle (other than the futures contract) would give rise to a long-term capital loss—the loss recognized on the termination of the gold forward contract is treated as 40 percent short-term and 60 percent long-term capital loss.[59]

Example 54-10

Assume that the facts are the same as in Example 54-9 above, except that on August 11, 1985, the taxpayer disposes of the short gold futures contract at a gain. Under these circumstances, the gain is still treated as 60 percent long-term and 40 percent short-term capital gain because the holding period rules of the regulations do not apply to section 1256 contracts.[60]

The implications of the rules presented in Examples 54-9 and 54-10 set forth above (these examples were taken from the temporary Treasury regulations), can be astounding—when there is a preferential tax rate for long-term capital gains—for an active trader of section 1256 contracts and offsetting non-section 1256 property. For example, an options dealer that routinely trades both stock options and the underlying stock can have a large number of his stock losses recharacterized as 60/40 losses, thereby offsetting the 60/40 treatment derived from his stock option gains. A commodity futures trader that actively trades the underlying property could also lose the benefit of the blended tax rate—when there is a preferential tax rate for long-term capital gains—generated by the 60/40 Rule for his futures contract gains.

Example 54-11

Throughout 1985, the taxpayer, an active options dealer, enters into thousands of mixed straddle transactions involving stock options and the underlying stock. The taxpayer did not hold any position for more than six months, did make the straddle-by-straddle identification, and did not elect a mixed straddle account. These transactions, prior to the application of the rules in the temporary Treasury regulations, resulted in 60/40 gains and losses from the options and

---

[59] Temp. Treas. Reg. § 1.1092(b)-2T(f), Example (5) (1986).
[60] Temp. Treas. Reg. § 1.1092(b)-2T(f), Example (6) (1986).

short-term capital gains and losses from the stock. The results of the mixed straddles are presented below in gross totals for each item traded:

Corporation Name	Gross Stock Gains	Gross Stock Losses	Gross Option Gains	Gross Option Losses
XYZ	$50,000	$40,000	$50,000	$50,000
ABC	40,000	40,000	40,000	35,000
ZZZ	40,000	25,000	40,000	40,000
Total	$130,000	$105,000	$130,000	$125,000

The taxpayer's net options gain from these transactions (generally qualifying for 60/40 treatment) is $5000, and his net stock gain is $25,000 for an overall economic gain of $30,000. He also actively traded AAA options during 1985 (although he did not acquire or sell any AAA stock) deriving a net gain, generally qualifying for 60/40 treatment, of $100,000. All gains and losses are recognized at year-end. Under these circumstances, the taxpayer's gross stock losses are recharacterized as 60/40 losses because they resulted from mixed straddles in which no positions were held for the long-term holding period. The resulting tax computation is as follows:

60/40 RESULTS

Net Option Gains Qualifying for 60/40 Treatment	100,000
Gross Option Losses from Mixed Straddles	(125,000)
Gross Option Gains from Mixed Straddles	130,000
Recharacterized Stock Losses from Mixed Straddles	(105,000)
Net 60/40 Gains Qualifying for Blended Tax Rate	-0-

SHORT-TERM CAPITAL RESULTS

Gross Stock Gains	130,000
Net Short-Term Capital Gain Taxable at 50 Percent Rate	130,000

The taxpayer could have protected the 60/40 treatment of his net option gains by making either a straddle-by-straddle identification[61] or a mixed straddle account election.[62]

The provisions of the temporary Treasury regulations apply to positions in a straddle established after June 23, 1981, in taxable years ending after such date,[63] and to positions in a mixed straddle established on or after January 1, 1984.[64] These provisions do not apply to positions that (1) constitute part of a hedging transaction, (2) are included in a straddle consisting only of section 1256 contracts, or (3) are included in a mixed straddle account.[65]

(b) MIXED STRADDLES

Significant questions as to the scope of the modified short sales rule are raised with a mixed straddle—a straddle where one, but not all, of the positions of a straddle is a section 1256 contract that is subject to the Mark-to-Market Rule and the 60/40 Rule.[66] Before enactment of the DRA in 1984, it had been argued that the purpose of the modified short sales rule was to prevent taxpayers from generating long-term capital gain from the sale of personal property (or to require that they report a short-term capital loss on the sale of loss positions) if they hold other positions that protect them from the risk of loss. The 1981 legislative history of ERTA, explaining the intended scope of the modified short sales rule, envisioned only the suspension or elimination of the holding period with respect to property that is part of a straddle. The problem was that 60/40 treatment from the section 1256 elements does not depend upon a holding period computation and thus it was unclear whether 60/40 treatment was

---

[61] *See* section 57.3.
[62] *See* section 57.4.
[63] Temp. Treas. Reg. § 1.1092(b)-2T(e)(1) (1986).
[64] Temp. Treas. Reg. § 1.1092(b)-2T(e)(2) (1986).
[65] Temp. Treas. Reg. § 1.1092(b)-2T(c) (1986).
[66] *See generally* Part Ten.

compromised by holding offsetting non-section 1256 positions.[67] The DRA's expansion in 1984, however, of the Treasury's authority to regulate offsetting positions to carry out the purposes of the Straddle Rules, and the principles of the short sales rule, make it possible for the Treasury to prevent conversions, by limiting the availability of 60/40 treatment on mixed straddles. The same analysis should apply to prevent conversion of long-term capital loss into short-term capital loss using straddles.

In addition, the DRA grants the Treasury authority to issue regulations for mixed straddles to apply in lieu of the modified short sales rule—if so elected by a taxpayer.[68] For an analysis of these elective rules to adopt section 1092(b)(2) identified mixed straddles or mixed straddle accounts, see generally Chapter 57.

Losses are treated as 60/40 on the disposition of one or more positions that are part of a mixed straddle and that are not section 1256 contracts, if three requirements are met. First, the gain or loss from the disposition of one or more of the section 1256 contract straddle positions would be considered gain or loss from the sale or exchange of a capital asset. Second, the disposition of non-section 1256 contract positions of the straddle would not generate long-term capital gain or loss. And third, neither a straddle-by-straddle identification of section 1092(b)(2) identified mixed straddles nor a mixed straddle account election is made.

(c) REGULATED INVESTMENT COMPANIES

The temporary Treasury regulations apply a special rule to positions held by RICs,[69] which—in order to qualify as such for tax purposes—must derive less than 30 percent of their gross incomes from the disposition of

---

[67] Upon review of ERTA's legislative history, it was argued that if a taxpayer holds a position with a long-term capital loss but sells another offsetting position that would generate short-term capital loss, the loss on the sale is converted to long-term capital loss. What would happen, however, if the offsetting position was a section 1256 contract eligible for 60/40 treatment? Loss on the position that is not a section 1256 contract might be treated as 60 percent long-term and 40 percent short-term loss. If this analysis were correct, a section 1256 contract subject to section 1256 treatment could shorten the holding period of another position (although the holding period of the section 1256 contract, itself, is immaterial).

On the other hand, it was also argued that as a position in a straddle, a section 1256 contract might cause 60 percent of the capital loss of the position that is not a section 1256 contract to be converted from short-term to long-term capital loss. The character of gain as 60 percent long-term and 40 percent short-term capital gain for the section 1256 contract itself, however, would not have been affected.

[68] I.R.C. § 1092(b)(2), *originally enacted as* DRA, *supra* note 3, § 103(a).

[69] *See* section 8.9.

securities held for less than three months.[70] The rule of Temp. Treas. Reg. § 1.1092(b)-2T(a), which provides that holding periods do not begin until the date the taxpayer no longer holds an offsetting position, is not applied for purposes of determining whether a RIC qualifies for the statutory definition.[71] If the short sales rule of I.R.C. § 1233(b) would have applied to the positions held by a RIC, these rules continue to apply.[72] Similarly, the regulations provide that the effect of daily marking-to-market provided under Temp. Treas. Reg. § 1.1092(b)-4T(c) is disregarded for purposes of I.R.C. § 851(b)(3), which is the statutory definition of a RIC.[73]

In LTR 8624067,[74] the IRS ruled that the holding periods of a short regulated futures contract and the underlying securities that formed a mixed straddle held by a RIC were determined under the modified short sales rule of I.R.C. § 1092(b). Gain was treated as having been derived from securities held for less than three months if less than three months had elapsed since the position was acquired and its holding period was determined under the modified short sales rule.[75]

(d) MARRIED PUT TRANSACTIONS

It is unclear whether the married put exception, provided in the short sales rule for capital assets,[76] is available as an exemption from the Straddle Rules.[77] Married put transactions were not addressed in the Code, or the legislative history in enacting the Straddle Rules. Nevertheless, married put options might be exempt from the Straddle Rules. Nothing in the legislative history of the DRA indicates that Congress intended to repeal the married put exception contained in I.R.C. § 1233(c) when it extended the scope of the Straddle Rules to publicly traded options.

In a married put transaction under I.R.C. § 1233(b), the short sales rule does not apply if a put option is acquired on the same day as property identified as the property to be used in exercising the put—and which, if exercised, is exercised through the sale of the property. For a put to be deemed "married" to stock for purposes of the short sales rule under

[70] I.R.C. § 851(b)(3).
[71] Temp. Treas. Reg. § 1.1092(b)-2T(d) (1986).
[72] *Id.*
[73] *Id.*
[74] (Mar. 17, 1986).
[75] LTR 8624067 (Mar. 17, 1986).
[76] I.R.C. § 1233(c).
[77] *See* section 18.4(d).

I.R.C. § 1233(b), the put option must be acquired on the same day as the stock, and the stock must be identified on the put holder's records as the stock to be delivered upon exercise of the put. Furthermore, it may be possible that the married put criteria can be met only by delivering the married stock, or by allowing the put to expire. If the put expires, the cost of the put is added to the stock's tax basis. Treasury regulations or clarifying legislation is needed to resolve the issue.[78] The better view at present appears to be to allow the married put exception for put option positions. Accordingly, a married put transaction should be able to provide a taxpayer with some downside protection, upside potential, and the accrual of the holding period for long-term capital gain purposes.

It is unclear whether the married put exception provided in the short sales rule of I.R.C. § 1233(c) is an exemption from the Straddle Rules. In fact, Temp. Treas. Reg. § 1.1092(b)-2T(a) suggests that married puts are not exempt from the Straddle Rules. Temp. Treas. Reg. § 1.1092(b)-2T(a) appears to eliminate the married put exception contained in I.R.C. § 1233(c) for transactions that meet the straddle definition. In particular, any pair of positions otherwise qualifying under I.R.C. § 1233(c)—that is, a put option and an underlying long position identified as intended to be used in exercising that option—constitute offsetting positions as long as the underlying long position is "actively traded" within the meaning of I.R.C. § 1092(d)(1). Under Temp. Treas. Reg. § 1.1092(b)-2T(a)(1), the holding period of the positions making up a straddle does not begin until the straddle is terminated. The temporary regulation does not contain an exception for straddles that consist of an underlying long position and a put option or other position "married" to the long position. As a result, further clarification is needed in final regulations.

---

[78] Treasury regulations could incorporate the married put exception and confirm that the short sales rule of Temp. Treas. Reg. § 1.1092(b)-2T does not apply to qualified married puts.

Fifty-five

Capitalization of Straddle Interest and Carrying Charges

Deductions are not allowed for interest and carrying charges that are allocable to personal property which is part of a straddle that does not consist solely of section 1256 positions.[1] The capitalization requirement applies to positions of a straddle consisting of non-section 1256 positions and does not apply to a straddle consisting solely of section 1256 positions.[2] As a result, the loss deferral rule and the modified wash sales and short sales rules also apply to "cash and carry transactions" and other straddle positions entered into after June 23, 1981.[3]

Under current law, when a taxpayer enters into a cash and carry transaction where not all of the positions are section 1256 contracts, the transaction is a mixed straddle subject to the mixed straddle rules.[4] Of course, because the capitalization requirements only apply to straddle transactions, they do not apply to property that is not part of a straddle, or to hedging transactions.[5] This chapter first discusses pre-ERTA cash and carry transactions and then discusses the current requirements to capitalize interest and carrying charges.

[1] I.R.C. § 263(g)(1).
[2] I.R.C. § 1256(a)(4).
[3] *See generally* Part Eleven. For a discussion of cash and carry transactions, see section 4.3(d).
[4] *See generally* Chapter 57.
[5] *See generally* Chapter 23.

§ 55.1 PRE-ERTA TRANSACTIONS

Under the law in effect prior to the enactment of ERTA[6] in 1981, taxpayers established cash and carry transactions in an attempt to convert ordinary income into long-term capital gain.[7] A taxpayer holds a cash and carry straddle if he acquires a physical commodity and enters into a short position to sell the commodity at a future date, preferably in excess of the long-term capital gain holding period.[8] In addition, if a taxpayer enters into long and short futures contract positions, subsequently takes delivery of the underlying property under the long position, and continues to maintain his short position, this is referred to as a "full carry straddle." Cash and carry straddles and full carry straddles are referred to collectively in this chapter as "cash and carry straddles." This section discusses the law in effect prior to the enactment of ERTA in 1981, which helps put the current law into perspective.[9]

Cash and carry straddles were used under pre-ERTA law to defer the payment of tax and to convert ordinary income into long-term capital gain.[10] Carrying charges—such as storage, transportation, insurance, and interest expense incurred (or continued) to purchase or carry a commodity held for investment—were deductible under pre-ERTA law by investors as section 212 expenses (paid or incurred for the management, conservation, or maintenance of property held for the production of income) and by traders and dealers as ordinary business expenses.[11]

Under pre-ERTA law, a taxpayer would deduct the interest and carrying charges associated with holding (referred to as carrying) the physical commodity, and to minimize his risk, the taxpayer would establish an

---

[6] Pub. L. No. 97-34, 95 Stat. 172 (1981) [hereinafter ERTA].

[7] STAFF OF THE JOINT COMM. ON TAXATION, 97TH CONG., 1ST SESS., GENERAL EXPLANATION OF THE ECONOMIC RECOVERY TAX ACT OF 1981, at 292 (Joint Comm. Print 1981) [hereinafter General Explanation of ERTA]; HOUSE WAYS AND MEANS COMM. REPORT, TAX INCENTIVE ACT OF 1981, H.R. REP. NO. 201, 97th Cong., 1st Sess. 203 (1981) [hereinafter H.R. REP. NO. 201]; SENATE FINANCE COMM. REPORT, ECONOMIC RECOVERY TAX ACT OF 1981, S. REP. NO. 144, 97th Cong., 1st Sess. 153, *reprinted in* 1981 U.S. CODE CONG. & ADMIN. NEWS 105, 252 [hereinafter S. REP. NO. 144].

[8] General Explanation of ERTA, *supra* note 7; H.R. REP. NO. 201, *supra* note 7; S. REP. NO. 144, *supra* note 7.

[9] For a discussion of current law, see section 55.2.

[10] General Explanation of ERTA, *supra* note 7, at 292; H.R. REP. NO. 201, *supra* note 7, at 203; S. REP. NO. 144, *supra* note 7, at 153.

[11] General Explanation of ERTA, *supra* note 7, at 292; H.R. REP. NO. 201, *supra* note 7, at 203; S. REP. NO. 144, *supra* note 7, at 153.

offsetting short position.[12] Under pre-ERTA law, closing a short position by delivering the property held by the taxpayer (long position) was not a short sale and would generate long-term capital gain if the property had been held for more than one year, which was the long-term capital gain holding period in effect for the period immediately prior to enactment of ERTA.[13] In addition, a taxpayer typically financed the purchase with borrowed funds and deducted the interest expense, subject to the investment interest limitations.[14] Assuming the commodity was a capital asset in the hands of the taxpayer (investor or trader), the taxpayer attempted to convert ordinary income into long-term capital gain.

In *Mortensen v. Comm'r*,[15] the Tax Court held, in a memorandum decision, that interest expenses incurred to finance cash and carry silver purchases were prepaid interest that materially distorted income. As a result, the interest deductions were attributable to a later tax year.[16] The interest deduction was reallocated over the life of the loan.

Cash and carry transactions were frequently established with commodities in which the price differential between the delivery months for the futures contracts were primarily a function of the cost of interest and other carrying charges, and the contract price for the futures contract was "approximately equal to the total payment for the physical commodity plus interest and carrying charges."[17] The commodity also had to be able to be stored and held for the time period necessary to obtain long-term capital gain and, if desired, used to satisfy delivery obligations under the short position.

To obtain long-term capital gain, the underlying property had to be a capital asset in the hands of the taxpayer.[18] An investor not otherwise required to inventory property would deduct interest and carrying charges under I.R.C. § 212(2) as ordinary and necessary expenses for the management, conservation, or maintenance of property held for the production of income.[19] Traders that are not required to inventory prop-

---

[12] General Explanation of ERTA, *supra* note 7, at 292; H.R. REP. No. 201, *supra* note 7, at 203; S. REP. No. 144, *supra* note 7, at 153.

[13] I.R.C. § 1233(e), *prior to amendment by* ERTA, *supra* note 6, § 501(c), which amended I.R.C. § 1233(e)(2)(A) to apply to property acquired or positions established after June 23, 1981, in tax years ending after that date. *See generally* Chapter 18.

[14] I.R.C. § 163(d) (Supp. IV 1980); *see* sections 9.2(e) and 10.2(e).

[15] 49 T.C.M. (CCH) 94 (1984).

[16] *Id.* at 103–104.

[17] General Explanation of ERTA, *supra* note 7, at 292; H.R. REP. No. 201, *supra* note 7, at 203; S. REP. No. 144, *supra* note 7, at 153.

[18] *See generally* Part Three.

[19] *See* section 9.1.

erty would deduct interest and carrying charges under I.R.C. § 162(a) as trade or business expenses.[20] In *Higgins v. United States*,[21] a taxpayer that was neither a commodities trader nor dealer was allowed to deduct storage and insurance expenses. The Court of Claims found in *Higgins* that storage and insurance expenses were properly classified as ordinary and necessary, rather than capital items, and were not part of either the purchase or sale of the commodity.[22] Rather, such expenses were incurred after the time the purchase was completed and prior to the time the sales transaction began.[23]

Example 55-1

Assume that in 1979—under the law in effect before enactment of ERTA—a taxpayer owns 100,000 ounces of gold for which he paid $350 per ounce and sells 100 short gold futures contracts (the amount of gold underlying each futures contract is 100 ounces per contract) for $375 per ounce, thereby agreeing to sell all of his gold at the futures contract price in the future. The short position calls for delivery at a date in excess of the long-term capital gain holding period. The taxpayer locks in a "profitable" sales price for his gold, and his position is essentially riskless (he owns the physical gold and holds a short gold futures contract). Historically, the difference between the gold's purchase price and the sales price of the futures contract was a function of carrying the gold until the delivery date.

The taxpayer has established a cash and carry straddle. When the gold was held for the long-term holding period, the gold could be delivered to satisfy the taxpayer's obligation under the short position, thereby obtaining long-term capital gain in 1980. On the other hand, if the price of gold increased, the taxpayer could sell the gold in the cash market for long-term capital gain, while closing the short futures contract position at a short-term capital loss.[24] In 1979 and 1980, investment income was taxed at rates of up to 70 percent. With the requisite profit motive, a taxpayer could attempt to defer investment income from 1979 to 1980 and convert it into long-term capital

---

[20] *See* section 10.1.
[21] 75 F. Supp. 252 (Ct. Cl. 1948).
[22] *Id.* at 255.
[23] *Id.*
[24] *See* sections 4.2(a) and 4.3(d).

gain taxable at maximum rates of up to 28 percent.[25] For a discussion of investment interest limitations, see section 9.2(e).

Example 55-2

In June 1979—under the law in effect prior to enactment of ERTA—a taxpayer established a long futures position to acquire silver for delivery in October 1979 and a short futures position to sell silver for delivery in July 1980. If the taxpayer took delivery of the silver under his long position in October 1979 and continued to hold the short position, he had established a full carry straddle. Holding the physical gold for a full year and a day from the date the long futures position was acquired generated long-term capital gain.

The holding period for the long futures contract position was "tacked on to" the holding period of the property acquired under it.[26]

Full carry straddles generated less carrying charges than other cash and carry transactions. The tacked holding period for the long futures contract position allowed the taxpayer to add the time period when the futures contract position was held to his holding period for the underlying property. As a result, the actual property did not need to be "carried" for a full year.

To provide the hoped for tax benefits under pre-ERTA law (which claimed capital gain treatment on the underlying property), taxpayers had to be careful not to execute sufficient transactions so as to be required to maintain an inventory for tax purposes. Inventories are deemed necessary at the beginning and end of each taxable year to clearly reflect income in those situations where the production, purchase, or sale of property is an income-producing factor.[27] If a taxpayer takes delivery of property underlying futures contracts and sells the property on a regular basis, he might be required to inventory the underlying property, which might include interest and other carrying charges.[28] The IRS takes the position that the need to maintain inventories is not confined to a

---

[25] *See* General Explanation of ERTA, *supra* note 7, at 292-93; H.R. Rep. No. 201, *supra* note 7, at 203–04; S. Rep. No. 144, *supra* note 7, at 153–54.

[26] I.R.C. § 1223(8). A tacked on holding period is still available under current law for property acquired pursuant to a futures contract that is not subject to section 1256 treatment. *See* section 17.3(b).

[27] Treas. Reg. § 1.471-1 (1958).

[28] *See* Rev. Rul. 74-226, 1974-1 C.B. 119.

taxpayer that technically qualifies either as a dealer or manufacturer, and the purchase or sale of commodities can be an income-producing factor for taxpayers engaged in cash and carry transactions.[29]

Where the taxpayer holds the underlying property (long position), an economic consideration for cash and carry transactions is the possibility that the long position increases in value. This would result in a margin call on the short futures contract position because the short position declines in value as the long position increases in value. Although documents of title or warehouse receipts for the underlying property can probably be used instead of cash for initial margin deposits, additional maintenance and mark-to-market payments must be made in cash.[30]

The first court cases, decided in 1984, directly addressing cash and carry transactions under pre-ERTA law were found to be without profit motive. In *Julien v. Comm'r*[31] and *Hirai v. Comm'r*,[32] the Tax Court denied interest deductions because the taxpayers did not prove that the transactions actually took place, the taxpayers had no profit motive, and the taxpayers did not establish an economic purpose for the transactions. In *Ostrower v. Comm'r*,[33] the Tax Court, in a memorandum decision, denied interest deductions on transactions it found to be shams designed solely to achieve interest deductions, short-term capital losses, and the conversion of ordinary income into capital gain. These cases should not control in situations where taxpayers can show that actual transactions were entered into for economic purposes to obtain profit.

In *Julien*, *Hirai*, and *Ostrower*, the taxpayers entered into cash and carry silver transactions marketed by a London brokerage firm as a way to convert ordinary income into long-term capital gain; the taxpayers acquired silver and entered into forward contracts to sell the silver in the future. The promotional materials included in the sales package provided by the broker discussed only contemplated tax results and did not refer to any profit potential. "Loans" to finance the purchase of the silver were obtained by a London finance company that would be repaid only out of the proceeds of the sale of silver.[34] The loans were without recourse against the taxpayers.[35]

---

[29] *Id.*
[30] *See* section 4.4(b).
[31] 82 T.C. 492 (1984).
[32] 48 T.C.M. (CCH) 1134 (1984).
[33] 48 T.C.M. (CCH) 1144 (1984).
[34] *Julien*, 82 T.C. at 497; *Hirai*, 48 T.C.M. (CCH) at 1138; *Ostrower*, 48 T.C.M. (CCH) at 1146.
[35] *Julien*, 82 T.C. at 507; *Hirai*, 48 T.C.M. (CCH) at 1142; *Ostrower*, 48 T.C.M. (CCH) at 1147.

In denying all of the interest deductions, the court discussed those circumstances in which interest on pre-ERTA cash and carry transactions is deductible. As a starting point, taxpayers defending pre-ERTA transactions must prove the transactions were bona fide. It also appears that transactions entered into in the domestic commodity markets might be more supportable than offshore transactions of the type addressed in *Julien, Hirai*, and *Ostrower*. Domestic transactions may be less suspicious, and the taxpayers may be better able to provide third party evidence that the transactions actually took place.[36] In *Julien*, the Tax Court stated "that the paucity of proven facts from overseas" fully justifies IRS skepticism "that an investment prospectus, cancelled checks, and confirmation statements issued in connection with an investment in futures contracts with a foreign investment firm are insufficient to substantiate the existence of transactions entitling the taxpayer to a loss deduction."[37]

The sole issue before the court in *Hirai* was the deductibility of interest expenses to finance silver while holding an offsetting short position to deliver silver in the future. The Tax Court, in a memorandum decision, analyzed I.R.C. § 163, which provides a deduction for "interest paid or accrued within the taxable year on indebtedness."[38] For purposes of I.R.C. § 163, the term "interest" denotes "that which is paid for the use of borrowed funds or compensation for the use or forbearance of money."[39] The "indebtedness" on which such a payment is made must be an "existing, unconditional, and legally enforcible [sic] obligation."[40] In determining whether a payment constitutes interest on indebtedness, economic realities govern over the form in which a transaction is cast.[41] The taxpayer must prove that the cash and carry transactions served some purpose beyond generating an interest deduction.[42]

---

[36] *But see* Brown v. Comm'r, 85 T.C. 968 (1985), *aff'd sub nom.* Sochin v. Comm'r, 842 F.2d 351 (9th Cir.), *cert. denied*, 109 S. Ct. 72 (1988) (where a United States government securities market was held to be a sham).

[37] *Julien*, 82 T.C. at 501–02; *see* Rev. Rul. 80-324, 1980-2 C.B. 340.

[38] *Hirai*, 48 T.C.M. (CCH) at 1141.

[39] *Id.* (citing Old Colony R. Co. v. Comm'r, 284 U.S. 552, 560 (1932), *rev'g* 50 F.2d 896 (1st Cir. 1931), *rev'g* 18 B.T.A. 267 (1929); Deputy v. Du Pont, 308 U.S. 488, 498 (1940), *rev'g* 103 F.2d 257 (3d Cir. 1939), *modifying* 22 F. Supp. 589 (D.C. Del. 1938)).

[40] *Id.* (citing Kovtun v. Comm'r, 54 T.C. 331, 338 (1970), *aff'd per curiam*, 448 F.2d 1268 (9th Cir. 1971), *cert. denied*, 405 U.S. 1016 (1972); Titcher v. Comm'r, 57 T.C. 315, 322 (1971)).

[41] *See* Knetsch v. United States, 364 U.S. 361, 365–66 (1960), *aff'g* 272 F.2d 200 (9th Cir. 1959); Goldstein v. Comm'r, 364 F.2d 734, 740 (2d Cir. 1966), *aff'g* 44 T.C. 284 (1965), *cert. denied*, 385 U.S. 1005 (1967).

[42] *See Hirai*, 48 T.C.M. (CCH) at 1142; Welch v. Helvering, 290 U.S. 111, 115 (1933), *aff'g* 63 F.2d 976 (8th Cir. 1933), *dismissing petition* 25 B.T.A. 117 (1932).

In *Ostrower*, the Tax Court, in a memorandum decision, noted that "amounts denominated as interest cannot be deducted where the underlying transaction was a sham."[43] In addition, the court noted that I.R.C. § 163(a) "does not 'intend' that taxpayers should be permitted deductions for interest paid on debts that were entered into solely in order to obtain a deduction."[44]

In light of the *Julien*, *Hirai*, and *Ostrower* cases, taxpayers seeking to support the deductibility of interest on pre-ERTA cash and carry transactions would need to demonstrate the following. First, the transactions were not prearranged at the outset so that there was no risk to the taxpayer and the broker.[45] Second, the commodity was actually purchased and the offsetting short sales position established.[46] Third, the taxpayer had the potential for making money as a result of various market forces and some risk of losing money.[47] Fourth, there was some economic purpose (such as the procurement of a profit) to support the acquisition of the commodity and to support the interest deduction.[48] And fifth, the interest payments were actually made.[49]

Although *Hirai* and *Ostrower* were both decided after the DRA was enacted July 18, 1984, neither case mentioned whether Section 108[50] might apply to limit the IRS's positions to the profit motive test. It is possible that the court did not feel it was necessary to address this issue because it concluded that the transactions were shams and did not take place.[51]

In *King v. Comm'r*,[52] the Tax Court held that interest expense incurred by a commodities trader to carry a physical commodity is part of his trade or business so the investment interest limitations of I.R.C. § 163(d) do not limit his interest deduction. In *King*, the taxpayer, who had spent his entire career in the commodity futures business, primarily traded for his own account in the years before the court. In 1978, the taxpayer took delivery of 10,000 ounces of gold under 100 long gold futures contracts.[53]

---

[43] *Ostrower*, 48 T.C.M. (CCH) at 1152 (citing Derr v. Comm'r, 77 T.C. 708, 730 (1981)).

[44] *Id.* (citing *Goldstein*, 364 F.2d 734 (2d Cir. 1966), *aff'g* 44 T.C. 284 (1965), *cert. denied*, 385 U.S. 1005 (1967)).

[45] *See Julien*, 82 T.C. at 505–06.

[46] *See id.* at 506.

[47] *Id.* at 508.

[48] *Hirai*, 48 T.C.M. (CCH) at 1143.

[49] *Id.* at 1143–44.

[50] Pub. L. No. 98-369, § 108, 98 Stat. 494, 630–31 (1984) [hereinafter DRA].

[51] *See* section 47.2(c).

[52] 89 T.C. 445 (1987), *acq.* 1988-2 C.B. 1, *action on decision*, 1988-009 (Apr. 11, 1988), *related reference* King v. Comm'r, 87 T.C. 1213 (1986).

[53] 89 T.C. at 454.

To finance this acquisition, he borrowed the delivery price and executed a promissory note in the amount of the loan, with interest, due on December 4, 1979.[54] The note was replaced on its due date by a replacement note with a higher interest rate. In 1980, the replacement note was paid in full.[55] The total interest paid on the debt incurred to purchase the gold was over $350,000.[56]

The IRS denied the taxpayer's deduction for interest on the grounds that the investment interest limitations of I.R.C. § 163(d) prohibited a deduction for the full amount of the interest expense. The IRS asserted that the taxpayer was not in the trade or business of trading physical commodities and that the gold transactions were not part of his trade or business of trading futures.[57]

In allowing the deduction, the Tax Court examined the legislative history of I.R.C. § 163(d), concluding that the taxpayer's trading activities did not fall within the abuse Congress intended to curb by its enactment.[58] The Tax Court rejected the IRS's argument that the taxpayer's interest expense was used to shelter noninvestment income from taxation. That is, the court rejected the IRS's argument that interest deductions should be limited where a taxpayer can postpone capital gain.[59] The court found that the investment interest limitations contained in I.R.C. § 163(d) do not apply to the ordinary trading activities that are part of a taxpayer's trade or business.

The Tax Court found that the taxpayer was in the trade or business of trading commodity futures and that the physical gold transactions were part of his trade or business.[60] The court said it was "not aware of any case which has held that a taxpayer may hold property both as a trader of commodity futures and as an investor in commodities. Past cases have held that a taxpayer may be both a trader and a dealer with respect to securities, but these cases have not dealt with the issue of whether the taxpayer therein was a trader or investor."[61] Under this analysis, the taxpayer was allowed to deduct his interest expenses.

---

[54] *Id.*

[55] *Id.* at 455.

[56] During 1979 and 1980, the taxpayer also took delivery under 34 futures contracts and held the underlying commodities for a period of time. He also had purchased some commodities in the cash market. *Id.* at 463.

[57] *Id.* at 457.

[58] *Id.* at 460.

[59] *Id.*

[60] *Id.* at 463–65.

[61] *Id.* at 465 (citations omitted).

§ 55.2 CAPITALIZATION REQUIREMENTS

Congress believed that the use of cash and carry straddle transactions executed with deductible interest and carrying charges was "a serious tax-avoidance problem threatening substantial revenue losses."[62] To discourage these transactions, Congress enacted I.R.C. § 263(g) as part of ERTA in 1981, which requires the capitalization of "certain otherwise deductible expenditures for personal property if the property is held as part or all of an offsetting position belonging to a straddle."[63]

Notwithstanding the ERTA capitalization requirements, cash and carry transactions continue to be established to seek a profit, irrespective of potential tax detriments. These transactions continue to be used as a form of arbitrage by market participants, not by taxpayers simply seeking tax deductions. An example of a typical cash and carry transaction follows.

Example 55-3

Assume that on September 15 cash soybeans are trading at $6 per bushel. In addition, interest rates are at 12 percent. Other carrying charges total $.05 per bushel per month. November futures are trading at $6.22 per bushel. The cost of borrowing $6 per bushel for two months is approximately $.12 per bushel. Therefore, the total cost to buy cash soybeans and carry them to delivery under the futures contract in November is $6.22 ($6 + $.12 + $.10 = $6.22). This provides an effective ceiling on November soybean futures prices, because if they traded at a price higher than $6.22 it would be profitable to buy cash soybeans and deliver them pursuant to the November futures contract. Market participants would willingly do this arbitrage trade until the guaranteed profit was gone.[64]

The November futures market, trading at $6.22, is said to be at "full carry." Traders buy the cash position and sell the futures position at full carry, because they are locking in, under the worst case, a break even transaction. If nothing happens, or if the futures price increases more than the cash position, they deliver their

---

[62] General Explanation of ERTA, *supra* note 7, at 292; H.R. REP. NO. 201, *supra* note 7, at 203; S. REP. NO. 144, *supra* note 7, at 153. For a discussion of cash and carry transactions, see sections 4.3(d) and 55.1.

[63] General Explanation of ERTA, *supra* note 7, at 293; H.R. REP. NO. 201, *supra* note 7, at 204; S. REP. NO. 144, *supra* note 7, at 154.

[64] *See generally* section 8.7.

soybeans pursuant to the November futures contract. If, on the other hand, futures happen to decline or increase less than the cash market, they unwind the trade (sell the cash soybeans and buy back the November futures) at a profit.

(a) IN GENERAL

In general, a taxpayer cannot deduct "interest and carrying charges" allocable to personal property that is part of a straddle.[65] Interest and carrying charges include (1) the amount of interest incurred or continued to purchase or carry personal property; (2) all amounts paid or incurred to store, insure, or transport personal property; and (3) any amounts paid or incurred in connection with personal property used in a short sale.[66] The types of nondeductible expenses have increased since ERTA. First, the definition of interest and carrying charges was expanded to include—for property acquired and positions established after September 22, 1982—all charges for the temporary use of a commodity in a short sale.[67] When it became clear that this definition was not broad enough, "interest" was redefined by the DRA in 1984 to include "any amount paid or incurred in connection with personal property used in a short sale."[68] Interest and carrying charges are capitalized and added to the basis of the property, thereby reducing the gain or increasing the loss upon its disposition. Without a rule requiring capitalization of interest and carrying charges, a taxpayer could otherwise generate deductions against ordinary income. And, assuming the taxpayer is not a dealer in the property, the taxpayer could obtain long-term capital gain on the sale of the property.[69]

If a taxpayer holds a short position, this position could be used to require capitalization of interest and carrying charges on any offsetting long position with which it could be paired, regardless of whether the long position is the position with which the short contract is paired for purposes of terminating the holding period under the modified short sales rule.[70] In other words, it is possible for a short position to terminate the

---

[65] I.R.C. § 263(g)(1). The capitalization requirement does not apply to a straddle consisting solely of section 1256 positions. I.R.C. § 1256(a)(4).
[66] I.R.C. § 263(g)(2); *see generally* Chapter 18.
[67] Pub. L. No. 97-448, § 105(b), 96 Stat. 2365, 2385 (1983) [hereinafter TCA '82].
[68] DRA, *supra* note 50, § 102(e)(7).
[69] *See* section 55.1.
[70] *See* section 54.4.

holding period of another short position while also being paired with a long position to require capitalization of interest and carrying charges.

Example 55-4

Assume that in June 1985, a taxpayer enters into a short futures contract position to deliver silver in February 1986 at $10 per ounce and simultaneously purchases silver ingots (long position) for $9 per ounce. The taxpayer incurs interest and carrying charges of $1 per ounce to hold the silver ingots from June through December 31, 1985, and an additional $.50 per ounce from January through February 1986. Assume further that the market price of the taxpayer's positions does not change during 1985, so under I.R.C. § 1256 there is no mark-to-market gain or loss on the short futures contract position held at the end of December 1985. The taxpayer must capitalize the entire $1 per ounce interest and carrying charges in 1985, as well as the $.50 per ounce charge incurred in 1986. The $1.50 per ounce of interest and carrying charges is added to the basis of the silver ingots, irrespective of whether the silver is used to satisfy the short futures contract position or it is sold in the cash market.

Example 55-5

In February 1986, a taxpayer buys gold bullion at $400 per ounce and enters into a short gold futures contract position to deliver gold 16 months later for $475 per ounce. The taxpayer holds a mixed straddle. A mixed straddle identification is not made and the taxpayer does not have a mixed straddle account for gold.[71] To purchase and carry the gold bullion, the taxpayer incurs expenses of $30.

Assume further that at the end of 1986, the price of gold increases so that there is a $30 unrealized gain on the gold bullion and a $40 loss on the futures contract position. The $40 loss (60 percent long-term and 40 percent short-term capital loss under I.R.C. § 1256) is deferred under the loss deferral rule.[72] The $30 paid to purchase and carry the gold bullion is added to its basis, thereby eliminating the $30 unrealized gain on the gold bullion position.[73]

---

[71] For a discussion of mixed straddle elections, see sections 57.4(g), 57.4(h), and 57.4(i).
[72] I.R.C. § 1092(a)(1).
[73] I.R.C. § 263(g)(1).

(b) STRADDLE INCOME

Interest and carrying charges that are capitalized and added to the basis of property are reduced to the extent that the straddle position generates certain income from interest, discount income, and dividends.[74] Amounts that must be capitalized are reduced by the sum of the following: (1) interest income (including OID)[75] includable in gross income earned on the property;[76] (2) any amounts of acquisition discount or market discount with respect to such property;[77] and (3) the excess of any dividends includable in gross income with respect to such property minus, for corporate shareholders, the amount of the intercorporate dividends received deduction.[78] Therefore, interest and carrying charges are currently deductible only to the extent that a straddle position generates interest and dividend income of the three types previously outlined. DRA added items (2) and (3)[79] for property acquired and positions established after July 18, 1984, in tax years ending after that date.[80]

A lender of securities used in a short sale receives compensation from the borrower to replace interest, dividends, and other compensating amounts on loaned property.[81] The lender can also incur interest and other carrying costs for the loaned securities. As initially enacted, I.R.C. § 263(g) did not provide for the inclusion of compensating payments to the lender of securities in those taxable amounts that reduce interest and other costs required to be capitalized under I.R.C. § 263(g). This problem was retroactively corrected by TRA '86. Compensating payments received by a lender of securities used in a short sale are treated as income and are used to reduce the amount of expenses (i.e., interest and other carrying charges) that must be capitalized under I.R.C. § 263(g).[82] This amendment is treated as if it had been included in the DRA when it was enacted in 1984. In other words, the amendment applies to positions established after July 18, 1984, in tax years ending after that date.

---

[74] I.R.C. § 263(g)(2)(B).
[75] I.R.C. §§ 1271–1275; *see generally* Chapter 25; *see also* section 31.2.
[76] I.R.C. § 263(g)(2)(B)(i).
[77] I.R.C. § 263(g)(2)(B)(ii); *see* sections 31.2 and 31.3.
[78] I.R.C. § 263(g)(2)(B)(iii); *see* section 24.9.
[79] DRA, *supra* note 50, § 102(e)(7).
[80] *Id.* § 102(f)(1).
[81] *See generally* Chapter 26.
[82] I.R.C. § 263(g)(2)(B)(iv).

Example 55-6

To speculate on interest rate movements, a taxpayer purchases a call option (long position), sells stock short (short position), and sells a put option (short position), all in XYZ Corporation. The taxpayer incurs interest expense on the call position and income from the short stock position (consisting of the short stock rebate received, less any payments made in lieu of dividends). Prior to amendment by TRA '86, the income received from the short stock position was not "interest" as defined in I.R.C. § 263(g)(2) and, therefore, could not have been used before amendment to reduce the amount of interest and carrying charges that otherwise must be capitalized. This result was retroactively changed by TRA '86 to cover all positions established after June 18, 1984, in tax years ending after that date.[83] As a result, the income must be capitalized.

(c) SHORT SALES

For positions established after September 22, 1982, charges for the temporary use of personal property in a short sale must be capitalized.[84] The capitalization requirement was extended in 1982, once Congress determined that a taxpayer could, for example, sell short a borrowed government security and buy another similar security to obtain long-term capital gain.[85] A taxpayer would pay the owner of a borrowed security (e.g., a Treasury bond) a charge equal to interest due on the bond. But because this charge was not "interest," it was not subject to I.R.C. § 263(g) and was deducted from ordinary income.[86] I.R.C. § 263(g), therefore, was modified to require capitalization of interest equivalent charges.[87]

The DRA further amended I.R.C. § 263(g) in 1984 to make it clear that "interest" that must be capitalized "includes any amount paid or incurred in connection with personal property used in a short sale."[88] This

---

[83] I.R.C. § 263(g)(2)(B)(iv).

[84] TCA '82, *supra* note 67, § 105(b); SENATE FINANCE COMM. REPORT, TECHNICAL CORRECTIONS ACT OF 1982, S. REP. NO. 592, 97th Cong., 2d Sess. 28, *reprinted in* 1982 U.S. CODE CONG. & ADMIN. NEWS 4149, 4174.

[85] *Tax Report*, Wall St. J., Oct. 13, 1982, at 1, col. 5.

[86] *Id.*

[87] TCA '82, *supra* note 67, § 105(b).

[88] I.R.C. § 263(g)(2).

applies—after July 18, 1984—to any amount paid or incurred in a short sale.[89]

One final point is that I.R.C. § 263(g) applies to short sales only after the application of I.R.C. § 263(h), which denies deductions for certain payments incurred in connection with short sales.[90]

(d) MIXED STRADDLE ACCOUNTS

If a taxpayer identifies individual straddles, it is possible to identify the expenses incurred in holding offsetting positions and the amount of income received from the straddle. On its face, I.R.C. § 263(g) appears to assume that all positions of the straddle can be identified and that interest income and expense with respect to such positions can be identified. However, this assumption is not correct in many cases. If a taxpayer establishes a mixed straddle account for mixed straddle positions, individual straddles are not identified.[91] In providing the election for a mixed straddle account, Congress recognized that identifying individual straddle transactions is difficult (and perhaps impossible) for certain taxpayers.[92] If a taxpayer maintains a mixed straddle account, the capitalization requirement is applied to the account rather than to individual straddles held within the account.[93]

The temporary Treasury regulations originally issued on January 18, 1985 (and as subsequently amended on October 11, 1985), provide some guidance on whether interest expense attributable to the account should be netted against all gains in the account or only netted against that portion of the gain generated from debt-financed assets.[94] The temporary Treasury regulations apply I.R.C. § 263(g) to a mixed straddle account as if the account contains only one straddle.[95] The gross expenses and income of the mixed straddle account are netted on an annual basis, and any excess expense from the mixed straddle account is capitalized to prevent excess expense from reducing ordinary income unrelated to the

---

[89] DRA, *supra* note 50, § 102(f)(1).

[90] I.R.C. § 263(g)(4)(A); *see* sections 18.6(e) and 55.2(e).

[91] I.R.C. § 1092(b)(2)(A)(i); *see* section 57.4.

[92] House Conference Report, Deficit Reduction Act of 1984, H.R. Conf. Rep. No. 861, 98th Cong., 2d Sess. 913 (1984).

[93] Temp. Treas. Reg. § 1.1092(b)-4T(c)(3) (1985).

[94] Temp. Treas. Reg. § 1.1092(b)-4T(c)(3)(i) (1985), T.D. 8008, 1985-1 C.B. 276, *amended by* T.D. 8058, 1985-2 C.B. 183; *see* section 57.4(d).

[95] *See* Temp. Treas. Reg. § 1.1092(b)-4T(c)(3) (1985).

account positions.[96] The temporary Treasury regulations further provide that no deduction is allowed for interest and carrying charges that are "properly allocable" to a mixed straddle account.[97] Interest and carrying charges properly allocable to a mixed straddle account are defined as the excess of (1) the sum of (a) interest (including short sale expenses) on debt incurred to purchase or carry any position in the account, and (b) all amounts paid or incurred to insure, store, transport, etc., personal property with respect to a position in the account; *over* (2) the sum of (a) interest includable in gross income with respect to all positions in the account, (b) ordinary income from the holding, retirement, or sale of debt securities in the account, and (c) dividends received with respect to positions in the account, net of certain dividend deductions.[98] Any nondeductible interest and carrying charges are capitalized by treating such charges as an adjustment to the annual mixed straddle account net gain or loss and are allocated on a pro rata basis between net short-term and long-term capital gain or loss.[99]

Example 55-7

Assume that a taxpayer has a mixed straddle account for ABC stock and options. During the taxable year he incurs $40 of net interest expense properly allocable to positions in the ABC mixed straddle account. Under these circumstances, the $40 of net interest expense is not deductible but is allocated to the annual net gain or loss of the ABC mixed straddle account. The $40 of interest expense proportionately reduces the long-term and short-term elements of the ABC capital gain, or increases proportionately the long-term and short-term elements of the ABC capital loss.

(e) APPLICATION AFTER CERTAIN PROVISIONS

Other Code provisions take priority over application of the capitalization requirement established in I.R.C. § 263(g).[100] In the case of any short sale, I.R.C. § 263(g) applies after application of I.R.C. § 263(h), which denies deductions for payments made in lieu of dividends on short sales of

---

[96] *Id.*
[97] *Id.*
[98] *Id.*
[99] *Id.*
[100] I.R.C. § 263(g)(4).

stock.¹⁰¹ For securities subject either to the market discount rules under I.R.C. § 1277 (for the deferral of net direct interest on indebtedness with respect to market discount bonds) or the rules under I.R.C. § 1282 (with respect to deferral of interest on indebtedness with respect to short-term obligations), the provisions of I.R.C. § 263(g) apply after application of these other provisions.¹⁰²

(f) HEDGING TRANSACTIONS

When Congress enacted ERTA in 1981, it recognized that certain legitimate business transactions that result only in ordinary income or loss lacked sufficient tax avoidance potential to be covered by I.R.C. § 263(g).¹⁰³ Hedging transactions that qualify for the statutory hedging exemption are exempt from the capitalization requirements.¹⁰⁴ This means that interest and carrying charges incurred to purchase and carry positions qualifying for the statutory hedging exemption can be deducted currently and need not be added to the basis of the property. If the hedging exemption is not properly elected, however, capitalization is required in otherwise exempt ordinary income dealer transactions.¹⁰⁵

Example 55-8

The taxpayer, a dealer in securities, is a general partnership. It borrows money and incurs expenses to finance its inventory and its ordinary income trading accounts. The taxpayer qualifies as a hedger for those positions entered into to hedge its inventory and for its ordinary income trading account positions. All transactions qualify as hedges. Interest and other carrying charges incurred by the taxpayer are deductible.¹⁰⁶

---

[101] I.R.C. § 263(g)(4)(A); *see* section 18.6(e).
[102] I.R.C. § 263(g)(4)(B); *see* sections 31.2(d) and 31.3.
[103] General Explanation of ERTA, *supra* note 7, at 293; H.R. REP. No. 201, *supra* note 7, at 204; S. REP. No. 144, *supra* note 7, at 154.
[104] I.R.C. § 263(g)(3); *see generally* Chapter 23.
[105] *See* section 23.2(g).
[106] *See* General Explanation of ERTA, *supra* note 7, at 293; H.R. REP. No. 201, *supra* note 7, at 204; S. REP. No. 144, *supra* note 7, at 154. *See* discussion in sections 8.4 and 8.4(d) for possible application of Arkansas Best v. Comm'r, 485 U.S. 212 (1988), *aff'g* 800 F.2d 215 (8th Cir. 1986), *aff'g in part, rev'g in part* 83 T.C. 640 (1984).

Example 55-9

A farmer borrows money and incurs other expenses to finance, store, and transport his corn and wheat crops. The farmer does not hedge his corn crop and does not enter into any short positions (e.g., options, futures, or forward contracts) for the sale of corn. The farmer holds no offsetting positions with respect to his corn. Under these circumstances, the farmer can deduct his interest and carrying charges incurred on his corn crop without regard to I.R.C. § 263(g). The expenses are not attributable to a position that is part of a straddle as is required for capitalization under I.R.C. § 263(g).

Assume, on the other hand, that with respect to his wheat crop the farmer enters into short futures contracts to sell his wheat crop for delivery after it is harvested. The farmer holds a straddle. As long as the transactions are properly identified as hedge transactions, the farmer can currently deduct his costs.[107] If the transactions do not meet the statutory hedging exemption, however, capitalization is required.[108]

For taxable years beginning after December 31, 1986, section 988 hedging transactions that qualify for section 988 treatment are exempt from the capitalization requirements under I.R.C. § 263(g). For a discussion of those foreign currency transactions that qualify for section 988 hedging treatment, see section 59.3.

---

[107] *See* I.R.C. § 263(g)(3).
[108] For a discussion of the qualifications for a valid hedging transaction, see generally section 23.2(b).

Fifty-six
Exceptions to Application of the Straddle Rules

Certain transactions are exempt from the Straddle Rules—identified straddles, hedging transactions, qualified covered calls, certain stock positions, section 988 hedging transactions of foreign currencies (for taxable years beginning after December 31, 1986), and straddles made up exclusively of section 1256 contracts. In addition, certain exchange-traded stock options established prior to July 18, 1984, are exempt from the Straddle Rules. This section discusses those transactions that are exempt from the Straddle Rules.

§ 56.1 IDENTIFIED STRADDLES

(a) REQUIREMENTS

Identified straddles are exempt from the Straddle Rules and are subject to special rules[1] if the positions qualify for and are properly designated as identified straddles under the rules set out in I.R.C. § 1092(a)(2). To qualify as an identified straddle, the offsetting positions must meet four conditions. First, the straddle must be clearly identified as an identified straddle on the taxpayer's records before the close of the day on which the

[1] I.R.C. § 1092(a)(2)(A).

straddle is acquired (or an earlier time if required by Treasury regulations).[2] Second, all of the original positions in the straddle must be acquired on the same day.[3] Third, either (1) all of the positions in the straddle must be disposed of on the same day during the taxable year, or (2) none of the positions are disposed of as of the close of the taxable year.[4] Fourth, the straddle must not be part of a larger straddle (e.g., a butterfly spread, box spread, conversion, or reverse conversion).[5]

Identified straddles must be clearly identified on the taxpayer's records as an identified straddle before the close of the day on which the straddle is acquired, or earlier if required by Treasury regulations. To date, such regulations have not been issued and guidance is needed as to how a taxpayer must comply with this identification requirement. Of course, where the taxpayer's own records are used to designate identified straddles, the problem of verification may be raised on audit. Presumably, a taxpayer would need to demonstrate that the records were kept in a manner contemplated by I.R.C. § 1092(a)(2)(B)(i).

The advantage to making an identified straddle designation is that a taxpayer can segregate his identified straddle transactions from his nonstraddle transactions. Identified straddle positions are not treated as offsetting any positions that are not identified as part of the identified straddle.[6] Therefore, positions that are part of an identified straddle will not (1) affect the holding periods (by application of the modified short sales rule) of other positions which are not part of the identified straddle; (2) defer the recognition of losses (by application of the modified wash sales rule); (3) cause the deferral of losses on positions that are not part of the identified straddle; or (4) cause the capitalization of interest and carrying charges on positions that are not part of the identified straddle. Any loss sustained with respect to an identified straddle position, however, is treated as sustained not earlier than the day on which all of the positions making up the identified straddle are disposed of.[7]

Example 56-1

Assume a taxpayer acquires gold bullion (long position), enters into a forward contract to sell gold (short position) on the same day, and

---

[2] I.R.C. § 1092(a)(2)(B)(i).
[3] I.R.C. § 1092(a)(2)(B)(ii).
[4] I.R.C. §§ 1092(a)(2)(B)(ii)(I), (II).
[5] I.R.C. § 1092(a)(2)(B)(iii).
[6] I.R.C. § 1092(c)(2)(C).
[7] I.R.C. § 1092(a)(2)(A)(ii).

properly designates the straddle as an identified straddle. Assume further that the taxpayer subsequently acquires additional gold that could be viewed as offsetting and at the end of the year he continues to hold the identified straddle. Because the taxpayer properly identified the two original positions as an identified straddle and both positions remained open at year-end, those positions do not offset any of the other gold positions held by the taxpayer.

(b) SUBSEQUENT TRANSACTIONS

Because all of the positions in an identified straddle must be acquired on the same day, a straddle ceases to be an identified straddle if a successor or substitute position is acquired to replace an original straddle position. In addition, it appears that no loss can be claimed on any positions that were once part of an identified straddle until all of the remaining positions are disposed of. This results even if a loss is disallowed because of the application of the modified wash sales rule.[8] If a taxpayer disposes of a position at a loss and the loss is disallowed under the modified wash sales rule (because the original position is replaced), other losses sustained on positions not part of the identified straddle may be disallowed because of unrealized gain on positions making up the identified straddle.[9]

An identified straddle no longer qualifies as an identified straddle in a subsequent tax year if, after having been kept open through the end of the tax year in which it was established, one of the straddle positions is closed out in the subsequent tax year before the remaining identified straddle positions are also closed out.[10] Neither the Code nor the legislative history of ERTA, when it was enacted in 1981, indicate directly whether the identified straddle designation applies to the first year in such a situation. One possible reading is that since none of the positions were disposed of as of the close of the first taxable year, the straddle qualifies as an identified straddle in the first, but not the second, tax year.

Finally, although a taxpayer must generally disclose unrecognized gains on his tax return, identified straddles need not be disclosed.[11] In addition, if a taxpayer initially designates offsetting positions as an

---

[8] *See generally* Chapter 54.

[9] STAFF OF THE JOINT COMM. ON TAXATION, 97TH CONG., 1ST SESS., GENERAL EXPLANATION OF THE ECONOMIC RECOVERY TAX ACT OF 1981, at 284 (Joint Comm. Print 1981) [hereinafter General Explanation of ERTA].

[10] *Id.*

[11] *See id.* at 286; *see generally* Chapter 52 and section 53.1.

identified straddle in the first year and the straddle no longer qualifies in a subsequent year, the taxpayer must disclose any unrecognized gains on the open positions.[12]

§ 56.2 HEDGING TRANSACTIONS

Hedging transactions that qualify for the statutory hedging exemption are exempt from the Straddle Rules and from section 1256 treatment. This means that qualified hedging transactions are exempt from the loss deferral rule,[13] modified wash sales rule,[14] modified short sales rule,[15] the requirement to capitalize interest and carrying charges,[16] the Mark-to-Market Rule,[17] and the 60/40 Rule.[18] For a detailed discussion of the hedging exemption, see generally Chapter 23. Although a taxpayer must generally disclose unrecognized gains on his tax returns, hedging transactions need not be disclosed.[19]

TRA '86[20] introduced a new hedging exemption for certain foreign currency transactions that qualify for section 988 treatment. This means that a taxpayer has some flexibility in identifying transactions as section 988 hedging transactions to avoid application of the Straddle Rules. For a discussion of foreign currency transactions eligible for section 988 hedging treatment, see section 23.3.

If a transaction does not comply with the specific requirements of I.R.C. § 1256(e)(2)—but is subject to ordinary treatment under the *Corn Products*[21] doctrine—the transaction nevertheless generates ordinary income or loss while remaining subject to the Straddle Rules and section 1256 treatment. In other words, the gains and losses from a *Corn Products*-type hedge transaction are always ordinary, rather than capital.

---

[12] *See* General Explanation of ERTA, *supra* note 9, at 286.
[13] *See* section 49.1.
[14] *See* section 54.3.
[15] *See* section 54.4.
[16] *See* section 55.2.
[17] *See* section 45.1.
[18] *See* section 45.2.
[19] *See generally* Chapter 52 and section 53.1.
[20] Pub. L. No. 99-514, 100 Stat. 2085 (1986) [hereinafter TRA '86].
[21] Corn Prods. Ref. Co. v. Comm'r, 350 U.S. 46 (1955), *aff'g* 215 F.2d 513 (2d Cir. 1954), *aff'g* 20 T.C. 503 (1953), *aff'g* 11 T.C.M. (CCH) 721 (1952), *aff'g* 16 T.C. 395 (1951), *reh'g denied*, 350 U.S. 943 (1956).

In 1988, the Supreme Court held in *Arkansas Best Corp. v. Comm'r*,[22] that a taxpayer's assets are to be classified as capital or ordinary based on the literal language of I.R.C. § 1221. Under the *Corn Products* doctrine, it had been generally assumed that assets falling squarely under the Code's definition of capital assets are nevertheless to be treated as ordinary assets if they are "integrally related" to the taxpayer's business operations. For a discussion of the application of *Arkansas Best* to hedging transactions, see generally Chapter 23.

§ 56.3 QUALIFIED COVERED CALLS

Taxpayers frequently write (sell) covered call options to enhance the return on their investments in the stocks and securities underlying the call options. A covered call has been described as a call option "that is written with respect to stock that is held by the taxpayer (or acquired by the taxpayer in connection with the granting of the option)."[23] In addition, writing (selling) a covered call option "does not substantially reduce a taxpayer's risk of loss with respect to holding the underlying long stock position unless the option is deep-in-the-money."[24]

(a) SCOPE OF EXEMPTION

Taxpayers entering into qualified covered call transactions established after December 31, 1983, need not postpone the deduction of losses on call option positions even if there is unrecognized gain in the underlying corporate stock position.[25] The qualified covered call exemption is limited to the disposition of qualified covered call options written on corporate stock and is not available for options on other securities, stock indexes, or foreign currencies.[26] This means that the positions are not subject to the Straddle Rules if all of the positions making up a straddle consist of qualified covered call options and the corporate stock under-

---

[22] 485 U.S. 212 (1988), *aff'g* 800 F.2d 215 (8th Cir. 1986), *aff'g in part, rev'g in part* 83 T.C. 640 (1984).

[23] REPORT OF THE COMM. ON WAYS AND MEANS, DEFICIT REDUCTION ACT OF 1984, H.R. REP. NO. 432, Pt. II, 98 Cong., 2d Sess. 1268, *reprinted in* 1984 U.S. CODE CONG. & ADMIN. NEWS 697, 930.

[24] *Id.* at 1268.

[25] I.R.C. § 1092(c)(4)(A).

[26] I.R.C. § 1092(c)(4)(B).

lying the options, and the straddle is not part of a larger straddle (e.g., a conversion or reverse conversion transaction, a butterfly, or box).[27]

(b) DEFINITION

A taxpayer holds a qualified covered call option if five conditions are met at the time the option is written. First, the option has more than 30 days before its expiration.[28] Second, it is traded on a national securities exchange.[29] Third, it is not deep-in-the-money.[30] Fourth, it is not granted by an options dealer in the course of his dealer activity.[31] And fifth, gain or loss with respect to the option is capital gain or loss.[32]

Whether an option is deep-in-the-money is determined by reference to the strike price of the option and, generally, the closing stock price on the last day the stock was traded before the option was written. A deep-in-the-money option is defined as an option with a strike price lower than the lowest qualified bench mark,[33] which generally means the highest available strike price below the applicable stock price.[34] Applicable stock price is defined as either (1) the closing price of the stock on the most recent day the stock was traded before the option was sold, or (2) the opening price of the stock on the day on which the option was granted if this price exceeds by 110 percent the price under clause (1).[35] Under current securities exchange rules, the lowest qualified bench mark for stock trading below $25 is $2.50 in-the-money, for stock trading between $25 and $200 is $5 in-the-money, and for stock trading above $200 is $10 in-the-money.[36]

Example 56-2

Assume a stock is trading at $48 per share and call options overlaying the stock are trading with strike prices of $30, $35, $40, $45, $50, and $55. Because the qualified covered call exemption does not

---

[27] I.R.C. § 1092(c)(4)(A).
[28] I.R.C. § 1092(c)(4)(B)(ii).
[29] I.R.C. § 1092(c)(4)(B)(i).
[30] I.R.C. § 1092(c)(4)(B)(iii).
[31] I.R.C. § 1092(c)(4)(B)(iv).
[32] I.R.C. § 1092(c)(4)(B)(v).
[33] I.R.C. § 1092(c)(4)(C).
[34] I.R.C. § 1092(c)(4)(D)(i).
[35] I.R.C. § 1092(c)(4)(G).
[36] CBOE Rule 5.5, Interpretation .01.

apply if the option's strike price is more than one bench mark below the stock's closing price, options with a strike price of $30, $35, and $40 are deep-in-the-money and, therefore, are not eligible for the qualified covered call exemption. Options with a strike price of $45, $50, and $55 are eligible for the exemption.

(c) EXCEPTIONS TO THE GENERAL RULE TO DETERMINE THE LOWEST QUALIFIED BENCH MARK

There are three exceptions to the general rule for determining the lowest qualified bench mark. First, in the case of an option that is granted more than 90 days before its date of expiration and has a strike price in excess of $50, the lowest qualified bench mark is the second highest available strike price below the applicable stock price.[37] Second, if the applicable stock price is $25 or less and the highest available strike price below the stock price is less than 85 percent of the stock price, the lowest qualified bench mark is 85 percent of the stock price.[38] Third, if the applicable stock price is $150 or less and the highest available strike price below the stock price is less than the stock price reduced by $10, the lowest qualified bench mark is equal to the stock price minus $10.[39]

Example 56-3

Assume that a stock is trading at $48 per share and call options overlaying it are trading with strike prices of $30, $35, $40, $45, $50, and $55. Assume further that the stock price increases to $53 per share. Options are not deep-in-the-money if these were written when the stock was trading at $48 more than 90 days before expiration with strike prices of $45, $50, or $55.

(d) LIMITATIONS ON THE EXEMPTION

In addition to the requirements set out above, two other conditions must be met for a qualified covered call to be exempt from the Straddle Rules. These conditions are discussed in the remainder of this section.

---

[37] I.R.C. § 1092(c)(4)(D)(ii).
[38] I.R.C. § 1092(c)(4)(D)(iii).
[39] I.R.C. § 1092(c)(4)(D)(iv).

(1) SUBSEQUENT STOCK SALE

First, under the law in effect prior to the enactment of TRA '86, the loss deferral rule applied to a loss realized on the call option if the underlying stock was sold in a subsequent tax year within 30 days after the call option position is closed out.[40] In determining whether a taxpayer held the stock for 30 days after closing the call option, the rules of I.R.C. § 246(c), which address the holding period of stock for purposes of the intercorporate dividends received deduction, were applied.[41] Under pre-TRA '86 law, stock that was offset by a qualified covered call was exempt from the Straddle Rules *unless* (1) gain from the disposition of the underlying stock was included in gross income in a taxable year after the year in which the option was closed, and (2) the stock was not held for more than 30 days following the date on which the option was closed. These conditions apply to positions established before December 31, 1986.

TRA '86 further narrows the availability of the qualified covered call exemption for positions established after December 31, 1986. The qualified covered call exemption from the Straddle Rules is not available after December 31, 1986, if three conditions are met. First, the stock is sold at a loss. Second, the related option is not held for 30 days after the sale. And third, the gain is included in the subsequent year.[42] A sale that meets each of these requirements is subject to the Straddle Rules.

(2) IN-THE-MONEY CALL OPTIONS ESTABLISHED AFTER JUNE 30, 1984

Second, a qualified covered call option that was in-the-money when written and was established after June 30, 1984, is subject to the modified short sales rule that (1) suspends, but does not eliminate, the holding period in the underlying stock,[43] and (2) treats any loss on the option position as a long-term loss if the underlying stock had a long-term holding period at the time the loss on the call option was realized.[44] The

---

[40] I.R.C. § 1092(c)(4)(E), *prior to amendment by* TRA '86, *supra* note 20, §§ 331(a)(1), (2), (3).
[41] *Id.*; *see* sections 17.7 and 24.9.
[42] I.R.C. § 1092(c)(4)(E); STAFF OF THE JOINT COMM. ON TAXATION, 99TH CONG., 2D SESS., TAX REFORM BILL OF 1986, FINAL CONFERENCE COMM. DECISIONS II-108 (Joint Comm. Print 1986).
[43] I.R.C. § 1092(f)(2).
[44] I.R.C. § 1092(f)(1).

DRA Conference Report provides that these rules apply in lieu of the modified short sales rule of I.R.C. § 1092(b)(1).[45]

(3) TREASURY REGULATIONS

The Treasury has broad authority to issue regulations necessary or appropriate to carry out the qualified covered call exemption from the Straddle Rules.[46] The Treasury regulations, when issued, can include modifications to the statutory provisions, if appropriate, to take into account changes in the practices of national securities exchanges (e.g., modification of designated strike price intervals) or to prevent the use of option transactions for tax avoidance purposes.[47]

§ 56.4 MARRIED PUT TRANSACTIONS

It is unclear whether the married put exception, provided in the short sales rule for capital assets,[48] is available as an exemption from the Straddle Rules.[49] Married put transactions were not addressed in the Code or the legislative history in enacting the Straddle Rules. Nevertheless, married put options might be exempt from the Straddle Rules. Nothing in the legislative history of the DRA[50] indicates that Congress intended to repeal the married put exception contained in I.R.C. § 1233(c) when it extended the scope of the Straddle Rules to publicly traded options.

In a married put transaction under I.R.C. § 1233(b), the short sales rule does not apply if a put option is acquired on the same day as property identified as the property to be used in exercising the put—and which, if exercised, is exercised through the sale of the property. For a put to be deemed "married" to stock for purposes of the short sales rule under I.R.C. § 1233(b), the put option must be acquired on the same day as the stock, and the stock must be identified on the put holder's records as the stock to be delivered upon exercise of the put. Furthermore, it may be possible that the married put criteria can be met only by delivering the

---

[45] HOUSE CONFERENCE REPORT, DEFICIT REDUCTION ACT OF 1984, H.R. CONF. REP. NO. 861, 98th Cong., 2d Sess. 908 (1984). *See generally* Chapter 54.
[46] I.R.C. § 1092(c)(4)(H).
[47] *Id.*
[48] I.R.C. § 1233(c).
[49] *See* section 18.4(d).
[50] Pub. L. No. 98-369, 98 Stat. 494 (1984) [hereinafter DRA].

married stock or by allowing the put to expire. If the put expires, the cost of the put is added to the stock's tax basis. Treasury regulations or clarifying legislation is needed to resolve the issue.[51] The better view at present appears to be to allow the married put exception for put option positions. Accordingly, a married put transaction should be able to provide a taxpayer with some downside protection, upside potential, and the accrual of the holding period for long-term capital gain purposes.

It is unclear whether the married put exception provided in the short sales rule of I.R.C. § 1233(c) is an exemption from the Straddle Rules. In fact, Temp. Treas. Reg. § 1.1092(b)-2T(a) suggests that married puts are not exempt from the Straddle Rules. Temp. Treas. Reg. § 1.1092(b)-2T(a) appears to eliminate the married put exception contained in I.R.C. § 1233(c) for transactions that meet the straddle definition. In particular, any pair of positions otherwise qualifying under I.R.C. § 1233(c)—that is, a put option and an underlying long position identified as intended to be used in exercising that option—constitute offsetting positions as long as the underlying long position is "actively traded" within the meaning of I.R.C. § 1092(d)(1). Under Temp. Treas. Reg. § 1.1092(b)-2T(a)(1), the holding period of the positions making up a straddle does not begin until the straddle is terminated. The temporary regulation does not contain an exception for straddles that consist of an underlying long position and a put option or other position "married" to the long position. As a result, further clarification is needed in final regulations.

§ 56.5 CERTAIN STOCK POSITIONS

Certain stock positions are exempt from the Straddle Rules. Prior to enactment of the DRA in 1984, stock was explicitly excluded from the definition of personal property, thereby excluding stock entirely from the application of the Straddle Rules. Personal property was defined as "any personal property (other than stock) of a type which is actively traded."[52] This explicit exclusion was narrowed significantly by a DRA amendment in 1984 that brought actively traded stock into the definition of personal property.[53]

There are exceptions to the general rule that actively traded stock is within the definition of personal property of the sort that is subject to the

---

[51] Treasury regulations could incorporate the married put exception and confirm that the short sales rule of Temp. Treas. Reg. § 1.1092(b)-2T does not apply to qualified married puts.

[52] I.R.C. § 1092(d)(1), *ior to amendment by* DRA, *supra* note 50, § 101(b)(1).

[53] *See* section 48.2(c).

Straddle Rules.[54] First, the definition of personal property does not include stock positions unless the stock is part of a straddle where at least one of the offsetting positions is either (1) an option on the same stock (or substantially identical stock or securities), or (2) characterized by Treasury regulations as a position with respect to property other than stock that is substantially similar or related property.[55] Second, stock is personal property if it is part of a straddle where the offsetting position is stock in a corporation "formed or availed of" to take positions which offset positions established by any stockholder ("offsetting position stock").[56]

In other words, the Straddle Rules apply to straddles where at least one of the positions is a stock position, unless the positions offsetting the stock are other stock positions or the short sale of stock. Hence, a short sale against the box is not subject to the Straddle Rules, although it may be subject to the wash sales or short sales rules.[57] TRA '86 amended I.R.C. § 1092(d)(3)(A) to "clarify" that the exemption for stock does not operate to exclude straddles of exchange-traded stock options (other than qualified covered calls that offset stock).[58]

The Treasury has broad authority to issue regulations to identify which stock positions are offset by property other than actual stock that is substantially similar or related to the stock.[59] The regulations, when promulgated, will not apply to mixed straddles where all of the positions were established prior to January 1, 1984.[60]

§ 56.6 SHORT-TERM STOCK OPTION POSITIONS ESTABLISHED BEFORE JULY 18, 1984

Prior to July 18, 1984, positions in exchange-traded stock options with a maximum exercise period that was less than the then current holding period to obtain long-term capital gain (referred to as "short-term stock options") were exempt from the Straddle Rules. An exemption was available because a short-term stock option was excluded from the

---

[54] I.R.C. § 1092(d)(3)(B).
[55] I.R.C. § 1092(d)(3)(B)(i).
[56] I.R.C. § 1092(d)(3)(B)(ii).
[57] *See* section 19.3(f); *see generally* Chapter 18.
[58] TRA '86, *supra* note 20, § 1808(c).
[59] I.R.C. § 1092(d)(3)(B)(i)(II).
[60] DRA, *supra* note 50, § 103(c).

§ 56.7   Financial Products: Taxation, Regulation, and Design   1304

definition of a "position."[61] Because all stock options traded on domestic securities exchanges before July 18, 1984, had exercise periods of less than the then applicable long-term capital gain holding period (i.e., more than one year), all such stock options were exempt from the Straddle Rules before July 18, 1984.

This exemption, originally granted in 1981, was provided for short-term stock options on the belief that the use of straddle transactions to defer taxes prevalent in the commodity markets was not occurring in exchange-traded stock options. The Treasury expressed concern at the commodity straddle hearings held in 1981 that straddles in the commodity markets might be shifted to the stock option markets if exchange-traded stock options were exempt from the legislation.[62] Several legislative proposals after ERTA was enacted in 1981 would have completely eliminated the exclusion for stock options in I.R.C. § 1092.[63] But it was not until enactment of the DRA in 1984 that the short-term stock options exemption from the Straddle Rules was eliminated.

Despite the exemption for short-term stock options entered into prior to July 18, 1984, the pre-DRA use of short-term stock option straddles to defer the payment of tax on capital gains (for investors and traders) or ordinary income (for dealers and hedgers) is subject to IRS attack. Transactions have been challenged if there was no profit motive and under the rationale of Rev. Rul. 77-185.[64] In addition, it is important to note that for dealers in those stocks underlying short-term stock options, the hedging exemption may be available, under certain circumstances, to exempt their stock option transactions from the Straddle Rules.[65]

§ 56.7   STRADDLES MADE UP EXCLUSIVELY OF SECTION 1256 CONTRACTS

If all positions in a straddle consist of section 1256 contracts, the Straddle Rules do not apply,[66] and the positions are subject to section 1256 treatment. For a discussion of section 1256 treatment, see generally Part

---

[61] I.R.C. § 1092(d)(2)(B) (1982).

[62] *Commodity Tax Straddles: Hearing on S. 626 before the Subcomm. on Taxation and Debt Management and the Subcomm. on Energy and Agricultural Taxation of the Senate Comm. on Finance*, 97th Cong., 1st Sess. 48–66 (1981).

[63] *See, e.g.*, S. 2062, 98th Cong., 1st Sess. § 105 (1983).

[64] 1977-1 C.B. 48, *amplified by* Rev. Rul. 78-414, 1978-2 C.B. 213; Laureys v. Comm'r, 92 T.C. 101 (1989), *acq. and nonacq.* 1990-1 C.B. 1; *see* sections 30.2(b)(2) and 47.2.

[65] *See generally* Chapter 23.

[66] I.R.C. §§ 1092(d)(5)(A), 1256(a)(4).

Ten. In addition, the requirement to capitalize interest and carrying charges is not applied.[67] According to the legislative history of ERTA, Treasury regulations (yet to be promulgated) will define the manner in which straddle positions in section 1256 contracts are to be matched.[68]

This exemption from the Straddle Rules for straddles made up exclusively of section 1256 contracts is consistent with the policy behind the Straddle Rules. There is no opportunity to defer income with section 1256 contracts. All offsetting positions comprising a straddle made up exclusively of section 1256 contracts, are subject to section 1256 treatment, which means that recognized and unrecognized gains and losses are reported for tax purposes at year-end.[69]

---

[67] I.R.C. § 263(g).
[68] SENATE FINANCE COMM. REPORT, ECONOMIC RECOVERY TAX ACT OF 1981, S. REP. NO. 144, 97th Cong., 1st Sess. 148, *reprinted in* 1981 U.S. CODE CONG. & ADMIN. NEWS 105, 248.
[69] *See* Chapter 45.

Fifty-seven

Mixed Straddles

A mixed straddle is comprised partially of section 1256 contracts and partially of other positions.[1] The concern with mixed straddles has been the disparity in 60/40 treatment for section 1256 contracts[2] and short-term capital gain or loss for non-section 1256 positions. This disparity—when there was a preferential tax rate for long-term capital gains and there were no rules to prevent conversion—provided taxpayers with an incentive to convert short-term capital gain into 60/40 gain by mixed straddles that offered the opportunity to accomplish this conversion. Basically, without rules to prevent conversion, a mixed straddle (or a series of increasingly larger mixed straddles) could have been used to generate short-term loss in the non-section 1256 property with an offsetting 60/40 gain. The short-term loss could eliminate either unrelated short-term gain (leaving the taxpayer with only 60/40 gain) or the 40 percent short-term gain element (leaving the taxpayer only long-term capital gain). Without a preventive rule, mixed straddles could have been used to convert all short-term capital gain into 60/40 gain and, ultimately, into long-term capital gain.

Example 57-1

Assume there are no rules in place to prevent the conversion of short-term capital gain into 60/40 gain or long-term capital loss into 60/40 loss. A taxpayer with an unrelated short-term gain of $100 for the tax year sells a section 1256 contract and buys the underlying property

---

[1] I.R.C. § 1256(d)(4)(A).
[2] For a discussion of section 1256 treatment, see Part Ten.

(which is not a section 1256 position). The taxpayer holds a mixed straddle. If the price of the underlying property falls, producing a $100 loss, the taxpayer could close out both positions—claiming a $100 60/40 gain on the section 1256 contract and a short-term loss of $100 on the non-section 1256 position. The short-term capital loss would be deductible against the unrelated short-term capital gain, leaving only a $100 60/40 gain for the year.

On the other hand, if the value of the underlying property increased by $100, the taxpayer would incur a $100 short-term gain on the underlying property and a $100 60/40 loss on the section 1256 position. This result would be detrimental to a taxpayer with long-term capital gain for the year; the $100 short-term gain and the $100 60/40 loss would convert $40 of the long-term gain into short-term gain. A short-term gain and a 60/40 loss, however, might not pose a problem for those taxpayers that enter into additional mixed straddles in larger sizes to generate gains on the section 1256 positions, thereby converting short-term capital gain into 60/40 gain. Of course, long-term losses could be converted to 60/40 losses in the same manner.

Although Congress recognized the possibility of conversion using mixed straddles in 1981, the possibility was not precluded by the Straddle Rules as enacted by ERTA. Rather, ERTA authorized a mixed straddle election under I.R.C. § 1256(d) that allows taxpayers to forgo application of section 1256 treatment for futures contracts and certain foreign currency contracts that are part of a section 1256(d) identified mixed straddle.[3]

It was possible with unidentified mixed straddles to convert short-term gain into 60/40 gain and long-term loss into 60/40 loss. Although some commentators speculated that the modified short sales rule, once it was promulgated by the Treasury, would convert long-term capital loss into 60/40 loss, the first indication of the Treasury's position was an internal memorandum of the IRS. The memorandum asserted that 60/40 treatment should not be available for those section 1256 contracts that

---

[3] *See* I.R.C. § 1256(d).

were part of an unidentified mixed straddle.[4] This position was not supported at that time by the language of the Code. The problem has since been addressed by the DRA amendments to the Code.

If a taxpayer made no election, the section 1256 contract positions that were part of the mixed straddle were subject to both the Mark-to-Market and the 60/40 Rules, while the non-section 1256 positions were not subject to such treatment. Gain or loss on the section 1256 contract positions were taxed at year-end, although no such rule applied to the unrealized gain or loss in the non-section 1256 positions. Further, taxpayers would report 60/40 gain or loss with respect to the section 1256 positions and (depending on the taxpayer's holding period) 100 percent short-term or long-term capital gain or loss on the non-section 1256 positions.[5] It was quite possible that taxpayers that failed to make a mixed straddle election would be subject to the modified short sales rule,[6] which would convert a short-term capital loss to a 60/40 loss when offset by a 60/40 gain in a mixed straddle. Without Treasury regulations to establish prohibitive rules, however, taxpayers used mixed straddles—subject to the possibility of denial on audit—to convert short-term gains into 60/40 gains.

In extending section 1256 treatment to dealer equity options in 1984,[7] Congress extended such treatment to products that are frequently traded in combination with stock, which is not eligible for section 1256 treatment. As a result, the mixed straddle issue had to be addressed in 1984 to prevent rampant conversion of short-term gain and long-term loss into 60/40 gain and loss. The DRA thus continued the one-time section 1256(d) mixed straddle election established in 1981 by ERTA, but added an anticonversion rule and two additional elections for netting straddle gains and losses.[8] The new rules are intended to prevent the conversion of

> Because section 1092 provides that in the case of an unidentified mixed straddle the provisions of section 1092 apply to any regulated futures contract, the short sales, as well as wash sales, rules are to be applied to each futures contract and thus the 60/40 rule of section 1256(a)(3) is not to apply. If the 60/40 rule were to apply there would be a chance for a taxpayer to convert a short-term gain into a long-term gain and a long-term loss into a short-term loss. Consequently, the reason sections 1233(b) and (d) were enacted are applicable here and it logically follows that section 1233 needs to, and therefore should, apply in the case of the regulated futures contract portion of an unidentified mixed straddle.

G.C.M. 39,151 (June 17, 1983) (footnote omitted); *see* LTR 8348033 (Aug. 30, 1983).

[5] For a discussion of holding period, see Chapter 17.

[6] *See* section 54.4.

[7] *See* section 44.4.

[8] I.R.C. § 1092(b)(2)(A).

short-term capital gain into long-term capital gain while taking into consideration the administrative burdens imposed on taxpayers that enter into a large volume of mixed straddle transactions.[9]

The DRA provides two netting rules for taxpayers holding mixed straddles. Taxpayers can elect to either (1) offset gains against losses by separately identifying each mixed straddle,[10] or (2) establish a "mixed straddle account" for each class of activities in which trading gains and losses would be recognized and offset on a periodic basis.[11] Under either of these elections, 60/40 treatment is available only for the net gain or loss from the straddle transactions attributable to section 1256 contracts. Under the rules applicable to a mixed straddle account election, not more than 50 percent of any net gain derived from any positions in the account (whether or not qualified for section 1256 treatment) can be treated as long-term capital gain, and not more than 40 percent of any net loss can be treated as short-term capital loss.[12] In addition, TMRA '88[13] authorized the Treasury to issue regulations relating to the treatment of mixed straddles where at least one position is ordinary and at least one position is capital.[14]

The DRA required the Treasury to issue regulations governing these new mixed straddle netting provisions within six months after the date the DRA was enacted (i.e., by January 18, 1985).[15] On January 18, 1985, the Treasury met the deadline and issued temporary regulations addressing the election for straddle-by-straddle identification and mixed straddle accounts. These temporary Treasury regulations affect all taxpayers that trade section 1256 contracts in combination or simultaneously with offsetting positions in non-section 1256 contracts (whether or not any coordination of these positions is intended by the taxpayer).

The netting rules authorized by the DRA are in lieu of having the modified short sales rule apply to a taxpayer's mixed straddle positions.[16] The modified short sales rule provides that losses on the disposition of one or more positions that are part of a mixed straddle and are non-section

---

[9] *See* STAFF OF THE JOINT COMM. ON TAXATION, 98TH CONG., 2D SESS., GENERAL EXPLANATION OF THE REVENUE PROVISIONS OF THE DEFICIT REDUCTION ACT OF 1984, at 316–17 (Joint Comm. Print 1984).

[10] *See* section 57.3.

[11] *See* section 57.4.

[12] Temp. Treas. Reg. § 1.1092(b)-4T(c)(4) (1985).

[13] Pub. L. No. 100-647, 102 Stat. 3342 (1988) [hereinafter TMRA '88].

[14] *See* section 57.7 for a discussion of these mixed straddles.

[15] Pub. L. No. 98-369, § 103(b), 98 Stat. 494, 628 (1984) [hereinafter DRA].

[16] Temp. Treas. Reg. § 1.1092(b)-2T(b)(2)(iii) (1986).

1256 positions are treated as 60 percent long-term and 40 percent short-term capital loss, unless the taxpayer elects to either (1) offset gains or losses from positions that are part of a mixed straddle by separately identifying the positions of each straddle for which offset treatment is elected, or (2) establish a mixed straddle account for determining gains or losses from all positions in a designated class of activities.[17] If a taxpayer fails to elect either of these rules—or fails to apply them properly—the Treasury can apply the modified short sales rule to the mixed straddle.[18] This means that a loss on a non-section 1256 contract can be converted to 60/40 loss, without any corresponding conversion of section 1256 contract losses to short-term capital losses. This one-way conversion (sometimes referred to as the "killer rule") can have a punitive effect—when there is a differential in the tax rate between long-term and short-term capital gains—a taxpayer that has a series of mixed straddles could have the short-term losses from the straddle converted to 60/40 loss when the loss was from the non-section 1256 position but would have short-term gain and 60/40 loss when the gain from the straddle was from the non-section 1256 position and the loss was from the section 1256 position. A taxpayer that has a mixed straddle that produces a loss on the section 1256 contract position, a short-term gain on the non-section 1256 contract position, and that has a long-term capital gain from other sources unrelated to the straddle, effectively converts the long-term capital gain to short-term gain.[19] For a taxpayer with a substantial volume of mixed straddles, the killer rule could eliminate the possible tax benefit of 60/40 treatment. The killer rule does not apply to positions that (1) are part of a hedging transaction,[20] or (2) are a part of a straddle consisting solely of section 1256 contracts.[21]

To be subject to the killer rule, a position must be part of a mixed straddle. The Code authorizes the Secretary of the Treasury to issue regulations appropriate to carry out the purposes of the Straddle Rules under I.R.C. § 1092(b)(1) and for mixed straddles under I.R.C. § 1092(b)(2). The Code does not give the Treasury the authority to impose the killer rule on positions cther than mixed straddles. Neither the Commissioner of the IRS nor the Secretary of the Treasury can "promulgate a regulation adding provisions [by regulation] that he believes

---

[17] *Id.*

[18] *See id.*

[19] *See* HOUSE CONFERENCE REPORT, DEFICIT REDUCTION ACT OF 1984, H.R. CONF. REP. NO. 861, 98th Cong., 2d Sess. 912 (1984) [hereinafter H.R. CONF. REP. NO. 861].

[20] Temp. Treas. Reg. § 1.1092(b)-2T(c)(1)(i) (1986); *see generally* Chapter 23.

[21] Temp. Treas. Reg. § 1.1092(b)-2T(c)(1)(ii) (1986); *see* sections 45.3 and 56.7.

Congress should have included [in the Code]."[22] A statute cannot be amended by regulation.[23]

The temporary Treasury regulation that sets out the killer rule—Temp. Treas. Reg. § 1.1092(b)-2T(b)(2)—only applies to mixed straddles where "an election under section 1092(b)(2)(A)(i)(I) (relating to straddle-by-straddle identification) or 1092(b)(2)(A)(i)(II) (relating to mixed straddle accounts) has not been made."[24] It is the author's view that the IRS cannot reassign positions of a cash spread position or straddle, pairing them with futures contracts or other section 1256 contracts to create a mixed straddle, if both the cash spread position or straddle and the futures position constituted bona fide trading strategies (verified by contemporaneous trading records).

Example 57-2

The taxpayer holds a short position of $570 million 9-7/8 percent Treasury bonds payable in 30 years, and also holds 600 long March Treasury bond futures contracts. The taxpayer is short $570 million 9-7/8 percent Treasury bonds payable in 30 years as part of a spread in an account that consists of a long position of $560 million 10-5/8 percent Treasury bonds payable in 30 years. The spread was a trading strategy where the taxpayer was long the new Treasury bond issue and short the old Treasury bond issue. The long futures position was not a component of the spread.

The taxpayer does not hold a mixed straddle. The taxpayer holds a cash straddle as part of a trading strategy, and the killer rule does not apply to cash straddles.

Example 57-3

The taxpayer holds a short position of $77 million 9-1/8 percent Treasury notes payable in five years and also holds 800 long March Treasury bond futures contracts. The taxpayer was short the 9-1/8 percent five-year Treasury notes as part of a spread in a trading account. The taxpayer's trading strategy reflected his belief that short-term interest rates were going to go down. The long futures contract position reflected the taxpayer's bias in the market at the

---

[22] Arrow Fastener Co. v. Comm'r, 76 T.C. 423, 431 (1981).
[23] Koshland v. Helvering, 298 U.S. 441, 447 (1936), *rev'g* 81 F.2d 641 (9th Cir. 1936).
[24] Temp. Treas. Reg. § 1.1092(b)-2T(b)(2)(iii) (1986).

time—it was not a component of the spread. On January 26, 1986, the taxpayer entered into a short position of March call options on Treasury bond futures. The taxpayer was in a spread of regulated futures contracts and nonequity call options.

The taxpayer did not hold a mixed straddle. First, the taxpayer was in a cash spread and the killer rule does not apply to cash spreads. In addition, the taxpayer was in a spread consisting of long Treasury bond futures contracts and short call options on Treasury bond futures. The futures contracts and the call options are both section 1256 contracts. Under the temporary Treasury regulations, positions that "are included in a straddle consisting only of section 1256 contracts" are exempt from application of the killer rule.[25]

For years where there is no preferential tax rate for long-term capital gains, this reduced the significance of the characterization of gains as long-term or short-term. Nevertheless, the loss deferral rule and the rules on the capitalization of interest and carrying charges still can be quite significant. As a result, taxpayers have reasons to use mixed straddle accounts, or to identify section 1092(b)(2) identified mixed straddles.

§ 57.1 SUMMARY OF CHOICES AVAILABLE WHEN HOLDING A MIXED STRADDLE

A taxpayer that holds mixed straddles essentially has five choices:

- First, the taxpayer can do nothing, in which case the killer rule applies to convert any short-term loss from a non-section 1256 position in a mixed straddle to 60/40 loss.[26] Short-term gains offset by 60/40 losses are left unchanged. The killer rule "converts" only one way—in the government's favor—and it is a "killer" to any taxpayer with a substantial volume of mixed straddles if there is a tax differential between long-term and short-term capital gains.[27]

---

[25] Temp. Treas. Reg. § 1.1092(b)-2T(c)(1)(ii) (1986).
[26] *See* Temp. Treas. Reg. § 1.1092(b)-2T(b)(2) (1986). For a discussion of the killer rule, see *supra* text beginning at note 19.
[27] It can be avoided by making the separate section 1092(b)(2) straddle-by-straddle identification election or the mixed straddle account election.

- The mixed straddle is subject to the Straddle Rules, including the requirement to capitalize interest and carrying charges,[28] and the modified wash sales and short sales rules.[29]
- Second, the taxpayer can make the one-time section 1256(d) identified mixed straddle election under section 1256(d) and identify each separate straddle that makes up a mixed straddle.[30] In this case, the section 1256 contracts of an identified mixed straddle are excluded from section 1256 treatment but remain subject to the Straddle Rules. Mixed straddle positions not so identified are subject to the modified wash sales and short sales rules.[31]
- Third, a taxpayer can identify straddles as section 1092(b)(2) identified mixed straddles, netting gains and losses in accordance with the Treasury regulations.[32] In this case, the taxpayer is subject to straddle-by-straddle netting of gains and losses and the modified wash sales and short sales rules apply to realized losses and the remaining open position.[33]
- Fourth, if the straddle otherwise qualifies as an identified straddle under I.R.C. § 1092 (where all of the positions are acquired on the same day),[34] the taxpayer can designate the straddle as a mixed straddle and further identify the straddle as an identified straddle under I.R.C. § 1092(a)(2). In this case, the section 1256 positions are not subject to section 1256 treatment and the straddle is not subject to the loss deferral rule of I.R.C. § 1092. The straddle, however, remains subject to the identified straddle, modified wash sales, and modified short sales rules. Interest and carrying charges incurred to carry identified straddles are required to be capitalized.[35]
- And fifth, the taxpayer with a large number of transactions can establish a mixed straddle account maintained in accordance with the Treasury regulations.[36]

---

[28] *See* section 55.2.
[29] *See generally* Chapter 54.
[30] *See* section 57.2.
[31] *See generally* Chapter 54.
[32] *See* section 57.3.
[33] *See generally* Chapter 54.
[34] *See* section 56.1.
[35] *See* section 55.2.
[36] *See* section 57.4.

The section 1092(b)(2) mixed straddle election does not provide any exemption from the loss deferral or modified wash sales rules.[37] In fact, Temp. Treas. Reg. § 1.1092(b)-3T(c)[38] provides that these rules apply after the application of certain computational rules contained in the temporary regulations. Also, the loss deferral and modified wash sales rules may be applied to positions that, although not identified as being part of the mixed straddle, are in fact offsetting to those in the identified mixed straddle. This means that a mixed straddle identified under I.R.C. § 1092(b)(2) cannot be segregated completely from other unidentified positions held by a taxpayer.

§ 57.2 IDENTIFIED SECTION 1256(d) MIXED STRADDLES

A taxpayer can elect to identify mixed straddle positions on a straddle-by-straddle basis under I.R.C. § 1256(d), referred to as "identified section 1256(d) mixed straddles." If such an election is in effect and the straddle was properly identified, the section 1256 positions are excluded from section 1256 treatment.[39] This election is not attractive for many taxpayers because section 1256 contracts receive short-term (rather than 60/40 treatment) and are still subject to the Straddle Rules.[40]

(a) ONE-TIME MIXED STRADDLE ELECTION

To remove identified section 1256(d) mixed straddles from section 1256 treatment, a taxpayer must make a one-time, mixed straddle election.[41] Once made, this election can be revoked only with the consent of the Treasury.[42] Thereafter, the section 1256 positions are subject to all of the Straddle Rules,[43] and long-term capital gain treatment is only available if the section 1256 positions were not part of a straddle for a period in excess of the long-term capital gain holding period.[44]

---

[37] *See* Chapters 49 and 54.
[38] (1985).
[39] I.R.C. § 1256(d)(1).
[40] *See generally* Part Eleven.
[41] I.R.C. § 1256(d)(1).
[42] I.R.C. § 1256(d)(3).
[43] *See generally* Part Eleven.
[44] *See* Temp. Treas. Reg. § 1.1092(b)-2T(a) (1986).

(b) LIMITED SCOPE OF ELECTION

The section 1256(d) mixed straddle election is quite restrictive. It is not available to a taxpayer that has "legged into" a mixed straddle after first acquiring the section 1256 position.[45] In addition, taxpayers that cannot identify all of their mixed straddle transactions run the risk of having their characterizations challenged on audit and having the killer rule applied to certain transactions.[46] Also, those taxpayers that enter into thousands of mixed straddle transactions might find it impossible to comply with the identification requirements necessary to identify mixed straddles.

A taxpayer cannot elect to bring any positions in personal property within the Mark-to-Market and the 60/40 Rules. Only section 1256 contract positions are eligible for section 1256 treatment.[47]

One final point is that an identified section 1256(d) mixed straddle may also qualify as an identified straddle under I.R.C. § 1092(a)(2) if the identified straddle provisions are complied with.[48]

Example 57-4

Assume that a taxpayer purchases a United States treasury bond position at $1000. Assume further that on day two the long bond position depreciates to $700. To "hedge" the position, the taxpayer sells bond futures contracts. The taxpayer can make a section 1256(d) election on day two by clearly identifying the positions of the straddle. If at the end of the tax year the bond is valued at $900 and the future has lost $200, the loss on the futures contract position is not marked-to-market. If the futures position is sold on the last day of the year, the taxpayer should be able to deduct the $200 loss because there is no unrealized gain in the bond position. (Of course, the question here is where there is an unrealized gain because the bond position increased in value after the futures position was established.)

---

[45] I.R.C. § 1256(d)(4)(B).
[46] For a discussion of the killer rule, see *supra* text beginning at note 19.
[47] For a discussion of section 1256 treatment, see generally Part Ten.
[48] *See* section 56.1.

(c) MIXED STRADDLES CREATED BY TAKING DELIVERY UNDER OR EXERCISING A LONG SECTION 1256 CONTRACT

There is an exception to the requirement that an identified section 1256(d) mixed straddle election must be made before the close of the day on which the first section 1256 contract forming the straddle is acquired. The exception is provided for mixed straddles created by taking delivery under (or exercising) a long section 1256 contract.[49] This special rule allows a taxpayer to (1) make a section 1256(d) mixed straddle election on the date of delivery or exercise, and (2) treat the remaining section 1256 contract positions as if they were terminated and new section 1256 contract positions were acquired on that date.[50] If a taxpayer (1) takes delivery of property under a section 1256 position, or (2) exercises a section 1256 contract position that is part of a straddle that includes section 1256 contracts, each of the remaining section 1256 contracts is treated as if terminated and sold for its fair market value on the day the taxpayer takes delivery under (or exercises) the long section 1256 contract.[51]

Example 57-5

Assume a taxpayer holds a straddle position in silver consisting of long and short section 1256 contracts, and he takes delivery of the silver under the long position. The section 1256 contract positions are treated as if sold for their fair market value on the delivery date.[52] On the day the taxpayer takes delivery of the silver, the taxpayer can make an identified section 1256(d) mixed straddle election for the new straddle consisting of the actual silver (long position) and the short section 1256 contract position.

---

[49] I.R.C. § 1256(c)(2).
[50] SENATE FINANCE COMM. REPORT, TECHNICAL CORRECTIONS ACT OF 1982, S. REP. No. 592, 97th Cong., 2d Sess. 27, *reprinted in* 1982 U.S. CODE CONG. & ADMIN. NEWS 4149, 4173.
[51] I.R.C. § 1256(c)(2).
[52] *Id.*

§ 57.3 STRADDLE-BY-STRADDLE NETTING WITH SECTION 1092(b)(2) IDENTIFIED MIXED STRADDLES

A taxpayer can elect to identify individual mixed straddles when they are established and have them treated under separate netting rules provided in Treasury regulations.[53] Such straddles are referred to as "section 1092(b)(2) identified mixed straddles" because this method is authorized in I.R.C. § 1092(b)(2). If elected, it prevents application of the killer rule to the positions held in the section 1092(b)(2) identified mixed straddles. A taxpayer identifies each section 1092(b)(2) identified mixed straddle when the straddle is established. The offsetting gains and losses from the straddle positions are netted together, with the excess of section 1256 gain or loss over non-section 1256 gain or loss treated as 60/40 gain or loss. The utility of this election for active investors and traders depends largely on their ability to comply with the complex rules for matching up straddle positions. One obvious advantage of the netting provision is that it allows taxpayers to make mixed straddle identifications in situations where the straddles are legged into, unlike the identified section 1256(d) mixed straddle election.

A taxpayer's determination of what constitutes a mixed straddle will generally be accepted by the IRS if the taxpayer adopts a reasonable and consistently applied method of identifying straddle positions and the method clearly reflects income.[54] The taxpayer's identification need not be accepted if the circumstances indicate that the taxpayer did not properly identify the straddles pursuant to such a method.[55]

(a) CLEAR IDENTIFICATION

After making a section 1092(b)(2) identified mixed straddle election, a taxpayer must clearly identify each position that is part of the mixed straddle on a "reasonable and consistently applied economic basis" before the "close of the day" on which the straddle is established.[56] There is no specific requirement in the Treasury regulations for labeling the section 1092(b)(2) mixed straddles as such. As a result, there appears to be no requirement to label the mixed straddle positions as "section 1092(b)(2) mixed straddles."

---

[53] I.R.C. § 1092(b)(2)(A)(i).
[54] H.R. Conf. Rep. No. 861, *supra* note 19, at 912.
[55] *Id.*
[56] Temp. Treas. Reg. § 1.1092(b)-3T(d)(1) (1985).

For a taxpayer that is an individual, the "close of the day" is midnight (local time) in the location of the taxpayer's principal residence. For all other taxpayers, the "close of the day" is midnight (local time) in the location of the taxpayer's principal place of business.[57] If the taxpayer disposes of part of the mixed straddle before the close of the day on which the straddle was established, identification must be made at or before the time the taxpayer disposes of the position. Identification and calculation of gain or loss on "day trades" is unclear. Only the person or entity that directly holds all of the positions of a straddle can make this election.[58] The regulations do not provide any guidance for determining what is a reasonable and consistently applied economic basis for identification.

Mixed straddles must be properly identified to make a valid section 1092(b)(2) identified mixed straddle election. The legs of the straddle must be identified for a section 1092(b)(2) identified straddle. The Conference Report that accompanied the enactment of the DRA in 1984 provides:

> [T]he determination ... of what constitutes a mixed straddle generally will be accepted by the IRS if the taxpayer has adopted a reasonable and consistently applied method of identifying straddle positions which clearly reflects income in the absence of circumstances indicating that the taxpayer has not properly identified straddles pursuant to such method.[59]

Temp. Treas. Reg. § 1.1092(b)-3T(d)(1) provides that "to elect [section 1092(b)(2) identified straddles] ... taxpayer must clearly identify on a reasonable and consistently applied economic basis each position that is part of the section 1092(b)(2) identified mixed straddle before the close of the day on which the section 1092(b)(2) identified straddle is established." The essence of the straddle-by-straddle election for a section 1092(b)(2) identified mixed straddle is whether the positions were identified.

It is recommended that a taxpayer check the appropriate box on IRS Form 6781, although there is no affirmative obligation in the Code, the legislative history, or Temp. Treas. Reg. § 1.1092(b)-3T[60] to check a box on the tax return to have a valid election—or to do anything other than make a contemporaneous "election" by identifying the straddle positions. In addition, the instructions to IRS Form 6781 do not require a checked election box for a valid election. Failure to check the box on IRS

---

[57] Id.
[58] Id.
[59] H.R. Conf. Rep. No. 861, *supra* note 19, at 912.
[60] (1985).

Form 6781 does not preclude a valid section 1092(b)(2) identified mixed straddle election. Rather, checking the box merely indicates that an election was made—checking the box is not the election.

The IRS has taken the position on audit that a taxpayer must comply with the Treasury regulations for proper calculation of the netting rules to make a proper section 1092(b)(2) election. It is the author's view that proper calculation is not required for a valid election under section 1092(b)(2). Rather, if there is an error, the taxpayer must recompute the calculation for the year in question. In addition, if the taxpayer does not comply with the requirement in I.R.C. § 263(g) to capitalize interest and carrying charges, it is the author's view that this does not mean an election under I.R.C. § 1092(b)(2) is not valid. Rather, the taxpayer must recompute the calculation to reflect net interest that must be capitalized and reduce interest expense as an ordinary deduction on the relevant tax returns.

The mixed straddle account election—as opposed to the section 1092(b)(2) identified mixed straddle election—does require an affirmative election by the taxpayer by checking a box on Form 6781 that is made a part of the taxpayer's tax return. Temp. Treas. Reg. § 1.1092(b)-4T(f)(2)[61] specifically requires the mixed straddle account election to be made on IRS Form 6781 in the manner prescribed by the form. As a result, the election requirement is different for mixed straddle accounts than it is for section 1092(b)(2) identified mixed straddles.

A taxpayer is presumed to have timely identified a section 1092(b)(2) mixed straddle only if he receives "independent verification" of the identification.[62] Under temporary Treasury regulations, independent verification is generally deemed to have occurred if the taxpayer causes the position to be placed in a separate account maintained by a broker or FCM, or when the taxpayer receives a written confirmation from a broker or FCM that identifies the positions of a mixed straddle. These methods of verification—as well as other acceptable methods—are discussed in the remainder of this section.

(1) SEPARATE ACCOUNTS

Independent verification includes placement of one or more positions of a section 1092(b)(2) identified mixed straddle in a separate account designated as a "section 1092(b)(2) identified mixed straddle account" that is maintained by a broker, FCM, or similar person by whom notations are

[61] (1985).
[62] Temp. Treas. Reg. § 1.1092(b)-3T(d)(2) (1985).

made identifying all positions of the identified mixed straddle and stating the date the straddle was established.[63]

(2) CONFIRMATIONS

Independent verification includes written confirmation from a broker, FCM, or similar person. It also includes a written confirmation from the party from whom one or more of the positions of the section 1092(b)(2) identified mixed straddle are acquired. Confirmation must state the date the straddle is established and identify the other positions of the straddle.[64]

(3) OTHER METHODS

Independent verification includes such other methods of independent verification as the Commissioner of Internal Revenue approves in his discretion.[65]

For example, if a taxpayer has ample written evidence (including, for example, trade tickets and computer-generated reports) that indicate that positions of mixed straddles were matched on a timely basis, the taxpayer should be able to meet the burden of proving that the transactions were identified.

The presumption that a taxpayer timely identified a mixed straddle by independent verification can be rebutted by clear and convincing evidence to the contrary.[66] If the presumption does not apply, the burden is on the taxpayer to establish that he made a timely identification by the time specified. In the absence of independent verification, the taxpayer must prove that timely identification was made and must present evidence other than his own testimony, unless he shows good cause for failure to produce additional evidence.[67]

Notwithstanding the identification rules and required time periods, a taxpayer can identify mixed straddles that were established before February 25, 1985, as section 1092(b)(2) identified mixed straddles if he adopts a "reasonable and consistent economic basis" for identifying the positions of such straddles.[68]

[63] Temp. Treas. Reg. § 1.1092(b)-3T(d)(4)(i) (1985).
[64] Temp. Treas. Reg. § 1.1092(b)-3T(d)(4)(ii) (1985).
[65] Temp. Treas. Reg. § 1.1092(b)-3T(d)(4)(iii) (1985).
[66] Temp. Treas. Reg. § 1.1092(b)-3T(d)(2) (1985).
[67] Temp. Treas. Reg. § 1.1092(b)-3T(d)(3) (1985).
[68] Temp. Treas. Reg. § 1.1092(b)-3T(d)(5) (1985).

(b) SUMMARY OF RULES TO NET GAINS AND LOSSES

The DRA in 1984 authorized the promulgation of Treasury regulations to establish how a taxpayer can offset gains and losses that are part of a section 1092(b)(2) identified mixed straddle on a straddle-by-straddle basis.[69] Under this netting rule, the gain or loss on the section 1256 contract positions are netted with the gain or loss on the non-section 1256 contract positions for the purpose of testing whether gain or loss on a closed position should be given 60/40 treatment or short-term treatment. If gain or loss is attributable to section 1256 contract positions, the resulting amount is a 60/40 gain or loss.[70] If gain or loss is attributable to positions that are non-section 1256 contracts, the resulting amount is a short-term capital gain or loss.[71]

Six rules in the Conference Report of the DRA identify those situations to be addressed in regulations where one position of a mixed straddle is acquired before another and where one position is disposed of before the other position.[72] These situations have been addressed by the temporary Treasury regulations.

First, any pre-straddle gain or loss with respect to a position of a straddle is recognized at the time the straddle is established. The character is either 60/40 gain or loss or short-term or long-term capital gain or loss, as the case may be.[73]

Second, if a taxpayer disposes of the section 1256 position at a loss and retains the non-section 1256 position, the loss is recharacterized as a short-term capital loss to the extent of the offsetting gain, and the positions are subject to the Straddle Rules. Any excess loss is treated as a 60/40 loss.[74]

Third, if a taxpayer disposes of the section 1256 position at a gain and retains the non-section 1256 position, the gain is recharacterized as a short-term capital gain to the extent of the offsetting loss. Any excess gain is treated as 60/40 gain.[75]

Fourth, if a taxpayer disposes of the non-section 1256 position and retains the section 1256 position, the gain or loss on the two positions is

---

[69] I.R.C. § 1092(b)(2)(A)(i).
[70] Temp. Treas. Reg. § 1.1092(b)-3T (1985).
[71] Id.
[72] H.R. Conf. Rep. No. 861, *supra* note 19, at 912–13.
[73] Temp. Treas. Reg. § 1.1092(b)-3T(b)(6) (1985).
[74] Temp. Treas. Reg. § 1.1092(b)-3T(b)(4) (1985).
[75] Id.

realized and netted at the time the non-section 1256 position is disposed of by the taxpayer.[76]

Fifth, the holding period for the non-section 1256 position is eliminated.[77]

Sixth, for mixed straddles held at the end of the tax year, gain or loss on the non-section 1256 contract is not recognized. Any gain on the section 1256 contract is recognized as short-term capital gain to the extent of the offsetting loss, and any loss on the section 1256 contract is treated as short-term capital loss to the extent of offsetting non-section 1256 gain and is subject to the Straddle Rules. Excess gain or loss, if any, is treated as 60/40 gain or loss.[78]

(c) ACCRUED GAIN AND LOSS ON ESTABLISHING STRADDLES

The regulations provide that positions that were held by a taxpayer prior to the day on which the identified mixed straddle was established are deemed sold at fair market value on the last business day before the straddle was established.[79] The regulations provide that the loss deferral and modified wash sales rules apply to the gains or losses from this deemed sale.[80] The intention of this rule is to provide a clean slate for the computation of gains and losses accrued while the mixed straddle is in place. A clean slate is important so that any losses can be deferred to the extent that gain is accrued in the offsetting position *after* the straddle is established (even if the offsetting position is in an overall loss position from the date it was acquired).

If one or more positions of a section 1092(b)(2) identified mixed straddle were held by the taxpayer on the day prior to the day the straddle was established, such position or positions must be marked to the market as of the last business day before the day the straddle is established.[81] An adjustment (through an adjustment to basis or otherwise) will be made to any subsequent gain or loss realized (or deemed realized) with respect to such position or positions. Accordingly, gain or loss in a non-section 1256

---

[76] Temp. Treas. Reg. § 1.1092(b)-3T(b)(3) (1985).
[77] Temp. Treas. Reg. § 1.1092(b)-3T(b)(7) (1985).
[78] Temp. Treas. Reg. §§ 1.1092(b)-3T(b)(3), (4), (7) (1985).
[79] Temp. Treas. Reg. § 1.1092(b)-3T(b)(6) (1985).
[80] Temp. Treas. Reg. § 1.1092(b)-3T(c) (1985).
[81] *Id.*

position offset by a section 1256 contract position is realized when the section 1256 contract position is realized.[82]

Example 57-6

On January 1, 1985, a taxpayer establishes a non-section 1256 position. As of the close of the day on July 9, 1985, there is $500 of unrealized long-term capital gain in the non-section 1256 position. On July 10, 1985, the taxpayer enters into an offsetting section 1256 contract and makes a valid election to treat the straddle as a section 1092(b)(2) identified mixed straddle by designating it to an account marked "section 1092(b)(2) identified mixed straddles." Under these circumstances, on July 9, 1985, the taxpayer recognizes $500 of long-term capital gain on the non-section 1256 position.[83]

Example 57-7

Assume that a taxpayer purchased a United States Treasury bond position for $1000. Assume further that on the fifth day after the purchase the bond position depreciated in value to $700. On day six, the taxpayer entered into a short Treasury bond futures contract position when the bond's value remained at $700. On day six, the taxpayer also identified the straddle as a section 1092(b)(2) identified mixed straddle. On day five, the $300 loss on the bond position is *recognized* by the taxpayer. If on the last day of the tax year, the long bond position increased in value to $900 and the futures contract declined in value by $200, then the futures contract is marked-to-market, but the loss is offset against the "deemed" $200 gain on the bond. If, on the other hand, the futures contract had been sold before year-end at a $200 loss, the loss would have been offset against the unrealized $200 "deemed" gain on the bond position. In either case, the overall result should be a $300 capital loss.

If a taxpayer holds a securities position that has unrealized losses in it at the time he enters into an offsetting position, and he properly identifies the positions as a section 1092(b)(2) identified straddle, it is possible that the IRS will seek to challenge these losses by either objecting to the validity of the elections (as discussed above) or asserting that the wash

---

[82] *Id.*

[83] Temp. Treas. Reg. § 1.1092(b)-3T(b)(6), Example (1) (1985).

sales rule in I.R.C. § 1091 or the modified wash sales rule should disallow the losses.

It is the author's view that neither the modified wash sales rule in I.R.C. § 1092(b)(1) and the regulations promulgated thereunder, nor the wash sales rule in I.R.C. § 1091 applies to the accrued losses marked-to-market on the day before a straddle is established pursuant to the regulations under Temp. Treas. Reg. § 1.1092(b)-3T.[84] The modified wash sales rule in Temp. Treas. Reg. § 1.1092(b)-1T(a)(1)[85] provides that losses sustained from the disposition of "securities that constitute positions of a straddle" will not be taken into account if, within a period beginning 30 days before the date of such disposition and ending 30 days after such date, the taxpayer has acquired (by purchase or by an exchange in which the entire amount of gain or loss is recognized by law), or has entered into a contract or option to acquire, substantially identical securities. Any loss sustained by a taxpayer from the deemed sale of the pre-straddle position, however, will not be sustained from the disposition of securities that constitute positions of a straddle; the deemed sale will occur the day before the straddle is acquired.

I.R.C. § 1091 provides that losses sustained from "any sale or other disposition" of securities will not be taken into account if, within a period beginning 30 days before the date of such disposition and ending 30 days after such date, the taxpayer has "acquired (by purchase or by [a taxable] exchange . . .), or has entered into a contract or option so to acquire" substantially identical securities. The taxpayer may sustain a loss from the deemed disposition of the pre-straddle position, but the taxpayer will not, and will not be deemed to, acquire substantially identical securities within the 61-day period. Pursuant to Temp. Treas. Reg. § 1.1092(b)-3T(b)(6),[86] the pre-straddle position will be deemed sold, but the regulations do not provide that the pre-straddle position will be deemed reacquired. The wash sales rule specifically provides that for a loss to be disallowed, the security (or a substantially identical security) must be acquired "by purchase or by [a taxable] exchange." But no such purchase or taxable exchange will take place or will be deemed to take place in connection with the marking-to-market required under Temp. Treas. Reg. § 1.1092(b)-3T(b)(6).[87] Furthermore, to apply I.R.C. § 1091 to disallow the recognition of accrued losses through the mark-to-market mechanism prior to entering into a mixed straddle would be directly contrary to

---

[84] (1985). The Treasury may address this in amended regulations or future pronouncements.
[85] (1986).
[86] (1985).
[87] (1985).

the language and purpose of the section 1092(b)(2) identified mixed straddle regulations. Thus, the caption to Treas. Reg. § 1.1092(b)-3T(b)(6)[88] specifically envisions the recognition of both gain and loss. The Conference Report that accompanied the Deficit Reduction Act of 1984 clearly supports the conclusion that all accrued gains and losses are to be recognized at the time that a taxpayer enters into a section 1092(b)(2) identified mixed straddle.

> It is intended that the offset for gains and losses from mixed straddles under the regulations prescribed under the conference agreement may apply in cases where the taxpayer holds either section 1256 contracts or other positions before a mixed straddle is established. In such cases, it is intended that the regulations will require the pre-straddle gains and losses accrued at the time the mixed straddle is created to be recognized at such time.[89]

In accordance with the intention of I.R.C. § 1092(b)(2)(A), the taxpayer will have a "clean tax slate" in computing gains and losses on the positions composing the straddle after it is established. The "clean slate" is necessary to assure that all such losses on any of the positions composing the straddle will be deferred to the extent of any such gain on any offsetting position.

In addition to recognizing any accrued gain or loss on the pre-straddle position upon establishing the straddle, the taxpayer will be required to make an adjustment (through a basis adjustment or otherwise) in reporting any subsequently realized gain or loss on the pre-straddle position.[90] This basis or other adjustment is required to "exclude pre-existing gains and losses from the mixed straddle offsetting rules."[91]

(d) SAME DAY DISPOSITION OF ALL POSITIONS

If all positions of a section 1092(b)(2) identified mixed straddle are disposed of on the same day, section 1256 gains and losses are netted and non-section 1256 gains and losses are netted.[92] First, net section 1256 contract gain or loss is determined by netting all section 1256 gains and losses. Second, non-section 1256 gain or loss is determined by netting all non-section 1256 gains or losses. Third, the net section 1256 gain or loss is offset against the net non-section 1256 gain or loss to determine the net

---

[88] (1985).
[89] H.R. CONF. REP. NO. 861, *supra* note 19, at 912.
[90] Temp. Treas. Reg. § 1.1092(b)-3T(b)(6) (1985).
[91] H.R. CONF. REP. NO. 861, *supra* note 19, at 912.
[92] Temp. Treas. Reg. § 1.1092(b)-3T(b)(2) (1985).

straddle gain or loss. And fourth, the net straddle gain or loss is short-term if the non-section 1256 gain or loss is greater than the section 1256 gain or loss. The net straddle gain or loss is treated as 60/40 gain or loss if the section 1256 contract gain or loss is greater than the non-section 1256 gain or loss. If both the section 1256 and non-section 1256 legs of the straddle result in either gain or loss, gain or loss derived from section 1256 contracts is given 60/40 treatment and non-section 1256 gain or loss is treated as short-term.

Example 57-8

On April 1, 1985, a taxpayer enters into a non-section 1256 position and an offsetting section 1256 position and makes a valid election to treat the straddle as a section 1092(b)(2) identified mixed straddle. On April 10, 1985, the taxpayer disposes of the non-section 1256 position at a $600 loss and the section 1256 contract at a $600 gain. Under these circumstances, the $600 loss on the non-section 1256 position is offset against the $600 gain on the section 1256 contract, and the net gain or loss from the straddle is zero.[93]

(e) NON-SECTION 1256 POSITIONS DISPOSED OF FIRST

If all of the non-section 1256 positions of a section 1092(b)(2) identified mixed straddle are disposed of on the same day, five rules are applied. First, the gain or loss realized from the non-section 1256 positions disposed of is netted.[94]

Second, the net section 1256 gain or loss is determined by netting section 1256 gains and losses for all positions disposed of during the day and all of the positions that have not been disposed of (i.e., the section 1256 gain or loss includes realized and unrealized gains and losses).

Third, the net section 1256 gain or loss and the net non-section 1256 gain or loss is offset to determine the net straddle gain or loss.

Fourth, the net gain or loss from the straddle attributable to the non-section 1256 position is recognized and treated as short-term capital gain or loss. Only the net amount is realized; the part of the non-section 1256 gain or loss offset by section 1256 gain or loss is eliminated. Net gain or loss from the straddle attributable to section 1256 contracts is realized

---

[93] Temp. Treas. Reg. § 1.1092(b)-3T(b)(2), Example (1) (1985).
[94] Temp. Treas. Reg. § 1.1092(b)-3T(b)(3) (1985).

and treated as 60 percent long-term and 40 percent short-term capital gain or loss.

And fifth, any gain or loss subsequently realized on the remaining section 1256 contracts is adjusted (through an adjustment to basis or otherwise) to take into account the extent to which gain or loss was used to offset the gain or loss of the previously disposed of non-section 1256 or the section 1256 contracts.

Example 57-9

On July 20, a taxpayer enters into a section 1256 contract and an offsetting non-section 1256 position, and he makes a valid election to treat the straddle as a section 1092(b)(2) identified mixed straddle. On July 27, the taxpayer disposes of the non-section 1256 position at a $1500 loss, at which time there is $1500 of unrealized gain in the section 1256 contract. The taxpayer holds the section 1256 contract at year-end at which time there is $1800 of gain. On July 27, the taxpayer offsets the $1500 loss of a non-section 1256 position against the $1500 gain of the section 1256 contract and realizes no gain or loss. On December 31, the taxpayer realizes a $300 gain on the section 1256 contract when the position is marked-to-market. The $300 gain is equal to $1800 of gain minus a $1500 adjustment for unrealized gain offset against the loss realized in a non-section 1256 position on July 27. The gain is treated as 60/40 gain.[95]

(f) SECTION 1256 POSITIONS DISPOSED OF FIRST

If all of the section 1256 contracts of a section 1092(b)(2) identified mixed straddle are disposed of on the same day before all of the offsetting non-section 1256 positions are disposed of, the gain or loss that is realized is netted.[96] Realized and unrealized gain or loss with respect to the non-section 1256 positions of the straddle is netted in that day by marking-to-market the non-section 1256 position of the straddle. Net gain or loss from section 1256 contracts will then be treated as short-term capital gain or loss to the extent of the net gain or loss from the non-section 1256 positions. Net gain or loss on the section 1256 contracts in excess of the net gain or loss on the non-section 1256 positions of the straddle are treated as 60 percent long-term and 40 percent short-term capital gain or loss. When

---

[95] Temp. Treas. Reg. § 1.1092(b)-3T(b)(3), Example (1) (1985).
[96] Temp. Treas. Reg. § 1.1092(b)-3T(b)(4) (1985).

the remaining non-section 1256 positions are disposed of, the gain or loss is realized and treated as short-term to the extent that the gain or loss is attributable to the period when the non-section 1256 contract positions were part of the straddle. The treatment of the remaining gain or loss depends upon the holding period of the non-section 1256 position.

Example 57-10

On July 20, 1987, a taxpayer enters into a straddle with a section 1256 position and an offsetting non-section 1256 position. The taxpayer makes a valid election to treat this straddle as an identified section 1092(b)(2) mixed straddle. On July 27, 1987, the taxpayer disposes of the section 1256 position at a $1400 loss, at which time there is $1500 of unrealized gain in the non-section 1256 contract. On July 27, 1987, the taxpayer treats the $1400 loss on the section 1256 position as a short-term capital loss.

(g) PARTIAL DISPOSITION OF STRADDLE POSITIONS

Where one or more, but not all, of the positions of a section 1092(b)(2) identified mixed straddle are disposed of on the same date, gain or loss from each of the non-section 1256 positions disposed of on that date is netted and the gain and loss from each of the section 1256 contracts that are disposed of on that date are also netted.[97] First, net gain or loss from the non-section 1256 positions that are disposed of is netted.

Second, the gain or loss from the section 1256 positions disposed of is netted.

Third, the net gain or loss from non-section 1256 positions disposed of is offset against the net section 1256 gain or loss from section 1256 positions disposed of.

Fourth, if net gain or loss from the dispositions is attributable to non-section 1256 positions, the realized and unrealized gains and losses from all section 1256 contracts in the straddle are netted. The net non-section 1256 gain or loss from non-section 1256 positions disposed of is offset against the net section 1256 gain or loss from positions retained as well as disposed of. Net gain or loss that is attributable to non-section 1256 positions is recognized and treated as short-term capital gain or loss. Net gain or loss attributable to realized gain or loss with respect to section 1256 contracts is recognized and treated as 60/40 gain or loss.

[97] Temp. Treas. Reg. § 1.1092(b)-3T(b)(5) (1985).

Fifth, if net gain or loss from dispositions is attributable to section 1256 contracts that are disposed of, realized and unrealized gain or loss with respect to the non-section 1256 positions of the straddle is netted by marking-to-market the entire non-section 1256 leg of the straddle. Realized net gain or loss from section 1256 contracts actually disposed of is then treated as short-term to the extent of the net gain or loss from the non-section 1256 positions to determine the net gain or loss from the straddle. If gain or loss on the section 1256 contracts exceeds the net gain or loss from the non-section 1256 positions of the straddle, the excess is treated as 60/40 gain or loss. Net gain or loss attributable to the non-section 1256 positions is treated as short-term capital gain or loss.

Sixth, if the net gain or loss from both the section 1256 and the non-section 1256 contract positions disposed of are either both gains or losses, the net section 1256 gain or loss is treated as described in point five, above. The net non-section 1256 gain or loss is treated as described in point four, above. The gain or loss later realized on the remaining straddle positions must be adjusted so that any gain or loss previously used for offset purposes is not used for that purpose again.

Example 57-11

On July 15, 1985, a taxpayer enters into a straddle consisting of four non-section 1256 positions and four section 1256 contracts. The taxpayer designates the straddle as a section 1092(b)(2) identified mixed straddle. On July 20, 1985, the taxpayer disposes of one non-section 1256 position at a gain of $800 and one section 1256 contract at a loss of $300. On the same day there is $400 of unrealized net loss on the section 1256 contracts retained by the taxpayer and $100 of unrealized net loss on his non-section 1256 positions. Under these circumstances, the $300 loss on the section 1256 contract disposed of is offset against the $800 gain on the non-section 1256 position that is disposed of. The $500 net gain is attributable to the non-section 1256 position. Therefore, the net mark-to-market loss of $700 on the section 1256 contracts is offset against the net gain of $800 attributable to the non-section 1256 position that was disposed of. The net gain of $100 is treated as short-term capital gain because it is attributable to the non-section 1256 position that was disposed of. Gain or loss subsequently realized on the section 1256 contracts will be adjusted to take into account the unrealized loss of $400 that was offset against the $800 gain attributable to the disposed of non-section 1256 position.[98]

Assume the facts are the same as in the previous situation, except that the section 1256 contract was disposed of at a $500 gain. Under these circumstances, there is a $500 gain attributable to the disposed of section 1256 contract and a gain of $800 attributable to the non-section 1256 position. Therefore, the realized and unrealized gains and losses on the section 1256 contracts are netted, resulting in a net gain of $100 ($500 minus $400). The section 1256 net gain does not offset the gain on the disposed of non-section 1256 position. Therefore, the gain of $800 on the disposed of non-section 1256 position is treated as a short-term capital gain because there is no net loss on the section 1256 contracts. In addition, the realized and unrealized gains and losses in the non-section 1256 positions are netted, resulting in a non-section 1256 net gain of $700 ($800 minus $100). Because there is no net loss on the non-section 1256 positions, the $500 gain realized on the section 1256 contract is treated as 60/40 gain.[99]

(h) LOSS DEFERRAL AND HOLDING PERIOD RULES

Any loss realized under the rules for section 1092(b) identified mixed straddles can be recognized at year-end only if there is no unrecognized gain in (1) any position offsetting to the loss position, (2) any successor position, or (3) any position that offsets a successor position.[100] A successor position is defined in the temporary Treasury regulations as a position that is or was at any time offsetting to a second position offsetting to any loss position disposed of, and the position is entered into during a period commencing 30 days before and ending 30 days after the disposition of the loss position.[101]

Gain or loss on a non-section 1256 position that is part of a section 1092(b)(2) identified mixed straddle and that is held after all section 1256 contracts in the straddle are disposed of, is treated as short-term capital gain or loss to the extent the gain or loss is attributable to the period when the positions were part of the mixed straddle.[102]

---

[98] Temp. Treas. Reg. § 1.1092(b)-3T(b)(5), Example (1) (1985).
[99] Temp. Treas. Reg. § 1.1092(b)-3T(b)(5), Example (3) (1985).
[100] Temp. Treas. Reg. § 1.1092(b)-3T(c) (1985).
[101] Temp. Treas. Reg. § 1.1092(b)-5T(n) (1986).
[102] Temp. Treas. Reg. § 1.1092(b)-3T(b)(7) (1985).

These rules apply to loss positions disposed of on or after January 24, 1985. Losses from positions disposed of before that date in straddles established after December 31, 1983, can be recognized only if there is no unrecognized gain in an offsetting position at the end of the year. Disallowed losses are treated as occurring in the next taxable year unless there is unrecognized gain inherent in an offsetting position.

Example 57-12

Assume a taxpayer enters into a section 1092(b)(2) identified mixed straddle on December 1, 1985. On December 31, 1985, the last day of the taxpayer's tax year, the taxpayer disposes of the section 1256 contract leg of the straddle at a $1000 loss. On the same day, there is $1000 of unrecognized gain in the non-section 1256 position. Under these circumstances, the $1000 loss is disallowed in 1985. On July 15, 1986, the taxpayer disposes of the non-section 1256 position at a $1500 gain, $500 of which is attributable to the post-straddle period. Under these circumstances, $1000 of the gain on the non-section 1256 positions is treated as short-term capital gain because that amount of the gain is attributable to the period when the position was part of a section 1092(b)(2) identified mixed straddle. The remaining $500 of the gain is long-term capital gain. The disallowed loss of $1000 from 1985 is allowed as a short-term capital loss in 1986.[103]

§ 57.4 MIXED STRADDLE ACCOUNTS

In 1984, the DRA introduced the concept of a mixed straddle account as a new method for netting gains and losses with respect to mixed straddles.[104] The need for mixed straddle accounts was suggested by option dealers[105] (as well as other taxpayers) that engage in frequent transactions in section 1256 contracts and the non-section 1256 property underlying such contracts. The purpose of a mixed straddle account is to accommodate taxpayers with such a large volume of transactions that identification of specific mixed straddles is impractical.[106] Mixed straddle

---

[103] Temp. Treas. Reg. § 1.1092(b)-3T(b)(7), Example (1985).
[104] DRA, *supra* note 15, § 103(a) (codified at I.R.C. § 1092(b)).
[105] *See* sections 8.2(b), 8.3(c), and 8.3(d).
[106] H.R. CONF. REP. NO. 861, *supra* note 19, at 913.

accounts provide simplification because taxpayers can avoid the daily identification of straddles and the application of the loss deferral and netting rules.[107]

To reduce the possibilities of conversion of short-term capital gain into 60/40 gain within a mixed straddle account, a compromise solution was reached. Not more than 50 percent of the annual net gain derived from any positions in a mixed straddle account (whether or not qualified for section 1256 treatment) can be treated as long-term capital gain, and not more than 40 percent of the annual net loss from positions in a mixed straddle account can be treated as short-term capital loss.[108]

A taxpayer can establish mixed straddle accounts in which both section 1256 and non-section 1256 property are traded. Within the account, the positions are marked-to-market daily. (An adjustment to the account through a basis adjustment or otherwise is made to prevent double counting of gains or losses realized on previous days.)[109]

An account gain or loss for each day is computed by (1) netting section 1256 gains and losses, (2) netting non-section 1256 gains and losses, and (3) offsetting the net section 1256 gain or loss against the net non-section 1256 gain or loss, with the excess treated as 60/40 (if from section 1256 contracts) or as short-term (if from non-section 1256 positions).[110]

The gains and losses from each day are then combined on an annual basis and adjusted for the capitalization of net interest and expenses under I.R.C. § 263(g).[111] If the aggregate net gain for the year from all accounts is greater than 50 percent long-term, the excess over 50 percent is converted to short-term gain. Similarly, if over 40 percent of a net loss for the year from all accounts is short-term, the excess is recharacterized as long-term loss.[112]

A taxpayer can elect to establish one or more mixed straddle accounts for determining gains and losses from all positions in a designated class of activities.[113]

The temporary Treasury regulations explain how to make the election and provide rules for determining gains and losses from positions in a

---

[107] There is some question as to whether net section 1256 losses incurred in a mixed straddle account are available to be carried back to prior years under I.R.C. § 1212(c). *See* section 45.4 for a discussion of this question.

[108] Temp. Treas. Reg. § 1.1092(b)-4T(c)(4) (1985).

[109] Temp. Treas. Reg. § 1.1092(b)-4T(c)(1) (1985).

[110] *Id.*

[111] Temp. Treas. Reg. §§ 1.1092(b)-4T(c)(2), (3) (1985).

[112] I.R.C. § 1092(b)(2)(B); Temp. Treas. Reg. § 1.1092(b)-4T(c)(4) (1985).

[113] Temp. Treas. Reg. § 1.1092(b)-4T(a) (1985).

mixed straddle account. A taxpayer can "designate as a class of activities the types of positions that a reasonable person, on the basis of all facts and circumstances, would ordinarily expect to be offsetting positions."[114] A separate mixed straddle account is required for each designated class of activities. A class of activities for option positions, for example, is on a symbol-by-symbol basis.[115]

Gains and losses from positions that are offsetting with respect to positions in more than one straddle account must be allocated among the accounts under a "reasonable and consistent method that clearly reflects income."[116]

A taxpayer's mixed straddle account must include all positions of a type ordinarily considered offsetting and cannot include nonoffsetting positions. An advantage of mixed straddle accounts over section 1092(b)(2) identified mixed straddles is that the long and short positions making up the mixed straddle account need not be straddle positions and simply must be property of the type contained in the account. The temporary Treasury regulations give the IRS broad authority to remove or include positions in the mixed straddle account if a taxpayer's designations are considered improper.[117]

The taxpayer's gain or loss from positions in his mixed straddle accounts is determined by applying the operating rules set out in the remainder of this section.

(a) ACCOUNT CONTENTS

A taxpayer can elect on a yearly basis to establish one or more mixed straddle accounts for all positions held as capital assets in a designated class of activities where gains and losses are determined in accordance with the rules established in Treasury regulations.[118] A mixed straddle account is established as of the first day of the taxable year for which the election is made.[119] In addition, a separate mixed straddle account must be established for each separate designated class of activities.[120] A taxpayer can designate as a class of activities those positions that "a reasonable person, on the basis of all the facts and circumstances, would

---

[114] Temp. Treas. Reg. § 1.1092(b)-4T(b)(2) (1985).
[115] Temp. Treas. Reg. § 1.1092(b)-4T(b)(1) (1985).
[116] Temp. Treas. Reg. § 1.1092(b)-4T(b)(3) (1985).
[117] Temp. Treas. Reg. § 1.1092(b)-4T(b)(4) (1985).
[118] *See* section 57.4(g).
[119] Temp. Treas. Reg. § 1.1092(b)-4T(a) (1985).
[120] Temp. Treas. Reg. § 1.1092(b)-4T(b)(1) (1985).

ordinarily expect to be offsetting positions."[121] The taxpayer will need to establish—to the satisfaction of the IRS, subject to judicial review—that the class of activities designated is appropriate and complies with the regulations. For example, an options market maker with 10 transactions in different listed opions and underlying stock must set up 10 mixed straddle accounts.

Example 57-13

Assume an options dealer[122] trades dealer equity options[123] on XYZ Corporation stock, stock in XYZ Corporation, dealer equity options on ABC Corporation stock, and stock in ABC Corporation. If the taxpayer makes a mixed straddle account election for all positions, he must designate two accounts—one for XYZ Corporation stock and options and the other for ABC Corporation stock and options—and he must maintain two separate mixed straddle accounts. The taxpayer can elect to trade one symbol in a mixed straddle account and the other symbol as an identified mixed straddle. ABC and XYZ cannot be traded in the same account.[124]

Certain positions that would be expected to offset more than one mixed straddle account are required to be allocated among all such accounts under a "reasonable and consistent method that clearly reflects income."[125] Index options that offset the positions in more than one account must be allocated among the accounts on a reasonable basis.[126] The regulations do not explain when an index position should be considered offsetting to positions in the mixed straddle accounts.[127]

If a taxpayer makes a mixed straddle account designation to include positions in an account that the IRS determines a reasonable person would not expect to be offsetting, the IRS can amend the class of activities designated by the taxpayer and either (1) remove the positions from the account that are not within the amended designated class of activities, or (2) establish two or more mixed straddle accounts.[128] On the other hand, if

---

[121] Temp. Treas. Reg. § 1.1092(b)-4T(b)(2) (1985).
[122] *See* sections 8.2(b) and 8.3(d).
[123] *See* section 44.4.
[124] Temp. Treas. Reg. § 1.1092(b)-4T(b)(2), Example (1985).
[125] Temp. Treas. Reg. § 1.1092(b)-4T(b)(3) (1985).
[126] Temp. Treas. Reg. § 1.1092(b)-4T(b)(3), Example (1985).
[127] *See* section 48.2(c).
[128] Temp. Treas. Reg. § 1.1092(b)-4T(b)(4)(i) (1985).

the IRS determines that positions not included in an account should be included in the account, the IRS can amend the class of activities designated by the taxpayer to (1) include the positions within the account, or (2) to exclude from the account those types of positions that offset positions that are not included in the account.[129] In other words, the IRS has broad discretion to move positions into a mixed straddle account, move positions from one account to another, or to remove positions from accounts altogether. The taxpayer's own designation will be respected, however, if a reasonable person would have designated the positions in the same manner that the taxpayer did.[130]

(b) DAILY MARK-TO-MARKET

The temporary Treasury regulations provide that all mixed straddle account positions, whether or not composed of section 1256 contracts, are marked-to-market at the close of each business day.[131] A daily non-section 1256 net gain or loss is determined for each account by netting all non-section 1256 gains and losses from positions disposed of during the day or marked-to-market at the close of the day. A daily section 1256 contract net gain or loss is determined for each account in the same manner.

The net non-section 1256 gain or loss is offset against net section 1256 gain or loss to determine the daily account net gain or loss for each account.[132] The net gain or loss is treated as 60/40 gain or loss if the section 1256 gain exceeds the non-section 1256 loss or the section 1256 loss exceeds the non-section 1256 gain.[133]

Similarly, the net gain or loss is short-term if the non-section 1256 gain exceeds the section 1256 loss or the non-section 1256 loss exceeds the section 1256 gain.[134] If both the section 1256 and non-section 1256 contracts result in net gains or net losses, the non-section 1256 gain or loss is short-term and the section 1256 gain or loss is 60 percent long-term and 40 percent short-term.[135]

---

[129] Temp. Treas. Reg. § 1.1092(b)-4T(b)(4)(ii) (1985).
[130] *See* Temp. Treas. Reg. §§ 1.1092(b)-4T(b)(4)(i), (ii) (1985).
[131] Temp. Treas. Reg. § 1.1092(b)-4T(c)(1) (1985).
[132] *Id.*
[133] *Id.*
[134] *Id.*
[135] *Id.*

(c) ANNUAL ACCOUNT NET GAIN OR LOSS

An annual account net gain or loss is determined for each mixed straddle account on the last business day of the taxable year by netting all of the daily mark-to-market results for that year.[136] This annual netting is done under the regular capital gain and loss netting rules. To accomplish this, 60/40 gains and losses are separated into their long-term and short-term components. Long-term gains and losses are then netted. In addition, short-term gains and losses are netted to arrive at net short-term and long-term results for each account. Long-term gains or losses in each account are then offset against short-term gains or losses.

No more than 50 percent of total aggregate, annual account net gain from all accounts for the taxable year is treated as long-term capital gain.[137] Any long-term gain in excess of the 50 percent limit is treated as short-term capital gain.[138] In addition, no more than 40 percent of total aggregate, annual account net loss from all accounts for the taxable year is treated as short-term capital loss, and any short-term loss in excess of the 40 percent limit is treated as long-term capital loss.[139] I.R.C. § 1092(b)(2)(B) appears to impose the percentage limitation on an account-by-account basis, while examples in Temp. Treas. Reg. § 1.1092(b)-4T(c)(6) appear to impose the percentage limitation on an aggregate basis.

Example 57-14

The taxpayer, an options market maker that specializes in ABC and XYZ options and stock, elects to establish mixed straddle accounts for each of his two specialty symbols. The taxpayer's stock option trading qualifies for 60/40 treatment, while his stock transactions are generally given short-term capital gain or loss treatment. For simplicity, only four consecutive trading days are illustrated. They are intended to represent the entire 1986 trading year. The rules illustrated here are equally applicable to a futures trader that trades the underlying commodity and elects to use a mixed straddle account. Short-term capital gain and loss are referred to in this example as "STCG" and "STCL," respectively.

---

[136] Temp. Treas. Reg. § 1.1092(b)-4T(c)(2) (1985).
[137] I.R.C. § 1092(b)(2)(B)(i); Temp. Treas. Reg. § 1.1092(b)-4T(c)(4) (1985).
[138] Temp. Treas. Reg. § 1.1092(b)-4T(c)(4) (1985).
[139] I.R.C. § 1092(b)(2)(B)(ii); Temp. Treas. Reg. § 1.1092(b)-4T(c)(4) (1985).

ABC MIXED STRADDLE ACCOUNT

	Non-Section 1256 Stock	Section 1256 Options	Daily Net	Character
December 28	(150)	(50)	(200)	(150) STCL (50) 60/40
December 29	160	(100)	60	60 STCG
December 30	(150)	300	150	150 60/40
December 31	50	150	200	50 STCG 150 60/40

XYZ MIXED STRADDLE ACCOUNT

	Non-Section 1256 Stock	Section 1256 Options	Daily Net	Character
December 28	(100)	150	50	50 60/40
December 29	100	(50)	50	50 STCG
December 30	(50)	(50)	(100)	(50) STCL (50) 60/40
December 31	(100)	50	(50)	(50) STCL

ANNUAL ABC ACCOUNT GAIN OR LOSS

60/40	Short-Term	Long-Term
(50)	(20)	(30)
150	60	90
150	60	90
—	(150)	—
—	60	—
—	50	—
Total	60	150

Under these circumstances, because no more than 50 percent of the net gain from a mixed straddle account can be treated as long-term capital gain, only 105 of the 210 net gain from the ABC account will be characterized as long-term and 105 will be characterized as short-term.

ANNUAL XYZ ACCOUNT GAIN OR LOSS

60/40	Short-Term	Long-Term
(50)	(20)	(30)
50	20	30
—	(50)	—
—	50	—
—	(50)	—
Total	(50)	0

Under I.R.C. § 1092(b)(2)(B), no more than 40 percent of a mixed straddle account net loss can be treated as a short-term capital loss, and as a result, 20 of the 50 net loss will be treated as short-term capital loss and 30 as long-term capital loss. The taxpayer's net results for the trading year will be as follows:

TAXPAYER TOTALS

Short-Term	Long-Term
105	105
(20)	(30)
85	75

The taxpayer's net long-term gain of 75 is subject to tax at the rate for long-term capital gain, while his short-term gain of 85 can be taxed at ordinary rates.

The Treasury regulations appear to call for a different result by applying the limitations of I.R.C. § 1092(b)(2)(B) only after netting the results of all of the mixed straddle accounts.[140] If that rule were applied to this example, the taxpayer's total annual account net gain or loss would total 160 net gain including 150 LTCG. Applying the limitations at this aggregate level, the LTCG would be limited to 80 (50 percent of the net gain).

---

[140] *See, e.g.,* Temp. Treas. Reg. § 1.1092(b)-4T(c)(6), Example (2) (1985).

The netting procedures in the temporary Treasury regulations, to the extent that they apply the I.R.C. § 1092(b)(2)(B) limitations at the aggregate and not the individual account level, clearly conflict with the language of the Code, which demands that the limitations be applied at the individual account level. This inconsistency may permit taxpayers to effectively select the more beneficial treatment, although the better answer is that the Code provision should control.

Example 57-15

Assume that a taxpayer with a Treasury bond mixed straddle account purchases a Treasury bond for $1000 on day one and designates it as belonging in its mixed straddle account. By day two, the bond has depreciated to $700 and the taxpayer enters into an offsetting position with a short futures contract position. On day two, the taxpayer marks the bond and the futures contract to market, recognizing a $300 loss. On day three, the bond appreciates to $900 and the futures contract generates a $200 loss. The taxpayer marks-to-market the bond and futures positions on day three and recognizes a $200 gain from the bond and offsets it against a $200 loss from the futures contracts. The taxpayer's net result for all three days is a $300 loss.

(d) CAPITALIZATION OF INTEREST AND CARRYING CHARGES

The Treasury is responsible for establishing rules to capitalize interest and carrying charges for mixed straddle accounts to the extent such charges exceed income on such positions.[141] The purpose of capitalizing excess straddle expenses (after netting the expenses and income of a straddle) is to prevent conversion of unrelated ordinary income into long-term capital gain. The income and expense items include interest, carrying charges, dividends, payments in lieu of dividends, and short stock rebates. To prevent this conversion, I.R.C. § 263(g) requires excess straddle expenses to be capitalized rather than deducted as ordinary expense deductions. This means that no expense attributable to a straddle can be used to reduce ordinary income that is unrelated to the straddle.[142]

---

[141] I.R.C. § 1092(b)(1).
[142] *See* section 55.2.

On its face, I.R.C. § 263(g) assumes that all positions of a straddle can be identified and that the interest income and interest expenses with respect to such positions can also be identified. In providing the election for a mixed straddle account, however, Congress recognized that identifying individual straddle transactions would be difficult (and perhaps impossible) for certain taxpayers.[143] If a taxpayer maintains a mixed straddle account, he may be required to capitalize interest and carrying charges allocable to the account, rather than to individual straddles held, but not otherwise identified, within the account.[144]

The regulations provide that no deduction is allowed for interest and carrying charges that are "properly allocable" to a mixed straddle account.[145] Interest and carrying charges "properly allocable" to a mixed straddle account are defined as the excess of (1) the sum of (a) interest (including short sale expenses) on debt incurred to purchase or carry any position in the account, and (b) all amounts paid or incurred to insure, store, transport, etc., personal property with respect to a position in the account; over (2) the sum of (a) interest includable in gross income with respect to all positions in the account, (b) ordinary income from the holding, retirement, or sale of debt securities in the account; and (c) dividends received with respect to positions in the account, net of certain dividends received deductions.[146]

The temporary Treasury regulations provide some guidance as to whether the interest expense attributable to the account should be netted against all gains in the account, or only against that portion generated from assets that are debt financed. The temporary Treasury regulations apply I.R.C. § 263(g) to a mixed straddle account as if the account contains one straddle.[147]

First, income and expense items are allocated to each account pursuant to a reasonable method. Second, income and expense items are netted for the year within each account. Third, net expense is capitalized by reducing the annual account net gain or increasing the annual account net loss. Fourth, any interest and carrying charges disallowed under this rule are capitalized, that is, they are treated as an adjustment to the annual account net gain or loss and are allocated pro rata between net short-term and long-term capital gain or loss.[148]

---

[143] H.R. CONF. REP. NO. 861, *supra* note 19, at 913.
[144] *See* Temp. Treas. Reg. § 1.1092(b)-4T(c)(3) (1985).
[145] *Id.*
[146] *Id.*
[147] *Id.*
[148] *Id.*

Example 57-16

Assume the same facts as in Example 57-14, except that the taxpayer also incurred $40 of net interest expense properly allocable to positions in the ABC mixed straddle account. Under these circumstances, the $40 of net interest expense is not deductible but must be allocated to the annual results of the ABC mixed straddle account. The $40 of interest expense reduces proportionately the long-term and short-term elements of the ABC capital gain. Therefore, $11.42 (60/210 times $40) of the interest expense reduces the taxpayer's ABC short-term capital gain and $28.57 (150/210 times $40) reduces the taxpayer's ABC long-term capital gain.

(e) TOTAL ANNUAL ACCOUNT NET GAIN OR LOSS

The results of all mixed straddle accounts for the year are netted to yield the total annual account net gain or loss.[149] Thus, for the year, the taxpayer has a single result from trading in all mixed straddle accounts of (1) long-term gain or loss, (2) short-term gain or loss, (3) a combination of long-term and short-term gains, or (4) a combination of long-term and short-term losses.

(f) ACCOUNT CAP

The annual total from all mixed straddle accounts for each year cannot exceed 50 percent long-term gain or 40 percent short-term loss.[150] Thus, if the total of all accounts is a gain, then the long-term portion is limited to 50 percent. If the total of all accounts is a loss, the short-term portion is limited to 40 percent.

(g) YEARLY MIXED STRADDLE ELECTIONS

The temporary Treasury regulations issued on January 18, 1985, provided that section 1092(b)(2) identified straddles or mixed straddle accounts, once made, were effective for all subsequent tax years unless the IRS consented to their revocation.[151] Revised temporary regulations

---

[149] Temp. Treas. Reg. § 1.1092(b)-4T(c)(2) (1985).
[150] Temp. Treas. Reg. § 1.1092(b)-4T(c)(4) (1985).
[151] Temp. Treas. Reg. § 1.1092(b)-4T(f)(3) (1985); T.D. 8008, 1985-1 C.B. 276.

issued October 11, 1985, however, provided that an election is effective only for the taxable year for which it is made.[152]

The election must be made by the due date (without regard to extensions) of the taxpayer's income tax return for the immediately preceding taxable year.[153] This means that individual taxpayers on a calendar year must make their elections by April 15 of the year in which the election is to be effective. Similarly, corporate taxpayers on the calendar year must make their elections by March 15 of the year in which the election is to be effective.

If an election is made after the times specified in Temp. Treas. Reg. § 1.1092(b)-4T(f)(1), the election is permitted only if the IRS concludes that the taxpayer had reasonable cause for failing to make a timely election.[154] In LTR 8847030,[155] the IRS found reasonable cause for failing to make timely mixed straddle account elections for the taxable year. The IRS granted a 30-day extension of time to file the elections.

In conclusion, taxpayers have until the date their tax return is due for the preceding taxable year (without extensions) to consider whether they should choose the mixed straddle account election or the section 1092(b)(2) identified mixed straddle election to comply with the regulations, taking into account their trading practices for the year and the nature of their accounting records. Elections after that date must be approved by the IRS.[156] Many taxpayers have found that they prefer the section 1092(b)(2) identified mixed straddle method, if they could track mixed straddles using their accounting systems on a day-by-day basis. However, many of these same taxpayers discovered that their accounting records as they existed for 1984 did not allow them to make the tax computations required by the section 1092(b)(2) identified mixed straddle method and, as a result, they preferred the mixed straddle account election for 1984 only. The amended temporary Treasury regulations issued October 17, 1985, make it clear that taxpayers can use the mixed straddle account election for purposes of convenience in filing their 1984 tax returns but thereafter may elect straddle-by-straddle identifica-

---

[152] Temp. Treas. Reg. § 1.1092(b)-4T(f)(4) (1985); see T.D. 8008, 1985-1 C.B. 276.
[153] Temp. Treas. Reg. § 1.1092(b)-4T(f)(1) (1985).
[154] Id.; LTR 8847030 (Aug. 25, 1988).
[155] (Aug. 25, 1988). See also LTR 8833042 (May 25, 1988); LTR 8938016 (June 23, 1989).
[156] Temp. Treas. Reg. § 1.1092(b)-4T(f)(1) (1985).

tion.¹⁵⁷ The temporary regulations extended the date for making the election generally until December 31, 1985.¹⁵⁸

If a taxpayer begins trading or investing in positions in a new class of activities during a taxable year, the election for the new class of activities must be made by the taxpayer by the later of the due date of the taxpayer's income tax return for the immediately preceding taxable year (without any extensions) or 60 days after the first mixed straddle in the new class of activities is entered into.¹⁵⁹

In addition, if on or after the date the taxpayer made a mixed straddle account election he begins trading positions that were not specified in the original election but are includable in a mixed straddle account, the taxpayer must make an amended election by the later of the due date of his income tax return for the immediately preceding taxable year (without any extensions) or 60 days after the acquisition of the first of the positions.¹⁶⁰ An election made after the specified time is permitted only if the taxpayer had reasonable cause for failing to make a timely election.¹⁶¹

Example 57-17

A calendar year taxpayer holds only a few positions in one class of activities prior to April 15 of a taxable year. He greatly increases his trading activity in this type of position after April 15. The IRS can conclude that the taxpayer had reasonable cause for failing to make a timely election and allow him to make a mixed straddle account election for that year.¹⁶²

(h) MANNER FOR MAKING ELECTION

A taxpayer must make a mixed straddle election on IRS Form 6781, in the manner prescribed therein, by attaching the form to his income tax return for the immediately preceding taxable year (or to his request for an automatic extension).¹⁶³ The taxpayer must also attach a statement to

---

[157] T.D. 8008, 1985-1 C.B. 276, also provided that taxpayers that already filed their 1985 returns without making a mixed straddle account election could make the election by filing an amended return on or before October 15, 1985.
[158] Temp. Treas. Reg. § 1.1092(b)-4T(f)(3) (1985).
[159] Temp. Treas. Reg. § 1.1092(b)-4T(f)(1) (1985).
[160] *Id.*
[161] *Id.*
[162] *Id.*
[163] Temp. Treas. Reg. § 1.1092(b)-4T(f)(2)(i) (1985).

Form 6781 designating the class of activities for which a mixed straddle account election is established. The designation must provide sufficient detail so that the IRS can determine, on the basis of the designation, whether specific positions are includable in the mixed straddle account.[164] If a taxpayer establishes more than one mixed straddle account, the IRS must be able to determine that specific positions are placed in the appropriate account.[165] An election applies to all positions held in the designated class of activities during the taxable year.

Amended elections and elections made for new classes of activities in which the taxpayer begins trading during a taxable year are to be made on Form 6781. The election must be made by the later of the due date of the taxpayer's return for the preceding taxable year (without extensions), or 60 days after the first of the positions is acquired.[166] The activity designation statement must be attached.

An election to establish a mixed straddle account, including any amendments to the election, is effective only for the taxable year for which the election is made. Once made, the election for that year can only be revoked during the taxable year with the consent of the IRS. One item that must be provided with the application for consent to revoke a mixed straddle account is a statement that the taxpayer's volume or nature of trading activities has changed substantially and that his activities no longer warrant the use of a mixed straddle account.[167]

(i) TRANSITIONAL ELECTIONS PROVIDED IN 1984

Special transitional rules apply to mixed straddle accounts. First, a calendar year taxpayer can retroactively apply the mixed straddle account rules to all positions established after December 31, 1983, and before January 1, 1985.[168] In general, all positions held on December 31, 1983, that are brought into a mixed straddle account on January 1, 1984, are marked-to-market on December 31, 1983. The resulting gains and losses are included in 1984 and are subject to the 60/40 Rule. Although the temporary regulations are not clear, the Treasury apparently intends that the pre-1984 gains and losses not be included in the account computations. Account positions held at the end of 1984 are marked-to-market on December 31, 1984. These mark-to-market gains and losses are

---

[164] *Id.*
[165] *Id.*
[166] Temp. Treas. Reg. § 1.1092(b)-4T(f)(2)(ii) (1985).
[167] *Id.*
[168] Temp. Treas. Reg. § 1.1092(b)-4T(f)(3) (1985).

combined with the gains and losses from account positions disposed of in 1984 and are netted and offset as if the entire 1984 period was a single day. After December 31, 1984, the daily marking rules apply to each account.

Second, because section 1256 treatment applies retroactively to 1984, the regulations permit the account rules to be applied to 1984 on a simplified basis.[169] The regulations are not entirely clear on the treatment of the pre-1984 gain or loss on the positions that are included in an account. It appears as if the intention under the regulations was to leave the pre-1984 gain or loss outside the mixed straddle account. Therefore, gain or loss remaining unrecognized at the end of 1983 is recognized in 1984 and is subject to section 1256 treatment. Thus, the section 1256 gain or loss is treated as 60/40 and the non-section 1256 gain or loss is treated as short-term. The cross-netting rules do not apply. All account positions are marked-to-market at the end of 1984. The 1984 gains and losses for each account are combined as if the entire period was one day.

Third, there is a special transitional rule for mixed straddle accounts. An election to establish a mixed straddle account for any taxable year that includes July 17, 1984, and any taxable year that ends before September 1, 1986 (or in the case of a corporation, October 1, 1986), must be made by the later of December 31, 1985, or the due date for the taxpayer's 1984 tax return (without extensions) if the due date is after December 31, 1985.[170] The election is made by attaching both Form 6781 and the required statement to the taxpayer's income tax return, amended return, or other form filed on or before the deadline date. The statement must designate with specificity the class of activities for which the account is established.[171]

Example 57-18

The tax return for a fiscal year taxpayer with a taxable year that ended September 30, 1985, is due (without regard to extensions) on January 15, 1986. The mixed straddle election must be made on or before January 15, 1986, with the taxpayer's tax return, or his request for an automatic extension.[172]

---

[169] *Compare* Temp. Treas. Reg. § 1.1092(b)-4T(f)(3) (1985) *with* Temp. Treas. Reg. §§ 1.1092(b)-4T(f)(1), (2) (1985).
[170] Temp. Treas. Reg. § 1.1092(b)-4T(f)(3) (1985).
[171] *See* section 57.4(h).
[172] Temp. Treas. Reg. § 1.1092(b)-4T(f)(3) (1985).

Example 57-19

A calendar year taxpayer that filed his 1984 income tax return before October 15, 1985, without making a mixed straddle account election for either 1984 or 1985 (or both years) can make the mixed straddle account election for either or both of the years with an amended return filed on or before December 31, 1985.[173]

A mixed straddle account elected on an amended return is effective for all positions in the designated class of activities even if the taxpayer elected straddle-by-straddle netting.[174] For taxable years beginning in 1984 and 1985, the election is effective for the entire year. For taxable years beginning in 1983, the election is effective for those days of the year after December 31, 1983, for which a DRA carry-back election is made.[175]

§ 57.5 METHODS OF IDENTIFYING AND NETTING MIXED STRADDLES MAY NOT BE MUTUALLY EXCLUSIVE

A taxpayer may be able to use more than one method of identifying and netting mixed straddles if the designations are proper and taxpayers only make one election for any straddle. Taxpayers need not use mixed straddle accounts if they can comply with other mixed straddle rules.

Temp. Treas. Reg. § 1.1092(b)-3T(a)[176] provides that an election cannot be made for a section 1092(b)(2) identified mixed straddle "for any straddle composed of one or more positions that are includible in a mixed straddle account (as defined in paragraph (b) of § 1.1092(b)-4T) or for any straddle for which an election under section 1256(d) has been made." The temporary Treasury regulations provide that once a mixed straddle account is established, it can only be terminated with IRS consent.[177]

Of course, given the broad discretion granted to the IRS to move positions into and out of accounts, any accounting system that allows the taxpayer to pick and choose the location of positions to achieve favorable tax treatment runs the risk of being challenged by the IRS.

---

[173] *Id.*
[174] *See* section 57.3.
[175] *See* section 44.5.
[176] (1985).
[177] Temp. Treas. Reg. § 1.1092(b)-4T(f)(4) (1985).

It has been suggested that it would be "incongruent" for a taxpayer to make both a section 1092(b)(2) identified mixed straddle election, as well as an identified straddle election under I.R.C. § 1256(d).[178]

> It would be incongruent for Section 1256 contracts to be marked to market upon disposition of Section 1256 positions and for 60/40 treatment to be so broadly applied under Temp. Reg. section 1.1092(b)-3T without Section 1256 contracts being marked to market and receiving 60/40 treatment at year-end under Section 1256(a).[179]

§ 57.6 LIMITATIONS ON WHO CAN MAKE SECTION 1092(b)(2) IDENTIFIED MIXED STRADDLE AND MIXED STRADDLE ACCOUNT ELECTIONS

The temporary Treasury regulations provide requirements as to how a taxpayer can identify section 1092(b)(2) identified mixed straddles and establish mixed straddle accounts. The remainder of this section addresses the limitations on these elections.

(a) SECTION 1092(b)(2) IDENTIFIED MIXED STRADDLES

Turning first to identification of section 1092(b)(2) identified mixed straddles, the temporary regulations provide that only the person or entity that *directly* holds *all* positions of a straddle can make the identification.[180] This requirement of direct ownership of all positions is too narrow, because it does not apply to all positions that should be eligible for identification as section 1092(b)(2) identified straddles. For purposes of defining a straddle, a taxpayer is treated as holding any position held by a related person.[181]

Related persons are defined to include a taxpayer's spouse, another corporation that files a consolidated return with the taxpayer, and certain flow-through entities (e.g., trusts, partnerships, and S corporations). If only taxpayers directly holding all straddle positions can make section 1092(b)(2) identified mixed straddle elections, however, then those taxpayers subject to aggregation of their positions under I.R.C.

---

[178] American Bar Association, Tax Section, *Comments on Proposed Regulations Relating to the Treatment of Positions Identified as Mixed Straddles*, reprinted in 4 DAILY TAX HIGHLIGHTS & DOCUMENTS 1959 (1987).

[179] *Id.* at 1960.

[180] Temp. Treas. Reg. § 1.1092(b)-3T(d)(1) (1985).

[181] I.R.C. § 1092(d)(4)(A); *see generally* Chapter 51.

§ 1092(d)(4) with positions held by related persons cannot make section 1092(b)(2) identified straddle elections with respect to those straddles that are deemed to be held by them under I.R.C. § 1092(d)(4). Under the temporary regulations, related persons cannot jointly make a section 1092(b)(2) election.

Because corporations filing consolidated returns within I.R.C. § 1502 are "related persons" under I.R.C. § 1092(d)(4), the section 1092(b)(2) identified straddle election should be available to the members of a consolidated group (or any group to which the rules of I.R.C. § 1092(d)(4) apply) even if different members of the group hold the positions making up the straddle. A joint election is unavailable, however, under a literal reading of the temporary regulations. Hence, the scope of the temporary regulations is too limited to cover all of the transactions for which the section 1092(b)(2) identified mixed straddle election should be available.

(b) MIXED STRADDLE ACCOUNTS

A less restrictive standard from the one for identified straddles[182] appears to apply to taxpayers that establish mixed straddle accounts. The temporary Treasury regulations do not specifically address the issue of whether the person or entity directly holding all of the positions must make the mixed straddle account election. Rather, the temporary regulations provide that the election must be made by the "taxpayer."[183] If the taxpayer that must make a mixed straddle account election is not required to directly hold all of the positions of a straddle, a more liberal standard than the one established for section 1092(b)(2) identified mixed straddles is available to him.

(c) CONCLUSION

Different standards for electing section 1092(b)(2) identified mixed straddles and mixed straddle accounts are not appropriate, despite the Treasury's broad authority to promulgate regulations under I.R.C. § 1092(b)(2). In fact, it should be possible to assert that both section 1092(b)(2) identified straddles and mixed straddle account elections should be available to any taxpayer for positions that are attributed to him under I.R.C. § 1092(d)(4).

---

[182] *See* discussion at section 57.6(a).
[183] Temp. Treas. Reg. § 1.1092(b)-4T(f)(2)(i) (1985).

§ 57.7 TREATMENT OF MIXED STRADDLES WHERE AT LEAST ONE POSITION IS CAPITAL AND AT LEAST ONE POSITION IS ORDINARY

TMRA '88 established new definitions of section 988 foreign currency transactions and altered the scope of the section 1256 carve-out to section 988 treatment.[184] Because the TMRA '88 changes allow taxpayers with foreign currency transactions to treat their positions as either capital or ordinary, a mixed straddle can have at least one position that is capital (i.e., a section 1256 foreign currency contract subject to the 60/40 treatment), while another position is ordinary (i.e., section 988 transactions that are not carved out by the narrower section 1256 carve-out—e.g., foreign currency-related bank forward contracts). As a result, Congress established I.R.C. § 1092(b)(2)(D), which enables the Treasury to issue regulations on the proper treatment of a mixed straddle where at least one position is capital and at least one position is ordinary.[185] Clearly, the legislation is intended to address the anomaly that can occur as a result of the changes to the I.R.C. § 988 provisions, but the statutory language apparently does not prevent the application of these regulations to nonforeign currency-related transactions.

The Conference Report that accompanied TMRA '88[186] provides that the section 1092(b) mixed straddle regulations will apply to such transactions with appropriate modifications to take into account the fact that one or more positions would ordinarily give rise to ordinary income or loss.[187] The Conference Report specifies that the Conferees expect that "as under the current regulations, 60/40 treatment will apply only to net gain or loss from the transactions included in the identified mixed straddle or the account and only to the extent attributable to section 1256 contracts giving rise to capital gain or loss."[188] Thus, the 60/40 application will apply in the same manner as it currently applies to both identified mixed straddle transactions and mixed straddle account transactions. The Conferees also specify that with respect to mixed straddle account transactions, the 40 percent restriction relating to short-term capital losses will also apply to ordinary losses.[189] Thus, no more than 40 percent

---

[184] *See* Chapter 59 for a discussion of the TMRA '88 changes to section 988 transactions.
[185] TMRA '88, *supra* note 13, § 6130(b)(2)(D).
[186] HOUSE CONFERENCE REPORT, H.R. CONF. REP. NO. 1104, 100th Cong., 2d Sess. 194, *reprinted in* 1988 U.S. CODE CONG. & ADMIN. NEWS 5048, 5254.
[187] *Id.*
[188] *Id.*
[189] *Id.*

of net foreign exchange loss from a mixed straddle account may be ordinary.

§ 57.8 SUMMARY OF EFFECTIVE DATES

The temporary Treasury regulations provide various effective dates that are summarized in this section. Application of the loss deferral rule under Temp. Treas. Reg. § 1.1092(b)-1T[190] applies to loss positions on or after January 24, 1985.

The holding period rule contained in Temp. Treas. Reg. § 1.1092(b)-2T[191] applies to positions of straddles, except for straddles made up exclusively of section 1256 positions, established after June 23, 1981, in taxable years ending after that date.

The killer rule contained in Temp. Treas. Reg. § 1.1092(b)-2T(b)(2)[192] applies to mixed straddle positions established after January 1, 1984.

The straddle-by-straddle netting rule for section 1092(b)(2) identified mixed straddles under Temp. Treas. Reg. § 1.1092(b)-3T[193] applies to positions established after January 1, 1984.

Finally, the mixed straddle account rules under Temp. Treas. Reg. § 1.1092(b)-4T[194] apply to positions held on or after January 1, 1984.

---

[190] (1986).
[191] (1986).
[192] (1986).
[193] (1985).
[194] (1985).

Part Twelve

Treatment of Gain or Loss on Terminations of Certain Contract Rights and Obligations

If a taxpayer's rights or obligations with respect to personal property that is a capital asset in the hands of the taxpayer are terminated by cancellation, lapse, expiration, or any other termination,[1] gain or loss is treated as from the sale of a capital asset.

---

[1] I.R.C. § 1234A.

Fifty-eight

Terminations of Contract Rights and Obligations

§ 58.1 PRE-ERTA CANCELLATION TRANSACTIONS

Under the law in effect prior to the enactment of ERTA in 1981, a taxpayer with the requisite profit motive could seek to obtain ordinary losses on certain dispositions of capital assets which, if sold at a gain, would produce capital gain. Some of the more typical of these transactions involved cancellations of forward contracts for government securities or foreign currency.[1]

One of the most common methods of closing out a forward contract is to enter into an offsetting contract, which requires the consent of both parties. Thus, if a taxpayer enters into a long (short) forward contract and he wants to terminate his obligations, he can enter into an offsetting short (long) contract with the same party, assuming the other party consents to the termination. The obligations of the two contracts offset each other and neither party is obligated to go through the formality of taking or making delivery. The taxpayer's gain or loss is determined by the difference in the price of the underlying property for each contract.

A forward contract is an executory contract. General principles of contract law allow the rights and obligations of a party to an executory contract to be assigned to a third party if the terms of the contract so

---

[1] For a discussion of forward contracts, see generally section 4.3(b).

permit. Further, since the rights in a forward contract can constitute capital assets, it appears that such an assignment would constitute the sale or exchange of a capital asset and, therefore, give rise to capital gain or loss. The IRS has taken this position with regard to the assignment of a long futures contract.[2] If a taxpayer holds a long contract for more than the long-term holding period (more than one year for transactions immediately prior to enactment of ERTA in 1981), he obtains long-term gain whether he assigns the contract or purchases an offsetting short contract. There is no possibility for manipulation of the holding period rules. An entirely different situation occurs when a taxpayer assigns a short contract. If the taxpayer subsequently closed the short contract by offsetting it with a substantially identical long contract, he recognizes short-term capital gain regardless of the length of time he held the short contract before acquiring the long contract.

Under the law in effect before enactment of ERTA, a disposition of a capital asset could be structured as a lapse or cancellation to obtain ordinary, rather than capital loss treatment. Such a disposition was not considered to be a sale or exchange. In addition, a straddle could have been established to minimize the taxpayer's risk of loss in holding the positions. The taxpayer could attempt to generate ordinary loss on the cancellation (by payment of an amount in settlement of his obligation to the other party to the contract), and a corresponding long-term capital gain on the sale or assignment of the contract. Closing out the two positions in different manners could possibly generate a different tax result.[3]

Example 58-1

Under the law in effect prior to the enactment of ERTA in 1981, a taxpayer entered into short and long forward contracts to buy and sell Deutsche marks. The taxpayer held a straddle. If the price of Deutsche marks declined, the taxpayer could sell or assign his short contract to a bank or other financial institution for a capital gain (equal to the excess of the forward contract price over the market price) and cancel his long contract for a capital loss (by payment of an amount in settlement of his obligation to the other party of the contract). The taxpayer would report the sales proceeds as capital

---

[2] *See* Rev. Rul. 78-414, 1978-2 C.B. 213.
[3] *See* Stoller v. Comm'r, Tax Ct. Mem. Dec. (CCH) 47,063 (Dec. 31, 1990).

gain but would treat the amount paid to terminate his obligation to buy as an ordinary loss.[4]

Several cases hold that when a contract is cancelled, the mutual rights and obligations of the parties simply "disappear," and there is no sale or exchange of any assets.[5] Accordingly, taxpayers took the position under pre-ERTA law that the cancellation of a forward contract generated ordinary income or loss. In *Hoover Co. v. Comm'r*,[6] the taxpayer—seeking ordinary loss on forward contract transactions—asserted that it had cancelled some of its contracts. Taxpayers reported ordinary loss treatment on the grounds that a release from their obligations under the forward contracts was not a sale or exchange and no property rights were transferred. The legal theory was that the mere relinquishment of simple contract rights did not constitute a sale or exchange and gives rise to ordinary income or loss.[7] The Tax Court found as a question of fact, however, that the contracts had been offset rather than cancelled, noting in a footnote the potential applicability of ordinary income treatment upon the cancellation of a forward contract.[8]

In *Foote v. Comm'r*,[9] the Tax Court held that an agreement to terminate tenure rights entered into by a college professor did not constitute a sale or exchange. The Tax Court stated that the agreement "simply terminated petitioner's rights; his tenure did not pass to the University, but was extinguished."[10] The agreement released the University of its obligations. Rights were not transferred but merely came to an end and

---

[4] *See* JOINT COMM. ON TAXATION, 97TH CONG., 1ST SESS., GENERAL EXPLANATION OF THE ECONOMIC RECOVERY TAX ACT OF 1981, at 313–14 (Joint Comm. Print 1981) [hereinafter General Explanation of ERTA]; HOUSE WAYS AND MEANS COMM. REPORT, TAX INCENTIVE BILL OF 1981, H.R. REP. NO. 201, 97th Cong., 1st Sess. 213 (1981) [hereinafter H.R. REP. NO. 201]; SENATE FINANCE COMM. REPORT, ECONOMIC RECOVERY TAX ACT OF 1981, S. REP. NO. 144, 97th Cong., 1st Sess. 171, *reprinted in* 1981 U.S. CODE CONG. & ADMIN. NEWS 105, 267 [hereinafter S. REP. NO. 144].

[5] Commissioner v. Starr Bros., Inc., 204 F.2d 673, 674 (2d Cir. 1953), *rev'g* 18 T.C. 149 (1959), *nonacq.* 1952-2 C.B. 6; General Artists Corp. v. Comm'r, 205 F.2d 360 (2d Cir. 1953), *aff'g* 17 T.C. 1517 (1952), *cert. denied*, 346 U.S. 866 (1953).

[6] 72 T.C. 206, 228 (1979), *acq.* 1984-2 C.B. 1.

[7] 72 T.C. at 248.

[8] *Id.* at 249 n.7.

[9] 81 T.C. 930, 936 (1983).

[10] *Id.*

vanished. Citing other cases, the Tax Court stated that there was no sale or exchange upon execution of the termination agreement.[11]

At this writing, only one case, *Stoller v. Comm'r*,[12] addresses the issue of whether the cancellation of certain pre-ERTA forward contracts results in an ordinary or a capital loss.[13] In *Stoller*, a partnership entered into various spreads using forward contracts. One of the issues in *Stoller* was whether fees the partnership paid to cancel certain forward contracts were deductible as ordinary losses or as capital losses. The Tax Court found that the cancellation fees paid for one cancellation transaction were deductible as an ordinary loss, but that all other cancellation fees were deductible as capital losses.

In the one instance in which cancellation fees were treated as an ordinary loss, the partnership cancelled all of the legs of a spread and claimed the net loss on the cancellation as an ordinary loss. In that transaction, the entire spread consisted of the four cancelled contracts. After the cancellation, the partnership did not enter into any new contracts to replace the cancelled contracts. The partnership realized and recognized a net $10,000 loss, which it then passed through to its partners as ordinary loss.

The Tax Court reviewed prior cases which treated the cancellation of a contract as producing ordinary income or loss rather than producing capital gain or loss.[14] In those cases, the courts had found no sale or exchange which would produce capital gain or loss because the effect of the cancellation was to completely terminate the taxpayer's rights under the cancelled contract. The Tax Court noted that in the transaction in which the partnership cancelled all of the legs of the spread, a complete

---

[11] *See* Billy Rose's Diamond Horseshoe, Inc. v. United States, 448 F.2d 549 (2d Cir. 1971), *aff'g* 322 F. Supp. 76 (S.D.N.Y. 1971); United States Freight Co. v. United States, 422 F.2d 887 (Ct. Cl. 1970); Commissioner v. Pittston Co., 252 F.2d 344 (2d Cir. 1958), *rev'g* 26 T.C. 967 (1956), *nonacq.* 1957-1 C.B. 5, *cert. denied*, 357 U.S. 919 (1958); Starr Bros., Inc., 204 F.2d 673 (2d Cir. 1953); Leh v. Comm'r, 27 T.C. 892 (1957), *aff'd*, 260 F.2d 489 (9th Cir. 1958); *see also* Rev. Rul. 56-531, 1956-2 C.B. 983, *clarified by* Rev. Rul. 72-85, 1972-1 C.B. 234; Rev. Rul. 75-527, 1975-2 C.B. 30.

[12] Tax Ct. Mem. Dec. (CCH) 47,063 (Dec. 31, 1990).

[13] Congress viewed certain of these forward contracts transactions as "abusive" when it enacted I.R.C. § 1234A. To prevent tax avoidance transactions, Congress enacted I.R.C. § 1234A as a change in the general sale or exchange requirement for capital gain or loss under I.R.C. § 1222. *See* General Explanation of ERTA, *supra* note 4, at 313; H.R. REP. NO. 201, *supra* note 4, at 212; S. REP. NO. 144, *supra* note 4, at 170.

[14] Leh v. Comm'r, 27 T.C. 892 (1957), *aff'd*, 260 F.2d 489 (9th Cir. 1958) (cancellation fee paid as a result of the termination of a gasoline purchase contract); Commissioner v. Pittston Co., 252 F.2d 344 (2d Cir. 1958), *rev'g* 26 T.C. 967 (1956), *nonacq.* 1957-1, C.B. 5, *cert. denied*, 357 U.S. 919 (1958) (involved termination of the right to purchase coal).

termination of the taxpayer's rights occurred. As a result, the Tax Court upheld treating the net loss on the spread as an ordinary loss.

The Tax Court held that the cancellation fees paid by the partnership in all of the other cancellation transactions were capital losses. In those other transactions, the partnership cancelled the losing leg of the spread and paid a cancellation fee. The partnership claimed the cancellation fees as ordinary losses, which it passed through to its partners. The partnership replaced the cancelled forward contracts with new contracts which were identical to the cancelled contracts, except for the delivery date. The Tax Court found that the partnership changed the delivery dates to shorten the window of risk of the spread.

The Tax Court called these transactions "switch transactions." A switch transaction is a transaction which "does not extinguish all rights of the parties to the transaction, but rather switches or exchanges those rights."[15]

In analyzing the switch transactions, the Tax Court stated that the substance of a transaction, and not its form, determined the tax incidence of the transaction. The Tax Court found that since the cancellations in the switch transactions were to shorten the partnership's window of risk of the spread, the cancellations really were part of an ongoing straddle. The partnership did not intend to terminate those straddles, but rather intended to replace the former contract. The Tax Court treated the switch transactions, in substance, as if the partnership entered into offsetting contracts to close out the loss legs and simultaneously entered into replacement contracts.[16]

In drawing a distinction between the cancellation transaction which resulted in ordinary loss and the cancellations which resulted in capital loss, the Tax Court determined whether "after the cancellation, any rights or property interests created by the contract remained."[17] Where all rights of the contracting parties came to an end and vanished, the cancellation was treated as creating ordinary income or loss. Under those circumstances, no transfer of any property rights occurs. On the other hand, where substantial rights remained after the cancellation, the Tax Court found a transfer of rights or an exchange. As a result, that cancellation resulted in capital loss.

---

[15] *Stoller*, Tax Ct. Mem. Dec. (CCH) 47,063, at 1566 (Dec. 31, 1990).

[16] The Tax Court also noted that the partnership did not bargain for the replacement contracts separately. Rather, the contracts were priced according to the spread in price between the legs of the straddle. The cancellation fee was based on the price of similar offsetting contracts in the futures market. *Stoller*, Tax Court Mem. Dec. (CCH) 47,063, at 1566 (Dec. 31, 1990).

[17] *Id.* at 1567.

One reason only one case addresses the issue of whether the cancellation results in ordinary or capital loss is that the courts have generally denied taxpayers deductions for any losses from the cancellation of pre-ERTA forward contracts because the taxpayers failed to prove that the forward contract transaction met three conditions.[18] First, the taxpayer must establish that the transaction actually occurred. Second, the transaction must not lack economic substance. And third, the transaction must have been entered into with the requisite profit motive.[19] When transactions take place on regulated markets, the courts focus their attention on the third element—the taxpayer's profit motive. When the market is limited to transactions between customers and the market maker (referred to as "off-market transactions"), however, the courts first focus on whether the transactions are shams.[20] If the transaction does not, in fact, occur, the transaction is referred to as a "factual sham." If the transaction lacks economic substance, it is referred to as a "legal sham."[21]

If an off-market transaction is not viewed as a factual or legal sham, it is possible that Section 108 of the DRA[22] may apply to the forward contract cancellation. This would limit IRS arguments on audit and subsequent litigation to the amount of loss, the character of loss (ordinary or capital), and whether the taxpayer had the requisite profit motive.[23]

Early cases discussed the nature of the profit motive that is required before any deduction is allowed. In *Wehrly v. United States*,[24] the taxpayers sued the government for refunds after they paid tax assessments imposed by the IRS on their pre-ERTA forward contract cancellation transactions. A three-judge panel of the Ninth Circuit Court of Appeals held that the taxpayers' pre-ERTA straddle losses were covered by Section 108 and were deductible if the straddle trades were real transactions (i.e., were not shams) and were entered into with "a reasonable prospect of profit."

The court in *Wehrly* focused on the nature of the profit motive required before Section 108 would apply. The court rejected the IRS's argument that the straddle transactions had to be entered into "primarily for

---

[18] The Tax Court in *Stoller* found all three conditions satisfied.

[19] Glass v. Comm'r, 87 T.C. 1087 (1986), aff'd sub nom. Herrington v. Comm'r, 854 F.2d 755 (5th Cir. 1988), and aff'd sub nom. Yosha v. Comm'r, 861 F.2d 494 (7th Cir. 1988), cert. denied, 1989 U.S. LEXIS 2370; Marcus v. Comm'r, 54 T.C.M. (CCH) 1452 (1988).

[20] Freytag v. Comm'r, 89 T.C. 849 (1987), aff'd, 904 F.2d 1011 (5th Cir. 1990), reh'g denied, 1990 U.S. App. LEXIS 15152, cert. granted, 1991 U.S. LEXIS 645. See also Thurner v. Comm'r, 60 T.C.M. (CCH) 961 (1990).

[21] *Glass*, 87 T.C. 1087 (1986).

[22] Pub. L. No. 98-369, § 108, 98 Stat. 494, 630–31 (1984) [hereinafter DRA]; see section 47.2(c).

[23] *See* section 47.2(c).

[24] 808 F.2d 1311 (9th Cir. 1986).

profit" to be deductible. The court held that the requisite profit motive was present if the taxpayer had only a *reasonable expectation of profit*. The IRS asked the full Ninth Circuit Court of Appeals to review and reconsider the decision of the three-judge panel. On December 23, 1986, the Ninth Circuit denied the IRS's motion for reconsideration and rehearing. This taxpayer victory was later lost, however, when *Wehrly* was overruled by the Ninth Circuit in *Landreth v. Comm'r*,[25] which held that the correct profit motive standard is the *primarily for profit* standard.[26]

In *Forseth v. Comm'r*,[27] the Tax Court found that the forward contract market in which the taxpayer had traded was a factual sham. In *Forseth*, the taxpayers entered into forward contract straddle transactions in gold and platinum futures contracts, which were executed in London between November 1980 and July 1981. The taxpayers reported ordinary losses on the cancellation of their forward contract positions. The Tax Court denied the taxpayers' losses and found the forward contracts in which the taxpayers traded a factual sham for the following reasons. First, the reported losses achieved a high degree of correlation to the taxpayers' tax "shelter" needs, offsetting 55 percent to 94 percent of their adjusted gross incomes.[28] Second, the predicted losses contained in promotional material were remarkably close to the actual losses reported.[29] Third, throughout the period of years during which the accounts were open, no margin calls or additional deposits were made—even though the forward contracts were not subject to any limits on price movements and there was no limit on the amount of losses that might be sustained.[30] Fourth, some trading occurred in accounts before margin was deposited.[31] Fifth, the taxpayers reported gains roughly equal to the difference between their reported losses minus the margin deposits they made with the dealer.[32] Sixth, there was no evidence that the dealer was "laying off" its positions

---

[25] 859 F.2d 643 (9th Cir.), *vacating* 845 F.2d 828 (1988).

[26] For a discussion of the provisions of Section 108, see section 47.2(c).

[27] 85 T.C. 127 (1985), *aff'd sub nom.* Mahoney v. Comm'r, 808 F.2d 1219 (6th Cir. 1987), *and aff'd sub nom.* Enrici v. Comm'r, 813 F.2d 293 (9th Cir. 1987), *and aff'd*, 845 F.2d 746 (7th Cir. 1988).

[28] 85 T.C. at 151.

[29] *Id.* at 152–53.

[30] *Id.* at 157.

[31] *Id.* at 154–55.

[32] *Id.* at 158–59.

with other dealers to reduce risk.[33] And seventh, the court found an apparent manipulation of trading records.[34]

Another example of a forward contract market that was found to be a factual sham is *Brown v. Comm'r*.[35] In *Brown*, the taxpayers entered into forward contract straddle transactions in GNMA and FHLMC securities with a government securities dealer. The taxpayers received offering memoranda predicting that a minimum margin deposit of $10,000 would generate ordinary losses on the cancellation of the contracts of $100,000. The Tax Court held that the program existed solely to provide tax benefits and denied the taxpayers' deductions.[36] The court based its decision on three facts that it believed to be relevant. First, the taxpayers did not prove that the prices for the contracts were determined in the open market.[37] Second, the dealer did not follow industry standards of the securities industry.[38] Third, the court found that contract cancellations in the securities industry were generally used only to correct errors, not as a trading strategy.[39]

In both *Forseth* and *Brown* the taxpayers were assessed penalties for underpayment of tax liability.[40] In *Brown*, however, the Tax Court initially imposed damages under I.R.C. § 6673 in the amount of $5000 against each taxpayer for filing Tax Court petitions primarily for the purpose of delaying the payment of tax.[41] The Tax Court in *Brown* found that the taxpayers were sufficiently sophisticated in business and tax matters to have known—and actually did know—at the time the dis-

---

[33] *Id.* at 161–63. A dealer "lays off" its risk by hedging its position in a forward contract either in the futures market, or with another investor with an offsetting forward contract. For example, if the dealer has a forward contract to deliver U.S. Treasury bills six months in the future, it can lay off the risk of that contract by buying (i.e., entering into a long position) Treasury bills for delivery within six months in the futures market.

[34] 85 T.C. at 163–64.

[35] 85 T.C. 397 (1985), *withdrawn and reissued at* 85 T.C. 968 (1985), *aff'd sub nom.* Sochin v. Comm'r, 842 F.2d 351 (9th Cir.), *cert. denied*, 109 S. Ct. 72 (1988).

[36] 85 T.C. 968, 976 (1985).

[37] *Id.* at 1000.

[38] *Id.*

[39] *Id.* at 994.

[40] I.R.C. § 6653(a).

[41] The initial Tax Court decision assessing a penalty under I.R.C. § 6673 was withdrawn and when the decision was reissued, the penalty assessment under I.R.C. § 6673 had been removed. TRA '86 expands the scope of I.R.C. § 6673. Prior to amendment, I.R.C. § 6673 assessed damages for proceedings instituted or maintained by a taxpayer for delay, or if a taxpayer's position is found to be frivolous or groundless. As amended by TRA '86, I.R.C. § 6673 also sanctions a taxpayer's unreasonable failure to pursue available administrative remedies.

puted transactions were entered into that the transactions were shams.[42] The court used its opinion in *Brown* to serve notice to other taxpayers that it will assess this penalty against taxpayers that file Tax Court petitions—or maintain tax positions—based on transactions that they knew or reasonably should have known to be factual shams.[43]

Glass v. Comm'r[44] involved straddles of options and futures contracts on the LME. The losing leg of the straddle would be offset in the first year and the taxpayers would claim an ordinary loss. Unlike the United States markets on which trading is regulated by the CFTC, the LME does not operate as a guarantor and clearing organization for the trades. Rather, all transactions are executed on a principal-to-principal basis.[45] Because the LME—like the United States forward contract market—was not a regulated market, the court addressed the issue of whether the transaction was a sham. Although the IRS argued that the transactions were factual shams, the Tax Court assumed, without deciding, that the options and futures contracts entered into were actual contracts. As a result, the Tax Court did not focus its attention on whether each petitioner sufficiently authenticated his transactions. Rather, the court focused on whether the transactions—even if factually bona fide—were legally sufficient to accomplish the desired tax results.[46]

The Tax Court in *Glass* rejected the premise that formal compliance with the literal provisions of the Code ends any discussion of the deductibility of losses. The Tax Court held that the transactions lacked economic substance and were, therefore, legal shams. The court observed that the one consistent thread that ran through all of the consolidated cases was that the losses were intentionally incurred in year one, followed by countervailing gains in the following or later years. The Tax Court found, after considering the entire transaction, that the intentional skewing of the transaction to realize a loss in the first year introduced an additional negative element that "prohibitively stacks the deck against the chances

---

[42] *Brown*, 85 T.C. at 1001.

[43] *Id.*

[44] 87 T.C. 1086 (1986), *aff'd sub nom.* Herrington v. Comm'r, 854 F.2d 755 (5th Cir. 1988), *and aff'd sub nom.* Yosha v. Comm'r, 861 F.2d 494 (7th Cir. 1988), *cert. denied*, 1989 U.S. LEXIS 2370.

[45] 87 T.C. at 1158.

[46] The *Glass* case was a consolidation of more than 1400 petitioners and is said to be the largest single consolidation of cases in the history of the Tax Court. *Glass*, 87 T.C. at 1153. Given the large number of petitioners, the Tax Court may have taken the approach of a legal sham to avoid reviewing the factual bona fides of each of the petitioners' separate transactions.

of significant financial success."[47] The Tax Court asked whether the petitioners could have profited from their transactions if they had not *in every instance* closed a leg of the straddle in the first tax year. The Tax Court found the answer to be yes, and it therefore concluded that no business or profit-making purpose was behind closing a leg in the first year above and beyond the tax deductions. As a result, the court held that the transactions lacked economic substance and were legal shams.

The Tax Court in *Glass* remarked that prior cases hold that Section 108 of the DRA[48] is not available to taxpayers in straddle cases involving factual shams.[49] The Tax Court in *Glass* held that Section 108 is also not available to permit loss deductions in the first year of a straddle transaction where "the sham involves a series of transactions having no business or profit making function apart from obtaining tax deductions."[50] The absence of economic substance in the structure of the transaction negated the existence of any profit motive.

Later cases involving contract cancellations deny any loss deductions on the grounds that the transactions were both factual shams and lacked economic substance.[51]

§ 58.2 CAPITAL GAIN OR LOSS ON TERMINATIONS

Congress viewed as inappropriate the tax result sought by some taxpayers on pre-ERTA contract cancellation transactions.[52] As a result, I.R.C. § 1234A was enacted as part of ERTA in 1981 so that gains and losses from economically equivalent transactions are taxed the same way. Congress considered ordinary income treatment inappropriate if a transaction was economically equivalent to a sale or exchange of the contract.[53]

The definition of a capital gain and loss requires a sale or exchange of a capital asset to generate a capital gain or loss.[54] In 1981, ERTA expanded

---

[47] *Glass*, 87 T.C. at 1174.

[48] DRA, *supra* note 22.

[49] For a discussion of Section 108, see section 47.2(c).

[50] *Glass*, 87 T.C. at 1176.

[51] *See Freytag*, 89 T.C. 849 (1987), *aff'd*, 904 F.2d 1011 (5th Cir. 1990), *reh'g denied*, 1990 U.S. App. LEXIS 15152, *cert. granted*, 1991 U.S. LEXIS 645; Maring v. Comm'r, 56 T.C.M. (CCH) 343 (1988). In *Maring*, the Court supported its finding of a factual sham, in part, by finding that the taxpayers submitted their tax loss goals to the promoter.

[52] For a discussion of pre-ERTA cancellation transactions, see section 58.1.

[53] *See* General Explanation of ERTA, *supra* note 4, at 313; H.R. REP. NO. 201, *supra* note 4, at 212; S. REP. NO. 144, *supra* note 4, at 170–71.

[54] *See* I.R.C. § 1222.

capital treatment to include the cancellation, lapse, expiration, or other termination of personal property (as defined in I.R.C. § 1092(d)(1)) that is (or would be on acquisition) a capital asset in the hands of the taxpayer.[55] ERTA also extended capital treatment to include a section 1256 contract that is not (or acquisition of which would not be) personal property if the contract is a capital asset in the hands of the taxpayer.[56]

Despite the statement in I.R.C. § 1234A that its provisions cover section 1256 contracts, the rules of domestic commodity and securities exchanges provide that contracts traded on the exchanges can only be terminated by offset or by making or taking delivery of the underlying property. Therefore, as a legal matter, domestic exchange rules prohibit termination of section 1256 contracts by cancellation. Nevertheless, I.R.C. § 1234A includes such contracts to assure that taxpayers do not seek to manipulate the termination of section 1256 contracts to obtain ordinary losses.

All personal property of a type that is actively traded is subject to I.R.C. § 1234A. As a result, I.R.C. § 1234A also includes stock as covered under I.R.C. § 1092(d)(3)(B) that is (or would be) a capital asset in the hands of the taxpayer. This provision generally applies to property acquired and positions established after June 23, 1981.

The scope of I.R.C. § 1234A was amended in 1984 by the DRA to exclude from its application the retirement of any debt instrument (whether or not through a trust or other participation agreement, such as a mortgage pass-through certificate).[57] The General Explanation of the DRA, prepared by the Joint Committee, states that I.R.C. § 1234A was not intended to change the longstanding ordinary income tax treatment of market discount on residential mortgage investments and other obligations of natural persons. Therefore, the DRA amendment clarifies that ordinary income is also obtained when the holder's interest is an indirect one, such as an interest in a fixed investment trust.[58] The DRA amendment is applied retroactively and is effective as if it had been included as part of ERTA in 1981.[59]

---

[55] I.R.C. § 1234A(1).

[56] I.R.C. § 1234A(2).

[57] DRA, *supra* note 22, § 102(e)(9); HOUSE CONFERENCE REPORT, DEFICIT REDUCTION ACT OF 1984, H.R. CONF. REP. NO. 861, 98th Cong., 2d Sess. 911 (1984); for a discussion of asset-backed securities including mortgage pass-through certificates see Part Eight.

[58] *See* JOINT COMM. ON TAXATION, 98TH CONG., 2D SESS., GENERAL EXPLANATION OF THE REVENUE PROVISIONS OF THE DEFICIT REDUCTION ACT OF 1984, at 316 (Joint Comm. Print 1984); *see also* section 36.2.

[59] DRA, *supra* note 22, § 102(f)(4).

Part Thirteen
Foreign Currency

Fifty-nine

Foreign Currency Transactions

§ 59.1 INTRODUCTION

Under the law in effect prior to TRA '86,[1] there were no express statutory rules for determining the amount and timing of gain or loss from fluctuations in the value of foreign currency. In addition, there were no rules for determining when the results of a foreign operation could be measured in a foreign currency before being translated into U.S. dollars.[2] TRA '86 introduced a new set of comprehensive rules contained in Subpart J of the Code for the treatment of foreign currency transactions.[3] Subpart J attempts to bring some clarity to foreign currency transactions, although it also creates some confusion over the appropriate tax treatment of certain transactions.

Subpart J now provides rules for (1) determining the functional currency of a business unit, (2) treating a business unit's gains and losses from transactions in a currency other than its functional currency, and (3) translating into U.S. dollars the profits of a business unit that keeps its books in a foreign currency when the profits are distributed to a United States taxpayer. The new rules basically adopt the financial accounting concept of "functional currency" and require all income tax determina-

---

[1] Pub. L. No. 99-514, 100 Stat. 2085 (1986) [hereinafter TRA '86].
[2] STAFF OF THE JOINT COMM. ON TAXATION, 99TH CONG., 2D SESS., TAX REFORM BILL OF 1986, FINAL CONFERENCE COMM. DECISIONS II-659 (Joint Comm. Print 1986) [hereinafter TRA '86 Conf. Rep.].
[3] I.R.C. §§ 985–989.

tions to be made in a taxpayer's functional currency (which for United States taxpayers is usually the U.S. dollar).[4]

The new rules generally apply after December 31, 1986. Positions established prior to December 31, 1986, that were open on January 1, 1987, are also subject to the new rules. In other words, no grandfather rules apply to foreign currency positions open on December 31, 1986—such positions are subject to the new rules.

Rules also set out how to claim a foreign tax credit. Subpart J is effective only with respect to foreign taxes paid or accrued with respect to earnings and profits for taxable years beginning after December 31, 1986.[5] Under this rule, post-1986 earnings and profits include earnings and profits accumulated by a second-tier or third-tier foreign subsidiary in taxable years beginning before January 1, 1987, if the second-tier or third-tier corporation distributes the earnings and profits to a first-tier corporation for any taxable year of the first-tier corporation beginning after December 31, 1986.[6]

§ 59.2 GENERAL RULES FOR FOREIGN CURRENCY TRANSACTIONS

(a) IN GENERAL

New I.R.C. § 988 generally treats foreign exchange gains and losses incurred by a United States taxpayer as domestic source ordinary income or loss, which is realized when the taxpayer sells, exchanges, or disposes of the position.[7]

(1) SECTION 988 TRANSACTIONS DEFINED

A section 988 transaction is defined as a transaction described in I.R.C. § 988(c)(1)(B), where the amount the taxpayer is entitled to receive (or is required to pay) is denominated in a foreign currency (i.e., a nonfunctional currency), or is determined by reference to the value of one

---

[4] TRA '86 Conf. Rep., *supra* note 2, at II-659. For a discussion of functional currency, see section 59.2(g).

[5] TRA '86, *supra* note 1, § 1261(e)(2).

[6] Notice 87-6, 1987-1 C.B. 417 (Jan. 20, 1987).

[7] For a discussion of section 988 treatment, see O'Neill & Lee, *Federal Income Tax Treatment of Foreign Currency Transactions After the Tax Reform Act of 1986*, Special Report, 33 TAX NOTES 185 (1986).

or more foreign currencies.[8] Section 988 principally focuses on the character, timing, and source of foreign currency gains and losses. Types of section 988 transactions described in I.R.C. § 988(c)(1)(B) include (1) loans; (2) expense or income items paid or received after the date of accrual; (3) dispositions of nonfunctional currencies; (4) any forward contract, futures contract, option, or similar financial instrument that is not a foreign currency-based RFC or nonequity option; and (5) futures and nonequity options subject to I.R.C. § 1256 that are brought into section 988 treatment under the election provided in I.R.C. § 988(c)(1)(D)(ii).[9] In LTR 8818010,[10] the IRS ruled that foreign currency swaps fall within section 988. As a result of the legislative broadening of section 988 transactions by TMRA '88,[11] section 988 generally includes all types of "positions," except RFCs and nonequity options subject to section 1256 treatment.[12] In addition, a taxpayer may elect under I.R.C. § 988(c)(1)(D)(ii) to have section 988 apply to those futures and nonequity options that are subject to section 1256 treatment.[13]

Under the temporary Treasury regulations, a forward contract, futures contract, option, warrant, or similar financial instrument is considered to be a section 988 transaction only if the underlying property to which the instrument ultimately relates is either (1) a nonfunctional currency, or (2) is described in Temp. Treas. Reg. § 1.988-1T(a)(1)(ii)[14] (involving transactions in which the payments are denominated in terms of a nonfunctional currency, or are determined by reference to the value of one or more nonfunctional currencies).[15]

Thus, a forward contract to purchase wheat denominated in a nonfunctional currency is not a section 988 transaction because the underlying property to which the contract relates (i.e., wheat) is not a nonfunctional currency. The fact that the payments under the contract are denominated in a nonfunctional currency is not relevant.

---

[8] I.R.C. § 988(c)(1); Temp. Treas. Reg. § 1.988-1T(a)(1) (1989).

[9] For a discussion of section 1256 treatment, see Part Ten.

[10] (Feb. 4, 1988).

[11] Pub. L. No. 100-647, 102 Stat. 3342 (1988) [hereinafter TMRA '88]. For a discussion of swaps, see generally Chapter 6.

[12] This "carve-out" of certain section 1256 contracts from the scope of the section 988 transactions was established by TMRA '88 and is significantly narrower than the original TRA '86 "carve-out" of all section 1256 contracts in I.R.C. § 988(c)(1)(B)(iii). TMRA '88, *supra* note 11, § 6130.

[13] TMRA '88, *supra* note 11, § 6130.

[14] (1989).

[15] Temp. Treas. Reg. § 1.988-1T(a)(2)(iii) (1989).

The acquisition of, or becoming the obligor under, a debt instrument is a section 988 transaction.[16] Debt instruments are defined to include bonds, debentures, notes, certificates, or other evidence of indebtedness.[17] Preferred stock can be treated as debt instruments to the extent provided in Treasury regulations,[18] although the legislative history provides no guidance on the circumstances in which preferred stocks might be treated as debt instruments.

Section 988 transactions include accrual of any item of expense, gross income, or receipt that is to be paid or received on a later date.[19] The Treasury can provide exceptions to inclusion of these items, if taking the items into account is not necessary to "carry out the purposes" of section 988 "by reason of the small amounts or short periods involved, or otherwise."[20] The Conference Report to TRA '86 also provides that Treasury regulations could provide exceptions for "small amounts or short periods."[21] Examples of items within the scope of this regulatory authority include short-term trade receivables and payables with maturities of 120 days or less.[22]

Section 988 transactions also include the disposition of nonfunctional currency,[23] which is defined to include coin or currency, and demand or time deposits and "similar instruments" issued by a bank or other financial institution if denominated in a nonfunctional currency.[24] Using a nonfunctional currency to establish a demand or time deposit denominated in the same currency, or the conversion of a nonfunctional currency deposit to another deposit in the same currency, is not a disposition for purposes of section 988.[25]

Section 988 transactions also include forward contracts, futures contracts, options, and similar financial instruments.[26] RFCs and nonequity options, that would be marked-to-market under I.R.C. § 1256 if held on the last day of the tax year are not treated as section 988 transactions

---

[16] I.R.C. § 988(c)(1)(B)(i).
[17] I.R.C. § 988(c)(4).
[18] *Id.*
[19] I.R.C. § 988(c)(1)(B)(ii).
[20] I.R.C. § 988(c)(1)(B).
[21] TRA '86 Conf. Rep., *supra* note 2, at II-662 to II-663.
[22] SENATE FINANCE COMM. REPORT, S. REP. NO. 313, 99th Cong., 2d Sess. 460 (1986) [hereinafter S. REP. NO. 313].
[23] I.R.C. § 988(c)(1)(C)(i).
[24] I.R.C. § 988(c)(1)(C)(ii). For a discussion of nonfunctional currency, see section 59.2(g)(2).
[25] TRA '86 Conf. Rep., *supra* note 2, at II-663.
[26] I.R.C. § 988(c)(1)(B)(iii), *as amended by* TMRA '88, *supra* note 11, § 6130.

unless the taxpayer elects into section 988 treatment.[27] A forward contract, futures contract, option, warrant, or similar financial instrument that is not a foreign currency-based RFC or nonequity option, is within the definition of a section 988 transaction only if the underlying property to which it relates is a nonfunctional currency or is otherwise described in Temp. Treas. Reg. § 1.988-1T(a)(1)(ii).[28] In addition, the amount required to be paid, or entitled to be received, must be denominated in a nonfunctional currency or must be determined by reference to the value of the foreign currency.[29] The term "similar financial instrument" includes notional principal contracts (e.g., swaps, caps, collars, and floors) and similar financial products, if the payments required to be made or received under the contract are determined with reference to a nonfunctional currency.[30]

The Treasury also has the authority to prescribe regulations for treatment under the Straddle Rules of I.R.C. §§ 1092 and 263(g) if a taxpayer holds mixed straddle positions, one of which is capital and one of which is ordinary in character.[31]

Prior to the passage of TMRA '88, the IRS ruled in LTR 8818010[32] that foreign currency swap agreements are not "foreign currency contracts" subject to section 1256 treatment.[33] Swaps are not foreign currency contracts under I.R.C. §§ 1256(g)(2)(A)(ii) and (iii) because they are distinguishable from bank forward contracts in the way interest rate differentials are accounted in the underlying currencies.[34] Currency swaps typically account for interest rate differentials through a present and continuing exchange of notional interest payments over the life of the agreements, while bank forward contracts typically account for such differences at maturity. LTR 8818010 was effectively codified by the passage of TMRA '88, which provided that only RFCs and nonequity

---

[27] I.R.C. § 988(c)(1)(D)(i), (ii).

[28] (1989).

[29] Temp. Treas. Reg. § 1.988-1T(a)(2)(iii)(A) (1989).

[30] Temp. Treas. Reg. § 1.988-1T(a)(2)(iii)(B) (1989). For a discussion of notional principal contracts, see Chapter 6.

[31] House Conference Report, H.R. Conf. Rep. No. 1104, 100th Cong., 2d Sess. 193–94, reprinted in 1988 U.S. Code Cong. & Admin. News 5048, 5253 [hereinafter TMRA '88 Conf. Rep.]. For a discussion of the Straddle Rules, see generally Part Eleven. For a discussion of mixed straddles, see generally Chapter 57.

[32] (Feb. 4, 1988).

[33] Prior to TMRA '88, all section 1256 contracts were "carved-out" from section 988 treatment. For a discussion of those foreign currency contracts subject to section 1256 treatment, see section 44.2.

[34] LTR 8818010 (Feb. 4, 1988).

options subject to section 1256 treatment would be excluded from section 988 treatment.[35] Thus, even if a swap were covered by I.R.C. § 1256, it would still be subject to section 988 treatment because it is not an RFC or a nonequity option.

Many transactions are not covered by section 988. Section 988 does not apply to equity investments.[36] Similarly, gains or losses on capital equipment, inventory, or real property carried in a nonfunctional currency are not section 988 transactions. In addition, the Treasury has the authority to issue regulations that exclude certain transactions from section 988 treatment, including those transactions where there are small amounts or periods involved (e.g., trade receivables and payables that mature in 120 days or less, or receivables and payables that mature in six months or less, if eligible for exclusion under I.R.C. § 1274).[37] Section 988 does, on the other hand, apply to debt securities.[38] And, to the extent provided in Treasury regulations, it can apply to preferred stock.[39]

Because section 988 is limited in scope, there is an opportunity for abuse. Transactions not covered by section 988 continue to be taxed under prior law principles. Therefore, economically equivalent transactions can have different tax characterizations. Because TRA '86 eliminated the preference for long-term capital gain, exchange gains and losses are now taxed at the same rate without regard to their different characters. RRA '90[40] provided a preferential maximum tax rate for the capital gains of individuals. If future legislation expands this preference or changes the tax rates for capital assets and reestablishes a long-term capital gains preference, different tax characterizations may once again have a significant tax effect.

(2) QUALIFIED FUNDS

TMRA '88 provides special rules for transactions in forward contracts, futures, options, and similar instruments held by "qualified funds."[41] These "qualified funds" are basically foreign currency commodity funds or similar partnerships that can elect to be treated as "qualified funds" to obtain capital treatment for instruments falling within a broader defini-

---

[35] I.R.C. § 988(c)(1)(D)(i).
[36] I.R.C. § 988(c)(1)(B).
[37] Id.
[38] Id.
[39] I.R.C. § 988(c)(4).
[40] Pub. L. No. 101-508, 104 Stat. 1388 (1990).
[41] For a detailed discussion of qualified funds, see section 59.2(i).

tion of the term "section 1256 contract."[42] All of such section 1256 contracts of "qualified funds" are marked-to-market under I.R.C. § 1256. The 60/40 Rule (60 percent long-term and 40 percent short-term capital gain or loss), however, is only accorded to those instruments falling within the general definition of a "section 1256 contract."[43] Those instruments falling within the broader definition of "section 1256 contracts" as a result of the special expansion for qualified funds, receive 100 percent short-term capital gain or loss treatment.[44]

(3) PERSONAL TRANSACTIONS

Section 988 does not apply to "personal transactions" entered into by an individual that do not meet the requirements of I.R.C. §§ 162 (for trade or business expenses) or 212 (for expenses incurred to produce income other than incurred in connection with the determination, collection, or refund of taxes).[45] Whether expenses are attributable to the production of income is determined without regard to the rule that limits the deduction of certain miscellaneous itemized deductions to the amount in excess of two percent of a taxpayer's adjusted gross income.[46]

For personal transactions, the functional currency of a United States individual residing abroad is always the U.S. dollar.[47] This means that exchange gain or loss could arise as a result of repayment of a foreign currency-denominated mortgage on a person's principal residence, without being subject to the statutory rule that mandates ordinary income or loss treatment.[48] A United States citizen that purchases foreign currency for use on a foreign vacation is not subject to I.R.C. § 988.[49] In addition, a United States citizen residing outside of the United States is exempt from I.R.C. § 988 upon repayment of a foreign currency-denominated mortgage on the taxpayer's principal residence.[50]

---

[42] I.R.C. § 988(c)(1)(E)(iv)(I).
[43] I.R.C. § 988(c)(1)(E)(iv)(II).
[44] *Id.*
[45] I.R.C. § 988(e); Temp. Treas. Reg. § 1.988-1T(a)(6)(i) (1989). For a discussion of trade or business expenses, see generally section 10.1(a). For a discussion of investment expenses and expenses to produce income, see section 9.1.
[46] I.R.C. § 67(a).
[47] I.R.C. § 985.
[48] *See* TRA '86 Conf. Rep., *supra* note 2, at II-669.
[49] Temp. Treas. Reg. § 1.988-1T(a)(6)(ii), Example (2) (1989).
[50] TRA '86 Conf. Rep., *supra* note 2, at II-669.

The exception for personal transactions of individuals is supported by the law in effect prior to enactment of I.R.C. § 988. In Rev. Rul. 74-7,[51] the IRS ruled that exchanging foreign currency back to the U.S. dollar after a portion was used for personal expenses generated exchange gains or losses which were generally treated as gain or loss from the sale of property. Exchange gain (or loss) also results on the use of appreciated (or depreciated) foreign currency to make personal purchases, which were generally treated as capital gain (or loss).[52]

(4) REALIZATION OF EXCHANGE GAINS AND LOSSES

The realization of exchange gain or loss with respect to various section 988 financial instruments, is governed by specific provisions of the temporary Treasury regulations.

First, gain or loss on forward contracts, futures, options, and similar financial instruments is realized in accordance with the applicable realization sections of the Code (including I.R.C. §§ 988(c)(5), 1001, 1092, and 1256). For purposes of determining the timing of the realization of exchange gain or loss, I.R.C. §§ 1092 and 1256 take precedence over I.R.C. § 988(c)(5) (which provides special rules for when a taxpayer takes or makes delivery).[53] Thus, gain or loss is generally recognized only upon a sale or exchange of the product and not solely because the product is offset by another transaction.[54] Moreover, extension of the time for making or taking delivery of such a product is treated as a realization event.[55]

Second, gain or loss with respect to certain narrowly defined currency swaps and other notional principal contracts is generally determined in accordance with the taxpayer's method of accounting if income is clearly reflected.[56] Moreover, special timing and computation rules apply with respect to currency swap income and expense. These rules adopt concepts applicable to debt instruments.[57] Finally, special rules are provided for the amortization of currency swap premium or discount with respect to

---

[51] 1974-1 C.B. 198.
[52] Rev. Rul. 74-7, 1974-1 C.B. 198.
[53] Temp. Treas. Reg. § 1.988-2T(d)(2)(i) (1989).
[54] Temp. Treas. Reg. § 1.988-2T(d)(2)(ii) (1989).
[55] Temp. Treas. Reg. § 1.988-2T(d)(2)(v) (1989).
[56] Temp. Treas. Reg. § 1.988-2T(e)(1) (1989). For a discussion of notional principal contracts, see generally Chapter 6.
[57] Temp. Treas. Reg. § 1.988-2T(e)(2) (1989).

"off-market" currency swap transactions entered into after September 21, 1989.[58]

If the taxpayer makes or takes delivery in connection with any section 988 transaction after October 21, 1988, that is a forward contract, futures contract, option, or similar financial instrument treated as a section 988 transaction, any gain or loss is recognized in the same manner as if the contract was sold.[59]

(b) CHARACTER OF GAINS AND LOSSES

(1) IN GENERAL

Section 988 is based on the premise that exchange rate changes are principally a function of interest rates.[60] As a result, section 988 generally treats exchange gains and losses as ordinary income or expense (unless Treasury regulations, when issued, specifically classify the gains and losses as interest income or expense).[61] Characterizing foreign exchange gains and losses as ordinary was viewed as a "pragmatic solution" to the fact that exchange rate gains and losses might not always be a function of interest rate changes.[62] Characterizing foreign exchange gains and losses as interest was reserved for those cases where the equivalency to "interest" is clear. The Treasury can also selectively exercise its authority to characterize exchange gain or loss as interest income or expense.[63] To the extent a taxpayer locks in an interest rate differential by buying or selling a foreign currency to hedge another position, the section 988 classification as either ordinary income or interest appears appropriate.

Basically, the differences between the foreign exchange markets can be viewed as a function of interest rate differentials. If, on the other hand, a taxpayer does not hedge a foreign currency risk, the basic premise of section 988 does not apply because changes in the value of a particular currency are not necessarily related to interest rate changes. With a naked (i.e., nonoffsetting) position, a taxpayer has not locked in or guaranteed an exchange gain or loss. Thus, it would appear that the

---

[58] Temp. Treas. Reg. §§ 1.988-2T(e)(3), (e)(6) (1989).

[59] I.R.C. § 988(c)(5).

[60] S. REP. NO. 313, *supra* note 22, at 452. Under prior law, foreign currency gain or loss was generally treated as gain or loss from the sale of property. This characterization was abandoned by TRA '86 for section 988 transactions.

[61] I.R.C. § 988(a)(2); TRA '86 Conf. Rep., *supra* note 2, at II-665.

[62] S. REP. NO. 313, *supra* note 22, at 452.

[63] I.R.C. § 988(a)(2); TRA '86 Conf. Rep., *supra* note 2, at II-665.

TMRA '88 broadening of the transactions covered by section 988 runs counter to this reasoning.

The character of foreign currency gain or loss on an investment in a foreign currency-denominated debt security may not match the character of gain or loss on certain instruments used to hedge such foreign currency positions, although the changes made by TMRA '88 do allow a taxpayer to match transactions through the proper election. Under I.R.C. § 988(c)(1)(B), a section 988 transaction includes the acquisition of any debt instrument denominated in foreign currency. Accordingly, foreign currency gain or loss is treated as ordinary. Entering into or acquiring any forward contract, futures contract, option, or similar financial instrument denominated in or determined by reference to foreign currency is treated as a section 988 transaction, giving rise to ordinary income or loss, unless the position is an RFC or nonequity option marked-to-market under I.R.C. § 1256 (and the taxpayer has not elected to have such RFCs or nonequity options treated as section 988 transactions).[64] As a result, an RFC on foreign currency or a nonequity option that is marked-to-market at the close of the taxable year is not generally a section 988 transaction; all gain or loss continues to be treated as capital, unless an appropriate election is made under I.R.C. § 988(c)(1)(D)(ii).

A taxpayer realizes ordinary income or loss on his debt portfolio, and he may realize capital gain or loss on the positions used to hedge the portfolio if he hedges a portion of the foreign currency risk inherent in debt securities denominated in foreign currencies for which RFCs are also traded.[65] Furthermore, the Treasury has authority to prescribe regulations under I.R.C. § 1092(b) for a mixed straddle account and the extent to which the gains and losses on the debt portfolio can be netted against the gains and losses on the hedging positions.[66]

(2) REGULATED INVESTMENT COMPANIES

Possible mismatching of income and expense for foreign currency transactions under section 988 can have potentially significant and adverse consequences for a RIC. This mismatching does not reflect the economic income derived by a RIC and thwarts the statutory authorization to invest in foreign currency transactions. Ninety percent of the ordinary

---

[64] For a discussion of section 1256 contracts, see generally Part Ten. For a discussion of the election to treat RFCs and nonequity options as section 988 transactions, see section 59.2(b)(4).

[65] *See* section 44.2.

[66] TMRA '88 Conf. Rep., *supra* note 31, at 193–94.

income earned by a RIC during its taxable year must be distributed to maintain its tax-qualified status and 97 percent of its ordinary income for the calendar year must be distributed to avoid the four percent excise tax imposed by TRA '86. For a discussion of RICs, see section 8.9. For a discussion of the four percent excise tax, see section 8.9(b).

(3) ELECTION TO TREAT CERTAIN GAINS OR LOSSES AS CAPITAL

Section 988 generally treats gains and losses on nonfunctional currency transactions as ordinary.[67] It also provides an election—available on a transaction-by-transaction basis—to treat foreign currency gain or loss attributable to a forward contract, futures contract, or an option that is neither an RFC nor a nonequity option as capital gain or loss if three conditions are met. First, the position must be a capital asset in the hands of the taxpayer. Second, the position must not be part of a straddle. And third, the taxpayer must elect out of section 988.[68] To make the election, the taxpayer elects and identifies the transaction before the close of the day on which the transaction is entered into.

The election under I.R.C. § 988(a)(1)(B) to treat forward contracts, futures, and options as capital is consistent with the view that foreign exchange gains are equivalent to interest because the gains or losses on a naked position are due to currency movements, thereby making such gains or losses speculative, rather than equivalent to interest income or expense.

(4) ELECTION TO TREAT REGULATED FUTURES CONTRACTS AND NONEQUITY OPTIONS AS SECTION 988 TRANSACTIONS

RFCs and nonequity options, as defined in I.R.C. § 1256, are not section 988 transactions if the contracts would be marked-to-market under I.R.C. § 1256 if held on the last day of the taxable year. Nevertheless, the taxpayer may elect, under I.R.C. § 988(c)(1)(D)(ii), to treat such RFCs and nonequity options as section 988 transactions. Moreover, RFCs and nonequity options that are carved out of section 988 treatment may still be subject to the hedging exemption in I.R.C. § 988(d). Under this election, gains and losses are treated as ordinary and the Mark-to-Market

---

[67] I.R.C. § 988(a)(1)(A).

[68] I.R.C. § 988(a)(1)(B). For fully hedged foreign currency transactions, the exchange gain or loss is treated as domestic source interest income or expense that is realized on the accrual basis.

Rule applies. For a discussion of foreign currency hedging, see section 23.3.

Foreign currency products that are covered by I.R.C. § 988(a) include:

1. Bank forward contracts in major currencies as defined in I.R.C. § 1256(g)(2)
2. All other forward contracts in foreign currency and futures contracts that are not RFCs
3. Foreign currency swaps and all other foreign currency-related financial instruments that are similar to forwards, futures, and options[69]

If a foreign currency futures contract or option is subject to section 1256 treatment, it can be exempt from such treatment by the hedging exemption under I.R.C. § 1256(e).[70]

Section 988 transactions do not generally include any RFCs or non-equity options that would be marked-to-market under I.R.C. § 1256 if held on the last day of the taxable year.[71] For a discussion of this election, see section 59.2(j).

(c) TIMING

(1) IN GENERAL

Under section 988, exchange gains and losses are not included in income until they are realized, except for section 988 hedging transaction treatment.[72] This means that exchange gains or losses are realized only on closed and completed transactions—when the positions are sold, exchanged, or otherwise disposed of.[73] The Senate Report that accompanied TRA '86 provides that "the recognition of exchange gain or loss generally requires a closed and completed transaction (e.g., the actual

---

[69] *See also* LTR 8818010 (Feb. 4, 1988) (issued prior to enactment of TMRA '88).

[70] For a discussion of the tax treatment of hedging transactions, see generally Chapter 23.

[71] I.R.C. § 988(c)(1)(D)(i).

[72] For a discussion of section 988 hedging treatment, see section 23.3(b).

[73] Anderson, Clayton & Co. v. United States, 562 F.2d 972 (5th Cir.), *reh'g denied*, 565 F.2d 1215 (1977), *cert. denied*, 436 U.S. 944 (1978); Theodore Tiedemann & Sons v. Comm'r, 1 B.T.A. 1077 (1925); Rev. Rul. 75-108, 1975-1, C.B. 69; Rev. Rul. 75-109, 1975-1 C.B. 69. For a discussion of the special rules that apply to deliveries, see section 59.2(c)(2).

payment of a liability).'"[74] Treasury regulations, when issued, should provide guidance as to the application of the OID provisions to foreign currency-denominated transactions.

The payment date is defined as the date on which the payment is made or received.[75] The IRS has addressed the appropriate payment date under I.R.C. § 988(c)(3)(B) to determine the timing of gain or loss in LTR 8818010.[76] In the private ruling, the IRS considered the situation of a taxpayer with foreign currency swap positions. The taxpayer intended to enter into mirror swap positions (reverse mirror swaps) with the original swap counterparties.[77] The taxpayer, faced with substantial losses on its original swaps, wanted to limit its foreign currency exposure. The IRS ruled that I.R.C. § 988 did not generally change prior law principles as to timing of exchange gains or losses for section 988 transactions. The IRS, citing the statement in the Senate Report on TRA '86 that "the recognition of exchange gain or loss generally requires a closed or completed transaction (e.g., the actual payment of a liability),"[78] found that establishing a mirror swap is not a realization event under I.R.C. § 1001 because the taxpayer has not extinguished its positions under the original currency swaps.[79] The IRS based its private ruling on the fact that all of the taxpayer's swap positions remained open after the mirror swap was established.

(2) DELIVERIES

Special rules apply if a taxpayer takes or makes delivery after June 10, 1987, in connection with any section 988 transaction described in I.R.C. § 988(c)(1)(B)(iii) ("entering into or acquiring any forward contract, futures contract, option, or similar financial instrument").[80] Any gain or loss (determined as if the taxpayer sold the contract, option, or instrument on the date on which he took or made delivery for its fair market value on such date) is recognized in the same manner as if such contract, option, or instrument were so sold.[81]

---

[74] S. REP. NO. 313, *supra* note 22, at 459.

[75] I.R.C. § 988(c)(3).

[76] (Feb. 4, 1988).

[77] For a discussion of swaps generally, see Chapter 6. For a discussion of mirror swaps and reverse mirror swaps, see section 6.2(g).

[78] S. REP. NO. 313, *supra* note 22, at 459.

[79] LTR 8818010 (Feb. 4, 1988).

[80] I.R.C. § 988(c)(5), *added to the Code by* TMRA '88, *supra* note 11, § 1012(v)(2)(A).

[81] *Id.*

(3) EXCEPTION WHERE ECONOMIC BENEFIT IS DERIVED

If a section 988 forward contract, futures contract, option, warrant, or similar financial instrument, is offset by another transaction or transactions, exchange gain is realized to the extent the taxpayer derives, by pledge or otherwise, an economic benefit from any gain inherent in such offsetting positions. Temp. Treas. Reg. § 1.988-2T(d)(2)(ii)(B) provides that the effective date of this provision is for transactions creating an offset after September 21, 1989.

(d) SOURCE

Section 988 views the source (domestic or foreign) of exchange gains or losses as the residence of the taxpayer.[82]

(1) EXCHANGE GAINS AND LOSSES

Exchange gains and losses realized by United States corporations are generally treated as United States source income, with the exception of a QBU.[83] The source of an exchange gain or loss of a QBU is in the country in which the QBU's principal place of business is located.[84]

The source of foreign currency gain or loss has an impact on the utilization of foreign tax credits because the use of foreign tax credits is limited to the United States tax attributable to foreign source income.[85] The residence of the taxpayer or the QBU on whose books the section 988 transaction is properly reflected is treated as the source for foreign currency gain, losses, and financial instruments covered by elections to treat the gain or loss as capital.[86] This means that most United States taxpayers treat foreign currency gain and loss as domestic source income.

If a taxpayer is a nonresident alien or a foreign corporation that is engaged in a United States trade or business, exchange gain or loss is treated as "fixed or determinable annual or periodic income" from United States sources to determine whether the exchange gain or loss is effectively connected with the United States business.[87]

---

[82] I.R.C. § 988(a)(3)(A); Temp. Treas. Reg. § 1.988-4T(a) (1989).
[83] I.R.C. § 988(a)(3)(B). For a discussion of QBUs, see section 59.2(g)(3).
[84] Temp. Treas. Reg. § 1.988-4T(b)(1) (1989).
[85] I.R.C. § 904(a).
[86] I.R.C. § 988(a)(3)(A).
[87] Temp. Treas. Reg. § 1.988-4T(c) (1989).

(2) RESIDENCE

(i) Individuals

For sourcing purposes, the residence of an individual is the country in which the individual's tax home (as defined in I.R.C. § 911(d)(3)) is located.[88] In general, an individual's tax home is the place where expenses incurred in traveling elsewhere on business are deductible trade or business expenses under I.R.C. § 162(a)(2) as expenses away from home.[89] If an individual does not have a tax home (as defined in I.R.C. § 911(d)(3)), the residence of the individual is the United States if the individual is a United States citizen or a resident alien.[90] If an individual without a tax home is not a United States citizen or a resident alien, the individual's residence is not treated as the United States.[91]

(ii) Corporations

For sourcing purposes, the residence of a corporation that is a United States person (as defined in I.R.C. § 7701(a)(30)) is the United States.[92] In other words, corporations organized under the laws of the United States, the District of Columbia, or one of the states are treated as United States residents. All other corporations are treated as residents of foreign countries.[93]

(iii) Partnerships

For sourcing purposes, partnerships that are United States persons (as defined in I.R.C. § 7701(a)(30)) are residents of the United States.[94] A partnership is a United States resident if it is organized under the laws of the United States, the District of Columbia, or one of the states. All other partnerships are residents of foreign countries.[95]

If a partnership is "formed or availed of to avoid tax by altering the source of exchange gain or loss," the partnership's residence is ignored for

---

[88] I.R.C. § 988(a)(3)(B)(i)(I).
[89] I.R.C. § 911(d)(3); Temp. Treas. Reg. § 1.988-4T(d)(1) (1989).
[90] I.R.C. § 988(a)(3)(B).
[91] Id.
[92] I.R.C. § 988(a)(3)(B)(i)(II).
[93] I.R.C. § 988(a)(3)(B)(i)(III).
[94] I.R.C. § 988(a)(3)(B)(i)(II).
[95] I.R.C. § 988(a)(3)(B)(i)(III).

tax purposes.⁹⁶ In addition, each partner's distributive share of the partnership's exchange gain or loss has its source in the residence country of the partner.⁹⁷

(iv) Estates and Trusts

For sourcing purposes, the residence of estates and trusts that are United States persons (as defined in I.R.C. § 7701(a)(30)) is the United States.⁹⁸ All other estates and trusts are not treated as residents of the United States.⁹⁹

(e) SEPARATELY COMPUTED GAIN OR LOSS

Exchange gains or losses are generally computed separately from the gain or loss arising from the underlying transaction.¹⁰⁰ In other words, I.R.C. § 988 generally retains the case law principle that exchange gains and losses are accounted for apart from any gain or loss attributable to the underlying transaction. The amount of foreign currency gain or loss is limited to the total gain or loss, thereby taking into account gain or loss on an underlying transaction.¹⁰¹

(f) FOREIGN CURRENCY GAIN OR LOSS

Foreign currency gains or losses on a nonfunctional currency are the gains (losses) from section 988 transactions to the extent the gains (losses) do not exceed gains (losses) realized by reason of changes in exchange rates on or after the "booking date" and before the "payment date."¹⁰² If the amount attributable to exchange rate fluctuations exceeds the total gain or loss on the transaction, the amount of the overall gain or loss is reported as a section 988 foreign currency gain or loss. If, on the other hand, the foreign currency gain or loss is less than the total gain or loss on the transaction, the remaining gain or loss is reported as gain or loss on the underlying transaction outside of, and not subject to, section 988.

---

⁹⁶ Temp. Treas. Reg. § 1.988-4T(d)(1) (1989).
⁹⁷ *Id.*
⁹⁸ I.R.C. § 988(a)(3)(B)(i)(II).
⁹⁹ I.R.C. § 988(a)(3)(B)(i)(III).
¹⁰⁰ I.R.C. § 988(a)(1)(A); TRA '86 Conf. Rep., *supra* note 2, at II-663. For a discussion of foreign currency hedging gains and losses, see section 23.3.
¹⁰¹ TRA '86 Conf. Rep., *supra* note 2, at II-664.
¹⁰² I.R.C. §§ 988(b)(1), (2).

A special rule is provided in I.R.C. § 988(b)(3) for any section 988 transaction described in I.R.C. § 988(c)(1)(B)(iii) (entering into or acquiring any forward contract, futures contract, option, or similar financial instrument). In the case of such a section 988 transaction, "any gain or loss from such transaction shall be treated as foreign currency gain or loss (as the case may be)."[103]

(1) BOOKING DATE

The "booking date" is the date accrued or otherwise taken into account for any item of expense or gross income or receipts which is to be paid or received after the date on which it is so accrued or taken into account.[104] If an expense or income item is paid or taken into account after the date of accrual, the booking date is the date it is accrued or otherwise taken into account.[105] The booking date for a loan is the date a creditor-taxpayer acquires the debtor's obligation, or a debtor-taxpayer becomes the obligor.[106] For transactions involving forward contracts, future contracts, or options, the "booking date" is the date the contract is entered into.[107]

(2) PAYMENT DATE

The payment date is the date on which payment is made or received.[108] In the case of futures, forward, or option contracts, the payment date is the date on which the position is terminated.

(3) COMPUTING GAIN OR LOSS

To compute the amount of foreign currency gain or loss, a taxpayer multiplies the difference in exchange rates between the booking date and the payment date by the units of functional currency originally booked.[109] The appropriate exchange rate is usually the free market rate.[110] Foreign

---

[103] I.R.C. § 988(b)(3).
[104] I.R.C. § 988(c)(2)(B).
[105] *Id.*
[106] I.R.C. § 988(c)(2)(A).
[107] S. REP. NO. 313, *supra* note 22, at 461.
[108] I.R.C. § 988(c)(3).
[109] TRA '86 Conf. Rep., *supra* note 2, at II-664.
[110] S. REP. NO. 313, *supra* note 22, at 459–60.

currency gain or loss is recognized only to the extent of the total gain or loss derived from a transaction.[111]

Example 59-1

For example, if a taxpayer whose functional currency is the U.S. dollar acquires a debt obligation that is not part of a section 988 hedging transaction for 100 British pounds when the exchange rate is 1 British pound = $1, and sells the obligation for 200 British pounds when the exchange rate is 1 British pound = $2, $100 of the taxpayer's $300 gain ($400 sales price less $100 basis) is foreign currency gain. This is calculated by multiplying the difference in exchange rates between the booking date and the payment date by the units of functional currency originally booked by the taxpayer. The foreign currency gain or loss is recognized only to the extent of the total gain or loss, taking into account gain or loss on an underlying transaction. Thus, in the above example, if the exchange rate had fallen to 1 British pound = $.50, the taxpayer would have had no foreign currency gain or loss; if the exchange rate had fallen to 1 British pound = $.75, the taxpayer would have had a $50 nonforeign currency gain; if the exchange rate had fallen to 1 British pound = $.25, the taxpayer would have had a $50 foreign currency loss.[112]

On the disposition of a nonfunctional currency, a different calculation applies to foreign currency gain or loss. In the case of any disposition of a nonfunctional currency, the disposition is treated as a section 988 transaction and any gain or loss is treated as foreign currency gain or loss.[113] For these purposes, nonfunctional currency includes coin or currency, and nonfunctional currency-denominated demand and time deposits or similar instruments issued by a bank or other financial institution.[114] Foreign currency gain or loss on a nonfunctional currency is the gain or loss realized because of changes in exchange rates between the currency's acquisition date and its disposition.

---

[111] TRA '86 Conf. Rep., *supra* note 2, at II-664.
[112] *Id.*
[113] I.R.C. § 988(c)(1)(C)(i).
[114] I.R.C. § 988(c)(1)(C)(ii). Prior to retroactive amendment by TMRA '88, the concept of the "booking date" was replaced with the "acquisition date" for a nonfunctional currency, and the concept of the "payment date" was replaced with "disposition." I.R.C. § 988(c)(1)(C)(i)(II), *repealed by* TMRA '88, *supra* note 11, § 1012(v)(3)(B).

(g) FUNCTIONAL CURRENCY RULES

Congress determined that the financial accounting concept of functional currency was an appropriate way to calculate the timing of exchange gains and losses—measured in the currency of the taxpayer's main economic environment. As a result, I.R.C. § 985(a) provides that all income tax determinations are made in a taxpayer's functional currency. The remainder of this section addresses the definitions and considerations for functional currency, nonfunctional currency, and QBUs.

(1) FUNCTIONAL CURRENCY

TRA '86 introduced the concept of a functional currency to identify the base currency against which all other currencies create exchange gains or losses for United States tax purposes. This means that the functional currency of a United States resident or corporation is the U.S. dollar, and transactions denominated in nondollar currencies can create exchange gains and losses. If a QBU or branch of a United States business has a nondollar currency as its functional currency, transactions denominated in U.S. dollars can create exchange gains and losses. To the extent provided in Treasury regulations, a taxpayer can elect to use the U.S. dollar as the functional currency of a QBU if certain conditions are met.[115]

Any change in a functional currency, once designated, is treated as a change in the taxpayer's method of accounting for purposes of I.R.C. § 481, which provides procedures for making adjustments required by changes in a taxpayer's method of accounting.[116] Any change in the choice of a functional currency is subject to such conditions as the Treasury prescribes by regulation.[117]

(i) In General

All determinations under the Code are made in a taxpayer's functional currency.[118] Because the Code heavily favors the use of the U.S. dollar as a taxpayer's functional currency, functional currency is generally defined

---

[115] I.R.C. § 985(b)(3).
[116] I.R.C. § 985(b)(4).
[117] TRA '86 Conf. Rep., *supra* note 2, at II-661.
[118] I.R.C. § 985(a).

as the U.S. dollar.[119] Taxpayers are required to use the U.S. dollar as their functional currency unless otherwise provided in the Code.[120]

Every taxpayer must determine its functional currency for United States tax purposes. Taxpayers with transactions in foreign currencies may find that the determination of a functional currency is a key issue affecting their United States tax liability.

(ii) Application of Treasury Regulations

On September 19, 1989, the Treasury issued final and temporary regulations under I.R.C. § 985.[121] Under Treas. Reg. § 1.985-1(a)(2), the final regulations generally apply to tax years beginning after December 31, 1986. Taxpayers can elect to apply the temporary regulations under sections 1.985-0T through 1.985-4T in lieu of the final regulations "on a consistent basis" for the period from December 31, 1986, to October 20, 1989.[122]

(iii) U.S. Dollar Functional Currency

Under the Treasury regulations, the U.S. dollar is the functional currency of a taxpayer or QBU in the following situations "regardless of the currency used in keeping its books and records":

1. A taxpayer that is not a QBU[123]
2. A QBU that conducts its activities primarily in U.S. dollars[124]
3. In general, a QBU that has the United States as its residence[125]
4. A QBU that elects to use, or is otherwise required to use, the U.S. dollar as its functional currency[126]

---

[119] I.R.C. § 985(a)(1)(A).
[120] For a discussion of nonfunctional currency, see section 59.2(g)(2). For a discussion of QBUs, see section 59.2(g)(3).
[121] T.D. 8263, 1989-2 C.B. 145.
[122] Treas. Reg. § 1.985-1(a)(2) (1989). The text of the temporary Treasury regulations can be found in 53 Fed. Reg. 20,308 (1988).
[123] Treas. Reg. § 1.985-1(b)(1) (1989).
[124] Treas. Reg. § 1.985-1(b)(2) (1989).
[125] Treas. Reg. § 1.985-1(b)(3) (1989).
[126] Treas. Reg. § 1.985-1(b)(4) (1989).

5. A QBU that does not keep its books and records in the currency of any economic environment in which a significant part of its activities is conducted[127]

6. Any activity (wherever conducted and regardless of its frequency) that produces income or loss that is, or is treated as, effectively connected with the conduct of a trade or business within the United States[128]

Regardless of any change in circumstances, a QBU can change its functional currency only if it complies with the provisions of Treas. Reg. § 1.985-4[129] for changing functional currencies.

The U.S. dollar is the functional currency of taxpayers if their operations are conducted in the United States. In addition, the U.S. dollar is the functional currency of a taxpayer if a foreign operation is an "integral extension of a United States operation."[130] Examples in the Conference Report that accompanied TRA '86 include (1) foreign finance operations of United States companies, (2) foreign holding companies used to hold passive assets (such as portfolio stock investments or similar passive assets that could be readily carried on its parent's books), and (3) foreign corporations with limited durations (such as, offshore construction operations undertaken by a United States taxpayer).[131]

(iv) Economic Environment

Identification of a taxpayer's functional currency is based on the facts and circumstances of the economic environment in which a significant part of a QBU's activities are conducted. The facts and circumstances considered by the Treasury regulations include the following:

1. The currency of the country in which the QBU is a resident, as determined under I.R.C. § 988(a)(3)(B)[132]

2. The currencies of the QBU's cash flows[133]

---

[127] Treas. Reg. § 1.985-1(b)(5) (1989).
[128] Treas. Reg. § 1.985-1(b)(6) (1989). The activity is treated as a separate QBU with the U.S. dollar as its functional currency. *Id.*
[129] (1989).
[130] TRA '86 Conf. Rep., *supra* note 2, at II-660.
[131] *Id.*
[132] Treas. Reg. § 1.985-1(c)(2)(i)(A) (1989).
[133] Treas. Reg. § 1.985-1(c)(2)(i)(B) (1989).

3. The currencies in which the QBU generates revenues and incurs expenses[134]
4. The currencies in which the QBU borrows and lends[135]
5. The currencies of the QBU's sales markets[136]
6. The currencies in which pricing and other financial decisions are made[137]
7. The duration of the QBU's business operations[138]
8. The significance and/or volume of the QBU's independent activities[139]

For purposes of determining a QBU's economic environment, the rate of inflation is not a factor to be considered.[140] In addition, a taxpayer must consistently apply the facts and circumstances in evaluating the economic environment of QBUs—such as its branches—that engage in the same or similar businesses.[141]

If a QBU has more than one currency that satisfies the requirements of Treas. Reg. § 1.985-1(c)(1)[142] (the currency of the economic environment in which a substantial part of its activities are conducted), the QBU can choose any of the currencies that satisfy the requirement.[143]

(v) Single Functional Currency of a Foreign Corporation

If a foreign corporation has two or more QBUs that do not have the same functional currency, the foreign corporation is treated as having a single functional currency for the corporation as a whole that is different from the functional currency of one or more of its QBUs.[144] The determination of the foreign corporation's functional currency is made in two steps.

[134] Treas. Reg. § 1.985-1(c)(2)(i)(C) (1989).
[135] Treas. Reg. § 1.985-1(c)(2)(i)(D) (1989).
[136] Treas. Reg. § 1.985-1(c)(2)(i)(E) (1989).
[137] Treas. Reg. § 1.985-1(c)(2)(i)(F) (1989).
[138] Treas. Reg. § 1.985-1(c)(2)(i)(G) (1989).
[139] Treas. Reg. § 1.985-1(c)(2)(i)(H) (1989).
[140] Treas. Reg. § 1.985-1(c)(2)(ii) (1989).
[141] Treas. Reg. § 1.985-1(c)(2)(iii) (1989).
[142] (1989).
[143] Treas. Reg. § 1.985-1(c)(4) (1989).
[144] Treas. Reg. § 1.985-1(d)(1) (1989).

Step 1   Each QBU of the foreign corporation determines its functional currency in accordance with the rules set out in Treas. Reg. §§ 1.985-2(b) and (c).[145]

Step 2   The foreign corporation determines its functional currency (applying the principles of Treas. Reg. §§ 1.985-1(b) and (c))[146] to the corporation's activities as a whole.[147] This means that a foreign corporation with two branches, for example, determines its functional currency by applying the principles of Treas. Reg. §§ 1.985-1(b) and (c) to the combined activities of the corporation and the branches.[148]

For purposes of determining a single functional currency for a foreign corporation, a QBU of such a corporation with the U.S. dollar as its functional currency is considered dollar activities of the corporation.[149]

Where the functional currency of a foreign corporation as a whole differs from the functional currency of one or more of its QBUs, each QBU determines the amount of its income or loss or earnings and profits (or deficit in earnings and profits) in its functional currency under the principles of I.R.C. § 987 (relating to branch transactions).[150] The amount of income or loss or earnings and profits (or deficit in earnings and profits) of each QBU in its functional currency is then translated into the foreign corporation's functional currency, using the appropriate exchange rate, as defined in I.R.C. § 989(b)(4).[151]

(2) NONFUNCTIONAL CURRENCY

A nonfunctional currency is any currency other than the functional currency of the taxpayer or QBU entering into the transaction. The disposition of a nonfunctional currency is generally treated as a section

---

[145] Treas. Reg. § 1.985-1(d)(1)(i) (1989).
[146] (1989).
[147] Treas. Reg. § 1.985-1(d)(1)(ii) (1989).
[148] *Id.*
[149] Treas. Reg. § 1.985-1(d)(1) (1989).
[150] Treas. Reg. § 1.985-1(d)(2) (1989).
[151] *Id.*

988 transaction.[152] It should be noted that this requirement can be satisfied by transactions of a U.S. dollar taxpayer where all payments are to be made in U.S. dollars, if the number of dollars to be paid or received varies with the exchange rate for a foreign currency. Examples of such transactions include cash settlement foreign currency futures contracts and certain U.S. dollar debt obligations (if the redemption price corresponds to the dollar value of a stated amount of foreign currency on the redemption date).

A nonfunctional currency includes coin or currency, and nonfunctional currency-denominated demand or time deposits or similar instruments issued by a bank or other financial institution.[153]

The temporary Treasury regulations define a nonfunctional currency as "a currency (including the European Currency Unit) other than the taxpayer's or the qualified business unit's functional currency as defined in [I.R.C.] section 985 and the regulations thereunder."[154] It is I.R.C. § 988 and the regulations thereunder that set out the treatment of nonfunctional currency transactions.[155]

A section 988 transaction is defined in temporary Treasury regulations as any of the following transactions:

1. A disposition of nonfunctional currency as defined in Temp. Treas. Reg. § 1.988-1T(c),[156] or

2. Any transaction described in Temp. Treas. Reg. § 1.988-1T(a)(2)[157] if any amount that the taxpayer is entitled to receive or is required to pay by reason of such transaction is denominated in terms of a nonfunctional currency, or is determined by reference to the value of one or more nonfunctional currencies[158]

The amount of nonfunctional currency gain or loss on a nonfunctional currency transaction is generally the total gain or loss, but not in excess of the gain or loss due to the changes in exchange rates on or after the booking date and before the payment date. For a discussion of nonfunctional currency gain or loss, see sections 59.2(b)(3) and 59.2(f)(3).

[152] For a discussion of section 988 transactions, see section 59.2(a)(1).
[153] I.R.C. § 988(c)(1)(C)(ii); TRA '86 Conf. Rep., *supra* note 2, at II-663.
[154] Temp. Treas. Reg. § 1.988-1T(c) (1989).
[155] Treas. Reg. § 1.985-1(e) (1989).
[156] Temp. Treas. Reg. § 1.988-1T(a)(1)(i) (1989).
[157] (1989).
[158] Temp. Treas. Reg. § 1.988-1T(a)(1)(ii) (1989).

(3) QUALIFIED BUSINESS UNITS

Whether an operation meets the definition of a QBU must first be determined before the operation's functional currency can be determined. The remainder of this section addresses QBUs.

(i) In General

On January 3, 1990, the Treasury issued final regulations under Treas. Reg. § 1.989(a)-1[159] defining a QBU.[160] Prior to that date, temporary regulations under I.R.C. § 989 were issued on June 3, 1988,[161] and September 19, 1989.[162] The final regulations define a QBU as any separate and clearly identified unit of a taxpayer's trade or business as long as separate books and records are maintained.[163]

(ii) Corporations

A corporation is treated as a QBU.[164] Activities of a corporation qualify as a QBU (separate from the corporation itself) if two conditions are met. First, the activities must constitute a trade or business.[165] Second, the corporation must maintain a complete and separate set of books and records with respect to the QBU's activities.[166]

(iii) Individuals

An individual is not treated as a QBU.[167] Activities of an individual qualify as a QBU, however, if two conditions are met. First, the activities must constitute a trade or business.[168] Second, the individual must maintain a complete and separate set of books and records with respect to the QBU's activities.[169]

---

[159] (1990).
[160] T.D. 8279, 1990-1 C.B. 151.
[161] T.D. 8207, 1988-2 C.B. 297.
[162] T.D. 8263, 1989-2 C.B. 145.
[163] Treas. Reg. § 1.989(a)-1(b)(1) (1990).
[164] Treas. Reg. § 1.989(a)-1(b)(2)(i) (1990).
[165] Treas. Reg. § 1.989(a)-1(b)(2)(ii)(A) (1990).
[166] Treas. Reg. § 1.989(a)-1(b)(2)(ii)(B) (1990).
[167] Treas. Reg. § 1.989(a)-1(b)(2)(i) (1990).
[168] Treas. Reg. § 1.989(a)-1(b)(2)(ii)(A) (1990).
[169] Treas. Reg. § 1.989(a)-1(b)(2)(ii)(B) (1990).

(iv) Partnerships, Trusts, and Estates

A partnership, trust, or estate is a QBU of a partner or beneficiary.[170] Activities of a partnership, trust, or estate qualify as a QBU if two conditions are met. First, the activities must constitute a trade or business.[171] Second, the entity must maintain a complete and separate set of books and records with respect to the QBU's activities.[172]

(v) Trade or Business

Whether activities constitute a trade or business depend on the facts and circumstances.[173] In general, a trade or business for purposes of I.R.C. § 989(a) is a specific unified group of activities that constitutes (or could constitute) an independent economic enterprise carried on for profit, the expenses related to which are deductible under I.R.C. § 162 or I.R.C. § 212 (other than the part of I.R.C. § 212 dealing with expenses incurred in connection with taxes.[174] A "group of activities" must ordinarily include every operation that forms a part of, or serves as a step in, a process by which an enterprise may earn income or profit.[175] In addition, the group of activities must ordinarily include the collection of income and the payment of expenses.[176]

A QBU does not need to conduct activities that constitute a different trade or business than those carried out by other QBUs of the taxpayer.[177] A vertical, functional, or geographical division of the same trade or business may qualify as a trade or business if the activities otherwise qualify as a trade or business.[178] Activities that are merely ancillary to a trade or business do not constitute a trade or business.[179]

---

[170] Treas. Reg. § 1.989(a)-1(b)(2)(i) (1990).
[171] Treas. Reg. § 1.989(a)-1(b)(2)(ii)(A) (1990).
[172] Treas. Reg. § 1.989(a)-1(b)(2)(ii)(B) (1990).
[173] Treas. Reg. § 1.989(a)-1(c) (1990).
[174] *Id.*
[175] *Id.*
[176] *Id.*
[177] *Id.*
[178] *Id.*
[179] *Id.*

Example 59-2

Assume a domestic corporation manufactures a product in the United States for sale worldwide, and all of its sales functions are conducted exclusively in the United States. If the corporation employs a courier to deliver sales documents to customers in a foreign country, the courier's activities do not constitute a QBU because the activities are merely ancillary to the corporation's manufacturing and selling business.[180]

An individual's activities as an employee do not by themselves constitute a trade or business.[181]

Example 59-3

Assume an individual that is a resident of the United States, markets and sells products in a foreign country and the United States. Assume further that the products are produced in the United States, and the individual has an office, employs a salesman in the foreign country, and maintains a separate set of books. The individual is treated as being in a trade or business and his activities in the foreign country are a QBU.[182]

Example 59-4

Assume an individual that is a resident of the United States is engaged in a trade or business which is wholly unrelated to any type of investment activity. Assume further that the individual also maintains a portfolio of foreign currency-denominated investments through a foreign broker, and the broker is responsible for all activities necessary to the management of the individual's investments. The broker also maintains separate books and records with respect to the individual's investment activities. The individual's investment activities qualify as a QBU to the extent the activities engaged in by the individual generate expenses that are deductible

---

[180] Example taken from Treas. Reg. § 1.989(a)-1(e), Example (3) (1990).
[181] Treas. Reg. § 1.989(a)-1(c) (1990).
[182] Example taken from Treas. Reg. § 1.989(a)-1(e), Example (8) (1990).

under I.R.C. § 212 (other than that part of I.R.C. § 212 dealing with expenses incurred in connection with taxes).[183]

It appears as if the standard for a trade or business is viewed more liberally than the standard for determining separate trades or businesses under I.R.C. § 446(d) (separate accounting methods for separate trades or businesses) or I.R.C. § 355 (separate trades or businesses prior to a tax-free split-up or spin-off). As a result, the fact that a group of activities is a QBU does not necessarily mean that the QBU would qualify as a separate trade or business for other purposes under the Code.

The "trade or business" requirement contained in I.R.C. § 989(a) raises a question as to the appropriate treatment for passive activities of a QBU. Unfortunately, this issue is not expressly resolved in the Code or the legislative history. The tax bill, originally reported in 1985 by the House Ways and Means Committee, required the operation of an "active" trade or business.[184] The Senate bill and the final legislation for TRA '86 dropped the "active" requirement, thereby reflecting a legislative intent to apply a more liberal definition.[185]

(vi) Separate Books and Records

A QBU must have separate books and records, which include "books of original entry" and "ledger accounts," both general and subsidiary, or similar records.[186] For a cash basis taxpayer using the cash receipts and disbursements method of accounting, books of original entry include a cash receipts and disbursements journal where each receipt and disbursement is recorded.[187] For an accrual basis taxpayer, books of original entry include a journal to record sales (accounts receivable) and a journal to record expenses incurred (accounts payable).[188]

A journal is defined in the regulations as a chronological account of all transactions entered into for an accounting period.[189] A ledger account chronicles, for an accounting period, the specific transactions recorded in the journal for that period upon the various items shown on the entity's

---

[183] Example taken from Treas. Reg. § 1.989(a)-1(e), Example (6) (1990).
[184] HOUSE WAYS AND MEANS COMM. REPORT, H.R. REP. NO. 426, 99th Cong., 1st Sess. 472 (1985).
[185] TRA '86 Conf. Rep., *supra* note 2, at II-660.
[186] Treas. Reg. § 1.989(a)-1(d)(1) (1990).
[187] *Id.*
[188] *Id.*
[189] *Id.*

balance sheet (i.e., assets, liabilities, and capital accounts) and income statements (i.e., revenues and expenses).[190]

Books and records also include books and records used to determine income or loss that is, or is treated as, effectively connected with the conduct of a trade or business within the United States.[191]

(vii) Transitional Rules for Certain QBUs Using a Profit and Loss Method of Accounting Before January 1, 1987

Temporary and proposed regulations have been issued under I.R.C. § 987, relating to accounting methods employed by QBUs in determining exchange gain or loss on remittances in excess of post-1986 earnings.[192] Transitional rules are also provided for QBUs that used a profit or loss method of accounting before enactment of TRA '86 and do not elect (or are not required) to use the U.S. dollar approximate separate transactions method for taxable years beginning after December 31, 1986.[193] Transitional rules are also provided for changes from the net worth method to the profit and loss method.[194]

(viii) Functional Currency of a QBU

All determinations under the Code are made in a taxpayer's functional currency.[195] Because the Code favors the use of the U.S. dollar as a taxpayer's functional currency, functional currency is generally defined as the U.S. dollar.[196] Taxpayers are generally required to use the U.S. dollar as their functional currency unless otherwise provided in the Code.

In the case of a QBU, on the other hand, functional currency is defined as "the currency of the economic environment in which a significant part of such unit's activities are conducted and which is used by such unit in keeping its books and records."[197] If I.R.C. § 985(b)(1)(B) can support the use of either of two foreign currencies as a functional currency of the taxpayer, the legislative history to TRA '86 indicates that the taxpayer may adopt either of such currencies as a QBU's functional currency. For a

---

[190] *Id.*
[191] Treas. Reg. § 1.989(a)-1(d)(2) (1990).
[192] T.D. 8220, 1988-2 C.B. 292.
[193] Temp. Treas. Reg. §§ 1.987-0T (1988) to 1.987-1T (1988).
[194] Temp. Treas. Reg. § 1.989(c)-1T (1988).
[195] I.R.C. § 985(a). For a discussion of functional currency, see section 59.2(g).
[196] I.R.C. § 985(a)(1)(A).
[197] I.R.C. § 985(b)(1)(B).

discussion of the Treasury regulations that address the economic environment of a QBU, see section 59.2(g)(l)(iv).

(h) MIXED STRADDLES

TMRA '88 added I.R.C. § 1092(b)(2)(D), providing that the Treasury could issue regulations relating to the timing and character of gains and losses in cases of straddles where at least one position is ordinary and at least one position is capital.[198] The legislative history provides that the TMRA '88 Conferees expect that in situations involving such mixed straddles, 60/40 treatment provided under I.R.C. § 1256 will apply only to the net gain (loss) from the transactions included in the identified mixed straddle or mixed straddle account and only to the extent attributable to section 1256 foreign currency contracts (as modified by the new TMRA '88 provisions).[199] Moreover, the TMRA '88 Conferees stated that, as under the prevailing regulations, they anticipate that not more than 40 percent of any net foreign exchange loss from a mixed straddle account may be treated as ordinary loss.[200]

After TRA '86 enacted the foreign currency rules contained in Subpart J of the Code, and before enactment of I.R.C. § 1092(b)(2)(D) by TMRA '88, there was a question as to the availability of a mixed straddle account election under Temp. Treas. Reg. § 1.1092(b)-4T[201] for straddles involving both section 988 transactions and section 1256 contracts.[202] This is because Temp. Treas. Reg. § 1.1092(b)-4T, issued before enactment of section 988, does not provide rules governing section 988 positions within a mixed straddle account. As a result, there were at least three possibilities as to how positions in a mixed straddle account should have been handled. First, all gains and losses from the account were treated as ordinary income or loss because the section 1256 foreign currency contracts within the account become section 988 transactions once the account is elected. Such foreign currency positions would be marked-to-market under Temp. Treas. Reg. § 1.1092(b)-4T rather than "under section 1256" as is provided in I.R.C. § 988(c)(1)(B)(iii). The foreign currency gain or loss on other positions would have been ordinary gain or loss under the general rules of I.R.C. § 988(a)(1)(A).

---

[198] TMRA '88, *supra* note 11, § 6130(c).
[199] TMRA '88 Conf. Rep., *supra* note 31, at 194.
[200] *Id.*
[201] (1985).
[202] For a discussion of mixed straddle accounts generally, see section 57.4.

A second possible way to treat section 988 positions within a mixed straddle account was that gain and loss generated in the mixed straddle account were all capital because the rules of Temp. Treas. Reg. § 1.1092(b)-4T so provide. This possibility was supported by the view that a mixed straddle account election is an agreement between the taxpayer and the government.

A third possibility was that gain and loss on section 1256 contracts in a mixed straddle account were capital assets while the foreign currency gain and loss on section 988 transactions were ordinary assets. Assuming ordinary income and loss is not netted against capital gain and loss (under the general rules of I.R.C. § 1211 in the absence of any direction under Temp. Treas. Reg. § 1.1092(b)-4T to net ordinary and capital transactions), an account might produce substantial ordinary loss (gain) and capital gain (loss). The appropriate treatment of section 988 contracts was clarified by TMRA '88 and will be fleshed out by the Treasury in future regulations.

(i) FOREIGN CURRENCY TRANSACTIONS OF CERTAIN COMMODITY FUNDS

(1) IN GENERAL

There are special rules for transactions in forward contracts, futures, options, and similar instruments held by "qualified funds." These "qualified funds" are basically foreign currency commodities pools or similar partnerships that can elect to be treated as "qualified funds" to obtain capital treatment for products falling within a broader definition of the term "section 1256 contract." All of such section 1256 contracts of "qualified funds" are subject to the Mark-to-Market Rule under I.R.C. § 1256.[203] The 60/40 Rule—which provides for 60 percent long-term and 40 percent short-term capital gain or loss—only applies to those instruments falling within the general definition of "section 1256 contracts."[204] Those instruments falling within the definition of "section 1256 contracts" as a result of the special expansion for "qualified funds" receive 100 percent short-term capital gain or loss treatment.

---

[203] For a discussion of the Mark-to-Market Rule, see section 45.1.

[204] For a discussion of the 60/40 Rule, see section 45.2.

(2) EXPANDED DEFINITION OF SECTION 1256 CONTRACTS

The expanded definition of "section 1256 contracts" includes all section 1256 futures and options as set forth in the general carve-out to section 988 transactions applicable to all taxpayers. The expanded definition of section 1256 contracts also includes the following:

1. All bank forward contracts held by qualified funds (even contracts that would not be classified as foreign currency contracts (as defined in I.R.C. § 1256(g)(1)) because they involve a foreign currency that is *not* also traded on a qualified board or exchange through RFCs)

2. All foreign currency-related futures contracts, including RFCs that would normally be treated as section 1256 contracts, as well as other futures contracts involving nonfunctional currencies that are not traded on or subject to the rules of a qualified board or exchange

3. All other contracts that the Treasury prescribes by regulations to be treated as section 1256 contracts (including options but not swaps). The Treasury has the authority to exclude futures and option contracts from the expanded "section 1256 contract" definition in cases where the contracts are thinly traded or "there are insufficient non-tax-motivated checks on the valuation process."[205]

Moreover, the TMRA '88 Conferees anticipated that futures contracts will be eligible for treatment as section 1256 contracts if the particular board or exchange at which the contracts are traded has (1) an appropriate daily marking-to-market system in place, or (2) the daily or month-end values of outstanding contracts are otherwise readily ascertainable on a consistent and reliable basis.[206]

(3) REQUIREMENTS FOR A QUALIFIED FUND

A qualified fund must meet three tests to qualify as such for a particular taxable year—it must meet an ownership test, an activity test, and an income test. In addition, the partnership must have met these tests in all

---

[205] TMRA '88 Conf. Rep., *supra* note 31, at 190.
[206] *Id.*

prior taxable years beginning with the first year that the partnership elected to be treated as a qualified fund.[207]

Turning first to the ownership test, the partnership must have at least 20 unrelated partners during the entire tax year.[208] If one of the partners is a partnership, the members of that partnership will each count toward the 20-partner requirement. This means that the partnership interest held by a partnership includes the number of partners in the partnership that owns the partnership interest. None of the partners may own more than 20 percent of the capital or profit interests in the partnership, although there are certain transitional rules for existing partnerships. The 20 percent capital or profit interests requirement is not violated if a *general* partner with a greater than 20 percent interest has no income or loss from section 988 transactions. In addition, the 20 percent limit does not apply to *any* partner, general or limited, whose share of the partnership tax attributes are not subject to federal income taxation. Further, in computing a partner's interest in profits, income applicable to a general partner as incentive compensation and not deductible by the partnership is disregarded.[209]

The second test, the activity test, requires that a qualified fund's principal activity be the buying and selling of options, futures, or forwards with respect to commodities. No more than a de minimis amount of gross income can be derived from the buying or selling of actual commodities or debt instruments. Nevertheless, this test can be met even if the partnership holds a substantial amount of debt instruments—for example, debt instruments required to fund guaranteed payments to limited partners, or to collateralize obligations on margin accounts.

The third test, the income test, requires that at least 90 percent of the gross income of a qualified fund be from "interest, dividends, gain from the sale or disposition of capital assets held for the production of interest or dividends, and income and gains from commodities, futures, forwards, and options with respect to commodities." The TMRA '88 Conferees state that the qualified fund shall have no more than a de minimis amount of income from buying and selling commodities or from debt instruments that are section 988 transactions. The de minimis requirement is not violated in cases where commodities are acquired for a short period of time for reasons beyond the control of the fund—for example, the exercise of a put option on a commodity that leaves the partnership in actual possession of a commodity for a short period of time until it can be

---

[207] *Id.*
[208] Whether a partner is a related person is determined under I.R.C. §§ 267(b) and 707(b).
[209] TMRA '88 Conf. Rep., *supra* note 31, at 190.

disposed of. In addition, for partnerships in existence prior to the enactment of the law, the violation of the de minimis rule in periods prior to the date of enactment does not violate the rule.

(4) ELECTION

The election to be treated as a qualified fund must be made on or before the later of the first day of the taxable year, or the first day in the taxable year that the partnership holds a section 1256 contract defined under the expanded definition of such contracts. The TMRA '88 Conferees specifically provided that an existing partnership that decides to make a qualified fund election must mark-to-market all contracts held at the beginning of the year of the election.

The TMRA '88 Conferees also stated that a partnership that fails to meet the qualified fund definition during the tax year must treat as ordinary income the net gains on all its section 1256 contracts (defined under the expanded definition of such contracts). If the section 1256 contracts result in a net loss, the loss is characterized under the rules that would have applied if the partnership had not ceased to be a qualified fund. The loss would be subject to the 60/40 rule if the instruments would generally fall within the unexpanded definition of "section 1256 contract" and would be accorded 100 percent short-term losses if falling within the special expanded definition of "section 1256 contracts" for "qualified funds." Inadvertent failure may be exempt from this rule.

On December 2, 1988, the IRS issued Notice 88-124,[210] to set out the way in which a taxpayer can make a qualified fund election under I.R.C. § 988(c)(1)(E)(iii)(V). The remainder of this section sets out the provisions contained in Notice 88-124.

(i) Procedure

A partnership can make a qualified fund election by sending to the IRS Service Center in Kansas City, Missouri, a statement entitled "Qualified Fund Election under Section 988(c)(1)(E)(iii)(V)," that contains the following information:

1. The partnership's name, address, and TIN[211]

---

[210] 1988-2 C.B. 534 (Dec. 2, 1988).
[211] Notice 88-124, 1988-2 C.B. 534 (Dec. 2, 1988).

2. The name, address, and TIN of the general partner making the election on behalf of the partnership[212]
   3. The date the notice is mailed or otherwise delivered to the IRS Service Center[213]
   4. A brief description of the activity of the partnership[214]
   5. A statement that the partnership is making the election provided in I.R.C. § 988(c)(1)(E)(iii)(V)[215]
   6. The date of the beginning of the taxable year for which the election is being made[216]
   7. If the election is filed after the first day of the taxable year, a statement as to whether the partnership previously held an instrument described in I.R.C. § 988(c)(1)(E)(i) during such taxable year, and if so, the first date during the taxable year on which such contract was held[217]
   8. The signature of the general partner making the election[218]

The election must be made by the general partner with management responsibility of the partnership's activities. In addition, a copy of the election must be attached to the partnership's income tax return (IRS Form 1065) for the first year it is effective.[219]

(ii) Time for Making the Election

In general, the election under I.R.C. § 988(c)(1)(E)(iii)(V) for any tax year must be made on or before the first day of the taxable year or, if later, on or before the first day during the year on which the partnership holds an instrument described in I.R.C. § 988(c)(1)(E)(i).[220]

The election under I.R.C. § 988(c)(1)(E)(iii)(V) applies to the taxable year for which it is made and for all succeeding tax years. The election can only be revoked with the consent of the IRS.[221] In determining whether to

---

[212] *Id.*
[213] *Id.*
[214] *Id.*
[215] *Id.*
[216] *Id.*
[217] *Id.*
[218] *Id.*
[219] *Id.*
[220] *Id.*
[221] *Id.*

grant revocation of the election, the IRS will consider recapture by the partners of the tax benefit derived from the election in previous years.[222]

(iii) Transitional Rule for the 1988 Calendar Year

A calendar year partnership can make the election to be treated as a qualified fund under I.R.C. § 988(c)(1)(E)(iii)(V) for the 1988 taxable year on or before December 31, 1988.[223] A fiscal year partnership can make the election to be treated as a qualified fund for its 1988 tax year or its 1989 tax year on or before December 31, 1988.[224] Such an election (1) will only apply to instruments entered into or acquired after October 21, 1988, and (2) will apply to the tax year for which it is made and all succeeding tax years.[225] Because December 31, 1988, was a Saturday, followed by the New Year's holiday, the IRS said the actual filing deadline was January 3, 1989.[226]

(j) ELECTION INTO SECTION 988 TREATMENT FOR REGULATED FUTURES CONTRACTS AND NONEQUITY OPTIONS

TMRA '88 changes to I.R.C. § 988 allow taxpayers to elect to have RFCs and nonequity options (as defined in I.R.C. §§ 1256(g)(1) and (3)) treated as section 988 transactions without regard to whether they are (or would be) marked-to-market at the end of the year. As result, a taxpayer can elect to obtain ordinary income treatment with respect to all foreign currency transactions by electing into section 988 treatment.

I.R.C. § 988(c)(1)(D)(ii) provides—for RFCs and nonequity options entered into after October 21, 1988—that the taxpayer can elect into section 988 treatment for the sourcing and characterization rules. The election applies to contracts held at any time during the taxable year for which the election is made, or any succeeding taxable year unless the election is revoked with the consent of the IRS.[227] Once the election is made, the gains and losses on all RFCs and nonequity options held by the taxpayer are ordinary, not capital. The positions remain subject to the Mark-to-Market Rule in I.R.C. § 1256.

---

[222] *Id.*
[223] *Id.*
[224] *Id.*
[225] *Id.*
[226] *How and When to Make the TAMRA-Enacted Foreign Currency Elections*, 69 Fed. Taxes Rep. Bull. (P-H) ¶ 60,548 (Dec. 8, 1988).
[227] I.R.C. § 988(c)(1)(D)(ii)(I).

Except as provided in regulations, an election into section 988 treatment must be made on or before the first day of the taxable year for which the election is made (or if later, on the first day during such year on which the taxpayer holds such an RFC or nonequity option that would be marked-to-market under I.R.C. § 1256 if held on the last day of the taxable year).[228]

For a partnership or S corporation, each partner or S corporation shareholder must make the election separately.[229] The election into section 988 treatment is not available to any partnership that made an election to be treated as a qualified fund under I.R.C. § 988(c)(1)(E)(iii)(V).[230]

On December 2, 1988, the IRS issued Notice 88-124[231] to set out the way in which a taxpayer can elect into section 988 treatment for RFCs and nonequity options. This procedure was superseded by Temp. Treas. Reg. § 1.988-1T(a)(4)(iii).[232] An election made prior to September 21, 1989, that satisfied the requirements of Notice 88-124, is deemed to satisfy the requirements of Temp. Treas. Reg. § 1.988-1T(a)(4)(iii).[233] The remainder of this section addresses the election into section 988 treatment as provided in Temp. Treas. Reg. § 1.988-1T(a)(4)(iii).

(1) PROCEDURE

A taxpayer can make an election into section 988 under I.R.C. § 988(c)(1)(D)(ii) by sending to the IRS Service Center in Kansas City, Missouri, a statement entitled "Election to Treat Regulated Futures Contracts and Nonequity Options as Section 988 Transactions under Section 988(c)(1)(D)(ii)," which contains the following information:

1. The taxpayer's name, address, and TIN[234]

2. The date the notice is mailed or otherwise delivered to the IRS Service Center[235]

---

[228] I.R.C. § 988(c)(1)(D)(ii)(II).
[229] I.R.C. § 988(c)(1)(D)(ii)(III).
[230] I.R.C. § 988(c)(1)(D)(iii). For a discussion of qualified funds, see sections 59.2(a)(2) and 59.2(i).
[231] 1988-2 C.B. 534 (Dec. 2, 1988).
[232] (1989).
[233] Temp. Treas. Reg. § 1.988-1T(a)(4)(v) (1989).
[234] Temp. Treas. Reg. § 1.988-1T(a)(4)(iii)(A) (1989).
[235] Temp. Treas. Reg. § 1.988-1T(a)(4)(iii)(B) (1989).

3. A statement that the taxpayer (including all members of the taxpayer's affiliated group as defined in I.R.C. § 1504, or in the case of an individual, all persons filing a joint return with such individual) elects to have I.R.C. § 988(c)(1)(D)(i) and Temp. Treas. Reg. § 1.988-1T(a)(4)(i)[236] not apply[237]

4. The date of the beginning of the taxable year for which the election is being made[238]

5. If the election is filed after the first day of the taxable year, a statement as to whether the taxpayer has previously held an RFC or nonequity option described in I.R.C. § 988(c)(1)(D)(i) or Temp. Treas. Reg. § 1.988-1T(a)(4)(i) during such taxable year, and if so, the first date during the taxable year on which such contract was held[239]

6. The signature of the person making the election (in the case of individuals filing a joint return, the signature of all persons filing the return)[240]

Those taxpayers that can make the election are as follows:

> in the case of an individual, by such individual; in the case of a partnership, by each partner separately; in the case of an S corporation, by each shareholder separately; in the case of a trust (other than a grantor trust) or estate, by the fiduciary of such trust or estate; in the case of any corporation other than an S corporation, by such corporation; in the case of a controlled foreign corporation, by its controlling United States shareholders under [I.R.C.] § 1.964-1(c)(3). With respect to a corporation (other than an S corporation), the election shall be binding on all members of such corporation's affiliated group as defined in section 1504.[241]

In addition, once the election is made, it is "binding on any income or loss derived from all contracts described in [I.R.C.] section 988(c)(1)(D)(i) or [Temp. Treas. Reg. § 1.988-1T](a)(4)(i) . . . in which the taxpayer holds a direct interest or indirect interest through a partnership or S corporation."[242]

---

[236] (1989).
[237] Temp. Treas. Reg. § 1.988-1T(a)(4)(iii)(C) (1989).
[238] Temp. Treas. Reg. § 1.988-1T(a)(4)(iii)(D) (1989).
[239] Temp. Treas. Reg. § 1.988-1T(a)(4)(iii)(E) (1989).
[240] Temp. Treas. Reg. § 1.988-1T(a)(4)(iii)(F) (1989).
[241] Id.
[242] Id.

The election into section 988 treatment cannot be made by a partnership that has elected to be a "qualified fund" under I.R.C. § 988(c)(1)(E)(iii)(V).[243]

A copy of the election must be attached to the taxpayer's income tax return for the first year it is effective.

(2) TIME FOR MAKING THE ELECTION

In general, the election under I.R.C. § 988(c)(1)(D)(ii) for any taxable year is made on or before the first day of the taxable year or, if later, on or before the first day during such year on which the taxpayer holds a contract described in I.R.C. § 988(c)(1)(D)(i).[244] The election applies to all contracts entered into or acquired after October 21, 1988, and held on or after the effective date of the election.[245]

The election is effective as of the beginning of the taxable year and it is binding for all succeeding years unless revoked with the consent of the IRS.[246] In determining whether to grant revocation of the election, recapture of the tax benefit derived from the election in previous taxable years will be considered.[247]

(3) LATE ELECTIONS

There is a special rule for certain late elections. A taxpayer can make an election within 30 days after the first day of the taxable year or, if later, on or before the thirtieth day on which the taxpayer holds such a contract.[248] This late election will be effective as of the beginning of the taxable year. Any losses recognized during the tax year on contracts described in I.R.C. § 988(c)(1)(D)(i) that were entered into or acquired after October 21, 1988, and held on or before the date on which the late election is mailed or otherwise delivered to the IRS Service Center, will not be treated as having been from a section 988 transaction.[249] In other words, RFCs and nonequity options entered into or acquired after October 21, 1988, and held on or before the date on which the late election is made, will be marked-to-market and treated as 60 percent long-term and 40 percent

---

[243] For a discussion of qualified funds, see sections 59.2(a)(2) and 59.2(i).
[244] Temp. Treas. Reg. § 1.988-1T(a)(4)(iv) (1989).
[245] *Id.*
[246] *Id.*
[247] *Id.*
[248] Temp. Treas. Reg. § 1.988-1T(a)(4)(iv)(B) (1989).
[249] *Id.*

short-term capital gain or loss (under the Mark-to-Market Rule and the 60/40 Rule).[250]

A late election must comply in all respects with the election procedure set out in Temp. Treas. Reg. § 1.988-1T(a)(4)(iii).[251]

(4) TRANSITIONAL RULE FOR THE 1988 CALENDAR YEAR

A calendar year taxpayer can make the election under I.R.C. § 988(c)(1)(D)(ii) for the 1988 taxable year on or before December 31, 1988.[252]

A fiscal year taxpayer can make the election under I.R.C. § 988(c)(1)(D)(ii) for its 1988 or 1989 taxable year on or before December 31, 1988.[253]

A transitional rule election made under Notice 88-124 (1) will only apply to contracts entered into or acquired after October 21, 1988, (2) will apply to the taxable year for which made and to all succeeding taxable years, and (3) will not be considered a late election.[254] For a discussion of late elections, see section 59.2(j)(3).

§ 59.3 FOREIGN CURRENCY HEDGING TRANSACTIONS

Foreign currency hedging transactions are discussed in detail in section 23.3.

§ 59.4 STEPS TO ANALYZE FOREIGN CURRENCY TRANSACTIONS

In summary, it is possible to analyze foreign currency transactions by conducting the following steps. First, the taxpayer's functional currency must be determined. Once determined, it is possible to identify whether a particular foreign currency transaction is denominated in a functional or nonfunctional currency.

---

[250] For a discussion of the Mark-to-Market Rule, see section 45.1. For a discussion of the 60/40 Rule, see section 45.2.

[251] (1989). For a discussion of this procedure, see section 59.2(j)(1).

[252] Temp. Treas. Reg. § 1.988-1T(a)(4)(v) (1989); Notice 88-124, 1988-2 C.B. 534 (Dec. 2, 1988).

[253] Notice 88-124, 1988-2 C.B. 534 (Dec. 2, 1988).

[254] *Id.*

Second, if a foreign currency transaction is denominated in a nonfunctional currency, the transaction must be analyzed to determine whether it is a so-called section 988 transaction. Section 988 transactions are subject to the provisions of I.R.C. § 988. Transactions that are not section 988 transactions are subject to pre-TRA '86 tax principles.

Third, the translation rules of I.R.C. §§ 986 and 987, if they are applicable, must be applied.

The remainder of this section summarizes the rules that apply to RFCs and nonequity options, foreign currency contracts defined in I.R.C. § 1256(g)(2), and forward contracts not defined in I.R.C. § 1256(g)(2).

(a) REGULATED FUTURES CONTRACTS AND NONEQUITY OPTIONS

RFCs (defined in I.R.C. § 1256(b)(1)) and nonequity options (defined in I.R.C. § 1256(b)(3)) can be part of foreign currency transactions that are not part of hedges.[255] The remainder of this section summarizes the tax rules that apply to RFCs and nonequity options that are not part of hedging transactions.

(1) POSITIONS ENTERED INTO BEFORE 1986

For RFC and nonequity option positions entered into before enactment of I.R.C. § 988, the character of the positions is capital and the positions are subject to the 60/40 Rule in I.R.C. § 1256 and the transactions are subject to the Mark-to-Market Rule in I.R.C. § 1256.[256]

(2) POSITIONS ENTERED INTO AFTER ENACTMENT OF I.R.C. § 988 AND BEFORE OCTOBER 22, 1988

For RFC and nonequity option positions entered into after enactment of I.R.C. § 988 and before October 22, 1988, the character of the positions is capital under I.R.C. § 1221, and subject to the 60/40 Rule in I.R.C. § 1256. Gains and losses are marked-to-market under the Mark-to-Market Rule in I.R.C. § 1256. This provision is effective for tax years beginning after December 31, 1986. It also applies to transactions entered into in tax years beginning before December 31, 1986, if closed in tax years beginning after December 31, 1986.

---

[255] For a discussion of RFCs, see section 44.1. For a discussion of nonequity options, see section 44.3. For a discussion of foreign currency hedging transactions, see section 23.3.

[256] For a discussion of section 1256 treatment, see generally Part Ten.

(3) POSITIONS ENTERED INTO AFTER OCTOBER 21, 1988

For RFC and nonequity option positions entered into after October 21, 1988, the character is capital under I.R.C. § 1221, and subject to the 60/40 Rule in I.R.C. § 1256. Gains and losses are marked-to-market under the Mark-to-Market Rule in I.R.C. § 1256.

For RFC and nonequity option positions entered into after October 21, 1988, taxpayers can elect under I.R.C. § 988(c)(1)(D) to have their RFC and nonequity option positions treated as ordinary income assets under I.R.C. § 988. The positions remain subject to the Mark-to-Market Rule in I.R.C. § 1256. For a discussion of the election under I.R.C. § 988(c)(1)(D), see section 59.2(j).

(b) FUTURES AND OPTIONS THAT ARE NOT SECTION 1256 CONTRACTS

Futures and options that are not section 1256 contracts can be part of foreign currency transactions that are not part of hedges.[257] The remainder of this section summarizes the tax rules that apply to futures and options that are not section 1256 options and that are not part of hedging transactions.

(1) POSITIONS ENTERED INTO BEFORE 1986

For futures and options not subject to section 1256 treatment because they are neither RFCs nor nonequity options, the character of gain or loss is capital under I.R.C. § 1221, while the timing of gains or losses depends on when the positions are sold, exchanged, or otherwise disposed of.

(2) POSITIONS ENTERED INTO AFTER ENACTMENT OF I.R.C. § 988 AND BEFORE OCTOBER 22, 1988

For futures contracts and options that are not section 1256 contracts entered into after enactment of I.R.C. § 988 and before October 22, 1988, the character is ordinary under I.R.C. § 988, while the timing of gains and losses depends on when they are sold, exchanged, or otherwise disposed of. This provision is effective for tax years beginning after December 31, 1986. It also applies to transactions entered into in tax years beginning

---

[257] For a discussion of RFCs, see section 44.1. For a discussion of nonequity options, see section 44.3.

before December 31, 1986, if closed in tax years beginning after December 31, 1986.

(3) POSITIONS ENTERED INTO AFTER OCTOBER 21, 1988

For futures contracts and options that are not section 1256 contracts entered into after October 21, 1988, the character of gain or loss is ordinary under I.R.C. § 988, while the timing of gains and losses depends on when the positions are sold, exchanged, or otherwise disposed of.

(4) ELECTION AVAILABLE FOR TAX YEARS BEGINNING AFTER SEPTEMBER 20, 1989

An election is available under I.R.C. § 988(a)(1)(B) for futures and options that are not section 1256 contracts. This election treats as capital the gain or loss arising from futures and options that are neither RFCs nor nonequity options. Under this election, gain or loss from non-section 1256 futures and options would be characterized as capital and would be recognized when the contract is closed and completed—except for delivery under I.R.C. § 988(c)(5) and where economic benefit is derived under Temp. Treas. Reg. § 1.988-2T(d)(2)(ii)(C).[258] The effective date of this election is for taxable years beginning on or after September 21, 1989.

(c) FOREIGN CURRENCY CONTRACTS THAT ARE SECTION 1256 CONTRACTS

Forward contracts defined as foreign currency contracts in I.R.C. § 1256(g)(2) are section 1256 contracts. These foreign currency contracts can be part of foreign currency transactions that are not part of hedges.[259] The remainder of this section summarizes the tax rules that apply to foreign currency contracts that are not part of hedges.

(1) POSITIONS ENTERED INTO BEFORE 1986

For foreign currency forward contract positions entered into before enactment of I.R.C. § 988, the character is capital under I.R.C. § 1221 and subject to the 60/40 Rule and the transactions are subject to the Mark-to-Market Rule in I.R.C. § 1256.

---

[258] (1989).

[259] For a discussion of foreign currency contracts subject to section 1256 treatment, see section 44.2. For a discussion of foreign currency hedging transactions, see section 23.3.

(2) POSITIONS ENTERED INTO AFTER ENACTMENT OF I.R.C. § 988 AND BEFORE OCTOBER 22, 1988

For foreign currency forward contract positions entered into after enactment of I.R.C. § 988 and before October 22, 1988, the character is capital under I.R.C. § 1221 and subject to the 60/40 Rule in I.R.C. § 1256 and the transactions are subject to the Mark-to-Market Rule in I.R.C. § 1256. This provision is effective for tax years beginning after December 31, 1986. It also applies to transactions entered into in tax years beginning before December 31, 1986, if closed in tax years beginning after December 31, 1986.

(3) POSITIONS ENTERED INTO AFTER OCTOBER 21, 1988

For foreign currency forward contract positions entered into after October 21, 1988, the character is ordinary under I.R.C. § 988, while the transactions are marked-to-market under the Mark-to-Market Rule in I.R.C. § 1256.[260]

(4) ELECTION AVAILABLE FOR TAX YEARS BEGINNING AFTER SEPTEMBER 20, 1989

An election under I.R.C. § 988(a)(1)(B) is available for foreign currency contracts defined in I.R.C. § 1256(g)(2). This election treats gain or loss from foreign currency contracts, other than RFCs and nonequity options, as capital. Under this election, forward contracts defined under I.R.C. § 1256(g)(2) as foreign currency contracts, are treated as 60/40 assets under I.R.C. § 1256 and subject to the Mark-to-Market Rule.[261]

---

[260] *See* Temp. Treas. Reg. § 1.988-2T(d)(2)(ii)(B) (1989) for the exception where the economic benefit is derived, for transactions creating an offset after September 21, 1989. If a "section 988" forward contract, futures contract, option, warrant, or similar financial instrument, is offset by another transaction or transactions, exchange gain is realized to the extent the taxpayer derives, by pledge or otherwise, an economic benefit from any gain inherent in such offsetting positions.

[261] All other forward contracts under this election would be characterized as capital and timed when the contract is closed and completed, except for delivery under I.R.C. § 988(c)(5) where economic benefit is derived under Temp. Treas. Reg. § 1.988-2T(d)(2)(ii)(C) (1989). The effective date of this election is for taxable years beginning on or after September 21, 1989. For prior taxable years, any reasonable, contemporaneous election meeting the requirements of I.R.C. § 988(a)(1)(B) is permissible.

(d) FORWARD CONTRACTS THAT ARE NOT SECTION 1256 CONTRACTS

Forward contracts that do not meet the definition of foreign currency contracts under I.R.C. § 1256(g)(2) can be part of foreign currency transactions that are not hedges.[262] The remainder of this section summarizes the tax rules that apply to forward contracts that are not section 1256 contracts under I.R.C. § 1256(g)(2).

(1) POSITIONS ENTERED INTO BEFORE 1986

For forward contract positions entered into before enactment of I.R.C. § 988, the character of gain or loss is capital under I.R.C. § 1221, while the timing of gains and losses depends on when the positions are sold, exchanged, or otherwise disposed of.

(2) POSITIONS ENTERED INTO AFTER ENACTMENT OF I.R.C. § 988 AND BEFORE OCTOBER 22, 1988

For forward contract positions entered into after enactment of I.R.C. § 988 and before October 22, 1988, the character of gain or loss is ordinary under I.R.C. § 988, while the timing of gains and losses depends on when the positions are sold, exchanged, or otherwise disposed of.

(3) POSITIONS ENTERED INTO AFTER OCTOBER 21, 1988

For forward contract positions entered into after October 21, 1988, the character is ordinary under I.R.C. § 988, while the timing of gains and losses depends on when the positions are sold, exchanged, or otherwise disposed of—except for delivery under I.R.C. § 988(c)(5) and where economic benefit is derived under Temp. Treas. Reg. § 1.988-2T(d)(2)(ii)(B).[263]

(4) ELECTION AVAILABLE FOR TAX YEARS BEGINNING AFTER SEPTEMBER 20, 1989

An election is available under I.R.C. § 988(a)(1)(B) for forward contracts not defined in I.R.C. § 1256(g)(2). This election treats gain or loss from forward contracts that are not section 1256 contracts as capital. Under

---

[262] For a discussion of foreign currency hedging transactions, see section 23.3.
[263] (1989).

this election, forward contracts not defined as foreign currency contracts in I.R.C. § 1256(g)(2) are characterized as capital, and gain or loss would be recognized when the contract is closed and completed. The effective date of this election is for taxable years beginning on or after September 21, 1989.

(e) SPOT CONTRACTS

A spot contract is defined under Temp. Treas. Reg. § 1.988-1T(b), as a contract to buy or sell nonfunctional currency on or before two business days following the date of the execution of the contract. Under Temp. Treas. Reg. § 1.988-2T(d)(1)(ii), a spot contract is not considered a forward contract or similar transaction unless the spot contract is disposed of prior to making or taking delivery of the currency. For example, if a taxpayer with the dollar as its functional currency enters into a spot contract to purchase British pounds, and takes delivery of such pounds under the contract, the delivery of the pounds is not a realization event. However, if the taxpayer sells or otherwise terminates the contract before taking delivery of the pounds, exchange gain or loss is realized and recognized. Under Temp. Treas. Reg. § 1.988-3T(b), the election under I.R.C. § 988(a)(1)(B) to treat certain foreign currency contracts as capital instead of ordinary is not available for spot contracts unless the spot contract is disposed of prior to making or taking delivery. Under Temp. Treas. Reg. § 1.988-1T(a)(1)(i), gain or loss results from a spot contract in which currency was acquired through delivery when the currency is disposed of and is treated as ordinary under I.R.C. § 988.

For spot contracts closed before January 1, 1987, the tax character is capital under I.R.C. § 1221 and is taxed under I.R.C. § 1001 when the contracts are closed. For spot contracts entered into after December 31, 1986, the tax character is ordinary under I.R.C. § 988 and is taxed under I.R.C. § 1001 when the contracts are closed.

§ 59.5 TRANSLATION RULES

The Code provides rules to convert a nonfunctional currency into a functional currency and a functional currency (other than the U.S. dollar) into U.S. dollars.[264] These rules, referred to as "translation rules," apply to foreign subsidiaries and foreign branches. Although a detailed discus-

---

[264] For a discussion of functional currency, see section 59.2(g).

sion of the translation rules is beyond the scope of this book, this section generally addresses the statutory translation rules. I.R.C. § 986 addresses foreign subsidiaries, while I.R.C. § 987 addresses foreign branches.

(a) FOREIGN SUBSIDIARIES

Translation rules are provided in I.R.C. § 986 for two issues concerning foreign subsidiaries—distributions to United States shareholders and foreign taxes paid for purposes of foreign tax credits.

Turning first to distributions to United States shareholders, I.R.C. § 986(a)(1) sets out the general rule that for purposes of determining the amount of the foreign tax credit, any foreign taxes must be translated into U.S. dollars, using the exchange rates as of the time such taxes were paid to the foreign country or possession of the United States, and any adjustment to the amount of foreign income taxes must be translated into dollars, using the exchange rate as of the time when the adjustment is paid to the foreign country or possession unless—in the case of a refund or credit of foreign income taxes—using the exchange rate as of the time of the original payment of such foreign income taxes.[265] For these purposes, foreign income taxes are defined to mean "any income, war profits, or excess profits taxes paid to any foreign country or to any possession of the United States."[266]

For purposes of determining the foreign taxes of any shareholder of any foreign corporation, the earnings and profits of the corporation must be determined in the corporation's functional currency.[267] For purposes of determining foreign taxes in the case of any United States person, the earnings and profits determined for the shareholder (when distributed, deemed distributed, or otherwise taken into account) must (if necessary) be translated into U.S. dollars using the appropriate exchange rate.[268]

Functional currency earnings and profits are generally translated into U.S. dollars. In addition, foreign currency gain or loss is not generally recognized by either the distributing corporation or its shareholders on distributions to shareholders. There is an exception for distributions of previously taxed earnings and profits (described in I.R.C. §§ 959 or 1293(c)).[269] For distributions of previously taxed earnings and profits, foreign currency gain or loss attributable to the change in exchange rates

---

[265] I.R.C. § 986(a)(1).
[266] I.R.C. § 986(a)(2).
[267] I.R.C. § 986(b)(1). For a discussion of functional currency, see section 59.2(g).
[268] I.R.C. § 986(b)(2).
[269] I.R.C. § 986(c)(1).

between the time it was previously taxed and the time it was distributed to the shareholder is recognized by the shareholder. Such foreign currency gain or loss is recognized and treated as ordinary income or loss.[270]

I.R.C. § 986 provides rules for translating into U.S. dollars the amount of foreign taxes deemed paid for foreign tax credit purposes. Foreign taxes are generally translated using the exchange rate at the time of payment.[271] If, on the other hand, taxes are refunded or credited, the refund or credit is translated using the exchange rates at the time the original payment is made for such foreign taxes.[272]

It is interesting to note that under the law in effect prior to TRA '86, foreign taxes were generally translated into U.S. dollars using the same exchange rate used for translating the earnings to which the tax was related.[273] As a result, the foreign tax rate did not vary with exchange rates. Under I.R.C. § 986, however, taxes are generally translated using the exchange rates in effect when the taxes are paid, and earnings are translated using the exchange rates in effect when the earnings are distributed, deemed distributed, or otherwise taken into account.[274] This means that taxes can be translated at rates that are very different from those rates used to translate the earnings to which they relate. As exchange rates vary, the effective foreign tax rate can be increased or decreased.

(b) FOREIGN BRANCHES

Translation rules for foreign branches are contained in I.R.C. § 987. In the case of any taxpayer with one or more QBUs with a functional currency other than the U.S. dollar, taxable income is determined under the rules set out in I.R.C. § 987. Each QBU foreign branch separately computes its taxable income or loss in its functional currency.[275] It then translates any income or loss into U.S. dollars at the weighted average exchange for its taxable year.[276] As a result, it is generally not possible for a taxpayer to

---

[270] *Id.*

[271] I.R.C. § 986(a)(1)(A).

[272] I.R.C. § 986(a)(1)(B)(ii).

[273] Bon Ami Co. v. Comm'r, 39 B.T.A. 825 (1939); Rev. Rul. 74-230, 1974-1 C.B. 187 (declared obsolete by Rev. Rul. 80-367, 1980-2 C.B. 386).

[274] I.R.C. § 986(b)(2).

[275] I.R.C. § 987(1). For a discussion of functional currency, see section 59.2(g).

[276] I.R.C. §§ 987(2), 989(b)(4).

recognize unrealized foreign currency gains or losses on a foreign branch's assets and obligations.[277]

When the profits are actually distributed, gain or loss attributable to the change in exchange rates between the time profits were earned and distributed is recognized by the corporation receiving the distribution.[278] The amount of gain or loss is based on the amount of foreign currency remitted, multiplied by the difference between the weighted average rate used to translate the profits on inclusion into income and the exchange rate on the date remitted.[279] The gain or loss is ordinary income, and it has the same source as the income to which it relates.

On June 26, 1989, the IRS issued Notice 89-74[280] to provide rules for translating the income of a foreign branch of a United States taxpayer (a QBU) that has a functional currency other than the U.S. dollar when the taxpayer credits, rather than deducts, foreign taxes. When Treasury regulations are issued, the rules in Notice 89-74 will be incorporated into the regulations.[281]

§ 59.6 MARK-TO-MARKET ACCOUNTING

At the end of the "Explanation of Provisions" section of proposed and temporary Treasury regulations issued on September 20, 1989, the Treasury stated that it was considering the adoption of a mark-to-market method of accounting for dealers in nonfunctional currency-denominated financial products.[282] The Treasury solicited comments on

---

[277] Because such gains or losses can only be effectively determined by using the spot or current rate, the use of the weighted average exchange rate (which takes into account exchange rate fluctuations throughout the year) prevents recognition of the effective unrealized gain or loss.

[278] I.R.C. § 987(3).

[279] TRA '86 Conf. Rep., *supra* note 2, at II-674 to II-675.

[280] 1989-1 C.B. 739 (June 26, 1989).

[281] Notice 89-74, 1989-1 C.B. 739 (June 26, 1989).

[282] T.D. 8265, 1989-2 C.B. 160.

the scope and methodology of such a procedure, and whether the methodology should be applied to taxpayers that were not dealers.[283]

The author believes that an election to use a mark-to-market method of accounting for all taxpayers (not just dealers) that engage in a large amount of foreign currency transactions would be a useful election. It could provide a simple solution to the difficult issues of timing gains and losses for foreign currency products.

§ 59.7 STRADDLE RULES

The foreign currency rules enacted as part of TRA '86 reflect a Congressional concern about identifying positions that are part of a straddle. The Conference Report to TRA '86 provided that "the Act clarifies the interaction of these rules and the tax straddle provisions, with a view towards providing an incentive for taxpayers to properly identify transactions that are part of a tax straddle."[284]

For a discussion of the Straddle Rules, see generally Part Eleven.

---

[283] *See* letter from Frank N. Panza, Vice President and General Tax Counsel, Fireman's Fund, to Commissioner of Internal Revenue (Dec. 19, 1989) (San Francisco Reinsurance Company's Comments on the Treasury Department's Proposed and Temporary Regulations Relating to the Taxation of Gains and Losses from Certain Foreign Currency Transactions under Section 988 of the Code), *reprinted in* 16 DAILY TAX HIGHLIGHTS & DOCUMENTS 105 (1990). *See also* letter from John F. Rolph III, Vice President & Director of Government Relations for Tax Legislation and Regulation, Citicorp, to Commissioner of Internal Revenue (Dec. 11, 1989) (discussing Section 988 Proposed and Temporary Regulations—Foreign Currency Transactions), *Foreign Currency Transactions*, Daily Tax Rep. (BNA) No. 238, at G-5 (Dec. 13, 1989).

[284] TRA '86 Conf. Rep., *supra* note 2, at II-667.

Part Fourteen
Notional Principal Contracts

Sixty

Notional Principal Contracts

§ 60.1 INTRODUCTION

The term "notional principal contract" is used to describe a wide variety of financial products.[1] What they all have in common is that they are bilateral agreements where one party agrees to pay another party, at specified intervals, amounts that are calculated by reference to a notional amount and a specified index, or one party pays an amount at the inception of the contract in return for payments to be made at specified intervals. These products are referred to as "notional principal" contracts because the principal amount is merely specified, rather than representing a real or actual amount of money. The contract has a notional principal amount because that amount is simply a "notion" or an "idea," for there is no actual exchange, investment, or borrowing of that amount. Common notional principal contracts include interest rate swaps, foreign currency swaps, forward rate agreements (although not technically notional principal contracts), interest rate caps, interest rate floors, and interest rate collars.

Established tax rules have not kept up with the development of notional principal contracts. In fact, at the date of this writing, the Treasury and the IRS have released temporary regulations and notices

---

[1] For a discussion of notional principal contracts, see generally Chapter 6.

that address only narrow issues for specific products and transactions.[2] As a result, the principal tax issues for evaluating notional principal contracts must be considered by making analogies to other areas of the tax laws.

The principal tax issues for financial products fall into five major categories.

- First, what is the character (capital or ordinary) of the income or loss from the product or transaction?
- Second, when is tax imposed? That is, when should a taxpayer report gain or loss?
- Third, how is the amount of the gain or loss calculated?
- Fourth, for transactions with a non-United States party, is the income from the financial product treated as United States-source income or foreign-source income?
- Fifth, are hybrid products issued by corporations more properly characterized as debt or equity interests?

The answers to many of these questions depend on how a financial product (or the taxpayer using the product) fits into certain established tax categories and rules. Therefore, frequent questions include:

- Is the product a section 1256 contract?
- Is the product an interest in actively traded property and, thus, do the Straddle Rules apply?
- Is the product a foreign currency transaction subject to the foreign currency tax provisions?
- Is the taxpayer a hedger, dealer, investor, or trader?

The problem with the taxation of notional principal contracts is that many of these products do not fit neatly into established tax categories

[2] Temp. Treas. Reg. § 1.988-1T(a)(2)(iii)(B)(2) (1989) defines a notional principal contract, for purposes of I.R.C. § 988 and the regulations promulgated thereunder, as "an interest rate swap, cap, floor, collar, or similar financial instrument that provides for the payment of amounts by one party to another at specified intervals measured by interest rates and notional principal amounts in exchange for specified consideration or a promise to pay similar amounts." For a discussion of I.R.C. § 988, see generally Chapter 59. Treas. Reg. § 1.863-7(a)(1) (1991) defines a notional principal contract as "a financial instrument that provides for the payment of amounts by one party to another at specified intervals calculated by reference to a specified index upon a notional principal amount in exchange for specified consideration or a promise to pay similar amounts."

and therefore it is unclear which tax rules apply to the product in question. To address the tax issues, the IRS's Office of the Chief Counsel formed a "Financial Products Group," which was announced on April 28, 1988.[3] This special interdisciplinary team of attorneys was directed to identify and analyze the "tax consequences associated with the new financial products being offered." On October 1, 1988, pursuant to a reorganization of the Treasury Department, the Financial Products Group was replaced with a new Treasury Department division known as the Office of the Assistant Chief Counsel—Financial Products and Institutions.

The accounting rules are also unclear. At the date of this writing, FASB has established the Emerging Issues Task Force, which devotes a significant amount of time addressing accounting issues with respect to financial products. In addition, in November 1987, FASB issued an 80-page "Exposure Draft" addressing "Disclosures about Financial Instruments," thereby launching a major project on financial instruments and off-balance-sheet financing.[4] A Revised Exposure Draft entitled "Disclosure of Information about Financial Instruments with Off-Balance-Sheet Risk and Financial Instruments with Concentrations of Credit Risk" was issued on July 21, 1989.[5] Further, in March 1990, FASB released Statement of Financial Accounting Standards No. 105, Disclosure of Information about Financial Instruments with Off-Balance-Sheet Risk and Financial Instruments with Concentrations of Credit Risk. Statement No. 105 is effective for fiscal years ending after June 15, 1990. Finally, on December 20, 1990, FASB announced that it will shortly propose that all companies disclose the market value, "if practicable to estimate," of all financial instruments (assets and liabilities).[6]

In addition, the Supreme Court decision of *Arkansas Best Corp. v. Comm'r*[7] leaves substantial uncertainty as to the correct tax treatment (capital or ordinary) for a number of financial hedging transactions. For a detailed discussion of *Arkansas Best*, see sections 8.4(d), 14.1, and 23.2(c)(4).

Unfortunately, needed guidance on the taxation of new financial products has not been and is not likely to be forthcoming in a timely manner. The issues are too complex and important to be resolved without careful

---

[3] Announcement 88-77, 1988-20 I.R.B. 48 (May 16, 1988).
[4] The comment period on the Exposure Draft ended, after one extension, on April 30, 1988.
[5] The comment period on the Revised Exposure Draft ended on September 19, 1989.
[6] Daily Tax Rep. (BNA) No. 246, at G-3 (Dec. 21, 1990).
[7] 485 U.S. 212 (1988), *aff'g* 800 F.2d 215 (8th Cir. 1986), *aff'g in part, rev'g in part* 83 T.C. 640 (1984).

consideration and deliberation. The best one can hope for is that, with time, sensible guidelines will ultimately be established.

This chapter addresses the tax considerations for notional principal contracts. It addresses swap transactions; interest rate caps, floors, and collars; and forward rate agreements.

§ 60.2 SWAP TRANSACTIONS

In general, a swap is an agreement between two parties to exchange a series of payments calculated on different bases: fixed rate interest payments exchanged for floating rate payments, U.S. dollar-denominated payments for nondollar-denominated payments, or payments tied to the price of one index for payments tied to the price of another index. All swap terms are negotiated between the parties, offering almost unlimited possibilities for future development as companies and financial institutions seek more effective ways of increasing their return on assets, decreasing their liabilities, and managing their balance sheet risks. For a discussion of swaps, see generally section 6.2.

The remainder of this section addresses the tax considerations for swap transactions. It addresses interest rate swaps, foreign currency swaps, commodity swaps, swap options, and zero coupon swaps. It also sets out withholding tax considerations.

(a) INTRODUCTION

In general, the relevant tax issues under a swap are the timing, character, and source of the gain or loss.

With respect to interest rate swaps—with the exception of Notice 89-21[8] (addressing the treatment of lump-sum payments with respect to notional principal contracts) and Treasury regulations dealing with the sourcing of interest rate swap income[9]—there is no direct authority on the income tax treatment of interest rate swap payments and receipts. Until the taxation of interest rate swaps is clarified in future legislation, Treasury pronouncements, and judicial decisions, swaps must be analyzed under general principles of tax law and by analogy to the treatment of similar financial instruments.

Analysis of the tax issues begins with the question: What is a swap? A number of definitions have been advanced. First, a swap might be viewed

---

[8] 1989-1 C.B. 651 (Feb. 9, 1989).
[9] Temp. Treas. Reg. § 1.861-9T (1989); Treas. Reg. § 1.863-7 (1991).

as a series of forward contracts (or futures contracts). Second, a swap might be viewed as a contract that is similar to a forward contract with a number of interim margin payment dates. Third, a swap might be viewed as a back-to-back loan transaction in which the parties have dispensed with the exchange of principal.[10] If swaps are viewed as forwards or futures, the tax rules applicable to forward contracts and futures would be the most analogous. If swaps are viewed as a forward-like contract with a number of interim margin payment dates, the transaction would remain open until the final payment date. If swaps are viewed as back-to-back loans, the interim payments would be accounted for as interest is accounted for.

With respect to foreign currency swaps, I.R.C. § 988, Notice 89-90,[11] and temporary Treasury regulations provide intricate tax rules for the treatment of foreign currency swaps. Although the principles of I.R.C. § 988 do not apply to interest rate swaps (because such swaps do not involve foreign currency), it is likely that interest rate swaps will be treated in a manner generally consistent with the treatment of foreign currency swaps. As a result, the rules that apply to foreign currency swaps are of great interest in examining other types of swaps.

The remainder of this section looks first at interest rate swaps and then at foreign currency swaps.

(b) INTEREST RATE SWAPS

An interest rate swap is a bilateral agreement whereby one party agrees to pay the other party, at specified intervals, amounts that are calculated by multiplying the notional principal amount by a specified index.[12] In return, the other party agrees to pay at specified intervals (which dates may or may not coincide with the dates set for payment by the first party) amounts that are calculated by multiplying the same notional amount by a different specified index. The most common interest rate swap is a fixed-for-floating swap. The party obligated to make the payment based on a fixed interest rate pays the same amount each payment date. The party obligated to make the payment based on a floating index (frequently LIBOR) calculates the payment to be made by multiplying the notional principal amount by the floating index on the specified date. When the specified intervals are the same for both parties, the payments are

---

[10] For a discussion of back-to-back loans, see section 6.2(b)(4).

[11] 1989-2 C.B. 407 (Aug. 14, 1989).

[12] For a discussion of interest rate swaps, see generally section 6.2(a).

typically netted, with the amount paid (or received) as the difference between the two payments.

Parties typically use interest rate swaps to synthetically convert interest income or interest expense from one index to another. For example, if a party has borrowed money at a floating rate, such as LIBOR plus one percent, and would rather fix its interest rate exposure, it could enter into a swap, under the terms of which it receives payments based on a floating rate and makes payments based on a fixed rate. The floating rate payments that it receives under the swap contract will match its interest obligation on the debt. Although the party remains obligated to make floating interest payments, the swap contract assures the availability of those funds. As long as the swap is in effect, the party's net exposure is the fixed payments that it is obligated to make under the swap contract. In this way, interest rate swaps alter the manner in which each party calculates its net economic interest expense or income for the period covered by the swap agreement.

In a typical interest rate swap, a borrower with a fixed rate liability (or whose most attractive direct borrowing opportunity is on a fixed rate basis) enters into an agreement with another party with a floating rate liability (or whose most attractive direct borrowing opportunity is on a floating rate basis) to swap interest payments equal to their respective interest payments for the terms of the borrowing. Thus, a party with a floating rate liability synthetically converts it into a fixed rate liability and vice versa. In effect, each party is servicing some, all, or more than the other party's interest obligation with payments calculated on the same basis as that obligation. Typically, the parties exchange only the net difference in the gross interest rate payments on the stated notional principal amount.[13] As a result—assuming payment dates match—only a net amount is due from one party to the other on any payment date. The parties can, however, agree to exchange gross interest rate payments, although this is much less common. For a discussion of interest rate swaps, see section 6.2(a). The remainder of this section addresses the tax considerations of interest rate swaps.

---

[13] The notional principal amount is usually the amount of the underlying liability (or asset).

(1) INTEREST RATE SWAP HEDGE TRANSACTIONS

Where an interest rate swap is entered into as a hedge, its income tax treatment must be analyzed in light of existing case law.[14] The vast majority of interest rate swaps are entered into as "hedges" of future interest income or expense. Many interest rate swaps are entered into simultaneously with a borrowing or lending transaction to produce an "integrated transaction" with a determinable series of cash flows. Other interest rate swaps "hedge" the net interest rate exposure of a taxpayer (rather than as a hedge of a single, specific transaction).

At the date of this writing, interest rate swaps are not "positions" in "actively traded personal property" subject to the Straddle Rules, because interest rate swaps are privately negotiated agreements between two parties and the underlying property is the U.S. dollar, which is not "personal property."[15] To the extent that the terms of interest rate swap agreements become standardized, such swaps may more closely resemble actively traded personal property. If interest rate swaps become actively traded, swaps could be viewed as positions in personal property.[16] As a result, interest rate swaps would then become subject to the Straddle Rules, except for those interest rate swaps that qualify as "hedges," which would be exempt from the Straddle Rules under I.R.C. §§ 1092(e) and 1256(e).[17]

(i) Periodic Swap Payments Prior to Swap Maturity

Interest rate swaps typically consist of the periodic "exchanges" of the notional principal amount multiplied by the specified rates. These interim payments could be viewed as:

1. Cash settlements with respect to a series of forward contracts that compose the swap contract

---

[14] For a discussion of the application of Arkansas Best Corp. v. Comm'r, 485 U.S. 212 (1988), aff'g 800 F.2d 215 (8th Cir. 1986), aff'g in part, rev'g in part 83 T.C. 640 (1984), to interest rate swap transactions, see section 60.2(b)(1)(i).

[15] For a discussion of the Straddle Rules as they may apply to notional principal contracts, see section 60.7. For a discussion of the Straddle Rules, see generally Part Eleven. For a discussion of "personal property," see section 48.2. For a discussion of "positions" in personal property, see section 48.3. For a discussion of "actively traded property," see section 48.2(a). For a discussion of "cash," see section 48.2(b).

[16] *See generally* Chapter 48.

[17] For a discussion of the hedging exemption, see generally section 23.2.

2. Interim payments with respect to a single forward contract that matures on the final payment date

3. Interest-like income that is properly accounted for under economic accrual principles,[18] or

4. An offset to the interest income or expense that the swap contract hedges

The tax consequences of the various characterizations are quite different. If the swap is viewed as a series of forward contracts, the interim payments are included in income when they are received. If the swap is viewed as a single forward contract, the interim payments would not be currently included in income, but rather the net receipts would be included when the swap contract ends. If the swap contract were viewed as a back-to-back loan, the interim payment would be recognized when interest income would be recognized (that is, a payment spanning tax years would be annualized—part reported in the first year, part the next year). If the swap contract were viewed as a hedge of an interest-bearing obligation, the interim payments could be viewed as adjustments to the interest on the hedged obligation. The interim payment would not be separately accounted for, but would instead offset the interest reported with respect to the hedged obligation.

At the date of this writing, there does not appear to be a consensus about what a swap is, but there does appear to be a consensus that interim payments are taxed periodically. The difference between treating interim payments as cash settlements with respect to a series of forward contracts and treating the interim payments as interest-like income is that under the former, the full amount of each payment is reported on the payment date, while under the latter, payments that span different tax years would be partially reported in two tax years.[19] The difference between treating the interim payments as interest-like income and treating the interim payments as an offset to interest income or expense is that under the former, the payments would be separately reported and (to the extent there is a difference between interest and other ordinary income) differently treated from the interest income or expense being hedged, while under the latter, the interim swap payments and the interest obligation that is being hedged creates synthetic interest. As of the date of this writing, the IRS has been considering treating the interim payments as

---

[18] "Economic accrual" is most likely an amortization method that is similar to the principles of OID as applied to debt securities. For a discussion of OID, see section 31.2.

[19] See Matthews, *Financial Product Guidance: Hedge Your Bets*, 42 TAX NOTES 910 (1989).

interest-like income—apparently because officials at the IRS consider economic accrual as the clearest reflection of income. Although some officials at the IRS are said to believe that treating interim payments as an offset to interest income or expense is appropriate when a swap is used as a hedge,[20] this application—along with other hedging issues—is currently stalled by the stalemate on the scope and application of *Arkansas Best Corp. v. Comm'r*.[21] It appears that interest rate swaps are taxed periodically (i.e., as payments are received by each party), rather than at the time the contract is offset or settled by delivery. These payments are viewed as ordinary income—whether part of a hedge or not—because there is no sale or exchange of property.[22] It also appears that periodic payments received under a swap must be accounted for as income by the recipient, despite the fact that in the next payment period, the amount of such payment—or a greater amount—may have to be returned to the other party.

Instead of payment on a gross basis, the offsetting amounts are generally netted so that only the difference is paid. Under the principles of the *Corn Products* doctrine, as limited by the Supreme Court decision in *Arkansas Best*,[23] these net payments or receipts should represent ordinary expense or income in the years paid or received if the swap is a hedge of interest income or expense.[24] Prior to *Arkansas Best*, many taxpayers reported the net payments under interest rate swaps as direct adjustments to their interest income or expense in the year received or paid. It is unclear whether the *Arkansas Best* decision has changed this result. Even a swap entered into to convert a fixed rate debt obligation into a floating rate obligation might reasonably be treated as an ordinary income transaction under an integration theory. For example, the economic substance of the combination of the fixed rate debt and the fixed-to-floating rate swap is a floating rate debt. The net periodic cash flow from the combined transactions could reasonably be viewed as interest expense.

---

[20] This is the approach that the Treasury has taken in foreign currency transactions where the Treasury has the statutory authority to adopt broad regulations under I.R.C. § 988.

[21] 485 U.S. 212 (1988), *aff'g* 800 F.2d 215 (8th Cir. 1986), *aff'g in part, rev'g in part* 83 T.C. 640 (1984).

[22] The "item" being exchanged is the U.S. dollar, and if dollars are the taxpayer's functional currency, they are not property for purposes of the Code.

[23] 485 U.S. 212 (1988), *aff'g* 800 F.2d 215 (8th Cir. 1986), *aff'g in part, rev'g in part* 83 T.C. 640 (1984).

[24] For a discussion of the *Corn Products* doctrine, see sections 8.4(d) and 23.2(d)(3)(i). For a discussion of *Arkansas Best*, see sections 8.4(d), 14.1, and 23.2(c)(4).

(ii) Up-Front and Assignment Fees

In Notice 89-21,[25] the IRS concluded that, with respect to notional principal contracts, up-front or lump-sum payments—including assignment fees received in connection with an assignment of a right to receive payments without a corresponding assumption of the obligation to make payments—must be recognized over the life of the contract (i.e., these payments must be amortized). In Notice 89-21, the IRS found that

> [I]n the case of a payment received during one taxable year with respect to a notional principal contract where such payment relates to the obligation to make a payment or payments in other taxable years under the contract, a method of accounting that properly recognizes such payment over the life of the contract clearly reflects income. Moreover, including the entire amount of such payment in income when it is received or deferring the entire amount of such payment to the termination of the contract does not clearly reflect income and is an impermissible method of accounting. The method of accounting prescribed in cases such as *Schlude v. Commissioner*, 372 U.S. 128 (1963), and *American Automobile Association v. United States*, 367 U.S. 687 (1961) does not clearly reflect income in the case of notional principal products.

Because the requirements for clear reflection of income are rules of general application, the amortization requirements of Notice 89-21 are required for all taxable years—even tax years prior to the date the notice was issued.

Notice 89-21 states that "no inference should be drawn" as to the treatment of transactions not properly characterized as notional principal contracts "to the extent that such transactions are in substance characterized as loans . . . [or] as an insurance contract or annuity contract."[26] The notice does not define notional principal contracts, other than to mention that they are "interest rate and currency swap contracts, interest rate cap contracts, and similar financial products." Treasury regulations, when issued, will need to define these terms and identify when a product is a notional principal contract rather than a loan,

---

[25] 1989-1 C.B. 651 (Feb. 9, 1989). For a discussion of Notice 89-21, see Winkler, *IRS Acts to Plug Big Loophole on Interest-Rate Swaps*, Wall St. J., Feb. 13, 1989, at C1, col. 1; letter and memorandum from Randall K.C. Kau to Dana L. Trier, Tax Legislative Counsel, U.S. Treasury Department (Apr. 3, 1989) (discussing interpretation and application of notional principal contract guidance in Notice 89-21), *reprinted in* 12 DAILY TAX HIGHLIGHTS & DOCUMENTS 605 (1989); Matthews, *Neff Defends Retroactive Notice on Notional Principal Contracts*, 43 TAX NOTES 390 (1989); Cantrell, Hanna & Kurtz, *Notice 89-21 Crashes the Interest Rate Swap Party, Special Report*, 45 TAX NOTES 337 (1989).

[26] Notice 89-21, 1989-1 C.B. 651 (Feb. 9, 1989).

insurance contract, annuity, or another contract that is not treated as a notional principal contract.

With respect to assignment fees where both the right to receive payments and the obligation to make payments are assigned, it appears that amortization is not required and that the taxpayer must include in income or expense such amounts when received or paid. The payments are lump-sum payments as to the taxpayer taking over the swap position, but they are termination payments to the taxpayer getting out of the swap. Lump-sum payments must be amortized, while termination payments are deductible when paid.

Notice 89-21 requires the use of a "reasonable amortization method." The exact method required is not clear, although at the date of this writing it is the author's understanding that Treasury officials are considering "economic accrual" as the appropriate amortization method for swaps. "Economic accrual" is most likely an amortization method that is similar to the principles of OID as applied to debt securities.[27] Until the Treasury sets out an amortization method that taxpayers must follow, Notice 89-21 allows a taxpayer to use any method that will clearly reflect the taxpayer's income. The IRS "will generally treat a method of accounting as clearly reflecting income if it takes such payments into account over the life of the contract under a reasonable amortization method, whether or not the method satisfies the specific rules in the forthcoming [Treasury] regulations."[28] The notice concludes that including the entire amount of an up-front or assignment fee in income when it is received—or deferring the entire amount of such payment to the termination of the contract—does not clearly reflect income and is viewed as an impermissible method of accounting.[29]

(iii) Termination Payments

Many of the provisions in swap agreements are designed to preserve the economic benefits of the contract if either party terminates the swap prior to its termination date. For example, a common termination clause provides that in the event of an early termination, the net "present value" of each payment stream under the swap is determined using the corresponding market interest rate prevailing on the termination date. The difference between these net present values is paid by the party required

---

[27] For a discussion of OID, see section 31.2.
[28] Notice 89-21, 1989-1 C.B. 651 (Feb. 9, 1989).
[29] *Id.*

to make the more valuable payment stream to the party required to make the less valuable payment stream.

There are no reported rulings, Treasury regulations, or other authority on the proper treatment of a termination payment by either the payor or the recipient. In an interest rate swap entered into as an "integrated hedge," a taxpayer might reasonably rely on an integration approach (similar to that applied to foreign currency swaps)[30] to treat the termination payment according t its economic substance.

If a floating rate borrower enters into a floating-to-fixed rate swap and the underlying borrowing and the swap are simultaneously terminated prior to maturity, any net termination payments under the swap might be treated as a deductible retirement premium with respect to the "synthetic fixed rate debt."[31] Any swap termination payment received might be treated as income from the partial discharge of the "synthetic fixed rate debt."

If an integration approach cannot be applied,[32] a party paying a swap termination payment could seek to deduct the payment as an ordinary and necessary business expense under I.R.C. § 162 by analogy to cases dealing with payments for release from business contracts.[33] Of course, *Arkansas Best*[34] must be considered to determine whether termination payments on swaps that are hedge transactions are treated as capital, rather than ordinary.

At the date of this writing, some taxpayers that are not swap dealers are finding on audit that IRS agents are treating termination payments as capital loss transactions when paid to close out unfavorable swap positions. The IRS has asserted that under I.R.C. § 1234A, capital gains and losses are recognized when a right or an obligation with respect to "actively traded personal property" that is a capital asset is cancelled, lapses, expires, or terminates. For I.R.C. § 1234A to apply to swap termination payments, however, swaps must first be capital assets, and second, they must be personal property of a type that is actively traded.[35]

---

[30] *See* section 60.2(c)(4).

[31] Treas. Reg. § 1.163-4(c) (1973).

[32] The Treasury has broad statutory authority under I.R.C. § 988 to adopt regulations. The IRS has not generally accepted integration theories absent a specific statutory grant of authority. *See* Monfort of Colorado, Inc. v. United States, 561 F.2d 190 (10th Cir. 1977), *aff'g* 406 F. Supp. 701 (D. Colo. 1976).

[33] *See* Pressed Steel Car Co. v. Comm'r, 20 T.C. 198 (1953), *acq.* 1956-2 C.B. 198.

[34] 485 U.S. 212 (1988), *aff'g* 800 F.2d 215 (8th Cir. 1986), *aff'g in part, rev'g in part* 83 T.C. 640 (1984).

[35] For a discussion of actively traded property, see section 48.2(a). For a discussion of personal property, see section 48.2.

Interest rate swaps might not be viewed as capital assets because the swap payments are made pursuant to a contract right and not as a sale or exchange of a capital asset. In addition, at the date of this writing, swaps are not personal property of the type that is actively traded.[36]

If the swap termination is a straight "unwind" with the payment of a termination fee, it is likely that the fee is taxable and reportable at that time. If, on the other hand, the swap termination is a "reverse mirror swap" (which means that two "reverse" swap transactions are in place simultaneously), the taxpayer should account for the existing swap and the new swap separately, which effectively amortizes the gain or loss on the transaction over the remaining swap term.[37] With a reverse mirror swap, the reverse swap is viewed as a separate transaction and the taxpayer has two separate transactions in place. Entering into a reverse mirror swap rather than terminating a losing swap can be used by a taxpayer to reduce the audit risk of having swap termination fees treated as capital losses. With two swaps in place, one produces a stream of ordinary income while the other swap produces a stream of ordinary expenses.

(2) INTEREST RATE SWAPS THAT ARE NOT HEDGE TRANSACTIONS

Swaps are also entered into by dealers in swaps, parties not eligible for hedging treatment, and (conceivably) parties that seek to speculate on interest rate movements.

At the date of this writing, interest rate swaps that are not hedges are exempt from the Straddle Rules. This is because interest rate swaps are not positions in actively traded personal property. For a discussion of the Straddle Rules, see section 60.7 and Part Eleven.

(i) Periodic Swap Payments for Swaps That Are Not Hedges

(a) CHARACTER OF PERIODIC SWAP PAYMENTS

Banks and dealers that, in the ordinary course of business, make a "market" in swaps, probably generate ordinary income or loss on the net periodic swap payments made or received under these swaps.

---

[36] For a discussion of the Straddle Rules, see section 60.7.

[37] For a discussion of reverse mirror swaps, see sections 6.2(g) and 60.2(b)(2)(ii).

The character of such income for traders and investors (assuming there are any investors in swaps) that enter into swaps to speculate on interest rate movements is not clear. The swap could arguably be viewed as analogous to a series of forward contracts, generating ordinary gain or loss on each periodic exchange because the "item" being exchanged is U.S. dollars, and if dollars are the taxpayer's functional currency, they are not property for purposes of the Code. The contractual right to receive a periodic swap payment in exchange for the specified swap payment could be viewed as a sale or exchange.[38] If the contractual right to receive periodic swap exchanges is not deemed to be a capital asset (or the net periodic payment is not deemed to constitute a sale or exchange of a capital asset), any gain or loss is treated as ordinary income for contracts on U.S. dollars.

A swap may also be viewed as analogous to gambling or wagering income, subject to the limitations under I.R.C. § 165(d).

Under either of those theories, the periodic payments are viewed as ordinary income.

(1) *Swap Payments Are Not Interest*

Swap payments should not be considered interest. Although swap payments appear to be similar to interest, any underlying debt obligations are not transferred to the other party and the swap parties do not establish a debtor–creditor relationship with each other. The classic definition of interest, as originally set out in *Old Colony R. Co. v. Comm'r*[39] and *Deputy v. Du Pont*,[40] limits interest to situations where there is an underlying indebtedness, defined as a "borrowing." In *Old Colony*, the Supreme Court defined interest as "the amount one has contracted to pay for the use of borrowed money." The Supreme Court's *Du Pont* decision relied on the definition of interest stated in *Old Colony*. The tax definition has not changed since these old Supreme Court cases.[41] In the Joint Committee Report that accompanied TRA '86, swap payments are described as follows: "Although in an interest rate swap . . . payments are

---

[38] *See* I.R.C. §§ 1001, 1221; National-Standard Co. v. Comm'r, 80 T.C. 551 (1983), *aff'd*, 749 F.2d 369 (6th Cir. 1984).

[39] 284 U.S. 552 (1932), *rev'g* 50 F.2d 896 (1st Cir. 1931), *rev'g* 18 B.T.A. 267 (1929).

[40] 308 U.S. 488 (1940), *rev'g* 103 F.2d 257 (3d Cir. 1939), *modifying* 22 F. Supp. 589 (D.C. Del. 1938).

[41] For a discussion of interest, see generally Chapter 25.

measured by interest payments, they are not viewed as interest because these are not paid as compensation for the use or forbearance of money."[42]

Although swap payments are not interest because there is no borrowing, the payments might be viewed—in some circumstances—as "synthetic interest" that is integrated with an existing debt obligation creating an offset to interest. This analysis would allow a taxpayer to get a net number. In addition, swap income might also be viewed as a substitute for interest, under an expansive reading of *Arkansas Best*. Finally, swap income might also be viewed as analogous to the "stream of income cases," which are also excepted from capital treatment under footnote five in the *Arkansas Best* decision that provides for ordinary income treatment for certain transactions.[43]

In Rev. Rul. 87-5,[44] the IRS considered whether a swap generated interest income. The IRS determined that a swap does not generate interest. Rather, swap payments were treated as payments other than interest. In Rev. Rul. 87-5, the IRS found that amounts received by a non-United States bank under a swap were exempt from United States tax because they were "industrial or commercial profits" exempt under the applicable tax treaty. Basically, the IRS used the process of elimination to reach its decision. Interest income is covered by the specific provisions of the tax treaty, and the IRS concluded that swap payments are not interest. The IRS found that swap payments were derived from the active conduct of a business and were not covered by other articles of the tax treaty—including the article that addressed interest income.[45]

Because a swap does not provide for the future advance of money other than the swap payments, a swap is not viewed as a standby commitment loan. In addition, swap payments are not viewed as the payment of interest on the other party's underlying indebtedness (if any). Rather, the payments are made pursuant to a contractual obligation established between the swap parties.

---

[42] STAFF OF THE JOINT COMM. ON TAXATION, 99TH CONG., 2D SESS., GENERAL EXPLANATION OF THE TAX REFORM ACT OF 1986, at 1077 (Joint Comm. Print 1986); *see also* SENATE FINANCE COMM. REPORT, S. REP. NO. 313, 99th Cong., 2d Sess. 142 (1986).

[43] For a discussion of footnote five in *Arkansas Best*, see section 14.1.

[44] 1987-1 C.B. 180.

[45] In the context of international transactions, the government has treated swap payments as equivalent to interest for purposes of I.R.C. § 863(e). For a discussion of the temporary Treasury regulations issued under I.R.C. § 863, see Temp. Treas. Reg. §§ 1.861-8T through 14T.

(2) *Swap Payments Are Not Made for the Purchase of Property*

Swap payments are not made for the purchase of property because they are made to purchase U.S. dollars.

(3) *Swap Payments Might Be Made for the Rendering of Services*

Swap payments may be viewed as payments for rendering services. In a swap, each party assumes a particular interest rate risk in exchange for the other party agreeing to assume the other party's interest rate risk. The parties are actually paying each other for providing a service of risk reduction. This makes swaps similar to guarantees, insurance, indemnities, and other services. In fact, the IRS has treated the assumption of credit risk through the guarantee of a loan as a personal service.[46]

(4) *Income Equivalent to Interest*

The IRS concluded in Notice 89-90,[47] that in certain instances where notional principal contracts are entered into for speculative purposes, the income attributable to the contract will be treated as income equivalent to interest under the Subpart F rules of I.R.C. § 954. In Notice 89-90, the IRS announced rules to be incorporated in final regulations with respect to the treatment under I.R.C. § 954(c)(1)(E) of income attributable to notional principal contracts that is denominated in the functional currency of, and that is earned by, a QBU (as defined in I.R.C. § 989(a)). Notional principal contracts subject to Notice 89-90 include an "interest rate swap agreement, an interest rate cap or floor agreement, or other similar contract."[48] The temporary regulations issued under I.R.C. § 861 address this issue.

(b) Timing and Amount of Periodic Swap Payments

It appears that net periodic payments are treated as ordinary income or loss in the year of each exchange. This is because the "item" being exchanged is U.S. dollars and if the dollars are the taxpayer's functional currency, they are not "property" for purposes of the Code.

---

[46] *See, e.g.,* LTR 8508003 (Nov. 9, 1984); LTR 7822005 (Feb. 22, 1978).
[47] 1989-2 C.B. 407 (Aug. 14, 1989).
[48] Notice 89-90, 1989-2 C.B. 407 (Aug. 14, 1989).

For accrual basis taxpayers, periodic swap payments should be included in income, or deducted, when the amount is fixed and determinable. For cash basis taxpayers, such periodic payments should be included in income or deducted when paid or received.[49]

(c) Up-Front and Assignment Fees

As in the case of swaps entered into to hedge other assets, up-front swap fees, as well as certain assignment fees for speculative swaps, must be amortized under the provisions of Notice 89-21.[50]

(d) Source of Income for Periodic Swap Payments

For a discussion of the source rules for notional principal contracts, see generally section 60.5(a).

(ii) Treatment of Termination of Swaps That Are Not Hedges

Termination payments made or received in the ordinary course of business by a swap dealer are probably treated as ordinary income or loss. If a taxpayer is a dealer in swaps, the taxpayer might be able to elect, on a consistent basis, to inventory its swaps at the lower of cost or market. It is possible, however, that swaps cannot be treated as "inventory" in the common tax meaning, because it is not clear whether a swap is an asset or a liability.[51] In addition, swap dealers do not buy and sell swaps. Rather, they act as principals in the swap market, and their dealer function comes from taking both sides of the market.[52]

Swap dealers may argue that their swap positions can be inventoried. To do so, however, the swap dealer would have to meet one of two requirements. First, the swap dealer would need to qualify as a "dealer in securities" under Treas. Reg. § 1.471-5.[53] Second, the swap dealer would need to qualify as a taxpayer for whom "the production, purchase, or sale

---

[49] It is the author's understanding that there have been discussions at the Treasury over treating cash basis taxpayers as if they are accrual basis taxpayers for purposes of periodic swap payments.

[50] 1989-1 C.B. 651 (Feb. 9, 1989). For a discussion of Notice 89-21, see section 60.2(b)(1)(ii).

[51] For a discussion of inventory methods, see generally section 22.2.

[52] For a discussion of dealers, see generally section 8.3 and Chapter 11.

[53] (1987). For a discussion of dealers in securities, see section 8.3(a).

of merchandise is an income-producing factor" under the general provisions of Treas. Reg. § 1.471-1.[54]

There is an additional problem faced by swap dealers. It may not be possible for a swap dealer to assign a purchase cost to a swap that is both an asset and a liability in the swap dealer's hands.

The IRS could attempt to assert, under the principles of G.C.M. 39,198,[55] that swaps generate ordinary gain or loss because they are "held for sale to customers" but are not "inventory" under the statutory construction of I.R.C. § 1221(1) (which uses the disjunctive to distinguish between inventory property and property held for sale to customers in the ordinary course of business).

For traders and investors, the tax treatment of termination payments made or received by parties entering into interest rate swaps is less clear. The swap termination might not be a sale or exchange, even if the swap party's rights under the agreement constitute a capital asset. I.R.C. § 1234A does not appear to treat the swap termination as a sale or exchange, because the swap agreement is not a section 1256 contract under I.R.C. § 1234A(2), and it is arguably not a "right or obligation with respect to personal property" (because it only contemplates the delivery of U.S. dollars) under I.R.C. § 1234A(1).[56]

Further, the swap termination payment would not be treated as a sale or exchange to the recipient under I.R.C. § 1271(a)(1) because the swap does not constitute a debt obligation. In the absence of a sale or exchange, any gain or loss on the termination would presumably be ordinary.

A swap termination can be viewed as the termination of an executory contract, and the termination fee consists of liquidated damages for the cancellation. The settlement amount is frequently calculated in the same way as expectation damages.[57]

Many taxpayers take the position that termination payments are currently includable and deductible as ordinary and necessary business expenses (under I.R.C. § 162) for expenses incurred in a trade or business—by analogy to cases dealing with payments for releases from disadvantageous business contracts.[58] If a payment does not qualify as an ordinary and necessary business expense under I.R.C. § 162, the payment

---

[54] (1958).

[55] (Apr. 5, 1984).

[56] For a discussion of I.R.C. § 1234A, see section 58.2.

[57] Under the analysis in footnote five of the *Arkansas Best* decision, income is treated as ordinary because it represents the present fair market value of the forgone income stream.

[58] *See, e.g., Pressed Steel Car Co.*, 20 T.C. 198 (1953), *acq.* 1956-2 C.B. 198. For a discussion of ordinary and necessary business expenses under I.R.C. § 162, see section 10.1.

might be deductible under I.R.C. § 212 (as investment expenses or expenses incurred to produce income)—subject to the two percent floor on section 212 expenses under I.R.C. § 67 (for tax years beginning after December 31, 1986).[59] As a result, a taxpayer may be able to deduct these payments under I.R.C. §§ 162 or 212. If the taxpayer has been integrating net swap income or expense against its interest income or expense, the termination payment should be integrated as well—that is, amortized over the remaining life of the underlying debt obligation.[60]

This treatment appears to depend on the argument that the swap contract itself is not a capital asset and therefore entitled to ordinary treatment.[61] But, as a result of *Arkansas Best*, ordinary income may not be generated—even if the swap is intricately connected to the taxpayer's trade or business. If a payment is not deductible under either I.R.C. § 162 or I.R.C. § 212, the payment might be viewed as a capital loss subject to the limitations on capital losses,[62] or as a capital expenditure that might be deductible as depreciation or amortization.

If—instead of terminating the swap—the dealer, trader, or investor sold its rights under the swap (or paid a third party to assume its obligation under the swap), a different treatment might be in order. Notice 89-21 provides that where a taxpayer receives a lump-sum payment in connection with an assignment of its right to receive payments, but without a corresponding assignment of the obligation to make payments, the taxpayer must amortize the fees received over the life of the contract. Notice 89-21 provides that this result is required by the "clear reflection of income" rule in I.R.C. § 446(b).[63]

Notice 89-21 does not address the tax treatment of lump sums received where both the right to receive and the obligation to pay are simultaneously assigned. Presumably, in such instances, the full amount must be immediately included in income by the party terminating the swap position. The party taking over the swap position is treated as making (or receiving) a lump-sum payment at that time. In situations not covered by

---

[59] For a discussion of so-called section 212 expenses, see section 9.1. For a discussion of the two percent floor, see section 9.1(d).

[60] However, the IRS has not generally accepted integration theories absent a specific statutory grant of regulatory authority. *See* I.R.C. § 988; *Monfort of Colorado, Inc.*, 561 F.2d 190 (10th Cir. 1977), *aff'g* 406 F. Supp. 701 (D. Colo. 1976).

[61] This analysis addresses the swap contract itself, not the periodic payments that are ordinary because they cover U.S. dollars.

[62] For a discussion of the limitation on capital losses, see sections 15.4(b) and 15.5(b).

[63] Because the requirements for clear reflection of income are rules of general application, the amortization requirements of Notice 89-21 are required for all taxable years—even years prior to the date of the notice.

Notice 89-21, the disposition of the swap might be considered a sale or exchange, and the party terminating the swap position would treat any gain or loss as capital. If a third party receives a payment to assume a "below water" swap (i.e., a losing swap position), the third party might have to amortize the amount received because it would probably be covered by Notice 89-21—the lump sum would represent amounts to be paid in other taxable years under the swap.

Finally, there is the question of the tax treatment of a reverse mirror swap. A "reverse mirror swap" is simply a method by which a party gets out of a swap by entering into another swap with a third party, which is the reverse position of the original swap. The tax treatment should be the same as that of the original swap, because the reversal of a swap consists of establishing a second swap. It does not close out or affect the first swap. The reasons for entering into the swap are the same—the parties to the swap perform the same service of assuming interest rate risks for their counterparties. The obligations each party undertakes in a mirror swap are identical to the obligations each has undertaken in a primary swap. The only difference is that the reversing party enters into a contract with another party to assume the risk of an opposite movement in rates.[64]

(c) FOREIGN CURRENCY SWAPS

(1) INTRODUCTION

Foreign currency swaps generally involve the purchase of one currency and the sale of, or investment in, a second currency. The basic foreign currency swap is essentially a repurchase agreement and is typically recorded as two foreign exchange contracts. Foreign currency swaps are routinely used by banks and other financial institutions in setting their rates for forward foreign exchange transactions. In addition, they are essential to multinational corporations in hedging their foreign exchange exposures.

In a typical foreign currency swap, the parties buy and sell currencies (e.g., Japanese yen for U.S. dollars) in the spot market and agree to sell and buy the currencies at a future date. At the future date, the parties settle the forward contract either by re-exchanging the principal amounts in the respective currencies at the agreed rate, or paying the difference to the "winning" party in the specified currency.

---

[64] Of course, looked at economically, the taxpayer has terminated the liability under the swap contract and his profit or loss can be calculated.

If a foreign currency is selling at a premium to the U.S. dollar in the forward market, a swap out of the U.S. dollar into that currency (through a spot sale and forward purchase) will produce a gain, while a swap out of that currency into the U.S. dollar will produce a loss. If, on the other hand, a foreign currency is selling at a discount in the forward market, a swap out of the U.S. dollar will produce a loss, while a swap into the U.S. dollar will produce a gain. The gain or loss inherent in such a currency swap can be calculated at the time the transaction is entered into at an annualized percentage rate. For a discussion of foreign currency swaps, see generally section 6.2(b). The taxation of foreign currency swaps is generally governed by I.R.C. § 988 and temporary Treasury regulations.[65] The remainder of this section addresses those rules.

(2) DEFINITION OF FOREIGN CURRENCY SWAPS

A foreign currency swap is defined in Temp. Treas. Reg. § 1.988-5T(a)(4)(ii)[66] as a contract involving two different currencies between two or more parties to (1) exchange periodic interim payments at the swap exchange rate on or prior to maturity of the contract, and (2) exchange the swap principal amount upon maturity of the agreement. In addition, a currency swap can also require an exchange of the swap principal amount on commencement of the agreement.[67] The definition of a foreign currency swap contained in the temporary Treasury regulations can be applied by a taxpayer in lieu of the definition of a swap agreement set out in Notice 87-11,[68] to those transactions entered into after December 31, 1986.[69]

(3) FOREIGN CURRENCY SWAPS ARE NOT SECTION 1256 CONTRACTS

A foreign currency swap is not a section 1256 contract[70] and therefore is subject to ordinary treatment.[71] The IRS ruled in LTR 8818010[72] that a

---

[65] For a discussion of I.R.C. § 988, see generally Chapter 59.
[66] (1989).
[67] Temp. Treas. Reg. § 1.988-5T(a)(4)(ii) (1989).
[68] 1987-1 C.B. 423 (Jan. 26, 1987).
[69] Temp. Treas. Reg. § 1.988-5T(a)(4)(iv) (1989).
[70] For a discussion of section 1256 contracts, see generally Part Ten.
[71] I.R.C. § 988 (as clarified by TMRA '88, Pub. L. No. 100-647, 102 Stat. 3342 (1988) [hereinafter TMRA '88]).
[72] (Feb. 4, 1988).

nonfunctional currency swap is not a section 1256 contract, but is rather a financial instrument similar to a forward contract, futures contract, or option and thus is considered a section 988 transaction.[73] In addition, the IRS ruled that foreign currency swap agreements are not "foreign currency contracts" subject to section 1256 treatment.[74] Swaps are not foreign currency contracts under I.R.C. §§ 1256(g)(2)(A)(ii) and (iii) because they are distinguishable from bank forward contracts in the way interest rate differentials are accounted in the underlying currencies.[75] Currency swaps typically account for interest rate differentials through a present and continuing exchange of notional interest payments over the life of the agreements, while bank forward contracts typically account for such differences at maturity. LTR 8818010 was effectively codified by the passage of TMRA '88, which provided that only RFCs and nonequity options subject to section 1256 treatment would be excluded from section 988 treatment.[76] Thus, even if a swap were covered by I.R.C. § 1256, it would still be subject to section 988 treatment because it is neither an RFC nor a nonequity option.[77]

(4) SECTION 988 TREATMENT

Foreign currency swaps are subject to section 988 treatment. As a result, the foreign currency gain or loss on such transactions is treated as domestic source ordinary income or loss that is realized when the taxpayer sells, exchanges, or disposes of the position. The capital gain election under I.R.C. § 988(a)(1)(B) is not available.[78]

Section 988 transactions include forward contracts, futures contracts, options, and similar financial instruments.[79] A forward contract, futures contract, option, warrant, or similar financial instrument that is not a foreign currency-based RFC or nonequity option is within the definition

---

[73] For a discussion of section 988 transactions, see section 59.2.

[74] Prior to TMRA '88, *supra* note 71, all section 1256 contracts were "carved-out" from section 988 treatment. For a discussion of foreign currency contracts subject to section 1256 treatment, see section 44.2.

[75] LTR 8818010 (Feb. 4, 1988).

[76] I.R.C. § 988(c)(1)(D)(i). For a discussion of RFCs, see section 44.1. For a discussion of nonequity options, see section 44.3.

[77] If the swap market were to evolve to the point of centralized clearing and margining, the CFTC might seek jurisdiction over swaps as futures contracts. For a discussion of "what is a futures contract," see section 4.1(b).

[78] Currency swaps are not "described in [Temp. Treas. Reg.] § 1.988-2T(d)," a requirement for this election. Temp. Treas. Reg. § 1.988-3T(b) (1989). For a discussion of the election available under I.R.C. § 988(a)(1)(B), see section 59.2(b)(3).

[79] I.R.C. § 988(c)(1)(B)(iii) (*as amended by* TMRA '88, *supra* note 71, § 6130).

of a section 988 transaction[80] if the underlying property to which it relates is a nonfunctional currency, or it is otherwise described in Temp. Treas. Reg. § 1.988-1T(a)(1)(iii).[81] In addition, the amount required to be paid, or entitled to be received, must be denominated in a nonfunctional currency or must be determined by reference to the value of the foreign currency.[82] The term, "similar financial instrument," includes notional principal contracts (e.g., swaps, caps, collars, and floors) and "similar financial products," if the payments required to be made or received under the contract are determined with reference to a nonfunctional currency.[83]

If a foreign currency swap qualifies as a section 988(d) hedge (including the various identification requirements), the swap and the underlying transaction qualify for integrated treatment as a single synthetic debt instrument.[84] If a foreign currency swap is improperly identified as a section 988 hedge, it would presumably be treated under the general section 988 transaction provisions.[85]

(5) TIMING OF INCOME AND EXPENSES

(i) Lump-Sum Payments

Under Notice 89-21,[86] lump-sum payments or receipts received in one taxable year, but attributable to another year, must be amortized over the life of the contract.[87] The temporary Treasury regulations elaborate on Notice 89-21 as it relates to "off-market currency swaps." In Temp. Treas. Reg. § 1.988-2T(e)(3),[88] an off-market currency swap is defined as a currency swap "under which the present value of the payments to be made is not equal to that of the payments to be received on the day the taxpayer enters into or acquires the contract (exclusive of the swap premium or discount, as defined in [Temp. Treas. Reg. § 1.988-2T](e)(3)(ii))."[89] In an off-market currency swap, to the extent a lump-sum amount is attributable to the difference between the swap exchange rate

---

[80] For a discussion of section 988 transactions, see section 59.2.
[81] For a discussion of nonfunctional currency, see section 59.2(g)(2).
[82] Temp. Treas. Reg. § 1.988-1T(a)(2)(iii)(A) (1989).
[83] Temp. Treas. Reg. § 1.988-1T(a)(2)(iii)(B) (1989).
[84] For a discussion of section 988(d) hedging transactions, see section 23.3.
[85] For a discussion of section 988 transactions, see generally section 59.2.
[86] 1989-1 C.B. 651 (Feb. 9, 1989).
[87] For a discussion of Notice 89-21, see generally sections 60.2(b)(1)(ii) and 60.2(b)(2)(ii).
[88] (1989).
[89] Temp. Treas. Reg. § 1.988-2T(e)(3)(i) (1989).

and the spot rate, the lump-sum amount is taken into account on the date the final exchange of principal amounts is taken into account. If the lump-sum amount is attributable to the difference in values of the periodic payments, the lump-sum amount is amortized under economic accrual concepts.[90]

(ii) Periodic Interim Payments

For purposes of determining the timing of income and expense for periodic interim payments in a foreign currency swap, payments made under the swap are treated "as payments made pursuant to a hypothetical borrowing that is denominated in the currency in which payments are required to be made (or are determined with reference to) under the swap."[91] Payments received under the swap are treated as "payments received pursuant to a hypothetical loan that is denominated in the currency in which payments are received (or are determined with reference to) under the swap."[92] This means that each stream of payments under the currency swap is treated as a hypothetical loan in the currency of the periodic interim payments. The hypothetical issue price of the hypothetical borrowing and loan is the swap principal amount.[93] The hypothetical stated redemption price at maturity is the total of all payments (excluding any exchange of the swap principal amount at the inception of the contract) provided under the hypothetical borrowing or loan, other than periodic interest payments under the principles of I.R.C. § 1273.[94]

For purposes of determining the timing and amount of the periodic interim payments, the principles regarding the amortization of interest[95] apply to the hypothetical interest expense and income of the hypothetical borrowing and loan.[96] The principles regarding the amortization of inter-

---

[90] The principles used in the OID rules, including the concept of "yield to maturity," reflect economic accrual. *See generally* I.R.C. §§ 1271–1274. Under Prop. Treas. Reg. § 1.1272-1(f) (1986), "yield to maturity" is defined as "that interest rate that when used in computing the present value of all payments of principal and interest to be paid in connection with a debt instrument produces an amount equal to the issue price."

[91] Temp. Treas. Reg. § 1.988-2T(e)(2)(ii)(A)(1) (1989).

[92] Temp. Treas. Reg. § 1.988-2T(e)(2)(ii)(A)(2) (1989).

[93] Temp. Treas. Reg. § 1.988-2T(e)(2)(ii)(A) (1989).

[94] *Id.*

[95] *See generally* I.R.C. §§ 163(e), 1272–1275.

[96] Temp. Treas. Reg. § 1.988-2T(e)(2)(ii)(A)(2) (1989).

est do not apply to determine the time when principal is deemed to be paid on the hypothetical borrowing and loan.⁹⁷

The amount that is treated as exchange gain or loss by the taxpayer (with respect to the periodic interim payments for the taxable year) is the amount of hypothetical interest income and exchange gain or loss attributable to the interest income from the hypothetical borrowing and loan for the year, minus the amount of hypothetical interest expense and exchange gain or loss attributable to the interest expense from the hypothetical borrowing and loan for such year.⁹⁸

(iii) Principal Payments

Exchange gain or loss with respect to the principal amount of a currency swap is realized on the day the units of swap principal in each currency are exchanged—that is, at the maturity of the swap agreement.⁹⁹ Under Temp. Treas. Reg. § 1.988-5T(a)(4)(ii)(A)(2),¹⁰⁰ the entire swap principal amount must be exchanged upon maturity of the contract.

Gain or loss on the exchange of the swap principal amount is determined "on the date of the exchange by subtracting the value (on such date) of the units of swap principal paid, from the value of the units of swap principal received."¹⁰¹ These provisions do not apply to an equal exchange of the swap principal amount at the commencement of the agreement at a market exchange rate.¹⁰²

(iv) Anti-Abuse Rule

If the taxpayer's method of accounting for income, expense, gain, or loss attributable to a foreign currency swap does not clearly reflect income, the IRS can "apply principles analogous to those of [I.R.C.] section 1274 or such other rules as the Commissioner deems appropriate to determine the hypothetical issue price, the hypothetical stated redemption price at

---

[97] Temp. Treas. Reg. § 1.988-2T(e)(2)(ii)(A), referring to Temp. Treas. Reg. §§ 1.988-2T(d)(2)(iii) and 1.988-2T(d)(5), Example (2), with respect to the time when principal is deemed to be paid.

[98] Temp. Treas. Reg. § 1.988-2T(e)(2)(ii)(A) (1989). The general rule under Temp. Treas. Reg. § 1.988-2T(b) is that interest income or expense is determined in units of nonfunctional currency and is translated into functional currency at the average spot rate over the interest period.

[99] Temp. Treas. Reg. § 1.988-2T(e)(2)(iii) (1989).

[100] (1989).

[101] Temp. Treas. Reg. § 1.988-2T(e)(2)(iii) (1989).

[102] *Id.*

maturity, and the amounts required to be taken into account within a taxable year."[103]

(v) Disposition or Termination

Any gain or loss on the disposition or termination of a currency swap is treated as exchange gain or loss.[104]

(6) SOURCE

Exchange gains or losses in section 988 transactions are subject to a residence-based source rule. In fact, I.R.C. § 988(b)(3) provides that all gain or loss from notional principal contracts involving nonfunctional currency is treated as exchange gain or loss and is to be sourced by reference to the taxpayer's residence. For a discussion of the source rules under I.R.C. § 988, see section 59.2(d).

The temporary Treasury regulations generally extend the residence-based source rules to all notional principal contracts, irrespective of whether the contracts are denominated in a nonfunctional currency.[105] For a discussion of the sourcing rules for notional principal contracts, see section 60.5(a).

(7) CHARACTER

All currency exchange gain or loss is treated as ordinary income or expense under I.R.C. § 988. For a detailed discussion of the character of gains and losses under I.R.C. § 988, see section 59.2(b). The temporary Treasury regulations issued under I.R.C. § 988 incorporate this rule for currency swaps as defined in Temp. Treas. Reg. § 1.988-5T(a)(4)(ii).[106]

(d) COMMODITY SWAPS

A commodity swap is simply a variation on a plain vanilla interest rate swap[107]—the only difference being that the index is the spot price of a commodity index, and the notional principal amount is expressed in terms of an agreed-to quantity of the given commodity. As with many

---

[103] Temp. Treas. Reg. § 1.988-2T(e)(2)(iv) (1989).
[104] Temp. Treas. Reg. § 1.988-2T(e)(4) (1989).
[105] Temp. Treas. Reg. § 1.988-4T(a) (1989).
[106] Temp. Treas. Reg. § 1.988-2T(e)(2)(i) (1989).
[107] For a discussion of plain vanilla interest rate swaps, see section 6.2(a)(1).

interest rate and foreign currency swaps, commodity swaps are typically entered into as hedges or risk-shifting transactions by producers and users.

(1) COMMODITY SWAP HEDGE TRANSACTIONS

When a commodity swap is used to hedge a commodity that is an inventory item in the taxpayer's hands, the income or loss with respect to the commodity swap is treated as ordinary under the *Corn Products* doctrine as limited by *Arkansas Best*.[108]

Certain financial intermediations that run "matched books" of commodity swaps would not be hedging inventories of commodities. Rather, they are using the offsetting swap positions to hedge other commodity swap positions. There is an open question as to whether these activities constitute hedging under the *Arkansas Best* decision.

Commodity swaps are "positions" in "actively traded personal property" subject to the Straddle Rules if the commodity upon which the swap is based is an actively traded commodity. For a discussion of application of the Straddle Rules to notional principal contracts, see section 60.7. For a discussion of the Straddle Rules, see generally Part Eleven.

(i) Periodic Swap Payments Prior to Swap Maturity

There are a number of ways to analyze a commodity swap. First, a commodity swap can be viewed as a series of forward contracts. Second, it can be viewed as a single forward contract with interim payments. Third, it can be viewed as interest-like payments with respect to hypothetical back-to-back loans of the commodity.

Periodic payments are currently included in income if the commodity swap is viewed as a series of forward contracts or as interest-like payments with respect to back-to-back loans of the commodity. Arguably, the periodic payments are not included in income until maturity of the swap if it is viewed as a single forward contract with interim payments.

---

[108] 485 U.S. 212 (1988), aff'g 800 F.2d 215 (8th Cir. 1986), aff'g in part, rev'g in part 83 T.C. 640 (1984). For a discussion of the *Corn Products* doctrine, see section 23.2(d)(3)(i). For a discussion of *Arkansas Best*, see sections 8.4(d), 14.1, and 23.2(c)(4).

(ii) Up-Front and Assignment Fees

Up-front or lump-sum payments made with respect to notional principal contracts must be recognized over the life of the contract.[109]

(iii) Termination Payments

If the swap is hedging a commodity that is inventory in the hands of the taxpayer, the termination payment would be treated as ordinary under the *Corn Products* decision[110] as limited by *Arkansas Best*.[111] Both the payor and the recipient would currently include the termination payments.

Certain financial intermediations that run "matched books" of commodity swaps would not be hedging inventories of commodities, but are using the offsetting positions to hedge other commodity swaps. There is an open question as to whether these activities constitute hedging under the *Arkansas Best* decision.

(2) COMMODITY SWAPS NOT USED AS HEDGES

Commodity swaps are entered into by taxpayers that are not hedgers. Banks and dealers make "markets" in commodity swaps, while investors and traders could conceivably enter into commodity swaps for speculative purposes.

(i) Periodic Swap Payments

For traders and investors, the character of such income is not clear. The swap could arguably be viewed as analogous to a series of forward contracts generating capital gain or loss on each periodic exchange. The contractual right to receive a periodic swap payment in exchange for the specified swap payment could be viewed as a sale or exchange. Any gain or loss could also possibly be treated as ordinary income, under an analogy to gambling and wagering income (subject to the limitation on losses under I.R.C. § 165(d)).

---

[109] Notice 89-21, 1989-1 C.B. 651 (Feb. 9, 1989). For a discussion of Notice 89-21, see sections 60.2(b)(1)(ii) and 60.2(b)(2)(ii).

[110] Corn Prods. Ref. Co. v. Comm'r, 350 U.S. 46 (1955), *aff'g* 215 F.2d 513 (2d Cir. 1954), *aff'g* 20 T.C. 503 (1953), *aff'g* 11 T.C.M. (CCH) 721 (1952), *aff'g* 16 T.C. 395 (1951), *reh'g denied*, 350 U.S. 943 (1956).

[111] 485 U.S. 212 (1988), *aff'g* 800 F.2d 215 (8th Cir. 1986), *aff'g in part, rev'g in part* 83 T.C. 640 (1984).

(ii) Timing and Amount

The net periodic payments under commodity swaps are likely to be treated as income or loss as paid or received by the taxpayer. If so, the issue would be whether there are intraperiod allocations under economic accrual principles. Up-front and assignment fees must be amortized under the provisions of Notice 89-21.[112] Termination payments are taken into account when they are received by the taxpayer.

(e) SWAP OPTIONS

(1) IN GENERAL

Swap options, or "swaptions," are swaps that include option features. The most common option features are straightforward put or call options to hedge against interest rate swings. But swaptions are an area of enormous innovation and now include options on the spread, as well as options to enter, extend, or cancel a swap.

The swaption market takes its terminology from the options market. In general, a swaption buyer ("holder") has the right, but not the obligation, for a specified period of time, to pay or receive a fixed swap rate. A swaption seller ("writer") is obligated to perform if and when the holder exercises the option. Calls and puts are the two "types" of options. A swaption call, for example, provides the holder with a right to receive the fixed rate stream of payments. A swaption put provides the holder with the right to pay the fixed rate stream of payments. If the holder exercises its option, the parties enter into a swap on the terms specified in the option contract. If the holder does not exercise its option prior to the expiration date, the option expires and the parties have no further obligations under the swaption. For a discussion of swaptions, see section 6.2(d).

The basic tax issue with a swaption is whether a swaption should be treated as a type of a swap, or as a traditional option (albeit on a nontraditional product). If a swaption is treated as a type of swap, the premium paid would be an up-front payment that must be amortized under the provisions of Notice 89-21[113] from the time the option is entered into.[114] If, on the other hand, a swaption is treated as a traditional option,

---

[112] 1989-1 C.B. 651 (Feb. 9, 1989). For a discussion of Notice 89-21, see sections 60.2(b)(1)(ii) and 60.2(b)(2)(ii).

[113] 1989-1 C.B. 651 (Feb. 9, 1989).

[114] For a discussion of Notice 89-21, see generally sections 60.2(b)(1)(ii) and 60.2(b)(2)(ii).

the premium is not accounted for until the option lapses or is exercised. If the swaption is exercised, the taxpayer enters into a swap and the premium will be amortized over the life of the swap entered into after exercise.

If a swaption is viewed as an option, Notice 89-21[115]—with its requirement to amortize up-front payments under interest rate caps or floors and front-loaded or back-loaded payments under interest rate swaps—does not apply to swaptions prior to exercise. As a result, even if swaptions provide economic results similar to interest rate caps, floors, or swaps, they may provide different tax results.

The remainder of this section addresses the tax considerations for swaptions. Obviously, because the taxation of interest rate swaps is unresolved at the date of this writing, the tax considerations of swaptions—which incorporate elements of both swaps and options—can be even more complicated.

(2) CHARACTER

Under I.R.C. §§ 1234(a) and 1234A, one looks to the character of the underlying property to determine the character of the option. This provision applies to swaptions. For an interest rate swap, the underlying property is cash and, therefore, the character is ordinary. Commodity swaps are more problematic, however, but if the underlying commodity is part of the taxpayer's inventory, the character is probably treated as ordinary.[116]

If swaptions are viewed as options, the character of gain or loss on certain types of options is addressed in I.R.C. § 1234. For a discussion of the tax rules that apply to options, see generally Chapter 30.

(3) TIMING

If a swaption is viewed as an option, it is treated as open until the option is exercised, lapses, or is terminated.[117]

If, on the other hand, the swaption is treated as a swap, Notice 89-21[118] would apply to require amortization of the swaption premium.[119] Of

---

[115] 1989-1 C.B. 651 (Feb. 9, 1989).

[116] For a discussion of inventory methods, see section 22.2.

[117] See Rev. Rul. 58-234, 1958-1 C.B. 279; Rev. Rul. 78-182, 1978-1 C.B. 265. For a discussion of the tax rules that apply to options, see generally Chapter 30.

[118] 1989-1 C.B. 651 (Feb. 9, 1989).

[119] For a discussion of Notice 89-21, see sections 60.2(b)(1)(ii) and 60.2(b)(2)(ii).

course, the appropriate amortization schedule raises real unresolved questions. If Notice 89-21 applies to require amortization, must the swap premium be amortized over the life of the option portion, the life of the swap, or the life of both the option and the swap?

When a swaption is exercised, it appears that the premium must be amortized over the life of the swap under the provisions of Notice 89-21. It also appears that the writer takes the premium into income and the holder deducts the premium from income over the life of the swap that is entered into on exercise.

As of the date of this writing, many taxpayers defer recognition of the swaption premium until the swaption is exercised or lapses. If the swaption lapses, the premium is recognized at that time. If the swaption is exercised, the premium is amortized over the life of the swap that is entered into after the exercise of the swaption.

(4) SOURCE

The source of a swaption is probably the residence of the taxpayer. For a discussion of the source rules that apply to notional principal contracts, see generally section 60.5(a).

(f) ZERO COUPON SWAPS

In a zero coupon swap, the party making the fixed rate payments either pays the present value of the fixed rate payments at the beginning of the swap ("front-loaded payments") or makes the payment in a lump sum at the maturity of the swap ("back-loaded payments"). Notice 89-21[120] provides that the lump-sum payment received under a zero coupon swap is not fully includable in income upon receipt. Rather, it must be amortized.[121]

---

[120] 1989-1 C.B. 651 (Feb. 9, 1989). The concern Notice 89-21 addressed was the use of lump-sum payments to offset expiring net operating losses to reduce or eliminate tax on the lump-sum payment. In addition, if the swap party with the net operating loss had taxable income in future years of the swap, it could offset the income with deductions for the floating rate payments it made during the remaining swap term.

[121] For a discussion of Notice 89-21, see sections 60.2(b)(1)(ii) and 60.2(b)(2)(ii).

Notice 89-21 does not require amortization of amounts characterized as a loan, so it might be argued that any prepayment is a "loan," but where would the Treasury draw that line?[122]

Notice 89-21 provides that Treasury regulations, when issued, will apply prospectively. Nevertheless, the notice provides that a method of accounting used by a taxpayer will only clearly reflect income "if the payments are taken into account over the life of the contract using a reasonable method of amortization."[123] As a result, the provisions of the notice actually apply retroactively.

(g) WITHHOLDING TAX OBLIGATIONS

In the absence of a tax treaty, the Code imposes a 30 percent withholding tax on the gross amount of "fixed or determinable, annual or periodical income" ("FDAPI") paid to foreign persons to the extent that the payments are from United States sources and not effectively connected with a United States trade or business.[124] I.R.C. §§ 871(a)(1)(A) and 881(a)(1) set out a list of items treated as FDAPI, including interest, dividends, rents, salaries, wages, premiums, annuities, compensations, remunerations, and emoluments. FDAPI describes items that are subject to withholding.[125] In general, "[i]ncome is fixed when it is to be paid in amounts definitely predetermined. Income is determinable whenever there is a basis of calculation by which the amount to be paid may be ascertained. The income need not be paid annually if it is paid periodically."[126]

(1) ON FIXED OR DETERMINABLE, ANNUAL OR PERIODICAL INCOME

For swap payments made by a United States counterparty to be subject to withholding, the payments must be FDAPI from a United States source. The source of foreign currency gain or loss is the residence of the party on whose books the financial asset or liability giving rise to the gain or loss is reflected.[127] The same transaction can give rise to gain or loss with a

---

[122] It is the author's understanding that there has been a continuing debate at the Treasury over whether a prepayment can be too large. Theoretically, any prepayment is really a "loan," but if the government does not adopt the position that any prepayment is a loan, how large must the "loan" be for the government to view it as such?

[123] Notice 89-21, 1989-1 C.B. 651 (Feb. 9, 1989).

[124] I.R.C. §§ 871(a)(1)(A), 881(a)(1), 1441(a), 1442(a).

[125] Treas. Reg. § 1.1441-2(a)(1) (1984).

[126] Treas. Reg. § 1.1441-2(a)(2) (1984).

[127] I.R.C. § 988(a)(3).

source in different jurisdictions for different taxpayers. Notice 87-4,[128] as supplemented by Temp. Treas. Reg. § 1.861-7T, resolved the issue of withholding tax for notional principal contracts that do not generate foreign currency gains or losses.

(2) WITHHOLDING UNDER TEMPORARY TREASURY REGULATION § 1.861-7T

The temporary Treasury regulations under I.R.C. § 861 are effective for swap income includable on or after December 24, 1986. The regulations only apply to notional principal contracts if the payments under the contracts are denominated in terms of and are determined by reference to the taxpayer's functional currency. The regulations modify Notice 87-4[129] (which provided that residence-based sourcing would only be applicable where at least one party to the swap is a United States resident with the U.S. dollar as its functional currency). For a discussion of Notice 87-4, and the sourcing rules, see section 60.5. The regulations do not apply to income or expense from the disposition of a swap, or to swap fees.

§ 60.3 INTEREST RATE CAPS, FLOORS, AND COLLARS

Interest rate caps, floors, and collars are notional principal contracts that provide some interest rate protection. Interest rate caps ("caps") protect a buyer against increasing interest rates without fixing the rate. Caps effectively guarantee a party's maximum borrowing costs, thereby protecting against interest rates increasing over an agreed-to level. Caps do not limit the benefits that may be derived from declining interest rates.

A cap is an agreement whereby one party ("seller"), for an up-front fee, agrees to compensate another party ("buyer") if an interest rate index rises above a certain specified rate ("strike level" or "cap level"). A cap places an upper limit on the interest rate to be paid on a floating rate debt obligation. At the time the cap is issued, its strike level is usually greater than the current rate in the fixed interest rate market. A cap agreement has a notional principal amount, by reference to which periodic payments are calculated. The purchase of a cap usually picks as the notional principal amount an amount equal to all or a portion of its obligations. If interest rates rise, the seller pays the buyer the difference between the strike level and the specified indexed interest rate, multiplied by the

---

[128] 1987-1 C.B. 416 (Jan. 19, 1987).
[129] *Id.*

notional principal amount. If interest rates do not rise by more than the specified amount, the seller simply keeps the fee. A cap protects the buyer because it establishes a maximum interest rate, while enabling the buyer to benefit from lower interest rates if rates decline.

Typically, the up-front cap fee is payable in a lump sum, although periodic payments of the fee can sometimes be negotiated. The up-front fee is determined by the cap level, the length of the agreement, the floating rate index that is being hedged, and current market conditions. Generally, the up-front payment represents the present value of the expected future payments (based on the current yield curve) plus the writer's profit. For a discussion of caps, see generally section 6.3.

Interest rate floors ("floors") protect a party against declining interest rates. The seller of a floor ("seller"), for a fee, agrees to make a cash payment to the purchaser ("buyer") equal to the difference between the prevailing market interest rate and the specified rate if, on an agreed-upon date, interest rates fall below the specified level (referred to as the "floor level"). The buyer of a floor is typically hedging against a decrease in interest rates on a floating rate asset. (These buyers may, in turn, sell caps to other parties.) The owner of a floating rate asset can assure a minimum return by purchasing a floor. Typically, the floor fee is paid up-front in a lump sum, although periodic payments of the premium can sometimes be negotiated. The fee is determined by the floor level, the length of the agreement, the floating rate index that is being hedged, and current market conditions. For a discussion of floors, see generally section 6.4.

An interest rate collar ("collar") is an agreement whereby a party buys a cap and sells a floor. If market rates exceed the cap level, the cap seller will make payments to the cap buyer sufficient to bring the rate back to the cap level. If market rates fall below the floor level, the floor seller makes payments to the floor buyer to bring the rates back to the floor level. The collar establishes a ceiling and a floor on the interest rate index the collar holder pays. A party can finance a portion of a cap's cost by selling a floor at the same time it purchases the cap. In return for lowering the cost of the cap, the party forgoes participating in a favorable market move below the floor level. Of course, the same thing holds true for a party that buys a floor and sells a cap.

A collar with a very narrow "band" has the same economic effect as a swap. If the strike price of the cap and the floor is equal, the collar—often referred to as a "tight collar"—is identical to an interest rate swap. In fact, a typical swap agreement could be characterized as a cap and a floor based on the current market rate, rather than on an agreed-to "out-of-the-money" rate. For a discussion of collars, see generally section 6.5.

The remainder of this section addresses the tax considerations of interest rate caps, floors, and collars.

(a) CAPS, FLOORS, AND COLLARS ENTERED INTO TO HEDGE

(1) UP-FRONT FEES

(i) Timing

Under Notice 89-21,[130] taxpayers must amortize the up-front fees paid by the buyer of a cap, floor, or collar over the term of the product (deferred up-front fees would presumably be amortized as well). The exact method of amortizing these fees, however, is still unsettled, although it is the author's understanding that the drafters of Notice 89-21 anticipated that the up-front fees should be amortized in the same manner in which the product was priced. If caps or floors are viewed as a series of options, the method of allocating the total option premium among the different periods is not clear. Although a straight-line method seems reasonable (and administratively simple), the IRS—at the date of this writing—appears to be attracted to an "economic basis" allocation that would allocate larger premium amounts to the later periods, thereby back-loading deductions for the buyer and income for the seller.

At the date of this writing, the Treasury has not decided on an appropriate method and it is not likely that guidelines will be forthcoming in the near future. Therefore, Notice 89-21,[131] which requires a reasonable amortization method that clearly reflects income, is the only guidance currently available to taxpayers. In the case of amortization of up-front fees, whether for interest rate swaps or caps, floors, and collars, the Treasury has received several suggestions for the appropriate methods of amortization. In general, the users of notional principal contracts have indicated to the Treasury that they prefer a straight-line method. Commercial banks have suggested that a method that more closely approximates the yield adjustment for the underlying loan involved would be preferred. Others have suggested that the seller (usually a broker-dealer) must report the method that it used to price the cap or the

[130] 1989-1 C.B. 651 (Feb. 9, 1989).
[131] *Id.*

floor to both the buyer and the IRS. The buyer would use the amount so reported as the amount to be amortized. Still others have suggested that the Treasury or the IRS should issue amortization tables similar to the types of tables issued under the OID rules. Finally, others have suggested the use of an options pricing model (for example, the Black-Scholes option valuation model) to determine the proper amortizable amounts. Variations on these methods have been suggested by other groups.

In general, there are many ways to amortize up-front fees. The easiest way is to adopt a straight-line method of amortization. The drawbacks of such a method are that it does not follow the economics of the transaction and it does not follow the way in which the product was priced. It gets more complicated to adopt an option pricing model. Under a mark-to-market pricing method, the last year's premium would be used up first and there would be large front-loaded deductions. Buyers would welcome such a method, but the Treasury would most likely object, given the negative revenue effect. Under a pricing method that attempts to follow how the product is priced, this would back-load the deductions. Buyers would object to this method, but the Treasury would welcome it.

(ii) Character

A reasonable approach for the character of caps, floors, and collars is to permit the integration of caps and floors with the assets and liabilities to which they relate, thereby generating ordinary gain or loss as adjustments to interest income or expense. Integration would not create any tax incentives, but would simply permit taxpayers to adjust their interest income or expense to match the economic performance of their transactions. One potential obstacle to this treatment, however, is the possible application of *Arkansas Best Corp. v. Comm'r*[132] to effectively bifurcate the character (ordinary or capital) of deductions relating to, say, a floating rate loan and a corresponding cap. In the unlikely event that *Arkansas Best* forces the taxpayer to view the cap as a capital transaction, it would not be possible to integrate the cap with the interest deductions on the underlying loan. Even if the cap generates ordinary income, however, there is no authority for integration (in the sense of an adjustment to interest income or expense). The integration approach has been applied in connection with Treasury regulations dealing with the sourcing of notional principal contract income where the contract is entered into to

---

[132] 485 U.S. 212 (1988), *aff'g* 800 F.2d 215 (8th Cir. 1986), *aff'g in part, rev'g in part* 83 T.C. 640 (1984).

hedge a liability.[133] These regulations result in interest equivalent treatment.

Despite *Arkansas Best*, it is difficult to justify capital treatment for up-front fees because they arguably do not involve the "sale or exchange" of property as is required for capital gain or loss. Because certain collars are economically identical to interest rate swaps, the tax treatment of collars should be the same as for interest rate swaps—that is, ordinary treatment. For a discussion of the tax treatment of interest rate swaps, see section 60.2(b).

(2) PERIODIC PAYMENTS

(i) Timing

Periodic payments should be recognized by the taxpayer based on its normal accounting method. Any amounts received by the buyer during the term (i.e., when the strike interest level is exceeded and the seller is committed to make a payment) should be recognized at that time. This amount would, of course, be offset by the amortizable portion of the premium attributable to that period. Furthermore, that net amount would be offset by the underlying deductions for interest payments due under the floating rate loan. The Straddle Rules generally will not apply to caps, floors, and collars.[134] In the case of a collar, payments by the buyer for drops in the interest rates below the floor would be recognized by the seller at the time of payment.

(ii) Character

Generally, the character of periodic payments on caps, floors, and collars should be treated as ordinary under two alternative theories. First, the "item" being exchanged is U.S. dollars and if the dollars are the taxpayer's functional currency, they are not property for purposes of the Code. The contractual right to receive a periodic payment in exchange for the specified payment could be viewed as a sale or exchange.[135] If the contractual right to receive periodic payments is not deemed to be a capital asset (or the net periodic payment is not deemed to constitute a

---

[133] Treas. Reg. § 1.863-7 (1991). For a discussion of the sourcing rules, see section 60.5(b).

[134] For a discussion of possible application of the Straddle Rules to notional principal contracts, see section 60.7.

[135] *See* I.R.C. §§ 1001, 1221; National-Standard Co. v. Comm'r, 80 T.C. 551 (1983), *aff'd*, 749 F.2d 369 (6th Cir. 1984).

sale or exchange of a capital asset), any gain or loss is treated as ordinary income for contracts on U.S. dollars.

Second, the cap, floor, or collar may also be viewed as analogous to gambling or wagering income, subject to the limitations on losses under I.R.C. § 165(d). Under either of these theories, the periodic payments are viewed as ordinary income.

(3) TERMINATION AND ASSIGNMENT FEES

(i) Timing

Certain assignment fees must be amortized by the party taking over the swap position.[136] All other termination and assignment fees are presumably recognized upon receipt. Such fees are currently recognized by the party getting out of the swap position.

(ii) Character

The character of termination and assignment fees probably depends on whether the cap, floor, or collar is terminated or assigned. Because termination involves a "sale or exchange of the contract," it is not clear if ordinary treatment is justified. Case law allows ordinary treatment of extinguishment payments paid to relieve oneself of a burdensome contract.[137] Nonetheless, since payments received for an assignment of a cap, floor, or collar appear to involve a property right that constitutes a capital asset, capital treatment would be justified.

(4) ANALOGY TO OPTIONS

Caps and floors entered into independently (as opposed to collars that might behave economically similar to interest rate swaps) can be analogized to options. For example, a cap by which the seller bears the risk of an increase in interest rates above a certain strike level, is very similar to the selling of a call option on interest rates. This analogy could lead to certain conclusions not likely to be palatable to taxpayers. Payments made by the seller of a cap or floor might not be deductible until the expiration of the term (the settlement date of the option).

Even with the option concept, caps and floors could also be viewed as a series of options that the holder (buyer) can choose to exercise on each

---

[136] Notice 89-21, 1989-1 C.B. 651 (Feb. 9, 1989).

[137] *See* Pressed Steel Car Co. v. Comm'r, 20 T.C. 198 (1953), *acq.* 1956-2 C.B. 198.

interest payment date. (It is the author's understanding that this view is currently being considered by Treasury officials.) Perhaps this approach would lead to the division of the payment for each of the "options" and the deductibility of each payment when that option is exercised. Basically, this could lead to a partial deduction by the buyer of the portion of the up-front fee paid for the particular option period and, as payments are made by the seller, the buyer would be entitled to deduct its expense with respect to that particular option period. These results would be in line with the amortization of up-front fees required by Notice 89-21.[138]

If the option analogy is used, I.R.C. §§ 1234(a) and 1234A provide that gain or loss from the sale of options has the same character as the property underlying the option.[139] Presumably, the underlying property—U.S. dollars—would be ordinary in character.

(b) CAPS, FLOORS, AND COLLARS NOT ENTERED INTO TO HEDGE

Caps, floors, and collars are not normally entered into for speculative purposes. Nevertheless, from a tax standpoint, the tax treatment for speculative positions should not be significantly different from those purchased as hedges. Notice 89-21[140] applies so that the fees are amortized over the life of the product. Presumably, the character would still be ordinary. If the option analogy is used, I.R.C. §§ 1234(a) and 1234A would still provide that the character is based on the underlying property involved—U.S. dollars—therefore, ordinary treatment would be appropriate.[141]

Periodic payments would be ordinary in character because there is still no "sale or exchange" of a capital asset and, therefore, no basis for capital treatment. Also, the periodic payments are still taken into income based on the normal accounting method used by the taxpayer.

As in the case of caps, floors, and collars used as hedges, termination and assignment fees are recognized at the time of payment, with the exception of those assignment fees that must be amortized as required by Notice 89-21.[142] The character of these fees depends on whether the

---

[138] 1989-1 C.B. 651 (Feb. 9, 1989). For a discussion of Notice 89-21, see sections 60.2(b)(1)(ii) and 60.2(b)(2)(ii).

[139] For a discussion of the taxation of options, see generally Chapter 30.

[140] 1989-1 C.B. 651 (Feb. 9, 1989).

[141] For a discussion of options, see generally Chapters 5 and 30.

[142] 1989-1 C.B. 651 (Feb. 9, 1989). For a discussion of Notice 89-21, see sections 60.2(b)(1)(ii) and 60.2(b)(2)(ii).

contract is terminated or assigned. Terminations might generate ordinary treatment, while assignments might generate capital treatment.[143] Moreover, I.R.C. §§ 1234(a) and 1234A (which would treat amounts as capital) do not appear to apply to these terminations because these agreements are not section 1256 contracts or rights or obligations with respect to "personal property" under I.R.C. § 1234A(1).[144]

§ 60.4 FORWARD RATE AGREEMENTS

In an FRA, one party agrees to "sell" ("seller") and another party agrees to "buy" ("buyer") a loan in a specified amount at a specified interest rate (the "forward rate") on a specified day in the future (the "contract period"). On the first day of the contract period ("settlement date"), the interest differential between interest on the principal amount at the forward rate and the then current index rate for the contract period is calculated. There is usually a single period for which a single payment will be made. If the index rate is above the forward rate on the settlement date, the seller pays the interest differential to the buyer. If the interest rate is below the forward rate on the settlement date, the buyer pays the interest differential to the seller.

An FRA is basically a "forward contract," for which the "commodity" is an interest rate. It is not technically a notional principal contract, although it is often referred to as such because the calculation of the forward rate is based on a notional principal amount. An FRA always involves cash settlement, and it does not require the delivery of any commodity or security.[145] FRAs typically call for an initial payment and a payment on termination (or at maturity). FRAs may also provide for periodic "margin" payments. For a discussion of FRAs, see section 6.7.

The relevant tax issues under an FRA are the timing, character, and source of gain or loss. The remainder of this section first looks at FRAs by comparing them to other financial products. It then looks at the tax considerations for character, timing, and source.

---

[143] For a discussion of the tax treatment of certain contract rights and obligations, see section 58.2.

[144] For a discussion of I.R.C. § 1234A, see section 58.2. For a discussion of "personal property," see section 48.2.

[145] FRAs are most commonly denominated in U.S. dollars, but FRAs can be denominated in foreign currencies. If denominated in foreign currencies, the foreign currency rules set out in Part Thirteen apply. Agreements to deliver a commodity or a security are forward contracts and are addressed in sections 6.7 and 42.1(b).

(a) IN GENERAL

The tax treatment of FRAs has not been explicitly addressed by the Code, Treasury pronouncements, or any United States court. Thus, the determination of how FRAs should be taxed depends on analogizing their taxation to the taxation of similar products and drawing conclusions from these analogies. Those products most similar to FRAs are futures contracts, forward contracts, and interest rate swaps. Such analogies may be of limited value to a taxpayer considering entering into FRAs, but they do provide an analytical starting point.

FRAs may be subject to the Straddle Rules.[146] The availability of the hedging exemption from the Straddle Rules for hedging transactions under I.R.C. §§ 1092(e) and 1256(e) depends on whether the FRA positions are established for speculative or hedging purposes.

(1) FORWARD RATE AGREEMENTS AS FUTURES CONTRACTS

FRAs are not exchange-traded futures contracts. As a result, even though they may have characteristics that are similar to futures contracts, they are not eligible for or subject to the 60/40 Rule and the Mark-to-Market Rule of I.R.C. § 1256.[147] Futures contracts that are not subject to the Mark-to-Market Rule of I.R.C. § 1256 are taxed only at the expiration of their terms, or when they are closed out. Like futures contracts, FRAs permit the parties to "speculate" on the price of a "commodity" in the future.

Upon the expiration of the term of an FRA, one party profits if prices have increased over a bench mark and the other party has a loss. Conceptually, this process is no different than if one party were forced to buy the "commodity" at the market price and deliver it at the contract price, just as with a futures contract held to maturity. Therefore, it stands to reason that FRAs should be taxed in the same manner as futures contracts that are not section 1256 contracts (i.e., only at the expiration or termination of the contracts) and that no gain should be recognized upon receipt of "margin payments."

---

[146] For a discussion of the Straddle Rules, see generally Part Eleven. For a discussion of possible application of the Straddle Rules to notional principal contracts, see section 60.7.

[147] Section 1256 contracts are defined in Chapter 44. For a discussion of the tax treatment of section 1256 contracts, see generally Part Ten.

(2) FORWARD RATE AGREEMENTS AS FORWARD CONTRACTS

FRAs have many characteristics of forward contracts. Both are privately negotiated contracts between two parties for payments in the future. Unlike forward contracts, however, FRAs do not generally contemplate delivery of an underlying product on termination of the contract, unless the interest differential is viewed as the "commodity." FRA margin payments are not expense or income items, but merely a good faith deposit. Therefore, the tax treatment of FRAs should follow closely the rules applicable to forward contracts.[148] In other words, gain or loss should be recognized only upon expiration of the term of the FRA and its final settlement.

Given the absence of precedent, it is possible that the IRS could attempt to tax gain on FRAs prior to their termination, at least to the extent that margin has been received by the taxpayer under the concept of constructive receipt. Although an accrual basis taxpayer does not generally include income until all events have occurred that fix the right to receive such income and the amount thereof can be determined with reasonable accuracy, an accrual basis taxpayer receiving a prepayment is generally not allowed to defer the income.[149] Under the theory that margin payments are prepayments of accrued gain, the IRS could attempt to assert that margin payments constitute prepayments of accrued gains and losses.

(3) FORWARD RATE AGREEMENTS AS INTEREST RATE SWAPS

An FRA can be viewed as similar to an interest rate swap because they both involve promises to make future payments based on a notional principal amount.[150] The principal amount is notional, so neither party makes a loan or borrows money from the other party. Neither FRA nor interest rate swap payments are "interest" on indebtedness, because they are not related to a debt or compensation for the use of someone else's

---

[148] For a discussion of forward contracts see sections 4.3(b) and 6.7.

[149] *See* Automobile Club of Michigan v. Comm'r, 353 U.S. 180 (1957), *aff'g* 230 F.2d 585 (6th Cir. 1956), *aff'g* 20 T.C. 1033 (1953), *reh'g denied*, 353 U.S. 989 (1957). *See also* Schlude v. Comm'r, 372 U.S. 128 (1963), *aff'g in part, rev'g in part* 296 F.2d 721 (8th Cir. 1961), *on remand* 368 U.S. 873 (1961), *denying reh'g to* 367 U.S. 911 (1961), *vacating* 283 F.2d 234 (8th Cir. 1960), *rev'g* 32 T.C. 1271 (1959); RCA Corp. v. United States, 664 F.2d 881 (2d Cir. 1981), *rev'g* 499 F. Supp. 507 (S.D.N.Y. 1980), *cert. denied*, 457 U.S. 1133 (1982).

[150] For a discussion of interest rate swaps, see section 60.2(b).

money. There is no exchange of principal amounts involved.[151] To cover more than one interest period, taxpayers may execute a series of FRAs at the outset. In this case, the FRAs would not be distinguishable from swaps and the tax treatment of swaps must be considered. Margin payments on FRAs—if viewed as periodic payments on a swap—would be subject to tax when they are paid or received by the taxpayer. For a discussion of the tax considerations that apply to interest rate swaps, see section 60.2(b).

(b) CHARACTER

The tax character of gain or loss on an FRA turns on whether the FRA was entered into as a hedge or for speculation purposes. If the FRA is entered into as a hedge, the gain or loss would most likely be treated as ordinary—subject, of course, to possible application of *Arkansas Best*.[152] If, on the other hand, an FRA is entered into for speculative purposes, gain or loss would be capital in nature.

(c) TIMING

Gain or loss on an FRA is most likely recognized when the FRA terminates or is disposed of by the taxpayer. For cash basis taxpayers, an amount is included in income or deductible when it is actually or constructively received or paid by the taxpayer.[153] For accrual basis taxpayers, an amount is includable in income "when all the events have occurred which fix the right to receive such income and the amount thereof can be determined with reasonable accuracy."[154] An amount is deductible for an accrual basis taxpayer for the taxable year "in which all the events have occurred which determine the fact of the liability and the amount thereof can be determined with reasonable accuracy."[155]

(d) SOURCE

The source of any payments made under an FRA is determined by the residence of the taxpayer. Income from the sale of personal property by a

---

[151] *See* section 60.2(b)(2)(i)(a)(1).

[152] 485 U.S. 212 (1988), *aff'g* 800 F.2d 215 (8th Cir. 1986), *aff'g in part, rev'g in part* 83 T.C. 640 (1984). For a discussion of possible application of *Arkansas Best* to financial products, see sections 23.2(c)(4) and 23.2(d)(3).

[153] I.R.C. §§ 451(a), 461(a); Treas. Reg. §§ 1.451-1(a) (1978), 1.461-1(a)(1) (1967).

[154] Treas. Reg. § 1.451-1(a) (1978); I.R.C. § 451(a).

[155] Treas. Reg. § 1.461-1(a)(2) (1967).

United States resident is sourced in the United States, while income from the sale of personal property by a nonresident is sourced outside of the United States.[156] Although I.R.C. § 865(j)(2) provides the Treasury with authority to issue regulations applying the rules of I.R.C. § 865 "to income derived from trading in futures contracts, forward contracts, options contracts, and other instruments," regulations have not been issued at the date of this writing.

(e) OFFSETTING POSITIONS WHERE ONE POSITION IS A FORWARD RATE AGREEMENT

FRAs are not actively traded. (In fact, there is no market at all in which to trade FRAs.) I.R.C. § 1092(d)(1) defines "personal property" for purposes of the Straddle Rules to mean property of a type that is actively traded. FRAs are not personal property for such purposes. Nevertheless, FRAs might be viewed as "positions" in personal property because I.R.C. § 1092(d)(2) does not require that the "positions" in personal property must be actively traded. Positions in personal property are subject to the Straddle Rules. For a discussion of the Straddle Rules, see generally Part Eleven.

It is possible that an FRA "hedge" will be treated as two offsetting positions and, thus, as a straddle subject to the Straddle Rules unless the I.R.C. § 1256(e) hedging exemption applies.[157] One of the requirements for a transaction to qualify as a hedging transaction is that the gain or loss on the transaction must receive ordinary income or loss treatment.[158]

(f) SPECULATIVE POSITIONS

If a trader or investor enters into "offsetting" FRAs, the taxpayer might be subject to the Straddle Rules (including the loss deferral rules of I.R.C. § 1092 and the capitalization rule of I.R.C. § 263(g)).[159] This is because the taxpayer is not engaged in a hedging transaction within the meaning of I.R.C. § 1092(e), which is exempt from the Straddle Rules. If FRAs are closed out at a loss before the end of the tax year, the loss is deferred to the extent there is an unrecognized gain in any offsetting positions. In addition, a trader or investor receives capital gain or loss on FRAs because the transactions do not come under the purview of the *Corn Products* doctrine

---

[156] I.R.C. § 865(a).
[157] For a discussion of the I.R.C. § 1256(e) hedging exemption, see section 23.2.
[158] I.R.C. § 1256(e)(2)(B).
[159] For a discussion of the Straddle Rules, see generally Part Eleven.

(as it was limited in *Arkansas Best*).[160] For a discussion of *Arkansas Best*, see generally sections 8.4(d), 14.1, and 23.2(c)(4).

§ 60.5 SOURCING RULES

The "source" of payments and receipts on notional principal contracts is important because many contracts are entered into with foreign counterparties, raising a withholding tax issue. In addition, the source may affect the taxpayer's calculation of foreign tax credits. This section addresses sourcing rules. In general, income is sourced from within or without the United States by reference to I.R.C. §§ 861 to 865 and the regulations promulgated thereunder.

(a) SOURCING RULES FOR NOTIONAL PRINCIPAL CONTRACTS

In Notice 87-4,[161] the IRS first addressed sourcing considerations with respect to certain interest rate swaps denominated in U.S. dollars. Notice 87-4 provided that the source of income and expense attributable to an interest rate swap denominated in U.S. dollars, where one party has its residence in the United States and the U.S. dollar as its functional currency, is determined by reference to the residence of the recipient of the swap income. It also provided that swap income attributable to a United States trade or business is sourced in the United States. Although Notice 87-4 did not set out the analysis used by the IRS to reach its conclusion, the notice eliminated the possibility of United States withholding for interest rate swaps denominated in U.S. dollars. It did not, however, address the source of income on other swap transactions. Notice 87-4 has been supplemented by Treas. Reg. § 1.863-7[162] and Temp. Treas. Reg. § 1.861-9T.[163] Temp. Treas. Reg. § 1.863-7T remains in effect for tax years between December 24, 1986, and February 13, 1991.

Notice 89-90[164] addresses those notional principal contracts that do not qualify for integration treatment as liability hedges or that are held by dealers in such contracts. Notice 89-90 provides that income attributable

---

[160] 485 U.S. 212 (1988), *aff'g* 800 F.2d 215 (8th Cir. 1986), *aff'g in part, rev'g in part* 83 T.C. 640 (1984).
[161] 1987-1 C.B. 416 (Jan. 19, 1987).
[162] (1991).
[163] (1989).
[164] 1989-2 C.B. 407 (Aug. 14, 1989).

to such contracts that is earned by a QBU (as defined in I.R.C. § 989(a) and the regulations issued thereunder) is treated as income equivalent to interest under I.R.C. § 954(c)(1)(E) of the Subpart F rules of the Code. Thus, such income would be subject to immediate United States taxation at the United States shareholder level.[165] As a result of Notice 89-90, income that is covered therein is characterized as passive income for foreign tax credit purposes.[166] Thus, such income is generally only exempt from United States taxation if it is subject to foreign taxation. Notional principal contracts denominated in, or the values of which are determined by reference to, a nonfunctional currency are generally subject to the provisions of I.R.C. §§ 954(c)(1)(D) and 988.

On January 11, 1991, the Treasury issued final regulations on the allocation of income attributable to notional principal contracts as foreign or United States source income under I.R.C. § 863(a). The regulations are generally effective on February 13, 1991.[167] A taxpayer can elect to apply the final regulations, on a consistent basis, in lieu of the temporary Treasury regulations. On or before May 15, 1991, a taxpayer had the opportunity to elect to apply the final regulations to all, but not part, of such taxpayer's notional principal contract income arising in open tax years (or portion thereof)[168] beginning before December 24, 1986.[169] This election is made by attaching a statement to a tax return or an amended tax return for each open tax year (or portion thereof) in which the electing taxpayer accrued or received notional principal contract income. The statement must (1) provide the taxpayer's name, address, and taxpayer identification number, (2) identify the election as a "Notional Principal Contract Election under § 1.863-7," and (3) specify each taxable year for which each election was made.[170]

In general, the final regulations provide that income on notional principal contracts will be sourced by reference to the residence of the recipient of the swap income. A notional principal contract is defined in the regulations as "a financial instrument that provides for the payment of amounts by one party to another at specified intervals calculated by reference to a specified index upon a notional principal amount in exchange for specified consideration or a promise to pay similar

---

[165] I.R.C. §§ 951(a)(1), 954(c)(1)(E).
[166] I.R.C. §§ 954(c)(1), 954(d)(2)(A)(i).
[167] Treas. Reg. § 1.863-7(a)(2) (1991).
[168] Open tax years are determined in accordance with I.R.C. § 6511(a).
[169] Treas. Reg. § 1.863-7(c).
[170] Treas. Reg. § 1.863-7(c)(3).

amounts."[171] The regulations provide that an agreement between a taxpayer and a QBU (as defined in I.R.C. § 989(a)) of the taxpayer, or between QBUs of the same taxpayer, is not a notional principal contract because a taxpayer cannot enter into such a contract with itself.[172] The definition of a notional principal contract is broad enough to cover interest rate, foreign currency, and commodity swaps.

In general, the source of notional principal contract income is determined by reference to the residence of the taxpayer as determined under I.R.C. § 988(a)(3)(B)(i).[173] Two exceptions are provided to this general rule. First, for a QBU of the taxpayer, the source is determined by reference to the residence of the QBU if four conditions are met: (1) the taxpayer's residence (as determined under I.R.C. § 988(a)(3)(B)(i)) is the United States; (2) the QBU's residence (as determined under I.R.C. § 988(a)(3)(B)(ii)) is outside of the United States; (3) the QBU is engaged in the conduct of a trade or business where it is a resident (as determined under I.R.C. § 988(a)(3)(B)(ii)); and (4) the notional principal contract is properly reflected on the books of the QBU.[174] Second, notional principal contracts that are entered into from the conduct of a United States trade or business are sourced in the United States, and such income is treated as effectively connected with the conduct of a United States trade or business for purposes of I.R.C. §§ 871(b) and 882(a)(1).[175]

The sourcing rules under Treas. Reg. § 1.863-7 do not apply to notional principal contracts that are nonfunctional currency transactions under I.R.C. § 988. Treas. Reg. § 1.863-7(e) provides a cross-reference to Temp. Treas. Reg. § 1.988-4T for section 988 transactions.[176]

---

[171] Treas. Reg. § 1.863-7(a)(1) (1991). The proposed regulations, which were issued on August 9, 1989, included in the definition of a notional principal contract, those amounts that were referenced to an interest rate index or were foreign currency-related. The final regulations are broader and include within the definition of a notional principal contract, those contracts that reference commodity indexes. The final regulations cover more products because of this change.

[172] Treas. Reg. § 1.863-7(a)(1) (1991).

[173] Treas. Reg. § 1.863-7(b)(1) (1991).

[174] Treas. Reg. § 1.863-7(b)(2) (1991). The fourth requirement mentioned in the text represents a relaxation of the rule set forth in the temporary regulation that preceded this final regulation. Taxpayers are permitted to elect this more liberal treatment, on a consistent basis, for income to which the temporary regulation would otherwise apply. Treas. Reg. § 1.863-7(a)(2) (1991).

[175] Treas. Reg. § 1.863-7(b)(3) (1991).

[176] For a discussion of section 988 transactions, see generally section 59.2.

(b) SOURCING RULES FOR LIABILITY HEDGES

(1) INTEREST EQUIVALENT TREATMENT FOR GAINS AND LOSSES FOR SWAPS AND OTHER FINANCIAL PRODUCTS

Temp. Treas. Reg. § 1.861-9T provides for the allocation of expenses to certain notional principal contracts. When a taxpayer enters into a transaction that involves a financial product that is used to alter its effective cost of borrowing with respect to an actual liability of the taxpayer, the gain or loss on the financial product will be integrated with the interest expense on the underlying liability, resulting in a reduction or increase in the amount of interest expense subject to the United States and foreign apportionment rules for interest expense.[177] The derivative financial products eligible for the liability hedge treatment include interest rate swaps, options, forward contracts, caps, and collars.[178]

To qualify for liability hedge treatment, the financial product and the underlying liability must be denominated in the same currency.[179] In addition, the financial product must be properly identified by the taxpayer as a liability hedge. In particular, the taxpayer must clearly identify the financial product as hedging a particular interest-bearing liability (or any group of liabilities) on its books and records on the same day that it becomes a party to the financial product.

A liability can be partially hedged through the use of a financial product, with the result that integration (i.e., treatment as interest equivalent) is obtained with respect to the portion of the liability hedged. A taxpayer can also enter into anticipatory hedges of liabilities. However, the liability being hedged must be incurred within 120 days after the taxpayer becomes a party to the hedge. Treatment as interest equivalent for liability hedges under Temp. Treas. Reg. § 1.861-9T in no way affects the status of the swap (or other financial product) for other purposes of the Code.

Liability hedge treatment is not available to taxpayers that constitute a "financial services" entity within the meaning of Treas. Reg. § 1.904-4(e)(3). Moreover, liability hedge treatment is not available to regular dealers in financial products.[180] Instead, "losses sustained by a regular

---

[177] Temp. Treas. Reg. § 1.861-9T (1989).
[178] Temp. Treas. Reg. § 1.861-9T(b)(6) (1989).
[179] *Id.*
[180] Temp. Treas. Reg. § 1.861-9T(b)(6)(vi) (1989).

dealer in connection with such financial products shall be allocated to the class of gross income from such arrangements.[181]

(2) TREATMENT WHERE LIABILITY HEDGES ARE NOT PROPERLY IDENTIFIED

With respect to losses, if the swap qualifies as a liability hedge, but the hedge is not properly identified and there is a loss on the swap, the loss is still apportioned in the same manner as interest expense.[182]

With respect to gains, if the swap qualifies as a liability hedge, but the hedge is not properly identified and there is a gain on the swap, the gain does not reduce the taxpayer's interest expense that is subject to the United States and foreign interest expense source apportionment rules. Rather, the gain is sourced under the basic Temp. Treas. Reg. § 1.861-7T rules, which generally rely on the residence of the taxpayer to determine source.

(c) SOURCING RULES FOR ASSET HEDGES

Where a taxpayer enters into a financial product used to hedge an interest-bearing asset (or group of such assets), if the taxpayer clearly identifies the financial product as an asset hedge on its books and records, there is a rebuttable presumption that the financial product is not an interest equivalent.[183] Therefore, the expense or loss on the swap is not subject to the United States and foreign interest expense source apportionment rules. Rather, gain on the swap is sourced based on residence, and loss is presumably fully deductible from United States source income.[184]

§ 60.6 MARK-TO-MARKET TREATMENT FOR DEALERS

Financial service firms, banks, and financial institutions act as dealers in notional principal contracts where they act as principals. One major concern for dealers in notional principal contracts is the fact that income and gains on the one hand, and deductions and losses on the other hand,

---

[181] *Id.* Gains of regular dealers in notional principal contracts are governed by the rules of Temp. Treas. Reg. § 1.863-7T(b).
[182] Temp. Treas. Reg. § 1.861-9T(b)(6)(iv)(A) (1989).
[183] Temp. Treas. Reg. § 1.861-9T(b)(6)(iv)(C) (1989).
[184] Treas. Reg. § 1.861-7 (1991).

may not be offset for tax purposes. Integration of notional principal contracts and related hedge transactions are also of concern. As a result, dealers have been working with the government to allow a mark-to-market accounting method for notional principal contracts and integrated hedge transactions entered into by dealers in the ordinary course of business.[185] Mark-to-market accounting for dealers could minimize the differences between financial and tax reporting of notional principal contracts.[186] In Notice 89-21,[187] the IRS stated that mark-to-market accounting for dealers in notional principal contracts is being considered by the Treasury. Until guidance is received from the Treasury, however, mark-to-market accounting is not available to dealers.

§ 60.7 STRADDLE RULES

The Straddle Rules apply to offsetting positions in personal property of a type that is actively traded.[188] The tax consequences of holding such offsetting positions are addressed in detail in Part Eleven. This section does not address the Straddle Rules in detail, but rather the possible application of the Straddle Rules to notional principal contracts on United States currency. It then addresses the application of the Straddle Rules to notional principal contracts on foreign currency.

(a) NOTIONAL PRINCIPAL CONTRACTS ON UNITED STATES CURRENCY

In general, notional principal contracts on United States currency do not meet the definition of "positions" in "personal property" because United States currency is not within the definition of personal property for purposes of the Straddle Rules.[189] The only reference to United States

---

[185] *See, e.g.*, letter and memorandum from Randall K.C. Kau to Dennis E. Ross, Deputy Assistant Secretary, Tax Policy, Treasury Department (Dec. 30, 1988) (discussing mark-to-market accounting by dealers), *reprinted in* 12 DAILY TAX HIGHLIGHTS & DOCUMENTS 577 (1989); letter and memorandum from Randall K.C. Kau to Dana L. Trier, Tax Legislative Counsel, Treasury Department (Apr. 3, 1989) (discussing interpretation and application of notional principal contract guidance in Notice 89-21), *reprinted in* 13 DAILY TAX HIGHLIGHTS & DOCUMENTS 605 (1989).

[186] *See, e.g.*, Statement of Financial Accounting Standards No. 96, Accounting for Income Taxes, Daily Tax Rep. (BNA) No. 250, at G-1 (Dec. 31, 1987).

[187] 1989-1 C.B. 651 (Feb. 9, 1989).

[188] I.R.C. § 1092(a).

[189] *See generally* section 48.2(b).

currency in the legislative history that accompanied ERTA in 1981[190] indicates that United States currency is not personal property. Personal property, as defined, only includes "property or interests in property that may result in gain or loss on their disposition."[191] There is no gain or loss on the disposition of United States currency.

In light of the rules under I.R.C. § 988—which contemplate foreign branches of United States taxpayers keeping their books in functional currencies other than the U.S. dollar—it is possible that United States currency may be treated as personal property for those United States taxpayers that have the U.S. dollar as a nonfunctional currency. For a discussion of I.R.C. § 988, see generally Chapter 59.

If the notional principal contracts themselves are actively traded at a future date, they may be viewed as personal property subject to the Straddle Rules. This is because a "position" may constitute "personal property" if it is "actively traded." If these contracts can be entered into or closed out based on publicly quoted prices, it is possible that they will be considered to be actively traded property subject to the Straddle Rules.

In other words, a notional principal contract can be subject to the Straddle Rules if it is either a "position"—that is, an interest—with respect to "personal property"—that is, personal property of a type that is actively traded—or if the swap is "actively traded" personal property. If this is the result, the exceptions to the Straddle Rules must be considered. For a discussion of the exceptions to application of the Straddle Rules, see generally Chapter 56.

(b) NOTIONAL PRINCIPAL CONTRACTS ON FOREIGN CURRENCY

The Straddle Rules apply to offsetting positions in personal property, including notional principal contracts on foreign currency. For a discussion of the Straddle Rules, see generally Part Eleven.

---

[190] Pub. L. No. 97-34, 95 Stat. 172 (1981).
[191] STAFF OF THE JOINT COMM. ON TAXATION, 97TH CONG., 1ST SESS., GENERAL EXPLANATION OF THE ECONOMIC RECOVERY TAX ACT OF 1981, at 239 (Joint Comm. Print 1981).

Table of Cases

(References are to book sections.)

Abeles v. Oppenheimer & Co., 834 F.2d 123 (7th Cir. 1987), *aff'g* 662 F. Supp. 290 (N.D. Ill. 1986), *granting summary judgment* 597 F. Supp. 532 (N.D. Ill. 1983)	2.2(b)
Ades v. Comm'r, 38 T.C. 501 (1962), *aff'd per curiam*, 316 F.2d 734 (2d Cir. 1963)	31.4(d), 34.3(e)
Adnee v. Comm'r, 41 T.C. 40 (1963)	10
Adrian & James, Inc. v. Comm'r, 4 T.C. 708 (1945), *acq.* 1945 C.B. 1	16.2(a), 31.8
Alamo Broadcasting Co. v. Comm'r, 15 T.C. 534 (1950), *acq.* 1951-1 C.B. 1	16.2(a)
Alverson v. Comm'r, 35 B.T.A. 482 (1937), *acq.* 1937-1 C.B. 1	10.1(b)
American Auto. Ass'n v. United States, 367 U.S. 687 (1961), *aff'g* 181 F. Supp. 255 (Ct. Cl. 1960), *reh'g denied*, 368 U.S. 870 (1961)	60.2(b)(1)(ii)
American Auto. Club of Mich. v. Comm'r, 353 U.S. 180 (1957), *aff'g* 230 F.2d 585 (6th Cir. 1956), *aff'g* 20 T.C. 1033 (1953), *reh'g denied*, 353 U.S. 989 (1957)	60.4(a)(2)
American Home Prods. Corp. v. United States, 601 F.2d 540 (Ct. Cl. 1979)	18.2(a)
American Hotels Corp. v. Comm'r, 46 B.T.A. 629 (1942), *aff'd on other grounds*, 134 F.2d 817 (2d Cir. 1943)	13.2(a)(1)
American Nat'l Bank of Austin v. United States, 421 F.2d 442 (5th Cir.), *cert. denied*, 400 U.S. 819 (1970)	31.11(b), 31.11(b)(1), 31.11(b)(2), 48.3(b)(2)(i)

Table of Cases

(References are to book sections.)

American Nat'l Bank of Austin v. United States, 573 F.2d 1201 (Ct. Cl. 1978), aff'g 77-1 U.S. Tax Cas. (CCH) ¶ 9316 (Ct. Cl. 1977)	31.11(b)
American Natural Gas Co. v. United States, 279 F.2d 220 (Ct. Cl.), cert. denied, 364 U.S. 900 (1960)	27.4(d)(2)
American Tobacco Co. v. Patterson, 456 U.S. 63 (1982), on remand, 691 F.2d 496 (1982), vacating 634 F.2d 744 (4th Cir. 1980)	23.2(d)(3)(ii)
AMF, Inc. v. United States, 476 F.2d 1351 (Ct. Cl. 1973), cert. denied, 417 U.S. 930 (1974)	34.2(b)
Anderson v. Comm'r, 527 F.2d 198 (9th Cir. 1975), aff'g in part, remanding in part 33 T.C.M. (CCH) 234 (1974)	17.1(a)
Anderson, Clayton & Co. v. United States, 562 F.2d 972 (5th Cir.), reh'g denied, 565 F.2d 1215 (1977), cert. denied, 436 U.S. 944 (1978)	59.2(c)(1)
Andrews v. Comm'r, 135 F.2d 314 (2d Cir. 1943), rev'g 46 B.T.A. 607 (1942), cert. denied, 320 U.S. 748 (1943)	17.4(a)
Anton v. Comm'r, 34 T.C. 842 (1960), aff'd sub nom. Estate of Smith v. Comm'r, 292 F.2d 478 (3d Cir. 1961), cert. denied, 368 U.S. 967 (1962)	24.7(c)
Apkin v. Comm'r, 86 T.C. 692 (1986)	32.1(b)(1)(iv)
Arkansas Best Corp. v. Comm'r, 485 U.S. 212 (1988), aff'g 800 F.2d 215 (8th Cir. 1986), aff'g in part, rev'g in part 83 T.C. 640 (1984)	8.4, 8.4(b), 8.4(d), 11.9(b), 12, 13.2(a), 14.1, 21.1, 23.2(a), 23.2(b)(3), 23.2(c)(4), 23.2(d)(3)(i), 23.2(e)(1), 23.3(b), 45.2(a), 55.2(f), 56.2, 60.1, 60.2(b)(1), 60.2(b)(1)(i), 60.2(b)(1)(iii), 60.2(d)(1), 60.2(d)(1)(iii), 60.3(a)(1)(ii), 60.4(b), 60.4(f)
Armstrong v. Comm'r, 6 T.C. 1166 (1946), aff'd, 162 F.2d 199 (3d Cir. 1947)	17.2(a)(1)
Arrow Fastener Co. v. Comm'r, 76 T.C. 423 (1981)	57
Atlantic City Elec. Co. v. United States, 161 F. Supp. 811 (Ct. Cl.), cert. denied, 358 U.S. 834 (1958)	24.4
Avery v. Comm'r, 111 F.2d 19 (9th Cir. 1940)	33.2

Table of Cases

(References are to book sections.)

Edward R. Bacon Co. v. Comm'r, 4 T.C.M. (CCH) 868 (1945), *aff'd per curiam*, 158 F.2d 981 (9th Cir. 1947)	17.2(c)(1)
Bagley & Sewall Co. v. Comm'r, 20 T.C. 983 (1953), *aff'd*, 221 F.2d 944 (2d Cir. 1955), *acq.* 1958-1 C.B. 3	21.1
Ball v. Comm'r, 54 T.C. 1200 (1970), *nonacq.* 1972-2 C.B. 3	9.3(b)(1), 9.3(b)(2)
Bankers Trust Co. v. United States, 284 F.2d 537 (2d Cir. 1960), *rev'g* 178 F. Supp. 267 (S.D.N.Y. 1959), *cert. denied*, 366 U.S. 903 (1961)	32.1(c)
Bank of America v. United States, 680 F.2d 142 (Ct. Cl. 1982), *aff'g in part, rev'g in part* 81-1 U.S. Tax Cas. (CCH) ¶ 9161 (Ct. Cl. 1981)	30.3(e)(1)(iv)
Barnes Group, Inc. v. United States, 697 F. Supp. 591 (D. Conn. 1988)	8.4(d), 23.2(e)(2)
Barnhill v. Comm'r, 241 F.2d 496 (5th Cir. 1957), *aff'g* Woodward v. Comm'r, 24 T.C. 883 (1955), *acq.* 1956-1 C.B. 6	31.4(a)(1)(i)
Barrett v. Comm'r, 58 T.C. 284 (1972), *acq.* 1974-1 C.B. 1	10.1(b)
Battelle v. Comm'r, 47 B.T.A. 117 (1942), *acq.* 1942-2 C.B. 2	18.11
Bazley v. Comm'r, 331 U.S. 737, *reh'g denied*, 332 U.S. 752 (1947)	27.3(c)(4)
Becker v. Comm'r, 378 F.2d 767 (3d Cir. 1967), *rev'g* 46 T.C. 613 (1966)	17.2(c)(2)
Becker Warburg Paribas Group, Inc. v. United States, 514 F. Supp. 1273 (N.D. Ill. 1981)	19.6(c)(3)
Behr-Manning Corp. v. United States, 196 F. Supp. 129 (D. Mass. 1961)	27.4(d)(2)
Belden v. Comm'r, 30 B.T.A. 601 (1934)	19.10(a)
Berckmans v. Comm'r, 20 T.C.M. (CCH) 458 (1961)	11.8(b)
Bethlehem Steel Corp. v. United States, 434 F.2d 1357 (Ct. Cl. 1970)	34.2(e)
Biggs v. Comm'r, 27 T.C.M. (CCH) 1177 (1968), *aff'd*, 440 F.2d 1 (6th Cir. 1971)	16.1
Billy Rose's Diamond Horseshoe, Inc. v. United States, 448 F.2d 549 (2d Cir. 1971), *aff'g* 322 F. Supp. 76 (S.D.N.Y. 1971)	58.1
Bingham v. Comm'r, 27 B.T.A. 186 (1932), *acq.* XII-1 C.B. 2	18.7
Black v. Comm'r, 45 B.T.A. 204 (1941)	11.9(c)
Blair v. Comm'r, 300 U.S. 5 (1937), *rev'g* 83 F.2d 655 (7th Cir. 1936)	24.7(c)
Bloch v. Comm'r, 148 F.2d 452 (9th Cir. 1945)	20.2(d)

Table of Cases

(References are to book sections.)

Board of Trade v. SEC, 677 F.2d 1137 (7th Cir.), *vacated as moot sub. nom.* Chicago Board Options Exch. v. Board of Trade, 459 U.S. 1026 (1982)	4.1(c)
Boehm v. Comm'r, 326 U.S. 287 (1945), *aff'g* 146 F.2d 553 (2d Cir. 1945)	27.8
Bogatin v. United States, 78-2 U.S. Tax Cas. (CCH) ¶ 9733 (W.D. Tenn. 1978)	36.5(d)
Bon Ami Co. v. Comm'r, 39 B.T.A. 825 (1939)	59.5(a)
Booth Newspapers, Inc. v. United States, 303 F.2d 916 (Ct. Cl. 1962)	23.2(d)(3)(i)
Boswell v. Comm'r, 91 T.C. 151 (1988)	47.2(e)
Bowersock Mills & Power Co. v. Comm'r, 172 F.2d 904 (10th Cir. 1949), *rev'g* 6 T.C.M. (CCH) 1106 (1947)	27.2, 27.3(b)(2)(ii)
Boykin v. Comm'r, 344 F.2d 889 (5th Cir. 1965), *rev'g* 22 T.C.M. (CCH) 1800 (1963)	17.2(a)(1)
Bradford v. Comm'r, 60 T.C. 253 (1973), *acq.* 1974-2 C.B. 1	9.3(b), 10.3(b), 11.3(b)(1)
Bradford v. United States, 444 F.2d 1133 (Ct. Cl. 1971)	10, 11.7(b), 17.2(a)(1)
Bramer v. United States, 259 F.2d 717 (3d Cir. 1958)	14.5(d)
Brewster v. Gage, 280 U.S. 327 (1930), *aff'g* 30 F.2d 604 (2d Cir. 1929), *rev'g* 25 F.2d 915 (W.D.N.Y. 1927)	17.3(c)(5)
Brochon v. Comm'r, 30 B.T.A. 404 (1934)	19.10(a)
Bronner v. Comm'r, 45 T.C.M. (CCH) 738 (1983)	18.11
Brown v. Comm'r, 85 T.C. 968 (1985), *aff'd sub nom.* Sochin v. Comm'r, 842 F.2d 351 (9th Cir.), *cert. denied*, 109 S. Ct. 72 (1988)	55.1, 58.1
Brown v. United States, 426 F.2d 355 (Ct. Cl. 1970)	8.3, 8.3(c), 9.4, 10.4, 11.4(a), 30.2(b)(4)
Bryant v. Comm'r, 111 F.2d 9 (9th Cir. 1940), *rev'g* 38 B.T.A. 618 (1938)	31.4(c)(2)
Bryant v. Comm'r, 2 T.C. 789 (1943), *acq.* 1944 C.B. 4	33.2
Busby v. United States, 679 F.2d 48 (5th Cir. 1982)	17.2(a)(2)(ii)
Business Roundtable v. SEC, 905 F.2d 406 (App. D.C. 1990)	1.1(a)
Byram v. United States, 705 F.2d 1418 (1983)	11.9(b)
Caldwell v. Comm'r, 202 F.2d 112 (2d Cir. 1953), *aff'g* 10 T.C.M. (CCH) 611 (1951)	22.3

Table of Cases

(References are to book sections.)

Campbell v. Comm'r, 39 B.T.A. 916 (1939), *aff'd sub nom.* Commissioner v. Gambrill, 112 F.2d 530 (2d Cir. 1940), *rev'd on other grounds sub nom.* Helvering v. Campbell, 313 U.S. 15, *reh'g denied*, 313 U.S. 598 (1941)	19.9(g)
Campbell Taggart, Inc. v. United States, 744 F.2d 442 (5th Cir. 1984), *aff'g* 552 F. Supp. 355 (N.D. Tex. 1982)	10.1
Cannon v. University of Chicago, 441 U.S. 677 (1979), *rev'g* 559 F.2d 1063 (7th Cir. 1976), *aff'g* 406 F. Supp. 1257 (N.D. Ill. 1976)	19.9(j)
Capek v. Comm'r, 86 T.C. 14 (1986)	30.2(b)(3)
Capento Sec. Corp. v. Comm'r, 47 B.T.A. 691 (1942), *nonacq.* 1943 C.B. 28, *aff'd*, 140 F.2d 382 (1st Cir. 1944)	34.2(e)
Carborundum Co. v. Comm'r, 74 T.C. 730 (1980), *acq.* 1984-2 C.B. 1	18.2(a)
Caruth v. United States, 688 F. Supp. 1129 (N.D. Tex. 1987), *aff'd*, 865 F.2d 644 (5th Cir. 1989)	24.7(c)
Case of State Tax on Foreign-Held Bonds, 82 U.S. 300 (1872)	48.3(b)(2)(i)
Caspe v. United States, 82-1 U.S. Tax Cas. (CCH) ¶ 9247 (S.D. Iowa 1982), *aff'd*, 694 F.2d 1116 (8th Cir. 1982)	17.1(a)
Centel Communications Co. v. Comm'r, 92 T.C. 612 (1989)	30.3(e)(1)(iv)
Central Elec. & Tel. Co. v. Comm'r, 47 B.T.A. 434 (1942), *acq.* 1942-2 C.B. 4	34.2(e)
CFTC v. CoPetro Mktg. Group, 680 F.2d 573 (9th Cir. 1982)	4.3(b)
Chamberlin v. Comm'r, 207 F.2d 462 (6th Cir. 1953), *rev'g* 18 T.C. 164 (1952), *cert. denied*, 347 U.S. 918 (1954)	27.3(b)(4)
Chang Hsiao Liang v. Comm'r, 23 T.C. 1040 (1955)	8.1
Chase v. Comm'r, 44 B.T.A. 39, *nonacq.* 1941-1 C.B. 13, *aff'd per curiam sub nom.* Helvering v. Chase, 128 F.2d 740 (2d Cir. 1942)	31.8
Chemical Bank & Trust Co. v. United States, 21 F. Supp. 167 (Ct. Cl. 1937)	8.2
Chesshire v. Comm'r, 11 T.C.M. (CCH) 146 (1952)	16.4(a)
Chicago Mercantile Exch. v. SEC, 883 F.2d 537 (7th Cir. 1989), *reh'g denied en banc*, 1989 U.S. App. LEXIS 16280, *cert. denied*, 1990 U.S. LEXIS 3165	4.1(c), 5.2(a)(2)
Chock Full O'Nuts Corp. v. United States, 453 F.2d 300 (2d Cir. 1971), *aff'g* 322 F. Supp. 772 (S.D.N.Y. 1971)	30.3(e)(2), 34.2(b)

Table of Cases

T-6

(References are to book sections.)

Citizens Nat'l Bank of Waco v. United States, 551 F.2d 832 (Ct. Cl. 1977)	31.11(b), 31.11(b)(2), 48.3(b)(2)(ii)
Citizens Nat'l Bank of Waco v. United States, 417 F.2d 675 (5th Cir. 1969), aff'g 68-2 U.S. Tax Cas. (CCH) ¶ 9484 (W.D. Tex. 1968)	17.3(c)(1)
City Bank Farmers Trust Co. v. Helvering, 313 U.S. 121 (1941), aff'g 112 F.2d 457 (2d Cir. 1940)	10.1(b)
City Bank Farmers Trust Co. v. Hoey, 52 F. Supp. 665 (S.D.N.Y. 1942), aff'd per curiam, 138 F.2d 1023 (2d Cir. 1943)	33.4
Clark Equip. Co. v. Comm'r, 89-2 U.S. Tax Cas. (CCH) ¶ 9471 (W.D. Mich. 1989), aff'd, 912 F.2d 113 (6th Cir. 1990)	34.2(f)
Claude Neon Elec. Prods. v. Comm'r, 35 B.T.A. 563 (1937), acq. 1937-2 C.B. 5, 1944 C.B. 5, nonacq. 1937-2 C.B. 34 withdrawn	22.2
Clyde E. Pierce Corp. v. Comm'r, 120 F.2d 206 (5th Cir. 1941)	33.3(a)(1)(i)(a)
Cole v. Helburn, 4 F. Supp. 230 (W.D. Ky. 1933)	19.10(b)
Colorado Nat'l Bank v. United States, 27 A.F.T.R.2d (P-H) ¶ 147,575 (D. Colo. 1971)	32.1(c)
Columbia Gas Sys. v. United States, 473 F.2d 1244 (2d Cir. 1973), aff'g 334 F. Supp. 1279 (S.D.N.Y. 1971)	34.2(e)
Comdisco, Inc. v. United States, 756 F.2d 569 (7th Cir. 1985), rev'g 83-2 U.S. Tax Cas. (CCH) ¶ 9245 (N.D. Ill. 1983)	36.5(b)
Commissioner v. Brown, 380 U.S. 563 (1965), aff'g 325 F.2d 313 (9th Cir. 1963), aff'g 37 T.C. 461 (1961)	36.5(c)
Commissioner v. Burnett, 118 F.2d 659 (5th Cir. 1941), aff'g in part, rev'g in part 40 B.T.A. 605 (1939)	8.3
Commissioner v. Charavay, 79 F.2d 406 (3d Cir. 1935)	8.3
Commissioner v. Court Holding Co., 324 U.S. 331 (1945), rev'g 143 F.2d 823 (5th Cir. 1944), rev'g 2 T.C. 531 (1943), acq. 1943 C.B. 5 (withdrawn in part), nonacq. 1968-2 C.B. 3, 1969-2 C.B. XXVI	36.5(b)
Commissioner v. Covington, 120 F.2d 768 (5th Cir. 1941), aff'g in part, rev'g in part 42 B.T.A. 601 (1940), cert. denied, 315 U.S. 822 (1942)	9.1(c)(1), 10, 10.1(d), 16.2(a), 42.1
Commissioner v. Danielson, 378 F.2d 771 (3d Cir. 1967), vacating 44 T.C. 549 (1965), cert. denied, 389 U.S. 858 (1967), on remand, 50 T.C. 782 (1968)	36.5(b)

(References are to book sections.)

Commissioner v. Dyer, 74 F.2d 685 (2d Cir.), *cert. denied*, 296 U.S. 586 (1935)	19.10(d)
Commissioner v. Farmers & Ginners Cotton Oil, 120 F.2d 772 (5th Cir. 1941), *rev'g* 41 B.T.A. 255 (1940), *superseding* 41 B.T.A. 1083 (1940), *nonacq.* 1940-2 C.B. 11, *cert. denied*, 314 U.S. 683 (1941)	18.11
Commissioner v. Fink, 483 U.S. 89 (1987), *rev'g* 789 F.2d 427 (6th Cir. 1986), *rev'g* 48 T.C.M. (CCH) 786 (1984)	16.4(a)
Commissioner v. Gambrill, 112 F.2d 530 (2d Cir. 1940), *rev'd on other grounds sub nom.* Helvering v. Campbell, 313 U.S. 15, *reh'g denied*, 313 U.S. 598 (1941)	19.9(g)
Commissioner v. Gillette Motor Transport Co., 364 U.S. 130 (1960), *rev'g* 265 F.2d 648 (5th Cir. 1959), *rev'g* 17 T.C.M. (CCH) 102 (1958)	14.1
Commissioner v. Groetzinger, 480 U.S. 23 (1987), *aff'g* 771 F.2d 269 (7th Cir. 1985), *aff'g* 82 T.C. 793 (1984)	8.2, 9.1(d), 10.1, 10.1(b), 11.9(c), 19.4(c)
Commissioner v. Guaranty Trust Co., 144 F.2d 756 (2d Cir. 1944), *rev'd sub nom.* Estate of Putnam v. Comm'r, 324 U.S. 393 (1945)	24.7(c)
Commissioner v. Johnston, 107 F.2d 883 (6th Cir. 1939)	19.10(c)
Commissioner v. P.G. Lake, Inc., 356 U.S. 260 (1958), *rev'g* 241 F.2d 71 (5th Cir. 1957), *aff'g* 24 T.C. 1016 (1955), *nonacq.* 1956-2 C.B. 10, *reh'g denied*, 356 U.S. 964 (1958)	14.1, 36.5(b)
Commissioner v. Leslie, 413 F.2d 636 (2d Cir. 1969), *rev'g* 50 T.C. 11 (1968), *cert. denied*, 396 U.S. 1007 (1970)	11.3(b)(1)
Commissioner v. Levis's Estate, 127 F.2d 796 (2d Cir.), *cert. denied*, 317 U.S. 645 (1942)	10.1(d), 18.2(c), 18.6(e)(1)
Commissioner v. Lincoln Sav. & Loan Ass'n, 403 U.S. 345 (1971), *rev'g* 422 F.2d 90 (9th Cir. 1970), *rev'g* 51 T.C. 82 (1968)	27.5(a)(3)
Commissioner v. Meridian & Thirteenth Realty Co., 132 F.2d 182 (7th Cir. 1942), *rev'g* 44 B.T.A. 865 (1941), *nonacq.* 1941-2 C.B. 21	27.3(b)(2)
Commissioner v. Motor Mart Trust, 156 F.2d 122 (1st Cir. 1946) *aff'g* 4 T.C. 931 (1945), *acq.* 1947-1 C.B. 3	34.2(d)
Commissioner v. North Am. Bond Trust, 122 F.2d 545 (2d Cir.), *cert. denied*, 314 U.S. 701 (1941)	29.1(a), 29.1(b), 36.2(a), 36.2(b)

Table of Cases   T-8

(References are to book sections.)

Commissioner v. Palmer, Stacy-Merrill, Inc., 111 F.2d 809 (9th Cir. 1940), aff'g 39 B.T.A. 636 (1939), nonacq. 1939-1 C.B. (1) 59, aff'g 37 B.T.A. 530 (1938)	27.2, 27.3(b)(2)(ii)
Commissioner v. Pittston Co., 252 F.2d 344 (2d Cir. 1958), rev'g 26 T.C. 967 (1956), nonacq. 1957-1 C.B. 5, cert. denied, 357 U.S. 919 (1958)	58.1
Commissioner v. Segall, 114 F.2d 706 (6th Cir. 1940), rev'g 38 B.T.A. 43 (1938), nonacq. 1938-2 C.B. 58, cert. denied, 313 U.S. 562 (1941)	36.5(c)
Commissioner v. Shapiro, 278 F.2d 556 (7th Cir. 1960)	16.4(a)
Commissioner v. Starr Bros., 204 F.2d 673 (2d Cir. 1953), rev'g 18 T.C. 149 (1959), nonacq. 1952-2 C.B. 6	58.1
Commissioner v. Turner, 410 F.2d 752 (6th Cir. 1969), aff'g 49 T.C. 356 (1968)	17.3(c)(1)
Commissioner v. Von Gunten, 76 F.2d 670 (6th Cir. 1935), aff'g 28 B.T.A. 702 (1933), acq. 1938-1 C.B. 32, nonacq. withdrawn, XII-2 C.B. 27	20.2(d)
Commissioner v. Wiesler, 161 F.2d 997 (6th Cir.), cert. denied, 332 U.S. 842 (1947)	18.6(d), 18.6(e)(1)
Commissioner v. Wilson, 163 F.2d 680 (9th Cir.), cert. denied, 332 U.S. 842 (1947)	18.6(a)
Connelly v. Comm'r, 45 T.C.M. (CCH) 49 (1982)	8.3(a)
Continental Ill. Nat'l Bank and Trust of Chicago v. Comm'r, 69 T.C. 357 (1977), acq. 1978-2 C.B.1	8.4
Cook v. Comm'r, 90 T.C. 975 (1988)	47.2(e)
Corbett v. Comm'r, 16 B.T.A. 1231 (1929), acq. VIII-2 C.B. 12	19.10(a)
Corn Prods. Ref. Co. v. Comm'r, 350 U.S. 46 (1955), aff'g 215 F.2d 513 (2d Cir. 1954), aff'g 20 T.C. 503 (1953), aff'g 11 T.C.M. (CCH) 721 (1952), aff'g 16 T.C. 395 (1951), reh'g denied, 350 U.S. 943 (1956)	8.4, 8.4(b), 8.4(d), 12, 12.3, 14.1, 19.6(c)(1), 21.1, 23.2(a), 23.2(b)(3), 23.2(c)(4), 23.2(d)(3), 45.2(a), 56.2, 60.2(d)(1)(iii)
Cortland Specialty Co. v. Comm'r, 60 F.2d 937 (2d Cir. 1932), aff'g 22 B.T.A. 808 (1931), cert. denied, 288 U.S. 599 (1933)	27.3(b)(2)(iii)
Cosgrove v. Comm'r, 54 T.C.M. (CCH) 136 (1987)	27.7

(References are to book sections.)

Cottage Sav. Ass'n v. Comm'r, ___ U.S. ___, 111 S. Ct. 1519 (1991) (59 U.S.L.W. 4314), rev'g ___ U.S. ___, 111 S. Ct. 383 (1990), granting motion to ___ U.S. ___, 111 S. Ct. 40 (1990), granting cert. to 1990 U.S. App. LEXIS 5151, denying reh'g en banc to 890 F.2d 848 (6th Cir. 1989), rev'g 90 T.C. 372 (1988)	19.9(j)
Coulter v. Comm'r, 32 B.T.A. 617 (1935)	10.1(b), 19.3(b), 19.4(c)
Cournan v. Comm'r, 58 T.C.M. (CCH) 219 (1989)	27.7
Craig v. Refco, Inc., 624 F. Supp. 944 (N.D. Ill. 1985), aff'd per curiam, 816 F.2d 347 (7th Cir. 1987)	9.2(c)(2)
Crown Iron Works Co. v. Comm'r, 245 F.2d 357 (8th Cir. 1957), aff'g 15 T.C.M. (CCH) 1046 (1956)	27.3(b)(2)
Cukor v. Comm'r, 27 T.C.M. (CCH) 89 (1968)	24.7(c)
Curtis v. Helvering, 101 F.2d 40 (2d Cir. 1939)	20.2(a)(1)(ii)
Dairy Queen of Okla. v. Comm'r, 18 T.C.M. (CCH) 322 (1959)	17.3(c)(3)
Darby Inv. Corp. v. Comm'r, 37 T.C. 839 (1962), aff'd per curiam, 315 F.2d 551 (6th Cir. 1963)	31.3(a)
Dart v. Comm'r, 74 F.2d 845 (4th Cir. 1935), rev'g 29 B.T.A. 125 (1933)	18.6(e)(1)
Davidson v. Comm'r, 305 U.S. 44 (1938), aff'g 94 F.2d 303 (8th Cir.), and aff'g 94 F.2d 300 (1938), aff'g 34 B.T.A. 555 (1936), acq. XV-2 C.B. 7, cert. denied, 304 U.S. 569 (1938)	20.2(a)(1)(ii)
Deely v. Comm'r, 73 T.C. 1081 (1980), acq. 1981-2 C.B. 1	9.1(c)(9)
DeMartino v. Comm'r, 51 T.C.M. (CCH) 1278 (1986), supp. op. 88 T.C. 583 (1987), aff'd without op. sub nom. McDonnell v. Comm'r, 862 F.2d 308 (3d Cir. 1988), and aff'd, 862 F.2d 400 (2d Cir. 1988)	9.2(g)
Denver & Rio Grande W.R.R. v. Comm'r, 32 T.C. 43 (1959), aff'd on other grounds, 279 F.2d 368 (10th Cir. 1960)	34.2(a)
Deputy v. Du Pont, 308 U.S. 488 (1940), rev'g 103 F.2d 257 (3d Cir. 1939), modifying 22 F. Supp. 589 (D.C. Del. 1938)	9.2(a), 10.1(b), 25.1, 30.3(d)(3), 55.1, 60.2(b)(2)(i)(a)(1)
Derr v. Comm'r, 77 T.C. 708 (1981)	55.1
Dillon, Read & Co. v. United States, 875 F.2d 293 (Fed. Cir. 1989), vacating and remanding 15 Cl. Ct. 246 (1988)	11.3(b)(1)
District Bond Co. v. Comm'r, 1 T.C. 837 (1943)	31.4(c)(2)
Dolin v. Comm'r, 54 T.C.M. (CCH) 1448 (1988)	9.1(c)(2)

Table of Cases

(References are to book sections.)

Donander Co. v. Comm'r, 29 B.T.A. 312 (1933)	19.4
Doyle v. Comm'r, 286 F.2d 654 (7th Cir. 1961), *rev'g* 19 T.C.M. (CCH) 677 (1960)	19.3(f)
Dunn Trust v. Comm'r, 86 T.C. 745 (1986)	27.4(b)
Dyer v. Comm'r, 352 F.2d 948 (8th Cir. 1965), *aff'g* 23 T.C.M. (CCH) 1208 (1964)	9.1(c)(4)
Dyke v. Comm'r, 6 T.C. 1134 (1946), *acq.* 1946-2 C.B. 2	17.2(a)(1)
Eastern Serv. Corp. v. Comm'r, 650 F.2d 379 (2d Cir. 1981), *rev'g* 73 T.C. 833 (1980)	27.5(a)(2), 27.5(a)(3)
Eder v. Comm'r, 9 T.C.M. (CCH) 98 (1950)	16.1
Edwards v. Hogg, 214 F.2d 640 (5th Cir. 1954), *aff'g in part, rev'g in part* Hogg v. Allen, 105 F. Supp. 12 (M.D. Ga. 1952)	17.3(c)(2)
Eisner v. Macomber, 252 U.S. 189 (1920)	9.2(c)(1), 19.9(j)
H. Elkan & Co. v. Comm'r, 2 T.C. 597 (1943), *acq.* 1943 C.B. 7	9.2(c)(1)
Elko Lamoilee Power Co. v. Comm'r, 50 F.2d 595 (9th Cir. 1931), *aff'g* 21 B.T.A. 291 (1930)	27.3(b)(2)
Emery v. Comm'r, 166 F.2d 27 (2d Cir. 1948), *aff'g* 8 T.C. 979 (1947)	31.9(b), 33.4
Emmer Bros. v. Comm'r, 57 T.C.M. (CCH) 952 (1989)	27.8
Enrici v. Comm'r, 813 F.2d 293 (9th Cir. 1987)	9.2(g), 10.2(g)
Epstein v. Comm'r, 36 B.T.A. 109 (1937), *acq.* 1938-1 C.B. 10	20.2(c)
Estate of Estroff v. Comm'r, 47 T.C.M. (CCH) 234 (1983)	19.8, 19.8(d)
Estate of Federman v. Comm'r, 11 T.C.M. (CCH) 686 (1952)	24.7(c)
Estate of Hirsch v. Comm'r, 46 T.C.M. (CCH) 559 (1983)	14.5(d)
Estate of Ingalls v. Comm'r, 45 B.T.A. 787 (1941), *nonacq.* 1942-1 C.B. 24, *aff'd*, 132 F.2d 862 (6th Cir. 1943)	19.10(d)
Estate of Laughlin v. Comm'r, 30 T.C.M. (CCH) 227 (1971)	18.11
Estate of Milner v. Comm'r, 1 T.C.M. (CCH) 513 (1943)	9.1(c)(1)
Estate of Mitchell v. Comm'r, 37 B.T.A. 161 (1938)	19.10(a)
Estate of Monroe v. Comm'r, 45 B.T.A. 1060 (1941), *acq.* 1942-1 C.B. 12, *aff'd per curiam sub nom.* Pinnell v. Comm'r, 132 F.2d 126 (3d Cir. 1942), *amended sub nom.* Pinnell v. Comm'r, 43-1 U.S. Tax Cas. (CCH) ¶ 9255 (3d Cir. 1943)	31.10

(References are to book sections.)

Estate of Parshelsky v. Comm'r, 303 F.2d 14 (2d Cir. 1962), rev'g 34 T.C. 946 (1960)	27.4(b)(2)
Estate of Piper v. United States, 57 A.F.T.R.2d (P-H) ¶ 148,833 (Ct. Cl. 1986)	32.1(c)
Estate of Putnam v. Comm'r, 324 U.S. 393 (1945), rev'g Commissioner v. Guaranty Trust Co., 144 F.2d 756 (2d Cir. 1944), rev'g Putnam v. Comm'r, 45 B.T.A. 517 (1941), nonacq. 1941-2 C.B. 19, 22	24.7(c)
Estate of Simmie v. Comm'r, 69 T.C. 890 (1978), aff'd, 632 F.2d 93 (9th Cir. 1980)	32.1(c)
Estate of Smith v. Comm'r, 292 F.2d 478 (3d Cir. 1961), aff'g Anton v. Comm'r, 34 T.C. 842 (1960), cert. denied, 368 U.S. 967 (1962)	24.7(c)
Estate of Smith v. Comm'r, 313 F.2d 724 (8th Cir. 1963), aff'g in part, rev'g in part 33 T.C. 465 (1959)	10
Etshokin v. Comm'r, 59 T.C.M. (CCH) 753 (1990)	47.2(e)
Evans v. Comm'r, 447 F.2d 547 (7th Cir. 1971), aff'g 54 T.C. 40 (1970), acq. 1978-2 C.B. 2	28.1(c)
Fabens v. Comm'r, 519 F.2d 1310 (1st Cir. 1975), aff'g in part, rev'g in part 62 T.C. 775 (1974)	9.3(a)
Factor v. Comm'r, 281 F.2d 100 (9th Cir. 1960), cert. denied, 364 U.S. 933 (1961)	8.3
Faroll v. Jarecki, 231 F.2d 281 (7th Cir.), cert. denied, 352 U.S. 830 (1956)	8.2, 8.2(a)
Fawsett v. Comm'r, 31 B.T.A. 139 (1934)	19.10(a)
Federal Deposit Ins. Corp. v. Philadelphia Gear Corp., 476 U.S. 426 (1986), on remand, 795 F.2d 903 (10th Cir. 1986), rev'g 474 U.S. 918 (1985), aff'g in part, rev'g in part 587 F. Supp. 294 (W.D. Okla. 1984)	33.3(a)(1)(ii)
Ferguson v. Comm'r, 33 T.C.M. (CCH) 1082 (1974)	8.2
First Fed. Sav. & Loan v. Oklahoma Tax Comm'n, 743 P.2d 640 (1987), cert. denied, 485 U.S. 901 (1988)	32.2(b)
First Kentucky Co. v. Gray, 190 F. Supp. 824 (W.D. Ky. 1960), aff'd, 309 F.2d 845 (6th Cir. 1962)	31.8
First Mortgage Corp. of Phila. v. Comm'r, 135 F.2d 121 (3d Cir. 1943)	27.3(b)(2)
First Nat'l Bank in Wichita v. Comm'r, 57 F.2d 7 (10th Cir. 1932), aff'g 19 B.T.A. 744 (1930), cert. denied, 287 U.S. 636 (1932)	31.11(b)
Fisher v. Comm'r, 209 F.2d 513 (6th Cir. 1954), aff'g 19 T.C. 384 (1952), cert. denied, 347 U.S. 1014 (1954)	31.8

Table of Cases

(References are to book sections.)

Fletcher v. Comm'r, Tax Ct. Rep. (CCH) 46,358 (Jan. 31, 1990)	32.1(b)(1)(iv)
Flint v. Stone Tracy Co., 220 U.S. 107 (1910)	10.1(b)
FNMA v. Comm'r, 90 T.C. 405 (1988), *aff'd*, 896 F.2d 580 (App. D.C. 1990)	19.9(j)
Foote v. Comm'r, 81 T.C. 930 (1983)	58.1
Ford v. Comm'r, 33 B.T.A. 1229 (1936), *acq.* 1937-1 C.B. 9	20.2(c)
Forrester v. Comm'r, 32 B.T.A. 745 (1935)	20.2(b)
Forseth v. Comm'r, 85 T.C. 127 (1985), *aff'd sub nom.* Mahoney v. Comm'r, 808 F.2d 1219 (6th Cir. 1987), *and aff'd sub nom.* Enrici v. Comm'r, 813 F.2d 293 (9th Cir. 1987), *and aff'd*, 845 F.2d 746 (7th Cir. 1988)	9.2(g), 10.2(g), 58.1
Fox v. Comm'r, 82 T.C. 1001 (1984)	30.2(b)(1), 47.2(b), 47.2(c), 47.2(d)(1), 47.2(d)(2)
Free v. Bland, 369 U.S. 663 (1962), *rev'g* 162 Tex. 72, 344 S.W.2d 435 (1961), *rev'g* 337 S.W.2d 805 (Tex. Civ. App. 1960)	32.1(b)(1)(iv)
Freytag v. Comm'r, 89 T.C. 849 (1987), *aff'd*, 904 F.2d 1011 (5th Cir. 1990), *reh'g denied*, 1990 U.S. App. LEXIS 15152, *cert. granted*, 1991 U.S. LEXIS 645	58.1
Frick v. Driscoll, 29 A.F.T.R. (P-H) 1298 (1941), *rev'd in part on other grounds*, 129 F.2d 148 (3d Cir. 1942)	19.9(g)
Frieder v. Comm'r, 27 B.T.A. 1239 (1933)	24.7(c)
FS Servs., Inc. v. United States, 413 F.2d 548 (Ct. Cl. 1969)	18.11
Fuller v. Comm'r, 81 F.2d 176 (1st Cir. 1936), *rev'g* 31 B.T.A. 154 (1934)	20.2(c)
Fulton Bag & Cotton Mills v. Comm'r, 22 T.C. 1044 (1954)	18.11
Gantner v. Comm'r, 91 T.C. 713 (1988), *later proceeding* Gantner v. Comm'r, 92 T.C. 192 (1989), *aff'd*, 905 F.2d 241 (8th Cir. 1990), *cert. denied*, 1990 U.S. LEXIS 5241	19.6(b), 19.6(c)(1)
Ganz v. Comm'r, 59 T.C.M. 604 (1990)	42.4
Gardens of Faith, Inc. v. Comm'r, 23 T.C.M. (CCH) 1045 (1964), *aff'd per curiam*, 345 F.2d 180 (4th Cir.), *cert. denied*, 382 U.S. 927 (1965)	16.4(a)
Garrett v. United States, 479 F.2d 598 (5th Cir. 1973), *aff'g* 73-2 U.S. Tax Cas. (CCH) ¶ 16,094 (N.D. Tex. 1972)	40.2(c)(4)

(References are to book sections.)

Gatlin v. Comm'r, 34 B.T.A. 50 (1936)	36.5(c)
General Artists Corp. v. Comm'r, 205 F.2d 360 (2d Cir. 1953), aff'g 17 T.C. 1517 (1952), cert. denied, 346 U.S. 866 (1953)	58.1
Giffin v. Comm'r, 19 B.T.A. 1243 (1930)	14.3
Gilman v. Comm'r, 53 F.2d 47 (8th Cir. 1931), aff'g 18 B.T.A. 1277 (1930)	25.1
Girard Trust Co. v. United States, 166 F.2d 773 (3d Cir. 1948), aff'g 69 F. Supp. 874 (E.D. Pa. 1946)	31.9(b), 33.4
Glass v. Comm'r, 87 T.C. 1087 (1986), aff'd sub nom. Herrington v. Comm'r, 854 F.2d 755 (5th Cir. 1988), and aff'd sub nom. Yosha v. Comm'r, 861 F.2d 494 (7th Cir. 1988), cert. denied, 1989 U.S. LEXIS 2370	30.2(b)(2), 31.11(b)(3), 47.2(c), 47.2(e), 58.1
Glensder Textile Co. v. Comm'r, 46 B.T.A. 176 (1942)	28.1(a)
Gold v. Comm'r, 41 T.C. 419 (1963)	18.6(a)
Goldin v. Baker, 809 F.2d 187 (2d Cir.), cert. denied, 484 U.S. 816 (1987)	33.3(a)(3)
Goldstein v. Comm'r, 364 F.2d 734 (2d Cir. 1966), aff'g 44 T.C. 284 (1965), cert. denied, 385 U.S. 1005 (1967)	9.2(a), 9.2(g), 10.2(g), 55.1
Graham v. Comm'r, 326 F.2d 878 (4th Cir. 1964), rev'g 40 T.C. 14 (1963)	9.1(c)(4)
Gregory v. Helvering, 293 U.S. 465 (1935), aff'g 69 F.2d 809 (2d Cir. 1934), rev'g 27 B.T.A. 223 (1932), nonacq. XII-2 C.B. 20	36.5(b)
Greiner v. Lewellyn, 258 U.S. 384 (1922)	33.3(a)(2)
Grodt v. McKay Realty v. Comm'r, 77 T.C. 1221 (1981)	36.5(c)
Groetzinger v. Comm'r, 771 F.2d 269 (7th Cir. 1985), aff'd, 480 U.S. 23 (1987)	10.1, 10.1(b), 19.5(c)
Gulftex Drug Co. v. Comm'r, 29 T.C. 118 (1957), aff'd per curiam, 261 F.2d 238 (5th Cir. 1958)	8.4
Gummey v. Comm'r, 26 B.T.A. 894 (1932)	19.10(a)
Gutmann v. Comm'r, 38 B.T.A. 679 (1938), acq. 1939-1 C.B. 15	19.8
Haft v. Comm'r, 20 B.T.A. 431 (1930)	16.4(a)
Haggard v. Comm'r, 24 T.C. 1124 (1955), aff'd, 241 F.2d 288 (9th Cir. 1956)	36.5(c)
Hale v. Comm'r, 44 T.C.M. (CCH) 1116 (1982)	9.1(c)
Hall v. Comm'r, 92 T.C. 1027 (1989)	16.2(b), 20.3
Handy Button Mach. Co. v. Comm'r, 61 T.C. 846 (1974), acq. 1974-2 C.B. 2	9.3(b)(1)
Hanes v. Comm'r, 1 T.C.M. (CCH) 634 (1943)	20.2(b)

Table of Cases

(References are to book sections.)

Hanlin v. Comm'r, 108 F.2d 429 (3d Cir. 1939), *aff'g* 38 B.T.A. 811 (1938), *nonacq.* 1939-1 C.B. (1) 55	19.9, 19.9(g), 19.9(j)
Harper v. Comm'r, 35 T.C.M. (CCH) 256 (1976)	11.9(b)
Harriss v. Comm'r, 143 F.2d 279 (2d Cir. 1944), *aff'g* 44 B.T.A. 999 (1941), *acq.* 1941-2 C.B. 6	47.2, 47.2(a)
Hart v. Comm'r, 54 F.2d 848 (1st Cir. 1932), *aff'g in part, rev'g in part* 21 B.T.A. (1930)	14.5(d)
Hart v. Comm'r, 41 T.C. 131 (1963), *aff'd*, 338 F.2d 410 (2d Cir. 1964)	18.6(a)
Harvey v. Comm'r, 2 B.T.A.M. (P-H) 639 (1933)	19.10(a)
Hastings v. Comm'r, 11 T.C.M. (CCH) 399 (1952)	24.7(c)
Hellman v. Helvering, 68 F.2d 763 (App. D.C. 1934)	16.4(l)
Helvering v. Campbell, 313 U.S. 15, *reh'g denied*, 313 U.S. 598 (1941)	19.9(g)
Helvering v. Chase, 128 F.2d 740 (2d Cir. 1942), *aff'g* 44 B.T.A. 39 (1941), *nonacq.* 1941-1 C.B. 13	
Helvering v. Fried, 299 U.S. 175 (1936), *aff'g* 83 F.2d 193 (2d Cir. 1936), *rev'g* 31 B.T.A. 638 (1934)	8.3(c), 11.9(c)
Helvering v. Horst, 311 U.S. 112 (1940), *rev'g* 107 F.2d 906 (2d Cir. 1939), *rev'g* 39 B.T.A. 757 (1939)	24.7(c), 24.7(d)
Helvering v. Janney, 311 U.S. 189 (1940), *aff'g* 108 F.2d 564 (3d Cir. 1939), *rev'g* 39 B.T.A. 240 (1939)	15.4(b), 15.4(d)
Helvering v. F. & R. Lazarus & Co., 308 U.S. 252 (1939), *aff'g* 101 F.2d 728 (6th Cir. 1939), *aff'g* 32 B.T.A. 633 (1935), *nonacq.* XIV-2 C.B. 35	36.5(b)
Helvering v. National Grocery Co., 304 U.S. 282 (1938), *rev'g* 92 F.2d 931 (3d Cir. 1937), *rev'g* 35 B.T.A. 163 (1936), *reh'g denied*, 305 U.S. 669 (1938)	47.2(d)(2)
Helvering v. Richmond, Fredericksburg & Potomac R.R., 90 F.2d 971 (4th Cir. 1937), *aff'g* 33 B.T.A. 895 (1936)	27.2
Helvering v. San Joaquim Fruit & Inv. Co., 297 U.S. 496 (1936), *rev'g* 85 F.2d 854 (9th Cir.), *and rev'g* 77 F.2d 723 (1935), *rev'g* 28 B.T.A. 395 (1933), *reh'g denied*, 297 U.S. 728 (1936)	17.2(c)(2)
Helvering v. Southwest Consol. Corp., 315 U.S. 194 (1942) *rev'g* 119 F.2d 561 (5th Cir. 1941), *reh'g denied*, 316 U.S. 710 (1942)	27.3(c)(2)
Helvering v. Stifel, 75 F.2d 583 (4th Cir. 1935)	20.2(d)
Helvering v. Stuart, 317 U.S. 154 (1942), *rev'g* 124 F.2d 772 (7th Cir. 1941), *modifying* 42 B.T.A. 1421 (1940)	32.1(b)(1)(iv)
Helvering v. Taylor, 128 F.2d 885 (2d Cir. 1942), *aff'g* 43 B.T.A. 563 (1941), *acq. and nonacq.* 1941-1 C.B. 10, 19	14.5(b)(1)

(References are to book sections.)

Helvering v. Union Pac. R.R., 293 U.S. 282 (1934), aff'g 69 F.2d 966 (2d Cir. 1934), denying reh'g to 69 F.2d 67 (2d Cir. 1934), rev'g 26 B.T.A. 1126 (1932), acq. and nonacq. XII-1 C.B. 13, 23	34.2(a)
Helvering v. Winmill, 305 U.S. 79 (1938), rev'g 93 F.2d 494 (2d Cir. 1937), rev'g 35 B.T.A. 804 (1937)	10.1, 10.1(d), 16.5
Henderson v. Comm'r, 27 T.C.M. (CCH) 109 (1968)	9.1(c)(5)
Hendrich v. Comm'r, 49 T.C.M. (P-H) 1448 (1980)	8.4(b)
Hendricks v. Comm'r, 51 T.C. 235 (1968), aff'd, 423 F.2d 485 (4th Cir. 1970)	18.2(c)
Herrington v. Comm'r, 854 F.2d 755 (5th Cir. 1988), cert. denied, 1989 U.S. LEXIS 2370	30.2(b)(2), 31.11(b)(3), 47.2(c), 47.2(e), 58.1
Hewitt v. Comm'r, 30 B.T.A. 962 (1934), acq. VIII-2 C.B. 9	31.8
Higgins v. Comm'r, 312 U.S. 212 (1941), aff'g 111 F.2d 795 (2d Cir. 1940), aff'g 39 B.T.A. 1005 (1939), acq. 1940-1 C.B. 3, reh'g denied, 312 U.S. 714 (1941)	8.1, 8.3, 10.1(b)
Higgins v. United States, 75 F. Supp. 252 (Ct. Cl. 1948)	55.1
Hirai v. Comm'r, 48 T.C.M. (CCH) 1134 (1984)	9.2(g), 10.2(g), 42.4, 55.1
Hogg v. Allen, 105 F. Supp. 12 (M.D. Ga. 1952), aff'd in part, rev'd in part sub nom. Edwards v. Hogg, 214 F.2d 640 (5th Cir. 1954)	17.3(c)(2)
Holmes v. Comm'r, 134 F.2d 219 (3d Cir. 1943)	20.2(a)(1)(ii)
R.O. Holton & Co. v. Comm'r, 44 B.T.A. 202 (1941)	31.8, 33.3(a)(1)(i)(a)
Honeywell Inc. v. Comm'r, 87 T.C. 624 (1986), acq. 1988-1 C.B. 1	34.2(b)
Honodel v. Comm'r, 722 F.2d 1462 (9th Cir. 1984), aff'g 76 T.C. 351 (1981)	9.1(c)(1)
Hoover Co. v. Comm'r, 72 T.C. 206 (1979), acq. 1984-2 C.B. 1	8.4(d), 18.11, 23.2(e)(2), 58.1
Horne v. Comm'r, 5 T.C. 250 (1945)	19.6(c)(3)
Hort v. Comm'r, 313 U.S. 28 (1941), aff'g 112 F.2d 167 (2d Cir. 1940), aff'g 39 B.T.A. 922 (1939), acq. 1939-2 C.B. 18	14.1
Hudspeth v. United States, 471 F.2d 275 (8th Cir. 1972), rev'g 335 F. Supp. 1401 (E.D. Mo. 1971)	24.7(c)
Huebschman v. Comm'r, 41 T.C.M. (CCH) 474 (1980)	10
Hummel-Ross Fibre Corp. v. Comm'r, 40 B.T.A. 821 (1939), acq. 1940-1 C.B. 3	34.2(e)
Hunt Foods & Indus. v. Comm'r, 57 T.C. 633 (1972), aff'd per curiam, 496 F.2d 532 (9th Cir. 1974)	34.2(b)

Table of Cases

T-16

(References are to book sections.)

Huntington Sec. Corp. v. Busey, 112 F.2d 368 (6th Cir. 1940), *rev'g* 26 F. Supp. 849 (S.D. Ohio 1939)	22.3
Husky Oil Co. v. Comm'r, 83 T.C. 717 (1984), *aff'd sub nom.* Marathon Oil v. Comm'r, 838 F.2d 1114 (10th Cir. 1987)	34.2(e)
Husted v. Comm'r, 47 T.C. 664 (1967), *acq.* 1968-1 C.B. 2	11.8(b)
Illinois Terminal R.R. v. United States, 375 F.2d 1016 (Ct. Cl. 1967)	9.3(b)(2)
Indian Trail Trading Post, Inc. v. Comm'r, 60 T.C. 497 (1973), *aff'd*, 503 F.2d 102 (6th Cir. 1974)	9.3(b)(2)
Industrial Research Prods., Inc. v. Comm'r, 40 T.C. 578 (1963), *acq.* 1966-1 C.B. 2	31.4(c)(1)
International Tel. & Tel. Corp. v. Comm'r, 77 T.C. 60, *supp. op.* 77 T.C. 1367 (1981), *aff'd per curiam*, 704 F.2d 252 (2d Cir. 1983)	34.3(e)
International Trading Co. v. Comm'r, 17 T.C.M. (CCH) 521 (1958), *aff'd*, 275 F.2d 578 (7th Cir. 1960), *and aff'd sub nom.* Commissioner v. Shapiro, 278 F.2d 556 (7th Cir. 1960)	16.4(a)
Jaglom v. Comm'r, 303 F.2d 847 (2d Cir. 1962), *aff'g* 36 T.C. 126 (1961)	31.8
Jemison v. Comm'r, 28 B.T.A. 514 (1933)	24.7(c)
Jewel Tea Co. v. United States, 90 F.2d 451 (2d Cir. 1937), *aff'g* 15 F. Supp. 56 (S.D.N.Y. 1936)	27.3(b)(3)
Johnson v. United States, 435 F.2d 1257 (4th Cir. 1971), *rev'g* 303 F. Supp. 1 (E.D. Va. 1971)	24.1(d)
Jordan Co. v. Allen, 85 F. Supp. 437 (M.D. Ga. 1949)	27.3(b)(3)
Julien v. Comm'r, 82 T.C. 492 (1984)	9.2(g), 10.2(g), 42.4, 55.1
Kaplan v. Comm'r, 21 T.C. 134 (1953)	19.10(d)
Kasle v. United States, 75 F. Supp. 341 (N.D. Ohio 1947)	16.4(a)
Keeler v. Comm'r, 86 F.2d 265 (8th Cir. 1936), *cert. denied*, 300 U.S. 373 (1937)	20.2(d)
Kelley v. Comm'r, 281 F.2d 527 (9th Cir. 1960), *aff'g* 18 T.C.M. 329 (1959)	11.9(b)
John Kelley Co. v. Comm'r, 326 U.S. 521 (1946), *rev'g* 146 F.2d 466 (7th Cir. 1944), *rev'g* 1 T.C. 457 (1943), *nonacq.* 1943 C.B. 34	27.3(b)(3)(iii)
Kemon v. Comm'r, 16 T.C. 1026 (1951)	8.2, 8.3, 8.3(a), 10, 11.9(c), 23.2(d)(3)(ii)

(References are to book sections.)

Kidder v. Comm'r, 30 B.T.A. 59 (1934)	19.9(c)
King v. Comm'r, 89 T.C. 445 (1987), *acq.* 1988-2 C.B. 1, *action on decision*, 1988-009 (Apr. 11, 1988), *related reference* King v. Comm'r, 87 T.C. 1213 (1986)	9.2(e), 10.1, 10.2(e), 42.4, 47.2(e), 55.1
King v. United States, 545 F.2d 700 (10th Cir. 1976)	47.2(d)(2)
Kinney v. Comm'r, 66 T.C. 122 (1976)	9.1(c)(5)
Kinsey v. Comm'r, 477 F.2d 1058 (2d Cir. 1973), *aff'g* 58 T.C. 259 (1972)	24.7(c)
Kistler v. Burnet, 58 F.2d 687 (App. D.C. 1932), *aff'g* 21 B.T.A. 433 (1930)	16.4(*l*)
Kluger Assocs., Inc. v. Comm'r, 69 T.C. 925 (1978), *aff'd*, 617 F.2d 323 (2d Cir. 1980)	20.2(a)(1)(i)
Knetsch v. United States, 364 U.S. 361 (1960), *aff'g* 272 F.2d 200 (9th Cir. 1959)	9.2(a), 9.2(g), 10.2(g), 55.1
Knight-Ridder Newspapers, Inc. v. United States, 743 F.2d 781 (11th Cir. 1984)	44.1
Knowlton v. Moore, 178 U.S. 41 (1900)	33.3(a)(2)
Knox v. Comm'r, 33 B.T.A. 972 (1936), *nonacq.* XV-1 C.B. 36	19.10(d)
Koebig & Koebig, Inc. v. Comm'r, 23 T.C.M. (CCH) 170 (1964)	22.3
Koshland v. Helvering, 298 U.S. 441 (1936), *rev'g* 81 F.2d 641 (9th Cir. 1936)	57
Kovner v. Comm'r, Tax Ct. Rep. (CCH) 46,664 (June 20, 1990)	8.2(c), 47.2(e)
Kovtun v. Comm'r, 54 T.C. 331 (1970), *aff'd per curiam*, 448 F.2d 1268 (9th Cir. 1971), *cert. denied*, 405 U.S. 1016 (1972)	9.2(a), 25.1, 55.1
Kraus v. Comm'r, 88 F.2d 616 (2d Cir. 1937), *aff'g* 33 B.T.A. 1088 (1936)	20.2(c), 20.2(d)
Kunau v. Comm'r, 27 B.T.A. 509 (1933), *acq.* XII-1 C.B. 7 (1933)	10.1(b), 19.4(c)
Kunze v. Comm'r, 19 T.C. 29 (1952), *aff'd per curiam*, 203 F.2d 957 (2d Cir. 1953)	24.7(f)
Kurtin v. Comm'r, 26 T.C. 958 (1956), *acq.* 1957-1 C.B. 4	8.4(b)
Kurtz v. Comm'r, 50 T.C.M. (CCH) 695 (1985), *rev'd sub nom.* Miller v. Comm'r, 836 F.2d 1274 (10th Cir. 1988)	47.2(e)
KVP Sutherland Paper Co. v. United States, 344 F.2d 377 (Ct. Cl. 1965)	15.1
La Grange v. Comm'r, 26 T.C. 191 (1956)	18.2(a)

Table of Cases

(References are to book sections.)

Landreth v. Comm'r, 50 T.C.M. (CCH) 728 (1985), *later proceeding* Landreth v. Comm'r, 51 T.C.M. (CCH) 1201 (1986), *aff'd*, 845 F.2d 828 (9th Cir.), *vacated*, 859 F.2d 643 (1988)	47.2(e), 58.1
Lang v. Comm'r, 46 T.C.M. (CCH) 335 (1983)	9.3(b)(2)
Larkin v. Comm'r, 46 B.T.A. 213, *appeal dismissed*, 129 F.2d 1020 (10th Cir. 1942)	14.5(d)
Larson v. Comm'r, 66 T.C. 159 (1976), *acq.* 1971-1 C.B. 1	28.1, 28.1(a), 28.1(d), 28.2(a)
Laureys v. Comm'r, 92 T.C. 101 (1989), *acq. and nonacq.* 1990-1 C.B. 1	8.2(b), 8.3(c), 11.9(c), 19.4(b), 30.2(b)(2), 30.2(b)(3), 30.2(b)(4), 44.4, 45.2(b), 56.6
Leach Corp. v. Comm'r, 30 T.C. 563 (1958), *acq.* 1959-1 C.B. 4	34.2(a)
Leader Fed. S & L Ass'n of Memphis v. Comm'r, 57 T.C.M. (CCH) 846 (1989)	19.9(j)
Leh v. Comm'r, 27 T.C. 892 (1957), *aff'd*, 260 F.2d 489 (9th Cir. 1958)	58.1
Levin v. United States, 597 F.2d 760 (Ct. Cl. 1979), *aff'g* 79-1 U.S. Tax Cas. (CCH) ¶ 9176 (Ct. Cl. Tr. Div. 1979)	8.2, 10.1(b), 19.4(c)
Levitt v. United States, 517 F.2d 1339 (8th Cir. 1975), *remanding* 368 F. Supp. 644 (S.D. Iowa 1974)	9.3(b)(1)
Lewis v. Comm'r, 176 F.2d 646 (1st Cir. 1949), *aff'g* 10 T.C. 1080 (1948)	27.4(b)(2)
Lewis v. Comm'r, 49 T.C.M. (P-H) ¶501 (1980)	8.4(b)
Lineaweaver v. Comm'r, 3 T.C.M. (CCH) 331 (1944)	16.4(c), 30.3(f)(1)
Lino v. City Investing Co., 487 F.2d 689 (3d Cir. 1973)	7.6(a)
Lloyd-Smith v. Comm'r, 116 F.2d 642 (2d Cir. 1941), *aff'g* 40 B.T.A. 214 (1939), *cert. denied*, 313 U.S. 588 (1941)	18.4(a)
Lorillard v. Pons, 434 U.S. 575 (1978), *aff'g* 549 F. 2d 950 (4th Cir. 1977), *vacating* 69 F.R.D. 576 (M.D.N.C. 1977)	19.9(j)
Lowell v. Comm'r, 30 B.T.A. 1297 (1934)	8.3(b)
MacDougald v. Comm'r, 44 B.T.A. 1046 (1941)	31.10
Mahoney v. Comm'r, 808 F.2d 1219 (6th Cir. 1987)	9.2(g), 10.2(g)
Main Line Distrib., Inc. v. Comm'r, 321 F.2d 562 (6th Cir. 1963), *aff'g* 37 T.C. 1090 (1962)	18.6(c)

(References are to book sections.)

Makransky v. Comm'r, 5 T.C. 397 (1945), *aff'd*, Makransky's Estate v. Comm'r, 154 F.2d 59 (3d Cir. 1946)	8.2, 10
Malat v. Riddell, 383 U.S. 569 (1966), *on remand*, 275 F. Supp. 358 (S.D. Cal. 1966), *vacating* 347 F.2d 23 (9th Cir. 1965), *aff'g* 64-1 U.S. Tax Cas. (CCH) ¶ 9432 (S.D. Cal. 1964)	11.9(b)
Mallinckrodt v. Comm'r, 2 T.C. 1128 (1943), *acq.* 1944 C.B. 18, *aff'd sub nom.* Mallinckrodt v. Nunan, 146 F.2d 1 (8th Cir.), *cert. denied*, 324 U.S. 781, *reh'g denied*, 325 U.S. 892 (1945)	9.1(b), 9.1(c), 9.3(a)
Mamula v. Comm'r, 346 F.2d 1016 (9th Cir. 1965), *rev'g* 41 T.C. 572 (1964)	32.1(b)(1)(ii)
Mansfield Journal Co. v. Comm'r, 31 T.C. 902 (1959), *aff'd*, 274 F.2d 284 (6th Cir. 1960)	18.11
Marathon Oil v. Comm'r, 838 F.2d 1114 (10th Cir. 1987), *aff'g* Husky Oil Co. v. Comm'r, 83 T.C. 717 (1984)	34.2(e)
Marchese v. Shearson Hayden Stone, Inc., 644 F. Supp. 1381 (C.D. Cal. 1986), *on remand*, 734 F.2d 414 (9th Cir. 1984), *aff'd*, 822 F.2d 876 (9th Cir. 1987)	9.2(c)(2)
Marcus v. Comm'r, 54 T.C.M. (CCH) 1452 (1988)	58.1
Maring v. Comm'r, 56 T.C.M. (CCH) 343 (1988)	58.1
Marr v. United States, 268 U.S. 536 (1925), *aff'g* 58 Ct. Cl. 658 (1923)	19.9(j)
Marsh v. Comm'r, 12 T.C. 1083 (1949), *acq.* 1949-2 C.B. 3	17.2(a)(1)
Masonite Corp. v. United States, 426 F. Supp. 469 (S.D. Miss. 1977)	9
Mather & Co. v. Comm'r, 171 F.2d 864 (3d Cir. 1949), *aff'g* 7 T.C. 1440 (1946), *acq.* 1947-1 C.B. 3, *cert. denied*, 337 U.S. 907 (1949)	27.3
Mathers v. Comm'r, 57 T.C. 666 (1972), *acq.* 1973-2 C.B. 2	36.5(c)
McCauslen v. Comm'r, 45 T.C. 588 (1966)	17.3(c)(2)
McClain v. Comm'r, 311 U.S. 527 (1941), *aff'g* 110 F.2d 878 (5th Cir. 1940)	31.10
McClure v. First Nat'l Bank, 497 F.2d 490 (5th Cir. 1974), *aff'g* 352 F. Supp. 454 (N.D. Tex. 1973), *reh'g denied*, 502 F.2d 1167 (1974), *cert. denied*, 420 U.S. 930 (1975)	7.6(a)
McCulloch v. Maryland, 17 U.S. (4 Wheat.) 316 (1819)	32.2

Table of Cases

(References are to book sections.)

McDonald's of Zion, 432, Ill., Inc. v. Comm'r, 76 T.C. 972 (1981), *rev'd sub nom.* McDonald's Restaurants of Ill., Inc. v. Comm'r, 688 F.2d 520 (7th Cir. 1982)	27.3(b)(2)(iii)
McDonnell v. Comm'r, 862 F.2d 308 (3d Cir. 1988)	9.2(g)
McDonough v. Comm'r, 577 F.2d 234 (4th Cir. 1978), *aff'g* 36 T.C.M. (CCH) 213 (1977)	9.3(b)(2), 9.3(b)(5)
McFeely v. Comm'r, 296 U.S. 102, *reh'g denied*, 296 U.S. 664 (1935)	17.2(c)(2)
McKean v. Comm'r, 6 T.C. 757 (1946), *acq.* 1947-1 C.B. 3	17.2(a)(1)
McWilliams v. Comm'r, 331 U.S. 694 (1947), *aff'g* 158 F.2d 637 (6th Cir. 1946), *rev'g* 5 T.C. 623 (1945), *nonacq.* 1945 C.B. 9	19.10(a)
Meade v. Comm'r, 42 T.C.M. (P-H) 205 (1973)	8.4(b)
Megargel v. Comm'r, 3 T.C. 238 (1944)	9.1(c)(3)
Mellon v. Comm'r, 36 B.T.A. 977 (1937)	19.3(g)
Memphis Bank & Trust Co. v. Garner, 459 U.S. 392 (1983), *rev'g* 459 U.S. 816 (1982)	32.2(a)
Merchants Nat'l Bank v. Comm'r, 9 T.C. 68 (1947)	8.8, 19.4
Merrill v. Comm'r, 40 T.C. 66 (1963), *aff'd per curiam*, 336 F.2d 771 (9th Cir. 1964)	17.2(a)(1)
Metropolitan Commercial Corp. v. Comm'r, 22 T.C.M. (CCH) 533 (1963)	19.3(g)
Microdot, Inc. v. United States, 728 F.2d 593 (2d Cir. 1984)	27.3(c)(4)
Miele v. Comm'r, 56 T.C. 556 (1971), *acq.* 1972-2 C.B. 2, *aff'd*, 474 F.2d 1138 (3rd Cir.), *cert. denied*, 414 U.S. 982, *reh'g denied*, 414 U.S. 1104 (1973)	27.3(b)(2)
Miller v. Comm'r, 70 T.C. 448 (1978)	9.2(e)
Miller v. Comm'r, 84 T.C. 827 (1985), *rev'd*, 836 F.2d 1274 (10th Cir. 1988)	47.2(c), 47.2(d), 47.2(d)(1), 47.2(d)(2), 47.2(e)
Mirro-Dynamics Corp. v. United States, 374 F.2d 14 (9th Cir. 1967), *aff'g* 247 F. Supp. 214 (S.D. Cal. 1965), *cert. denied*, 389 U.S. 896 (1967)	10
Moller v. United States, 721 F.2d 810 (Fed. Cir. 1983), *rev'g* 553 F. Supp. (Cl. Ct. 1982), *cert. denied*, 467 U.S. 1251 (1984)	8.1, 8.2, 2.1(c)(6)
Molsen v. Comm'r, 85 T.C. 485 (1985)	22.1(c)
Monfort of Colo., Inc. v. United States, 561 F.2d 190 (10th Cir. 1977), *aff'g* 406 F. Supp. 701 (D. Colo. 1976)	60.2(b)(1)(iii), 60.2(b)(2)(ii)
Montgomery Ward Life Ins. Co. v. State Dep't of Local Gov't Affairs, 89 Ill. App. 3d 292, 411 N.E.2d 973 (1980)	32.2(a)

(References are to book sections.)

Morgan v. Comm'r, 46 T.C. 878 (1966), *acq.* 1967-1 C.B. 2	27.7
Morris v. Comm'r, 38 B.T.A. 265 (1938), *acq.* 1938-2 C.B. 22	8.2(a), 10.1(b), 19.4(c)
Morrissette v. United States, 342 U.S. 246 (1952), *rev'g* 187 F.2d 427 (6th Cir. 1951)	23.2(d)(3)(ii)
Morse v. Comm'r, 34 B.T.A. 943 (1936)	19.10(a)
Mortensen v. Comm'r, 49 T.C.M. (CCH) 94 (1984)	42.4, 55.1
Muchnic v. Comm'r, 29 B.T.A. 163 (1933), *acq.* XIII-1 C.B. 11	27.3(c)(2)
Mutual Loan & Sav. Co. v. Comm'r, 184 F.2d 161 (5th Cir. 1950), *rev'g* 8 T.C.M. (CCH) 203 (1949)	31.9(a), 33.4
Natco Corp. v. United States, 240 F.2d 398 (3d Cir. 1956), *aff'g* 56-2 U.S. Tax Cas. (CCH) ¶ 9642 (W.D. Pa. 1956)	34.2(e)
National Can Corp. v. United States, 687 F.2d 1107 (7th Cir. 1982), *aff'g* 520 F. Supp. 567 (N.D. Ill. 1981)	31.4(d), 34.2(c)(2), 34.2(f), 34.3(b)
National-Standard Co. v. Comm'r, 80 T.C. 551 (1983), *aff'd*, 749 F.2d 369 (6th Cir. 1984)	15.1, 60.2(b)(2)(i)(a), 60.3(a)(2)(ii)
Nevitt v. Comm'r, 20 T.C. 318 (1953)	19.4
New Mexico *ex rel.* New Mexico State Highway Dept. v. Goldschmidt, 629 F.2d 665 (10th Cir. 1986)	23.2(d)(3)(ii)
Nichols v. Comm'r, 22 T.C.M. (CCH) 698 (1963)	9.1(c)
Nidetch v. Comm'r, 37 T.C.M. (CCH) 1309 (1978)	9.1(c)(4)
Nielsen v. United States, 212 F. Supp. 801 (M.D. Tenn. 1962), *aff'd in part, modified in part*, 333 F.2d 615 (6th Cir. 1964)	11.7(b)
1955 Prod. Expo., Inc. v. Comm'r, 41 T.C. 85 (1963)	18.6(c)
Noll v. Comm'r, 43 B.T.A. 496 (1941)	31.8
Northeastern Sur. Co. v. Comm'r, 29 B.T.A. 297 (1933)	8.3(a)
Northern Refrigerator Line, Inc. v. Comm'r, 1 T.C. 824 (1943)	27.2, 27.3(b)(2)(ii)
Northern Trust Co. of Chicago v. United States, 193 F.2d 127 (7th Cir. 1951), *rev'g* 100 F. Supp. 177 (N.D. Ill. 1950), *cert. denied*, 343 U.S. 956 (1952)	24.7(c)
Old Colony R. Co. v. Comm'r, 284 U.S. 552 (1932), *rev'g* 50 F.2d 896 (1st Cir. 1931), *rev'g* 18 B.T.A. 267 (1929)	9.2(a), 25.1, 30.3(d)(3), 55.1, 60.2(b)(2)(i)(a)(1)

Table of Cases

(References are to book sections.)

Oringderff v. Comm'r, 38 T.C.M. 402 (CCH) (1979), aff'd, 81-2 U.S. Tax Cas. (CCH) ¶ 9642 (10th Cir. 1981)	18.11
Ostrower v. Comm'r, 48 T.C.M. 1144 (1984)	42.4, 55.1
Otto v. Comm'r, 37 B.T.A. 479 (1938), remanded, 101 F.2d 1017 (4th Cir. 1939)	17.2(a)(1), 17.2(a)(5)
Pacific Affiliate, Inc. v. Comm'r, 18 T.C. 1175 (1952), aff'd, 224 F.2d 578 (9th Cir. 1955), cert. denied, 350 U.S. 967 (1956)	31.4(c)(2)
Page v. Rhode Island Hosp. Trust Co., 88 F.2d 192 (1st Cir. 1937), aff'g 14 F. Supp. 481 (D.C.R.I. 1936)	14.5(d)
Pagel, Inc. v. Comm'r, 91 T.C. 200 (1988), aff'd, 905 F.2d 1190 (8th Cir. 1990)	11.8(c), 30.3(e)(1)(iv)
Pan-American Bank & Trust Co. v. Comm'r, 5 B.T.A. 839 (1926)	8.3
Paoli v. Comm'r, 54 T.C.M. (CCH) 1574 (1988)	8.1, 8.2
Patterson v. Anderson, 20 F. Supp. 799 (S.D.N.Y. 1937)	17.4(a)
Patterson v. Comm'r, 50 T.C.M. (P-H) 122 (1981)	8.4(b), 18.11
Paulsen v. Comm'r, 469 U.S. 131 (1985), aff'g 716 F.2d 563 (9th Cir. 1983), rev'g 78 T.C. 291 (1982)	27.4(b)(2)
Peerless Stages v. Railroad Com., 296 U.S. 663 (1936), denying reh'g to 296 U.S. 540 (1935)	17
Pennroad Corp. v. Comm'r, 29 T.C. 914 (1958), aff'd, 261 F.2d 325 (3d Cir. 1958), cert. denied, 359 U.S. 958 (1959)	11.9(c)
Pennsylvania Co. for Ins. on Lives and Granting Annuities v. United States, 146 F.2d 392 (3d Cir. 1944), aff'g 48 F. Supp. 972 (E.D. Pa.), and aff'g 48 F. Supp. 969 (1942)	29.1(b), 36.2(b)
Perlin v. Comm'r, 86 T.C. 388 (1986)	20.2(f), 47.2(c), 47.2(e)
Piekarczyk v. Comm'r, 52 T.C.M. (CCH) 128 (1986)	27.8
Pierce v. Underwood, 487 U.S. 552 (1988)	19.9(j)
Pierce v. United States, 49 F. Supp. 324 (Ct. Cl. 1943)	16.2(a)
Pinellas Ice & Cold Storage Co. v. Comm'r, 287 U.S. 462 (1933), aff'g 57 F.2d 188 (5th Cir. 1932), denying petition to 21 B.T.A. 425 (1930)	18.4(a)
Pinnell v. Comm'r, 132 F.2d 126 (3d Cir. 1942), amended per curiam, 43-1 U.S. Tax Cas. (CCH) ¶ 9255 (1943)	31.10

(References are to book sections.)

Piper v. Chris-Craft Indus., 430 U.S. 1 (1977), *rev'g* 516 F.2d 172 (2d Cir. 1975), *aff'g in part, rev'g in part and vacating* 384 F. Supp. 507 (S.D.N.Y. 1974), *on remand,* 414 U.S. 924 (1973), *denying cert.* to 414 U.S. 910 (1973), *rev'g* 337 F. Supp. 1128 (S.D.N.Y. 1971), *reh'g denied,* 430 U.S. 976 (1977)	23.2(d)(3)(ii)
Pointer v. Comm'r, 48 T.C. 906 (1967), *aff'd,* 419 F.2d 213 (9th Cir. 1970)	11.9(c)
Polachek v. Comm'r, 22 T.C. 858 (1954)	8.3, 10
Pressed Steel Car Co. v. Comm'r, 20 T.C. 198 (1953), *acq.* 1956-2 C.B. 198	60.2(b)(1)(iii), 60.2(b)(2)(ii), 60.3(a)(3)(ii)
Price v. Comm'r, 88 T.C. 860 (1987)	31.11(a), 31.11(b)(3)
Provost v. United States, 269 U.S. 443 (1926), *aff'g* 60 Ct. Cl. 49 (1924)	18.2(a)
Prudential Ins. Co. of Am. v. SEC, 326 F.2d 383 (3d Cir.) *cert. denied,* 377 U.S. 953 (1964)	7.6(d)
Purvis v. Comm'r, 530 F.2d 1332 (9th Cir. 1976), *aff'g* 33 T.C.M. (CCH) 702 (1974)	8.1, 8.2, 8.3(a), 10.1(b), 19.4(c), 23.2(d)(3)(ii)
Ragland Inv. Co. v. Comm'r, 52 T.C. 867 (1969), *aff'd,* 435 F.2d 118 (6th Cir. 1970)	27.2, 27.3(b)(2), 27.3(b)(2)(i)
Raynor v. Comm'r, 50 T.C. 762 (1968)	25.1
RCA Corp. v. United States, 664 F.2d 881 (2d Cir. 1981), *rev'g* 499 F. Supp. 507 (S.D.N.Y. 1980), *cert. denied,* 457 U.S. 1133 (1982)	60.4(a)(2)
Redding v. Comm'r, 630 F.2d 1169 (7th Cir. 1980), *rev'g* 71 T.C. 597 (1979), *cert. denied,* 450 U.S. 913 (1981)	24.2(b)(7), 30.3(f)(2)
Reed v. Comm'r, 723 F.2d 138 (1st Cir. 1983), *rev'g* 45 T.C.M. (CCH) 398 (1982)	17.2(a)(2)(ii)
Reinach v. Comm'r, 373 F.2d 900 (2d Cir. 1967), *aff'g* 24 T.C.M. (CCH) 1605 (1965), *cert. denied,* 389 U.S. 841 (1967)	8.3, 8.3(c)
Richardson v. Smith, 23 A.F.T.R. (P-H) 1264 (D.C. Conn. 1938), *rev'd on other grounds,* 102 F.2d 697 (2d Cir. 1939)	20.2(b)
Richmond, Fredericksburg & Potomac R.R. v. Comm'r, 528 F.2d 917 (4th Cir. 1975), *aff'g* 62 T.C. 174 (1974)	27.2, 27.3(b)(2)(ii)
Rickaby v. Comm'r, 27 T.C. 886 (1957), *acq.* 1960-2 C.B. 6	31.8
Rivera v. Comm'r, 89 T.C. 343 (1987)	48.2(c)(1)

Table of Cases

T-24

(References are to book sections.)

Roberts v. United States, Nos. 86 C 9934, 86 C 9935, 86 C 9936 (N.D. Ill. Sept. 19, 1988)	45.4(b)
Roberts v. United States, 734 F. Supp. 314 (N.D. Ill. 1990), *adopting* 1988 U.S. Dist. LEXIS 17336, *rereporting* 1988 U.S. Dist. LEXIS 17334	45.4(b)
Rockford Life Ins. Co. v. Ill. Dept. of Revenue, 482 U.S. 182 (1987), *aff'g* 479 U.S. 947 (1986), *noting jur.* 112 Ill. 2d 174, 492 N.E.2d 1278 (1986), *aff'g* 128 Ill. App. 3d 302, 470 N.E.2d 596 (1984)	32.2(c)
R.O. Holton & Co. v. Comm'r, 44 B.T.A. 202 (1941)	31.8, 33.3(a)(1)(i)(a)
Rose v. Trust Co. of Ga., 77 F.2d 355 (5th Cir. 1935)	27.3(c)(5), 34.3(e)
Rosenberg v. United States, 481 U.S. 107 (1987)	33.3(a)(2)
Rothstein v. Comm'r, 90 T.C. 488 (1988)	36.5(b)
Royalty Participation Trust v. Comm'r, 20 T.C. 466 (1953), *acq.* 1953-2 C.B. 6	29.1(b)
San Antonio Sav. Ass'n v. Comm'r, 887 F.2d 577 (5th Cir. 1989), *aff'g* 55 T.C.M. (CCH) 813 (1988), *reh'g denied en banc*, 894 F.2d 1335 (1990)	19.9(j)
Schaeffer v. Comm'r, 41 T.C.M. (CCH) 752 (1981)	36.5(d)
Schafer v. Helvering, 299 U.S. 171 (1936), *aff'g* 83 F.2d 317 (App. D.C. 1936), *aff'g* 32 B.T.A. 289 (1935)	8.3(a)
Scheuber v. Comm'r, 371 F.2d 996 (7th Cir. 1967), *rev'g* 25 T.C.M. 559 (1966)	11.9(b)
Schley v. Comm'r, 375 F.2d 747 (2d Cir. 1967), *aff'g* 24 T.C.M. (CCH) 588 (1965)	10.1(b)
Schlude v. Comm'r, 372 U.S. 128 (1963), *aff'g in part, rev'g in part* 296 F.2d 721 (8th Cir. 1961), *on remand* 368 U.S. 873 (1961), *denying reh'g to* 367 U.S. 911 (1961), *vacating* 283 F.2d 234 (8th Cir. 1960), *rev'g* 32 T.C. 1271 (1959)	60.2(b)(1)(ii), 60.4(a)(2)
Schwinn v. Comm'r, 9 B.T.A. 1304 (1928), *acq.* VII-1 C.B. 28	10.1(b)
Scott Paper Co. v. Comm'r, 74 T.C. 137 (1980)	34.2(e)
Seas Shipping Co. v. Comm'r, 371 F.2d 528 (2d Cir. 1967), *aff'g* 24 T.C.M. (CCH) 1222 (1965), *cert. denied*, 387 U.S. 943 (1967)	34.2(d)
Securities Allied Corp. v. Comm'r, 95 F.2d 384 (2d Cir. 1938), *aff'g* 36 B.T.A. 168 (1937), *cert. denied*, 305 U.S. 617 (1938)	8.3
Security First Nat'l Bank of Los Angeles v. Comm'r, 28 B.T.A. 289 (1933)	19.10(d)
Seeley v. Helvering, 77 F.2d 323 (2d Cir. 1935)	8.2, 10.1(e)
Seroussi v. Comm'r, 22 T.C.M. (CCH) 1186 (1963)	8.2, 8.2(a), 10
S & H, Inc. v. Comm'r, 78 T.C. 234 (1982)	11.9(c)

(References are to book sections.)

Shafer v. United States, 204 F. Supp. 473 (S.D. Ohio 1962), *aff'd per curiam*, 312 F.2d 747 (6th Cir.), *cert. denied*, 373 U.S. 933 (1963)	31.6(b)(1)
Shamrock Oil & Gas Co. v. Comm'r, 42 B.T.A. 1016 (1940), *acq.* 1940-2 C.B. 6	34.2(e)
Shanis v. Comm'r, 19 T.C. 641 (1953), *aff'd per curiam*, 213 F.2d 151 (3d Cir. 1954)	17.2(a)(6), 27.3(d)
Shapiro v. Comm'r, 40 T.C. 34 (1963)	18.6(b)
Sheldon v. Comm'r, Tax Ct. Rep. (CCH) 46,602 (May 29, 1990)	31.11(b)(2), 31.11(b)(3), 31.11(b)(4), 32.1(a)(3), 48.3(b)(2)(ii)
Shethar v. Comm'r, 28 T.C. 1222 (1957)	19.10(a)
Shillinglaw v. Comm'r, 99 F.2d 87 (6th Cir. 1938), *aff'g* 32 B.T.A. 1235 (1935), *cert. denied*, 306 U.S. 635 (1939)	17.2(a)(1)
Shober v. Comm'r, Tax Court Dkt. No. 10806-85 (July 17, 1987)	20.2(f)
Shoenberg v. Comm'r, 77 F.2d 446 (8th Cir.), *cert. denied*, 296 U.S. 586 (1935)	19.10(d)
Sicanoff Veg. Oil Corp. v. Comm'r, 27 T.C. 1056 (1957), *rev'd on other grounds*, 251 F.2d 764 (7th Cir. 1958)	19.6(c)(1)
Singer v. Comm'r, 32 B.T.A. 177 (1935)	19.10(a)
Smith v. Comm'r, 33 T.C. 465 (1959), *aff'd in part, rev'd in part sub nom.* Estate of Smith v. Comm'r, 313 F.2d 724 (8th Cir. 1963)	10
Smith v. Comm'r, 78 T.C. 350 (1982), *aff'd without op.* 820 F.2d 1220 (4th Cir. 1987)	19.6(c)(1), 30.2(b)(1), 47.2, 47.2(b), 47.2(c), 47.2(d)(2)
Smith v. Davis, 323 U.S. 111 (1944), *aff'g* 197 Ga. 95, 28 S.E.2d 148 (1943)	32.2(a), 32.2(c)
Snow v. Comm'r, 416 U.S. 500 (1974), *rev'g* 482 F.2d 1029 (6th Cir. 1973), *aff'g* 58 T.C. 585 (1972)	10.1(b)
Snyder v. Comm'r, 295 U.S. 134 (1935), *aff'g* 73 F.2d 5 (3d Cir. 1934), *aff'g* 29 B.T.A. 39 (1933), *reh'g denied*, 295 U.S. 769 (1935)	10.1(b)
Snyder v. Comm'r, Tax Ct. Rep. (CCH) 46,137 (Nov. 2, 1989)	27.3(a)
Sochin v. Comm'r, 842 F.2d 351 (9th Cir.), *cert. denied*, 109 S. Ct. 72 (1988)	9.4, 10.4, 11.4(a)
Sommers v. Comm'r, 22 B.T.A. 1241 (1931), *aff'd*, 63 F.2d 551 (10th Cir. 1933)	17.2(c)(1)

Table of Cases

(References are to book sections.)

South Carolina v. Baker, 485 U.S. 505, *reh'g denied*, 486 U.S. 1062 (1988)	31.12(a), 33.3(a)(1)(i), 33.3(a)(1)(iii)
Southern Bancorporation v. Comm'r, 67 T.C. 1022 (1977)	8.8
Southern Natural Gas Co. v. United States, 412 F.2d 1222 (Ct. Cl. 1969)	34.2(d)
Spreckels v. Helvering, 315 U.S. 626 (1942), *aff'g* 119 F.2d 667 (9th Cir. 1941), *aff'g in part, rev'g in part* 41 B.T.A. 1204 (1940), *nonacq.* 1940-2 C.B. 14	9.1(c)(1), 10.1(d)
Spring v. United States, 38 A.F.T.R.2d (P-H) ¶ 76-5149 (E.D. Tex. 1976)	8.2
Stanley v. United States, 436 F. Supp. 581 (N.D. Miss. 1977), *aff'd*, 599 F.2d 672 (5th Cir. 1979)	17.2(c)(2)
Stavisky v. Comm'r, 34 T.C. 140 (1960), *aff'd*, 291 F.2d 48 (2d Cir. 1961)	17.2(a)(6), 18.4(b), 27.3(d)
Stein v. Director of Internal Revenue, 135 F. Supp. 356 (E.D.N.Y. 1955)	36.5(c)
Stephens, Inc. v. United States, 464 F.2d 53 (8th Cir. 1972), *rev'g in part, dismissing appeal in part*, 321 F. Supp. 1159 (E.D. Ark. 1970), *cert. denied*, 409 U.S. 1118 (1973)	8.3, 11.7(d)
Stewart Silk Corp. v. Comm'r, 9 T.C. 174 (1947)	8.4(b), 18.11
St. Louis Union Trust Co. v. Comm'r, 30 B.T.A. 370 (1934), *acq.* XIII-I C.B. 14 (1934)	16.4(c), 30.3(f)(1)
Stokes v. Rothensies, 61 F. Supp. 444 (E.D. Pa. 1945), *aff'd per curiam*, 154 F.2d 1022 (3d Cir. 1946)	8.3(b), 8.3(c)
Stoller v. Comm'r, Tax Ct. Mem. Dec. (CCH) 47,063 (Dec. 31, 1990)	58.1
Strauss v. Comm'r, 168 F.2d 441 (2d Cir.), *cert. denied*, 335 U.S. 858, *reh'g denied*, 335 U.S. 888 (1948)	16.2(a)
Surasky v. United States, 325 F.2d 191 (5th Cir. 1963), *rev'g* 62-2 U.S. Tax Cas. (CCH) ¶ 9836 (M.D. Fla. 1962)	9.1(c)(4)
Swenson v. Comm'r, 309 F.2d 672 (8th Cir. 1962), *rev'g* 37 T.C. 124 (1961)	17.2(c)(2)
Tandy Corp. v. United States, 79-1 U.S. Tax Cas. (CCH) ¶ 9160 (N.D. Tex. 1979), *aff'd*, 626 F.2d 1186 (5th Cir. 1980)	34.2(e)
Taylor v. Comm'r, 43 B.T.A. 563 (1941), *acq. and nonacq.* 1941-1 C.B. 10, 19, *aff'd*, Helvering v. Taylor, 128 F.2d 885 (2d Cir. 1942)	14.5(b)(1)

(References are to book sections.)

Taylor v. Comm'r, 76 F.2d 904 (2d Cir.), *cert. denied*, 296 U.S. 594 (1935), *reh'g denied*, 296 U.S. 663 (1936)	17
Textron, Inc. v. United States, 561 F.2d 1023 (1st Cir. 1977), *aff'g* 418 F. Supp. 39 (D.C.R.I. 1976)	27.8(f)
Theodore Tiedemann & Sons v. Comm'r, 1 B.T.A. 1077 (1925)	59.2(c)(1)
Thermoid Co. v. Comm'r, 4 T.C.M. (CCH) 412 (1945), *aff'd*, 155 F.2d 589 (3d Cir. 1946)	27.3(c)(2)
L.A. Thompson S.R. Co. v. Comm'r, 9 B.T.A. 1203 (1928), *acq.* VII-1 C.B. 31	38.2
Thompson v. Comm'r, 322 F.2d 122 (5th Cir. 1963), *aff'g in part, rev'g in part* 38 T.C. 153 (1962)	21.6
Thurner v. Comm'r, 60 T.C.M. (CCH) 961 (1990)	58.1
Titcher v. Comm'r, 57 T.C. 315 (1971)	9.2(a), 25.1, 55.1
Tobey v. Comm'r, 26 T.C. 610 (1956), *acq.* 1956-2 C.B. 8	31.8
Town & Country Food Co. v. Comm'r, 51 T.C. 1049 (1969), *acq.* 1969-2 C.B. XXV	36.5(c)
Tracy v. Comm'r, 70 T.C. 397 (1978), *acq.* 1978-2 C.B. 3	32.1(b)(1)(iv)
Trenton Cotton Oil Co. v. Comm'r, 148 F.2d 208 (6th Cir. 1945), *denying reh'g to* 147 F.2d 33 (1945)	19.6(c)(1)
Union Pac. R.R. v. United States, 524 F.2d 1343 (Ct. Cl. 1975), *cert. denied*, 429 U.S. 827 (1976), *later proceeding* Union Pac. R.R. v. United States, 9 Cl. Ct. 702 (1986), *aff'd*, 847 F.2d 1567 (Fed. Cir. 1988)	8.4
Union Planters Nat'l Bank of Memphis v. United States, 426 F.2d 115 (6th Cir. 1970), *rev'g* 295 F. Supp. 1151 (W.D. Tenn. 1968), *cert. denied*, 400 U.S. 827 (1970)	31.11(b)(1)
United Nat'l Corp. v. Comm'r, 33 B.T.A. 790 (1935), *nonacq.* XV-1 C.B. 47	36.5(c)
United States Freight Co. v. United States, 422 F.2d 887 (Ct. Cl. 1970)	58.1
United States v. American Trucking Ass'ns, 310 U.S. 534 (1940), *rev'g* 31 F. Supp. (D.C. Cir. 1939), *reh'g denied*, 311 U.S. 724 (1940)	23.2(d)(3)(ii)

Table of Cases

T-28

(References are to book sections.)

Case	Section
United States v. Centennial Sav. Bank FSB (Resolution Trust Corp., Receiver), ___ U.S. ___, 111 S. Ct. 1512 (1991) (59 U.S.L.W. 4319), *aff'g in part, rev'g in part*, ___ U.S. ___, 111 S. Ct. 40 (1990), *granting cert. to* 894 F.2d 1335 (5th Cir. 1990), *denying reh'g to* 887 F.2d 595 (5th Cir. 1989), *aff'g in part, rev'g in part* 682 F. Supp. 1389 (N.D. Tex. 1988)	19.9(j)
United States v. Chandler, 410 U.S. 257 (1973), *rev'g* 460 F.2d 1281 (9th Cir. 1972), *aff'g* 312 F. Supp. 1263 (N.D. Cal. 1970)	32.1(b)(1)(iv)
United States v. Chinook Inv. Co., 136 F.2d 984 (9th Cir. 1943), *aff'g* 42-2 U.S. Tax Cas. (CCH) ¶ 9575 (D.C. Or. 1942)	8.3
United States v. Davis, 397 U.S. 301 (1970), *rev'g* 408 F.2d 1139 (6th Cir. 1969), *aff'g* 274 F. Supp. 466 (M.D. Tenn. 1967), *reh'g denied*, 397 U.S. 1071 (1970)	24.2(b)(3)
United States v. Isaak, 400 F.2d 869 (9th Cir. 1968), *rev'g* 267 F. Supp. 595 (E.D. Wash. 1967)	21.7
United States v. Langston, 308 F.2d 729 (5th Cir. 1962), *rev'g* 62-1 U.S. Tax Cas. (CCH) ¶ 9243 (S.D. Fla. 1961)	31.8
United States v. Midland-Ross Corp., 381 U.S. 54 (1965), *rev'g* 335 F.2d 561 (6th Cir. 1964), *aff'g* 214 F. Supp. 631 (N.D. Ohio 1963)	14.1, 31.2(d)(2)(i)
United States v. Mississippi Chem. Corp., 405 U.S. 298 (1972), *rev'g* 431 F.2d 1320 (5th Cir. 1970), *aff'g* 69-1 U.S. Tax Cas. (CCH) ¶ 9266 (S.D. Miss. 1969)	27.5(a)(3)
United States v. Phellis, 257 U.S. 156 (1921), *rev'g* 56 Ct. Cl. 157 (1921)	19.9(j)
United States v. Pyne, 313 U.S. 127 (1941), *vacating* 35 F. Supp. 81 (Ct. Cl. 1940)	10.1(b)
United States v. Seattle First Int'l Corp., 79-2 U.S. Tax Cas. (CCH) ¶ 9495 (W.D. Wash. 1979)	8.8
United States v. Wells Fargo Bank, 485 U.S. 351 (1988), *rev'g* Rosenberg v. United States, 481 U.S. 107 (1987)	33.3(a)(2)
United Surgical Steel Co. v. Comm'r, 54 T.C. 1215 (1970), *acq.* 1971-2 C.B. 3	36.5(c)
Universal Castings Corp. v. Comm'r, 37 T.C. 107 (1961), *aff'd*, 303 F.2d 620 (7th Cir. 1962)	34.2(a)

(References are to book sections.)

Valley Waste Mills v. Page, 115 F.2d 466 (5th Cir. 1940), *aff'g* 40-1 U.S. Tax Cas. (CCH) ¶ 9382 (M.D. Ga. 1940), *cert. denied*, 312 U.S. 68 (1941)	47.2, 47.2(a)
Vancoh Realty Co. v. Comm'r, 33 B.T.A. 918 (1936), *nonacq.* XV-2 C.B. 49	31.3(a)
Vaughn v. Comm'r, 87 T.C. 164 (1986), *supplementing* 81 T.C. 893 (1983)	17.2(a)(2)(ii)
Verito v. Comm'r, 43 T.C. 429 (1965), *acq.* 1965-2 C.B. 7	8.3
Vickers v. Comm'r, 80 T.C. 394 (1983)	8.2(a), 10
Victorson v. Comm'r, 326 F.2d 264 (2d Cir. 1964), *aff'g* 21 T.C.M. (CCH) 1238 (1962)	11.8(a)
Eli Wallach and Anne (Jackson) Wallach v. United States, 8 Ct. Cl. 631 (1985), *aff'd*, 800 F.2d 1121 (Fed. Cir. 1986)	15.4(a)(2)(ii)(b), 31.11(c)
Jim Walter Corp. v. United States, 498 F.2d 631 (5th Cir. 1974), *aff'g* 73-2 U.S. Tax Cas. (CCH) ¶ 9682 (M.D. Fla. 1973)	30.3(e)(2)
Walters v. Comm'r, 28 T.C.M. (CCH) 22 (1969)	9.1(c)(5)
Warner Co. v. Comm'r, 11 T.C. 419 (1948), *aff'd*, 181 F.2d 599 (3d Cir. 1950)	31.8
Waterman, Largen & Co. v. United States, 419 F.2d 845 (Ct. Cl. 1969), *cert. denied*, 400 U.S. 869 (1970)	21.1
Wehrly v. United States, 808 F.2d 1311 (9th Cir. 1986)	47.2(e), 58.1
Weigl v. Comm'r, 84 T.C. 1192 (1985)	11.8(a), 30.3(e)(1)(iii)
Weinstein v. United States, 420 F.2d 700 (Ct. Cl. 1970)	9.1(c)(5)
Weir v. Comm'r, 109 F.2d 996 (3d Cir. 1940), *aff'g* 39 B.T.A. 400 (1939), *cert. denied*, 310 U.S. 637 (1940)	47.2(d)(2)
Weir v. Comm'r, 10 T.C. 996 (1948), *aff'd per curiam*, 173 F.2d 222 (3d Cir. 1949)	17.1(a), 30.3(b)(1)(iv), 30.3(c)(2)(iv), 47.2(d)(2)
Weiss v. Comm'r, 24 T.C.M. (CCH) 79 (1965)	9
Weiss v. Stearn, 265 U.S. 242 (1924), *aff'g* 285 F. 689 (6th Cir. 1923)	19.9(j)
Welch v. Helvering, 290 U.S. 111 (1933), *aff'g* 63 F.2d 976 (8th Cir. 1933), *dismissing petition* 25 B.T.A. 117 (1932)	27.8, 55.1
West v. United States, 701 F. Supp. 695 (W.D. Ark. 1988)	32.1(b)(1)(ii)

Table of Cases

(References are to book sections.)

Case	Section
Western Wine & Liquor Co. v. Comm'r, 18 T.C. 1090 (1952), *appeal dismissed*, 205 F.2d 420 (8th Cir. 1953), *acq.* 1958-1 C.B. 6	21.1
West Mo. Power Co. v. Comm'r, 18 T.C. 105 (1952)	33.4
Whittemore v. United States, 383 F.2d 824 (8th Cir. 1967), *rev'g* 257 F. Supp. 1008 (E.D. Mo. 1966)	9.3(a)
W.H. Wilson, Inc. v. Comm'r, 5 T.C.M. (CCH) 592 (1946), *aff'd per curiam*, 161 F.2d 556 (4th Cir.), *cert. denied*, 332 U.S. 769 (1947)	18.11
Willcuts v. Bunn, 282 U.S. 216 (1931), *rev'g* 35 F.2d 29 (8th Cir. 1929), *aff'g* 29 F.2d 132 (D.C. Minn. 1928)	33.3(a)(1)(i)(d), 33.3(a)(2)
Willock v. Comm'r, 6 T.C.M. (CCH) 487 (1947)	20.2(c)
W.W. Windle Co. v. Comm'r, 65 T.C. 694 (1976), *appeal dismissed*, 550 F.2d 43 (1st Cir.), *cert. denied*, 431 U.S. 966 (1977)	8.4
Wisconsin Cheeseman, Inc. v. United States, 388 F.2d 420 (7th Cir. 1968), *aff'g in part, rev'g in part* 265 F. Supp. 168 (W.D. Wis. 1967)	9.3(b)(2), 11.3(b)(1)
Wood v. Comm'r, 197 F.2d 859 (5th Cir. 1952), *aff'g* 9 T.C.M. (CCH) 142 (1950)	22.3
Woodward v. Comm'r, 397 U.S. 572 (1970), *aff'g* 410 F.2d 313 (8th Cir. 1969), *aff'g* 49 T.C. 377 (1968)	9.1(c)(1), 10.1, 16.5
Woodward v. Comm'r, 24 T.C. 883 (1955), *acq.* 1956-1 C.B. 6	31.4(a)(1)(i)
Wool Distrib. Corp. v. Comm'r, 34 T.C. 323 (1960), *acq.* 1961-2 C.B. 5	18.11
Wynn v. United States, 411 F.2d 614 (3d Cir. 1969), *aff'g* 288 F. Supp 797 (E.D. Pa. 1968), *cert. denied*, 396 U.S. 1008 (1970)	9.3(b)(2)
Yosha v. Comm'r, 861 F.2d 494 (7th Cir. 1988), *aff'g* Glass v. Comm'r, 87 T.C. 1087 (1986)	30.2(b)(2), 31.11(b)(3), 58.1
Young v. Comm'r, 34 B.T.A. 648 (1936), *acq.* 1940-1 C.B. 5	19.10(a)
Young v. Comm'r, 123 F.2d 597 (2d Cir. 1941)	27.8
Zambakian v. Comm'r, 51 T.C.M. (CCH) 1101 (1986), *aff'd without op.* 815 F.2d 697 (1987)	15.4(a)(2)(ii)(c)
Zilkha & Sons, Inc. v. Comm'r, 52 T.C. 607 (1969), *acq.* 1970-1 C.B. XVI, 7	27.3(b)(2), 27.3(b)(3)
Zuckman v. United States, 524 F.2d 729 (Ct. Cl. 1975)	28.1, 28.1(a), 28.1(b), 28.1(d)

Table of Internal Revenue Code Sections

(References are to book sections.)

I.R.C.	
1(i)(7)(A)(i)	24.5(b)
3	31.4(a)(1)(i)
11(b)	15.5(a)(2)(i), 15.5(c), 36.8(i)
22	24.8, 25.2
25(d)(2)(A)	33.2(c)(2)(ii)(a)
25(e)(10)	36.8(d)(1)(i)
25(f)(2)	33.2(c)(2)(ii)(a)
25(h)	33.2(c)(2)(ii)(a)
55	15.4(a)(2)(ii)(b), 15.5(d), 25.4(c)
55(a)	15.4(a)(2)(ii)(a)
55(b)	15.4(a)(2)(ii)(a)
55(f)	15.4(a)(2)(ii)(a)
56(a)	15.5(c)
56(b)(1)(C)(iii)	25.4(c), 33.1, 33.7
56(c)(1)	15.5(d), 25.4(c), 33.1, 33.7
57	15.4(a)(2)(ii)(b), 15.5(c)
57(a)(5)	31.8
57(a)(5)(C)(ii)	33.7
57(a)(5)(C)(iii)	33.7
57(a)(9)(A)	15.4(a)(2)(ii)(a)
57(a)(9)(B)	15.5(c)
59A	25.4(c), 33.1, 33.2(a), 33.12

I.R.C.	
61(a)(3)	15.4(a)(1), 33.3(c)
61(a)(4)	9.2(c)(2), 28.4(d)(2)(i)
61(a)(7)	28.4(d)(2)(ii)
61(4)	25.1
62(3)	15.4(a)(2)(i)
64	21.1
65	21.1
67	9.1(a), 9.1(c), 9.1(d), 29.1(d), 37.1, 60.2(b)(2)(ii)
67(a)	59.2(a)(3)
67(b)(9)	9.1(d)
67(b)(12)	9.1(d)
67(c)	8.9(c), 9.1(d)
72(o)(5)	16.3(c)
75	11.4(b), 31.4(a)(2)(ii)
75(a)	11.4(b), 16.4(l)
75(a)(1)	11.4(b), 31.4(a)(2)(ii)
75(a)(2)	11.4(b), 31.4(a)(2)(ii)
75(b)	31.4(a)(2)(ii)
75(b)(1)	11.4(b), 31.4(a)(2)(ii)
75(b)(2)	31.4(a)(2)(ii)
77	21.6

Table of Internal Revenue Code Sections

(References are to book sections.)

I.R.C.	
83	11.8(a), 11.8(c), 24.7(f), 30.3(e)(1)(iv)
83(h)	30.3(e)(1)(iv)
86(a)	33.3(a)(3)
86(b)(1)	33.3(a)(3)
86(b)(2)	33.3(a)(3)
86(d)(1)	33.3(a)(3)
103	3.1, 9.3(b), 25.1, 26.2(e), 31.2(e)
103(a)	25.4(a), 25.4(b), 25.4(c), 31.2(n)(3), 31.12(a), 33.1, 33.2(c)(2)(i), 33.2(c)(2)(iii), 33.2(c)(2)(iv), 33.3(a)(1)(i), 33.3(a)(2)
103(a)(1)	25.4(a)(1), 33.1
103(b)	25.4(a)(1), 25.4(b), 25.4(c), 33.2(c)(2)
103(b)(1)	3.2(c), 25.4(b)
103(b)(2)	33.3(a)(1)(vi)
103(b)(4)	25.4(b)
103(b)(6)	25.4(b)
103(j)	25.4(d), 31.12(c)
108(b)	47.2(c)
108(e)(10)	34.2(d)
108(e)(10)(c)	34.2(d)
108(f)	47.2(c)
116(a)	24.8
116(a)(2)	24.8
116(b)	24.8
116(b)(1)	25.2
116(c)(1)	24.8
116(c)(2)	24.8
135	32.1(b)(1)(v)(a), 32.1(b)(1)(v)(d), 32.1(b)(1)(v)(e)
141	3.1, 3.2(c), 11.3(b)(3)(ii)(b), 25.4(b), 25.4(c), 33.2(b)
141(a)	3.2(c), 33.2(c)(1)
141(b)	33.2(c)(1)
141(b)(3)	33.2(c)(1)(i)
141(b)(4)	33.2(c)(1)(i)
141(b)(5)	33.2(a)
141(c)	33.2(c)(1)(i)
141(e)	3.2(c), 33.2(c)(2)
141(e)(1)(A)	33.2(c)(2)
141(e)(1)(B)	33.2(c)(2)
141(e)(1)(C)	33.2(c)(2)

I.R.C.	
141(e)(1)(D)	33.2(c)(2)
141(e)(1)(E)	33.2(c)(2)
141(e)(1)(F)	33.2(c)(2)
141(e)(1)(G)	33.2(c)(2)
142	3.2(c), 33.2(c)(2), 33.2(c)(2)(i)
142(a)(1)	33.2(c)(2)(i)
142(a)(2)	33.2(c)(2)(i)
142(a)(3)	33.2(c)(2)(i)
142(a)(4)	33.2(c)(2)(i)
142(a)(5)	33.2(c)(2)(i)
142(a)(7)	33.2(c)(2)(i)
142(a)(8)	33.2(c)(2)(i)
142(a)(9)	33.2(c)(2)(i)
142(a)(10)	33.2(c)(2)(i)
142(a)(11)	33.2(c)(2)(i)
142(b)	33.2(c)(2)(i)
142(b)(2)(A)	33.2(c)(2)(i)
142(b)(2)(B)	33.2(c)(2)(i)
142(c)	33.2(c)(2)(i)
142(d)	33.2(c)(2)(i)
142(e)	33.2(c)(2)(i)
142(f)	33.2(c)(2)(i)
142(g)	33.2(c)(2)(i)
142(h)	33.2(c)(2)(i)
142(i)	33.2(c)(2)(i)
143	3.2(c), 33.2(c)(2)(ii)
143(a)	33.2(c)(2), 33.2(c)(2)(ii), 33.2(c)(2)(ii)(a)
143(a)(1)(B)	33.2(c)(2)(ii)(a)
143(a)(2)(A)(i)	33.2(c)(2)(ii)(a)
143(a)(2)(D)	33.2(c)(2)(ii)(a)
143(b)	33.2(c)(2), 33.2(c)(2)(ii)
143(b)(1)	33.2(c)(2)(ii)(b)
143(b)(2)	33.2(c)(2)(ii)(b)
143(c)	33.2(c)(2)(ii)(a), 33.2(c)(2)(ii)(b)
143(d)	33.2(c)(2)(ii)(a)
143(e)	33.2(c)(2)(ii)(a)
143(f)	33.2(c)(2)(ii)(a)
143(g)	33.2(c)(2)(ii)(b)
143(h)	33.2(c)(2)(ii)(a)
143(i)	33.2(c)(2)(ii)(a)
143(i)(1)	33.2(c)(2)(ii)(b)
143(j)	33.2(c)(2)(ii)(a)
143(l)(2)	33.2(c)(2)(ii)(b)

(References are to book sections.)

I.R.C.	
143(*l*)(4)	33.2(c)(2)(ii)(b)
143(m)	33.2(c)(2)(ii)(a)
144	3.2(c), 31.4(a)(1)(i)
144(a)	33.2(c)(2), 33.2(c)(2)(iii)
144(a)(4)	33.2(c)(2)(iii)
144(a)(4)(A)(ii)	33.2(c)(2)(iii)
144(a)(10)	33.2(c)(2)(iii)
144(a)(12)(A)	33.2(c)(2)(iii)
144(a)(12)(B)	33.2(c)(2)(iii)
144(a)(12)(C)	33.2(c)(2)(iii)
144(b)	33.2(c)(2)
144(b)(1)(A)	33.2(c)(2)(iv)
144(b)(1)(B)	33.2(c)(2)(iv)
144(b)(2)(A)	33.2(c)(2)(iv)
144(b)(2)(B)	33.2(c)(2)(iv)
144(c)	33.2(c)(2), 33.2(c)(2)(v)
144(c)(1)	33.2(c)(2)(v)
144(c)(2)(B)	33.2(c)(2)(v)
144(c)(3)(B)	33.2(c)(2)(v)
144(c)(4)(A)	33.2(c)(2)(v)
144(c)(4)(B)	33.2(c)(2)(v)
144(c)(4)(C)	33.2(c)(2)(v)
144(c)(4)(D)	33.2(c)(2)(v)
144(c)(5)	33.2(c)(2)(v)
144(c)(6)	33.2(c)(2)(v)
144(c)(8)	33.2(c)(2)(v)
145	3.2(c), 33.2(c)(2)
145(a)	33.2(c)(2)(vi)(a)
145(a)(2)(A)	33.2(c)(2)(vi)(a)
145(b)	33.2(c)(2)(vi)(a), 33.2(c)(2)(vi)(b)
145(b)(3)	33.2(c)(2)(vi)(c)
145(b)(4)	33.2(c)(2)(vi)(a)
145(d)	33.2(c)(2)(vi)(e)
145(e)	33.2(c)(2)(vi)(a)
146	3.2(c), 33.2(c)(1)(ii), 33.2(c)(2), 33.2(c)(2)(i), 33.2(c)(2)(ii)(a), 33.2(c)(2)(ii)(b), 33.2(c)(2)(iii), 33.2(c)(2)(iv), 33.2(c)(2)(v)
146(b)	33.2(c)(1)(ii)
146(c)	33.2(c)(1)(ii)
146(d)(1)	33.2(c)(1)(ii)
146(d)(2)	33.2(c)(1)(ii)
146(d)(3)	33.2(c)(1)(ii)
146(d)(4)	33.2(c)(1)(ii)

I.R.C.	
146(f)	33.2(c)(1)(ii)
146(g)(1)	33.2(c)(1)(ii)
146(g)(2)	33.2(c)(1)(ii), 33.2(c)(2)(vi)(d)
146(g)(3)	33.2(c)(1)(ii), 33.2(c)(2)(i)
146(h)	33.2(c)(1)(ii)
146(i)	33.2(c)(1)(ii)
147	3.2(c), 33.2(c)(1)(i), 33.2(c)(2)
147(a)	33.2(c)(1)(i)
147(b)	33.2(c)(1)(i)
147(b)(3)(B)	33.2(c)(2)(vi)(f)
147(c)	33.2(c)(2)(v), 33.2(c)(2)(vi)(f)
147(c)(1)	33.2(c)(1)(i)
147(c)(2)	33.2(c)(1)(i)
147(c)(3)	33.2(c)(1)(i)
147(d)	33.2(c)(1)(i)
147(e)	33.2(c)(1)(i)
147(f)	33.2(c)(1)(i)
147(g)	33.2(c)(1)(i)
147(h)(1)	33.2(c)(1)(i)
147(h)(2)	33.2(c)(2)(f)
148	3.1, 3.2(c), 33.2(c)(2)(ii)(a), 33.2(c)(2)(iv), 33.3(a)(1)(vi)
148(a)	33.3(a)(1)(vi)
148(b)(2)(E)	33.2(c)(2)(vi)(a), 33.2(c)(2)(vi)(e)
148(c)	33.3(a)(1)(vi)
148(d)	33.3(a)(1)(vi)
148(d)(3)	33.3(a)(1)(vi)
148(e)	33.3(a)(1)(vi)
148(f)	33.3(a)(1)(vi)
148(f)(4)(C)	33.3(a)(1)(vi)
148(f)(4)(D)	33.2(c)(2)(iv)
148(f)(6)	33.3(a)(1)(vi)
148(g)	33.2(c)(2)(iv)
148(h)	33.3(a)(1)(vi)
149	3.1, 3.2(c), 25.4(d)
149(a)	3.1, 31.12(d)(1), 33.3(a)(1)(iii)
149(a)(2)	31.12(b)(1), 33.3(a)(1)(iii)
149(a)(3)(A)	31.12(b)(3)
149(a)(3)(B)	31.12(b)(3), 33.3(a)(1)(ix)
149(b)	33.3(a)(1)(ii)
149(b)(2)(A)	33.3(a)(1)(ii)

Table of Internal Revenue Code Sections

(References are to book sections.)

I.R.C.	
149(b)(2)(B)	33.3(a)(1)(ii)
149(b)(2)(C)	33.3(a)(1)(ii)
149(b)(3)(B)	33.3(a)(1)(ii)
149(b)(3)(C)(ii)	33.3(a)(1)(ii)
149(c)(2)	33.3(a)(1)(ii)
149(d)	33.3(a)(1)(vii)
149(d)(2)	33.3(a)(1)(vii)
149(d)(3)(A)	33.3(a)(1)(vii)
149(d)(3)(A)(ii)	33.3(a)(1)(vii)
149(d)(3)(A)(iii)	33.3(a)(1)(vii)
149(d)(3)(A)(iv)	33.3(a)(1)(vii)
149(d)(3)(A)(v)	33.3(a)(1)(vii)
149(d)(3)(B)(ii)	33.3(a)(1)(vii)
149(d)(4)	33.3(a)(1)(vii)
149(d)(6)	33.3(a)(1)(vii)
149(e)(1)	33.3(a)(1)(viii)
149(e)(2)	33.3(a)(1)(viii)
149(f)(3)	33.3(a)(1)(ix)
149(g)	33.3(a)(1)(ix)
149(g)(1)(B)	33.3(a)(1)(ix)
149(g)(2)(A)	33.3(a)(1)(ix)
149(g)(2)(B)	33.3(a)(1)(ix)
149(g)(2)(C)	33.3(a)(1)(ix)
149(g)(2)(D)	33.3(a)(1)(ix)
149(g)(3)(A)(i)	33.3(a)(1)(ix)
149(g)(3)(A)(ii)	33.3(a)(1)(ix)
149(g)(3)(C)(i)	33.3(a)(1)(ix)
149(g)(3)(C)(ii)	33.3(a)(1)(ix)
149(g)(3)(C)(iii)	33.3(a)(1)(ix)
149(g)(4)(A)	33.3(a)(1)(ix)
150	3.2(c)
150(b)	33.10
150(c)	33.10
162	9.1(c), 9.1(c)(10), 9.1(d), 10.1, 10.1(a), 10.1(c), 11.1(a), 13.1, 13.2(a)(1), 13.2(a)(2), 18.6(a), 19.4(c), 29.1(d), 30.3(e)(1)(iv), 59.2(a)(3), 59.2(g)(3)(v), 60.2(b)(1)(iii), 60.2(b)(2)(ii)
162(a)	9.1(a), 10.1(c), 11.1(a), 11.1(b), 12.1, 18.6(a), 18.6(e)(1), 55.1
162(a)(1)	10.1(a), 12.1
162(a)(2)	10.1(a), 59.2(d)(2)(i)
162(a)(3)	10.1(a)
162(c)	9.1(b), 10.1(c)

I.R.C.	
162(d)	27.5(a)(2)
162(f)	9.1(b), 10.1(c)
162(g)	9.1(b), 10.1(c)
162(*l*)	27.3(b)(4)
163	9.2(a), 9.2(b), 25.1, 25.5, 55.1
163(a)	9.2(a), 10.2(a), 31.2(d)(1), 34.2(e), 34.5, 55.1
163(d)	9.2(e), 9.2(h), 10.2(e), 28.4(g)(1), 31.4(b), 42.2, 55.1
163(d)(1)	9.2(e)
163(d)(2)	9.2(e)
163(d)(3)	9.2(e)
163(d)(3)(A)	10.2(e)
163(d)(3)(B)(i)	9.2(e)
163(d)(3)(B)(ii)	9.2(e)
163(d)(3)(D)(ii)	18.6(e)(1)
163(d)(4)	9.2(e)
163(d)(4)(B)	9.2(e), 10.2(e)
163(d)(4)(C)	10.2(e)
163(d)(4)(D)	28.4(g)(1)
163(e)	11.3(b)(3)(ii)(c), 23.3(g)(1)(v)(d), 31.2(a), 31.3(a), 31.6(c)(3), 60.2(c)(5)(ii)
163(e)(2)(C)	31.2(d)
163(e)(3)(A)	31.2(f)
163(e)(5)	31.2(g)(1), 31.2(g)(2), 31.2(g)(3)(ii), 31.2(g)(3)(iii), 31.2(g)(4), 31.2(g)(5), 31.5
163(e)(5)(B)	31.2(g)(4)
163(e)(5)(B)(i)	31.2(g)(4)
163(e)(5)(B)(ii)	31.2(g)(4)
163(e)(5)(C)	31.2(g)(3)(i)
163(e)(5)(D)	31.2(g)(3)(iii)
163(e)(5)(E)	31.2(g)(3)(ii)
163(f)	31.12(c), 31.12(d)(1)
163(f)(1)	31.12(f)
163(f)(2)	31.12(b)(1)
163(f)(2)(A)	31.12(f)
163(f)(2)(B)	31.12(a), 31.12(b)(1), 31.12(b)(4)(i), 31.12(e), 31.12(f)
163(f)(2)(B)(i)	31.12(a)
163(f)(2)(B)(ii)	31.12(a)
163(f)(2)(C)	31.12(b)(2)
163(f)(3)	31.12(b)(3)
163(h)(1)	9.2(h)

Table of Internal Revenue Code Sections

(References are to book sections.)

I.R.C.	
163(h)(2)	9.2(h)
163(h)(6)	9.2(h)
163(i)	31.2(g)(1), 31.2(g)(2), 31.2(g)(5), 31.5
163(i)(1)	31.2(g)(2)
163(i)(1)(B)	31.2(g)(2)(i), 31.2(g)(3)(i)
163(i)(1)(C)	31.2(g)(2)(ii)
163(i)(2)	31.2(g)(2)(ii)
163(i)(2)(A)	31.2(g)(2)(ii), 31.2(g)(2)(ii)(a)
163(i)(2)(B)	31.2(g)(2)(ii)
163(i)(3)	31.2(g)(2)(ii)
163(i)(3)(A)	31.2(g)(2)(i), 31.2(g)(2)(ii)(b)
163(i)(3)(B)	31.2(g)(2)(i)
165	8.7(d), 19.3(a), 19.9(j), 47.2(b)
165(a)	12.1, 13.2(a)(2), 27.8(a), 27.8(b), 27.8(c), 30.3(e)(2)
165(b)	27.8(b)
165(c)	47.2(a)
165(c)(2)	19.11, 47.2(b), 47.2(c), 47.2(d)(1), 47.2(e)
165(d)	60.2(b)(2)(i)(a), 60.2(d)(2)(i), 60.3(a)(2)(ii)
165(g)	27.3(d), 27.8, 27.8(d)
165(g)(1)	17.1(c), 27.8, 27.8(a)
165(g)(3)	27.8(a), 27.8(b)
165(g)(3)(B)	27.8(a)
165(j)	31.12(c), 31.12(d)(1), 31.12(d)(2), 31.12(e)
165(j)(1)	33.3(a)(1)(iii)
165(j)(3)	31.12(d)(1)
165(j)(3)(A)	31.12(d)(1)
165(j)(3)(B)	31.12(d)(1)
165(j)(3)(C)	31.12(d)(1)
165(j)(3)(D)	31.12(d)(1)
168	33.9
168(g)(1)(C)	33.9
168(g)(5)	33.9
171	9.1(d), 31.4, 31.4(a)(2)(i), 31.7(c), 34.3(c), 37.3, 38.3, 41.1(b)
171(a)	9.4, 10.4, 31.4(a)(1)(i), 31.4(b)
171(a)(1)	31.4(a)(1)

I.R.C.	
171(a)(2)	16.4(g), 31.4(a)(2)(ii), 33.5(c)
171(b)	31.4(d), 34.3(c)
171(b)(1)	31.4(b), 31.4(c)(1), 34.2(c)(3)
171(b)(1)(C)	31.4(a)(1)(i)
171(b)(2)	31.4(b), 31.4(c)(1)
171(b)(3)	31.4(b), 38.3
171(b)(3)(B)	31.4(b)
171(b)(4)	31.4(b)
171(c)	31.4(a)(1), 31.4(a)(1)(i)
171(c)(2)	31.4(a)(1)(i)
171(d)	31.4, 31.4(a)(2)(ii), 31.4(b), 37.3, 38.3
171(e)	9.4, 10.4, 31.4(b)
171(f)	11.4(b), 31.4(a)(2)(ii)
172(b)	45.4(c)
172(c)	45.4(c)
172(d)	45.4(c)
172(d)(2)	45.4(c)
183	31.11(b)(4)
212	8.9(c), 9.1(a), 9.1(c), 9.1(c)(3), 9.1(d), 18.6(a), 18.6(e)(1), 29.1(d), 37.1, 41.2(e), 59.2(a)(3), 59.2(g)(3)(v), 60.2(b)(2)(ii)
212(1)	9.1(a)
212(2)	9.1(a), 55.1
212(3)	9.1(a)
216	36.8(d)(1)(i)
243	16.6(f), 17.7(a), 24.9(a)(1), 29.3(b)(2), 31.2(g)(4)
243(a)	24.7(c), 24.9(b)(3), 27.6(c), 30.3(d)(2)(ii)
243(a)(1)	24.9(a)(1)
243(a)(2)	24.9(a)(2)
243(a)(3)	24.9(a)(2)
243(b)(1)	24.9(a)(2)
243(b)(1)(B)(i)	24.9(a)(2)
243(b)(1)(B)(ii)	24.9(a)(2)
243(b)(1)(C)	24.9(a)(2)
243(b)(2)	24.9(a)(2)
243(b)(5)	24.9(a)(2)
243(c)	24.9(a)(1)
243(c)(1)	24.9(a)(2)
244	17.7(a), 24.9(a)(1), 24.9(a)(2)

Table of Internal Revenue Code Sections

T-36

(References are to book sections.)

I.R.C.	
245	17.7(a), 31.2(g)(4)
246	24.9(a)(1), 31.2(g)(4)
246(a)(2)(B)	24.9(d), 27.5(b)
246(a)(4)	27.3(b)(3)
246(b)	24.9(a)(1)
246(b)(2)	24.9(a)(1)
246(b)(3)	24.9(a)(1)
246(c)	19.9(f), 24.5(a), 24.9(b), 24.9(b)(1), 27.3(b)(3), 56.3(d)(1)
246(c)(1)(A)	17.7(a), 17.7(b), 24.9(b), 27.3(b)(3)(iii), 48.4(b)
246(c)(1)(B)	24.9(b), 24.9(b)(2)
246(c)(2)	17.7(a), 24.9(b)
246(c)(3)	17.7(c), 17.9, 19.9(f)
246(c)(3)(A)	17.7(a)
246(c)(3)(B)	17.7(a), 17.7(c), 17.9
246(c)(3)(C)	17.7(a)
246(c)(4)	16.6(a), 17.7(a), 17.7(c), 17.9, 27.3(b)(3)(iii)
246(c)(4)(A)	24.9(b)(1)
246(c)(4)(C)	27.3(b)(2)(ii), 27.3(b)(3)(iii)
246A	17.7(b), 24.9(c)(1), 24.9(c)(4), 31.2(g)(4)
246A(a)	24.9(c)(1), 24.9(c)(3), 27.3(b)(3)
246A(b)	24.9(c)(2)
246A(c)(2)	24.9(c)(2), 24.9(c)(4)
246A(c)(3)	24.9(c)(2)
246A(c)(4)	24.9(c)(2)
246A(d)(1)	24.9(c)(3)
246A(d)(3)(A)	24.9(c)(4)
246A(e)	24.9(c)(2)
246A(f)	24.9(c)(3)
247	24.4
247(a)	24.4
247(b)(1)	24.4
249	34.2(f)
249(a)	31.4(d), 34.2(f)
249(b)(2)	34.2(f)
263	10.1(c)
263(g)	8.4(d), 9.7, 10.2(f), 10.7, 11.13, 12.1, 18.6(e)(5), 23.3(g)(1)(v)(a), 23.3(g)(2)(viii)(f), 26.5, 45.2(a), Part Eleven, 48.3(b)(2), 55.2, 55.2(b),

I.R.C.	
	55.2(c), 55.2(d), 55.2(e), 55.2(f), 56.7, 57.3(a), 57.4(d), 59.2(a)(1), 60.4(f)
263(g)(1)	9.2(f), 42.3, 42.4, 45.3, 48.3(b)(3), 55, 55.2(a)
263(g)(2)	55.2(a), 55.2(b), 55.2(c)
263(g)(2)(B)	55.2(b)
263(g)(2)(B)(i)	55.2(b)
263(g)(2)(B)(ii)	55.2(b)
263(g)(2)(B)(iii)	55.2(b)
263(g)(2)(B)(iv)	26.5, 55.2(b)
263(g)(3)	9.2(g), 12.1, 12.3, 23.1, 55.2(f)
263(g)(4)	55.2(e)
263(g)(4)(A)	55.2(e)
263(g)(4)(B)	55.2(e)
263(h)	18.6(b), 18.6(d), 18.6(e)(5), 55.2(e)
263(h)(1)	18.6(e)(1)
263(h)(2)	18.6(e)(2)
263(h)(3)	18.6(e)(2)
263(h)(4)	18.6(e)(3)
263(h)(5)	18.6(e)(4)
263(h)(5)(A)	18.6(e)(4)
263(h)(5)(B)	18.6(e)(4)
263(h)(6)	18.6(e)(5)
263A	22.4
263A(b)(2)(B)	22.4
263A(h)	22.4
263A(h)(2)	22.4
265	9.1(a), 11.3(a), 11.3(b)(3)(ii)(c), 33.5(c)
265(1)	9.1(b)
265(3)	33.5(c)
265(4)	33.5(c)
265(a)	11.3(b)(3)(ii)(c)
265(a)(1)	9.3, 9.3(b)(5), 10.3(a), 18.6(e)(1)
265(a)(2)	9.3, 9.3(b)(5), 10.3(a), 10.3(b), 11.3(b)(1), 33.3(d)
265(a)(3)	9.3(b)(3)
265(a)(5)	31.3(m)(1)
265(b)	11.3(b)(3)(ii)(a), 11.3(b)(3)(ii)(c), 11.3(b)(3)(ii)(d), 11.3(b)(3)(ii)(g), 33.6
265(b)(1)	11.3(b)(3)(ii)

(References are to book sections.)

I.R.C.	
265(b)(2)	11.3(b)(3)(ii)(a), 11.3(b)(3)(ii)(c)
265(b)(3)	11.3(b)(3)(ii)(b), 33.6
265(b)(3)(B)	11.3(b)(3)(ii)(b)
265(b)(4)(A)	11.3(b)(3)(ii)(c)
265(b)(4)(B)	11.3(b)(3)(ii)(b)
265(b)(5)	11.3(b)(3)(ii)(d)
267	19.10(a)
267(b)	23.3(f)(1), 23.3(g)(1)(i)(c), 23.3(g)(2)(iii), 23.3(g)(3), 28.2(b), 28.4(c)(5), 28.4(c)(5)(ii), 28.4(c)(6)(ii), 59.2(i)(3)
267(c)(4)	28.4(c)(6)(ii)
269A	9.8
274(h)	9.1(c)(10)
274(h)(7)	9.1(c)(10)
280A(a)	9.1(c)(6)
280A(c)	9.1(c)(6)
291	15.5(c)
291(a)(3)	11.3(b)(3)(i), 33.6
291(e)(1)(B)	11.3(b)(3)(i)
291(e)(1)(B)(ii)	11.3(b)(3)(i)
301	16.6(a), 24.1(f), 24.2(b)(2), 30.3(e)(2), 30.3(f)(2), 34.3(d)
301(b)(1)(A)	24.1(f)(1), 29.2(a)
301(b)(1)(B)	24.1(f)(2), 29.2(a)
301(b)(2)	16.4(c)
301(c)(1)	24.1(e)
301(c)(2)	16.4(k), 29.2(a)
301(c)(3)	24.1(d), 29.2(a)
301(d)(1)	24.2(b)(7), 30.3(f)(2)
301(d)(2)	24.2(b)(7), 30.3(f)(2)
301(d)(2)(A)	24.1(f)(2)
301(d)(3)	24.1(f)(2)
301(d)(4)	24.1(f)(2)
301(e)(2)	24.1(f)(2)
302	24, 27.3(b)(3)(vii), 27.3(b)(5), 27.3(c)(5), 30.3(e)(2)
302(a)	30.3(e)(2)
302(b)(1)	24.2(b)(3)
302(b)(2)	17.7(b), 24.2(b)(3)
302(b)(2)(A)	24.2(b)(3)
302(b)(2)(B)	24.2(b)(3)
302(b)(2)(C)	24.2(b)(3)
302(b)(2)(D)	24.2(b)(3)

I.R.C.	
303	30.3(e)(2)
304	16.4(l), 30.3(e)(2)
305	16.4(b), 16.4(c), 24.2, 27.3(a), 27.3(b)(1), 27.3(b)(3)(vi), 27.3(c)(1), 30.3(e)(2)
305(a)	16.4(b)
305(b)	16.4(b), 16.4(l), 24.2(b)
305(b)(1)	24.2(b)(1)
305(b)(2)	24.2(b)(2), 34.3(d)
305(b)(3)	24.2(b)(4)
305(b)(4)	24.2(b)(5)
305(b)(5)	24.2(b)(6)
305(c)	24.2(b)(2), 27.3(b)(4), 27.3(b)(5), 27.3(c)(1), 27.3(c)(3), 34.3(d)
305(d)	27.3(c)(1)
305(d)(1)	24.2
305(e)	24.2, 24.4
305(e)(7)	24.4
305(e)(9)(A)	24.4
305(e)(9)(B)	24.4
306	24, 27.3(b)(5), 27.3(c)(3), 27.3(c)(8), 30.3(e)(2)
306(a)(1)	27.3(b)(5)
306(a)(2)	27.3(b)(5)
306(b)(4)	27.3(b)(5)
306(c)	27.3(b)(5), 27.3(c)(3)
306(c)(1)(A)	27.3(c)(3)
306(c)(1)(B)	27.3(c)(3)
306(c)(2)	27.3(b)(5)
306(e)(2)	27.3(c)(3)
307	16.4(b), 30.3(e)(2)
307(a)	16.4(c), 30.3(f)(1)
307(b)	30.3(e)(1)(i)
307(b)(1)	16.4(c), 30.3(f)(1)
307(b)(2)	30.3(f)(1)
308	30.3(e)(2)
309	30.3(e)(2)
310	30.3(e)(2)
311	29.2(a), 29.2(b), 30.3(c)(3), 30.3(e)(2)
311(b)	27.3(a)
311(d)(1)	29.2(a), 29.2(b)
312	30.3(e)(2)
312(a)	24.1(b)

Table of Internal Revenue Code Sections

(References are to book sections.)

I.R.C.	
312(a)(3)	24.1(f)(1)
312(m)	31.12(c)
312(n)	29.2(b)
313	30.3(e)(2)
314	30.3(e)(2)
315	30.3(e)(2)
316	24.1(a), 24.1(e), 30.3(e)(2)
316(b)(2)	24.3
317	30.3(e)(2)
317(a)	24.1(b)
318	30.3(e)(2)
318(a)	30.3(e)(2)
318(a)(4)	17.7(b), 19.9(a)
332	17.3(c)(4)
333	17.3(c)(4)
334(b)	17.3(c)(4)
334(c)	17.3(c)(4)
335	27.3(b)(5)
337(d)	8.9
338	11.3(b)(3)(ii)(g)
338(a)(2)	11.3(b)(3)(ii)(a)
351	14.4, 17.3(a)(4), 17.3(c)(3), 18.4(a), 19.6(a), 21.4, 27.3(b)(3)(v), 27.4(a), 28.4(e), 31.3(d), 34.2(a)
354	14.4, 17.3(a)(1), 18.4(a), 19.6(a), 21.4, 31.2(a), 31.9(b)
354(a)(1)	19.9(d), 27.3(c)(2)
354(a)(2)	26.2(g), 27.2
354(a)(2)(B)	27.3(c)(4)
355	14.4, 16.4(*l*), 21.4, 27.3(a), 27.4(a), 27.4(b), 59.2(g)(3)(v)
355(a)(3)(B)	27.4(b)
356	14.4, 17.3(a)(1), 21.4
356(d)	27.3(c)(4)
358(a)	17.3(a)(1), 17.3(a)(4)
361	18.4(a), 19.6(a)
362(a)	17.3(c)(3)
368	27.3(b)(2)(iii), 27.3(b)(5), 27.4(a), 31.9(a)
368(a)	26.2(g), 31.2(n)(2)
368(a)(1)	26.2(g), 27.4(b), 31.3(e), 31.9(b), 33.4, 34.2(a)
368(a)(1)(A)	27.4(b)
368(a)(1)(B)	27.4(b)
368(a)(1)(C)	27.4(b)
368(a)(1)(D)	27.4(b)
368(a)(1)(E)	27.3(c)(1), 27.3(c)(2), 27.3(c)(4), 27.4(b)
368(a)(1)(F)	27.4(b)
368(a)(1)(G)	27.4(b)(1)
368(a)(3)	31.2(g)(5)
368(c)	16.4(a)
368(c)(1)	34.2(f)
371	31.9(a)
382	27.3(c)(2)
382(e)	27.3(c)(2)
382(k)	27.3(c)(2)
382(k)(6)(A)	27.3(c)(2)
385	27.2, 27.3(b)(2)(i), 34.2(a)
385(a)	34.2(a), 34.4
385(b)	27.2, 34.2(a)
385(b)(1)	27.2, 34.2(a)
385(b)(2)	27.2, 34.2(a)
385(b)(3)	27.2, 34.2(a)
385(b)(4)	27.2, 34.2(a)
385(b)(5)	27.2, 34.2(a)
401(a)	16.3(c), 28.4(c)(6)(ii)
446	11.5, 30.3(e)(1)(iv), 32.1(b)(1)(ii)
446(a)	11.5, 22.1(a)
446(b)	22.1(a), 23.2(f), 60.2(b)(2)(ii)
446(c)	11.5, 22.1(a)
446(d)	22.1(a), 59.2(g)(3)(v)
446(e)	22.2
448	39.2(b)
451(a)	25.2, 60.4(c)
453	14.5(b)(1), 28.4(c)(6), 34.2(a), 34.3(e)
453(a)	17.2(a)(2)(i)(c)
453(b)(1)	17.2(a)(2)(i)(a)
453(b)(2)(A)	17.2(a)(2)(i)(a)
453(b)(2)(B)	17.2(a)(2)(i)(a)
453(c)	17.2(a)(2)(i)(c)
453(d)(1)	17.2(a)(2)(i)(c)
453(d)(3)	17.2(a)(2)(i)(c)
453(f)(1)	31.2(g)(2)(i)
453(k)	17.2(a)(i)(b)
453(k)(2)	14.5(b)(2)
453A	17.2(a)(2)(i)(b)

Table of Internal Revenue Code Sections

(References are to book sections.)

I.R.C.	
453B	31.3(b)
454	32.1(a)(1), 32.1(b)(1)(ii), 32.1(b)(1)(iii)
454(a)	32.1(b)(1)(ii), 32.1(b)(1)(iv), 32.1(b)(3)
454(b)	48.3(b)(2)(iii)
454(c)	32.1, 32.1(b)(1)(iii), 32.1(d), 32.1(d)(2)(i)
461	30.3(e)(1)(iv)
461(a)	60.4(c)
461(g)	9.2(d), 10.2(d)
464	23.2(c)(2)(ii), 45.2(c)(1)
464(e)	23.2(c)(2)(ii), 45.2(c)(1)
464(e)(2)	23.2(c)(2)(ii), 45.2(c)(1)
465	30.2(b)(3)
465(b)	30.2(b)(3)
465(b)(1)	30.2(b)(3)
465(b)(4)	30.2(b)(3), 45.2(c)(1)
469	9.8, 25.5, 28.4(b)(3), 28.4(g)(1)
469(a)(2)	9.8
469(c)	9.8
469(e)(1)	28.4(g)(1)
469(e)(1)(A)(i)(I)	9.9
469(e)(1)(A)(i)(II)	9.9
469(g)	9.8
469(g)(1)	28.4(g)(1)
469(k)	28.4(g)(1), 28.4(g)(2)
469(k)(1)	28.4(g)(1)
469(k)(2)	28.4(c)(6)(ii)
469(*l*)	9.8
471	22.2(a), 22.3
481	59.2(g)(1)
483	16.4(f), 27.3(b)(3)(vi)
501	24.8
501(a)	29.2(c), 31.2(n)(3)
501(b)	29.2(c)
501(c)(3)	3.1, 33.2(c)(1), 33.2(c)(2)(vi)(a), 33.2(c)(2)(vi)(b)
511	36.8(e), 41.2(g)(2), 41.2(g)(4)
512(a)	26.2(f)
512(a)(5)	26.2(f), 28.4(d)(2)(viii)
512(b)	26.2(f)
512(b)(2)	29.2(c)
512(b)(12)	28.4(h)
512(c)	28.4(h)

I.R.C.	
512(c)(2)	28.4(c)(6)(ii)
512(c)(2)(A)	28.4(h)
512(c)(2)(B)	28.4(h)
512(c)(3)	28.4(h)
513(a)	33.2(c)(2)(vi)(a)
514	26.2(f), 29.2(c)
514(c)(1)	26.2(f)
514(c)(8)	26.2(f)
514(c)(8)(A)	26.2(f)
514(c)(8)(B)	26.2(f)
514(c)(8)(C)	26.2(f)
521	24.8, 36.8(e)
541	24.3
542	11.10, 13.6, 24.3
542(a)(2)	24.3
542(b)(2)	24.3
543	24.3
543(a)(1)	24.3
543(a)(2)	24.3
545	24.3
547	24.3
547(a)	24.3
547(d)	24.3
561	8.9(a), 24.3, 24.5(c)
561(a)	24.5(c)
561(a)(l)	24.3
561(a)(3)	24.3
562	8.9(a), 24.3, 24.5(c)
562(b)	24.3
562(c)	24.3, 24.5(c)
562(d)	24.3
563	24.3
581	8.8, 11.3(b)(3)(i), 11.3(b)(3)(ii)(d), 23.2(d)(1), 23.2(d)(3)(i)
582	8.4(d), 8.8, 23.2(d)(3), 23.2(d)(3)(i), 27.6(c)
582(c)	8.8, 23.2(c)(4), 23.2(d)(3), 23.2(d)(3)(i), 23.2(d)(3)(ii), 27.6(c), 41.4
582(c)(1)	8.8, 33.6, 41.4
582(c)(5)	8.8
584(a)	31.2(n)(3)
585	8.10
585(a)(2)	11.3(b)(3)(ii)(d)

Table of Internal Revenue Code Sections

(References are to book sections.)

I.R.C.	
586	8.10
591	24.8
591(a)	37.1, 41.4
593	8.10, 11.3(b)(3)(ii)(d)
593(a)	11.3(b)(3)(i)
593(b)(1)	37.1
593(d)	41.4
593(d)(4)	36.8(d)(2)(ii)(b), 36.8(n), 41.4
596	24.9(a)(2)
612	29.1(e)
613	29.1(e)
613A	29.1(e)
631(c)	8.10(a)
664(c)	31.2(n)(3)
671	29.1, 29.1(a), Part Eight, 36.2(a)
672	29.1, 29.1(a), Part Eight, 36.2(a)
673	29.1, 29.1(a), Part Eight, 36.2(a)
674	29.1, 29.1(a), Part Eight, 36.2(a)
674(a)	29.1(a), 36.2(a)
675	29.1, 29.1(a), Part Eight, 36.2(a)
676	29.1, 29.1(a), Part Eight, 36.2(a)
677	29.1, 29.1(a), Part Eight, 36.2(a)
678	29.1, 29.1(a), Part Eight, 36.2(a)
679	29.1, 29.1(a), Part Eight, 36.2(a)
691	18.2(c)
691(a)(1)(B)	32.1(b)(1)(iv)
702(a)	28.4(g)(2)
703(a)(2)	41.2(e)
704(b)	28.2(b)
704(c)	28.2(b)
705(a)	33.5(a)
707(b)	28.2(b), 59.2(i)(3)
707(b)(1)	23.3(f)(1), 28.2(b), 28.4(c)(5), 28.4(c)(5)(ii), 28.4(c)(6)(ii)
707(c)	28.2(b)

I.R.C.	
708	28.4(b)(3)
708(b)(1)(B)	36.2(e)
723	17.3(c)(2)
731	28.4(e)
732	28.4(c)(6)(ii), 28.4(e)
735(b)	17.3(c)(2)
761(a)	36.1
832(b)(5)(B)(i)	33.8
851	8.9(a), 24.5, 31.11(a)(2), 36.7
851(a)	28.4(d)(1)
851(b)(1)	8.9(a), 8.9(a)(1)
851(b)(2)	8.9(a), 8.9(a)(2), 28.4(d)(2)(viii)
851(b)(3)	8.9(a), 8.9(a)(2), 8.9(a)(3), 8.9(d), 36.8(d)(2)(ii)(d), 54.4(c)
851(b)(4)	8.9(a)(4)
851(b)(4)(A)	8.9(a), 8.9(a)(4)
851(b)(4)(B)	8.9(a), 8.9(a)(5)
851(c)	8.9(c), 8.9(a)(5)
851(d)	8.9(a)(4), 8.9(a)(5)
851(e)	8.9(a), 8.9(a)(4)
851(g)	8.9(a)(3), 8.9(e)
851(g)(2)	8.9(e)
851(h)	8.9(d)
851(h)(1)	8.9(d)
851(h)(3)(A)(i)	8.9(d)
851(h)(3)(A)(ii)	8.9(d)
851(h)(3)(B)	8.9(d)
851(h)(3)(C)	8.9(d)
851(q)	8.9(d)
852	8.9(a), 8.9(f), 24.5(a), 24.5(d), 31.11(a)(2), 36.7
852(a)(1)	8.9(a), 8.9(a)(6)
852(a)(2)	8.9(a), 8.9(a)(6)
852(b)	33.5(c)
852(b)(1)	8.9(a)
852(b)(2)(D)	24.5(c)
852(b)(3)	8.9(a), 17
852(b)(3)(B)	8.9(c), 24.5(a)
852(b)(3)(C)	24.5(b)
852(b)(3)(D)	9.3(b)(3), 20.2(f)
852(b)(3)(D)(iii)	16.4(*l*)
852(b)(4)	8.9(c), 17.6, 24.5(b)
852(b)(4)(A)	24.5(a)
852(b)(4)(B)	33.5(c)

Table of Internal Revenue Code Sections

(References are to book sections.)

I.R.C.	
852(b)(4)(E)	8.9(c), 17.6, 24.5(b)
852(b)(5)	8.9(a), 8.9(c), 9.3(b)(3), 33.5(c)
852(b)(5)(A)	33.5(c)
852(b)(6)	8.9(c)
852(b)(7)	8.9(c), 24.5(b)
852(c)(1)	8.9(f)
852(c)(2)	8.9(f)
853	8.9(a), 24.5, 31.11(a)(2), 36.7
853(c)	8.9(c)
854	8.9(a), 24.5, 24.8, 31.11(a)(2), 36.7
855	8.9(a), 24.5, 24.5(b), 31.11(a)(2), 36.7
856	24.6, 31.2(n)(3), 36.7
856(a)	8.10, 24.6
856(a)(1)	8.10
856(a)(2)	8.10
856(a)(3)	8.10
856(a)(4)	8.10, 31.11(a)(2)
856(a)(5)	8.10
856(a)(6)	8.10
856(b)(3)	8.10(d)
856(b)(3)(B)	8.10(d)
856(c)(2)	8.10(b), 28.4(d)(2)(viii)
856(c)(3)	8.10(b), 37.1
856(c)(3)(B)	7.2(i), 36.7, 41.3(a)
856(c)(4)	8.10(b), 41.3(a)
856(c)(5)	31.11(a)(2), 36.7, 41.3(a)
856(c)(5)(A)	7.2(i), 8.10(a), 36.7, 41.3(a)
856(c)(5)(B)	8.10(a)
856(c)(6)	41.3(a)
856(c)(6)(B)	8.10(a)
856(c)(6)(C)	8.10(a)
856(c)(6)(E)	36.8(d)(2)(ii)(b), 36.8(n)
856(d)	28.4(d)(2)(iii)
856(d)(1)(B)	28.4(d)(2)(iii)
856(d)(1)(C)	28.4(d)(2)(iii)
856(d)(2)(B)	28.4(d)(2)(iii)
856(d)(2)(C)	28.4(d)(2)(iii)
856(d)(3)	28.4(d)(2)(iii)
856(e)	8.10(b), 36.8(d)(2)(iii)
856(f)	28.4(d)(2)(i)

I.R.C.	
856(h)	8.10
856(i)	8.10(f)
856(i)(2)	8.10(f)
856(j)	8.10(g)
857	24.6, 36.7
857(a)(1)	36.7
857(b)	8.10(c)
857(b)(2)	8.10(e), 41.3(b)
857(b)(3)	17
857(b)(4)(B)	36.8(i)
857(b)(5)	8.10(c)
857(b)(6)	8.10(c), 28.4(d)(2)(viii), 41.3(b)
857(b)(6)(C)	8.10(c)
857(c)(7)	8.10(c)
858	24.6, 36.7
859	24.6, 36.7
860A	36.8(a)
860A(a)	36.8(a)
860B	36.8(a)
860B(a)	36.8(c)(1)(ii), 41.1(a)
860B(b)	41.1(a), 41.1(a)(1)
860B(c)	41.1(a)(1), 41.1(c)
860C	36.8(a)
860C(a)(1)	41.2(a)
860C(a)(2)	41.2(a)
860C(b)	36.8(k)
860C(b)(1)	41.2(e)
860C(b)(1)(A)	41.2(e)
860C(b)(1)(B)	41.2(e)
860C(b)(1)(C)	41.2(e)
860C(b)(1)(D)	41.2(e)
860C(b)(1)(E)	41.2(e)
860C(c)(1)	41.2(b)
860C(c)(2)	41.2(b)
860C(d)(1)	41.2(f)
860C(d)(2)	41.2(f)
860D	31.12(f), 36.8(a)
860D(a)	36.8(d), 36.8(n)
860D(a)(1)	36.8(a), 36.8(k)
860D(a)(2)	36.8(a)
860D(a)(3)	36.8(a), 36.8(c)(1)(i)
860D(a)(4)	36.8(a), 36.8(d), 36.8(n)
860D(a)(5)	36.8(a), 36.8(j)(1)
860D(a)(6)	36.8(e)

Table of Internal Revenue Code Sections

(References are to book sections.)

I.R.C.	
860D(b)(1)	36.8(k)
860D(b)(2)	36.8(f)
860D(b)(2)(A)	36.8(k)
860D(b)(2)(B)	36.8(f)
860D(b)(2)(B)(ii)	36.8(f)
860D(b)(2)(B)(iv)	36.8(f)
860E	36.8(a), 41.2(a)
860E(a)	41.2(g)(2)
860E(a)(1)	41.2(g)(2)
860E(a)(2)	41.2(g)(2)
860E(b)	41.2(g)(2), 41.2(g)(4)
860E(c)	36.8(o), 41.2(g)(2)
860E(c)(1)	41.2(g)(4)
860E(c)(2)	41.2(g)(3)
860E(c)(2)(C)	41.2(g)(3)
860E(d)	36.8(o), 41.3(b)
860E(d)(1)	41.3(b)
860E(d)(2)	41.3(b)
860E(e)	36.8(e)
860E(e)(5)	36.8(e)
860E(e)(5)(B)	36.8(e)
860E(e)(5)(C)	36.8(e)
860F	36.8(a)
860F(a)(1)	36.8(g)
860F(a)(2)	36.8(g)
860F(a)(2)(A)	36.8(g), 36.8(m)
860F(a)(2)(A)(i)	36.8(g)
860F(a)(2)(A)(ii)	36.8(g)
860F(a)(2)(A)(iii)	36.8(g)
860F(a)(2)(A)(iv)	36.8(g)
860F(a)(2)(B)	36.8(g)
860F(a)(2)(C)	36.8(g)
860F(a)(2)(D)	36.8(g)
860F(a)(3)	36.8(g)
860F(a)(4)	36.8(m)
860F(a)(4)(A)(i)	36.8(m)
860F(a)(4)(A)(ii)	36.8(m)
860F(a)(4)(A)(iii)	36.8(m)
860F(a)(4)(B)	36.8(m)
860F(a)(5)	36.8(g)
860F(a)(5)(B)	36.8(g)
860F(d)	19.9(i), 41.2(j)
860F(d)(1)	19.6(a), 19.9(i), 41.2(j)
860F(d)(2)	19.6(a)
860F(d)(2)(A)	19.9(i), 41.2(j)

I.R.C.	
860F(e)	36.8(j)(1)
860G	31.12(f), 36.8(a)
860G(a)	36.8(d)(1)(i)
860G(a)(1)	36.8(c)(1)(ii), 36.8(c)(1)(vi)
860G(a)(1)(A)	36.8(c)(1)(ii), 36.8(c)(1)(vi)
860G(a)(1)(B)	36.8(c)(1)(ii), 36.8(c)(1)(iii), 36.8(c)(1)(iv), 36.8(c)(1)(vi)
860G(a)(1)(B)(ii)	36.8(c)(1)(vi)
860G(a)(2)	36.8(c)(2)
860G(a)(3)	31.12(f), 36.8(c)(2), 36.8(d)(1)(i)
860G(a)(3)(A)	36.8(d)(1)(i)
860G(a)(3)(B)	36.8(d)(1)(iii)
860G(a)(3)(C)	36.8(d)(1)(ii)
860G(a)(4)	36.8(g)
860G(a)(4)(B)	36.8(d)(1)(iii)
860G(a)(5)	36.8(d)(2)
860G(a)(6)	36.8(d)(2)(i)
860G(a)(7)	36.8(d)(2)(ii)
860G(a)(7)(A)	36.8(d)(2)(ii)(b)
860G(a)(7)(B)	36.8(d)(2)(ii)(a), 36.8(d)(2)(ii)(c)
860G(a)(7)(C)	36.8(d)(2)(ii)(d)
860G(a)(8)	36.8(d)(2)(iii)
860G(a)(9)	31.2(n)(1), 36.8(a), 36.8(c)(2), 36.8(d)(1)(i)
860G(b)(2)	41.2(g)(2)
860G(c)	41.2(e)
860G(c)(1)	36.8(i)
860G(c)(2)	36.8(i)
860G(d)	36.8(h)
860G(d)(1)	36.8(h)
860G(d)(2)(A)	36.8(h)
860G(d)(2)(B)	36.8(h)
860G(d)(2)(C)	36.8(h)
860G(d)(2)(D)	36.8(h)
860G(d)(2)(E)	36.8(h)
860G(e)(1)	36.8(d)(2)(ii)(c)
861	60.2(b)(2)(i)(a)(4), 60.2(g)(2), 60.5
861(a)(1)	23.3(g)(1)(v)(e)
862	60.5

Table of Internal Revenue Code Sections

(References are to book sections.)

I.R.C.	
862(a)(1)	23.3(g)(1)(v)(e)
863	60.2(b)(2)(i)(a)(1), 60.5
863(e)	60.2(b)(2)(i)(a)(1)
864	60.5
865	60.4(d), 60.5
865(a)	60.4(d)
865(j)(2)	60.4(d)
871(a)	23.3(g)(1)(v)(c)
871(a)(1)(A)	60.2(g)
871(a)(1)(C)	31.2(f)
871(b)	60.5(a)
881	23.3(g)(1)(v)(c)
881(a)(1)	60.2(g)
881(a)(3)	31.2(f)
882(a)(1)	60.5(a)
884	25.4(c), 33.1, 33.2(a), 33.11
895	31.12(b)(4)(ii)
904(a)	59.2(d)(1)
911(d)(3)	23.3(c), 59.2(d)(2)(i)
936	24.9(a)(2)
951(a)(1)	60.5(a)
954	60.2(b)(2)(i)(a)(4)
954(c)(1)	60.5(a)
954(c)(1)(D)	60.5(a)
954(c)(1)(E)	60.2(b)(2)(i)(a)(4), 60.5(a)
954(d)(2)(A)(i)	60.5(a)
959	59.5(a)
961	16.4(*l*)
985	23.3(a), 59.1, 59.2(a)(3), 59.2(g)(1)(ii), 59.2(g)(2)
985(a)	59.2(g), 59.2(g)(1)(i), 59.2(g)(3)(viii)
985(a)(1)(A)	59.2(g)(1)(i), 59.2(g)(3)(viii)
985(b)(1)(B)	59.2(g)(3)(viii)
985(b)(3)	59.2(g)(1)
985(b)(4)	59.2(g)(1)
986	23.3(a), 59.1, 59.4, 59.5, 59.5(a)
986(a)(1)	59.5(a)
986(a)(1)(A)	59.5(a)
986(a)(1)(B)(ii)	59.5(a)
986(a)(2)	59.5(a)
986(b)(1)	59.5(a)

I.R.C.	
986(b)(2)	59.5(a)
986(c)(1)	59.5(a)
987	23.3(a), 59.1, 59.2(g)(1)(v), 59.2(g)(3)(vii), 59.4, 59.5, 59.5(a), 59.5(b)
987(1)	59.5(b)
987(2)	59.5(b)
987(3)	59.5(b)
988	8.9(b)(1), 21.9, 23.2(e)(2), 23.3, 23.3(a), 23.3(g)(1)(i)(c), 23.3(g)(1)(ii), 31.7, 31.7(a), 44.6, 57.7, 59.1, 59.2(a), 59.2(a)(3), 59.2(c)(1), 59.2(e), 59.2(g)(2), 59.2(j), 59.4, 59.4(a)(1), 59.4(a)(2), 59.4(a)(3), 59.4(b)(2), 59.4(b)(3), 59.4(c)(1), 59.4(c)(2), 59.4(c)(3), 59.4(d)(1), 59.4(d)(2), 59.4(d)(3), 59.4(e), 60.1, 60.2(a), 60.2(b)(1)(i), 60.2(b)(1)(iii), 60.2(b)(2)(ii), 60.2(c)(1), 60.2(c)(6), 60.2(c)(7), 60.5(a), 60.7(a)
988(a)	59.2(b)(4), 60.5(a)
988(a)(1)	21.9, 23.3(c)
988(a)(1)(A)	23.3(e), 59.2(b)(3), 59.2(e), 59.2(h)
988(a)(1)(B)	23.3(a), 23.3(b), 23.3(c), 23.3(e), 59.2(b)(3), 59.4(b)(4), 59.4(c)(4), 59.4(d)(4), 59.4(e), 60.2(c)(4)
988(a)(2)	23.3(c), 59.2(b)(1)
988(a)(3)	60.2(g)(1)
988(a)(3)(A)	23.3(c), 59.2(d), 59.2(d)(1)
988(a)(3)(B)	23.3(g)(1)(i)(c), 23.3(g)(2)(iii), 23.3(g)(3), 59.2(d)(1), 59.2(d)(2)(i), 59.2(g)(1)(iv)
988(a)(3)(B)(i)	60.5(a)
988(a)(3)(B)(ii)	60.5(a)
988(a)(3)(B)(i)(I)	23.3(c), 59.2(d)(2)(i)
988(a)(3)(B)(i)(II)	23.3(c), 59.2(d)(2)(ii), 59.2(d)(2)(iv)
988(a)(3)(B)(i)(III)	23.3(c), 59.2(d)(2)(ii), 59.2(d)(2)(iv)
988(b)(1)	59.2(f)
988(b)(2)	59.2(f)

Table of Internal Revenue Code Sections

(References are to book sections.)

I.R.C.	
988(b)(3)	59.2(f), 60.2(c)(6)
988(c)(1)	59.2(a)(1)
988(c)(1)(B)	59.2(a)(1), 59.2(b)(1)
988(c)(1)(B)(i)	59.2(a)(1)
988(c)(1)(B)(ii)	59.2(a)(1)
988(c)(1)(B)(iii)	59.2(a)(1), 59.2(c)(2), 59.2(f), 59.2(h)
988(c)(1)(C)(i)	59.2(a)(1), 59.2(f)(3)
988(c)(1)(C)(i)(II)	59.2(f)(3)
988(c)(1)(C)(ii)	59.2(a)(1), 59.2(f)(3), 59.2(g)(2)
988(c)(1)(D)	59.4(a)(3)
988(c)(1)(D)(i)	59.2(a)(1), 59.2(b)(4), 59.2(j)(1), 59.2(j)(2), 59.2(j)(3), 60.2(c)(3)
988(c)(1)(D)(ii)	59.2(a)(1), 59.2(b)(1), 59.2(j), 59.2(j)(2), 59.2(j)(4)
988(c)(1)(D)(ii)(I)	59.2(j)
988(c)(1)(D)(ii)(II)	59.2(j)
988(c)(1)(D)(ii)(III)	59.2(j)
988(c)(1)(D)(iii)	59.2(j)
988(c)(1)(E)(i)	59.2(i)(4)(i), 59.2(i)(4)(ii)
988(c)(1)(E)(iii)(V)	59.2(i)(4), 59.2(i)(4)(i), 59.2(i)(4)(ii), 59.2(i)(4)(iii), 59.2(j)(1)
988(c)(1)(E)(iv)(I)	59.2(a)(2)
988(c)(1)(E)(iv)(II)	59.2(a)(2)
988(c)(2)(A)	59.2(f)(1)
988(c)(2)(B)	59.2(f)(1)
988(c)(3)	59.2(c)(1), 59.2(f)(2)
988(c)(3)(B)	59.2(c)(1)
988(c)(4)	59.2(a)(1)
988(c)(5)	59.2(a)(4), 59.2(c)(2), 59.4(b)(4), 59.4(c)(4), 59.4(d)(3)
988(d)	21.5, 22.1(b), 23.1, 23.3(g), 30.2, 44.2(b), 45.1(b), 46.2(b), 59.2(b)(4)
988(d)(1)	23.3(a), 23.3(b), 23.3(g), 45.1, 46.2(b)
988(d)(2)	23.3(a), 23.3(b)
988(d)(2)(B)	23.3(a), 23.3(b)
988(e)	59.2(a)(3)
989	23.3(a), 59.1, 59.2(g)(3)(i)

I.R.C.	
989(a)	59.2(g)(3)(v), 60.2(b)(2)(i)(a)(4), 60.5(a)
989(b)(4)	59.2(g)(1)(v), 59.5(b)
1001	16.4, 26.3, 27.4(b)(3), 31.9(a), 31.10(c), 33.4, 59.2(a)(4), 59.2(c)(1), 59.4(e), 60.2(b)(2)(i)(a), 60.3(a)(2)(ii)
1001(a)	14.3, 19.9(j), 21.3, 33.3(c), 33.4
1001(c)	9.2(c)(1), 14.4, 21.4
1002	27.3(e)(5)
1011	11.3(b)(3)(ii)(e)
1012	16.4(b), 30.5(b)(3)
1014(a)(1)	16.3(b)
1014(a)(2)	16.3(b)
1014(a)(3)	16.3(b)
1015(a)	16.3(a)
1015(c)	16.3(a)
1015(d)(1)(A)	16.3(a)
1015(d)(6)(A)	16.3(a)
1016	11.3(b)(3)(ii)(e)
1016(a)	31.4(a)(2)(i)
1016(a)(4)	16.4(k)
1016(a)(5)	11.4(b), 16.4(g), 16.4(*l*), 31.4(a)(1)(i), 31.4(a)(2)(ii)
1016(a)(6)	31.4(a)(2)(ii)
1023	16.3(b)
1031	14.4, 21.4, 27.4(d)(1)
1031(a)(2)	31.9(a)
1031(b)	32.1(d)(1)
1031(c)	32.1(d)(1)
1031(d)	17.3(a)(2), 32.1(d)(1)
1032	27.3(a), 27.3(c)(1), 34.2(a)
1032(a)	30.3(c)(3), 30.3(e)(2), 30.5(c)
1033	27.4(c), 27.4(d), 27.4(d)(1)
1033(a)	27.4(d), 27.4(d)(1), 27.4(d)(2)
1036	14.4, 17.3(a)(2), 21.4, 27.3(c)(2), 27.4(a)
1036(a)	27.3(c)(2)
1037	14.4, 32.1, 32.1(b)(3), 32.1(d), 32.1(d)(1)
1037(a)	32.1(d), 32.1(d)(1), 32.1(d)(2)
1037(b)(1)	32.1(d)(2)(i)

(References are to book sections.)

I.R.C.	
1037(b)(1)(B)	32.1(d)(2)(i)
1037(b)(2)	32.1(d)(2)(ii)
1041(a)	32.1(b)(1)(iii)
1041(b)(1)	32.1(b)(1)(iii)
1042(a)	16.4(e)
1042(b)	16.4(e)
1042(d)	16.4(e)
1054	27.5(a)(2)
1056(d)(3)	17.7(c)
1058	17.8, 18.6(d), 24.9(b)(3), 26.1, 26.2, 26.2(e), 26.2(g), 26.3, 31.11(b)(1), 31.11(b)(2), 48.3(b)(2)(ii)
1058(a)	26.2, 26.2(e)
1058(b)	26.3
1058(b)(1)	26.2(b)
1058(b)(2)	26.2(b)
1058(b)(3)	26.2(b), 31.11(b)(1)
1058(b)(4)	26.2(b)
1058(c)	26.2(b)
1059	16.6(a), 16.6(b), 16.6(g), 16.6(h), 17.7(c), 27.3(b)(3), 31.2(g)(4)
1059(a)	16.6(a), 16.6(b), 18.6(e)(2)
1059(a)(1)	16.6(g)
1059(a)(2)	16.6(b), 17.7(c)
1059(b)(1)	16.6(a)
1059(b)(2)	16.6(a)
1059(c)	18.6(e)(2)
1059(c)(2)(A)	16.6(a)
1059(c)(2)(B)	16.6(a)
1059(c)(3)	16.6(d)
1059(c)(3)(A)	16.6(a), 16.6(e)
1059(c)(3)(B)	16.6(a), 16.6(e)
1059(c)(3)(C)	16.6(e)
1059(c)(4)	16.6(b), 16.6(d), 16.6(e), 18.6(e)(2)
1059(d)(2)	16.6(a)
1059(d)(3)	16.6(a)
1059(d)(5)	16.6(b)
1059(d)(6)	16.6(b)
1059(d)(6)(A)(ii)	16.6(b)
1059(d)(6)(B)	16.6(b)
1059(d)(6)(B)(ii)	16.6(b)
1059(e)(1)	16.6(b)
1059(e)(2)	16.6(f)
1059(e)(3)(A)	16.6(c)

I.R.C.	
1059(e)(3)(B)(i)	16.6(c)
1059(e)(3)(B)(ii)	16.6(c)
1059(e)(3)(C)	16.6(c)
1059(f)	16.6(g), 16.6(h)
1059(f)(2)(A)	16.6(g)
1059(f)(2)(B)	16.6(g)
1059(f)(2)(C)	16.6(g)
1059(g)	16.6(h)
1059(g)(1)	16.6(h)
1059(g)(2)	16.6(h)
1071	27.4(b), 27.4(c)
1081	27.4(b), 27.4(c)
1082	27.4(b), 27.4(c)
1083	27.4(b), 27.4(c)
1091	8.8, 9.5, 10.5, 11.11, 17.4(b), 19.2, 19.3(a), 19.3(b), 19.6(a), 19.6(b), 19.9, 19.9(i), 19.9(j), 19.11, 21.10, 24.9(b)(2), 26.3, 30.3(g)(2), 41.2(j), Part Eleven, 47.2, 47.2(b), 54.1, 54.2, 54.3, 57.3(c)
1091(a)	19.2, 19.3(a), 19.4, 19.4(b), 19.6(a), 19.6(b), 19.6(c)(1), 19.8, 19.8(f), 19.11, Part Eleven, 54, 54.2
1091(d)	16.4(i), 16.4(*l*), 19.3(a), 19.3(c), 54
1091(e)	19.3(f)
1092	8.4(d), 9.7, 10.7, 11.13, 12.1, 23.3(g), 23.3(g)(1)(v)(a), 23.3(g)(2)(viii)(f), 30.3(d)(2)(i), 30.5(b)(5), 42.1(b), 45.2(a), 45.3, Part Eleven, 48.2(c)(1), 49.2, 54.2, 56.6, 57, 57.1, 59.2(a)(1), 59.2(a)(4), 60.4(f)
1092(a)	60.7
1092(a)(1)	14.6, 48.3(b)(3), 55.2(a)
1092(a)(1)(A)	14.6, 21.2, Part Eleven, 48.4, 48.4(b), 48.5, 49.1, 52.3
1092(a)(1)(B)	Part Eleven, 50
1092(a)(2)	45.3, 56.1(a), 57.1, 57.2(b)
1092(a)(2)(A)	56.1(a)
1092(a)(2)(A)(ii)	56.1(a)
1092(a)(2)(B)(i)	56.1(a)
1092(a)(2)(B)(ii)	56.1(a)
1092(a)(2)(B)(ii)(I)	56.1(a)
1092(a)(2)(B)(ii)(II)	56.1(a)

Table of Internal Revenue Code Sections

(References are to book sections.)

I.R.C.

1092(a)(2)(B)(iii) ....56.1(a)
1092(a)(2)(C) ....56.1(a)
1092(a)(3) ....23.2(c)(3)(iv)
1092(a)(3)(A)(i) ....23.2(c)(3)(iv), 48.5
1092(a)(3)(A)(ii) ...23.2(c)(3)(iv), 48.5
1092(a)(3)(B) ...12.3, 23.2(e)(1), 52.1, 53.1(a)
1092(a)(3)(B)(i) ....52.1, 53.1(a)
1092(a)(3)(B)(ii)(I) 52.2
1092(a)(3)(B)(ii)(II) 52.2, 52.3
1092(a)(3)(B)(ii)(III) 52.2
1092(b) ...17.4(d), 18.1, 19.2, 19.6(a), 42.1(a), 45.2(b), Part Eleven, 49.2, 54.1, 54.4(c), 59.2(b)(1)
1092(b)(1) ....11.11, 18.1, 18.4(f), 19.8(e), 54, 57, 57.3(c), 57.4(d)
1092(b)(2) ....54.4(b), 57, 57.2(b), 57.3, 57.3(a), 57.6(a), 57.6(c)
1092(b)(2)(A) ....57, 57.3(c)
1092(b)(2)(A)(i) ....57.3, 57.3(b)
1092(b)(2)(A)(i)(I) 57
1092(b)(2)(A)(i)(II) 57
1092(b)(2)(B) ....30.4, 45.1, 57.4, 57.4(c)
1092(b)(2)(B)(i) ....57.4(c)
1092(b)(2)(B)(ii) ....57.4(c)
1092(b)(2)(D) ....57.7, 59.2(h)
1092(c) ......23.3(a), 23.3(b), 23.3(c), 23.3(e), 23.3(g)(1)(iii), 53.2
1092(c)(1) ......30.5(b), 45.6(c), 48.1, 49.2
1092(c)(2)(A) ......48.3, 48.4(a), 49.2
1092(c)(2)(B) ....48.4(c)
1092(c)(3)(A) ....48.4(a), 48.4(c), 49.1
1092(c)(3)(B) ....48.4(a)
1092(c)(4) ....18.4(c)
1092(c)(4)(A) ....17.9, 56.3(a)
1092(c)(4)(B) ....56.3(a)
1092(c)(4)(B)(i) ....56.3(b)
1092(c)(4)(B)(ii) ....56.3(b)
1092(c)(4)(B)(iii) ....56.3(b)
1092(c)(4)(B)(iv) ....56.3(b)
1092(c)(4)(B)(v) ....56.3(b)
1092(c)(4)(C) ....56.3(b)
1092(c)(4)(D)(i) ....56.3(b)

I.R.C.

1092(c)(4)(D)(ii) ....56.3(c)
1092(c)(4)(D)(iii) ....56.3(c)
1092(c)(4)(D)(iv) ....56.3(c)
1092(c)(4)(E) ....17.9, 56.3(d)(1)
1092(c)(4)(E)(i) 17.9
1092(c)(4)(E)(ii) 17.9
1092(c)(4)(E)(iii) 17.9
1092(c)(4)(G) ....56.3(b)
1092(c)(4)(H) ....56.3(d)(3)
1092(d) ....30.3(d)(2)(i), 53.2
1092(d)(1) ...12.3, 23.2(a), 23.2(e)(1), 23.2(e)(2), 23.3(d), 27.9, Part Eleven, 48.2, 48.2(c)(1), 48.3(b)(2)(i), 48.4(b), 48.4(c), 54.4(d), 56.4, 56.5, 58.2, 60.4(e)
1092(d)(2) ....Part Eleven, 48.3, 48.3(b)(2)(i), 48.4(b), 60.4(e)
1092(d)(2)(B) 56.6
1092(d)(2)(B)(ii) 30.2
1092(d)(3) ....48.2(c)(1)
1092(d)(3)(A) ....48.2(c)(1), 56.5
1092(d)(3)(B) 56.5, 58.2
1092(d)(3)(B)(i) ....48.2(c)(1), 56.5
1092(d)(3)(B)(i)(I) ....30.5(b)
1092(d)(3)(B)(i)(II) 56.5
1092(d)(3)(B)(ii) ....48.2(c)(1), 48.2(c)(4), 56.5
1092(d)(4) ......23.2(c)(1), 51.1, 54.3, 54.4(a), 57.6(a), 57.6(c)
1092(d)(4)(A) ....23.2(c)(1), 51.1, 57.6(a)
1092(d)(4)(B) 51.1, 51.4
1092(d)(4)(C) 51.1, 51.3, 51.4
1092(d)(5)(A) ......45.3, Part Eleven, 48.4(a), 48.4(b), 49.1, 56.7
1092(d)(5)(B) 45.3
1092(d)(7) ....48.3(c)
1092(d)(7)(A) ....48.3(c)
1092(d)(7)(B) ....48.2(a), 48.2(b), 48.3(c)
1092(e) ......12.3, 23.1, 48.4(a), 52.3, 60.2(b)(1), 60.4(a), 60.4(f)
1092(f) 17.9
1092(f)(1) ....56.3(d)(2)
1092(f)(2) ....17.9, 56.3(d)(2)

Table of Internal Revenue Code Sections

(References are to book sections.)

I.R.C.	
1101	27.4(b), 27.4(c)
1102	27.4(b), 27.4(c)
1103	27.4(b), 27.4(c)
1201	15.5(a)(1)
1201(a)	15.5(a)(2)(i), 15.5(c)
1201(a)(2)	15.5(a)(2)(i)
1202	15.4(a)(2)(i), 45.2
1202(a)	Part Ten
1211	8.4(d), 15.4(c), 23.2(c)(4), 27.8(a), 45.4(c), 59.2(h)
1211(a)	15.5(b)
1211(b)	15.4(b)
1211(b)(1)	15.4(b), 15.4(c)
1211(b)(1)(A)	15.4(b)
1211(b)(1)(c)(ii)	15.4(b)
1211(b)(2)	15.4(b)
1211(b)(2)(B)	15.4(b)
1211(b)(3)	15.4(b)
1212	27.8(a), 45.4(b)
1212(a)(1)	45.4(c)
1212(a)	15.5(b), 45.4(c)
1212(a)(1)(A)(ii)	15.5(b)
1212(b)	15.4(c), 45.4(a), 45.4(c)
1212(b)(1)	15.4(c)
1212(b)(1)(A)	45.4(c)
1212(b)(1)(B)	45.4(c)
1212(b)(2)	15.4(b), 15.4(c)
1212(c)	45.4(a), 45.4(b), 45.4(c), 57.4
1212(c)(1)	45.4(a)
1212(c)(2)	45.4(a)
1212(c)(3)	45.4(a)
1212(c)(4)	45.4(a), 45.4(c)
1212(c)(4)(A)	45.4(a)
1212(c)(4)(B)	45.4(a)
1212(c)(5)	45.4(a)
1212(c)(6)(A)	45.4(a), 45.4(c)
1221	8.4, 8.4(d), 9, 12, Part Three, 14.1, 18.2(b), 21.1, 23.2(b)(3), 23.2(c)(4), 23.2(d)(3)(i), 30.4, 32.1(a)(3), 45.4(a), 56.2, 59.4(a)(2), 59.4(a)(3), 59.4(b)(1), 59.4(c)(1), 59.4(c)(2), 59.4(d)(1), 59.4(e), 60.2(b)(2)(i)(a), 60.3(a)(2)(ii)

I.R.C.	
1221(1)	8.4, 8.4(d), 9, 11, 11.9(b), 11.9(c), 14.1, 15.2, 21.1, 23.2(b)(3), 28.4(d)(2)(iv), 60.2(b)(2)(ii)
1221(2)	8.4, 8.4(d), 14.1, 15.2, 21.1, 23.2(b)(3)
1221(3)	8.4, 8.4(d), 14.1, 21.1, 23.2(b)(3)
1221(4)	8.4, 8.4(d), 14.1, 21.1, 23.2(b)(3)
1221(5)	8.4, 8.4(d), 14.1, 21.1, 23.2(b)(3)
1222	Part Three, 15.1, 15.2, 30.5(b)(5), 42.1(e), 47.2, 58.2
1222(1)	45.4(c)
1222(2)	47.1
1222(3)	15.2, 47.1
1222(4)	15.2, 47.1
1223	8.9(a)(3), Part Three, 17.3(c)(2), 17.3(c)(4)
1223(1)	17.3(a), 17.3(a)(1), 17.3(a)(4), 17.3(c)(3)
1223(2)	17.3(c), 17.3(c)(1), 17.3(c)(5)
1223(4)	17.4(b), 17.7(a), 19.3(a), 19.3(d)
1223(5)	17.4(a)
1223(6)	17.2(c)(3)
1223(8)	17.3(b), 17.5, 42.1(a), 42.1(e), 45.6(a), 55.1
1223(11)	17.1(d)
1231	17.3(a), 23.2(e)(2), 28.4(d)(2)
1231(b)	21.1, 28.4(d)(2)(vi)
1232	27.3(c)(4), 31.10
1232(a)	31.10
1232(b)(2)	27.3(c)(4)
1232(c)	31.6(c)(4)
1232A(a)(2)(A)	31.2(d)(1)
1232A(a)(2)(B)(ii)	31.2(d)(1)
1232A(a)(2)(C)	31.2(d)(1)
1232B	31.6(c)
1232B(a)	31.6(c)(2)
1232B(b)(1)	31.6(c)(1)
1232B(b)(2)	31.6(c)(1)
1232B(b)(3)	31.6(c)(1)
1232B(b)(4)	3.16(c)(1)

Table of Internal Revenue Code Sections

(References are to book sections.)

I.R.C.	
1233	8.7(d), 9.6, 10.6, 11.12, 14.5(b)(1), 17.4(c), 18.1, 18.4(a), 18.4(e)(4), 18.4(f), 18.5, 24.9(b)(2), 30.3(g)(3), 47.2, 54.1, 54.4, 54.4(a), 57
1233(b)	18.4(c), 30.3(c)(1)(ii), 47.1, 54, 54.4(a), 54.4(c), 54.4(d), 56.4, 57
1233(b)(1)	18.2, 18.3(a), 18.4(c)
1233(b)(2)	18.2, 18.3(b), 18.7
1233(c)	18.4(d), 54.4(d), 56.4
1233(d)	18.2, 18.3(c), 18.4(c), 54, 54.4(a), 57
1233(e)	55.1
1233(e)(1)	18.2, 18.3(a), 18.3(c)
1233(e)(2)	18.1, 18.4(a), 18.4(e), 18.8, 30.3(g)(3), 54.1
1233(e)(2)(A)	18.2(b), 18.4, 18.4(b), 55.1
1233(e)(2)(B)	18.4(e)
1233(e)(3)	18.4(e)(4), 18.10
1233(e)(4)	18.4(a), 18.9
1233(e)(4)(B)(ii)	18.9
1233(f)	18.4(e)(4), 18.10
1233(f)(1)	18.10
1233(f)(2)	18.10(a)
1233(f)(4)	18.10
1233(g)	18.4(e)(1), 18.11
1234	14.5(b)(1), 19.8(f), 19.9(f), 27.3(d), 30.3(e)(1)(ii), 30.3(e)(2), 35.2, 43.1, 44.3(b), 44.3(c), 44.3(c)(1)(i), 44.3(c)(2), 60.2(e)(2)
1234(a)	8.3(a), 30.3(b)(1)(ii), 30.3(b)(1)(iii), 30.4, 30.5(b)(2), 44.3(c)(1)(ii), 44.3(c)(2), 60.2(e)(2), 60.3(a)(4), 60.3(b)
1234(a)(1)	30.3(b)(1), 30.3(b)(1)(ii), 30.4, 45.2(b)
1234(a)(2)	30.3(b)(1)(iii)
1234(a)(3)	30.3(b)(1)(iii)
1234(b)	8.3(c), 30.3(b)(2)(iii), 30.3(e)(2), 30.4, 44.3(c)(1)(i)
1234(b)(3)	8.3(c), 11.9(c)
1234(c)(2)	30.3(a), 30.4, 30.5(b)
1234A	15.1, 27.3(d), 30.5(b)(2), Part Twelve, 58.2, 60.2(b)(1)(iii), 60.2(b)(2)(ii), 60.2(e)(2), 60.3(a)(4), 60.3(b)
1234A(1)	58.2, 60.2(b)(2)(ii), 60.3(b)
1234A(2)	58.2, 60.2(b)(2)(ii)
1236	8.1, 8.3(c), 11.7(a), 11.7(c), 11.7(f), 18.9, 44.4
1236(a)	11.7(a)
1236(c)	8.3(c), 11.7(a), 18.4(a), 19.2, 19.6(a), 54.2
1236(d)	11.7(a)
1236(e)	11.7(c)
1242	18.2(a), 27.6(a), 27.6(b)
1243	27.6(a), 27.6(c)
1244	27.7
1244(b)	27.7
1244(c)(1)(A)	27.7
1244(c)(1)(B)	27.7
1244(c)(1)(C)	27.7
1244(c)(3)(A)	27.7
1246(e)(1)	16.4(*l*)
1256	8.9(a)(2), 9.2(c)(1), 10.1, 12.3, 17.3(b), 23.2(a), 23.3(a), 23.3(b), 23.3(c), 23.3(g), 23.3(g)(1)(v)(a), 23.3(g)(2)(viii)(f), 35.1, 43.3(a), 44.1, 44.1(a), 44.1(b), 44.3(b), 44.3(c)(1)(i), 44.3(c)(1)(ii), 44.3(c)(2), 44.4, 44.6, 45.6(a), 46.2(b), Part Eleven, 55.2(a), 59.2(a)(1), 59.2(a)(2), 59.2(a)(4), 59.2(b)(1), 59.2(b)(4), 59.2(h), 59.2(i)(1), 59.2(j), 59.4(a)(1), 59.4(a)(2), 59.4(a)(3), 59.4(c)(1), 59.4(c)(2), 59.4(c)(3), 59.4(c)(4), 60.2(c)(3), 60.4(a)(1)
1256(a)	14.2, 17.5, 45.3
1256(a)(1)	9.2(c)(1), 43.1, 45.1
1256(a)(2)	45.1(b)
1256(a)(3)	30.4, 44.3(c)(1)(ii), 45.2, 45.4(a), 57
1256(a)(4)	9.2(f), 10.2(f), 45.3, Part Eleven, 48.4(b), 49, 55, 55.2(a), 56.7
1256(b)	42.3, 44, 44.2(a), 45.2
1256(b)(1)	44.1, 59.4(a)
1256(b)(3)	35.2, 44.1, 44.3, 44.3(a), 59.4(a)

(References are to book sections.)

I.R.C.	
1256(b)(4)	44.4, 45.4(a)
1256(c)	9.2(c)(1), 42.1(e)
1256(c)(1)	45.1, 45.5, 45.6(a)
1256(c)(2)	42.1(a), 45.6(c), 57.2(c)
1256(c)(3)	45.1, 45.6(c)
1256(d)	30.4, 57, 57.2, 57.5
1256(d)(1)	30.4, 45.1, 45.1(b), 45.2(a), 57.2, 57.2(a)
1256(d)(3)	57.2(a)
1256(d)(4)	42.3, 46.1
1256(d)(4)(A)	57
1256(d)(4)(B)	57.2(b)
1256(e)	12.3, 14.6, 21.5, 22.1(b), 23.2, 23.2(a), 23.2(b)(4)(iii), 23.2(c), 23.2(c)(1), 23.2(c)(2)(ii), 23.2(c)(4), 23.2(d)(3)(ii), 23.2(e)(1), 23.2(g), 23.3(b), 23.3(g)(1)(i)(c), 30.4, 45.1, 45.1(b), 45.2(a), 45.2(c)(1), 46.2(a), 52.3, 59.2(b)(4), 60.2(b)(1), 60.4(a), 60.4(e)
1256(e)(1)	23.1, 45.2(a)
1256(e)(2)	12.2, 23.1, 23.2(b), 31.2(d)(2)(i), 56.2
1256(e)(2)(A)	23.2(b), 23.2(b)(1), 23.2(d)(1)
1256(e)(2)(A)(i)	23.2(b), 23.2(b)(2), 23.2(d)(1)
1256(e)(2)(A)(ii)	23.2(b), 23.2(b)(2), 23.2(d)(1)
1256(e)(2)(B)	23.2(b), 23.2(b)(3), 60.4(e)
1256(e)(2)(C)	23.2(b), 23.2(b)(4)(i), 23.2(e)(1)
1256(e)(3)	23.2(a), 23.2(c)(2)(i), 23.2(c)(2)(ii)
1256(e)(3)(C)	23.2(c)(2)(iii)
1256(e)(3)(C)(i)	23.2(c)(2)(iii)
1256(e)(3)(C)(ii)	23.2(c)(2)(iii)
1256(e)(3)(C)(iii)	23.2(c)(2)(iii)
1256(e)(3)(C)(iv)	23.2(c)(2)(iii)
1256(e)(3)(C)(v)	23.2(c)(2)(iii)
1256(e)(4)	23.2(c)(3)(i), 23.2(d)(1)
1256(e)(4)(A)(i)	23.2(c)(3)(ii)
1256(e)(4)(A)(ii)	23.2(c)(3)(iii)
1256(e)(4)(B)	23.2(c)(3)(iv)

I.R.C.	
1256(e)(4)(C)	23.2(c)(3)(ii)(b)
1256(e)(4)(D)	23.2(c)(3)(ii)
1256(e)(4)(E)	23.2(c)(3)(iv)
1256(e)(5)	23.2(c)(3)(i)
1256(e)(5)(A)(i)	23.2(c)(3)(ii)
1256(e)(5)(B)	23.2(c)(3)(iv)
1256(f)(1)	12.3, 23.2(a), 23.2(b)(4)(iii), 23.2(c)(4), 23.2(e)(1), 23.2(e)(2)
1256(f)(2)	21.5, 23.2(b)(4)(iii), 23.2(e)(1), 30.4, 45.2(a)
1256(f)(3)	10.1, 23.2(d)(3), 23.2(d)(3)(ii), 23.2(d)(3)(iii), 45.2(b)
1256(f)(3)(A)	23.2(d)(3)(ii), 45.2(b)
1256(f)(3)(B)	23.2(d)(3)(ii), 45.2(a)
1256(f)(3)(C)	8.3(e), 45.2(a), 45.2(b)
1256(f)(4)	44.4, 45.2(c)
1256(g)	44.2(a)
1256(g)(1)	59.2(i)(2), 59.2(j)
1256(g)(1)(A)	44.1
1256(g)(1)(B)	44.1
1256(g)(2)	59.2(b)(4), 59.4, 59.4(c), 59.4(c)(4), 59.4(d), 59.4(d)(4)
1256(g)(2)(A)	44.2(a)
1256(g)(2)(A)(i)	44.2(a)
1256(g)(2)(A)(ii)	44.2(a), 59.2(a)(1), 60.2(c)(3)
1256(g)(2)(A)(iii)	44.2(a), 59.2(a)(1), 60.2(c)(3)
1256(g)(2)(B)	44.2(a)
1256(g)(3)	30.3(a), 35.2, 44.3, 44.3(a), 59.2(j)
1256(g)(4)	8.3(d), 30.1(d), 30.3(a), 44.4
1256(g)(4)(B)	44.4
1256(g)(4)(C)	44.4
1256(g)(5)	30.1(a), 30.3(a), 30.3(e)(1)(ii), 35.2, 43.1, 44.3, 44.4
1256(g)(6)	30.1(a)
1256(g)(6)(A)	30.1(c), 44.3, 44.4
1256(g)(6)(B)	30.1(c), 44.3, 44.3(a)
1256(g)(7)	9.2(c)(2), 35.2, 43.1, 44.1
1256(g)(7)(B)	44.1(b)
1256(g)(7)(C)	44.1(b)
1256(g)(8)	8.2(b), 45.2(b)

Table of Internal Revenue Code Sections

(References are to book sections.)

I.R.C.	
1256(g)(8)(A)	45.5
1256(g)(8)(B)	44.4
1271	31.2(d)(4), 31.10, 34.2(b), 55.2(b), 60.2(c)(5)(i)
1271(a)	37.4(a)
1271(a)(1)	31.10, 37.4(a), 60.2(b)(2)(ii)
1271(a)(2)	31.10
1271(a)(2)(A)	31.2(a)
1271(a)(2)(B)	31.2(d), 31.10
1271(a)(3)	31.2(d)
1271(a)(3)(A)	31.2(d)(4)
1271(a)(3)(B)	31.2(d), 31.2(d)(4)
1271(a)(3)(E)	31.2(d)(4)
1271(a)(4)	31.2(d), 31.2(d)(4)
1271(a)(4)(C)	31.2(d)(4)
1271(a)(4)(D)	31.2(d)(4)
1271(b)	31.6(e)(1), 31.10
1271(b)(1)	37.4(a)
1271(c)(1)	31.10
1271(c)(2)	31.2(c)
1271(c)(2)(A)	31.2(c), 31.10(a), 34.3(b)
1272	16.4(f), 23.3(g)(1)(v)(d), 27.3(b)(3)(vi), 31.2(a), 31.2(g)(4), 31.2(n)(3), 31.6(e)(2)(iii), 34.2(b), 37.4, 37.5(b), 55.2(b), 60.2(c)(5)(i), 60.2(c)(5)(ii)
1272(a)	27.3(b)(5), 31.2(g)(3)(ii), 31.2(g)(4), 31.3(f)(2)(ii), 31.6(c)(3)
1272(a)(1)	31.2(a), 31.2(b), 31.3(a), 34.3(b), 38.4
1272(a)(2)	31.2(n), 32.1(a)(1)
1272(a)(2)(C)	31.2(d)
1272(a)(3)	31.2(a)
1272(a)(4)	31.2(a)
1272(a)(5)	23.3(g)(1)(v)(d)(2), 31.2(a), 31.2(g)(2)(ii), 31.2(g)(2)(ii)(a)
1272(a)(6)	31.2(m), 31.2(n), 31.2(n)(4), 31.6(a)(2)(iii), 37.3, 37.4(a), 37.5(b), 41.1(a)(3)
1272(a)(6)(A)	31.2(m), 41.1(a)(3)
1272(a)(6)(B)(iii)	31.2(m), 31.2(n)(1), 41.1(a)(3)
1272(a)(6)(C)	31.2(m), 31.2(n)(4), 31.3(*l*), 41.1(a)(3)
1272(a)(6)(C)(i)	37.4(a)
1272(a)(6)(C)(ii)	36.8(j)(4)
1272(a)(7)	31.2(a)
1272(b)(1)	31.2(b), 34.3(b)
1272(b)(4)	31.2(b)
1272(d)(1)	31.6(c)(2)
1272(d)(2)	16.4(*l*), 31.2(a), 31.2(b)
1273	23.3(g)(1)(v)(d), 34.2(b), 55.2(b), 60.2(c)(5)(i), 60.2(c)(5)(ii)
1273(a)	31.2(n)(2)
1273(a)(1)	31.2, 31.2(n)(1), 31.3(a)
1273(a)(2)	23.3(g)(1)(v)(d)(4)
1273(a)(3)	27.2, 27.3(b)(5), 31.2(a), 31.2(e), 31.10(a)
1273(b)	31.2(g)(2)(ii), 31.2(j), 31.2(n)(2), 31.12(a), 41.1(b)
1273(c)	31.2(j)
1273(c)(2)	31.2(j)
1273(c)(2)(A)	31.2(j)
1273(c)(2)(B)	31.2(j)
1273(c)(2)(C)	31.2(j)
1274	23.3(g)(1)(v)(d), 34.2(b), 55.2(b), 59.2(a)(1), 60.2(c)(5)(i), 60.2(c)(5)(ii), 60.2(c)(5)(iv)
1274(a)	31.2(g)(2)(ii)
1274(d)	41.1(c), 41.2(g)(3)
1275	23.3(g)(1)(v)(d), 31.2(i), 34.2(b), 41.1(a), 55.2(b), 60.2(c)(5)(ii)
1275(a)(1)(A)	31.2(d), 31.3(b)
1275(a)(2)	31.2(n), 31.2(n)(1)
1275(a)(3)	31.2(d)(2)(i), 31.2(e), 31.3(b), 31.6(d)(2)(i)
1275(a)(3)(A)	31.2(e)
1275(a)(3)(B)	31.2(e)
1275(a)(4)	31.2(h)
1275(c)(1)(A)	31.2(n)(1)
1275(c)(1)(B)	31.2(n)(1)
1276	23.3(g)(1)(v)(d), 31.3(c), 37.4, 37.4(b), 38.4
1276(a)	31.3(h), 31.3(i), 41.2(e)
1276(a)(1)	31.3(f)(1), 37.4(a)
1276(a)(2)	31.3(f)(2)(ii)

Table of Internal Revenue Code Sections

(References are to book sections.)

I.R.C.

1276(a)(3) .... 31.3(a), 31.3(f)(1), 31.3(h)
1276(a)(3)(A) .... 37.4(b)
1276(a)(3)(B) .... 31.3(i)
1276(a)(4) .... 31.3(a), 31.3(f)(*l*)
1276(b) ... 31.3(g), 31.3(m)(1), 41.1(b)
1276(b)(1) ...... 31.3(f)(1), 31.3(f)(2), 31.3(f)(2)(i), 31.3(f)(2)(ii)
1276(b)(2) ...... 31.3(f)(1), 31.3(f)(2), 31.3(f)(2)(ii), 41.2(e)
1276(b)(2)(A) .... 31.3(f)(2)(ii)
1276(b)(2)(B) .... 31.3(f)(2)(ii)
1276(b)(2)(C) .... 31.3(f)(2)(ii)
1276(b)(3) .... 31.3(i), 31.3(*l*)
1276(c)(2) .... 31.3(m)(2)(iii)
1276(d)(1)(C) .... 31.3(d)
1276(e) .... 31.3(h)
1277 .... 23.3(g)(1)(v)(d), 31.3(a), 31.3(m)(1), 31.3(m)(2), 37.4, 37.4(b), 38.4, 41.2(e), 55.2(e)
1277(a) .... 31.3(m)(1), 37.4(b)
1277(b)(1) .... 31.10(b)
1277(b)(1)(A) .... 31.3(m)(2)(i)
1277(b)(1)(B) .... 31.3(m)(2)(i)
1277(b)(1)(C) .... 31.3(m)(2)(i)
1277(b)(2)(A) .... 31.3(m)(1), 31.3(m)(2)(ii)
1277(b)(2)(B) .... 31.3(m)(2)(iii)
1277(c) .... 31.2(d)(3), 31.3(m)(1)
1277(c)(1) .... 31.3(m)(2)(i)
1277(c)(2) .... 31.3(m)(2)(i)
1277(d) .... 31.3(m)(1), 31.10(b)
1278 ... 23.3(g)(1)(v)(d), 31.3(a), 37.4, 37.4(b), 38.4
1278(a)(1) .... 31.3(b), 31.3(c), 37.4(b)
1278(a)(1)(B) .... 31.10(b)
1278(a)(1)(B)(i) .... 31.3(b)
1278(a)(1)(B)(ii) .... 31.3(b)
1278(a)(1)(B)(iii) .... 31.3(b)
1278(a)(1)(B)(iv) .... 31.3(b)
1278(a)(1)(C)(i) .... 31.3(e)
1278(a)(1)(C)(ii) .... 31.3(c)
1278(a)(1)(C)(iii) ...... 31.3(c), 31.3(e)
1278(a)(2) .... 31.3(b), 31.7(b)
1278(a)(2)(A) .... 31.3(b), 37.4(b)

I.R.C.

1278(a)(2)(A)(ii) .... 16.4(e)
1278(a)(2)(B) .... 37.4(b)
1278(a)(2)(C) .... 31.3(b), 31.3(c), 31.10(b)
1278(a)(3) .... 31.3(b)
1278(a)(5) .... 31.3(a)
1278(b) ...... 31.3(g), 31.3(h), 31.7(b), 37.4(b), 41.1(b)
1278(b)(1) .... 31.3(g)
1278(b)(2) .... 31.3(g)
1278(b)(3) .... 31.3(g)
1278(b)(4) .... 31.3(g)
1279 .... 23.3(g)(1)(v)(d)
1280 .... 23.3(g)(1)(v)(d)
1281 .... 23.3(g)(1)(v)(d), 31.2(d), 31.2(d)(1), 31.2(d)(3), 31.2(d)(4)
1281(b)(1)(A) .... 31.2(d)(2)(i)
1281(b)(1)(C) .... 31.2(d)(2)(i)
1281(b)(1)(D) .... 31.2(d)(2)(i)
1281(b)(1)(E) .... 31.2(d)(2)(i)
1281(b)(1)(F) .... 31.2(d)(2)(i)
1281(b)(2)(A) .... 31.2(d)(2)(i)
1281(b)(2)(C) .... 31.2(d)(2)(i)
1281(b)(2)(D) .... 31.2(d)(2)(i)
1282 .... 23.3(g)(1)(v)(d), 31.2(d), 31.2(d)(3), 55.2(e)
1282(a)(1) .... 31.2(d)(3)
1282(a)(2) .... 31.2(d)(3)
1282(b) .... 31.2(d)(2)(ii)
1282(b)(2) ... 31.2(d)(1), 31.2(d)(2)(ii), 31.11(b)(4)
1283 .... 23.3(g)(1)(v)(d), 31.2(d)
1283(a)(1)(A) .... 31.2(d), 31.2(d)(2)(i)
1283(a)(1)(B) .... 31.2(d)(2)(i)
1283(a)(2) .... 31.2(d)(2)(i)
1283(b)(1) .... 31.2(d)(2)(i), 31.2(d)(2)(ii)
1283(b)(2) .... 31.2(d)(2)(ii)
1283(c) .... 31.2(d)(1)
1283(d) .... 31.2(d)(4)
1284 .... 23.3(g)(1)(v)(d)
1285 .... 23.3(g)(1)(v)(d)
1286 .... 23.3(g)(1)(v)(d), 29.1(c), 31.6(b)(1), 31.6(c), 31.6(c)(3), 31.6(e)(2)(i), 31.6(e)(2)(ii),

Table of Internal Revenue Code Sections

(References are to book sections.)

I.R.C.	
31.6(e)(2)(iii), 31.6(f), 36.2(c), 36.2(d), 36.8(d)(1)(iii), 37.5, 37.5(a), 37.5(b), 38.5	
1286(a)	31.6(c), 31.6(c)(2), 31.6(d)(2)(i), 31.6(e)(2)(iii), 37.4(a), 37.5(b)
1286(b)	31.6(d)(1), 31.6(d)(2)(i), 31.6(e)(2)(ii), 37.5(a)
1286(b)(1)	31.6(c)(1), 31.6(c)(4), 31.6(e)(2)(ii), 37.5(a)
1286(b)(2)	31.6(c)(1), 31.6(e)(2)(ii), 37.5(b)
1286(b)(3)	31.6(c)(1), 31.6(e)(2)(ii), 37.5(b)
1286(b)(4)	31.6(c)(1)
1286(c)	31.6(c)(4)
1286(d)	31.6(c)(4), 31.6(d)(1), 31.6(d)(2)(i), 31.6(d)(2)(ii)
1286(d)(1)	31.6(c)(4), 31.6(d)(2)(i)
1286(d)(2)	31.6(c)(4), 31.6(d)(2)(ii)
1286(d)(3)	31.6(c)(4)
1286(e)(1)	31.6(e)(1), 31.6(e)(2)(ii), 37.5(a)
1286(e)(2)	31.6(a), 31.6(c), 31.6(e)(2)(ii), 31.6(e)(2)(iii), 31.6(g), 37.5, 37.5(a), 37.5(b), 38.5
1286(e)(3)	31.6(c), 31.6(e)(2)(iii), 37.5(b)
1286(e)(5)	31.6(a), 31.6(e)(2)(ii), 31.6(f), 37.5, 37.5(a), 38.5
1286(e)(6)	31.6(c)(2)
1287	23.3(g)(1)(v)(d), 31.12(c), 31.12(d)(1), 31.12(e), 33.3(a)(1)(iii)
1288	23.3(g)(1)(v)(d), 31.2(e)
1288(a)	31.2(e), 33.3(a)(4)
1288(b)(1)	31.2(e)
1288(b)(2)	31.2(e)
1293(c)	59.5(a)
1301	15.4(e)(2), 45.4(a)
1302	45.4(a)
1302(a)	15.4(e)(2)
1302(c)	15.4(e)(2)
1303	45.4(a)
1303(a)	15.4(e)(2)
1304	45.4(a)

I.R.C.	
1305	45.4(a)
1362(d)	28.4(f)
1367(a)(1)	16.4(h), 33.5(b)
1367(a)(2)	16.4(h)
1367(b)	16.4(h)
1368	16.4(h)
1381(a)(2)(C)	36.8(e)
1401	8.2(c), 47.2(e)
1402	8.2(c), 47.2(e)
1402(i)	8.2(b), 8.2(c), 8.3(d), 47.2(e)
1402(i)(2)(B)	8.2(b), 8.3(e), 45.2(b)
1403	8.2(c), 47.2(e)
1441	23.3(f)(5), 23.3(g)(1)(v)(c)
1441(a)	60.2(g)
1441(c)(9)	23.3(f)(5)
1442	23.3(f)(5), 23.3(g)(1)(v)(c)
1442(a)	60.2(g)
1501	51.1
1502	11.3(b)(3)(ii)(a), 27.3(b)(3), 57.6(a)
1503(f)	27.3(b)(3)
1504	11.3(b)(3)(ii)(a), 11.3(b)(3)(ii)(f), 59.2(j)(1)
1504(a)	24.9(a)(2), 27.3(b)(3), 27.3(c)(2), 27.8(b)
1504(a)(2)	27.3(b)(3)
1504(a)(4)	27.3(b)(3), 27.3(c)(2)
2031	32.1(b)(1)(iv)
2031(1)	33.3(a)(2)
2032A(e)(1)	17.1(d)
2033	32.1(b)(1)(iv), 33.3(a)(2)
2040	32.1(b)(1)(iv)
3406	13.4, 31.2(a)
3406(a)(1)	13.4
3406(a)(1)(A)	13.4
3406(a)(1)(B)	13.4
3406(a)(1)(C)	13.4
3406(a)(1)(D)	13.4
3406(b)(2)	13.4
3406(b)(3)(C)	13.4
3406(c)	13.4
3406(h)(5)	13.4
4701	31.12(c), 31.12(f)
4701(a)	31.12(c)
4974(a)(1)	31.2(n)(3)

Table of Internal Revenue Code Sections

(References are to book sections.)

I.R.C.	
4981(a)	8.10(e)
4981(b)	8.10(e)
4981(b)(3)	8.10(e)
4981(c)	8.10(e)
4981(d)	8.10(d)
4981(e)	8.10(e)
4982	8.9(b), 8.9(b)(1), 8.9(b)(2), 8.9(b)(3)
4982(b)(1)	8.9(b)
4982(b)(1)(B)	8.9(b)(2)
4982(b)(2)	8.9(b)
4982(b)(2)(A)	8.9(b)(2)
4982(c)(1)(B)	8.9(b)
4982(e)(2)	8.9(b)
4982(e)(4)	8.9(b)(1), 8.9(b)(3)
6001	9.3(a)
6031(b)	28.3
6031(c)	28.3
6042	24.10
6044	24.10
6045	13.3, 14.5(b)(2)
6045(a)	13.3
6045(c)(1)	13.4
6049	23.3(g)(1)(v)(c), 24.10, 31.2(n)(3)
6049(b)(2)(A)	31.2(n)(3)
6049(b)(2)(B)	31.2(n)(3)
6049(b)(4)	31.2(n)(3)
6049(b)(5)	31.2(n)(3)
6049(c)	31.2(n)(3)
6049(d)(1)	3.12(n)(3)
6049(d)(6)	31.2(n)(3)
6049(d)(6)(i)	31.2(n)(3)
6049(d)(6)(ii)	31.2(n)(3)
6049(d)(7)	31.2(n)(4)
6049(d)(7)(A)	36.8(j)(2)
6049(d)(7)(B)	36.8(j)(2), 36.8(j)(3)
6049(d)(7)(D)	36.8(j)(3)
6050N	24.10
6072(a)	36.8(k)
6110	29.3(b)(1)
6163	9.2(h)
6166	9.2(h)
6312	32.1(c)
6312(a)	32.1(a)(2)

I.R.C.	
6411(a)	45.4(c)
6411(a)(1)	45.4(c)
6411(a)(2)	45.4(c)
6511(a)	60.5(a)
6511(d)(1)	17.1(c)
6601(a)	53.2
6611	45.4(c)
6611(a)	45.4(c)
6611(b)(1)	45.4(c)
6611(e)	45.4(c)
6611(f)	45.4(c)
6611(f)(1)	45.4(c)
6611(f)(3)(C)	45.4(c)
6621	9.2(g)
6621(b)	53.2
6621(c)	9.2(g), 10.2(g), 53.2
6621(c)(3)(A)(v)	9.2(g), 10.2(g)
6621(d)	53.2
6621(d)(1)	53.2
6621(d)(2)	53.2
6621(d)(3)(A)	53.2
6652	24.10
6652(a)(1)	31.11(d)
6652(a)(2)	31.11(d)
6652(a)(3)	31.11(d)
6653	53.1(b)
6653(a)	53.1(b), 58.1
6653(a)(1)	53.1(a)
6653(a)(2)	53.1(a)
6653(a)(2)(B)	53.1(a)
6653(a)(3)	53.1(b)
6653(f)	12.3, 23.2(e)(1), 53.1(a), 53.1(b)
6673	58.1
6706(a)	31.2(n)(1)
6706(b)	31.2(n)(2)
6723	24.10
6723(a)(2)	24.10
7701	29.3
7701(a)(1)	9.1(a)
7701(a)(3)	23.3(c), 28.1, 29.1(a), 36.2(a)
7701(a)(18)	31.12(b)(4)(ii)
7701(a)(19)	36.8(d)(2)(ii)(b), 36.8(o)
7701(a)(19)(C)	36.8(n)

Table of Internal Revenue Code Sections

(References are to book sections.)

I.R.C.	
7701(a)(19)(C)(xi)	36.8(d)(2)(ii)(b)
7701(a)(30)	59.2(d)(2)(ii), 59.2(d)(2)(iii), 59.2(d)(2)(iv)
7701(c)	28.4(e)
7701(e)	7.2(g), 36.8(o)
7701(i)	36.8(o)
7701(i)(1)	36.8(o)
7701(i)(2)(A)(i)	36.8(o)
7701(i)(2)(A)(ii)	36.8(o)
7701(i)(2)(A)(iii)	36.8(o)
7701(i)(2)(C)	36.8(o)
7701(i)(2)(D)	36.8(o)
7704	28.2(b), 28.4(a), 28.4(b)(3), 28.4(d)(2)(i), 28.4(d)(2)(iv), 28.4(g)(2)
7704(a)	28.4(b)(1), 28.4(e)
7704(b)	28.4(b)(1), 28.4(c), 28.4(c)(1), 28.4(c)(6)(ii)
7704(b)(1)	28.4(c)(2)
7704(b)(2)	28.4(c)(3), 28.4(c)(4)
7704(c)	28.4(b)(2)
7704(c)(1)	28.4(d)(1)
7704(c)(2)	28.4(d)(1), 28.4(f)
7704(c)(3)	28.4(d)(1), 28.4(d)(2)(vii)
7704(d)	28.4(b)(3), 28.4(d)(2), 28.4(d)(2)(viii)
7704(d)(1)	28.4(d)(2)

I.R.C.	
7704(d)(1)(A)	28.4(d)(2)(i)
7704(d)(1)(B)	28.4(d)(2)(ii)
7704(d)(1)(C)	28.4(d)(2)(iii)
7704(d)(1)(D)	28.4(d)(2)(iv)
7704(d)(1)(E)	28.4(d)(2)(v)
7704(d)(1)(F)	28.4(d)(2)(vi)
7704(d)(1)(G)	28.4(d)(2)(vii)
7704(d)(2)(A)	28.4(d)(2)(i)
7704(d)(2)(B)	28.4(d)(2)(i)
7704(d)(3)	28.4(d)(2)(iii)
7704(d)(4)	28.4(d)(2)(viii)
7704(d)(5)	28.4(d)(2)(iv)
7704(e)(2)	28.4(f)
7704(e)(3)	28.4(f)
7704(e)(4)	28.4(f)
7704(f)(1)	28.4(e)
7704(f)(2)	28.4(e)
7805	23.2(e)(1)
7805(b)	23.2(e)(1)
7872	9.2(c)(2), 16.4(f)
7872(c)(1)(B)	9.2(c)(2)
7872(c)(1)(D)	9.2(c)(2)
7872(c)(1)(E)	9.2(c)(2)
7872(c)(2)	9.2(c)(2)
7872(g)	9.2(c)(2)

Table of Statutory Sections

(References are to book sections.)

BANK HOLDING COMPANY ACT OF 1956, AS AMENDED
Pub. L. No. 84-511, ch. 240, 70 Stat. 133 (1956)

Bank Holding Company Act	
	27.4(c)

BANKRUPTCY TAX ACT OF 1980
Pub. L. No. 96-589, 94 Stat. 3389

Bankruptcy Tax Act of 1980	
4(a)	27.4(b)

COMMODITY EXCHANGE ACT, AS AMENDED
Ch. 545, 49 Stat. 1491 (1936)

CEA	
2(a)(1)(A)	4, 4.1(a), 4.1(b), 4.3(b)
2(a)(1)(B)	4, 4.1(a), 4.1(c)
4(a)	4.1(a), 4.1(b), 4.2(b)
4(a)(2)	4.2(b)
4b	4.3(f)
4c	5.2(b)
4c(a)	4.3(f)
4c(b)	4.1(a)
4d(2)	4.4(b)
4e	4.2(b)
5	5.2(b)

CEA	
5a(8)	4
5(g)	4.2(b)
6(b)	4.1(a)
6d	4
8a(9)	4.4(b)(1)
9	4.1(a)
12(e)	4
17	4
17(m)	4
19	4.1(a)

CRUDE OIL WINDFALL PROFIT TAX ACT OF 1980, AS AMENDED
Pub. L. No. 96-223, 94 Stat. 229 (1980)

Crude Oil Windfall Profit Tax Act

401(a)	16.3(b)
404(a)	24.8, 25.3

DEFICIT REDUCTION ACT OF 1984, AS AMENDED
Pub. L. No. 98-369, 98 Stat. 494 (1984)

DRA		DRA	
	1.1(i), 8.2(b), 17.7(b), 19.4, 24.1(c), 27.5(b), 31.2(d)(1), 34.2(d), 35.1, 43.1, 45.2(a), 54, 56.4	102(c)	8.2(c)
		102(c)(2)	8.2(c), 8.3(e)
		102(e)(7)	55.2(a), 55.2(b)
41(a)	31.2(d)(3), 31.6(c), 33.3(a)(4), 37.4(a)	102(e)(9)	58.2
		102(f)(1)	45.4(a), 55.2(c)
42(a)	31.2(d)(1)	102(g)	44.5
42(a)(1)	31.6(c), 31.6(c)(1), 31.6(c)(2)	102(h)(1)(A)	44.5
		102(h)(1)(B)(ii)(II)	44.5
44(e)(2)	31.2(d)(2)(ii)	103(a)	54.4(b), 57.4
44(f)	31.5	103(b)	Part Eleven, 57
51(a)	24.9(c)(1)	103(c)	48.2(c)(3), 56.6
53	29.2(b)	106(b)	19.4, 19.5(b)
53(b)(1)	24.9(b)	108	47.2(c), 55.1, 58.1
54	29.2(b)	108(b)	47.2(c)
57(a)	30.3(e)(2)	108(c)	47.2(c)
59	34.2(d)	108(h)	47.2(c)
101(a)(1)	30.2, Part Eleven	144(a)	53.2
101(b)(1)	27.9, 48.2(c)(1), 56.5	144(c)	53.2
101(b)(2)	51.3	177	2.1(b)(4), 27.5(b)
101(e)	30.3(g)(1)	177(a)	2.1(b)(4)
101(e)(1)	44.5	481	27.7
101(e)(2)	48.2(c)(1)	631(c)(1)	33.3(a)(1)(ii)
102(a)(2)	43.3(a), Part Ten, 44.3, 44.4	1001	15.2
		1001(a)	47.2
102(a)(3)	44.1, 44.2(a)	1001(b)(11)	24.5(a)
102(b)	45.2(b)		

DEPARTMENT OF ENERGY ACT OF 1978—CIVILIAN APPLICATIONS, AS AMENDED
Pub. L. No. 95-238, 92 Stat. 47 (1978)

Dep't of Energy Act of '78
Title V .... 33.3(a)(1)(ii)

ECONOMIC RECOVERY TAX ACT OF 1981, AS AMENDED
Pub. L. No. 97-34, 95 Stat. 172 (1981)

ERTA	ERTA
.... 30.2, 32.1(a)(3), 43.3(a), 44.1, 45, 54, 55.1, 60.7(a)	504 .... Part Eleven
	505 .... 32.1(a)(3), Part Eleven
501 .... Part Eleven	506 .... Part Eleven
501(a) 54	507 .... Part Eleven
501(c) 55.1	508 .... Part Eleven
502 .... 42.4, Part Eleven	508(c) 51.2
503 .... Part Eleven	509 .... Part Eleven, 51.2
503(a) 45.3	509(a)(1) .... 44.1, 47.2(c)

FEDERAL HOME LOAN MORTGAGE CORPORATION ACT, AS AMENDED
Pub. L. No. 91-351, 84 Stat. 450 (1970)

FHLMC Act
303 .... 2.1(b)(4)

FINANCIAL INSTITUTIONS REFORM, RECOVERY, AND ENFORCEMENT ACT OF 1989
Pub. L. No. 101-73, 103 Stat. 183 (1989)

FIRREA	FIRREA
.... 2.1(b)(1), 7.2(c)(2)(iii)	512 .... 2.1(b)(8)
204(b) .... 7.2(c)(2)(iii)	704(a) .... 2.1(b)(1)
301(t)(1)(A) .... 7.2(c)(2)(iii)	706 .... 2.1(b)(1)
501(b) .... 2.1(b)(7)	731 .... 2.1(b)(4)
511 .... 2.1(b)(7)	

FUTURES TRADING ACT OF 1978, AS AMENDED
Pub. L. No. 95-405, 92 Stat. 865 (1978)

Futures Trading Act of '78

3(3) .... 5.2(b)

GOVERNMENT SECURITIES ACT OF 1986
Pub. L. No. 99-571, 100 Stat. 3208 (1986)

Gov't Sec. Act of '86

101 2

HIGHER EDUCATION ACT OF 1965, AS AMENDED
Pub. L. No. 89-329, 79 Stat. 1219 (1965)

Higher Education Act of '65

.... 33.2(c)(2)(iv)

HOMEOWNERS' LOAN ACT OF 1933, AS AMENDED
48 Stat. 128 (1933)

Homeowners' Loan Act of '33

5 .... 7.2(c)(2)(iii)

HOUSING AND COMMUNITY DEVELOPMENT AMENDMENTS OF 1979, AS AMENDED
Pub. L. No. 96-153, 93 Stat. 1101 (1979)

Hous. & Community Dev. Amendments of '79

316(b) .... 2.1(b)(4)

INTEREST AND DIVIDEND TAX COMPLIANCE ACT OF 1983
Pub. L. No. 98-67, 97 Stat. 369 (1983)

Interest and Dividend Tax Compliance Act of '83

104 .... 13.4

INTERNAL REVENUE CODE, AS AMENDED
(See Table of Internal Revenue Code Sections.)

INVESTMENT COMPANY ACT OF 1940, AS AMENDED
54 Stat. 789 (1940)

ICA	
.... 31.2(n)(3)	
3(a)(1) .... 7.6(d)	
3(a)(2) .... 7.6(d)	
3(a)(3) .... 6.6(a), 7.6(d)	
3(a)(5) .... 7.6(d)	
3(c)(1) .... 7.6(d)	
3(c)(2) .... 7.6(d)	

ICA	
3(c)(3) .... 7.6(d)
3(c)(4) .... 7.6(d)
3(c)(5) .... 7.6(d)
6(c) .... 7.6(d)
8 .... 1.4(b)(2), 7.4(b)(2), 7.6(d)
18 .... 7.6(d)

OMNIBUS BUDGET RECONCILIATION ACT OF 1987, AS AMENDED
Pub. L. No. 100-203, 101 Stat. 1330 (1987)

OBRA	
.... 8.9(c), 9.1(d), 28.4	
10104 .... 8.9(c)	
10104(a) .... 9.1(d)	
10104(a)(2)(A) .... 9.1(d)	
10211(c)(1)(B) .... 28.4(b)(3)	
10211(c)(2) .... 28.4(b)(3), 28.4(e)	

OBRA	
10211(c)(2)(B) .... 28.4(b)(3)
10212 .... 28.4(g)(1)
10212(a) .... 28.4(g)(1)
10213 .... 28.4(h)
10221 .... 24.9(a)(1)
10225 .... 27.8(f)

PUBLIC DEBT ACT OF 1941, AS AMENDED
Ch. 7, 55 Stat. 7 (1941)

Public Debt Act of '41
4(a) 32.1

PUBLIC DEBT LIMIT—INTEREST RATE—SOCIAL SECURITY WAGE BASE ACT
Pub. L. No. 92-5, 85 Stat. 5 (1971)

Public Debt Limit—Interest Rate—Social Security Wage Base Act
4(a)(2) .... 32.1(c)

PUBLIC DEBT ACT OF 1942
Pub. L. No. 77-510, ch. 205, 56 Stat. 189 (1942)

Public Debt Act of '42
.... 27.5

REVENUE ACT OF 1978, AS AMENDED
Pub. L. No. 95-600, 92 Stat. 2763 (1978)

Revenue Act of '78
.... 30.2(b)(3)
345 .... 27.7

REVENUE RECONCILIATION ACT OF 1989
Pub. L. No. 101-239, 103 Stat. 2301 (1989)

RRA '89	
.... 16.6(g), 27.2, 31.2(g)(1), 33.3(a)(1)(vii), 34.1	
7201(a) .... 27.3(b)(3)	
7202(c)(2) .... 31.2(g)(5)	
7202(c)(2)(A)(i) .... 31.2(g)(5)	
7202(c)(2)(A)(ii) .... 31.2(g)(5)	
7202(c)(2)(A)(iii) .... 31.2(g)(5)	
7202(c)(2)(B) .... 31.2(g)(5)	

RRA '89	
7202(c)(2)(C) .... 31.2(g)(5)
7202(c)(2)(D) .... 31.2(g)(5)
7204(a)(1) .... 8.9(b)
7204(c)(1) .... 24.5(a)
7206(a) .... 16.6(g), 16.6(h)
7206(b) .... 16.6(g)
7206(b)(2) .... 16.6(h)
7208(a) 27.2

REVENUE RECONCILIATION ACT OF 1989 *(Continued)*
Pub. L. No. 101-239, 103 Stat. 2301 (1989)

RRA '89	
7208(a)(1)	34.2(a)
7208(a)(2)	27.2, 34.2(a)
7651(b)(1)	33.3(a)(1)(ix)
7651(b)(2)	33.3(a)(1)(ix)

RRA '89	
7651(b)(3)	33.3(a)(1)(ix)
7651(b)(4)	33.3(a)(1)(ix)
7651(b)(5)	33.3(a)(1)(ix)

REVENUE RECONCILIATION ACT OF 1990
Pub. L. No. 101-508, 104 Stat. 1388 (1990)

RRA '90	
	Part Two, Part Three, 15.4(a)(2)(i), 27.2, 31.2(g), Part Ten, 45.2, 59.2(a)(1)
11322(a)	24.2(b)(2)
11408	33.2(c)(2)(ii)(a), 33.2(c)(2)(iii)

SECONDARY MORTGAGE MARKET ENHANCEMENT ACT OF 1984
Pub. L. No. 98-440, 98 Stat. 1689 (1984)

SMMEA	
	7.4(a)(3)

SECOND LIBERTY BOND ACT, AS AMENDED
Ch. 56, 40 Stat. 288 (1917)

Second Liberty Bond Act	
	31.12(a)
28(b)(2)	31.12(e)

SECURITIES ACT OF 1933, AS AMENDED
48 Stat. 74 (1933)

Securities Act	
Preamble	7.6(a)
2(1)	5.2(a), 5.2(a)(3), 5.2(a)(4), 5.5(a), 7.6(a), 7.6(b)
2(4)	7.6(a)
3(a)(2)	3.1, 7.3(a)(3), 7.6(a)
3	2.1(b)
4	8.9(c), 9.1(d)
4(2)	6.6(a), 7.3(a)(2), 7.6(d)
4(5)(A)	7.3(a)(3)

Securities Act	
5	7.4(b)(5)
5(a)	5.2(a), 5.3(a)
5(c)	7.6(a)
6	7.3(a)(3)
7	7.3(a)(1), 7.6(a)
17	2
8	7.3(a)(1)
10	7.3(a)(1), 7.6(a)

SECURITIES EXCHANGE ACT OF 1934, AS AMENDED
48 Stat. 881 (1934)

SEA	
Preamble	7.6(b)
3(a)(5)	8.7(b)
3(a)(10)	5.2(a), 5.2(a)(3), 5.2(a)(4), 5.5(a), 6.6(a), 7.4(a)(1), 7.6(b)
3(a)(12)	1.4(a), 7.4(a)(1), 7.4(b)(3)
3(a)(12)(A)	1.4(a), 2.3
3(a)(12)(C)	1.4(a)
3(a)(29)	1.4(a)
3(a)(38)	8.3(c)
3(a)(41)	7.4(b)(5), 7.4(b)(6)
3(a)(41)(A)	7.4(a)(2)
3(a)(41)(B)	7.4(a)(2)
3(a)(42)	1.4(a)
3(a)(42)(A)	2.3
5	28.4(c)(3)
6	1.2(a), 28.4(c)(3)
7	1.4, 2.3, 5.5(a), 7.4, 7.4(a)(3)
7(a)	7.4(b)(1)

SEA	
7(c)	7.4(b)(1)
8(a)	7.4(a)(3)
10	2
10(b)	7.6(b)
11(d)	7.4(a)(1), 7.4(a)(3)
12(a)	1.2(a), 5.3(a), 7.3(b)(1), 7.6(b)
12(b)	5.3(a), 7.6(b)
12(f)	1.2(a), 7.3(b)(1)
12(g)(1)	7.6(b)
12(h)	7.6(b)
15(a)(1)	1.2(a), 1.2(b)
15(b)(8)	1.2(a), 1.2(b)
15(d)	7.6(b)
16	8.7(b)
16(e)	8.7(b)
17A	2.1(b)(2)
19	3.1

SHERMAN ANTI-TRUST ACT, AS AMENDED
Ch. 647, 26 Stat. 209 (1890)

Sherman Act	
	27.4(d)(2)

SMALL BUSINESS INVESTMENT ACT OF 1958, AS AMENDED
Pub. L. No. 85-699, 72 Stat. 689 (1958)

SBIA	
	27.6(a)
301(a)	27.6(a)
303	27.6(c)

SUBCHAPTER S REVISION ACT OF 1982, AS AMENDED
Pub. L. No. 97-354, 96 Stat. 1669 (1982)

Subchapter S Revision Act of '82	
	27.7

TAX EQUITY AND FISCAL RESPONSIBILITY ACT OF 1982, AS AMENDED
Pub. L. No. 97-248, 96 Stat. 324 (1982)

TEFRA	
.... 29.2(a), 33.3(a)(1)(i)	
232 .... 31.5(a), 31.6(c)	
310 .... 31.12(a)	
310(a) .... 31.12(c)	

TEFRA	
310(b)(1) ...... 31.12(a), 33.3(a)(1)(i), 33.3(a)(1)(iii)	
310(d)(1) ...... 31.12(a), 33.3(a)(1)(iii)	
310(d)(2) .... 31.12(a)	
310(d)(3) .... 31.12(a)	

TAX REFORM ACT OF 1969, AS AMENDED
Pub. L. No. 91-172, 83 Stat. 487 (1969)

TRA '69	
421(b)(1) .... 24.2(b)	
421(b)(4) .... 24.2(b)	

TAX REFORM ACT OF 1976, AS AMENDED
Pub. L. No. 94-455, 90 Stat. 1520 (1976)

TRA '76	
.... 30.2(b)(3)	
1402(b)(1)(U) .... 30.3(e)(2)	
1402(b)(2) .... 30.3(e)(2)	
2136(a) .... 30.3(e)(2)	
2137(c) .... 33.5(c)	

TAX REFORM ACT OF 1986, AS AMENDED
Pub. L. No. 99-514, 100 Stat. 2085 (1986)

TRA '86	
.... 1.1(i), Part Two, 9.1(d), 11, 15.4(a)(2)(i), 16.6(a), 17, 19.9(j), 23.2(b)(2), 24.3, 25.1, 27.3(b)(3), 29.2(a), 31.2(d)(4), 33.2(a), Part Eight, 44.2(b), 45.1(b), 47.2(c), 48.2(c)(1), 53.1(a), 56.2, 59.1	
141(a) .... 15.4(e)(1), 15.4(e)(2)	
301(a) .... 15.4(a)(2)(i)	
301(b)(10) .... 15.4(b)	
301(b)(11) .... 15.4(b)	
311(a) .... 15.5(a)(1), 15.5(a)(2)(i)	
331(a)(1) .... 56.3(d)(1)	
331(a)(2) .... 56.3(d)(1)	
331(a)(3) .... 56.3(d)(1)	
511(a) .... 9.2(e)	
601(a) .... 15.5(a)(2)(i)	
611(a)(1) .... 24.9(a)(1)	

TRA '86	
611(a)(4) .... 24.9(c)(3)	
612(a) 24.8	
613 .... 27.3(b)(4)	
614(a)(1) .... 16.6(a)	
614(a)(3) .... 16.6(a)	
621(e)(1) .... 34.2(d)	
631(c) .... 29.2(b)	
631(e)(4)(B) .... 17.3(c)(4)	
651(b)(1)(A) .... 8.9(c)	
654(a) .... 8.9(d)	
654(b)(2)(A) .... 8.9(d)	
654(b)(2)(B) .... 8.9(d)	
671(b)(4) 8.8	
675(a) .... 36.8(j)(3)	
675(c)(2) .... 36.8(o)	
675(c)(3) .... 19.9(j), 41.2(j)	
701(a) .... 15.4(a)(2)(ii)(a), 15.5(c)	

TAX REFORM ACT OF 1986, AS AMENDED (Continued)
Pub. L. No. 99-514, 100 Stat. 2085 (1986)

TRA '86	
803(d)(1)	22.4
803(d)(2)	22.4
803(d)(2)(B)	22.4
901(d)(3)(A)	8.8
901(d)(3)(B)	8.8
902(c)(1)	11.3(b)(3)(i)
902(c)(2)(A)	11.3(b)(3)(i)
902(c)(2)(B)	11.3(b)(3)(i)
902(c)(2)(C)	11.3(b)(3)(i)
902(f)	11.3(b)(3)(ii)(g)
902(f)(2)	11.3(b)(3)(ii)(g)
1018(g)(4)(B)(i)	31.6(c)(4), 31.6(d)(2)(i)
1018(g)(4)(B)(ii)	31.6(c)(4), 31.6(d)(2)(i)
1202(a)	Part Ten
1261(a)	23.3(a)
1261(c)	23.2(b)(2), 23.2(c)(3)(i), 23.2(c)(3)(ii), 23.2(d)(1)
1261(e)(2)	59.1
1301	3.1
1301(a)	25.4(a), 25.4(b), 25.4(d)
1302	3.1
1311	3.1
1312	3.1, 25.4(d), 33.2(c)(2)
1313	3.1, 25.4(d), 33.2(c)(2)
1314	3.1, 25.4(d), 33.2(c)(2)
1315	3.1, 25.4(d), 33.2(c)(2)
1316	3.1, 25.4(d), 33.2(c)(2)
1317	3.1, 25.4(d), 33.2(c)(2)
1318	3.1, 25.4(d)
1503(a)	53.1(a)
1503(c)	53.1(a)

TRA '86	
1503(c)(3)	53.1(a)
1511(a)	53.2
1511(a)(1)(a)	53.2
1511(c)(1)(A)	53.2
1511(c)(1)(B)	53.2
1511(c)(1)(C)	53.2
1511(c)(11)	53.2
1803(a)	31.2(d)(4)
1803(a)(3)	31.2(d)(4)
1803(a)(4)	31.6(c)(3)
1803(a)(5)	31.3(d)
1803(a)(6)	31.3(c)
1803(a)(11)	31.4(b)
1803(a)(11)(B)	31.4, 37.3
1803(a)(12)	31.4(b)
1803(a)(13)	31.6(d)(1)
1803(a)(13)(A)	31.3(i)
1803(a)(13)(A)(i)	31.3(a), 31.3(f)(1)
1803(a)(13)(B)	31.6(d)(2)(i)
1803(a)(13)(B)(i)	31.6(c)(1)
1803(a)(13)(B)(ii)	31.6(c)(1)
1804(a)(1)	24.9(c)(3)
1804(a)(2)	24.9(c)(3)
1804(b)(1)(B)	16.6(a)
1804(c)	17.6
1804(f)(1)(D)	29.2(b)
1808(c)	48.2(c)(1), 56.6
1808(d)	47.2(c)
1810(e)	31.2(f)
1810(e)(1)(A)	31.6(c)(3)
1810(e)(1)(B)	31.6(c)(3)
1810(e)(2)(B)	31.2(f)
1879(s)(1)	31.6(c)(4)

TECHNICAL AND MISCELLANEOUS REVENUE ACT OF 1988, AS AMENDED
Pub. L. No. 100-647, 102 Stat. 3342 (1988)

TMRA '88	
	9.1(d), 16.6(b), 19.6(a), 23.3(a), 24.3, 28.4(b)(3), 33.2(c)(2)(v)(e), 44.1, 45.1, 57, 59.2(a)(1), 60.2(c)(3)

TMRA '88	
1005(c)(2)	9.2(e)
1006(c)(2)	16.6(b)
1006(c)(3)	16.6(b)
1006(c)(4)	16.6(b)

TECHNICAL AND MISCELLANEOUS REVENUE ACT OF 1988, AS AMENDED (Continued)
Pub. L. No. 100-647, 102 Stat. 3342 (1988)

TMRA '88	
1006(c)(5)	16.6(f)
1006(c)(7)	16.6(c)
1006(c)(9)	16.6(h)
1006(j)(1)(A)	31.4(b)
1006(*l*)(1)(A)	8.9(c)
1006(*l*)(9)(A)	8.9(c)
1006(*l*)(9)(B)	8.9(c)
1006(*l*)(9)(C)	8.9(c)
1006(*l*)(9)(D)	8.9(c)
1006(*o*)(1)	8.9(d)
1006(*o*)(2)	8.9(d)
1006(t)(5)(A)	36.8(c)(1)(ii), 36.8(c)(1)(vi)
1006(t)(5)(E)	36.8(d)(1)(i)
1006(t)(5)(F)	36.8(d)(1)(i)
1006(t)(8)(B)	36.8(i)
1006(t)(16)(B)	36.8(e)
1006(t)(19)	36.8(e)

TMRA '88	
1012(v)(2)(A)	59.2(c)(2)
1012(v)(3)(B)	59.2(f)(3)
2004(f)(1)	28.4(f)
2004(f)(4)	28.4(d)(2)(v)
2004(f)(5)	28.4(d)(2)(iii)
2004(g)	28.4(g)(1)
4011	8.9(c), 9.1(d)
5053(c)(3)	33.3(a)(1)(vii)
5075	19.6(c)(1)
5075(a)	19.6(a)
6006	24.5(b)
6009	2.1(a)(4)(i), 32.1(b)(1)(v)(a)
6130	59.2(a)(1), 60.2(c)(4)
6130(b)(2)(D)	57.7
6130(c)	59.2(h)
6279(a)	11.10, 13.6, 24.3
6279(b)	11.10, 13.6, 24.3

TECHNICAL CORRECTIONS ACT OF 1982, AS AMENDED
Pub. L. No. 97-448, 96 Stat. 2365 (1983)

TCA '82	
	27.3(c)(4)
105(a)(1)	48.5
105(a)(1)(A)	50
105(b)	55.2(a), 55.2(c)
105(c)(4)	42.1(a)
105(c)(5)	44.2(a)
105(d)(1)	11.7(c)

TCA '82	
306(a)(9)	27.3(c)(4)
306(a)(9)(c)(ii)	31.2(b)
306(b)(2)	31.12(a), 33.3(a)(1)(iii)
105(c)(5)(A)	44.1, 44.1(a), 44.1(b)
105(c)(5)(B)	Part Ten
105(c)(5)(D)(ii)(I)	44.1, 44.1(a)

TRUST INDENTURE ACT OF 1939, AS AMENDED
53 Stat. 1149 (1939)

TIA	
	7.6(c)

Table of Treasury Pronouncements

(References are to book sections.)

Treas. Reg.	
1.61-6(a)	31.6(b)(1)
1.61-7(a)	25.1, 25.2
1.61-7(c)	31.8, 33.3(a)(1)(i)(a)
1.61-9(b)	24.7(b)
1.61-9(c)	16.4(d), 24.7(a), 24.7(c), 24.7(d)
1.61-12	16.4(a), 31.7(c)
1.61-12(c)(1)	34.2(a)
1.61-12(c)(2)	34.2(c)(1)
1.61-12(c)(6)	34.2(c)(1)
1.61-13(b)	36.5(c)
1.61-15(b)(2)	11.8(a)
1.75-1(a)(2)	31.4(a)(2)(ii)
1.75-1(a)(3)	31.4(a)(2)(ii)
1.75-1(b)(2)	31.4(a)(2)(ii)
1.75-1(c)	31.4(a)(2)(ii)
1.77-1	21.6
1.77-2	21.6
1.83-6(a)(3)	30.3(e)(1)(iv)
1.83-7	11.8(c), 30.3(e)(1)(iv)
1.83-7(b)	11.8(c), 30.3(e)(1)(iv)
1.103-1(b)	33.2
1.103-2	27.5
1.103-10(b)(1)(ii)	33.2(c)(2)(iii)

Treas. Reg.	
1.103-13(a)(2)(i)	33.3(a)(1)(vi)
1.103-13(a)(2)(ii)(B)	33.3(a)(1)(vi)
1.103-13(a)(2)(ii)(F)	33.3(a)(1)(vi)
1.118-1	16.4(a)
1.162-1(a)	10.1, 10.1(c), 11.1(b)
1.162-2	10.1(c)
1.162-4	10.1(c)
1.162-7	10.1(a), 10.1(c)
1.162-9	10.1(a)
1.162-11	10.1(a)
1.162-18	10.1(c)
1.162-21	10.1(c)
1.162-22	10.1(c)
1.163-3(a)(1)	34.2(b)
1.163-4(a)(1)	34.2(b)
1.163-4(c)	60.2(b)(1)(iii)
1.163-5(c)	31.12(f)
1.163-5(c)(2)(i)(A)	31.12(b)(4)(i), 31.12(b)(4)(v)
1.163-5(c)(2)(i)(B)	31.12(b)(4)(i), 31.12(b)(4)(v)
1.163-5(c)(2)(i)(D)	31.12(b)(4)(i), 31.12(b)(4)(v)
1.163-5(c)(2)(i)(D)(1)(i)	31.12(b)(4)(ii)
1.163-5(c)(2)(i)(D)(1)(ii)(A)	31.12(b)(4)(ii)

TREASURY REGULATIONS (Continued)
(References are to book sections.)

Treas. Reg.	Treas. Reg.
1.163-5(c)(2)(i)(D)(1)(ii)(B) .... 31.12(b)(4)(ii)	1.165-5(d)(1) .... 27.8(b)
1.163-5(c)(2)(i)(D)(1)(iii)(A)........... 31.12(b)(4)(ii)	1.165-5(d)(2)(i) .... 27.8(b)
	1.165-5(d)(2)(i)(a) .... 27.8(b)
1.163-5(c)(2)(i)(D)(3)(i)............... 31.12(b)(4)(iv)(a)	1.165-5(d)(2)(ii) .... 27.8(b)
	1.165-5(d)(2)(iii) .... 27.8(b)
1.163-5(c)(2)(i)(D)(3)(i)(A)........... 31.12(b)(4)(iv)(a)	1.165-5(e) .... 27.8(c)
1.163-5(c)(2)(i)(D)(3)(i)(B)........... 31.12(b)(4)(iv)(a)	1.165-5(f) 27.8
	1.165-5(g) .... 27.8(d)
1.163-5(c)(2)(i)(D)(3)(i)(C)........... 31.12(b)(4)(iv)(a)	1.165-5(h) .... 27.8(d)
1.163-5(c)(2)(i)(D)(3)(ii).............. ...31.12(b)(4)(iv)(a), 31.12(b)(4)(iv)(b)	1.165-12(c)(1) .... 31.12(d)(1)
	1.165-12(c)(1)(ii) .... 31.12(d)(2)
	1.165-12(c)(1)(iv) .... 31.12(d)(2)
	1.165-12(c)(1)(v) .... 31.12(d)(1), 31.12(d)(2)
1.163-5(c)(2)(i)(D)(3)(iii)(A)........... 31.12(b)(4)(iv)(c)	1.165-12(c)(2) .... 31.12(d)(1)
1.163-5(c)(2)(i)(D)(3)(iii)(B).......... 31.12(b)(4)(iv)(c)	1.165-12(c)(3) .... 31.12(d)(1)
	1.165-12(c)(4) .... 31.12(d)(1)
1.163-5(c)(2)(i)(D)(3)(iii)(C).......... 31.12(b)(4)(iv)(c)	1.171-1(b)(1) .... 31.4(a)(2)(i)
	1.171-1(b)(2) ..31.4(a)(1), 31.4(a)(1)(i)
1.163-5(c)(2)(i)(D)(3)(iii)(D) .... 31.12(b)(4)(iv)(c)	1.171-1(b)(3) .... 31.4(a)(1)(i)
	1.171-1(b)(3)(ii) .... 31.4(a)(1)
1.163-5(c)(2)(i)(D)(3)(iii)(E).......... 31.12(b)(4)(iv)(c)	1.171-1(b)(5) .... 31.4(a)(1)(i)
	1.171-1(c)(1) .... 31.4(a)(1)(ii)
1.163-5(c)(2)(i)(D)(3)(iii)(F).......... 31.12(b)(4)(iv)(c)	1.171-1(c)(3) .... 31.4(a)(1)(ii)
	1.171-2(a) .... 31.4(b)
1.163-5(c)(2)(i)(D)(3)(iii)(G) .... 31.12(b)(4)(iv)(c)	1.171-2(a)(2)(i) .....31.4(b), 31.4(c)(1)
	1.171-2(a)(2)(iii) .... 31.4(c)(1)
1.163-5(c)(2)(i)(D)(3)(iii)(H) .... 31.12(b)(4)(iv)(c)	1.171-2(a)(4) .... 31.4(a)(1)(i)
	1.171-2(a)(6) .... 31.4(b)
1.163-5(c)(2)(i)(D)(5) ...31.12(b)(4)(ii)	1.171-2(b) .... 31.4(c)(1)
1.163-5(c)(2)(i)(D)(6)................. 31.12(b)(4)(iv)(a)	1.171-2(b)(2) .... 31.4(c)(1)
	1.171-2(c)(1) ......31.4(d), 34.2(c)(2), 34.3(c)
1.163-5(c)(2)(i)(D)(6)(i) .31.12(b)(4)(ii)	1.171-2(c)(2) ......31.4(d), 34.2(c)(2), 34.3(c)
1.163-5(c)(2)(i)(D)(7) ...31.12(b)(4)(ii), 31.12(b)(4)(iii)	1.171-2(d)(1) .... 31.4(e)
1.163-5(c)(3)(ii) ....31.12(b)(4)(v)	1.171-2(d)(2)(i) .... 31.4(e)
1.165-1(b) ....9.2(c)(1), 19.11, 27.8(c)	1.171-2(d)(2)(iii) .... 31.4(e)
1.165-1(d) .... 27.8(c)	1.171-2(f) 38.3
1.165-4 .... 27.8	1.171-3(a) .... 31.4(a)(1)(i)
1.165-5(a) 27.8	1.171-4(a) 31.4
1.165-5(b) .... 27.8(a)	1.171-4(c) 31.4
1.165-5(c) .... 27.8(a)	1.172-2(f)(1) 38.3
1.165-5(c)(3) .... 27.8(a)	1.212-1(b) .... 9.1(a)

TREASURY REGULATIONS (Continued)
(References are to book sections.)

Treas. Reg.		Treas. Reg.	
1.212-1(d)	9.1(a)	1.305-5(b)(1)	24.2(b)(5)
1.212-1(e)	9.1(b)	1.305-5(b)(2)	24.2(b)(5)
1.212-1(g)	9.1(c), 9.1(c)(2)	1.305-6(a)(2)	24.2(b)(6)
1.212-1(i)	9.1(a)	1.305-7	27.3(c)(1)
1.243-4(c)(1)	24.9(a)(2)	1.307-1	16.4(b)
1.246-3(c)(2)	24.9(b)(2)	1.307-1(a)	16.4(c), 30.3(f)(1)
1.246-3(c)(3)	24.9(b)(3)	1.307-2	16.4(c), 30.3(f)(1)
1.249-1	34.2(f)	1.312-6(b)	25.4(b), 33.5(c)
1.249-1(a)	31.4(d), 34.2(f)	1.316-1(a)(1)	24.1(a)
1.249-1(b)	31.4(d)	1.351-1(a)(1)	18.4(a), 19.6(a)
1.249-1(d)(1)	34.2(f)	1.351-1(a)(1)(ii)	30.3(e)(2)
1.249-1(d)(2)	34.2(f)	1.354-1(e)	18.4(a), 30.3(e)(2)
1.249-1(e)	34.2(f)	1.355-1(a)	30.3(e)(2)
1.249-1(e)(1)	34.2(f)	1.355-2(b)(1)	27.4(b)(1)
1.249-1(e)(2)	34.2(f)	1.355-2(b)(2)	27.4(b)(1)
1.265-1(a)(1)	9.3(a)	1.368-1(b)	18.4(a), 27.4(b)(1)
1.265-1(b)	9.3(a)	1.368-1(d)(5), Example (4)	27.4(b)(2)
1.265-1(c)	9.3(a)	1.368-2(a)	27.4(b)(2)
1.265-1(d)(1)	9.3(a)	1.368-2(e)(2)	27.3(c)(2)
1.265-1(d)(2)	9.3(a)	1.368-2(g)	27.3(c)(2)
1.265-2(a)	9.3(b)	1.402(a)-1(b)(1)	16.3(c)
1.265-3(a)	9.3(b)(3)	1.446-1(c)(1)	24.7(f)
1.265-3(b)(1)	9.3(b)(3)	1.446-1(c)(1)(i)	14.5(a), 24.7(a), 24.7(f)
1.265-3(b)(2)	9.3(b)(3)	1.446-1(c)(1)(ii)	14.5(a), 24.7(a), 25.1
1.301-1(b)	14.5(a), 24.7(a), 30.3(e)(1)(i)	1.446-1(c)(2)(i)	11.5, 22.1(a)
1.305-1(c)	27.3(b)(3)(vi)	1.446-1(d)(1)	22.1(a)
1.305-2(a)(1)	24.2(b)(1)	1.446-1(d)(2)	22.1(a)
1.305-2(a)(2)	24.2(b)(1)	1.446-1(d)(3)	22.1(a)
1.305-2(a)(3)	24.2(b)(1)	1.446-1(e)	22.2, 22.2(a)
1.305-2(a)(4)	24.2(b)(1)	1.446-1(e)(3)(ii)	32.1(b)(1)(ii)
1.305-2(a)(5)	24.2(b)(1)	1.451-1(a)	13.5, 25.1, 60.4(c)
1.305-2(b), Example (2)	24.2(b)(1)	1.451-2(a)	25.2
1.305-3(a)	24.2(b)(1)	1.451-2(b)	14.5(a), 24.7(a), 25.2
1.305-3(b)(5)	34.3(d)	1.454-1(a)	32.1(b)(1)(ii)
1.305-3(c)	24.2(b)(3)	1.454-1(a)(2)	32.1(b)(1)(ii)
1.305-3(c)(1)	24.2(b)(3)	1.461-1(a)(1)	60.4(c)
1.305-3(d)	24.2(b)(2)	1.461-1(a)(2)	60.4(c)
1.305-3(d)(1)(i)	34.3(d)	1.471-1	55.1, 60.2(b)(2)(ii)
1.305-3(e)	24.2(b)(2)	1.471-2(c)	22.2(a)
1.305-4(a)	24.2(b)(4)	1.471-2(d)	22.2(b), 22.2(c)
1.305-4(b), Example (1)	24.2(b)(4)	1.471-5	8.3, 8.3(a), 8.3(c), 8.8, 22.2(a), 22.2(b), 22.2(c), 27.8(d), 60.2(b)(2)(ii)
1.305-5(a)	24.2(b)(5), 27.3(b)(1)		
1.305-5(b)	27.2		

TREASURY REGULATIONS (Continued)
(References are to book sections.)

Treas. Reg.	
1.472-1(a)	22.2(b)
1.472-2(b)	22.2(b)
1.472-8(a)	22.2(b)
1.547-2(b)(1)	24.3
1.561-1	24.5(c)
1.582-1	27.8(e)
1.582-1(d)	27.6(c)
1.671-3(a)	29.1(a), 29.1(d), 36.2(a), 37.1
1.671-4(a)	29.1(a)
1.705-1(a)(1)	33.5(a)
1.761-2	36.1
1.761-3(a)	36.1
1.761-4(a)	36.2(a)
1.852-4(a)(1)	8.9(c)
1.852-4(b)	17
1.852-4(b)(1)	8.9(c)
1.852-4(c)(1)	17
1.852-4(d)	17.6
1.856-1(e)(1)	8.10(d)
1.856-2(d)(1)	8.10(a)
1.856-4(b)(1)	28.4(d)(2)(iii)
1.857-6(a)	8.10(d)
1.857-6(b)	17
1.857-6(e)(1)	17
1.861-7	60.5(c)
1.863-7	60.2(a), 60.3(a)(1)(ii), 60.5(a)
1.863-7(a)(1)	60.1, 60.5(a)
1.863-7(a)(2)	60.5(a)
1.863-7(b)(1)	60.5(a)
1.863-7(b)(2)	60.5(a)
1.863-7(b)(3)	60.5(a)
1.863-7(c)	60.5(a)
1.863-7(c)(3)	60.5(a)
1.863-7(e)	60.5(a)
1.882-5	23.3(g)(1)(i)(c), 23.3(g)(1)(v)(b), 23.3(g)(1)(v)(e)
1.904-4(e)(3)	60.5(b)(1)
1.964-1(c)(3)	59.2(j)(1)
1.985-1(a)(2)	59.2(g)(1)(ii)
1.985-1(b)	59.2(g)(1)(v)
1.985-1(b)(1)	59.2(g)(1)(iii)
1.985-1(b)(2)	59.2(g)(1)(iii)
1.985-1(b)(3)	59.2(g)(1)(iii)

Treas. Reg.	
1.985-1(b)(4)	59.2(g)(1)(iii)
1.985-1(b)(5)	59.2(g)(1)(iii)
1.985-1(b)(6)	59.2(g)(1)(iii)
1.985-1(c)	59.2(g)(1)(v)
1.985-1(c)(1)	59.2(g)(1)(iv)
1.985-1(c)(2)(i)(A)	59.2(g)(1)(iv)
1.985-1(c)(2)(i)(B)	59.2(g)(1)(iv)
1.985-1(c)(2)(i)(C)	59.2(g)(1)(iv)
1.985-1(c)(2)(i)(D)	59.2(g)(1)(iv)
1.985-1(c)(2)(i)(E)	59.2(g)(1)(iv)
1.985-1(c)(2)(i)(F)	59.2(g)(1)(iv)
1.985-1(c)(2)(i)(G)	59.2(g)(1)(iv)
1.985-1(c)(2)(i)(H)	59.2(g)(1)(iv)
1.985-1(c)(2)(ii)	59.2(g)(1)(iv)
1.985-1(c)(2)(iii)	59.2(g)(1)(iv)
1.985-1(c)(4)	59.2(g)(1)(iv)
1.985-1(d)(1)	59.2(g)(1)(v)
1.985-1(d)(1)(i)	59.2(g)(1)(v)
1.985-1(d)(1)(ii)	59.2(g)(1)(v)
1.985-1(d)(2)	59.2(g)(1)(v)
1.985-1(e)	59.2(g)(2)
1.985-4	59.2(g)(1)(iii)
1.989(a)-1	59.2(g)(3)(i)
1.989(a)-1(b)(1)	59.2(g)(3)(i)
1.989(a)-1(b)(2)(i)	59.2(g)(3)(ii), 59.2(g)(3)(iv)
1.989(a)-1(b)(2)(ii)(A)	59.2(g)(3)(ii), 59.2(g)(3)(iii), 59.2(g)(3)(iv)
1.989(a)-1(b)(2)(ii)(B)	59.2(g)(3)(ii), 59.2(g)(3)(iii), 59.2(g)(3)(iv)
1.989(a)-1(c)	59.2(g)(3)(v)
1.989(a)-1(d)(1)	59.2(g)(3)(vi)
1.989(a)-1(d)(2)	59.2(g)(3)(vi)
1.989(a)-1(e), Example (3)	59.2(g)(3)(v)
1.989(a)-1(e), Example (6)	59.2(g)(3)(v)
1.1001-1	19.9(j)
1.1001-1(a)	21.3, 26.3
1.1001-2	21.6
1.1012-1(c)	16.2(b), 20.3
1.1012-1(c)(1)	16.2(b), 20.2(a)(1)(i), 20.2(a)(1)(ii), 20.2(b), 20.3

TREASURY REGULATIONS (Continued)
(References are to book sections.)

Treas. Reg.	
1.1012-1(c)(2)	20.2(a)(1)(i), 20.2(a)(1)(ii)
1.1012-1(c)(3)(i)	16.2(b), 20.2(a)(2)
1.1012-1(c)(3)(ii)	20.2(a)(1)(iii)
1.1012-1(c)(3)(ii)(a)	20.2(a)(1)(iii)
1.1012-1(c)(3)(ii)(b)	20.2(a)(1)(iii)
1.1012-1(c)(4)	20.2(a)(3)
1.1012-1(c)(4)(i)	20.2(a)(3)
1.1012-1(c)(4)(ii)	20.2(a)(3)
1.1012-1(c)(7)	20.2(e)
1.1012-1(c)(7)(i)	20.2(e), 22.2(c)
1.1012-1(c)(7)(i)(b)	20.2(e)
1.1012-1(c)(7)(ii)(a)	20.2(e)
1.1012-1(c)(7)(ii)(b)	20.2(e)
1.1012-1(c)(7)(iii)(a)(1)	20.2(e)
1.1012-1(c)(7)(iii)(b)	20.2(e)
1.1012-1(e)(1)(i)	20.2(f)
1.1012-1(e)(3)	20.2(f)
1.1012-1(e)(4)	20.2(f)
1.1012-1(e)(6)(i)	20.2(f)
1.1012-1(e)(6)(ii)	20.2(f)
1.1015-1(a)(1)	16.3(a)
1.1015-1(a)(2)	16.3(a)
1.1016-5(b)	16.4(g), 31.4(a)(1)(i)
1.1032-1	30.3(c)(3)
1.1037-1(a)	32.1(d)(1)
1.1037-1(a), Example (1)	32.1(d)(1)
1.1037-1(a)(3), Example (2)	32.1(d)(1), 32.1(d)(2)
1.1037-1(b)	32.1(d)(2)
1.1037-1(b)(2)(ii)	32.1(d)(2)(i)
1.1037-1(b)(5)	32.1(d)(2)(ii)
1.1037-1(c)	32.1(d)(1)
1.1037-1(d)	32.1(d)(1)
1.1091-1(a)	19.4(b)
1.1091-1(b)	19.3(b)
1.1091-1(c)	19.3(b)
1.1091-1(f)	19.8
1.1091-1(g)	19.3(f)
1.1091-2	19.3(a), 19.3(c)
1.1211-1(b)(6)(iii)	15.4(b)
1.1212-1(a)(3)(iv), Example (3)	15.5(b)

Treas. Reg.	
1.1212-1(c)(1)(i)	15.4(d)
1.1212-1(c)(1)(iii)	15.4(d)
1.1212-1(c)(1)(v)	15.4(d)
1.1223-1(b)	17.3(c)(1)
1.1232	34.2(b)
1.1232-3(b)(1)(iv)	31.2(h)
1.1232-3(b)(2)	31.10(a)
1.1232-3(b)(2)(i)	30.3(e)(1)(iii), 34.2(b)
1.1232-3(b)(2)(ii)	30.3(e)(1)(iii), 30.3(e)(2)
1.1232-3(c)	31.2(c)
1.1232-3A(a)(2)	31.2(b)
1.1232-3A(a)(3)	31.2(b)
1.1233-1(a)(1)	18.2(c)
1.1233-1(b)	18.4(e)(1)
1.1233-1(c)(2)	18.2
1.1233-1(c)(3)	18.4(c), 18.4(d)
1.1233-1(c)(4)	18.2, 18.4(c)
1.1233-1(c)(6), Example (6)	18.10(c), 19.9(d), 19.9(e)
1.1233-1(d)	19.9, 19.9(a)
1.1233-1(d)(1)	18.5, 18.10(c), 19.9, 19.9(d)
1.1233-1(d)(2)(i)	18.4(e), 18.4(e)(1), 18.4(e)(2), 18.4(e)(3)
1.1233-1(d)(2)(ii)	18.4(e)(4)
1.1233-1(f)(1)(ii)	18.10(b)
1.1233-1(f)(1)(iii), Example (1)	18.10(b)
1.1233-1(f)(1)(iii), Example (2)	18.10(b)
1.1233-1(f)(3)	18.10
1.1233-1(f)(4)	18.10
1.1234-1(a)(1)	30.3(b)(1)(ii), 44.3(c)(1)(ii)
1.1234-1(b)	30.3(b)(1)(ii), 30.3(b)(1)(iii)
1.1234-3(c)	8.3(c)
1.1236-1(c)(1)	19.2
1.1236-1(d)(1)	11.7(c)
1.1242-1(c)	27.6(b)
1.1243-1	27.6(c)
1.1243-1(b)	27.6(c)

TREASURY REGULATIONS (Continued)
(References are to book sections.)

Treas. Reg.	
1.1244(a)-1(b)	27.7
1.1244(a)-1(b)(2)	27.7
1.1244(b)-1(a)	27.7
1.1441-2(a)(1)	60.2(g)
1.1441-2(a)(2)	60.2(g)
1.1502-13(g)	11.3(b)(3)(ii)(a)
1.6042-2(a)(1)(ii)	13.3
1.6042-3(a)(2)	13.3
1.6045-1(c)(2)	13.3
1.6045-1(c)(3)	13.3
1.6045-1(c)(5)(i)	13.3
1.6045-1(c)(6)(i)(a)	13.3
1.6045-1(d)(4)	13.3
1.6045-1(d)(4)(i)	13.3, 14.5(b)(2)
1.6045-1(*l*)	13.3
1.6045-2(c)	13.3
1.6049-2(a)(5)	13.3
1.6049-4(b)(2)	31.2(n)(3)
1.6049-6(a)	31.2(a), 31.2(b)
1.6049-6(b)(1)(iv)	31.2(n)(3)
1.9100-1	24.3
5f.103-1(a)	25.4(d)
5f.103-1(b)(1)	25.4(d)
5f.103-1(b)(2)	25.4(d)
5f.103-1(b)(3)	25.4(d)
5f.103-1(b)(4)	25.4(d)
5f.103-1(c)(1)(i)	25.4(d)
5f.103-1(c)(1)(ii)	25.4(d)
5f.6045-1(c)(3)(iii)	13.3
20.2033-1(a)	33.3(a)(2)
20.6151-1(c)	32.1(c)
25.2511-1(a)	33.3(a)(2)
46.4701-1	31.12(a), 31.12(c)

Treas. Reg.	
46.4701-1(c)	31.12(a)
46.4701-1(e)	31.12(a)
301.7701-2	28.2(b), 36.2(e)
301.7701-2(a)	1.1(h)
301.7701-2(a)(1)	28.1
301.7701-2(a)(3)	28.1
301.7701-2(b)	28.2(b)
301.7701-2(b)(1)	28.1, 28.1(a)
301.7701-2(b)(3)	28.1(a)
301.7701-2(c)	28.2(b)
301.7701-2(c)(1)	28.1(b)
301.7701-2(c)(4)	28.1(b)
301.7701-2(d)	28.2(b)
301.7701-2(d)(1)	28.1(d)
301.7701-2(d)(2)	28.1(d)
301.7701-2(e)(1)	28.1(c)
301.7701-3(b)(2), Example (2)	28.1(b)
301.7701-4	29.1(c), 36.2(a), 36.2(c)
301.7701-4(c)	36.2(a), 36.5(c)
301.7701-4(c), Example (4)	31.6(e)(2)(i)
301.7701-4(c)(1)	29.1(a), 29.1(c), 29.3(b)(1), 36.2(c), 36.3
301.7701-4(c)(2), Example (1)	29.1(c), 36.2(c), 36.2(e)
301.7701-4(c)(2), Example (2)	29.1(c), 36.2(c), 36.2(e), 36.8(c)(1)(v)
301.7701-4(c)(2), Example (3)	29.1(c), 29.3(b)(1)
301.7701-4(c)(2), Example (4)	29.1(c), 36.2(c), 36.2(d)

TEMPORARY TREASURY REGULATIONS
(References are to book sections.)

Temp. Treas. Reg.	
1.56-1T(c)(2)	15.5(d)
1.56-1T(c)(3)	15.5(d)
1.56-1T(c)(3)(iii)(A)	15.5(d)
1.56-1T(d)(4)(i)	15.5(d)
1.56-1T(d)(4)(ii)	15.5(d)

Temp. Treas. Reg.	
1.56-1T(d)(4)(iii)	15.5(d)
1.56-1T(d)(4)(iv)	15.5(d)
1.67-1T	9.1(d)
1.67-1T(b)	9.1(d)
1.67-1T(c)	9.1(d)

TREASURY REGULATIONS (Continued)
(References are to book sections.)

Treas. Reg.	
1.67-2T	9.1(d)
1.67-2T(e)	8.9(c), 9.1(d)
1.67-2T(g)(1)	8.9(c), 9.1(d)
1.67-2T(g)(3)(ii)	8.9(c)
1.67-2T(i)	8.9(c)
1.67-3T	9.1(d), 36.8(j)(4)
1.67-3T(a)(1)	36.8(*l*)
1.67-3T(a)(2)(i)(A)	36.8(*l*)
1.148-0T	33.3(a)(1)(vi)
1.148-1T	33.3(a)(1)(vi)
1.148-2T	33.3(a)(1)(vi)
1.148-3T	33.3(a)(1)(vi)
1.148-4T	33.3(a)(1)(vi)
1.148-5T	33.3(a)(1)(vi)
1.148-6T	33.3(a)(1)(vi)
1.148-7T	33.3(a)(1)(vi)
1.148-8T	33.3(a)(1)(vi)
1.148-9T	33.3(a)(1)(vi)
1.149(b)(3)-1T	33.3(a)(1)(ii)
1.150-0T	33.3(a)(1)(vi)
1.163-5T(c)	33.3(a)(1)(iii)
1.163-5T(e)(3)	31.12(f)
1.163-5T(e)(4)	31.12(f)
1.163-8T	25.5, 28.4(g)(1)
1.163-9T	9.2(h), 25.5
1.163-10T	9.2(h), 25.5
1.163-11T	25.5
1.165-5T(e)(1)	31.12(f)
1.165-5T(e)(2)	31.12(f)
1.165-13T	47.2(c), 47.2(d)(1), 47.2(e)
1.165-13T (Q-2)	47.2(d)(2)
1.165-13T (A-2)	47.2(d)(1), 47.2(d)(2)
1.165-13T (Q-5)	47.2(e)
1.165-13T (A-5)	47.2(e)
1.263A-1T	22.4
1.382-2T(f)(18)(ii)	27.3(c)(2)
1.382-2T(f)(18)(ii)(A)	27.3(c)(2)
1.382-2T(f)(18)(ii)(B)	27.3(c)(2)
1.382-2T(f)(18)(ii)(C)	27.3(c)(2)
1.382-2T(h)(4)(v)	27.3(c)(2)
1.469-0T	25.5
1.469-1T	25.5
1.469-1T(e)(6)	9.8
1.469-2T	25.5

Treas. Reg.	
1.469-3T	25.5
1.469-4T	25.5
1.469-5T	25.5
1.469-11T	25.5
1.860-1T	36.8(j)(4)
1.860D-1T(a)	36.8(k)
1.860F-4T	36.8(j)(4)
1.860F-4T(b)	36.8(k)
1.860F-4T(e)(4)	36.8(*l*)
1.861-7T	60.2(g)(1), 60.2(g)(2), 60.5(b)(2)
1.861-7T(b)	60.5(b)(1)
1.861-8T	23.3(g)(1)(v)(e), 60.2(b)(2)(i)(a)(1)
1.861-9T	23.3(g)(1)(v)(e), 60.2(a), 60.2(b)(2)(i)(a)(1), 60.5(a), 60.5(b)(1)
1.861-9T(b)(6)	60.5(b)(1)
1.861-9T(b)(6)(iv)(A)	60.5(b)(2)
1.861-9T(b)(6)(iv)(C)	60.5(c)
1.861-9T(b)(6)(vi)	60.5(b)(1)
1.861-10T	23.3(g)(1)(v)(e), 60.2(b)(2)(i)(a)(1)
1.861-11T	23.3(g)(1)(v)(e), 60.2(b)(2)(i)(a)(1)
1.861-12T	23.3(g)(1)(v)(e), 60.2(b)(2)(i)(a)(1)
1.861-13T	60.2(b)(2)(i)(a)(1)
1.861-14T	60.2(b)(2)(i)(a)(1)
1.863-7T	60.5(a)
1.863-7T(b)	60.5(b)(1)
1.985-0T	59.2(g)(1)(ii)
1.985-1T	59.2(g)(1)(ii)
1.985-2T	59.2(g)(1)(ii)
1.985-3T	59.2(g)(1)(ii)
1.985-4T	59.2(g)(1)(ii)
1.987-0T	59.2(g)(3)(vii)
1.987-1T	59.2(g)(3)(vii)
1.988-1T(a)(1)	59.2(a)(1)
1.988-1T(a)(1)(i)	59.2(g)(2), 59.4(e)
1.988-1T(a)(1)(ii)	23.3(g)(2)(iv)(a), 23.3(g)(3), 59.2(a)(1), 59.2(g)(2)
1.988-1T(a)(1)(iii)	59.2(a)(1), 60.2(c)(4)
1.988-1T(a)(2)	59.2(g)(2)

Table of Treasury Pronouncements

TREASURY REGULATIONS (*Continued*)
(References are to book sections.)

Treas. Reg.	
1.988-1T(a)(2)(i)	23.3(g)(3), 31.7(c)
1.988-1T(a)(2)(iii)	23.3(g)(2)(iv)(a), 59.2(a)(1), 60.1
1.988-1T(a)(2)(iii)(A)	59.2(a)(1), 60.2(c)(4)
1.988-1T(a)(2)(iii)(B)	59.2(a)(1), 60.2(c)(4)
1.988-1T(a)(4)(i)	59.2(j)(1)
1.988-1T(a)(4)(iii)	59.2(j), 59.2(j)(3)
1.988-1T(a)(4)(iii)(A)	59.2(j)(1)
1.988-1T(a)(4)(iii)(B)	59.2(j)(1)
1.988-1T(a)(4)(iii)(C)	59.2(j)(1)
1.988-1T(a)(4)(iii)(D)	59.2(j)(1)
1.988-1T(a)(4)(iii)(E)	59.2(j)(1)
1.988-1T(a)(4)(iii)(F)	59.2(j)(1)
1.988-1T(a)(4)(iv)	59.2(j)(2)
1.988-1T(a)(4)(iv)(B)	59.2(j)(3)
1.988-1T(a)(4)(v)	59.2(j), 59.2(j)(4)
1.988-1T(a)(6)(i)	59.2(a)(3)
1.988-1T(a)(6)(ii), Example (2)	59.2(a)(3)
1.988-1T(b)	59.4(e)
1.988-1T(c)	59.2(g)(2)
1.988-1T(d)(4)(i)	59.2(a)(1)
1.988-2T(b)	23.3(g)(1)(i), 60.2(c)(5)(ii)
1.988-2T(b)(2)(i)	23.3(g)(1)(i)(a), 31.7(a)
1.988-2T(b)(3)	31.7(b)
1.988-2T(b)(8)	23.3(g)(1)(ii), 31.7(c)
1.988-2T(b)(10)	31.7(c)
1.988-2T(b)(11)	31.7(b)
1.988-1T(c)	59.2(g)(2)
1.988-2T(c)(2)	23.3(g)(2)(viii)(e)
1.988-2T(d)	60.2(c)(4)
1.988-2T(d)(1)(ii)	59.4(e)
1.988-2T(d)(2)(i)	59.2(a)(4)
1.988-2T(d)(2)(ii)	59.2(a)(4)
1.988-2T(d)(2)(ii)(B)	59.2(c)(3), 59.4(c)(3), 59.4(d)(3)
1.988-2T(d)(2)(ii)(C)	59.4(b)(4), 59.4(c)(4)
1.988-2T(d)(2)(iii)	60.2(c)(5)(ii)
1.988-2T(d)(2)(iii)(D)	23.3(g)(2)(iv)(d)

Treas. Reg.	
1.988-2T(d)(2)(v)	23.3(g)(2)(iv)(c)(3), 59.2(a)(4)
1.988-2T(d)(5), Example (2)	60.2(c)(5)(ii)
1.988-2T(e)(1)	59.2(a)(4)
1.988-2T(e)(2)	59.2(a)(4)
1.988-2T(e)(2)(i)	60.2(c)(7)
1.988-2T(e)(2)(ii)(A)	60.2(c)(5)(ii)
1.988-2T(e)(2)(ii)(A)(1)	60.2(c)(5)(ii)
1.988-2T(e)(2)(ii)(A)(2)	60.2(c)(5)(ii)
1.988-2T(e)(2)(iii)	60.2(c)(5)(iii)
1.988-2T(e)(2)(iv)	60.2(c)(5)(iv)
1.988-2T(e)(3)	59.2(a)(4), 60.2(c)(5)(i)
1.988-2T(e)(3)(i)	60.2(c)(5)(i)
1.988-2T(e)(3)(ii)	60.2(c)(5)(i)
1.988-2T(e)(4)	60.2(c)(5)(v)
1.988-2T(e)(6)	59.2(a)(4)
1.988-3T(b)	23.3(e), 59.4(e), 60.2(c)(4)
1.988-3T(b)(2)	23.3(e)
1.988-4T	23.3(g)(1)(v)(c), 60.5(a)
1.988-4T(a)	59.2(d), 60.2(c)(6)
1.988-4T(b)(1)	59.2(d)(1)
1.988-4T(c)	59.2(d)(1)
1.988-4T(d)(1)	59.2(d)(2)(i), 59.2(d)(2)(iii)
1.988-5T	23.3(g)
1.988-5T(a)	23.3(g)(1)(i)(b), 23.3(g)(1)(ii), 23.3(g)(1)(iv)
1.988-5T(a)(1)	23.3(g)(1)(i)
1.988-5T(a)(3)	23.3(g)(1)(i), 23.3(g)(1)(i)(a)
1.988-5T(a)(4)	23.3(g)(1)(i)
1.988-5T(a)(4)(i)	23.3(g)(1)(i)(b)
1.988-5T(a)(4)(ii)	23.3(g)(1)(i)(b), 60.2(c)(2), 60.2(c)(7)
1.988-5T(a)(4)(ii)(A)	60.2(c)(5)(ii)
1.988-5T(a)(4)(ii)(A)(2)	60.2(c)(5)(ii), 60.2(c)(5)(iii)
1.988-5T(a)(4)(iv)	60.2(c)(2)
1.988-5T(a)(5)	23.3(g)(1)(i), 23.3(g)(1)(ii)
1.988-5T(a)(5)(i)	23.3(g)(1)(i)(c)
1.988-5T(a)(5)(ii)	23.3(g)(1)(i)(c)
1.988-5T(a)(5)(iii)	23.3(g)(1)(i)(c)

TREASURY REGULATIONS (*Continued*)
(References are to book sections.)

Treas. Reg.	Treas. Reg.
1.988-5T(a)(5)(iv) ...... 23.3(g)(1)(i)(c)	1.988-5T(b)(2)(i)(E) .... 23.3(g)(2)(iii), 23.3(g)(3)
1.988-5T(a)(5)(v) ...... 23.3(g)(1)(i)(c)	1.988-5T(b)(2)(i)(F) .... 23.3(g)(2)(iii), 23.3(g)(3)
1.988-5T(a)(5)(vi) ...... 23.3(g)(1)(i)(c)	1.988-5T(b)(2)(i)(G) .... 23.3(g)(2)(iii), 23.3(g)(3)
1.988-5T(a)(5)(vii) .... 23.3(g)(1)(i)(c), 23.3(g)(1)(v)(b)	1.988-5T(b)(2)(ii) .... 23.3(b), 23.3(g)(2)(ii), 23.3(g)(2)(iii)
1.988-5T(a)(6)(i) .... 23.3(g)(1)(ii), 23.3(g)(1)(iv)	1.988-5T(b)(2)(iii) ...... 23.3(g)(2)(iii), 23.3(g)(2)(viii)(d)
1.988-5T(a)(6)(ii) .... 23.3(g)(1)(ii)	1.988-5T(b)(2)(iii)(A) . 23.3(g)(2)(iv)(a)
1.988-5T(a)(6)(ii)(B) ..... 23.3(g)(1)(ii)	1.988-5T(b)(2)(ii)(B) ..... 23.3(g)(2)(ii)
1.988-5T(a)(6)(ii)(C) ..... 23.3(g)(1)(ii)	1.988-5T(b)(2)(iii)(B) . 23.3(g)(2)(iv)(b)
1.988-5T(a)(7) .... 23.3(g)(1)(iii)	1.988-5T(b)(2)(iii)(C)(1) ....
1.988-5T(a)(8) .... 23.3(g)(1)(i)(c), 23.3(g)(1)(iv)	.... 23.3(g)(2)(iv)(c)(1)
1.988-5T(a)(8)(i)(A) ..... 23.3(g)(1)(iv)	1.988-5T(b)(2)(iii)(C)(3) ....
1.988-5T(a)(8)(i)(B) ..... 23.3(g)(1)(iv)	.... 23.3(g)(2)(iv)(c)(3)
1.988-5T(a)(8)(i)(C) ..... 23.3(g)(1)(iv)	1.988-5T(b)(2)(iv) .... 23.3(g)(2)(v)
1.988-5T(a)(8)(i)(D) ..... 23.3(g)(1)(iv)	1.988-5T(b)(2)(v) .... 23.3(g)(2)(vi)
1.988-5T(a)(8)(i)(E) ..... 23.3(g)(1)(iv)	1.988-5T(b)(3) .... 23.3(g)(2)(iii), 23.3(g)(2)(vii), 23.3(g)(3)
1.988-5T(a)(8)(ii) ..... 23.3(g)(1)(v)(a)	1.988-5T(b)(3)(i) ..... 23.3(g)(2)(iv)(b), 23.3(g)(2)(vii)
1.988-5T(a)(9)(i)(A) ... 23.3(g)(1)(v)(a)	
1.988-5T(a)(9)(i)(B) ... 23.3(g)(1)(v)(b)	1.988-5T(b)(3)(ii) ...... 23.3(g)(2)(vii)
1.988-5T(a)(9)(i)(C) .... 23.3(g)(1)(v)(c)	1.988-5T(b)(4)(i) .... 23.3(g)(2)(viii)(a)
1.988-5T(a)(9)(ii)....................	1.988-5T(b)(4)(ii) ... 23.3(g)(2)(viii)(b)
.... 23.3(g)(1)(v)(a), 23.3(g)(1)(v)(d)	1.988-5T(b)(4)(iii)(A) ....
1.988-5T(a)(9)(ii)(A) ... 23.3(g)(1)(i)(b), 23.3(g)(1)(v)(d)(1)	.... 23.3(g)(2)(viii)(c)
1.988-5T(a)(9)(ii)(B)	1.988-5T(b)(4)(iii)(B) ....
.... 23.3(g)(1)(v)(d)(2)	.... 23.3(g)(2)(viii)(d)
1.988-5T(a)(9)(ii)(C)	1.988-5T(b)(4)(iv) ... 23.3(g)(2)(viii)(e)
.... 23.3(g)(1)(v)(d)(3)	1.988-5T(b)(4)(v) .... 23.3(g)(2)(viii)(f)
1.988-5T(a)(9)(ii)(D)	1.988-5T(b)(4)(vi) ... 23.3(g)(2)(viii)(e)
.... 23(g)(1)(v)(d)(4)	1.988-5T(c) ... 23.3(g)(2)(ii), 23.3(g)(3)
1.988-5T(a)(9)(iii) ..... 23.3(g)(1)(v)(e)	1.989(c)-1T .... 59.2(g)(3)(vii)
1.988-5T(b) .... 23.3(g)(2)(i), 23.3(g)(2)(iii), 23.3(g)(2)(iv)(a), 23.3(g)(2)(vii), 23.3(g)	1.1092(b)-1T 49.2, 54, 54.2, 57.8
	1.1092(b)-1T(a) .... Part Eleven, 49.2
1.988-5T(b)(1) .... 23.3(g)(2)(i)	1.1092(b)-1T(a)(1) ..... 49.2, 50, 54.2, 57.3(c)
1.988-5T(b)(2) ...... 23.3(g)(2)(viii)(f)	
1.988-5T(b)(2)(i)(A) ..... 23.3(g)(2)(iii)	1.1092(b)-1T(a)(2) 49.2, 54.2
1.988-5T(b)(2)(i)(B) ..... 23.3(g)(2)(iii)	1.1092(b)-1T(b) 49.2, 50, 54.2
1.988-5T(b)(2)(i)(C) ..... 23.3(g)(2)(iii)	1.1092(b)-1T(c)(1) 49.2, 50, 54.2
1.988-5T(b)(2)(i)(D) .... 23.3(g)(2)(iii), 23.3(g)(3)	1.1092(b)-1T(c)(2) 49.2, 50, 54.2
	1.1092(b)-1T(d) 54, 54.2

TREASURY REGULATIONS (*Continued*)
(References are to book sections.)

Treas. Reg.	
1.1092(b)-1T(d)(1)(i)	54
1.1092(b)-1T(d)(2)	54.2
1.1092(b)-1T(e)	19.2, 54.1
1.1092(b)-1T(g), Example (1)	49.1, 54.2
1.1092(b)-1T(g), Example (2)	54.2
1.1092(b)-1T(g), Example (4)	54.2
1.1092(b)-1T(g), Example (5)	54.2
1.1092(b)-1T(g), Example (10)	54.2
1.1092(b)-2T	54, 54.4(d), 56.4, 57.8
1.1092(b)-2T(a)	50, 54.4(c), 54.4(d), 56.4, 57.2(a)
1.1092(b)-2T(a)(1)	30.5(b)(1), Part Eleven, 54.4(a), 54.4(d), 56.4
1.1092(b)-2T(a)(2)	30.5(b)(1), 54.4(a)
1.1092(b)-2T(b)	50
1.1092(b)-2T(b)(1)	30.5(b)(1), 54.4(a)
1.1092(b)-2T(b)(2)	54.4(a), 57, 57.1, 57.8
1.1092(b)-2T(b)(2)(iii)	57
1.1092(b)-2T(c)	54.4(a)
1.1092(b)-2T(c)(1)(i)	57
1.1092(b)-2T(c)(1)(ii)	57
1.1092(b)-2T(d)	54.4(c)
1.1092(b)-2T(e)(1)	54.4(a)
1.1092(b)-2T(e)(2)	54.4(a)
1.1092(b)-2T(f), Example (1)	54.4(a)
1.1092(b)-2T(f), Example (4)	54.4(a)
1.1092(b)-2T(f), Example (5)	54.4(a)
1.1092(b)-2T(f), Example (6)	54.4(a)
1.1092(b)-2T(f), Example (7)	54.4(a)
1.1092(b)-3T	54, 57.3(a), 57.3(b), 57.3(c), 57.5, 57.8
1.1092(b)-3T(a)	57.5
1.1092(b)-3T(b)(2)	57.3(d)
1.1092(b)-3T(b)(2), Example (1)	57.3(e)
1.1092(b)-3T(b)(3)	57.3(b), 57.3(e)
1.1092(b)-3T(b)(3), Example (1)	57.3(e)
1.1092(b)-3T(b)(4)	57.3(b), 57.3(f)
1.1092(b)-3T(b)(5)	57.3(g)
1.1092(b)-3T(b)(5), Example (1)	57.3(g)

Treas. Reg.	
1.1092(b)-3T(b)(5), Example (3)	57.3(g)
1.1092(b)-3T(b)(6)	57.3(b), 57.3(c)
1.1092(b)-3T(b)(6), Example (1)	57.3(c)
1.1092(b)-3T(b)(7)	57.3(b), 57.3(h)
1.1092(b)-3T(b)(7), Example	57.3(h)
1.1092(b)-3T(c)	57.2(b), 57.3(c), 57.3(h)
1.1092(b)-3T(d)(1)	57.3(a), 57.6(a)
1.1092(b)-3T(d)(2)	57.3(a), 57.3(a)(3)
1.1092(b)-3T(d)(3)	57.3(a)(3)
1.1092(b)-3T(d)(4)(i)	57.3(a)(1)
1.1092(b)-3T(d)(4)(ii)	57.3(a)(2)
1.1092(b)-3T(d)(4)(iii)	57.3(a)(3)
1.1092(b)-3T(d)(5)	57.3(a)(3)
1.1092(b)-4T	45.4(b), 54, 54.2, 57.8, 59.2(h)
1.1092(b)-4T(a)	57.4, 57.4(a)
1.1092(b)-4T(b)	48.2(c)(3), 57.5
1.1092(b)-4T(b)(1)	57.4, 57.4(a)
1.1092(b)-4T(b)(2)	57.4, 57.4(a)
1.1092(b)-4T(b)(2), Example	57.4(a)
1.1092(b)-4T(b)(3)	57.4, 57.4(a)
1.1092(b)-4T(b)(3), Example	48.2(c)(3), 57.4(a)
1.1092(b)-4T(b)(4)	57.4
1.1092(b)-4T(b)(4)(i)	57.4(a)
1.1092(b)-4T(b)(4)(ii)	57.4(a)
1.1092(b)-4T(c)	54.4(c)
1.1092(b)-4T(c)(1)	57.4, 57.4(b)
1.1092(b)-4T(c)(2)	57.4, 57.4(c), 57.4(e)
1.1092(b)-4T(c)(3)	55.2(d), 57.4, 57.4(d)
1.1092(b)-4T(c)(3)(i)	55.2(d)
1.1092(b)-4T(c)(4)	57, 57.4, 57.4(c), 57.4(f)
1.1092(b)-4T(c)(6)	57.4(c)
1.1092(b)-4T(c)(6), Example (2)	57.4(c)
1.1092(b)-4T(f)	51.2
1.1092(b)-4T(f)(1)	57.4(g), 57.4(i)

TREASURY REGULATIONS (Continued)
(References are to book sections.)

Treas. Reg.	
1.1092(b)-4T(f)(2)	57.3(a), 57.4(i)
1.1092(b)-4T(f)(2)(i)	57.4(h), 57.6(b)
1.1092(b)-4T(f)(2)(ii)	57.4(h)
1.1092(b)-4T(f)(3)	57.4(g), 57.4(i)
1.1092(b)-4T(f)(4)	57.4(g), 57.5
1.1092(b)-5T	54
1.1092(b)-5T(a)	19.7
1.1092(b)-5T(j)	51.4
1.1092(b)-5T(n)	49.2, 54.2, 57.3(h)
1.1092(b)-5T(p)	19.2, 19.9, 54.2
1.1092(b)-5T(q)	19.2, 19.6(a), 54.2
1.1256(h)-2T(d)	44.5
1.1256(h)-3T(a)	44.5
1.1256(h)-3T(b)(1)	44.5
1.1256(h)-3T(b)(2)(ii)	44.5
1.1256(h)-3T(c)	44.5
1.1256(h)-3T(d)	44.5
1.6031(b)-1T	28.3
1.6031(b)-1T(a)	28.3
1.6031(b)-1T(a)(1)(ii)	28.3
1.6031(b)-1T(a)(2)(i)(A)	28.3
1.6031(b)-1T(a)(2)(i)(B)	28.3
1.6031(b)-1T(a)(2)(i)(C)	28.3
1.6031(b)-1T(b)	28.3
1.6031(b)-1T(c)	28.3
1.6031(c)-1T	28.3
1.6031(c)-1T(a)(1)(i)	28.3
1.6031(c)-1T(a)(3)	28.3
1.6049-7T	36.8(j)(4)
1.6049-7T(b)(1)	31.2(n)(4)
1.6049-7T(g)	31.2(n)(1)
1.6049-7T(g)(3)	31.2(n)(1)
1.6049-7T(g)(4)	31.2(n)(1)
1.6050N-1	13.4
1.6655-7T(a)	15.5(d)
1.6655-7T(c)(2)	15.5(d)
1.7872-5T	9.2(c)(2)
1.7872-5T(b)(13)	9.2(c)(2)
1.7872-5T(b)(13)(i)	9.2(c)(2)
1.7872-5T(b)(13)(ii)	9.2(c)(2)
5c.1256-2	44.1
5f.6045-1(c)(3)	13.3
7.1023(b)(3)-1	16.3(b)
15A.453-1(d)(2)(i)	17.2(a)(2)(i)(e)

Treas. Reg.	
15A.453-1(d)(2)(ii)(A)	17.2(a)(2)(i)(e)
15A.453-1(d)(3)(i)	17.2(a)(2)(i)(c)
15A.453-1(d)(3)(ii)	17.2(a)(2)(i)(c)
15A.453-1(e)(4)(iii)	28.4(c)(3), 28.4(c)(6)
15A.453-1(e)(4)(iv)	28.4(c)(3)
31.3406-0	13.4
31.3406(a)-1	13.4
31.3406(a)-2	13.4
31.3406(a)-3	13.4
31.3406(a)-4	13.4
31.3406(b)(1)-1	13.4
31.3406(b)(2)-1	13.4
31.3406(b)(2)-2	13.4
31.3406(b)(2)-3	13.4
31.3406(b)(2)-4	13.4
31.3406(b)(2)-5	13.4
31.3406(b)(3)-1	13.4
31.3406(b)(3)-2	13.4
31.3406(b)(3)-3	13.4
31.3406(b)(3)-4	13.4
31.3406(b)(4)-1	13.4
31.3406(c)-1	13.4
31.3406(d)-1	13.4
31.3406(d)-2	13.4
31.3406(d)-3	13.4
31.3406(d)-4	13.4
31.3406(d)-5	13.4
31.3406(e)-1	13.4
31.3406(f)-1	13.4
31.3406(g)-1	13.4
31.3406(g)-2	13.4
31.3406(g)-3	13.4
31.3406(h)-1	13.4
31.3406(h)-2	13.4
31.3406(h)-3	13.4
31.3406(i)-1	13.4
31.6011(a)-11	13.4
31.6051-4	13.4
31.6413(a)-3	13.4
35a.3406-1	13.4
35a.3406-2	13.4
35a.3406-2(b)(3)	13.4
35a.3406-2(c)(1)	13.4

TREASURY REGULATIONS (*Continued*)
(References are to book sections.)

Treas. Reg.	
35a.3406-2(d)	13.4
35a.3406-2(e)(1)	13.4
35a.3406-2(e)(2)	13.4
35a.9999-2 (A-15)	31.2(a)
35a.9999-3 (A-51)	13.4

Treas. Reg.	
55.6011-1	8.9(b)
55.6071-1(a)	8.9(b)
301.6621-2T (Q-5)	53.2
301.6676-2	13.4

PROPOSED TREASURY REGULATIONS
(References are to book sections.)

Prop. Treas. Reg.	
1.163-7	31.2(a)
1.385-10(b)	27.3(b)(2)(i)
1.464-2(a)(3)	23.2(c)(2)(ii), 45.2(c)(1)
1.613A-3(f)	29.1(e)
1.1058-1	31.11(b)(2)
1.1058-1(a)	26.2(a), 26.2(g)
1.1058-1(b)	26.2(b), 26.2(g), 26.3
1.1058-1(b)(3)	26.2(b), 31.11(b)(1)
1.1058-1(c)(1)	26.2(b)
1.1058-1(c)(2)	26.2(c)
1.1058-1(d)	18.6(a), 24.9(b)(3), 26.2(e), 26.4, 31.11(b)(1)
1.1058-1(e)(1)	26.3
1.1058(e)(2)	26.3
1.1058-1(f)	26.2(g)
1.1058-2, Example (1)	26.2(b)
1.1058-2, Example (2)	26.2(g)
1.1058-2, Example (4)	26.2(e)
1.1223-2(a)	17.8, 26.2(d)
1.1223-2(b)(1)	17.8, 26.3
1.1223-2(b)(2)	17.8, 26.3
1.1271-1	31.2(a)
1.1272-1(c)(2)(i)	37.4(a)
1.1272-1(d)	31.2(g)(2)(ii)(a)
1.1272-1(f)	31.2(n)(1), 60.2(c)(5)(i)
1.1273-1(a)	31.2(n)(1)
1.1273-1(b)(1)	36.8(c)(1)(iii)
1.1273-2	31.2(a)
1.1273-2(d)	31.2(j)
1.1273-2(d)(1)	31.2(j)
1.1273-2(e)	34.2(b)
1.1274-3(d)(1)(v), Example (2)	36.8(c)(1)(iv)
1.1275-1	31.2(a)

Prop. Treas. Reg.	
1.1275-1(c)	31.2(n)(1)
1.1275-1(d)(1)	27.3(b)(3)(vi)
1.1275-2	31.2(a)
1.1275-2(d)	31.6(e)(2)(iii), 37.5(b)
1.1275-3	31.2(a)
1.1275-3(a)	31.2(n)(1)
1.1275-3(b)(2)	31.2(n)(2)
1.1275-3(b)(3)	31.2(n)(2)
1.1275-3(b)(4)	31.2(n)(2)
1.1275-4	31.2(a), 31.2(i), 31.7(a)
1.1275-5	31.2(a)
1.1275-5(a)	31.2(n)(2), 36.8(c)(1)(iv)
1.1275-5(b)	36.8(c)(1)(iv)
1.1275-5(c)	36.8(c)(1)(iv)
1.1275-5(d)(4)	36.8(c)(1)(iv)
1.1275-5(d)(5), Example (5)	36.8(c)(1)(iv)
1.6042-5	13.4
1.6044-6	13.4
1.6045-1(a)(1)	13.3
1.6045-1(c)(6)(ii)	13.3
1.6049-5(c)	31.2(n)(3)
1.6049-6	13.4
1.7872-5	9.2(c)(2)
1.7872-5(b)(13)	9.2(c)(2)
31.6011(a)-5	13.4
31.6011(a)-6	13.4
31.6071(a)-1	13.4
31.6302(a)-1	13.4
31.6682-1	13.4
301.6109-1	13.4
INTL-53-86, 1987-7 I.R.B. 30	31.12(a)
LR-10-87, 1987-2 C.B. 1053	9.2(h)

TREASURY REGULATIONS (Continued)
(References are to book sections.)

Treas. Reg.		Treas. Reg.	
LR-55-87, 1988-1 C.B. 929	15.5(d)	LR-137-86, 1988-1 C.B. 926	9.2(h)
LR-14-88, 1988-1 C.B. 932	9.8	IA-224-82, 1990-43 I.R.B. 12	13.4
LR-107-86, 1987-1 C.B. 805	15.5(d)		

REVENUE RULINGS
(References are to book sections.)

Rev. Rul.		Rev. Rul.	
53-45, 1953-1 C.B. 178	24.7(g)	58-384, 1958-2 C.B. 410	18.4(c), 18.10, 19.9(f)
54-43, 1954-1 C.B. 119	36.5(c)	58-536, 1958-2 C.B. 21	31.6(b)(1)
55-68, 1955-1 C.B. 372	17.3(c)(2)	59-44, 1959-1 C.B. 205	19.9(g)
55-76, 1955-1 C.B. 239	25.4(a)	59-242, 1959-2 C.B. 125	18.4(c)
55-355, 1955-1 C.B. 418	20.2(d)	59-373, 1959-2 C.B. 37	25.4(a)
55-655, 1955-2 C.B. 253	32.1(b)(1)(ii)	59-387, 1959-2 C.B. 56	34.2(a)
55-717, 1955-2 C.B. 298	27.4(d)(2)	59-418, 1959-2 C.B. 184	19.3(e)
56-116, 1956-1 C.B. 164	27.3(b)(5)	60-17, 1960-1 C.B. 124	31.4(c)(2)
56-153, 1956-1 C.B. 166	24.7(c)	60-24, 1960-1 C.B. 171	8.4(b), 23.2(b)(3)
56-179, 1956-1 C.B. 187	27.3(c)(2)	60-177, 1960-1 C.B. 9	24.9(b)(3), 26.2(e), 26.4, 31.11(b)(1)
56-406, 1956-2 C.B. 523	19.6(a), 19.8(a), 19.9(b)		
56-431, 1956-2 C.B. 171	24.7(g)	60-195, 1960-1 C.B. 300	19.9(h)
56-435, 1956-2 C.B. 506	31.9(a), 33.4	60-284, 1960-2 C.B. 464	31.4
56-452, 1956-2 C.B. 525	19.8, 19.8(c)	60-321, 1960-2 C.B. 166	8.3(b)
56-510, 1956-2 C.B. 168	24.8, 27.5(a)(1)	60-331, 1960-2 C.B. 189	24.7(c)
56-531, 1956-2 C.B. 983	58.1	61-97, 1961-1 C.B. 394	20.2(a)(1)(ii), 20.2(a)(2)
56-602, 1956-2 C.B. 527	19.3(b)		
56-653, 1956-2 C.B. 185	20.2(c)	61-145, 1961-2 C.B. 21	25.4(a)
57-29, 1957-1 C.B. 519	17.2(a)(6), 27.3(d)	61-175, 1961-2 C.B. 128	29.1(a), 29.1(d), 29.1(e), 36.2(a)
57-103, 1957-1 C.B. 113	27.3(b)(5)	61-181, 1961-2 C.B. 21	25.4(a)
57-151, 1957-1 C.B. 64	25.4(a)	62-21, 1962-1 C.B. 37	9.1(c)(7)
57-167, 1957-1 C.B. 294	8.8	62-42, 1962-1 C.B. 133	18.6(d), 18.6(e)(1)
57-212, 1957-1 C.B. 114	27.3(b)(5)		
58-2, 1958-1 C.B. 236	32.1(b)(3)	62-58, 1962-1 C.B. 158	27.6(b)
58-11, 1958-1 C.B. 273	27.4(d)(2)	62-140, 1962-2 C.B. 181	17.3(a)(3)
58-40, 1958-1 C.B. 275	8.4	62-153, 1962-2 C.B. 186	17.3(a)(3), 18.2(c), 19.9(e)
58-210, 1958-1 C.B. 523	19.9(g)		
58-211, 1958-1 C.B. 529	19.9(g)	62-217, 1962-2 C.B. 59	30.5(c)
58-234, 1958-1 C.B. 265	30.3(b)(1)(i), 30.3(b)(1)(iv), 30.3(b)(2)(i), 30.3(b)(2)(ii), 30.3(b)(2)(iv), 30.3(c)(1)(iv), 30.3(c)(2)(i), 30.3(c)(2)(ii), 60.2(e)(3)	63-27, 1963-1 C.B. 57	9.3(a)
		63-65, 1963-1 C.B. 142	18.2(a), 27.6(b)
		63-225, 1963-2 C.B. 339	30.3(e)(1)(ii)
		64-85, 1964-1 C.B. 230	8.9(a)(4)

TREASURY REGULATIONS (Continued)
(References are to book sections.)

Treas. Reg.	
64-160, 1964-1 C.B. 306	11.7(c)
64-236, 1964-2 C.B. 64	9.1(c)(4)
64-237, 1964-2 C.B. 319	27.4(d)(1)
65-17, 1965-1 C.B. 207	21.7
65-291, 1965-2 C.B. 290	27.6(b)
66-7, 1966-1 C.B. 188	17.1(b)
66-97, 1966-1 C.B. 190	17.1(a), 17.2(a)(5), 31.4(b)
66-355, 1966-2 C.B. 302	27.4(d)(1)
67-419, 1967-2 C.B. 265	11.7(c)
67-436, 1967-2 C.B. 266	20.2(a)(2)
68-54, 1968-1 C.B. 69	34.5
68-126, 1968-1 C.B. 194	14.5(a), 24.7(a)
68-151, 1968-1 C.B. 363	30.3(b)(1)(i), 30.3(b)(1)(iv), 30.3(b)(2)(i), 30.3(b)(2)(ii), 30.3(b)(2)(iv), 30.3(c)(1)(iv), 30.3(c)(2)(i), 30.3(c)(2)(ii)
68-170, 1968-1 C.B. 71	34.2(e)
68-363, 1968-2 C.B. 336	27.4(d)(1)
68-601, 1968-2 C.B. 124	17.7(b), 19.9(a)
68-633, 1968-2 C.B. 329	29.3(b)(2)
69-15, 1969-1 C.B. 95	24.2(b)(3)
69-135, 1969-1 C.B. 198	27.3(c)(5), 27.3(c)(8), 34.3(e)
69-142, 1969-1 C.B. 107	27.4(b)(3)
69-171, 1969-1 C.B. 46	33.2
69-202, 1969-1 C.B. 95	17.4(a)
69-265, 1969-1 C.B. 109	27.3(c)(5), 27.3(c)(8)
69-416, 1969-2 C.B. 159	11.7(c)
69-489, 1969-2 C.B. 172	32.1(c)
69-550, 1969-2 C.B. 161	27.4(d)(2)
69-574, 1969-2 C.B. 130	29.2(c)
70-6, 1970-1 C.B. 172	17.3(c)(4)
70-33, 1970-1 C.B. 140	8.8
70-41, 1970-1 C.B. 77	27.4(b)(3)
70-108, 1970-1 C.B. 78	30.5(a)
70-221, 1970-1 C.B. 33	9.2(b)
70-231, 1970-1 C.B. 171	19.3(b), 19.3(e)
70-269, 1970-1 C.B. 82	27.4(b)(3)
70-291, 1970-1 C.B. 168	16.4(a), 16.4(*l*)
70-342, 1970-2 C.B. 32	10.1(c)
70-344, 1970-2 C.B. 50	14.5(d), 17.2(a)(2)(i)(f), 17.2(a)(5)
70-521, 1970-2 C.B. 72	24.2(b)(7), 30.3(e)(1)(ii)
70-544, 1970-2 C.B. 6	29.1(a), 29.1(d), 36.2(a), 36.7
70-545, 1970-2 C.B. 7	29.1(a), 29.1(b), 29.1(d), 36.2(a), 36.2(b), 36.7, 37.1
70-563, 1970-2 C.B. 108	8.8
70-597, 1970-2 C.B. 146	24.5(d)
70-598, 1970-2 C.B. 168	17.1(b), 17.2(a)(5), 30.5(b)(3)
70-627, 1970-2 C.B. 159	9.1(c)(8)
70-647, 1970-2 C.B. 38	9.2(b)
71-15, 1971-1 C.B. 149	11.7(c)
71-21, 1971-1 C.B. 221	20.2(e), 22.2(c)
71-30, 1971-1 C.B. 226	8.3(b), 11.7(f), 11.9(c)
71-316, 1971-2 C.B. 311	19.3(b), 19.7, 19.8
71-399, 1971-2 C.B. 433	29.1(a), 29.1(b), 29.1(d), 36.2(a), 36.2(b), 37.1
71-520, 1971-2 C.B. 311	19.8(a)
71-521, 1971-2 C.B. 313	30.3(b)(1)(i), 30.3(c), 30.3(c)(1)(iv), 30.3(f)(2)
71-568, 1971-2 C.B. 312	19.6(c)(1), 47.2
71-594, 1971-2 C.B. 91	25.4(a)
72-46, 1972-1 C.B. 50	31.10(a)
72-71, 1972-1 C.B. 99	17.4(a)
72-85, 1972-1 C.B. 234	58.1
72-134, 1972-1 C.B. 29	33.3(a)(1)(v)
72-179, 1972-1 C.B. 57	8.4(b), 8.4(c)(1), 8.4(c)(2), 12.1, 23.2(b)(3)
72-198, 1972-1 C.B. 223	30.3(b)(2)(i), 30.3(c)(2)(i), 30.3(e)(2)
72-224, 1972-1 C.B. 30	33.3(c)
72-264, 1972-1 C.B. 131	34.3(e)

TREASURY REGULATIONS (*Continued*)
(References are to book sections.)

Treas. Reg.		Treas. Reg.	
72-265, 1972-1 C.B. 222	...27.3(c)(2), 34.3(e)	74-221, 1974-1 C.B. 365	......29.1(a), 29.1(d), 36.2(a), 36.2(b), 37.1
72-359, 1972-2 C.B. 478	....17.3(c)(5)	74-223, 1974-1 C.B. 23	.......22.1(b)
72-376, 1972-2 C.B. 647	......29.1(a), 29.1(b), 29.1(d), 36.2(a), 36.2(b), 37.1	74-226, 1974-1 C.B. 119	.......9.2(e), 10.1(e), 22.1(b), 55.1
72-381, 1972-2 C.B. 233	....14.5(b)(1)	74-227, 1974-1 C.B. 119	......22.1(b), 22.2(a), 22.2(b)
72-415, 1972-2 C.B. 463	......20.2(a)(1)(iii)	74-230, 1974-1 C.B. 187	......59.5(a)
72-478, 1972-2 C.B. 487	......18.2(a)	74-300, 1974-1 C.B. 169	......29.1(a), 29.1(d), 36.2(a), 36.2(b), 36.7, 37.1
72-521, 1972-2 C.B. 178	......18.6(b), 18.6(c), 18.6(e)(1)	74-380, 1974-2 C.B. 32	..33.2(c)(2)(iii)
72-522, 1972-2 C.B. 215	....27.4(b)(3)	74-384, 1974-2 C.B. 152	.....9.1(c)(1)
72-575, 1972-2 C.B. 74	..33.3(a)(1)(v)	74-482, 1974-2 C.B. 267	......33.3(c)
72-587, 1972-2 C.B. 74	.....31.4(c)(2)	74-503, 1974-2 C.B. 117	......30.5(c)
73-13, 1973-1 C.B. 42	.......9.1(c)(2)	74-530, 1974-2 C.B. 188	......29.1(e)
73-27, 1973-1 C.B. 46	..........9.3(a)	74-562, 1974-2 C.B. 28	......24.7(c)
73-31, 1973-1 C.B. 217	.......20.2(e), 22.2(c)	75-13, 1975-1 C.B. 67	............8.4
73-37, 1973-1 C.B. 374	.......11.7(c), 20.2(e), 22.2(c)	75-33, 1975-1 C.B. 115	.......30.5(a)
		75-39, 1975-1 C.B. 272	.......31.2(a)
73-112, 1973-1 C.B. 47	........31.2(e), 33.3(a)(1)(i)(b), 33.3(a)(4)	75-57, 1975-1 C.B. 141	..........21.6
		75-108, 1975-1 C.B. 69	.....59.2(c)(1)
73-122, 1973-1 C.B. 66	..........34.5	75-109, 1975-1 C.B. 69	.....59.2(c)(1)
73-160, 1973-1 C.B. 365	.31.9(a), 33.4	75-117, 1975-1 C.B. 273	.....31.10(a)
73-328, 1973-2 C.B. 296	......31.9(a)	75-192, 1975-1 C.B. 384	......29.1(a), 36.2(a), 36.2(b), 36.2(e)
73-329, 1973-2 C.B. 302	......19.8(b)		
73-403, 1973-2 C.B. 308	......11.7(a)	75-236, 1975-1 C.B. 106	......27.3(a), 27.3(b)(1)
73-460, 1973-2 C.B. 424	......29.1(b), 36.2(b)	75-337, 1975-2 C.B. 124	....27.4(b)(1)
73-472, 1973-2 C.B. 114	.27.3(b)(3)(v)	75-360, 1975-2 C.B. 110	....27.4(b)(3)
73-524, 1973-2 C.B. 307	......16.3(b), 18.2(c)	75-513, 1975-2 C.B. 114	......34.3(d)
		75-523, 1975-2 C.B. 257	.......9.1(c)
73-563, 1973-2 C.B. 24	.......25.4(a)	75-527, 1975-2 C.B. 30	..........58.1
74-4, 1974-1 C.B. 51	............19.4	75-548, 1975-2 C.B. 331	....17.2(a)(5)
74-7, 1974-1 C.B. 198	......59.2(a)(3)	76-53, 1976-1 C.B. 87	.........20.2(f)
74-27, 1974-1 C.B. 24	.......31.11(b), 31.11(b)(4), 48.3(b)(2)(i)	76-78, 1976-1 C.B. 25	....33.3(a)(1)(v)
		76-265, 1976-2 C.B. 448	......36.5(c)
74-127, 1974-1 C.B. 47	.......34.2(e)	76-299, 1976-2 C.B. 211	......24.5(a)
74-169, 1974-1 C.B. 147	......29.1(a), 29.1(d), 36.2(a), 36.7	76-346, 1976-2 C.B. 247	......19.9(g)
		76-367, 1976-2 C.B. 259	......32.1(c)
74-172, 1974-1 C.B. 178	....31.4(c)(2)	76-387, 1976-2 C.B. 96	.......27.3(a)
74-177, 1974-1 C.B. 165	......24.5(d)	76-489, 1976-2 C.B. 250	......11.7(c)
74-197, 1974-1 C.B. 143	......29.2(c)	77-40, 1977-1 C.B. 248	..30.3(b)(2)(i), 30.3(e)(2)
74-218, 1974-1 C.B. 202	....19.6(c)(2)	77-55, 1977-1 C.B. 18	...33.2(c)(2)(iii)

TREASURY REGULATIONS (*Continued*)
(References are to book sections.)

Treas. Reg.	
77-59, 1977-1 C.B. 196	8.10(a), 31.11(a)(2), 31.11(b), 31.11(b)(4), 48.3(b)(2)(i)
77-108, 1977-1 C.B. 86	27.3(b)(2)(iii), 27.3(b)(5)
77-137, 1977-1 C.B. 178	28.1(c)
77-149, 1977-1 C.B. 82	20.2(f)
77-185, 1977-1 C.B. 48	30.2(b)(1), 47.2, 47.2(a), 47.2(b), 47.2(c), 56.6
77-199, 1977-1 C.B. 195	8.10(a)
77-201, 1977-1 C.B. 250	19.8(g), 19.9(a)
77-234, 1977-2 C.B. 39	33.2(c)(2)(iii)
77-238, 1977-2 C.B. 115	27.3(c)(2)
77-349, 1977-2 C.B. 20	29.1(a), 29.1(d), 36.2(a), 36.7, 37.1
77-415, 1977-2 C.B. 311	27.3(c)(4)
78-5, 1978-1 C.B. 263	17.2(b)
78-73, 1978-1 C.B. 265	30.3(e)(2)
78-94, 1978-1 C.B. 58	8.4
78-115, 1978-1 C.B. 85	27.3(b)(4)
78-117, 1978-1 C.B. 214	24.7(a)
78-142, 1978-1 C.B. 111	30.5(a)
78-149, 1978-1 C.B. 448	29.1(a), 29.1(b), 36.2(a), 36.2(b)
78-159, 1978-1 C.B. 27	33.2(c)(2)(iii)
78-182, 1978-1 C.B. 265	18.4(c), 30.3(b)(1)(i), 30.3(b)(1)(ii), 30.3(b)(1)(iii), 30.3(b)(1)(iv), 30.3(b)(2)(i), 30.3(b)(2)(iii), 30.3(b)(2)(iv), 30.3(c)(1)(ii), 30.3(c)(1)(iv), 30.3(c)(2)(i), 30.3(c)(2)(iv), 30.3(d)(1), 30.5(c), 60.2(e)(3)
78-270, 1978-2 C.B. 215	17.1(b)
78-375, 1978-2 C.B. 130	20.2(f)
78-408, 1978-2 C.B. 203	27.4(b)(3)
78-414, 1978-2 C.B. 213	30.2(b)(1), 32.1(a)(3), 47.2, 47.2(a), 47.2(c), 56.6, 58.1
79-42, 1979-1 C.B. 130	20.2(f)
79-80, 1979-1 C.B. 86	13.2, 13.2(a), 13.2(a)(1)

Treas. Reg.	
79-108, 1979-1 C.B. 75	33.3(a)(1)(vi), 48.3(b)(2)(i)
79-122, 1979-1 C.B. 204	29.2(c)
79-155, 1979-1 C.B. 153	27.3(c)(5), 27.3(c)(8), 31.9(a), 34.2(e)
79-163, 1979-1 C.B. 131	27.3(a), 27.3(b)(1)
79-195, 1979-1 C.B. 177	31.11(b), 31.11(b)(4)
79-269, 1979-2 C.B. 297	27.4(d)(2)
79-272, 1979-2 C.B. 124	9.3(b)(2)
80-19, 1980-1 C.B. 185	21.6
80-91, 1980-1 C.B. 29	33.3(a)(1)(vi)
80-92, 1980-1 C.B. 31	33.3(a)(1)(vi)
80-96, 1980-1 C.B. 317	29.1(a), 29.1(d), 36.2(a), 36.2(b), 37.1
80-134, 1980-1 C.B. 187	30.3(e)(2)
80-135, 1980-1 C.B. 18	26.2(e), 31.11(b)(1)
80-143, 1980-1 C.B. 19	31.4(c)(2)
80-161, 1980-1 C.B. 21	33.3(a)(1)(ii)
80-221, 1980-2 C.B. 107	27.3(b)(2)
80-238, 1980-2 C.B. 96	17.7(b), 19.9(f), 24.9(b)(1), 48.4(b)
80-292, 1980-2 C.B. 104	24.2(b)(7), 30.3(f)(2)
80-324, 1980-2 C.B. 340	55.1
80-328, 1980-2 C.B. 53	33.3(a)(1)(vi)
80-367, 1980-2 C.B. 386	59.5(a)
81-91, 1981-1 C.B. 123	27.3(a)
81-169, 1981-1 C.B. 429	11.3(b)(3)(ii)(a), 31.9(a), 33.4
81-203, 1981-2 C.B. 137	29.1(a), 29.1(d), 36.2(a), 36.2(b), 37.1
81-204, 1981-2 C.B. 157	19.9(j), 19.12, 29.1(a), 29.1(d), 36.2(a)
81-216, 1981-2 C.B. 21	33.2(c)(2)(iii)
81-298, 1981-2 C.B. 114	22.1(c)
82-101, 1982-1 C.B. 21	33.3(a)(1)(vi)
82-112, 1982-1 C.B. 59	16.4(a), 16.4(*l*)
82-144, 1982-2 C.B. 34	33.3(a)(1)(iv), 48.3(b)(2)(i)
82-163, 1982-2 C.B. 57	9.2(e)

TREASURY REGULATIONS (Continued)
(References are to book sections.)

Treas. Reg.	
82-227, 1982-2 C.B. 89	....14.5(b)(1), 17.2(a)(2)(i)(e)
83-98, 1983-2 C.B. 40	......27.3(c)(6), 34.2(a), 34.4, 34.5
83-119, 1983-2 C.B. 57	..........27.2
84-10, 1984-1 C.B. 155	.......29.1(a), 29.1(b), 29.1(d), 36.2(a), 36.2(b), 36.7, 37.1, 37.3
85-42, 1985-1 C.B. 36	........31.9(a)
85-65, 1985-1 C.B. 366	.......45.4(c)
85-87, 1985-1 C.B. 268	.......19.8(e), 19.9(f)
85-119, 1985-2 C.B. 60	.....1.1(g)(2), 34.2(a), 34.5
85-125, 1985-2 C.B. 180	......19.9(j), 19.12, 29.1(a), 29.1(b), 29.1(d), 36.2(a)
85-164, 1985-2 C.B. 117	....17.3(a)(3)
85-182, 1985-2 C.B. 39	..33.3(a)(1)(vi)
86-7, 1986-1 C.B. 295	.44.1(b), 44.2(a)
86-8, 1986-1 C.B. 295	...30.3(a), 44.3, 44.3(a)
86-27, 1986-1 C.B. 248	..........24.3
86-70, 1986-1 C.B. 83	..........9.2(e)
86-72, 1986-1 C.B. 253	.......44.2(a)
86-80, 1986-1 C.B. 79	........10.1(c)
86-92, 1986-2 C.B. 214	.......29.1(b), 36.2(b)
86-104, 1986-2 C.B. 80	..........24.3
87-5, 1987-1 C.B. 180	...............60.2(b)(2)(i)(a)(1)
87-17, 1987-1 C.B. 20	..........21.6

Treas. Reg.	
87-19, 1987-1 C.B. 249	............11.3(b)(3)(ii)(a), 31.9(a)
87-43, 1987-1 C.B. 252	..........44.3
87-63, 1987-2 C.B. 210	.......10.1(b)
87-67, 1987-2 C.B. 212	..........44.3
87-68, 1987-2 C.B. 378	..........8.4
87-103, 1987-2 C.B. 41	..........21.6
87-112, 1987-2 C.B. 207	......................32.1(b)(1)(iii)
88-31, 1988-1 C.B. 302	....30.3(c)(3), 30.5, 30.5(a), 30.5(b), 30.5(b)(1), 30.5(b)(2), 30.5(b)(3), 30.5(b)(5)
88-49, 1988-1 C.B. 297	.......16.6(e)
88-66, 1988-2 C.B. 34	........17.7(b), 24.9(c)(4)
88-81, 1988-2 C.B. 127	.......16.4(a), 16.4(l)
88-95, 1988-2 C.B. 28	...........21.7
89-20, 1989-1 C.B. 170	..........24.3
89-63, 1989-1 C.B. 90	......27.3(b)(5)
89-64, 1989-1 C.B. 91	.17.7(b), 19.9(a)
89-81, 1989-1 C.B. 226	.......24.5(d)
89-122, 1989-2 C.B. 200	.....................11.3(b)(3)(ii)(a)
90-7, 1990-1 C.B. 153	........29.1(a)
90-27, 1990-1 C.B. 50	...27.3(b)(3)(iii)
90-44, 1990-1 C.B. 54	......11.3(b)(3)(ii)(a), 11.3(b)(3)(ii)(c), 11.3(b)(3)(ii)(d), 11.3(b)(3)(ii)(e)
90-57, 1990-28 I.R.B. 7	.....8.9(b)(3)

REVENUE PROCEDURES
(References are to book sections.)

Rev. Proc.	
65-29, 1965-2 C.B. 1023	....30.3(d)(1)
69-18, 1969-2 C.B. 300	.......32.1(c)
72-13, 1972-1 C.B. 735	.......28.2(a), 28.2(b)
72-18, 1972-1 C.B. 740	........9.3(b), 9.3(b)(4), 9.3(b)(5), 10.3(b), 11.3(b)(1), 11.3(b)(2)

Rev. Proc.	
74-8, 1974-1 C.B. 419	......9.3(b)(4), 9.3(b)(5), 11.3(b)(1)
74-17, 1974-1 C.B. 438	.......28.2(a), 28.2(b)
75-16, 1975-1 C.B. 676	.......28.2(b)
77-37, 1977-2 C.B. 568	............27.3(b)(2)(iii), 27.4(b)(2)
79-14, 1979-1 C.B. 496	.27.3(b)(2)(iii)

TREASURY REGULATIONS (*Continued*)
(References are to book sections.)

Treas. Reg.	
80-55, 1980-2 C.B. 849	.....9.3(b)(4), 9.3(b)(5), 11.3(b)(1), 11.3(b)(3)(i)
81-16, 1981-1 C.B. 688	.....9.3(b)(4), 9.3(b)(5), 11.3(b)(1), 11.3(b)(3)(i)
83-11, 1983-1 C.B. 674	.......29.1(b)
83-22, 1983-1 C.B. 680	.......29.1(c), 36.2(c)
83-52, 1983-2 C.B. 569	.......29.1(c), 36.2(c)
83-55, 1983-2 C.B. 572	..33.3(a)(1)(iv)
84-22, 1984-1 C.B. 449	..33.3(a)(1)(iv)
86-3, 1986-1 C.B. 416	.29.1(c), 36.2(c)

Treas. Reg.	
86-29, 1986-1 C.B. 659	.......29.1(c), 36.2(c)
87-33, 1987-2 C.B. 402	.......16.6(d)
87-59, 1987-2 C.B. 764	..........27.2
88-44, 1988-2 C.B. 634	.......28.2(a)
89-1, 1989-1 C.B. 740	........28.2(b)
89-3, 1989-1 C.B. 761	.29.1(c), 36.2(c)
89-12, 1989-1 C.B. 798	.......28.2(b)
89-30, 1989-1 C.B. 895	.....27.3(b)(5)
89-46, 1989-2 C.B. 597	..32.1(b)(1)(ii)
90-6, 1990-1 C.B. 430	.........26.2(e)

GENERAL COUNSEL'S MEMORANDA
(References are to book sections.)

G.C.M.	
17,322, XV-2 C.B. 151	........8.4(b), 23.2(b)(3)
18,436, 1937-1 C.B. 101	...27.3(c)(2), 34.3(e)
28,274 (June 14, 1954)	.......19.9(b)
34,602 (Sept. 9, 1971)	........36.5(c)
36,132 (Jan. 8, 1975)	.........36.2(b)
37,004 (Feb. 15, 1977)	........19.9(a)
37,332 (Nov. 25, 1977)	.......19.9(e), 19.9(f)
37,848 (Feb. 5, 1979)	.........36.5(c)
38,178 (Nov. 27, 1979)	.8.4(b), 8.4(c), 8.4(d), 23.2(b)(3)
38,285 (Feb. 22, 1980)	.......18.4(c), 19.9(f)
38,311 (Mar. 19, 1980)	.......36.2(e)
38,369 (May 9, 1980)	......19.6(c)(1)
38,574 (Dec. 3, 1980)	......19.6(c)(1)
38,597 (Dec. 30, 1980)	..33.2(c)(2)(iii)

G.C.M.	
39,036 (Sept. 22, 1983)	.......19.9(b)
39,040 (Sept. 27, 1983)	.......36.2(e)
39,151 (June 17, 1983)	57
39,198 (Apr. 5, 1984)	....60.2(b)(2)(ii)
39,304 (Nov. 5, 1984)	.........8.7(d)
39,316 (July 31, 1984)	......8.9(a)(4)
39,447 (Dec. 5, 1984)	.......8.9(a)(4)
39,493 (Apr. 10, 1986)	......8.9(a)(3)
39,520 (June 16, 1986)	........24.7(f)
39,526 (July 8, 1986)	........8.9(a)(2)
39,543 (July 29, 1986)	.........31.10
39,551 (June 30, 1986)	........19.9(j)
39,570 (Nov. 28, 1986)	.8.9(f), 24.5(c)
39,584 (Oct. 10, 1986)	........36.5(c)
39,586 (June 24, 1986)	..............33.3(a)(1)(i)(a)
39,708 (Mar. 4, 1988)	.......8.9(a)(4)
39,749 (Aug. 3, 1988)	......24.9(c)(4)

INCOME TAX UNIT RULINGS
(References are to book sections.)

I.T.	I.T.
1353, I-1 C.B. 150 .... 19.3(e)	3858, 1947-2 C.B. 71 .... 19.9(e)
3721, 1945 C.B. 164 .... 17.2(a)(6), 27.3(d)	3985, 1949-2 C.B. 51 .... 17.1(a)

INTERNAL REVENUE NEWS RELEASES
(References are to book sections.)

I.R.	I.R.
IR-81-42, 10 Stand. Fed. Tax Rep. (CCH) ¶ 6552 (Apr. 9, 1981)............ .... 11.3(b)(3)(i)	IR-82-145, 10 Stand. Fed. Tax Rep. (CCH) ¶ 6851 (Dec. 16, 1982) .... 28.2(a)
IR-81-102, 10 Stand. Fed. Tax Rep. (CCH) ¶ 6750 (Sept. 3, 1981)........... .... 33.2(c)(2)(iii)	IR-83-92, 10 Stand. Fed. Tax Rep. (CCH) ¶ 6630 (June 30, 1983) .. 31.11(d)
IR-82-13, 10 Stand. Fed. Tax Rep. (CCH) ¶ 6330 (Jan. 22, 1982)........... .... 51.2	IR-86-177, 10 Stand. Fed. Tax Rep. (CCH) ¶ 6328 (Dec. 31, 1986) 9.8
	IR-87-56, 10 Stand. Fed. Tax Rep. (CCH) ¶ 6454 (Apr. 16, 1987) .... 47.2(c)
IR-82-51, 10 Stand. Fed. Tax Rep. (CCH) ¶ 6488 (Apr. 30, 1982) .... 33.3(a)(1)(vi)	IR-87-57, 10 Stand. Fed. Tax Rep. (CCH) ¶ 6455 (Apr. 16, 1987) .... 47.2(c)
	IR-88-80, 10 Stand. Fed. Tax Rep. (CCH) ¶ 6533 (May 2, 1988) ..... 47.2(e)

INTERNAL REVENUE ANNOUNCEMENTS
(References are to book sections.)

Announcement	Announcement
Announcement 86-58, 1986-17 I.R.B. 35 (Apr. 28, 1986) .... 44.1(b), 44.3	Announcement 88-13, 1988-3 I.R.B. 53 (Jan. 19, 1988) .... 8.9(a)
Announcement 86-92, 1986-32 I.R.B. 46 (Aug. 11, 1986) .... 31.7(a)	Announcement 88-18, 1988-5 I.R.B. 29 (Feb. 1, 1988) .... 36.8(j)(5)
Announcement 87-4, 1987-3 I.R.B. 17 (Jan. 20, 1987) 9.8, 25.5	Announcement 88-77, 1988-20 I.R.B. 48 (May 16, 1988) 60.1
Announcement 87-17, 1987-10 I.R.B. 26 (Mar. 9, 1987) 24.10	Announcement 88-83, 1988-21 I.R.B. 32 (May 23, 1988) .... 36.8(j)(5)
Announcement 88-6, 1988-3 I.R.B. 52 (Jan. 19, 1988) .... 13.3, 14.5(b)(2)	Announcement 88-118, 1988-38 I.R.B. 25 (Sept. 19, 1988) .... 28.2(a)
Announcement 88-10, 1988-3 I.R.B. 53 (Jan. 19, 1988) .... 8.9(c)	Announcement 91-20, 1991-7 I.R.B. 31 (Feb. 19, 1991) 13.3

INTERNAL REVENUE NOTICES
(References are to book sections.)

Notice	
Notice 86-8, 1986-1 C.B. 393 (June 12, 1986)	27.4(b)
Notice 87-4, 1987-1 C.B. 416 (Jan. 19, 1987)	60.2(g)(1), 60.5(a)
Notice 87-6, 1987-1 C.B. 417 (Jan. 20, 1987)	59.1
Notice 87-11, 1987-1 C.B. 423 (Jan. 26, 1987)	23.3(b), 23.3(f), 23.3(f)(1), 23.3(f)(2), 23.3(f)(3), 23.3(f)(4), 23.3(f)(5), 23.3(g), 60.2(c)(2)
Notice 87-41, 1987-1 C.B. 500 (June 15, 1987)	36.8(c)(1)(iv), 36.8(d)(1)(i)
Notice 87-67, 1987-2 C.B. 377 (Oct. 5, 1987)	36.8(c)(1)(iv)
Notice 87-76, 1987-2 C.B. 384 (Nov. 30, 1987)	22.4
Notice 88-4, 1988-1 C.B. 474 (Jan. 11, 1988)	8.9(b)(1), 8.9(b)(2)
Notice 88-19, 1988-1 C.B. 486 (Feb. 4, 1988)	8.9
Notice 88-20, 1988-1 C.B. 487 (Feb. 29, 1988)	28.4(g)(1)
Notice 88-23, 1988-1 C.B. 490 (Mar. 7, 1988)	22.4
Notice 88-37, 1988-1 C.B. 522 (Apr. 11, 1988)	28.4(g)(1)
Notice 88-67, 1988-1 C.B. 555 (June 20, 1988)	27.3(c)(2)
Notice 88-75, 1988-2 C.B. 368 (July 4, 1988)	28.4(b)(3), 28.4(c), 28.4(c)(1), 28.4(c)(4), 28.4(c)(5), 28.4(c)(5)(i), 28.4(c)(5)(ii), 28.4(c)(6)(i), 28.4(c)(6)(ii), 28.4(c)(6)(iii), 28.4(c)(6)(iii)(a), 28.4(c)(6)(iii)(b), 28.4(g)(1), 28.4(h)
Notice 88-78, 1988-2 C.B. 394 (July 11, 1988)	22.4
Notice 88-86, 1988-2 C.B. 401 (Aug. 22, 1988)	22.4
Notice 88-88, 1988-2 C.B. 412 (Aug. 22, 1988)	8.9(c), 9.1(d)
Notice 88-89, 1988-2 C.B. 413 (Aug. 22, 1988)	13.4
Notice 88-92, 1988-2 C.B. 416 (Aug. 22, 1988)	22.4
Notice 88-96, 1988-2 C.B. 420 (Aug. 11, 1988)	8.9
Notice 88-99, 1988-2 C.B. 422 (Sept. 6, 1988)	22.4
Notice 88-104, 1988-2 C.B. 443 (Sept. 19, 1988)	22.4
Notice 88-124, 1988-2 C.B. 534 (Dec. 2, 1988)	59.2(i)(4), 59.2(i)(4)(i), 59.2(j), 59.2(j)(4)
Notice 89-21, 1989-1 C.B. 651 (Feb. 9, 1989)	60.2(a), 60.2(b)(1)(ii), 60.2(b)(2)(i)(c), 60.2(b)(2)(ii), 60.2(c)(5)(i), 60.2(d)(1)(ii), 60.2(d)(2)(ii), 60.2(e)(1), 60.2(e)(3), 60.2(f), 60.3(a)(1)(i), 60.3(a)(3)(i), 60.3(a)(4), 60.3(b), 60.6
Notice 89-72, 1989-1 C.B. 738 (June 26, 1989)	36.8(j)(4), 36.8(j)(5)
Notice 89-74, 1989-1 C.B. 739 (Jan. 26, 1989)	59.5(b)
Notice 89-90, 1989-2 C.B. 407 (Aug. 14, 1989)	60.2(a), 60.2(b)(2)(i)(a)(4), 60.5(a)
Notice 90-7, 1990-3 I.R.B. 5 (Jan. 16, 1990)	2.1(a)(4)(i), 32.1(b)(1)(v)(a), 32.1(b)(1)(v)(b), 32.1(b)(1)(v)(d)

TREASURY DECISIONS
(References are to book sections.)

T.D.	
7747, 1981-1 C.B. 141	...27.3(b)(2)(i)
7920, 1983-2 C.B. 69	.....27.3(b)(2)(i)
8008, 1985-1 C.B. 276	.......55.2(d), 57.4(g)
8058, 1985-2 C.B. 183	........55.2(d)
8070, 1986-1 C.B. 291	..19.2, 54, 54.1
8080, 1986-1 C.B. 371	........29.1(c), 36.2(c), 36.2(e)
8102, 1986-2 C.B. 182	......31.12(a), 31.12(c)
8110, 1987-1 C.B. 81	........31.12(a)
8111, 1987-1 C.B. 69	........31.12(a)
8137, 1987-1 C.B. 302	..........13.4
8138, 1987-1 C.B. 3	..........15.5(d)
8145, 1987-2 C.B. 47	..........9.2(h)
8163, 1987-2 C.B. 226	..........13.4
8168, 1988-1 C.B. 80	..........9.2(h)
8175, 1988-1 C.B. 191	............9.8
8180, 1988-1 C.B. 363	........8.9(b), 8.9(b)(1)
8186, 1988-1 C.B. 37	......36.8(j)(4), 36.8(j)(5)
8189, 1988-1 C.B. 24	..........9.1(d)
8197, 1988-1 C.B. 18	.........15.5(d)
8203, 1988-1 C.B. 77	........31.12(a)
8207, 1988-2 C.B. 297	....59.2(g)(3)(i)
8220, 1988-2 C.B. 292	..59.2(g)(3)(vii)
8225, 1988-2 C.B. 346	..........28.3
8248, 1989-1 C.B. 280	..........13.4
8253, 1989-1 C.B. 121	............9.8
8263, 1989-2 C.B. 145	..59.2(g)(1)(ii), 59.2(g)(3)(i)
8265, 1989-2 C.B. 160	........23.3(g)
8279, 1990-1 C.B. 151	....59.2(g)(3)(i)
8300, 1990-1 C.B. 31	.......31.12(a), 31.12(b)(4)(i), 31.12(f)
8313, 1990-44 I.R.B. 7	..33.3(a)(1)(ii)

PRIVATE LETTER RULINGS
(References are to book sections.)

LTR	
7101131330A (Jan. 13, 1971)	..22.2(c)
7107230380A (July 23, 1971)	..11.7(e)
7601140600A (Jan. 14, 1976)	..11.7(c)
7729003 (Apr. 19, 1977)	....32.1(b)(3)
7752001 (Aug. 25, 1977)	....17.3(c)(1)
7801017 (Oct. 7, 1977)	..33.3(a)(1)(v)
7816004 (Jan. 17, 1978)	.33.3(a)(1)(v)
7822005 (Feb. 22, 1978)	.............60.2(b)(2)(i)(a)(3)
7902002 (June 29, 1978)	......31.9(a)
7929061 (Apr. 19, 1979)	......33.5(a)
7948011 (Aug. 24, 1979)	......33.5(a)
8011067 (Dec. 20, 1979)	..........8.8
8037096 (June 20, 1980)	......27.3(a)
8044023 (Aug. 5, 1980)	.......28.4(h)
8104098 (Oct. 30, 1980)	......28.4(h)
8107114 (Nov. 24, 1980)	......28.4(h)
8110164 (Dec. 15, 1980)	......28.4(h)
8111056 (Dec. 16, 1980)	...24.2(b)(3)
8113068 (Dec. 31, 1980)	......29.1(e)
8142048 (July 21, 1981)	.........33.2
8210065 (Dec. 10, 1981)	......27.3(a)
8223015 (Feb. 26, 1982)	......29.1(b)
8234122 (May 27, 1982)	............33.2(c)(2)(iii)
8247025 (Aug. 18, 1982)	............33.3(a)(1)(iv)
8317017 (Jan. 21, 1983)	.33.3(a)(1)(iv)
8327008 (Mar. 28, 1983)	......19.9(j)
8331065 (May 2, 1983)	......29.1(b), 29.1(e)
8338138 (June 24, 1983)	......28.4(h)
8345007 (Aug. 5, 1983)	.33.2(c)(2)(iii)
8347040 (Aug. 22, 1983)	............33.2(c)(2)(iii)

TREASURY REGULATIONS (*Continued*)
(References are to book sections.)

Treas. Reg.	Treas. Reg.
8347043 (Aug. 22, 1983) .... 33.2(c)(2)(iii)	8621113 (Feb. 28, 1986) 24.4
8347050 (Aug. 22, 1983) .... 33.2(c)(2)(iii)	8624017 (Mar. 10, 1986) .... 9.3(b)(5)
8347058 (Aug. 25, 1983) . 33.3(a)(1)(v)	8624067 (Mar. 17, 1986) ...... 54.4(c)
8348033 (Aug. 30, 1983) 57	8625048 (Mar. 24, 1986)............ 31.6(e)(2)(ii), 37.5(a)
8406039 (Nov. 7, 1983) . 33.2(c)(2)(iii)	8625080 (Mar. 27, 1986) ...... 24.7(f)
8411017 (Dec. 7, 1983) .... 29.1(e)	8630035 (Apr. 29, 1986) 24.4
8435054 (May 29, 1984) ...... 8.4(d), 23.2(b)(3)	8637061 (June 12, 1986) .... 9.3(b)(5)
8437122 (June 18, 1984) ...... 44.1(b)	8640012 (June 30, 1986)............ 31.6(e)(2)(ii), 37.5(a)
8447010 (Aug. 9, 1984) .... 8.7(d)	8640075 (July 10, 1986) ..... 8.9(a)(2)
8503016 (Oct. 9, 1984) .... 24.7(c), 24.9(b)(2)	8713006 (Dec. 15, 1986) .... 8.9(d)
8508003 (Nov. 9, 1984)............ 60.2(b)(2)(i)(a)(3)	8713015 (Dec. 23, 1986) .... 8.9(d)
	8713025 (Dec. 24, 1986) .... 8.9(d)
	8713075 (Dec. 31, 1986) .... 8.9(d)
8517029 (Jan. 29, 1985) ...... 19.8(f), 19.9(f)	8713076 (Dec. 19, 1986) .... 8.9(d)
8519038 (Feb. 12, 1985) ...... 24.7(g)	8720014 (Feb. 11, 1987) .... 8.9(a)(2), 8.9(a)(4)
8523009 (Feb. 25, 1985) .... 27.2, 27.3(c)(6), 34.2(a), 34.4, 34.5	8721040 (Feb. 19, 1987) ..... 8.9(a)(2)
8526035 (Apr. 1, 1985) .... 44.3(a)	8722083 (Mar. 3, 1987) .... 27.4(d)(2)
8527041 (Apr. 8, 1985) .. 4.3(a), 4.3(b)	8737033 (June 15, 1987)............ 11.3(b)(3)(ii)(g)
8529095 (Apr. 25, 1985) .... 27.3(b)(3)(iii)	8741062 (Oct. 16, 1987) ...... 24.5(c)
8535010 (May 28, 1985) ...... 24.7(c), 24.9(b)(2)	8742045 (July 21, 1987) ..... 8.9(a)(2)
8548016 (Aug. 29, 1985) ..... 8.9(a)(4)	8742061 (July 23, 1987) .... 8.4(b), 23.2(b)(3)
8551025 (Sept. 23, 1985) 31.10	8744025 (Aug. 3, 1987)............ 11.3(b)(3)(ii)(g)
8610016 (Nov. 29, 1985) ..... 17.7(b), 24.9(b)(1), 27.3(b)(3)(iii)	8746045 (Nov. 19, 1987) ...... 24.5(c)
8612054 (Dec. 23, 1985) 24.3	8751046 (Sept. 23, 1987)............ 17.2(a)(2)(i)(c)
8614009 (Dec. 31, 1985) ..... 8.9(a)(2)	8753029 (Oct. 5, 1987) ...... 8.9(a)(4)
8616021 (Jan. 14, 1986) ..... 8.9(a)(3)	8806044 (Feb. 19, 1988) ...... 24.5(c)
8616066 (Jan. 22, 1986) 24.4	8810007 (Mar. 21, 1988) ...... 24.5(c)
8616079 (Jan. 24, 1986) 24.4	8810023 (Dec. 7, 1987) ...... 8.9(a)(4)
8617095 (Jan. 29, 1986) 24.4	8814041 (Jan. 11, 1988) .... 11.3(b)(3)(ii)(a)
8618065 (Feb. 7, 1986) .. 31.6(e)(2)(i), 36.2(d)	8818010 (Feb. 4, 1988) .... 23.3(f)(4), 59.2(a)(1), 59.2(b)(4), 59.2(c)(1), 60.2(c)(3)
8620016 (Feb. 7, 1986) .. 31.6(e)(2)(ii), 37.5(a)	8819068 (Feb. 17, 1988) 31.8
8621025 (Feb. 18, 1986) ...... 27.4(c)	8821018 (Feb. 23, 1988) 31.8
8621075 (Feb. 25, 1986) 24.4	8830039 (May 2, 1988) ..... 28.4(b)(3)
8621095 (Feb. 27, 1986) 24.4	8832017 (May 13, 1988) . 36.8(d)(1)(i)

TREASURY REGULATIONS (Continued)
(References are to book sections.)

Treas. Reg.	
8833042 (May 25, 1988)	57.4(g)
8837050 (June 20, 1988)	28.4(b)(3)
8847030 (Aug. 25, 1988)	57.4(g)
8849033 (Sept. 12, 1988)	36.8(d)(1)(i)
8851047 (Sept. 27, 1988)	31.2(j)
8852028 (Sept. 29, 1988)	16.2(b), 20.2(a)(2)
8906010 (Nov. 7, 1988)	24.9(c)(4)
8916009 (Jan. 13, 1989)	28.4(c)(4)
8917059 (Jan. 31, 1989)	24.2(a)
8918026 (May 9, 1989)	29.1(b), 36.2(b)
8918045 (Feb. 6, 1989)	36.2(e), 36.8(c)(1)(v), 36.8(d)(1)(iii), 36.8(d)(2)(ii)(a), 36.8(d)(2)(ii)(b), 36.8(i), 36.8(n)
8921018 (Feb. 16, 1989)	36.8(d)(1)(i)
8929030 (dated Apr. 21, 1989 and issued July 21, 1989)	36.2(e)
8938016 (June 23, 1989)	57.4(g)
8939014 (June 30, 1989)	31.6(a)
8942076 (July 26, 1989)	28.4(b)(3)
8946013 (Aug. 15, 1989)	36.8(d)(1)(i)
9016059 (Jan. 23, 1990)	28.4(b)(3), 28.4(c)(4)
9019012 (Feb. 8, 1990)	28.4(b)(3)
9019037 (Feb. 11, 1990)	28.4(b)(3)

TECHNICAL ADVICE MEMORANDA
(References are to book sections.)

TAM	
7845001 (June 29, 1978)	33.5(a)
8052023 (Sept. 25, 1980)	33.5(a)
8131008 (Apr. 4, 1981)	11.7(f)
8141035 (June 30, 1981)	8.3(c), 11.9(c)
8342005	19.9(j)
8347005 (July 25, 1983)	19.9(j)
8347006 (July 25, 1983)	19.9(j)
8350015 (Aug. 31, 1983)	19.9(j)
8422004 (Nov. 16, 1983)	19.9(j)
8422009 (Jan. 27, 1984)	19.9(j)
8426002 (Mar. 16, 1984)	19.9(j)
8451012 (Aug. 23, 1984)	33.5(a)
8538001 (June 6, 1985)	24.9(b)(3), 26.4
8538004 (May 24, 1985)	19.9(j)
8604004 (Oct. 21, 1985)	19.9(j)
8620004 (Feb. 3, 1986)	44.1
8622003 (Feb. 21, 1986)	13.5, 22.1(b)
8623003 (Feb. 11, 1986)	8.4(b), 8.4(d), 23.2(b)(4)(i), 23.2(d)(3)(i)
8641004 (June 30, 1986)	19.9(j)
8644002 (July 17, 1986)	30.3(e)(2)
8735008 (May 22, 1987)	27.2
8742005 (June 30, 1987)	44.1
8827002 (Mar. 30, 1988)	31.6(b)(1)
8828003 (Apr. 6, 1988)	24.9(b)(3), 26.4
8939001 (June 9, 1989)	27.8(a)
9024002 (Feb. 26, 1990)	30.3(e)(1)(iv)
9034002 (May 9, 1990)	27.2, 27.3(b)(2)

Table of Legislative History

COMMODITY FUTURES IMPROVEMENTS ACT OF 1989
(References are to book sections.)

H.R. 2869, 101st Cong., 1st Sess. (1989)	4.2(b)

DEFICIT REDUCTION ACT OF 1984
(References are to book sections.)

HOUSE WAYS AND MEANS COMM. REPORT, DEFICIT REDUCTION ACT OF 1984, H.R. REP. NO. 432, 98th Cong., 2d Sess., *reprinted in* 1984 U.S. CODE CONG. & ADMIN. NEWS 697	27.7, 31.2(e), 31.3(a), 33.3(a)(4), 45.2(b), 56.3
HOUSE CONFERENCE REPORT, DEFICIT REDUCTION ACT OF 1984, H.R. CONF. REP. NO. 861, 98th Cong., 2d Sess., *reprinted in* 1984 U.S. CODE CONG. & ADMIN. NEWS 1445	8.2(c), 8.3(c), 9.2(c)(2), 19.4(b), 23.2(b)(4)(i), 23.2(b)(4)(ii), 23.2(d)(2), 24.9(c), 27.3(b)(3)(iii), 31.2(e), 31.3(m)(1), 33.3(a)(4), 44.3(a), 44.4, 45.2(a), 45.2(b), 47.2(c), 47.2(d)(1), 47.2(e), 48.2(c)(2), 48.3(b)(2)(iii), 55.2(d), 56.3(d)(2), 57, 57.3, 57.3(a), 57.3(b), 57.3(c), 57.4, 58.2

STAFF OF THE JOINT COMM. ON TAXATION, 98TH CONG., 2D SESS., GENERAL EXPLANATION OF THE REVENUE PROVISIONS OF THE DEFICIT REDUCTION ACT OF 1984 (Joint Comm. Print 1984)

8.3(c), 16.6(a), 16.6(e), 17.7(a), 17.7(b), 23.2(c)(3)(i), 23.2(c)(3)(ii), 23.2(c)(3)(ii)(a), 23.2(c)(3)(iv), 23.2(d)(3)(ii), 24.1(c), 24.1(f)(2), 24.5(a), 24.9(b), 24.9(b)(1), 24.9(c)(1), 24.9(c)(2), 24.9(c)(4), 24.9(d), 31.2(d)(2)(ii), 45.3, 57, 58.2

ECONOMIC RECOVERY TAX ACT OF 1981
(References are to book sections.)

HOUSE WAYS AND MEANS COMM. REPORT, TAX INCENTIVE ACT OF 1981, H.R. REP. NO. 201, 97th Cong., 1st Sess. (1981)

23.2(b)(4)(ii), 55.1, 55.2, 55.2(f), 58.1, 58.2

SENATE FINANCE COMM. REPORT, ECONOMIC RECOVERY TAX ACT OF 1981, S. REP. NO. 144, 97th Cong., 1st Sess., *reprinted in* 1981 U.S. CODE CONG. & ADMIN. NEWS 105

12.1, 23.2(a), 23.2(d)(2), 45.3, 45.5, 47.2, 47.2(c), 48.4(a), 48.4(c), 50, 51.1, 53.1(a), 54.3, 54.4(a), 55.1, 55.2, 55.2(f), 56.7, 58.1, 58.2

SENATE CONFERENCE REPORT, ECONOMIC RECOVERY TAX ACT OF 1981, S. CONF. REP. NO. 176, 97th Cong., 1st Sess. (1981)

47.2(c)

STAFF OF THE JOINT COMM. ON TAXATION, 97TH CONG., 1ST SESS., GENERAL EXPLANATION OF ECONOMIC RECOVERY TAX ACT OF 1981 (Joint Comm. Print 1981)	8.4, 8.4(d), 23.2(a), 23.2(b)(3), 23.2(b)(4)(ii), 23.2(c)(2)(i), 23.2(c)(ii), 23.2(d)(1), 23.2(d)(2), 23.2(e)(2), 23.2(f), 44.1(a), 44.3(c)(1)(ii), 45.1, 45.2(a), 45.4(a), 45.6(a), 47.2, 47.2(c), 48.2(a), 48.3(b)(2)(i), 48.4(a), 48.4(b), 48.4(c), 49.1, 50, 51.1, 52.2, 53.1(a), 54.3, 54.4(a), 55.1, 55.2, 55.2(f), 56.1(b), 58.1, 58.2, 60.7(a)

INTERNAL REVENUE BILL OF 1921
(References are to book sections.)

HOUSE WAYS AND MEANS COMM. REPORT, INTERNAL REVENUE BILL OF 1921, H.R. REP. No. 350, 67th Cong., 1st Sess. (1921)	19.1
SENATE FINANCE COMM. REPORT, INTERNAL REVENUE BILL OF 1921, S. REP. No. 275, 67th Cong., 1st Sess. (1921)	19.1

INTERNAL REVENUE CODE OF 1939
(References are to book sections.)

S. REP. No. 648, 76th Cong., 1st Sess. (1939), 1939-2 C.B. 524	21.6

INTERNAL REVENUE CODE OF 1954
(References are to book sections.)

HOUSE WAYS AND MEANS COMM. REPORT, INTERNAL REVENUE CODE OF 1954, H.R. REP. No. 1337, 83rd Cong., 2d Sess., *reprinted in* 1954 U.S. CODE CONG. & ADMIN. NEWS 4019	30.3(b)(1)

OMNIBUS BUDGET RECONCILIATION ACT OF 1987
(References are to book sections.)

HOUSE CONFERENCE REPORT, H.R. CONF. REP. NO. 495, 100th Cong., 1st Sess., *reprinted in* 1987 U.S. CODE CONG. & ADMIN. NEWS 2313-1245 [hereinafter OBRA Conf. Rep.]	28.4(b)(3), 28.4(c), 28.4(c)(1), 28.4(c)(2), 28.4(c)(3), 28.4(c)(4), 28.4(c)(5), 28.4(c)(6), 28.4(d)(1), 28.4(d)(2)(i), 28.4(d)(2)(iii), 28.4(d)(2)(iv), 28.4(d)(2)(v), 28.4(d)(2)(vii), 28.4(e), 28.4(g)(1), 28.4(h)
HOUSE WAYS AND MEANS COMM. REPORT, H.R. REP. No. 391, 100th Cong., 1st Sess. (1987) [hereinafter H.R. REP. NO. 391]	28.4(a), 28.4(d)(1), 28.4(d)(2)(ii), 28.4(d)(2)(iv), 28.4(e), 28.4(f), 28.4(g)(1), 28.4(h)
SENATE FINANCE COMM. REPORT, S. REP. No. 76, 100th Cong., 1st Sess. (1987) [hereinafter S. REP. No. 76]	28.4(g)(1)

REVENUE ACT OF 1950
(References are to book sections.)

HOUSE WAYS AND MEANS COMM. REPORT, REVENUE ACT OF 1950, H.R. REP. No. 2319, 81st Cong., 2d Sess. (1950)	19.9(b)
SENATE FINANCE COMM. REPORT, REVENUE ACT OF 1950, S. REP. No. 2375, 81st Cong., 2d Sess., *reprinted in* 1950 U.S. CODE CONG. & ADMIN. NEWS 3053	18, 18.4(b), 19.9(d)

REVENUE ACT OF 1978
(References are to book sections.)

HOUSE WAYS AND MEANS COMM. REPORT, REVENUE ACT OF 1978, H.R. REP. No. 1445, 95th Cong., 2d Sess., *reprinted in* 1978 U.S. CODE CONG. & ADMIN. NEWS 7046	30.2(b)(3)
HOUSE CONFERENCE REPORT, REVENUE ACT OF 1978, H.R. CONF. REP. No. 1800, 95th Cong., 2d Sess., *reprinted in* 1978 U.S. CODE CONG. & ADMIN. NEWS 7198	30.2(b)(3)

REVENUE RECONCILIATION ACT OF 1989
(References are to book sections.)

HOUSE CONFERENCE REPORT, REVENUE RECONCILIATION ACT OF 1989, H.R. CONF. REP. No. 386, 101st Cong., 1st Sess. 521, *reprinted in* 1989 U.S. CODE CONG. & ADMIN. NEWS 3124 [hereinafter RRA '89 Conf. Rep.]	31.2(g)(3)(iii)
HOUSE WAYS AND MEANS COMM. REPORT, REVENUE RECONCILIATION ACT OF 1989, H.R. REP. No. 247, 101st Cong., 1st Sess. 1222, *reprinted in* 1989 U.S. CODE CONG. & ADMIN. NEWS 2692	27.2

SECONDARY MORTGAGE MARKET ENHANCEMENT ACT OF 1984
(References are to book sections.)

S. REP. No. 293, 98th Cong., 2d Sess., *reprinted in* 1984 U.S. CODE CONG. & ADMIN. NEWS 2809	7.4(a)(3)

TAX EQUITY AND FISCAL RESPONSIBILITY ACT OF 1982
(References are to book sections.)

SENATE FINANCE COMM. REPORT, TAX EQUITY AND FISCAL RESPONSIBILITY ACT OF 1982, S. REP. No. 494, 97th Cong., 2d Sess. (1982), *reprinted in* 1982 U.S. CODE CONG. & ADMIN. NEWS 781	31.6(a), 31.6(c), 31.6(c)(1), 31.6(c)(2), 31.6(c)(4)
HOUSE CONFERENCE REPORT, TAX EQUITY AND FISCAL RESPONSIBILITY ACT OF 1982, H.R. CONF. REP. No. 760, 97th Cong., 2d Sess. (1982), *reprinted in* 1982 U.S. CODE CONG. & ADMIN. NEWS 1190	31.6(c)

TAX REFORM ACT OF 1969
(References are to book sections.)

HOUSE CONFERENCE REPORT, TAX REFORM ACT OF 1969, H.R. CONF. REP. NO. 782, 91st Cong., 1st Sess., *reprinted in* 1969 U.S. CODE CONG. & ADMIN. NEWS 2392	34.3(d)
SENATE FINANCE COMM. REPORT, TAX REFORM ACT OF 1969, S. REP. No. 552, 91st Cong., 1st Sess., *reprinted in* 1969 U.S. CODE CONG. & ADMIN. NEWS 2027	34.3(d)

TAX REFORM ACT OF 1976
(References are to book sections.)

HOUSE WAYS AND MEANS COMM. REPORT, TAX REFORM ACT OF 1976, H.R. REP. No. 658, 94th Cong., 2d Sess., *reprinted in* 1976 U.S. CODE CONG. & ADMIN. NEWS 2897	23.2(c)(2)(ii)
HOUSE WAYS AND MEANS COMM. REPORT, TAX TREATMENT OF GRANTOR OF CERTAIN OPTIONS, H.R. REP. No. 1192, 94th Cong., 2d Sess. (1976), *reprinted in* 1976-3 C.B. (Vol. 3) 19	8.3(c)
SENATE FINANCE COMM. REPORT, TAX REFORM ACT OF 1976, S. REP. No. 938, 94th Cong., 2d Sess., *reprinted in* 1976 U.S. CODE CONG. & ADMIN. NEWS 3439	30.2(b)(3)
STAFF OF THE JOINT COMM. ON TAXATION, REPORT ON THE TAX REFORM ACT OF 1976, H.R. REP. No. 10612, 94th Cong., 2d Sess. (1976), *reprinted in* 1976-3 C.B. (Vol. 2) 1	11.9(c)

TAX REFORM ACT OF 1985
(References are to book sections.)

H.R. 3838, 99th Cong., 1st Sess. (1985)	33.2(c), 33.2(c)(2)(vi)(a), 33.2(c)(2)(vi)(b)

TAX REFORM ACT OF 1986
(References are to book sections.)

HOUSE WAYS AND MEANS COMM. REPORT, H.R. REP. No. 426, 99th Cong., 1st Sess. (1985) [hereinafter H.R. REP. No. 426]	24.9(d), 33.2(c)(2)(vi)(a), 33.2(c)(2)(vi)(b), 33.2(c)(2)(vi)(c), 47.2(c), 47.2(e), 59.2(g)(3)(v)
SENATE FINANCE COMM. REPORT, S. REP. No. 313, 99th Cong., 2d Sess. (1986) [hereinafter S. REP. No. 313]	9.9, 14.5(b)(2), 23.3(c), 24.8, 24.9(b), 24.9(b)(1), 24.9(d), 31.7(a), 31.7(c), 48.3(c), 48.5, 59.2(a)(1), 59.2(b)(1), 59.2(c)(1), 59.2(f)(1), 59.2(f)(3), 60.2(b)(2)(i)(a)(1)
STAFF OF THE JOINT COMM. ON TAXATION, 99TH CONG., 2D SESS., SUMMARY OF CONFERENCE AGREEMENT ON H.R. 3838 (TAX REFORM ACT OF 1986) (Joint Comm. Print 1986)	9.1(d)
STAFF OF THE JOINT COMM. ON TAXATION, 99TH CONG., 2D SESS., SUMMARY OF H.R. 3838 (TAX REFORM ACT OF 1986) AS PASSED BY THE SENATE (Joint Comm. Print 1986)	9.1(c)(6), 15.4(e)(3)

Table of Legislative History

STAFF OF THE JOINT COMM. ON TAXATION, 99TH CONG., 2D SESS., TAX REFORM BILL OF 1986, FINAL CONFERENCE COMM. DECISIONS (Joint Comm. Print 1986) [hereinafter TRA '86 Conf. Rep.]

8.10(g), 8.10(h), 8.10(i), 9.4, 9.8, 11.3(b)(3)(i), 11.3(b)(3)(ii), 11.3(b)(3)(ii)(a), 11.3(b)(3)(ii)(b), 15.4(a)(2)(i), 15.5(a)(2)(i), 17.2(a)(2)(i)(b), 22.4, 23.3(a), 23.3(b), 23.3(c), 23.3(d), 24.3, 24.10, 29.2(a), 29.2(b), 31.2(m), 31.3(i), 31.4(b), 31.6(d)(2)(i), 31.6(d)(2)(ii), 33.2(c)(1)(i), 33.2(c)(2)(vi)(b), 33.11, 36.8(a), 36.8(c), 36.8(c)(1)(i), 36.8(c)(1)(ii), 36.8(c)(1)(v), 36.8(c)(2), 36.8(d), 36.8(d)(1), 36.8(d)(1)(i), 36.8(d)(1)(iii), 36.8(d)(2)(i), 36.8(d)(2)(ii)(a), 36.8(f), 36.8(g), 36.8(j)(2), 36.8(j)(3), 36.8(m), 36.8(p), 37.3, 37.4(b), 41, 41.1(a), 41.1(a)(3), 41.1(b), 41.2(c), 41.2(d), 41.2(e), 41.2(g)(2), 41.2(g)(4), 41.2(h), 41.2(i), 41.3(a), 47.2(c), 53.1(b), 56.3(d)(1), 59.1, 59.2(a)(1), 59.2(a)(3), 59.2(b)(1), 59.2(e), 59.2(f)(3), 59.2(g)(1), 59.2(g)(1)(iii), 59.2(g)(2), 59.2(g)(3)(v), 59.2(h), 59.2(i)(2), 59.5(b), 59.7

STAFF OF THE JOINT COMM. ON TAXATION, 99TH CONG., 2D SESS., GENERAL EXPLANATION OF THE TAX REFORM ACT OF 1986 (Joint Comm. Print 1986) [hereinafter General Explanation of TRA '86]	7.2(g), 36.8(a), 36.8(c)(1)(i), 36.8(c)(1)(v), 36.8(c)(2), 36.8(d)(1)(iii), 36.8(m), 36.8(o), 60.2(b)(2)(i)(a)(1)

TECHNICAL AND MISCELLANEOUS REVENUE ACT OF 1988
(References are to book sections.)

HOUSE CONFERENCE REPORT, H.R. CONF. REP. NO. 1104, 100th Cong., 2d Sess., *reprinted in* 1988 U.S. CODE CONG. & ADMIN. NEWS 5048 [hereinafter TMRA '88 Conf. Rep.]	57.7, 59.2(a)(1)
SENATE FINANCE COMM. REPORT, S. REP. NO. 445, 100th Cong., 2d Sess., *reprinted in* 1988 U.S. CODE CONG. & ADMIN. NEWS 4515 [hereinafter S. REP. No. 445]	28.4(d)(2)(v), 28.4(f), 36.8(c)(1)(vi)
HOUSE WAYS AND MEANS COMM. REPORT, H.R. REP. No. 795, 100th Cong., 2d Sess. (1988)	36.8(c)(1)(vi)

TECHNICAL CORRECTIONS ACT OF 1982
(References are to book sections.)

HOUSE WAYS AND MEANS COMM. REPORT, TECHNICAL CORRECTIONS ACT OF 1982, H.R. REP. No. 794, 97th Cong., 2d Sess. (1982)	23.2(c)(3)(i), 42.1(a), 44.2(a), 45.5
SENATE FINANCE COMM. REPORT, TECHNICAL CORRECTIONS ACT OF 1982, S. REP. No. 592, 97th Cong., 2d Sess., *reprinted in* 1982 U.S. CODE CONG. & ADMIN. NEWS 4149	23.2(c)(3)(i), 42.1(a), 44.2(a), 45.5, 45.6(c), 48.5, 55.2(b), 57.2(c)
HOUSE CONFERENCE REPORT, TECHNICAL CORRECTIONS ACT OF 1982, H.R. CONF. REP. No. 986, 97th Cong., 2d Sess., *reprinted in* 1982 U.S. CODE CONG. & ADMIN. NEWS 4203	44.2(a)

TECHNICAL CORRECTIONS BILL OF 1988
(References are to book sections.)

H.R. 4333, 100th Cong., 2d Sess. (1988)	28.4(f)
S. 2238, 100th Cong., 2d Sess. (1988)	28.4(f)

REGULATION OF GOVERNMENT SECURITIES
(References are to book sections.)

REPORT OF THE JOINT TREASURY-SEC-FEDERAL RESERVE STUDY OF THE GOVERNMENT-RELATED SECURITIES MARKETS, 96TH CONG., 2D SESS. (Comm. Print 1980)	2.2(b)
HOUSE COMM. ON ENERGY AND COMMERCE, GOVERNMENT SECURITIES ACT OF 1985, H.R. REP. No. 258, 99th Cong., 1st Sess. (1985)	2.1(a)(1)
Regulating Government Securities Dealers: Hearings Before the Subcomm. on Telecommunications, Consumer Protection and Finance of the Comm. on Energy and Commerce of the U.S. House of Representatives, 99th Cong., 1st Sess. (1985)	2
H.R. 2032, 99th Cong., 1st Sess. (1985)	2
S. 936, 99th Cong., 1st Sess. (1985)	2
S. REP. No. 426, 99th Cong., 2d Sess. (1986)	2

SPECIAL REPORTS, STUDIES, AND LEGISLATION
(References are to book sections.)

SENATE COMM. ON AGRICULTURE AND FORESTRY, TRADING IN ONION FUTURES—PROHIBITION, S. REP. No. 1631, 85th Cong., 2d Sess., *reprinted in* 1958 U.S. CODE CONG. & ADMIN. NEWS 4210	4.1(a)
REPORT OF THE SPECIAL STUDY OF THE SECURITIES MARKETS OF THE SECURITIES AND EXCHANGE COMMISSION, H.R. Doc. No. 95, Pt. 2, 88th Cong., 1st Sess. (1963) [hereinafter Special Securities Study]	1.2(a), 1.2(b), 7.3(b)(1), 7.3(b)(2), 8.2(a), 8.3(b)
SENATE FINANCE COMM. REPORT, INTERNAL REVENUE CODE OF 1954, NONMEMBER TELEPHONE COMPANIES—INCOME, S. REP. No. 762, 95th Cong., 2d Sess., *reprinted in* 1978 U.S. CODE CONG. & ADMIN. NEWS 1286	26.1, 26.2, 26.2(f), 31.11(b)(1)
REPORT OF THE SPECIAL STUDY OF THE OPTIONS MARKETS TO THE SECURITIES AND EXCHANGE COMMISSION, 96TH CONG., 1ST SESS. (Comm. Print 1978) [hereinafter Special Options Study]	5.1, 5.3(a), 5.4(a), 5.4(e)(1), 5.4(e)(3), 8.3(c), 30.1(f)

Commodity Tax Straddles: Hearing on S. 626 Before the Subcomm. on Taxation and Debt Management and the Subcomm. on Energy and Agricultural Taxation of the Senate Comm. on Finance, 97th Cong., 1st Sess. (1981)	47.1, 56.6
S. 981, 99th Cong., 1st Sess. (1981)	33.2(c)
S. 2062, 98th Cong., 1st Sess. (1983)	56.6
JOINT COMM. ON TAXATION, 98TH CONG., 1ST SESS., DESCRIPTION OF S. 1822 (RELATING TO TRUSTS FOR INVESTMENTS IN MORTGAGES) (Joint Comm. Print 1983) [hereinafter Joint Comm. Description of S. 1822]	36.8(b)
STAFF OF THE JOINT COMM. ON TAXATION, 98TH CONG., 1ST SESS., BACKGROUND ON TAX SHELTERS, in *Abusive Tax Shelters: Hearing Before the Subcomm. on Oversight of the Internal Revenue Service of the Senate Comm. on Finance*, 98th Cong., 1st Sess. (1983)	30.2(a)
STAFF OF SENATE COMM. ON FINANCE, 98TH CONG., 2D SESS., PRELIMINARY REPORT ON THE REFORM AND SIMPLIFICATION OF THE INCOME TAXATION OF CORPORATIONS (Comm. Print 1983)	29.2(b)
STAFF OF THE BOARD OF GOVERNORS OF THE FEDERAL RESERVE SYSTEM, A REVIEW AND EVALUATION OF FEDERAL MARGIN REGULATIONS (1984) [hereinafter FRB Margin Study]	1.4(b)(3), 1.4(b)(4), 4.4(b), 4.4(b)(1), 4.4(b)(1)(i), 7.4(b)(1)
S. 1959, 99th Cong., 1st Sess., 131 CONG. REC. 36,864-70 (1985)	36.8(b)
S. 1978, 99th Cong., 1st Sess., 131 CONG. REC. 17,984-86 (1985)	36.8(b)
H.R. 1767, 99th Cong., 1st Sess. (1985)	33.2(c)
H.R. 2551, 99th Cong., 1st Sess. (1985)	33.2(c)
H.R. 3092, 99th Cong., 1st Sess. (1985)	33.2(c)
STAFF OF THE JOINT COMM. ON TAXATION, DESCRIPTION OF BILLS RELATING TO THE TAX TREATMENT OF MORTGAGE RELATED SECURITIES (S. 1959 AND S. 1978) AND ENVIRONMENTAL ZONES (S. 1839) (JCS-3-86) Jan. 30, 1986, *reprinted in* Daily Tax Rep. (BNA) No. 21, at J-1 (Jan. 31, 1986)	36.8(b)
H.R. 5215, 100th Cong., 2d Sess. (1988)	33.2(c)
H.R. 157, 101st Cong., 1st Sess. (1989)	33.2(c)

HOUSE WAYS AND MEANS COMM., 101ST CONG., 2D   33.1
SESS., OVERVIEW OF THE FEDERAL TAX SYSTEM,
(Comm. Print 1990), *reprinted in Special
Supplement,* 17 DAILY TAX HIGHLIGHTS &
DOCUMENTS S1 (1990)

HOUSE WAYS AND MEANS COMM., 101ST CONG., 2D   33.3(a)(1)(vi)
SESS., WRITTEN PROPOSALS ON TAX SIMPLIFICATION
(Comm. Print 1990), *reprinted in* 17 DAILY TAX
HIGHLIGHTS & DOCUMENTS 2871 (1990)

Index

(References are to book sections.)

A

ABCZ structure, *see* Collateralized mortgage obligations (CMOs), ABCZ structure
ACC, *see* AMEX Commodities Corporation (ACC)
Account equity, 4.4(b)(1)(ii)
Accounting method(s):
  accrual basis, 9.2(a), 10.2(a), 11.5, 14.5(a), 14.5(c), 17.2(a)(2)(i)(e), 21.7, 22.1(a), 22.3, 23.3(g)(2)(v), 24.7(a), 25.1, 29.1(a), 31.2(d), 59.2(g)(3)(vi), 60.2(b)(2)(i)(b), 60.4(a)(2), 60.4(c)
    decedents:
      amortizable bond premium, 31.4(a)(1)(ii)
      debt securities, 31.4(a)(1)(ii)
      futures commission merchants, 22.1(b)
      futures contracts, 22.1(b)
  accuracy, 22.3
  cash basis:
    decedents:
      amortizable bond premium, 31.4(a)(1)(ii)
      debt securities, 31.4(a)(1)(ii)
      interest, 31.4(a)(1)(ii)
    expenses, 14.5(c), 31.2(c), 31.2(d), 31.3(f)
    generally, 2.1(a)(4)(i), 10.2(a), 11.5, 14.5(a), 14.5(b), 17.1(b), 17.2(a)(2)(i)(e), 22.1(a), 23.3(g)(3), 24.7(a), 25.2, 29.1(a), 48.3(b)(2)(iii), 59.2(g)(3)(vi), 60.2(b)(2)(i)(b), 60.4(c)
    hedge gain or loss, 23.3(g)(3)
    income, 14.5(a)
    interest expenses, 9.2
    interest income, 25.2
  clearly reflects income, 22.1(a), 22.1(c), 22.3, 23.2(f), 57.4(a), 60.2(b)(1)(ii), 60.2(b)(2)(ii), 60.2(c)(5)(iv), 60.3(a)(1)(i)
  "clearly," defined, 22.3
  commodities, 20.1, 47.2(e)
  commodities actually on hand, 22.1(b)
  dealers, 11.5, 22.1(a)
    mark-to-market method, 59.6, 60.6
  discount accrual, change in accounting method, 31.2(d)
  financial products, 60.1
  first-in, first-out (FIFO), 19.9(g), 20.1, 20.2(b), 20.2(d), 20.2(f), 22.2(b), 47.2(e)
  functional currency rules, 23.3(a), 59.2(g)
  impermissible method of accounting, 60.2(b)(1)(ii)
  last-in, first-out (LIFO), 22.2(b)
  mark-to-market method, 22.1(d), 59.6, 60.6
  multiple trade or business, 22.1(a)
  nonfunctional currency-denominated financial products, 59.6, 60.6

I-1

Index

Accounting method(s) (*Continued*)
  notional principal contracts, 22.1(d), 60.1, 60.2(b)(1)(ii)
  regular interests, REMICs, 41.1(a), 41.1(a)(1)
  REMIC regular interests, 41.1(a), 41.1(a)(1)
  standard accounting practices, federal regulatory agencies, 23.2(d)(2)
  swaps, 22.1(d)
Accreting bond, 2.1(b)(4)
Accrual basis, *see* Accounting methods, accrual basis
Accrual basis taxpayer, *see* Accounting methods, accrual basis
Accrual bond, 2.1(b)(4)
Acquisition date, 11.3(b)(3)(ii)(a)
ACRNs, *see* Convertible debt securities, adjustable rate convertible notes (ACRNs); *see also* Stock, adjustable rate convertible notes (ACRNs)
Active interests, 23.2(c)(2)(iii), 45.2(c)
Actively traded property:
  asset-backed securities, 7.3(b)(1)
  foreign currency, 48.2(a)
  hedging, 23.1
  interest in property, 48.3(a)
  interests in personal property as positions, 48.2(a)
  not generally thought of as actively traded, 48.2(a)
  options, 48.4(b)
  personal property, 48.2, 48.3(a), 60.1, 60.2(b)(1), 60.2(b)(1)(iii), 60.2(b)(2), 60.2(d)(1), 60.4(e), 60.7, 60.7(a)
  securities, 1.2(a)
Actual rate of return, 16.6(b)
Add-on minimum tax, corporate, 15.5(c)
  tax method, 15.5(c)
  tax rate, 15.5(a)(2)
Adjustable rate convertible notes (ACRNs), *see* Convertible debt securities, adjustable rate convertible notes (ACRNs); *see also* Stock, adjustable rate convertible notes (ACRNs)
Adjustable rate mortgages (ARMs), 2.1(b)(2); *see also* Asset-backed securities
Adjustable rate preferred stock (ARPS), 1.1(g)(3), 27.3(b)(3)(ii)
ADRs, 1.1(f)

Affiliated groups, *see* Corporations, affiliated groups
Agency securities, *see* Federal agency securities
Agents, Part Two, 8.3, 8.5, 13, 29.1(a), 36.2(a) remarketing, 1.1(g)(3)
Alphabet stock, 1.1(g)(9), 27.3(a)
Alternative minimum tax:
  corporate, 9.8, 15.5(d), 33.7
    adjusted book income, 27.3(b)(3)
    adjustments, prevent exclusion or duplication, 15.5(d)
    annualization method, computing estimated taxes, 15.5(d)
    book income preference, 15.5(d)
    calculation, 15.5(d)
    earnings and profits preference, 15.5(d)
    pre-tax book income, 15.5(d)
    stated rate of return, 16.6(b)
    tax preference, 15.5(c), 15.5(d)
  municipal securities, 3.1, 25.4(c), 33.1, 33.2(b), 33.7
  noncorporate, 15.4(a)(2)(ii), 31.11(c), 33.6, 33.7
  preferred stock, 27.3(b)(3)
  REIT, 33.7
  REMIC, 33.7
  repurchase transactions, 31.11(c)
  RIC, 33.7
  S corporation, 33.7
American depository receipts (ADRs), 1.1(f)
American Express Company, *see* Preferred stock, American Express Company, dutch-auction rate preferred
American Stock Exchange (AMEX), 1.3(d), 5.2(a)(4), 29.3(b)(1)
American-style options, 5.1, 5.2(a)(3), 6.2(d)
American Telephone & Telegraph, divestiture, *see* When-issued securities, American Telephone & Telegraph, divestiture
Americus trust(s):
  AMEX trading, 29.3(b)(1)
  arbitrage opportunity, 29.3(a)
  classification, 29.3(b)(1)
  intercorporate dividends received deduction, 29.3(b)(2)
  investment trust, grandfathered, 29.3(b)(1), 29.3(b)(2)
  IRS ruling, 29.3(b)(2)

PRIME unit, 29.3(a), 29.3(b)(2)
recombined units, 29.3(b)(2)
SCORE unit, 29.3(a), 29.3(b)(2)
tax considerations, 29.3(b)
tax issues, 29.3(b)(2)
termination of trust, 29.3(b)(2)
trust structure, 29.3(a)
26 corporate "blue-chip" stock issues, 29.3
AMEX, *see* American Stock Exchange (AMEX)
AMEX Commodities Corporation (ACC), 5.2(b)
AMEX Institutional Index, *see* Indexes
Amnesty provisions, DRA, Section 108, 30.2, 47.2, 47.2(c), 58.1
Amount realized, 14.3, 21.3
Amount recognized, 14.4, 21.4
Anti-abuse rule, 60.2(c)(5)(iv)
Applicable high yield discount obligation(s):
  bifurcation, 31.2(g)(2)
  effective date, 31.2(g)(5)
  exceptions, 31.2(g)(5)
  generally, 31.2(g)(2)
  nondeductible return on equity, portion, 31.2(g)(3)(i)
  PIK bonds, 31.2(g)(1), 31.2(g)(2)(i)
  RRA '89 provisions, 31.2(g)(1)
  significant OID:
    accrual period, 31.2(g)(2)(ii)(a)
    calculation, 31.2(g)(2)(ii)(b)
    defined, 31.2(g)(2)(ii)
  taxation of issuers, 31.2(g)(3)
    earnings and profits, 31.2(g)(3)(ii)
    OID, 31.2(g)(3)(i)
    S corporations, exempt, 31.2(g)(3)(iii)
Applicable stock price, 56.3(b)
Arbitrage:
  arbitrageurs, 8.7
    securities arbitrageurs, *see* Securities arbitrageurs
  bonds, 3.1, 25.4(a), 33.3(a)(1)(vi)
  certificates, 33.3(a)(1)(vi)
  commodities futures, arbitrage transactions, 18.4(e)(4), 18.10
  discounting, 5.4(e)(1)
  dividend arbitrage, 5.4(e)(2)
  in general, 8.7(a)
  intermarket arbitrage, 8.7
  intramarket arbitrage, 8.7
  of not substantially identical securities, 18.10(c)

operations in stocks or securities, 18.4(e)(4)
options:
  arbitrage transactions, 5.4(e), 30.3(d)(2)
  box spreads, 5.4(e)(4), 30.3(d)(3)
  conversions, 5.4(e)(3), 30.3(d)(2)
  discounting, 5.4(e)(1)
  dividend arbitrage, 5.4(e)(2)
  put and call arbitrage, 5.4(e)(1)
  reverse conversions, 5.4(e)(3), 30.3(d)(2)
opportunities, 6.2(b)(1)
put and call arbitrage, 5.4(e)(1)
risk arbitrage, 8.7, 8.7(c)
  block positioning, 8.7(c)
  confidential treatment, security positions, 8.7(c)
  defined, SEC, 8.7(c)
  Form 13F procedures for confidential treatment, 8.7(c)
  market for target shareholders, 8.7(c)
  net capital rule, 11.9(c)
  occurrences, 8.7(c)
  pro rata rules revised, 8.7(c)
  public investors, 8.7(c)
  Rule 10b-13, 8.7(c)
  Rule 14d-8, 8.7(c)
  Rule 16e-1, 8.7(b)
securities arbitrage transactions, defined by SEC, 18.10
  classical securities arbitrage, 8.7(b)
  exemptions as securities dealers, 8.7(b)
  holding period, 18.10(a)
  merger plans, 18.10(c)
  modified short sales rule, 18.10
  property not substantially identical, 18.10(c)
  Regulation T, 8.7(b)
  Regulation U, 8.7(b)
  Rule 16e-1 exemption, 8.7(b)
  short sale, deemed, 18.10(b)
  short sales rule, 18.10(c)
  substantially identical property, 18.10
tax considerations, 8.7(d)
  broker-dealers, 8.7(d)
  merchandising function, 8.7(d)
techniques, 5.4(e)
Arbitrageurs, 8.7
  securities arbitrageurs, *see* Securities arbitrageurs

Index

ARPS, 1.1(g)(3), 27.3(b)(3)(ii)
As of trades, 4.5(b)
Asset-backed securities:
 adjustable rate mortgages (ARMs), 2.1(b)(2), 7.2(c)(1)
 aircraft loans and leases, 7.1
 antifraud provisions of Securities Exchange Act, 7.6(b)
 asset-collateralized securities, 1.1(e)
 asset test, 36.8(d)
 automobile loans and leases, 7.1
 automobile receivables:
  CARS, Salomon Brothers, Inc., 7.2(c)(1)
  GMAC certificates, 7.2(c)(4)
  pass-through certificates, 7.2(c)(4)
  pay-through bonds, 7.2(d)(10)
  prepayment rates, 7.2(d)(4)
 cash flow bonds, 1.1(e), 2.1(b)(4)
 cash flow investments, 36.8(d)(2)(i)
 cash flow shortfalls, 7.2(c)(1)
 certificated mortgage-backed securities, 7.5(b)
 clearance and settlement, 7.5
 collateralized debt securities, 1.1(e), 7.2(a)
 collateralized mortgage obligations (CMOs), see Collateralized mortgage obligations (CMOs)
 collateralized mortgage securities (CMSs), see Collateralized mortgage obligations (CMOs)
 corporation electing REMIC status, 7.3(b)(1)
 corporations, equity interests, pay-throughs, 39.1
 credit card receivables:
  CARDS, Salomon Brothers, Inc., 7.2(c)(1)
  pass-through certificate, 7.2(c)(5)
  pay-through bonds, 7.2(d)(11)
 credit enhancements, see Credit enhancements
 credit ratings, 7.1(b)
 credit regulation, 7.4
  after distribution, 7.4(b)
  during distribution, 7.4(a)
  good faith margin, defined, 7.4(b)(3)
 "Dean Witter regulations," 36.2(c)
 direct investment standard, examples, 36.2(c)
 entities issuing pay-through bonds, equity interests, 1.1(e), 7.2(e), 36.4
 entities pooling asset-backed securities, 36
 equipment loans and leases, 7.1
 equity interests, corporations, 39.1
 equity interests, owner trusts, 39.2
 excess inclusions, taxed to residual interest holders, 41.2(g)(2)
 excess servicing transactions, 7.2(c)(2)(i)
 exchange trading, 7.3(b)(1)
 exempted securities, 7.4(b)(3)
 failure to deliver, 7.5(c)
 Farmer Mac MBSs, 2.1(b)(9)
 fast pay/slow pay bonds, 2.1(b)(4), 7.2(d)(1), 36.2(c), 36.3
 federal long-term rate, 41.2(g)(3)
 FFIEC supervisory policy statement, 7.2(c)(2)(iii)
 FHLMC/CMOs, 2.1(b)(4)
 FHLMC/MCFs, 2.1(b)(4)
 FHLMC/PCs, 2.1(b)(4), 7.2(b), 7.3(b)(2)
 financial institutions, 7.2(c)(2)(iii), 41.4
 FIRREA regulations, 7.2(c)(2)(iii)
 fixed payment bonds, 7.2(a)(1)
 fixed rate regular interests, 36.8(c)(1)(iii)
 floating rate tranches, 7.2(d)(2), 7.2(d)(8)
 FNMA/MBSs, 2.1(b)(3)
 FNMA/REMICs, 2.1(b)(3)
 FNMA/SMBSs, 2.1(b)(3)
 foreclosure properties, 36.8(d)(2)(iii)
 form over substance, 36.5(b)
 Freddie Mac Giants, 7.2(b)
 generally, 1.1(e), 1.1(g), 2.2(b), 7, 31.11(a), Part Eight
 GMAC certificates, 7.2(c)(4)
 GNMA/GPMs, 2.1(b)(2)
 GNMA/MBSs, 2.1(b)(2), 7.2(c)(1)
 government agency pass-throughs, 7.2(c)(1), 7.3(b)(2)
 graduated payment mortgages, special considerations, 37.7
 guarantee alternatives, protections, 7.1(b)
 guaranteed investment contracts, 36.8(d)(2)(i)
 home equity lines of credit, 7.1
 initial offerings, 7.3(a)
 innovation, restraints 7.1(c)
 interest only (IO) strips, 2.1(b)(4), 7.2(c)(2)(ii)
 interest rate:
  caps, 36.8(c)(1)(iv)

federal rate, 41.2(g)(3)
floors, 36.8(c)(1)(iv)
interests in REMICs, 1.1(e)
introduction, 7.1
investment companies, 7.6(d)
Investment Company Act of 1940, 7.6(d)
investment expenses, allocable, treatment of, 36.8(*l*)
investment trusts, 7.2(c)(1), 29.1, 29.1(a), Part Eight, 36.2, 36.4(b), 39.2(a)
  multiple interests prohibited, 7.2(c)(1), 36.2(c)
  nontaxable conduit, 36.2(a)
  tax qualification, 36.4(b)
  varying investments prohibited, 36.2(b)
investor interests, 36.8(c)
LBO debt obligations, 7.1
legislative proposals, pre-REMIC, 36.8(b)
liquidation period, defined, 36.8(m)
loan participations, 2.1(b)(4), 7.2(b), 36.1
loan syndications, 7.2(b)
market discount:
  calculation, 41.1(a)(3)
  pass-through certificates, 31.3(j)
  pay-through bonds, 31.3(k)
  premiums, reporting, 36.8(j)(3)
  REMIC regular interests, 31.3(*l*)
  rules, 37.4(b)
markets, types, 7.3
master limited partnership listing, 7.3(b)(1)
mortgage-backed bonds (MBBs), 7.2(a), 7.2(d)(1)
mortgage-backed securities (MBSs), 7.1(c), 7.2(c)(2)(iii), 7.2(g), 7.4(a)(2), 7.6(d)
mortgage cash flow obligations, 2.1(b)(4)
mortgage, disposition not prohibited transaction, 36.8(g)
mortgage pool provisions, taxable, 36.8
mortgage related securities:
  credit regulation, 7.4(a)(3)
  described, 2.1(b)(4), 7.4(a)(2), 7.4(b)(5), 36.8(b)
mortgages, qualified replacement, 36.8(d)(1)(iii)
multiple classes, 31.6(e)(2)(i)

multiple interests, prohibited, 7.2(c)(1), 36.2(c), 31.6(e)(2)(i)
multitranche securities, 8.11
net income from foreclosure property, taxed, 36.8(i)
New York Stock Exchange, requirements, 7.4(b)(6)
nonconvertible debt securities, registered, 7.4(b)(4)
nonmortgage asset pools, REMIC treatment, 36.8(p)
objective interest index, 36.8(c)(1)(iv)
OID, 37.4(a)
  calculation, 41.1(a)(3)
  negative, never, 41.1(a)(3)
  reporting, 36.8(j)(2)
OTC margin bonds, 7.4(b)(2), 7.4(b)(5)
other than exempted securities, 7.4(b)(2)
overcollateralization, 7.1(b), 7.2(a)
over-the-counter market, 7.3(b)(2)
owner trusts, 7.2(e), 7.2(e)(2), 36.4(b), 39.2(a), 39.2(b)
PACs, *see* planned amortization class bonds (PACs)
participation certificates, 2.1(b)(4), 7.2(b), 36.1
partnerships, 39.2(b)
  tax qualification, 36.4(b)
  tax status, 36.5(d)
pass-through certificates:
  automobile receivables, 7.2(c)(1), 7.2(c)(4)
  credit card receivables, 7.2(c)(1), 7.2(c)(5)
  debt certificates, 1.1(e), 7.2(f), 36.5, 40
    owner taxation, 40
  financial institutions considerations, 7.2(c)(2)(iii), 41.4
  generally, 1.1(e), 2.1(b)(2), 2.1(b)(3), 7.2(c)(1), 7.2(d)(2), 36.2, 58.2
  government agency pass-throughs, 7.2(c)(1), 7.3(b)(1) secondary market, 7.3(b)(2)
  interest only (IO), 2.1(b)(4), 7.2(c)(2)(ii)
  multiple classes, 31.6(e)(2)(i)
  owners, taxation, 37
  principal only (PO), 2.1(b)(4), 7.2(c)(2)(ii)
  private pass-through certificates, 7.2(c)(1)

Index

Asset-backed securities (*Continued*)
  prohibition against multiple interests, 7.2(c)(1), 31.6(e)(2)(i), 36.2(c)
  purchased at discount, 37.4
  purchased at premium, 31.4(f), 37.3
  purchased at principal amount, 37.2
  senior, 7.2(c)(3), 7.2(d)(9), 36.2(e), 37.6
  stripped:
    current law, 31.6(e)(2)
    generally, 7.2(c)(2), 7.2(c)(2)(i), 36.2(d)
    pre-July 18, 1984 law, 31.6(e)(1)
    taxation of taxpayer, owning, 31.6(e)(2)(iii), 37.5(b)
    taxation of taxpayer, stripping, 31.6(e)(2)(ii), 37.5(a)
  subordinated, 7.2(c)(3), 7.2(d)(9), 36.2(e), 37.6
  pay-through bonds:
    automobile receivables, 7.2(d)(10)
    characteristics of collateralized debt securities and pass-through certificates, 7.2(d)(1)
    collateralized mortgage obligations, 7.2(d)(2), 36.3
    credit card receivables, 7.2(d)(11)
    debt securities, structured, 36.3
    equity interests in entities issuing, 1.1(e), 7.2(e), 36.4, 39
    fast pay/slow pay bonds, 2.1(b)(4), 7.2(d)(1), 36.2(c), 36.3
    floating rate tranches, 7.2(d)(8)
    generally, 1.1(e), 1.1(g), 7.2(d), 36.3
    owners, taxation, 38
    owner trusts, issued by, 7.2(e)(2), 36.4(b)
    planned amortization class (PAC), 7.2(d)(2), 7.2(d)(5), 7.2(d)(6)
    prepayment rates, 7.2(d)(3)
    PSA model, 7.2(d)(4)
    purchased at discount, 38.4
    purchased at premium, 31.4(g), 38.3
    purchased at principal amount, 38.2
    RepublicBank Delaware, 7.2(d)(11)
    senior, 7.2(d)(9), 38.6
    special purpose corporations, issued by, 1.1(e), 7.2(e)(1), 7.2(e)(2), 36.4(a)
    stripped, 7.2(d)(7), 31.6(f), 38.5
      multiple classes, 31.6(e)(2)(i)
      prohibition against multiple interests, 31.6(e)(2)(i)
    subordinated, 7.2(d)(9), 38.6

targeted amortization class (TAC), 7.2(d)(2), 7.2(d)(6)
taxed, 37.5(a)
taxpayer owning, 37.5(b)
tax principles, generally, 38.1
permitted investments, 36.8(d)(2)
phantom income considerations, 9.1(d), 36.4(c), 39.2(c), 41.2(k)
planned amortization class bonds (PACs), 7.2(d)(2), 7.2(d)(5), 7.2(d)(6)
pooled assets, 7.1(a)
pooled property bonds, 7.2(a)(3)
potential problems, 36.8(d)(2)(ii)(b)
prepayment rates, 7.2(d)(3)
pricing considerations, 7.2(d)(4)
principal and interest payment aggregation, 37.5(b)
principal only (PO) strips, 2.1(b)(4), 7.2(c)(2)(ii)
private pass-throughs, 7.2(c)(1)
private placements, 7.3(a)(2)
prohibited transaction, defined, 36.8(g)
property specific bonds, 7.2(a)(2)
public offerings, 7.3(a)(1)
qualified periodic interest payment (QPIP), 37.4(a)
rating organizations, requirements, 7.1(b)
real estate investment trusts (REITs), *see* Real estate investment trusts (REITs)
real estate mortgage investment conduits, *see* Real estate mortgage investment conduits (REMICs)
reasonable arrangement rules, 36.8(e)
reductions, prompt and appropriate, 36.8(d)(2)(ii)(c)
REIT listing, 7.3(b)(1)
registered nonconvertible debt securities, 7.4(b)(2)
regulated investment companies (RICs), *see* Regulated investment companies (RICs)
Regulation T, 7.4
Regulation U, 7.4
reserve assets, 36.8(d)(2)(ii)
  active trading prohibited, 36.8(d)(2)(ii)(d)
reserve fund, defined, 36.8(d)(2)(ii)(a)
reserve funds, 7.1(b), 7.2(c)(3)
risk-based capital requirement, 7.2(c)(2)(iii)
restraints on innovation, 7.1(c)

sale or secured loan tax
  characterization, 36.5(c)
"Sears regulations," 36.2(c)
secondary market transactions, 7.3(b)
secured debt, varying forms, 7.2
Securities Act of 1933, 7.6(a)
Securities Exchange Act of 1934, 7.6(b)
securities law considerations, 7.6
securities sold in exempted
  transactions, 7.3(a)(3)
securities, types of:
  collateralized debt securities, 7.2(a)
  equity interests in entities issuing
    pay-through bonds, 7.2(e)
  participation certificates, 7.2(b)
  pass-through certificates, 7.2(c)
  pass-through debt certificates, 7.2(f)
  pay-through bonds, 7.2(d)
  real estate investment trusts (REITs),
    7.2(h)
  real estate mortgage investment
    trusts (REMICs), 7.2(g)
  regulated investment companies
    (RICs), 7.2(i)
securitization:
  asset classification, 7.2
  considerations, 7.1(a)
  corporate assets, 1.1(e), 7.1
  risks to investors, 7.1(b)
senior and subordinated ownership
  interests, 7.1(b)
servicing, excess, 7.2(c)(2)(i)
SMMEA, 7.4(a)(3)
special purpose corporations, 7.2(e)(1),
  36.4(a)
special purpose entities, 1.1(e), 7.2(a)
statistical rating organizations, 7.1(b)
stripped mortgage-backed securities,
  2.1(b)(3), 2.1(b)(4)
TACs, *see* targeted amortization class
  bonds (TACs)
targeted amortization class bonds
  (TACs), 7.2(d)(2), 7.2(d)(6)
taxation, *see* specific entries under
  Asset-backed securities
tax avoidance at pool level, 36.2(a)
tax treatment, general, 36
terminations, inadvertent, 36.8(f)
TIMs, 36.8(b)
TMP(s):
  defined, 7.2(g), 36.8(*o*)
  substantially identical property,
    19.9(i)

trade receivables, 7.1
trading markets, 7.3
Trust Indenture Act of 1939, 7.6(c)
types of securities, 7.2
variable rate regular interests,
  36.8(c)(1)(iv)
Zero coupon bonds, *see* Zero coupon
  securities, bonds
zero coupon CMOs, *see* Zero coupon
  securities, CMOs
Asset-collateralized securities, *see* Asset-
  backed securities
Asset hedges, 23.2(e)(2), 60.5(c)
Asset ownership requirements, 8.10(a),
  17.2(c)(2)
Assignee, limited partner, 28.1(c)
Assignment of income doctrine, 24.7(c)
Associated person, 8.2(c)
Associations, 28.1, 29.2, 29.1(a), 36.2
At-risk rules, 30.2(b)(3)
At-the-money options, 24.9(b)(1)
Attribution rule(s):
  general rules, 51.1
  mixed straddles, 51.4
  modified short sales rule, used to apply,
    54.4(a)
  modified wash sales rule, used to apply,
    54.3
  related parties, 51.1
  S corporations, 51.1
  section 1256 contracts, 51.3
  Straddle Rule statutory elections, 51.2
Auction rate preferred stock, 1.1(g)(3),
  27.3(b)(3)(iii)
Automobile receivable(s):
  pass-through certificates, 7.2(c)(1),
    7.2(c)(4)
  pay-through bonds, 7.2(d)(10)

B

Baby bonds, 31.2(g)(2)(i)
Backspreads, 5.4(c)(3)
Back-to-back loans, 6.2, 6.2(b)(4),
  60.2(b)(1)(i)
Backup withholding, 13.4
Bank holding companies, *see* Financial
  institutions, bank holding companies
Bankruptcy proceedings, 31.9(c)
Banks, *see* Financial institutions, banks
Banks for Cooperatives, 2.1(b), 2.1(b)(5)

Index

Basis:
  adjusted basis:
    corporate transactions, 16.4(*l*)
    generally, 11.3(b)(3)(ii)(e), 14.3, 16.1, 16.4, 21.3
    nontaxable transactions, 16.4
    paid-in surplus, 16.4(k)
    short sales, 18.6(e)(2)
    wash sales, 16.4(i), 19.3(c)
  adjustment for property received from decedent, 16.3(b)
  adjustments, 16.4, 19.3(c)
  allocation rules, 31.6
  alternative valuation date, 16.3(b)
  amortizable bond premium, 16.4(g)
  basis risk, 8.4(b)
  beneficiary's basis, 17.3(c)(5)
  bequests, 16.3(b)
  bond premium, amortizable, 31.4(a)(1)
  bulk purchase, 16.2
  capital contributions, 16.4(a)
  carry-over basis, 17.3(c)(3), 17.3(c)(4), 17.3(c)(5), 24.2(b)(7)
  changes, 17.3(a)(1)
  commission(s):
    added to cost of property, 16.5
    buying and selling, 16.5
  contingent payment right, 30.5(b)(3)
  controlled corporations, 16.4(a), 17.3(c)(3)
  corporate liquidations, 17.3(c)(3)
  corporate reorganizations, 17.3(a)(1)
  corporate shareholder's basis, 24.1(f)(2)
  corporate transactions, 16.4(*l*)
  cost basis, 16.2
  determination:
    of basis other than cost, 16.3
    of cost basis, 16.2
    of cost basis (purchase), 16.2, 16.3(b)
  distributions in excess of earnings and profits, 16.4(k)
  dividends received on stock sold, 16.4(d)
  donee's basis for loss transactions, 16.3(a)
  election by executor, 16.3(b)
  employee stock option plans, 16.3(c), 16.4(e)
  extraordinary dividends, 16.6
  gifts, 16.3(a)
  hedge transactions, 8.4(b), 23.2(a)
  inheritances, 16.3(b)
  intercorporate dividends received deduction, 16.6(a)
  modified wash sales rule, 16.4(j)
  noncash capital contribution, 16.4(a)
  nontaxable stock dividends, 16.4(b)
  nontaxable stock rights, 16.4(c)
  nontaxable transactions, 16.4
  OID securities, 16.4(f), 31.2(a)
  partner's basis, 17.3(c)(2)
  partnership interests, 33.5(a), 28.3
  pension and profit sharing plans, 16.3(c)
  qualified loan agreements, 26.2(c)
  redemptions, 16.4(*l*)
  S corporation stock, 16.4(h), 33.5(b)
  shareholder and corporate transactions, 16.4
  shareholder's stock basis, 16.4
  stepped-up basis, 16.3(a), 16.3(b), 17.3(c)(5)
  stock dividends, 16.4(b)
  stock rights:
    allocation election, 16.4(c)
    disposed of, 16.4(c)
    exercised, 16.4(c)
    expired unexercised, 16.4(c)
  subpart F income, 16.4(*l*)
  substituted basis, 16.3(a), 17.3(a)(1), 17.3(a)(2), 17.3(a)(4)
  tax basis of asset, 16.1, 17.3(a), 45.6(a)
  Treasury security exchange, 32.1(d)(1)
  valuation rules, 16.3(b)
  wash sales, 16.4(i)
BBA short forms, *see* Swaps, BBA short forms
Bearer bonds, 1.1(b), 17.2(a)(2)(i), 31.12(a)
Bear spreads, 5.4(c)(1)(ii), 5.4(c)(1)(iii), 5.4(c)(3), 30.3(d)(3)
Below market interest rules, 9.2(c)(2)
Below market loan(s):
  below market interest rules, 9.2(c)(2)
  commodities margin, 9.2(c)(2)
  compensation-related loan, 9.2(c)(2)
  exempted loans, 9.2(c)(2)
  margin, commodity futures and options prior to July 1, 1986, 9.2(c)(2)
Best efforts underwritings, 1.2(b), 8.6, 11.8(a), 27.7
Black-Scholes option valuation model, 60.3(a)(1)(i)
Board of Trade Gratuity Fund, *see* Traders, Board of Trade Gratuity Fund

Bond premium(s):
　amortizable bond premium(s):
　　amount amortizable, 31.4(a)(1)
　　as itemized deduction, 31.4(a)(1)
　　basis reduction, 16.4(g)
　　determination of, 31.4(b)
　　generally, 9.1(d), 9.4, 10.4, 31.4(a)(1), 31.4(a)(2), 31.4(a)(2)(ii)
　　on callable securities, 31.4(c)(1)
　amortization:
　　capitalized expenses, 31.4(e)
　　not required, 11.4(a)
　　premiums, 31.4, 31.4(a)(1)
　basis adjustment, 31.4(a)(1)
　callable taxable securities, 31.4(c)(1)
　callable tax-exempt securities, 31.4(c)(2)
　capitalized expenses, 31.4(e)
　constant yield method, 31.4(a)(2)
　convertible debt securities, 31.4(d), 34.2(c), 34.3(c)
　　conversion feature, 34.2(c)(2)
　　general rule, 34.2(c)(1)
　　unamortized premium at conversion, 34.2(c)(3)
　corporate income, prorated, 34.2(c)(1)
　dealers, 11.4
　　generally, 11.4(a), 31.4(a)(1)
　　tax-exempt securities, 11.4(b), 31.4(a)(2)(ii)
　decedents, special rules, 31.4(a)(1)(ii)
　de minimis exception, OID, 31.2(e)
　　market discount bonds, 31.10(b)
　　OID securities, 31.10(a)
　　tax-exempt securities, unavailable, 31.2(e)
　determination of amortizable bond premiums, 31.4(b)
　election to amortize bond premiums, 31.4(a)(1)
　expense deduction, 9.4
　foreign currency transactions, 31.7
　investment interest limitations, 9.4, 31.4(a)(2)
　investors, 9.4
　paid by issuing corporation, 31.4(d)
　pass-through certificates, 31.4(f)
　pay-through bonds, 31.4(g)
　premium runoff, municipal securities, 11.4(b)
　purchase premiums, 31.4
　redemption premiums, reasonable, 24.2(b)(5)
　redemptions, 31.10
　REMIC regular interests, 31.4(h)
　retirements, 31.10
　sales to customers, 31.4
　securities, 31.4(a)(1)
　taxable securities, 31.4(a)(1)
　tax-exempt securities, 9.4, 11.4(b), 31.4(a)(2), 31.4(a)(2)(i)
　traders, 10.4
　TRA '86 changes,
　yield-to-maturity method of amortization, 31.4(a)(1)
Bonds, *see* Asset-backed securities; Convertible debt securities; Debt securities; Federal agency securities; Government securities; Municipal securities; Treasury securities
Book-entry:
　corporate stock, 1.1(a)
　Fedwire transfers, 2.4
　FRB, *see* Federal Reserve Board (FRB), book-entry system
　GNMA securities, 2.1(b)(2)
　securities, 11.7(c), 20.2(e), 31.12(b)
　　identification requirements, 20.2(e)
　system, 2.1(a)(1), 2.1(b)(5), 2.4, 22.2(c), 25.4(d)
　transfers, 1.5, 2.4
　Treasury securities, 2.1(a)(1)
Box spreads, 5.4(e)(4), 30.2(b), 30.3(d)(3), 56.1(a), 56.3(a)
Branch profits tax:
　municipal securities, 25.4(c), 33.1, 33.2(a), 33.11
Brent oil contracts, 4.1(b), 4.3(b)
British Bankers Association (BBA) short forms, *see* Swaps, BBA short forms
Broad-based stock indexes, *see* Indexes
Brokerage accounts, 10.1(b), 19.5(c)
Broker-dealers, *see* Brokers, broker-dealers
Broker(s):
　as agents, 20.2(a)(1)(ii), 20.2(a)(2)
　backup withholding requirements, 13.4
　　"B" notices, 13.4
　　modified regulations, 13.4
　　"C" notices, 13.4
　　reportable payments, 13.4
　　temporary exemptions, 13.3
　　withholding procedures, 13.4
　　withholding triggered, 13.4
　broker-dealer(s):
　　below market interest rules, 9.2(c)(2)
　　Cheeseman rule, 11.3(b)(1)

Index

Broker(s) (*Continued*)
    credit regulation, 1.4, 7.4
    Federal Reserve Board, 1.4
    government securities, 2
    market makers, 1.2(b)
    notional principal contracts, 60.3(a)(1)(i)
    Regulation T, 1.4, 7.4
    Regulation U, 1.4, 7.4
    SEC registration, 1, 2
        brokers that represent customers, 1.2(b)
        government securities, 2
        national exchange members, 1.2(a)
        over-the-counter market makers, 1.2(b)
        securities arbitrageurs, 11.9(a)
        stock specialists, 8.3(b)
        underwriters, 1.2(b)
    securities, 11.9(c)
    stock specialists, 8.3(b)
    when-distributed securities, 1.3(g)
    when-issued securities, 1.3(f)
  commodity futures commission income, 13.5
  dealers, 8.3
  defined, 13.3, 13.4
  discrepancies, 13.2(b)
  exchange markets, 4.2(b)
  expenses, *see* Expenses, brokers
  floor brokers, 1.2(a), 4.2(b)
  futures contracts, 18.4(e)(2)
  generally, 1.3(i), 1.4, 2, Part Two, 8.5, 13, 18.4(e)(2)
  information returns, 13.3
  interest expense, 11.3(b)(1)
  introducing brokers (IBs), 4
  mistakes, 13.2(a)
  nominees, 20.2(a)(1)(ii), 20.2(a)(2)
  order errors and differences, 13.2
  over-the-counter brokers, 1.2(b), 5.1
  personal holding companies, 13.6
  reporting requirements, 13.3
    agricultural products or commodities, sales, 13.3
    Commodity Credit Corporation products, 13.3
    information return, 13.3
        certain dividends and interest, 13.3
        filed on magnetic media, 13.3
        reporting period, 13.3
        sales proceeds reported, trade date basis, 13.3, 14.5(b)
    securities broker, 11.3(b)(1)
  selling expenses, deductible, 11.1(b)
  short sales, 1.3(i), 18.4(e)(2)
  stock specialists, 8.3(b), 8.5
Building and loan associations, *see* Financial institutions, building and loan associations
Bull spreads, 5.4(c)(1)(i), 5.4(c)(1)(iii), 5.4(c)(3), 30.3(d)(3)
Business development companies:
  denied capital gain or loss on certain debt transactions, 8.8
  regulated investment companies, 8.9(a), 33.6
Business expenses, *see* Expenses, business
Butterfly spreads:
  audit issues, pre-DRA, 30.2(b)
  commission costs, 5.4(c)(1)(iii)
  explained, 5.1
  generally, 5.4(c)(1)(iii), 5.4(c)(3)
  identified straddles, 56.1(a)
  put and call option combination, 5.4(c)(1)(iii)
  qualified covered calls, 56.3(a)
Buyer's option (deferred payment) transactions, 1.3(e)
Buying hedges, 8.4(c), 8.4(c)(1), 8.4(d)

C

Calendar spreads, 5.4(c)
Callable debt securities:
  bond premiums, 31.4(c)(1)
  buy back agreements, 31.4(c)(1)
  call dates:
    multiple call dates, 31.4(c)(1)
    municipal securities, 31.4(a)(2)(ii)
  disposition, 31.10
  earlier call date, 31.4(c)(1)
  intent to call securities, 31.2(a)
  multiple call dates, 31.4(c)(1)
  put options, 31.4(c)(1)
  redemption, 31.10
  retirement, 31.10
  tax-exempt securities, bond premium, 31.4(c)(2)
Call markets, 1.2(a)
Call options, *see* Options, call options
Cancellation transactions, *see* Contract cancellation transactions
Capital asset(s):
  acquired between June 23, 1984 and December 31, 1987, 15.2, 17

actively traded personal property, 60.2(b)(1)(iii)
capital asset or property
  considerations, 11.9(b)
  collateral, used as, 11.7(a)
  computation of gain or loss, 15
  controlled corporation, transfer to, 17.3(c)(3)
  dealer investment accounts, *see* Investment accounts
  dealers, 11.7(a), 11.7(b), 18.9
  defined, 8.4, 8.4(d), 14.1, 21.1, 23.2(b)(3)
  exchange of, 14.1
  excluded from definition, 8.4(d), 9, 11.9(b), 14.1, 18.2(b)
  gain, 14.5(b)
  general principles, 14.1
  government securities, 32.1(a)(3)
  identification, 20, 20.2, 20.2(a)(1)(i), 20.2(c), 20.2(e)
  ordinary course of business, 11.9(b)
  portfolio investments, 9.3(b)
  purchased on last day of month, 17.1(b)
  records, adequate, 20.1
  sale or exchange, 14.1, 14.3, 15.1, 16.1
  section 1256 contracts, 14.2, 15.3, 17.5
  short sales, 18, 18.2(b)
  specific identification, 20.1
  tacked holding period, 17.3(c)(3)
  trade or business, 14.1
  Treasury bills, 32.1(a)(3)
Capital gain(s) and loss(es):
  after 1986, 14.5(b)(2)
  basis, *see* Basis
  before 1986, 14.5(b)(1)
  capital treatment expanded by ERTA, 58.2
  contract terminations, *see* Contract cancellation transactions
  corporate taxpayers, 15.5
    gains, 15.5(a)
    losses, 15.5(b)
  election, 59.2(b)(3)
  excess net capital losses, 15.4(b)
  foreign subsidiaries and branches, 23.2(e)(2)
  futures contracts, 15.1
  holding period requirements, 17.1, 17.2, 17.3, 17.4
  long-term and short-term transactions, 15.2
  long-term capital gains, 15.2
  losses, 15.4(b), 16.3(a)
  carried back for three years, 15.5(b), 45.4(a)
  carried forward for five years, 15.5(b)
  carry-overs of noncorporate taxpayers, 15.4(c)
  corporate taxpayers, 15.5
  joint returns, 15.4(d)
  section 1256 contract losses, 14.2, 45.4
  net adjustments to income, 31.2(d)
  net capital loss carry-back, 45.4(c)
  net long-term capital gain or loss, 15.4, 15.5, 45.4(c)
  net short-term capital gain or loss, 15.4, 15.5, 45.4(c)
  noncorporate taxpayers, 15.4
    capital gains deduction, 15.4(a)(2)(i)
    capital loss carry-backs, not applicable, 45.4(c)
    capital loss carry-overs, 15.4(c)
    gains, 15.4(a)
    losses, 15.4(b)
  nonfunctional currency transactions, 59.2(b)(3)
  sale or exchange requirement, 15.1
  section 1256 contracts, 14.1, 15.3, 45.4
  settlement date, 14.5(b)(1)
  short-term capital gain, 15.2
  termination payment, 60.2(b)(2)(ii)
Capital gains deduction, 15.4(a)(2)(ii)(a)
  repealed, 15.4(a)(2)(i)
  tax preference item, 15.4(a)(2)(ii)(a)
Capitalization of straddle interest and carrying charge(s):
  capitalization requirement, 10.2(f), 55.2(f)
  capitalized amounts reduced, 55.2(b)
  carrying charges, 55.1
  interest expenses capitalized, 48.3(b)(2)
  interest income, 55.2(b)
  market discount bonds, net direct interest deferred, 55.2(e)
  mixed straddle accounts, 57.4, 57.4(d)
  payments in lieu of dividends, 55.2(e)
  pre-ERTA expenses, 55.1
  pre-ERTA transactions, 55.1
  requirements, in general, 55.2(a)
  section 1256 contract straddles, capitalization not required, 56.7
  security loans, 26.5, 55.2(b)
  short sales expenses, 55.2(a), 55.2(c)
  statutory exemption, 55.2(f)
  straddle income:
    acquisition discount, 55.2(b)

Index

Capitalization of straddle interest and carrying charge(s) *(Continued)*
  compensating payments to lender of securities, 55.2(b)
CAPS, 1.1(g)(4), 17.7, 24.9(b), 24.9(b)(1), 27.3(b)(3)(iii), 27.3(b)(3)(vii)
Cap(s):
  hedge use:
    assignment fees, 60.3(a)(3)
    cap level, 6.3
    cash settlement option structure, 6.6(a)
    character, 60.3(a)(1)(ii)
    defined, 60.3
    gambling or wagering income analogy, 60.3(a)(2)(ii)
    generally, 6.3, 60.3(a)
    integration, 60.3(a)(1)(ii)
    interest rate, 36.8(c)(1)(iv)
    ISDA Interest Rate and Currency Exchange Agreement, 6.3
    ISDA Interest Rate Swap Agreement, 6.3
    Notice 89-21, 60.3(a)(1)(i)
    Notice 89-90, 60.2(b)(2)(i)(a)(4)
    notional principal amount, 6.3, 60.3
    notional principal contract, 60.3
    objective interest index rates, 36.8(c)(1)(iv)
    option analogy, 60.3(a)(4)
    periodic payments, 60.3(a)(2)(i)
      character, 60.3(a)(2)(ii)
      normal accounting method, 60.3(a)(2)(i)
      ordinary income, 60.3(a)(2)(ii)
    Straddle Rules, generally inapplicable, 60.3(a)(2)(i)
    termination fees, 60.3(a)(3)
    underlying property, 60.3(a)(4)
    up-front fee, 6.3, 60.3(a)(1)
      amortization, 60.3(a)(1)(i), 60.3(a)(4)
      defined, 6.1
      pricing methods, 60.3(a)(1)(i)
    variable rate debt instruments, 36.8(c)(1)(iv)
  liability hedge treatment, 60.5(b)(1)
  nonhedge use, 60.3(b)
CARDS, 7.2(c)(1), 7.2(c)(5), 7.2(d)(11)
CARS, 7.2(c)(1), 7.2(c)(4), 7.2(d)(10)
Cash accounts, 1.4(a), 5.5(a), 7.4
Cash basis, *see* Accounting methods, cash basis
Cash basis taxpayers, *see* Accounting methods, cash basis
Cash and carry transactions, 4.3(d), 42.4, 55.1, 55.2
Cash markets, 1.3(b), 2.2(a), 4, 4.2(a), 4.5(a)
Cash on delivery (COD) transactions, 1.3(c)
Cash receipts and disbursements, *see* Accounting methods, cash basis
Cash settlement contracts, 44.1(a)
Cash transactions, 1.3(b), 2.2(a), 14.5(b), 17.2(a)(5)
CATS, *see* Certificate of Accrual on Treasury Securities (CATS)
CBOE, *see* Chicago Board Options Exchange, Inc. (CBOE)
CCC, *see* Commodity Credit Corporation (CCC)
C corporations, 9.8
  hedging loss limitation, 23.2(c)(3)(ii)(b)
  passive losses, 9.8
  portfolio income, 9.8
  related parties, 23.3(g)(2)(iii)
  RICs, 8.9
CDCs, *see* Certified development companies (CDCs)
Central Bank for Cooperatives, 2.1(b)(5)
Certificated:
  beneficial interests, 1.1(i)
  corporate stock, 1.1(a)
Certificate of Accrual on Treasury Securities (CATS), 2.2(e)
Certified development companies (CDCs), 2.1(b)(10)
CFTC, *see* Commodity Futures Trading Commission (CFTC)
Cheeseman rule, 11.3(b)(1)
Chicago Board Options Exchange, Inc. (CBOE), 5.1, 5.2(a)(3), 5.2(a)(4)
Chicago Mercantile Exchange (CME), 44.3
Clearance and settlement:
  asset-backed securities, 7.5
  commodities, 4.5
    cash markets, 4.5(a)
    futures markets, 4.5(b)
  government securities, 2.4
  options, 5.6
  stock, 1.5
  Treasury securities, 2.4
Clearing banks, *see* Financial institutions, clearing banks
Clearing organization(s):

below market interest rules, 9.2(c)(2)
commodities, 4.2(b), 4.4(b)(3), 4.5(b)
Government Securities Clearing
  Corporation (GSCC), 2.4
margin requirements, 5.6
National Securities Clearing
  Corporation (NSCC), 2.4
options, 5.1, 5.2(a), 5.2(a)(2), 5.3(a),
  5.4(a)(1), 5.6
Options Clearing Corporation (OCC), 5.6
Participants Trust Company (PTC),
  2.1(b)(2)
securities, 1.5
Clear reflection of income, 22.1(a), 22.3,
  23.2(f), 60.2(b)(2)(ii)
Close of the day, 57.3(a)
Closing transaction(s):
commodities, 4.3(c)
generally, 42.1(a), 45.5
options, 5.1
CME, see Chicago Mercantile Exchange
  (CME)
CMO structure, see Collateralized
  mortgage obligations, CMO structure
CMSs, see Collateralized mortgage
  obligations (CMOs)
COD transactions, 1.3(c), 1.4(a)
Collar(s):
hedge use:
  assignment fees, 60.3(a)(3)
  character, 60.3(a)(1)(ii)
  defined, 6.5, 60.3
  economic effect of swap, 60.3,
    60.3(a)(4)
  gambling or wagering income
    analogy, 60.3(a)(2)(ii)
  generally, 6.5, 60.3(a)
  ISDA Interest Rate and Currency
    Exchange Agreement, 6.5
  ISDA Interest Rate Swap Agreement,
    6.5
  narrow band, 6.5, 60.3
  Notice 89-21, 60.3(a)(1)(i)
  Notice 89-90, 60.2(b)(2)(i)(a)(4)
  notional principal contract, 60.3
  periodic payments, 60.3(a)(2)(i)
  character, 60.3(a)(2)(ii)
  normal accounting method,
    60.3(a)(2)(i)
  ordinary income, 60.3(a)(2)(ii)
  Straddle Rules, generally inapplicable,
    60.3(a)(2)(i)
  termination fees, 60.3(a)(3)

tight collar, 60.3
up-front fee, 60.3(a)(1)
  amortization, 60.3(a)(1)(i)
  defined, 6.1
  pricing methods, 60.3(a)(1)(i)
  liability hedge treatment, 60.5(b)(1)
  nonhedge use, 60.3(b)
Collateralized debt securities:
  fixed payment bonds, 7.2(a)(1)
  generally, 1.1(e), 7.2(a), 7.2(d)(1)
  pooled property bonds, 7.2(a)(3)
  property specific bonds, 7.2(a)(2)
Collateralized mortgage obligation(s)
  (CMOs):
  ABCZ structure, 7.2(d)(2)
  accreting bond, 2.1(b)(4)
  accrual bonds, 2.1(b)(4)
  CMO structure, 7.2(d)(2)
  collateralized mortgage securities
    (CMSs), 36.8(b)
  floating rate tranches, 7.2(d)(1)
  generally, 2.1(b)(4), 7.2(d)(1), 7.2(d)(2),
    36.3, 36.8(c)(1)(i)
  pay-through bonds, see Asset-backed
    securities, pay-through bonds
  planned amortization class bonds
    (PACs), 7.2(d)(2), 7.2(d)(5), 7.2(d)(6)
  prepayment rates, 7.2(d)(3)
  pricing considerations, 7.2(d)(4)
  targeted amortization class bonds
    (TACs), 7.2(d)(2), 7.2(d)(6)
  tranches, 7.2(d)(1)
  Z bond, 2.1(b)(4), 7.2(d)(1), 7.2(d)(2)
  zero coupon CMO, 2.1(b)(4), 7.2(d)(2)
Collateralized mortgage securities
  (CMSs), see Collateralized mortgage
  obligations (CMOs)
COMEX, see Commodity Exchange, Inc.
  (COMEX)
Commercial banks, see Financial
  institutions, commercial paper
Commercial paper, see Debt securities,
  commercial paper
Commission(s):
  buying and selling costs, 8.5, 9.1(c)(1),
    16.5
  commodity futures commission income,
    13.5
  fees and, 10.1(d), 12.1
  futures contracts, half-turn, 13.5,
    22.1(b)
  futures contracts, round-turn, 11.1(c),
    12.1, 13.5

Index   I-14

Commission(s) (*Continued*)
  half-turn, futures transactions, 13.5, 22.1(b)
  noncapitalized commissions, 10.1(c)
  purchases and sales, 10.1(d)
  round-turn, futures transactions, 11.1(c), 12.1, 13.5, 22.1(b)
  selling commission(s):
    as ordinary and necessary business expenses, 11.1(b)
    reducing sales price, 16.5
Commodities:
  accounting method, futures, 20.1, 47.2(e)
  acquisition:
    pursuant to long call options position, 42.1(c)
    pursuant to long forward contract position, 42.1(b)
    pursuant to long futures contract position, 42.1(a)
    pursuant to short put options position, 42.1(d)
  board of trade, 18.4(e), 44.1
  brokerage services, 4
  cash markets, 4, 4.2(a), 4.4(a), 4.5(a)
  Central Securities Administrators Council (CSAC), 4
  clearance and settlement, 4.5
    cash markets, 4.5(a)
    futures markets, 4.5(b)
  clearing members, 4.4(b)
  clearing organization, 4.5(b)
  commodity dealers, 8.2(c), 8.3(e), 45.2(b), 47.2(c)
    dealer options, 5.2(b)
    hedged accounts, 23.2(b)(4)(ii)
    leverage transaction merchants, 4.3(e)
  commodity market(s):
    cash markets, 4, 4.2(a), 4.4(a), 4.5(a)
    commodity option market, exchange traded, 5.3(a)
    exchange markets, 4.2(b), 4.4(b), 4.5(b)
    off-exchange markets, 4.2(a)
    regulation, 4
    SEC jurisdiction, 4.1(c)
    Shad-Johnson Accord, 4.1(c), 5.2
    types of, 4.2
  commodity pool programs, 4
  commodity swaps, *see* Commodity swaps
  contract market, 4.2(b), 8.3(c)
  contract price, 4.3(c)
  daily cash settlement system, 45.1(a)
  daily mark-to-market, 4.4(b)(1), 4.4(b)(1)(ii), 4.4(b)(2), 4.4(b)(3), 4.5(b), 45.1(a)
  daily variation settlement, 4.4(b)(3)
  exchange markets, 4.2(b)
  exchange of futures for physicals, 4.3(f)
  ex-pit transactions, 4.2(b)
  financed purchases, 42.2
  forward contracts, 4, 4.1(b), 4.3(b)
    distinctions between futures, 4.3(b)
  forward rate agreements, 60.4
  futures arbitrage, 18.4(e)(4), 18.10
  futures contracts, 4, 4.3(c), 44.1
    defined, 4.1(b)
    distinctions between forwards, 4.3(b)
    mark-to-market payments, 9.2(c)(1)
    off-exchange trading, illegal, 4.1(b)
  futures market, 4.4(b)
  GNMAs, 4.1(a)
  hybrid instruments, 4.1(b)
  margin:
    below market loans, characterization as, 9.2(c)(2)
    broker-dealer, 9.2(c)(2)
    calls, 55.1
    cash market, 4.4(a)
    clearing margin, 4.4(b), 4.4(b)(3)
    clearing organization, 9.2(c)(2)
    customer margin, 4.4(b)(1)
    daily settlement, 4.4(b)(3)
    debtor–creditor relationship, 9.2(c)(2)
    deposits and credits, 4.4(b), 9.2(c)(1)
    emergency margin, 4.4(b)(3)
    FCM, 9.2(c)(2)
    forward contracts, 4.3(b), 4.4(a), 6.2(c)
    futures margin, 4.4(b), 9.2(c), 10.2(c)
    futures options, *see* Options, futures options
    initial clearing margins, 4.4(b)(3)
    initial margin, 4.3(b), 4.3(c), 4.4(b)(1), 4.4(b)(1)(i), 4.4(b)(3), 9.2(c)(2), 55.1
    long positions, 9.2(c)(1)
    maintenance margin, 4.3(b), 4.4(b)(1), 4.4(b)(1)(ii)
    margin credit, 9.2(c)(1)
    margined to the market, 4.4(b)(2)
    margining system, 4.3(c)
    margin payments, 60.4, 60.4(a)(1)
    member margin, 4.4(b)
    nonclearing member margin, 4.4(b)(2)

option-against-futures spreads, 5.5(b)
option-against-option spreads, 5.5(b)
options margin, 5.5(b), 9.2(c)(1)
original margin, 4.4(b)(1)(i), 4.4(b)(3)
performance bond, 9.2(c)(1)
prior to July 1, 1986, 9.2(c)(2)
receipt of futures margin, 9.2(c)(1)
requirements, 4.4
risk analysis program, 5.5(b)
settlement variation, 4.4(b)(3)
short positions, 9.2(c)(1)
speculative positions, 4.4(b)(1)
spot margin, 4.3(a), 4.4(a)
spreads, margin requirements, 48.4(a)
standing margin, 4.4(b)(3)
stock indexes, 4
super-margin, 4.4(b)(3)
tax-avoidance loans, 9.2(c)(2)
Treasury bills as collateral, 9.2(c)(1)
Treasury securities margin, 4.4(b)(1)(i)
unrealized gain, 9.2(c)(1)
variation deposits, 4.4(b)(3)
variation margin, 4.3(b), 4.4(b)(3), 9.2(c)(1)
variation settlement, 4.4(b)(3)
North American Securities Administrators Association (NASAA), 4
office transfers, 4.2(b)
offsetting positions, 42.3, 48.2, 48.3
off-shore commodity transactions, 55.1
on-call purchase contracts, 22.1(c)
options, *see* Options, commodity options; Options, futures options
physical commodities, 6.2(c), 10.2(e), 18.4(f), 20.2, 42, 48.2(d), 48.3(a)
pit, 4.2(b)
regulated futures contracts, 44.1
round-turn commissions, 11.1(c), 12.1
section 1256 treatment, 42.1(a), 45.1, 45.2
spot market, 4, 4.3(a), 42.1
  delivery, 4.2(a)
  transactions, 4.3(a)
spreads, 4.3(c), 4.4(b)(1)
state law, application, 4
transactions, types of, 4.3
transfer trades, 4.2(b)
types of, 4.1(a)
variation settlement, 4.4(b)(3)
Commodities amnesty provision, 30.2(b), 47.2(c), 58.1

Deficit Reduction Act (DRA) Section 108, 30.2(b), 47.2(c), 58.1
pre-ERTA straddles, 58.1
Commodity Credit Corporation (CCC):
  first handler payments, 21.7
  generally, 13.3, 21.6
  inventory protection payments, 21.7
  sales subject to broker reporting, 13.3
Commodity credit loans, 21.6
  commodity pledged as security, 21.6
  election, section 77, 21.6
  generic commodity certificates, 21.6
  income recognition, 21.6
  loans treated as income, 21.6
Commodity dealers, 8.2(c), 8.3(e)
  associated persons excluded from definition, 8.2(c)
Commodity Exchange, Inc. (COMEX), 5.2(b), 43.3
Commodity exchange memberships, 19.6(c)(3)
  self-regulatory jurisdiction over members, 4.2(b)
Commodity exchanges, 4, 4.2(b), 9.2(c)(2), 18.4(e), 30.1(a), 44.1, 58.2
Commodity futures commission income, *see* Brokers, commodity futures commission income
Commodity futures contract options, 44.3
Commodity futures traders, 8.2, 8.3(c), 54.4(a)
Commodity Futures Trading Commission (CFTC):
  Brent oil contracts, 4.1(b), 4.3(b)
  CEA enforcement, 4
  contract market designation, 4.2(b)
  forward contracts excluded from jurisdiction, 4.1(b)
  forward rate agreements, 6.7
  futures commission merchants, 4, 8.1, 22.1(b)
  generally, 1.1(g)(5), 4, 4.1, 5.5(b), 8.2(c), 44.1(b), 44.3(a)
  introducing brokers, 4
  jurisdiction, 4.1
    between SEC and CFTC, 4.1(c)
  leverage transaction regulation, 4.3(e)
  Shad-Johnson Accord, 4.1(c), 5.2
  Statement of Policy, 6.6(b)
  statutory interpretation concerning forward transactions, 4.1(b), 4.3(b)
  swap transactions, 6.6(b)

Index

Commodity options, *see* Options, commodity options
Commodity pools, publicly traded, 28.4(b)(2), 28.4(d)(2)(vii)
Commodity-product spread, 4.3(c)
Commodity swap(s):
  financial intermediations, 60.2(d)(1), 60.2(d)(1)(iii)
  forward contracts, 6.2(c)
  generally, 6.2(c), 60.2(d), 60.2(e)(2)
  hedge transactions, 60.2(d)(1)
    financial intermediations, 60.2(d)(1)(iii)
    inventories of commodities, not hedged, 60.2(d)(1)
    matched books, 60.2(d)(1), 60.2(d)(1)(iii)
    other commodity swap positions hedged, 60.2(d)(1), 60.2(d)(1)(iii)
    periodic swap payments prior to maturity, 60.2(d)(1)(i)
    spot price, 60.2(d)
    termination payments, 60.2(d)(1)(iii)
    up-front and assignment fees, 60.2(d)(1)(ii)
  nonhedge transactions, 60.2(d)(2)
    periodic swap payments, 60.2(d)(2)(i)
    termination payments, 60.2(d)(2)(ii)
    timing and amount, 60.2(d)(2)(ii)
  notional amount, 6.2(c)
  physical commodities, 6.2(c)
  positions in actively traded personal property, 60.2(d)(1)
Commodity traders, 8.2(a), 8.2(c), 8.3(e), 10.1(c)
  defined as commodity dealers, 8.3(e)
  professional commodity traders, 10.1
Common stock:
  convertible into preferred stock, 27.3(c)(3)
  defined, 1.1(a), 27.3(a)
  distributions of, 24.2(b)(4)
  dividends, 18.6(e)(2), 24.2
  equity interests, 27.1
  nonvoting, 2.1(b)(6)
  securities convertible into common stock, 1.1(d)
  short sale, 17.7(b)
  tax classification, 27.3(a)
  voting, 2.1(b)(6)
  warrants, 1.1(c)
Common trust funds, 8.9, 31.2(d)
Compensation-related loans, 9.2(c)(2)

Compound interest bonds, 2.1(b)(4)
Comptroller of the Currency, 1.1(d), 7.2(b)
  regulation of government securities brokers and dealers, 2
Condor options, 5.4(d)
Consolidated returns, *see* Corporations, consolidated returns
Constructive receipt:
  accrued interest, 25.2
  actually received, 24.7(a)
  cash basis taxpayers, 25.2
  constructively received, 24.7(a)
  dividends, 24.7(f)
  interest, 9.2(b), 25.2
  Mark-to-Market Rule, 45.1(a)
  proceeds, 17.2(a)(2)(ii)
  regulated futures contracts, 44.1
  reporting income, 24.7(f)
Contingent and adjustable preferred stock, 27.3(b)(3)(vi)
Contingent payment right(s):
  cash settlement put option, 30.5(b)
  characterization, 30.5(a)
  holder, tax consequences, 30.5(b)
  holding period, 30.5(b)(3)
  investment units, 30.5, 30.5(a)
  issuer, tax consequences, 30.5(b)
  lapse, 30.5(b)(2)
  minimum payment, 30.5(b)(2)
  OID rules, not applicable, 31.2(i)
  payment date, 30.5(b)(3)
  receipt of payment, 30.5(b)(3)
  sale, 30.5(b)(1)
  sale of stock, 30.5(b)(4)
  stock and contingent payment right owned, 30.5(b)(4)
  Straddle Rules, 30.5(b)(5)
  tax basis, stock payment, 30.5(b)(3)
Contingent promissory notes, *see* Debt securities, contingent promissory notes
Contingent takedown options, *see* Debt securities, contingent takedown options
Contract cancellation transaction(s):
  assignment of contract, 58.1
  audit issues, 58.1
  capital treatment, 58.2
  current law, 58.2
  pre-ERTA transactions, 58.1
  retirement of debt instruments, 58.2
  terminations, 58.2
  when-issued contracts, 27.3(d)

Contribution:
  partnership, 28.4(b)(3)
Controlled corporations, see Corporations, controlled corporations
Conventional options, 5.1, 5.3(b)
Conventions; deductions, 9.1(c)(10)
Conversion transactions, 5.4(e)(3), 56.1(a), 56.3(a)
Convertible adjustable preferred stocks (CAPS), 1.1(g)(4), 17.7(b), 24.9(b), 24.9(b)(1), 27.3(b)(3)(iii), 27.3(b)(3)(vii)
Convertible common stocks, 27.3(c)(3)
Convertible debt instruments, 8.9(a)(2)
Convertible debt securities:
  accrued interest on conversion, 34.2(e)
  acquisition of, 34.3(a)
  adjustable rate convertible notes (ACRNs), 27.3(c)(6), 34.4
  bond premiums, 31.4(d), 34.3(c)
  bonds, 1.1(b), 1.1(d), 25.1
  cancellation income, 34.2(d)
  change in conversion ratio or conversion price, 34.3(d)
  conversion, 56.3(a)
  conversion feature, 27.3(c)(2), 31.4(d), 34.2(b), 34.2(c)(2)
  conversion into common stock, 1.1(d), 34.3(e)
  conversion option, 1.1(d), 1.1(g)(8)
  conversion price, 1.1(d), 34.3(d)
  conversion ratio, 34.3(d)
  conversion right, exercise of, 34.2(d)
  convertible securities, 1.1(d)
  convertible subordinated debentures, noncallable, 17.2(a)(2)(i)(c)
  creditor relationship, 1.1(d)
  debentures, debt or equity evaluation, 27.2
  debt-equity exception, 34.2(d)
  debt instruments, 8.9(a)(2)
  debt subordinated or with preference, 34.2(a)
  defined, 1.1(d)
  discount convertible debt securities, 34.7
  exercise of conversion right, 34.2(d)
  exchange for stock, 34.3(e)
  floating rate convertible notes (FRCNs), 34.4
  holding period:
    intercorporate dividends received, 17.7
    tacked, 17.3(a)(3)
  issuance, 34.2(a)
  issuer:
    accrual basis interest deduction, 34.2(e)
    accrued interest, 34.2(e)
    interest paid to parent corporation of, 34.2(e)
    redemption premium, 34.2(f)
    repurchase by, 34.2(f)
    retirement premium, 34.2(f)
    tax treatment for issuing corporation, 34.2
  mandatory convertible notes, 1.1(g)(1), 34.5
  market discount, 31.3(f)
  normal call premium, 31.4(d), 34.2(f)
  offsetting positions, 48.2(c)
  original issue discount, 31.10(a), 34.2(b)
  repurchase by issuer, 34.2(f)
  stock acquired, 17.3(a)(3)
  tacked holding period, 17.3(a)(3)
  tax treatment for issuer, 34.2
  unamortized bond premium at conversion, 34.2(c)(3)
  underwriters' options, 11.8(a)
  value of conversion feature, 34.2(c)(2)
  wash sales, 19.9(a)
  tax treatment for owner, 34.3
Convertible exchangeable preferred stock, 1.1(g)(8), 27.3(b)(3)(vii)
Convertible notes, see Convertible debt securities
Convertible preferred stock, 1.1(d), 8.9(a)(2), 17.7(b), 18.2(c), 19.8(g), 27.3(b)(3)(vii), 27.3(c)(1), 27.3(c)(2), 27.3(c)(7)
Convertible securities, see Convertible stock
Convertible stock:
  common stock convertible into preferred, 27.3(b)(4)
  convertible ACRNs, 27.3(c)(6)
  convertible adjustable preferred stock (CAPS), 1.1(g)(4), 17.7, 27.3(b)(3)(vii)
  convertible debt instruments, 8.9(a)(2)
  convertible exchangeable preferred stock, 1.1(g)(8), 27.3(b)(3)(vii)
  convertible preferred stock, 1.1(d), 8.9(a)(2), 17.7, 18.2(c), 27.3(b)(3)(vii), 27.3(c)(1), 27.3(c)(2), 27.3(c)(7)
  with contingent payment right, 30.5(a)

Index

Convertible stock (*Continued*)
  defined, 1.1(d)
  dividends, 24.2
  generally, 1.1(d), 27.3(c)(1)
  holding period, tacked, 17.3(a)(3)
  intercorporate dividends received, 27.3(b)(2)
  offsetting positions, 48.2(c)
  preferred stock convertible into common stock, 27.3(c)(2)
    issued after July 20, 1988, new rules, 27.3(c)(2)
    Notice 88-67, 27.3(c)(2)
    with contingent payment right, 30.5(a)
  pure preferred, 27.3(c)(2)
  receipt in recapitalizations, 27.3(c)(8)
  stock convertible into another corporation, 27.3(c)(5)
  stock convertible into debt securities, 27.3(c)(4)
  synthetic convertibles, 8.9(a)(2)
  tacked holding period, 17.3(a)(3)
  tax considerations, 27.3(c)
  unamortized premium at conversion, 34.2(c)(3)
  underwriters' options, 11.8(a)
  wash sales, 19.9(a)
Cooperative banks, *see* Financial institutions, cooperative banks
Corn Products doctrine, 8.4, 8.4(d), 12, 23.1, 23.2(a), 23.2(b)(3), 23.2(d)(3)(i), 23.2(e), 45.2(a), 56.2, 60.4(f)
  Arkansas Best interpretation, 8.4, 8.4(d), 12, 23.2(b)(3)
Corporate bonds, 1.1(b), 25.1
Corporate securities:
  asset-backed securities, *see* Asset-backed securities
  basis, 16.4(*l*)
  cash market, 1.3(b)
  cash transactions, 1.3(b)
  clearance and settlement, 1.5
  commercial paper, 1.1(b), 1.1(g)(2)
  credit regulation, 1.4, 7.4
  debentures, 1.1(b)
  equity interests in entities issuing pay-through bonds, 7.2(e), 36.4
  initial margin requirements, 1.4(b)
  installment transaction, 1.3(h)
  liquidations, 17.3(c)(4)
  maintenance margin requirements, 1.4(b)
  margin, *see* Securities, margin
  markets, 1.2
    exchange trading, 1.2(a)
    over-the-counter, 1.2(b)
  notes, *see* Debt securities, corporate notes
  offsetting positions, 48.2(c)
  offsetting position stock, *see* Offsetting position stock
  original issue discount, *see* Original issue discount (OID)
  settlement date, 1.3
  settlement of, 1.5
  stock, *see* Stock
  trade date, 1.3
  transactions, types of, 1.3
  types, 1.1
  zero coupon securities, *see* Zero coupon securities
  see also Debt securities; Securities; Stock
Corporate takeovers, 8.7(c), 27.3(c)(7)
Corporation(s):
  affiliated corporations, defined, 27.8(b)
  affiliated group, hedging exemption, 23.2(c)(1)
  affiliated groups, 11.3(b)(3)(ii)(a), 11.3(b)(3)(ii)(f), 23.2(c)(1), 24.9(a)(2), 27.3(b)(3)
  basis, noncash capital contributions, 16.4(a)
  business development corporations, 33.6
  capital contributions, 16.4(a)
  capital gain transactions, 15.5(a)
  capital loss transactions, 15.5(b)
  C corporations, *see* C corporations
  consolidated groups, 23.2(c)(1), 51.2
  consolidated returns, 23.2(c)(1), 24.9(a)(2), 27.3(b)(3), 57.6(a)
    special purpose subsidiary, 27.3(b)(3)
  contributions to capital, 17.3(a)(4)
  controlled corporations, 16.4(a), 17.3(a)(3), 17.3(c)(3), 19.10(d)
    section 988 election, 59.2(j)(1)
    spin-off of controlled corporation, 16.4(*l*)
    transfers to controlled corporations, holding period, 17.3(c)(3)
  debt equity:
    considerations, 27.2
    equity interests in entities issuing pay-through bonds, 7.2(e), 36.4

evaluation factors, 27.2
leveraged buy out, 27.2, 34.4
ratio of debt to equity, 34.2(a)
defined, 28.1
dividend(s):
  intercorporate dividends received, *see* Intercorporate dividends received deduction
  noncash dividends, 24.1(f)(2)
domestic corporations, 24.9(a)
earnings and profits, 24.1(c), 27.3(b)(5)
foreign corporations, 24.1(f)(2)
holding period:
  contributions to capital, 17.3(a)(4)
  noncash dividends, 24.1(f)(2)
  transferred property, 17.3(a)(4)
incorporation, tax-free, 17.3(a)(4)
intercorporate dividends received, *see* Intercorporate dividends received deduction
investment units, 30.5
liquidation(s):
  corporate, 17.3(c)(4)
  corporate subsidiary, 17.3(c)(4)
  liquidating distributions, complete or partial, 18.6(c)
  liquidating dividends, 18.6(c)
  one-month liquidations, 17.3(c)(4)
  partial liquidations, 16.4(*l*)
  taxable liquidations, 17.2(a)(3)
margin accounts, 24.9(b)(3)
net operating losses, 15.5(b)
personal service corporations, 9.8
qualified business units, 59.2(g), 59.2(g)(3)
recapitalizations, *see* Reorganizations, recapitalizations
reorganizations, *see* Reorganizations
residence, 23.3(c)
S corporations, *see* S corporations
security loans, *see* Security loans
special purpose corporations, issuing asset-backed securities, 7.2(e), 36.4(a)
special purpose entities, 1.1(e), 7.2(a), 7.2(g), 27.3(b)(3)
special purpose subsidiary, 27.3(b)(3), 27.3(b)(3)(iii)
taxable liquidations, 17.2(a)(3)
taxable purchases, 17.2(a)(3)
taxable reorganizations, 17.2(a)(3)
tax-free incorporations, 17.3(a)(4)
tax preference items, 15.5(c)

see also Regulated investment companies (RICs)
Cotton industry, 22.1(c)
Coupon bonds, 1.1(b), 25.1
Covered calls, 5.4(a)(2), 5.4(a)(2)(ii), 56.3
  regulated investment company, 8.9(a)(2)
Credit card asset-backed securities:
  pass-through certificates, 7.2(c)(1), 7.2(c)(5)
  pay-through bonds, 7.2(d)(11)
Credit card receivables, *see* Asset-backed securities, credit card receivables
Credit enhancement(s):
  asset-backed securities, 7.1(b), 36.8(d)(1)(iv)
  debt securities, 1.1(g)(12)
  guarantees, 7.1(b)
  insurance policies, 7.1(b)
  letters of credit, 7.1(b)
  overcollateralization, 7.1(b), 7.2(a)
  REMICs, 36.8(n)
  statistical rating organizations, 7.1(b), 7.2(a), 27.3(b)(3)
Credit for the elderly (or disabled), 24.8, 25.3
Credit option spreads, 5.4(c)
Credit regulation:
  asset-backed securities, 7.4
    after distribution, 7.4(b)
    during distribution, 7.4(a)
  corporate securities, 1.4
  exempted securities, 7.4(b)(3)
  good faith margin, defined, 7.4(b)(3)
  government securities, 2.3
  options, 5.5(a)
  OTC margin bonds, 7.4(b)(5)
  registered nonconvertible debt securities, 7.4(b)(4)
  securities other than exempted securities, registered nonconvertible debt securities, or over-the-counter margin bonds, 7.4(b)(2)
Credit unions, *see* Financial institutions, credit unions
Current income bonds, 2.1(a)(4)(ii)
Customers, 1.2(b), 11, 11.9(b), 11.9(c), 21.1, 24.10, 25.6, 31.2(d), 31.4, 60.2(b)(2)(ii)

Index

D

Day trades, 57.3(a)
Dealer equity option(s):
  active participation in entity management, 45.2(c)
  defined, 30.1(d), 30.4, 44.4
  enterprise, 45.2(c)(2)
  entity, 45.2(c)(2)
  limited entrepreneurs, 45.2(c)
  option dealers, 8.2(b), 8.3(d)
  S corporations, 44.4
  section 1256 treatment, 44.4, 57
Dealer option(s):
  over-the-counter market, 5.2(b), 5.3(b)
  settlement, 5.6
Dealer(s):
  accounting methods, see Accounting methods, dealers
  arbitrageur, 8.7(d)
  bank dealers, municipal securities, 11.3(b)(3)
  block positioner, 8.3(c)
  bond premiums, 11.4
  brokers, 8.3
  character of assets, capital or ordinary, 11
  commodities dealers, 23.2(b)(4)(ii), 45.2(b), 47.2(c)
  dealer equity options, see Dealer equity options
  debt securities, 31.1, 31.2(c), 31.2(d), 31.4, 31.4(a)(1), 31.6(b)(1)
  determination of dealer status, 8.3(a)
  expenses, see Expenses, dealers
  factors determinative of dealer status, 8.3
  floor specialists, 1.2(a), 8.3(b)
  futures contract transactions, 11.1(c)
  government securities, 2, 8.4(c)(1)
  hedged accounts, 23.2(b)(4)(ii)
  hedgers, see Hedgers
  inventory methods, see Inventory methods, dealers
  inventory securities, 11.11, 11.12
  investment accounts, see Investment accounts, securities dealer
  investment interest limitations, 11.7(a)
  investment positions, 18.9
  investment securities, 11.7(c)
  investor, 8.1, 11.7(b)
  liability hedge treatment unavailable, 60.5(b)(1)
  market makers, see Market makers
  merchandising function, 8.3, 8.7(d), 11.7(b), 11.9(a)
  modified wash sales rule, 11.11, 54.3
  municipal securities, 11.3, 31.4(a)(2)(ii)
  nonbank dealers, 11.3(b)(3)
  notional principal contracts, 60.5(a), 60.6
  options dealer, 8.2(b), 44.4, 45.2(b), 54.4(a)
  ordinary course of business, 8.3, 11.1, 19.5(c), 21.1, 48.4(a)
  ordinary income transactions, 21.1, 21.3, 21.4, 22.1, 22.2
  personal holding companies, 11.10
  pre-ERTA option transactions, 30.2(b)
  principals, Part Two, 8.3
  professional dealers, 8.3(b)
  sales to customers, 11.9(c)
  securities dealers, see Securities dealers
  short sales of capital assets, 18.9
  short sales rule exemption, 11.12
  special provisions for, 11.4(b), 16.5
  stock specialists, 8.3(b), 11.9(c)
  stripped bonds, 31.6(b)(1)
  substantially identical property, 18.9
  swap dealers, 60.2(b)(1)(iii), 60.2(b)(2), 60.2(b)(2)(i)(a), 60.2(b)(2)(ii)
  swap intermediaries, 6.2, 60.2(b)(2)(ii)
  tax-exempt securities, 11.4(b), 16.4(*l*), 31.4(a)(2)(ii)
  trader, 8.3(d), 11.7(b)
  underlying property, dealers in, 45.2(a)
  wash sales, exemption, 11.11, 19.4, 19.5(a), 19.5(b)
Debentures, 1.1(b), 18.4(a), 25.1
Debt financed portfolio stock:
  allowable deduction, 24.9(c)(3)
  average indebtedness ratio, 24.9
  defined, 24.9(c)(1)
  intercorporate dividends received deduction, 24.9(c)
  portfolio indebtedness, defined, 24.9(c)(4)
Debt flavored preferred stock products, 27.3(b)(3)
Debt instruments, 59.2(a)(1)
Debt obligation(s):
  individuals, 31.2(d), 37.3, 37.4(a)
  natural persons, 31.2(d), 37.4(a)
Debt option(s):
  nonequity options, 44.3
  post-DRA transactions, 35.2

pre-DRA transactions, 35.1
securities, 5.2(a)(2)
Treasury securities, 5.2(a)(2)
Debt refundings, 31.9(a)
Debt securities:
accreting bonds, 2.1(b)(4)
accrual bonds, 2.1(b)(4)
actively traded, 48.4(c)
agency securities, see Federal agency securities
applicable high yield discount obligations, 31.2(g)
arbitrage bonds, 3.1, 25.4(a), 33.3(a)(1)(vi)
asset-backed securities, see Asset-backed securities
bearer bonds, 1.1(b), 17.2(a)(2)(i), 31.12(a)
bond premiums, see Bond premiums
callable debt securities, 31.10
classified as equity, 34.2(a)
collateralized, 1.1(e), 7.2(a)
commercial paper, 1.1(b), 1.1(g)(2), 1.1(g)(12), 23.2(b)(3)
compound interest bonds, 2.1(b)(4)
Comptroller of the Currency, 1.1(d)
contingent promissory notes, 1.1(g)
contingent takedown options, 1.1(g)
convertible debt securities, see Convertible debt securities
corporate bonds, 1.1(b), 25.1
  issued by insolvent corporation, 27.8(c)
corporate notes, 1.1(b), 18.4(a)
coupon bonds, 1.1(b), 25.1
credit enhancements, 1.1(g)(1); see also Credit enhancements
current income bonds, 2.1(a)(4)(ii)
debentures, 1.1(b), 18.4(a), 25.1
debt instruments, defined, 59.2(a)(1)
debt refundings, 31.9(a)
defaulted securities, see Defaulted securities
different issuers, 48.4(c)
discount notes, see Federal Home Loan Mortgage Corporation (FHLMC) (Freddie Mac) securities, discount notes
dispositions, 31.10
District of Columbia securities, 33.1
early redemption (put) options, 1.1(g)(11)
equity, classification, 34.2(a)

exchangeable debt securities, 34.6(a)
exchange(s):
  debt securities, 31.9, 31.9(a), 34.3(e)
  defeasance, in substance, 31.9(a)
  for stock, 34.3(e)
  interest adjustment waiver, 31.9(a)
exempt facility bonds, see Municipal securities
extendible debt securities, 1.1(g)(13)
fast pay/slow pay bonds, 2.1(b)(4), 7.2(d)(1), 36.2(c), 36.3
federal agency securities, see Federal agency securities
fixed payment bonds, 7.2(a)(1)
flat bonds, 31.8
flexible rate bonds, 3.3
floating rate bonds, 3.3
floating rate notes, 2.1(b)(6)
floating rate tranches, 7.2(d)(8)
flower bonds, 32.1(c)
foreign currency-denominated debt security, 59.2(b)(1)
futures characteristics, 1.1(g)(5)
general obligation bonds, see Muncipal securities
hedge bonds, 33.3(a)(1)(ix)
high yield OID securities, 31.2(g)
hybrid debt instruments, 34.4
indexed debt securities, 1.1(g)(5)
indemnity bonds, 9.1(c)(7)
industrial development bonds, see Industrial development bonds (IDBs)
installment bonds, 31.3
installment notes, 9.3(b)(1)
installment sales, 1.3(h), 17.2(a)(2)(i)(c)
issued at face value, 34.2(a)
market discount bonds, 31.3(m), 31.10(b)
mortgage-backed bonds, 7.2(a), 7.2(d)(1)
multiple tranche, 7.2(d)(1)
municipal securities, see Municipal securities
offsetting positions, 48.4(a), 48.4(c)
option characteristics, 1.1(g)(5)
options on, 35.2
original issue discount, see Original issue discount (OID)
originally issued at a discount, 31.10(a)
OTC margin bonds, 7.4(b)(2), 7.4(b)(2)
pass-through debt certificates, 7.2(f), 36.5

Index

Debt securities (*Continued*)
  payment-in-kind (PIK) bonds, 31.2(g)(1), 31.2(g)(2)(i)
  pay-through bonds, 7.2(d), 36.3
  performance bonds, 4.3(c), 9.2(c)(1)
  PERLS, 1.1(g)(6), 2.1(b)(6)
  PIK bonds, 31.2(g)(1), 31.2(g)(2)(i)
  planned amortization class bonds, 7.2(d)(2), 7.2(d)(5), 7.2(d)(6)
  pooled property bonds, 7.2(a)(3)
  portfolio exchangeables, 34.6(b)
  portfolio of, 48.4(c)
  preferred stock, 59.2(a)(1)
  premiums, *see* Bond premiums
  principal exchange rate linked securities (PERLS), 1.1(g)(6), 2.1(b)(6)
  private activity bonds, *see* Private activity bonds (PABs)
  promissory notes, 14.5(d), 25.1
  property specific bonds, 7.2(a)(2)
  put options, 1.1(g)(11)
  redemption of, 1.1(g)(13), 31.10
  refunding, 31.9(a)
  registered debt securities:
    nonconvertible, 7.4(b)(4)
    registered as to principal and stated interest, 25.4(d)
    registered bonds, 1.1(b)
    registered form, 25.4(d), 31.2(a), 31.12(b), 33.3(a)(1)
      definition clarified, 31.12(a)
    registered owner, 31.2(a)
    registration requirements, 31.12, 31.12(a), 33.3(a)(1)(iii)
    tax-exempt securities, 31.12(c)
  registration-required securities, *see* Registration-required securities
  reissuances, 31.10(c)
  REIT debt securities, 8.10(i)
  reset notes, 31.2(j)
  retirement, 31.10
  retirement bonds, 2
  reverse principal exchange rate linked securities (reverse PERLS), 1.1(g)(6), 2.1(b)(6)
  same issuer, 48.4(c)
  savings bonds, *see* Savings bonds
  section 988 transactions, 59.2(a)(1)
  securities in default, 31.8
  short-term debt securities:
    corporate, 31.2
    government securities, 31.2, 31.3, 48.3(b)(2)(iii)
    issued at discount, 31.3, 32.1(a)(1)
    market discount bonds, exempt, 31.10(b)
    market discount obligations, 48.3(b)(2)(iii)
    original issue discount, 31.2(d)
    registration not required, 31.12(b)
  similar maturities, 48.4(a), 48.4(c)
  state debt securities, 33.1
    registered form, 31.12(a)
  stock convertible into, 27.3(c)(4)
  stripped bonds, *see* Stripped bonds
  targeted amortization class bonds, 7.2(d)(2), 7.2(d)(6)
  tax considerations, Part Seven
  tax-exempt securities, *see* Tax-exempt securities
  Treasury securities, *see* Government securities
  United States debt securities, *see* Government securities
  United States possessions securities, 33.1
  United States territory securities, 33.1
  variable rate demand, 1.1(g)(3)
  wash sales rule:
    not substantially identical, 19.9(h)
    substantially identical, 19.9(g)
    with OID, information reporting, 31.2(n)
  zero coupon bonds, *see* Zero coupon securities
  see also Asset-backed securities; Federal agency securities; Government securities; Municipal securities; Treasury securities
Decedent(s):
  amortizable bond premium, 31.4(a)(1)(ii)
  cash basis, 31.4(a)(1)(ii)
  debt securities, 31.4(a)(1)(ii)
  interest, 31.4(a)(1)(ii)
Deep-in-the-money option(s):
  defined, 56.3(b)
  intercorporate dividends received, holding period, 17.7
  lowest qualified bench mark, 56.3(b)
    determination, exceptions to rule, 56.3(c)
  pre-DRA audit issues, 30.2(a)
  qualified covered calls, 56.3(b)

substantially similar or related property, 17.7(b)
Defaulted securities:
　principal/interest proration, 31.8
　redemption, 31.8
　resale, 31.8
　short sales, 31.8
　tax-exempt securities, 31.8, 33.4
Deferred delivery (seller's option) transactions, 1.3(e), 14.5(b)
Deferred payment (buyer's option) transactions, 1.3(e)
Deficit Reduction Act (DRA):
　commodities amnesty provision, 30.2(b), 47.2, 47.2(c), 58.1
　date of enactment election, 44.5
　full year election, 44.5
　pre-DRA audit issues, options, 27.2
　pre-ERTA straddles, 58.1
　Section 108, 30.2(b), 47.2(c)
　short-term stock options exemption, 56.6
　transitional year elections for section 1256 options, 44.5
Delivery:
　against cash transactions, 1.3(c)
　against payment transactions, 1.3(c)
　before regular way transactions, 1.3(d)
　between next day and regular way transactions, 1.3(d)
　(buyer's option) transactions, 1.3(e)
　deferred transactions, 1.3(e)
　failure to deliver, 7.5(c)
　(seller's option) transactions, 1.3(e)
　versus payment transactions, 1.3(c), 7.5(b)
Department of Energy Act of 1978, 33.3(a)(1)(ii)
Depository institutions, *see* Financial institutions, depository institutions
Depreciation:
　depreciation deductions, 16.4
　property used in taxpayer's trade or business, 52.2
　termination payment, 60.2(b)(2)(ii)
Diagonal spreads, 5.4(c)(3)
Direct ownership requirement, 57.6(a)
Disclosure Guidelines for Offerings of State and Local Government Securities, *see* Municipal securities
Disclosure of unrecognized gain:
　examples, 52.3
　exceptions, 52.2
　penalties for failure, 53.1

requirements, 52.1
Discount convertible debt securities, 34.7
Discounting arbitrage transactions, 5.4(e)(1)
Disqualified preferred stock, 16.6(g)
Distribution(s):
　common and preferred stock, 24.2(b)(4)
　convertible preferred stock, 24.2(b)(6), 27.3(c)(7)
　deemed distributions, 24.2(b)(2)
　disproportionate distributions, 24.2(b)(2), 34.3(d)
　estates and trusts, 17.3(c)(5)
　in excess of earnings and profits, 16.4(k), 24.1(d)
　in lieu of money, 24.2(b)(1)
　of property, 24.1(a)
　partial liquidation distribution, 16.6(b)
　preferred stock, 24.2(b)(4), 24.2(b)(5), 24.2(b)(6), 27.3(c)(7)
　tax-free, 27.4(b)
　see also Dividends
Distribution trusts, 1.1(i), 29
Dividend aggregation rules, 16.6(e)
Dividend announcement date, 16.6(b), 27.3(b)(3)
Dividend arbitrage transactions, 5.4(e)(2)
Dividend exclusion, 24.8
　repealed, 24.8
Dividend(s):
　adjusted basis, 16.4(b)
　adjust to money market rate, 1.1(g)(3), 27.3(b)(3)(ii)
　affiliated groups, 24.9(a)
　aggregation rules, 16.6(e)
　announcement date, 18.6(e)(2)
　defined, 16.6(b)
　arbitrage transactions, 5.4(e)(2)
　auction process, 1.1(g)(3), 27.3(b)(3)
　AA Composite Commercial Paper Rate, 27.3(b)(3)(iii)
　basis, 16.4(b)
　building and loan associations, 24.8, 24.9(a)
　capital gains dividends, 8.9(b)(3), 8.10(d), 17.6, 24.5
　cash dividends, 14.5(a), 18.6(d), 24.1, 24.2
　C corporation stock, 9.9
　common and preferred stock, 24.2(b)(4)
　common stock, 18.6(e)(2)
　convertible preferred stock, 24.2(b)(6), 27.3(c)(7)

Index

Dividend(s) (*Continued*)
  convertible securities, 24.2, 24.2(b)(2)
  cooperative banks, 24.8, 24.9(a)
  corporations exempt from tax, 24.8
  credit for the elderly (or disabled), 24.8
  deemed distributions, 24.2(b)(2), 34.3(d)
  deemed dividends, 16.4(*l*)
  deficiency determination, 24.3
  delivery before regular way transactions, 1.3(d)
  delivery between next day and regular way transactions, 1.3(d)
  disproportionate distributions, 24.2(b)(2), 24.2(b)(6)
  dutch-auction process, 1.1(g)(3), 27.3(b)(3)(iii)
  earnings and profits, 16.4(k), 24.1(c), 24.1(d), 24.1(f)
  85-day aggregation period, 16.6(e)
  exclusion, 24.8
  exempt-interest dividends, 8.9(a), 8.9(c), 9.3(b)(3)
  extraordinary dividends, *see* Extraordinary dividends
  FHLMC dividends, 24.9(d)
  fractional shares of stock, 17.4(a), 24.2(b)(3)
  holding period, 17.4(a)
  income, 24.1(e), 24.2(a), 28.4(d)(2)(ii)
  in excess of earnings and profits, 16.4(k), 24.1(d)
  information reports, 24.10
  in lieu of money, 24.2(b)(1)
  intercorporate dividends received, *see* Intercorporate dividends received deduction
  interest and carrying charges, 57.4(d)
  interest on debt securities, 9.9
  liquidating distributions, 18.6(c)
  liquidating dividends, 18.6(c)
    payments in lieu of liquidating dividends, 18.6(c)
  money in lieu of fractional shares, 24.2(b)(3)
  mutual savings banks, 24.8, 24.9(a)
  noncash capital contributions, 16.4(a)
  noncash dividend(s):
    corporate taxpayers, 24.1(f)(2)
    identification of stock dividends, 20.2(c)
    identification of stock splits, 20.2(c)
    noncorporate taxpayers, 24.1(f)(1)
    valuation, 14.5(a)
  noncash property dividends, 24.7(a)
  noncorporate shareholders, 24.1(f), 24.1(f)(1), 24.2(b)(7)
  nondividend distributions, basis, 24.1(d)
  nonqualifying dividends, 24.5
  nontaxable stock dividends, 16.4(b), 17.4(a), 18.6(c)
  nontaxable stock rights, 16.4(c), 17.4(a)
  ordinary income dividends, 8.9(c)
  paid by borrower in short sales, 1.3(i), 18.6(a)
  partially in lieu of money, 24.2(b)(1)
  pegged to performance of subsidiary, 1.1(g)(9)
  periodically reset, 1.1(g)(3), 27.3(b)(3)(iii)
  periodic redemption, 24.5
  personal holding companies, 18.6(e)(2), 24.3
  portfolio income, 9.9
  possessions corporation credit, 24.9(a)
  preference in, 17.7, 24.9(b)
  preferential dividends, 24.3, 24.5
  preferred stock, 18.6(e)(2), 24.2(b)(5)
  preferred stock redemptions deemed distributions, 27.3(b)(4)
  premium rate, 1.1(g)(3)
  property dividends, 17.2(a)(4), 24.1(a), 24.2
  public utilities, 24.4
  qualified preferred dividends, 16.6(c)
  rate, 27.3(b)(3)(iii)
  real estate investment trusts, 24.6
  received on stock sold, 16.4(d)
  record date, 1.3(d)
  record owner, 24.7(d)
  redemption, periodic, 24.5
  redemption premiums, 24.2(b)(5)
  regulated investment companies:
    capital gain dividends, 8.9(a), 8.9(c), 17.6, 24.5
    exempt-interest dividends, 8.9(a), 8.9(c), 9.3(b)(3)
    nonqualifying dividends, 24.5
  reinvestment, 24.4
  REIT, 9.9
  reporting income, 24.7(a), 24.7(b), 24.7(d)
  reporting requirements, 24.10
  return of capital, 16.4(k), 24.1(d), 24.5
  RIC, 9.9, 24.5
  royalties, 9.9
  savings institutions, 24.8, 24.9(a)

short sales expenses, *see* Short sales expenses
small business, 24.9(c)
small business investment companies, 24.9(a)
statement mailings, 24.10
statutory concepts, 24.1(a)
stock dividends, 1.3(e), 16.4(b), 18.6(c), 34.3(d)
stock redemptions as, 24
stock right(s):
　for other property, 24.2(b)(7)
　general rule, 24.2(a)
　taxable distributions, 24.2(b)
stock splits, 20.2(c)
straddle income, 55.2(b)
stripping, 16.6(c), 16.6(e), 24.9(b)
substantially disproportionate distribution, 24.2(b)(3)
substantially similar or related property, 17.7(b)
taxable distributions, 17.2(a)(4)
taxable purchases, 17.2(a)(4)
365-day aggregation period, 16.6(e)
time of reporting, 14.5(a)
triple taxation prevented, 24.9(a)
waivers, 24.7(g)
warrants, 17.4(a)
see also Distributions
Dividends paid deduction(s):
　personal holding companies, 24.3
　real estate investment trusts, 8.10(c)
　regulated investment companies, 8.9(f), 24.5(c)
Dividends received deduction, *see* Intercorporate dividends received deduction
Dividend stripping, 16.6(c), 16.6(e), 24.9(b)
Dividend waivers, 24.7(g)
Division:
　partnership, 28.4(b)(3)
Domestic building and loan associations, *see* Financial institutions, domestic building and loan associations
DRA, *see* Deficit Reduction Act (DRA)
Duff & Phelps, 7.1(b)
Dutch-auction rate preferred stock, 1.1(g)(3) 27.3(b)(3)(iii)

E

Earnings and profits:
　accumulated and current earnings and profits, 16.4(k)
　defined, 24.1(c)
　dividends, 24.1(a), 24.1(f)(1), 27.3(b)(3)
　foreign currency, 59.1
　preferred stock:
　　bailouts, 27.3(b)(5)
　　redemptions, 27.3(b)(4)
　qualified corporations, 16.6(b)
　registration-required securities, effect on, 31.12(c)
　regulated investment companies, 8.9(a), 8.9(f)
　statutory definitions, 24.1(c)
Economic accrual:
　amortization method, similar to OID rules, 60.2(b)(i), 60.2(c)(5)(ii)
　described, 60.2(b)(1)(i)
　Notice 89-21, 60.2(b)(1)(ii)
　swaps, appropriate amortization method, 60.2(b)(1)(ii)
Economic Recovery Tax Act (ERTA):
　commodity provisions, 47.2(c)
　Mark-to-Market Rule, 45.1
　pre-ERTA law, *see* Pre-ERTA law
　regulated futures contracts, 44.1
　60/40 Rule, 45.1, 45.2
ECUs, *see* European currency units
EFP transactions, *see* Exchange of futures for physicals (EFPs)
Employee benefit plans, 29.2(c)
Employee stock ownership plans, 16.3(c), 16.4(e)
Equity option(s):
　dealer equity options, *see* Dealer equity options
　defined, 30.1(c)
　equity call options, 30.3(b)
　　purchasers, 30.3(b)(1)
　　　commissions, 30.3(b)(1)(i)
　　　dispositions, 30.3(b)(1)(ii)
　　　exercise, 30.3(b)(1)(iv)
　　　fees, 30.3(b)(1)(i)
　　　lapse of long position, 30.3(b)(1)(iii)
　　　premiums, 30.3(b)(1)(i)
　　sellers, 30.3(b)(2)
　　　commissions, 30.3(b)(2)(ii)
　　　exercise, 30.3(b)(2)(iv)
　　　fees, 30.3(b)(2)(ii)
　　　lapse of short position, 30.3(b)(2)(iii)
　　　premiums, 30.3(b)(2)(i)
　equity put options, 30.3(c)

Equity option(s) (*Continued*)
  purchasers, 30.3(c)(1)
    commissions, 30.3(c)(1)(i)
    dispositions, 30.3(c)(1)(ii)
    exercise of long position, 30.3(c)(1)(iv)
    fees, 30.3(c)(1)(i)
    lapse of long position, 30.3(c)(1)(iii)
    premiums, 30.3(c)(1)(i)
  sellers, 30.3(c)(2)
    assignment, 30.3(c)(2)(iv)
    commissions, 30.3(c)(2)(ii)
    fees, 30.3(c)(2)(ii)
    lapse of short position, 30.3(c)(2)(iii)
    premiums, 30.3(c)(2)(i)
Escrow accounts, 17.2(a)(1), 17.2(a)(2)(ii)
Escrow agreements, 17.2(a)(2)(ii)
Esoteric securities, 1.1(g)
Estate, residence, 23.3(c)
European currency units (ECUs), 5.2(a)(3)
European-style options, 5.1, 5.2(a)(3), 6.2(d)
Exchangeable debt securities, 34.6(a)
Exchanged securities, 17.3(a)
Exchange gains and losses, 59.2(a)(4), 59.2(d)(1), 60.2(c)(5)(ii), 60.2(c)(5)(iii), 60.2(c)(5)(v), 60.2(c)(6), 60.2(c)(7)
  FDAPI, 59.2(d)(1)
  foreign currency transactions, 59.2(d)(1)
  functional currency rules, 59.2(g)
  notional principal contracts, 60.2(c)(6)
  section 988 transactions, 59.2(a), 59.2(a)(4), 59.2(c), 59.2(d)(1), 60.2(c)(6)
    special rule, 59.2(f)
  separately computed, 59.2(e)
Exchange of futures for physicals (EFPs), 4.3(f), 42.6
  regulation of EFPs, 4.3(f)
Exchange trading, 1.2(a)
Excise tax:
  capital gains dividend, defined, 8.9(b)(3)
  real estate investment trusts, 8.10(e)
  regulated investment companies, 8.9(b), 8.9(b)(1), 8.9(b)(2)
    calculation, 8.9(b)(1)
    grossed up required distribution, 1986, 8.9(b)(2)
    nondeductible, 8.9(b)(1)
Ex-dividend date:
  delivery between next day and regular way, 1.3(d)

  generally, 1.3(d), 5.1, 16.6(a), 17.6, 24.7(c), 24.9(b)(3)
  income, reporting, 24.7(a)
  intercorporate dividends received, holding period, 17.7
  sales and gifts after, 24.7(d)
  sales and gifts before, 24.7(c)
Executory contracts, 23.3(g)(2)(ii)
Exempted securities:
  defined, 7.4(a)(1)
  generally, 1.3(h), 2.3, 7.4(b)(3)
  good faith margin, defined, 7.4(b)(3)
Exempted transactions, 7.3(a)(3)
Exempt facility bonds, municipal securities, 33.2(c)(2)(vi)
Exempt-interest dividends, *see* Dividends, exempt-interest dividends
Expense(s):
  accounting fees, 9.1(c)(1)
  administrative, 9.1(a)
  advertising, 10.1(c)
  against public policy, 10.1(c)
  allocable to taxable (nontaxable) income, 9.1(b)
  amortized bond premiums, 9.1(d), 9.4
  antitrust damages, 10.1(c)
  automatic dividend reinvestment plan, 9.1(c)(8)
  automobiles, 10.1(c)
  Board of Trade Gratuity Fund, 10.1(c)
  bond premiums, 9.4
  brokerage fees, 9.1(c)(1)
  brokers, 13.1, 13.2
  business expenses, 10.1(a), 11.1(a), 12.1, 13.1, 18.6, 18.6(e)(1), 60.2(b)(2)(ii)
  buying and selling costs, 9.1(c)(1)
  capitalization of short sale payments, 18.6(e)(1)
  carrying charges, 55.1
  clerical help, 9.1(c)
  commissions, 9.1(c)(1), 10.1(d), 12.1
  computer-generated commodity price information, 10.1(c)
  conventions, 9.1(c)(10)
  covered expenses, types, 9.1(c)
  custodial fees, 9.1(c)
  dealer(s):
    banks, 11.3(b)(3)
    deductible selling expenses, 11.1(b)
    futures contract transactions, 11.1(c)
    interest expenses, 11.2; *see also* Interest expense
    relating to tax-exempt income, 11.3

selling commissions, 11.1(b)
tax avoidance, 18.6(a)
tax-exempt income, 11.3(a)
trade or business expenses, 11.1(a)
types of expenses, 11.3(a)
deductible losses, 13.2(a)(2)
disallowed deductions, 9.1(a), 9.3(b)(2)
educational, 32.1(b)(1)
fees, 10.1(d), 12.1
fiduciary fees, 9.1(a)
fines and penalties, 9.1(a), 10.1(c)
generally, 9.1(a)
hedgers, 12.1
home office expenses, 9.1(c)(6)
illegal bribes, 9.1(a), 10.1(c)
indemnity bonds, 9.1(c)(7)
insurance, 10.1(c)
interest expenses, *see* Interest expense
investment advisory fees, 9.1(c), 9.1(c)(2)
investment counsel, 9.1(c)(2)
investment expenses, 8.9(c), 9.1, 9.1(d), 60.2(b)(2)(ii)
investment interest expense, 9.2(b), 9.2(e), 9.2(h), 10.2(e), 42.2, 55.1
  tax preference item, 15.4(a)(2)(ii)(c)
investment promotion expenses, 9.1(c)(9)
investors, 9.1(c), 9.3, 18.6(e)(1)
kickbacks, 9.1(a), 10.1(c)
labor expenses, 10.1(c)
legal fees, 9.1(c)
limitations, 9.1(d)
litigation expenses, 9.1(a), 9.1(c)(3)
margin interest, 9.2(b), 9.3(b)(5)
meetings, 9.1(d)(10)
miscellaneous itemized deductions, 9.1(d)
noncapitalized commissions, 10.1(c)
nondeductible expenses, 10.1(c), 55.2(a)
nontrade or nonbusiness expenses, 9.1(a)
office rent, 10.1(a)
order errors, 13.2(a)(2)
penalties and fines, 9.1(a), 10.1(c)
periodicals and books, 9.1(c)
personal, 10.1(c)
personal interest, 9.2(h)
prepaid interest, 10.2(d)
production (collection) of taxable income, 9.1(a)
promotion expenses, 9.1(c)(9), 10.1(c)
proxy contest expenses, 9.1(c)(4)
quotation display systems, 9.1(c)(5)
rental expenses, 10.1(a), 10.1(c)
repair expenses, 10.1(c)
replacement of stock certificates, 9.1(c)(7)
research expenses, 9.1(c)
salaries, 9.1(c), 10.1(a)
section 212 expenses, *see* Section 212 expenses
selling expense(s):
  dealers, 11.1(b)
  traders, 10.1(d)
seminars, 9.1(c)(10)
service charges, 9.1(c)(8)
short sales, expenses and payments, 9.1(d), 18.6(a)
stock certificates, replacement, 9.1(c)(7)
storage and insurance expenses, 55.1, 55.2
supplies, 10.1(c)
tax-exempt income, 9.3, 10.3, 11.3
temporary use of property, fees, 18.6(a) 24.9(b)(3), 26.2(e)
termination payments, 60.2(b)(2)(ii)
traders:
  Board of Trade Gratuity Fund, 10.1(c)
  business expenses, 10.1(c)
  commissions, 10.1(d)
  computer-generated commodity price information, 10.1(c)
  deductible expenses, 10.1(a), 10.1(b), 10.1(c)
  direct expenses recharacterized, 10.1
  indirect expenses, 10.1
  interest expenses, 10.2, 10.2(e); *see also* Interest expense
  trade or business expenses, 10.1(a)
  transporation expenses, 9.1(c)(5)
  travel expenses, 9.1(c)(5), 10.1(a), 10.1(c)
  educational travel expenses, 9.1(c)(9)
treble damages, 9.1(a)
trustees' fees and commissions, 9.1(c)
two percent floor, 9.1(d)
Extendible debt securities, 1.1(g)(13)
Extraordinary dividend(s):
  actual rate of return, 16.6(c), 18.6(e)(2)
  aggregation rules, 16.6(e)
  automatic valuation procedure, 16.6(d)
  basis reduction, 16.6, 16.6(b)
  de minimis amount, earnings and profits, 16.6(b)
  disqualified preferred stock, 16.6(g)
  dividend announcement date, 16.6(b)

Index

Extraordinary dividend(s) (*Continued*)
  definition clarified by TMRA '88, 16.6(b)
  dividends declared:
    after March 1, 1984 and before July 18, 1986, 16.6(a)
    on and after July 18, 1986, 16.6(b)
  dividend stripping, 16.6(c), 16.6(e),
  election statement, section 1059(c)(4), 16.6(d)
  extraordinary dividend treatment avoidance, 16.6(b), 18.6(e)(2)
  fair market value established, 16.6(d)
  generally, 16.6, 16.6(b), 17.7(c), 18.6(b), 18.6(e)(2), 18.6(e)(4)
  holding period, 17.7(c)
  intercorporate dividends received, 16.6(f), 17.7(c)
  multiple dividends, 16.6(e)
  non-pro rata redemptions, 16.6(b)
  nonpublic trading procedures, 16.6(d)
  nontaxed portion of, 16.6(b), 18.6(e)(2)
  one-year holding period, 16.6(a)
  partial liquidation distribution, 16.6(b)
  qualified corporation, defined, 16.6(b)
  qualified preferred dividends, 16.6(b), 16.6(c), 18.6(e)(2)
  regulatory authority, 16.6(h)
  stated rate of return, 16.6(c), 18.6(e)(2)
  taxable portion, 16.6
  two-year holding period, 16.6(b)

F

Fails, 7.5(c)
Fail sale transactions, 24.9(b)(3), 26, 26.4
Farm Credit Administration, 2.1(b)(4)
Farm Credit Agencies' securities, *see* Federal agency securities, Farm Credit Agencies' securities
Farm Credit Bank, 2.1(b), 2.1(b)(5)
Farmer Mac, *see* Federal agency securities, Federal Agricultural Mortgage Corporation (Farmer Mac) securities
FASB Emerging Issues Tax Force, 60.1
Fast pay/slow pay bonds, 2.1(b)(4), 7.2(d)(1), 36.2(c), 36.3
FCMs, *see* Futures commission merchants (FCMs)
FDAPI, *see* Fixed or determinable, annual or periodical income (FDAPI)
Federal Agricultural Mortgage Corporation (Farmer Mac) securities, *see* Federal agency securities, Federal Agricultural Mortgage Corporation (Farmer Mac) securities
Federal agency securities, 2, 2.1(b), 48.4(c)
  Banks for Cooperatives securities, 2.1(b)
  book-entry securities, 20.2(e)
  debt securities, 32.2
    state and local tax, test for exemption, 32.2(a)
  exempt from SEC registration, 2.1(b)
  Farm Credit Agencies' securities, 2.1(b)(5), 8.9(a)(4)
  Farm Credit Banks securities, 2.1(b)
  Federal Agricultural Mortgage Corporation (Farmer Mac) securities, 2.1(b)(9)
  Federal Home Loan Bank (FHLB) securities, 2.1(b)(1)
    intercorporate dividends received deduction, 24.9(d)
  Federal Home Loan Mortgage Corporation (FHLMC) (Freddie Mac) securities, *see* Federal Home Loan Mortgage Corporation (FHLMC) (Freddie Mac) securities
  Federal Intermediate Credit Banks securities, 2.1(b)
  Federal Land Banks securities, 2.1(b)
  Federal National Mortgage Association (FNMA) (Fannie Mae) securities, *see* Federal National Mortgage Association (FNMA) (Fannie Mae) securities
  Financing Corporation (FICO) securities, 2.1(b)(8)
  government agency pass-through certificates, 7.2(c)(1), 7.3(b)(2)
  Government National Mortgage Association (GNMA) (Ginnie Mae) securities, *see* Government National Mortgage Association (GNMA) (Ginnie Mae) securities
  income, taxable, 32.2
  Resolution Funding Corporation (Refcorp) securities, 2.1(b)(7)
  Small Business Administration (SBA) securities, 2.1(b)(10)
  Student Loan Marketing Association (SLMA) (Sallie Mae) securities, *see* Student Loan Marketing

Association (SLMA) (Sallie Mae) securities
test for exemption from state and local tax, 32.2(a)
Federal Communications Commission (FCC), 27.4(c)
Federal Deposit Insurance Corporation (FDIC), 2, 31.5(a), 33.3(a)(1)(ii)
Federal Financial Institutions Examination Council (FFIEC), 7.2(c)(2)(iii)
Federal Financing Bank, 2.1(b)
Federal Home Loan Banks, 2.1(b), 24.9(d)
  Federal Home Loan Bank Board, replaced by Federal Housing Finance Board, 2.1(b)(1)
  Federal Housing Finance Board supervision, 2.1(b)(1)
  FHLB system, 12 FHLBs, 2.1(b)(1), 2.1(b)(4)
Federal Home Loan Bank (FHLB) securities, *see* Federal agency securities, Federal Home Loan Bank (FHLB) securities
Federal Home Loan Mortgage Corporation (FHLMC) (Freddie Mac) securities:
  CMOs, 2.1(b)(4)
  contract cancellation transactions, 58.1
  debentures, 2.1(b)(4)
  discount notes, 2.1(b)(4)
  dividends, 24.9(d)
  fast pay/slow pay bonds, 2.1(b)(4), 36.3
  FIRREA, 2.1(b)(4)
  forward market, 2.2(b)
  Freddie Mac Giants, 7.2(b)
  guaranteed mortgage certificates, 2.1(b)(4)
  guarantor swap program, 7.5(b)
  HUD regulatory authority, 2.1(b)(4)
  intercorporate dividends received deduction, 24.9(d)
  MCFs, 2.1(b)(4)
  mortgage participation certificates, 2.1(b)(4)
  municipal securities, federal guarantee, 33.3(a)(1)(ii)
  nonvoting common stock, 27.5(b)
  participating preferred stock, 2.1(b)(4), 27.5(b)
  participation certificates, 2.1(b)(4), 7.2(b), 7.3(b)(2)
  pay-through securities, 1.1(e), 2.1(b)(4), 36.3
  post-1984 income, 24.9(d)
  preferred stock, 24.9(d), 27.5(b)
  pre-1985 income, 24.9(d)
  REMICs, 2.1(b)(4)
  Security Sales and Trading Group, 7.3(b)(2)
  senior participating preferred stock, 2.1(b)(4)
  stock, 27.5(b)
  strip PCs, 2.1(b)(4)
Federal Housing Administration (FHA), 2.1(b)(2), 33.3(a)(1)(ii)
Federal Housing Finance Board, 2.1(b)(1)
Federal Intermediate Credit Banks, 2.1(b), 2.1(b)(5)
Federal Land Bank, 2.1(b), 2.1(b)(5)
  substantially identical property, 19.9(g), 19.9(h)
Federal National Mortgage Association (FNMA) (Fannie Mae) securities:
  bonds, 32.2(b)
  capital contributions to FNMA, 27.5(a)(2)
  common stock, 27.5
  debentures, 2.1(b)(3)
  FNMA/MBSs, 2.1(b)(3)
  FNMA/REMICs, 2.1(b)(3)
  FNMA/SMBSs, 2.1(b)(3)
  FNMA strip PCs, 2.1(b)(4)
  intercorporate dividends received deduction, 24.9(d), 34.4
  IO/PO strip offering, 7.2(c)(2)(ii)
  LIBOR-based MBSs, 2.1(b)(3)
  municipal securities, federal guarantee, 33.3(a)(1)(ii)
  pass-through securities, 2.1(b)(3)
  stock dispositions, 27.5(a)(3)
  traded on NYSE, 2.1(b)(3)
  types of, 2.1(b)(3)
Federal Public Housing Administration, 19.9(h)
Federal Reserve Board (FRB):
  book-entry system, 2.1(a)(1), 2.1(b)(2), 2.1(b)(3), 2.1(b)(4), 2.4
  depository institutions, 2.1(a)(1)
  generally, 1.4, 2, 2.1(a)(1), 3.1, 27.4(c)
  New York Federal Reserve Bank, 2
  open market operations, 2
  Regulation D, 7.6(d)
  Regulation G, 7.4(b)(1)

Index

Federal Reserve Board (FRB) (*Continued*)
  Regulation T, 1.4, 2.3, 7.4, 7.4(b)(3), 7.4(b)(6), 8.7(b)
  Regulation U, 1.4, 2.3, 7.4, 7.4(b)(1), 7.4(b)(3), 8.7(b)
Federal Reserve Board bank (FRBB), 20.2(e)
Federal Reserve Board margin regulations, 1.4, 5.5(a)
Federal Savings and Loan Insurance Corporation (FSLIC), 2.1(b)(7), 2.1(b)(8)
FICO, *see* Federal agency securities, Financing Corporation (FICO) securities
FIFO, *see* First-in, first-out (FIFO)
Financial institution(s):
  automatic investment service, 17.2(a)(5)
  bank deposits, 25.1
  bank holding companies, 11.3(b)(3)(ii)(g), 27.4(c)
    installment sale, 17.2(a)(2)(i)(c)
  bank holding company stock, 1.1(g), 24.9(c)
  bank letters of credit, 1.1(g)(12), 7.1(b)
  bank regulatory agencies, 2, 3.1
  banks, 2, 8.8, 11.3(b)(3), 27.5(a)(1)
    definition, general, 23.2(d)(1)
    hedge accounts, 23.2(d)(2)
    hedging transactions, 23.2(d)
    market in interest rate swaps, 60.2(b)(2)(i)(a)
    worthless securities, 27.8(e)
  bond premiums, 31.4(a)(1)
  building and loan associations, 11.3(b)(3), 24.8, 24.9(a)
  business development companies, 8.8
  capital asset treatment, limitation, 8.8
  cash accounts, 1.4(a)
  clearing banks, 2.4
  commercial banks, 2.1(a)(1), 8.8, 33.6, 60.3(a)(1)(i)
  Comptroller of the Currency ruling, 1.1(d)
  consolidated net income, 8.8
  cooperative banks, 8.8, 11.3(b)(3), 24.8, 24.9(a), 33.6
  credit unions, 2.1(a)(1)
  dealers, 11.1, 11.3(b)(3)
  debt securities, special rules, 1.1(d), 11.3(b)(3), 31.1
  defined, 8.8, 11.3(b)(3)(ii)(d)
  depository institutions, 2.1(a)(1)

dividend(s):
  building and loan associations, 24.8
  cooperative banks, 24.8
  dividends received deduction, reduction, 24.9(a)(2)
  mutual savings banks, 24.8
  savings institutions, 24.8, 24.9(a)
domestic building and loan associations, 8.8, 11.3(b)(3), 24.8, 24.9(a)
farm credit agencies, 2.1(b)(5)
federal agencies, 2.1(b)
Federal Financial Institutions Examination Council (FFIEC), 7.2(c)(2)(iii)
FFIEC policy statement, 7.2(c)(2)(iii)
Financial Institutions Reform, Recovery, and Enforcement Act of 1989 (FIRREA), 7.2(c)(2)(iii)
FIRREA capital standards, 7.2(c)(2)(iii)
FNMA stock, 27.5(a)(1)
foreign central banks, 2
forward foreign exchange transactions, 60.2(c)(1)
government securities brokers and dealers, 2
hedging transaction(s):
  futures contracts, 8.4(d)
  identification, 23.2(b)(4)
  special rules, 23.2(d)
    qualified tax-exempt obligations, 33.6
  repeal, 23.2(d)
Home Owners' Loan Act of 1933, 7.2(c)(2)(iii)
interest expense, special rules, 11.3(b)(3), 11.3(b)(3)(ii)(e)
inventory rules, 8.8
investment accounts, 8.8
  loss denial, ordinary income treatment, exceptions, 31.12(d)(2)
Investment Company Act of 1940, exemption, 7.6(d)
investment positions, 8.8
investments, tax-exempt securities, 11.3(b)(3), 33.6
letters of credit, 1.1(g), 7.1(b), 33.3(a)(1)(ii)
limitations on capital treatment, 8.8
mortgage-backed bonds (MBBs), *see* Asset-backed securities, mortgage-backed bonds (MBBs)
municipal securities, 3.3, 33.6

mutual savings banks, 8.8, 11.3(b)(3), 24.8, 33.6
national banks, 1.1(d)
Office of Thrift Supervision, 7.2(c)(2)(iii)
original issue discount, 31.2(c), 31.2(d)
portfolio stock, 24.9(c)(2)
post-FIRREA capital requirements, 7.2(c)(2)(iii)
qualified tax-exempt obligations, 33.6
real estate mortgage investment conduits, 41.4
registration requirements, exceptions, 31.12(d)
Regulation U, 1.4, 7.4
REMICs, 41.4
savings and loan association(s):
  FFIEC policy statement, 7.2(c)(2)(iii)
  FIRREA capital standards, 7.2(c)(2)(iii)
  generally, 2, 2.1(a)(1), 7.2(c)(2)(iii), 7.6(d), 8.8, 27.5(a)(1), 33.6
  hedging transactions, 8.4(d), 23.2(b)(3)
  stripped pass-through certificates, 7.2(c)(2)(iii)
  supervision by FHLBs, FDIC, and OTS, 2.1(b)(1)
savings banks, 2.1(a)(1)
savings deposits, 25.1
securities purchases, 17.2(a)(5)
small business investment companies, 8.8
special rules, 8.8, 11.3(b)(3), 31.12(d)
stock in banks, 24.9(c)
stripped pass-through certificates, 7.2(c)(2)(iii)
subordinate governmental entities, 11.3(b)(3)(ii)(b)
tax-exempt securities, 11.3(b)(3), 33.6(e)
  acquired after August 7, 1986, 11.3(b)(3)(ii)
  acquired before August 8, 1986, 11.3(b)(3)(i)
thrift institutions, 7.2(c)(2)(iii)
transitional rules, 11.3(b)(3)(ii)(g)
trust companies, 8.8, 11.3(b)(3)
wholly owned subsidiary of bank, 8.8
Financial Institutions Reform, Recovery, and Enforcement Act of 1989 (FIRREA), 2.1(b)(4), 7.2(c)(2)(iii)
Financial intermediations, 60.2(d)(1), 60.2(d)(1)(iii)

Financial Products and Institutions, Office of Chief Counsel, 60.1
Financial Products Group, 60.1
Financing Corporation (FICO) securities, see Federal agency securities, Financing Corporation (FICO) securities
Financing trusts, 1.1(i)
Firm commitment underwritings, 1.2(b), 8.6, 11.8(a), 23.2(c)(3)
First-in, first-out (FIFO), 19.3(b), 19.9(g), 20.2, 20.2(b), 20.2(d), 20.2(f), 22.2(b), 47.2(e)
Fitch Investors Service, 7.1(b)
Five year phase-in period, 9.2(h)
Fixed investment trust, 58.2
Fixed mortgage pool, 36.8(a)
Fixed or determinable, annual or periodical income (FDAPI), 59.2(d)(1), 60.2(g)
Fixed payment bonds, 7.2(a)(1)
Flat bonds, 31.8
Flexible rate bonds, 3.3
Floaters, see Asset-backed securities, floating rate tranches
Floating rate bonds, 3.3
Floating rate convertible notes (FRCNs), see Convertible debt securities, floating rate convertible notes (FRCNs)
Floating rate index, see Indexes
Floating rate notes, see Debt securities, floating rate notes
Floating rate preferred stock, 1.1(g)(2), 27.3(b)(3)(i)
Floating rate tranches, see Asset-backed securities, floating rate tranches
Floor brokers, 1.2(a)
Floor(s):
  hedge use:
    assignment fees, 60.3(a)(3)
    character, 60.3(a)(1)(ii)
    defined, 6.4, 60.3
    gambling or wagering income analogy, 60.3(a)(2)(ii)
    generally, 6.4, 60.3(a)
    integration, 60.3(a)(1)(ii)
    ISDA Interest Rate and Currency Exchange Agreement, 6.4
    ISDA Interest Rate Swap Agreement, 6.4
    Notice 89-21, 60.3(a)(1)(i)
    Notice 89-90, 60.2(b)(2)(i)(a)(4)

Index   I-32

Floor(s) (*Continued*)
  notional principal contract, 60.3
  objective interest index rates, 36.8(c)(1)(iv)
  option analogy, 60.3(a)(4)
  periodic payments, 60.3(a)(2)(i)
    character, 60.3(a)(2)(ii)
    normal accounting method, 60.3(a)(2)(i)
    ordinary income, 60.3(a)(2)(ii)
    Straddle Rules, generally inapplicable, 60.3(a)(2)(i)
    termination fees, 60.3(a)(3)
    underlying property, 60.3(a)(4)
  up-front fee, 60.3(a)(1)
    amortization, 60.3(a)(1)(i), 60.3(a)(4)
    defined, 6.1
    lump-sum payment, 60.3
    pricing methods, 60.3(a)(1)(i)
  variable rate debt instruments, 36.8(c)(1)(iv)
  nonhedge use, 60.3(b)
Floor specialists as dealers, 8.3(b)
Floor traders, 4.2(b), 8.2(a), 10.1(d)
Flower bonds, 32.1(c)
Flow-through entities, 8.9, 9.3(b)(3), 33.5, 44.5, 51.1, 51.4, 54.4(a)
Foreign corporations, 24.1(f)(2)
  American depository receipts (ADRs), 1.1(f), 51.1, 51.4
Foreign currency:
  actively traded, 48.2(a)
  contracts, *see* Foreign currency contracts
  gains or losses, 59.1
  hedging transactions, 23.3, 55.2(f), 59.3; *see also* Section 988 hedging transactions
  options, 23.3(c), 23.3(e)
    futures, 5.2(b), 23.3(c), 23.3(e)
    nonequity options, 44.3
    securities, 5.2(a)(3)
  personal property, 48.2(d)
  positions in personal property, 30.3(d)(1)
  straddles, 48.3(c)
  swaps, *see* Foreign currency swaps
  transactions, *see* Foreign currency transactions
Foreign currency contract(s):
  arm's length price, 44.2(a)
  bank forward contracts, 59.2(a)(1)
    foreign currency-related, 23.3(e)
  "carve-out," section 988 transactions, 44.2(b)
  foreign currency swaps, excluded, 59.2(a)(1)
  forward contracts that are section 1256 contracts:
    cancellations, 58.1
    nonhedge transactions, 59.4(c)
      post-October 21, 1988 positions, 59.4(c)(3)
      post-section 988 positions, 59.4(c)(2)
      pre-1986 positions, 59.4(c)(1)
      pre-October 22, 1988 positions, 59.4(c)(2)
      section 988(a)(1)(B) election, available September 21, 1989, 59.4(c)(4)
    short sales rule, not applicable, 18.2(a)
  generally, 23.3(c), 23.3(e), 44.2, 44.2(a), 44.2(b), 44.6, 45.1(a), 59.2(h), 59.4(c)
  identified mixed straddles, 23.3(e), 57, 59.2(h)
  interbank forward contracts, 44.2, 44.2(a)
  interbank market requirement, 44.2(a)
  mixed straddle account, 57
  mixed straddle election under section 1256(d), 57
  pre-TRA '86, 44.2(b)
  section 1256 foreign currency contracts, 23.3(c), 23.3(e), 44.2, 44.2(a), 44.2(b), 44.6, 45.1(a), 57, 59.2(h), 59.4(c)
  TRA '86; TMRA '88, treatment, 44.2
Foreign currency swap(s):
  amortization of lump-sum payments, 60.2(c)(5)(i)
  anti-abuse rule, 60.2(c)(5)(iv)
  back-to-back loans, 6.2(b)(4)
  character, 60.2(c)(7)
  cross-currency interest rate swap, 6.2(b)(2)
  currency swap, 23.3(g)(1)(i)(b), 60.2(c)(5)(i)
  debt swaps, 6.2(b)(3)
  definition, 60.2(c)(2)
  disposition, 60.2(c)(5)(v)
  domestic source ordinary income, 60.2(c)(4)
  exchange gain or loss, 60.2(c)(5)(ii), 60.2(c)(5)(iii), 60.2(c)(5)(v), 60.2(c)(6), 60.2(c)(7)

exchange of swap principal amount, 60.2(c)(2)
foreign currency contract, excluded as, 59.2(a)(1), 60.2(c)(3)
foreign currency gain or loss, 60.2(c)(4)
foreign currency, selling at discount, 60.2(c)(1)
foreign currency, selling at premium, 60.2(c)(1)
forward market, 60.2(c)(1)
functional currency, 60.2(c)(5)(ii)
generally, 6.2(b), 23.3(f)(4), 59.2(a)(1), 60.2(c)(1)
hypothetical borrowing, 60.2(c)(5)(ii)
hypothetical exchange gain (loss), 60.2(c)(5)(ii)
hypothetical interest income, 60.2(c)(5)(ii)
hypothetical issue price, 60.2(c)(5)(ii), 60.2(c)(5)(iv)
hypothetical loan, 60.2(c)(5)(ii)
hypothetical stated redemption price, 60.2(c)(5)(ii), 60.2(c)(5)(iv)
income and expenses, 60.2(c)(5)
lump-sum payments, 60.2(c)(5)(i)
market exchange rate, 60.2(c)(5)(iii)
nonfunctional currency, 59.2(a)(1), 60.2(c)(3), 60.2(c)(4), 60.2(c)(5)(ii), 60.2(c)(6)
Notice 89-21, 60.2(c)(5)(i)
off-market currency swap, defined, 60.2(c)(5)(i)
parallel loans, 6.2(b)(4)
periodic interim payments, 60.2(c)(5)(ii)
plain vanilla swap, 6.2(b)(1)
principal payments, 60.2(c)(5)(iii)
repurchase agreement, 60.2(c)(1)
section 988 treatment, 59.2(a)(1), 60.2(c)(3), 60.2(c)(4)
  residence-based source rule, 60.2(c)(6)
section 988(d) hedge, 60.2(c)(4)
section 1256 contract, excluded as, 60.2(c)(3)
selling at a discount, 60.2(c)(1)
selling at a premium, 60.2(c)(1)
source rules, 60.2(c)(6)
  residence-based source rules, 60.2(c)(6)
spot market, 60.2(c)(1)
swap principal amount, 60.2(c)(5)(iii)
synthetic debt instrument, 60.2(c)(4)
termination, 60.2(c)(5)(v)
Foreign currency transaction(s):
acquisition dates, 59.2(f)
analysis, three steps, 59.4
bond premiums, 31.7(c)
booking dates, 59.2(f)
borrowings, 31.7(a)
commodity funds, 59.2(i)
debt instruments, defined, 59.2(a)(1)
domestic source ordinary income, 21.9
earnings and profits, 59.1
exception where economic benefit derived, 59.2(c)(3)
exchange gains and losses, 59.2(a), 59.2(a)(3), 59.2(c)(3), 59.2(f)
  FDAPI, 59.2(d)(1)
  separately computed, 59.2(e)
exchange rate, appropriate, 59.5(a)
expense or income items, 59.2(a)(1)
FDAPI, 59.2(d)(1)
financial instruments, 59.2(a)(1), 59.2(c)(3)
foreign:
  branches, 59.2(g), 59.5, 59.5(b)
  currency, actively traded, 48.2(a)
  currency contracts, *see* Foreign currency contracts
  currency futures, 23.3(e)
  currency positions, 23.3(a), 59.1
  currency risks hedged, 23.3(a)
  currency swaps, *see* Foreign currency swaps
  income taxes, defined, 59.5(a)
  subsidiaries, 59.1, 59.5(a)
  tax credits, 59.1, 59.2(d)(1), 59.5(a)
forward contracts that are not section 1256:
  contracts, nonhedge transactions, 59.4(d)
    post-October 21, 1988 positions, 59.4(d)(3)
    post-section 988 positions, 59.4(d)(2)
    pre-1986 transactions, 59.4(d)(1)
    pre-October 22, 1988 positions, 59.4(d)(2)
    section 988(a)(1)(B) election, available September 21, 1989, 59.4(d)(4)
  generally, 59.2, 59.2(c), 59.2(f)
functional currency, *see* Functional currency
futures contracts, 59.2, 59.2(c), 59.2(f)

Index

Foreign currency transaction(s) (*Continued*)
  gain or loss, 59.2(a)(3), 59.2(b), 59.2(c)(3), 59.2(f), 59.2(h), 59.5(b)
    booking date, 59.2(f)(1)
    computation, 59.2(f)(3)
    payment date, 59.2(f)(2)
  generally, 21.9, 23.3, 59
  hedging transactions, 59.3; *see also* Section 988 hedging transactions
    superseded, 23.3(g)
  loans, 59.2
  market discount, 31.7(b)
  mark-to-market accounting method, dealers, 59.6
  nonequity options, *see* Nonequity options
  nonfunctional currency, *see* Nonfunctional currency
  non-section 1256 contracts, futures and options, 59.4(b)
  Notice 87-11, 23.3(f)
  offsetting position, after September 21, 1989, 59.2(c)(3)
  options, 59.2(a)(1), 23.3(e)
  ordinary income or loss, 21.9, 23.3(c)
  original issue discount, 31.7(a)
  personal transactions, 59.2(a)(3)
  premiums, 31.7(c)
  qualified business units, *see* Qualified business units
  qualified funds, *see* Qualified funds
  regulated futures contracts, *see* Regulated futures contracts
  regulations, 23.3(g)
  residence, 23.3(c), 59.2(d)(2)(i)
  section 988 hedging transactions, *see* Section 988 hedging transactions
  section 988 transactions, *see* Section 988 transactions
  section 1256 "carve-out," 44.2(b), 44.6, 57.7, 59.2(a)(1)
  separately computed gains or losses, 59.2(e)
  source of income, 59.2(d)
  spot contract:
    defined, 59.4(e)
    forward contract considerations, 59.4(e)
    tax character, 59.4(e)
  Straddle Rules, 59.7
  Subpart J, 59.1
  effective, post-1986 taxable years, 59.1
  foreign subsidiary, pre-1987 taxable years, 59.1
  swaps, *see* Foreign currency swaps
  synthetic foreign currency transactions, 23.3(a)
  timing, 59.2(c), 59.2(h)
  TMRA '88, special rules, 44.6, 59.2
  translation rules, 59.5
  United States shareholders, distributions, 59.5(a)
  warrants, 5.2(a)(3), 5.2(a)(4)
  wash sales, 19.6(c)(2)
  withholding requirements, 23.3(f)(5)
Foreign exchange:
  gains and losses, 59.2(a)
  risks, 23.2(e)(2)
Foreign exchanges, 17.3(b), 44.1(b)
Foreign income taxes, defined, 59.5(a)
Foreign investment companies, 16.4(*l*)
Foreign investors, 31.5
Foreign tax credits, 59.1, 59.2(d)(1), 59.5(a), 60.5
Forms, IRS, *see* IRS forms
Forward contract(s):
  acquisition pursuant to long position, 42.1(b)
  assignment, 58.1
  bank forward contracts, 59.2(a)(1)
  Brent oil contracts, 4.1(b), 4.3(b)
  cancellation fees, 58.1
  CFTC statutory interpretation, 4.1(b)
  closing out, 58.1
  commodity swap, 60.2(d)(1)(i)
  defined, 4.3(b)
  distinctions between futures contracts, 4.3(b)
  exchange gains and losses, 59.2(a)(4)
  executory contracts, 58.1
  foreign currency contracts, *see* Foreign currency contracts; *see also* Foreign currency transactions
    cancellation, 58.1
  forward contract exclusion, 4.1(b)
  forward delivery, 4.2(a)
  forward foreign exchange transactions, 60.2(c)(1)
  forward market, 2.2(b)
  forward rate agreements, 60.4(a), 60.4(a)(2)
    see also Forward rate agreements (FRAs)

forward transactions, 2.2(b), 4.1(b), 4.3(b)
generally, 60.2(d)(2)(i)
hedges, 12.1
liability hedge treatment, 60.5(b)(1)
margin, 4.3(b), 4.4(a)
mark-to-market, 4.3(b)
offsetting contract, 58.1
physical commodities swapped, 6.2(c)
repos, economic equivalents, 48.3(b)(2)(ii)
section 1256 contracts, 44.2, 59.2(c)
switch transactions, 58.1
with interim payments, 60.2(d)(1)(i)
Forward rate agreement(s) (FRAs):
cash settlement, 60.4
character, 60.4(b)
contract period, 60.4
disadvantages, 6.7
forward contracts, 60.4(a)(2)
offsetting positions, 60.4(e)
futures contracts, 60.4(a), 60.4(a)(1)
generally, 6.7, 60.4, 60.4(a)
hedge purposes, 60.4(b)
interest rate swaps, 60.4(a)(3)
legal status, 6.7
LIBOR rate, 6.7
margin payments, 60.4, 60.4(a)(1), 60.4(a)(3)
Mark-to-Market Rule, ineligible, 60.4(a)(1)
notional principal amount, 60.4(a)(3)
single period interest rate swap, 60.4(a)(3)
60/40 Rule, ineligible, 60.4(a)(1)
source of payments, 60.4(d)
speculative positions, 60.4(b), 60.4(f)
taxation, 60.4(a)(1), 60.4(b)
timing, 60.4(c)
Fox Television Stations, Inc., *see* Preferred stock, Fox Television Stations, Inc., increasing rate exchangeable guaranteed preferred stock
Fractional shares of stock, 17.4(a), 24.2(b)(3)
Fractional stock dividends, *see* Dividends, fractional stock dividends
FRAs, *see* Forward rate agreements (FRAs)
Fraudulent transactions, 10.2(g)
increased interest rate, 53.2
FRB, *see* Federal Reserve Board (FRB)

FRCNs, *see* Convertible debt securities, floating rate convertible notes (FRCNs)
FSLIC, *see* Federal Savings and Loan Insurance Corporation (FSLIC)
regulation, government securities brokers and dealers, 2
Full carry straddles, 4.3(d), 55.1, 55.2
Functional currency:
accounting method, 23.3(a), 59.2(g)
Code determinations made in functional currency, 59.2(g)(1)(i)
defined for QBUs, 59.2(g)(3)(viii)
earnings and profits, 59.5(a)
foreign corporations, 59.2(g)(1)(v)
foreign operation, 59.2(g)(1)(iii)
generally, 23.3(a), 23.3(f)(1), 59.1, 59.2(a)(3), 59.2(f), 59.2(g), 60.2(b)(1)(i), 60.2(b)(2)(i)(a), 60.2(b)(2)(i)(a)(4), 60.2(b)(2)(i)(b), 60.2(c)(5)(ii), 60.3(a)(ii), 60.5(a)
generally defined as U.S. dollar, 59.2(g)(3)(viii)
identification of a functional currency, 59.2(g)(1)(iv)
notional principal contracts, 60.2(g)(2)
personal transactions, 59.2(a)(3)
qualified business units, *see* Qualified business units
rules, 59.2(g)
single functional currency, 59.2(g)(1)(v)
spot contracts, 59.4(e)
TRA '86, 59.2(g)(1)
translation rules, 59.5
Treasury regulations, final, September 1989, 59.2(g)(1)(ii)
U.S. dollar application, when used, 59.2(g)(1)(iii)
Futures arbitrage transactions, 18.4(e)(4)
Futures commission merchant(s) (FCMs):
below market interest rules, 9.2(c)(2)
CFTC-imposed disclosure obligations, 5.3(a), 5.3(b)
generally, 4, 8.1, 9.2(c)(1), 9.2(c)(2), 13.5, 22.1(b)
Futures contract(s):
acquisition pursuant to long options position, 42.1(a)
arbitrage transactions, 18.4(e)(4)
characteristics, 1.1(g)(5)
commissions, 13.5
commodities acquired, 17.3(b)
commodities, types of, 4.1, 4.3(c)

Index

Futures contract(s) (*Continued*)
 currency positions, 18.11
 dealers, 11.1(c)
 delivery under, 4.3(c), 4.5(b), 45.6(a)
 distinctions between forward contracts, 4.3(b)
 exchange gains and losses, 59.2(a)(4)
 exchange markets, 4.2(b)
 executory contracts, 4.3(c)
 forward rate agreements, 60.4(a), 60.4(a)(1)
 futures markets, 4.2(b), 4.3(c), 4.4(b), 4.5(b)
 GNMA securities, 8.9(a)(4)
 hedge transactions, 8.4(d), 12.1, 18.4(e)(1), 18.11
 holding period of property acquired, 17.3(b), 42.1(a)
 identification, 20.1, 22.1(b)
 index participations, 4.1(c)
 inventory, 18.11
 margin, 4.3(c), 4.4(b), 9.2(c), 10.2(c)
 margin deposits and credits, 9.2(c)(1)
 mark-to-market payments, 4.3(c), 4.4(b)(1), 4.4(b)(3), 9.2(c)(1), 55.1
 mark-to-market system, 44.1
 modified short sales rule, 18.4(e)(4)
 non-section 1256 futures contracts, 15.2, 42.1(a)
  foreign currency transaction(s):
   post-October 21, 1988, 59.4(b)(3)
   post-section 988, 59.4(b)(2)
   pre-1986 transactions, 59.4(b)(1)
   pre-October 22, 1988, 59.4(b)(2)
   section 988(a)(1)(B) election, effective September 21, 1989, 59.4(b)(4)
 offsetting positions, 48.2(d), 48.3(a)
 performance bond, 4.3(c)
 regulated futures contracts, *see* Regulated futures contracts (RFCs)
 round-turn commissions, 11.4, 12.1
 section 1256 contracts, *see* Section 1256 contract(s)
 settlement, 5.6
 short sales, 18.2(b), 18.4, 18.4(e), 18.11
 spreads, 4.3(c)
 substantially identical property, 18.4(e)(1), 18.4(e)(3)
 swaps, 6.2(c), 6.2(f)
 traded on different markets, 18.4(e)(3)
 traders, 8.2

 unlawful off-exchange futures contracts, 4.1(b), 6.7
 wash sales, 19.6(c)(1)
Futures margin, *see* Commodities, margin, futures margin
Futures market, 4.4(b)
 hedgers, 8.4
Futures option(s):
 after October 31, 1983, 43.3(b), 44.3(b)
 before November 1, 1983, 43.3(a), 44.3(c)
 contradictory reporting positions, 44.3(c)
 eligible for 60/40 treatment, 44.3(c)(1)
 ineligible for 60/40 treatment, 44.3(c)(2)
 generally, 5.2(b), 42.1(a), 42.1(c), 43.1

G

Gambler, professional, *see* Trade or business, professional gambler
Gambling or wagering income, 9.1(d), 10.1(b), 60.2(b)(2)(i)(a), 60.2(d)(2)(i), 60.3(a)(2)(ii)
General Motors Acceptance Corporation (GMAC), certificates, 7.2(c)(4)
General Motors Class E shares, *see* Stock General Motors Class E shares, alphabet stock
General obligation bonds, 3.1, 3.2(a), 33.2(a), 33.2(b)
General Utilities doctrine, 8.9, 28.4(a), 29.2(b)
Gifts:
 after ex-dividend date, 24.7(d)
 before ex-dividend date, 24.7(c)
 determination of basis other than cost, 16.3(a)
 gift taxes, 16.3(a), 33.3(a)(2)
Government Finance Officers Association, *see* Municipal securities
Government National Mortgage Association (GNMA) (Ginnie Mae) securities:
 book-entry form, 2.1(b)(2)
 certificates, 32.2(c)
 clearance and settlement, 2.4
 commodities, 4.1(a), 4.3(b)
 contract cancellation transactions, 58.1
 futures contracts, 8.9(a)(4)
 GNMA/ARMs, 2.1(b)(2), 7.2(c)(1)
 GNMA/GEMs, 2.1(b)(2)

GNMA/GPMs, 2.1(b)(2)
GNMA/MBSs, 2.1(b)(2)
GNMA I, 2.1(b)(2)
GNMA II, 2.1(b)(2)
graduated payment mortgages, 2.1(b)(2)
growing equity mortgages, 2.1(b)(2)
municipal securities, federal guarantees, 33.3(a)(1)(ii)
pass-through securities, 2.1(b)(2), 2.1(b)(4)
PSA good delivery guidelines, 2.1(b)(2)
sale and repurchase, 19.9(j)
substantially identical property, 19.9(j)
types of, 2.1(b)(2), 2.2(b)
VA, 2.1(b)(2)
wash sales rule, 19.9(j)
Government securities:
  agency securities, see Federal agency securities
  broker-dealers, 2
  brokers, 2
  cash transactions, 2.2(a)
  clearance and settlement, 2.4
  credit regulation, 2.3
  dealers, 2, 8.4(c)(1)
  exempted securities, 2.3
  federal agency securities, see Federal agency securities
  flower bonds, 32.1(c)
  government securities market, 2, 2.2
  individual retirement plan bonds, 2
  margin:
    credit regulation, 2.3
    exempted securities, 1.4(b)
    maintenance margin requirements, 2.3
    options margin, 5.3(a)
    Treasury securities margin, 4.4(b)(1)(i)
  marketable, 2, 2.1(a)
  nonmarketable, 2, 2.1(a)(4)
  offsetting positions, 48.2(d)
  original issue discount, 31.2
  over-the-counter, 2
  regulation, brokers and dealers, 2
  repos and reverse repos, 31.11(a)
  retirement plan bonds, 2
  same day settlement, 2.2(a)
  savings bonds, see Savings bonds
  secondary market, 2
  short sales, capitalization requirements, 55.2(c)
  transactions, types of, 2.2
  Treasury rules, 2
  Treasury securities, see Treasury securities
  types of, 2.1
Government Securities Act of 1986, 2
  regulation, government securities brokers and dealers, 2
Government Securities Clearing Corporation (GSCC), 2.4
Graduated payment mortgages (GPMs), see Government National Mortgage Association (GNMA) (Ginnie Mae) securities, GNMA/GPMs
Grantor trusts, 1.1(i), 29.1, 36.2
Growing equity mortgages (GEMs), see Government National Mortgage Association (GNMA) (Ginnie Mae) securities, GNMA/GEMs

H

Half-turn commissions, 13.5
Hedge bonds, 33.3(a)(1)(ix)
Hedged executory contracts, 23.3(g)(2)(i)
  accrual date, 23.3(g)(2)(ii), 23.3(g)(2)(iv)(b)
  defined, 23.3(g)(2)(v)
  defined, 23.3(g)(2)(iii)
  disposition before accrual date, 23.3(g)(2)(viii)(c)
  executory contract, defined, 23.3(g)(2)(ii)
  exception to definition, 23.3(g)(2)(ii)
  gain or loss, 23.3(g)(3)
  hedge disposition:
    before accrual date, 23.3(g)(2)(viii)(d)
    on or after accrual date, 23.3(g)(2)(viii)(e)
  historical rate rollover, 23.3(g)(2)(iv)(c)(1)
  hedge, 23.3(g)(2)(iv)(c)(2)
  interest income or expense, 23.3(g)(2)(iv)(c)(3)
  identification requirements, 23.3(g)(2)(vii)
  integration, 23.3(g)(2)(i), 23.3(g)(2)(viii)(a)
  nonfunctional currency, 23.3(g)(2)(ii)
  ordinary course of business, 23.3(g)(2)(ii)
  partially hedged, 23.3(g)(2)(viii)(b)
  payment date, defined, 23.3(g)(2)(vi)
  qualified business unit, 23.3(g)(3)

Index

Hedged executory contracts (*Continued*)
  requirements, 23.3(g)(2)(iii)
  section 1256 treatment, 23.3(g)(2)(viii)(f)
  series of hedges, 23.3(g)(2)(iv)(b)
  settlement date, 23.3(g)(3)
  Straddle Rules, 23.3(g)(2)(viii)(f)
  taxation, 23.3(g)(2)(viii)(a)
  trade date, 23.3(g)(3)
Hedger(s):
  Arkansas Best decision, 8.4, 8.4(d), 12
    stream of income cases, 60.2(b)(2)(i)(a)(1)
  banks, 23.2(b)(4)(ii), 23.2(d)(1)
  basis risk, 8.4(b)
  character of assets, capital or ordinary, 8.4, 8.4(d)
  defined, 8.4
  expenses, *see* Expenses, hedgers
  interest costs, 12.2
  interest deductions, 12.2
  inventories, Part Two, 8.4(d), 23.1
  notional principal contracts, 8.4, 12.2
  ordinary income and loss, 12, 21.1
  original issue discount, 31.2(c), 31.2(d)
  raw materials, 23.1
  trade or business, 8.4(b), 12.1
Hedge(s):
  accounting methods, futures, 22.1(b)
  actively traded property, 48.2(a)
  agricultural hedges, 8.4(d)
  asset hedges, 60.5(c)
  buying hedges, 8.4(c), 8.4(c)(1), 8.4(d), 23.2(a)
  capital assets, defined, 8.4, 8.4(d)
  commercial hedges, 23.3(e)
  commercial paper transactions, 23.2(b)(3)
  contract rights, 12.1
  definition, 23.2(a), 23.3(g)(2)(iv)(a)
  executory contracts, *see* Hedged executory contracts
  financial futures contracts, 8.4(d)
  foreign currency hedges, *see* Section 988 hedging transactions
  forward contracts, 12.1
  futures contracts, 12.1, 18.11
  futures markets, 8.4
  hedged accounts, 23.2(b)(4)(ii), 23.2(d)(2)
  hedged property, 8.4, 8.4(b), 23.2(b)(4), 23.2(d)
  hedge positions, 4.4(b), 8.4(b)

historical rate rollover, 23.3(g)(2)(iv)(c)(3)
identification, 12.3, 23.2(a), 23.2(b)(4)(i)
integral part of business, 8.4, 12, 23.2(a), 23.2(b)
  Arkansas Best decision, 8.4, 8.4(d), 12, 23.2(b)(3)
interest rate hedges, 8.4(d), 23.2(a), 23.2(b), 23.2(b)(3)
interest rate swap hedge transactions, *see* Interest rate swaps, hedge transactions
inventory-purchase system, 8.4(d)
investment motive, 8.4
liability hedges, 23.2(c)(4), 60.5(a), 60.5(b)(1)
long futures contract buying hedge, 8.4(c)(1)
long hedges, 8.4(c), 8.4(c)(1), 23.2(a)
long put option position selling hedge, 8.4(c)(2)
nonstatutory hedges, 23.2(g)
normal course of business, 23.2(a), 23.2(b)(2)
notional principal contracts, 8.4, 12.1
options, 8.4, 12.1, 23.2(a)
REIT, 8.4(d)
requirements for a hedge, 23.2(b)(4)(i)
reverse hedge (option), 5.4(a)(1)
section 1256(e) hedge, requirements, 23.2(b)
selling hedges, 8.4(c), 8.4(c)(2), 23.2(a)
selling interest rate hedges, 8.4(d)
short hedges, 8.4(c), 8.4(c)(2), 23.2(a)
short sales, 12.1, 18.4(e)(1), 18.11
see also Hedging transactions
Hedging exemption:
  affiliated groups, 23.2(c)(1)
  clear reflection of income, 23.2(f)
  determination of exemption, 12.3
  foreign branches, 23.2(e)(2)
  foreign currency transactions, 23.3, 46.2(b), 55.2(f)
  foreign subsidiaries, 23.2(e)(2)
  section 988 hedging transactions, 23.3(b), 55.2(f), 59.3
    fully hedged currency transactions, 23.3(f)
    identification, 23.3(f)(2)
  section 1256 treatment, 23.2
  section 1256(e), requirements, 23.2(a)
  syndicates, excluded, 23.2(a), 23.2(c)(2)(i)

Hedging transaction(s):
  active interests, 23.2(c)(2)(iii)
  affiliated groups, 23.2(c)(1)
  Arkansas Best impact, 8.4, 8.4(d), 12, 23.2(b)(3), 23.2(c)(4), 60.2(b)(1)(i)
    capital assets, defined, 8.4(d)
    financial products, taxation, 8.4, 60.2(b)(1)(i)
    open issues, 23.2(c)(4)
  bank(s):
    hedged accounts, 23.2(b)(4)(ii), 23.2(d)(2)
    repeal of special rule, 23.2(d)(1)
    special rule, 23.2(d)
  capital gain unavailable, 23.2(e)
  capital transactions, 8.4(d)
  character of gain, 23.2(c)(4)
  clear reflection of income, 23.2(f)
  Corn Products doctrine, 23.2(d)(3)(i)
  defined, 23.2(c)(1)
  designated hedging transactions, 8.9(e)
  disclosure of unrecognized gain, exempt, 52.2
  exempt from capitalization requirements, 55.2(f)
  exempt from section 1256 treatment, 46.2
  exempt from Straddle Rules, 12.3, 23.2(a), 56.2
  factors, 8.4(b)
  financial product hedges, 23.2(d)(3)
  flow-through entities, 23.2(a), 23.2(c)(2)
  foreign branches, 23.2(e)(2)
  foreign currencies, 23.1, 55.2(f), 59.3
    foreign currency-related, tax treatment, 23.3
    synthetic foreign currency transactions, 23.3
  foreign currency risks, 46.2
  foreign exchange risks, 23.2(e)(2)
  foreign subsidiaries, 23.2(e)(2)
  forwards, 23.2(a)
  futures transactions, 4.3(c), 23.2(a), 23.2(b)(3)
  hedgers, *see* Hedgers
  hedges as insurance, 23.2(c)(4)
  hedging foreign currency risks, 45.1(b)
  hedging gains (losses), 23.2(c)(3)
    carried forward, 23.2(c)(3)(iii)
    economic losses, 23.2(c)(3)(iv)
    flow-through losses, 23.2(c)(3)(i)
    limitation on deductions, 23.2(c)(3)(ii)
    limited partners and limited entrepreneurs, 23.2(c)(3)
    ordinary income (loss), 23.2(b)(3)
    property other than stock or securities, 23.2(c)(3)(ii)(b)
    reallocation to other participants prohibited, 23.2(c)(3)
    stock or securities, 23.2(c)(3)(i)(c)
    trade or business, 23.2(c)(3)(ii)(a)
  identification, 12.3, 23.2(a), 23.2(b)(4)(i), 23.2(b)(4)(iii), 23.2(e)
    improper identification, 23.2(b)(4)(iii), 23.2(e)(i)
  integral part of taxpayer's business, 23.2(a)
  interest rate hedges, 8.4(d), 23.2(a), 23.2(b), 23.2(b)(3)
  interest rate swap hedge transactions, *see* Interest rate swaps, hedge transactions
  inventory-purchase system, 8.4(d)
  liability hedges, 23.2(c)(4)
  limitation(s):
    hedging losses, 23.2(c)(3)
    limited entrepreneurs, 23.2(a), 23.2(c)(2), 23.2(c)(3)
    limited partners, 23.2(a), 23.2(c)(2), 23.2(c)(3)
    related persons, 23.2(c)(1)
    syndicates, 23.2(a), 23.2(c)(2)
    trade or business interpretation, 23.2(c)(3)(ii)(a)
    unrecognized gain, 23.2(c)(3)
    who can qualify, 23.2(c)(1)
  limited entrepreneurs, 23.2(a), 23.2(c)(2)(ii), 23.2(c)(3)
  limited partners, 23.2(a), 23.2(c)(2), 23.2(c)(3)
  marked-to-market, 12.3
  Mark-to-Market Rule, 23.2(a), 23.2(b)(4)(iii), 45.1, 45.1(b)
  net worth of foreign branches, 23.2(e)
  nonpassive interests, 23.2(c)(2)(iii)
  non-section 1256 positions, 23.2(a)
  nonstatutory hedges, 23.2(g)
  normal course of business, 23.2(b)(1)
  notional principal contracts, 8.4, 12.2
  options, 23.2(a)
  ordinary income or loss, 21.8, 23.2(b)(3), 23.2(b)(4)(iii), 23.3(c)
  ordinary income transactions, 23.2(d)(3)
  participation in enterprise, 23.2(c)(2), 45.2(c)(2)

Index

I-40

Hedging transaction(s) (*Continued*)
  passive investors, 23.2(c)(2)(ii)
  personal property positions, 23.2(a)
  pre-DRA stock option transactions, 30.2
  primarily to reduce certain risks, 23.2(a), 23.2(b)(2)
  qualified hedging transactions, *see* Qualified hedging transactions
  real economic losses, 23.2(c)(3)
  regulated investment companies, 8.9(e)
  rules for banks, 23.2(d)(1)
  savings and loan futures position, 23.2(b)(3), 23.2(d)(3)(i)
  section 988 hedging transactions, *see* Section 988 hedging transactions
  section 1256 treatment, exempt from, 12, 12.3, 23.1, 23.2(a), 46.2(a), 46.2(b)
  section 1256(e) transactions, 23.2(a)
  short sales rule, 18.4(e)(2)
  statutory requirements, 23.2(b)
  Straddle Rules, 8.4(d), 12, 12.3, 23.2(a), 23.2(g), 56.2
  syndicates, 23.2(a), 23.2(c)(2)
  trade or business, 23.2(c)(3)(ii)(a)
  under section 1256(e), 23.2(a)
  whipsaw under section 1256(f)(1), 23.2(c)(4), 23.2(e)(1)
  see also Hedges
Historical rate rollovers, 23.3(g)(2)(iv)(c)(1)
Holding period:
  acquisition and disposition date(s):
    computation, 17.1(a)
    date capital asset is acquired, 17.2(a)(1)
    date option holder gives notice of exercise, 17.2(c)(2)
    date securities are issued, 17.2(c)(2)
    date title to asset passes, 17.2(a)(1)
    determination, 17.2
    escrow must be established, 17.2(a)(2)(ii)
    general rule, 17.2(a)(1)
    more than six-month capital asset, 17.1(b)
    more than 12-month capital asset, 17.1(b)
    purchase from another holder, 17.2(a)
    taxable distributions, 17.2(a)(3), 17.2(a)(4)
    taxable exchanges, 17.2(a)(3)
    taxable transactions, 17.2(a)(3)

    Treasury securities, 17.2(b)
  arbitrage transactions, 18.10(a)
  automatic investment service, 17.2(a)(5)
  boot, 17.3(a)
  cash basis taxpayer, 17.1(b)
  commodities, acquired pursuant to futures contracts, 17.3(b)
  computation, 17.1
  contingent payment right, 30.5(b)(3)
  corporate reorganization, 17.3(a)(1)
  corporate shareholder's holding period, 24.1(f)(2)
  corporate stock, determination, 17.7(a)
  date capital asset is acquired, 17.2(a)(1)
  date option holder gives notice of exercise, 17.2(c)(2)
  date securities are issued, 17.2(c)(2)
  date taxpayer becomes shareholder, 17.2(c)(1)
  date title to asset passes, 17.2(a)(1)
  determined by reference to other property, 17.4
  direct purchases of securities from issuing corporation, 17.2(c)
  donor's holding period tacked, 17.3(c)(1)
  escrow account, 17.2(a)(1)
  exception for losses, 17.3(c)(1)
  exception, killer rule, 54.4(a)
  exchanged securities, 17.3(a)
  executory contract, 17.2(a)(1)
  exercise of warrants or options, 17.2(c)(2)
  extraordinary dividends, 17.7(c)
  FIFO, 20.2(b)
  fractional share of stock, 17.4(a)
  gifts, 17.3(c)(1)
  installment method, 17.2(a)(2)(i)
  intercorporate dividends received, 16.6(a), 17.7, 19.9(f), 24.9, 24.9(b)(1)
  leap year computation, 17.1(a)
  long contract position, 17.2(a)(6)
  loss securities, 17.4(b)
  method of computation, 17.1(b)
  modification of sales agreement, 17.2(a)(2)(ii)
  modified wash sales and short sales, 17.4(d)
  non-section 1256 futures contract, 17.3(b)
  nontaxable stock dividends, 17.4(a)
  one-year holding period, 16.6(a)
  option exercise, 17.2(c)(2)

property acquired from a decedent, 17.1(d)
property contributed to partnership, 17.3(c)(2)
property dividends, 17.2(a)(4)
put feature, 17.2(a)(2)(i)
qualified corporation, 16.6(b)
qualified covered calls, 17.7(a), 17.9
qualifying purchaser evidences of indebtedness, 17.2(a)(2)(i)
regulated investment companies, 17.6, 54.4(c)
reorganization plan, 17.3(a)(1)
rules, not applicable to section 1256 contracts, 54.4(a)
section 1092(b)(2) identified mixed straddles, 57.3(h)
section 1256 contracts, 17.3(b), 17.5
security arbitrage transactions, 18.10(a)
security loan transactions, 17.8
seller's option transactions, 17.2(a)(5)
shares of stock represented by cash payment, 17.3(a)(3)
shares of stock represented by convertible securities, 17.3(a)(3)
short sales, 17.4(c), 17.7(a), 18.3(b)
   suspension of holding period, 17.4(c), 18.6(e)(3)
stock dividends, 17.4(a)
stock rights, 17.2(a)(4), 17.2(c)(3), 17.4(a)
stock scrip, 17.4(a)
stock with debentures, 17.2(a)(2)(i)
straddles, holding period:
   effective date, 57.8
   suspended, 54.4(a)
subscription for securities, 17.2(c)(1)
subsidiary's holding period, 17.3(c)(4)
substantially identical property, 17.4(b), 17.7(a)
substituted basis, tacked, 17.3(a)(2), 17.3(a)(4)
suspension of, short sales, 17.4(c), 18.6(e)(3)
tacked holding period, 17.3, 17.3(a)(2), 17.3(c)(3), 17.3(c)(4), 17.4(b), 17.7, 20.2(b)
   carry-over basis, 17.3(c)
   contribution to capital, 17.3(a)(4)
   controlled corporations, transfers, 17.3(c)(3)
   convertible securities, 17.3(a)(3)
   estates or trusts, 17.3(c)(5)
   exchanged securities, 17.3(a)
   futures contracts, 17.3(b)
   gifts, 17.3(c)(1)
   liquidations, 17.3(c)(4)
   of another person, 17.3(c)
   partnership transactions, 17.3(c)(2)
   reorganizations, 17.3(a)(1)
   rule for wash sales, 17.7(a)
   stock exchanged for stock, 17.3(a)(2)
   substituted basis, 17.3(a)(2), 17.3(a)(4)
   wash sales, 17.7(a)
title to asset, date passed, 17.2(a)(1)
trade date, 17.2(a)(5)
two-year holding period, 16.6(b)
warrants, acquisition date, 17.2(c)(2)
wash sales, 17.4(b), 17.7(a), 19.3(d)
worthless securities, 17.1(c)
writing call options, 17.7(b)
year-end transactions, 17.2(a)(2)
Horizontal spreads, 5.4(c)
Hybrid securities, 1.1(g)
Hypothetical back-to-back loans, *see* Commodity Swaps
Hypothetical borrowing, *see* Foreign currency swaps
Hypothetical exchange gain (loss), *see* Foreign currency swaps
Hypothetical interest income, *see* Foreign currency swaps
Hypothetical issue price, *see* Foreign currency swaps
Hypothetical loan, *see* Foreign currency swaps
Hypothetical stated redemption price, *see* Foreign currency swaps

I

IDBs, *see* Industrial development bonds (IDBs); *see also* Private activity bonds (PABs)
Identification of securities:
   acquisition date, 20.2(b)
   actual delivery of certificates, 20.2(a)(1)(ii)
   adequately identified, 20.2(a)(1)(i), 20.2(e)
   adequate records, 20.1
   book-entry securities, 11.7(c), 20.2(e), 22.2(c)
   capital assets, 20.1
   certificated and uncertificated, no distinction, 16.2(b), 20.3

Index

Identification of securities (*Continued*)
  clearing facility, 11.7(c)
  confirmation statements, 20.2(a)(1)
  confirmed by FRB bank acknowledgment, 20.2(e)
  dealer(s):
    accounting methods, *see* Accounting methods, dealers
    inventory methods, *see* Inventory methods, dealers
    investment securities, 11.7(c)
    specific identification by dealers, 11.7(c), 22.2(c)
  distributed to beneficiary, 20.2(a)(3)
  fiduciaries, held by, 20.2(a)(3)
  first-in, first-out rule, 20.2, 20.2(b), 20.2(d)
  for allocation of basis, 16.2(b)
  hedging transactions, 23.2(b)(4)(i)
  identification procedure, 20.2(a)(2)
  incorrect identification of investments by dealers, 11.7(d)
  investment account identification, *see* Investment accounts
  institutional investor, 20.2(a)(2)
  lot numbers and numerical sequences, 20.2(e)
  mistaken delivery by broker or agent, 20.2(a)(1)(ii)
  mutual fund shares, 16.2(b), 20.3
  noncash dividends, 20.2(c)
  particular securities, 20.2(a)(1)(iii)
  physical commodities, 20.2(f)
  purchased through broker or another agent, 20.2(a)(1)
  records, 20.1, 20.2
  registered securities, 20.2(a)(1)
  regulated investment companies:
    double-category method, 20.2(f)
    single-category method, 20.2(f)
  securities, 20.2
  single certificate representing two or more lots, 20.2(a)(1)(iii)
  specific identification, 20.2(a), 20.2(f), 22.2(b), 22.2(c)
  specific instructions, 20.2(a)(1)(ii)
  street name securities, 20.2(a)(2)
  uncertificated mutual fund, 16.2(b)
  warehouse receipts, 20.2(f)
  written confirmations, 20.2(a)(1)(iii), 20.2(e)
Identified section 1092(b)(2) mixed straddle(s):
  attribution rules, 51.4
  clear identification, 57.3(a)
  close of the day, 57.3(a)
  direct ownership requirement, 57.6(a)
  election, 45.4(b), 57.1
    carry-back provisions, affected, 45.4(b)
    joint election, unavailable, 57.6(a)
    limitations on election, 57.6
  flow-through entity, 51.4
  gains and losses:
    accrued, 57.3(c)
    netted, 57.3(b)
  generally, 51.4, 57.1, 57.6(a), 57.6(b)
  holding period rules, 57.3(h)
  identification, 51.4, 57.6(a)
  independent verification, 57.3(a), 57.3(a)(3)
  killer rule, inapplicable, 57.3
  labelling requirements, 57.3(a)
  loss deferral rules, 57.3(h)
  matched on timely basis, 57.3(a)(3)
  methods of verification, 57.3(a)(1), 57.3(a)(2), 57.3(a)(3)
  non-section 1256 positions, disposition, 57.3(e)
  partial disposition of positions, 57.3(g)
  related persons, 51.4, 57.6(a)
  same day disposition, 57.3(d)
  section 1092(b)(2) identified mixed straddle account, 57.3(a)(1)
  section 1256 positions, disposition, 57.3(f)
  separate accounts, 57.3(a)(1)
  straddle-by-straddle netting, 57.3
  Treasury regulations, requirements, 57.6
Identified section 1256(d) mixed straddle(s):
  delivery under long section 1256 contracts, 57.2(c)
  exercise of long section 1256 contracts, 57.2(c)
  futures contracts, tacked holding period, 17.3(b)
  generally, 17.3(b), 42.1(a), 45.1, 45.1(b), 45.6(c), 51.2, 54.4(b), 57.1, 57.2, 57.2(a), 57.2(b), 57.3
  limited scope of election, 57.2(b)
  mixed straddle election under section 1256(d), one-time, 57
  not attractive for most taxpayers, 57.2
Identified straddle(s):

box spread, 56.1(a)
butterfly spread, 56.1(a)
generally, 45.3, 52.2, 56, 56.1, 57.1, 57.2(b)
not part of larger straddle, 56.1(a)
original positions acquired on same day, 56.1(a)
requirements, 56.1(a)
Straddle Rules, exemption, 56.1(a)
subsequent transactions, 56.1(b)

Income:
capital transactions, 14.5
cash basis taxpayer, 14.5(a)
constructive receipt, 24.7(f)
defined for purposes of section 212 expenses, 9.1(a)
foreign persons, 23.3(g)(1)(v)(c)
gambling or wagering income, 9.1(d), 10.1(b), 60.2(b)(2)(i)(a), 60.2(d)(2)(i), 60.3(a)(2)(ii)
gifts:
 after ex-dividend date, 24.7(d)
 before ex-dividend date, 24.7(c)
in respect of a decedent, 18.2(c)
interest, *see* Interest income
interest-like, 60.2(b)(1)(i), 60.2(d)(1)(i)
investment interest income, 9.2(e), 10.2(e)
loans outstanding, 14.5(d)
losses, settlement date, 14.5(d)
loss on closing short sale of property, 14.5(d)
ordinary income, *see* Ordinary income or loss, ordinary income
personal holding company income, 13.6
phantom income, 9.1(d), 19.9(i), 36.4(c), 39.2(c), 41.2(k)
preferred stock, 24
qualified hedging transaction, 23.3(g)(1)(v)(c)
receipt of futures margin, 9.2(c)(1)
recognition of gain, 14.5(b)
reflected with accuracy, 22.3
REMIC regular interests, 2.1(b)(4), 7.2(g), 36.8(c)(1)
REMIC residual interests, 2.1(b)(4), 7.2(g), 36.8(c)(2)
reporting income, 14.5, 24.7(a)
 accrual basis, 24.7(a)
 characterization of interest, 25.5
 dealers, *see* Accounting methods, dealers
 deductions, 14.5(c)
 dividends, 14.5(a), 24.7(a), 24.7(b), 24.7(d)
 dividends received deduction, 24.9(b)(1), 24.9(b)(2), 24.9(b)(3)
 expenses, *see* Expenses
 gain, 14.5(b)
 income, 14.5(a)
 intercorporate dividends received, 24.9(b)(1), 24.9(b)(2), 24.9(b)(3)
 interest, 25.1
 losses, 14.5(d)
 record date, 24.7(a)
 regular way transactions, 24.7(c), 24.7(d)
 sale(s):
  after ex-dividend date, 24.7(d)
  before ex-dividend date, 24.7(c)
  generally, 14.1, 14.4
  of commodity, 42.1(e)
  or disposition, 19.7
 settlement date, 14.5(b), 17.2(a)(5)
  gain on securities, 14.5(b)
  losses on securities, 14.5(d)
 stock held as collateral for loan, 24.7(c)
 swap income, 60.2(g)(2)
  stream of income cases, analogy, 60.2(b)(2)(i)(a)(1)
  substitute for interest, 60.2(b)(2)(i)(a)(1)
 tax-exempt income:
  defined, 9.3(a)
  expenses, 9.3, 10.3
 tax-exempt securities, sales, 33.3(c)
 trade date, 14.5(b), 17.2(a)(5)
Income averaging:
 current law, 15.4(e)(1)
 generally, 15.4(e)
 pre-TRA '86 law, 15.4(e)(2)
 repealed, 15.4(e)(1)
 retained for qualified farmers, 15.4(e), 15.4(e)(3)
 section 1256 contract losses, 45.4(a)
Increasing rate exchangeable guaranteed preferred stock, 1.1(g)(7), 27.2, 27.3(b)(3)(v)
Indexed debt securities, 1.1(g)(5)
Index(es):
 AMEX Institutional Index, 44.3
 broad-based index, 30.1, 30.4, 44.3
 floating rate index, 6.4
 interest rate index, 6.1, 60.5(a)
 Major Market Index, 5.2(a)(4)
 municipal bond index, 8.9(a)(2)

Index

Index(es) (*Continued*)
  narrow-based index, 30.3(a)
  NASDAQ 100 Index, 5.2(b), 5.3(b)
  Nikkei Stock Average, 5.2(a)(4)
  NYSE Composite Index, 5.2(a)(4)
  objective interest index, 36.8(c)(1)(iv)
  PSE High Technology Index, 44.3
  rate indexes, 6.1
  S&P 100 Index, 5.2(a)(4), 48.2(c)(2)
  S&P 500 Index, 1.1(g)(5), 5.2(a)(4), 5.2(b), 48.2(c)(2)
  S&P 500 stock index futures, 5.2(b), 48.2(c)(2)
  stock indexes, 5.2(a)(4), 17.7, 48.2(c), 48.2(d)
  United States Treasury security index, 1.1(g)(3), 1.1(g)(4)
  Value Line Composite Index, 5.2(a)(4)
Index participations (IPs), 4.1(c)
Individual retirement bonds, *see* Government securities, individual retirement bonds
Industrial development bonds (IDBs), 3.1, 3.2(c), 25.1, 25.4(b)
see also Private activity bonds
Information network:
  partnerships, 28.4(c)(4)
Information return(s):
  dividends, 13.3, 24.10
  exempt recipients, 13.3
  failure to file, 13.3
  interest, 13.3, 24.10
Installment bonds, 31.3
Installment method:
  cash basis taxpayer, 14.5(b)(1), 17.2(a)(2)(i)(e)
  defined, 17.2(a)(2)(i)(c)
  electing out of installment method, 17.2(a)(2)(i)(d), 17.2(a)(2)(i)(e)
  examples, 17.2(a)(2)(i)(d)
  gain, 14.5(b)(1), 14.5(b)(2)
  general considerations, 17.2(a)(2)(i)(c)
  holding period, 17.2(a)(2)(i)
  intermediaries, 17.2(a)(2)(i)
  late election, 17.2(a)(2)(i)(c)
  losses, 17.2(a)(2)(i)(f)
  pass-through entities, 17.2(a)(2)(i)
  property traded on established market, 14.5(b)
  publicly traded property, 14.5(b)(2), 17.2(a)(2)(i)(b)
  qualifying purchaser evidences of indebtedness, 17.2(a)(2)(i)(c)
  regular way trades, 17.2(a)(2)(i)(e)
  related parties, 17.2(a)(2)(i)
  reporting gain, 1.3(h)
  revolving credit plans, 17.2(a)(2)(i)(b)
  sales after December 31, 1986, 17.2(a)(2)(i)(b)
  sales before January 1, 1987, 17.2(a)(2)(i)(a)
  Schedule D, 17.2(a)(2)(i)(c)
  stock and securities, 1.3(h), 14.5(b), 17.2(a)(2)(i)
  TRA '86 limitations, 17.2(a)(2)(i)(b)
Installment notes, *see* Debt securities, installment notes
Installment sales:
  bank holding company, 17.2(a)(2)(i)(c)
  defined, 17.2(a)(2)(i)(a)
  generally, 1.3(h), 14.5(b), 17.2(a)(2)(i)
Insurance companies, 1.4(a), 27.5(a)(1)
Insurance on securities, 1.1(g), 3.3, 33.3(a)(1)(v)
Integrated economic transaction(s):
  defined, 23.3(g)(1)(i)(c)
  identification requirements, 23.3(g)(1)(iv)
  interest rate swap hedge transactions, 60.2(b)(1)
  legging in (legging out), special rules, 23.3(g)(1)(ii)
  qualifying debt instrument, 23.3(g)(1)(i)(c)
  section 1.988-5T(a) hedge, 23.3(g)(1)(i)(c)
  section 1256 contract treatment, 23.3(g)(1)(v)(a)
  Straddle Rules, 23.3(g)(1)(v)(a)
Integration treatment, 60.2(b)(1), 60.2(b)(1)(i), 60.2(b)(1)(iii), 60.2(b)(2)(i)(a)(1), 60.2(b)(2)(ii), 60.2(c)(4), 60.3(a)(1)(ii), 60.5(a), 60.5(b)(1), 60.6
Interbank market, 44.2, 44.2(a)
Intercommodity spread, 4.3(c)
Intercorporate dividends received deduction(s):
  adjustable rate preferred stock (ARPS), 1.1(g), 27.3(b)(3)(ii)
  affiliated group deduction, 24.9(a)(2)
  Americus trusts, 29.3(b)(2)
  convertible adjustable preferred stock (CAPS), 17.7(b), 24.9(b), 24.9(b)(1), 27.3(b)(3)(iii), 27.3(b)(3)(vii)
  debt financed portfolio stock, 24.9(c)

dividend stripping, 16.6(c), 16.6(e), 24.9(b)
domestic corporations, 24.9(a)
80 percent deduction, 24.9(a)(1)
85 percent deduction, 24.9(a)(1)
fail sales, 24.9(b)(3), 26.4
Federal Home Loan banks, 24.9(d)
generally, 1.3(d), 16.6, 16.6(a), 16.6(f), 17.7, 24.7, 24.9, 24.9(a), 27.2, 27.3(b)(2), 29.2(b), 48.2(c)(2), 48.4(b), 55.2(b), 56.3(d)
general rule, 24.9(a)(1)
holding period requirement, 17.7(a), 19.9(f)
  reduced, 24.9(b)(1)
limitations, 24.9(a)
loaned stock, 24.9(b)(3)
net operating loss, 24.9(a)(1)
OBRA, corporate shareholders, 24.9(a)
100 percent deduction, 24.9(a)(2)
ordinary income dividends, 8.9(c)
out-of-the-money call options, 24.9(b)(1)
preferred stock, 27.3(b)(3)
publicly traded partnerships, 28.4(e)
reduced, certain corporate shareholders, 24.9(a)
reporting income, 24.9(b)(1), 24.9(b)(3)
70 percent deduction, 24.9(a)(1)
short sales, 18.6(a), 24.9(b)(3)
short sales, used to cover, 26.4
small business investment companies, 24.9(a)(2), 24.9(c)(2), 27.6(c)
special 100 percent exclusion, 24.9(a)(2)
stock in bank holding companies, 24.9(c)
stock in banks, 24.9(c)
stock options, 30.3(d)(2)(ii)
substantially identical property, 24.9(b)(2)
substantially similar or related property, 17.7(b)
taxable years after 1987, 24.9(a)
  holding period requirements, 16.6(b), 16.6(c), 17.7, 24.9(b)
20 percent owned corporations, 24.9(a)(1)
underlying interest, option, stock, 30.3(d)(2)(ii)
Interest, *see also* Interest and carrying charges; Interest expense; Interest income
characterization:
  investment interest, 25.5
  passive activities, 42.2
  personal interest, 25.5
  portfolio interest, 25.5, 42.2
  restricted, 45.4(c)
  synthetic interest, 60.2(b)(1)(i), 60.2(b)(2)(i)(a)(1)
constructive receipt, 25.2
definition, 30.3(d)(3)
dividends, 24.10
information reports, 24.10
overpayment of tax, 45.4(c)
reporting, 25.6
statement mailing, 24.10
Interest and carrying charge(s):
capitalization, 9.2(f), 11.7(f), 12.1, 18.6(e)(5), 23.2(g), 48.3(b)(2), 55.2(a)
carrying charge(s):
  defined, 55.1, 57.4(d)
  insurance expenses, 55.1, 55.2
  storage, 55.1
  transportation, 55.1
insurance expenses, 55.1, 55.2
mixed straddles, 57.4(d)
  allocable to account, 57.4(d)
  dividends, 57.4(d)
  net interest and expenses, 57.4
  netted for year, 57.4(d)
offsetting long positions, 55.2(a)
section 1256 contract straddles, exemption, 56.7
storage, 55.1, 55.2
straddle positions, 9.2(f), 10.2(f)
tax-exempt securities, 18.6(e)(1)
temporary use of property, 18.6(a), 24.9(b)(3), 26.2(e), 55.2(c)
transportation, 55.1
Interest-bearing asset, 60.5(c)
Interest-bearing liability, 60.5(b)(1)
Interest deferral, market discount bonds, 31.3(m)
Interest equivalent treatment, 60.3(a)(1)(ii), 60.5(b)(1), 60.5(c)
Interest exclusion, 25.3, 33.2(c)(2)(iv), 33.3(a)(1)
Interest expense(s):
accrual basis taxpayer, 9.2(a)
accrued interest, 34.2(e), 55.1
allowable deductions for carrying tax-exempt securities, 9.3(b)(1)
capitalized, 48.3(b)(2)
cash basis taxpayer, 9.2(a)
character, 9.2(a)
constructively paid, 9.2(b)

Index

Interest expense(s) (*Continued*)
  corporate dealers, 11.3(b)(2)
  dealers, costs, 11.2
  deducted, 31.2(a), 55.1
  deductibility, 10.2(a)
  financial institutions, special rules, 11.3(b)(3), 11.3(b)(3)(ii)(e)
  flat bonds, interest on, 31.8
  foreign apportionment rules, 60.5(b)(1)
  foreign person, 23.3(g)(1)(v)(b)
  generally, 9.2(a), 9.3(b)(5), 10.2(a), 11.3(b)(3)(ii)(c), 12.1, 55.1
  hedgers, 12.2
  historical rate rollovers, 23.3(g)(2)(iv)(c)(3)
  inability to deduct, 48.3(b)(3)
  interest on indebtedness, 10.2(a)
  investment interest, *see* Investment interest
  investors, 9.2
  issuer payments made to parent corporation, 34.2(e)
  issuers of zero coupon securities, 31.5(a)
  margin account interest, 9.2(b), 9.2(e), 9.3(b)(5)
  margin accounts, 9.2(b), 9.3(b)(5)
  mixed straddle account, 55.2(d)
  noncorporate dealers, 11.3(b)(2)
  passive activities, 9.2(a), 9.2(e), 10.2(a)
  personal interest, 9.2(a), 9.2(b), 9.2(e), 9.2(h)
  portfolio interest, 9.2(a), 10.2(a)
  pre-ERTA business expenses, 55.1
  prepaid interest, 9.2(d), 10.2(d)
  qualified hedging transaction, 23.3(g)(1)(v)(b)
  securities broker, 11.3(b)(1)
  short sales, 55.2(c)
  short-term obligations, 55.2(e)
  synthetic debt instrument, 23.3(g)(1)(v)(e)
  tax-exempt securities, 9.3(b), 9.3(b)(5), 10.3(b), 11.3(b), 18.6(e)(1), 33.2, 33.3(d), 33.6
    dealers, de minimis exception unavailable to, 11.3(b)(2)
    de minimis exception, 9.3(b)(4), 10.3(b), 11.3(b)(2)
  trade or business interest, 10.2(a), 55.1
  traders, 10.2
Interest income:
  accrual basis taxpayer, 25.1
  cash basis taxpayer, 25.2
  constructive receipt, 25.2
  credited to taxpayer, 25.1, 33.3(a)
    market discount, 31.3, 48.3(b)(2)(iii)
    received by taxpayer, 25.1
    reporting, 31.5(a)
    tax-exempt interest, 25.4(a)
      debt securities, 16.4(*l*)
      financial institution, 11.3(b)(3)(ii)(e)
  credit for the elderly (or disabled), 25.3
  foreign person, 23.3(g)(1)(v)(b)
  historical rate rollovers, 23.3(g)(2)(iv)(c)(3)
  interest-like income, 60.2(b)(1)(i), 60.2(d)(1)(i)
  municipal securities, 3.1, 33.3(a)
  nonfunctional currency, 23.3(g)(2)(iv)(d)
  passive activities, 25.5, 42.2
  portfolio income, 9.8, 25.5, 42.2
  qualified hedging transactions, 23.3(g)(1)(v)(b)
  registration requirements, 25.4(d), 31.12, 33.3(a)(1)(iii)
  reporting, 31.5(a)
  short sales, 1.3(i)
  straddle expenses, capitalized, 55.2(b)
  stripped bonds, 31.6
  synthetic debt instrument, 23.3(g)(1)(v)(e)
  Treasury securities, 2.1(a)(4)(i), 2.1(a)(4)(ii), 32.1, 32.1(b)(1)
Interest on flat bonds, 31.8
Interest only strips, *see* Asset-backed securities interest only (IO) strips
Interest on tax-exempt securities:
  de minimis exception, 10.3(b)
  unavailable to dealers, 11.3(b)(2)
  sufficiently direct relationship, 9.3(b)(2)
Interest rate:
  caps, *see* Caps
  collars, *see* Collars
  compound interest rate, 31.3(f)
  constant (based on yield to maturity), 31.2(d)
  constant interest rate, 31.3(f)
  economic interest method, 31.2(e)
  federal rate, 41.2(g)(3)
  fence, *see* Floors
  floors, *see* Floors
  resetting, 1.1(g)(3)
  swaps, *see* Interest rate swaps
Interest rate hedges, *see* Hedges, interest rate hedges
Interest rate index, *see* Indexes

Index

Interest rate-sensitive products, 8.4(d)
Interest rate swap(s):
  Arkansas Best decision, 60.2(b)(1)(i), 60.2(b)(1)(iii)
  basis swaps, 6.2(a)(2)
  cross-currency interest rate swaps ("circuses"), 6.2(b)(2)
  defined, 6.2(a)
  exchanges of notional principal amount, 60.2(b)(1)(i)
  fixed-for-floating rate swap, 60.2(b)
  fixed rate liability, 60.2(b)
  floating index, 60.2(b)
  floating rate liability, 60.2(b)
  floating-to-fixed rate swap, 60.2(b)(1)(iii)
  forward rate agreements, 60.4(a), 60.4(a)(3)
  functional currency, 60.2(b)(1), 60.2(b)(2)(i)(a), 60.2(b)(2)(i)(a)(4), 60.2(b)(2)(i)(b)
  generally, 6.2(a), 60.2(b)
  hedge transactions, 60.2(b)(1)
    capital assets, 60.2(b)(1)(iii)
    cash settlements, 60.2(b)(1)(i)
    economic accrual, 60.2(b)(1)(i)
    integrated transaction, 60.2(b)(1), 60.2(b)(1)(iii)
    interest-like income, 60.2(b)(1)(i)
    interest rate exposure, 6.2(a)
    interim payments, 60.2(b)(1)(i)
    liability hedge treatment, 60.5(b)(1)
    offset to interest income or expense, 60.2(b)(1)(i)
    periodic swap payments prior to maturity, 60.2(b)(1)(i)
    synthetic fixed rate date, 60.2(b)(1)(iii)
    synthetic interest, 60.2(b)(1)(i)
    termination payments, 60.2(b)(1)(iii)
    up-front and assignment fees, 60.2(b)(1)(ii)
      amortized, 60.2(b)(2)(i)(c)
  interest rate index, 6.1
  LIBOR, 60.2(b)
  nonhedge transactions, 60.2(b)(2)
    cross-currency interest rate swap, 6.2(b)(2)
    exempt from Straddle Rules, 60.2(b)
    functional currency, 60.2(b)(2)(i)(a)
    gambling or wagering income analogy, 60.2(b)(2)(i)(a)
    interest rate movements, 60.2(b)(2)
    periodic swap payments, 60.2(b)(2)(i)
    active conduct of business, 60.2(b)(2)(i)(a)(1)
    character, 60.2(b)(2)(i)(a)
    described, 60.2(b)(2)(i)(a)(1)
    international transactions, 60.2(b)(2)(i)(a)(1)
    not considered interest, 60.2(b)(2)(i)(a)(1)
    ordinary income, 60.2(b)(2)(i)(a)
    purchase of U.S. dollars, 60.2(b)(2)(i)(a)(2)
    source of income for periodic swap payments, 60.2(b)(2)(i)(d)
    synthetic interest, 60.2(b)(2)(i)(a)(1)
    termination treatment, 60.2(b)(2)(ii)
    time and amount, 60.2(b)(2)(i)(b)
    up-front and assignment fees, 60.2(b)(2)(i)(c)
      amortized, 60.2(b)(2)(i)(c)
  Notice 87-4, 60.2(g)(1), 60.2(g)(2), 60.5(a)
  Notice 89-21, 60.2(a)
  notional principal amount, 60.2(b)
  plain vanilla swaps, 6.2(a)(1), 60.2(d)
  section 988, not applicable, 60.2(a)
  sourcing rules, 60.5(a)
  taxation, 60.2(a), 60.2(e)(1)
  underlying property, cash, 60.2(b)(1), 60.2(e)(2)
  U.S. dollar-denominated, sourcing, 60.5(a)
Intergovernmental tax immunity, doctrine of, 31.12(a), 32.2
Intermarket arbitrage, 8.7
Intermarket spread, 4.3(c)
International Primary Market Association (IPMA) disclosure standards, *see* Swaps, IPMA disclosure standards
International Swap Dealers Association (ISDA) Code, *see* Swaps, ISDA Code
In-the-money options, 17.7, 24.9(b)(1), 48.4(b)
Intramarket arbitrage, 8.7
Intramarket spread, 4.3(c)
Intrinsic value, options, 5.1
Inventory:
  bond premiums, 31.4
  clearly reflects income, 22.3
  dealers, 8.3, 11.4(b)
  exclusion, 8.4(d)
  futures contracts, 18.11
  hedging, 8.4(d), 23.1
  inventory items, 52.2
  inventory-purchase system, 8.4(d)

Index

Inventory (*Continued*)
  lower of cost or market, 11.4(b)
  market value, 11.4(b)
  methods, *see* Inventory methods
  necessary under certain circumstances, 55.1
  not confined to dealer or manufacturer, 55.1
  options market maker, 11.9(c)
  ordinary income or loss, 21.1
  personal holding company income, 13.6
  pre-ERTA, interest and carrying charges, 55.1
  securities, 11.11, 11.12
  short positions, 22.2(d)
  special rule for inventories not valued at cost, 11.4(b)
  swaps, 60.2(b)(2)(ii)
  traders, unavailable, 10.1(e)
  see also Inventory methods
Inventory method(s):
  amount realized, 21.3
  capitalization of certain direct and indirect costs, 22.4
    comprehensive IRS Notices, clarifying, 22.4
    costs identified, 22.4
  clear reflection of income, 22.3
  cost flow assumptions, 22.2
  cost flow methods, 22.2(b), 22.3
  dealers, 11.6, 22.2(c), 60.2(b)(2)(ii)
  dealer valuation basis, 22.2(d)
  lower of cost or market, 11.4(b), 22.2(a)
  opening inventory, 22.2
  short positions, 22.2(d)
  simplified method, 22.4
  specific identification, 22.2(c)
  uniform inventory capitalization, 22.4
  valuation bases, 22.2, 22.2(a), 22.3
    cost, 22.2(a)
    lower of cost or market, 22.2(a)
  valuation methods, 22.2(a)
  verification methods, 22.2(c)
Investment account(s):
  financial institutions, 8.8
  investment activities, 8.1
  investment interest limitations, 11.7(a)
  investment positions, 8.8, 18.9
  passive income, 11.7(a)
  passive loss limitations, 11.7(a)
  securities dealer investment accounts, *see* Securities dealers, investment accounts
  securities used as collateral, 11.7(a)
  underwriters, 11.8(b)
Investment Company Act of 1940:
  asset-backed securities, application, 7.6(d)
  disclosure requirements, 7.6(d)
  partnership, 28.4(d)(1)
  RICs, 7.6(d), 8.9(a), 8.9(a)(2)
Investment company, defined, 7.6(d)
Investment expenses, *see generally* Expenses; *see also* Section 212 expenses
Investment interest:
  generally, 9.2(b), 9.2(e), 9.2(h), 10.2(e), 15.4(a)(2)(ii)(c), 18.6(e)(1), 42.2, 55.1
  securities margin accounts, 9.2(b)
  short sales, 18.6(e)(1)
  tax preference item, 15.4(a)(2)(ii)(c)
Investment interest limitations, bond premiums, 31.4(a)(2)
Investment property, *see* Capital assets, investment property
Investment trust(s):
  actively traded trust interests, 29.1(e)
  generally, 7.2(c)(1), 29.1, Part Eight, 36.2, 36.4(b), 39.2(a)
  grandfather provision, Americus trusts, 29.3(b)(1)
  multiple ownership classes, prohibited, 29.1(c)
  taxation of certificate owners, 29.1(d)
  tax considerations, 29.1, 29.1(a), 29.1(c)
  trust certificates, 29.1(a), 29.1(d)
  trustee powers, 29.1(a), 29.1(b)
  varying investments, prohibited, 29.1(b)
Investment units, 30.5
  original issue discount, 31.2(j)
  preferred stock, 31.2(j)
  reset notes, 31.2(j)
Investor(s):
  arbitrageur, 8.7(d)
  associated person, 8.2(c)
  character of assets, capital or ordinary, 9
  defined, 8.1
  expenses, *see* Expenses, investors; *see also* Section 212 expenses
  generally, 1.4, 7.2(c)(1), 8.1, 9.1, 9.1(d), 9.2, 9.3, 11, 11.7(b), 31.1, 31.2(c), 31.2(d)
  institutional investors, 8.1, 20.2(a)(2)
  interest expense, *see* Interest expenses
  interest rate swaps, 60.2(b)(2)(i)(a)

passive activities, 9.8
portfolio investments, 9.9
registered as associated person, 8.2(c)
short sales rule, 9.4
Straddle Rules, 9.7
swap payments, 60.2(b)(2)(ii), 60.2(d)(2)(i)
trade or business, 8.1
traders, 8.2
wash sales rule, 9.5, 19.4
Involuntary conversions, 27.4(d), 27.4(d)(2)
IO strips, *see* Asset-backed securities, interest only (IO) strips
IPMA disclosure standards, *see* Swaps, IPMA disclosure standards
IRS form(s):
 IRS Form W-2, 24.10
 IRS Form W-2P, 24.10
 IRS Form W-8, 24.10
 IRS Form W-9, 24.10
 IRS Form 720, 31.12(a)
 IRS Form 1041, 36.2(a)
 IRS Form 1065, 59.2(i)(4)(i)
 IRS Form 1066, 36.8(j)(5), 36.8(k)
 IRS Form 1098, 24.10
 IRS Form 1099, 24.10
 IRS Form 1099-B, 13.3
 IRS Form 1099-DIV, 8.9(c), 9.1(d)
 IRS Form 1099-INT, 31.11(d)
 IRS Form 1099-OID, 31.2(a), 31.2(b)
 IRS Form 1120-RIC, 8.9(a)
 IRS Form 5498, 24.10
 IRS Form 6781, 52.1, 57.4(h), 57.4(i)
 IRS Form 8281, 31.2(n)(3)
 IRS Form 8613, 8.9(b)
 IRS Form 8811, 36.8(j)(5)
ISDA Code, *see* Swaps, ISDA Code

J

Joint Commission on Accreditation of Hospitals (JCAH), 33.2(c)(2)(vi)
Joint return(s):
 capital loss carry-overs, 15.4(d)
 generally, 2.1(a)(4)(i), 15.4(d)
 separate returns filed in subsequent tax years, 15.4(d)

K

Killer rule:
 applicable only to mixed straddles, 57

 avoidance, 57.1
 cash spreads, inapplicable, 57
 converts in favor of government, 57.1
 effective date, 57.8
 generally, 54.4(a)
 holding period, exception, 54.4(a)
 inadequate identification prompts application of killer rule, 57.2(b)
 section 1092(b)(2) election, prevents killer rule application, 57.3
 section 1256 contract straddle, exempt from killer rule application, 57

L

Last-in, first-out (LIFO), 22.2(b)
 dollar-value method, 22.2(b)
 unit-value method, 22.2(b)
Leg-out date, 23.3(g)(1)(ii)
Lenders of securities:
 compensating payments, 55.2(b)
 security loan transactions, *see* Security loans
 stock, 24.9(b)(3)
 used in short sales, 55.2(b)
Letters of credit, 1.1(g)(2), 7.1(b), 33.3(a)(1)(ii)
Leverage contract transactions, 4.1, 4.3(e), 42.5
Leverage transaction merchants (LTMs), 4.3(e)
Liability hedges, 60.5(a), 60.5(b), 60.5(b)(2)
 anticipatory hedges of liabilities, 60.5(b)(1)
 identification, improper, 60.5(b)(2)
 sourcing rules, 60.5(b)
Liability hedge treatment, 60.5(b)(1)
 qualification for, 60.5(b)(1)
LIFO, *see* Last-in, first-out (LIFO)
Limited entrepreneur(s), 23.2(a), 23.2(c)(2), 23.2(c)(3), 44.4, 45.2(c)
Limited partner(s), 23.2(a), 23.2(c)(3), 44.4, 45.2(c), 45.2(c)(1)
 assignee, 28.1(c)
 substituted, 28.1(c)
Limited partnership interests, 1.1(h), 9.9
 real estate, 9.8
Limited partnership(s):
 advance ruling requests, 28.2
  post-February 13, 1989
  pre-February 14, 1989
 asset-backed securities, 7.3(b)(1)

Index

Limited partnership(s) (*Continued*)
  capitalization, minimum requirement, 28.2
  centralized management, 28.1(b)
  continuity of life, 28.1(a)
  factors in determining tax status, 28.1
  free transferability of interests, 28.1(c)
  interests in, 1.1(h)
  limited liability, 21.8(d)
  limited partner:
    assignee, 28.1(c)
    substituted, 28.1(c)
  passive activities, 9.8
  publicly traded, *see* Publicly traded partnerships after December 31, 1987
  publicly traded limited partnerships, 1.1(h), 28
  securities law, 1.1(h)
Liquidation(s):
  corporate, 17.3(c)(4)
  liquidating distributions, 18.6(c)
  liquidating dividends, 18.6(c)
  of subsidiary, 17.3(c)(4)
  one-month liquidations, 17.3(c)(4)
  partial liquidations, 16.4(*l*)
  taxable liquidations, 17.2(a)(3)
Listed options, *see* Options, listed options
Listing agreements, *see* Markets, listing agreements
London options, 47.2(e)
Loss deferral rule:
  application, 14.6, 21.2
  capital transactions, 14.6
  coordination with modified wash sales rule, 49.2
  coordination with wash sales rule, 19.2
  generally, 48.5, 49.1, 54.2, 55, 60.4(f)
  ordinary income and loss, 21.2
  section 1092(b)(2) identified mixed straddles, 57.3(h)
  straddles, effective date, 57.8
Loss(es):
  carried back, 45.4(a), 57.4
  carried forward, 50, 27.8(f)
  date sustained, 19.3(e)
  deductible, 13.2(a)(2)
  generally, 14.5(d), 48.4
  holding period exception, 17.3(c)(1)
  loss carry-back election, 45.4(a)
  offsetting positions, 48.4
  premium runoff, 11.4(b)
  publicly traded securities, 14.5(d)
  sale of stocks and bearer bonds, 17.2(a)(2)(i)(f)
  section 1256 contracts, 45.4(a)
  settlement date, 14.5(d)
  sham transactions, 19.12
  worthless securities, 27.8
Lots, securities:
  assigned numbers and numerical sequence, 20.2(e)
  identification of capital assets, 20.1
  single certificate representing several, 20.2(a)(1)(iii)
Lower of cost or market, 22.2(a)
Lowest qualified bench mark, 56.3(b)
  general rule, exceptions, 56.3(c)
LTMs, *see* Leverage transaction merchants (LTMs)

M

Major market index, *see* Indexes
Mandatory convertible notes, *see* Convertible debt securities, mandatory convertible notes
Margin, *see* Commodities, margin; Government securities, margin; Options, margin; Securities, margin
Margin account(s):
  basic requirements, 1.4(b)(2)
  calculation, 1.4(b)(2)
  CFTC authority, 5.5(b)
  clearing organizations, 5.6
  COD transactions prohibited, 1.4(a)
  commodities margin, tax effect, 9.2(c)(1), 10.2(c)
  commodity option margin, subject to CFTC authority, 5.5(b)
  corporate shareholders, 24.9(b)(3)
  debt financed portfolio stock, 24.9(c)
  debtor-creditor relationship, 9.2(b)
  delivery against payment, prohibited, 1.4(a)
  FRB requirements, 1.4(b)(2), 5.5(a), 5.5(b)
  generally, 1.4, 1.4(b), 5.5(a), 7.4, 9.2(b), 9.3(b)(5), 10.2(b), 13.6, 14.5(d)
  initial margin requirements, 4.3(b), 4.4(b)
  interest income and expenses, 9.3(b)(5), 10.2(b)
  long position, 1.4(b)(3)
  margin borrowing, as portfolio indebtedness, 24.9(c)

NYSE requirements, 1.4(b)(2), 7.4(b)(6)
principal customer account, 1.4(b)(1)
securities margin accounts, 10.2(b)
self-regulatory organizations, 1.4(b)(2)
short positions in options, 5.5(a)
short sales, 1.4(b)(4)
Marketable government securities, *see* Government securities
Market auction preferred stock, 27.3(b)(3)(iii)
Market discount bond(s):
  accrued, market discount, 31.3(f)
    election to accrue, 31.3(f)(1)
  acquisition discount, 31.2(d), 55.2(b)
  compound interest method, 31.3(f)
  constant interest rate, 31.3(f)
  current market discount, election, 31.3(g)
  debt securities, 31.3(*l*)
  defined, 31.3(b)
  de minimis exception, 31.2(a), 31.2(e), 31.3, 31.10(a)
  disallowed deductions, 31.3(m)(2)
  disposition, 31.2(m)(2)(ii)
  exclusions, 31.3(b)
  gain on sale, 31.3(h)
  generally, 31.3(a)
  installment instruments, 31.3(i)
  installment obligations, 31.3(i)
  installment obligations, exempt, 31.10(b)
  interest:
    additional, 48.3(b)(2)(iii)
    deferral, 31.3(m)(1)
    disallowed interest expense, 31.3(m)(2)
    election, 31.3(m)(2)(i)
    incurred to purchase or carry, 31.3, 48.3(b)(2)(iii)
  net direct interest on indebtedness, 55.2(e)
  nonrecognition transactions, 31.3(m)(2)(iii)
  original issue discount, 31.3(c)
  pass-through certificates, 31.3(j)
  pay-through bonds, 31.3(k)
  plan of reorganization, 31.3(e)
  purchase premiums, 31.4
  redemption, 31.10
  REMIC regular interests, 31.3(*l*)
  retirement, 31.10
  savings bonds, exempt, 31.10(b)
  short-term obligations, exempt, 31.10(b), 48.3(b)(2)(iii)
  swapping bonds, 31.3(c)
  tax-exempt securities, exempt, 31.10(b)
  TRA '86 changes, 31.2(d)(2)
  transfers to controlled corporations, 31.3(d)
Market discount, defined, 31.3(b)
Market exchange rate, 60.2(c)(5)(iii)
Market maker(s):
  broker-dealers, 1.2(b)
  defined, 8.3(c)
  generally, 1.2(a), 5.5(a), 8.2(b), 8.3(c), 11.7(f), 44.4
  merchandising function, 8.3(c)
  net income from self-employment, 8.3(d)
  option dealers, 8.2(b), 8.3(d), 44.4, 45.2(b), 57.4
  option market makers, 5.3(a), 5.5(a), 8.2(b), 8.3(c), 8.3(d), 11.9(c), 19.5(b), 45.2(b)
  dealer status, 30.2(b)(4)
  over-the-counter market, 1.2(b)
  pre-DRA option transactions, 8.3(c), 19.5(b), 30.2
  treated as traders, 8.3(c)
Market(s):
  exchange trading, 1.2(a), 5.3(a), 7.3(b)(1)
  generally, 1.2
  listing agreement, 1.2(a), 7.3(b)(1)
  over-the-counter, 1.2(b), 5.3(b)
  types of, 1.2
  unlisted trading privileges, 1.2(a), 7.3(b)(1)
Mark-to-market payments, 4.3(b), 4.4(b)(3), 9.2(c)(1), 14.2
Mark-to-Market Rule, 21.5, 44.6, 45.1, 45.2, 45.4(a), 59.2(a)(2)
Married put transactions, 18.4(d), 18.9, 30.3(c)(1)(ii), 30.3(c)(1)(iv), 54.4(d), 56.4
  married put exception, 54.4(d)
  modified short sales rule, 54.4(d)
  short sales of capital assets, 18.4(d)
  Straddle Rules application, exception, 56.4
  married put options, 54.4(d)
Married stock transactions, 56.4
Massachusetts business trusts, *see* Regulated investment companies (RICs), Massachusetts business trusts
Matching service(s):
  affiliate, 28.4(c)(4)
  corporate affiliate, 28.4(c)(4)

Index

I-52

Matching service(s) (*Continued*)
  listing customer, 28.4(c)(4)
  operator, 28.4(c)(4)
  partnership, 28.4(c)(4)
MBBs, *see* Asset-backed securities, mortgage-backed bonds (MBBs)
MBSCC, *see* MBS Clearing Corporation (MBSCC)
MBS Clearing Corporation (MBSCC):
  depository division, purchased by PTC, 2.1(b)(2)
  generally, 2.4, 7.5(b)
MBSs, *see* Asset-backed securities, mortgage-backed securities (MBSs)
McCarthy, Crisanti & Maffei, 7.1(b)
MCFs, *see* Mortgage cash flow obligations (MCFs)
Meetings; deductions, 9.1(c)(10)
Merger:
  partnership, 28.4(b)(3)
  qualified loan agreements, 26.2(g)
Merrill Lynch, *see* Preferred stock, Merrill Lynch, remarketed preferred stock
Midwest Stock Exchange (MSE), 1.3(d)
Minimum tax:
  add-on minimum tax, corporate taxpayers, 15.5(c)
  alternative minimum tax, noncorporate, 15.4(a)(2)(ii), 31.11(c)
  corporate add-on tax:
    alternative tax computation, 15.5(a)(2)
    alternative tax method, 15.5(c)
    alternative tax rate, 15.5(a)(2)
    noncorporate taxpayers, 15.4(a)(2)(ii), 31.11(c)
Miscellaneous itemized deductions, 9.1(d)
Mixed straddle account(s):
  account cap, 57.4(f)
  account contents, 57.4(a)
  accounting method, 57.4(a)
  allocable to each account, 57.4(d)
  amended elections, 57.4(h)
  amended returns, 57.4(i)
  annual account net gain or loss, 57.4(c), 57.4(e)
  attribution rules, 51.2, 51.4
  capitalization of interest and carrying charges, 55.2(d), 57.4(d)
  class of activities, 57.4
  daily account net gain or loss, 57.4(b)
  daily mark-to-market, 57.4(b)
  daily non-section 1256 net gain or loss, 57.4(b)
  designated class of activities, 57.4
  election for post-1983 and prior to September 1, 1986, 57.4(i)
  elections, 45.4(b), 57.4(g), 57.4(h), 57.4(i), 57.6(b), 57.6(c), 59.2(h)
    effective date, 57.8
    limitation on elections, 57.6
    manner for making election, 57.4(h)
    revocation, 57.4(h), 57.5
  40 percent restriction, ordinary and short-term capital losses, 57.7
  gross expense of account, 55.2(d)
  gross income of account, 55.2(d)
  interest and carrying charges properly allocable, defined, 57.4(d)
  interest expense attributable to account, 55.2(d)
  introduced by DRA, 57.4
  modified short sales rule, 54.4(b)
  new classes of activities, 57.4(g)
  non-section 1256 contracts, 57.4
  ownership of positions, 57.6(b)
  related persons, elections, 57.6
  section 988 positions, 59.2(h)
  section 1256 contracts, 45.1, 57.4, 57.4(b), 59.2(h)
  separate account for each class of activities, 57.4, 57.4(a)
  single result from all, 57.4(e)
  timely identification, 57.3(a)(3)
  total annual account net gain or loss, 57.4(e)
  total result from all, 57.4(f)
  transitional rules, special, 57.4(i)
  yearly elections, 57.4(a), 57.4(g)
Mixed straddle(s):
  attribution rules, 51.2, 51.4, 57.6
  capitalization of interest and carrying charges, 55.2(d), 57.4(d)
  choices available, summary of, 57.1, 57.5
  composition, 57
  created by taking delivery (or exercising) long section 1256 contract, 57.2(c)
  effective dates, 57.8
  election under section 1256(d), 57
  foreign currency contracts, 59.2(h)
  foreign currency-related bank forward contract, 23.3(e)

foreign currency-related section 1256 futures contract, 23.3(e)
identified section 1256(d) mixed straddles, *see* Identified section 1256(d) mixed straddles
killer rule, 57, 57.1, 57.2(b), 57.3
  effective date, 57.8
  limitations on who can make elections, 57.6
  methods of identifying and netting mixed straddles, 57.5
mixed straddle accounts, *see* Mixed straddle accounts
  mixed straddle account rules, effective date, 57.8
mixed straddle election under section 1256(d), 57
  limited scope, 57.2(b)
modified short sales rule, 54.4(a), 54.4(b)
netting rules in lieu of modified short sales rule, 57
one-time mixed straddle election, 57.2(a)
positions, one capital, one ordinary, 23.3(e), 23.3(f)(4), 57.7, 59.2
related parties, elections, 51.2, 51.4, 57.6
section 988 transactions, 57.7, 59.2(h)
section 1092(b) regulations, 57.7
section 1092(b)(2) identified mixed straddle, *see* Identified section 1092(b)(2) mixed straddles
section 1092(b)(2)(D) treatment, 57.7
section 1256 "carve-out," 57.7
section 1256 contract loss, carried back, 45.4(b)
section 1256 treatment, exemption, 46.1
60/40 application, 57.7
straddle-by-straddle netting, *see* Straddle-by-straddle netting
  straddle-by-straddle netting rule, effective date, 57.8
timing of gains and losses, 59.2(h)
Modified short sales rule:
  application, 54.4(a)
  attribution rules, 54.4(a)
  coordination with loss deferral rule, 54.2
  futures contracts, part of mixed straddle, 18.4(e)(4)
  generally, 54.4, 55.2
  identified mixed straddles, 57.1

married put transactions, 54.4(d)
mixed straddles, 54.4(b), 57, 57.1
nonstatutory hedges, 23.2(g)
option positions, 18.4(c)
qualified covered calls, exempt, 18.4(c)
regulated investment companies, 54.4(c)
short sale, straddle, 18.1
special holding periods, straddles, 17.4(d)
straddles, 54.4
Modified wash sales rule:
  coordination with loss deferral rule, 49.2, 54.2
  coordination with wash sales rule, 19.2
  dealers, 11.11
  generally, 16.4(j), 17.4(d), 19.3(a), 19.9, 54.1, 54.3, 55
  loss deferral rule, coordination, 49.2, 54.2
  nonstatutory hedges, 23.2(g)
  offsetting positions, concept, 54.3
  4special holding periods, straddles, 17.4(d)
  stock or securities:
    loss deferral rule, coordination, 49.2, 54.2
    special rule, 54.2
    substantially identical securities, 54.2
  substantially identical property, concept, 54.3
  successor positions, 49.2, 54.2, 57.3(h)
  wash sales rule, coordination, 19.2
Money market preferred stock, 1.1(g), 27.3(b)(3)(iii)
Money spreads, 5.4(c)
Moody's Investors Service, 3.1, 7.1(b), 7.2(c)(4)
Mortgage-backed bonds (MBBs), *see* Asset-backed securities, mortgage-backed bonds (MBBs)
Mortgage-backed securities (MBSs), *see* Asset-backed securities, mortgage-backed securities (MBSs)
  qualified mortgage bonds, 3.2(b), 33.2(c)(2)(ii)
  qualified veterans' mortgage bonds, 3.2(d), 33.2(c)(2)(ii)
Mortgage cash flow obligations (MCFs), *see* Asset-backed securities, mortgage cash flow obligations (MCFs)
Mortgage companies, 27.5(a)(1)
Mortgage obligation(s):
  individuals, 31.2(d)
  natural persons, 31.2(d)

Index

Mortgage participation certificates (PCs), 2.1(b)(4), 7.2(b)
Mortgage pools, 7.1, 19.9(j), 31.6(e)(1), 36.8
Mortgage related security, *see generally* Asset-backed securities
Mortgage swaps, *see* Swaps, mortgage swaps
MSE, *see* Midwest Stock Exchange (MSE)
MSRB, *see* Municipal securities, Municipal Securities Rulemaking Board (MSRB)
Multiple-ownership interest market, 36.8(a)
Municipal securities:
  advance refunding bonds, 33.3(a)(1)(vii)
  advance refunding(s):
    limitations, 33.3(a)(1)(vii)
    qualified 501(c)(3) bonds, 33.3(a)(1)(vii)
  alternative depreciation system, 33.9
  alternative minimum tax, 3.1, 25.4(c), 33, 33.2(b)
  arbitrage bonds, 3.1, 25.4(a), 33.3(a)(1)(vi)
  arbitrage certificates, 33.3(a)(1)(vi)
  arbitrage restrictions, 33.2(a), 33.3(a)(1)(vi)
  backed by guarantees, 3.3, 33.3(a)(1)(ii)
  backed by insurance, 3.3, 33.3(a)(1)(v)
  backed by letters of credit, 3.3
  banks, investment in, 33.6
  branch profits tax, 25.4(c), 33, 33.2(a), 33.11
  Bonneville Power Authority, 33.3(a)(1)(ii)
  call date for callable municipal securities, 31.4(a)(2)(ii)
  credit enhancements, 3.3, 33.3(a)(1)(iv), 33.3(a)(1)(v), 33.3(a)(1)(vi)
  credit ratings, 3.1
  dealer in, 31.4(a)(2)(ii)
  dealers, premium run off, 11.4(b)
  defaulted securities, 33.3(a)(1)(i)(a), 33.4
  Disclosure Guidelines for Offerings of State and Local Government Securities, 3.1
  estate and gift taxes, 33.3(a)(2)
  exempt facility bonds, 33.2(c), 33.2(c)(2)(vi)
  exempt facility IDBs, 33.2(c)(2)(i)
  federal guarantee(s):
    geothermal energy, 33.3(a)(1)(ii)
    letters of credit, 33.3(a)(1)(ii)
  federal income tax, 33.3(a)(1)
  financial institutions, investment in, 33.6
  financing enhancement(s):
    generally, 3.3, 33.3(a)(1)(iv), 33.3(a)(1)(v)
    guarantees, 3.3, 33.3(a)(1)(ii)
    insurance, 3.3, 33.3(a)(1)(v)
    letters of credit, 3.3
    put options, 3.3, 33.3(a)(1)(iv)
    warrants, 3.3
  flow-through entities, 33.5
  general obligation bond(s):
    arbitrage restrictions, 33.2(a)
    generally, 3.1, 3.2(a), 3.2(c), 33.2(a)
    information reporting requirements, 33.2(a)
    private activity bonds, 33.2(a)
    restrictions on advance refundings, 33.2(a)
  general tax principles, 33.3
  gift tax, 33.3(a)(2)
  Government Finance Officers Association, 3.1
  guarantees, backed by, 3.3, 33.3(a)(1)(ii)
  hedge bonds, 33.3(a)(1)(ix)
  industrial development bonds, *see* Industrial development bonds (IDBs); *see also* Private activity bonds (PABs)
  information reporting, 33.3(a)(1)(viii)
  information reporting requirements, 33.2(a)
  interest expense, 9.3(b), 10.3(b), 11.3(b), 33.3(d), 33.6
  interest income, 3.1, 25.4, 33.3(a), 33.3(a)(1)
  interest in default, 33.3(a)(1)(i)(a)
  letters of credit, 1.1(g), 33.3(a)(1)(ii)
  long-term obligations, 3.1
  losses incurred by property and casualty insurance companies, 33.8
  market, 3.1
  Municipal Securities Rulemaking Board (MSRB), 3.1
  mutual funds, 8.9(a), 9.1(d), 24.5, 33.5(c)
    identification of mutual fund shares, 16.2(b), 20.3
  notes, 33
  original issue discount, 33.3(a)(4), 33.3(a)(1)(i)(b)
  partnerships, investment in, 33.5(a)

premiums, 33.3(a)(1)(i)(c)
project limitations, 3.1
proposals to limit tax exemption, 3.1
purchased when interest payments are in default, 33.3(a)(1)
put option features, 3.3, 33.3(a)(1)(iv)
put option, reissuance of securities, 3.3, 33.3(a)(1)(iv)
private activity bonds, 3.2(c), 25.4(a), 25.4(b), 25.4(c), 33.2(c)
  exempt facilities bonds, 33.2(c)(2)(i)
  exemption for first-time farmers, 33.2(c)
  mortgage revenue bonds, 33.2(c)
  qualified 501(c)(3) bonds, 33.2(c)(vi)
    qualified hospital bonds, 33.2(c)(2)(vi)
    qualified mortgage bonds, 33.2(c)(2)(ii)(a)
    qualified redevelopment bonds, 33.2(c)(2)(v)
    qualified student loan bonds, 33.2(c)(iv)
    qualified veterans' mortgage bonds, 33.2(c)(2)(ii)(b)
    small issue exemptions, 33.2(c)(2)(iii)
  tax exemptions, 33.2(c)
  use of bond proceeds, 33.10
  volume cap, expanded, 3.1
qualified 501(c)(3) bond(s):
  after October 21, 1988, 33.2(c)(2)(vi)
  generally, 3.1, 3.2(c), 25.4(c), 33.2(c)(2)(vi)(a), 33.3(a)(1)(vi), 33.6
  land acquisitions, 33.2(c)(2)(vi)(f)
  mixed-used facilities, 33.2(c)(2)(vi)(c)
  municipal securities, 25.4(c), 33
  qualified hospital bonds, 33.2(c)(2)(vi)(b)
  rental housing projects, 33.2(c)(2)(vi)(e)
  volume limitation, 33.2(c)(2)(vi)(d)
qualified exempt facility bonds, 33.2(c)(i)
qualified mortgage bond(s):
  generally, 33.2(c)(2)(ii)(a)
  tax-exempt, conditions, 33.2(c)(2)(ii)
    after December 31, 1988, 33.2(c)(2)(ii)
    after December 31, 1990, 33.2(c)(2)(ii)
  volume limitation, 33.2(c)(2)(ii)
qualified redevelopment bonds, 33.2(c), 33.2(c)(2)(v), 33.2(c)(2)(vi)
qualified small issue bonds, 33.2(c)
qualified student loan bonds, 33.2(c), 33.2(c)(2)(iv)
qualified tax-exempt obligation(s):
  defined, 11.3(b)(3)(ii)(b)
  financial institutions, special rules, 33.6
qualified veterans' mortgage bonds, 33.2(c)(2)(ii)(b)
recapitalization provisions, unavailable, 33.4
refinancing, 3.3, 33
refunding bonds, 33.2(c)
refunding issues, 33.3(a)(1)(vi)
registration requirements, 25.4(c)
regulated investment companies, 8.9, 33.5(c), 54.4(c)
reporting requirements, 33.3(a)(1)(viii)
repo transactions, 31.11(a)
restrictions on advance refundings, 33.2(a)
revenue bonds, 3.1, 3.2(b), 3.2(c), 33.2(b), 33.3
sales, 33.3(a)(1)(i)(d), 33.3(c)
S corporations, investment in, 33.5(b)
short-term anticipation obligations, 3.1
single-family housing bonds, 33.3(a)(1)(vi)
sinking fund provisions, 3.1
standby letters of credit, 1.1(g), 33.3(a)(1)(ii)
state taxation, 3.1, 33.3(b)
stepped coupon securities, 3.3
substantially identical property, 19.9(g)
Superfund environmental tax, 25.4(c), 33, 33.2(a), 33.12
taxable, 3.1
taxable municipal securities, 3.1, 33
tax-exempt interest, 33.3(a)(1)
tax-exempt revenue securities, 3.1
tax-free reorganizations, unavailable, 31.9(b)
types of, 3.2, 33.2
underwriters accountable, 3.1
underwritings, 11.4(b)
variable rate municipal securities, 3.3
volume cap, 3.1
voluntary disclosure guidelines, 3.1
warrants, 3.3
zero coupon municipal securities, *see* Zero coupon securities, municipal
see also Tax-exempt securities

Index

Municipal Securities Rulemaking Board (MSRB), see Municipal securities, Municipal Securities Rulemaking Board (MSRB)
Mutual funds, see Municipal securities, mutual funds
Mutual Offset System, 44.3
Mutual savings banks, see Financial institutions, mutual savings banks

N

Narrow-based index, see Indexes
NASD, see National Association of Securities Dealers (NASD)
NASDAQ market, 1.2(b), 2.1(b)(6), 5.2(a)(1), 5.3(b)
NASDAQ 100 index, see Indexes
NASDAQ system, 1.2(b), 5.1, 5.3(b), 16.6(d)
National Association of Securities Dealers (NASD), 1, 1.2(b), 3.1, 5.1, 5.5(a)
National Futures Association (NFA), 4
National Securities Clearing Corporation (NSCC), 2.4
Neutral spreads, 5.4(c)(2)
New York Stock Exchange (NYSE):
  generally, 2.1(b)(3), 2.1(b)(6), 5.2(b)(4), 17.2(a)(5)
  margin requirements, 7.4(b)(6)
Noncorporate taxpayer(s):
  alternative minimum tax, 15.4(a)(2)(ii), 31.11(c)
  capital gains deduction, 15.4(a)(2)(i)
  capital loss carry-overs, 15.4(a)(1), 15.4(c)
  generally, Part Two, 15.4, 24.8, 25.3
  interest exclusion, 25.3
  net operating loss deduction, 15.4(a)(2)(ii)(a)
  tax preference items, 15.4(a)(2)(ii)(a)
  traders prior to January 1, 1985, 19.5(b)
  wash sales rule, exemption, 19.5(b)
Noncorporate traders prior to January 1, 1985, 19.5(b)
Nonequity option(s):
  constructive receipt, 45.1(a)
  defined, 44.3
  foreign currency transactions, nonhedge, 59.4(a)
    post-October 21, 1988 positions, 59.4(a)(3)
    post-section 988 positions, 59.4(a)(2)
    pre-1986 positions, 59.4(a)(1)
    pre-October 22, 1988 positions, 59.4(a)(2)
  generally, 44.3
  Notice 88-124, 59.2(j)
  section 988 election, 59.2(b)(4), 59.2(j)
    information required, 59.2(j)(1)
    late election, 59.2(j)(3)
    1988 calendar year, transitional rule, 59.2(j)(4)
    procedure, 59.2(j)(1)
    time for making election, 59.2(j)(2)
  section 1256 option, 30.1(d), 59.2(a)(1), 60.2(c)(3)
Nonexempted security, 1.4(a)
Nonfunctional currency:
  debt instrument, 23.3(g)(1)(i)
  defined, 59.2(g)(2)
  disposition, section 988 transaction, 59.2(g)(2)
  gain or loss, 59.2(b)(3), 59.2(f)(3), 59.2(g)(2)
  generally, 21.9, 23.3(f)(1), 23.3(g)(1)(i)(a), 23.3(g)(2)(ii), 59.2(a)(1), 59.2(g)(2), 59.5, 60.2(c)(3), 60.2(c)(4), 60.2(c)(5)(ii), 60.2(c)(6), 60.5(a), 60.7(a)
  section 988 transactions, 59.2(a)(1)
  spot contracts, 59.4(e)
  translation rules, 59.5
Nonmarketable government securities, see Government securities, nonmarketable
Nonqualified loan transactions, 26.3
Nonrecognition treatment, 27.4(d), 27.4(d)(1)
Nontaxable income, 9.1(b)
Nontaxable stock dividends, see Dividends, nontaxable stock dividends
Nontaxable stock rights, 16.4(c), 17.4(a)
Nontaxable stock scrip, 17.4(a)
Nontaxable transactions, 16.4, 20.2(d)
Notes, see Debt securities; convertible notes, see Convertible debt securities
Notional principal contract election, 60.5(a)
Notional principal contracts:
  allocation of expenses, 60.5(b)(1)
  amortization methods for up-front fee(s):

Black-Scholes option valuation
  model, 60.3(a)(1)(i)
  economic basis, 60.3(a)(1)(i)
  option pricing model, 60.3(a)(1)(a)
  straight-line method, 60.3(a)(1)(i)
asset hedges, 60.5(c)
assignment fees, amortized,
  60.2(b)(1)(ii)
Assistant Chief Counsel—Financial
  Products and Institutions, 60.1
commodity index, referenced, 60.5(a)
dealers, 60.5(a)
  mark-to-market treatment, 60.6
defined, 6.1, 60.1, 60.5(a)
  broader definition, 60.5(a)
determination of income source, 60.5(a)
Disclosure of Information about
  Financial Instruments with Off-
  Balance-Sheet Risk and Financial
  Instruments with Concentrations of
  Credit Risk, 60.1
exchange gain or loss, 60.2(c)(6)
FASB Emerging Issues Task Force, 60.1
FDAPI, 60.2(g)
Financial Products Group, 60.1
financial products, principal tax issues,
  60.1
foreign currency, 60.7(b)
foreign currency-related, 60.5(a)
foreign source income, 60.5(a)
forward rate agreements (FRAs), *see*
  Forward rate agreements (FRAs)
generally, 6.1, 59.2(a)(1), 60.1
hedge transactions, 8.4, 12.2, 60.5(b),
  60.5(c)
integration treatment, 60.3(a)(1)(ii),
  60.5(a), 60.6
interest equivalent treatment,
  60.3(a)(1)(ii), 60.5(b)(1)
interest rate caps, *see* Caps
interest rate collars, *see* Collars
interest rate floors, *see* Floors
interest rate index, referenced, 6.1,
  60.5(a)
interest rate swaps, *see* Interest rate
  swaps
liability hedges, 60.3(a)(1)(ii), 60.5(b)
  anticipatory hedges of liabilities,
  60.5(b)(1)
liability hedge treatment, 60.5(b)(1)
lump-sum payments, amortized,
  60.2(b)(1)(ii)
market regulation, 6.6

mark-to-market accounting method
  sought, 22.1(d), 60.6
Notice 87-4, 60.2(g)(1), 60.2(g)(2), 60.5(a)
  supplemented by Temp. Treas. Reg.
  § 1.861-7T, 60.2(g)(1), 60.2(g)(2)
  supplemented by Temp. Treas. Reg.
  § 1.861-9T; Treas. Reg. § 1.863-7,
  60.5(a)
Notice 89-21, 60.2(b)(1)(i)
Notice 89-90, 60.2(b)(2)(i)(a)(4), 60.5(a)
notional principal amount, 6.1,
  7.2(c)(2)(ii), 60.1
notional principal contract election
  under Treas. Reg. § 1.863-7, 60.5(a)
  election deadline, May 15, 1991,
  60.5(a)
open tax years, 60.5(a)
QBUs, agreements with, 60.5(a)
rate indexes, 6.1
residence-based sourcing rules,
  60.2(c)(6)
sourcing rules, 60.5(a)
Statement of Financial Accounting
  Standards No. 105, 60.1
Straddle Rules, 60.2(b)(1), 60.2(d)(1),
  60.7
  exceptions, 60.7(a)
  when subject to, 60.7(a)
strike level, 6.1
Subpart F, 60.2(b)(2)(i)(a)(4)
swap transactions, *see* Swaps
tax issues, 60.1
termination payments, 60.2(b)(1)(ii)
United States currency, 60.7(a)
United States source income, 60.5(a)
up-front fee, 60.2(d)(1)(ii)
  amortized, 60.2(b)(1)(ii)
  defined, 6.1
withholding under Temp. Treas. Reg.
  § 1.861-7T, 60.2(g)(1), 60.2(g)(2)
NYSE, *see* New York Stock Exchange
  (NYSE)
NYSE composite index, *see* Indexes

O

OCC, *see* Options Clearing Corporation
  (OCC)
Office of Thrift Supervision (OTS), 2,
  7.2(c)(2)(iii), 11.3(b)(3)(ii)(e)
Offsetting position(s):
  altered form of property, 48.4(a)
  basket of stocks, 48.2(c)(2)

Index

Offsetting position(s) (*Continued*)
  debt securities, 48.4(c)
  defined, 48.3
  diversification of assets, 48.4(a)
  FRA hedge, treated as two offsetting positions, 60.4(e)
  hedging commodity swaps, 60.2(d)(1), 60.2(d)(1)(iii)
  modified wash sales rule, 54.3
  offsetting with respect to loss positions, 49.2
  offsetting with respect to successor positions, 49.2
  one position a forward rate agreement, 60.4(e)
  one position protects other, 48.1
  option writers, 48.4(b)
  options positions, 48.4(b)
  personal property, 10.7, 48.1
  portfolio of corporate stock, 48.2(d)
  portfolio of debt securities, 48.4(c)
  portfolio of stocks, 48.2(c)(2)
  purchases of commodities, 42.3
  rebuttable presumptions, 48.4(a)
  repurchase agreements, 48.3(b)
  short option positions, 48.4(b)
  sold or marketed as offsetting, 48.4(a)
  straddles, 10.7, 48.4(b)
  substantial diminution of risk of loss, 48.4(a)
Offsetting position stock, 48.2(c)(1), 48.2(c)(4), 51.1, 56.5
OID, *see* Original issue discount (OID)
Oil and gas property, 29.1(b)
  cost depletion deduction, 29.1(d)
Omnibus Budget Reconciliation Act of 1987 (OBRA),
  publicly traded partnerships, 28.4
On-call purchase contracts, 22.1(c)
Opening inventory, 22.2
Opening transaction(s):
  commodities, 4.3(c), 42.1(a)
  options, 5.1
  termination of section 1256 contracts, 45.5
Option dealers, *see* Market makers, option dealers
Option market makers, *see* Market makers, option market makers
Option premium(s):
  commodity options, 5.2(b)
  defined, 5.1
  foreign currency futures, 5.2(b)

  index option, 5.2(a)(4)
  purchasers of equity calls, 30.3(b)(1)
  purchasers of equity puts, 30.3(c)(1)(i)
  receipt of premiums on sale of equity options, 30.3(b)(2)(i)
  sellers of equity calls, 30.3(b)(2)(i), 30.3(b)(2)(ii)
  sellers of put and call straddles, 30.3(d)(1)
  standardized options, 5.2(a)(1)
Option(s):
  acquisition of put options, 33.3(a)(1)(iv)
  adjustment procedures, 5.1
  American-style, 5.1, 5.2(a)(3), 6.2(d)
  arbitrage transactions, *see* Arbitrage, options
  at-the-money options, 5.1, 24.9(b)(1)
  backspreads, 5.4(c)(3)
  bank discount rate, 5.2(a)(2)
  bear spreads, 5.4(c)(1)(ii), 5.4(c)(1)(iii), 5.4(c)(3)
  box spreads, 5.4(e)(4), 30.2(b), 30.3(d)(3), 56.1(a), 56.3(a)
  broad-based stock indexes, 5.5(a), 30.4, 44.3
  bull spreads, 5.4(c)(1)(i), 5.4(c)(1)(iii), 5.4(c)(3)
  butterfly spreads, 5.4(c)(1)(iii), 5.4(c)(3), 30.2(b), 47.1
    identified straddles, 56.1(a)
    qualified covered calls, 56.3(a)
  calendar spreads, 5.4(c)
  call options:
    acquisition pursuant to long position, 42.1(c)
    buying, 5.4(a)(1)
    covered calls, 5.4(a)(2)(ii), 56.3
    equity calls, *see* Equity options
    exchange-traded call options, 19.6(b)
    exercise of long position, 30.3(b)(1)(iv)
    generally, 5.1, 5.4(a), 18.4(c), 19.8(f), 24.9(b)(1), 45.6(b)
    lapse of long call option position, 30.3(b)(1)(iii)
    qualified covered calls, *see* Qualified covered calls
    ratio writing, 5.4(a)(2)(iii)
    regulated investment company, 8.9(a)(2)
    selling, 5.4(a)(2)
    selling hedge, 8.4(c)(2)
    substantially identical property, not viewed as, 18.4(c)

uncovered calls, 5.4(a)(2)(i)
cash options, 5.2(b), 43.1
CFTC pilot option program, 5.1, 5.2(b)
  terminated, 5.2(b)
characteristics, 1.1(g)(5)
classes of, 5.2
clearance and settlement, 5.6
clearing organizations, *see* Clearing organizations
closing short options position, 14.5(b)
closing transaction, 5.1
commissions and fees, 30.3(b)(1)(i)
commodity option(s):
  CFTC regulation, 5.2
  dealer options, 5.1, 5.2(b), 5.3(b), 5.6
  futures contracts options, *see* Options, futures options
  generally, 5.2(b), 5.3(b), 5.5(b), 43.1, 43.2, 44.3, 48.4(b)
  long call options position, 42.1(a), 42.1(c)
  margin, 5.5(b), 9.2(c)(1), 9.2(c)(2)
  CFTC authority, 5.5(b)
  pilot program, 5.1, 5.2(b)
  settlement, 5.6
  trade options, 5.1, 5.2(b), 5.3(b)
condor options, 5.4(d)
contingent payment rights, *see* Contingent payment rights
contract terms, 5.1
  adjustment procedure, 5.1
  exercise price, 5.1
  expiration date and time, 5.1
  premium, 5.1
  strike price, 5.1
  underlying interest, 5.1
  unit of trading, 5.1
conventional options, 5.1, 5.3(b)
conversion transactions, 5.4(e)(3), 56.1(a), 56.3(a)
convertible preferred stock, 19.8(g)
covered calls, 5.4(a)(2), 5.4(a)(2)(ii), 56.3
  regulated investment company, 8.9(a)(2)
credit spreads, 5.4(c)
dealer equity options, *see* Dealer equity options
dealer options, *see* Dealer options
debt options, *see* Debt options
deep-in-the-money options, *see* Deep-in-the-money options
Delta Government Options Corp., 5.2(a)(2)

diagonal spreads, 5.4(c)
discounting arbitrage, 5.4(e)(1)
dividend arbitrage, 5.4(e)(2)
DRA elimination of short-term stock options exemption, 56.6
equity options, *see* Equity options
European currency unit (ECU), 5.2(a)(3)
European-style options, 5.1, 5.2(a)(3), 6.2(d)
exchange gains and losses, 59.2(a)(4)
exchange-traded options, 5.3(c), 19.6(b), 20.1, 48.3(a), 56.6
exercise of option positions, 17.2(c)(2), 30.3(b)(1)(iv), 45.6(b)
exercise price, 5.1, 5.2(a)(2)
exercise value, 5.1
expiration date, 5.1
expiration time, 5.1
foreign currency, 5.2(a)(3), 5.2(a)(4), 48.4(b)
foreign currency futures options, 5.2(b)
futures option(s):
  exchange-traded options on futures, 5.1
  generally, 5.2(b), 42.1(a), 42.1(c), 43.1, 43.3, 48.4(b)
  nonagricultural, 5.2(b)
  positions after October 31, 1983, 43.3(b), 44.3(b)
  positions before November 1, 1983, 43.3(a), 44.3(c)
hedges, 12.1
holders, 5.1
horizontal spreads, 5.4(c)
hybrid options, 5.2(b)
index options, 5.2(a)(4)
in-the-money options, 5.1, 5.3(b), 8.4(c)(1), 17.7, 24.9(b)(1), 48.4(b)
intrinsic value, 5.1
lapse of long position, 30.3(b)(1)(iii)
liability hedge treatment, 60.5(b)(1)
listed options, 5.3(a), 30.1(a), 30.3(a), 43.1, 44.3, 44.4
  on commodities, 43.2(b)
  on debt securities, 35.2
listing process, 5.3(a)
long call option buying hedge, 8.4(c)(1)
long call options position, 42.1(a), 42.1(c)
long call position, exercise, 30.3(b)(1)(iv)
long put option position selling hedge, 8.4(c)(2)

Index

I-60

Option(s) (*Continued*)
　margin:
　　commodity options, 5.5(b)
　　Federal Reserve Board regulations, 1.4, 5.5(a)
　　futures style margining, 5.5(b)
　　generally, 5.5
　　securities, premium-plus method, 5.5(a)
　　security options, 5.2(a), 5.3(b), 5.5(a)
　　spreads, margin requirements, 48.4(a)
　margin accounts, *see* Margin accounts
　markets, 5.3
　married put transactions, *see* Married put transactions
　modified short sales rule, *see* Modified short sales rule
　modified wash sales rule, *see* Modified wash sales rule
　money spreads, 5.4(c)
　naked call position, 5.4(a)(2)(i)
　narrow-based index, 30.3(a)
　NASDAQ options, 5.1, 5.2(a)(1)
　neutral spreads, 5.4(c)(2)
　nonagricultural futures options, 5.2(b)
　nonequity options, 30.1(d), 44.3, 45.1(a)
　non-section 1256 option(s):
　　foreign currency transaction(s):
　　　post-October 21, 1988, 59.4(b)(3)
　　　post-section 988, 59.4(b)(2)
　　　pre-1986 transactions, 59.4(b)(1)
　　　pre-October 22, 1988, 59.4(b)(2)
　　　section 988(a)(1)(B) election, effective September 21, 1989, 59.4(b)(4)
　offsetting positions, 48.2(d), 48.4(b)
　on physicals, 5.2(b)
　opening transactions, *see* Opening transactions
　option markets, types of, 5.3
　option price information, 5.2
　OTC trading system, 5.1, 5.3(b)
　out-of-the-money options, 5.1, 5.5(a), 5.5(b), 8.4(c)(1), 24.9(b)(1), 48.4(b)
　over-the-counter markets, *see* Over-the-counter (OTC) markets
　over-the-counter options, 5.3(b)
　payoff diagram, 5.4(a)(2)(ii)
　perpendicular spreads, 5.4(c)
　physical commodities, 5.2(b), 5.3(b), 43.1, 43.2, 48.4(b)
　physical debt securities, 35.1, 35.2
　positions, 48.4(b)
　pre-DRA short-term stock option positions, 30.2, 56.6
　premiums, *see* Option premiums
　price spreads, 5.4(c)
　publicly traded options, 19.9(f)
　purchased spread, 5.4(c)(1)(i)
　purchaser of equity calls, *see* Equity options, equity call options
　purchaser of equity puts, *see* Equity options, equity put options
　put and call arbitrage, 5.4(e)(1)
　put and call straddles, 5.4(e)(1), 30.3(d)(1)
　put option municipal bonds, 3.3
　put option(s):
　　acquisition of, 18.4(c), 33(a)(1)(iv)
　　acquisition pursuant to short position, 42.1(d)
　　buying, 5.4(b)(1)
　　buying hedge, 8.4(c)(1)
　　cash settlement put option, 30.5, 30.5(b)(3)
　　exercise of long position, 30.3(c)(1)(iv)
　　married put exception, 54.4(d)
　　preferred stock, 24.9(b)(1)
　　purchaser of equity put, 30.3(c)(1)(iv)
　　regulated investment company, 8.9(a)(2)
　　selling, 5.4(b)(2)
　　short sale, 18.2(a), 18.4(c)
　　short synthetic put, 5.4(e)(3)
　　substantially identical property, 18.2(a)
　　synthetic put, 5.4(a)(1)
　　tax consequences, put option writer is issuer, 30.5(c)
　　wash sale, 19.8(e)
　put option writing programs, 5.4(b)(3), 18.4(c), 30.3(c)(3)
　qualified covered calls, *see* Qualified covered calls
　ratio spreads, 5.4(c)(3)
　ratio writing, 5.4(a)(2)(iii)
　registered exchanges, 5.3(a)
　reverse conversion transactions, 5.4(e)(3), 56.1(a)
　RMJ Options Trading Corp., 5.2(a)(2)
　secondary market, 5.1, 56.3(a)
　section 1256 options, 30.1(d), 30.4, 44.3, 44.4
　security/commodity distinction, 5.2
　security options, 5.2(a), 5.5(a)
　　SEC regulation, 5.2

Treasury securities, 5.2(a)(2)
seller of equity calls, *see* Equity options, equity call options, sellers
seller of equity puts, *see* Equity options, equity put options, sellers
sellers of put and call straddles, 30.3(d)(1)
semistandardized options, 5.2(a)(2)
series, 5.2
settlement:
  conventional commodity options, 5.6
  conventional stock options, 5.6
  futures option, 5.6
  security options, 5.6
  trade-plus-one settlement, 5.6
Shad-Johnson Accord, 4.1(c), 5.2
short sales rule, 18.4(c), 30.3(g)(3)
short selling, 5.4(b)(1)
short-term stock options, 30.2, 56.5, 56.6
simulated straddles, 5.4(a)(1)
sold spreads, 5.4(c)(1)(ii)
specialists in listed options, *see* Market makers
spread transactions, 5.4(c), 48.4(b)
  arbitrage transactions, 30.3(d)(2)
  bear put spread, 30.3(d)(3)
  box spreads, 5.4(e)(4), 30.2(b), 30.3(d)(3), 56.1(a), 56.3(a)
    described, 30.3(d)(3)
  bull call spread, 30.3(d)(3)
  combination transactions, 5.4(d)
  conversions, 30.3(d)(2)
  credit box spread, 30.3(d)(3)
  debit box spread, 30.3(d)(3)
  diagonal spreads, 5.4(c)(3)
  horizontal spreads, 5.4(c)(2)
  pre-DRA, 30.2
  reverse conversions, 30.3(d)(2)
  straddle transactions, 5.4(d), 30.3(d)(1), 30.3(d)(2)(i)
  vertical spreads, 5.4(c)(1)
standardized options, 5.1, 5.2(a)(1), 5.3(a)
stock groups, 48.4(b)
stock indexes, 48.4(b)
stock option plan, 19.8(c)
stock options, *see* Stock options
stock rights, *see* Stock rights
straddles and combinations, 5.4(d)
  synthetic straddles, 5.4(a)(1)
strangle, 5.4(d)
striking price, 5.1

sugar, 5.2(b)
swaps, *see* Swap options
swaptions, 60.2(e)(1)
time spreads, 5.4(c)
time value, 5.1
trade options, 5.2(b), 5.3(b)
trading strategies, 5.4
Treasury bond futures, 5.2(b)
types, 5.1
uncovered calls, 5.4(a)(2), 5.4(a)(2)(i)
uncovered puts, 5.4(b)(2)
underlying interest, 5.1, 5.4(a)(2)
underwriters' options, 11.8(a), 30.3(e)(1)(ii)
unit of trading, 5.1
unlisted cash options on physical commodities, 43.2(a)
unlisted debt security options, 35.2
unlisted options, 30.1(b), 30.3(a), 43.1
vertical spreads, 5.4(c)
  bear spreads, 5.4(c)(1)(ii), 5.4(c)(1)(iii), 5.4(c)(3)
  bull spreads, 5.4(c)(1)(i), 5.4(c)(1)(iii), 5.4(c)(3)
  butterfly spreads, *see* Butterfly spreads
warrants, *see* Warrants
wash sales rule, *see* Wash sales rule
writers, 5.1, 11.9(c), 48.4(b)
writing call options, 17.7
writing options, 8.3(c)
Options Clearing Corporation (OCC), 5.1, 5.2(a), 5.2(a)(4), 5.3(b), 5.6
Option specialists, *see* Market makers
Option writers, 5.1, 11.9(c), 48.4(b)
Order differences, *see* Order errors
Order error(s):
  accidentally receiving property, 13.2(b)
  deductible business expenses, 13.2(a)(1)
  deductible losses, 13.2(a)(2)
  discrepancies, 13.2(b)
  failing to detect, 13.2(b)
  mismatching of property, 13.2(b)
  mistakes, 13.2(a)
  over-delivering, 13.2(b)
  purchasing more than correct amount, 13.2(a)(2)
  purchasing wrong property, 13.2(a)(2)
  replacing property, 13.2(a)(2)
  selling more than correct amount, 13.2(a)(2)
  transferring property not subsequently returned, 13.2(b)
  transmitting wrong property, 13.2(b)

Index

Ordinary income or loss:
  Commodity Credit Corporation, 21.7
    loans, 21.6
  currency exchange gain or loss,
    60.2(c)(7)
  dealers, 21.1, 22, 45.2(a)
  defined, 21.1
  dividend income, 24.1(e)
  domestic source ordinary income (loss),
    21.9, 60.2(c)(3)
  foreign currency transactions, 21.9
  hedging transactions, 21.8, 23.2(b)(3)
  identification of ordinary income
    property, 22
  loss deferral rule, 21.2
  ordinary course of business, 19.5(c),
    21.1, 48.4(a)
  ordinary income, 8.10(e), 23.2(d)(3),
    24.1(e), 26.2(e), 60.2(b)(2)(i)(a),
    60.2(d)(1)(iii)
  ordinary income rates, 21.5
  ordinary loss, 21.1
  periodic swap payments, 60.2(b)(2)(i)(a)
  primarily for sale to customers, 11, 21.1
  section 1256 contracts, 21.5
  security loan transactions, *see* Security
    loans
  specific identification, 22.2(b), 22.2(c)
  swap income, substitute for interest,
    60.2(b)(2)(i)(a)(1)
    stream of income cases, analogy,
      60.2(b)(2)(i)(a)(1)
  trade or business expenses, 11.1(a), 12.1
  wash sales rule, possible application,
    21.10
Original issue discount (OID):
  accrual of discount as change in
    accounting method, 31.2(d)
  accrued market discounts, 31.3(i)
  accrued on daily basis, 31.2(d)
  acquisition discounts, 31.2(d)(4)
  acquisition premium, 31.2(a)
  adjusted issue price for any bond
    period, 31.2(a)
  applicable high yield discount
    obligations, *see* Applicable high
    yield discount obligations
  basis in OID security, 16.4(f), 31.2(a),
    31.2(b)
  bond period, 31.2(a)
  compound interest method, 31.2(e),
    31.3(f)
  constant interest rate formulas,
    31.2(d)(2)(ii), 31.2(d)(4)
  constant interest rates, 31.2(d)(2)(ii)
  contingent payment obligations, 31.2(i)
  convertible debt securities, 31.10(a),
    34.2(b), 34.3(b)
  corporate debt securities:
    issued after July 1, 1982, 31.2(a)
    issued after May 27, 1969 and before
      July 2, 1982, 31.2(b)
    issued before May 28, 1969, 31.2(c)
    short-term corporates, 31.2(d)
  corporate reorganizations, 31.2(h)
  corporate transactions, basis, 16.4(*l*)
  daily portion of OID, 31.2(a)
  deductible by corporation, 34.2(b)
  defer discount income, 31.2(c)
  de minimis exception, 31.2(a)
  discounts, 27.2, 31.3
  disposition of debt securities, 31.10
  economic interest method, 31.2(e)
  exchange, 31.2(c), 31.2(d)(4)
  foreign currency transactions, 31.7
  foreign investors, 31.2(f)
    related foreign lenders, 31.2(f)
  functional currency-denominated
    securities, 31.7
  gain, disposition of short-term
    obligations, 31.2(d)(4)
  government debt securities:
    issued after July 1, 1982, 31.2(a)
    issued before July 2, 1982, 31.2(c)
  hedgers, 31.2(c), 31.2(d)
  information reporting, 31.2(n)
    debt securities issued after May 8,
      1986, 31.2(n)(1)
    IRS form 8281, 31.2(n)(3)
    OID payments, 31.2(n)(3)
    publicly offered debt securities issued
      after August 16, 1984, 31.2(n)(2)
    REMIC regular interests, 31.2(n)(4)
  initial offering price, 31.3(c)
  installment instruments, 31.3(i)
    accrued market discount, 31.3(i)
  intent to call debt securities, 31.2(a)
  investment units, 31.2(j)
  irrevocable election to accrue
    acquisition discounts, 31.2(d)(4)
  issue price, 31.3(c)
  mandatory accrual, 31.2(d)
  market discount, 27.2, 31.3, 31.3(i)
    defined, 31.3(b)
  market discount bonds, 31.3(i)

defined, 31.3(b)
installment obligations, 31.3(i), 31.4(b)
market discount rules, 31.3(c), 31.3(d)
MBSs, *see* Asset-backed securities, mortgage-backed securities (MBSs)
municipal securities, 33.3(a)(4)
never negative, 31.2(m)
nonfunctional currency-denominated securities, 31.7
OID securities, 31.2(a), 31.6(c)(3)
  high yield OID securities, 31.2(g)(1)
pass-through certificates, 31.2(k), 37.4(a)
pay-through bonds, 31.2(*l*), 38.4
premiums, foreign currency transactions, 31.7(c)
ratable accrual, 31.2(d)
ratable monthly portion, 31.2(b)
ratable shares, 31.2(d)(4)
redemption, 31.2(c), 31.10(a)
regular interests, REMICs, 31.2(m)
  discount, 41.1(a)(3)
  IRS information reporting requirements, 31.2(n)(4)
  premium, 41.1(a)(2)
  principal amount, 41.1(a)(1)
REMIC regular interests, 31.2(m)
repurchase agreements, 48.3(b)(2)(iii)
retirement, 31.2(d)(4), 31.10(a)
sale, 31.2(d)(4)
  customers in ordinary course, 31.2(d)
  sales, 31.2(c)
security loans, 26.2(e)
short-term nongovernmental obligations, 31.2(d)(4)
short-term securities:
  accrues ratably on daily basis, 31.2(d)
  acquisition discount, 31.2(d)
  constant interest rate (based on yield to maturity), 31.2(d)
  corporate and government securities:
    issued after July 18, 1984, 31.2(d)(2)
      interest deferral, 31.2(d)(3)
      retirement or sale, 31.2(d)(4)
      transitional year election, 31.2(d)(2)(ii)
    issued before July 19, 1984, 31.2(d)(1)
  net adjustments to income, 31.2(d)
  net direct interest expense, 31.2(d)
  transitional year election, 31.2(d)
significant OID, 31.2(g)(2)(ii)
  accrual period, 31.2(g)(2)(ii)(a)
  calculation, 31.2(g)(2)(ii)(b)
stock, convertible into debt securities, 27.3(c)(4)
straddle income, 55.2(b)
straight-line basis, 31.3(f)
stripped bonds, 31.6(c)(4)
taxable securities, 31.2
taxable zero coupon securities, 31.5(a)
tax-exempt securities, 31.2(e)
  constant (compound) interest method, 31.2(e)
  economic interest method, 31.2(e)
  tax-free OID, 31.6(c)(4)
  zero coupon municipal securities, 31.5(b)
tax-free exchanges of Treasury securities, 32.1(d)(2)
Treasury securities, exchanges, 32.1(d)(2)
yield to maturity, 31.2(d)(2)(ii), 31.2(n)(1)
zero coupon securities, 31.5
OTC, *see* Over-the-counter (OTC) markets
OTS, *see* Office of Thrift Supervision (OTS)
Out-of-the-money options, 5.5(a), 24.9(b)(1), 48.4(b)
Out-trades, 4.5(b)
Over-the-counter brokers, 1.2(b)
Over-the-counter market(s):
  broker-dealers, 1.2(b), 5.1
  brokers, 1.2(b)
  customers' orders, 1.2(b)
  defined, OBRA Conferees, 28.4(c)(2)
  generally, 1.1(i), 1.2(b), 1.3(a), 2, 3.1, 5.1, 5.3(b), 7.3(b)(2), 14.5(d), 17.2(a)(5)
  government securities, marketable, 2
  inventory, 1.2(b)
  margin bonds, 1.4(b)(2), 7.4(b)(5), 7.4(b)(6)
  margin securities, 1.4(b)(2)
  margin stocks, 1.4(b)(2)
  market makers, 1.2(b)
  municipal securities, 3.1
  options, 5.1, 5.3(b)
  public offerings, 1.2(b)
  securities traded in over-the-counter market, 1.2(b), 2, 14.5(b)
  "upstairs" business, 1.2(b)
Owner trusts, *see* Asset-backed securities, owner trusts

Index

I-64

P

Pacific Stock Exchange (PSE), 44.3
Packages, *see* Integrated economic transactions
PACs, *see* Asset-backed securities, planned amortization class bonds (PACs)
Partially hedged executory contracts, 23.3(g)(2)(viii)(b)
Participants Trust Company (PTC), 2.1(b)(2), 2.4, 7.5(b)
Participation certificates (PCs), 2.1(b)(4), 7.2(b), 36.1
Partnership(s):
  assets distributed upon termination, 17.3(c)(2)
  association classification, 28.1
  attribution, Straddle Rules, 51.1, 51.2, 51.3
  basis, 28.3
  characterization of interest expense purchases, 25.5
  contribution, 28.4(b)(3)
  distributions, 17.3(c)(2)
  division, 28.4(b)(3)
  full redemption rights, 28.4(c)(5)
  general partners, 45.2(c)(2)
  hardship redemptions, 28.4(c)(5)
  hedging losses of limited entrepreneurs, 23.2(c)(3)
  hedging losses of limited partners, 23.2(c)(3)
  information network, 28.4(c)(4)
  interests, 28
  investment interest, 9.2(e)
  irregular redemptions, 28.4(c)(5)
  limited entrepreneurs, 23.2(a), 44.4, 45.2(c), 45.2(c)(1)
  limited partners, 23.2(a), 44.4, 45.2(c), 45.2(c)(1)
  limited partnerships, *see* Limited partnerships
  limited redemption programs, 28.4(c)(5)
  matching services, 28.4(c)(4)
  merger, 28.4(b)(3)
  municipal securities, 33.5(a)
  nonpublic, tax status, 28.1
  occasional redemptions, 28.4(c)(5)
  original issue discount, 31.2(d)
  publicly traded, *see* Publicly traded partnerships after December 31, 1987
  publicly traded limited partnerships, 1.1(h), 28
  qualified fund, election, 59.2(i)(4)(i)
    calendar year partnership, 59.2(a)(4)(iii)
    fiscal year partnership, 59.2(a)(4)(iii)
    section 988 election, unavailable, 59.2(j)
  redemptions, 28.4(c)(4), 28.4(c)(5)
  reporting requirements, 28.3
  residence, 23.3(c)
  secondary market, 28.4(c)(4)
  section 988 election, 59.2(j)
  street name interests, 28.3
  tacked holding periods, 17.3(c)(2)
  tax basis, 28.3
  tax status of partnerships not publicly traded, 28.1
  trading desk, 28.4(c)(4)
Passive activities:
  commodity pools, 9.8, 28.4(b)(2)
  generally, 9.2(e), 9.2(h), 9.8, 9.9, 14.5(d), 25.5, 59.2(g)(3)(v)
  interest expense, 9.2(a), 10.2(a)
  materially participates, 9.8
  new regulations controversial, 9.8
  personal service corporations, 9.8
  taxpayer does not materially participate, 9.8
Passive activity losses, 9.2(e), 9.2(h), 9.8
Pass-through certificates, *see* Asset-backed securities, pass-through certificates
Pass-through debt certificates, *see* Asset-backed securities, pass-through certificates, debt certificates
Pass-through entities, 9.1(d); *see also* Municipal securities, mutual funds; Real estate mortgage investment conduits (REMICs); Regulated investment companies (RICs)
Pass-through securities, 1.1(e); *see generally* Asset-backed securities
Payment-in-kind (PIK) bonds, 31.2(g)(1), 31.2(g)(2)(i)
Pay-through bonds, *see* Asset-backed securities, pay-through bonds
Pay-through (or cash flow) bond, 1.1(e), 36.3
Pay-through securities, 1.1(e); *see generally* Asset-backed securities
PCs, *see* Participation certificates (PCs)
Penalties:
  dividend(s):

information returns, 13.3, 24.10
    intentionally disregards rules, 24.10
  failure to disclose unrecognized gain, 53.1
    current law, requirements, 53.1(b)
    pre-TRA '86, requirements, 53.1(a)
  failure to file information returns, 13.3
  failure to include all required information, 13.3
  failure to report correct TINs, 13.4
  50 percent of interest payable on deficiency, 53.1
  five percent of amount of underpayment, 53.1
  for delays, 58.1
  fraud, 53.1
  frivolous or groundless positions, 58.1
  interest:
    information returns, 24.10
      intentionally disregards rules, 24.10
    reporting, 25.6
  negligent or intentional disregard, 53.1
  negligence, defined, 53.1(b)
  proceedings instituted, 58.1
  Tax Court petitions filed to delay payment of tax, 58.1
  underpayment of tax liability, 53.2, 58.1
  undistributed income, 11.10, 13.6
  unreasonable failure to pursue administrative remedies, 58.1
  unrecognized gains, 53.1
Pension and profit sharing plans, 1.4(a), 8.2(c), 16.3(c), 29.2(c)
Perpendicular spreads, 5.4(c)
PERLS, 1.1(g)(6), 2.1(b)(6)
Personal holding companies:
  adjusted ordinary gross income, requirement, 24.3
  affiliated group, 24.3
  broker, 13.6
  dealer, 11.10
  dividends, 24.3
    deficiency, 24.3
    dividends paid deduction, 24.3
    intercorporate dividends received, 24.3
  generally, 8.10, 11.10, 13.6
  income, 11.10, 13.6, 24.3
    definition modified, 11.10, 13.6, 24.3
  nonliquidating distributions, 24.3
  preferential dividends, 24.3
  tax rate, 24.3
  undistributed income, 11.10, 13.6, 24.3
Personal interest:
  defined, 9.2(h)
  five-year phase-in period, 9.2(h)
  nondeductible, 9.2(a), 9.2(e)
  qualified residence interest, 9.2(h)
  securities margin accounts, 9.2(b)
  see also Interest expense, personal interest
Personal property:
  actively traded, 48.2(a)
    commodity swaps, 60.2(d)(1)
    debt securities, 48.4(c)
    interests, 48.2(a), 48.3
    interests in property, 48.3(a)
    options, 48.4(b)
    property, 48.3(a)
    swaps, 60.2(b)(1)(iii)
  defined, 48.2, 48.2(c)(1)
    for purposes of Straddle Rules, 60.4(e), 60.7(a)
  FRAs, "positions" in personal property, 60.4(e)
  hedging transactions, 12.3, 23.2(a)
  offsetting positions, 48.4, 60.2(b)(1), 60.4(e), 60.7
  positions, 48.3, 60.2(b)(1), 60.4(e)
  stock positions, 48.2(c), 48.2(c)(1), 56.5
  straddles, 48.1
  swaps, 60.2(b)(1)(iii), 60.2(b)(2)(ii)
  United States currency, 48.2(b), 48.3(a), 48.3(b)(2)(i), 60.2(b)(1)
Personal transactions, 59.2(a)(3)
Phantom income, 9.1(d), 19.9(i), 36.4(c), 39.2(c), 41.2(k)
Philadelphia Stock Exchange (PHLX), 5.2(a)(3), 5.2(a)(4)
PHLX, see Philadelphia Stock Exchange (PHLX)
Physical commodity transactions, 18.4(f)
  identification, 20.2(f)
PIK bonds, see Payment-in-kind (PIK) bonds
Planned amortization class bonds (PACs), see Asset-backed securities, planned amortization class bonds (PACs)
Pooled property bonds, 7.2(a)(3)
Portfolio:
  exchangeables, 34.6(a)
  income, defined, 9.8
  indebtedness, defined, 24.9(c)(4), 27.3(b)(3)
  interest expense, 10.2(a)

Index

Portfolio (*Continued*)
   30 percent withholding obligation, exemption, 23.3(f)(5)
   investments, 9.8
   stock, defined, 24.9(c)(2)
Portfolio exchangeables, 34.6(a)
Position(s):
   actively traded, 48.2(a)
   balanced positions, 48.4(a)
   definition, 48.3(a)
   examples of, 48.3(a)
   foreign currencies, 48.3(c)
   offset successor position, 57.3(h)
   offsetting with respect to loss position, 49.2
   offsetting with respect to successor position, 49.2
   put option, 54.4(d)
   repurchase agreements, 48.3(b)
   reverse repurchase agreements, 48.3(b)
   sold or marketed as offsetting, 48.4(a)
PO strips, *see* Asset-backed securities, principal only strips
Pre-DRA law:
   broker-dealer treatment, 8.3(c)
   dealers for certain option transactions, 30.2(b)
   option audit issues, 30.2(b)
   option market maker's transactions, 8.2(b), 8.3(c), 30.2(b)(4)
   option spread transactions, 30.2(a), 30.2(b), 56.6
     at-risk rules, 30.2(b)(3)
     audit issues, 30.2(b)(1)
     option market makers, 30.2(b)(4)
     profit motive, 30.2(b)(2)
     specialists, 30.2(b)(4)
   stock positions, 48.2(c), 56.5
   transactions, 30.2, 35.1
Pre-ERTA law:
   background, 47.1, 47.2
   cancellation transactions, 58.1
   capitalization of interest and carrying charges, 55.1
   contract cancellations, 58.1
   DRA, Section 108, 30.2(b), 47.2(c), 47.2(d)
   interest and carrying charges, 55.1
   IRS settlement offer, pre-ERTA cases, 47.2(c)
   judicial decisions on pre-ERTA straddles, 47.2(e)
   legislative, judicial, and administrative solutions for certain straddles, 47.2(c)
   interpretation of Section 108:
     tax court decision, 47.2(d)(1)
     reversed, 47.2(d)(2)
     Tenth Circuit decision, 47.2(d)(2)
     IRS's attempted disallowance, 47.2(d)(1)
     issues clarified, 47.2(d)(1)
     primarily for profit, 47.2(d)(1)
     profit motive requirement, 47.2(d)(2)
   S corporations, 47.2(c)
   Section 108, 30.2(b), 47.2(c), 47.2(d)
     judicial decisions, 47.2(e)
     TRA '86, amended, 47.2(e)
   straddles, 47.2(c)
   tax rules in effect, 47.2, 47.2(e)
Pre-ERTA straddle(s):
   Deficit Reduction Act (DRA), 58.1
   generally, 58.1
   legislative, judicial, and administrative solutions, 47.2(c)
   Section 108, judicial decisions, 47.2(e)
Preferred stock:
   alternative minimum tax, 27.3(b)(3)
   American Express Company, dutch-auction rate preferred stock, 1.1(g)(3)
   adjustable rate preferred stock (ARPS), 1.1(g)(3), 27.3(b)(3)(ii)
   auction rate preferred, 1.1(g)(3), 27.3(b)(3)(iii)
   bailouts, 27.3(b)(5)
   bond premiums, 27.2
   consolidation test, 27.3(b)(3)
   contingent and adjustable preferred stock, 27.3(b)(3)(vi)
   convertible adjustable preferred stock (CAPS), 1.1(g)(4), 17.7, 24.9(b)(1), 27.3(b)(3)(iii), 27.3(b)(3)(vii)
     conversion option not option to sell, 24.9(b)(1)
     intercorporate dividends received deduction available, 24.9(b)(1)
   convertible exchangeable preferred stock, 1.1(g)(8)
   convertible preferred stock, 1.1(d), 17.7, 18.2(c), 27.3(c)(2), 27.3(b)(3)(vii)
   credit ratings, 27.3(b)(3)
   debt-equity considerations, 27.3(b)(2)

debt financed portfolio stock, 24.9(c), 27.3(b)(3); *see also* Debt financed portfolio stock
debt flavored preferred stock products, 27.3(b)(3)
debt instruments, 59.2(a)(1)
defined, 1.1(a), 27.3(b)(1)
disqualified preferred stock, 16.6(g)
distributions of convertible preferred stock, 27.3(c)(7)
distributions on, 24.2(b)(5)
dividends, 18.6(e)(2), 24.2, 24.2(b)(4), 24.2(b)(5)
dutch-auction rate preferred, 1.1(g)(3), 27.3(b)(3)(iii)
floating rate preferred, 1.1(g)(2), 27.3(b)(3)(i)
Fox Television Stations, increasing rate exchangeable guaranteed preferred stock, 1.1(g)(7), 27.3(b)(3)(v)
guarantees, 27.3(b)(2)(ii)
increasing rate exchangeable guaranteed preferred stock, 1.1(g)(7), 27.2, 27.3(b)(3)(v)
intercorporate dividends received deduction, 27.3(b)(3)
investment unit, 31.2(j)
issued with redemption premium, 27.3(b)(6)
mandatory redemption provisions, 27.3(b)(2)(i), 27.3(b)(3)(i), 27.3(b)(3)(ii)
mandatory sinking funds, 31.2(a)
market auction preferred stock, 27.3(b)(3)(iii)
Merrill Lynch, remarketed preferred stock, 1.1(g)(3), 27.3(b)(3)(iv)
money market preferred, 1.1(g)(3), 27.3(b)(3)(iii)
original issue discount, 27.2
participating preferred, 2.1(b)(4), 27.5(b)
periodic redemptions, 27.3(b)(4)
permanent preferred stock, 27.3(b)(2)(i)
perpetual preferred, 27.2
portfolio stock, 27.3(b)(3)
public utilities, 24.4, 24.9(a)
put option, 24.9(b)(1)
reasonable redemption premiums, 24.2(b)(5), 27.3(b)(6)
reclassified as debt securities, 27.3(b)(2)(i)
redemptions, 27.3(b)(2), 27.3(b)(2)(i), 27.3(b)(4), 31.2(a)
remarketed preferred, 1.1(g)(3), 27.3(b)(3)(iv)
sales or redemptions of shares of, 24
section 306 stock, *see* Section 306 stock
section 988 transactions, 59.2(a)(1)
security arrangements, 27.3(b)(4)
short sales, closing, 18.2(c)
sinking funds, 31.2(a)
special purpose subsidiary, 27.3(b)(3)
tax classification, 27.3(b)(1)
tax-free exchanges, 27.3(b)(2)(iii)
tax objectives, 27.3(b)(3)
with redemption premium, 27.3(b)(6)
Premium dividend rate, *see* Dividends, premium rate
Premium runoff, 11.4(b)
Premiums, *see* Option premiums or Bond premiums
Prepayment assumption, 7.2(d)(4), 31.2(m)
Price spreads, 5.4(c)
Primary dealers; government securities brokers and dealers, 2
PRIME units, *see* Americus trusts
Principal exchange rate linked securities (PERLS), 1.1(g)(6), 2.1(b)(6)
Private activity bond(s) (PABs):
aggregate amounts, limits, 33.2(c)(1)(ii)
exempt facilities, 33.2(c)(2)(i), 33.2(c)(2)(vi)(a)
financing, 33.2(c)(2)
generally, 3.1, 3.2(c), 25.4(a), 25.4(b), 25.4(c), 33.2(c)
municipal securities, 25.4(c)
post-August 16, 1986, 33.2(c)(1)(i)
qualified 501(c)(3) bonds, 33.2(c)(2)(vi)
qualified hospital bonds, 33.2(c)(2)(vi)(b)
qualified mortgage bonds, 33.2(c)(2)(ii)(a)
qualified redevelopment bonds, 33.2(c)(2)(v)
qualified student loan bonds, 33.2(c)(2)(iv)
qualified veterans' mortgage bonds, 33.2(c)(2)(ii)(b)
revenue bonds, 33.4, 33.2(c)
small issue exemptions, 33.2(c)(2)(iii)
use of bond proceeds, 33.10
Private mortgage pools, 29.1(a)
Private placements, securities:

Index

Private placements, securities (*Continued*)
  asset-backed securities, 7.3(a)(2),
    7.3(b)(2)
  Investment Company Act of 1940,
    exemption, 7.6(d)
  municipal securities, 3.1
Profit motive, 30.2(b)(4), 47.2, 47.2(a),
  47.2(b), 47.2(c), 47.2(d), 47.2(e), 55.1
Profits, *see* Earnings and profits
Program trading, 48.2(c)(2)
Prohibited transaction(s):
  REITs, safe harbor, 8.10(c)
Promissory notes, *see* Debt securities,
  promissory notes
Property, 16.2, 17.3(c)(2), 18.2(b), 19.6(b),
  24.1(b), 27.4(d)
  involuntary conversion, 27.4(d),
    27.4(d)(2)
    nonrecognition treatment, 27.4(d)(1)
    replacement property, 27.4(d)(1)
Property and casualty insurance
  companies:
  losses, 33.8
  municipal securities, 33.8
Property specific bonds, 7.2(a)(2)
PSA model, *see* Public Securities
  Association (PSA), PSA model
PSE High Technology Index, *see* Indexes
Publicly traded partnerships after
  December 31, 1987:
  accommodation trades, 28.4(c)(6)
  active business activity, 28.4(a)
  closed end partnerships, 28.4(c)(5)(ii)
  commodity pools, 28.4(b)(2),
    28.4(d)(2)(vii)
  commodity trading, exception,
    28.4(d)(1)
  corporate nontax characteristics, 28.4(a)
  corporate tax exception, 28.4(b)(2),
    28.4(d)(1)
  defined, 28.4(b)(1), 28.4(c), 28.4(c)(1)
  established securities market, trade,
    28.4(c)(2)
  existing partnership exemption,
    28.4(b)(3)
  General Utilities doctrine, 28.4(a)
  gross income requirement, 28.4(f)
  intercorporate dividends received
    deduction, 28.4(e)
  Investment Company Act of 1940,
    registered, 28.4(d)(1)
  matching services, defined, 28.4(c)(4)

new line of business, classification,
  28.4(b)(3)
90 percent test, 28.4(f)
OBRA grandfather provisions, 28.4(b)(3)
open end partnerships, 28.4(c)(5)(i)
partnerships, not PTPs, 28.4(g)(2)
passive loss rules, amended by OBRA,
  28.4(g), 28.4(g)(1)
  entire interest, disposed, 28.4(g)(1)
  interest expenses, 28.4(g)(1)
  investment income, 28.4(g)(1)
  losses (credits) suspended, 28.4(g)(1)
  partnerships, not PTPs, 28.4(g)(2)
  passive activity deduction, 28.4(g)(1)
  passive income, 28.4(g)(1)
  portfolio income, 28.4(g)(1)
  privately placed, 28.4(g)(2)
  publicly traded, 28.4(g)(1)
  $25,000 allowance, 28.4(g)(1)
private placements safe harbor,
  28.4(c)(6)(i)
qualifying income, defined, 28.4(d)(1),
  28.4(d)(2)
  active income, 28.4(d)(1)
  capital assets sales, 28.4(d)(2)(vi)
  commodities, 28.4(d)(2)(vii)
  dividends, 28.4(d)(2)(ii)
  exemptions, 28.4(b)(2)
  interest, 28.4(d)(2)(i)
  natural resources, 28.4(d)(2)(v)
  90 percent test, 28.4(f)
  passive-type, 28.4(d)(1)
  real property, rent, 28.4(d)(2)(iii)
  real property, sales, 28.4(d)(2)(iv)
  REITs and RICs, 28.4(d)(2)(vii)
readily tradable requirement, 28.4(c)(6)
redemption and repurchase safe harbor,
  28.4(c)(5)
safe harbors, 28.4(b)(3), 28.4(c)(5),
  28.4(c)(6)(iii), 28.4(c)(6)(iii)(a),
  28.4(c)(6)(iii)(b)
secondary market, substantial
  equivalent, trade, 28.4(c)(4),
  28.4(c)(5)
secondary market, trade, 28.4(c)(3)
special rule, different tax year, 28.4(h)
tax benefits, recapture, 28.4(e)
taxed as corporation, 28.4(a), 28.4(b)(1),
  28.4(e)
tax-exempt entities, 28.4(h)
tax treatment, 28.4(a), 28.4(e)
termination, inadvertent, 28.4(f)
trading desk, 28.4(c)(4)

trading volume safe harbors,
28.4(c)(6)(iii)
five percent, 28.4(c)(6)(iii)(a)
safe harbor selection, considerations,
28.4(c)(6)(iii)(c)
two percent, 28.4(c)(6)(iii)(b)
transfers without trading, 28.4(c)(6)(ii)
unrelated business taxable income,
28.4(h)
Publicly traded trust interest(s):
Americus trusts, see Americus trusts
certificates of beneficial interest, 1.1(i)
classification, 29.1
dividends and distributions,
distribution trusts, 1.1(i)
employee benefit plans, 29.2(c)
generally, 1.1(i), 29
nonoperating interests, 1.1(i)
pension and profit sharing plans, 29.2(c)
recent developments, 29.2(b)
tax status as trust, 29.1
use of trust to maximize shareholder
return, 29.2(a)
real estate investment trusts, see Real
estate investment trusts (REITs)
residence, 23.3(c)
royalty trusts, see Royalty trusts
tax-exempt securities held in, 9.3(a)
tax status, 29.1
TIMs, 36.8(b)
Treasury securities, 2
trustees, 20.2(a)(3)
trust investments, 36.8(b)
unit investment trusts, 8.9, 20.2(f), 24.5
voting trust certificates, 19.9(c)
see also Regulated investment
companies (RICs)
Public offerings, 1.2(b), 3.1, 8.9(c)
Public Securities Association (PSA):
CMOs, 7.2(d)(4)
generally, 2.4, 7.2(d)(4)
GNMA securities, 2.1(b)(2)
prepayment assumption, 7.2(d)(4),
31.2(m)
PSA model, 2.4, 7.2(d)(4)
Public utilities:
dividends, 24.4
electrical energy, 24.4
gas, 24.4
holding companies, 27.4(c)
mortgage bonds, 7.2(a)
preferred stock, 24.9(a)
qualified dividend reinvestment, 24.4

distributions, 24.4
regulated public utilities, 24.2(b)(3)
telephone service, 24.4
water, 24.4
Public utility holding companies, 27.4(c)
Purchase premiums, see Bond premiums
Put and call arbitrage, see Arbitrage, put
and call arbitrage
Put options, see Options, put options

Q

QBUs, see Qualified business units (QBUs)
QPIP, see Qualified periodic interest
payment (QPIP)
Qualified board or exchange, 30.1(a), 44.1,
44.2, 44.3, 44.4, 45.1
Qualified bonds, 3.2(c)
Qualified business unit(s) (QBUs):
accounting methods, 59.2(g),
59.2(g)(3)(vi), 59.2(g)(3)(vii)
accrual basis taxpayer, 59.2(g)(3)(vi)
activities constitute trade or business,
59.2(g)(3)(ii)
activities of:
corporation, 59.2(g)(3)(ii)
estates, partnerships, trusts,
59.2(g)(3)(iv)
individual, 59.2(g)(3)(iii), 59.2(g)(v)
books and records, separate,
59.2(g)(3)(vi)
cash basis taxpayer, 59.2(g)(3)(vi)
change functional currency,
59.2(g)(1)(iii)
corporations, 59.2(g)(3)(ii)
defined, 59.2(g)(3)(i)
economic environment, 59.2(g)(1)(i),
59.2(g)(3)(viii)
exchange gain or loss, source, 59.2(d)(1)
foreign branch, 59.5(b)
functional currency, 59.1, 59.2(g)(3)(i),
60.2(b)(2)(i)(a)(4)
change functional currency,
59.2(g)(1)(iii)
defined for QBUs, 59.2(g)(3)(viii)
generally, 23.3(d), 23.3(f)(1), 23.3(f)(2),
23.3(g)(1)(i)(c), 23.3(g)(2)(iii),
23.3(g)(3), 59.2(g)(1), 59.2(g)(3),
59.5(b), 60.5(a)
group of activities, described,
59.2(g)(3)(v)
journal, defined, 59.2(g)(3)(vi)
Notice 89-90, 60.2(b)(2)(i)(a)(4)

Index

I-70

Qualified business unit(s) (QBUs) (*Continued*)
  passive activities, 59.2(g)(3)(v)
  profit and loss, method, 59.2(g)(3)(vii)
  residence, 59.2(d)(1)
  separate books and records, 59.2(g)(3)(i), 59.2(g)(3)(ii), 59.2(g)(3)(iii), 59.2(g)(3)(iv)
  trade or business, 59.2(g)(2)(ii), 59.2(g)(3)(iii), 59.2(g)(iv), 59.2(g)(3)(v), 59.2(g)(3)(vi)
    "active" trade or business, 59.2(g)(3)(v)
    described, 59.2(g)(3)(v)
    separate and clearly identified unit, 59.2(g)(3)(i)
  transitional rules, before January 1, 1987, 59.2(g)(3)(vii)
Qualified corporation, defined, 16.6(b)
Qualified covered call(s):
  applicable stock price, 56.3(b)
  box spreads, 56.3(a)
  butterfly spreads, 56.3(a)
  covered calls, generally, 5.4(a)(2)(ii)
  deep-in-the-money options, 56.3, 56.3(b)
  definitions, 56.3(b)
  holding period, 17.9
  intercorporate dividends received, 17.7
  in-the-money when written, 56.3(d)
  limitations on exemption, 56.3(d)
  lowest qualified bench mark, 56.3(b)
    determination, exception to general rule, 56.3(c)
  modified short sales rule, exempt from, 18.4(c)
  offsetting stock, 56.5
  options dealers, 56.3(b)
  pre-DRA transactions, 30.2
  scope of exemption, 56.3(a)
  short sales, property covered, 18.4(c)
  stock price:
    $25 or less, 56.3(d)
    $150 or less, 56.3(d)
  Straddle Rules, qualified covered call exemption, 18.4(c), 23.3(c), 48.2(c)(1), 56.3
    limitations on exemption, 56.3(d)
      governing Treasury regulations, 56.3(d)(3)
      in-the-money call options, post-June 30, 1984, 56.3(d)(2)
      subsequent stock sale, 56.3(d)(1)
    scope of exemption, 56.3(a)
  straddles, exceptions, 48.2(c)(1)
  strike price, 17.9
    in excess of $50, 56.3(d)
  uncovered calls, generally, 5.4(a)(2)(i)
Qualified farmers, income averaging, 15.4(e)(3)
Qualified 501(c)(3) bond(s):
  after October 21, 1988, 33.2(c)(2)(vi)
  generally, 3.1, 3.2(c), 25.4(c), 33.2(c)(2)(vi)(a), 33.3(a)(1)(vi), 33.6
  land acquisitions, 33.2(c)(2)(vi)(f)
  mixed-used facilities, 33.2(c)(2)(vi)(c)
  municipal securities, 25.4(c), 33
  qualified hospital bonds, 33.2(c)(2)(vi)(b)
  rental housing projects, 33.2(c)(2)(vi)(e)
  volume limitation, 33.2(c)(2)(vi)(d)
Qualified funds:
  activity test, 59.2(i)(3)
  commodity partnerships, 45.1
  debt instruments, section 988 transactions, 59.2(i)(e)
  election, qualified fund, 59.2(i)(4)
    information required, 59.2(i)(4)(i)
    1988 calendar year, transitional rule, 59.2(i)(4)(iii)
    time for making election, 59.2(i)(4)(ii)
  foreign currency transactions, 59.2(i)(1)
  income test, 59.2(i)(3)
  IRS form 1065, 59.2(i)(4)(i)
  marked-to-market, 59.2(a)(2)
  ownership test, 59.2(i)(3)
  partnership, election by, 59.2(i)(4)(i)
    section 988 election unavailable, 59.2(j)
  qualified fund election under section 988(c)(1)(E)(iii)(V), 59.2(i)(4)(i)
  requirements, 59.2(i)(3)
  section 1256 contracts, expanded definition, 44.6
    foreign currency products, 45.1
    items included, 59.2(i)(2)
  TMRA '88 special rules, 44.6, 45.1, 46.2, 59.2(a)(2)
Qualified hedging transaction(s):
  defined, 23.3(f)(1)
  exchange rate, 23.3(f)(1)
  failure to qualify, 23.3(f)(4)
  foreign persons, special rules, 23.3(f)(3)
  functional currency, 23.3(f)(1)
  identification requirements, 23.3(f)(2)
  independent verification, 23.3(f)(2)

integrated economic transaction
  requirements, 23.3(f)(1), 23.3(g)(1)(i)
  income tax effect, 23.3(g)(1)(v)
interest rate, 23.3(f)(2)
marked-to-market, ineligible, 46.2(a)
mixed straddle provisions, 23.3(f)(4)
nonfunctional currency, 23.3(f)(1)
Notice 87-11, 23.3(f)(1), 23.3(f)(2),
    23.3(f)(3), 23.3(f)(4), 23.3(f)(5)
  superseded, 23.3(g)
package requirements, 23.3(f)(1)
qualified hedging account, 23.3(f)(2)
qualified transaction defined, 23.3(f)(1)
section 1.988-5T(a) qualified hedge, see
    Section 1.988-5T(a) hedges
section 1256 treatment, exempt,
    23.3(f)(3), 46.2(a)
settlement date, 23.3(f)(1)
60/40 treatment, ineligible, 46.2(a)
Straddle Rules, 23.3(f)(3), 23.3(g)(1)(iii)
taxation, 23.3(f)(3)
trade date, 23.3(f)(1), 23.3(f)(2)
United States source income, 23.3(f)(3)
withholding requirements, 23.3(f)(5)
Qualified heir, 17.1(d)
Qualified liquidations, 36.8(m)
Qualified loan agreements, 26.2
Qualified mortgage bonds, 3.2(c),
    33.2(c)(2)(ii)(a)
  municipal securities, 33.2(c)(2)(ii)
Qualified mortgages, 36.8(d)(1)
Qualified periodic interest payment
    (QPIP), 37.4(a)
Qualified redevelopment bonds,
    33.2(c)(2)(v)
  municipal securities, 33.2(c)(2)(v)
Qualified reserve assets, 36.8(d)(2)(ii)
Qualified reserve fund, 36.8(d)(2)(ii)(a)
Qualified residence interest, 9.2(e), 9.2(h)
Qualified securities, 16.4(e)
Qualified small issue bonds, 33.2(c)(2)(iii)
Qualified student loan bonds,
    33.2(c)(2)(iv)
Qualified tax-exempt obligation(s):
  defined, 11.3(b)(3)(ii)(b)
  financial institutions, special rules, 33.6
Qualified transaction, 23.3(f)(1)
Qualified veterans' mortgage bonds,
    33.2(c)(2)(ii)(b)
  municipal securities, 33.2(c)(2)(ii)
Qualifying debt instrument,
    23.3(g)(1)(i)(c), 23.3(g)(1)(ii)
  defined, 23.3(g)(1)(i)(a)

integrated economic transaction,
    23.3(g)(1)(i)
nonfunctional currency, 23.3(g)(1)(i)(a)
section 1.988-5T(a) qualified hedging
    transaction, 23.3(g)(1)(i)
Qualifying income, partnership, 28.4(b)(2)
Qualifying purchaser evidences of
    indebtedness, 17.2(a)(2)(i)(c)

R

Radio broadcasting corporations, 27.4(c)
Railroad retirement benefits, 33.3(a)(3)
Ratio spreads, 5.4(c)(3)
Ratio writing, 5.4(a)(2)(iii)
Real estate investment trust(s) (REITs):
  alternative minimum tax, 33.7
  asset-backed securities, 7.2(i), 8.10(a)
  asset ownership requirements, 8.10(a)
  associations, 24.6
  capital gains, 8.10(d)
  cash, 8.10(a)
  cash items, 8.10(a)
  convenience of tenants, 8.10(h)
  customary services, 8.10(h)
  debt obligation issues, 41.3(a)
  debt securities, 8.10(i)
  distributed amount, 8.10(e)
  distributions, 8.10(d), 24.6
  diversification requirements, 8.10(a)
  dividend deductions, 36.7
  dividends, 8.10(e)
  dividends paid deductions, 8.10
  equity investments, 8.10(i)
  excess inclusion allocation,
      shareholders, 41.3(b)
  excise tax, 8.10(e)
  financial institutions, qualifying real
      property loans, 41.4
  foreclosure properties, 8.10(b)
  generally, 7.2(i), 36.7
  grossed up required distribution, 8.10(e)
  hedging transaction, 8.4(d)
  income requirements, 8.10(b)
  independent contractors, 8.10(h)
  involuntary conversions, 8.10(b)
  losses, 8.10(d)
  MBS structures, 36.7
  nonqualifying securities, 8.10(a)
  100 shareholder requirement, 8.10
  ordinary income, 8.10(d)
  owner taxation, 36.7, 41.3
  parking facilities, 8.10(h)

Index

Real estate investment trust(s) (REITs) (*Continued*)
  pay-through bonds, 7.2(i)
  prohibited transactions, 8.10(c)
  qualification requirements for REITs, 8.10, 36.7
  qualified REIT subsidiaries, 8.10(f)
  qualifying income, publicly traded partnership, 28.4(d)(2), 28.4(d)(2)(viii)
  real estate assets, defined, 8.10(a)
  REMIC interests, 7.2(i), 41.3(a)
  rental of real properties, 8.10(h)
  repos, 31.11(a)(2)
  repurchase agreements, 8.10(a)
  required distribution, 8.10(e)
  safe harbors, 8.10(c)
  secured properties, 8.10(g)
  shared appreciation mortgages, 8.10(g)
  taxable income, 8.10(c), 8.10(e)
  taxation of shareholders, 8.10(d)
  TMP rules, exempt from, 36.8(*o*)
  undistributed earnings, 8.10(e)
  wholly owned subsidiaries, 8.10(f)
Real estate mortgage investment conduit(s) (REMICs):
  alternative minimum tax, 33.7
  asset test, 36.8(c)(1)(iv)
  books/records, calendar year, 36.8(j)(1)
  CMOs, 36.3, 36.8(c)(1)(i)
  CMSs, 36.8(b)
  compliance and reporting, 36.8(j)
  contributions, taxed after startup day, 36.8(h)
  credit enhancements, 36.8(d)(1)(iv), 36.8(n)
  election and termination, 36.8(k)
  excess inclusion rule, 19.9(i)
  financial institutions, 7.2(c)(2)(iii), 41.4
  FNMA, 2.1(b)(3)
  generally, 7.2(g)
  interest owners, taxation, 41
  interests in REMICs, 1.1(e), 7.2(g)
    real estate assets, 41.3(a)
  investment expenses, 36.8(*l*)
  IRS information, 36.8(j)(5)
  legislative proposals, pre-REMIC, 36.8(b)
  market discount, calculation, 31.3(*l*), 41.1(a)(3)
  multiple-class mortgage-backed securities, 1.1(e), 7.2(g), 8.11, 36.8(a)
  objective interest index, 36.8(c)(1)(iv)
  OID calculation, 31.2(m), 41.1(a)(3)
  pass-through interest holder, 36.8(*l*)
  pay-through bonds, 36.8(a)
  permitted investments, 36.8(d)(2)
  prohibited transactions, 36.8(g)
  qualified mortgages, 36.8(d)(1)
  regular interest(s):
    caps, 36.8(c)(1)(iv)
    debt security treatment, 41, 41.1(a)
    exchanged for property, 41.1(b)
    fixed rate, 36.8(c)(1)(iii)
    floors, 36.8(c)(1)(iv)
    gain on disposition, 41.1(c)
    generally, 2.1(b)(3), 7.2(g), 36.8(e)(1)
    holders, 41.1
    issue price, 41.1(b)
    OID rules, 41.1(a)(3)
      discount, 41.1(a)(3)
      premium, 41.1(a)(2)
      principal amount, 41.1(a)(1)
    owner, basis, 41.1(b)
    reports to, 36.8(j)(4)
    senior, 36.8(c)(1)(v)
    startup day, transfer, 36.8(d)(1)(ii)
    stripped, 36.8(c)(1)(vi)
    subordinated, 36.8(c)(1)(v)
    TMP rules, exceptions, 36.8(*o*)
    variable rate, 36.8(c)(1)(iv)
  REITs not eligible, 36.7
  reporting:
    market discount, 36.8(j)(3)
    OID, 36.8.(j)(2)
    premiums, 36.8(j)(2)
  residual interest(s):
    adjusted tax basis, 7.2(g)
    daily accrual, 41.2(g)(3)
    disallowed losses, 41.2(c)
    distributions to, 41.2(b)
    excess inclusions, 41.2(g)
    exchanged for property, 41.2(i)
    generally, 2.1(b)(3), 7.2(g), 19.6(a), 19.9(i), 36.8(c)(2)
    holders, 41.2
    income/loss calculation, general rule, 41.2(e)
    issue price, 41.2(h)
    phantom income, 19.9(i), 41.2(k)
    security treatment, 19.6(a), 41.2(j)
    subsequent holders, 41.2(d)
    substantially identical property, 19.9(i)
    taxation, 41.2(a), 41.2(f)

value determination, significant, 41.2(g)(4)
wash sales rule, 41.2(j)
segregated pool of assets, 36.8(a)
senior and subordinated classes, 7.2(g)
startup day, defined, 36.8(a), 36.8(c)(2)
substantially identical property, 19.9(i)
terminations, inadvertent, 36.8(f)
TIMs, 36.8(b)
TMP provisions, 7.2 (g), 36.8(o)
two percent floor, 9.1(d)
variable rate regular interests, 36.8(c)(1)(iv)
wash sales rule, 19.6(a), 19.9(i), 41.2(j)
Rebates, short stock, 18.6(e)(4), 57.4(d)
Recombined units, *see* Americus trusts
Reconstituted stripped bonds, 31.6(g)
Record dates, 1.3(d)
Record owners, 24.7(d)
Redemption(s):
  abnormal redemptions, 8.9(d)
  bond redemption transaction, 13.3
  partnership(s):
    full, 28.4(c)(5)
    hardship, 28.4(c)(5)
    irregular, 28.4(c)(5)
    limited, 28.4(c)(5)
    matching services, 28.4(c)(4)
    occasional, 28.4(c)(5)
  preferred stock, 27.3(b)(4)
  premium, 11.8(a)
  price of security, 31.3
  pursuant to mandatory sinking fund, 31.2(a)
  stock redemption, 16.4(*l*)
Refcorp securities, *see* Federal agency securities, Resolution Funding Corporation (Refcorp) securities
Registered owners, 31.2(a)
Registered securities:
  asset-backed securities, 7, 36
  municipal securities, 33.3(a)(1)(iii)
  registered form, 1.1(b), 20.2(a)(1), 25.4(c), 31.2(a), 31.12(b)
  definition clarified, 31.12(a)
  registered in taxpayer's name, 20.2(a)(1)
  registered owner, 31.2(a)
  registration-required securities, *see* Registration-required securities
  tax-exempt securities, 31.12(c)
  United States securities offered to public, 31.12(c)
Registration-required securities:
  capital gain treatment, 31.12(c)
  corporate issuer's earnings and profits, 31.12(c)
  defined, 31.12(b)
  exceptions to loss denial and ordinary income treatment, 31.12(d)(1)
  financial institutions, investment accounts, 31.12(d)(2)
  excise tax on issuers, 31.12(a), 31.12(c)
  foreign-issued obligations, 31.12(b)(4)(i)
    certification requirements, 31.12(b)(4)(iv)
    effective date, 31.12(b)(4)(v)
    electronic certification, 31.12(b)(4)(iv)(b)
    exceptions, 31.12(b)(4)(iv)(c)
    restrictions on delivery, 31.12(b)(4)(iii)
    restrictions on offers and sales, 31.12(b)(iv)(ii)
    special rules, 31.12(b)(4)(v)
  generally, 31.12(b)
  issuer's deduction for interest paid, 31.12(c)
  loss on sale, exchange, theft, loss, or other dispositions, 31.12(c)
  noncompliance with registration requirements, 31.12(c)
  obligation not registration-required, 31.12(a)
  registration requirements, generally, 31.12(a)
  REMICs, 31.12(f)
  short-term debt securities, 31.12(b)
Regular interests, *see* Real estate mortgage investment conduits (REMICs), regular interests
Regular way transactions, 1.3(a), 2.2(a), 17.2(a)(2)(i)(e), 24.7(a), 24.7(c), 24.7(d)
Regulated futures contract(s) (RFCs):
  cash settlement contracts, 44.1(a)
  foreign currency-related, 44.1, 44.6, 59.2(a)(1)
  foreign currency transactions, nonhedge, 59.4(a)
    post-October 21, 1988 positions, 59.4(a)(3)
    post-section 988 positions, 59.4(a)(2)
    pre-1986 positions, 59.4(a)(1)
    pre-October 22, 1988 positions, 59.4(a)(2)
  generally, 23.3(e), 44.1, 60.2(c)(3)
  Notice 88-124, 59.2(j)

Index

Regulated futures contract(s) (RFCs) (*Continued*)
  qualified boards or exchanges, 44.1(b)
  section 988 election, 59.2(b)(4), 59.2(j)
    information required, 59.2(j)(1)
    late election, 59.2(j)(3)
    1988 calendar year, transitional rule, 59.2(j)(4)
    procedure, 59.2(j)(1)
    time for making election, 59.2(j)(2)
  section 1256 treatment, 44.1, 44.1(a)
  transitional election requirements, 44.1
  United States currency, 44.1(a)
Regulated investment companies:
  alternative minimum tax, 33.7
  asset-backed securities, 7.2(h), 8.9, 36.6
  business development companies, 8.9(a)
  capital gain distributions, 24.5(a)
  capital gain net income, calculation, 8.9(b)(1), 8.9(b)(2)
  C corporation assets, 8.9
  dividends, 24.5
    capital gains dividends, 8.9(b)(3), 8.9(c), 17.6, 24.5
    dividend exclusion, 24.8
    exempt-interest dividends, 8.9(a), 8.9(c), 9.3(b)(3)
    nonqualifying dividends, 24.5
    ordinary income dividends, 8.9(c)
  dividends paid deduction, 8.9, 24.5(c), 27.3(b)(3)(iii)
    calculation, 24.5
  earnings and profits, 8.9(a), 8.9(f)
  election, 8.9(a), 8.9(a)(1)
  excise tax:
    calculation, 8.9(b)(1)
    capital gains dividend, defined for excise tax purposes, 8.9(b)(3)
    generally, 8.9(b), 59.2(b)(2)
    grossed up required distribution, 1986, 8.9(b)(2)
    nondeductible, 8.9(b)(1)
  financial statements, 8.9(c)
  foreign currencies, 8.9(a)
  foreign currency gains and losses, 59.2(b)(2)
  forward contracts, 8.9(a)
  futures, 8.9(a)
  gains and losses, receipt, 24.5(b)
  General Utilities doctrine, 8.9
  hedging transactions, 8.9(e)
  holding periods, 17.6, 54.4(c)
  Investment Company Act of 1940, registration, 7.6(d), 8.9(a)
  investment expenses, 8.9(c)
  losses, 17.6, 24.5(b)
  management companies, 8.9
  marking-to-market, 54.4(c)
  Massachusetts business trust, 8.9(d)
  minimum shareholder requirement, waiver, 8.9(c)
  modified short sales rule, application, 54.4(a)
    special rule, 54.4(c)
  multifund RIC, 8.9(d)
  multiple classes of stock, 24.5(d)
  municipal securities, flow-through, 33.5(c)
  mutual funds, 8.9(a), 9.1(d), 24.5, 33.5(c)
  nonpublic, 8.9(c), 9.1(d)
  Notice 88-4, 8.9(b)(1), 8.9(b)(2)
  Notice 88-88, 8.9(c)
  notices to shareholders, 8.9(c)
  offsetting positions, 48.2(c)(2)
  options, 8.9(a)
  ordinary income, calculation, 8.9(b)(1), 8.9(b)(2)
  original issue discount, 31.2(d)
  owner taxation, 7.6(d), 8.9(c), 36.6
  pass-through entities, 9.1(d)
  pass-through limitations, 8.9, 9.1(d)
  phantom income, 9.1(d)
  publicly offered, defined, 8.6(c), 9.1(d)
  publicly traded partnership, 28.4(d)(2), 28.4(d)(2)(viii)
  qualification requirements, 8.9(a)
    25 percent diversification, 8.9(a)(5)
    30 percent of gross income, 8.9(a)(3)
    50 percent diversification, 8.9(a)(4)
    90 percent of gross income, 8.9(a)(2)
    distribution requirements, 8.9(a)(6)
  qualified securities loans, 26.2
  relief provision, 8.9(d)
  section 988 transactions, 59.2(b)(2)
  security loans, 26.1
  series funds, 8.9(d)
  shareholders; expenses, 8.9(c)
    reporting requirements, new, 8.9(c)
      additional two-year delay, application, 8.9(c)
      erroneous removal, two percent floor, 8.9(c)
  share identification:
    average basis election, 20.2(f)
    double-category method, 20.2(f)

reinvestment of dividends, 20.2(f)
single-category method, 20.2(f)
short-short rule, 8.9(a)(3)
short sales rule, 54.4(c)
tax-exempt dividends, 8.9(c), 17.6
tax-exempt interest, 9.3(b)(3), 24.5
tax-exempt securities, 33.5(c)
third-party recordkeepers, 8.9(c)
two percent floor, 9.1(d)
undistributed capital gains, 16.4(*l*), 20.2(f)
unit investment trust, 8.9(a)
Regulation D, 7.6(d)
Regulation G, 7.4(b)(1)
Regulation S, 31.12(b)(4)(i)
Regulation T, 1.4, 2.3, 7.4, 7.4(b)(3), 7.4(b)(6), 8.7(b)
Regulation U, 1.4, 2.3, 7.4, 7.4(b)(1), 7.4(b)(3), 8.7(b)
REITs, *see* Real estate investment trusts (REITs)
Related parties:
  attribution rules, 51.1, 51.2, 51.3
  brothers and sisters, 19.10(c)
  controlled corporations, 19.10(d)
  hedging transactions, 23.2(c)(1)
  husbands and wives, 19.10(a)
  mixed straddles, 51.4, 57.6
  parents and children, 19.10(b)
  related persons, defined, 57.6(a)
  section 1092(b)(2) elections, 57.6(a)
  section 1256 contracts, 51.3
  statutory elections, 51.2
  wash sales of stock or securities, 19.10
Remarketed preferred stock, 1.1(g)(3), 27.3(b)(3)(iv)
Remarketing agent, 1.1(g)(3)
REMICs, *see* Real estate mortgage investment conduits (REMICs)
Reorganization(s):
  business purpose requirement, 27.4(b)(1)
  continuity of business enterprise, 27.4(b)(2)
  continuity of interest, 27.3(b)(2)(iii), 27.4(b)(2)
  exchanges of debt securities, 31.9(b)
  municipal securities, unavailability, 33.4
  recapitalizations, 20.2(d), 27.3(c)(2), 27.3(c)(8), 33.4
  security loans, 26, 26.2
  separable transactions, 27.4(b)(3)

spin-offs of controlled corporations, 16.4(*l*), 27.4(b)
stock exchanged solely for stock, 17.3(a)(2)
substantially identical property, wash sales rule, 19.9(d)
substituted basis, 17.3(a)(1), 17.3(a)(2)
tacked holding period, 17.3(a)(1)
taxable reorganizations, 17.2(a)(3)
tax-free exchanges, 17.3(a), 20.2(d), 27.4, 32.1(d)
  securities received in exchange, 17.3(a)
  stock exchanged solely for stock, 17.3(a)(2)
  Type A reorganizations, 27.4(b), 34.3(e)
  Type B reorganizations, 27.4(b)
  Type C reorganizations, 27.3(c)(5), 27.3(c)(8), 27.4(b)
  Type D reorganizations, 27.4(b)
  Type E recapitalizations, 27.3(c)(1), 27.3(c)(3), 27.3(c)(8), 27.4(b), 33.4
  Type F reorganizations, 27.4(b)
  Type G reorganizations, 27.4(b)
warrants, separable transactions, 27.4(b)(3)
Reporting income, *see* Income, reporting income
Reporting requirements:
  bond redemption transactions, 13.3
  broker, 13.3
  disclosure of unrecognized gain, 52.1
  dividends, 24.10, 13.3
  exceptions to, 52.2
  identifying owners of MLP shares, 28.3
  interest, 25.6
  municipal securities, 33.3(a)(1)(viii)
  partnerships, 28.3
Repurchase transaction(s):
  alternative minimum tax, 15.4(a)(2)(ii), 31.11(c)
  buyer-creditors, 31.11(a)
  cash basis taxpayers, 48.3(b)(2)(iii)
  characterized as a sale or loan, 31.11(b)
  deferral and conversion opportunities, 48.3(b)(2)(ii)
  economic equivalent of forward contract, 48.3(b)(2)(ii)
  economic substance, 31.11(b)(4)
  financing transactions, 31.11(b), 48.3(b)(2)(i)
  foreign currency swaps, 60.2(c)(1)

Index

Repurchase transaction(s) (*Continued*)
  generally, 31.11(a)
  government securities, 2.2(c)
  interest reporting requirements, 31.11(d)
  loans, 31.11(b)(1)
  market discount, additional interest, 48.3(b)(2)(iii)
  municipal securities, 31.11(a)
  nongovernmental short-term obligations, cash basis taxpayers, 48.3(b)(2)(iii)
  open repos, 2.2(c), 31.11(a)
  positions, Straddle Rules, 48.3(b)
  REITs, 31.11(a)(2)
  reporting requirements, 31.11(d)
  reverse repos, 2.2(c)
  sales transactions, 31.11(b)(2), 48.3(b)(2)(ii)
  security loan provisions, 31.11(b)(1)
  seller-debtors, 31.11(a), 48.3(b)(1), 48.3(b)(2)(i)
  sham transaction, 31.11(b)(3)
  Straddle Rules, 31.11(e), 48.3(b)(3)
  tax considerations, 31.11(a)(3)
  tax-exempt securities, 31.11(b)(1)
  tax preference items, 15.4(a)(2)(ii), 31.11(c)
  terminations, 31.11(a)(1)
  term repos, 2.2(c), 31.11(a), 31.11(b)(2)
  transactions, types of, 2.2(c), 31.11(a)(1)
Reset notes, 31.2(j)
Residence, 59.2(d)(2)
  corporations, 59.2(d)(2)(ii)
  estates and trusts, 59.2(d)(2)(iv)
  individuals, 59.2(d)(2)(i)
  partnerships, 59.2(d)(2)(iii)
  QBUs, 59.2(d)(1)
  residence-based source rule, 59.2(d)(2), 60.2(c)(6), 60.5(c)
  resident alien, 59.2(d)(2)(i)
Residual interests, *see* Real estate mortgage investment conduits (REMICs), residual interests
Resolution Funding Corporation (Refcorp) securities, *see* Federal agency securities, Resolution Funding Corporation (Refcorp) securities
Resolution Trust Corporation (RTC), 2.1(b)(7)
Retirement plan bonds, *see* Government securities, retirement plan bonds
Revenue bonds, 3.1, 3.2(b), 33.2(b), 33.3(b)

Reverse conversion transactions, 5.4(e)(3), 56.1(a), 56.3(a)
Reverse PERLS, *see* Debt securities, reverse PERLS
Reverse repurchase transactions, 31.11
RFCs, *see* Regulated futures contracts, RFCs
RICs, *see* Regulated investment companies (RICs)
Rights, *see* Stock rights
Risk analysis programs, margin, commodity options, 5.5(b)
Risk arbitrage, *see* Arbitrage, risk arbitrage
Risk management products, *see* Notional principal contracts
Round-turn commissions, 11.1(c), 12.1, 13.5
Royalty trust(s):
  distribution-type royalty trusts, 1.1(i), 29.2, 29.2(b)
  employee benefit plans, special considerations, 29.2(c)
  financing trusts, 1.1(i), 29.2
  reduced tax benefits, 29.2(b)
  shareholder return on investment, 29.2(a)
  tax status as trust, 29.1
  UBTI, 29.2(c)
RTC, *see* Resolution Trust Corporation (RTC)

S

S&P 100 index, *see* Indexes
S&P 500 index, *see* Indexes
S&P 500 stock index futures, *see* Indexes
Savings and loan associations, *see* Financial Institutions
Savings bond(s):
  cash basis taxpayer, 2.1(a)(4)(i)
  collateral, cannot be pledged, 2.1(a)(4)(i)
  college savings bonds, 32.1(b)(i)(v)
  current income bonds, 2.1(a)(4)(ii)
  dispositions, 32.1(b)(3)
  electronic funds transfer, 2.1(a)(4)(ii)
  exchanges, 32.1(d)
  exempt from market discount rules, 31.10(b)
  interest income, 2.1(a)(4)(i), 2.1(a)(4)(ii)
  market discount, exempt, 31.3, 31.10(b)

nonmarketable Treasury securities, 2.1(a)(4)
qualified savings bonds, 32.1(b)(1)(v)(b)
registered form, 2.1(a)(4)(i), 2.1(a)(4)(ii)
Series E savings bonds, 2.1(a)(4), 2.1(a)(4)(i)
Series EE savings bonds, 2.1(a)(4), 2.1(a)(4)(i), 32.1(b)(1)
  college savings bonds, 32.1(b)(1)(v)
  co-owners, 32.1(b)(1)(iv)
  educational expense exclusion, 32.1(b)(1)
  election to defer taxes, 32.1(b)(1)(ii)
  generally, 32.1(b)(1)(i)
  interest, amount excludable, 32.1(b)(1)(v)(d)
  interest taxable, redemption year, 32.1(b)(1)
  maturity extended, 2.1(a)(4), 2.1(a)(4)(i)
  qualified higher education expenses, 32.1(b)(1)(v)(c)
  qualified savings bonds, 32.1(b)(1)(v)(b)
  recordkeeping, 32.1(b)(1)(v)(e)
  transfer, divorce, 32.1(b)(1)(iii)
  transfer, spouses, 32.1(b)(1)(iii)
Series H savings bonds, 2.1(a)(4), 2.1(a)(4)(ii)
Series HH savings bonds, 2.1(a)(4), 2.1(a)(4)(i), 2.1(a)(4)(ii), 32.1(b)(2)
  disposition, 32.1(b)(3)
  transfer to grantor trust, 32.1(b)(3)
  zero coupon bonds, 2.1(a)(4)(i)
SBA, see Small Business Administration (SBA)
SCORE units, see Americus trusts
S corporations, 9.2(e), 9.8, 9.9
  attribution rules, 51.1
  basis, 16.4(h), 33.5(b)
  characterization of interest expense on stock purchase, 25.5
  dealer equity options, 44.4
  hedging loss limitation, 23.2(c)(3)(ii)
  limited entrepreneurs, see Limited entrepreneurs
  municipal securities, flow-through, 33.5(b)
  pre-ERTA transactions, 47.2(c)
  related parties, 23.3(g)(2)(iii)
  section 988 election, 59.2(j)
  60/40 rule, 45.2(c)
Scrip, stock, 17.4(a), 24.2(b)(3)

Secondary markets, 1.2, 2, 3.1, 5.1, 7.3(b)
  partnerships, 28.4(c)(4)
Secondary Mortgage Market Enforcement Act of 1984 (SMMEA), 7.4(a)(3)
Section 108, judicial decisions, 47.2(e)
Section 212 expense(s):
  additional two-year break, 9.1(d)
  administrative expenses, 9.1(a)
  against public policy, 9.1(a)
  amortized bond premiums, 9.1(d)
  automatic dividend reinvestment plans, 9.1(c)(8)
  buying and selling costs, 9.1(c)
  capitalization of short sale payments, 18.6(e)(1)
  clerical help, 9.1(c)
  covered expenses, 9.1(c)
  custodial fees, 9.1(c)
  defined, generally, 9.1(a)
  deductions disallowed, 9.1(a), 9.1(b)
  erroneous removal, two percent floor, 9.1(d)
  fiduciary fees, 9.1(a)
  generally, 9.1
  income defined for section 212 purposes, 9.1(a)
  investment advisory services, 9.1(c), 9.1(c)(2)
  investment expenses excluded, 9.1(d)
  limitation, 9.1(a)
  litigation expenses, 9.1(a), 9.1(c)(2)
  management of property, 9.1(a)
  miscellaneous itemized deductions, 9.1(d)
  mutual funds, 9.1(d)
  nonpublic RICs, 9.1(d)
  nontrade or nonbusiness expenses, 9.1(a)
  pass-through entities, 9.1(d)
  periodicals and books, 9.1(c)
  phantom income, 9.1(d)
  pre-ERTA law, 55.1
  production (collection) of taxable income, 9.1(a)
  promotion expenses, 9.1(c)(9)
  proxy contest expenses, 9.1(c)(4)
  public RICs, 9.1(d)
  reasonable in amount, 9.1(a)
  REITs, 9.1(d)
  REMICs, 9.1(d)
  replacement of stock certificates, 9.1(c)(7)
  service charges, 9.1(c)(8)

Index

Section 212 expense(s) (*Continued*)
  short sales expenses, 9.1(d), 18.6(a)
  tax-exempt income, 9.1(a)
  tax-exempt interest, 9.1(a)
  termination payments, swaps, 60.2(b)(2)(ii)
  transportation expenses, 9.1(c)(5)
  travel expenses, 9.1(c)(5)
  trusts, 9.1(d)
  trustees' commissions and fees, 9.1(c)
  two percent floor, 9.1(d), 60.2(b)(2)(ii)
Section 306 stock:
  bailouts, 27.3(b)(5)
  common stock convertible into preferred stock, 27.3(c)(3)
  dispositions, 27.3(b)(5)
  exchanges of, 27.3(b)(5)
  receipt, 27.3(b)(5)
  redemptions, 27.3(b)(5)
  tax-free exchanges, 27.3(b)(2)(iii)
Section 988 hedging transaction(s):
  after September 20, 1989, 23.3(g)
  asset and liability transactions, 23.3(a)
  currency exposure integration, 23.3(g)
  definition, 23.3(a), 23.3(b), 23.3(f)(1), 59.2
  election under section 988, 23.3(a), 23.3(d)
  exceptions, 59.2(a)(1)
  exchange gains and losses, 59.2(c)(1)
  integration, 23.3(a)
  exempt from Straddle Rules, 42.3
  foreign currency gains or losses, 23.3(c)
  foreign currency swap, 60.2(c)(4)
  fully hedged transactions, 23.3(a), 23.3(f), 23.3(g)
  exchange gain or loss, 59.2(b)(3)
  Notice 87-11, 23.3(f)
  superseded, 23.3(g)
  functional currency, 23.3(a)
  functional currency-denominated debt instrument, 23.3(f)(1)
  generally, 23.1, 23.3, 30.2, 42.1(e), 45.1, 45.2(a), 46.2, 55.2(f)
  hedged debt instruments, 23.3(a)
  hedged executory contracts, 23.3(a), 23.3(b), 23.3(g)(2); *see also* Hedged executory contracts
  hedging exemption, 23.3(d), 46.2(b)
  identification requirement, 23.3(a), 23.3(b), 23.3(f)(2), 46.2(b)
  independent verification, 23.3(f)(2)
  integrated transaction, 23.3(a), 23.3(d)
  integration of exchange gains or losses, 23.3(a)
  marked-to-market requirement, avoided, 23.3(a), 46.2(b)
  net hedge, 23.3(d)
  nonfunctional currency-denominated debt instrument, 23.3(f)(1), 23.3(g)
  integration, 23.3(g), 23.3(g)(1)(i)
  Notice 87-11, 23.3(f), 23.3(f)(1), 23.3(f)(2), 23.3(f)(3), 23.3(f)(4), 23.3(f)(5), 23.3(g)
  superseded, 23.3(g)
  ordinary income or loss, 23.3(c)
  package, 23.3(f)(1)
  partially hedged transactions, 23.3(d)
  qualified hedging accounts, 23.3(f)(2)
  qualified hedging transactions, *see* Qualified hedging transactions
  requirements defined, 46.2(b)
  section 1256 treatment, exempt, 23.3(b), 23.3(g), 46.2(b)
  60/40 treatment, avoided, 46.2(b)
  spot contract, 23.3(f)(1)
  Straddle Rules, 23.3(b), 23.3(d), 23.3(g)
  Subpart J, 23.3(a)
  synthetic dollar transactions, 23.3(a), 23.3(b)
  TMRA '88, special rules, 44.6, 45.1, 46.2
  trade date, 23.3(f)(2)
  trade date/settlement date hedges, 23.3(a), 23.3(g), 23.3(g)(3)
Section 988 transaction(s):
  caps, 59.2(a)(1)
  collars, 59.2(a)(1)
  debt instruments, defined, 59.2(a)(1)
  defined, 59.2(a)(1), 59.2(g)(2)
  deliveries, 59.2(c)(2)
  election under section 988, taxpayers eligible, 59.2(j)(1)
  exchange gain or loss, 59.2(a), 59.2(a)(4), 59.2(c), 59.2(d)(1), 60.2(c)(6)
  character, 59.2(a)(1), 59.2(b)
  separately computed, 59.2(e)
  source, 59.2(a)(1), 59.2(d)
  special rule, 59.2(f)
  timing, 59.2(a)(1), 59.2(c)
  executory contracts, 23.3(g)(2)(ii)
  expense or income items, 59.2(a)(1)
  financial instruments, 60.2(c)(4)
  floors, 59.2(a)(1)
  foreign currency gains and losses, 23.3(c), 59.2(a)(1)

capital gains and losses, election, 59.2(b)(3)
foreign currency-denominated debt security, 59.2(b)(1)
foreign currency positions, 59.2(a)(1)
foreign currency products covered, 59.2(b)(4)
foreign currency swaps, 59.2(a)(1), 60.2(c)(3), 60.2(c)(4)
forward contracts, 59.2(a)(1), 60.2(c)(4)
futures contracts, 59.2(a)(1), 60.2(c)(4)
hedges, see Section 988 hedging transactions
independent verification, 23.3(e)
integration, 23.3(b)
method of identification, 23.3(e)
nonequity options, 59.2(a)(1), 59.2(b)(4), 59.2(j)
nonfunctional currency, disposition, 59.2(a)(1), 59.2(g)(2)
notional principal contracts, 59.2(a)(1), 60.2(c)(4)
options, 23.3(e), 59.2(a)(1), 60.2(c)(4)
ordinary income or loss, 23.3(c)
partnerships, 59.2(j)
part of section 988 hedging transaction, 23.3(g)
payment date, 59.2(c)(1)
personal transactions, 59.2(a)(2)
preferred stock, 59.2(a)(1)
regulated futures contracts, 59.2(b)(4), 59.2(j)
regulated investment companies, 59.2(b)(2)
residence of taxpayer, 23.3(c)
S corporation, 59.2(j)
section 988 treatment, 59.2(j)
section 1256 contract "carve-out," 44.2(b), 44.6, 57.7, 59.2(a)(1)
short-term receivables (payables), 59.2(a)(1)
similar financial instrument, described, 59.2(a)(1)
source, 23.3(c), 59.2(d)
swaps, 59.2(a)(1)
timing, 59.2(c)
Temp. Treas. Reg. § 1.988-1T(a)(2), certain transactions, 59.2(g)(2)
types of section 988 transactions, 59.2(a)(1)
warrant, 59.2(a)(1)
see also Foreign currency transactions
Section 1.988-5T(a) hedge(s):
defined, 23.3(g)(1)(i), 23.3(g)(1)(i)(b)
hedged executory contracts, see Hedged executory contracts
integrated economic transaction, 23.3(g)(1)(i)
defined, 23.3(g)(1)(i)(c)
identification requirements, 23.3(g)(1)(iv)
income tax effect, 23.3(g)(1)(v)(d)
legging in and legging out rules, 23.3(g)(1)(ii)
leg-out date, 23.3(g)(1)(ii)
section 1256 contract treatment, 23.3(g)(1)(v)(a)
Straddle Rules, 23.3(g)(1)(v)(a)
requirements, 23.3(g)(1)(i)(c)
interest income, 23.3(g)(1)(v)(b)
qualifying debt instrument, defined, 23.3(g)(1)(i)(a)
synthetic debt instrument, 23.3(g)(1)(v)(d)
accrual period, 23.3(g)(1)(v)(d)(2)
allocation of expenses, 23.3(g)(1)(v)(e)
denomination, 23.3(g)(1)(v)(d)(1)
interest income, 23.3(g)(1)(v)(e)
issue price, 23.3(g)(1)(v)(d)(3)
stated redemption price, 23.3(g)(1)(v)(d)(4)
term, 23.3(g)(1)(v)(d)(2)
taxation, 23.3(g)(1)(v)(a)
United States source income, 23.3(g)(1)(v)(c)
United States trade or business, 23.3(g)(1)(v)(b), 23.3(g)(1)(v)(c)
Section 1092(b)(2) elections, 57.1, 57.3, 57.3(a), 57.6
Section 1092(b)(2) identified mixed straddles, see Identified section 1092(b)(2) mixed straddles
Section 1244 (small business) stock, 27.7
Section 1256 contract(s):
"carve-out," section 988 transactions, 44.2(b), 44.6, 57.7, 59.2(a)(1)
daily net gain or loss, 57.4(b)
dealer equity options, 44.4, 57
definition expanded, 44.6, 59.2(i), 59.2(a)(2)
delivery, 45.6(a)
DRA transitional year elections, 44.1, 44.5
exercises of, 45.6, 57.2(c)
foreign currency contracts, 44.2, 44.2(a), 44.2(b), 44.6, 59.2(h)

Index

Section 1256 contract(s) (*Continued*)
  foreign currency-related, 44.6, 45.2
  hedges, 23.1, 23.2(a), 23.2(g), 23.3(a)
  holding period, 17.3(b), 17.5
  loss carry-back rules, 45.4(a), 57.4
    restricted interest, 45.4(c)
  marked-to-market, 14.2, 23.3(a)
  Mark-to-Market Rule, 21.5, 23.2(a), 44.6, 45.1, 45.2, 59.2(a)(2)
  net section 1256 contract gain, 45.4(a), 45.4(c)
  net section 1256 contract loss:
    carry-back provisions, 45.4(b)
    carry-backs, available only to individuals, 45.4(c)
    defined, 45.4(c)
    generally, 45.4(a), 45.4(b), 45.4(c)
    mandatory payment rules, 45.4(c)
    net capital loss treatment, 45.4(b)
  nonequity options, 44.3
  100 percent short-term gain (loss), 44.6, 45.1, 45.2
  options, 30.1(d), 30.4
  ordinary income, 21.5, 22.1(b), 45.2(a)
  qualified funds, 44.6, 45.1, 45.2, 59.2(a)(2)
  regulated futures contracts, 44.1
    cash settlement contracts, 44.1(a)
    qualified boards or exchanges, 44.1, 44.1(b)
  restricted interest, 45.4(c)
  short sales rule, irrelevant, 18.4(e)(4)
  60/40 rule, 59.2(a)(2)
  straddles of, 30.2, 45.3, 45.5, 54.4, 56.7
  swap agreements, 60.2(b)(2)(ii)
  terminations prior to delivery or exercise date, 45.5
  three-year carry-back rule, 45.4(a)
  TMRA '88, special rules, 44.6
  traders, 8.2, 8.2(c)
  transfers of rights in, 45.5
Section 1256 options, 30.1(d), 30.4, 44.3, 44.4
Section 1256 treatment:
  commodities, 42.1(a)
  dealer equity options, 44.4, 57
  exceptions, 46
  executory contracts, 23.3(g)(2)(viii)(f)
  hedged executory contracts, 23.3(g)(2)(viii)(f)
  hedging transactions, 12.3, 23.1, 23.2(a), 46.2

  integrated economic transactions, 23.3(g)(1)(v)(a)
  interest rate hedges, 8.4(d)
  nonequity options, 44.3(a), 44.3(b)
  physical commodities, 42.1, 42.1(a)
  qualified hedging transactions, 23.3(f)(3)
  qualifying debt instrument, 23.3(g)(1)(v)(a)
  regulated futures contracts, 44.1
  section 988 hedging transactions, 23.3(b)
  section 1.988-5T(a) hedges, 23.3(g)(1)(v)(a)
  60/40 rule, 44.6, 45, 45.1, 45.2
  stock, ineligible, 57
  straddles made up exclusively of section 1256 contracts, 56.7
Section 1256(d) identified mixed straddles, *see* Identified section 1256(d) mixed straddles
Securities:
  actual securities, 17.2(a)(6)
  adequate identification, 20.2(a)(1)(i), 20.2(c)
  adjustable rate preferred stock (ARPS), 1.1(g), 27.3(b)(3)(ii)
  alphabet stock, 1.1(g)(9), 27.3(a)
  American depository receipts (ADRs), 1.1(f)
  arbitrage transactions, 18.10
    Rule 16e-1 exemption, 8.7(b)
  arbitrageur, *see* Securities arbitrageurs
  ARPS, 1.1(g), 27.3(b)(3)(ii)
  asset-backed securities, *see* Asset-backed securities
  auction rate preferred stock, 1.1(g)(3), 27.3(b)(3)(iii)
  book-entry securities, 20.2(e)
  bonds, 1.1(b)
  broker, 11.3(b)(1)
  broker-dealers, 1.2(a), 1.2(b), 1.3(f)
  buyer's option transactions, 1.3(e)
  cash accounts, short sales, 1.4(a)
  certificates of beneficial interest, 1.3(i)
  collateral for loan, 48.3(b)(2)(i)
  commercial paper, 1.1(b), 1.1(g)(2)
  common stock, *see* Common stock
  contingent and adjustable preferred stock, 27.3(b)(3)(vi)
  convertible adjustable preferred stock (CAPs), 1.1(g)(4), 17.7, 24.9(b),

24.9(b)(1), 27.3(b)(3)(iii), 27.3(b)(3)(vii)
convertible bonds, *see* Convertible debt securities, bonds
convertible exchangeable preferred stock, 1.1(g), 27.3(b)(3)(vii), 27.3(c)(2)
convertible preferred stock, 1.1(d), 17.7, 18.2(c), 27.3(c)(1), 27.3(c)(2), 27.3(b)(3)(vii)
convertible securities, *see* Convertible stock
convertible stock, *see* Convertible stock
corporate bearer bonds, 1.1(b)
corporate bonds, 1.1(b)
corporate cash market, 1.3(b)
corporate cash transactions, 1.3(b)
corporate commercial paper, 1.1(b)
corporate debentures, 1.1(b)
corporate installment transactions, 1.3(h)
corporate notes, *see* Debt securities, corporate notes
corporate registered bonds, 1.1(b)
corporate securities, 1.1(a)
  margin, 1.4(b)
  types of, 1.1
corporate settlement, 1.5
corporate settlement date, 1.3
corporate stock, 1.1(a), 48.2(d)
corporate trade date, 1.3
  date issued, 17.2(c)(2)
dealers, *see* Securities dealers
debt, *see* Debt securities
debt-equity considerations, 27.2
  evaluation factors, 27.2
debt financed portfolio stock, *see* Debt financed portfolio stock
debt flavored, 1.1(g), 27.3(b)(3)
debt options, 5.2(a)(2)
debt securities, *see* Debt securities
defaulted securities, *see* Defaulted securities
defined, 7.4(a)(1), 18.4(a), 19.6
discount convertible debt securities, 34.7
disqualified preferred stock, 16.6(g)
dividend income, 24.7(d)
dutch-auction rate preferred stock, 1.1(g)(3), 27.3(b)(3)(iii)
equity securities, 1.1(d)
esoteric securities, 1.1(g)
exchangeable debt securities, 34.6(a)

exchanged, 17.3(a)
exempted, 1.3(h), 7.4(b)(3)
  defined, 1.4(a), 7.4(a)(1)
extendible debt securities, 1.1(g)(13)
fiduciaries, held by, 20.2(a)(3)
financial institutions, *see* Financial institutions
floating rate preferred stock, 1.1(g)(2), 27.3(b)(3)(i)
gain on, 14.5(b)
General Motors Class E shares, alphabet stock, 1.1(g)(9), 27.3(a)
government securities, 2, 2.1
holding period, 1.3
hybrid securities, 1.1(g)
identification, *see* Identification of securities
identified on put holder's records, 56.4
increasing rate exchangeable guaranteed preferred stock, 1.1(g)(7), 27.2, 27.3(b)(3)(v)
in default, 31.8
indexed debt securities, 1.1(g)(5)
index options, 5.2(a)(4)
index participations, 4.1(c)
installment sales, 1.3(h)
limited, 28.3
limited partnership interests, *see* Limited partnership interests
listed securities, 1.2(a)
loans, *see* Security loans
loss deferral rule, coordination, 54.2
mandatory convertible notes, 1.1(g)(1)
margin accounts, *see* Margin accounts
margin requirements, 1.4
  basic requirements, 1.4(b)(2)
  credit regulation, corporate securities, 1.4
  credit regulation, government securities, 2.3
  extension, 1.4(b)(2)
  FRB requirements, 1.4(b)(2)
  initial margin, corporate securities, 1.4(b)(1)
  long margin securities, 1.4(b)
  maintenance margin, corporate securities, 1.4(b)(1), 2.3
  regular way short sale, 1.3(i)
  Regulation T, 1.4, 2.3, 7.4
  Regulation U, 1.4, 2.3, 7.4
margin securities, defined, 1.4(b)(2)
market auction preferred stock, 27.3(b)(3)(iii)

Index

Securities (*Continued*)
  markets, 1.2
  money market preferred stock, 1.1(g)(3), 27.3(b)(3)(iii)
  municipal, *see* Municipal securities
  NYSE rules, 1.4(b)(2)
  mortgage-backed securities, *see* Asset-backed securities, mortgage-backed securities (MBSs)
  multiple-class, 7.2(c)(1)
  national banks, 1.1(d)
  nominees, securities held by, 31.12(b)
  nonexempted, defined, 1.4(a)
  OID, *see* Original issue discount (OID)
  over-the-counter brokers, 1.2(b)
  over-the-counter market, 14.5(b)
  portfolio exchangeables, 34.6(b)
  portfolio stock, *see* Portfolio, stock
  preferred stock, *see* Preferred stock
  principal exchange rate linked securities, 1.1(g)(6), 2.1(b)(6)
  public offerings, 1.2(b)
  registration-required securities, *see* Registration-required securities
  regular way transactions, 1.3(a), 2.2(a), 17.2(a)(2)(i), 24.7(a), 24.7(c), 24.7(d)
  remarketed preferred stock, 1.1(g)(3), 27.3(b)(3)(iv)
  revenue securities, 3.1
  securitized corporate assets, *see* Asset-backed securities, securitization, corporate assets
  security exchange memberships, 1.2(a), 19.6(c)(3)
  seller's option transactions, 1.3(e)
  settlement:
    corporate, 1.5
    date, 1.3
    government securities, 2.4
  shareholders:
    corporate, 24.1(f)(2)
    date of acquisition, 17.2(c)(1)
    noncorporate, 24.1(f), 24.1(f)(1), 24.2(b)(7)
  sold in exempted transactions, 7.3(a)(3)
  specialists, *see* Specialists
  stock, *see* Stock
  stock bonus shares, 19.8(b)
  stock dividends, *see* Dividends, stock
  stock exchanges, *see* Stock exchanges
  stock indexes, *see* Indexes
  stock option plans, 19.8(c)
  stock options, 5.2(a)(1), 30.3(a), 56
  stock redemptions that have effect of dividends, 24
  stock rights, *see* Stock rights
  stock scrip, 17.4(a), 24.2(b)(3)
  stock specialists, *see* Specialists
  stock splits, 20.2(c)
  street name securities:
    identification, 20.2(a)(2)
    information return with IRS, 24.7(e)
    stock held in street name, 24.7(e)
  stripping, 2.2(e)
  subscription agreements, 17.2(c)(1)
  subscription basis, 17.2(b)
  subscription for securities, 17.2(c)(1)
  subscription rights, 19.8(a)
  tender offers, 1.3(b)
  trade date, 1.3, 14.5(b), 14.5(d), 17.2(a)(5), 20.2(a)(2)
  traditional, 1.1(g)
  transactions:
    trade-plus-two, 1.3(d)
    trade-plus-three, 1.3(d)
    trade-plus-four, 1.3(d)
  Treasury securities, *see* Treasury securities
  trust interests, 1.1(i)
  types of, 1.1
  unlisted trading privileges, 1.2(a)
  warrants, *see* Warrants
  when-issued contracts, *see* When-issued contracts
  when-issued securities, *see* When-issued securities
  with contingent note, 1.1(g)(10)
  worthless securities, 17.1(c), 27.8
  yield to maturity, 15.4(a)(2)(ii)(b)
Securities Act of 1933, 7.6(a)
Securities and Exchange Commission (SEC), *see* entries under specific subjects
Securities arbitrageur(s):
  broker-dealers, 11.9(a)
  capital asset, defined, 11.9(b)
  capital asset or property under section 1221(1), 11.9(b)
  capital or ordinary treatment, 11.9(a)
  classical arbitrageur, 8.7(b), 11.9(a)
  customers, 11.9(b), 11.9(c)
  dealer, 8.7(d), 11.9(a), 11.9(b)
  dealer status, specialists, 11.9(c)
  determination, dealer or trader status, 11.9(b)

exclusion from capital asset definition, 11.9(b)
exemption as securities dealer, 8.7(b)
investor, 8.7(d), 11.9(a), 11.9(b)
market-making function, 11.9(a)
merchandising function, 11.9(a)
property excluded from capital asset definition, 11.9(c)
risk arbitrageur, 8.7(c), 11.9(a)
   net capital rule, 11.9(c)
sales to customers, 11.9(c)
statutory framework and case law, 11.9(b)
stock specialist, 11.9(c)
tax character, dealer or investor, 11.9(b)
trade or business, 11.9(c)
trader, 8.7(d), 11.9(a)
trading activities of risk arbitrageur modified, 11.9(c)
Securities dealer(s):
  amortization of bond premiums, 11.4(a)
  defined, 8.3(a)
  generally, 8.3, 18.6(c), 18.9
  hedged accounts, 23.2(b)(4)(ii)
  hedging losses, 23.2(c)(3)(ii)(a)
  inventory valuation, 22.2(a)
  investment account(s):
    generally, 8.1, 11.7, 11.7(b), 18.4(a), 18.9
    identification requirements, 11.7(c)
    incorrect identification, 11.7(d)
    statutory requirements, 11.7(a)
    stock or securities, defined, 18.4(a), 18.9, 19.6(a)
    stock rights, 18.4(a)
    straddles with dealer accounts, 11.7(f)
    trade or business, 23.2(c)(3)(ii)(a)
    voluminous transactions, 11.7(e)
    warrants, 18.4(a)
  options market maker, 8.3(c), 11.9(c)
  stock specialists, 8.3(b)
  swap dealer, 60.2(b)(2)(ii)
  tax-exempt securities, 11.4(b)
  worthless securities, 27.8(d)
Securities Exchange Act of 1934, 7.6(b)
Securities exchanges, 1.1(f), 30.1(a), 44.1, 58.2
Securities in default, 31.8
Securities lending transactions, 26.1
Securities margin account(s):
  investment interest, 9.2(b)
  personal interest, 9.2(b)

Securitized corporate assets, 1.1(e), 7.1
Security loan(s):
  agreements, 48.3(b)(2)(ii)
  amounts received, treatment, 26.5, 55.2(b)
  debt financed portfolio stock, 24.9(b)(3), 24.9(c)
  discount securities, transferred, 26.2(e)
  fail sale transactions, 24.9(b)(3), 26.4
  failure to return identical securities, 26.3
  holding period, for nonidentical securities, 17.8
  identical securities, 26.2(b), 26.2(c)
  intercorporate dividends received, ineligible, 24.9(b)(3), 26.4
  introduction, 26.1
  lending transactions, 17.8, 26, 26.1, 31.11(b)(1)
  mergers, 26.2(g)
  nonqualified transactions, 26.3
  nonrecognition, 26.2(a)
  payments equivalent to all interest, dividends, and other distributions, 26.2(b)
  payments lose original character, 26.2(e)
  payments to lender, 26.2(e)
  qualified loan agreements, 26.2
  recapitalization, 26.2(g)
  recognition, 26.2
  reorganizations, 26.2(g)
  repos, 31.11(b)(1)
  security lenders, 31.11(b)(1)
  security lending transactions, 26.1, 31.11(b)(1)
  security loan agreement, 26.3
  in writing, 26.2(b)
  straddle income, 55.2(b)
  tax-exempt organizations, 26, 26.2(f)
  termination, 26.2(b)
  unrelated business taxable income, 26.2(f)
  written agreements, 26.2(b)
Security options, *see* Options
Self-employment income, 8.2(b), 8.2(c), 8.3(e)
Seller's option (deferred delivery) transactions, 1.3(e), 17.2(a)(5), 24.7(c), 24.9(b)(2)
Seminars; deductions, 9.1(c)(10)

Index

Senior pass-through certificates, *see* Asset-backed securities, pass-through certificates, senior
Senior pay-through bonds, *see* Asset-backed securities, pay-through bonds, senior
Separate Trading of Registered Interest and Principal of Securities (STRIPS), 2.2(e), 31.5(a)
Series funds, *see* Regulated investment companies (RICs), series funds
Settlement:
  asset-backed securities, 7.5(b)
  cash, 1.3(b), 6.2(c), 6.6(a), 6.7, 60.4
  commodities:
    cash market, 4.5(a)
    futures market, 4.5(b)
  conventional commodity options, 5.6
  conventional stock option, 5.6
  futures options, 5.6
  government securities, 2.4
  next day, 1.3(d)
  nonregular way, 1.3(d)
  physical delivery settlement, 1.5, 7.5(b)
  regular way, 1.3(b)
  securities, 1.5, 7.5(b)
  security options, 5.6
  skip day, 1.3(d)
  T-plus-one, 5.6, 14.5(b), 17.2(a)
  T-plus-two, 1.3(d)
  T-plus-three, 1.3(d)
  T-plus-four, 1.3(d)
  when-distributed contracts, 1.3(g)
Settlement date:
  gain on securities, 14.5(b)
  holding period, 17.2(a)(5), 17.2(a)(6)
  losses, 14.5(d)
  securities, 1.3
  short sale, 18.2(a)
Shad-Johnson Accord, 4.1(c), 5.2
Sham transaction(s):
  additional interest, 9.2(g)
  economic shams, 47.2(e)
  generally, 9.2(g), 10.2(g), 19.12, 58.1
  increased interest rates, 53.2
  interest on substantial underpayments, 10.2(g)
  pre-ERTA commodity transactions, 47.2(d)(1), 47.2(e)
  repurchase transactions, 31.11(b)(3)
Shareholder(s):
  corporate, 24.1(f)(2)
  date on which taxpayer becomes, 17.2(c)(1)
Short sale(s):
  adjusted basis, 18.6(e)(2)
  against the box, 1.4(b)(4), 18.2(a), 19.3(f), 56.5
  amounts paid or incurred, 55.2(a)
  borrowed securities, 1.3(i), 18.6(b)
  broker, 1.3(i)
  cannot sell stock, 24.9(b)
  capital assets, 18.4
  cash accounts, 1.4(a)
  cash dividends, 18.6(d)
  certificates of stock, 18.4(a)
  closing, 14.5(b), 18.2(c)
  closing short options position, 14.5(b)
  commodities arbitrage, 18.4(e)(4)
  common stock, 17.7(b)
  coverage, deemed, 18.10(b), 19.3(f)
  dealers, 11.12
  dealer transactions, 18.9
  debt securities, 31.14
  decedents, open at death, 16.3(b), 18.2(c)
  defined, 18.2(a)
  exemption, 11.12
  expenses, 18.6(d)
  futures contracts, 18.4
  gains on, 18.3(a)
  hedges, 12.1
  holding period, 17.4(c), 18.3(b)
  identified, 1.3(i)
  intercorporate dividends received deduction, 18.6(a)
  interest amounts, 55.2(c)
  investors, 9.6
  loan premiums, 18.6(b)
  loss on closing short sale of property, 14.5(d)
  losses, 18.3(c)
  margin requirements, 1.3(i), 1.4(b)(2), 1.4(b)(4)
  married put exception, 18.4(d), 18.9
  matching property, 18.7
  options, 30.3(g)(3)
  payments, 18.6(d), 18.6(e)(4)
    capitalization, 18.6(e)(5)
  property covered, 18.4
  put buying, 5.4(b)(1)
  put options, 18.2(a)
  regular way, 1.3(i)
  securities, 18.4
  securities arbitrage, 18.10

securities loan, 1.3(i), 18.6(b)
spouses, 18.8
stock, 18.4
stock or securities, 18.4(a)
stock specialists, 11.9(c)
straddle interest and carrying charges, 18.6(e)(5)
substantially identical property, 18.3(c), 18.9
tax avoidance, 18.6(a)
temporary use of personal property, capitalized, 55.2(c)
traders, 10.6
wash sales rule, 19.3(f)
when-issued securities, 18.4
see also Short sales rule

Short sales expense(s):
application before capitalization requirements, 18.6(e)(5)
capitalized, 18.6(e)
  extraordinary dividends, 18.6(e)(2)
  short stock rebates, 18.6(e)(4)
  suspension of holding period, 18.6(e)(3)
dividends or interest on borrowed securities, 1.3(i)
dividends paid by borrower in short sales, 18.6(a)
fee for temporary use of property, 18.6(a), 24.9(b)(3), 26.2(e)
general requirements, 18.6(e)(1)
in lieu of dividends, 18.6(e)
investment interest expense, 18.6(e)(1)
ordinary and necessary business expenses, 18.6(a), 18.6(e)(1)
section 212 expenses, 18.6(a)

Short sales rule:
commodities, 18.4(f)
commodity futures arbitrage, 18.10
consists of three separate rules, 18.2
dealer transactions, 18.9
debt securities, application, 31.1
deemed short sale, 18.10(b)
expenses, 18.6
foreign currency forward contract, 18.2(a)
futures arbitrage transactions, 18.4(e)(4)
futures contracts, 18.2(b)
hedges, commodities futures, 18.4(e)(1), 18.11
married put transactions, 18.4(d), 56.4
matching property, 18.7
mergers, 18.10(c)

modified short sales rule, see Modified short sales rule
coordination, 54.1
operation of, 18.2
payments, 18.6
positions, 30.3(g)(3)
pre-ERTA transactions, 47.2
property covered, 18.4
  futures contracts, 18.2(b)
  put options, 18.4(c)
  stock, 18.4(a)
  stock rights, 18.4(a)
  when-issued securities, 18.2(b), 18.4(b)
property subject to rule, 18.2(b)
put option, acquisition, 18.4(c)
scope substantially reduced, 18.1
  limited to short sales of stock, 54.1
securities arbitrage, 18.10
small business investment company, 18.2(a)
spouses, 18.8
stock or securities, not defined, 18.4(a)
substantially identical property, 18.2, 18.2(a), 18.2(c), 18.3(c), 18.5, 18.9
taxpayer or spouse, 18.8
up-tick, 1.3(i)
when-issued securities, 18.2(b), 18.4(b)
writing a put option, 18.4(c)
zero-plus-tick, 1.3(i)
see also Short sales

Short sales securities:
capitalization of interest and carrying charges, 55.2(b)

Short selling, 1.3(i), 5.4(b)(1)
Short-short rule, 8.9(a)(3), 8.9(e)
Short stock rebates, 18.6(e)(4), 57.4(d)
Short-term securities, 31.1
  corporate securities, 31.2(d)
  exempt, market discount bonds, 31.10(b)
  flat bonds, interest with respect to short-term obligations, 55.2(e)
  government securities, 31.2(d)
  interest on indebtedness, 55.2(e)
  issued at discount, 32.1(a)(1)
  market discount bonds, 31.3, 31.10(b), 48.3(b)(2)(iii)
  original issue discount, 31.2(d)
  registration not required, 31.12(b)
Short-term stock options, 30.2, 56.6
  DRA eliminated exemption for, 56.6
  pre-DRA, 56.6

Index

Short-term trade receivables (payables), 59.2(a)(1)
SIMEX, see Singapore International Monetary Exchange Limited (SIMEX)
Simulated straddles, 5.4(a)(1)
Singapore International Monetary Exchange Limited (SIMEX), 44.3
Sinking funds, mandatory, 31.2(a)
60/40 Rule:
 commodity dealers, 45.2(b)
 dealer equity options, 45.2(c)
 dealers in underlying property, 45.2(a)
 equity options, 45.2(c)
 generally, 44.6, 45.2, 59.2(a)(2)
 option dealers, 45.2(b)
 S corporations, 45.2(c)
60/40 treatment, 44.6, 45.2
SLMA securities, see Federal agency securities, Student Loan Marketing Association (SLMA) (Sallie Mae) securities
Small Business Administration (SBA), 2.1(b)(10), 27.6(a)
 CDC debentures, 2.1(b)(10)
 securities, see Federal agency securities, Small Business Administration securities
Small Business Investment Act of 1958 (SBIA), 24.9(a)(2), 27.6(a), 27.6(c)
Small business investment companies:
 as financial institutions, 8.8
 generally, 27.6(a)
 intercorporate dividends received, 24.9(a)(2)
 portfolio losses, 27.6(c)
 SBA licensing and regulation, 2.1(b)(10)
 short sales rule, 18.2(a)
 stock, 27.6(b)
 substantially identical stock, 18.2(a)
 tax-exempt securities, investments, 33.6
Small issue exemption, 33.2(c)(2)(ii)
SMMEA, see Secondary Mortgage Market Enforcement Act of 1984
Social security:
 benefits, 33.3(a)(3)
 net earnings from self-employment, 8.2(c)
 net income from self-employment, 8.2(b), 8.3(e)
Sourcing rule(s):
 asset hedges, 60.5(c)
 exchange gains and losses, 59.2(d)(1)
 foreign counterparties, 60.5
 foreign currency swaps, 60.2(c)(6)
 foreign currency transactions, 59.2(d)
 foreign tax credits, 60.5
 forward rate agreements, 60.4(d)
 interest equivalent treatment, 60.5(b)(1)
 liability hedges, 60.5(b)
 Notice 87-4, 60.2(g)(1), 60.2(g)(2), 60.5(a)
 notional principal contracts, 60.5(a)
 payments under FRAs, 60.4(d)
 periodic swap payments, 60.2(b)(2)(i)(d)
 residence, 59.2(d)(2)
  corporations, 59.2(d)(2)(ii)
  estates and trusts, 59.2(d)(2)(iv)
  individuals, 59.2(d)(2)(i)
  partnerships, 59.2(d)(2)(iii)
  QBUs, 59.2(d)(1)
  resident alien, 59.2(d)(2)(i)
 residence-based source rule, 59.2(d)(2), 60.2(c)(6), 60.5(c)
 section 988 transactions, 59.2(d)(1)
 swap option, 60.2(e)(4)
 United States source income, 23.3(f)(3), 23.3(f)(5), 23.3(g)(1)(v)(c), 59.2(d)(1)
 United States trade or business, 23.3(f)(1), 23.3(f)(3), 23.3(g)(1)(i)(c), 23.3(g)(1)(v)(b), 23.3(g)(1)(v)(c), 23.3(g)(2)(iv)(a), 23.3(g)(3)
Specialist(s):
 exchange trading corporate securities, 1.2(a)
 listed options, 8.2(b), 8.3(c), 8.3(d), 44.4
 obligations, 11.9(c)
 options, 5.3(a), 5.5(a), 8.2(b), 8.3(c), 8.3(d), 11.7(f), 30.2(b)(4), 44.4
 dealer status, 30.2(b)(4)
 stock specialists, 1.2(a), 8.3(b), 8.3(c), 8.5, 11.7(a), 11.9(c)
 broker-dealers, registration with SEC, 8.3(b)
 dealer, 11.9(c)
Special purpose accounts, 1.4, 7.4
Special purpose entities, see Corporations, special purpose entities
Special purpose subsidiaries, see Corporations, special purpose subsidiaries
Specific identification:
 cost flow methods, 22.2(b)
 methods, 20.2(f)
 requirements, 20.2(a)
Spot contracts, 23.3(f)(1), 59.4(e)
Spreads:
 backspreads, 5.4(c)(3)

bear spreads, 5.4(c)(1)(ii), 5.4(c)(1)(iii), 5.4(c)(3)
box spreads, 5.4(e)(4), 30.2(b), 56.1(a), 56.3(a)
bull spreads, 5.4(c)(1)(i), 5.4(c)(1)(iii), 5.4(c)(3)
butterfly spreads, *see* Butterfly spreads
combination transactions, 5.4(d)
credit ratio spread, 5.4(c)(1)(iii)
credit spread, 5.4(c)
debit, 5.4(c)
defined, 5.4(c)
diagonal spreads, 5.4(c)(3)
horizontal spreads, 5.4(c)(2)
intercommodity, 4.3(c)
intermarket, 4.3(c)
intramarket, 4.3(c)
option-against-futures spread, 5.5(b)
option-against-option spread, 5.5(b)
options spreads, 5.4(c)
  pre-DRA, 30.2
price spreads, 5.4(c)
ratio spreads, 5.4(c)(1)(iii)
reverse ratio spreads, 5.4(c)(3)
variable spreads, 5.4(c)(1)(iii)
vertical spreads, 5.4(c)(1)
Standard & Poor's, 3.1, 7.1(b), 7.2(c)(4)
see also S&P 100 index; S&P 500 index; S&P 500 stock index futures
Standardized options, 5.1, 5.3(a)
Statement mailing:
  dividends, 24.10
  interest, 24.10
Statistical rating organizations, 3.1, 7.1(b)
Stepped coupon securities, 3.3
Stock:
  accompanied by contingent promissory note, 1.1(g)
  acquired from convertible securities, 17.3(a)(3)
  adjustable rate convertible notes (ACRNs), 27.3(c)(6), 34.4
  adjustable rate preferred stock (ARPS), 1.1(g), 27.3(b)(3)(ii)
  alphabet stock, 1.1(g)(9), 27.3(a)
  as personal property, 48.2(c)(1), 48.2(c)(2)
  auction rate preferred stock, 1.1(g)(3), 27.3(b)(3)(iii)
  bank holding company, 24.9(c)
  banks, 24.9(c)
  book-entry, 1.1(a)
  cash on delivery (COD), 1.3(c)
  certificated, 1.1(a)
  clearance and settlement, 1.5
  clearing organizations, 1.5
  common stock, *see* Common stock
  contingent and adjustable preferred stock, 27.3(b)(3)(vi)
  convertible adjustable preferred stock (CAPS), 1.1(g)(4), 17.7, 24.9(b), 24.9(b)(1), 27.3(b)(3)(iii), 27.3(b)(3)(vii)
  convertible exchangeable preferred stock, 1.1(g)(8), 27.3(b)(3)(vii)
  convertible preferred stock, 1.1(d), 8.9(a)(2), 17.7, 18.2(c), 27.3(c)(1), 27.3(c)(2), 27.3(b)(3)(vii)
  convertible stock, 27.3(c), 27.3(c)(8)
  corporate bonds, debentures, notes and commercial paper, 1.1(b)
    issued by insolvent corporation, 27.8(c)
  corporate installment transaction, 1.3(h)
  corporate securities market, overview of, 1
  corporate stock, 1.1(a), 48.2(d)
  corporation formed or availed of to take positions which offset positions taken by any shareholder, 56.5
  credit regulation, 1.4, 7.4
  debt-equity considerations, 27.2, 34.2(a)
  debt financed portfolio stock, *see* Debt financed portfolio stock
  debt flavored, 1.1(g), 27.3(b)(3)
  defined, 18.4(a), 19.6, 27.3
  delivery:
    against cash, 1.3(c)
    against payment, 1.3(c)
    before regular way, 1.3(d)
    between next day and regular way, 1.3(d)
    buyer's option, 1.3(e)
    deferred payment, 1.3(e)
    failure to deliver, 7.5(c)
    nonregular way, 1.3(d)
    record date, 1.3(d)
    regular way, 1.3(d)
    seller's option, 1.3(e)
    trade-plus-two, 1.3(d)
    trade-plus-three, 1.3(d)
    trade-plus-four, 1.3(d)
    versus payment, 1.3(c), 7.5(b)
  disqualified preferred stock, 16.6(g)
  dividend income, 24.2(a)

Index

Stock (*Continued*)
  dividends, *see* Dividends
  dutch-auction rate preferred stock, 1.1(g)(3), 27.3(b)(3)(iii)
  exchanges, *see* Stock exchanges
  extension of credit on securities, 1.4
  floating rate preferred stock, 1.1(g)(2), 27.3(b)(3)(i)
  forced sales, 27.4(d)(2)
  for consolidation purposes, 27.3(b)(3)
  foreign corporations, stock in, 1.1(f), 23.2(e)
  for stock held in same corporation, 17.3(a)(2)
  fractional shares, 17.4(a), 24.2(b)(3)
  fractional stock dividends, 24.2(b)(3)
  held in street name, 24.7(e)
  hybrid and esoteric securities, 1.1(g)
  identified on put holder's records, 56.4
  in bank holding company, 24.9(c)
  in banks, 24.9(c)
  increasing rate exchangeable guaranteed preferred stock, 1.1(g)(7), 27.2, 27.3(b)(3)(v)
  installment sales, 1.3(h)
  loans, *see* Security loans
  loss deferred rule, coordination, 54.2
  lost certificates, expenses, 9.1(c)(7)
  margin:
    credit regulation, 1.4, 7.4
    initial margin requirements, long margin securities, 1.4(b)
  market auction preferred stock, 27.3(b)(3)(iii)
  markets, 1.2
  money market preferred stock, 1.1(g)(3), 27.3(b)(3)(iii)
  offsetting options, 48.2(c)(2)
  offsetting position stock, 56.5
  personal property, 48.2(c)(1)
  portfolio stock, *see* Portfolio, stock
  post-DRA stock positions, 56.5
  preferred stock, *see* Preferred stock
  purchased with debentures, 17.2(a)(2)(i)
  reasonable redemption premiums, 24.2(b)(5)
  rebates, short stock rebates, 18.6(e)(4), 57.4(d)
  remarketed preferred stock, 1.1(g)(3), 27.3(b)(3)(iv)
  rights, *see* Stock rights
  sales or redemptions, 24
  section 306 stock, *see* Section 306 stock
  section 1244 stock, 27.7
  section 1256 treatment, ineligible, 57
  short sales, *see* Short sales
  short stock rebates, 18.6(e)(4), 57.4(d)
  specialists in, *see* Specialists
  stolen shares of stock, 27.4(d)(1)
  street name securities, *see* Street name securities
  substantially identical property, 48.2(c)(2)
  surrender of, 16.4(*l*)
  transaction(s):
    buyer's option, 1.3(e)
    deferred delivery, 1.3(e)
    deferred payment, 1.3(e)
    seller's option, 1.3(e), 24.7(c)
    seller's option trade, 1.3(e), 24.9(b)(2)
    seller's option transactions, 17.2(a)(5), 24.9(b)(2)
  types of:
    ACRNs, 27.3(c)(6), 34.4
    common stock, *see* Common stock
    convertible stock, *see* Convertible stock
    preferred stock, *see* Preferred stock
    when-issued securities, *see* When-issued securities
    with contingent note, 1.1(g)(10)
    with dividends pegged to performance of subsidiary, 1.1(g)
    with dividends preference, 17.7
  see also Securities
Stock bonus shares, 19.8(b)
Stock, certain positions:
  straddles, exceptions, 48.2(c)(1)
Stock dividends, *see* Dividends, stock
  and liquidating dividends, 18.6(c)
  and stock rights, *see* Dividends
Stock exchange(s):
  holding period, 17.2(a)(5)
  interrogation devices, 1.3(a)
  listing agreements, 1.2(a)
  registered with SEC, 1.2(a)
  securities traded, 14.5(b)
  ticker tape, 1.3(a)
  see also specific entries under named exchanges
Stock index, *see* Indexes
Stock option plan, 19.8(c)
Stock options, 5.2(a)(1), 18.1, 19.6(b), 30, 30.1, 30.3(a), 30.3(g)(1), 48.4(b), 56
  intercorporate dividends received deduction, 30.3(d)(2)(ii)

Stock right(s):
  basis election, 16.4(c)
  disposed of, 16.4(c)
  exercise of, 16.4(c), 17.2(c)(3)
  expire unexercised, 16.4(c)
  general rule, 24.2(a)
  nontaxable, 16.4(c), 30.3(f)(1)
  shares of stock in foreign company, 1.1(f)
  taxable distributions, 24.2(b), 30.3(f)(2)
  to purchase other property, 24.2(b)(7)
  unexercised, 16.4(c)
Stock scrip, 17.4(a), 24.2(b)(3)
Stock specialists, *see* Specialists
Stock splits, 20.2(c)
Straddle-by-straddle netting:
  accrued gain and loss, 57.3(c)
  choices, summary of, 57.1
  clear identification, 57.3(a)
  disposition of positions, 57.3(d), 57.3(e), 57.3(f), 57.3(g)
  elections, 57.3(a)
  holding period rules, 57.3(h)
  independent verification of identification, 57.3(a)
  loss deferral rule, 57.3(h)
  mixed straddles, *see* Mixed straddles
  modified short sales rule, 54.4(b)
  net gains and losses, 57.3(b)
  reasonable and consistent economic basis, 57.3(a)
  related persons, elections, 57.6
  section 1092(b)(2) identified mixed straddles, 57.3
Straddle rule(s):
  attribution rule(s):
    general rules, 51.1
    mixed straddles, 51.4
    related parties, 51.1
    S corporation, 51.1
    section 1256 contracts, 51.3
  caps, 60.3(a)(2)(i)
  collars, 60.3(a)(2)(i)
  contingent payment right, 30.5(b)(5)
  corporate stock, 27.9
  dealers, 11.13
  debt securities, 31.1, 31.15
  definitions, 48
  disclosure of unrecognized gain:
    examples, 52.3
    exceptions, 52.2
    generally required, 52.1
    identified straddles, exempt, 56.1(b)
  effective dates, summary, 57.8
  exception(s):
    hedging transactions, 56.2
    identified straddles, 56.1(a)
    married put options, 54.4(d)
    married put transactions, 56.4
    married stock, 56.4
    nonhedge interest rate swaps, 60.2(b)
    qualified covered calls, 18.4(c), 23.3(c), 48.2(c)(1), 56.3
      defined, 56.3(b)
      limitation on exemption, 56.3(d)
      scope of exemption, 56.3(a)
    section 1256 straddles, 12.3, 56.7
    short-term stock options, pre-July 18, 1984, 56.6
    stock, certain positions, 48.2(c)(1), 56.5
  executory contracts, 23.3(g)(2)(viii)(f)
  floors, 60.3(a)(2)(i)
  foreign currency transactions, 23.3(b), 23.3(d), 23.3(f)(4)
  hedged executory contracts, 23.3(g)(2)(viii)(f)
  holding period rule, effective date, 57.8
  integrated economic transactions, 23.3(g)(1)(v)(a)
  interest rate hedges, 8.4(d)
  investors, 9.7
  loss deferral rule, 50
    effective date, 57.8
  mixed straddles, *see* Mixed straddles
  notional principal contracts, 60.2(b)(1), 60.2(d)(1), 60.7
  on United States currency, 60.7(a)
  offsetting positions in personal property, 10.7, 60.7
  personal property described for purposes of Straddle Rules, 60.4(e)
  qualified covered call exemption, 56.3(a)
    limitations, 56.3(d)
  qualified hedging transactions, 23.3(f)(3)
  qualifying debt instrument, 23.3(g)(1)(v)(a)
  repurchase agreements, 31.11(e), 48.3(b)(3)
  reverse repurchase agreements, 48.3(b)(3)
  section 988 hedging transactions, 23.3(b), 23.3(d)

Index

Straddle rule(s) (*Continued*)
  section 1.988-5T(a) hedge,
    23.3(g)(1)(v)(a)
  section 1256 treatment, 12.3
  short sale against the box, 56.5
  stock options, 18.1, 30.3(g)(1)
  stock positions subject to, 18.1, 48.2(c)
  straddle income, 55.2(b)
    dividends, 55.2(b)
    market discount, 55.2(b)
  straddles made up exclusively of
    section 1256 contracts, 45.3, 56.1
  traders, 10.6
  transactions, exempt, 56
Straddle(s):
  background on pre-ERTA rules, 47
    Section 108, judicial decisions, 47.2(e)
  balanced positions, 48.4(a)
  carrying charges, 18.6(e)(5), 55.1
  corporate stock as personal property,
    48.2(c)(1)
  defined, 48.1, 53.2
  delivery or exercise of part of, 45.6(c)
  foreign currencies, 48.3(c)
  full carry straddles, 4.3(d), 55.1, 55.2
  full carry transactions, 55.2
  holding period:
    effective date, 57.8
    position making up straddle, 54.4(d)
    suspended, 54.4(a)
  identified straddles, 56.1
    qualifications, 56.1(a), 56.1(b)
    successor positions, 56.1(b)
    tax return disclosure, 56.1(b)
  interest and carrying charges, 9.2(f),
    18.6(e)(5)
  investment accounts and dealer
    accounts, between, 11.7(f)
  limitation on straddle losses while
    holding offsetting positions, 49
  loss deferral rule, 50
    effective date, 57.8
  losses carried forward, 50
  Mark-to-Market Rule, 45.1
  mixed straddle account rules, effective
    date, 57.8
  modified short sales rule, 18.1, 54
  modified wash sales rule, 54
  one position protects other, 48.1
  option positions, substantially reduce
    risk of loss, 48.4(b)
  options, 5.4(d), 30.3(d)(1)
  partial disposition of straddle positions,
    57.3(g)
  personal property, 56.5
  qualified hedging transaction,
    23.3(g)(1)(iii)
  replacement position, 54.3
  reverse hedge (option), 5.4(a)(1)
  section 1256 contracts, Straddle Rules
    do not apply, 45.3
  section 1256 contract straddle, 54.4
  section 1256 straddles, 30.2, 45.3, 56.7
  section 1256 treatment, 45.3, 45.4
  sellers of put and call, 30.3(d)(1)
  short sale, 18.1
  simulated straddles, 5.4(a)(1)
  statutory attribution elections, 51.2
  stock and substantially similar or
    related property, examples,
    48.2(c)(2)
  stock not included if all positions are
    stock or short sale of stock,
    48.2(c)(1)
  stock options, Section 108 not
    applicable, 47.2(d)(1)
  straddle-by-straddle netting rules,
    effective date, 57.8
  straddle income, 55.2(b)
    dividends, 55.2(b)
    holding period, 54.4(a)
    market discount, 55.2(b)
  switch transactions, 47.1
  syndicates, 47.2(c)
  synthetic straddle, 5.4(a)(1)
  underpayment of tax, 53.2
Strangle options, 5.4(d)
Street name securities:
  identification, 20.2(a)(2)
  information return with IRS, 24.7(e)
  limited, 28.3
  stock held in street name, 24.7(e)
Stripped bond(s):
  accrued discounts, 31.6(d)(1)
  acquired post-October 22, 1986:
    taxable securities, 31.6(d)(1)
    tax-exempt securities, 31.6(d)(2)
    acquired post-June 10, 1987,
      31.6(d)(2)(ii)
    acquired pre-June 11, 1987,
      31.6(d)(2)(i)
  acquired pre-October 23, 1986:
    tax-exempt securities, 31.6(c)(4)
    treatment of issuer, 31.6(c)(3)
    treatment of purchaser, 31.6(c)(2)

treatment of seller, 31.6(c)(1)
basis allocation, 31.6
coupon bond rules, 31.5
disposed of:
  post-July 1, 1982:
    tax-exempt securities, 31.6(c)(4)
    treatment of issuer, 31.6(c)(3)
    treatment of purchaser, 31.6(c)(2)
    treatment of seller, 31.6(c)(1)
  pre-July 2, 1982:
    treatment of purchaser, 31.6(b)(2)
    treatment of seller, 31.6(b)(1)
government securities, 2.2(e)
gross income, 31.6(d)(1)
interest portion, 31.6
IO strips, *see* Asset-backed securities, interest only (IO) strips
issuer, 31.6(c)(3)
loss, computation, 31.6
mortgage pools, 31.6(e)(1)
original issue discount, 31.6(c)(2)
pass-through certificates, *see* Asset-backed securities, pass-through certificates, stripped
pay-through certificates, *see* Asset-backed securities pay-through certificates, stripped
PO strips, *see* Asset-backed securities, principal only (PO) strips
principal portion, 31.6
purchaser, 31.6(c)(2)
reconstituted, 31.6(g)
REMIC regular interests, 2.1(b)(3), 7.2(g), 36.8(c)(1)(vi)
seller, 31.6(c)(1)
tax-exempt securities, 31.6(c)(4)
Stripped mortgage-backed securities (SMBSs), *see* Asset-backed securities (SMBSs); *see also* Federal National Mortgage Association (FNMA) (Fannie Mae) securities
Stripping securities, 2.2(e)
STRIPS, *see* Separate Trading of Registered Interest and Principal of Securities (STRIPS)
Student Loan Marketing Association (SLMA) (Sallie Mae) securities, 2.1(b)(6), 33.3(a)(1)(ii)
Subordinated pass-through certificates, *see* Asset-backed securities, pass-through certificates, subordinated
Subordinate governmental entities:
  defined, 11.3(b)(3)(ii)(b)

Subordinated pay-through bonds, *see* Asset-backed securities, pay-through bonds, subordinated
Subpart F income, 16.4(*l*), 60.2(b)(2)(i)(a)(4), 60.5(a)
Subscription agreements, 17.2(c)(1)
Subscription for securities, 17.2(c)(1)
Subscription rights, 19.8(a)
Substantially identical property:
  brokers, different, 18.4(e)(2)
  call options, 18.4(c)
  debt securities:
    identical, 19.9(g)
    nonidentical, 19.9(h)
  Federal land bank securities, 19.9(g)
  futures contracts, 18.4(e)(2)
  gifts, 19.8
  GNMA certificates, 19.9(j)
  holding period, 17.4(b)
  intercorporate dividends received, 17.7, 24.9(b)(2)
  markets, different, 18.4(e)(3)
  modified wash sales rule, 19.9, 54.3
  mortgage swaps, 19.9(j)
  municipal securities, 19.9(g)
  option(s):
    publicly traded, 19.9(f)
    to purchase, 8.9(e)
  related property, 48.2(c)(2)
  REMICs, 19.9(i)
  reorganizations, 19.9(d)
  securities, 19.1, 19.8
  securities arbitrage transactions, 18.10, 18.10(c)
  short sales, 8.9(e), 18.2, 18.2(a), 18.2(c), 18.3(c), 18.5
  Straddle Rules, 48.1, 48.2, 48.3
  TMPs, 19.9(i)
  wash sales rule, 17.4(b), 19.9
  writing call options, 19.9(f)
Substantially similar or related property, 17.7(b), 48.2(c)(2)
Substituted limited partner, 28.1(c)
Successor position rule, 54.2
Successor positions, 49.2, 54.2, 57.3(h)
  hybrid rule, 54.2
  offsetting positions, 49.2
  positions that offset, 57.3(h)
Superfund environmental tax, municipal securities, 25.4(c), 33, 33.2(a), 33.12
Swap(s):
  American-style swaptions, 6.2(d)
  amortization method, 60.2(b)(1)(ii)

Index

Swap(s) (*Continued*)
  arbitrage, 6.2(a)(1), 6.2(b)(1)
  asset swaps, 6.2(a), 60.2(b)(2)(ii)
  back-to-back loans, 6.2, 6.2(b)(4),
      60.2(a), 60.2(b)(1)(i)
  basis swaps, 6.2(a)(2)
  BBA short forms, 6.2(f)
  below water swap, 60.2(b)(2)(ii)
  centralized clearing and margining,
      evolution, 60.2(c)(3)
  CFTC Statement of Policy, 6.6(b)
    CFTC description of swap
        transaction, 6.6(b)
    CFTC, not regulated by, 6.2(c), 6.6,
        60.2(c)(3)
    commodity regulation, 6.6(b)
  characterization of interim payments,
      60.2(b)(1)(i)
  commodity swaps, *see* Commodity
      swaps
  credit risk, 6.2(g)
  cross-currency interest rate swaps,
      ("circuses"), 6.2(b)(2)
  currency swap, 23.3(g)(1)(i)(b),
      60.2(c)(5)(i)
  dealers, 6.6(a), 60.2(b)(1)(iii), 60.2(b)(2)
  debt swaps, 6.2(b)(3)
  defined, 60.2(a)
  dollar-denominated interest payments,
      6.2
  economic accrual, 60.2(b)(1)(ii)
  European-style swaptions, 6.2(d)
  expectation damages, 60.2(b)(2)(ii)
  fixed or determinable, annual or
      periodical income (FDAPI), 60.2(g)
    description of items subject to
        withholding, 60.2(g)
    items treated as FDAPI, 60.2(g)
    swap payments, 60.2(g)(1)
  fixed rate interest payments, 6.2
  floating rate interest payments, 6.2
  floating swap, 6.2(a)(2)
  foreign currency swaps, *see* Foreign
      currency swaps
  forward contracts, 6.2(c)
  forward swaps, 6.2(e)
  futures-like, 6.6(b)
  generally, 6.2, 60.2
  generic swap, 6.2(a)(1)
  held for sale to customers, 60.2(b)(2)(ii)
  ICA exemptions, 6.6(a)
  interim payments taxed periodically,
      60.2(b)(1)(i)
  interest equivalent treatment, gains and
      losses, 60.5(b)(1)
  interest rate swaps, *see* Interest rate
      swaps
  intermediary dealer function, 6.2
  inventory, 60.2(b)(2)(ii)
  investors, 60.2(b)(2)(ii)
  IPMA disclosure standards, 6.2(f)
  ISDA Code, 6.2(f)
  liability, 60.2(b)(2)(ii)
  LIBOR, 6.1, 6.2
  liquidated damages, 6.2(g), 60.2(b)(2)(ii)
  lump-sum payment, tax treatment,
      60.2(b)(2)(ii)
  market regulation, 6.6
  mark-to-market accounting method
      sought, 22.1(d)
  mirror swaps, 6.2(g), 59.2(c)
  mortgage swaps, 19.9(j)
  nondollar-denominated interest
      payments, 6.2
  nonexclusive safe harbor, 6.6(b)
  Notice 89-21, 60.2(a), 60.2(b)(1)(i)
  Notice 89-90, 60.2(b)(2)(i)(a)(4)
  notional principal amount, 6.2(a), 6.2(c)
  notional principal contract, 6.1
  off-market currency swap, defined,
      60.2(c)(5)(i)
  offsetting swaps, 6.2(g)
  option-like, 6.6(b)
  out-of-the-money, 6.2(d)
  parallel loans, 6.2(b)(4)
  payments calculated on different
      indexes, 6.2(a)(2)
  payments tied to price of one index, 6.2
  personal property, actively traded,
      60.2(b)(1)(iii)
  physical commodities, 6.2(c)
  plain vanilla swap, 6.2(a)(1)
  primary swap, 60.2(b)(2)(ii)
  reverse mirror swaps, 6.2(g),
      60.2(b)(1)(iii), 60.2(b)(2)(ii)
  SEC, not regulated by, 6.6
  securities regulation, 6.6(a)
  settlement, 5.6
  split fee swaption, 6.2(d)
  standardization of swap terms and
      documents, 6.2(f)
  straight unwind, 60.2(b)(1)(iii)
  swap agreement not section 1256
      contract, 60.2(b)(2)(ii)
  swap fees, 60.2(g)(2)
  swap income, 60.2(g)(2)

swap option(s):
  calls, 60.2(e)(1)
  character, 60.2(e)(2)
  generally, 6.2(d), 60.2(e)(1)
  Notice 89-21, 60.2(e)(1)
  option features, 60.2(e)(1)
  puts, 60.2(e)(1)
  source, 60.2(e)(4)
  swap premium, amortized, 60.2(e)(3)
  swaptions, four types, 6.2(d)
  timing, 60.2(e)(3)
  up-front payments amortized, 60.2(e)(1)
synthetic interest, 60.2(b)(2)(i)(a)(1)
termination payments, 6.2(g), 60.2(b)(1)(iii), 60.2(b)(2)(ii)
  ordinary and necessary business expense, 60.2(b)(2)(ii)
terminations, 6.2(g), 60.2(b)(2)(ii)
trade or business, 60.2(b)(2)(ii)
traders, 60.2(b)(2)(ii)
transportation costs, 6.2(c)
United Kingdom exchange controls, 6.2(b)(4)
up-front fee, 6.1, 6.2(d)
U.S. dollars, functional currency, 60.2(b)(2)(i)(a)
wash sales rule, 19.11
withholding obligations, 60.2(g)
yield enhancement, 6.2(b)(1)
zero coupon swaps, *see* Zero coupon swaps
see also Notional principal contracts
Swaption market, 60.2(e)(1)
Swaptions, *see* Swaps, swap options
Switch transactions, 47.1, 58.1
Syndicate(s):
  defined, 23.2(a), 23.2(c)(2)(i)
  generally, 23.2(c)(2), 30.2(a), 47.2(c)
  hedging exemption, 23.2(c)(2)(i), 30.2(a)
Synthetic convertibles, 8.9(a)(2)
Synthetic debt instrument, 23.3(g)(1)(v)(d)
  accrual period, 23.3(g)(1)(v)(d)(2)
  allocation of expenses, 23.3(g)(1)(v)(e)
  character, 23.3(g)(1)(v)(e)
  denomination, 23.3(g)(1)(v)(d)(1)
  foreign currency swap, 60.2(c)(4)
  interest income, 23.3(g)(1)(v)(e)
  issue price, 23.3(g)(1)(v)(d)(3)
  section 988(d) hedge, 60.2(c)(4)
  source of income, 23.3(g)(1)(v)(e)
  stated redemption price, 23.3(g)(1)(v)(d)(4)
  term, 23.3(g)(1)(v)(d)(2)
Synthetic fixed rate debt instrument, 60.2(b)(1)(iii)
Synthetic interest, 60.2(b)(1)(i), 60.2(b)(2)(i)(a)(1)
Synthetic puts, *see* Options, put options, synthetic

T

Tacked holding period, *see* Holding period, tacked holding period
TACs, *see* Asset-backed securities, targeted amortization class bonds (TACs)
Takeovers, corporate, 8.7(c), 27.3(c)(7)
TAP, *see* Transaction adjustment payment (TAP)
Targeted amortization class bonds (TACs), *see* Asset-backed securities, targeted amortization class bonds (TACs)
Taxable mortgage pools (TMPs), *see* Asset-backed securities, TMPs
Tax-avoidance:
  loans, 9.2(c)(2)
  short sale, 18.6(a)
Tax-exempt entities, 26, 26.2(f), 29.2(c), 31.5
  income, publicly traded partnership, 28.4(h)
Tax-exempt income:
  defined, 9.3(a)
  deduction disallowed for section 212 expenses, 9.1(a)
  expenses, 9.3, 10.3
Tax-exempt interest:
  distribution of, 24.5
  financial institutions, 11.3(b)(3)
    transitional rules, 11.3(b)(3)(ii)(g)
  generally, 9.1(a), 25.4, 25.4(a), 31.4(a)(2)(i), 33
  on any debt security, 16.4(*l*)
  transferable only by surrender, 25.4(d)
Tax-exempt organizations, 1.4(a), 26, 26.2(f), 28.4, 29.2(c), 31.5
Tax-exempt securities:
  acquired before June 11, 1987, 31.6(d)(2)
  acquisition date determined, 11.3(b)(3)(ii)(a)
  actual yield to maturity, 31.6(d)(2)(i)
  affiliated group of corporations, 11.3(b)(3)(ii)(a)

Index

Tax-exempt securities (*Continued*)
  bond premiums, 9.4, 11.4(b), 31.4(a)(2), 31.4(a)(2)(i)
  callable securities, 31.4(c)(2)
  Cheeseman rule, 11.3(b)(1)
  coupon rates, 31.6(d)(2)(i)
  dealers, 11.4(b), 16.4(*l*)
  defaulted, material changes, 33.4
  District of Columbia securities, 33
  exchanges, 31.9(a)
  financial institutions, special rule, 11.3(b)(3), 33.6
  general principles, 31.1
  interest deduction(s):
    de minimis exception, 10.3(b)
      corporate taxpayers, 9.3(b)(4)
      noncorporate taxpayers, 9.3(b)(4)
      unavailable to dealers, 11.3(b)(2)
    interest incurred to purchase or carry, 11.3(b)(1), 11.3(b)(3), 18.6(e)(1), 33.3(d), 33.6
  interest on indebtedness, 9.3(b), 10.3(b), 11.3(b)
  interest to purchase or carry, 33.3(d)
  market discount bonds, 31.3, 31.10(b)
  municipal securities, *see* Municipal securities
  original issue discount, 31.2, 31.2(e), 31.6(c)(4), 31.6(d)
  premiums, 9.4, 11.4(b), 31.4(a)(2)(i)
  project limitations, 3.1
  purchasing or carrying tax-exempt securities, 9.3(b)
  registered form for interest to be exempt, 31.12(c)
  sales of tax-exempt securities, 33.3(c)
  savings bonds, 31.10(b)
  security loans, *see* Security loans
  state securities, 33
  stripped bonds, 31.6(c)(4)
  transitional rules, 11.3(b)(3)(ii)(g)
  trust, 9.3(a)
  United States territory securities, 33
  yield method, 31.4(a)(2)(i)
  zero coupon securities, 3.3, 31.5(b)
  see also Municipal securities
Tax-free exchanges, *see* Reorganizations, tax-free exchanges
Tax-free reorganizations, *see* Reorganizations
Tax-motivated transaction(s):
  increased interest rate, 53.2
  120 percent interest rate, 53.2
  tax-motivated underpayment, 48.2(c)(1), 53.2
Tax preference item(s):
  capital gains deduction, 15.4(a)(2)(ii)(a)
  corporate, 15.5(c)
  investment interest expense, 15.4(a)(2)(ii)(c)
  repo interest expense, 15.4(a)(2)(ii)(b), 31.11(c)
Temporary use of personal property:
  fee for temporary use of property, 18.6(a)
  in short sale must be capitalized, 55.2(c)
  short sales, *see* Short sales expenses
  treated as fee for temporary use of property, 24.9(b)(3), 26.2(e)
Tender offers, 1.3(b), 8.7(c), 27.3(c)(7)
Terminations, *see* Contract cancellation transactions
Term repos, 2.2(c), 31.11(a), 31.11(b)(2)
Thrift institutions, *see* Financial institutions, thrift institutions
Ticker tape, 1.3(a)
TIGRs, *see* Treasury Investment Growth Receipts (TIGRs)
Time of reporting:
  deductions, 14.5, 14.5(c)
  dividends, 14.5(a)
  income, gain, deductions, or losses, 14.5
Time value, options, 5.1
TMPs, *see* Taxable mortgage pools (TMPs)
Trade date, 1.3(a), 1.3(d), 1.4(a), 13.3, 14.5(b), 14.5(d), 17.2(a)(5), 20.2(a)(2), 23.3(f)(1), 23.3(f)(2), 23.3(g)(1)(i)(c), 23.3(g)(2)(ii), 23.3(g)(3)
Trade options, 5.2(b), 5.3(b)
Trade or business:
  block traders, 23.2(c)(3)(ii)(a)
  brokerage account, 10.1(b), 19.5(c)
  capital assets, 8.4, 8.4(d), 14.1, 21.1, 23.2(b)(3)
  dealers, securities, 8.3(a), 23.2(c)(3)(ii)(a)
  defined, 10.1(b)
  expenses, 10.1(a), 11.1(a), 12.1, 59.2(a)(3)
  gambler, professional, 9.1(d), 10.1(b)
  hedgers, 12.1, 23.2(b), 23.2(b)(1), 23.2(b)(3), 23.2(c)(3)(ii), 23.2(c)(3)(ii)(a), 23.2(c)(3)(iii), 23.2(c)(3)(iv), 23.2(d)(3)(i), 23.3(b)
  hedging exemption, 23.2(a)
  interest expenses, 10.2(a)

investors, 8.1
qualified business units, 59.2(g)(3)(v)
selling goods and services, 10.1(b)
substantial attention, 8.1
traders, 8.2, 10.1(a), 11.9(c)
types of activities, 9.1(d), 10.1(b)
underwriters, 23.2(c)(3)(ii)(a)
United States trade or business, 23.3(f)(1), 23.3(f)(3), 23.3(g)(1)(i)(c), 23.3(g)(1)(v)(b), 23.3(g)(1)(v)(c), 23.3(g)(2)(iv)(a), 23.3(g)(3)
Trade-plus-one, 5.6
Trade-plus-two, 1.3(d)
Trade-plus-three, 1.3(d)
Trade-plus-four, 1.3(d)
Trader(s):
 arbitrageuer, 8.7(d)
 basic definition of, 8.2
 block traders, 23.2(c)(3)
 Board of Trade Gratuity Fund, 10.1(c)
 character of assets, capital or ordinary, 10
 dealers, 8.3(d), 11
 debt securities, 31.1
 expenses, *see* Expenses, traders
 floor traders, 4.2(b), 8.2(a), 10.1(d)
 interest rate swaps, 60.2(b)(2)(i)(a)
 market makers, 8.3(c)
 markets, types of, 1.2(a)
 noncorporate traders, prior to January 1, 1985, 19.5(b)
 original issue discount, 31.2(c), 31.2(d)
 overview, 8.2
 professional investors, 8.2
 professional traders, 8.2(a), 47.2(c), 47.2(d)(1)
 section 1256 contracts, 8.2(c)
  and offsetting non-section 1256 property, 54.4(a)
 securities dealer, investment accounts, 11.7(b)
 short sales, 10.6
 swap payments, 60.2(b)(2)(ii), 60.2(d)(2)(1)
 tax basis, 10.1
 trade or business, 8.2, 9.1(d), 11.9(c)
 upstairs traders, 8.2(a)
 wash sales rule, 10.5
  exemption for noncorporate traders, 19.4, 19.5(b)
Trade tickets, 57.3(a)(3)
Trading desk:
 partnerships, 28.4(c)(4)

Trading floor, 1.2(a)
Trading markets, 1.2
Trading post, 1.2(a)
Transaction adjustment payment (TAP), 2.4
Treasury bills, 2.1(a)(1), 31.2(d), 32.1, 32.1(a), 48.3(b)(2)(iii)
Treasury bonds, 2.1(a)(3), 5.2(b), 19.9(h)
Treasury Department, 2
Treasury Investment Growth Receipts (TIGRs), 2.2(e)
Treasury notes, 2.1(a)(2)
Treasury securities:
 auctions, 2.1(a)(1), 17.2(b)
 bidding, competitive and noncompetitive, 2.1(a)(1), 2.1(a)(3)
 book-entry system, 2.1(a)(1)
 call option basis, 2.1(a)(3)
 certificated, 2.1(a)(3)
 clearance and settlement, 2.4
 debt securities, 2.1(a)(1), 2.1(a)(2)
 defined, 2.1(a), 32.1
 discount, 2.1(a)(1)
 estate tax payments, 32.1(c)
 exchanges of, 32.1(d)
 federal agencies, *see* Federal agency securities; debt securities
 flower bonds, 32.1(c)
 foreign central banks, 2
 holding period, 17.2(b)
 index, 1.1(g)(4)
 interest-bearing, 2.1(a)(1), 2.1(a)(2), 2.1(a)(3)
 interest income earned, 32.1
 margin, 4.4(b)(1)(i)
 marketable securities, 2, 2.1(a), 32.1
  issued at discount, 32.1(d)(2)(ii)
 noncertificated, 2.1(a)(1)
 noninterest-bearing, 2.1(a)(1)
 nonmarketable securities, 2, 2.1(a)(4), 32.1
  issued at discount, 32.1(d)(2)(i)
 nontaxable exchanges, 32.1(d)
 offsetting positions, 48.4(c)
 OID rules, 32.1(d)(2)
 physical form, 2.1(a)(3)
 receipt of cash, otherwise nontaxable exchange, 32.1(d)(1)
 repurchase agreements, 32.3
 reverse repurchase agreements, 32.3
 savings bonds, *see* Savings bonds
 state and local government, 2
 tax-free exchange(s):
  general rule, 32.1(d)(1)
  OID rules, 32.1(d)(2)

Index

Treasury securities (*Continued*)
  Treasury bills, 2.1(a)(1), 2.1(a)(4)(i), 31.2(d), 32.1, 32.1(a), 48.3(b)(2)(iii)
  Treasury bonds, 2.1(a)(3), 2.1(a)(4)(i), 5.2(b), 19.9(h)
  Treasury notes, 2.1(a)(2)
  trust funds, 2
  valued at par, 32.1(c)
  when-issued securities, 32.4
  zero coupon securities, 32.5
Treasury security exchanges, 32.1(d)
Trust(s):
  Americus trusts, *see* Publicly traded trust interests, Americus Trusts
  and estates, 19.10(e)
  attribution, Straddle Rules, 51.1
  certificate holders, 29.1(a)
  certificates, 29.1(a), 29.1(d)
  certificates of beneficial interest, 1.1(i)
  common trust funds, 8.9, 31.2(d)
  distribution trusts, 1.1(i), 29.1(b), 29.2
  financing trusts, 1.1(i), 29.2
  fixed investment trusts, 58.2
  fixed mortgage pools, 36.8(a)
  grantor trusts, 1.1(i), 29.1, 29.1(e), 36.2, 36.4(b), 39.2(a)
  interests, 1.1(i)
    actively traded, 29.1(e)
  investment trusts, *see* Investment trusts
  liquidating distributions, 29.2(a)
  Massachusetts business trusts, *see* Regulated investment companies (RICs), Massachusetts business trusts
  mortgage-backed securities (MBSs), *see* Asset-backed securities (MBSs)
  multiple classes, 31.6(e)(2)(i)
  nonliquidating distributions, 29.2(a)
  nonoperating mineral interests, 1.1(e)
  ownership interests in, 36.2, 36.2(b), 36.2(c)
  owner trusts, *see* Asset-backed securities, owner trusts
  prohibition against multiple interests, 31.6(e)(2)(i)
  publicly traded trust interests, *see* Publicly traded trust interests
  royalty trusts, *see* Royalty trusts
Trust companies, 2.1(b)(2), 11.3(b)(3)
Trustees, 20.2(a)(3)
Trust for investment in mortgages (TIMs), *see* Asset-backed securities, TIMs
Trust Indenture Act of 1939, 7.6(c)

U

UBTI, *see* unrelated business taxable income (UBTI)
Underpayments of tax liability, 53.2, 58.1
Underwriter(s):
  broker-dealers, 1.2(b)
  defined, 8.6
  firm-commitment underwriters, 23.2(c)(3)
  investment accounts, 11.8(b)
  members of NASD, 1.2(b)
  options issued in connection with offering of securities, 11.8(a)
  over-the-counter markets, 1.2(b)
  registered with SEC, 1.2(b)
  registration-required securities, 31.12(d)
  section 1244 stock, 27.7
  stock brokerage firm, 11.8(c)
  trade or business, 23.2(c)(3)(ii)(a)
  underwriters' options, 11.8(a), 30.3(e)(1)(ii)
  underwriting arrangements, 24.7(g)
Underwriters' options, 11.8(a), 30.3(e)(1)(ii)
Underwriting arrangements, 24.7(g)
Underwriting(s):
  best efforts underwritings, 1.2(b), 8.6, 11.8(a), 27.7
  firm commitment underwritings, 1.2(b), 8.6, 11.8(a), 23.2(e)(3)
  municipal securities underwritings, 11.4(b)
  section 1244 stock, 27.7
Unenforceable agreements, 19.8(d)
Unit investment trusts, 8.9(a), 20.2(f), 24.5
United States currency, 44.1(a), 48.2(b), 48.3(a), 48.3(b)(2)(i), 60.7(a)
United States Farm Credit System, 2.1(b)(5)
United States savings bonds, *see* Savings bonds
United States source income, 23.3(f)(3), 23.3(f)(5), 23.3(g)(1)(v)(c), 59.2(d)(1); *see also* Sourcing rules
United States trade or business, 23.3(f)(1), 23.3(f)(3), 23.3(g)(1)(i)(c), 23.3(g)(1)(v)(b), 23.3(g)(1)(v)(c), 23.3(g)(2)(iv)(a), 23.3(g)(3)
United States Treasury security index, *see* Indexes
Unlisted trading privileges, *see* Markets

Index

Unrecognized gain, 23.2(c)(3), 48.4, 48.5, 52.1, 52.2, 52.3, 53.1, 56.1(b)
  disclosure, 52.1
  penalties, failure to disclose, 53.1
    current law, requirements, 53.1(b)
    pre-TRA '86 law, requirements, 53.1(a)
Unrelated business taxable income (UBTI), 26.2(f), 28.4(h), 29.2(c)
Unrelated trade or business, 26.2(f)
Utility holding companies, 27.4(c)

V

Value Line Composite Index, *see* Indexes
Variable rate demand debt securities, 1.1(g)(3)
Variable rate municipal bonds, 3.3
Variation deposits, 4.4(b)(3)
Variation margin, *see* Commodities, margin, variation margin
Variation settlement, 4.4(b)(3)
Vertical spreads, 5.4(c)
Voting trust certificates, 19.9(c)

W

Warrant holders, 30.3(e)(1)(ii)
Warrant issuers, 30.3(e)(2)
Warrant owners, 30.3(e)(1)
Warrant(s):
  acquired by gift, 30.3(e)(1)(i)
  acquired by inheritance, 30.3(e)(1)(i)
  acquired by purchase, 30.3(e)(1)(i)
  acquisition of, 30.3(e)(1)(i)
  capitalization expense, 30.3(e)(2)
  common stock purchase right, 1.1(c)
  defined, 1.1(c), 30.1(e), 30.3(e)
  detachable, 1.1(c)
  exchange of, separable from reorganizations, 27.4(b)(3)
  exercise of, 1.1(c), 17.2(c)(2)
  foreign currency, 5.2(a)(3), 5.2(a)(4)
  guaranteed by third parties, 1.1(c)
  holding period, exercise, 17.2(c)(2)
  index, 5.2(a)(3), 5.2(a)(4)
  investment packages, 30.3(e)(1)(ii)
  issued by corporation, 1.1(c)
  issuers, 30.3(e)(2)
  listed options, 30.3(e)(1)(ii)
  municipal securities, 3.3
  nontaxable distributions, 30.3(e)(1)(i)
  ordinary income, sale, 30.3(e)(1)(ii)
  owner(s):
    acquisition, 30.3(e)(1)(i)
    disposition, 30.3(e)(1)(ii)
    exercise, 30.3(e)(1)(ii)
    lapse, 30.3(e)(1)(ii)
  perpetual, 1.1(c)
  premiums, 30.3(e)(1)(ii), 30.3(e)(2)
  premium valuations, 30.3(e)(1)(ii)
  prior to July 19, 1984, 30.3(e)(2)
  registration requirements, 31.12(a)
  repurchase by issuer, 30.3(e)(2)
  section 988 transaction, 59.2(a)(1)
  short sales rule, 18.4(a)
  similar to call options, 1.1(c)
  substantially identical property, 19.9(b)
  taxable transactions, 30.3(e)(1)(i)
  traded on stock exchanges, 30.3(e)(1)(ii)
  underwriters' options, 11.8(a)
  used as sweeteners, 1.1(c)
  wash sales, 19.8(a), 19.9(b)
Wash sale(s):
  acquisition of substantially identical securities, 19.8
  acquisition of substantially identical stock, 19.8(e)
  basis, adjusted, 16.4(i), 16.4(l), 19.3(c)
  convertible securities, 19.9(a)
  covered persons, 19.4
  date loss sustained, 19.3(e)
  dealers, 11.11
  debt securities, 31.13
  exemption, 19.5
  GNMA certificates, 19.9(j)
  holding period, 17.4(b)
  investors, 9.5
  matching dispositions and acquisitions, 19.3(b)
  modified wash sales rule, coordination, 19.2, 54.1
  mortgage swaps, 19.9(j)
  noncorporate traders prior to January 1, 1985, 19.5(b)
  property not deemed "stock or security," 19.6(c)
  put options, 19.8(e)
  related parties:
    brothers and sisters, 19.10(c)
    controlled corporations, 19.10(d)
    husbands and wives, 19.10(a)
  securities acquired in, 17.4(b)
  61-day prohibited period, 19.3(a), 19.3(f), 19.3(g), 19.8(e), 19.9
  stock or securities, 19, 19.6(b)
    defined, 19.6

Index

Wash sale(s) (*Continued*)
  substantially identical property:
    acquired, 19.8
    defined, 19.9
  tacked holding period, 17.7(a), 19.3(d)
  traders, 10.5, 19.5(b)
  warrants, 19.9(b)
  see also Wash sales rule
Wash sales rule:
  basis, adjusted, 16.4(i), 16.4(*l*)
  burden of proof, 19.3(g)
  commodities futures trading, 19.6(c)(1)
  convertible securities, 19.9(a)
  covered persons, 19.4
  dealers, exemption, 11.11, 19.4, 19.5(a)
  debt securities, application, 19.9(g), 19.9(h), 31.1
  exchange memberships, 19.6(c)(2)
  exemptions, 19.5
    dealers, 11.11, 19.4, 19.5(a)
    noncorporate traders prior to January 1, 1985, 19.5(b)
    ordinary course of business, transactions, 19.5(c)
  foreign currency transactions, 19.6(c)(2)
  futures contracts, 19.6(c)(1)
  investment accounts, financial institution, 8.8
  matching dispositions and acquisitions, 19.3(b)
  modified wash sales rule, coordination, 19.2, 54.1
  mortgage swaps, 19.9(j)
  noncorporate traders, 30.2(b)
    exemption, 19.4, 19.5(a)
  operation, wash sales rule, 19.3
  option market makers, 19.5(b)
  option(s):
    application to, 19.6(b), 30.3(g)(2)
    call options, 19.8(f)
    publicly traded, 19.6(b), 19.9(f)
    put options, 19.8(e)
  oral agreements, 19.8(e)
  ordinary income or loss, 21.10
  possible application of wash sales rule, 21.10
  property not deemed stock or securities, 19.6(c)
  purpose, 19.1
  real estate mortgage investment conduits, 41.2(j)
  related parties, 19.10
  REMICs, 19.6(a), 19.9(i), 41.2(j)
  reorganizations, 19.9(d)
  securities, 19.6(a)
  sham transactions, 19.12
  short sales coverage, 19.3(f)
  stock or securities, 19.6, 19.6(b)
    sale or disposition, 19.7
  substantially identical property, 19.3(d), 19.9(h)
  swap transactions, 19.11
  TMPs, 19.9(i)
  unenforceable agreements, 19.8(d)
  voting trust certificates, 19.9(c)
  warrants, 19.9(b)
  when-issued securities, 19.9(e)
  see also Wash sales
When-distributed:
  contracts, 1.3(g)
  defined, 1.3(g)
  settlement, 1.3(g)
  trading, 1.3(g)
When-issued contract(s):
  cancellation of contract rights, 27.3(d)
  disposed of prior to delivery, 17.2(a)(6)
  long position, 17.2(a)(6)
  securities subject contract, issued, 17.2(a)(6)
  short position, 17.2(a)(6)
When-issued securities:
  actual contracts, 17.2(a)(6)
  American Telephone & Telegraph, divestiture, 1.3(f)
  broker-dealers, 1.3(f)
  common stock, 18.2(c)
  defined, 1.3(f), 2.2(d), 27.3(d)
  holding period, 17.2(a)(6)
  modified short sales rule, 18.4(c)
  securities arbitrage, 18.10(c)
  settlement of when-issued transactions, 1.3(f)
  short sales, 18.2(b), 18.2(c), 18.4, 18.4(a), 18.4(b)
  substantially identical property, 19.9(e)
  wash sales, 19.9(e)
  wi market, 1.3(f), 2.2(d), 27.3(d), 32.4
Whipsaw, section 1256(f)(1), 23.2(c)(4), 23.2(e)(1)
Wi market, 1.3(f), 2.2(d), 27.3(d), 32.4
Withholding procedures, 13.3
Worthless securities, 17.1(c), 27.8
  affiliated corporations, 27.8(b)
  banks, 27.8(e)
  character of loss, 27.8(a)
  insolvent corporations, 27.8(c)

loss deduction, 28.8
securities dealers, 27.8(d)
stock deductions, 27.8(f)

Y

Year-end transactions, 17.2(a)(2)
  arm's length escrow agreements, 17.2(a)(2)(ii)
  escrow accounts, 17.2(a)(2)(ii)
  installment method, electing out, 17.2(a)(2)(i)
    sales after December 31, 1986, 17.2(a)(2)(i)(b)
    sales before January 1, 1987, 17.2(a)(2)(i)(a)
  modification of sales agreement, 17.2(a)(2)(ii)
  regular way trades, 17.2(a)(2)(i)(e)
Yield to maturity, 7.2(d)(4), 15.4(a)(2)(ii)(b), 23.3(g)(1)(i)(b), 31.2(d)(2)(ii), 31.2(m), 31.2(n)(1)

Z

Zero coupon bonds, *see* Zero coupon securities; *see also* Asset-backed securities
Zero coupon CMOs, *see* Zero coupon securities; *see also* Asset-backed securities
Zero coupon municipal securities, *see* Zero coupon securities, municipal

Zero coupon securities:
  bonds, 2.1(a)(4)(i), 2.1(b)(4), 7.2(d)(2), 9.3(b)(5)
    accreting bond, 2.1(b)(4)
    accrual bond, 2.1(b)(4)
  CATs, 2.2(e)
  CMOs, 2.1(b)(4), 7.2(d)(2)
  corporate, 31.5(a)
  deep discount, 31.5, 31.5(b)
  government securities, 2.2(e)
  interest deductions for issuers, 31.5(a)
  low bracket taxpayers, 31.5
  margin account, 9.3(b)(5)
  municipal securities, 3.3, 31.5(b)
  OID rule(s):
    taxable zeros, 31.5(a)
    tax-exempt zeros, 31.5(b)
  Series EE bonds, 2.1(a)(4)(i)
  STRIPS, 2.2(e)
  taxable, 31.5(a)
  tax-exempt, 3.3, 31.5(b)
  tax-exempt entities, 31.5
  TIGRs, 2.2(e), 31.5(a)
  Treasury bills, 2.1(a)(4)(i)
  Treasury securities, 32.5, 31.5
  see also Asset-backed securities
Zero coupon swap(s):
  back-loaded payments, 60.2(f)
  front-loaded payments, 60.2(f)
  generally, 60.2(f)
  lump-sum payment amortized, 60.2(f)
  Notice 89-21, 60.2(f)

About the Author

ANDREA S. KRAMER, a partner in the Chicago law firm of Coffield Ungaretti & Harris, is a graduate of the University of Illinois (B.A., summa cum laude) and of Northwestern University School of Law (J.D., cum laude). Ms. Kramer is a member of the Illinois Bar and is admitted to practice law before the United States Tax Court and the United States Court of Claims. She is a member of the Chicago Bar Association (Tax Committee: Division on Partnerships, Real Estate, and Other Tax Sheltered Investments; Commodities Law Committee) and International Bar Association (Committee on Issues and Trading in Securities). Ms. Kramer, recognized as a leading commentator on the taxation of financial products, has published numerous articles on the taxation and regulation of commodities, options, and other financial products, and has participated in continuing legal education programs in the areas of taxation and matters related to financial products and the financial services industry. Her national legal practice is primarily in the areas of taxation and general business representation of major corporations, money center banks, national and international trading firms, and many individuals and market participants in tax planning, contested tax matters, tax legislative counseling, and lobbying. Ms. Kramer has served as an arbitrator for the National Futures Association.